# HAMMOND'S
# WORLD ATLAS
## CLASSICS EDITION

*An Encyclopedic Atlas of the World*
**with**
**Latest and most Authentic**
**Geographical and Statistical Information**
*in*
**Map, Word and Picture**

*1958*

*Map Publishers Since 1900*

*C. S. Hammond & Company*
Maplewood, N. J.

*New York, N. Y.*                    *Chicago, Ill.*

# Contents

## PART I

## PART II

## PART III

# List of Modern Maps

# HAMMOND'S
# WORLD ATLAS AND GAZETTEER

Copyright MCMLVIII by C. S. Hammond & Co., New York. Printed in U.S.A.

## GAZETTEER-INDEX OF THE WORLD

This alphabetical list of grand divisions, countries, states, colonial possessions, etc., gives area, population, capital, seat of government or chief town, and index references and numbers of plates on which they are shown on the largest scale. The mother country of colonial possessions is indicated by abbreviations in parentheses. The index reference shows the square on the respective map in which the name of the country, state or colonial possession is located.

### ABREVIATIONS

| | | | | | | | |
|---|---|---|---|---|---|---|---|
| Aust. | — Australian | I. | — Island. | Pak. | — Pakistan. | Trust | — Trust Territory. |
| Belg. | — Belgian or Belgium. | Is. | — Islands. | pen. | — peninsula. | U. S. A. | — United States of America. |
| Br. | — British Commonwealth of Nations. | It. | — Italian or Italy | Port. | — Portugal or Portuguese. | U. S. Adm. | — U. S. Administration. |
| | | Jap. | — Japan or Japanese | Rep. | — Republic. | U.S.S.R. | — Union of Soviet Socialist Republics. |
| Dan. | — Danish or Denmark. | Mand. | — Mandate. | So. | — South. | | |
| E. | — East. | N. | — North. | Sp. | — Spain or Spanish. | U. of So. Africa | — Union of South Africa. |
| Fr. | — France or French. | Neth. | — Netherlands. | sq. mi. | — square miles. | | |
| Gr. | — Greece or Greek. | N. Z. | — New Zealand. | S. S. R. | — Soviet Socialist Republic. | W. | — West. |

| Country | Area (Sq. Miles) | Population | Capital or Chief Town | Index Ref. | Plate No. |
|---|---|---|---|---|---|
| **A**den (incl. Protectorate) (Br.) | 112,000 | 650,000 | Aden | E 7 | 26 |
| Aden Colony | 75 | 138,441 | Aden | E 7 | 26 |
| Admiralty Is. (Aust. Tr.) | 820 | 16,394 | Lorengau | E 6 | 37 |
| Afghanistan | 250,000 | 12,000,000 | Kabul | J 3 | 26 |
| Africa | 11,850,000 | 223,000,000 | | | 34, 35 |
| Alabama, U.S.A. | 51,078 | 3,061,743 | Montgomery | M 6 | 43 |
| Alaska, (U.S.A.) | 571,065 | 128,643 | Juneau | C 3 | 38 |
| Albania | 11,096 | 1,394,310 | Tiranë | E 5 | 21 |
| Alberta, Canada | 248,800 | 1,123,116 | Edmonton | G 4 | 40 |
| Aleutian Islands (U.S.A.) | 6,800 | 5,600 | | F 3 | 6 |
| Algeria (Fr.) | 851,284 | 9,528,670 | Alger (Algiers) | G 5 | 34 |
| Andaman Is. (India) | 2,508 | 21,316 | Port Blair | F 6 | 29 |
| Andorra | 191 | 5,664 | Andorra la Vieja | G 1 | 17 |
| Angola (Port.) | 481,351 | 4,280,000 | Luanda | K14 | 35 |
| Antarctica | 5,500,000 | | | | 8 |
| Antigua (Br.) (incl. Barbuda and Redonda) | 171 | 52,454 | St. Johns | G 3 | 45 |
| | | | | E 3 | 45 |
| Antilles, Greater, Lesser | | | | | |
| Arab Federation | 151,350 | 6,049,500 | Baghdad, Amman | C 3 | 26 |
| | | | | D 5 | 26 |
| Arabia | 1,000,000 | 10,700,000 | | | 8 |
| Arctic Ocean | | | | | 8 |
| Argentina | 1,078,266 | 16,108,573 | Buenos Aires | H10 | 47 |
| Arizona, U.S.A. | 113,580 | 749,587 | Phoenix | E 6 | 42 |
| Arkansas, U.S.A. | 52,725 | 1,909,511 | Little Rock | K 6 | 43 |
| Armenian S.S.R. (U.S.S.R.) | 11,500 | 1,345,000 | Yerevan (Erivan) | F 5 | 22 |
| Ascension Island (Br.) | 34 | 159 | Georgetown | D13 | 35 |
| Asia | 16,500,000 | 1,520,000,000 | | | 25 |
| Australia, Commonwealth of (Br.) | 2,974,581 | 8,986,530 | Canberra | | 36 |
| Australian Capital Territory | 939 | 30,315 | Canberra | J 7 | 36 |
| Austria | 32,369 | 6,918,959 | Wien (Vienna) | B-C 3 | 20 |
| Azerbaidzhan S.S.R. (U.S.S.R.) | 33,100 | 3,100,000 | Baku | F 5 | 22 |
| Azores Islands (Port.) | 890 | 287,091 | Ponta Delgada | B 4 | 34 |
| **B**ahama Islands (Br.) | 4,404 | 98,489 | Nassau | C 1 | 45 |
| Bahrein Islands (Br.) | 213 | 109,650 | Manama | F 4 | 26 |
| Balearic Islands (Sp.) | 1,936 | 422,127 | Palma | H 3 | 17 |
| Barbados (Br.) | 166 | 229,113 | Bridgetown | G 4 | 45 |
| Barbuda and Redonda Is. (Br.) | 63 | 979 | Codrington | F-G 3 | 45 |
| Basutoland (Br.) | 11,716 | 631,396 | Maseru | M17 | 35 |
| Bechuanaland Prot. (Br.) | 275,000 | 296,883 | Mafeking | L16 | 35 |
| Belgian Congo | 902,274 | 12,600,000 | Léopoldville | L12 | 35 |
| Belgium | 11,775 | 8,512,195 | Bruxelles (Brussels) | E 7 | 15 |
| Bermuda (Br.) | 21 | 41,160 | Hamilton | G 2 | 45 |
| Bhutan | 18,000 | 600,000 | Bumthang | F 3 | 29 |
| Bismarck Archipelago (Aust. Trust.) | 19,660 | 141,757 | Rabaul | E 6 | 37 |
| Bolivia | 412,777 | 3,019,031 | La Paz, Sucre | G 7 | 46 |
| Bonin Is. (U.S. Adm.) | 76 | | | E 3 | 37 |
| Borneo | 208,286 | | | E 5 | 31 |
| Brazil | 3,286,170 | 58,456,000 | Rio de Janeiro | K 6 | 46 |
| British Columbia, Canada | 359,279 | 1,398,464 | Victoria | F 4 | 40 |
| British Honduras | 8,867 | 80,888 | Belize | C 2 | 39 |
| Brunei (Br.) | 2,226 | 65,000 | Brunei | E 5 | 31 |
| Bulgaria | 42,796 | 7,629,254 | Sofiya | G 4 | 21 |
| Burma | 261,610 | 19,242,000 | Rangoon | C 2 | 30 |
| Byelorussian S.S.R. (White Russian S.S.R.) (U.S.S.R.) | 80,100 | 7,220,000 | Minsk | D 4 | 22 |
| **C**alifornia, U.S.A. | 156,803 | 10,586,223 | Sacramento | C 5 | 42 |
| Cambodia | 69,884 | 4,358,000 | Phnom Penh | E 4 | 30 |
| Cameroons (Br. Trust.) | 34,081 | 1,430,000 | Lagos | J10 | 34 |
| Cameroun (Fr. Trust.) | 161,787 | 3,065,800 | Yaoundé | J10 | 34 |
| Canada | 3,621,616 | 16,080,791 | Ottawa | | 40, 41 |
| Canal Zone (U.S.A.) | 362 | 52,822 | Balboa Heights | G 6 | 39 |
| Canary Islands (Sp.) | 2,894 | 776,912 | Las Palmas, Santa Cruz | B 4 | 17 |
| Cape of Good Hope, U. of So. Africa | 277,169 | 4,426,726 | Capetown | M18 | 35 |
| Cape Verde Islands (Port.) | 1,557 | 147,328 | Praia | N 5 | 6 |
| Caroline Islands (U.S. Trust.) | 525 | 36,980 | Moen, Ponape | E 5 | 37 |
| Cayman Is., Jamaica (Br.) | 100 | 8,266 | Georgetown | B 3 | 45 |
| Celebes | 72,986 | 5,500,000 | Makassar | G 6 | 31 |
| Central America | 217,813 | 10,196,000 | | | 39 |
| Ceylon | 25,332 | 8,103,648 | Colombo | D 7 | 29 |
| Channel Islands (Br.) | 75 | 102,776 | St. Helier | E 8 | 10 |
| Chatham Islands (N.Z.) | 372 | 505 | | J10 | 37 |
| Chile | 286,396 | 6,761,000 | Santiago | F10 | 47 |
| China: Mainland | 3,745,296 | 582,603,417 | Peiping | | 32 |
| China: Taiwan | 13,885 | 8,907,000 | Taipei | | 32 |
| Christmas Island (Br.) | 64 | 2,432 | | O11 | 25 |
| Colombia | 439,828 | 12,657,000 | Bogotá | F 3 | 46 |
| Colorado, U.S.A. | 103,967 | 1,325,089 | Denver | G 5 | 42 |
| Comoro Is. (Is. Comores) (Fr.) | 849 | 180,000 | Dzaoudzi | P14 | 35 |
| Connecticut, U.S.A. | 4,899 | 2,007,280 | Hartford | P 4 | 43 |
| Cook Islands (N.Z.) | 99 | 14,088 | Avarua | K 7 | 37 |
| Corsica (Corse) (Fr.) | 3,367 | 246,995 | Ajaccio | G 6 | 16 |
| Costa Rica | 19,238 | 951,000 | San José | E 5 | 39 |
| Cuba | 42,857 | 5,829,029 | Habana | 48 & B 2 | 45 |
| Curaçao (Neth. Antilles) | 173 | 95,195 | Willemstad | E 4 | 45 |
| Cyprus (Br.) | 3,572 | 527,000 | Nicosia | E 5 | 28 |
| Czechoslovakia | 49,356 | 13,089,000 | Praha (Prague) | D 2 | 20 |
| **D**ahomey (Fr.) | 42,471 | 1,614,000 | Porto Novo | G10 | 34 |
| Daito Is. (U.S. Adm.) | 18 | 2,691 | | M 6 | 32 |
| Damão (Port.) | 213 | 63,521 | | B 4 | 29 |
| Delaware, U.S.A. | 1,978 | 318,085 | Dover | P 5 | 43 |
| Denmark | 16,556 | 4,439,000 | København (Copenhagen) | E 9 | 13 |
| District of Columbia, U.S.A. | 61 | 802,178 | Washington | O 5 | 43 |
| Diu (Port.) | 12 | 19,731 | | B 4 | 29 |
| Dominica (Br.) | 305 | 63,000 | Roseau | G 4 | 45 |
| Dominican Republic | 19,129 | 2,539,325 | Ciudad Trujillo | D 6 48 & D 3 | 45 |
| **E**cuador | approx. 115,000 | 3,675,000 | Quito | E 4 | 46 |
| Egypt | 386,000 | 22,934,000 | Cairo | M 6 | 34 |
| England and Wales | 58,340 | 43,744,924 | London | | 10 |
| Eritrea, Ethiopia | 47,900 | 1,086,000 | Asmara | O 8 | 34 |
| Estonia (Estonian S.S.R.) (U.S.S.R.) | 17,400 | 1,000,000 | Tallin (Tallinn) | D 4 | 22 |
| Ethiopia (excl. Eritrea) | 409,266 | 15,000,600 | Addis Ababa | O 9 | 34 |
| Europe | 4,129,908 | 570,100,000 | | | 9 |
| **F**aerö Islands (Dan.) | 540 | 29,178 | Thorshavn | D 2 | 9 |
| Falkland Islands (Br.) (incl. S. Georgia) | 5,618 | 2,230 | Port Stanley | H14 | 47 |
| Fernando Póo (island) (Sp. Guinea) | 800 | 17,249 | Santa Isabel | H11 | 34 |
| Fiji (Br.) | 7,036 | 345,164 | Suva | H 7 | 37 |
| Finland | 130,500 | 4,288,521 | Helsinki | P 4 | 13 |
| Florida, U.S.A. | 54,262 | 2,771,305 | Tallahassee | N 7 | 43 |

| Country | Area (Sq. Miles) | Population | Capital or Chief Town | Index Ref. | Plate No. |
|---|---|---|---|---|---|
| Formosa (Taiwan) (China) | 13,885 | 8,907,000 | Taipei | K 7 | 32 |
| France | 212,736 | 42,734,445 | Paris | ........ | 16 |
| Franz Josef Land (Zemlya Frantsa Iosifa) | ........ | ........ | ........ | F 1 | 22 |
| French Equatorial Africa.... | 961,392 | 4,658,207 | Brazzaville | K10 | 34 |
| French Sudan | 584,942 | 3,642,000 | Bamako | F 8 | 34 |
| French West Africa | 1,814,852 | 18,729,000 | Dakar | G 8 | 34 |
| Gabon (Fr.) | 90,733 | 391,781 | Libreville | J12 | 35 |
| Galápagos Islands, Ecuador | 3,042 | 1,346 | Pto. Baquerizo | D 7 | 46 |
| Gambia (Br.) | 4,033 | 278,858 | Bathurst | C 9 | 34 |
| Gambier Islands (Fr.) | 6 | 1,569 | Rikitea | N 8 | 37 |
| Georgia, U.S.A. | 58,518 | 3,444,578 | Atlanta | N 6 | 43 |
| Georgian S.S.R. (U.S.S.R.) | 29,400 | 3,555,000 | Tbilisi (Tiflis) | F 5 | 22 |
| Germany, East (German Democratic Rep.) | 41,535 | 18,488,316 | Berlin | ........ | 14 |
| Germany, West (Federal Republic of) | 95,914 | 50,579,878 | Bonn | ........ | 14 |
| Ghana | 91,844 | 4,118,450 | Accra | F10 | 34 |
| Gibraltar (Br.) | 2 | 23,232 | ........ | D 4 | 17 |
| Gilbert, Ellice and Phoenix Islands | 369 | 36,000 | Bairiki | H 6 | 37 |
| Gôa (Port.) | 1,313 | 540,925 | Pangim | B 5 | 29 |
| Great Britain and Northern Ireland | 94,279 | 50,210,472 | London | E 3 | 9 |
| Greece | 51,182 | 7,856,000 | Athenai (Athens) | F 6 | 21 |
| Greenland (Dan.) | 839,999 | 26,192 | Godthaab | D22 | 8 |
| Grenada (Br.) | 133 | 88,215 | St. George's | G 4 | 45 |
| Guadaloupe and Dependencies (Fr.) | 688 | 229,120 | Basse Terre | F 3 | 45 |
| Guam (U.S.A.) | 203 | 59,498 | Agaña | E 4 | 37 |
| Guatemala | 45,452 | 3,258,000 | Guatemala | B 3 | 39 |
| Guiana, British | 89,480 | 492,980 | Georgetown | J 2 | 46 |
| Guiana, French | 35,135 | 27,863 | Cayenne | K 3 | 46 |
| Guiana, Netherlands (Surinam) | 54,300 | 219,000 | Paramaribo | J 3 | 46 |
| Guinea, French | 96,525 | 2,505,000 | Conakry | D 9 | 34 |
| Guinea, Portuguese | 13,948 | 510,736 | Bissau | C 9 | 34 |
| Guinea, Spanish | 10,830 | 161,032 | Santa Isabel | J 11 | 35 |
| Haiti | 10,714 | 3,305,000 | Port-au-Prince | C 5 48 & D 3 | 45 |
| Hawaii (U.S.A.) | 6,420 | 499,794 | Honolulu | L 3 | 37 |
| Holland (Netherlands)..land | 12,883 | 9,625,499 | 's Gravenhage, Amsterdam | F 4 | 15 |
| Honduras | 45,000 | 1,505,465 | Tegucigalpa | D 3 | 39 |
| Honduras, British | 8,867 | 59,220 | Belize | C 2 | 39 |
| Hong Kong (Br.) | 391 | 2,400,000 | Victoria | J 7 | 32 |
| Hungary | 35,875 | 9,805,000 | Budapest | E 3 | 20 |
| Iceland | 39,709 | 158,000 | Reykjavik | C 2 | 9 |
| Idaho, U.S.A. | 82,808 | 588,637 | Boise | E 3 | 42 |
| Ifni (Sp.) | 676 | 45,852 | Sidi Ifni | D 6 | 34 |
| Illinois, U.S.A. | 55,947 | 8,712,176 | Springfield | L 4 | 43 |
| India | 1,059,342 | 356,755,978 | New Delhi | ........ | 29 |
| India, Portuguese | 1,538 | 624,177 | Pangim | B 4-5 | 29 |
| Indiana, U.S.A. | 36,205 | 3,934,224 | Indianapolis | M 5 | 43 |
| Indochina (Fr.) | 285,927 | 26,876,510 | ........ | E 3 | 30 |
| Indonesia (East Indies) | 735,286 | 82,000,000 | Djakarta (Batavia) | F 7 | 31 |
| Iowa, U.S.A. | 55,986 | 2,621,073 | Des Moines | K 4 | 43 |
| Iran (Persia) | 628,000 | 19,000,000 | Teheran | H 4 | 27 |
| Iraq (Mesopotamia) | 116,600 | 5,200,000 | Baghdad | C 4 | 27 |
| Ireland (Eire) | 26,601 | 2,894,822 | Dublin (Baile Atha Cliath) | ........ | 12 |
| Ireland, Northern | 5,238 | 1,369,579 | Belfast | H 2 | 12 |
| Isle of Man (Br.) | 221 | 55,213 | Douglas | C 3 | 10 |
| Israel | 7,987 | 1,872,000 | Jerusalem | ........ | 24 |
| Italy | 116,000 | 47,489,636 | Roma (Rome) | ........ | 18 |
| Ivory Coast (Fr.) | 183,397 | 2,481,000 | Abidjan | E10 | 34 |
| Jamaica (Br.) | 4,411 | 1,579,620 | Kingston | 48 & C 3 | 45 |
| Jammu and Kashmir | 92,780 | 4,021,616 | Srinagar | C 2 | 29 |
| Japan | 142,272 | 89,275,529 | Tokyo | ........ | 33 |
| Java and Madura | 51,032 | 52,000,000 | Djakarta | K 2 | 31 |
| Jordan (Trans-Jordan) | 34,750 | 1,427,000 | Amman | D 4 | 24 |
| Kansas, U.S.A. | 82,113 | 1,905,299 | Topeka | J 5 | 42 |
| Kashmir and Jammu | 92,780 | 4,021,616 | Srinagar | C 2 | 29 |
| Kazakh S.S.R. (U.S.S.R.) | 1,061,600 | 6,000,000 | Alma-Ata | H 5 | 22 |
| Kentucky, U.S.A. | 40,109 | 2,944,806 | Frankfort | M 5 | 43 |
| Kenya (Br.) | 219,730 | 6,100,000 | Nairobi | O11 | 35 |
| Kerguelen Arch. (Fr.) | ........ | ........ | ........ | T 8 | 6 |
| Kirghiz S.S.R. (U.S.S.R.) | 76,100 | 1,490,000 | Frunze | J 5 | 22 |
| Korea, North | 49,096 | 6,474,000 | Pyongyang | C 4 | 33 |
| Korea, South | 36,152 | 21,526,374 | Seoul | C 5 | 33 |
| Krētē (Crete), Greece | 3,232 | 441,687 | Erákleion | G 8 | 21 |
| Kuria Muria Is. (Br.) | ........ | 70 | ........ | G 6 | 26 |
| Kuril Is. (Chishima) (U.S.S.R.) | 5,700 | 15,000 | Severo-Kuril'sk | R 5 | 23 |
| Kuwait | 8,000 | 203,000 | Al Kuwait | E 4 | 26 |
| Laccadive Islands (India) | 746 | 18,393 | ........ | B 6 | 29 |
| Laos | 89,343 | 1,425,000 | Vientiane | E 3 | 30 |
| Latvia (Latvian S.S.R.) (U.S.S.R.) | 24,600 | 1,800,000 | Riga | D 4 | 22 |
| Lebanon | 3,475 | 1,400,000 | Beirut | F 6 | 28 |
| Leeward Islands | ........ | ........ | ........ | G 3 | 45 |
| Liberia | 43,000 | 1,600,000 | Monrovia | E10 | 34 |
| Libya | 679,358 | 1,091,830 | Tripoli, Benghazi | K 6 | 34 |

| Country | Area (Sq. Miles) | Population | Capital or Chief Town | Index Ref. | Plate No. |
|---|---|---|---|---|---|
| Liechtenstein | 65 | 14,861 | Vaduz | J 2 | 19 |
| Lithuania (Lithuanian S.S.R.) (U.S.S.R.) | 31,200 | 2,700,000 | Vil'nyus (Vilna) | D 4 | 22 |
| Louisiana, U.S.A. | 45,177 | 2,683,516 | Baton Rouge | K 7 | 43 |
| Loyalty Islands (Fr.) | 800 | 11,854 | Chépénéhé | G 8 | 37 |
| Luxembourg | 999 | 309,000 | Luxembourg | J 9 | 15 |
| Macao (Port.) | 6 | 389,000 | Macao | H 7 | 32 |
| Madagascar (Fr.) | 241,094 | 4,776,000 | Tananarive | R15 | 35 |
| Madeira Islands (Port.) | 308 | 269,179 | Funchal | A 2 | 17 |
| Madura I. | 1,752 | 2,444,000 | Pamekasan | K 2 | 31 |
| Maine, U.S.A. | 31,040 | 913,777 | Augusta | R 3 | 43 |
| Malaya, Federation of | 50,690 | 6,152,099 | Kuala Lumpur | E 6 | 30 |
| Maldive Islands (Br.) | 115 | 81,950 | Malé | L 9 | 25 |
| Malta (Br.) | 122 | 313,955 | Valletta | E 7 | 18 |
| Manchuria (China) | 412,801 | 36,903,000 | Shenyang (Mukden) | K 2 | 32 |
| Manitoba, Canada | 219,723 | 850,040 | Winnipeg | L 3 | 40 |
| Mariana Is. (U.S. Trust.) | 142 | 6,286 | Garapan | E 4 | 37 |
| Marquesas Is. (Fr.) | 480 | 2,976 | Atuona | N 6 | 37 |
| Marshall Islands (U.S. Trust.) | 61 | 14,260 | Majuro | H 4 | 37 |
| Martinique (Fr.) | 425 | 239,130 | Fort de France | G 4 | 45 |
| Maryland, U.S.A. | 9,887 | 2,343,001 | Annapolis | O 5 | 43 |
| Massachusetts, U.S.A. | 7,907 | 4,690,514 | Boston | P 4 | 43 |
| Mauritania (Fr.) | 328,185 | 615,000 | St. Louis | D 8 | 34 |
| Mauritius (Br.) | 720 | 559,932 | Port Louis | S19 | 35 |
| Mesopotamia (See Iraq) | ........ | ........ | ........ | D 4 | 27 |
| Mexico | 760,373 | 29,679,000 | México | ........ | 44 |
| Michigan, U.S.A. | 57,022 | 6,371,766 | Lansing | M 3 | 43 |
| Midway Islands (U.S.A.) | 2 | 437 | ........ | J 3 | 37 |
| Minnesota, U.S.A. | 80,009 | 2,982,483 | St. Paul | K 3 | 43 |
| Mississippi, U.S.A. | 47,420 | 2,178,914 | Jackson | L 6 | 43 |
| Missouri, U.S.A. | 69,270 | 3,954,653 | Jefferson City | K 5 | 43 |
| Moldavian S.S.R. (U.S.S.R.) | 13,100 | 2,660,000 | Kishinev | D 5 | 22 |
| Molucca Islands | 30,168 | 544,302 | Ternate | C 6 | 37 |
| Monaco | 370 Acres | 20,422 | Monaco | G 6 | 16 |
| Mongolian Republic | 625,946 | 2,000,000 | Ulan Bator | F 2 | 32 |
| Montana, U.S.A. | 146,316 | 591,024 | Helena | F 3 | 42 |
| Montserrat (Br.) | 32 | 14,436 | Plmouth | G 3 | 45 |
| Morocco | 171,583 | 9,961,387 | Rabat | E 5 | 34 |
| Moyen Congo (Fr.) | 175,676 | 708,624 | Pointe Noire | J12 | 35 |
| Mozambique (Port.) | 297,731 | 5,730,930 | Lourenço Marques | O15 | 35 |
| Natal, U. of So. Africa | 35,284 | 2,415,318 | Pieter-maritzburg | N17 | 35 |
| Nauru (Austr.-N.Z.—Br. Tr. Terr.) | 8 | 3,676 | ........ | G 6 | 37 |
| Nebraska, U.S.A. | 76,653 | 1,325,510 | Lincoln | H 4 | 42 |
| Nepal | 54,000 | 8,431,537 | Katmandu | D 3 | 29 |
| Netherlands (Holland).land | 12,883 | 10,751,000 | Amsterdam, 's Gravenhage | F 4 | 15 |
| Netherlands Antilles | 383 | 189,000 | Willemstad | E 4 | 45 |
| Nevada, U.S.A. | 109,802 | 160,083 | Carson City | D 5 | 42 |
| New Britain (island) (Aust. Trust.) | 14,600 | 105,000 | Rabaul | F 6 | 37 |
| New Brunswick, Canada | 27,473 | 554,616 | Fredericton | G 4 | 41 |
| New Caledonia (Fr.) | 7,201 | 63,000 | Nouméa | G 8 | 37 |
| Newfoundland, Canada | 42,734 | 415,074 | St. John's | J 4 | 41 |
| New Guinea, Netherlands | 161,514 | 700,000 | Hollandia | K 6 | 31 |
| New Guinea, Territory of (Aust. Trust.) | 93,000 | 1,254,160 | Port Moresby | B 7 | 31 |
| New Hampshire, U.S.A. | 9,024 | 533,242 | Concord | R 3 | 43 |
| New Hebrides Islands (Br. and Fr.) | 5,700 | 52,920 | Vila | G 7 | 37 |
| New Ireland (island) (Aust. Trust.) | 3,800 | 33,960 | Kavieng | F 6 | 37 |
| New Jersey, U.S.A. | 7,522 | 4,835,329 | Trenton | P 5 | 43 |
| New Mexico, U.S.A. | 121,511 | 681,187 | Sante Fe | G 6 | 42 |
| New South Wales, Australia | 309,432 | 3,423,529 | Sydney | H 6 | 36 |
| New York, U.S.A. | 47,929 | 14,830,192 | Albany | P 4 | 43 |
| New Zealand, Dominion of (Br.) | 103,934 | 2,174,062 | Wellington | M 7 | 36 |
| Nicaragua | 57,143 | 1,245,000 | Managua | E 4 | 39 |
| Nicobar Islands (India) | 635 | 12,452 | Port Blair | F 7 | 29 |
| Nigeria (Br.) | 338,593 | 31,171,000 | Lagos | H10 | 34 |
| Niger Colony (Fr.) | 501,930 | 2,334,000 | Niamey | H 8 | 34 |
| Niue I. (Br.) | 100 | 4,253 | Alofi | K 7 | 37 |
| Norfolk Island (Aust.) | 13 | 942 | Kingston | G 8 | 37 |
| North America | 9,124,000 | 241,000,000 | ........ | ........ | 38 |
| North Borneo (Br.) | 29,387 | 377,324 | Jesselton | F 5 | 31 |
| North Carolina, U.S.A. | 49,142 | 4,061,929 | Raleigh | O 6 | 43 |
| North Dakota, U.S.A. | 70,054 | 619,636 | Bismarck | J 3 | 42 |
| Northern Ireland (Br.) | 5,238 | 1,369,579 | Belfast | H 2 | 12 |
| Northern Rhodesia (Br.) | 288,130 | 2,156,750 | Lusaka | M14 | 35 |
| Northern Territory, Algeria. | 80,117 | 8,706,257 | Alger | G 4 | 34 |
| Northern Territory, Aust. | 523,620 | 16,469 | Darwin | E 3 | 36 |
| Northwest Territories, Canada | 1,258,217 | 19,313 | Ottawa | F 1 | 40 |
| Norway | 124,560 | 3,425,000 | Oslo | F 6 | 13 |
| Nova Scotia, Canada | 20,743 | 694,717 | Halifax | H 4 | 41 |
| Nyasaland Prot. (Br.) | 36,879 | 2,616,330 | Zomba | N14 | 35 |
| Ohio, U.S.A. | 41,122 | 7,946,627 | Columbus | N 4 | 43 |
| Oklahoma, U.S.A. | 69,283 | 2,233,351 | Oklahoma City | J 6 | 42 |
| Oman, Sultanate of | 82,000 | 550,000 | Masqat | J 5 | 26 |
| Ontario, Canada | 363,282 | 5,404,933 | Toronto | C 3 | 41 |
| Orange Free State, U. of South Africa | 49,647 | 1,016,570 | Bloemfontein | M17 | 35 |

| Country | Area (Sq. Miles) | Population | Capital or Chief Town | Index Ref. | Plate No. |
|---|---|---|---|---|---|
| Oregon, U.S.A. | 96,350 | 1,521,341 | Salem | C 4 | 42 |
| Orkney Islands, Scotland | 376 | 21,258 | Kirkwall | J 1 | 11 |
| Oubangui-Chari (Fr.) | 239,382 | 1,104,836 | Bangui | K10 | 34 |
| Pacific Islands (excl. Australia) | 262,718 | 5,600,000 | | | 37 |
| Pacific Islands, Terr. of the (U.S.) Trust. | 680 | 64,290 | | E-F 5 | 37 |
| Pakistan | 364,218 | 75,843,000 | Karachi | A 3 & F 4 | 29 |
| Palau Islands (U.S. Trust) | 189 | 7,656 | Koror | D 5 | 37 |
| Palestine | | | | | 20 |
| Panama (excl. Canal Zone) | 28,575 | 910,000 | Panamá | G 6 | 39 |
| Papua Territory (Aust.) | 90,540 | 446,163 | Port Moresby | B 7 | 31 |
| Paraguay | 150,518 | 1,565,000 | Asunción | J 8 | 47 |
| Pennsylvania, U.S.A. | 45,045 | 10,498,012 | Harrisburg | O 4 | 43 |
| Persia (Iran) | 628,000 | 19,000,000 | Teheran | H 4 | 27 |
| Peru ... approx. | 513,000 | 9,396,000 | Lima | E 5 | 46 |
| Philippines, Republic of the | 115,600 | 21,039,000 | Quezon City | H 4 | 31 |
| Phoenix Is. (U.S. and Br.) | 16 | 984 | Canton I. | J 6 | 37 |
| Pitcairn Island (Br.) | 2 | 138 | | O 8 | 37 |
| Poland | 119,734 | 27,278,000 | Warszawa (Warsaw) | | 24 |
| Portugal | 35,413 | 8,765,000 | Lisboa (Lisbon) | B 3 | 17 |
| Prince Edward Island, Canada | 2,184 | 99,285 | Charlottetown | H 4 | 41 |
| Principe and S. Tomé (Port.) | 372 | 62,000 | São Tomé | H11 | 35 |
| Puerto Rico (U.S.A.) | 3,423 | 2,210,703 | San Juan | G 2 | 45 |
| Qatar | 5,000 | 34,000 | Doha | F 4 | 26 |
| Québec, Canada | 523,860 | 4,628,378 | Québec | G 3 | 41 |
| Queensland, Australia | 670,500 | 1,318,259 | Brisbane | G 4 | 36 |
| Réunion (Fr.) | 970 | 274,370 | St. Denis | R20 | 35 |
| Rhode Island, U.S.A. | 1,058 | 791,896 | Providence | R 4 | 43 |
| Rhodesia and Nyasaland, Federation of | 475,342 | 7,033,080 | Salisbury | M15 | 35 |
| Rio de Oro (Sp.) | 71,583 | 24,000 | Villa Cisneros | D 7 | 34 |
| Rio Muni (continental Sp. Guinea) | 10,040 | 142,237 | Bata | J11 | 35 |
| Ruanda-Urundi (Belg. Tr.) | 20,309 | 4,305,606 | Usumbura | M12 | 35 |
| Rumania | 91,671 | 17,489,794 | Bucureşti | G 3 | 21 |
| Russian S.F.S.R. (U.S.S.R.) | 6,501,500 | 111,000,000 | Moscow (Moskva) | E 4 | 22 |
| Ryukyu Islands (U.S. Adm.) | 921 | 914,462 | Naha | L 7 | 33 |
| Saguia el Hamra (Sp.) | 31,660 | 14,298 | Aiún | D 6 | 34 |
| St. Croix, Virgin Is. (U.S.A.) | 80 | 12,103 | Christiansted | H 2 | 45 |
| St. Helena I. (Br.) | 47 | 4,877 | Jamestown | E15 | 35 |
| St. John, Virgin Is. (U.S.A.) | 20 | 749 | | H 1 | 45 |
| St. Lucia (Br.) | 238 | 88,150 | Castries | G 4 | 45 |
| St. Pierre and Miquelon Is. (Fr.) | 93 | 4,354 | St. Pierre | J 4 | 41 |
| St. Thomas, Virgin Is. (U.S.A.) | 32 | 13,813 | Charlotte Amalie | G 1 | 45 |
| St. Vincent (Br.) | 150 | 76,778 | Kingstown | G 4 | 45 |
| Sakhalin (U.S.S.R.) | 35,400 | 300,000 | Yuzhno-Sakhalinsk | R 5 | 23 |
| Salvador, El | 13,176 | 2,193,000 | San Salvador | C 4 | 39 |
| Samoa, Western (N.Z. Tr.) | 1,133 | 96,678 | Apia | J 7 | 37 |
| Samoa, U.S.A. | 76 | 18,937 | Pago Pago | J 7 | 37 |
| San Marino | 38 | 12,100 | San Marino | D 2 | 18 |
| Santa Cruz Islands (Br.) | 375 | 5,000 | Peu | G 6 | 37 |
| Sarawak (Br.) | 47,071 | 613,879 | Kuching | E 5 | 31 |
| Sardinia (Sardegna) (It.) | 9,301 | 1,276,023 | Cagliari | B 4 | 18 |
| Saskatchewan, Canada | 237,975 | 880,665 | Regina | J 4 | 40 |
| Saudi Arabia, Kingdom of | 350,000 | 5,500,000 | Riyadh, Mecca | D 4 | 26 |
| Scotland | 30,405 | 5,095,969 | Edinburgh | | 11 |
| Senegal (Fr.) | 77,401 | 2,214,000 | St. Louis | D 9 | 34 |
| Seychelles (Br.) | 157 | 38,671 | Victoria | T 6 | 6 |
| Shetland Islands, Scotland | 550 | 19,343 | Lerwick | L 3 | 11 |
| Siam (Thailand) | 200,148 | 20,302,000 | Krung Thep (Bangkok) | D 3 | 30 |
| Sicily (It.) | 9,926 | 4,486,749 | Palermo | D 6 | 18 |
| Sierra Leone (Br.) | 27,925 | 2,260,000 | Freetown | D10 | 34 |
| Sikkim | 2,745 | 129,000 | Gangtok | E 3 | 29 |
| Singapore (Br.) | 220 | 1,261,677 | Singapore | F 6 | 30 |
| Sinkiang, China | 660,977 | 4,012,330 | Tihwa (Urumchi) | C 3 | 32 |
| Society Islands (Fr.) | 650 | 30,500 | Papeete | L 7 | 37 |
| Socotra (Br.) | 1,400 | 12,000 | Tamrida | J 8 | 25 |
| Solomon Islands (Aust. Tr.) | 4,070 | 49,067 | Sohano | F 6 | 37 |
| Solomon Islands Prot. (Br.) | 11,500 | 99,200 | Honiara | F 6 | 37 |
| Somaliland, French | 8,492 | 63,000 | Djibouti | P 9 | 34 |
| Somaliland (Italian Tr.) | 194,000 | 916,300 | Mogadiscio | R10 | 34 |
| Somaliland Prot. (Br.) | 68,000 | 700,000 | Hargeisa | R10 | 34 |
| South America | 6,894,000 | 125,000,000 | | | 46, 47 |
| South Australia, Australia | 280,070 | 794,094 | Adelaide | E 5 | 36 |
| South Carolina, U.S.A. | 30,594 | 2,117,027 | Columbia | N 6 | 43 |
| South Dakota, U.S.A. | 76,536 | 652,740 | Pierre | J 3 | 42 |
| Southern Rhodesia (Br.) | 150,333 | 2,260,000 | Salisbury | M15 | 35 |
| Southern Territories, Algeria | 767,435 | 822,413 | Alger | G 6 | 34 |
| South West Africa (U. of South Africa Mand.) | 317,725 | 418,104 | Windhoek | K16 | 35 |
| Spain | 195,258 | 29,446,789 | Madrid | | 17 |
| Spanish Sahara | 103,243 | 38,298 | Aiún | D 6 | 34 |
| Spanish West Africa | 103,919 | 84,150 | Sidi Ifni | D 6 | 34 |
| Sudan | 967,500 | 8,309,663 | Khartoum | M 9 | 34 |
| Sumatra | 164,148 | 12,000,000 | Padang | C 6 | 31 |
| Surinam (Netherlands Guiana) | 54,300 | 219,000 | Paramaribo | J 3 | 46 |
| Svalbard, Norway (Spitsbergen) | 24,294 | 1,539 | Longyearbyen | C 2 | 13 |
| Swaziland (Br.) | 6,704 | 241,865 | Mbabane | N17 | 35 |
| Sweden | 173,394 | 7,262,000 | Stockholm | J 6 | 13 |
| Switzerland | 15,944 | 4,977,000 | Bern | | 19 |
| Syria | 72,587 | 4,145,000 | Dimishq (Damascus) | H 5 | 28 |
| Tadzhik S.S.R. (U.S.S.R.) | 54,900 | 1,455,000 | Stalinabad | J 6 | 22 |
| Tahiti (island) (Fr.) | 600 | 29,684 | Papeete | M 7 | 37 |
| Taiwan (Formosa) | 13,885 | 8,907,000 | Taipei | | 32 |
| Tanganyika Territory (Br. Trust.) | 342,706 | 8,324,000 | Dar es Salaam | N13 | 35 |
| Tasmania, Australia | 26,215 | 308,752 | Hobart | J 8 | 36 |
| Tchad (Fr.) | 455,598 | 2,452,966 | Fort Lamy | K 8 | 34 |
| Tennessee, U.S.A. | 41,961 | 3,291,718 | Nashville | M 6 | 43 |
| Texas, U.S.A. | 263,644 | 7,711,194 | Austin | J 7 | 42 |
| Thailand (Siam) | 200,148 | 20,302,000 | Krung Thep | D 3 | 30 |
| Tibet, China | 469,413 | 2,000,000 | Lhasa | C 5 | 32 |
| Timor (Port.) | 7,332 | 424,132 | Dili | H 7 | 31 |
| Timor Archipelago (Indon.) | 24,450 | 1,657,376 | Kupang | G 8 | 31 |
| Togo (Fr. Trust.) | 20,733 | 1,080,000 | Lomé | G10 | 34 |
| Tokelau (Union Group) (N.Z. and U.S.) | 4 | 1,875 | Fakaofo | J 6 | 37 |
| Tonga, Friendly Is. (Br.) | 269 | 56,000 | Nukualofa | J 7 | 37 |
| Transvaal, Union of South Africa | 110,450 | 4,812,838 | Pretoria | N17 | 35 |
| Trinidad and Tobago (Br.) | 1,980 | 720,450 | Port of Spain | G 5 | 45 |
| Tristan da Cunha (Br.) | 38 | 230 | | N 7 | 6 |
| Trucial Oman | 12,000 | 95,000 | Sharja | F 5 | 26 |
| Tuamotu (Low) Arch. (Fr.) | 332 | 5,127 | Apataki | M 7 | 37 |
| Tunisia | 48,300 | 3,782,480 | Tunis | H 5 | 34 |
| Turkey | 296,185 | 20,934,670 | Ankara | | 28 |
| Turkmen S.S.R. (U.S.S.R.) | 187,200 | 1,170,000 | Ashkhabad | G 6 | 22 |
| Turks and Caicos Is., Jamaica (Br.) | 166 | 6,500 | Grand Turk | D 2 | 45 |
| Uganda Protectorate (Br.) | 80,301 | 5,508,000 | Entebbe | N11 | 35 |
| Ukrainian S.S.R. (U.S.S.R.) | 220,600 | 40,500,000 | Kiev | E 5 | 22 |
| Union of South Africa | 472,494 | 12,671,452 | Capetown, Pretoria | L18 | 35 |
| Union of Soviet Socialist Republics | 8,570,600 | 200,200,200 | Moscow (Moskva) | | 22, 23 |
| United Arab Republic | 458,587 | 22,222,304 | Cairo | A 4 & C 3 | 26 |
| United Kingdom | 94,279 | 50,210,472 | London | D 3 | 9 |
| United States of America land | 2,977,128 | 150,697,361 | Washington | | 42, 43 |
| land and water | 3,022,387 | | | | |
| Upper (Haute) Volta (Fr.) | | 3,324,000 | Ouagadougou | F 9 | 34 |
| Uruguay | 72,172 | 2,615,000 | Montevideo | J10 | 47 |
| Utah, U.S.A. | 82,346 | 688,862 | Salt Lake City | F 5 | 42 |
| Uzbek S.S.R. (U.S.S.R.) | 157,400 | 6,000,000 | Tashkent | H 5 | 22 |
| Vatican City | 109 Acres | 1,010 | | B 6 | 18 |
| Venezuela | 352,143 | 5,774,000 | Caracas | G 2 | 46 |
| Vermont, U.S.A. | 9,278 | 377,747 | Montpelier | P 4 | 43 |
| Victoria, Australia | 87,884 | 2,452,341 | Melbourne | G 7 | 36 |
| Vietnam | 126,700 | 26,300,000 | Saigon | E 3 | 30 |
| Virgin Islands (Br.) | 67 | 7,760 | Road Town | H 1 | 45 |
| Virgin Islands (U.S.A.) | 132 | 26,665 | Charlotte Amalie | H 1 | 45 |
| Virginia, U.S.A. | 39,899 | 3,318,680 | Richmond | O 5 | 43 |
| Volcano Is. (U.S. Adm.) | 29 | | | E 3 | 37 |
| Wake Island (U.S.A.) | 3 | | | G 4 | 37 |
| Wales (excluding Monmouthshire) | 7,466 | 2,172,339 | Cardiff | D 5 | 10 |
| Wallis and Futuna (Fr.) | 75 | 6,700 | Matautu | J 7 | 37 |
| Walvis Bay (Br.) | 430 | 2,263 | | J16 | 35 |
| Washington, U.S.A. | 66,977 | 2,378,963 | Olympia | C 3 | 42 |
| Western Australia, Australia | 975,920 | 639,777 | Perth | C 4 | 36 |
| West Indies | 90,000 | 17,000,000 | | | 45 |
| West Indies (Br. Fed.) | 8,005 | 2,974,226 | Port of Spain | H 3 | 45 |
| West Virginia, U.S.A. | 24,090 | 2,005,552 | Charleston | N 5 | 43 |
| White Russian S.S.R. (Byelorussian S.S.R.), (U.S.S.R.) | 80,100 | 7,220,000 | Minsk | D 4 | 22 |
| Windward Islands | | | | G 4 | 45 |
| Wisconsin, U.S.A. | 54,715 | 3,434,575 | Madison | L 3 | 43 |
| World ... land area | 57,500,000 | 2,691,000,000 | | | 6, 7 |
| Wyoming, U.S.A. | 97,506 | 290,529 | Cheyenne | G 4 | 42 |
| Yap (U.S. Trust.) | 87 | 5,102 | Yap | D 5 | 37 |
| Yemen | 75,000 | 4,500,000 | San'a | D 7 | 26 |
| Yugoslavia | 99,079 | 16,927,275 | Beograd (Belgrade) | C 3 | 21 |
| Yukon Territory, Canada | 205,346 | 12,190 | Whitehorse | C 1 | 40 |
| Zanzibar Prot. (Br.) | 1,020 | 278,000 | Zanzibar | P13 | 35 |

This alphabetical list of cities gives statistics of population based on the latest official reports. Each line begins with the name of a place, followed by the name of the country or state, the population, the index reference and the plate number. Different forms of names have been included to a large extent in the index.

Capitals are designated by asterisks *   † Including suburbs.   ‡ No room on map for name.

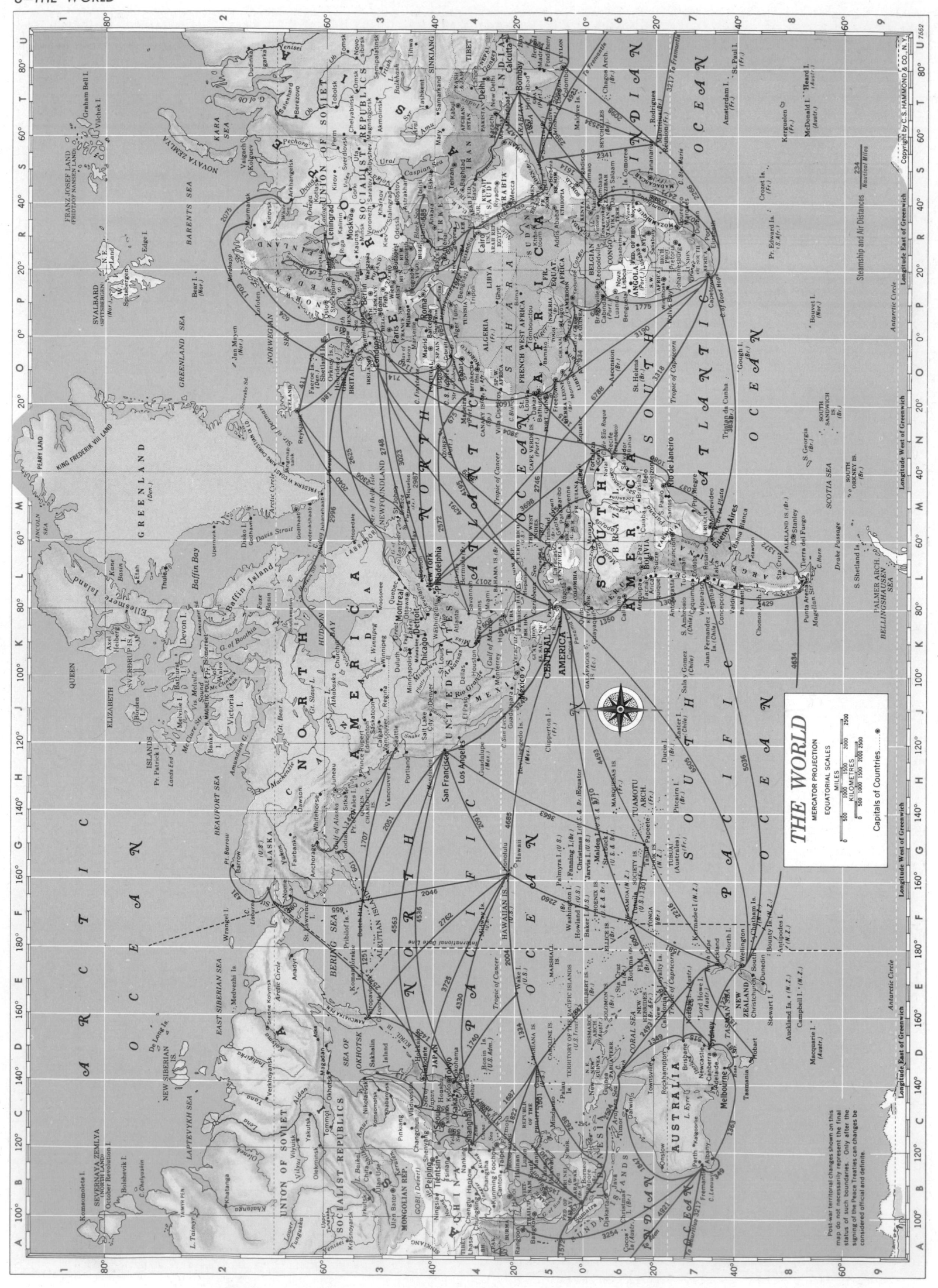

THE WORLD

MERCATOR PROJECTION

EQUATORIAL SCALES

Capitals of Countries......●

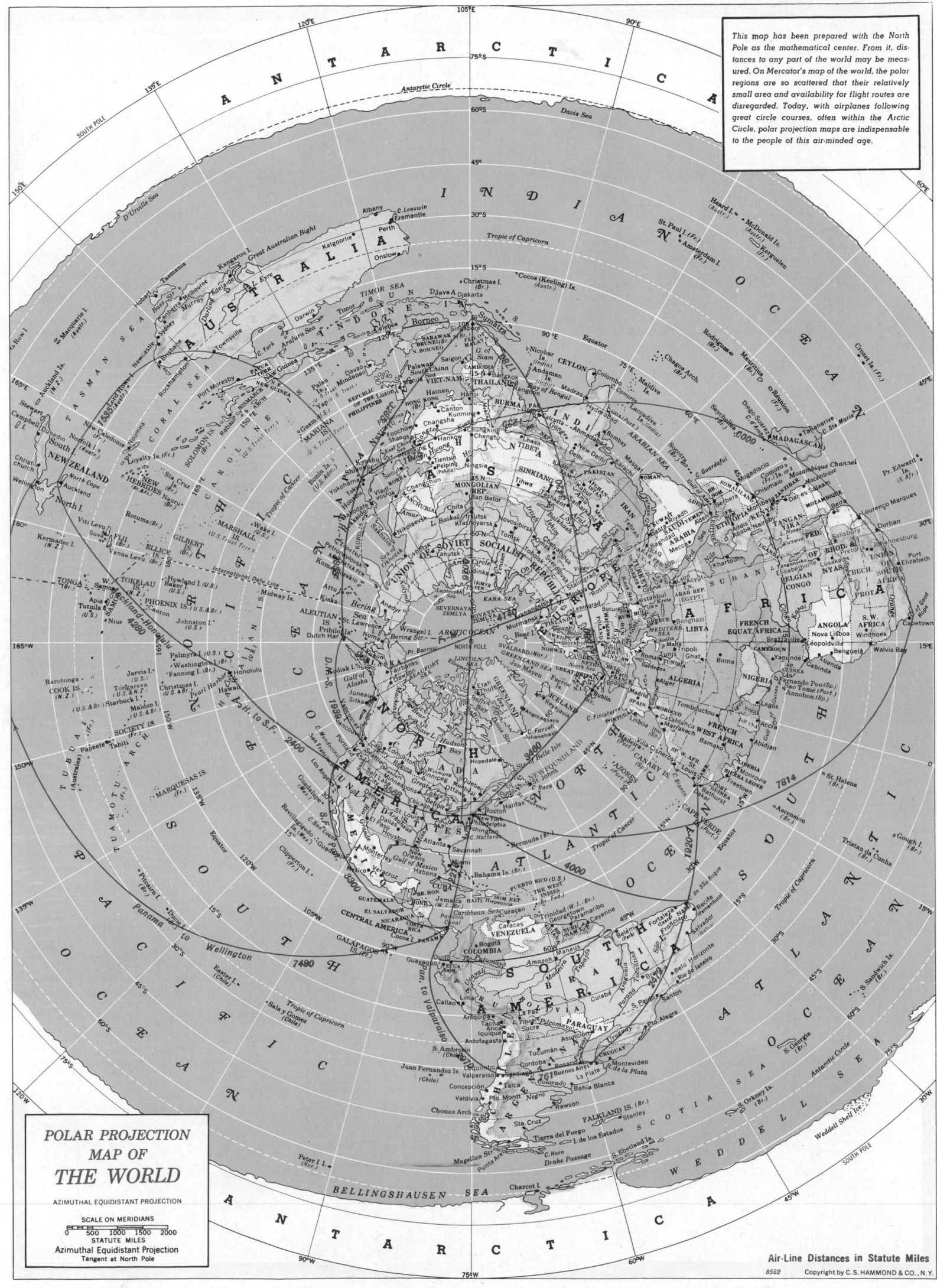

This map has been prepared with the North Pole as the mathematical center. From it, distances to any part of the world may be measured. On Mercator's map of the world, the polar regions are so scattered that their relatively small area and availability for flight routes are disregarded. Today, with airplanes following great circle courses, often within the Arctic Circle, polar projection maps are indispensable to the people of this air-minded age.

POLAR PROJECTION
MAP OF
THE WORLD

AZIMUTHAL EQUIDISTANT PROJECTION

SCALE ON MERIDIANS
0    500   1000   1500   2000
STATUTE MILES
Azimuthal Equidistant Projection
Tangent at North Pole

Air-Line Distances in Statute Miles

8552          Copyright by C. S. HAMMOND & CO., N.Y.

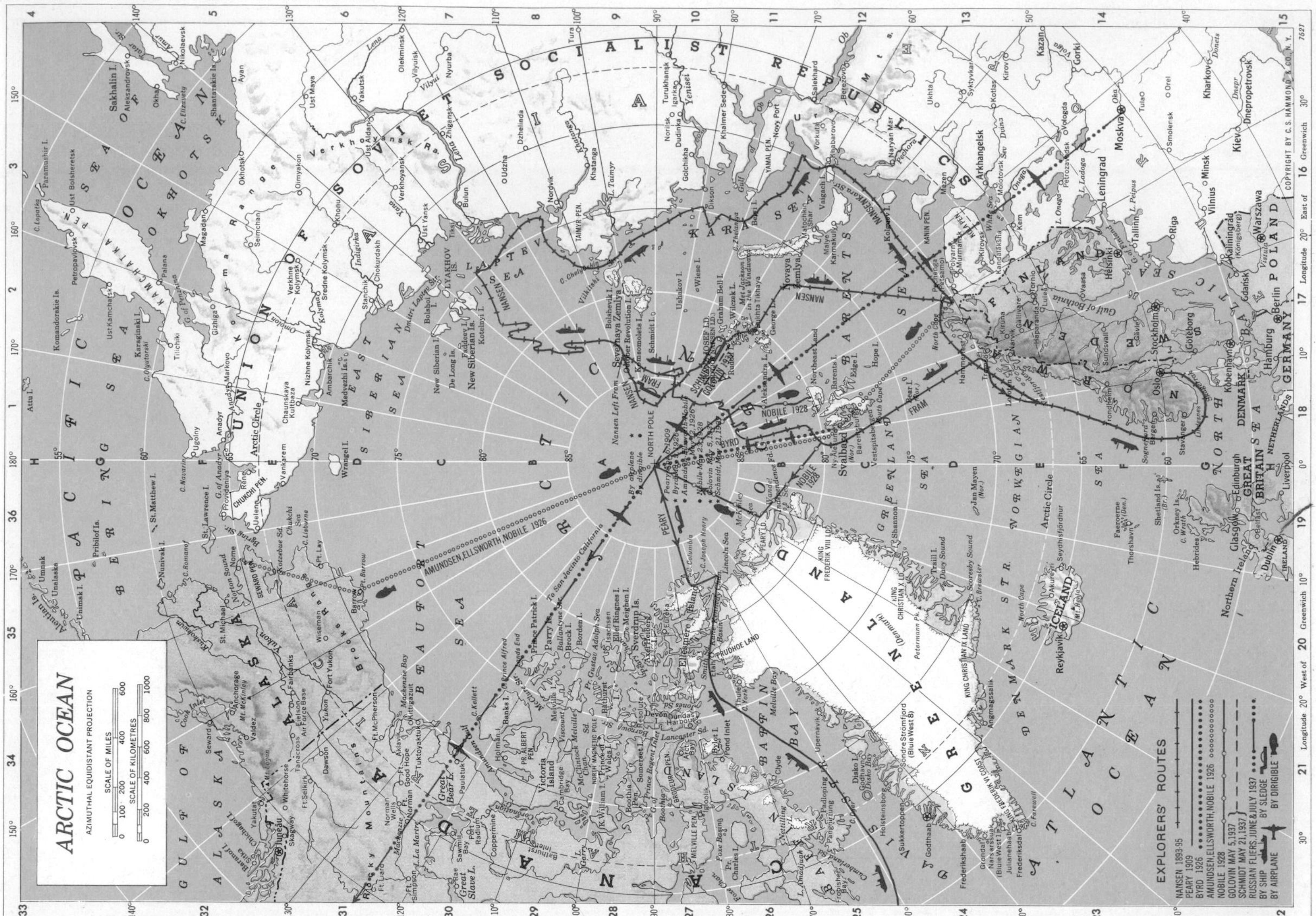

## ARCTIC OCEAN
AZIMUTHAL EQUIDISTANT PROJECTION

SCALE OF MILES
SCALE OF KILOMETERS

EXPLORERS' ROUTES

NANSEN 1893-95
PEARY 1909
BYRD 1926
AMUNDSEN,ELLSWORTH,NOBILE 1926
NOBILE 1928
GOLOVIN MAY 5, 1937
RUSSIAN FLIERS, JUNE & JULY 1937
SCHMIDT MAY 21, 1937
BY AIRPLANE
BY SHIP
BY DIRIGIBLE

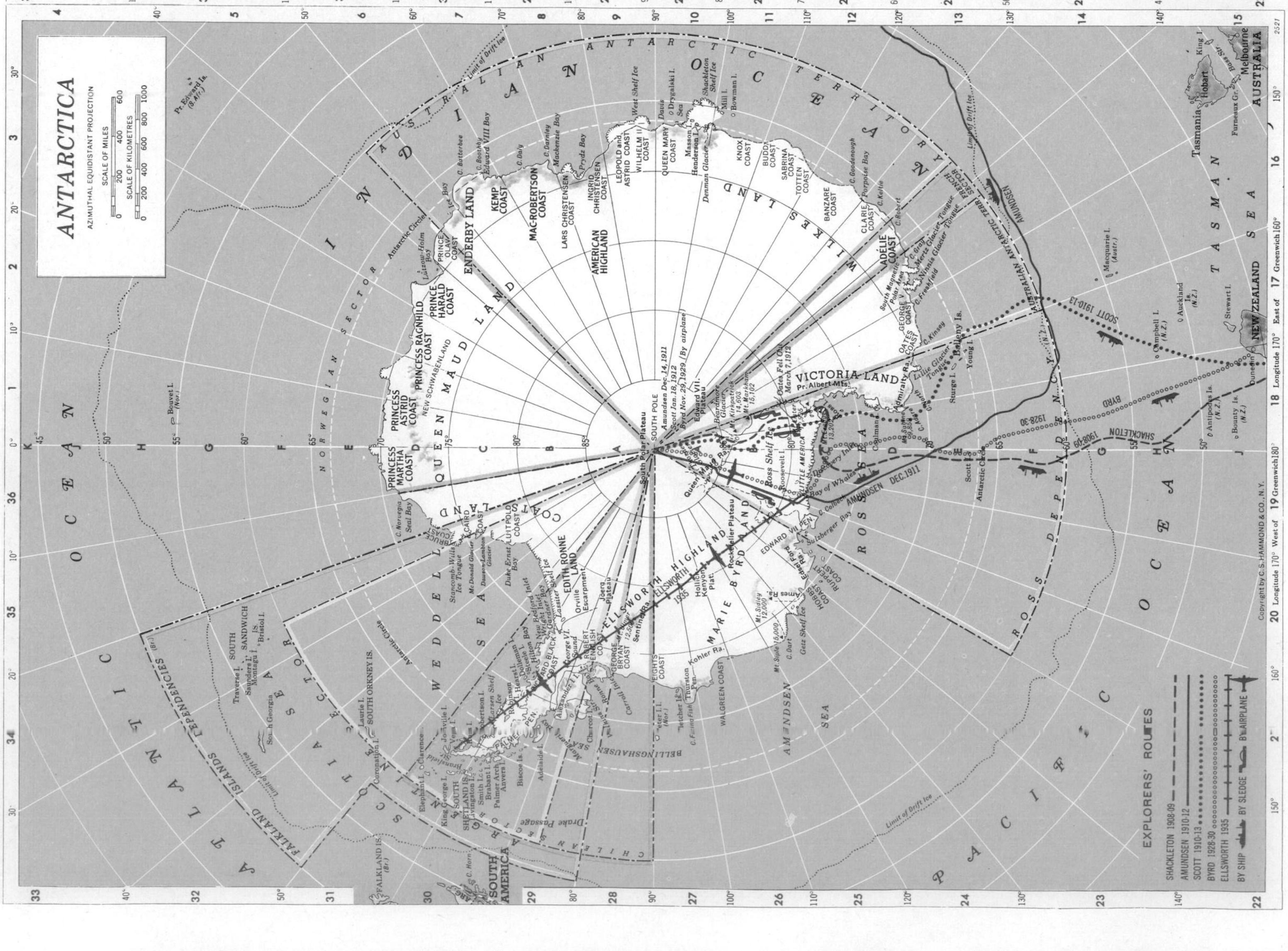

## ANTARCTICA
AZIMUTHAL EQUIDISTANT PROJECTION

SCALE OF MILES
SCALE OF KILOMETRES

EXPLORERS' ROUTES

SHACKLETON 1908-09
AMUNDSEN 1910-12
SCOTT 1910-13
BYRD 1928-30
ELLSWORTH 1935
BY SHIP
BY SLEDGE
BY AIRPLANE

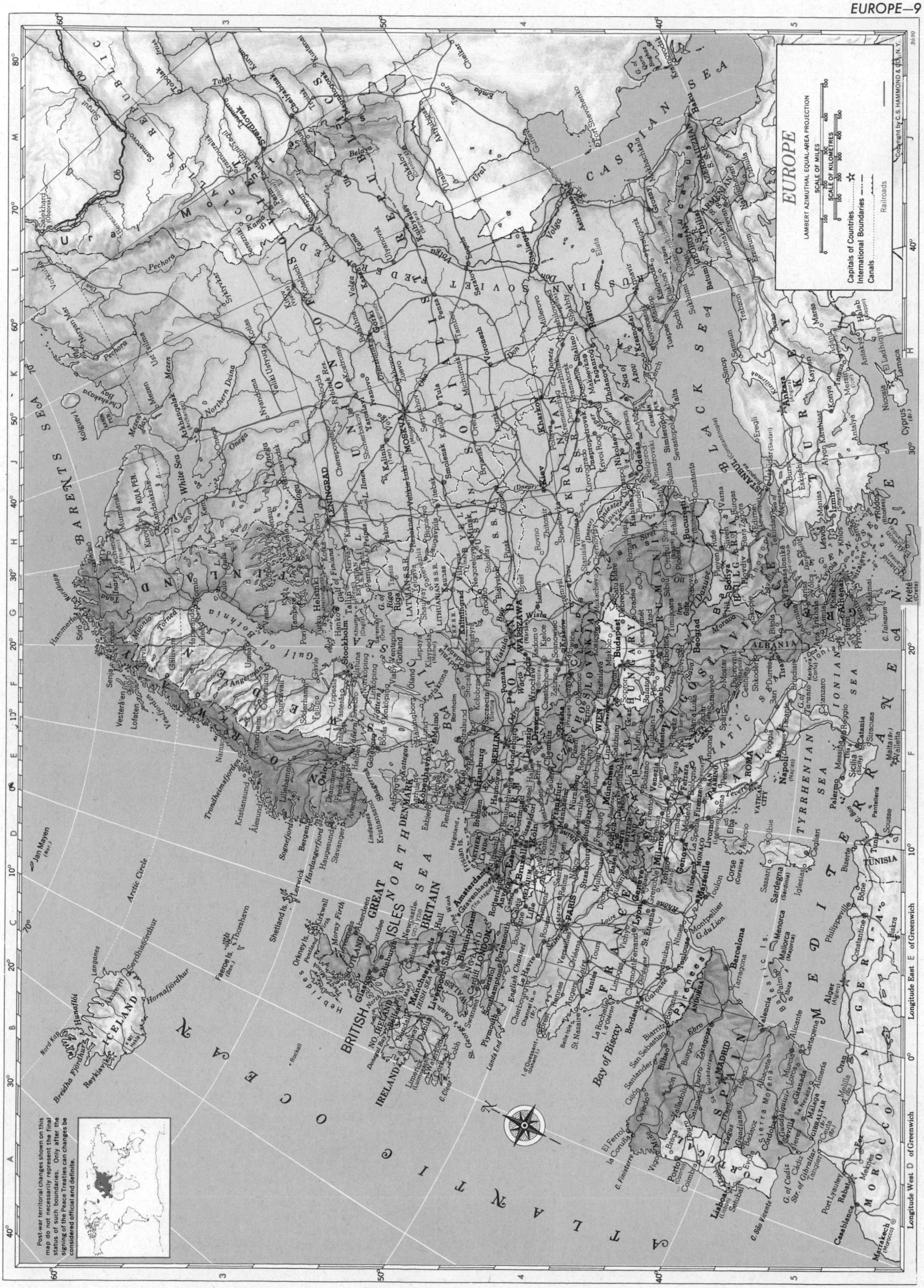

# EUROPE

LAMBERT AZIMUTHAL EQUAL-AREA PROJECTION

SCALE OF MILES

SCALE OF KILOMETRES

Capitals of Countries ............ ☆
International Boundaries ........
Canals ........................
Railroads

Post war territorial changes shown on this map do not necessarily represent the final status of such boundaries. Only after the signing of the Peace Treaties can changes be considered official and definite.

ARCTIC OCEAN

ATLANTIC OCEAN

BARENTS SEA

CASPIAN SEA

BLACK SEA

MEDITERRANEAN SEA

NORTH SEA

TYRRHENIAN SEA

IONIAN SEA

ADRIATIC SEA

RUSSIAN SOVIET FEDERATED SOCIALIST REPUBLIC

FINLAND

SWEDEN

NORWAY

DENMARK

GREAT BRITAIN

BRITISH ISLES

IRELAND

NO. IRELAND

SCOTLAND

ENGLAND

WALES

FRANCE

SPAIN

PORTUGAL

GERMANY

POLAND

CZECHOSLOVAKIA

HUNGARY

YUGOSLAVIA

ROMANIA

BULGARIA

ALBANIA

GREECE

ITALY

TURKEY

ALGERIA

MOROCCO

TUNISIA

ICELAND

NETHERLANDS

BELGIUM

LATVIAN S.S.R.

LITHUANIAN S.S.R.

UKRAINE

KRIM

LONDON

PARIS

MADRID

ROMA

WARSZAWA

MOSCOW

LENINGRAD

WIEN

BERLIN

BUDAPEST

Longitude West D of Greenwich

Longitude East E of Greenwich

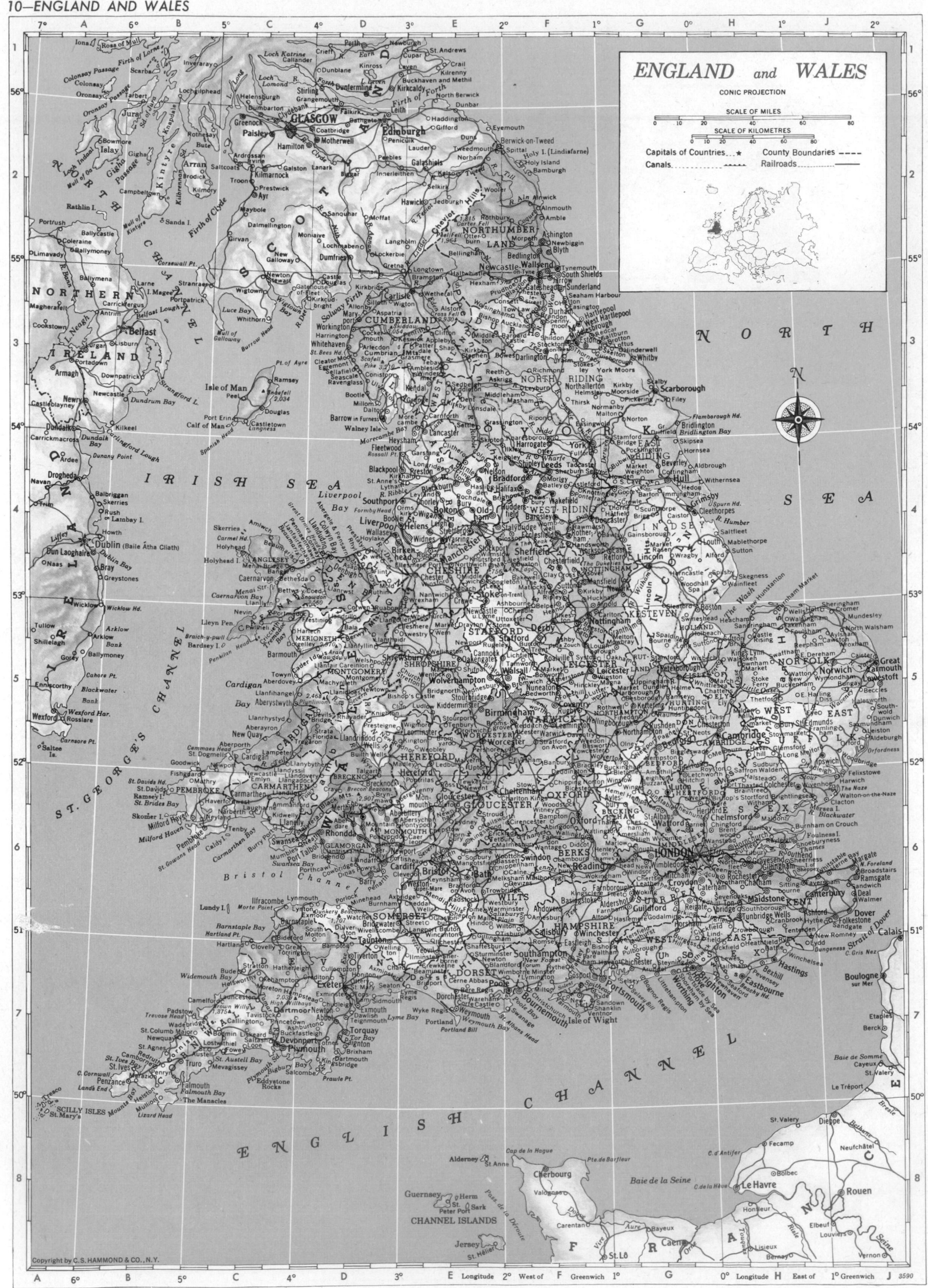

ENGLAND and WALES
CONIC PROJECTION
SCALE OF MILES
SCALE OF KILOMETRES

Capitals of Countries.....★     County Boundaries -----
Canals..............     Railroads_____

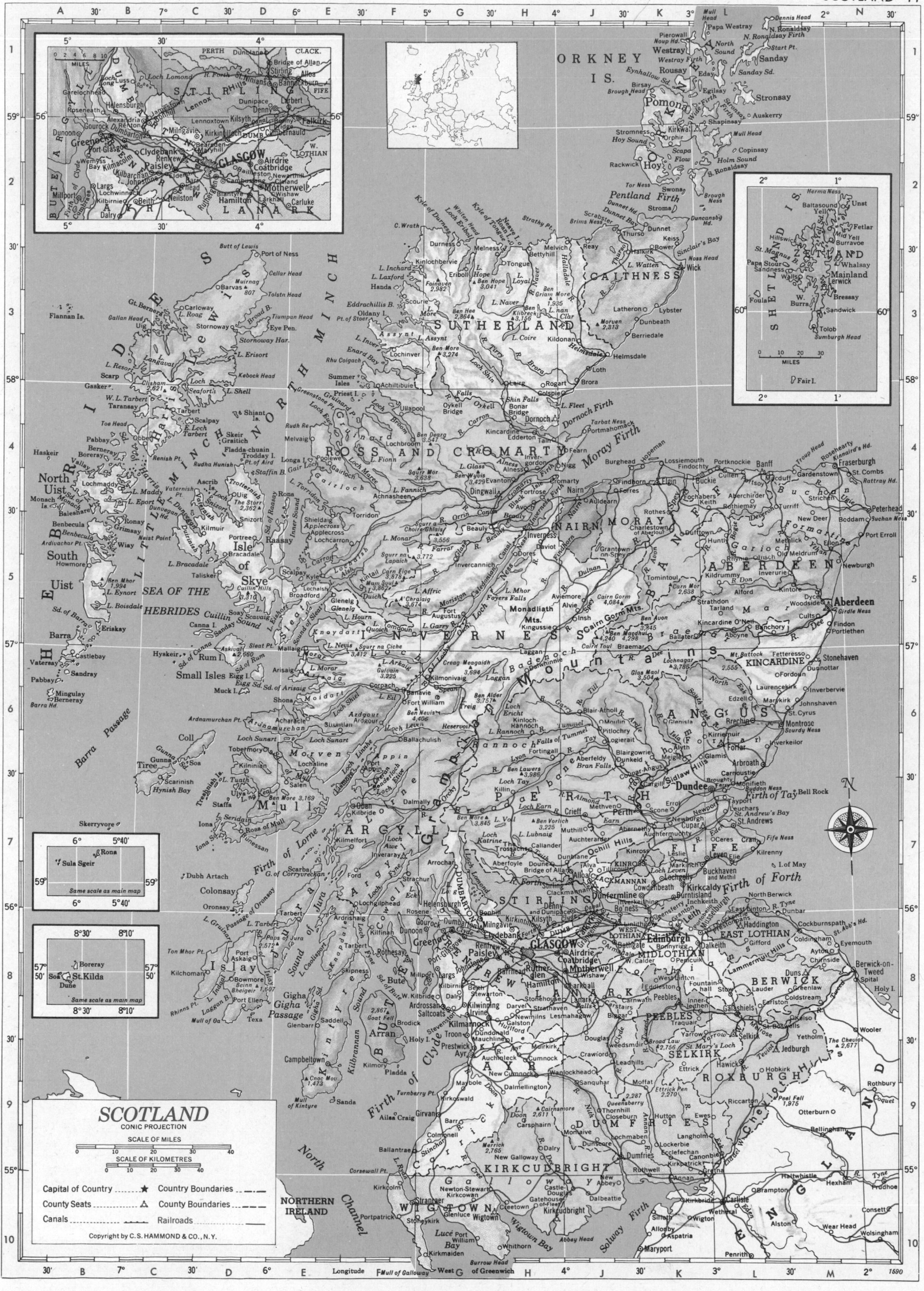

SCOTLAND
CONIC PROJECTION

SCALE OF MILES

SCALE OF KILOMETRES

Capital of Country .......... ★
County Seats .......... △
Canals ..........
Country Boundaries .......... ___
County Boundaries .......... ___
Railroads .......... ___

Copyright by C.S. HAMMOND & CO., N.Y.

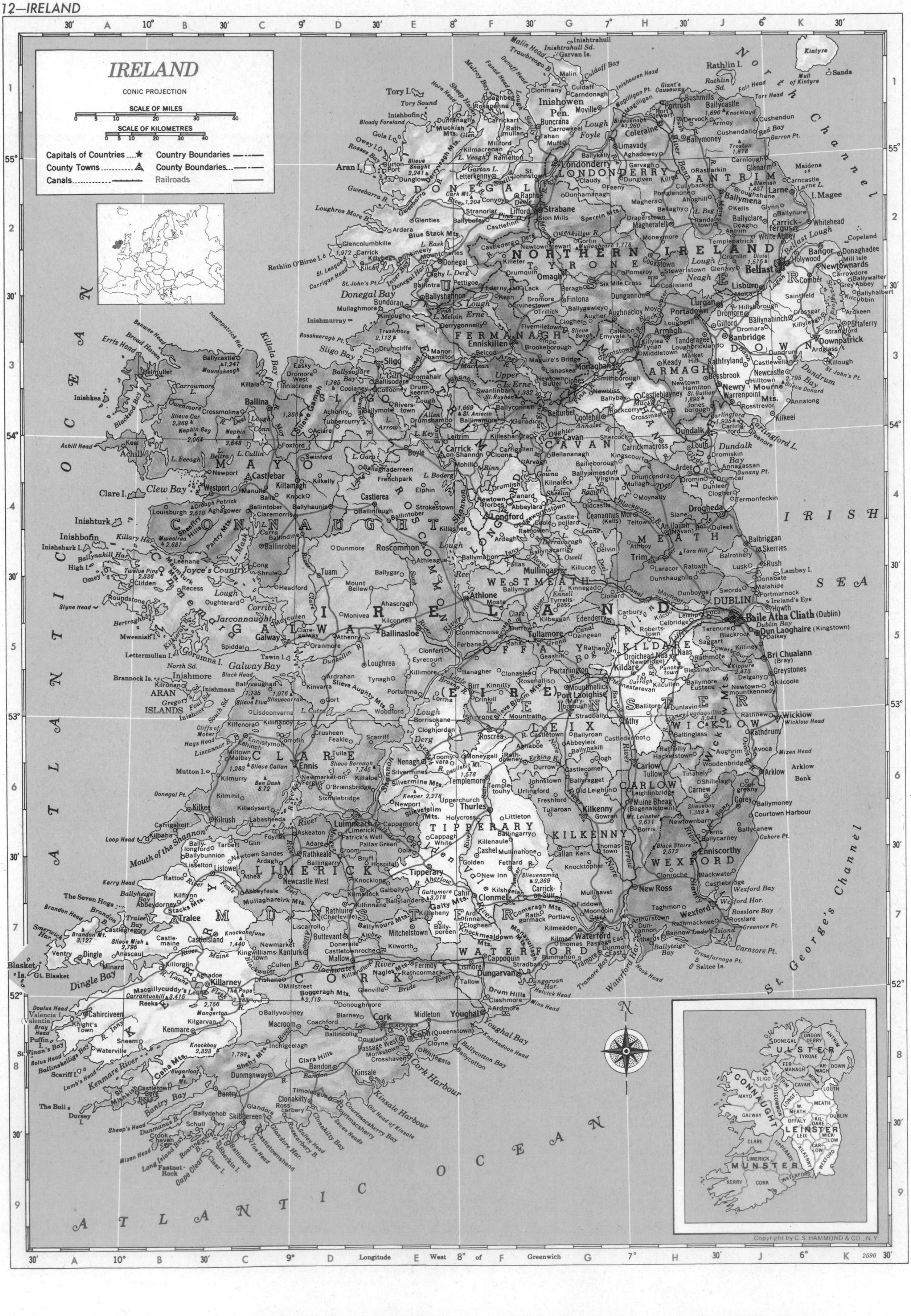

# IRELAND

CONIC PROJECTION

SCALE OF MILES

SCALE OF KILOMETRES

Capitals of Countries ......★  Country Boundaries ......———
County Towns ............△  County Boundaries......—··—
Canals..........————  Railroads ————

ATLANTIC OCEAN

NORTH CHANNEL

NORTHERN IRELAND

IRELAND (EIRE)

IRISH SEA

ST. GEORGE'S CHANNEL

DONEGAL

LONDONDERRY

ANTRIM

TYRONE

FERMANAGH

DOWN

ARMAGH

MONAGHAN

CAVAN

SLIGO

LEITRIM

MAYO

ROSCOMMON

LONGFORD

MEATH

WESTMEATH

CONNAUGHT

GALWAY

OFFALY

KILDARE

DUBLIN

LEIX

WICKLOW

CLARE

TIPPERARY

CARLOW

KILKENNY

WEXFORD

LIMERICK

MUNSTER

KERRY

CORK

WATERFORD

LEINSTER

ULSTER

Belfast

Londonderry

DUBLIN — Baile Atha Cliath (Dublin)

Dun Laoghaire (Kingstown)

ULSTER

CONNAUGHT

LEINSTER

MUNSTER

Copyright by C. S. HAMMOND & CO., N.Y.

Longitude West of Greenwich

2590

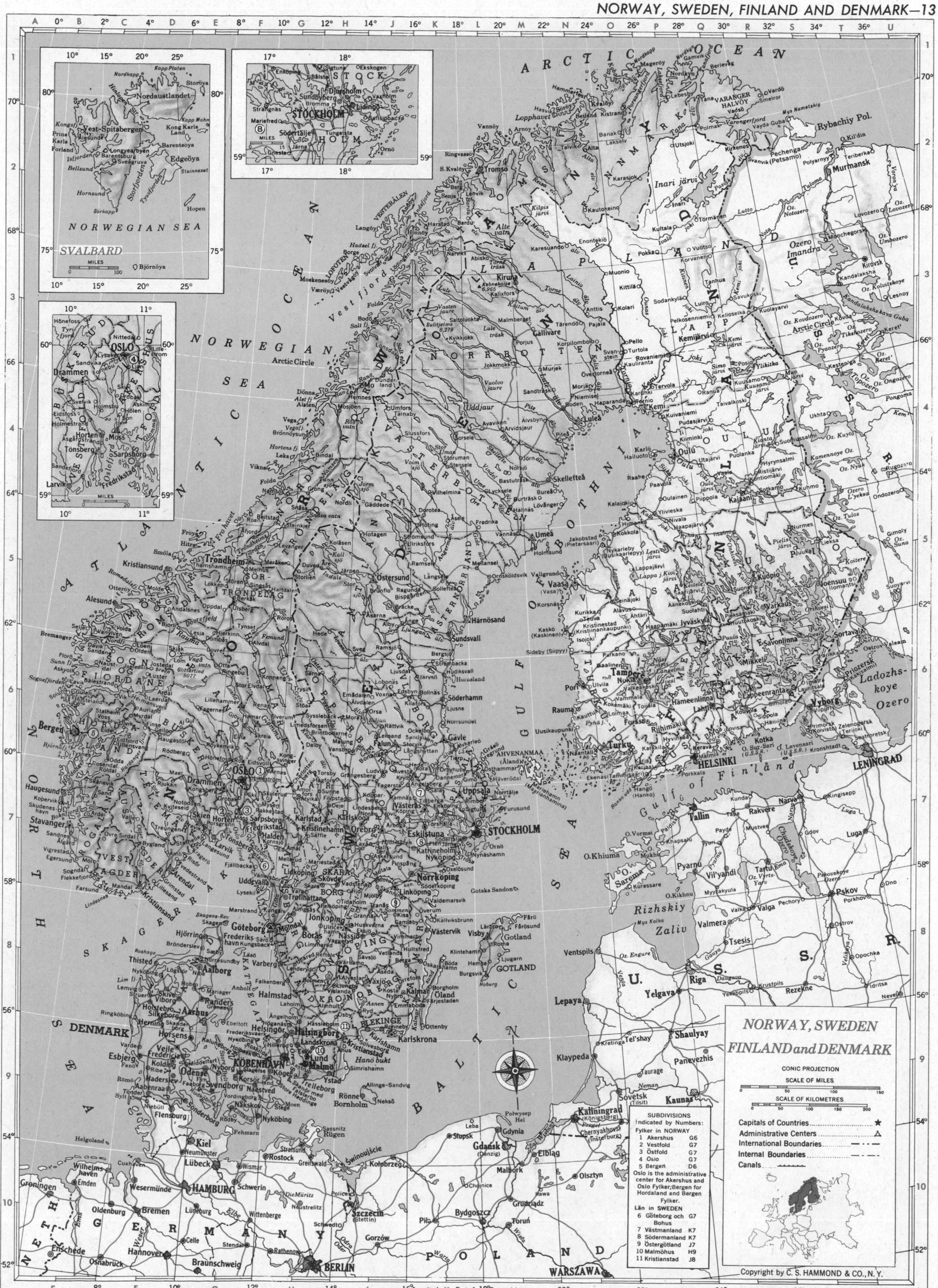

NORWAY, SWEDEN
FINLAND and DENMARK
CONIC PROJECTION
SCALE OF MILES
SCALE OF KILOMETRES
Capitals of Countries
Administrative Centers
International Boundaries
Internal Boundaries
Canals
SUBDIVISIONS
Indicated by Numbers:
Fylker in NORWAY
1 Akershus G6
2 Vestfold G7
3 Östfold G7
4 Oslo G7
5 Bergen D6
Oslo is the administrative center for Akershus and Oslo Fylker; Bergen for Hordaland and Bergen Fylker.
Län in SWEDEN
6 Göteborg och Bohus G7
7 Västmanland K7
8 Södermanland K7
9 Östergötland J7
10 Malmöhus H9
11 Kristianstad J8
SVALBARD
NORWEGIAN SEA
STOCKHOLM
OSLO
ARCTIC OCEAN
NORWEGIAN SEA
ATLANTIC OCEAN
NORTH SEA
SKAGERRAK
KATTEGAT
GULF OF BOTHNIA
BALTIC SEA
Gulf of Finland
DENMARK
GERMANY
POLAND
U.S.S.R.
HELSINKI
LENINGRAD
KØBENHAVN
BERLIN
WARSZAWA
Longitude East of Greenwich
Copyright by C. S. HAMMOND & CO., N.Y.
9511

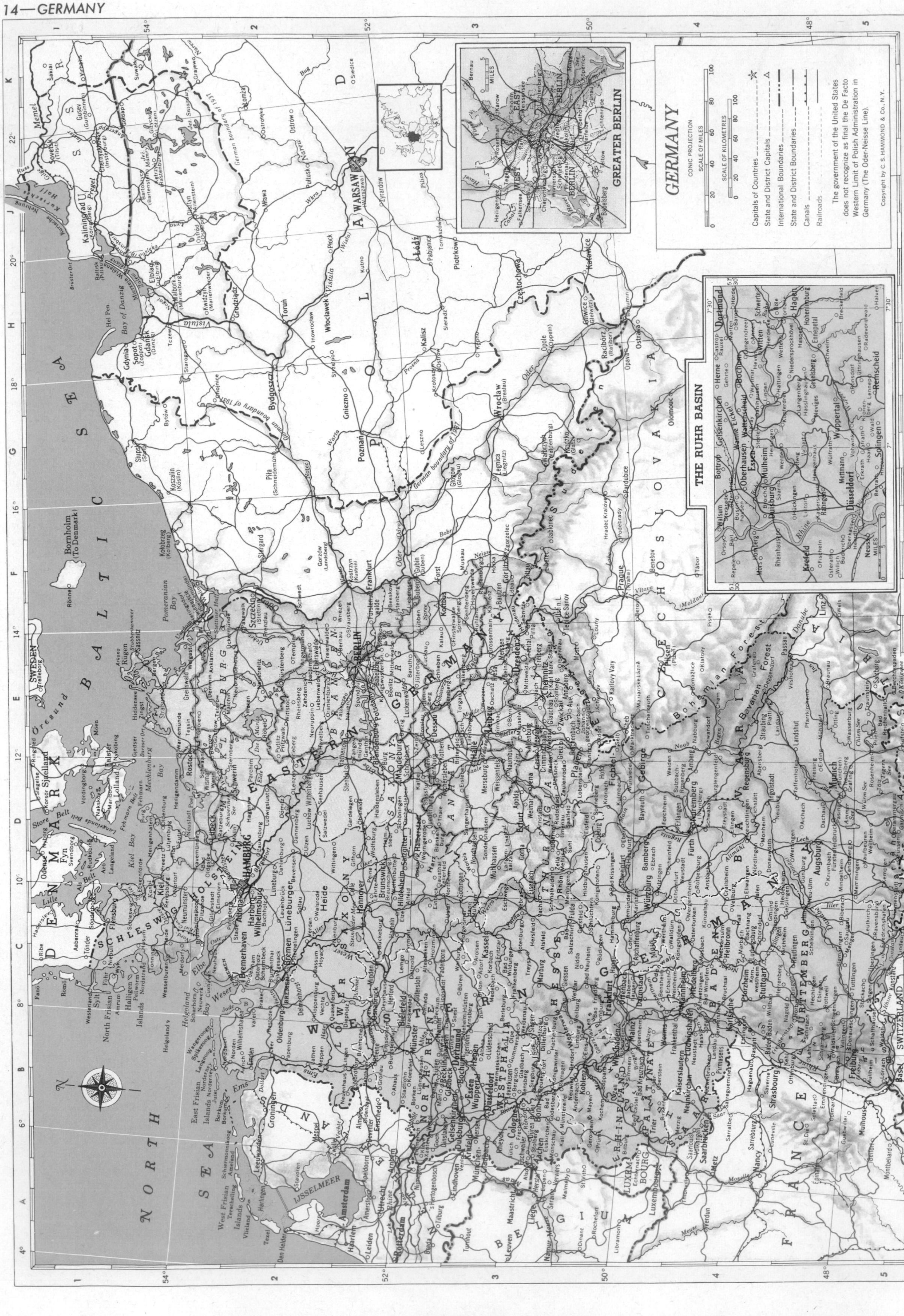

GERMANY
CONIC PROJECTION
SCALE OF MILES
SCALE OF KILOMETRES
Capitals of Countries
State and District Capitals
International Boundaries
State and District Boundaries
Canals
Railroads
The government of the United States does not recognize as final the De Facto Western Limit of Polish Administration in Germany (The Oder-Neisse Line).
Copyright by C. S. HAMMOND & Co., N.Y.
GREATER BERLIN
THE RUHR BASIN
NORTH SEA
BALTIC SEA
Longitude East of Greenwich

NETHERLANDS, BELGIUM
and LUXEMBOURG

CONIC PROJECTION

SCALE OF MILES

SCALE OF KILOMETRES

Capitals of Countries · · · · · · · · · · · · ★
Provincial Capitals · · · · · · · · · · · · ⊞
International Boundaries · · · · · · ·—··—··
Provincial Boundaries · · · · · · · · · · · —·—·—
Canals · · · · · · · · · · · · · · · · · · · · · · · ·
Railroads · · · · · · · · · · · · · · · · · · · · · ·

Elevations in Feet

AMSTERDAM

BRUXELLES (Brussel)

Longitude 5° East of Greenwich

Copyright by C. S. HAMMOND & CO., N. Y.

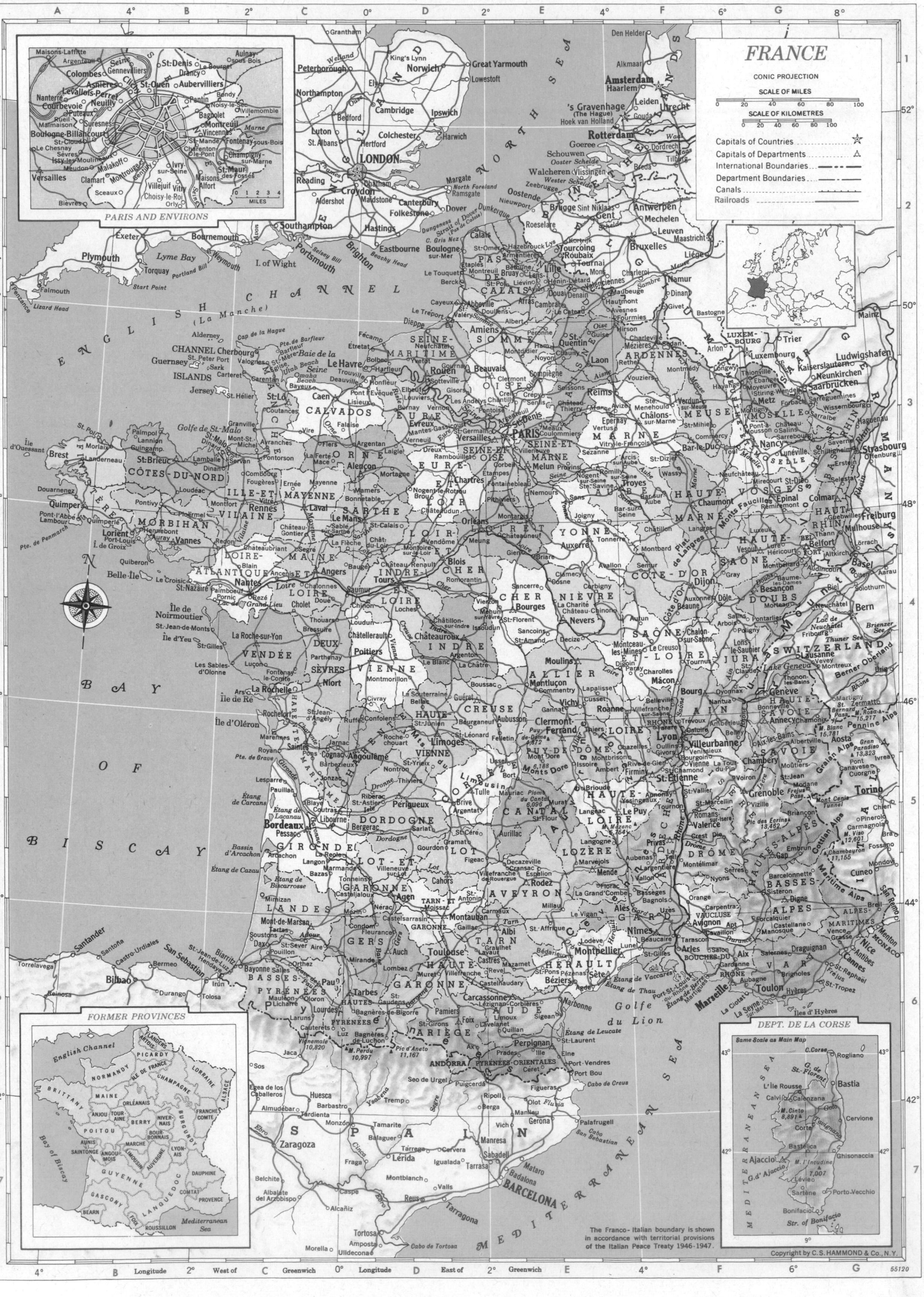

# FRANCE

CONIC PROJECTION

SCALE OF MILES

0  20  40  60  80  100

SCALE OF KILOMETRES

0  20  40  60  80  100

Capitals of Countries ........... ☆
Capitals of Departments ........ △
International Boundaries ....... — ·· —
Department Boundaries ......... — · —
Canals ..........................
Railroads .......................

**PARIS AND ENVIRONS**

**FORMER PROVINCES**

**DEPT. DE LA CORSE**

Same Scale as Main Map

The Franco-Italian boundary is shown in accordance with territorial provisions of the Italian Peace Treaty 1946-1947.

Copyright by C. S. HAMMOND & Co., N.Y.

Longitude 2° West of Greenwich 0° Longitude East of 2° Greenwich

55120

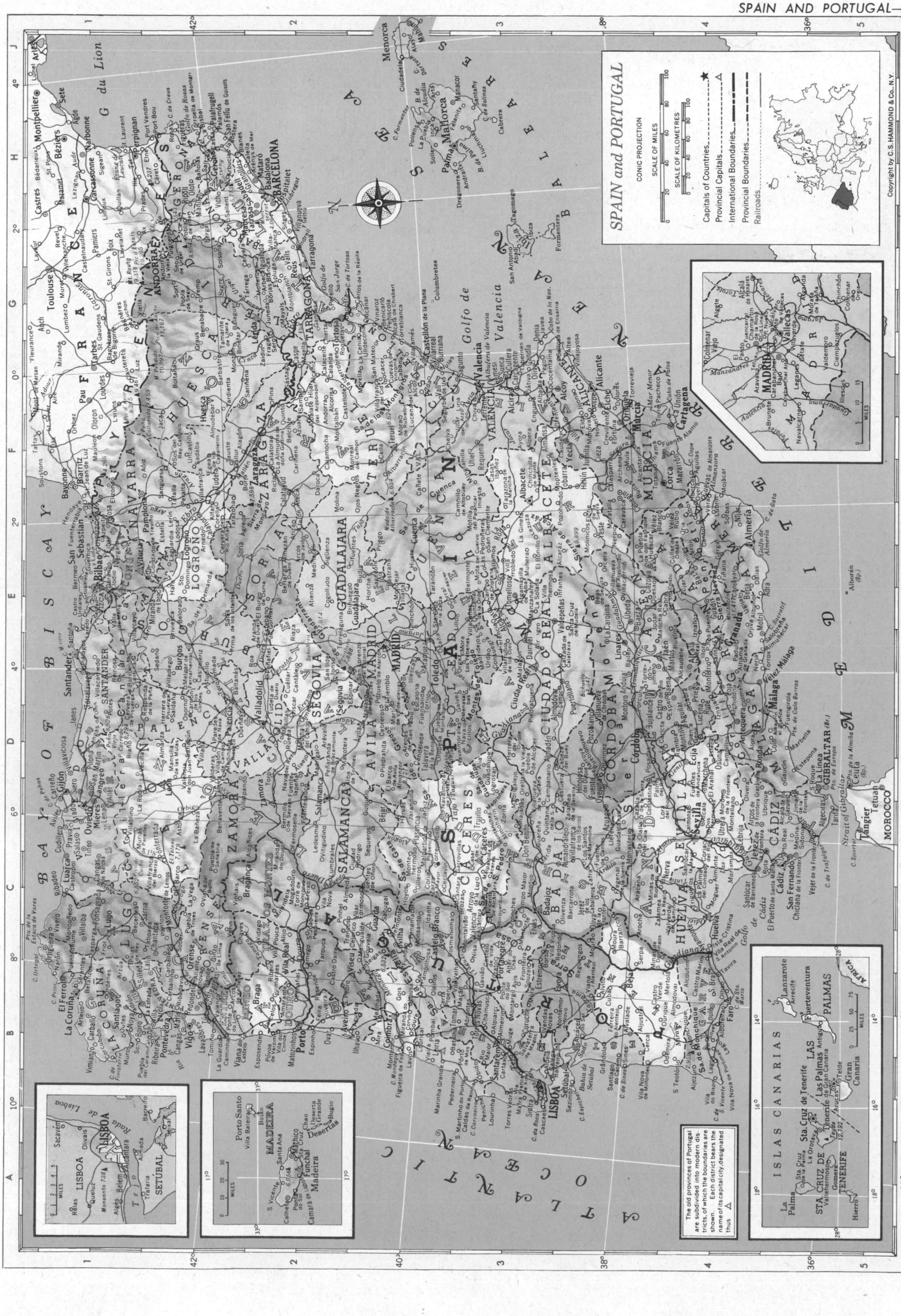

## SPAIN and PORTUGAL

CONIC PROJECTION

SCALE OF MILES

SCALE OF KILOMETRES

Capitals of Countries..........⊛
Provincial Capitals...............★
International Boundaries.......—·—·—
Provincial Boundaries...........
Railroads............................

Copyright by C.S. HAMMOND & Co., N.Y.

The old provinces of Portugal are subdivided into modern districts, of which the boundaries are shown. Each district bears the name of its capital city, designated thus △

ISLAS CANARIAS

LAS PALMAS

STA. CRUZ DE TENERIFE

MADEIRA

LISBOA — SETUBAL

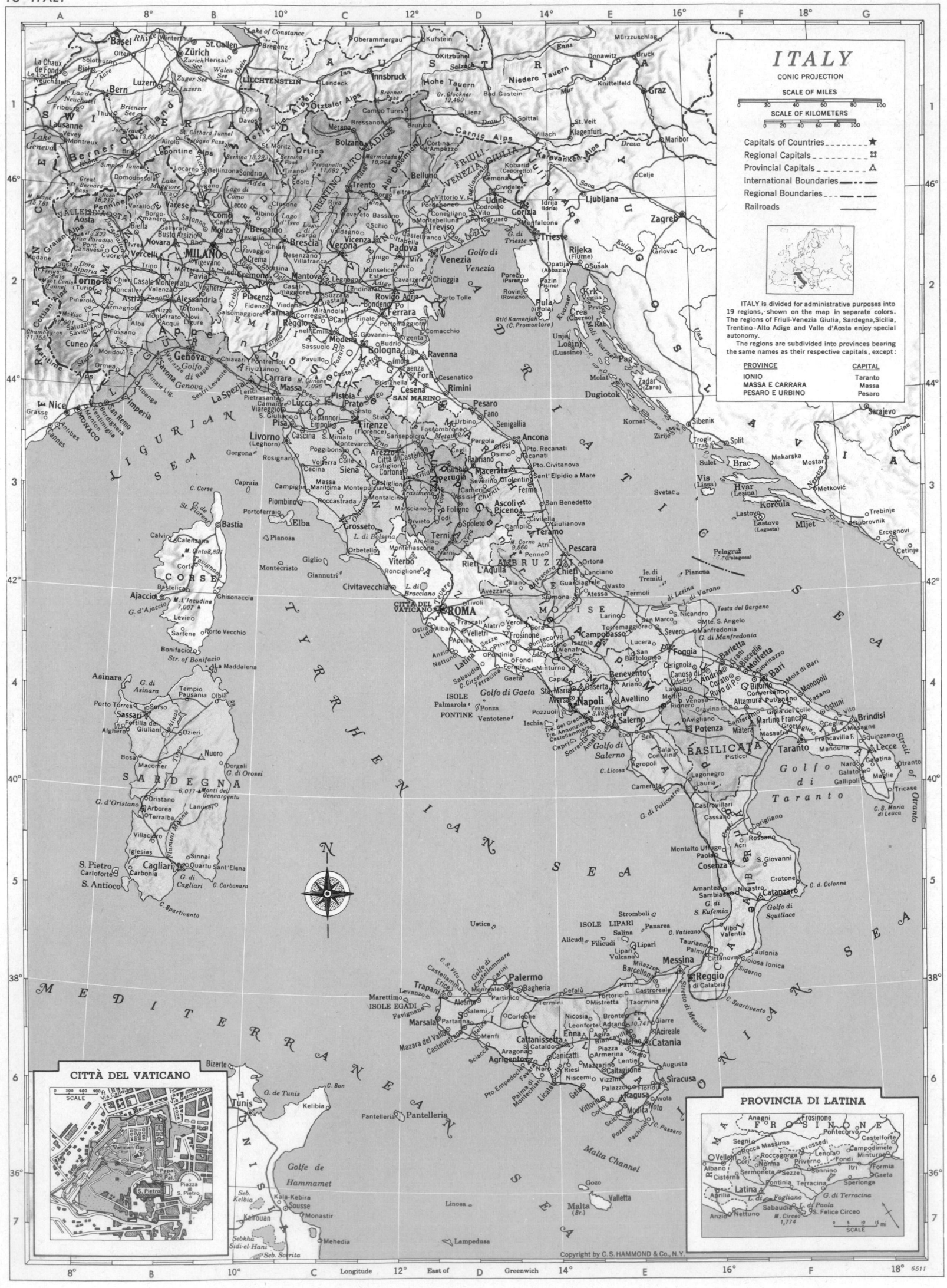

ITALY
CONIC PROJECTION
SCALE OF MILES
SCALE OF KILOMETERS

Capitals of Countries ........ ★
Regional Capitals ............ ⊞
Provincial Capitals .......... △
International Boundaries ...... — ·· —
Regional Boundaries .......... — · —
Railroads ....................

ITALY is divided for administrative purposes into 19 regions, shown on the map in separate colors. The regions of Friuli-Venezia Giulia, Sardegna, Sicilia, Trentino-Alto Adige and Valle d'Aosta enjoy special autonomy.

The regions are subdivided into provinces bearing the same names as their respective capitals, except:

| PROVINCE | CAPITAL |
|---|---|
| IONIO | Taranto |
| MASSA E CARRARA | Massa |
| PESARO E URBINO | Pesaro |

CITTÀ DEL VATICANO
SCALE

PROVINCIA DI LATINA
SCALE

Copyright by C. S. HAMMOND & Co., N.Y.

Longitude    East of    Greenwich

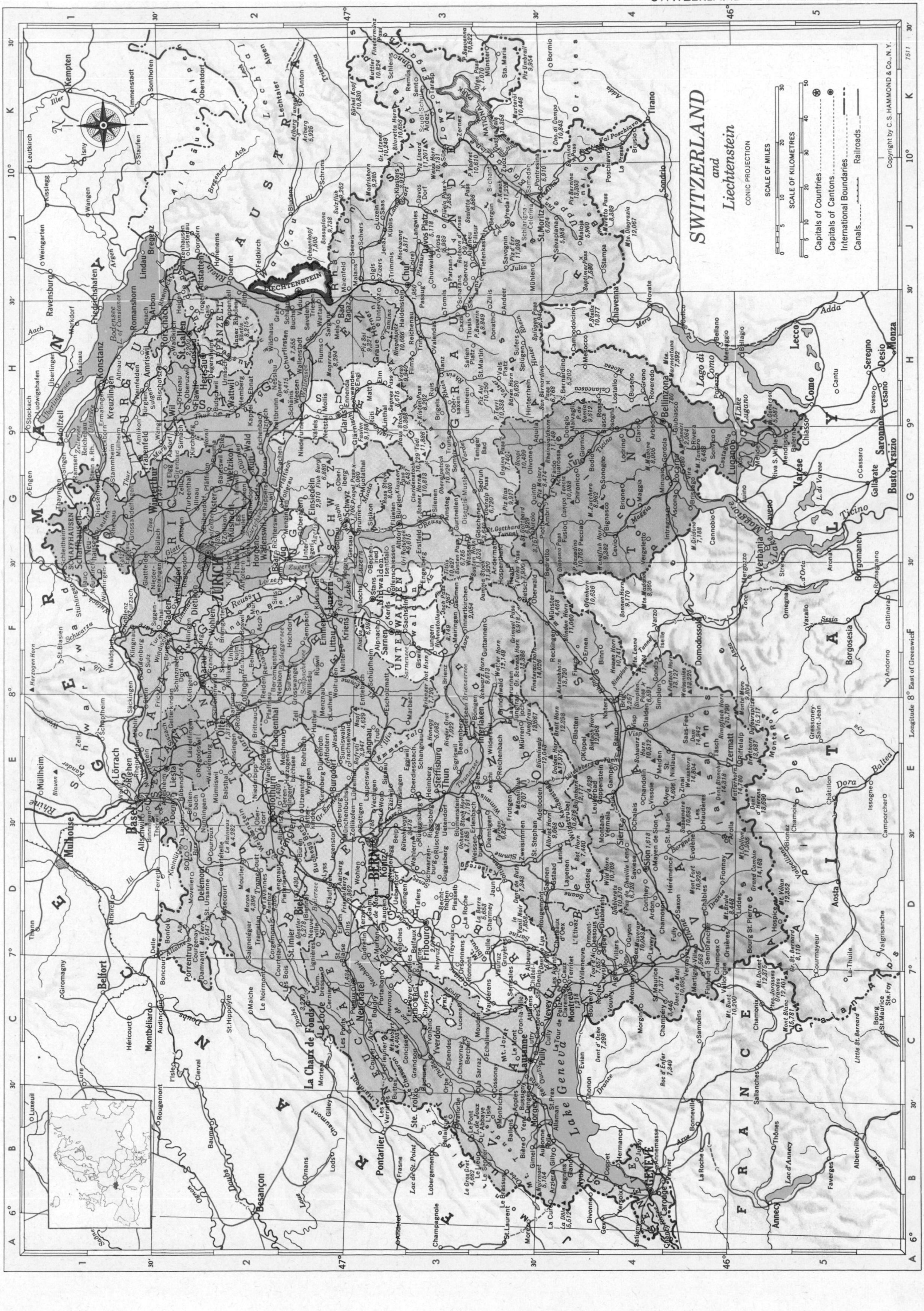

## SWITZERLAND
### *and*
### *Liechtenstein*

CONIC PROJECTION

SCALE OF MILES

SCALE OF KILOMETRES

⊛ Capitals of Countries
⊙ Capitals of Cantons
International Boundaries
Canals
Railroads

Copyright by C. S. HAMMOND & Co., N.Y.

Longitude 8° East of Greenwich

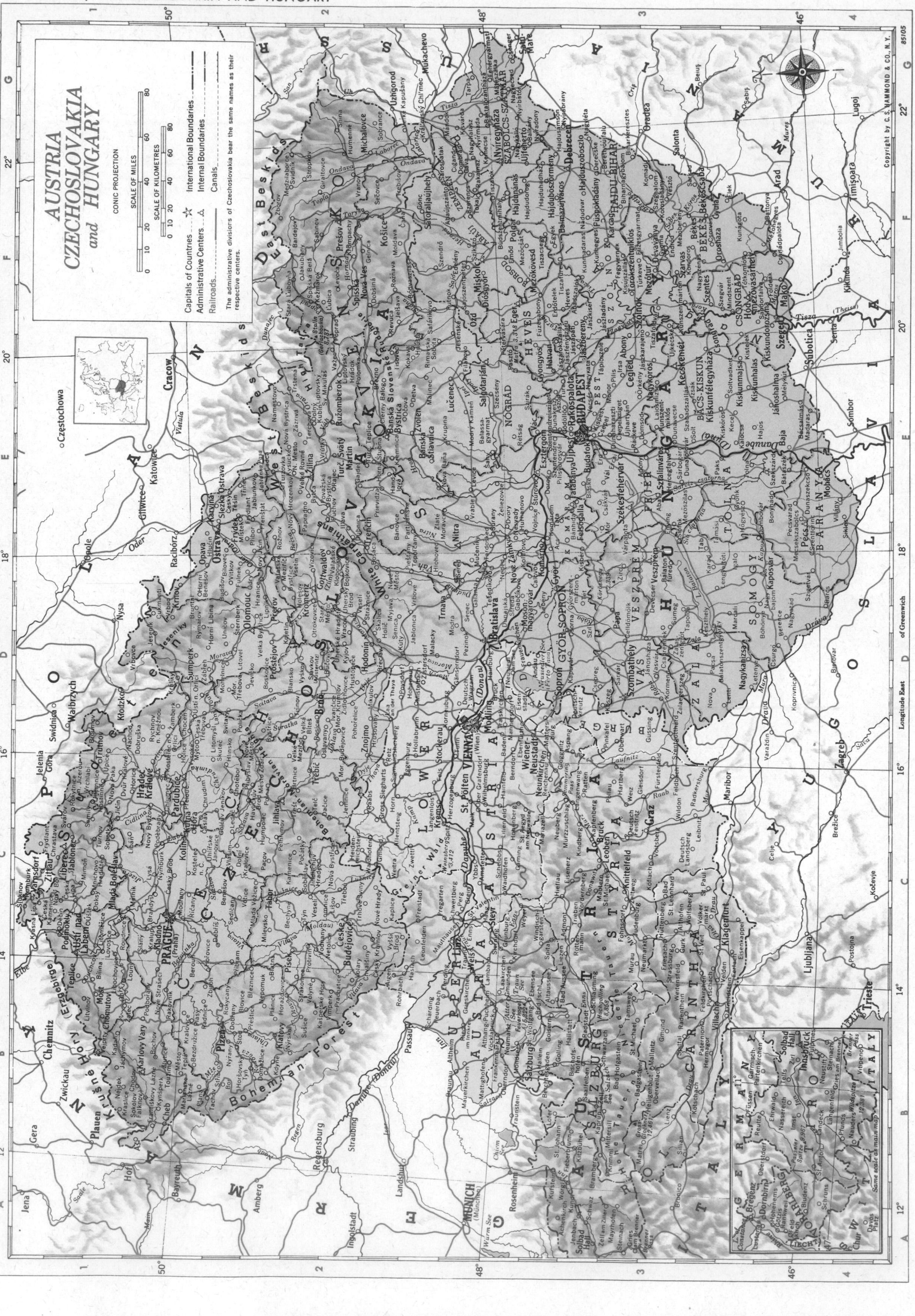

AUSTRIA
CZECHOSLOVAKIA
and HUNGARY

CONIC PROJECTION

SCALE OF MILES
0 10 20 40 60 80

SCALE OF KILOMETRES
0 10 20 40 60 80

Capitals of Countries ........ ☆
Administrative Centers ...... △
Railroads ................

International Boundaries ......
Internal Boundaries ..........
Canals ....................

The administrative divisions of Czechoslovakia bear the same names as their respective centers.

Copyright by C. S. HAMMOND & CO., N.Y.

85105

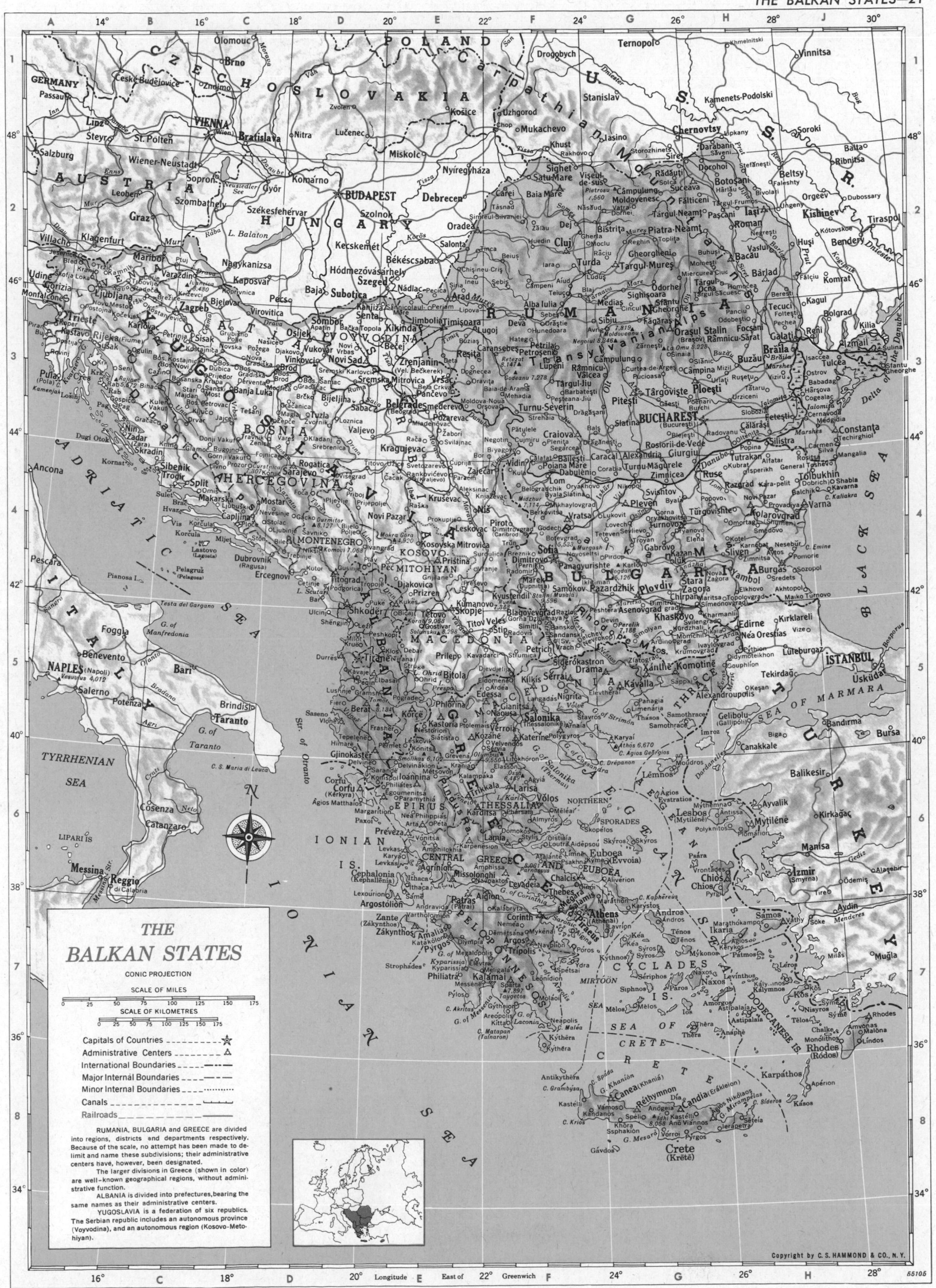

## THE BALKAN STATES

CONIC PROJECTION

SCALE OF MILES

0  25  50  75  100  125  150  175

SCALE OF KILOMETRES

0  25  50  75  100  125  150  175

Capitals of Countries  ⸻⸻☆

Administrative Centers  ⸻⸻△

International Boundaries  ⸻ ⸺ ⸻

Major Internal Boundaries  ⸻ ⸺ ⸻

Minor Internal Boundaries  ⸻ ⸺ ⸻

Canals  ⸻⸻⸻

Railroads  ⸻⸻⸻

RUMANIA, BULGARIA and GREECE are divided
into regions, districts and departments respectively.
Because of the scale, no attempt has been made to de-
limit and name these subdivisions; their administrative
centers have, however, been designated.
  The larger divisions in Greece (shown in color)
are well-known geographical regions, without administrative function.
  ALBANIA is divided into prefectures, bearing the
same names as their administrative centers.
  YUGOSLAVIA is a federation of six republics.
The Serbian republic includes an autonomous province
(Voyvodina), and an autonomous region (Kosovo-Meto-
hiyan).

Copyright by C. S. HAMMOND & CO., N.Y.

85105

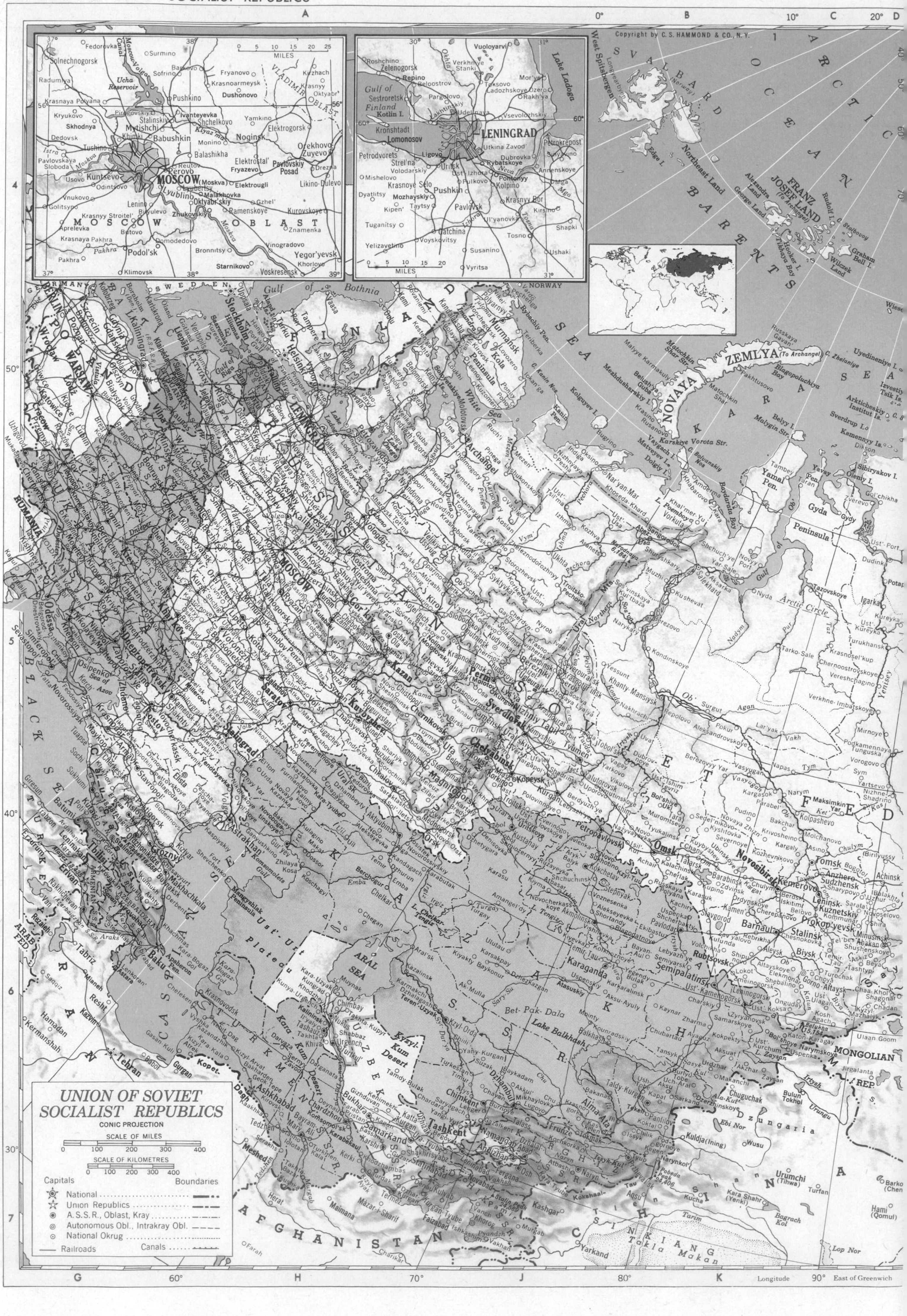

Copyright by C.S. HAMMOND & CO., N.Y.

**MOSCOW**

MOSCOW OBLAST

VLADIMIR OBLAST

Ucha Reservoir

MILES
0 5 10 15 20 25

**LENINGRAD**

Gulf of Finland

MILES
0 5 10 15 20

## UNION OF SOVIET SOCIALIST REPUBLICS

CONIC PROJECTION

SCALE OF MILES
0 100 200 300 400

SCALE OF KILOMETRES
0 100 200 300 400

| Capitals | | Boundaries |
|---|---|---|
| National | ⊛ | |
| Union Republics | ★ | |
| A.S.S.R., Oblast, Kray | ⊚ | |
| Autonomous Obl., Intrakray Obl. | ⊛ | |
| National Okrug | ⊙ | |
| Railroads | | Canals |

ARCTIC OCEAN

SVALBARD

FRANZ JOSEF LAND (To Archangel)

BARENTS SEA

NOVAYA ZEMLYA (To Archangel)

KARA SEA

WHITE SEA

GULF OF BOTHNIA

FINLAND

SWEDEN

NORWAY

BALTIC SEA

GERMANY

POLAND

RUMANIA

BLACK SEA

Sea of Azov

CASPIAN SEA

ARAL SEA

Kyzyl-Kum Desert

Kara-Kum

Ust'-Urt Plateau

IRAN

ARAB FED.

TURKEY

AFGHANISTAN

MONGOLIAN REP.

SINKIANG

Takla Makan

Lop Nor

Longitude 90° East of Greenwich

MOSCOW

LENINGRAD

Archangel

Murmansk

Kola Peninsula

Omsk

Novosibirsk

Stalinsk

Karaganda

Lake Balkhash

Alma Ata

Tashkent

Samarkand

Bukhara

Baku

Tbilisi

Erivan

Rostov

Stalingrad

Saratov

Kuybyshev

Kazan

Perm

Sverdlovsk

Chelyabinsk

Magnitogorsk

Ufa

Gor'kiy

## Administrative Divisions Legend

ADMINISTRATIVE DIVISIONS OF UNION REPUBLICS BEAR SAME
NAMES AS THEIR RESPECTIVE CAPITALS OR CENTERS, EXCEPT:

| Division | Capital | Ref. | Division | Capital | Ref. |
|---|---|---|---|---|---|
| Abkhaz A.S.S.R. | Sukhumi | F5 | Kashka-Dar'ya Oblast | Karshi | H6 |
| Adygey Aut. Oblast | Maykop | F5 | Khakass Aut. Oblast | Abakan | L4 |
| Adzhar A.S.S.R. | Batumi | F5 | Khorezm Oblast | Urgench | H5 |
| Aginsk Nat'l Okrug | Aginskoye | N4 | Komi A.S.S.R. | Syktyvkar | G3 |
| Altay Kray | Barnaul | K4 | Komi-Permyak Nat'l Okrug | Kudymkar | G4 |
| Amur Oblast | Blagoveshchensk | O4 | Koryak Nat'l Okrug | Palana | T4 |
| Bashkir A.S.S.R. | Ufa | F4 | Mari A.S.S.R. | Yoshkar-Ola | F4 |
| Buryat-Mongol A.S.S.R. | Ulan-Ude | M4 | Maritime Kray | Vladivostok | P5 |
| Chechen-Ingush A.S.S.R. | Groznyy | F5 | Mordvinian A.S.S.R. | Saransk | F4 |
| Cherkess Aut. Oblast | Cherkessk | F5 | Nagorno-Karabakh Aut. Oblast | Stepanakert | F6 |
| Chukchi Nat'l Okrug | Anadyr' | U3 | Nenets Nat'l Okrug | Nar'yan-Mar | G3 |
| Chuvash A.S.S.R. | Cheboksary | F4 | North Kazakhstan Oblast | Petropavlovsk | H4 |
| Crimean Oblast | Simferopol' | E5 | North Osetian A.S.S.R. | Ordzhonikidze | F5 |
| Dagestan A.S.S.R. | Makhachkala | F5 | South Kazakhstan Oblast | Chimkent | H5 |
| East Kazakhstan Oblast | Ust'-Kamenogorsk | K4 | South Osetian Aut. Oblast | Stalinir' | F5 |
| Evenki Nat'l Okrug | Tura | L3 | Surkhan-Dar'ya Oblast | Termez | H6 |
| Gorno-Altay Aut. Oblast | Gorno-Altaysk | K4 | Tatar A.S.S.R. | Kazan' | F4 |
| Gorno-Badakhshan Aut. Oblast | Khorog | J6 | Taymyr (Dolgano-Nenets) Nat'l Okr. | Dudinka | K3 |
| Issyk-Kul' Oblast | Przheval'sk | J5 | Trans-Carpathian Oblast | Uzhgorod | D5 |
| Jewish Aut. Oblast | Birobidzhan | O4 | Tuvinian Aut. Oblast | Kyzyl | L4 |
| Kabardin-Balkar A.S.S.R. | Nal'chik | F5 | Tyan'-Shan' Oblast | Naryn | J5 |
| Kalmuck Aut. Oblast | Elista | F5 | Udmurt A.S.S.R. | Izhevsk | G4 |
| Kamchatka Oblast | Petropavlovsk-Kam. | S4 | Volyn Oblast | Lutsk | D4 |
| Kamensk Oblast | Kamensk-Shakhtinskiy | F5 | West Kazakhstan Oblast | Ural'sk | G4 |
| Karachai-Cherkess Aut. Oblast | Cherkessk | F5 | Yakut A.S.S.R. | Yakutsk | O3 |
| Kara-Kalpak Oblast | Nukus | G5 | Yamal-Nenets Nat'l Okrug | Salekhard | H3 |
| Karelian A.S.S.R. | Petrozavodsk | E3 | | | |

Inset maps: UKRAINIAN S.S.R.; KAZAKH S.S.R.; KIRGHIZ S.S.R.; UZBEK S.S.R.; TADZHIK S.S.R. (Tashkent); KEMEROVO OBLAST; PERM OBLAST / SVERDLOVSK OBLAST.

Major labels: SEVERNAYA ZEMLYA, LAPTEV SEA, EAST SIBERIAN SEA, NEW SIBERIAN ISLANDS, Taymyr Peninsula, Cherskiy Range, Verkhoyansk Range, Vilyuy Range, Stanovoy Range, Yablonovyy Range, Baykal Range, Anadyr' Range, Koryak Range, Kamchatka Peninsula, SEA OF OKHOTSK, BERING SEA, CHUKCHI SEA, SEA OF JAPAN, KURIL ISLANDS, SAKHALIN, RUSSIAN SOVIET FEDERATED SOCIALIST REPUBLIC, MONGOLIAN PEOPLE'S REPUBLIC, CHINA, ALASKA (U.S.).

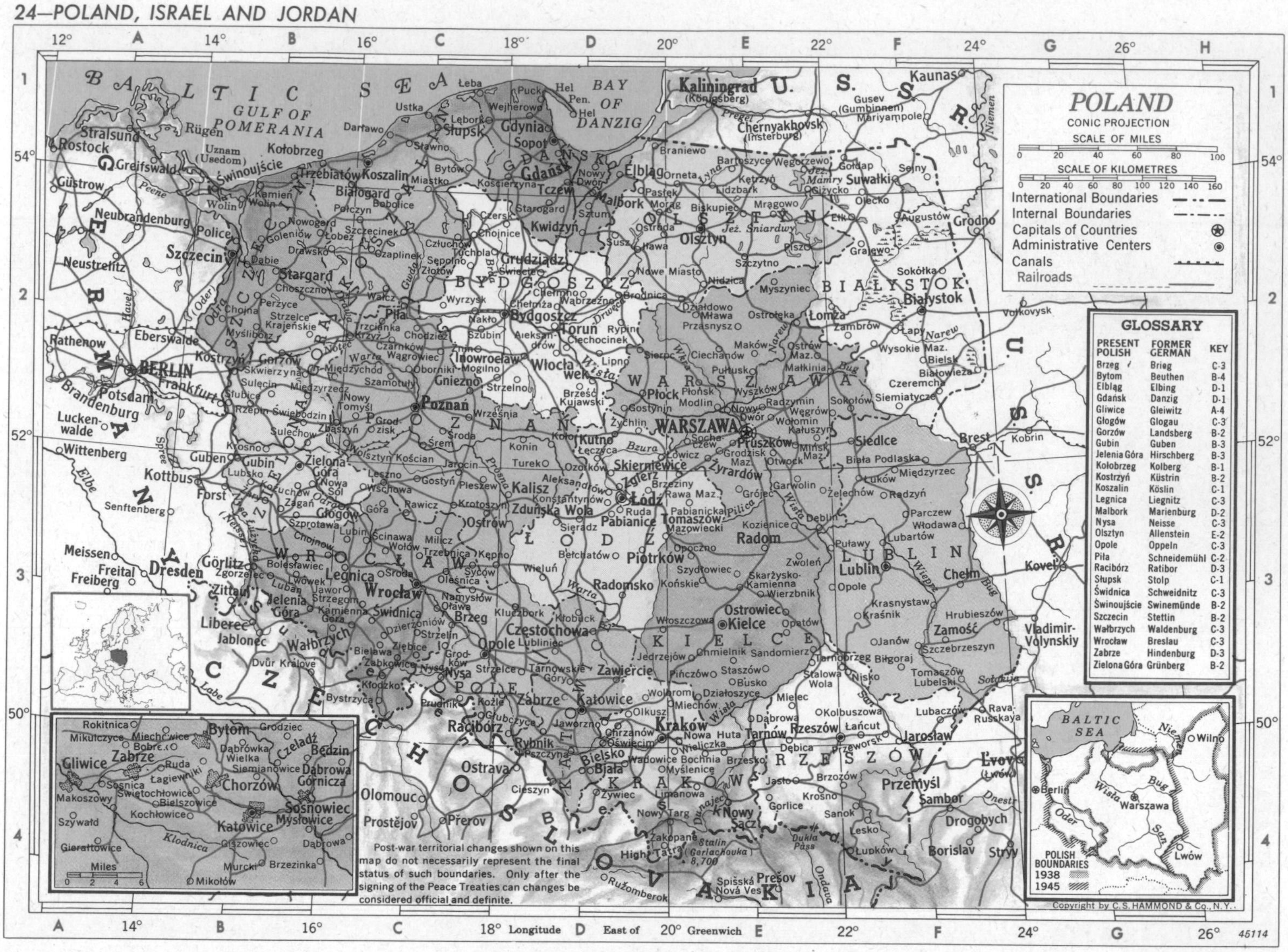

## POLAND
### CONIC PROJECTION
#### SCALE OF MILES
0 20 40 60 80 100
#### SCALE OF KILOMETRES
0 20 40 60 80 100 120 140 160

International Boundaries
Internal Boundaries
Capitals of Countries
Administrative Centers
Canals
Railroads

### GLOSSARY

| PRESENT POLISH | FORMER GERMAN | KEY |
|---|---|---|
| Brzeg | Brieg | C-3 |
| Bytom | Beuthen | B-4 |
| Elbląg | Elbing | D-1 |
| Gdańsk | Danzig | D-1 |
| Gliwice | Gleiwitz | A-4 |
| Głogów | Glogau | C-3 |
| Gorzów | Landsberg | B-2 |
| Gubin | Guben | B-3 |
| Jelenia Góra | Hirschberg | B-3 |
| Kołobrzeg | Kolberg | B-1 |
| Kostrzyn | Küstrin | B-2 |
| Koszalin | Köslin | C-1 |
| Legnica | Liegnitz | C-3 |
| Malbork | Marienburg | D-2 |
| Nysa | Neisse | C-3 |
| Olsztyn | Allenstein | E-2 |
| Opole | Oppeln | C-3 |
| Piła | Schneidemühl | C-2 |
| Racibórz | Ratibor | D-3 |
| Słupsk | Stolp | C-1 |
| Świdnica | Schweidnitz | C-3 |
| Świnoujście | Swinemünde | B-2 |
| Szczecin | Stettin | B-2 |
| Wałbrzych | Waldenburg | C-3 |
| Wrocław | Breslau | C-3 |
| Zabrze | Hindenburg | D-3 |
| Zielona Góra | Grünberg | B-2 |

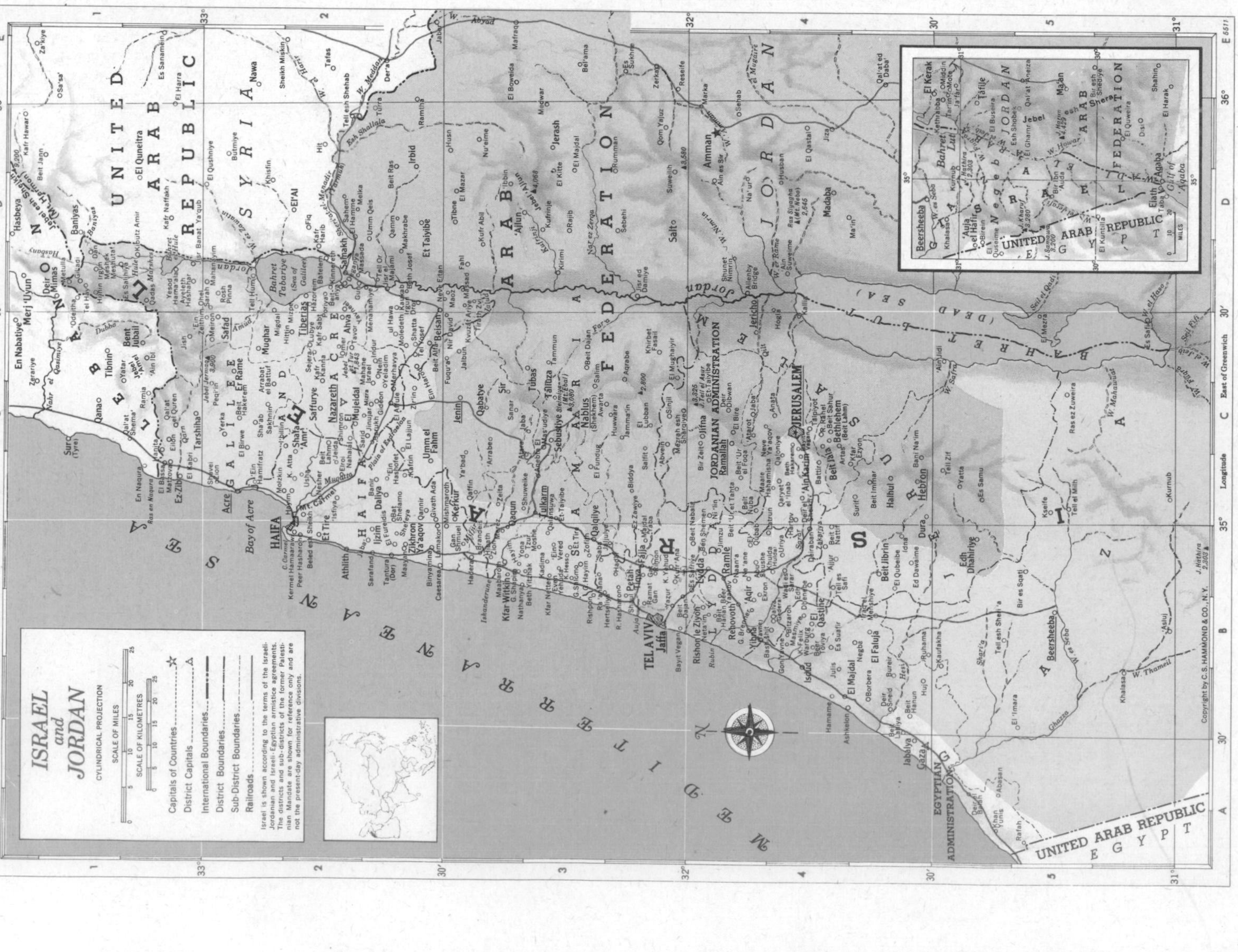

BALTIC SEA
POLISH BOUNDARIES
1938
1945

Copyright by C.S. Hammond & Co., N.Y.

Post-war territorial changes shown on this map do not necessarily represent the final status of such boundaries. Only after the signing of the Peace Treaties can changes be considered official and definite.

45114

### ISRAEL and JORDAN
#### CYLINDRICAL PROJECTION
SCALE OF MILES
SCALE OF KILOMETRES

Capitals of Countries
District Capitals
International Boundaries
District Boundaries
Sub-District Boundaries
Railroads

Israel is shown according to the terms of the Israeli-Jordanian and Israeli-Egyptian armistice agreements. The districts and sub-districts of the former Palestinian Mandate are shown for reference only and are not the present-day administrative divisions.

Copyright by C.S. Hammond & Co., N.Y.

E 6511

UNITED ARAB REPUBLIC
EGYPT

UNITED ARAB REPUBLIC
(EGYPT)

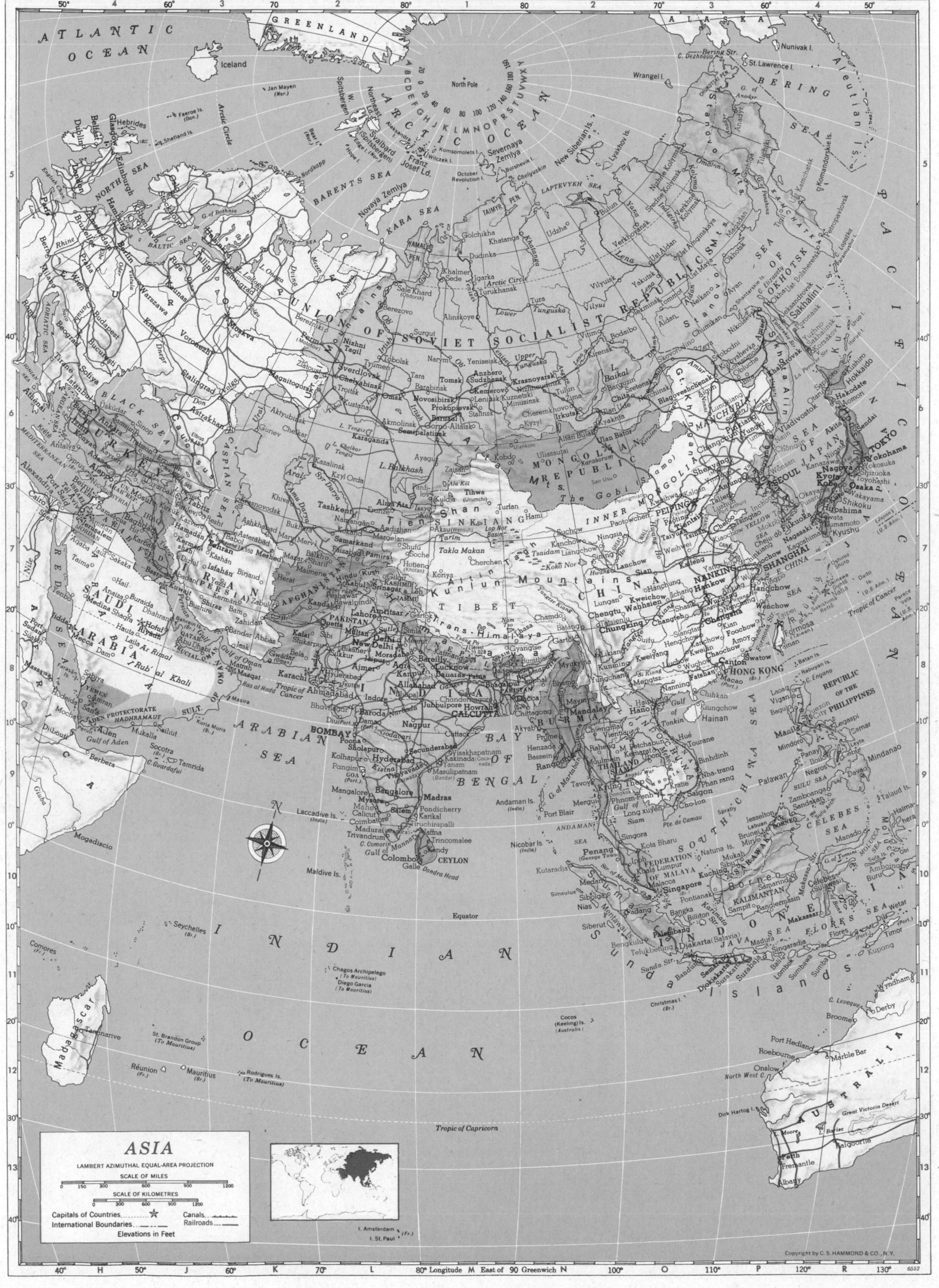

## ASIA

LAMBERT AZIMUTHAL EQUAL-AREA PROJECTION

SCALE OF MILES

150   300   600   900   1200

SCALE OF KILOMETRES

300   600   900   1200

Capitals of Countries .......... ★
International Boundaries ..........
Elevations in Feet
Canals ..........
Railroads ..........

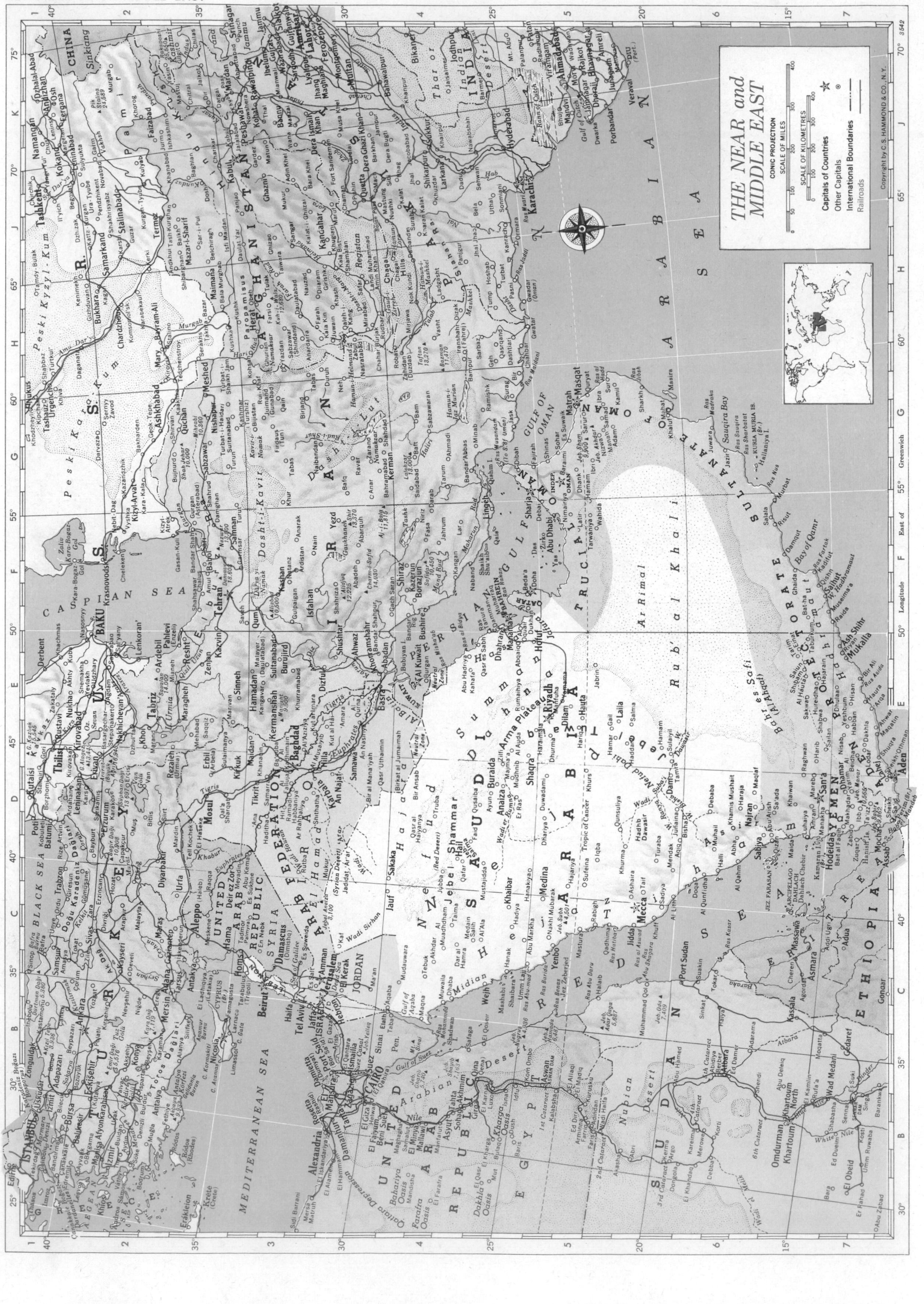

## THE NEAR and MIDDLE EAST

CONIC PROJECTION

SCALE OF MILES

SCALE OF KILOMETRES

★ Capitals of Countries
⊛ Other Capitals
International Boundaries
Railroads

Copyright by C. S. HAMMOND & CO., N.Y.

CHINA

U. R. S. S.

AFGHANISTAN

WEST PAKISTAN

INDIA

IRAN

IRAQ

SAUDI ARABIA

SYRIA

UNITED ARAB REPUBLIC

JORDAN

ISRAEL

LEBANON

TURKEY

CYPRUS

OMAN

SULTANATE OF OMAN

TRUCIAL OMAN PROTECTORATE

QATAR

KUWAIT

YEMEN

ADEN PROTECTORATE

ETHIOPIA

SUDAN

ERITREA

CASPIAN SEA

BLACK SEA

MEDITERRANEAN SEA

AEGEAN SEA

RED SEA

ARABIAN SEA

GULF OF OMAN

PERSIAN GULF

Rub' al Khali

Dasht-i-Kavir

Dasht-i-Lut

An Nefud

Jebel Shammar

Armand Plateau

CAIRO

BAGDAD

Tehran

Riyadh

Mecca

Medina

Jerusalem

Damascus

Beirut

Amman

Aden

Ankara

ISTANBUL

BAKU

Tbilisi

Kabul

Karachi

Khartoum

Tropic of Cancer

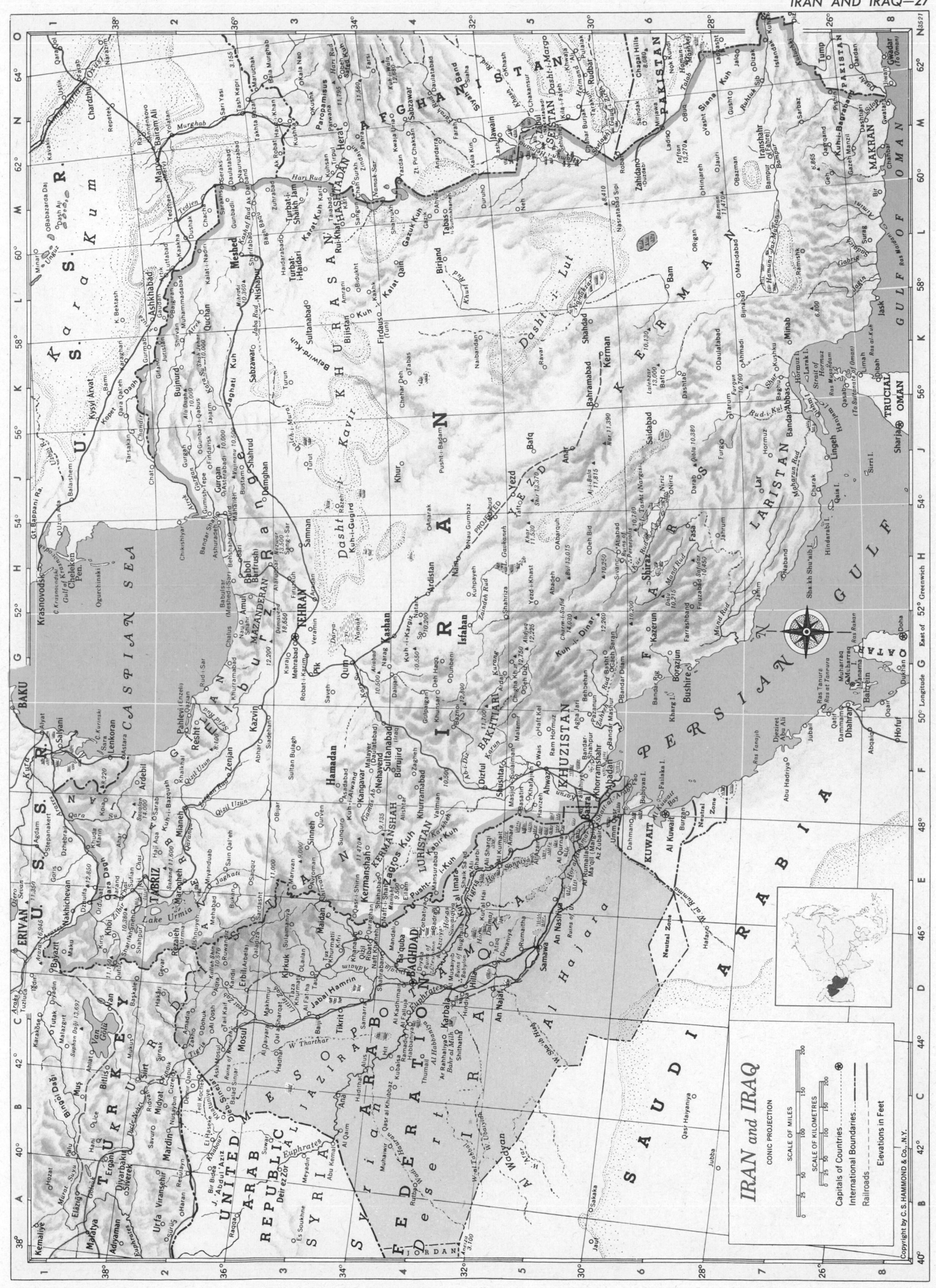

## IRAN and IRAQ

CONIC PROJECTION

SCALE OF MILES

SCALE OF KILOMETRES

⊕ Capitals of Countries
─ · ─ International Boundaries
── Railroads
── Elevations in Feet

Copyright by C. S. HAMMOND & Co., N.Y.

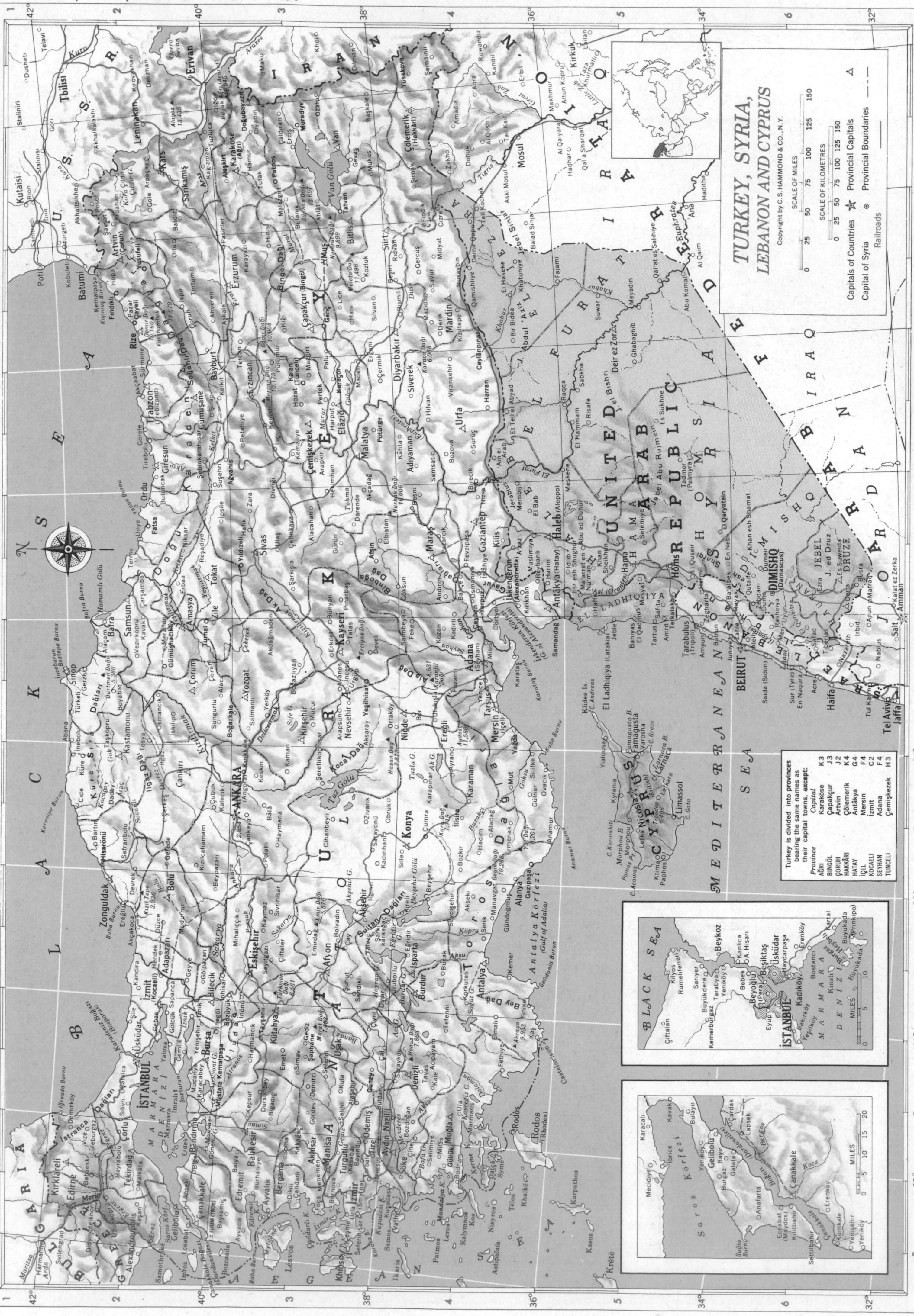
TURKEY, SYRIA,
LEBANON AND CYPRUS
Copyright by C.S. HAMMOND & CO., N.Y.
SCALE OF MILES
0 25 50 75 100 125 150
SCALE OF KILOMETRES
0 25 50 75 100 125 150
Capitals of Countries
Provincial Capitals
Capital of Syria
Provincial Boundaries
Railroads
Turkey is divided into provinces bearing the same names as their capital towns, except:
Province Capital
AĞRI Karaköse K3
BINGÖL Çapakçur J3
ÇORUH Artvin J2
HAKKÂRI Çölemerik K4
HATAY Antâkya G4
İÇEL Mersin F4
KOCAELI İzmit C2
SEYHAN Adana F4
TUNCELI Çemişkezek H3
BLACK SEA
İSTANBUL
MARMARA DENİZİ
MILES
MEDITERRANEAN SEA
BLACK SEA
U. S. S. R.
IRAN
IRAQ
JORDAN
UNITED ARAB REPUBLIC
CYPRUS

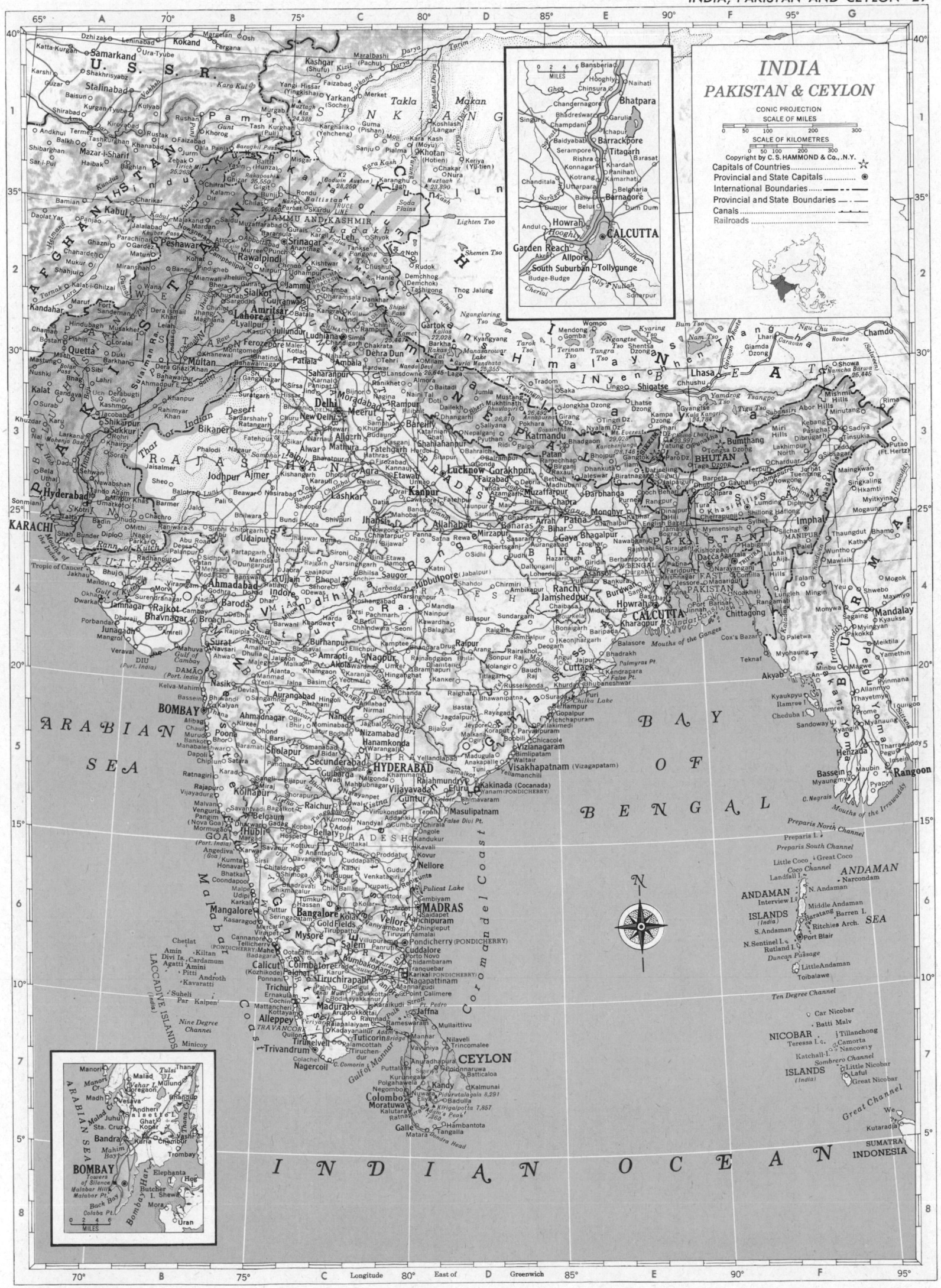

INDIA
PAKISTAN & CEYLON

CONIC PROJECTION
SCALE OF MILES
SCALE OF KILOMETRES
Copyright by C. S. HAMMOND & Co., N.Y.
Capitals of Countries ........................ ☆
Provincial and State Capitals ............ ◉
International Boundaries ...............
Provincial and State Boundaries .. _ _ _ _
Canals ..............................
Railroads ...........................

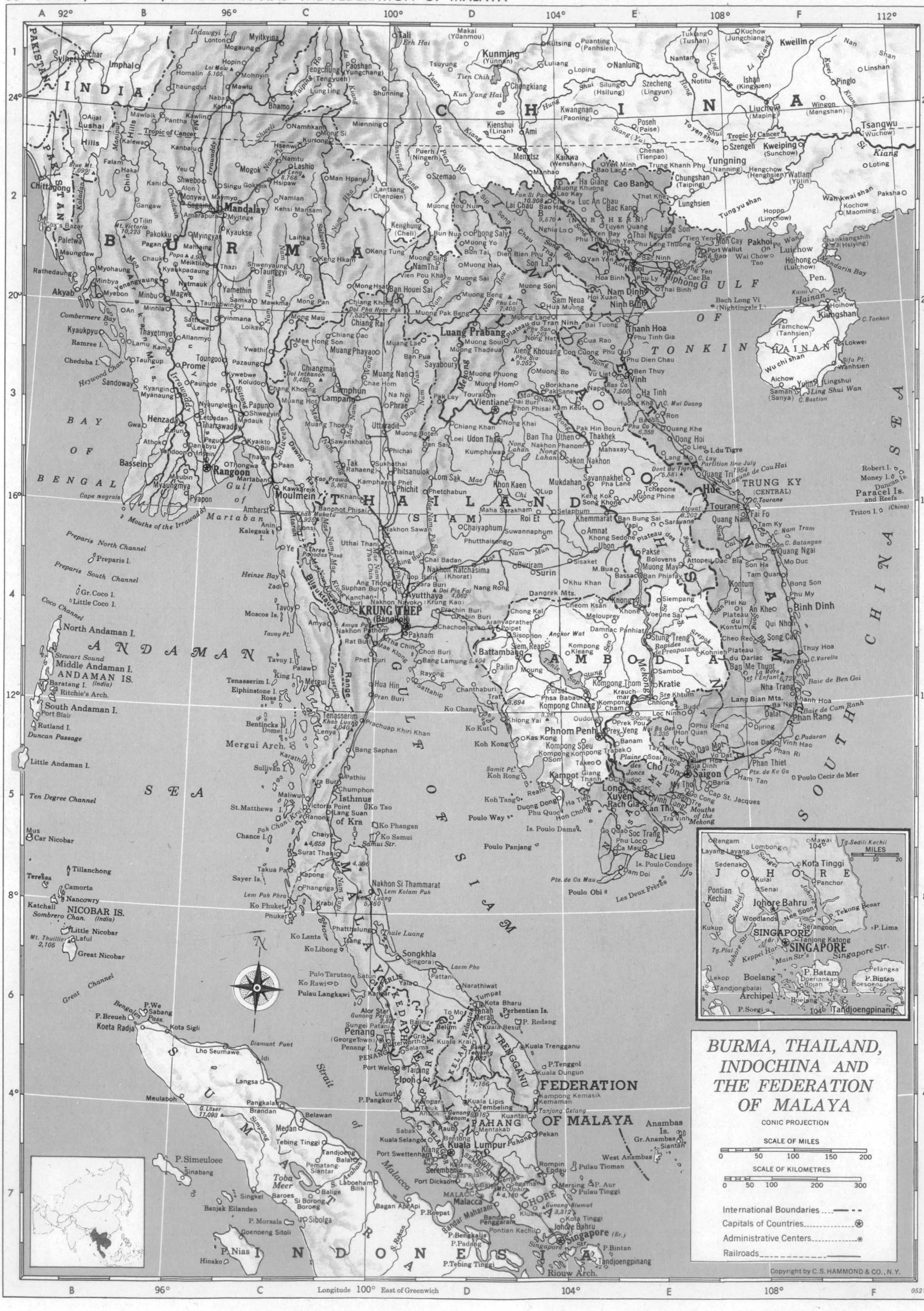

# BURMA, THAILAND, INDOCHINA AND THE FEDERATION OF MALAYA

CONIC PROJECTION

SCALE OF MILES

0  50  100  150  200

SCALE OF KILOMETRES

0  50  100  200  300

International Boundaries ........ — ∙∙ —

Capitals of Countries ............ ⊛

Administrative Centers ........... ⊛

Railroads ..................... ——

Copyright by C. S. HAMMOND & CO., N.Y.

0521

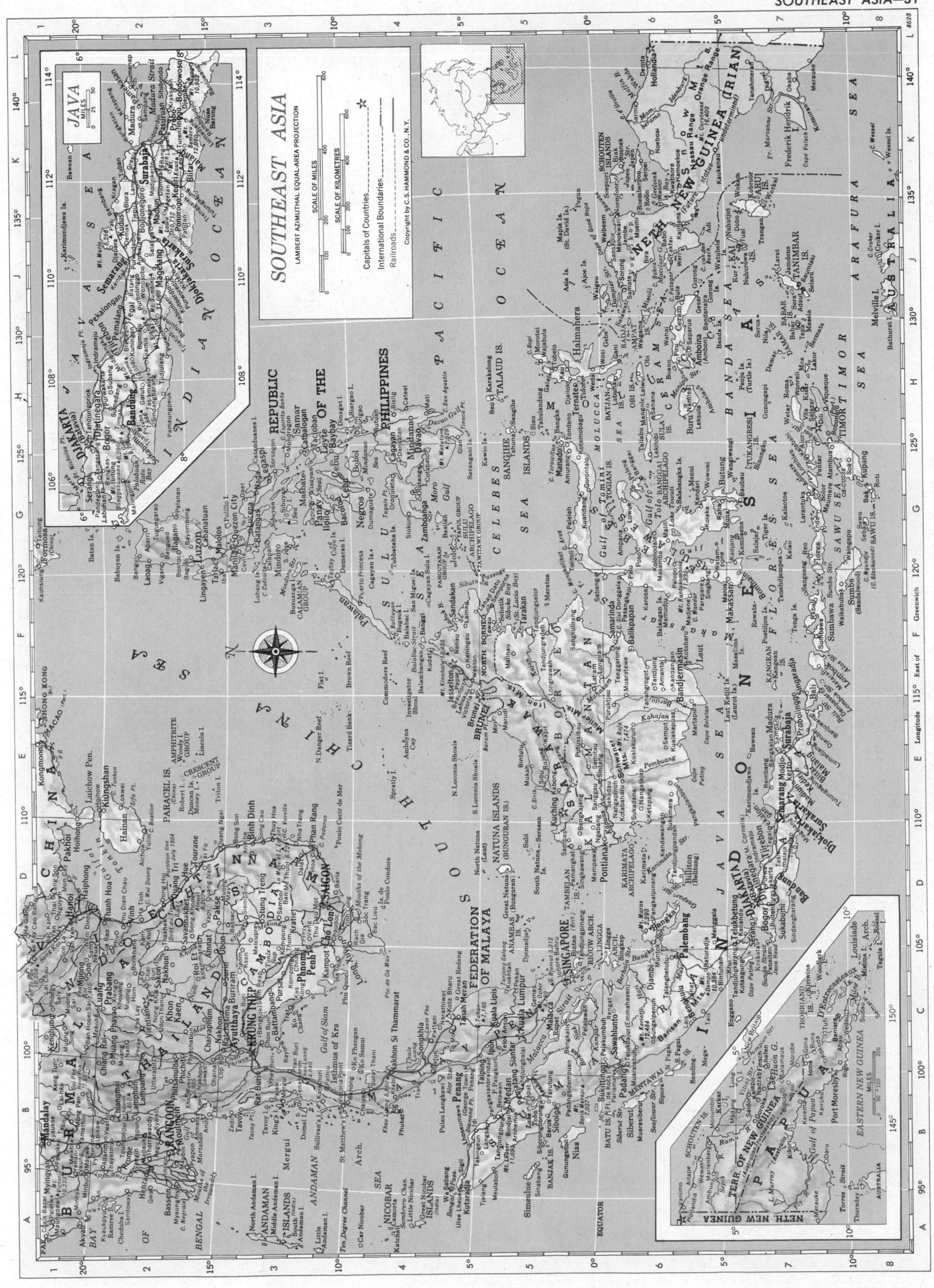

SOUTHEAST ASIA

LAMBERT AZIMUTHAL EQUAL-AREA PROJECTION

SCALE OF MILES

SCALE OF KILOMETRES

Capitals of Countries
International Boundaries
Railroads

Copyright by C. S. HAMMOND & CO., N.Y.

JAVA

MILES
0  25  50

CHINA, JAPAN, KOREA
and MONGOLIAN REPUBLIC

CONIC PROJECTION
SCALE OF MILES

SCALE OF KILOMETRES

Capitals of Countries........⊛
Provincial Capitals............⊙
Trade Routes.....................
Railroads..........................

International Boundaries........
Provincial Boundaries...........
Canals................................
(Projected)........................

Copyright by C.S. HAMMOND & CO., N.Y.

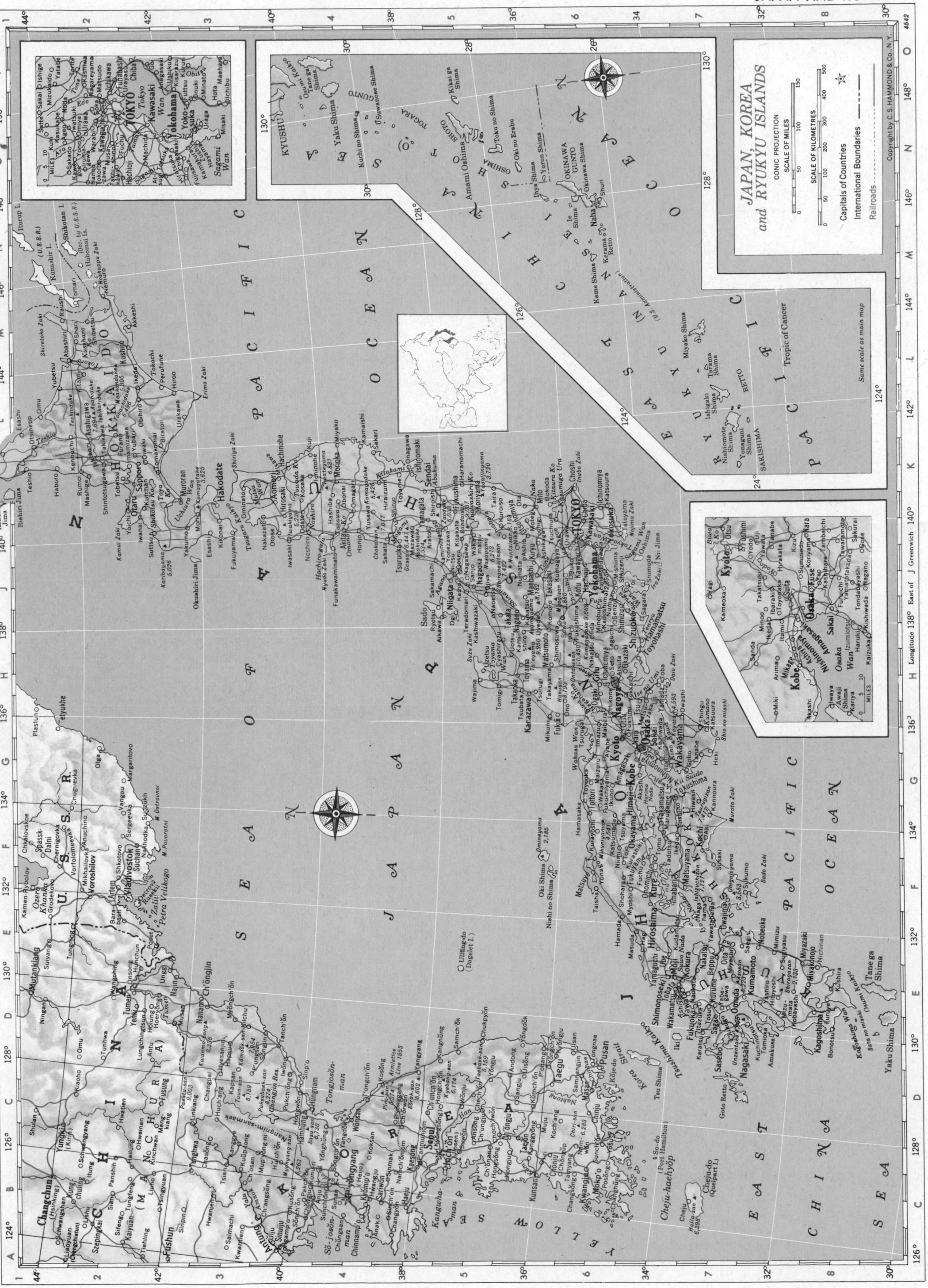

## JAPAN, KOREA and RYUKYU ISLANDS

CONIC PROJECTION

SCALE OF MILES

SCALE OF KILOMETRES

Capitals of Countries ............ ★

International Boundaries ........ ━━━

Railroads ........................ ━━━

Copyright by C. S. HAMMOND & Co., N. Y.

**Main map labels:**

PACIFIC OCEAN

SEA OF JAPAN

EAST CHINA SEA

YELLOW SEA

U. S. S. R.

C H I N A

M A N C H U R I A

K O R E A

HOKKAIDO

HONSHU

KYUSHU

RYUKYU ISLANDS

Tropic of Cancer

**Inset (top left):** TOKYO, Yokohama, Kawasaki, Chiba, Sagami Wan, MILES

**Inset (lower right):** Kyoto, Osaka, Kobe, Sakai, Osaka Wan, MILES

Tokyo, Nagoya, Sendai, Hakodate, Sapporo, Aomori, Hiroshima, Nagasaki, Kumamoto, Kagoshima, Fukuoka, Seoul, Pyongyang, Pusan, Taegu, Changchun, Vladivostok

SAKISHIMA

OKINAWA GUNTO

OSHIMA

Cheju-do (Quelpart I.)

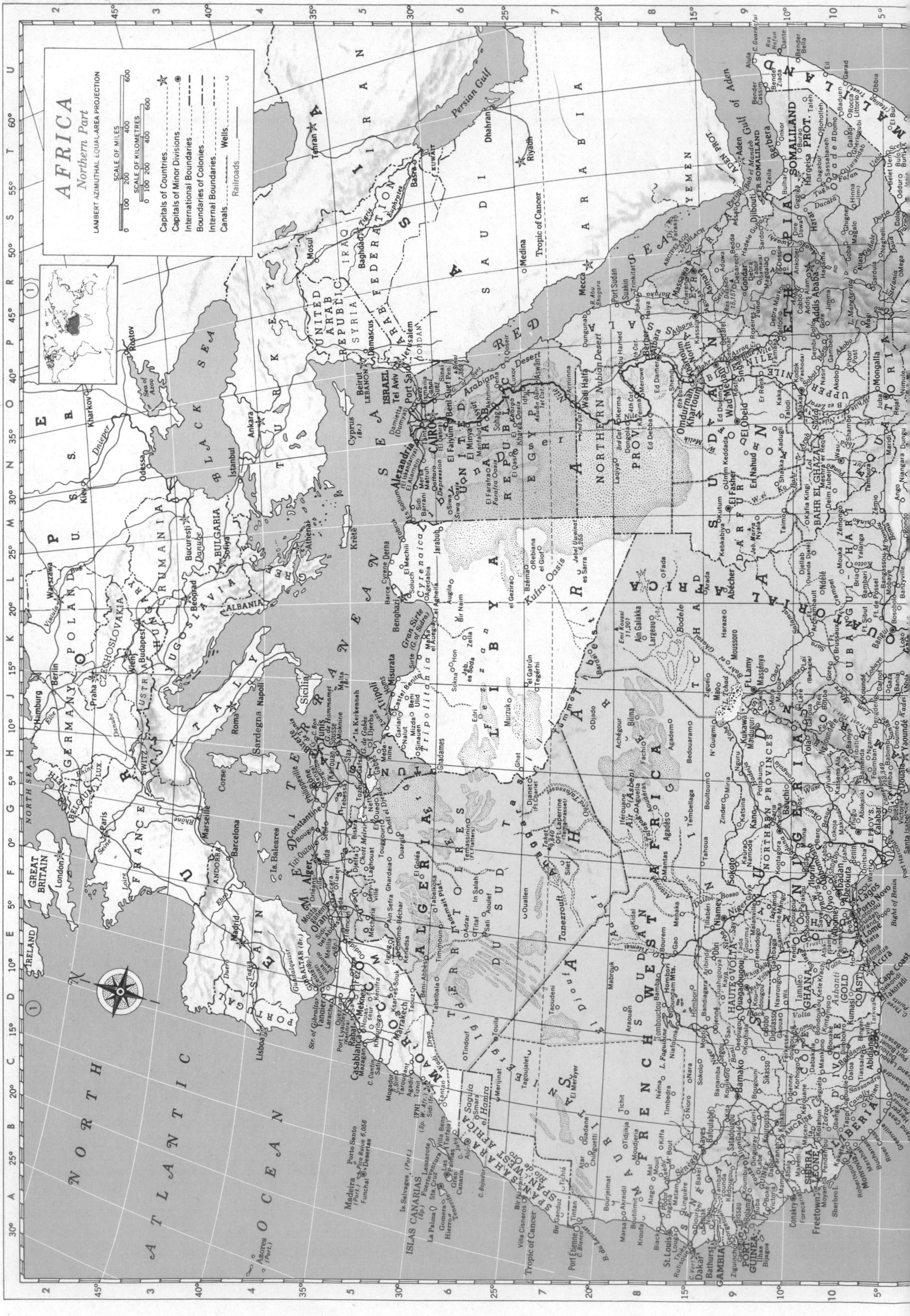

AFRICA
Northern Part
LAMBERT AZIMUTHAL EQUAL-AREA PROJECTION
SCALE OF MILES
0 100 200 400 600
SCALE OF KILOMETRES
0 100 200 400 600
Capitals of Countries
Capitals of Minor Divisions
International Boundaries
Boundaries of Colonies
Internal Boundaries
Canals
Wells
Railroads
NORTH ATLANTIC OCEAN
MEDITERRANEAN SEA
BLACK SEA
RED SEA
Persian Gulf
Gulf of Aden
Tropic of Cancer

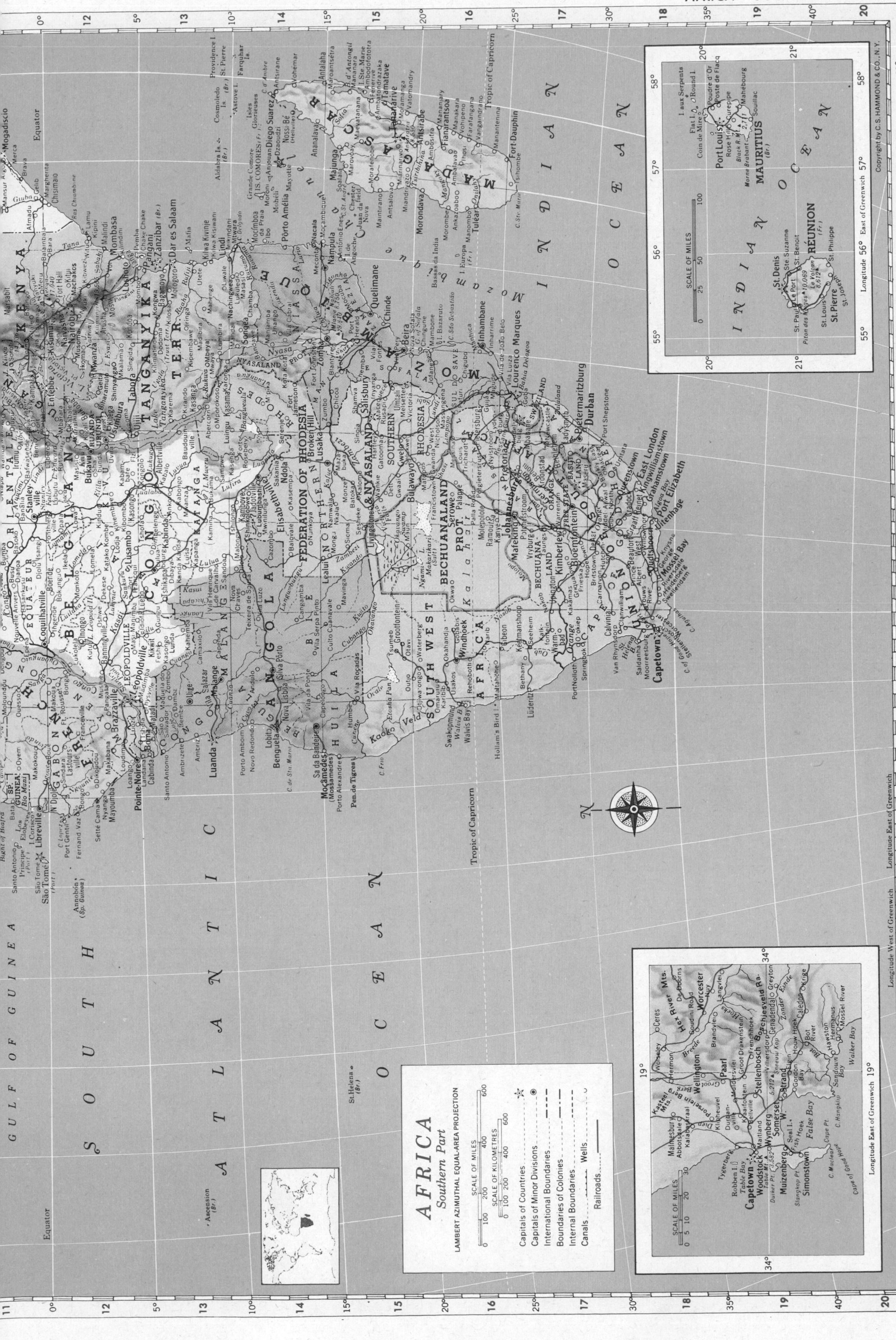

# AFRICA
## Southern Part
LAMBERT AZIMUTHAL EQUAL-AREA PROJECTION

SCALE OF MILES
0   100   200   400   600

SCALE OF KILOMETRES
0   100  200   400   600

Capitals of Countries ............ ⊛
Capitals of Minor Divisions ...... ⊙
International Boundaries .......... — — —
Boundaries of Colonies ........... — · —
Internal Boundaries .............. — — —
Canals ........................... Wells ... ○
Railroads ........................ ——————

Copyright by C.S. HAMMOND & CO., N.Y.

GULF OF GUINEA

SOUTH ATLANTIC OCEAN

INDIAN OCEAN

Tropic of Capricorn

Equator

KENYA

TANGANYIKA TERR.

BELGIAN CONGO

ANGOLA

RHODESIA

FEDERATION OF RHODESIA & NYASALAND

NORTHERN RHODESIA

SOUTHERN RHODESIA

NYASALAND

BECHUANALAND PROT.

SOUTH WEST AFRICA

UNION OF SOUTH AFRICA

ORANGE FREE STATE

CAPE OF GOOD HOPE

MADAGASCAR

MAURITIUS

RÉUNION (Fr.)

SCALE OF MILES
0   25   50   100

Longitude 56° East of Greenwich 57°

Longitude West of Greenwich    Longitude East of Greenwich

Longitude East of Greenwich 19°

SCALE OF MILES
0  5  10   20   30

Capetown

Durban

Mombasa

Dar es Salaam

Lourenço Marques

Johannesburg

Pretoria

Bloemfontein

Windhoek

Luanda

Leopoldville

Benguela

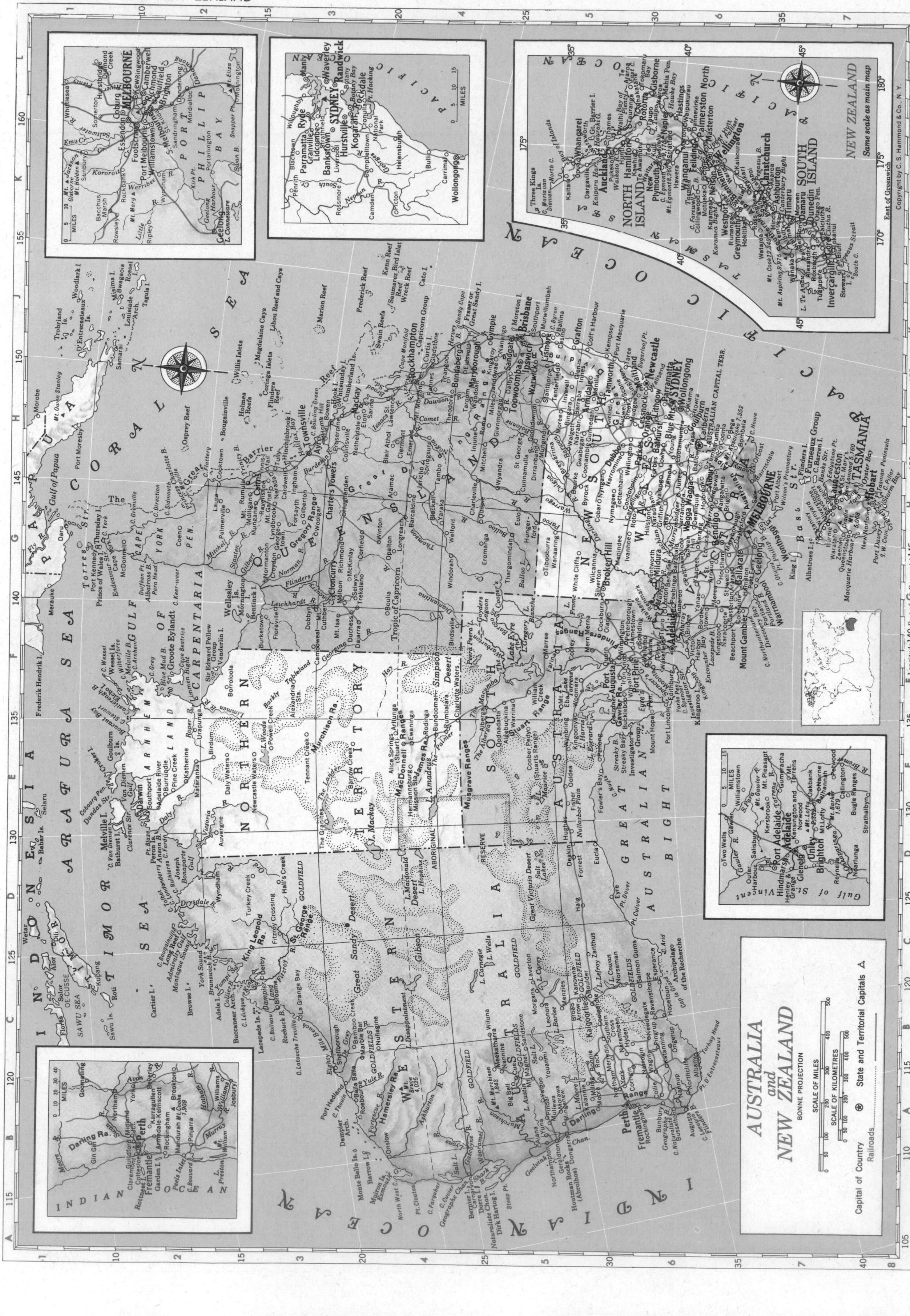

AUSTRALIA
and
NEW ZEALAND

BONNE PROJECTION

SCALE OF MILES

SCALE OF KILOMETRES

Capital of Country ⊛    State and Territorial Capitals △

Railroads

NEW ZEALAND
Same scale as main map

NORTH ISLAND

SOUTH ISLAND

PACIFIC OCEAN

INDIAN OCEAN

CORAL SEA

ARAFURA SEA

TIMOR SEA

GULF OF CARPENTARIA

INDONESIA

PAPUA

QUEENSLAND

NEW SOUTH WALES

VICTORIA

SOUTH AUSTRALIA

WESTERN AUSTRALIA

NORTHERN TERRITORY

TASMANIA

GREAT AUSTRALIAN BIGHT

Copyright by C. S. Hammond & Co., N.Y.

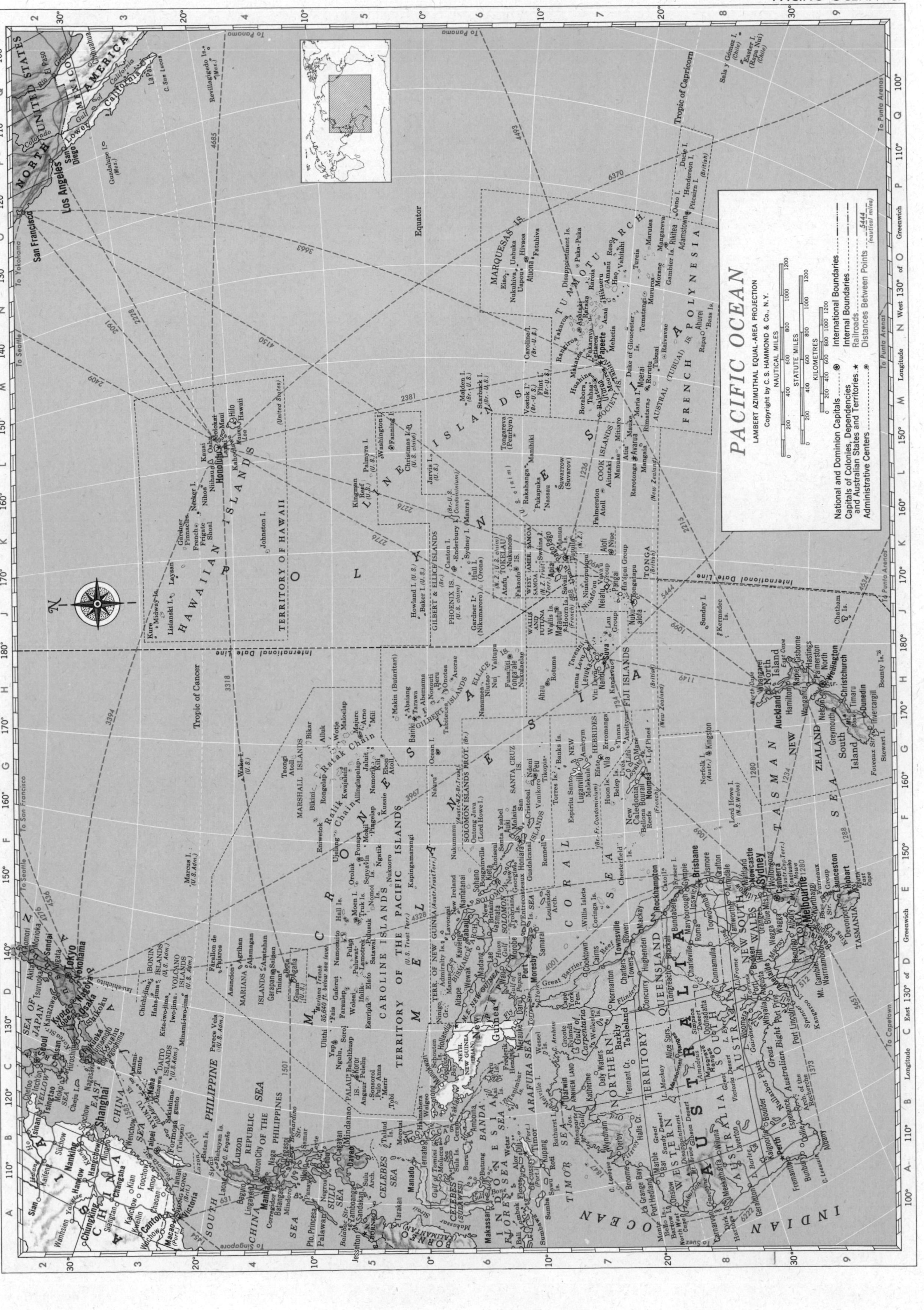

## PACIFIC OCEAN

LAMBERT AZIMUTHAL EQUAL-AREA PROJECTION

Copyright by C. S. HAMMOND & Co., N.Y.

NAUTICAL MILES

STATUTE MILES

KILOMETRES

National and Dominion Capitals ............... ⊛
Capitals of Colonies, Dependencies
and Australian States and Territories ... ⊛
Administrative Centers

International Boundaries .............
Internal Boundaries .............
Railroads .............
Distances Between Points ....★

NORTH AMERICA

UNITED STATES

MEXICO

Los Angeles
San Francisco
San Diego

Equator

Tropic of Cancer

Tropic of Capricorn

International Date Line

HAWAIIAN ISLANDS
TERRITORY OF HAWAII
Honolulu

POLYNESIA

MICRONESIA

MELANESIA

MARQUESAS IS.

FRENCH POLYNESIA

Papeete

TUAMOTU ARCH.

COOK ISLANDS

SOCIETY IS.

AUSTRAL (TUBUAI) IS.

GILBERT & ELLICE ISLANDS

PHOENIX IS.

LINE ISLANDS

CAROLINE ISLANDS
TERRITORY OF THE PACIFIC ISLANDS

MARSHALL ISLANDS

MARIANA ISLANDS

VOLCANO ISLANDS

BONIN ISLANDS

PALAU ISLANDS

PHILIPPINE SEA

REPUBLIC OF THE PHILIPPINES
Manila

CHINA

Shanghai
Canton
Hong Kong
Macao

JAPAN
Tokyo
Yokohama
Osaka
Kyoto
Nagoya

SEA OF JAPAN

YELLOW SEA

EAST CHINA SEA

SOUTH CHINA SEA

SULU SEA

CELEBES SEA

BORNEO
KALIMANTAN

INDONESIA

BANDA SEA

FLORES SEA

TIMOR SEA

ARAFURA SEA

CORAL SEA

TERR. OF NEW GUINEA

NETH. NEW GUINEA

SOLOMON ISLANDS PROT. (Br.)

NEW HEBRIDES

NEW CALEDONIA

FIJI ISLANDS

SAMOA

TONGA

NIUE

TOKELAU

SANTA CRUZ IS.

AUSTRALIA

WESTERN AUSTRALIA

NORTHERN TERRITORY

QUEENSLAND
Brisbane
Rockhampton
Townsville
Cairns

SOUTH AUSTRALIA

NEW SOUTH WALES
Sydney
Newcastle
Canberra

VICTORIA
Melbourne

TASMANIA
Hobart
Launceston

Darwin

Perth

Adelaide

TASMAN SEA

NEW ZEALAND
Auckland
Wellington
Christchurch
Dunedin
North Island
South Island

INDIAN OCEAN

PACIFIC OCEAN

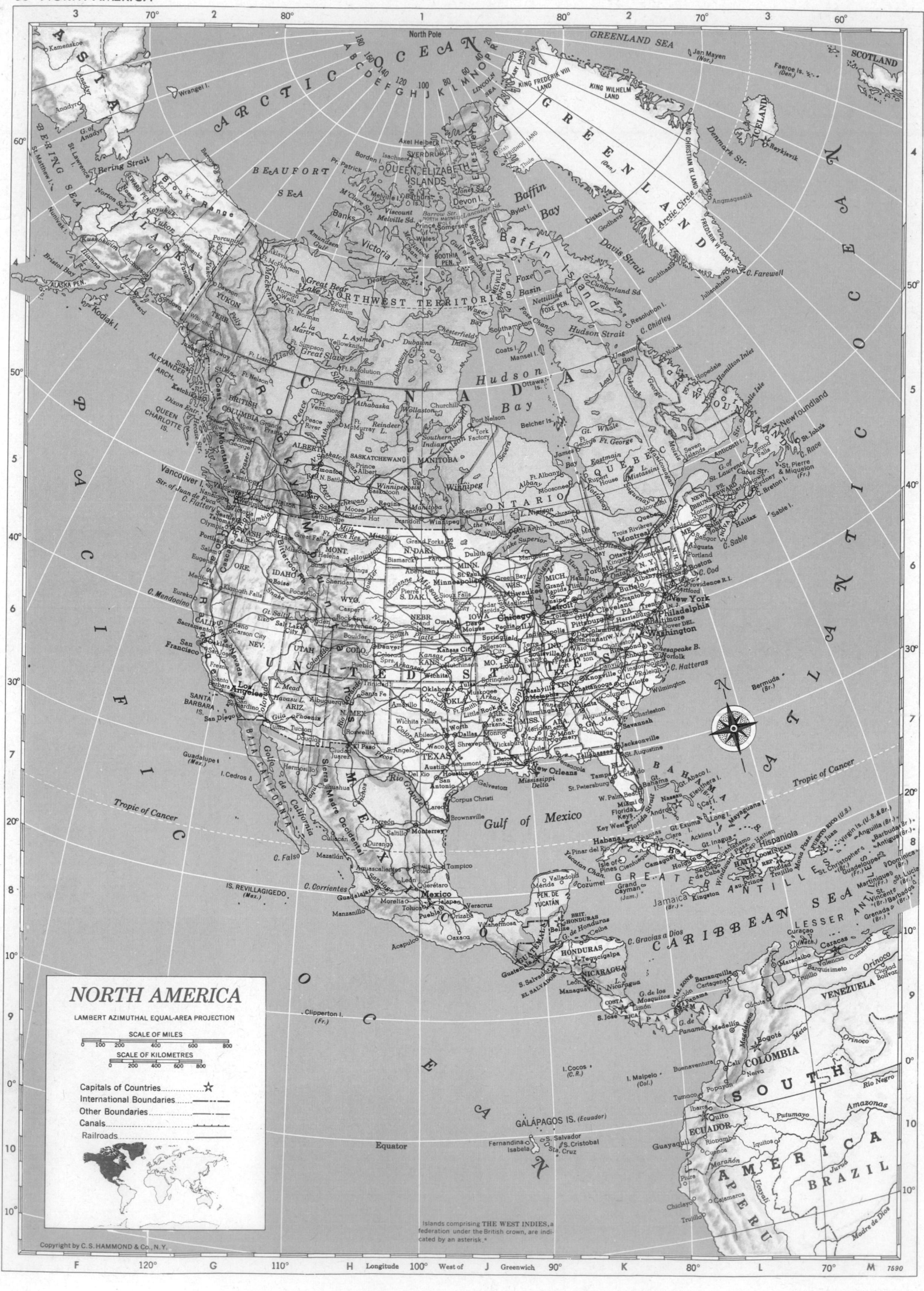

# NORTH AMERICA

LAMBERT AZIMUTHAL EQUAL-AREA PROJECTION

SCALE OF MILES

0    100    200    400    600    800

SCALE OF KILOMETRES

0    200    400    600    800

Capitals of Countries............☆
International Boundaries........—— ——
Other Boundaries..................—·—·—
Canals..................................— · —
Railroads...............................———————

Islands comprising THE WEST INDIES, a federation under the British crown, are indicated by an asterisk *

7590

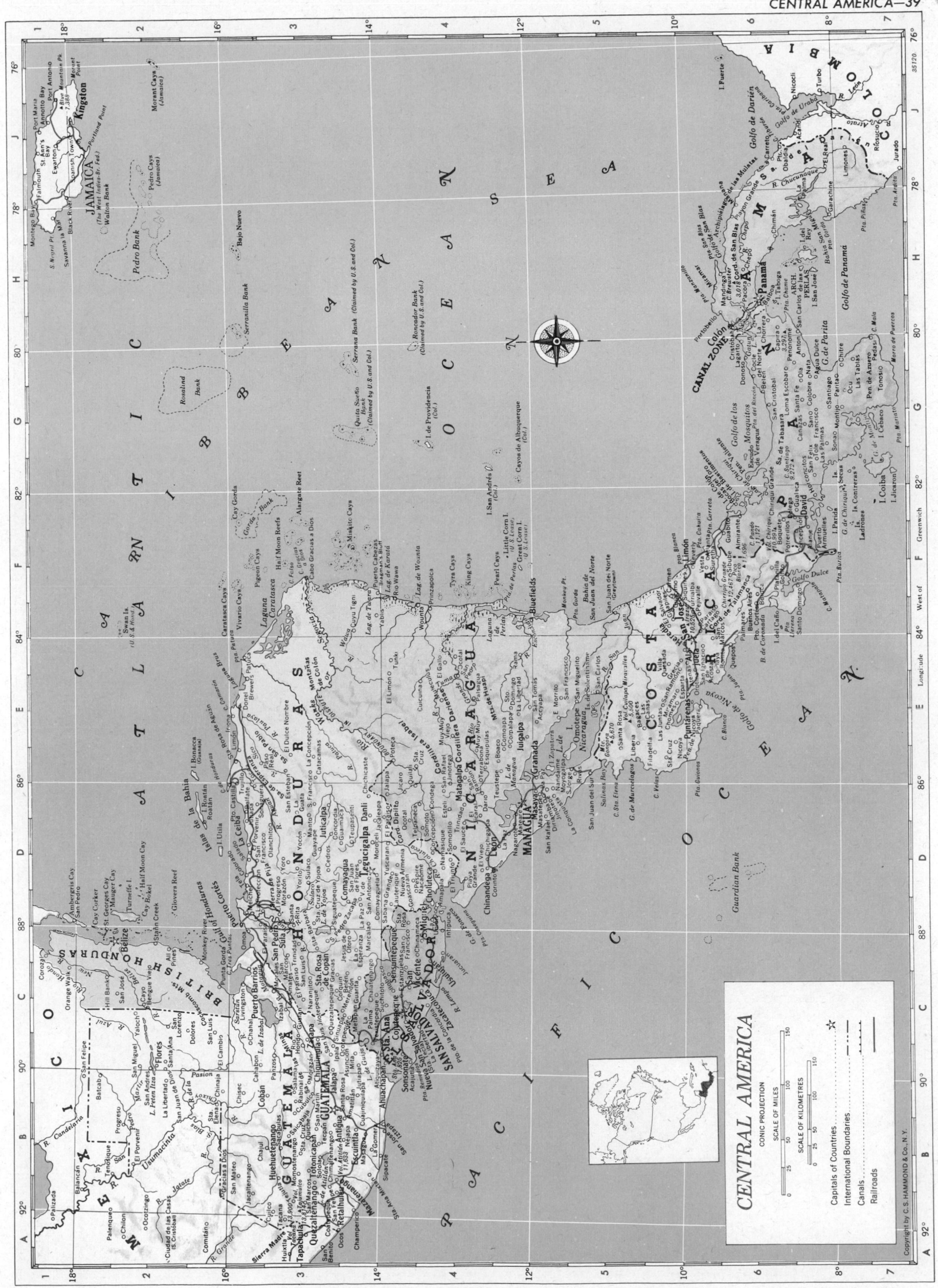

CENTRAL AMERICA

CONIC PROJECTION

SCALE OF MILES

SCALE OF KILOMETRES

Capitals of Countries ............ ★

International Boundaries ........

Canals ...................

Railroads ...............

Copyright by C.S. HAMMOND & Co., N.Y.

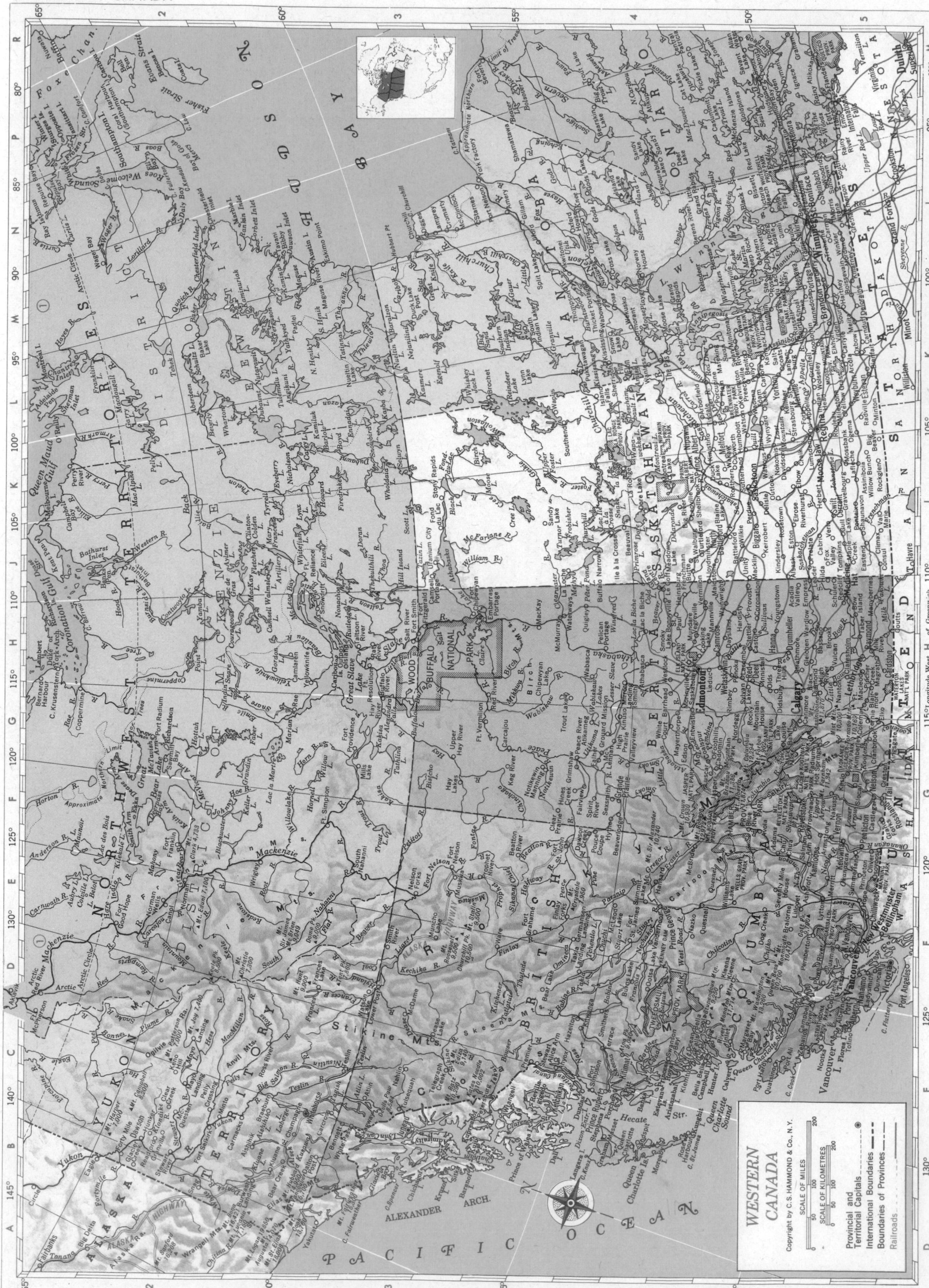

WESTERN CANADA

Copyright by C. S. Hammond & Co., N.Y.

SCALE OF MILES

SCALE OF KILOMETRES

Provincial and
Territorial Capitals
International Boundaries
Boundaries of Provinces
Railroads

NORTHWEST TERRITORIES

DISTRICT OF MACKENZIE

DISTRICT OF KEEWATIN

YUKON TERRITORY

BRITISH COLUMBIA

ALBERTA

SASKATCHEWAN

MANITOBA

ONTARIO

ALASKA

WASHINGTON

IDAHO

MONTANA

NORTH DAKOTA

MINNESOTA

Edmonton

Calgary

Regina

Winnipeg

Vancouver

Victoria

HUDSON BAY

Foxe Chan.

Fisher Strait

Roes Welcome Sound

Queen Maud Gulf

Coronation Gulf

Great Bear Lake

Great Slave Lake

Lake Athabasca

Reindeer Lake

Lake Winnipeg

Lake Manitoba

Lake Winnipegosis

WOOD BUFFALO NATIONAL PARK

JASPER NAT'L PARK

BANFF NAT'L PARK

WATERTON LAKES NAT'L PARK

ALASKA HIGHWAY

Mackenzie R.

Peace River

Churchill R.

Nelson R.

Hayes R.

Alexander Arch.

Queen Charlotte Is.

Vancouver I.

Hecate Str.

Queen Charlotte Sound

PACIFIC OCEAN

Stikine Mts.

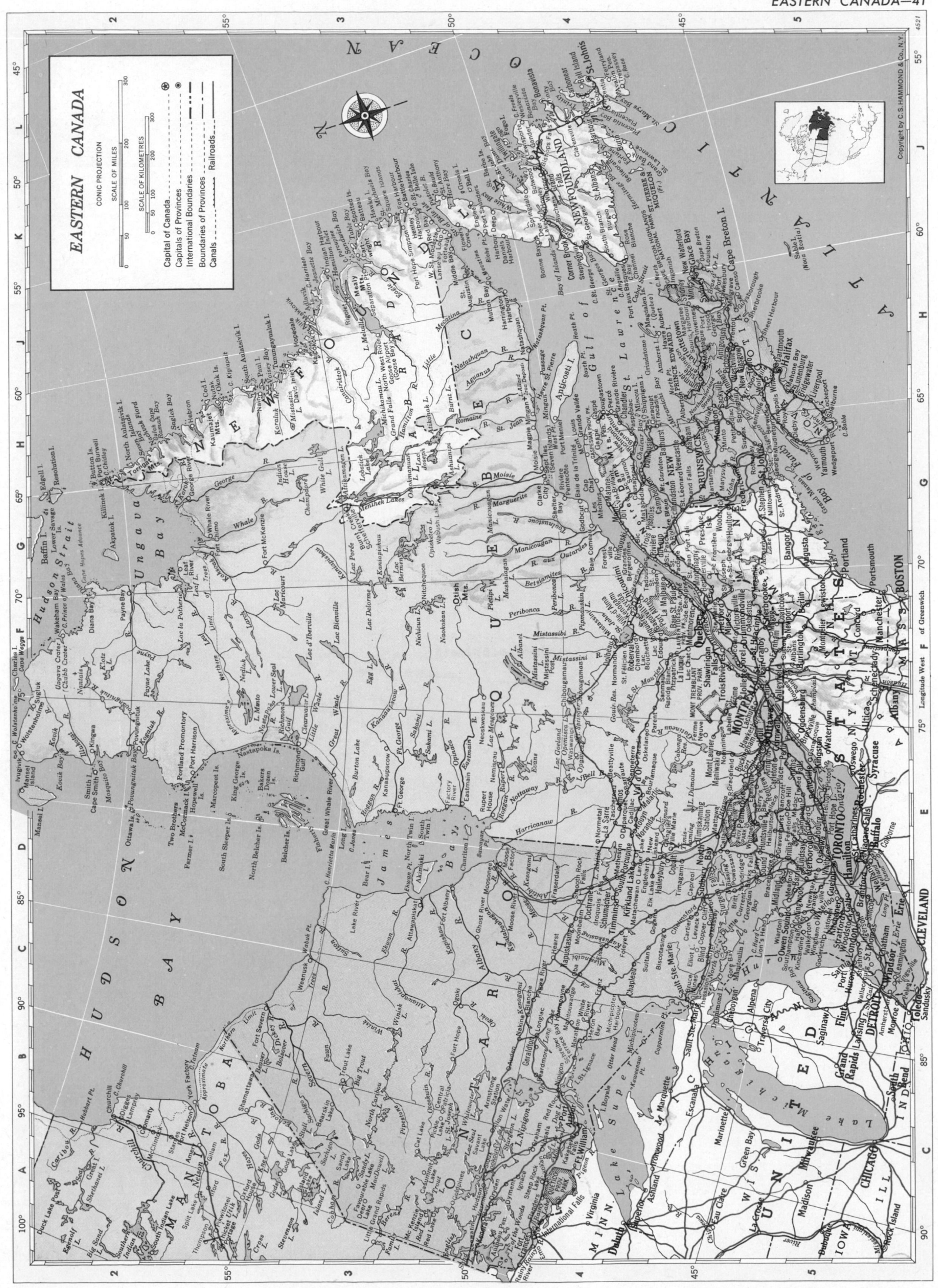

**EASTERN CANADA**

CONIC PROJECTION

SCALE OF MILES

SCALE OF KILOMETRES

Capital of Canada
Capitals of Provinces
International Boundaries
Boundaries of Provinces
Canals
Railroads

## UNITED STATES
### Western Part
POLYCONIC PROJECTION
SCALE OF MILES

SCALE OF KILOMETRES

See United States Eastern Part for legend.

Copyright by C. S. HAMMOND & Co., N.Y.

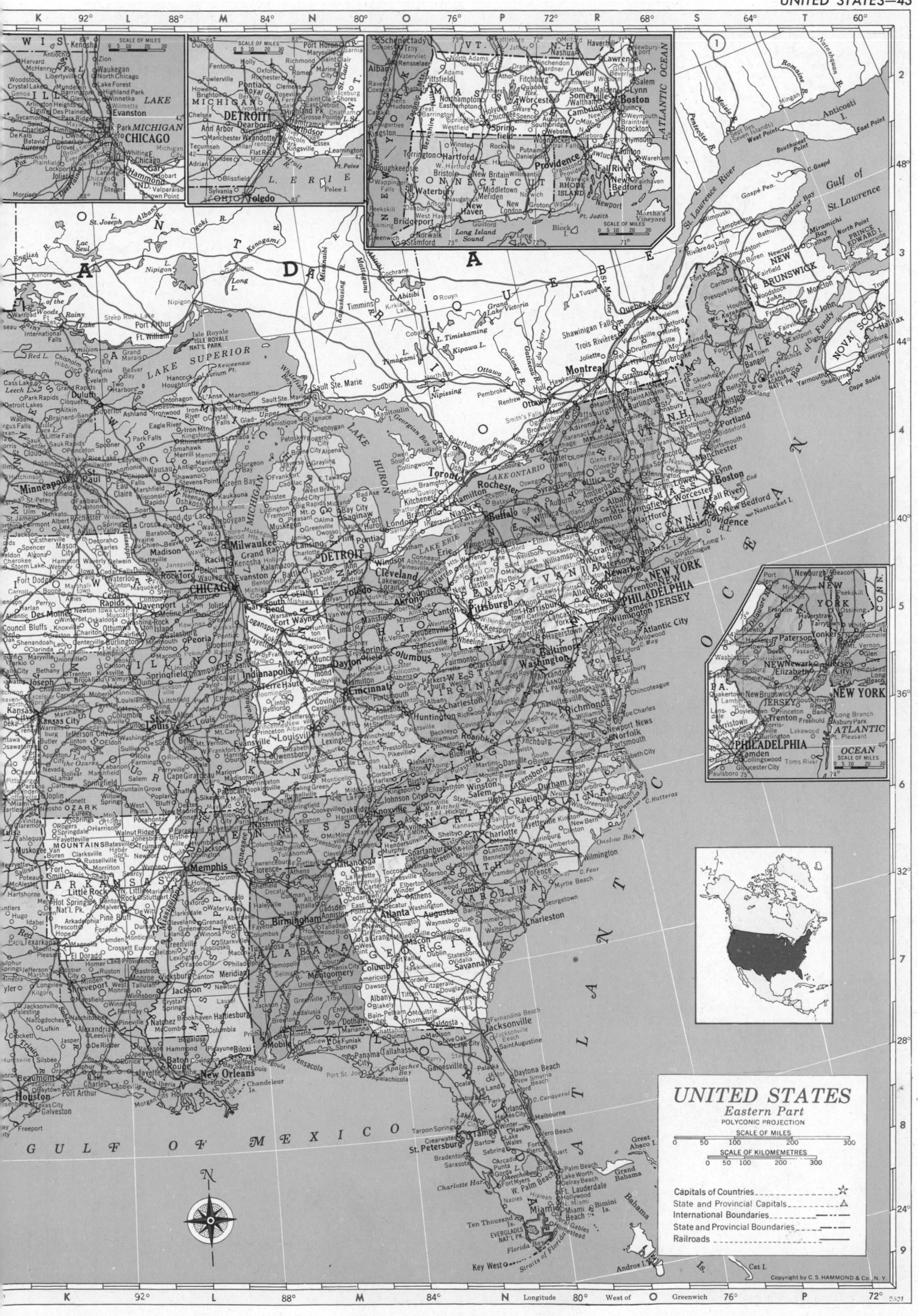

## UNITED STATES
### Eastern Part
POLYCONIC PROJECTION

SCALE OF MILES
0    50    100         200         300

SCALE OF KILOMEMETRES
0   50  100       200       300

Capitals of Countries
State and Provincial Capitals
International Boundaries
State and Provincial Boundaries
Railroads

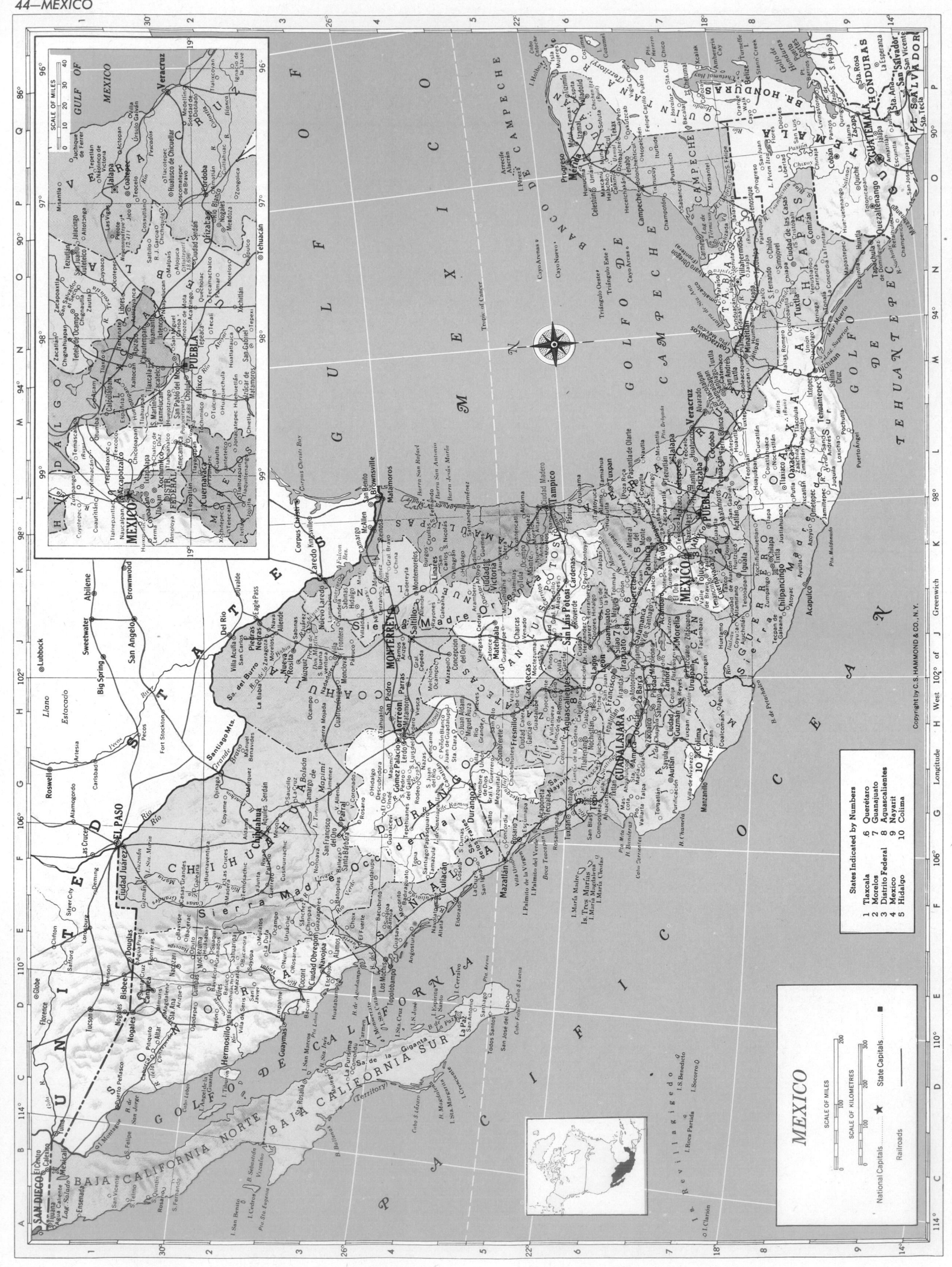

# MEXICO

SCALE OF MILES

SCALE OF KILOMETRES

★ National Capitals

★ State Capitals

■ Railroads

**States Indicated by Numbers**

1 Tlaxcala
2 Morelos
3 Distrito Federal
4 Mexico
5 Hidalgo
6 Querétaro
7 Guanajuato
8 Aguascalientes
9 Nayarit
10 Colima

Copyright by C. S. HAMMOND & CO., N.Y.

## THE WEST INDIES
CONIC PROJECTION

SCALE OF KILOMETRES
0  50  100  200  300

SCALE OF MILES
0  50  100  200

Distances are given in Nautical Miles

Capitals ........... ☆    Railroads _____

Copyright by C. S. HAMMOND & CO., N.Y.

### PUERTO RICO

San Juan
Pt. Borinquen, Aguadilla, Pt. Jiguero, Añasco, Mayagüez, San Germán, Boquerón, C. Rojo, Lares, Utuado, Adjuntas, Ponce, Camuy, Arecibo, Manati, Bayamón, Rio Piedras, Juncos, Caguas, Cayey, Jayuya, Coamo, Salinas, Guayama, Arroyo, Humacao, Guayanilla

ATLANTIC OCEAN

### VIRGIN ISLANDS
Anegada, Virgin Gorda, Jost Van Dyke, Tortola, Road Town, St. Peter I. (Br.), St. John, St. Thomas I. (U.S.), Culebra (P.R.), Vieques I. (P.R.), Charlotte Amalie, Christiansted, Frederiksted, St. Croix

### BERMUDA ISLANDS
North Rocks, N.E. Breakers, St. George, St. George's I., St. David's I., Castle Harbour, Hamilton, Main or Bermuda I., Somerset I., Harrington Sound, Great Sound, Ireland I., Little Flats, W. Ledge Flats (U.S. Leased Base), (U.S. Leased Base)

Islands and island groups, comprising THE WEST INDIES, a federation under the British crown, are indicated by an asterisk ✳

ATLANTIC OCEAN

GULF OF MEXICO

UNITED STATES
L. Okeechobee, W. Palm Beach, Miami, Key West, Dry Tortugas

MEXICO

### BAHAMAS
Grand Bahama, Great Abaco, The Biminis, Gun Cay, Berry Is., Great Isaac, Andros I., New Providence, Nassau, Eleuthera, Harbour I., Cat I., San Salvador, Watling I., Rum Cay, Long I., Exuma, Crooked I., Acklins I., Mayaguana, Great Inagua, Little Inagua, Caicos Is., Turks Is.

### CUBA
HAVANA, Matanzas, Cárdenas, Santa Clara, Cienfuegos, Trinidad, Sancti Spíritus, Ciego de Ávila, Camagüey, Manzanillo, Holguín, Santiago de Cuba, Guantánamo, Gibara, I. of Pines (I. de Pinos), Pinar del Río

GREATER ANTILLES

CAYMAN IS.
Grand Cayman, Little Cayman, Cayman Brac, Georgetown

### JAMAICA (Br.)
Kingston, Montego Bay, Port Antonio, Port Maria, Spanish Town, Blue Mountain Pk.

### HAITI
Port-au-Prince, Cap Haïtien, Gonaïves, Jérémie, Les Cayes, Jacmel, La Tortue, Île de la Gonâve

### DOMINICAN REPUBLIC
Ciudad Trujillo, Santiago de los Caballeros, Puerto Plata, Monte Cristi, Samaná, San Pedro de Macorís, La Romana, Barahona, Azua, San Francisco de Macorís

### PUERTO RICO
San Juan, Ponce, Mayagüez, Arecibo

### LEEWARD ISLANDS
Sombrero, Anguilla ✳, St. Martin, St. Barthélemy, Barbuda, Saba, St. Eustatius, St. Kitts ✳, Nevis ✳, Antigua ✳, St. Johns, Basseterre, Charlestown, Redonda, Montserrat ✳, Plymouth, Guadeloupe (Fr.), Basse Terre, Pointe-à-Pitre, Marie Galante

### WINDWARD ISLANDS
Dominica ✳ (Br.), Roseau, Martinique (Fr.), St. Pierre, Fort-de-France, St. Lucia ✳, Castries, St. Vincent ✳, Kingstown, Grenada ✳, St. George's, Barbados ✳, Bridgetown, Bequia, Union I., Carriacou, Tobago (Br.)

### NETH. ANTILLES
Aruba, Oranjestad, Curaçao, Willemstad, Bonaire, Kralendijk, Los Roques, La Orchila, Isla de Margarita, La Tortuga, La Blanquilla

### TRINIDAD (Br.)
Port of Spain, San Fernando, Serpents Mouth

CARIBBEAN SEA

VENEZUELA
CARACAS, Maracaibo, Barquisimeto, Valencia, Maracay, La Guaira, Puerto Cabello, Coro, Cumaná, Barcelona, Ciudad Bolívar, Orinoco Delta, L. de Maracaibo

COLOMBIA
Barranquilla, Cartagena, Santa Marta, Magdalena, Riohacha, Montería, Magangué

PANAMA
CANAL ZONE (U.S.), Colón, Cristóbal, Panamá, Balboa, Arch. de las Perlas

COSTA RICA
Puerto Limón

NICARAGUA
Puerto Cabezas (Bragmans Bluff), Bluefields, Corn Is., Swan Is. (U.S. & Hond.)

HONDURAS
C. Gracias a Dios

Florida Straits, Florida Channel, Old Bahama Channel, Santaren Channel, Nicholas Channel, Windward Passage, Mona Passage, Anegada Passage, Tropic of Cancer

New York — Havana 914
New York — San Juan 1,399
New York — La Guaira 1,847
New York — Kingston 1,474
Havana — San Juan 973
Kingston — Barranquilla 437
Ciudad Trujillo — La Guaira 501
Ciudad Trujillo — Curaçao 393
Colón — Kingston 551
Bridgetown — Georgetown 389
Port of Spain — Georgetown 378

ATLANTIC OCEAN

PACIFIC OCEAN

CARIBBEAN SEA

VENEZUELA

COLOMBIA

ECUADOR

PERU

BOLIVIA

BRAZIL

BRITISH GUIANA

SURINAM (Neth.)

FRENCH GUIANA

PANAMA

COSTA RICA

RIO AMAZONAS

Rio Negro

Rio Branco

MATO GROSSO

MINAS GERAES

BAHIA

PIAUHY

MARANHÃO

PERNAMBUCO

AMAPÁ

Serra Parima

Serra Pacaraima

MARTINIQUE (Fr.) — Fort de France
WINDWARD ISLANDS (Br.) — St. Lucia, St. Vincent, Grenadines
BARBADOS (Br.) — Bridgetown
St. George's — Grenada (Br.)
TRINIDAD (Br.) — Port of Spain
Tobago

Bogotá
Caracas
Medellín
Cali
Quito
Guayaquil
Lima
Callao
Arequipa
La Paz
Sucre
Cochabamba
Potosí
Oruro
Iquitos
Manáos
Belém
Fortaleza
Recife (Pernambuco)
Maceió
João Pessoa (Parahyba)
Natal
Aracaju
Salvador (Bahia)
Brasília
Georgetown
Paramaribo
Cayenne
Barranquilla
Cartagena
Santa Marta
Maracaibo
Valencia
Barquisimeto
Ciudad Bolívar
Cúcuta
Bucaramanga
Trujillo

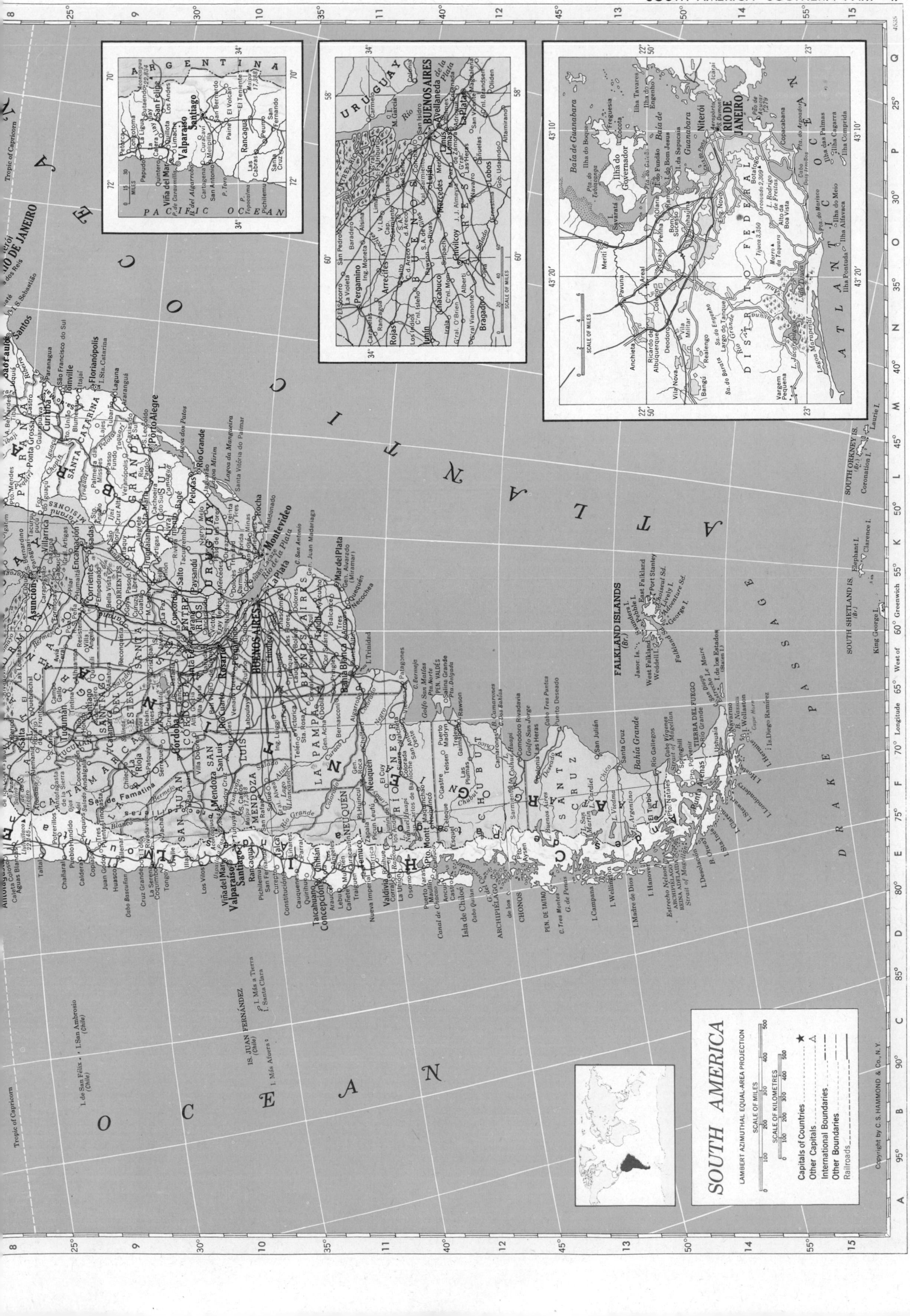

ARGENTINA

Aconcagua 22,834

Valparaíso
Santiago
Viña del Mar
Rancagua

PACIFIC OCEAN

URUGUAY

BUENOS AIRES
La Plata
Montevideo

SCALE OF MILES

Baía de Guanabara

RIO DE JANEIRO
Niterói
DISTRITO FEDERAL

ATLANTIC OCEAN

SCALE OF MILES

Curitiba
Florianópolis
Pôrto Alegre
Rio Grande
Pelotas

Montevideo
La Plata
BUENOS AIRES
Rosario
Córdoba
Santa Fé
Paraná
Mendoza
San Luis
San Juan
La Rioja
Catamarca
Tucumán
Salta

PARAGUAY
Asunción

LA PAMPA

RIO NEGRO
Neuquén

CHUBUT

SANTA CRUZ

ARGENTINA

TIERRA DEL FUEGO

Punta Arenas
Strait of Magellan

FALKLAND ISLANDS (Br.)
West Falkland
East Falkland
Port Stanley

SOUTH SHETLAND IS.
SOUTH ORKNEY IS.

DRAKE PASSAGE

Valdivia
Pto. Montt
Isla de Chiloé
ARCHIPIÉLAGO de los CHONOS

Concepción
Talcahuano
Temuco

Valparaíso
Santiago
Viña del Mar
Rancagua

IS. JUAN FERNÁNDEZ
I. Más a Tierra (Chile)
I. Santa Clara (Chile)

Tropic of Capricorn

PACIFIC OCEAN

ATLANTIC OCEAN

# SOUTH AMERICA

LAMBERT AZIMUTHAL EQUAL-AREA PROJECTION

SCALE OF MILES
SCALE OF KILOMETRES

Capitals of Countries ............ ★
Other Capitals ............ △
International Boundaries ............
Other Boundaries ............
Railroads ............

Copyright by C. S. HAMMOND & Co., N.Y.

## CUBA

## JAMAICA

## HISPANIOLA

LEGEND

Capitals of Countries..............☆
Colonial Capital..................◉
Provincial Capitals...............△
International Boundaries...........
Provincial Boundaries.............
Railroads.........................

Copyright by C.S. HAMMOND & Co., N.Y.

SCALE OF MILES
SCALE OF KILOMETRES

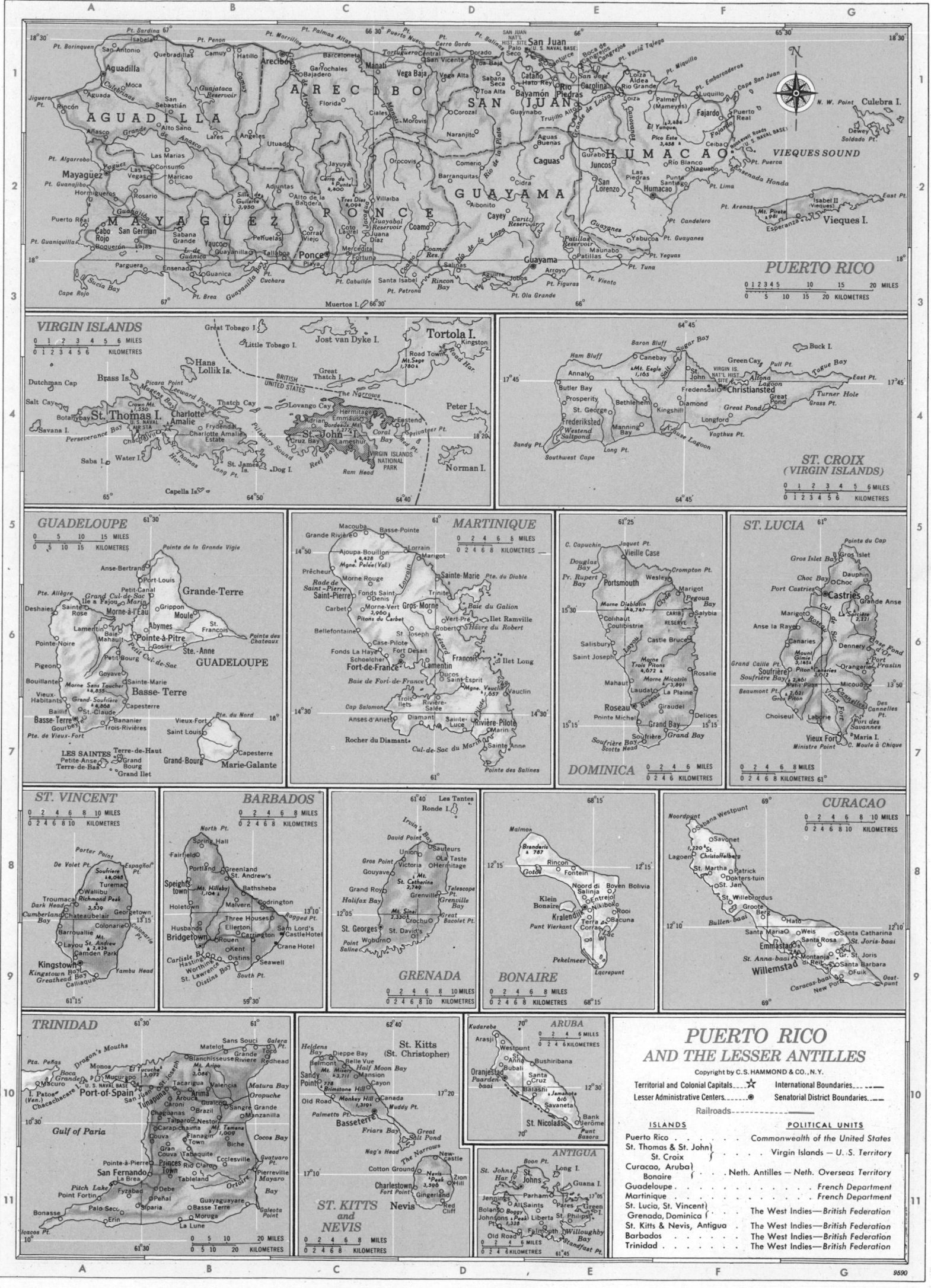

## PUERTO RICO

## PUERTO RICO
### AND THE LESSER ANTILLES
Copyright by C.S. HAMMOND & CO., N.Y.

Territorial and Colonial Capitals ☆   International Boundaries
Lesser Administrative Centers ◉   Senatorial District Boundaries
Railroads

| ISLANDS | POLITICAL UNITS |
|---|---|
| Puerto Rico | Commonwealth of the United States |
| St. Thomas & St. John | Virgin Islands – U.S. Territory |
| St. Croix | |
| Curacao, Aruba, Bonaire | Neth. Antilles – Neth. Overseas Territory |
| Guadeloupe | French Department |
| Martinique | French Department |
| St. Lucia, St. Vincent | The West Indies – British Federation |
| Grenada, Dominica | The West Indies – British Federation |
| St. Kitts & Nevis, Antigua | The West Indies – British Federation |
| Barbados | The West Indies – British Federation |
| Trinidad | The West Indies – British Federation |

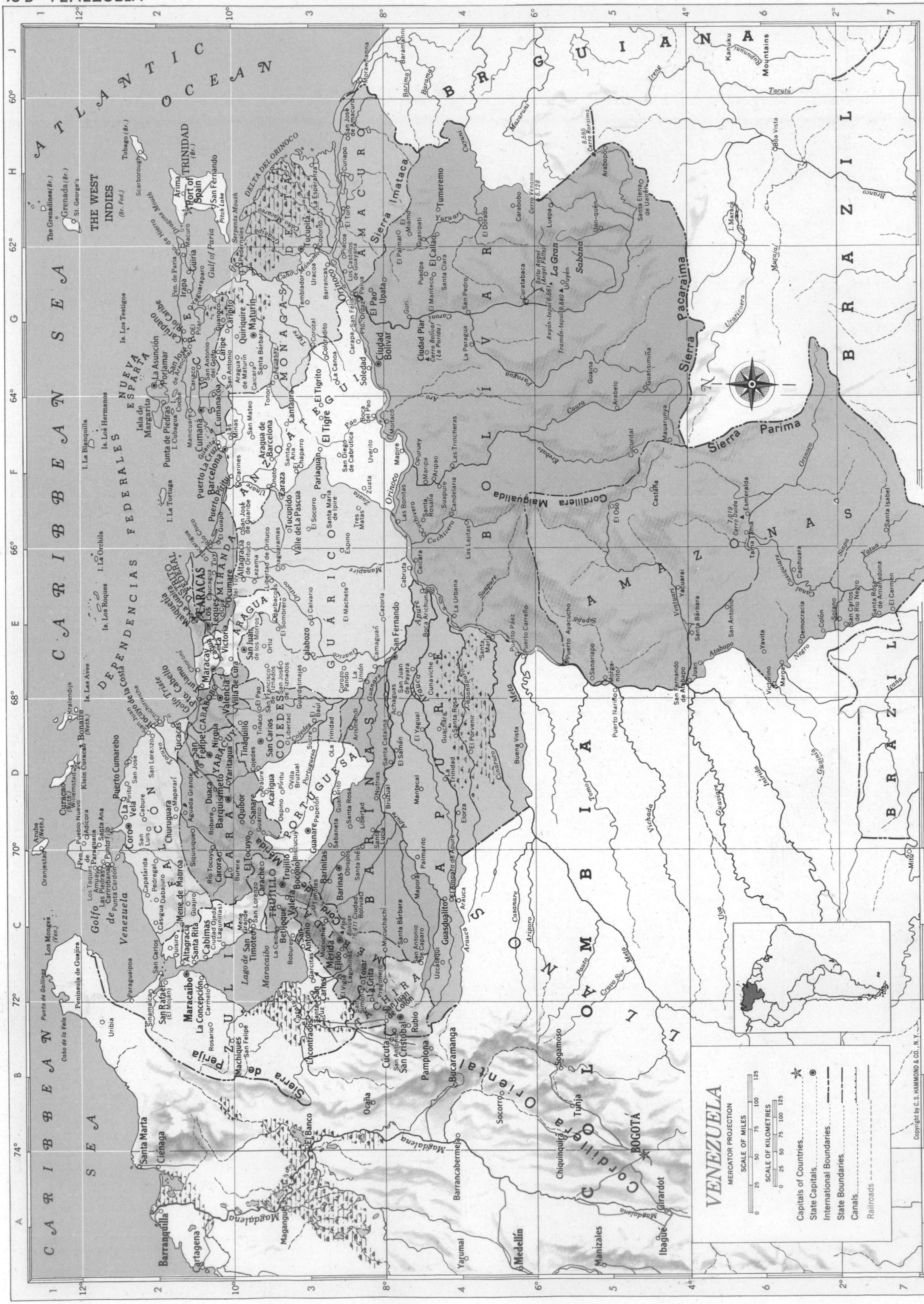

# VENEZUELA

MERCATOR PROJECTION

SCALE OF MILES
0   25   50   75   100   125

SCALE OF KILOMETRES
0   25   50   75   100   125

Capitals of Countries............
State Capitals............
International Boundaries............
State Boundaries............
Canals............
Railroads............

ATLANTIC OCEAN

CARIBBEAN SEA

THE WEST INDIES (Br. Fed.)

B R I T I S H   G U I A N A

B R A Z I L

C O L O M B I A

TRINIDAD

Tobago (Br.)

Grenada (Br.)
The Grenadines (Br.)
St. George's

Port of Spain

DELTA DEL ORINOCO

Gulf of Paria

NUEVA ESPARTA
Isla de Margarita
La Asunción
Porlamar

DEPENDENCIAS FEDERALES

I. La Blanquilla
I. La Tortuga
I. La Orchila
In. Los Roques
In. Los Hermanos
In. Los Testigos
I. Las Aves

Aruba (Neth.)
Curaçao (Neth.)
Bonaire (Neth.)
Oranjestad
Willemstad
Kralendijk

Golfo de Venezuela
Península de Guajira
Punta de Gallinas

CARACAS

MARACAIBO

Lago de Maracaibo

Z U L I A
F A L C O N
L A R A
Y A R A C U Y
C A R A B O B O
A R A G U A
M I R A N D A
D I S T R I T O   F E D E R A L
C O J E D E S
P O R T U G U E S A
G U A R I C O
B A R I N A S
A P U R E
T A C H I R A
M E R I D A
T R U J I L L O
A N Z O A T E G U I
S U C R E
M O N A G A S
A M A C U R O
B O L I V A R
A M A Z O N A S

Maracay
Valencia
Barquisimeto
Coro
San Felipe
San Carlos
San Juan de los Morros
San Fernando
Barinas
San Cristóbal
Mérida
Trujillo
Barcelona
Cumaná
Maturín
Ciudad Bolívar
San Fernando de Atabapo

Orinoco

Río Negro

Sierra Parima
Sierra Pacaraima
Sierra Imataca
Cordillera Maquarida

La Gran Sabana

Cerro Roraima
8,595

Auyán-tepui 9,094
(Angel Falls)

Cerro Yaví 5,128

Cordillera Oriental

BOGOTA

Medellín
Manizales
Ibagué
Girardot

Magdalena

Copyright by C. S. HAMMOND & CO., N.Y.

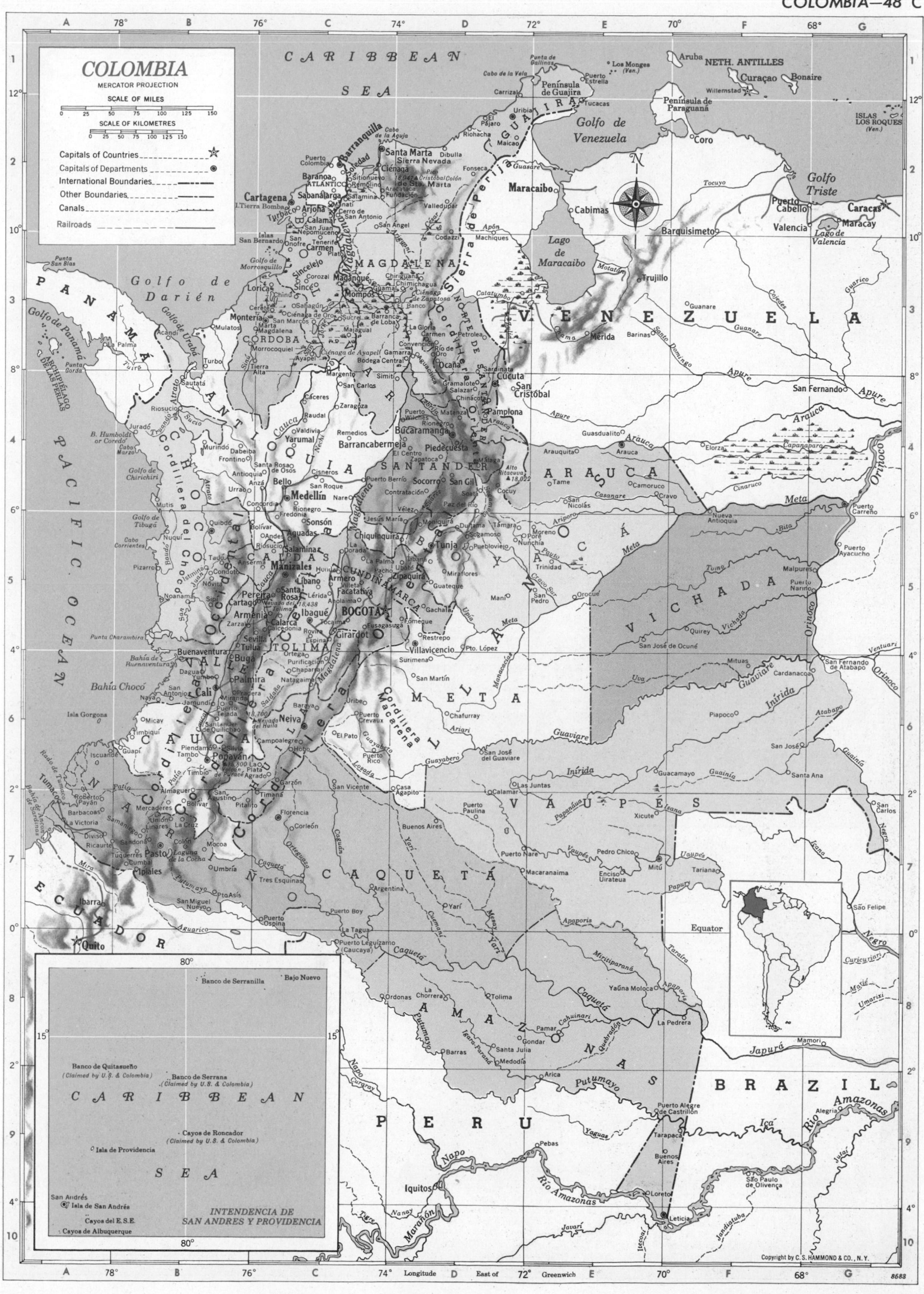

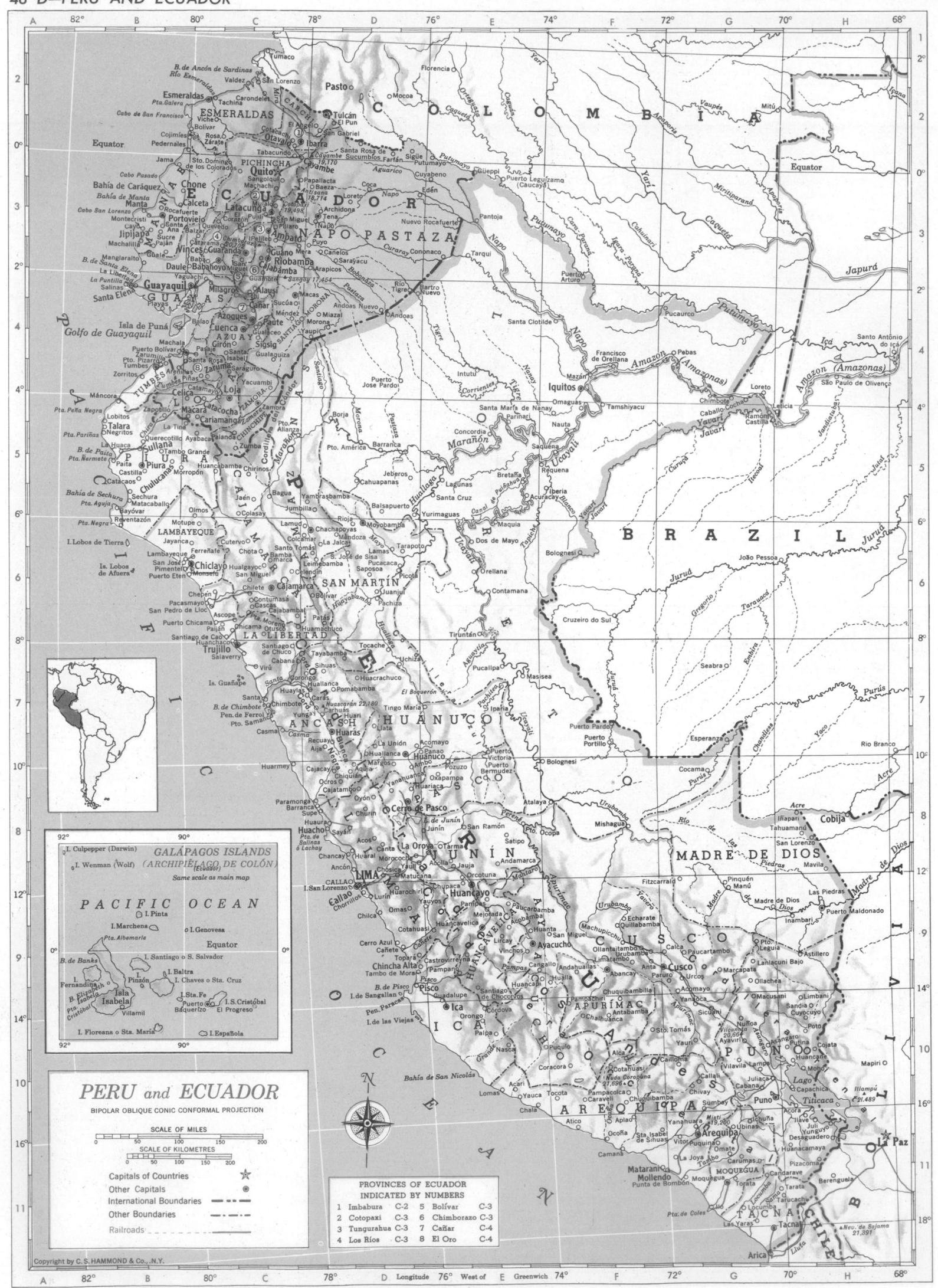

GALÁPAGOS ISLANDS
(ARCHIPIÉLAGO DE COLÓN)
(Ecuador)
Same scale as main map

PACIFIC OCEAN

PERU and ECUADOR

BIPOLAR OBLIQUE CONIC CONFORMAL PROJECTION

SCALE OF MILES
0    50    100    150    200

SCALE OF KILOMETRES
0    50    100    150    200

Capitals of Countries ............... ★
Other Capitals ............... ◉
International Boundaries ...... –––––
Other Boundaries ............... –·–·–
Railroads ............... ┼┼┼┼

PROVINCES OF ECUADOR
INDICATED BY NUMBERS

| 1 Imbabura | C-2 | 5 Bolívar | C-3 |
| 2 Cotopaxi | C-3 | 6 Chimborazo | C-3 |
| 3 Tungurahua | C-3 | 7 Cañar | C-4 |
| 4 Los Ríos | C-3 | 8 El Oro | C-4 |

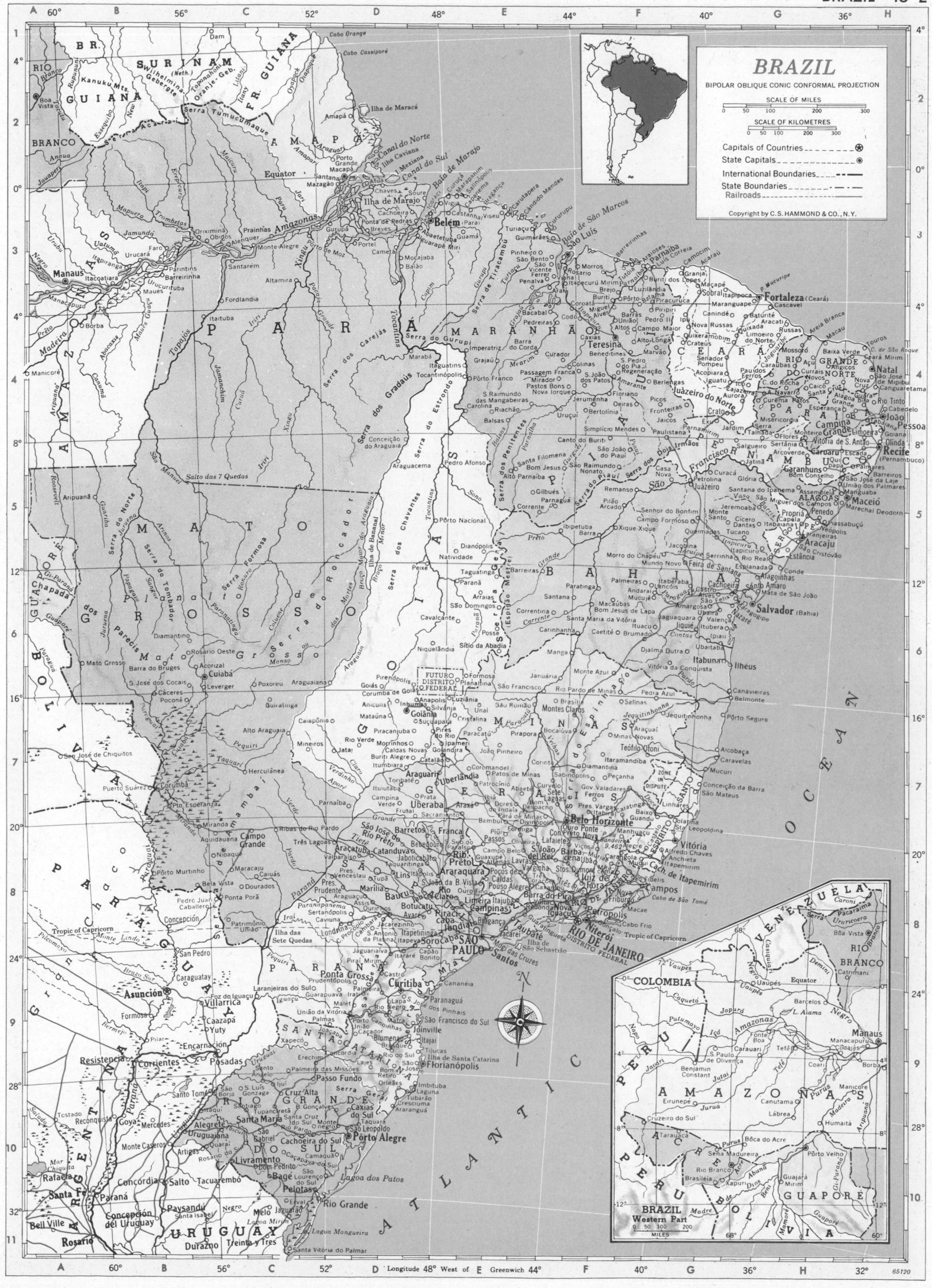

BRAZIL
BIPOLAR OBLIQUE CONIC CONFORMAL PROJECTION

SCALE OF MILES
0  50  100        200        300

SCALE OF KILOMETRES
0  50  100        200        300

Capitals of Countries _____ ⊗
State Capitals _____ ◉
International Boundaries _____
State Boundaries _____
Railroads _____

Copyright by C.S. HAMMOND & CO., N.Y.

BRAZIL
Western Part
0 50 100      200
MILES

Longitude 48° West of Greenwich 44°

65120

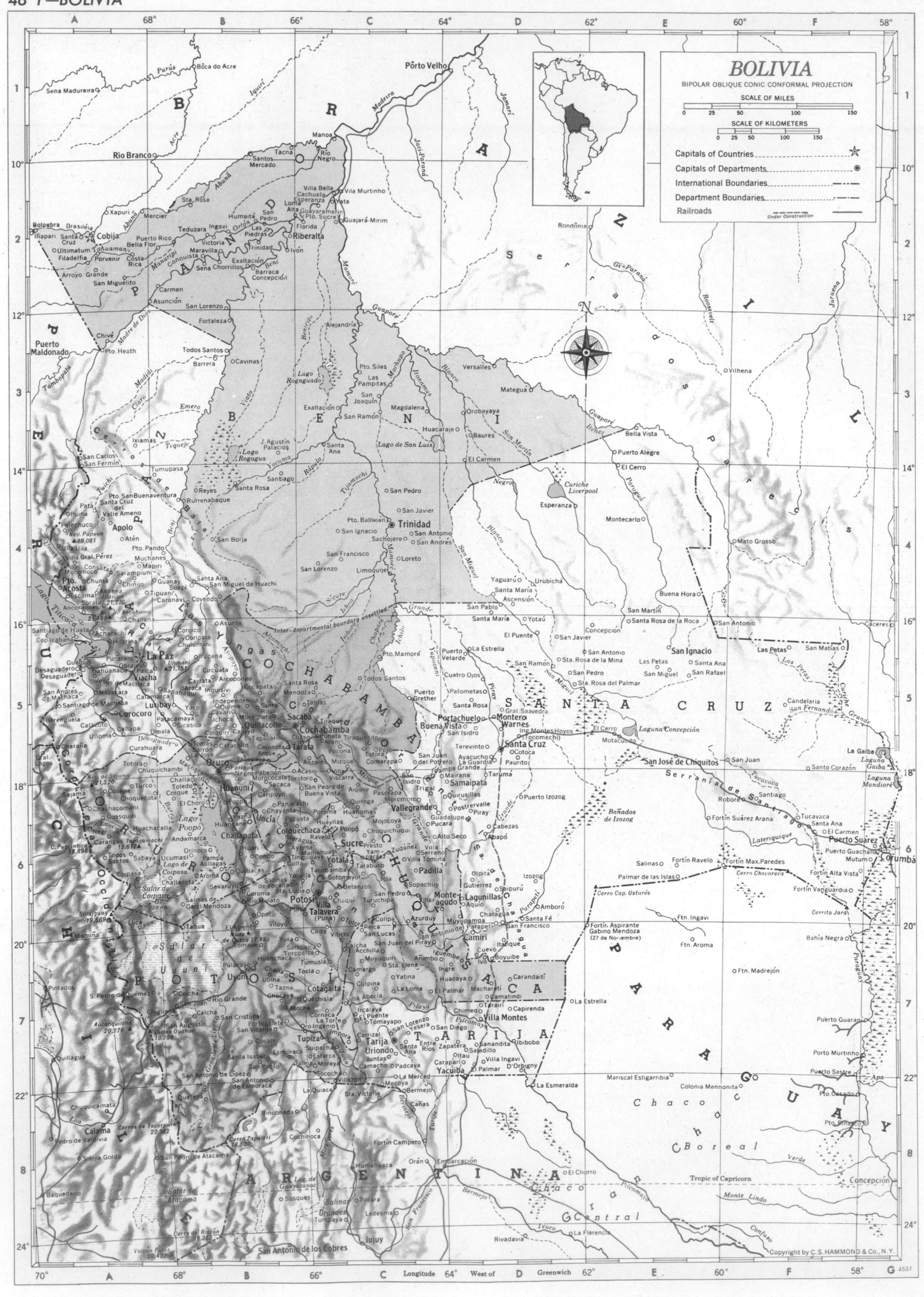

## BOLIVIA
BIPOLAR OBLIQUE CONIC CONFORMAL PROJECTION

SCALE OF MILES
0   25   50        100        150

SCALE OF KILOMETERS
0   25   50    100    150

Capitals of Countries ................................ ★
Capitals of Departments ........................... ◉
International Boundaries .....................
Department Boundaries ......................
Railroads ...................................
*Under Construction*

Longitude 64° West of Greenwich 62°

Copyright by C.S. HAMMOND & Co., N.Y.

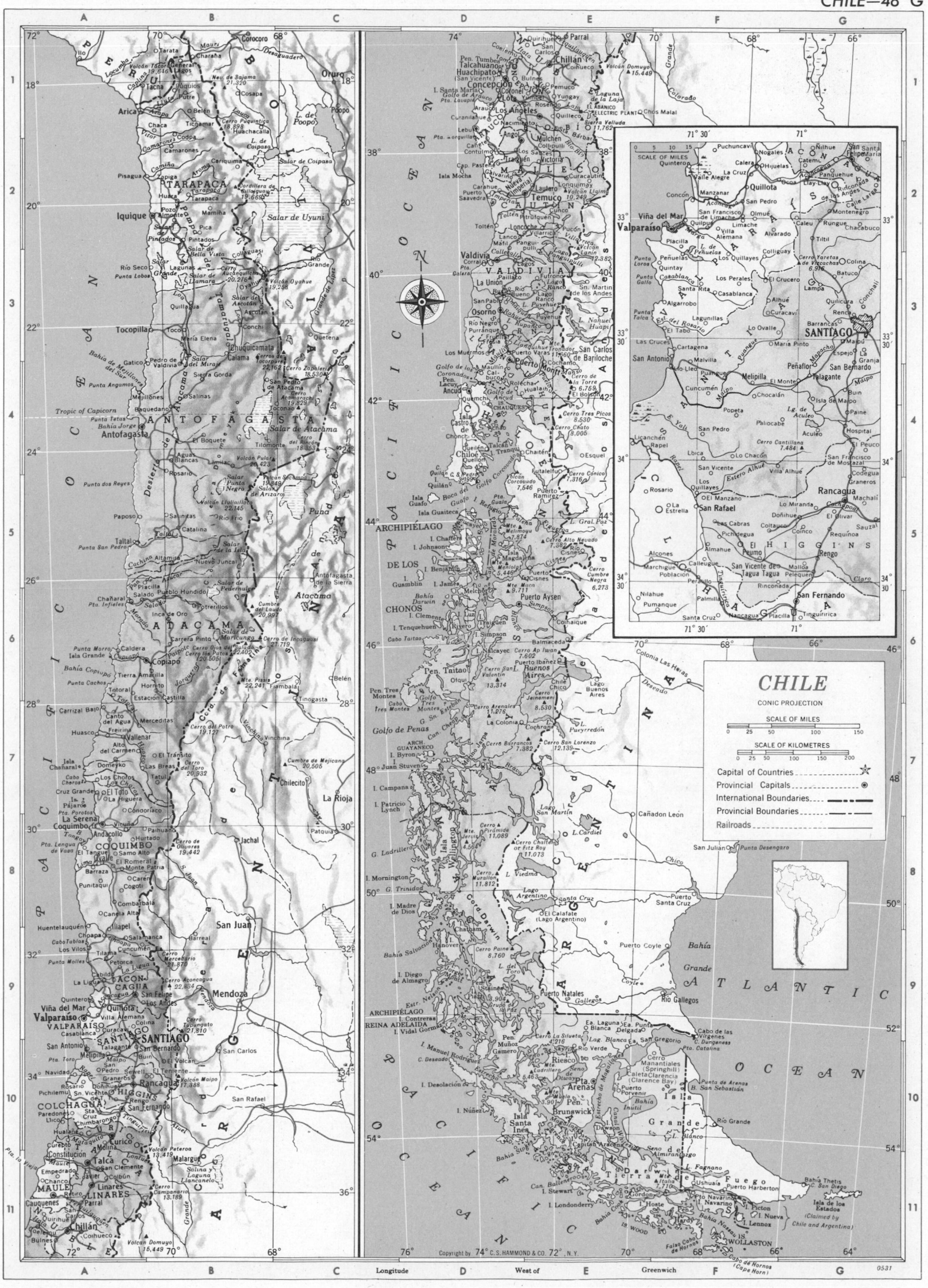

CHILE

CONIC PROJECTION

SCALE OF MILES
0    25    50    75    100    150

SCALE OF KILOMETRES
0  25  50   100   150   200

Capital of Countries ............ ⭐
Provincial Capitals ............ ⊙
International Boundaries ........
Provincial Boundaries ..........
Railroads ......................

Copyright by C. S. HAMMOND & CO., N.Y.

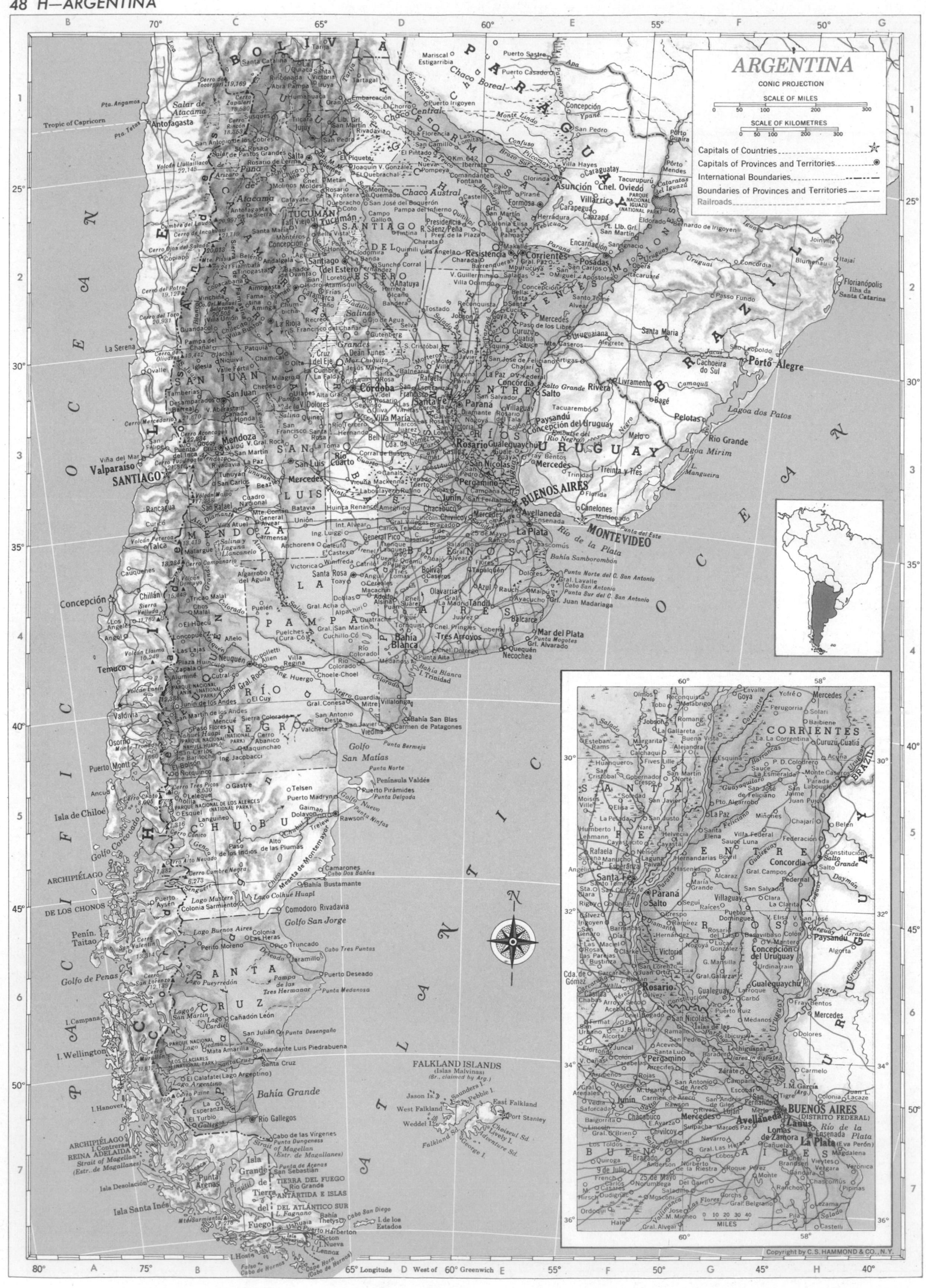

ARGENTINA

CONIC PROJECTION

SCALE OF MILES

SCALE OF KILOMETRES

Capitals of Countries
Capitals of Provinces and Territories
International Boundaries
Boundaries of Provinces and Territories
Railroads

Copyright by C. S. HAMMOND & CO., N. Y.

FALKLAND ISLANDS
(Islas Malvinas)
(Br., claimed by Arg.)

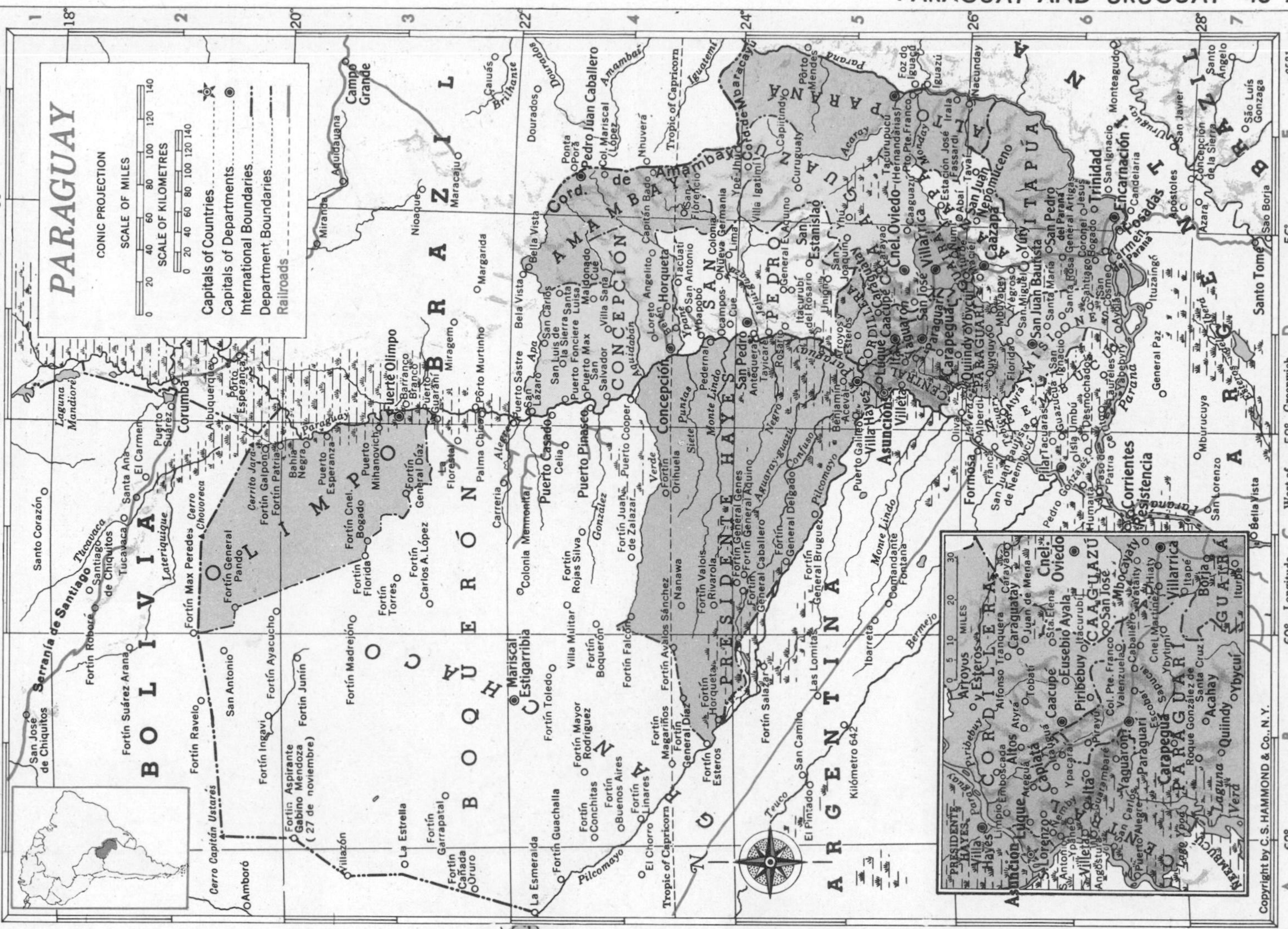

# PARAGUAY

CONIC PROJECTION

SCALE OF MILES

SCALE OF KILOMETRES

Capitals of Countries ......... ⊙
Capitals of Departments ...... ◉
International Boundaries ......
Department Boundaries ........
Railroads ........................

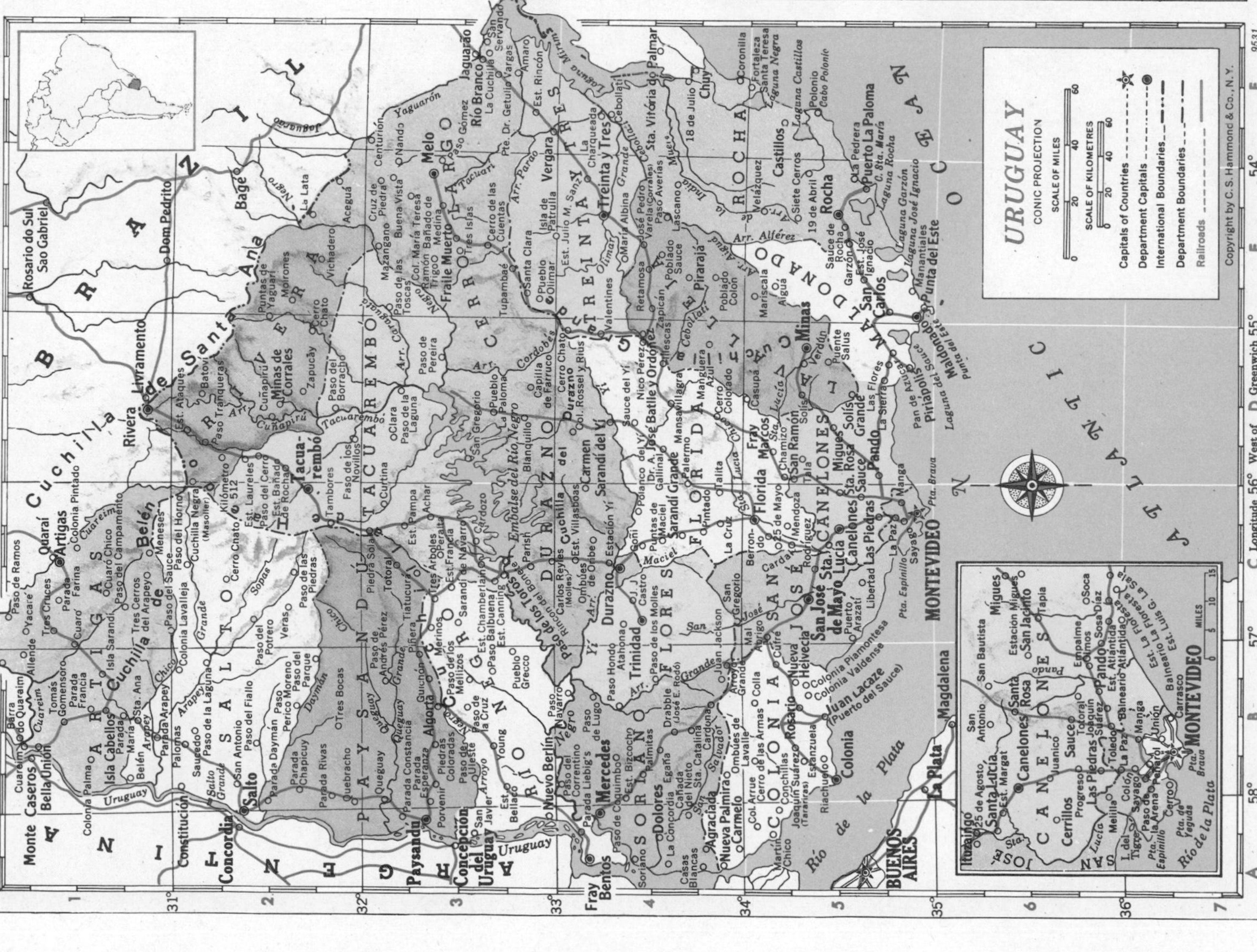

# URUGUAY

CONIC PROJECTION

SCALE OF MILES

SCALE OF KILOMETRES

Capitals of Countries ......... ⊛
Department Capitals ........... ◉
International Boundaries ......
Department Boundaries ........
Railroads ........................

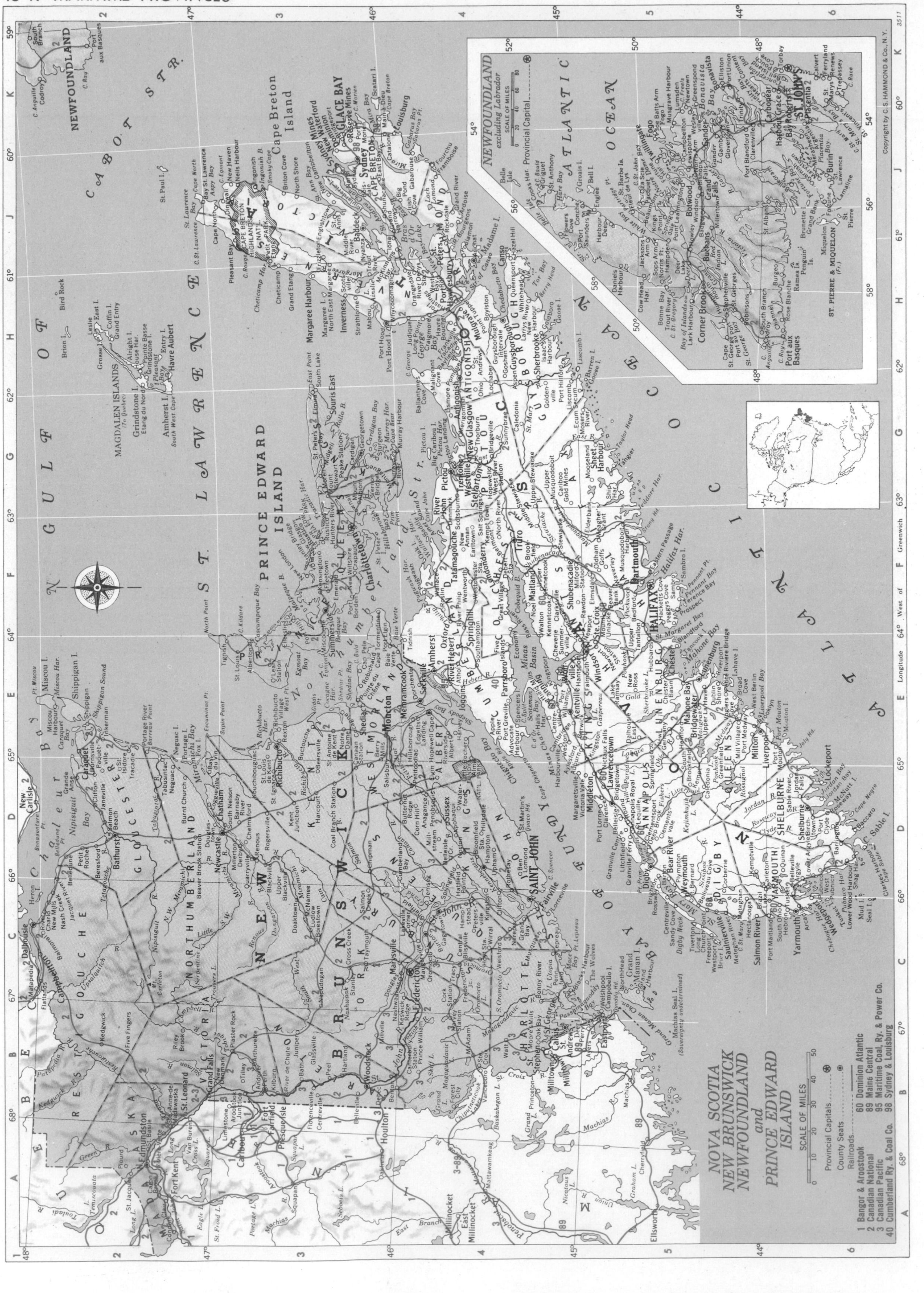

NEWFOUNDLAND
*excluding Labrador*

ST. PIERRE & MIQUELON (Fr.)

NOVA SCOTIA
NEW BRUNSWICK
NEWFOUNDLAND
and
PRINCE EDWARD
ISLAND

SCALE OF MILES
0   10   20   30   40   50

Provincial Capitals
County Seats
Railroads

1  Bangor & Aroostook
2  Canadian National
3  Canadian Pacific
40 Cumberland Ry. & Coal Co.
60 Dominion Atlantic
89 Mains Central
95 Maritime Coal, Ry. & Power Co.
98 Sydney & Louisburg

Copyright by C. S. HAMMOND & Co., N.Y.

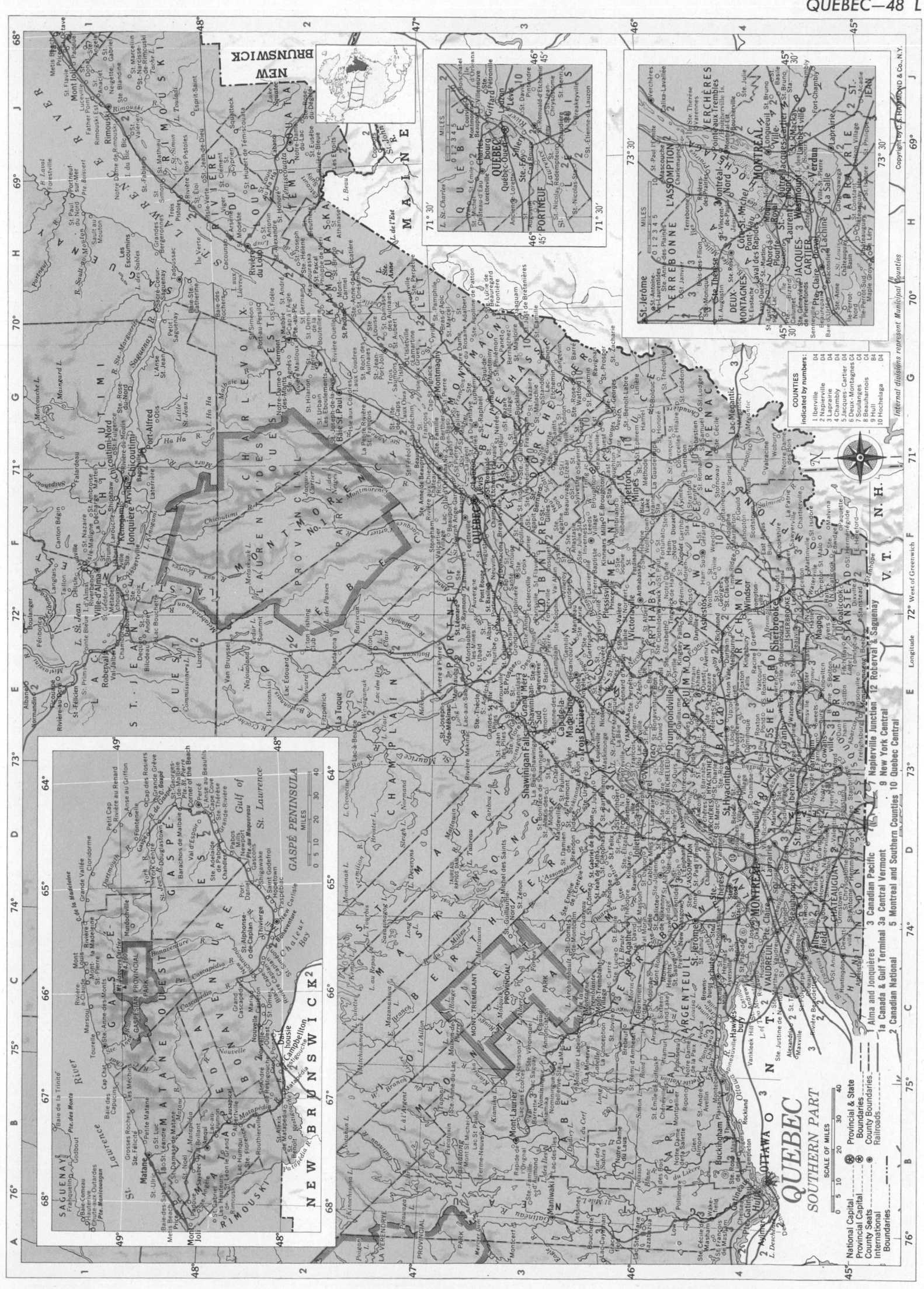

# QUEBEC
## SOUTHERN PART

SCALE OF MILES

National Capital ★
Provincial Capital ⊛
County Seats ⊙
International
Boundaries

Provincial & State
Boundaries
County Boundaries
Railroads

COUNTIES
indicated by numbers:

1 Iberville D4
2 Napierville D4
3 Laprairie D4
4 Chambly D4
5 St. Johns D4
6 Deux-Montagnes C4
7 Soulanges C4
8 Beauharnois C4
9 Hull A4
10 Hochelaga C4

Internal divisions represent Municipal Counties

1 Alma and Jonquières   2 Canada National
1a Canada & Gulf Terminal   3 Canadian Pacific
3a Central Vermont   5 Montreal and Southern Counties
7 Napierville Junction   9 New York Central
12 Roberval & Saguenay   10 Quebec Central

GASPÉ PENINSULA

Copyright by C. S. HAMMOND & Co., N.Y.

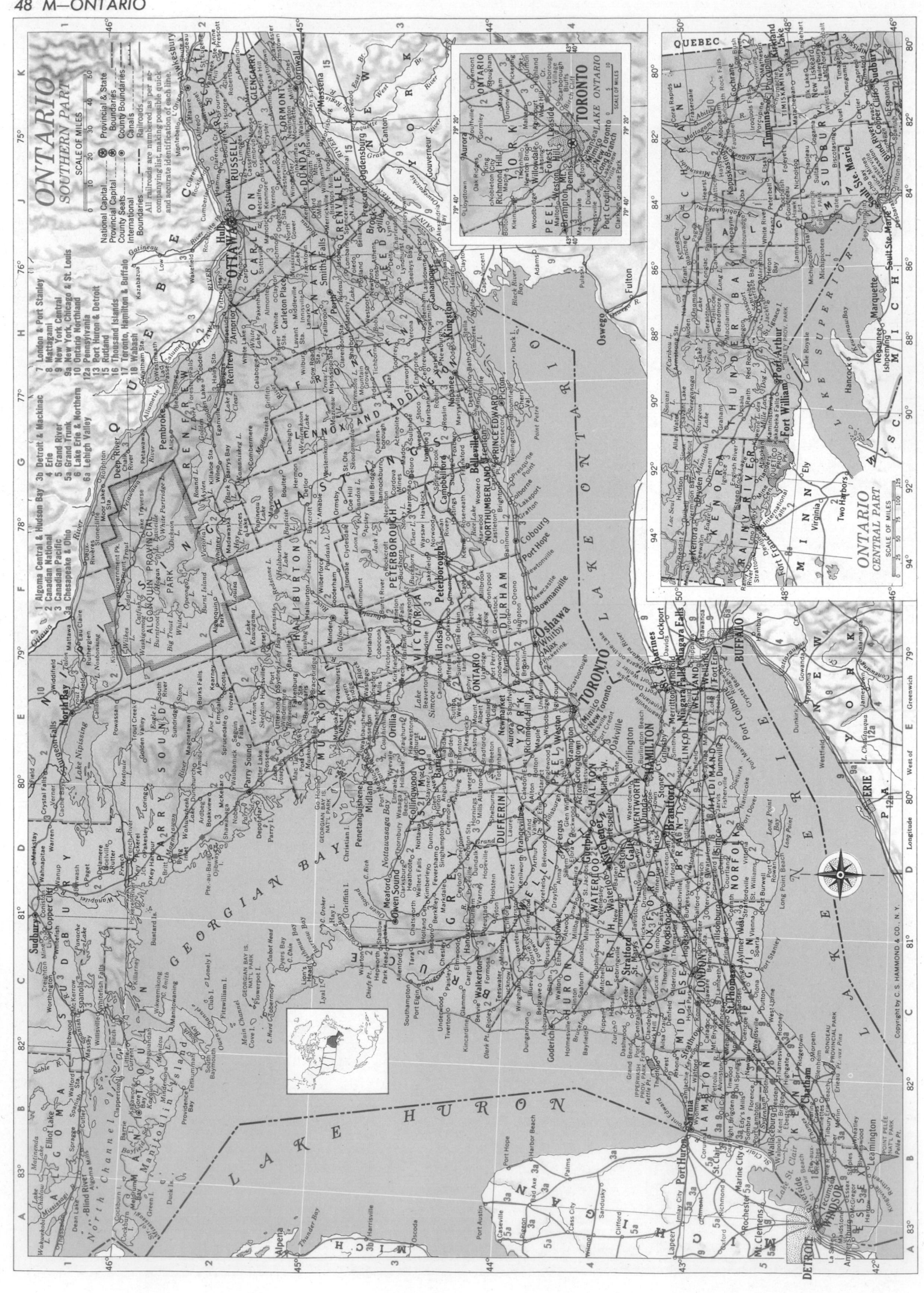

ONTARIO
SOUTHERN PART

SCALE OF MILES

Copyright by C. S. HAMMOND & CO., N.Y.

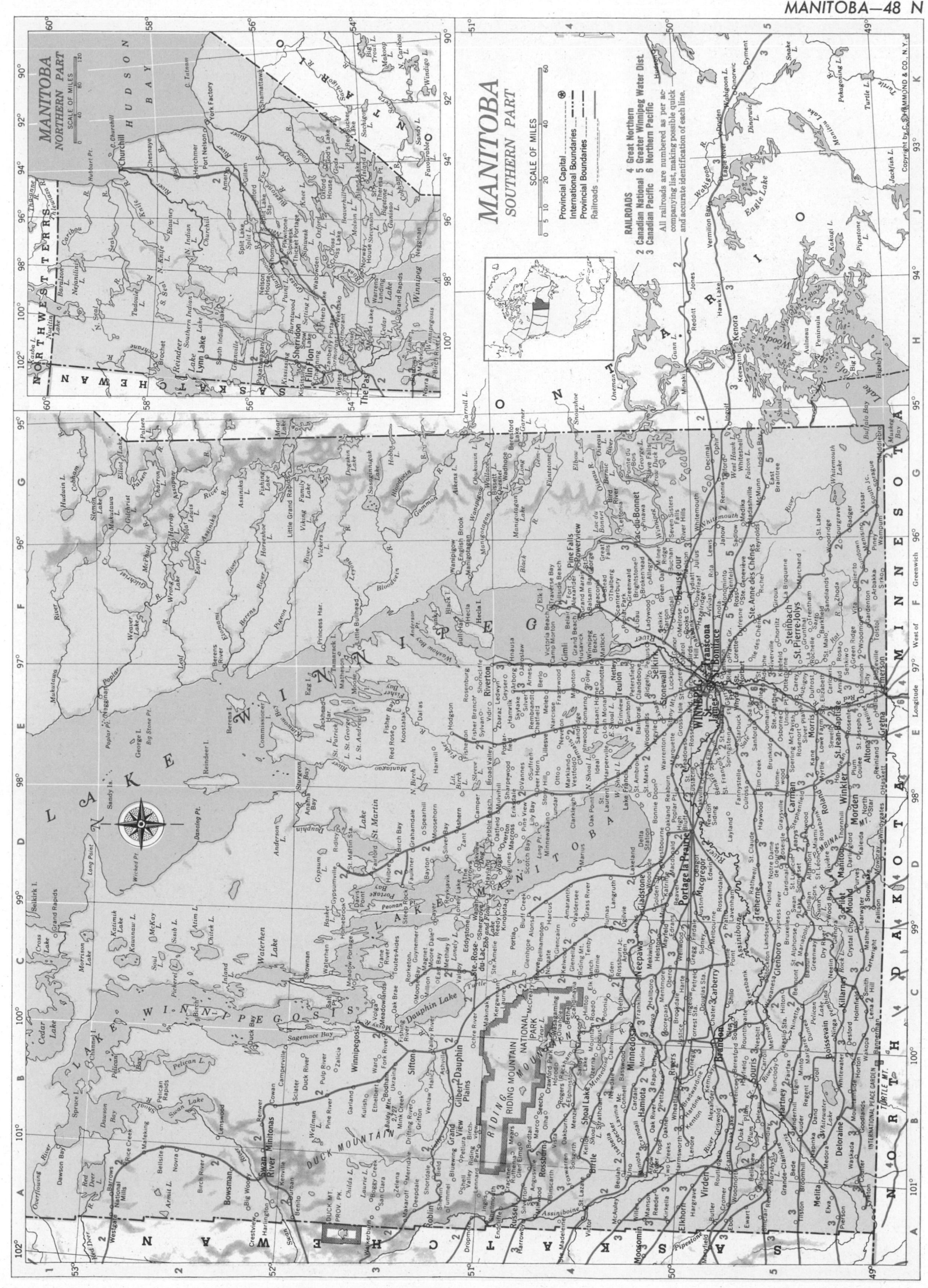

MANITOBA
NORTHERN PART
SCALE OF MILES

MANITOBA
SOUTHERN PART
SCALE OF MILES

RAILROADS  4 Great Northern
1 Canadian National  5 Greater Winnipeg Water Dist.
2 Canadian Pacific  6 Northern Pacific
3 Northern Pacific

Provincial Capital ⊛
International Boundaries
Provincial Boundaries
Railroads

All railroads are numbered as per accompanying list, making possible quick and accurate identification of each line.

Copyright by C. S. HAMMOND & CO., N. Y. C.

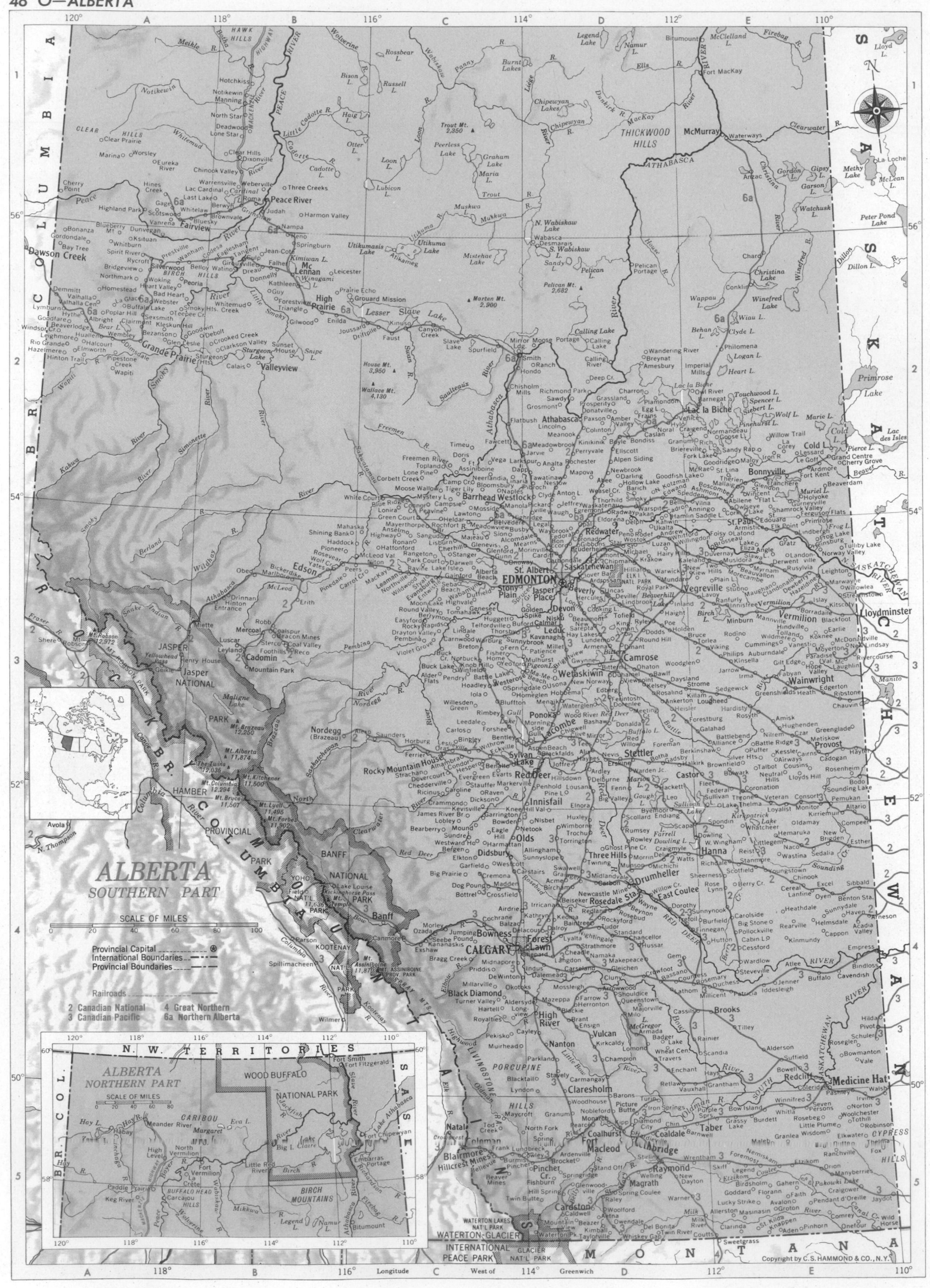

ALBERTA
SOUTHERN PART

SCALE OF MILES
0    20    40    60    80    100

⊗ Provincial Capital
Provincial Capital
International Boundaries
Provincial Boundaries

Railroads
2 Canadian National      4 Great Northern
3 Canadian Pacific        6a Northern Alberta

ALBERTA
NORTHERN PART

SCALE OF MILES
0   20   40   60   80

Copyright by C. S. HAMMOND & CO., N.Y.

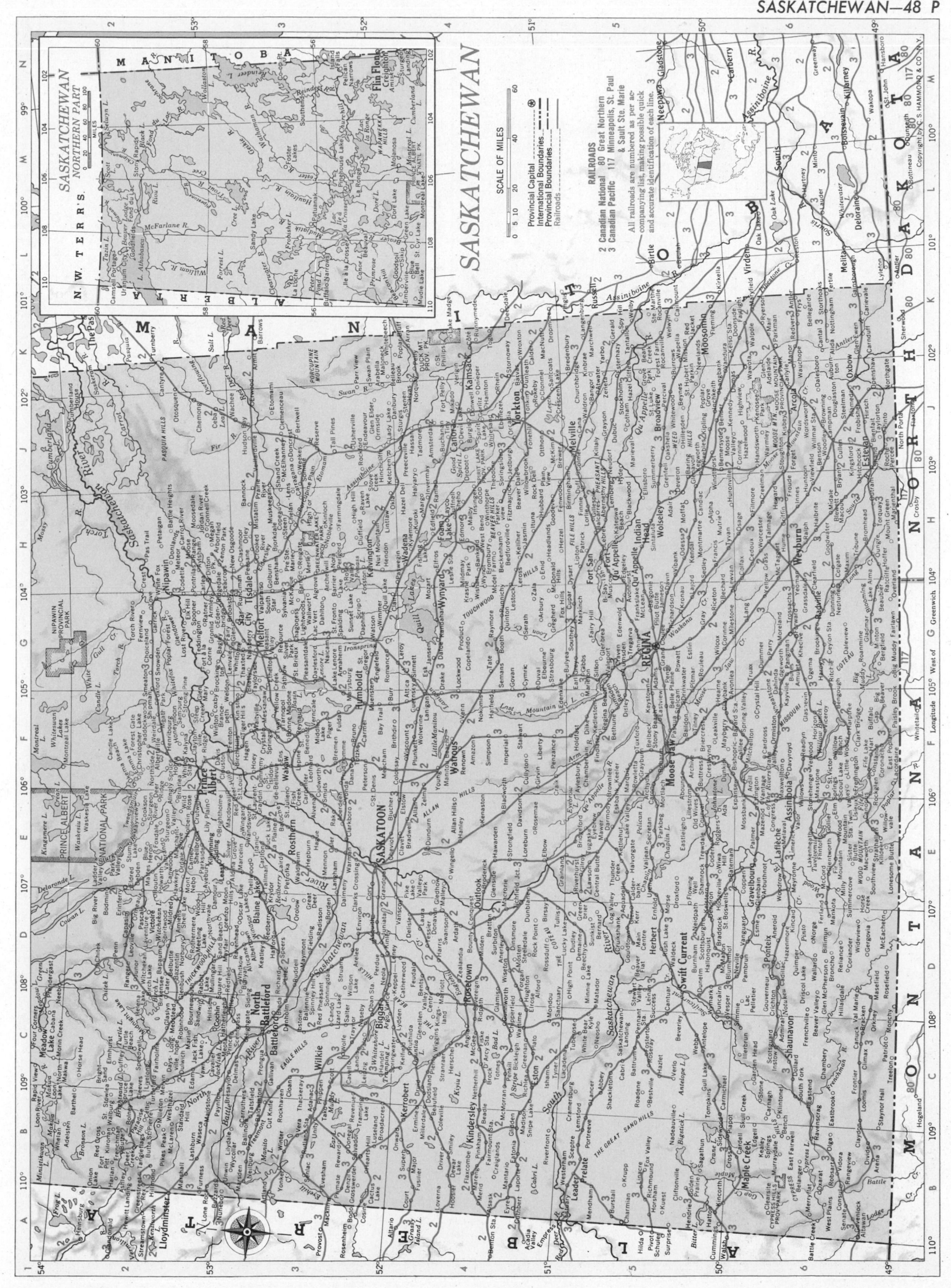

# SASKATCHEWAN

### SCALE OF MILES

Provincial Capital ⊛
International Boundaries — — —
Provincial Boundaries ..........
Railroads ———

### RAILROADS

2 Canadian National 80 Great Northern
3 Canadian Pacific 117 Minneapolis, St. Paul & Sault Ste. Marie

All railroads are numbered as per accompanying list, making possible quick and accurate identification of each line.

Copyright by C. S. HAMMOND & CO., N.Y.

### SASKATCHEWAN
### NORTHERN PART

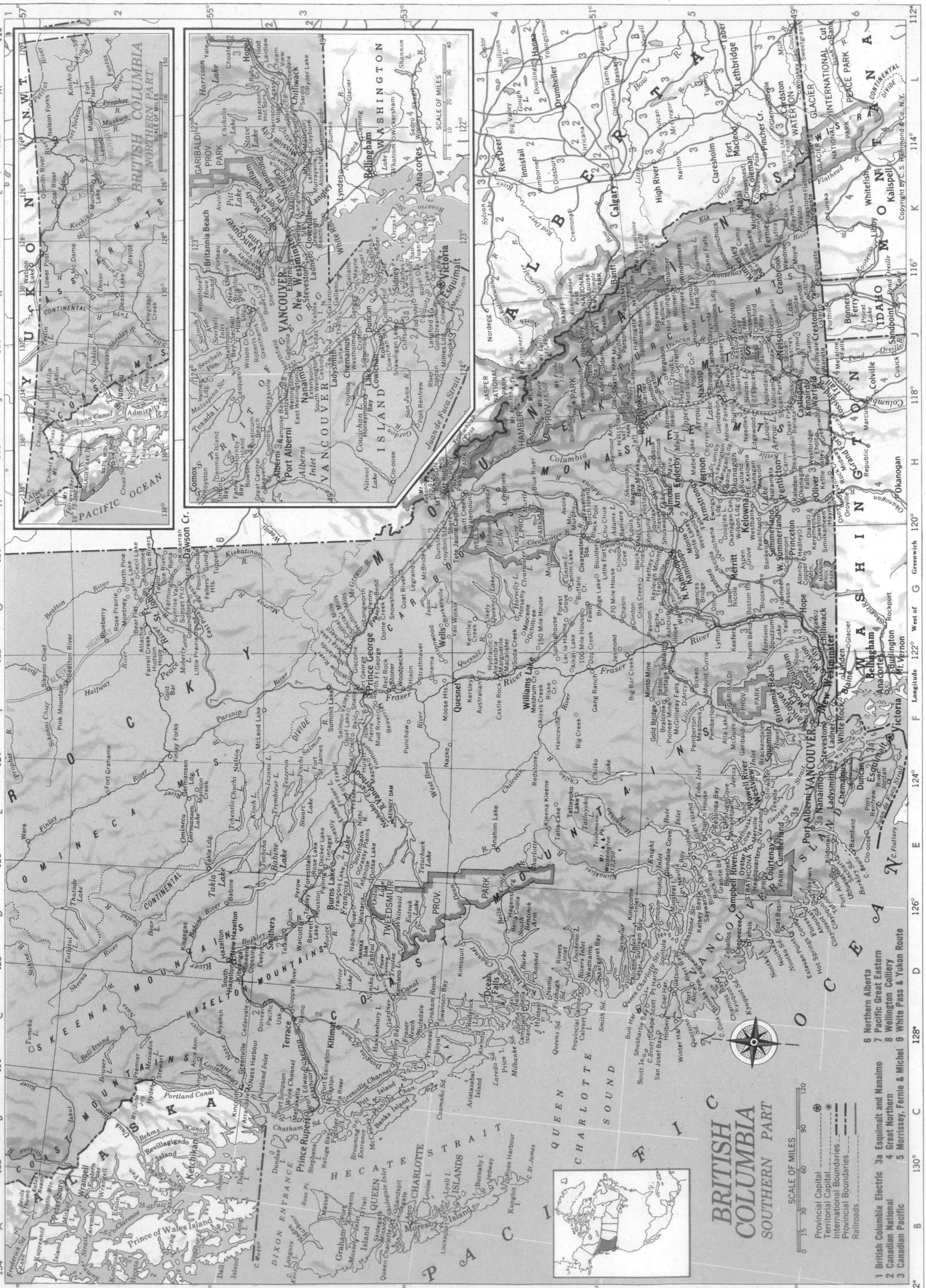

## BRITISH COLUMBIA
### NORTHERN PART
SCALE OF MILES

## BRITISH COLUMBIA
### SOUTHERN PART

SCALE OF MILES

**LEGEND**

1 British Columbia Electric
2 Canadian National
3 Canadian Pacific
3a Esquimalt and Nanaimo
4 Great Northern
5 Morrissey, Fernie & Michel
6 Northern Alberta
7 Pacific Great Eastern
8 Wellington Colliery
9 White Pass & Yukon Route

Provincial Capital
Territorial Capital
International Boundaries
Provincial Boundaries
Railroads

N.W.T.
YUKON
ALASKA
ALBERTA
WASHINGTON
IDAHO
MONTANA

PACIFIC OCEAN

ROCKY MOUNTAINS
COAST MOUNTAINS
SKEENA MOUNTAINS
CARIBOO MOUNTAINS
SELKIRK MOUNTAINS
MONASHEE MTS.
PURCELL MTS.
OMINECA MTS.
HAZELTON MOUNTAINS
CONTINENTAL DIVIDE

QUEEN CHARLOTTE ISLANDS
VANCOUVER ISLAND
HECATE STRAIT
QUEEN CHARLOTTE SOUND
DIXON ENTRANCE

Vancouver
Victoria
New Westminster
Nanaimo
Prince George
Prince Rupert
Kamloops
Kelowna
Penticton
Vernon
Revelstoke
Nelson
Cranbrook
Trail
Quesnel
Williams Lake
Terrace
Kitimat
Hazelton
Smithers
Calgary
Lethbridge
Red Deer

Copyright by C. S. Hammond & Co., N.Y.

TWEEDSMUIR PROV. PARK
TSEDISMUIR PROV. PARK
GARIBALDI PROV. PARK
JASPER NATIONAL PARK
BANFF NATIONAL PARK
GLACIER NATIONAL PARK
WATERTON

SCALE OF MILES

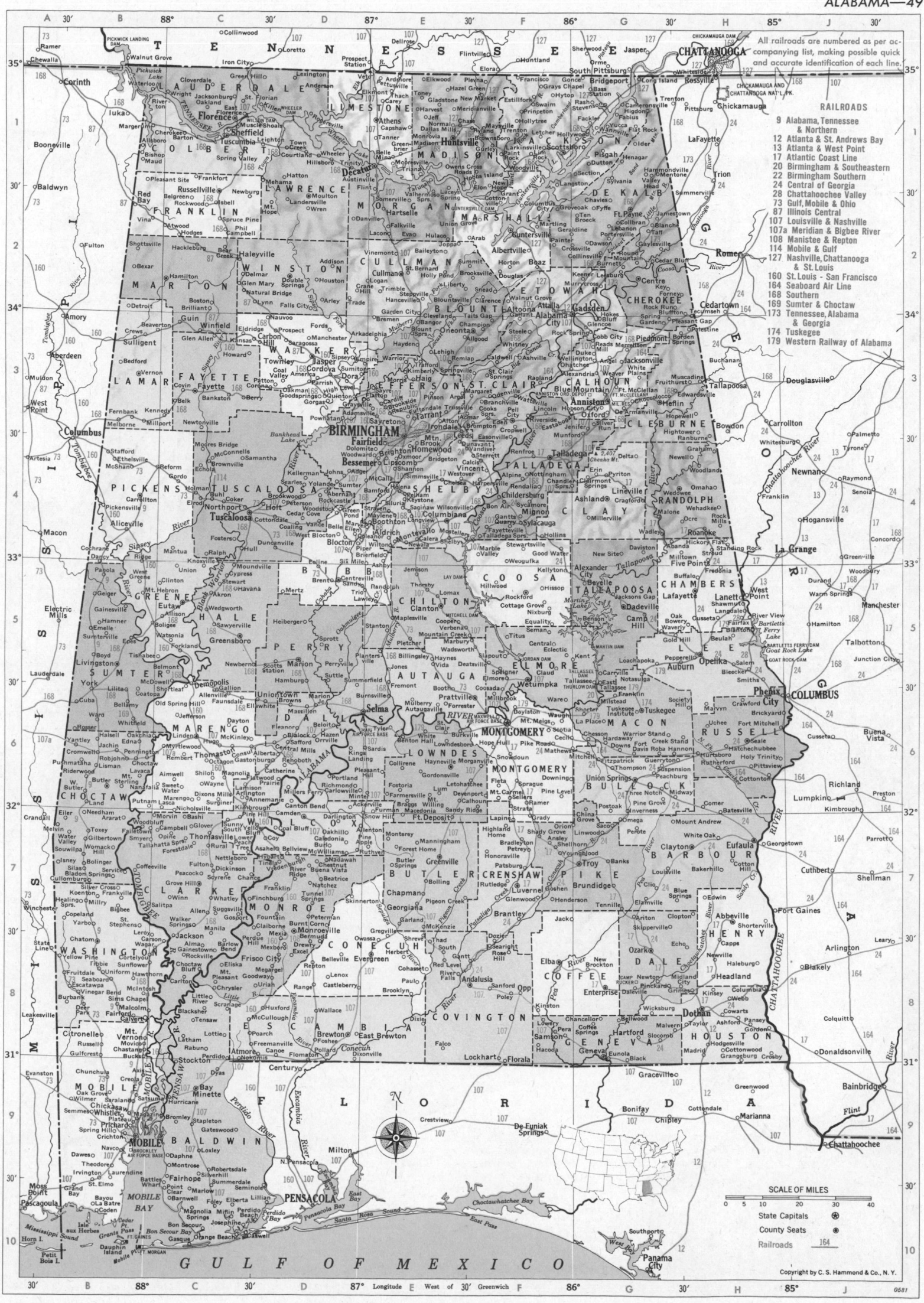

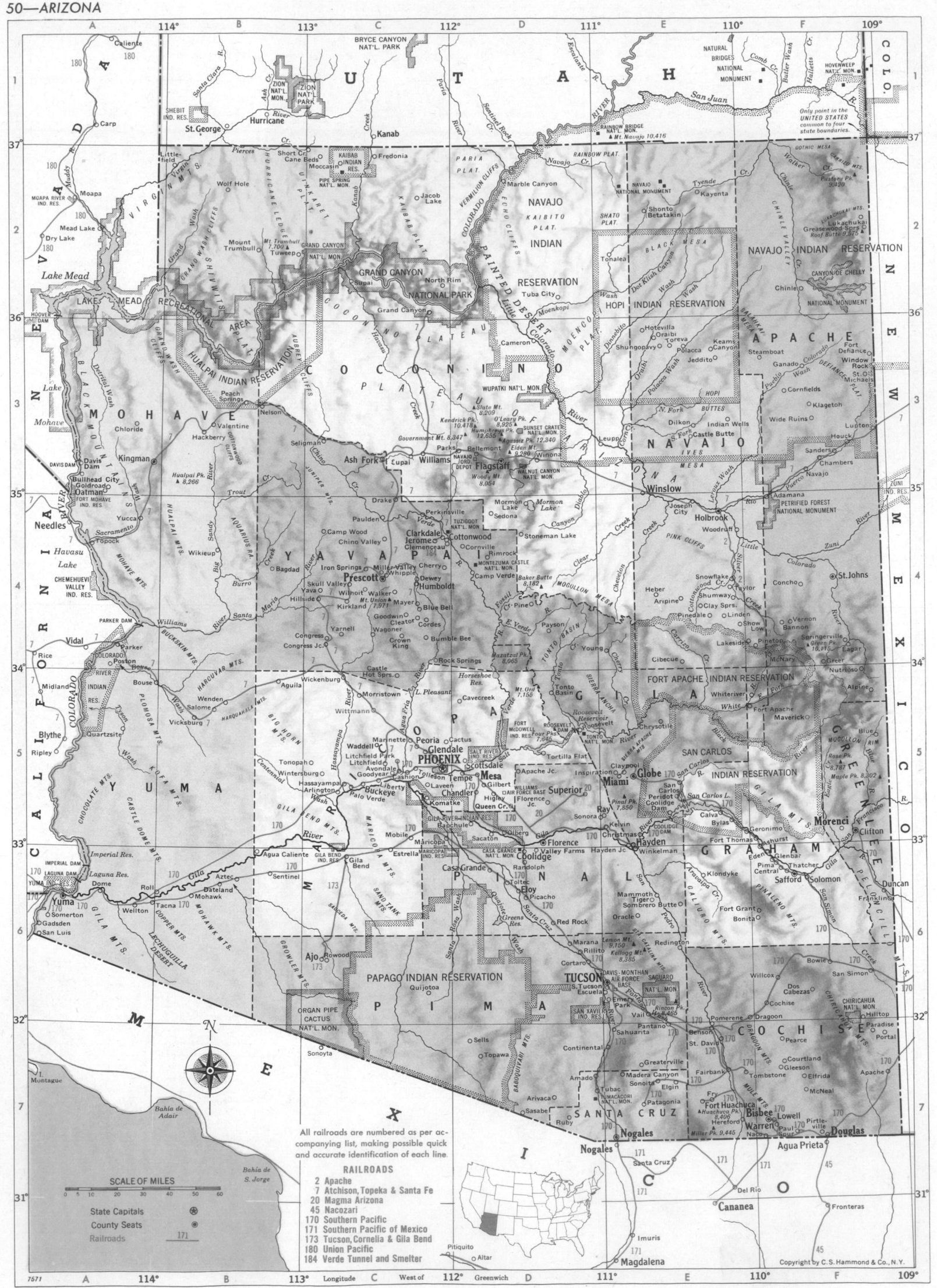

All railroads are numbered as per accompanying list, making possible quick and accurate identification of each line.

RAILROADS

2 Apache
7 Atchison, Topeka & Santa Fe
20 Magma Arizona
45 Nacozari
170 Southern Pacific
171 Southern Pacific of Mexico
173 Tucson, Cornelia & Gila Bend
180 Union Pacific
184 Verde Tunnel and Smelter

SCALE OF MILES

State Capitals
County Seats
Railroads

7571

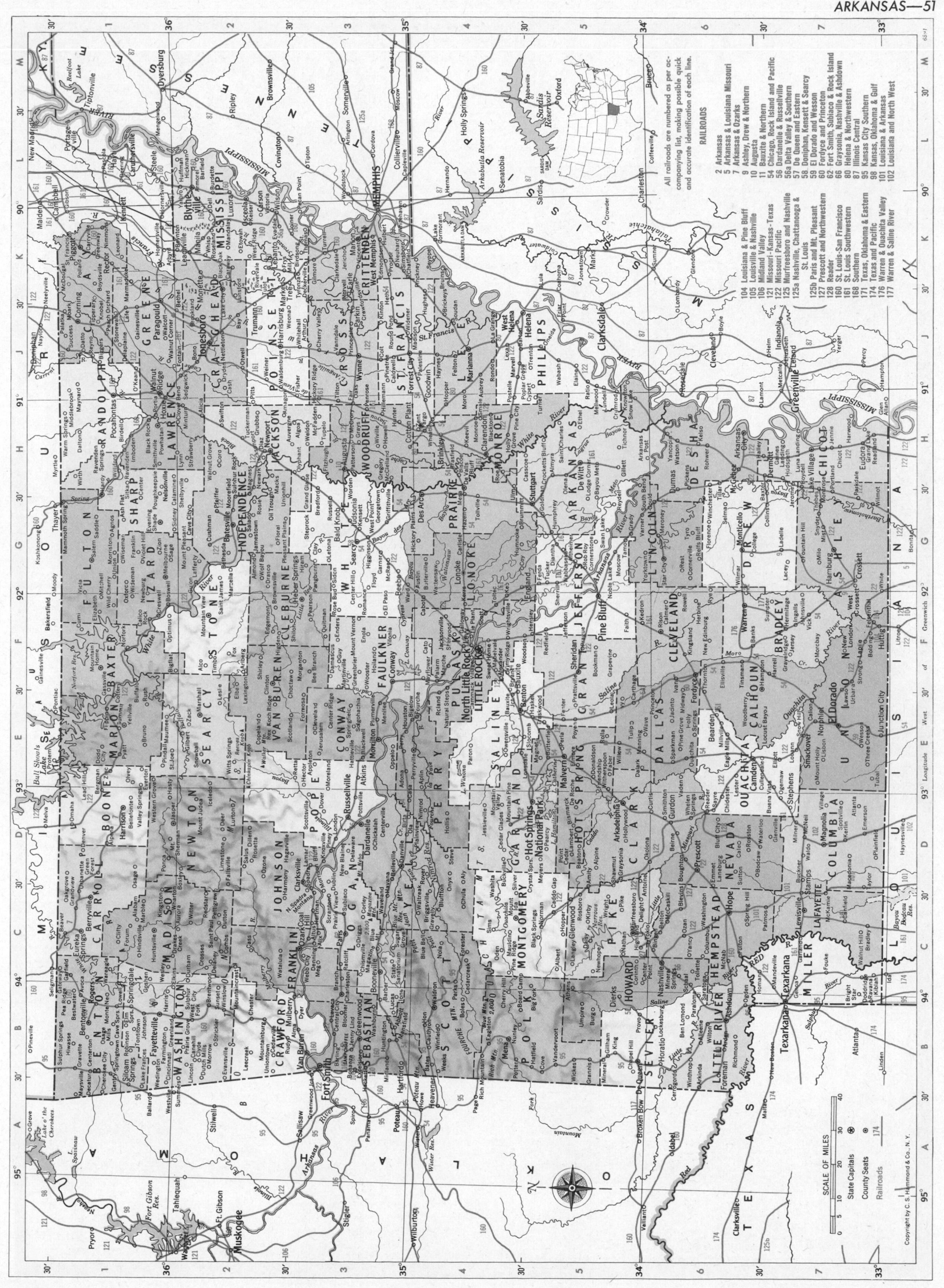

RAILROADS

2 Almanor
3 Amador Central
5 Arcata & Mad River
7 Atchison, Topeka & Santa Fe
12 California Western
13 Camino, Placerville & Lake Tahoe
13a Eagle Mountain (Kaiser Steel Corp.)
14 Feather River
17 Great Northern
37 Holton Inter-Urban
38 McCloud River
88 Northwestern Pacific
89 Oregon, California & Eastern
90 Petaluma & Santa Rosa
91 Quincy
94 Sacramento Northern
95 San Diego & Arizona Eastern
98 Santa Maria Valley
99 Sierra
170 Southern Pacific
172 Stockton Terminal & Eastern
174 Tidewater Southern
176 Trona
180 Union Pacific
183 Western Pacific
189 Yreka Western

All railroads are numbered as per accompanying list, making possible quick and accurate identification of each line.

SAN FRANCISCO AND VICINITY

SACRAMENTO AND VICINITY

LOS ANGELES AND VICINITY

SCALE OF MILES

State Capitals
County Seats
Canals
Railroads

Copyright by C. S. Hammond & Co., N.Y.

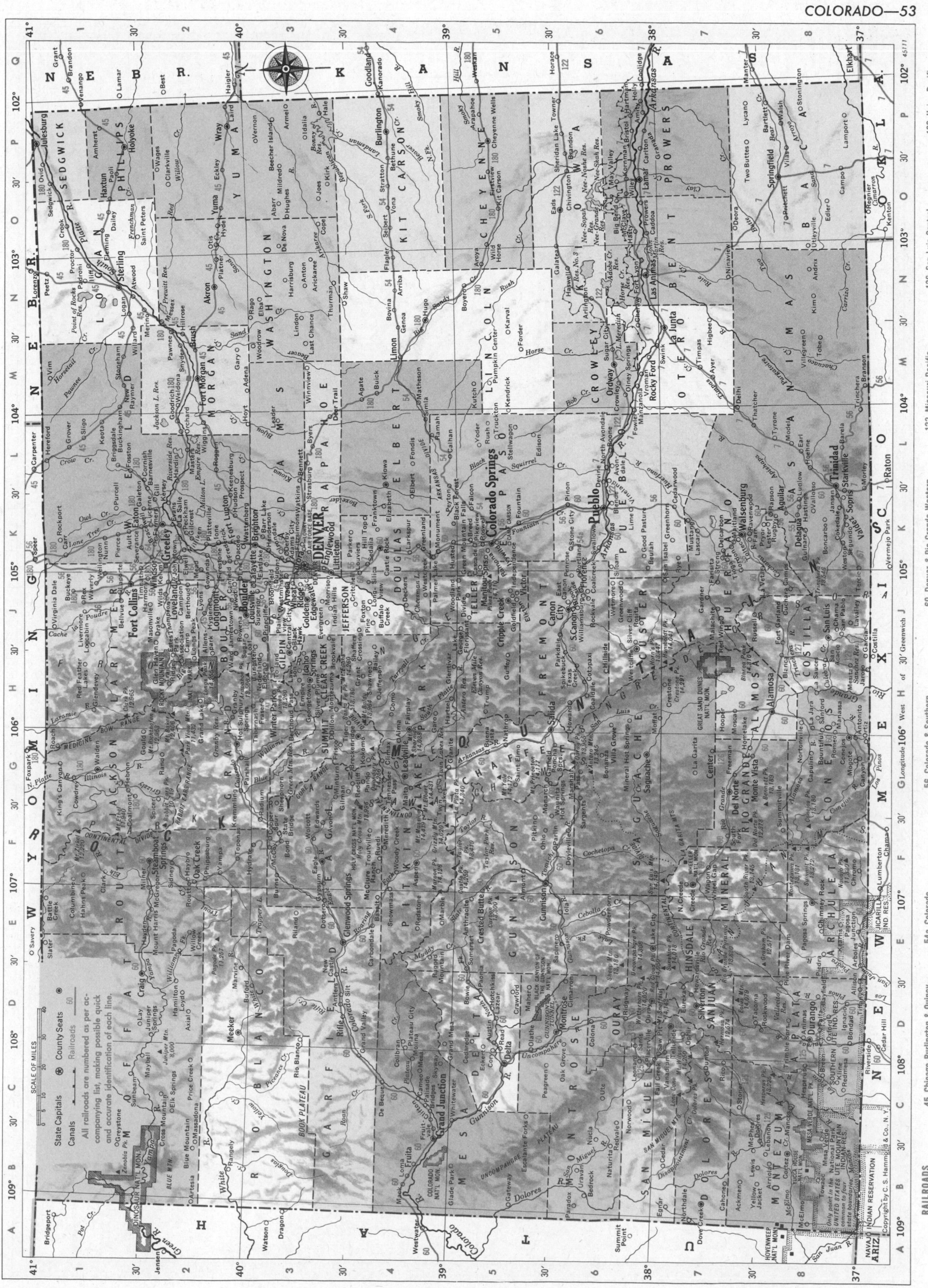

**RAILROADS**

| | | | |
|---|---|---|---|
| 7 Atchison, Topeka & Santa Fe | 45 Chicago, Burlington & Quincy<br>54 Chicago, Rock Island & Pacific | 54a Colorado<br>55 Colorado & South-Eastern<br>56 Colorado & Southern<br>57 Colorado & Wyoming | 60 Denver & Rio Grande Western<br>64 Great Western |
| | 122 Missouri Pacific<br>125 Rio Grande Southern | 126 San Luis Central<br>127 San Luis Valley Southern | 180 Union Pacific |

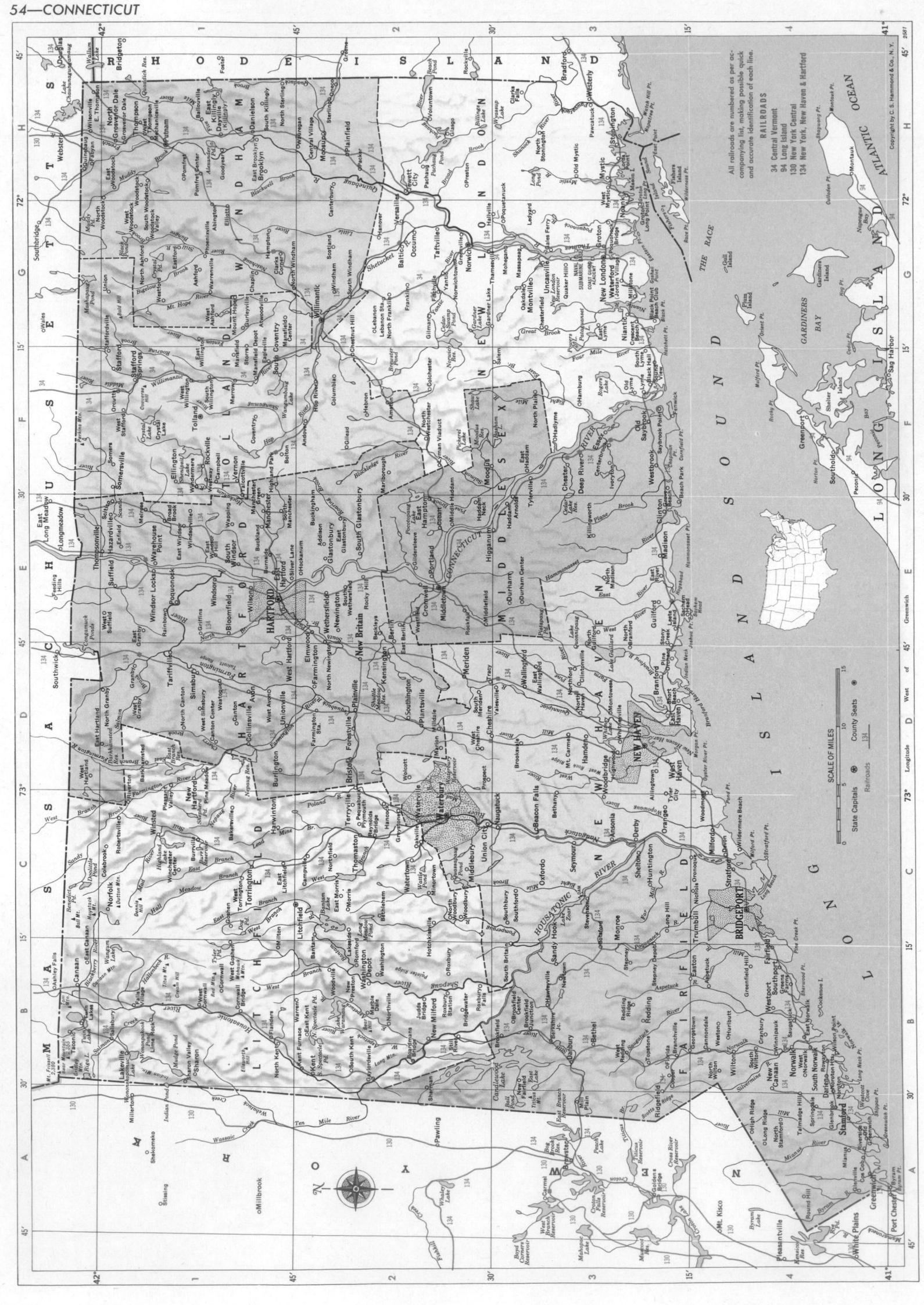

RAILROADS

All railroads are numbered as per accompanying list, making possible quick and accurate identification of each line.

34   Central Vermont
94   Long Island
130  New York Central
134  New York, New Haven & Hartford

SCALE OF MILES

State Capitals ⊛   County Seats ⊛
Railroads 134

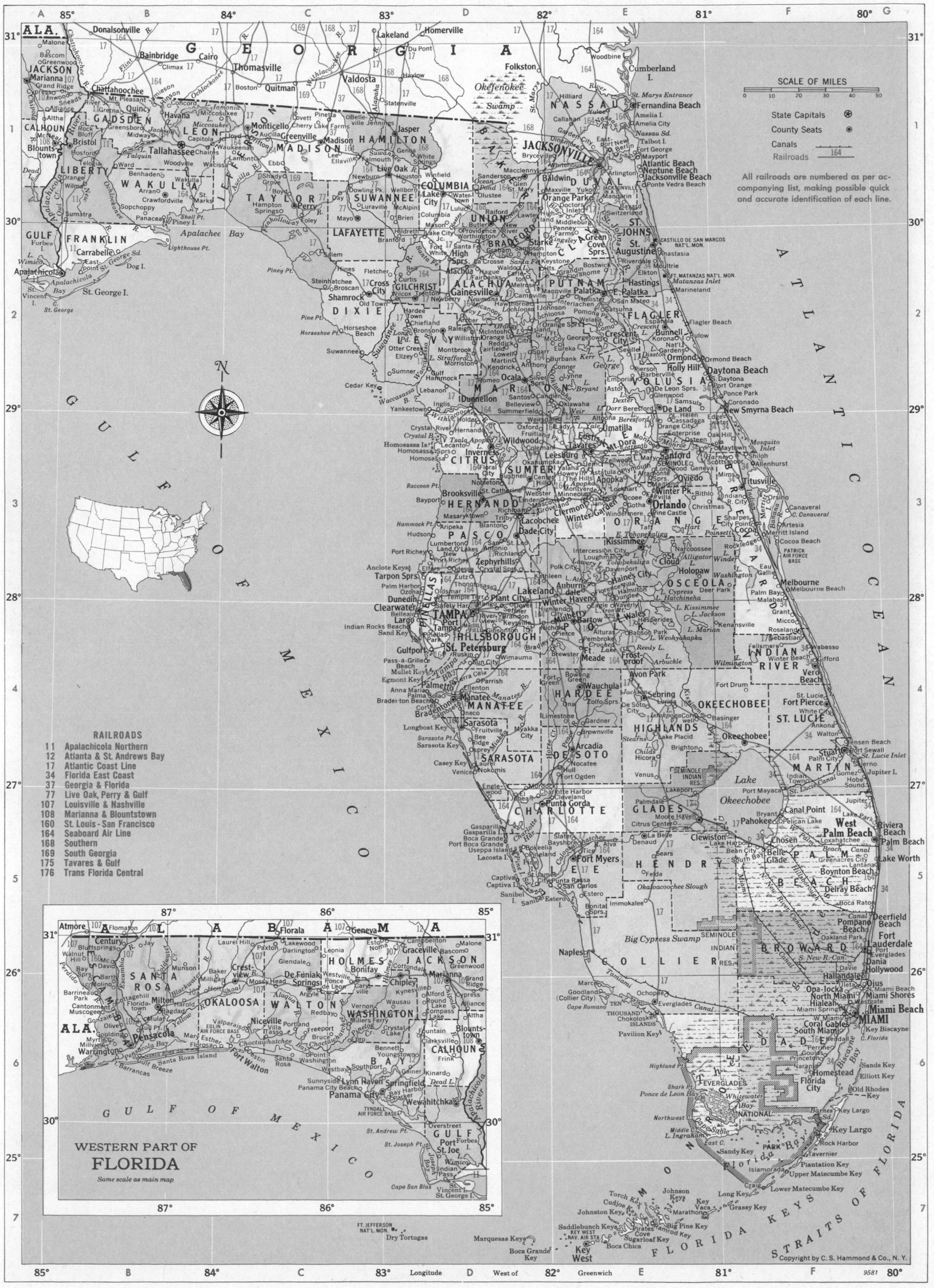

WESTERN PART OF
**FLORIDA**
*Same scale as main map*

RAILROADS
11 Apalachicola Northern
12 Atlanta & St. Andrews Bay
17 Atlantic Coast Line
34 Florida East Coast
37 Georgia & Florida
77 Live Oak, Perry & Gulf
107 Louisville & Nashville
108 Marianna & Blountstown
160 St. Louis - San Francisco
164 Seaboard Air Line
168 Southern
169 South Georgia
175 Tavares & Gulf
176 Trans Florida Central

SCALE OF MILES

State Capitals
County Seats
Canals
Railroads

All railroads are numbered as per accompanying list, making possible quick
and accurate identification of each line.

Copyright by C. S. Hammond & Co., N.Y.

9581

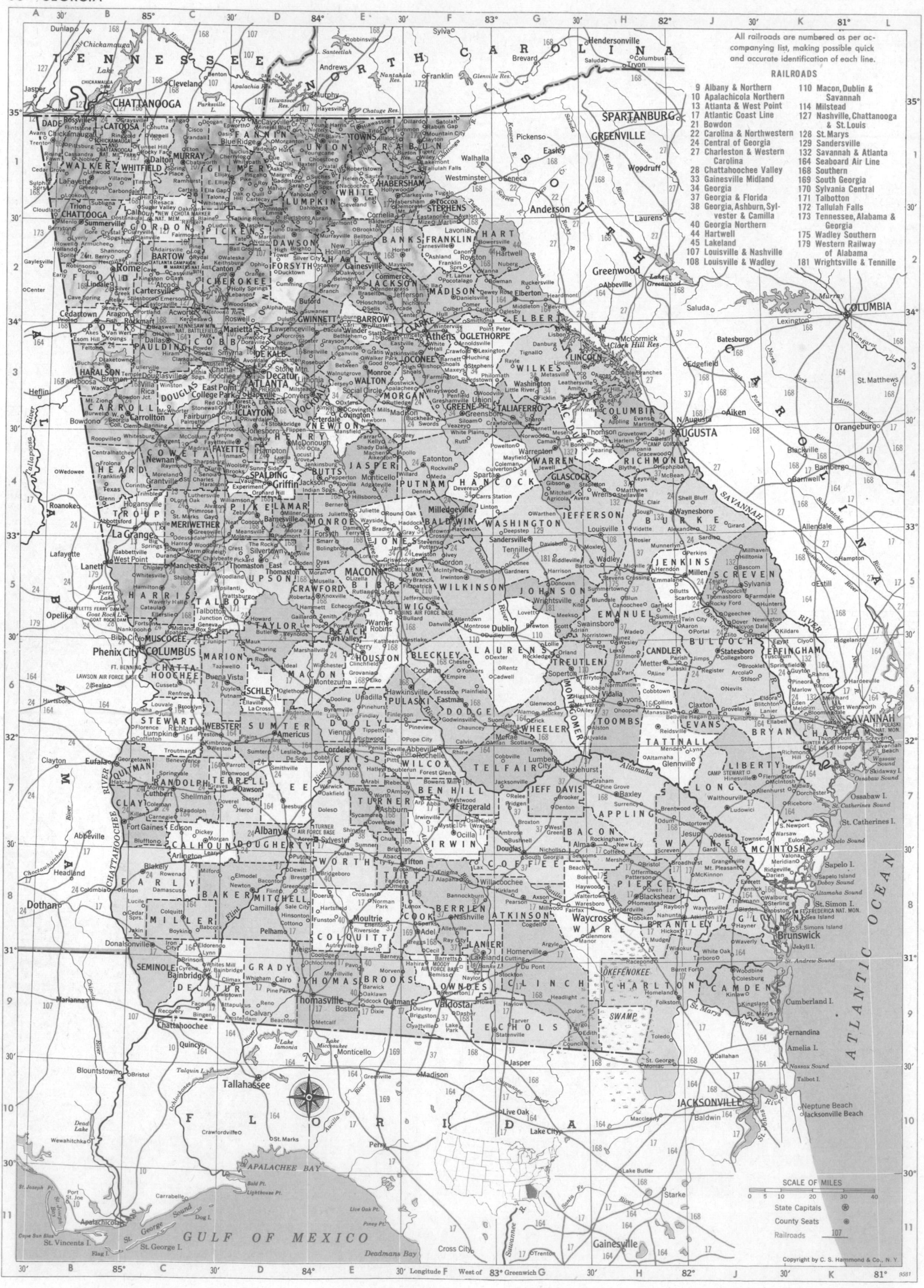

RAILROADS

All railroads are numbered as per accompanying list, making possible quick and accurate identification of each line.

| | |
|---|---|
| 9 Albany & Northern | 110 Macon, Dublin & |
| 10 Apalachicola Northern | Savannah |
| 13 Atlanta & West Point | 114 Milstead |
| 17 Atlantic Coast Line | 127 Nashville, Chattanooga |
| 21 Bowdon | & St. Louis |
| 22 Carolina & Northwestern | 128 St. Marys |
| 24 Central of Georgia | 129 Sandersville |
| 27 Charleston & Western | 132 Savannah & Atlanta |
| Carolina | 164 Seaboard Air Line |
| 28 Chattahoochee Valley | 168 Southern |
| 33 Gainesville Midland | 169 South Georgia |
| 34 Georgia | 170 Sylvania Central |
| 37 Georgia & Florida | 171 Talbotton |
| 38 Georgia, Ashburn, Syl- | 172 Tallulah Falls |
| vester & Camilla | 173 Tennessee, Alabama & |
| 40 Georgia Northern | Georgia |
| 44 Hartwell | 175 Wadley Southern |
| 45 Lakeland | 179 Western Railway |
| 107 Louisville & Nashville | of Alabama |
| 108 Louisville & Wadley | 181 Wrightsville & Tennille |

SCALE OF MILES

0 5 10 20 30 40

State Capitals

County Seats

Railroads ___107___

Copyright by C. S. Hammond & Co., N. Y.

Longitude F West of 83° Greenwich G

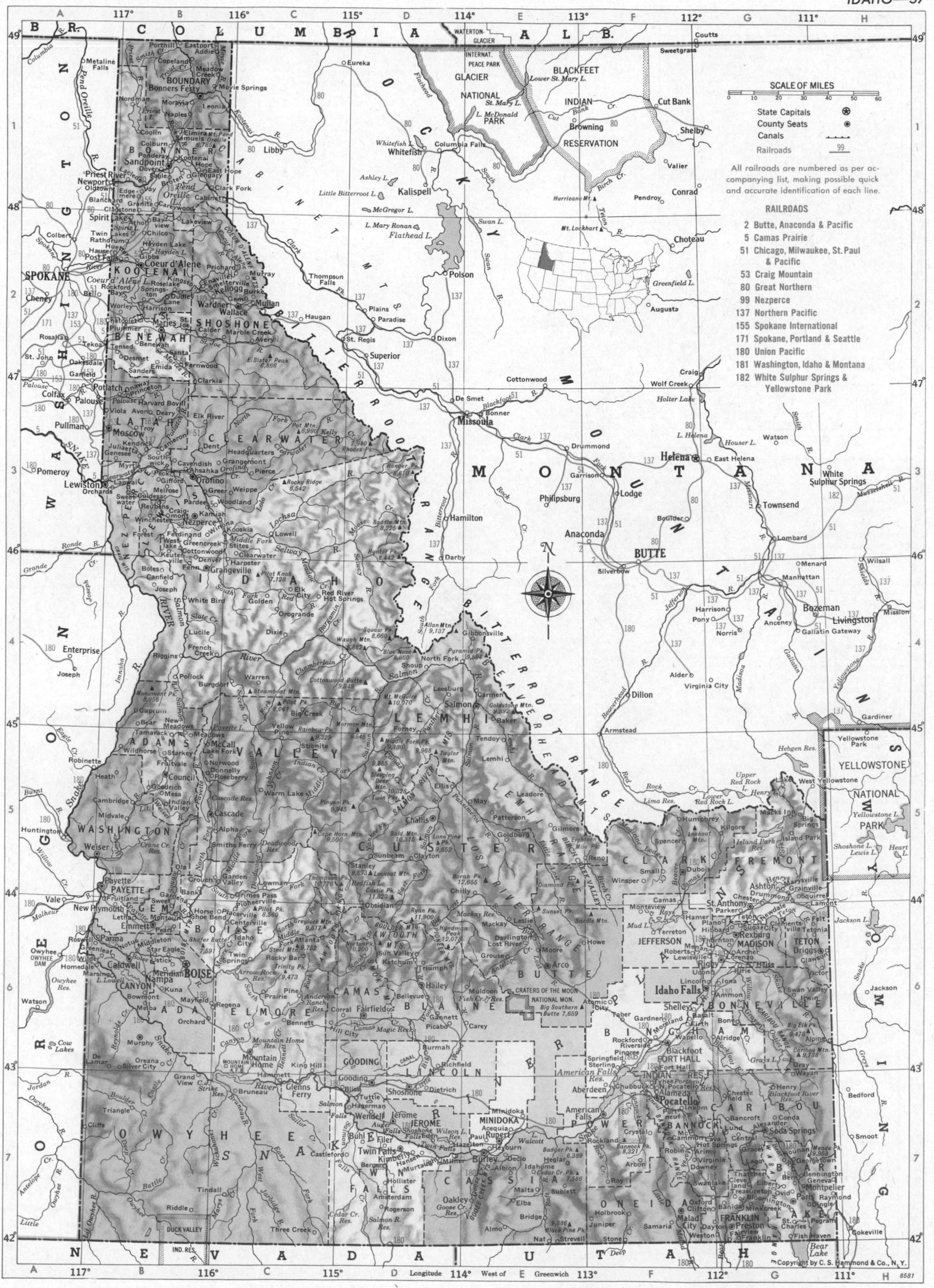

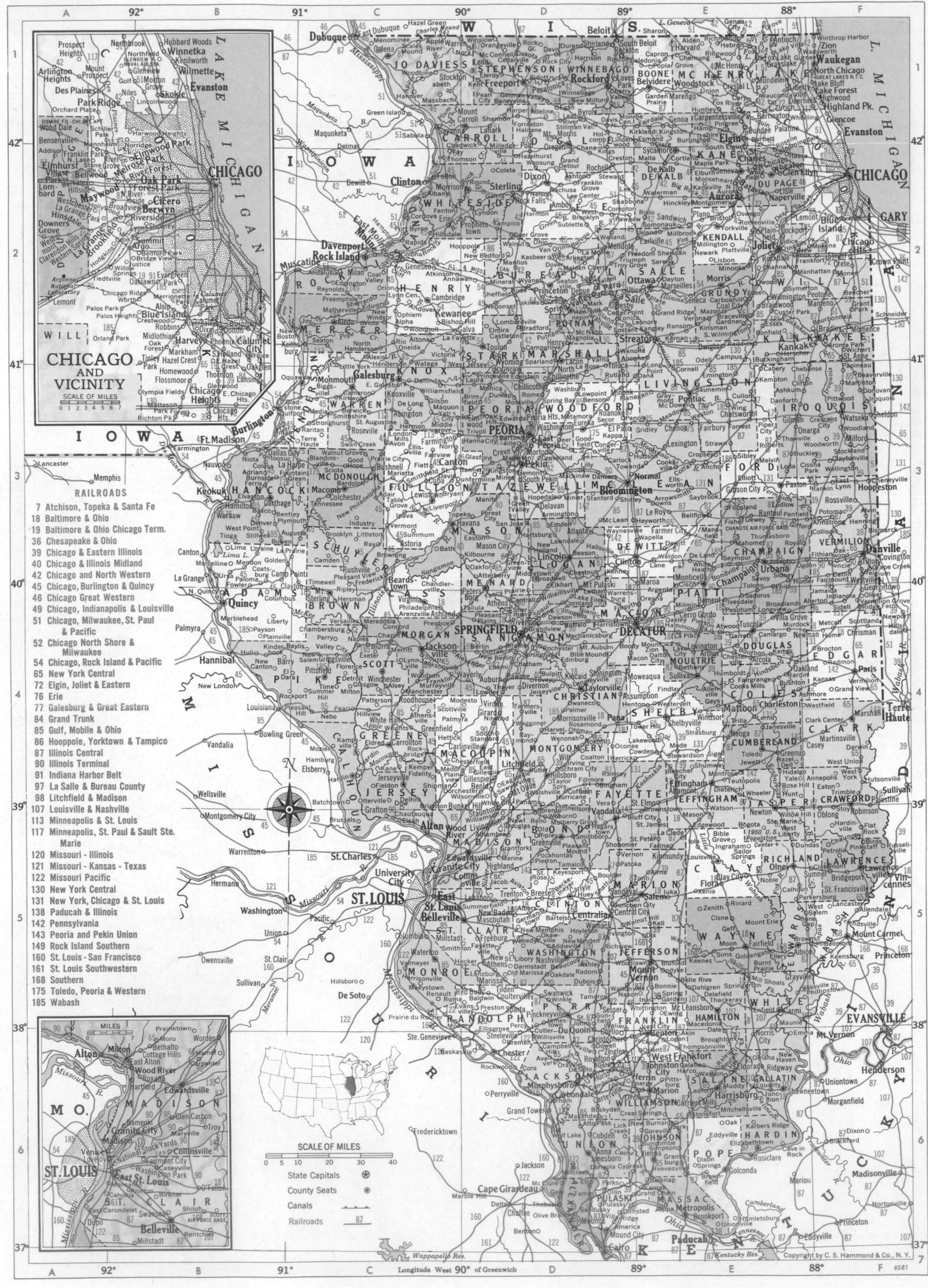

RAILROADS

7 Atchison, Topeka & Santa Fe
18 Baltimore & Ohio
19 Baltimore & Ohio Chicago Term.
36 Chesapeake & Ohio
39 Chicago & Eastern Illinois
40 Chicago & Illinois Midland
42 Chicago and North Western
46 Chicago, Burlington & Quincy
46 Chicago Great Western
49 Chicago, Indianapolis & Louisville
51 Chicago, Milwaukee, St. Paul
   & Pacific
52 Chicago North Shore &
   Milwaukee
54 Chicago, Rock Island & Pacific
65 New York Central
72 Elgin, Joliet & Eastern
76 Erie
77 Galesburg & Great Eastern
84 Grand Trunk
85 Gulf, Mobile & Ohio
86 Hooppole, Yorktown & Tampico
87 Illinois Central
90 Illinois Terminal
91 Indiana Harbor Belt
97 La Salle & Bureau County
98 Litchfield & Madison
107 Louisville & Nashville
113 Minneapolis & St. Louis
117 Minneapolis, St. Paul & Sault Ste.
    Marie
120 Missouri - Illinois
121 Missouri - Kansas - Texas
122 Missouri Pacific
130 New York Central
131 New York, Chicago & St. Louis
138 Paducah & Illinois
142 Pennsylvania
143 Peoria and Pekin Union
149 Rock Island Southern
160 St. Louis - San Francisco
161 St. Louis Southwestern
168 Southern
175 Toledo, Peoria & Western
185 Wabash

CHICAGO
AND
VICINITY
SCALE OF MILES
0 1 2 3 4 5 6 7

SCALE OF MILES
0 5 10    20    30    40

State Capitals ⊛
County Seats ⊙
Canals
Railroads    87

Longitude West 90° of Greenwich

Copyright by C. S. Hammond & Co., N.Y.

5581

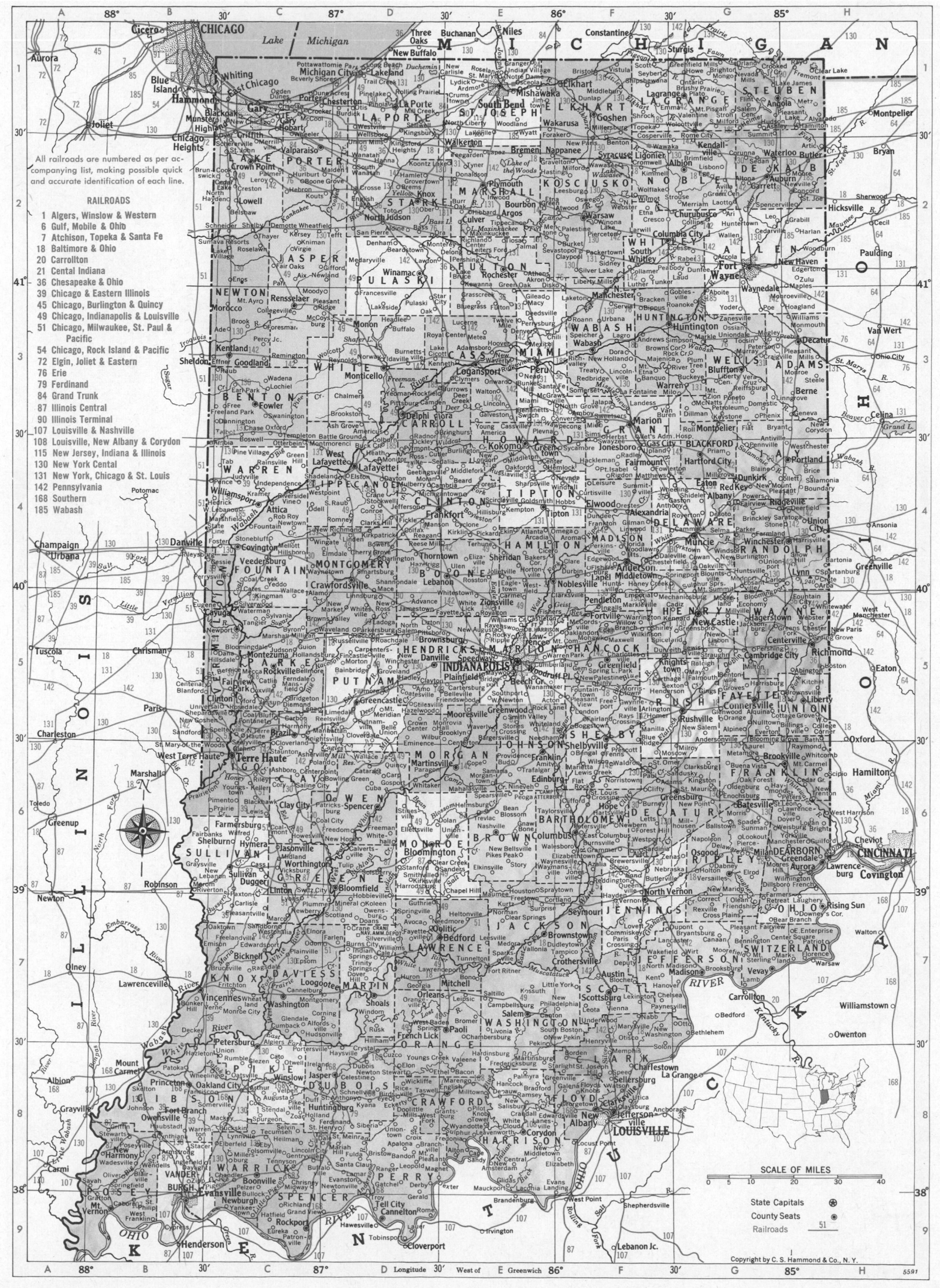

All railroads are numbered as per accompanying list, making possible quick and accurate identification of each line.

**RAILROADS**

1 Algers, Winslow & Western
6 Gulf, Mobile & Ohio
7 Atchison, Topeka & Santa Fe
18 Baltimore & Ohio
20 Carrollton
21 Cental Indiana
36 Chesapeake & Ohio
39 Chicago & Eastern Illinois
45 Chicago, Burlington & Quincy
49 Chicago, Indianapolis & Louisville
51 Chicago, Milwaukee, St. Paul & Pacific
54 Chicago, Rock Island & Pacific
72 Elgin, Joliet & Eastern
76 Erie
79 Ferdinand
84 Grand Trunk
87 Illinois Central
90 Illinois Terminal
107 Louisville & Nashville
108 Louisville, New Albany & Corydon
115 New Jersey, Indiana & Illinois
130 New York Central
131 New York, Chicago & St. Louis
142 Pennsylvania
168 Southern
185 Wabash

SCALE OF MILES
0  5  10  20  30  40

State Capitals
County Seats
Railroads    51

Copyright by C. S. Hammond & Co., N.Y.

5591

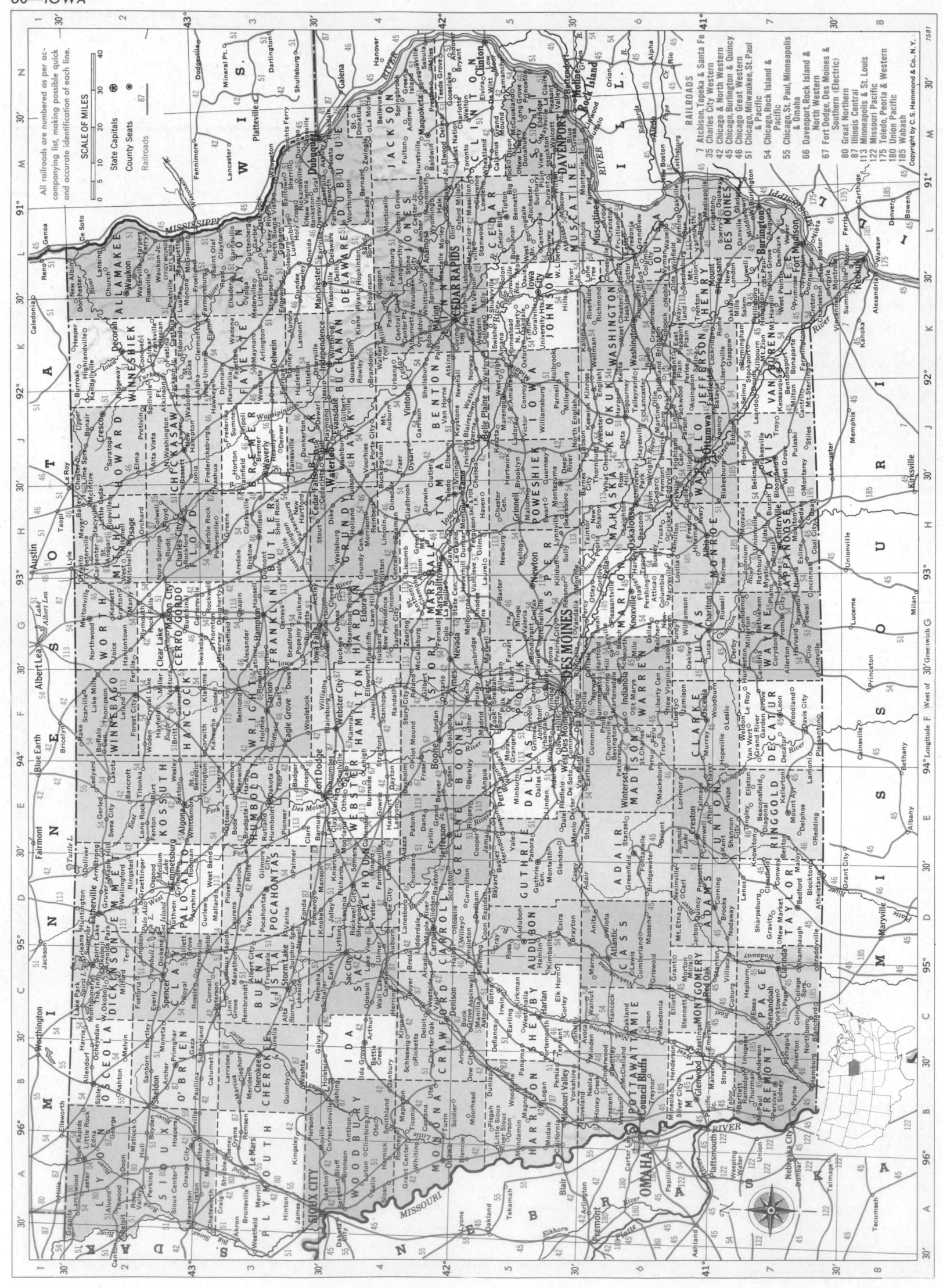

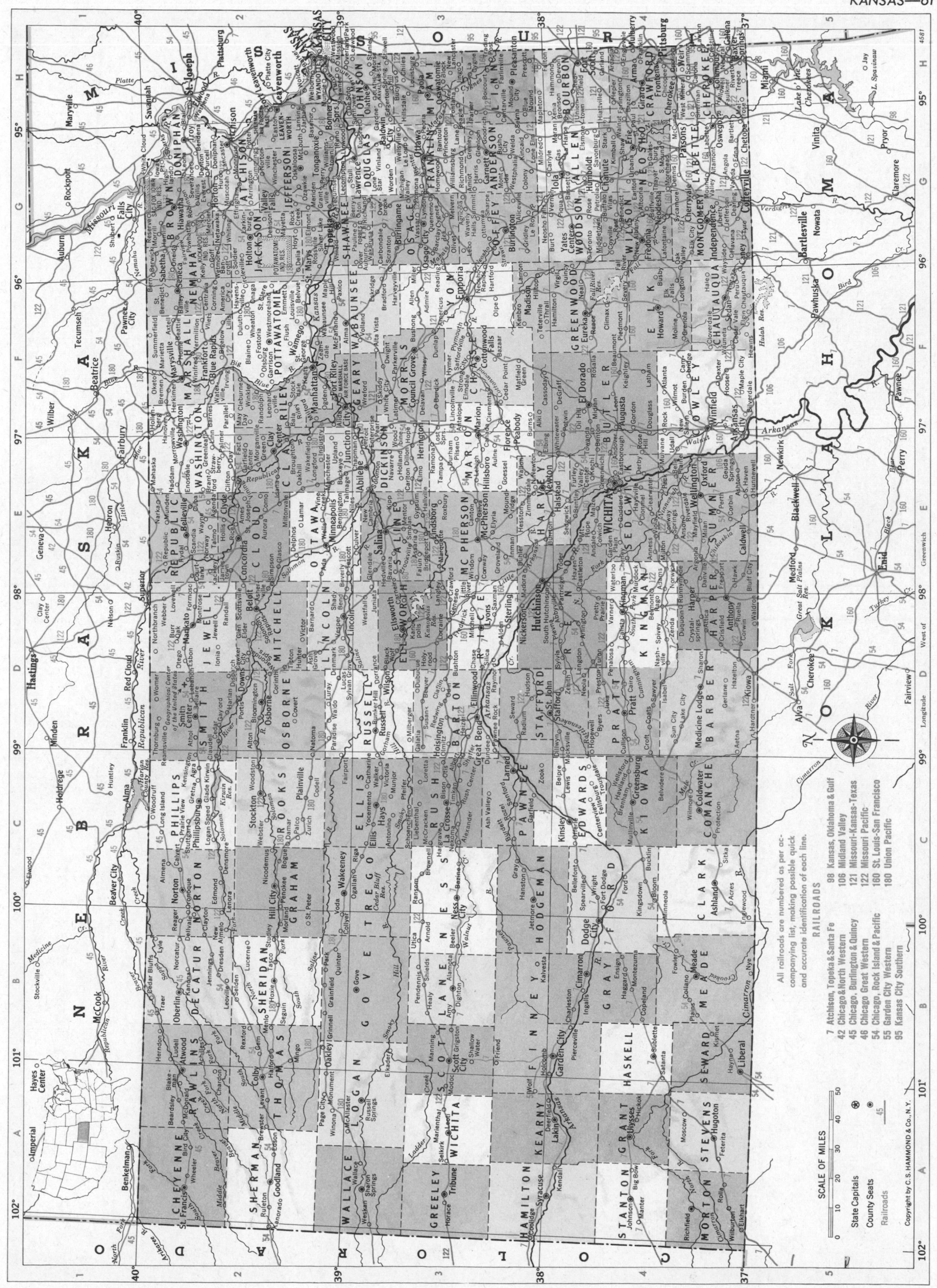

RAILROADS

All railroads are numbered as per accompanying list, making possible quick and accurate identification of each line.

| | |
|---|---|
| 7 Atchison, Topeka & Santa Fe | 98 Kansas, Oklahoma & Gulf |
| 42 Chicago & North Western | 106 Midland Valley |
| 45 Chicago, Burlington & Quincy | 121 Missouri-Kansas-Texas |
| 46 Chicago Great Western | 122 Missouri Pacific |
| 54 Chicago, Rock Island & Pacific | 160 St. Louis-San Francisco |
| 55 Garden City Western | 180 Union Pacific |
| 95 Kansas City Southern | |

SCALE OF MILES

0  10  20  30  40  50

State Capitals  ⊛
County Seats  ⊙
Railroads

Copyright by C. S. HAMMOND & CO., N.Y.

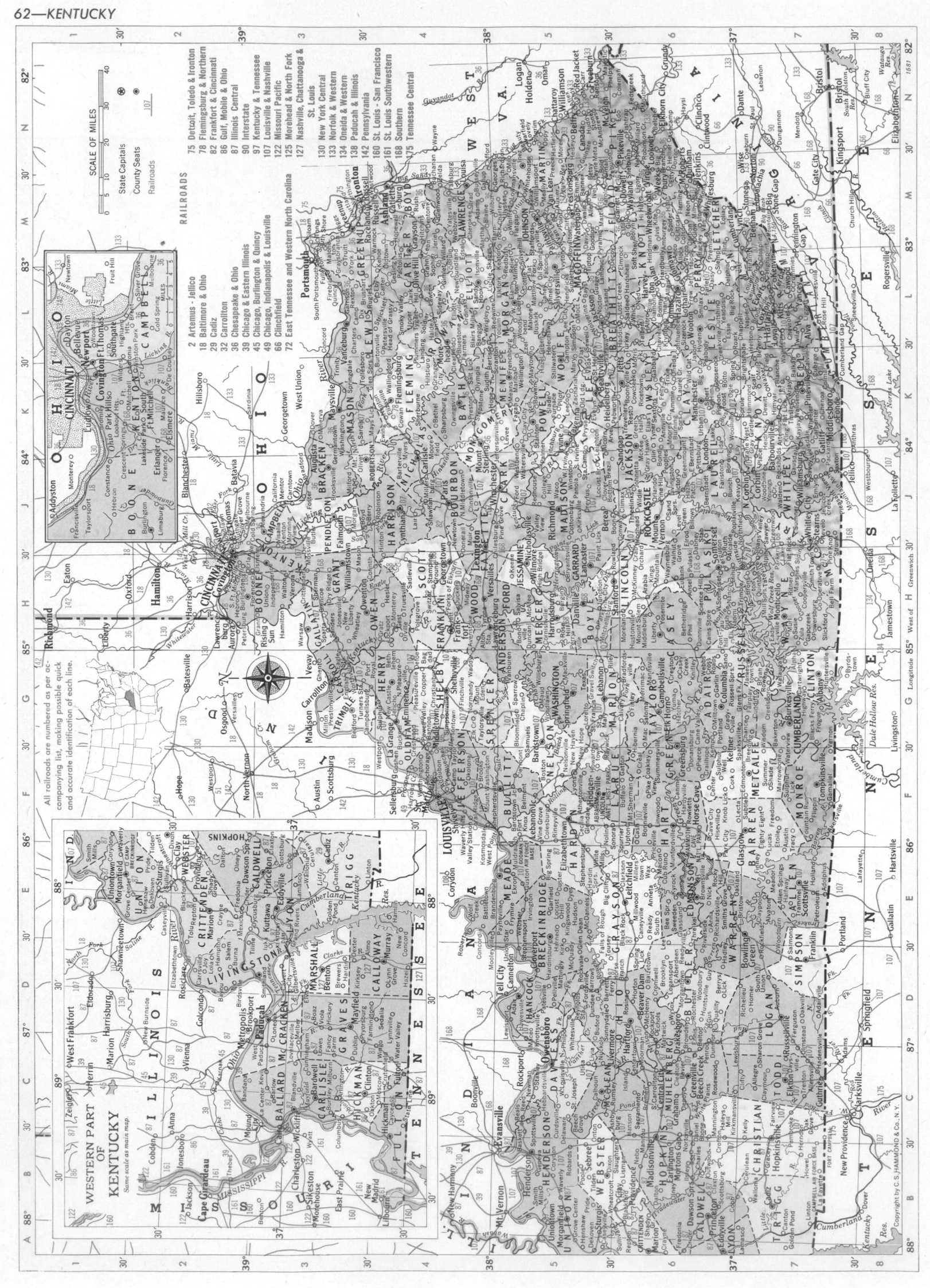

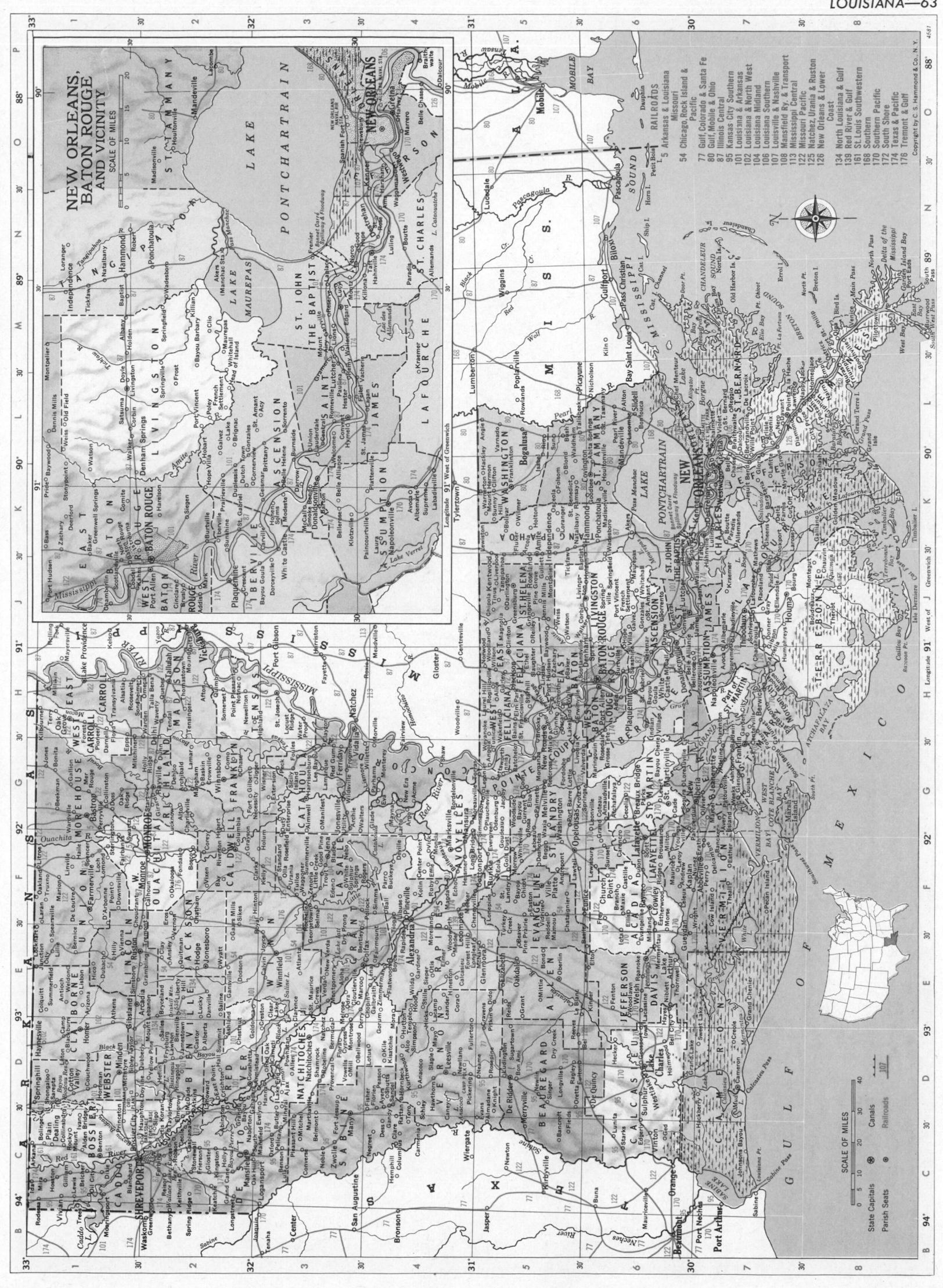

NEW ORLEANS,
BATON ROUGE
AND VICINITY
SCALE OF MILES

RAILROADS

5   Arkansas & Louisiana
54  Chicago, Rock Island &
      Pacific
77  Gulf, Colorado & Santa Fe
80  Gulf, Mobile & Ohio
87  Illinois Central
95  Kansas City Southern
101 Louisiana & Arkansas
102 Louisiana & North West
104 Louisiana Midland
106 Louisiana Southern
107 Louisville & Nashville
108 Mansfield Ry. & Transport
113 Mississippi Central
122 Missouri Pacific
125 Natchez, Urania & Ruston
126 New Orleans & Lower
      Coast
134 North Louisiana & Gulf
139 Red River & Gulf
161 St. Louis Southwestern
168 Southern
170 Southern Pacific
172 South Shore
174 Texas & Pacific
176 Tremont & Gulf

Copyright by C. S. Hammond & Co., N.Y.

SCALE OF MILES

State Capitals
Parish Seats

Canals
Railroads

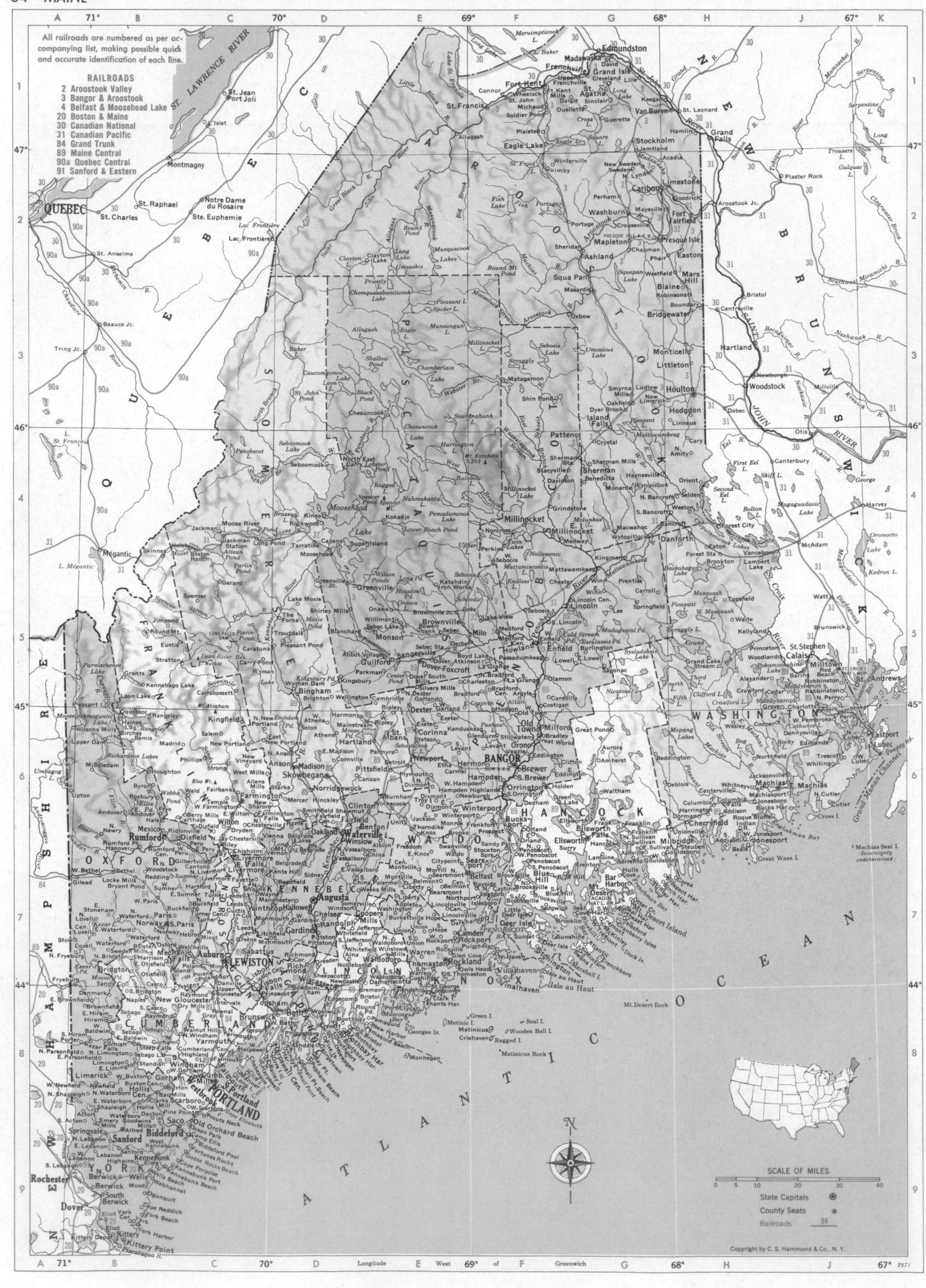

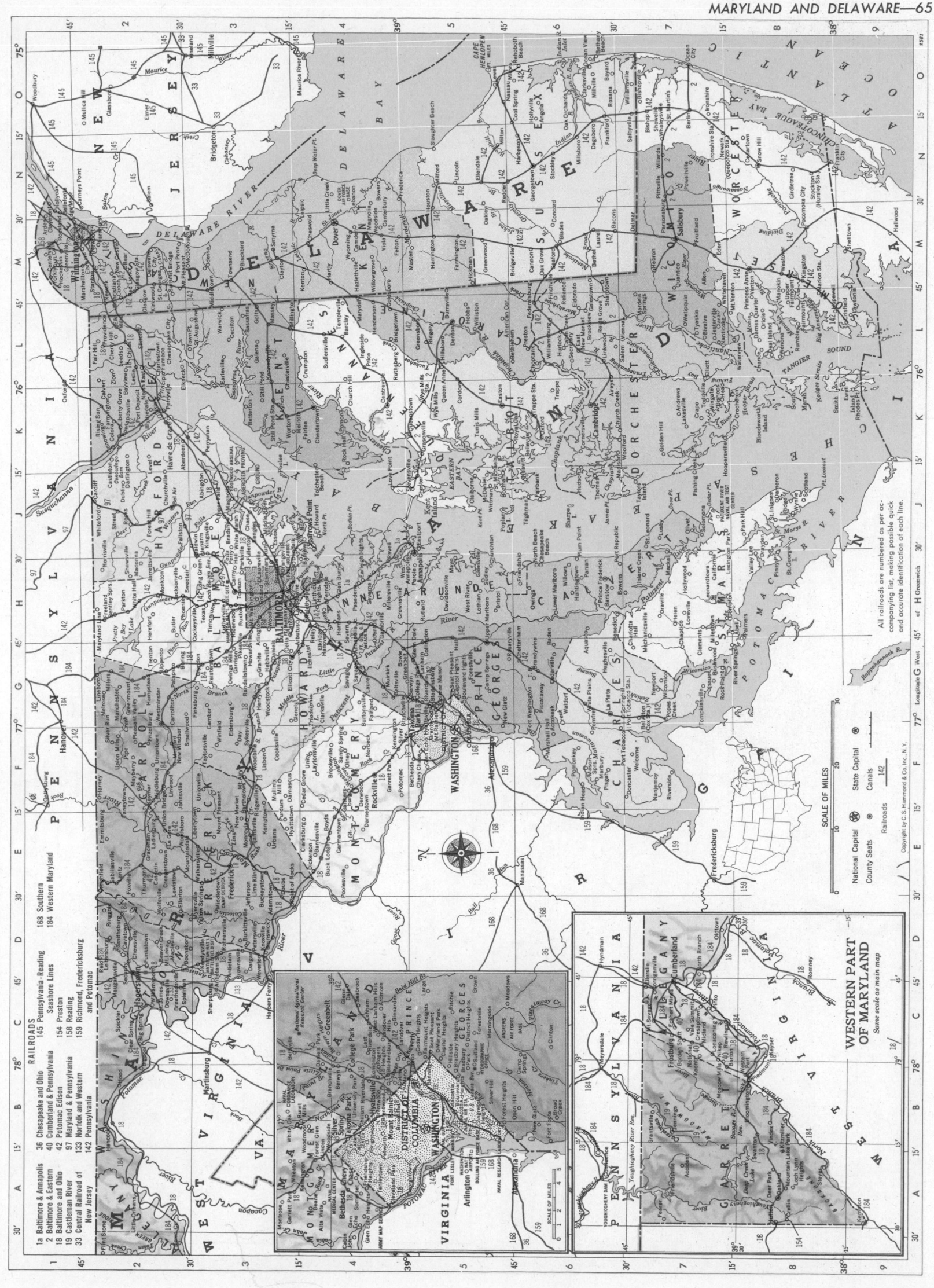

WESTERN PART
OF MARYLAND
*Same scale as main map*

Copyright by C. S. Hammond & Co. Inc., N. Y.

RAILROADS

| | | | |
|---|---|---|---|
| 1a | Baltimore & Annapolis | 145 | Southern |
| 2 | Baltimore & Eastern | 184 | Western Maryland |
| 18 | Baltimore and Ohio | 154 | Preston |
| 19 | Castleman River | 158 | Reading |
| 33 | Central Railroad of | 159 | Richmond, Fredericksburg |
| | New Jersey | | and Potomac |
| 36 | Chesapeake and Ohio | 145 | Pennsylvania-Reading |
| 40 | Cumberland & Pennsylvania | | Seashore Lines |
| 42 | Potomac Edison | 97 | Maryland & Pennsylvania |
| 97 | Maryland & Pennsylvania | 133 | Norfolk and Western |
| 133 | Norfolk and Western | 142 | Pennsylvania |

SCALE OF MILES

National Capital ⊛     State Capital ⊛

County Seats ○     Railroads ———

Canals  142

All railroads are numbered as per accompanying list, making possible quick
and accurate identification of each line.

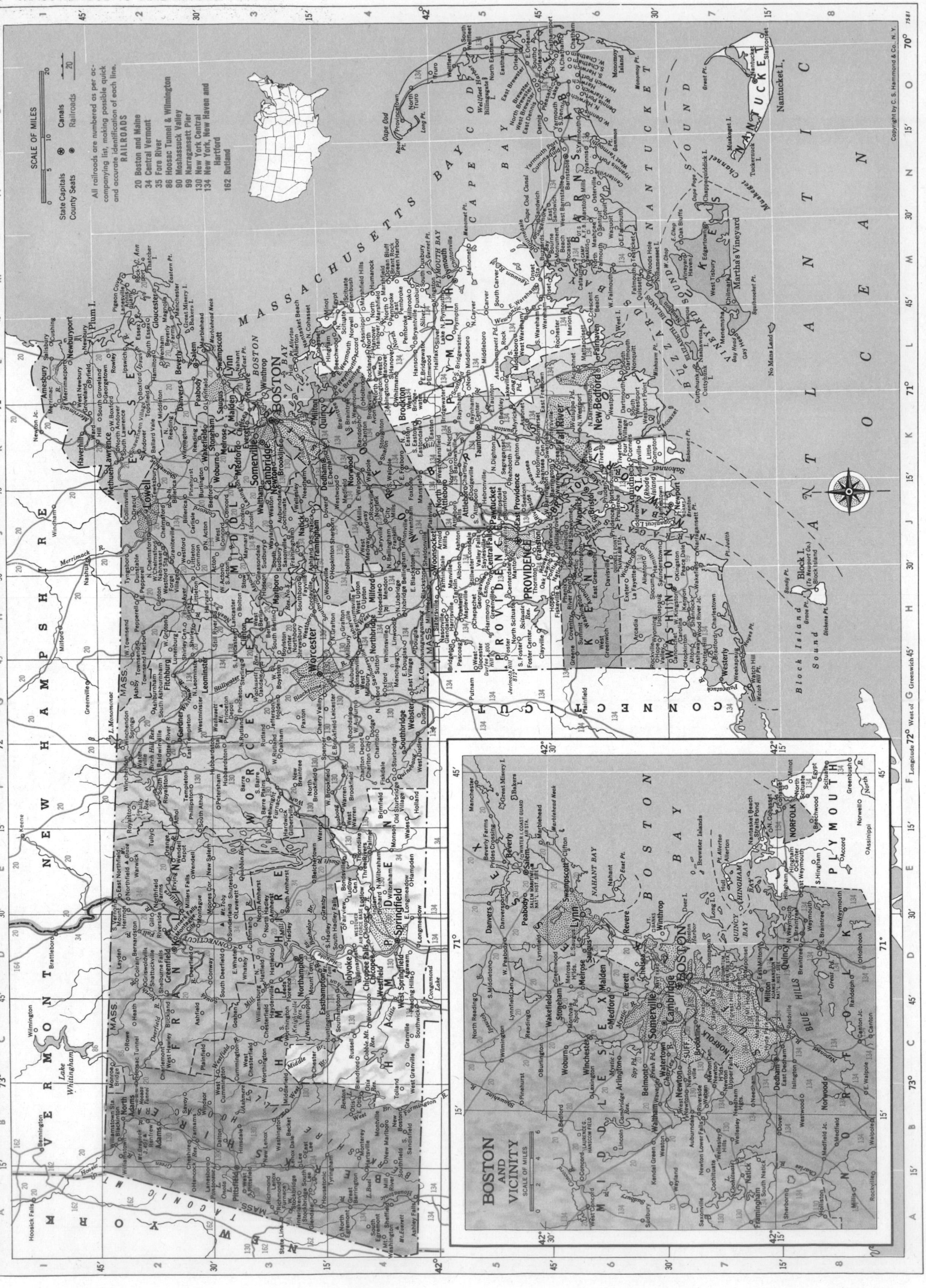
SCALE OF MILES
0 5 10 15 20
State Capitals
County Seats
Canals
Railroads
All railroads are numbered as per accompanying list, making possible quick and accurate identification of each line.
RAILROADS
20 Boston and Maine
34 Central Vermont
35 Fore River
86 Hoosac Tunnel & Wilmington
90 Moshassuck Valley
99 Narragansett Pier
130 New York Central
134 New York, New Haven and Hartford
162 Rutland
MASSACHUSETTS BAY
CAPE COD BAY
NANTUCKET SOUND
ATLANTIC OCEAN
NEW HAMPSHIRE
VERMONT
NEW YORK
CONNECTICUT
BOSTON AND VICINITY
Copyright by C. S. Hammond & Co., N. Y.

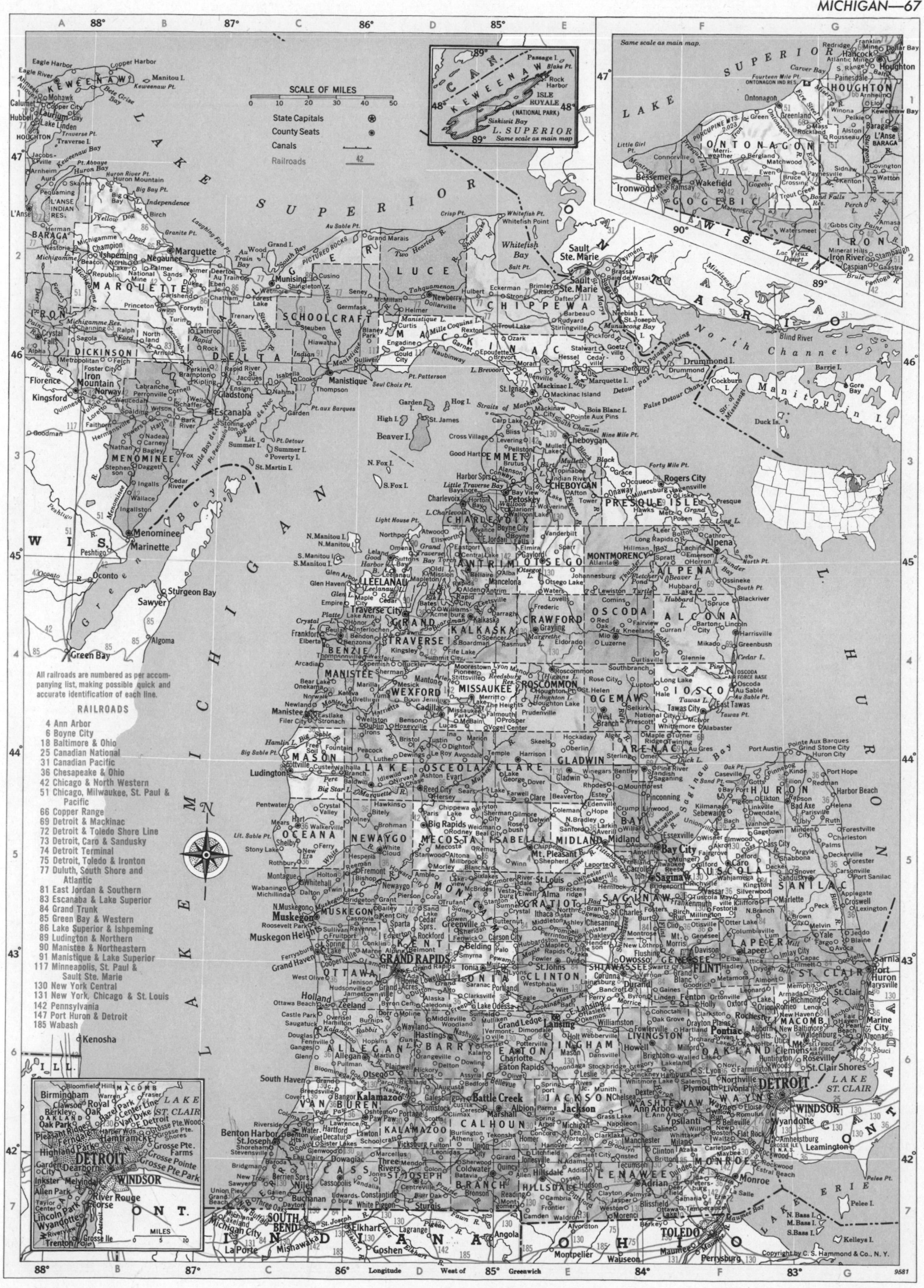

SCALE OF MILES

State Capitals
County Seats
Canals
Railroads

**RAILROADS**

4 Ann Arbor
6 Boyne City
18 Baltimore & Ohio
25 Canadian National
31 Canadian Pacific
36 Chesapeake & Ohio
42 Chicago & North Western
51 Chicago, Milwaukee, St. Paul & Pacific
66 Copper Range
69 Detroit & Mackinac
72 Detroit & Toledo Shore Line
73 Detroit, Caro & Sandusky
74 Detroit Terminal
75 Detroit, Toledo & Ironton
77 Duluth, South Shore & Atlantic
81 East Jordan & Southern
83 Escanaba & Lake Superior
84 Grand Trunk
85 Green Bay & Western
86 Lake Superior & Ishpeming
89 Ludington & Northern
90 Manistee & Northeastern
91 Manistique & Lake Superior
117 Minneapolis, St. Paul & Sault Ste. Marie
130 New York Central
131 New York, Chicago & St. Louis
142 Pennsylvania
147 Port Huron & Detroit
185 Wabash

All railroads are numbered as per accompanying list, making possible quick and accurate identification of each line.

Copyright by C. S. Hammond & Co., N.Y.

9581

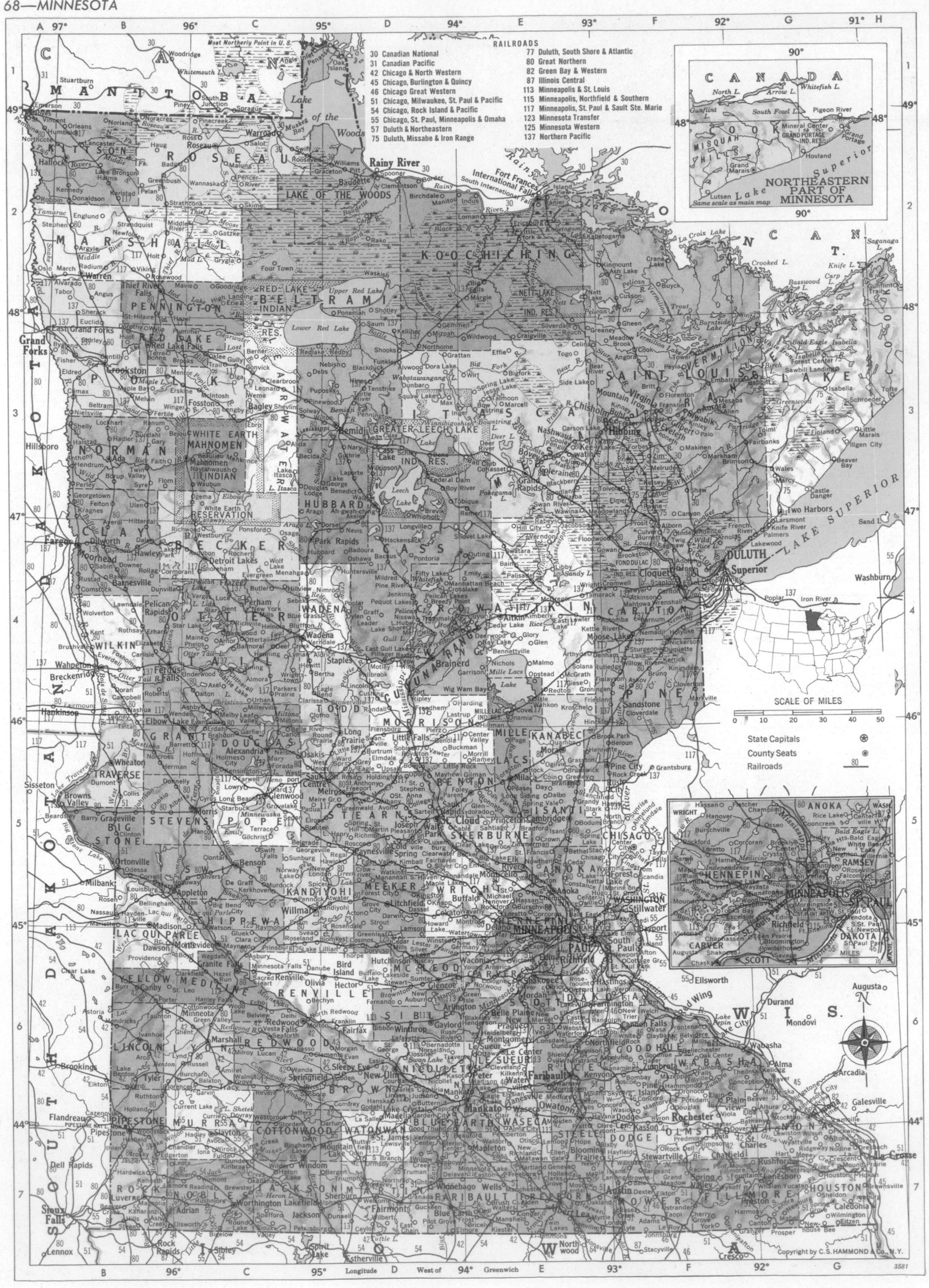

### RAILROADS

| | |
|---|---|
| 30 | Canadian National |
| 31 | Canadian Pacific |
| 42 | Chicago & North Western |
| 45 | Chicago, Burlington & Quincy |
| 46 | Chicago Great Western |
| 51 | Chicago, Milwaukee, St. Paul & Pacific |
| 54 | Chicago, Rock Island & Pacific |
| 55 | Chicago, St. Paul, Minneapolis & Omaha |
| 57 | Duluth & Northeastern |
| 75 | Duluth, Missabe & Iron Range |
| 77 | Duluth, South Shore & Atlantic |
| 80 | Great Northern |
| 82 | Green Bay & Western |
| 87 | Illinois Central |
| 113 | Minneapolis & St. Louis |
| 115 | Minneapolis, Northfield & Southern |
| 117 | Minneapolis, St. Paul & Sault Ste. Marie |
| 123 | Minnesota Transfer |
| 125 | Minnesota Western |
| 137 | Northern Pacific |

NORTHEASTERN PART OF MINNESOTA
Same scale as main map

SCALE OF MILES

State Capitals
County Seats
Railroads

Copyright by C. S. HAMMOND & CO., N. Y.

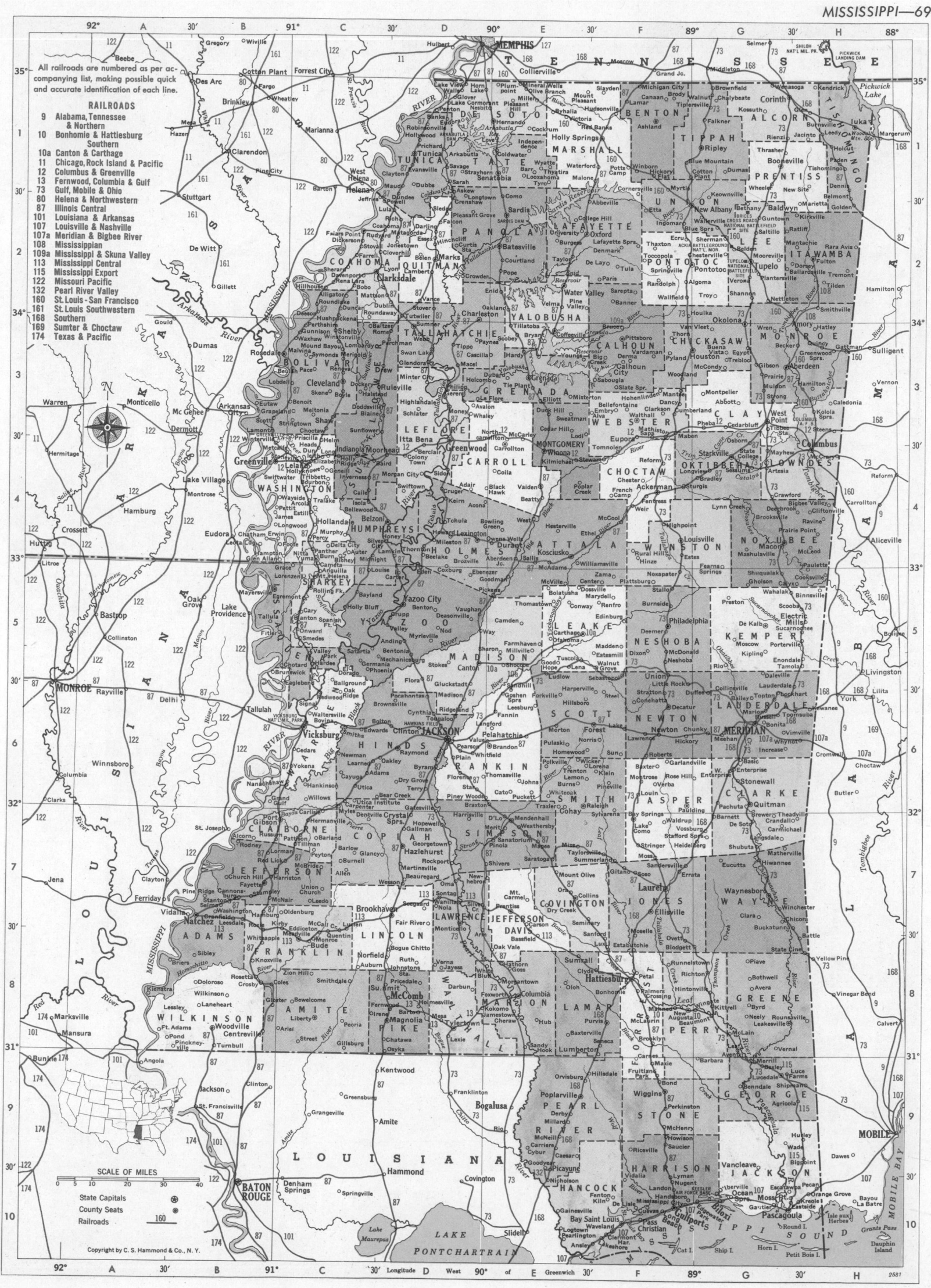

All railroads are numbered as per accompanying list, making possible quick and accurate identification of each line.

## RAILROADS

9 Alabama, Tennessee & Northern
10 Bonhomie & Hattiesburg Southern
10a Canton & Carthage
11 Chicago, Rock Island & Pacific
12 Columbus & Greenville
13 Fernwood, Columbia & Gulf
73 Gulf, Mobile & Ohio
80 Helena & Northwestern
87 Illinois Central
101 Louisiana & Arkansas
107 Louisville & Nashville
107a Meridian & Bigbee River
108 Mississippian
109a Mississippi & Skuna Valley
113 Mississippi Central
115 Mississippi Export
122 Missouri Pacific
132 Pearl River Valley
160 St. Louis-San Francisco
161 St. Louis Southwestern
168 Southern
169 Sumter & Choctaw
174 Texas & Pacific

SCALE OF MILES

State Capitals
County Seats
Railroads

Copyright by C. S. Hammond & Co., N.Y.

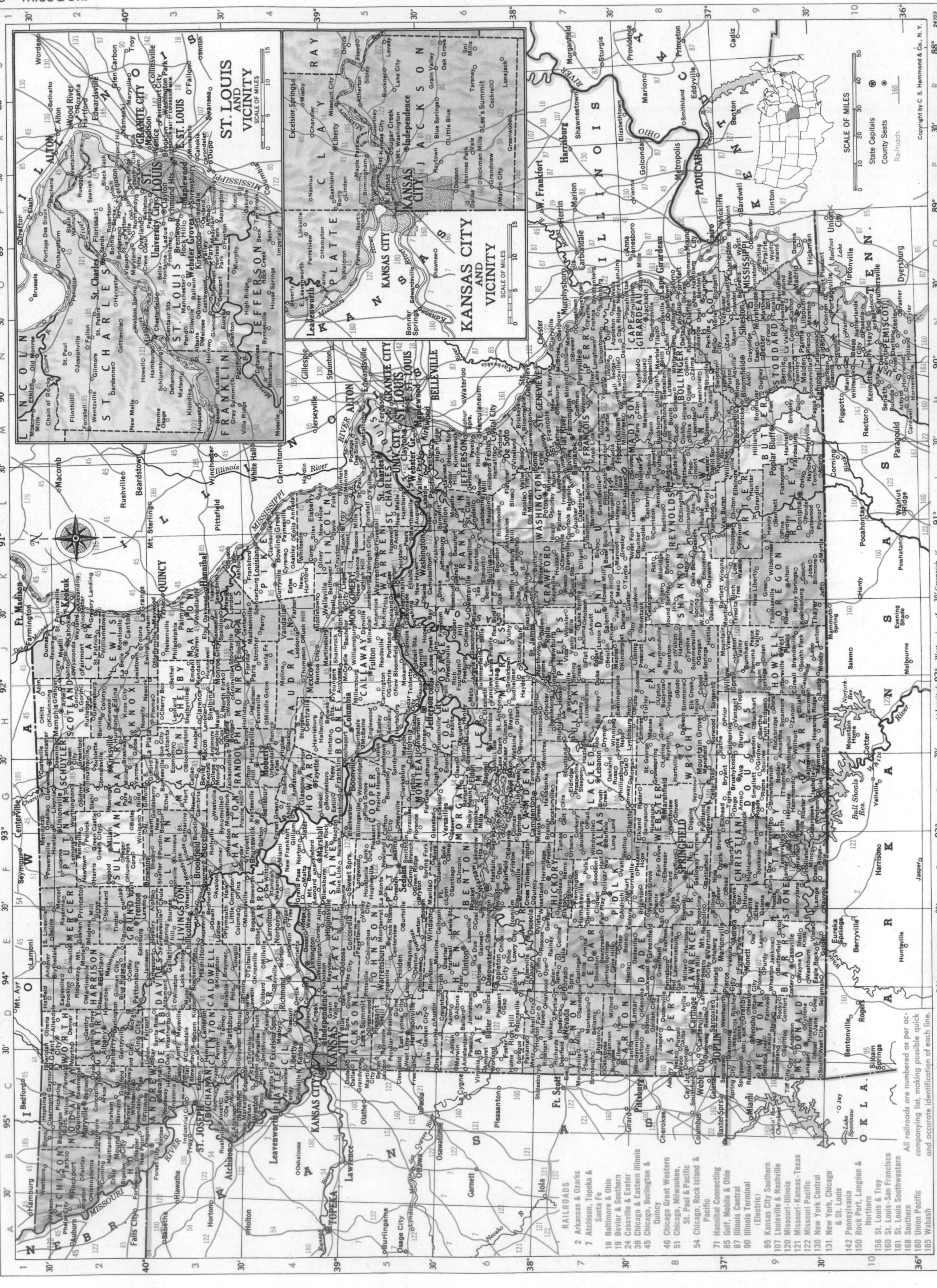

## ST. LOUIS AND VICINITY
SCALE OF MILES

## KANSAS CITY AND VICINITY
SCALE OF MILES

SCALE OF MILES

State Capitals ⊛
County Seats ⊙
Railroads

Copyright by C. S. Hammond & Co., N. Y.

### RAILROADS
2 Arkansas & Ozarks
7 Atchison, Topeka & Santa Fe
18 Baltimore & Ohio
19 Bevier & Southern
24 Cassville & Exeter
39 Chicago & Eastern Illinois
45 Chicago, Burlington & Quincy
46 Chicago Great Western
51 Chicago, Milwaukee, St. Paul & Pacific
54 Chicago, Rock Island & Pacific
71 Hannibal Connecting
85 Gulf, Mobile & Ohio
87 Illinois Central
90 Illinois Terminal (Electric)
95 Kansas City Southern
107 Louisville & Nashville
120 Missouri-Illinois
121 Missouri-Kansas-Texas
122 Missouri Pacific
130 New York Central
131 New York, Chicago & St. Louis
142 Pennsylvania
150 Rock Port, Langdon & Northern
156 St. Louis & Troy
160 St. Louis-San Francisco
161 St. Louis Southwestern
168 Southern
180 Union Pacific
185 Wabash

All railroads are numbered as per ac-companying list, making possible quick and accurate identification of each line.

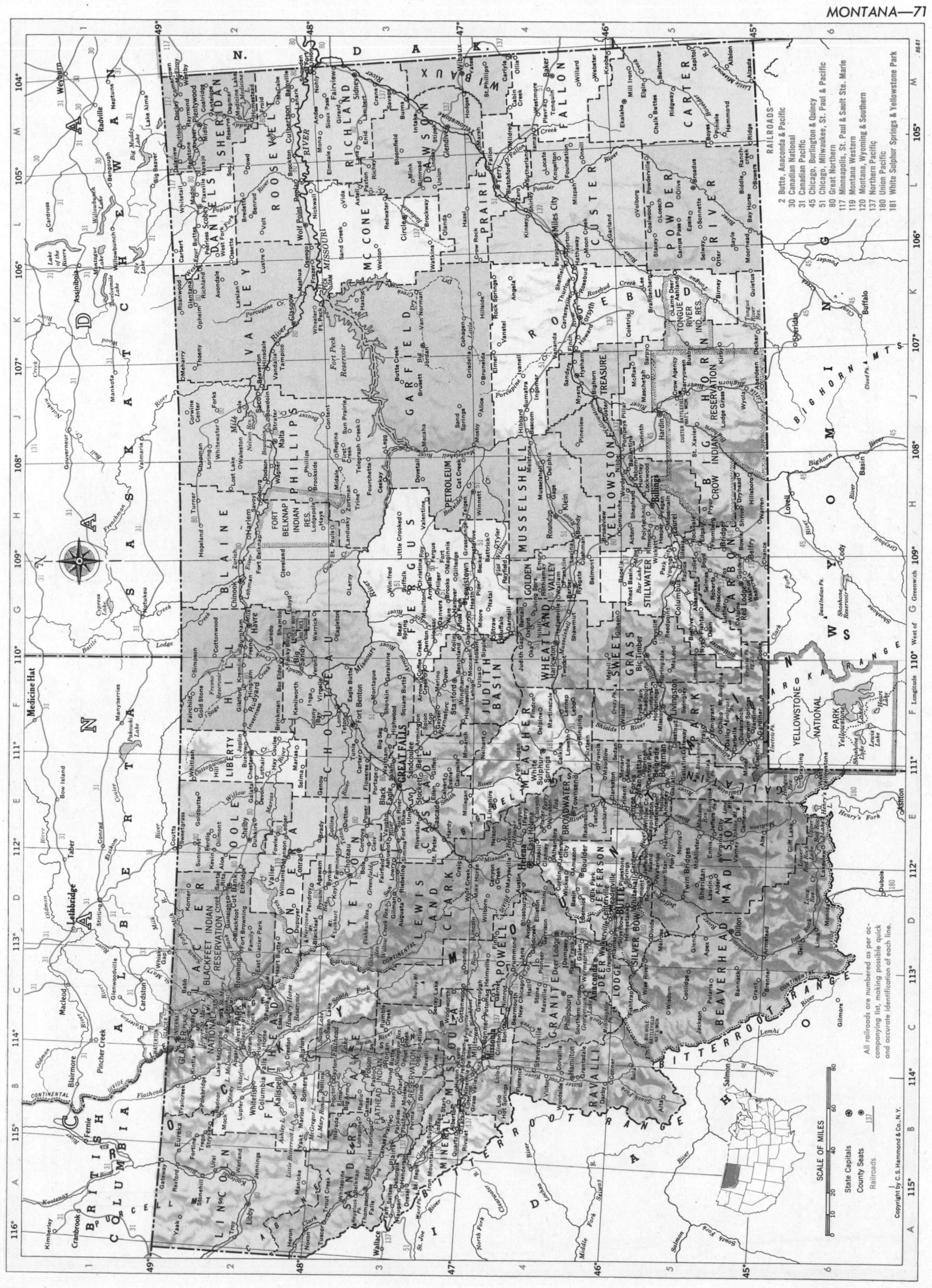

SCALE OF MILES

State Capitals
County Seats
Railroads

RAILROADS

2   Butte, Anaconda & Pacific
30  Canadian National
31  Canadian Pacific
45  Chicago, Burlington & Quincy
51  Chicago, Milwaukee, St. Paul & Pacific
80  Great Northern
117 Minneapolis, St. Paul & Sault Ste. Marie
119 Montana Western
120 Montana, Wyoming & Southern
137 Northern Pacific
180 Union Pacific
181 White Sulphur Springs & Yellowstone Park

All railroads are numbered as per accompanying list, making possible quick
and accurate identification of each line.

Copyright by C. S. Hammond & Co., N.Y.

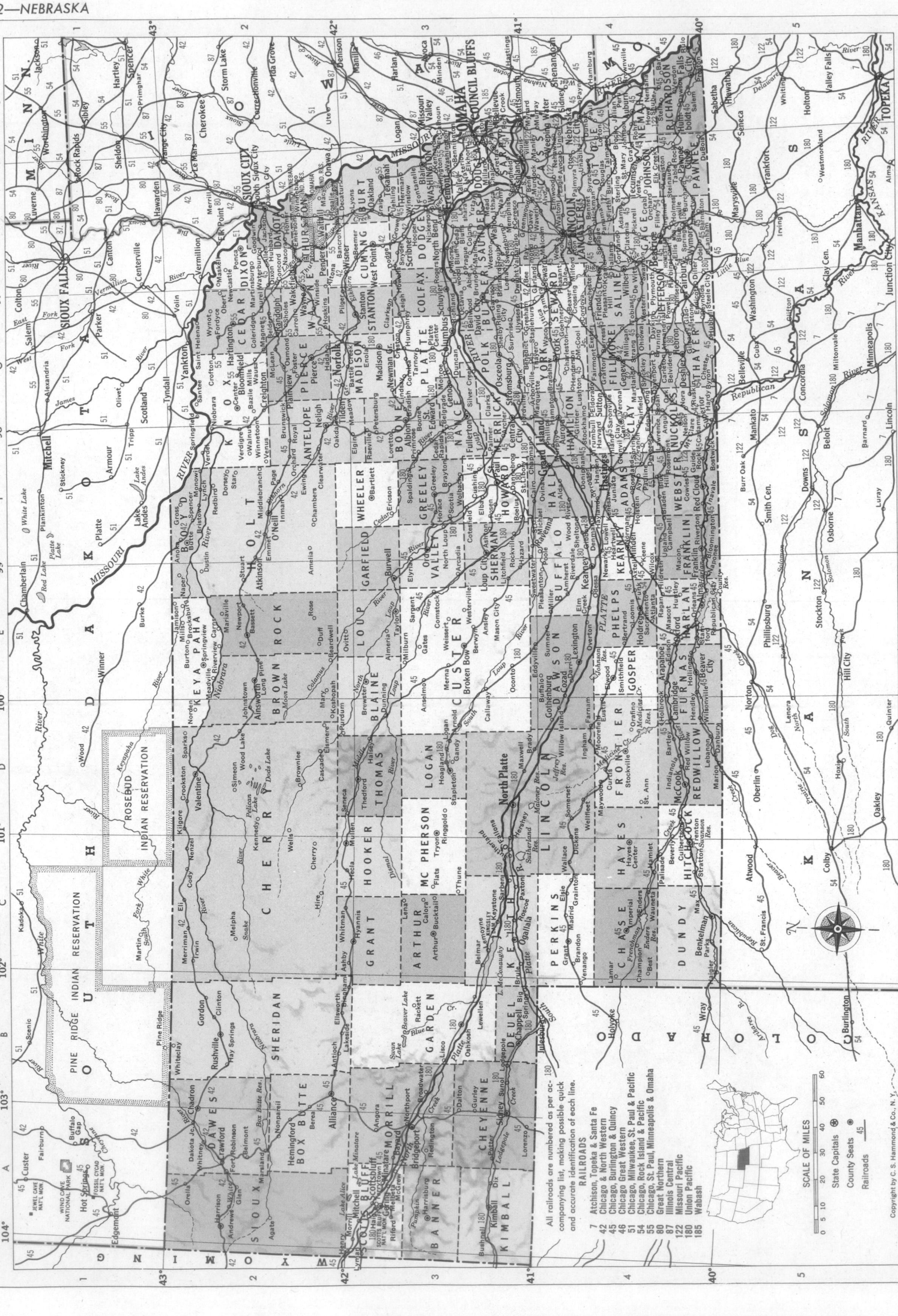

RAILROADS

All railroads are numbered as per accompanying list, making possible quick and accurate identification of each line.

| 7 | Atchison, Topeka & Santa Fe |
| 42 | Chicago & North Western |
| 45 | Chicago, Burlington & Quincy |
| 46 | Chicago Great Western |
| 51 | Chicago, Milwaukee, St. Paul & Pacific |
| 54 | Chicago, Rock Island & Pacific |
| 55 | Chicago, St. Paul, Minneapolis & Omaha |
| 80 | Great Northern |
| 87 | Illinois Central |
| 120 | Missouri Pacific |
| 122 | Union Pacific |
| 185 | Wabash |

SCALE OF MILES

0  5  10    20    30    40    50    60

State Capitals ⊛
County Seats ⊙
Railroads 45

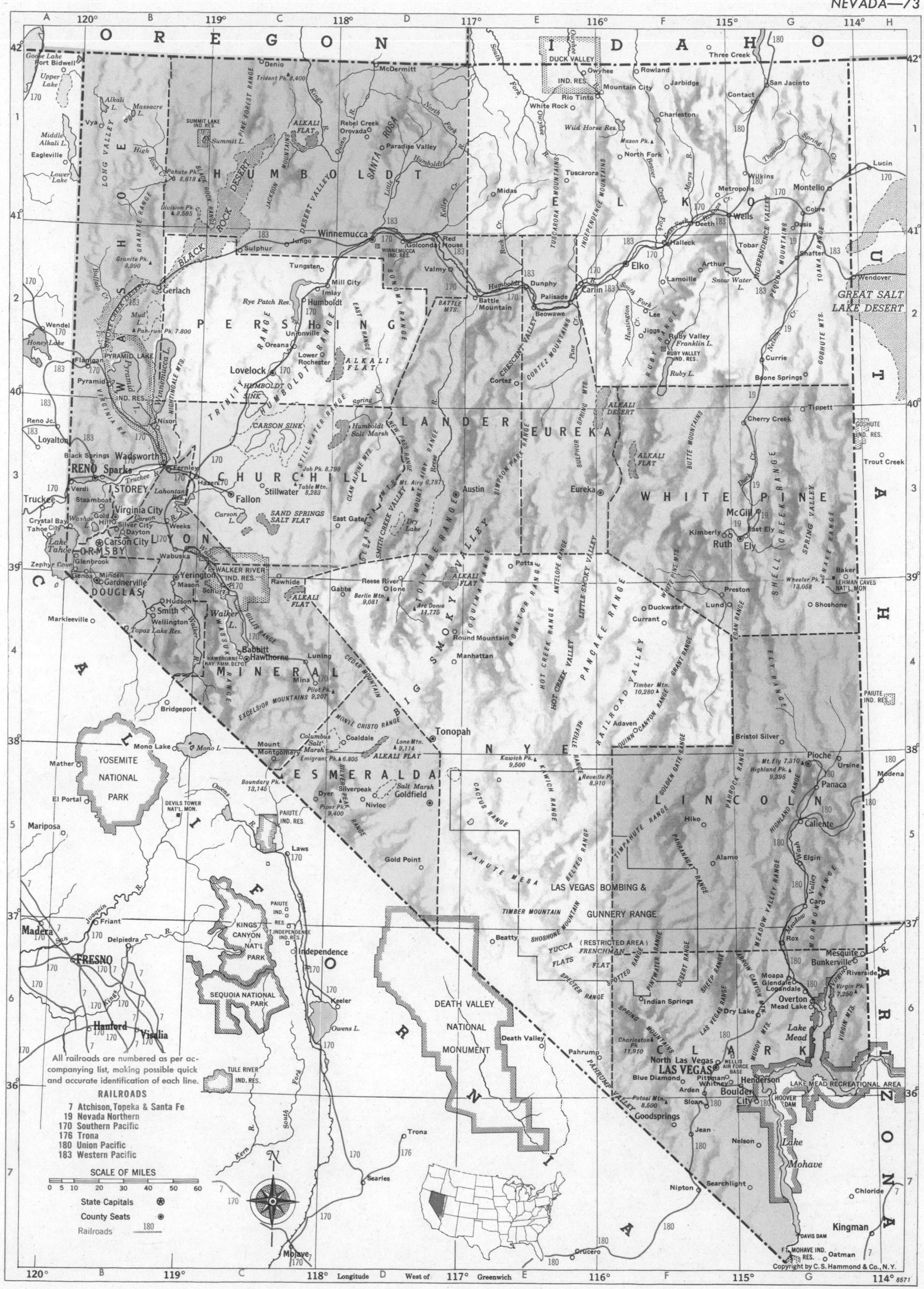

RAILROADS

7 Atchison, Topeka & Santa Fe
19 Nevada Northern
170 Southern Pacific
176 Trona
180 Union Pacific
183 Western Pacific

All railroads are numbered as per accompanying list, making possible quick and accurate identification of each line.

SCALE OF MILES
0 5 10    20    30    40    50    60

State Capitals
County Seats
Railroads

Copyright by C. S. Hammond & Co., N.Y.

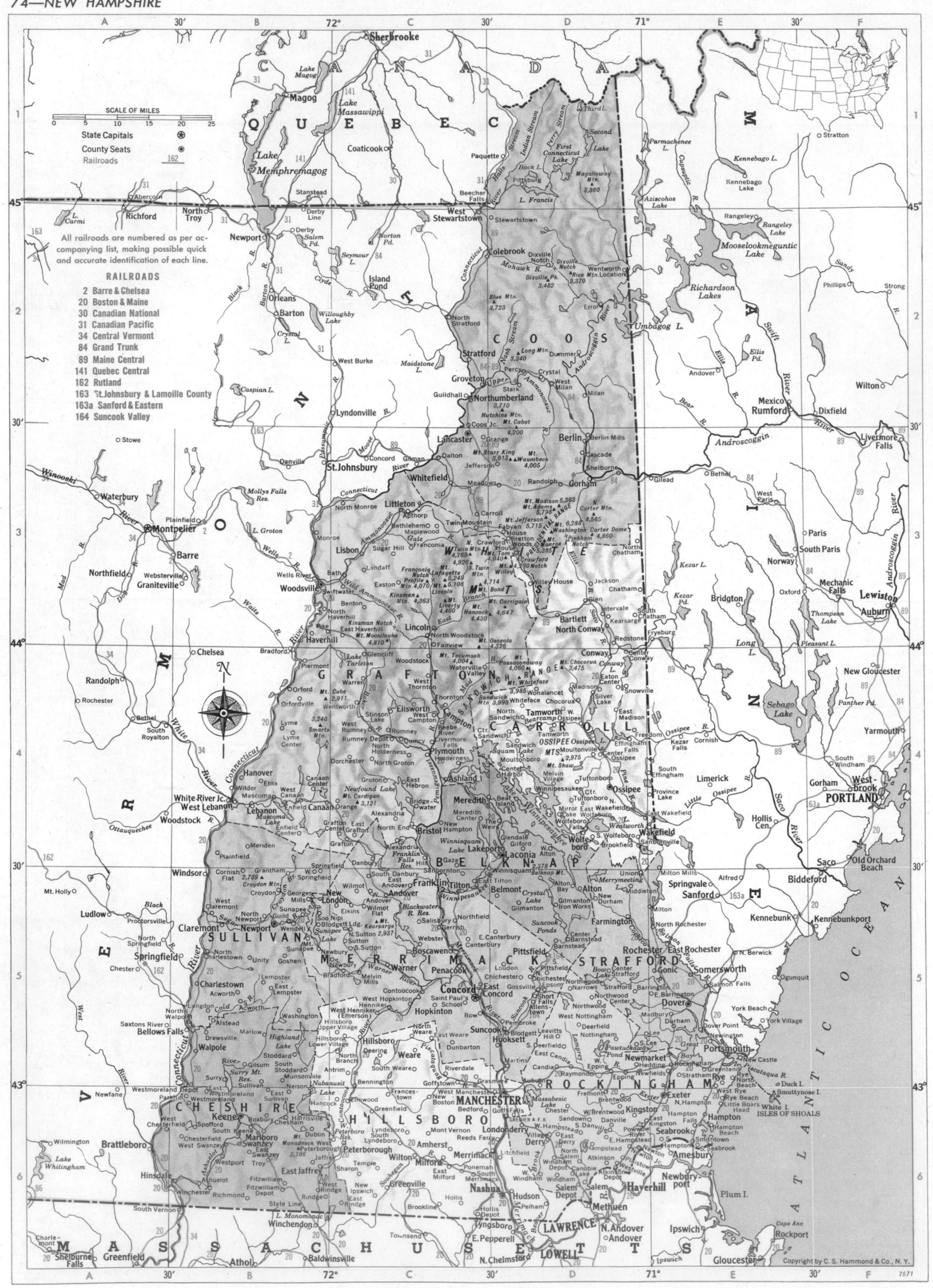

## RAILROADS

- 2 Barre & Chelsea
- 20 Boston & Maine
- 30 Canadian National
- 31 Canadian Pacific
- 34 Central Vermont
- 84 Grand Trunk
- 89 Maine Central
- 141 Quebec Central
- 162 Rutland
- 163 St. Johnsbury & Lamoille County
- 163a Sanford & Eastern
- 164 Suncook Valley

State Capitals ⊛
County Seats ⊚
Railroads 162

All railroads are numbered as per accompanying list, making possible quick and accurate identification of each line.

SCALE OF MILES
0 5 10 15 20 25

Copyright by C. S. Hammond & Co., N. Y.

7671

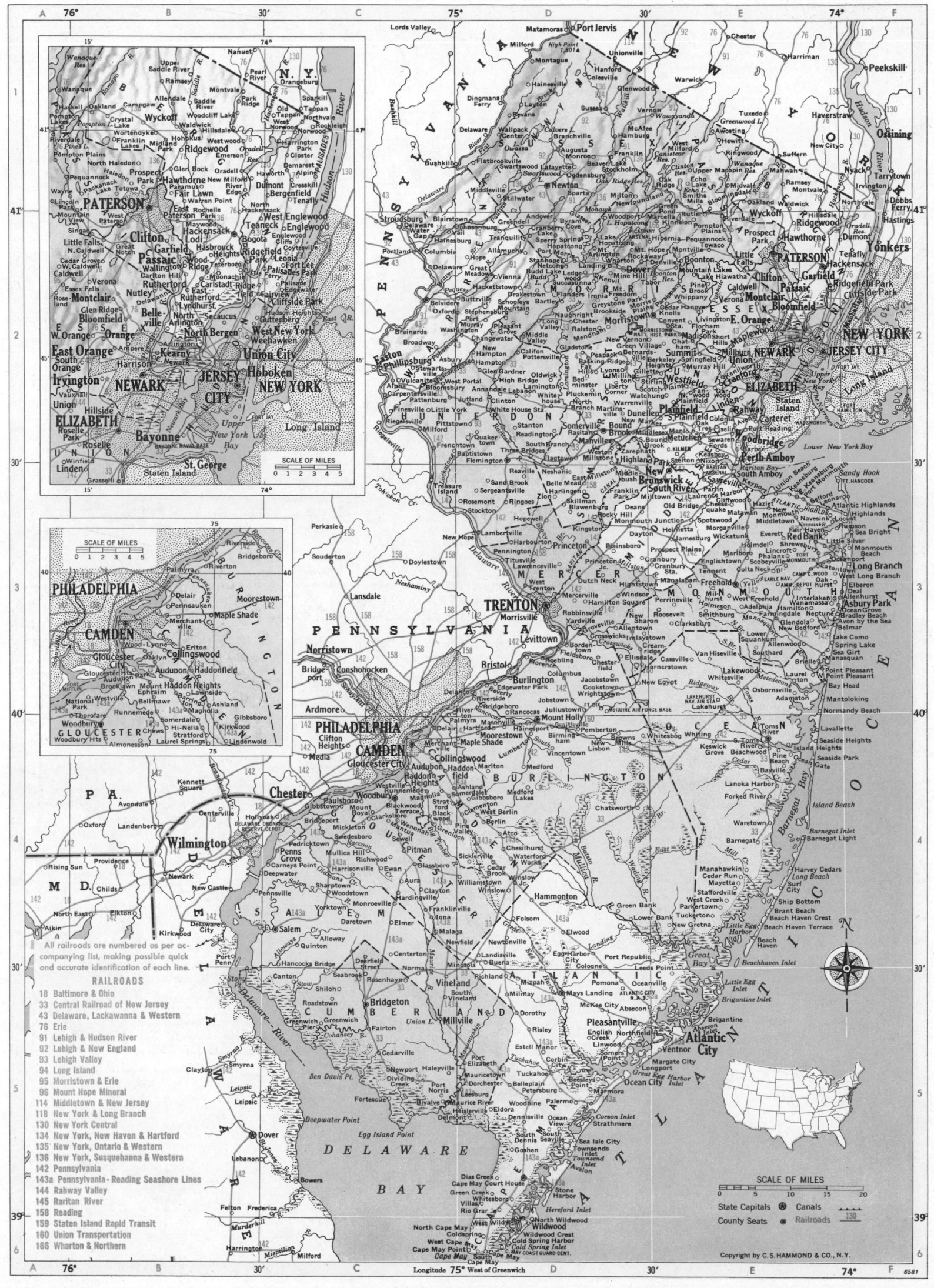

**RAILROADS**
- 18 Baltimore & Ohio
- 33 Central Railroad of New Jersey
- 43 Delaware, Lackawanna & Western
- 76 Erie
- 91 Lehigh & Hudson River
- 92 Lehigh & New England
- 93 Lehigh Valley
- 94 Long Island
- 95 Morristown & Erie
- 96 Mount Hope Mineral
- 114 Middletown & New Jersey
- 118 New York & Long Branch
- 130 New York Central
- 134 New York, New Haven & Hartford
- 135 New York, Ontario & Western
- 136 New York, Susquehanna & Western
- 142 Pennsylvania
- 143a Pennsylvania - Reading Seashore Lines
- 144 Rahway Valley
- 145 Raritan River
- 158 Reading
- 159 Staten Island Rapid Transit
- 160 Union Transportation
- 166 Wharton & Northern

All railroads are numbered as per accompanying list, making possible quick and accurate identification of each line.

State Capitals  Canals
County Seats  Railroads

Copyright by C.S. Hammond & Co., N.Y.

Longitude 75° West of Greenwich

8581

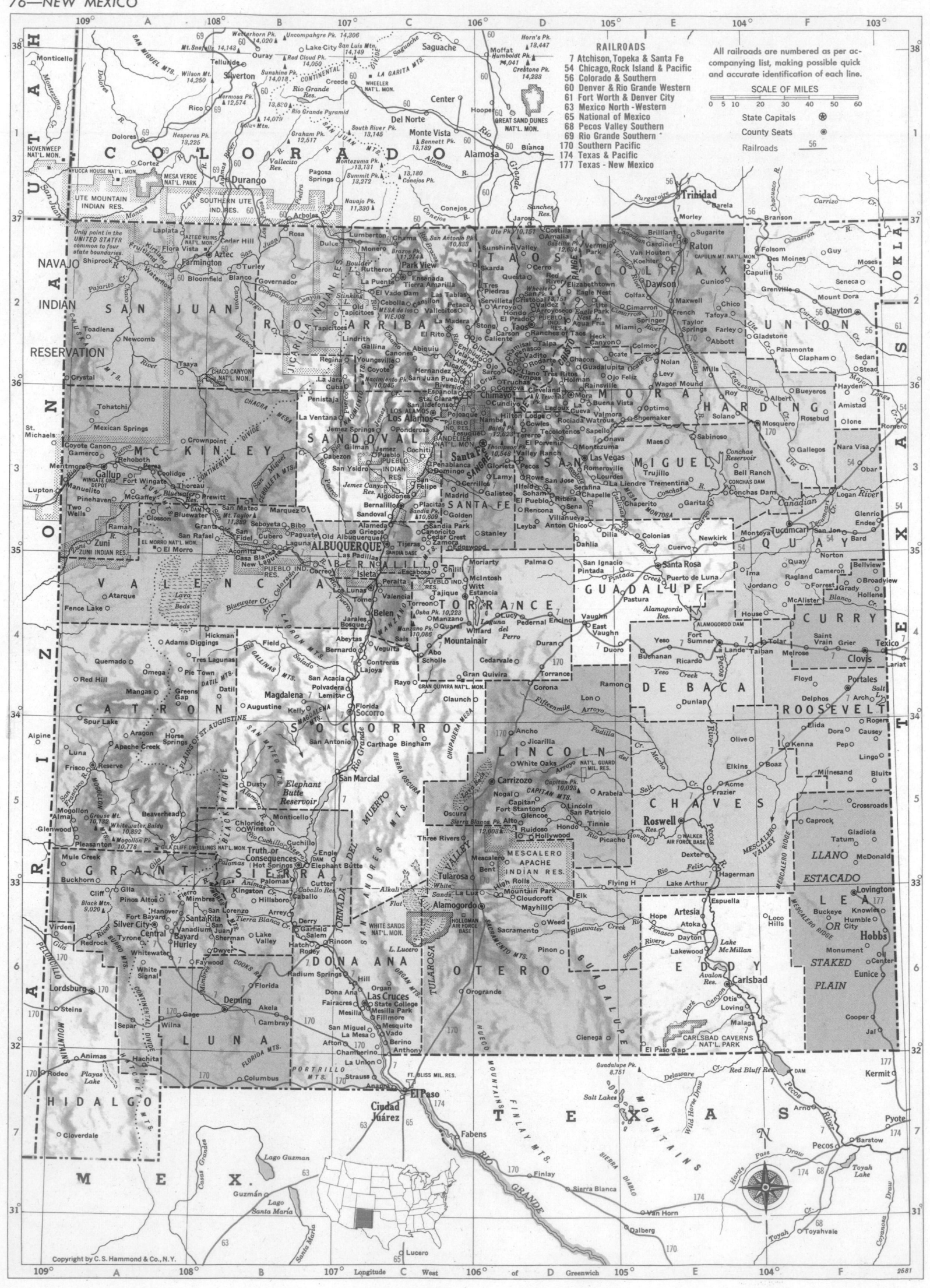

RAILROADS
7 Atchison, Topeka & Santa Fe
54 Chicago, Rock Island & Pacific
56 Colorado & Southern
60 Denver & Rio Grande Western
61 Fort Worth & Denver City
63 Mexico North-Western
65 National of Mexico
68 Pecos Valley Southern
69 Rio Grande Southern
170 Southern Pacific
174 Texas & Pacific
177 Texas - New Mexico

All railroads are numbered as per accompanying list, making possible quick and accurate identification of each line.

SCALE OF MILES

State Capitals ⊛
County Seats ⊚
Railroads

Copyright by C. S. Hammond & Co., N.Y.

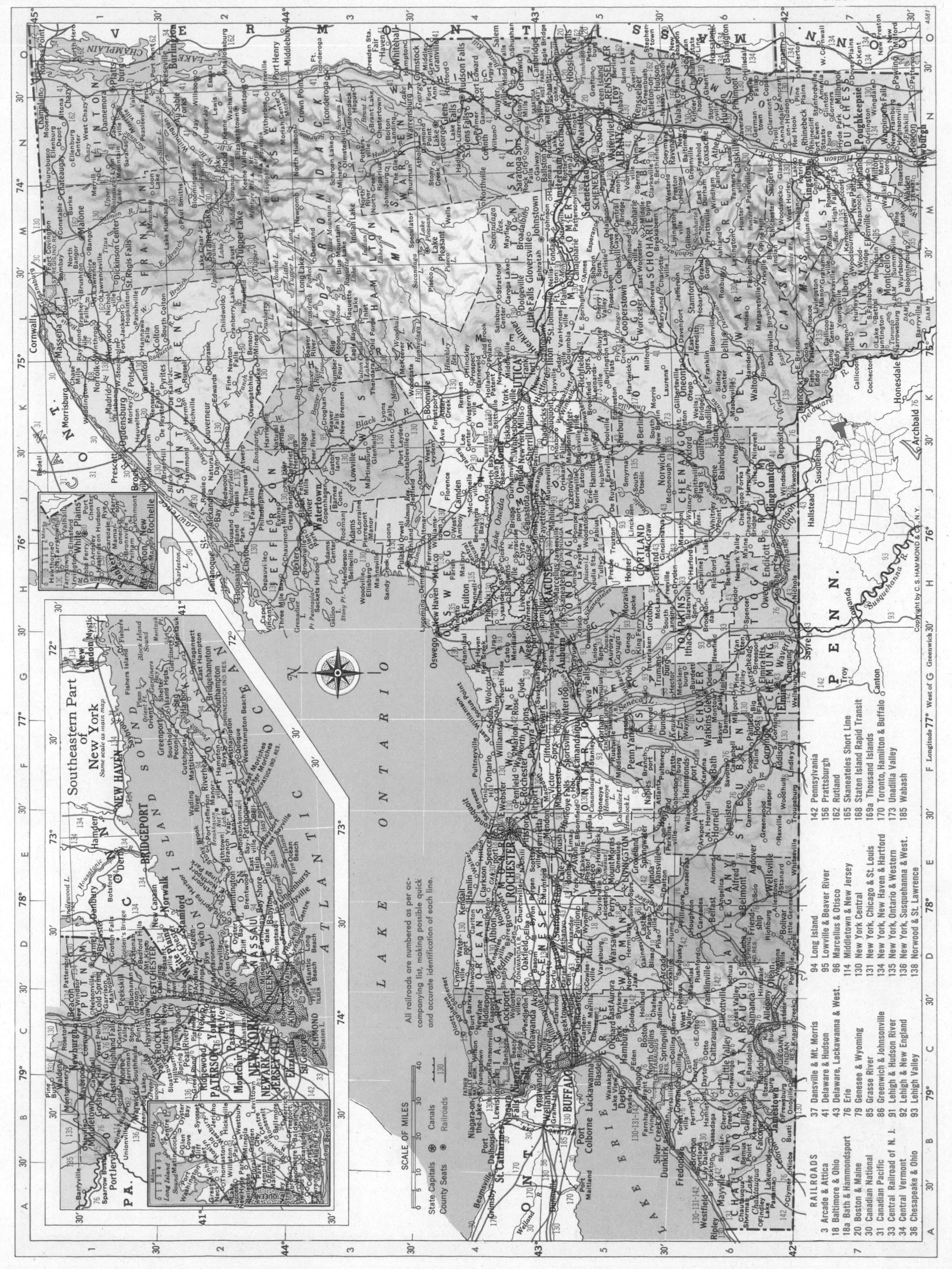

Southeastern Part of New York
Same scale as main map

All railroads are numbered as per accompanying list, making possible quick and accurate identification of each line.

SCALE OF MILES

State Capitals
County Seats
Canals
Railroads

**RAILROADS**

3 Arcade & Attica
18 Baltimore & Ohio
18a Bath & Hammondsport
20 Boston & Maine
30 Canadian National
31 Canadian Pacific
33 Central Railroad of N. J.
34 Central Vermont
36 Chesapeake & Ohio
37 Dansville & Mt. Morris
41 Delaware & Hudson
43 Delaware, Lackawanna & West.
76 Erie
79 Genesee & Wyoming
85 Grasse River
86 Greenwich & Johnsonville
91 Lehigh & Hudson River
92 Lehigh & New England
93 Lehigh Valley
94 Long Island
95 Lowville & Beaver River
96 Marcellus & Otisco
114 Middletown & New Jersey
130 New York Central
131 New York, Chicago & St. Louis
134 New York, New Haven & Hartford
135 New York, Ontario & Western
136 New York, Susquehanna & West.
138 Norwood & St. Lawrence
142 Pennsylvania
156 Prattsburg
162 Rutland
165 Skaneateles Short Line
168 Staten Island Rapid Transit
169a Thousand Islands
170 Toronto, Hamilton & Buffalo
173 Unadilla Valley
185 Wabash

Copyright by C. S. HAMMOND & CO., N. Y.

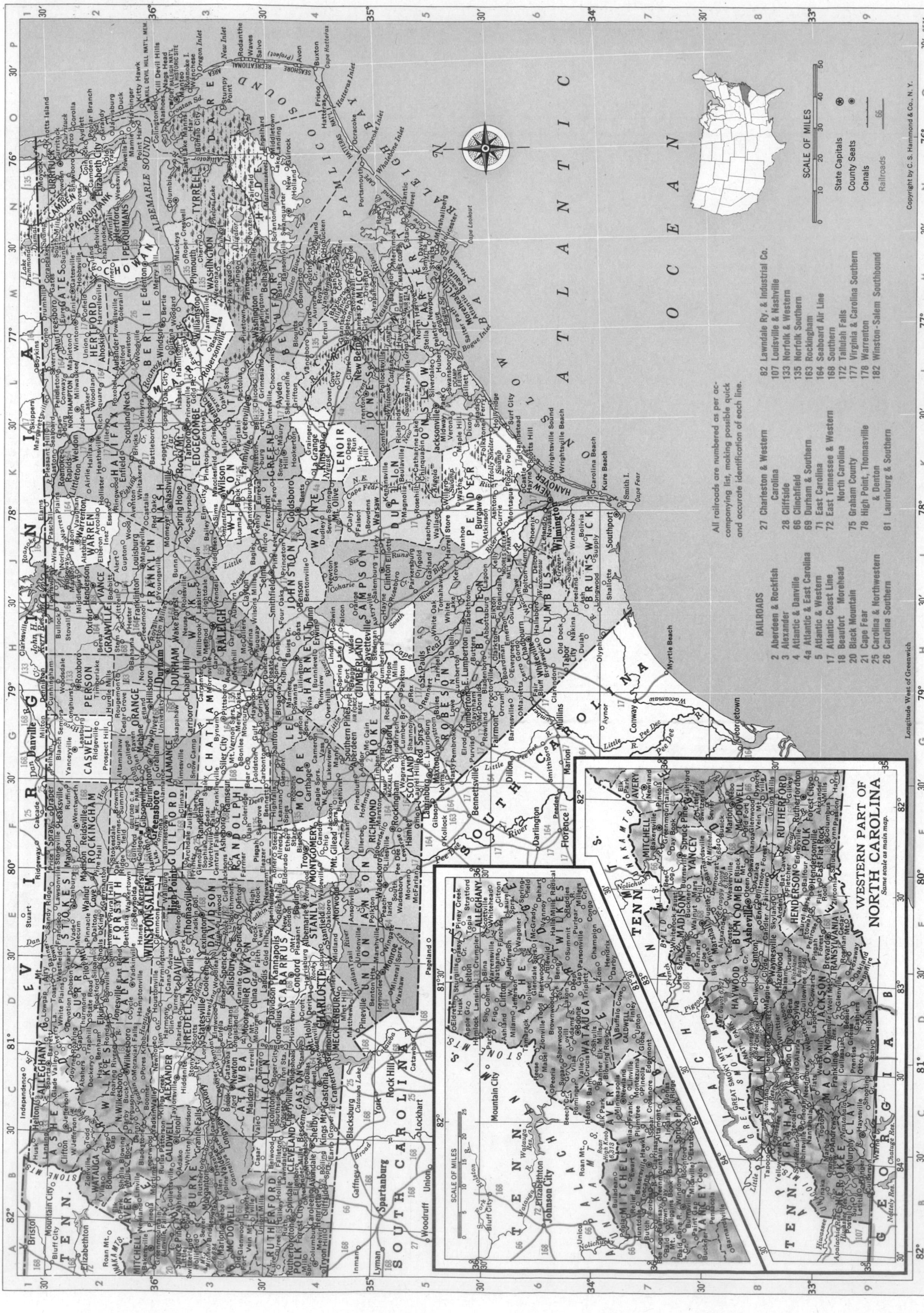

SCALE OF MILES

State Capitals ⊛
County Seats ◉
Canals
Railroads 66

All railroads are numbered as per accompanying list, making possible quick and accurate identification of each line.

**RAILROADS**

| | |
|---|---|
| 2 Aberdeen & Rockfish | 27 Charleston & Western Carolina |
| 3 Alexander | 28 Cliffside |
| 4 Atlantic & Danville | 66 Clinchfield |
| 4a Atlantic & East Carolina | 133 Norfolk & Western |
| 5 Atlantic & Western | 135 Norfolk Southern |
| 17 Atlantic Coast Line | 163 Rockingham |
| 18 Beaufort Morehead | 164 Seaboard Air Line |
| 20 Black Mountain | 168 Southern |
| 21 Cape Fear | 172 Tallulah Falls |
| 25 Carolina & Northwestern | 177 Virginia & Carolina Southern |
| 26 Carolina Southern | 178 Warrenton |
| | 182 Winston-Salem Southbound |
| 82 Lawndale Ry. & Industrial Co. | |
| 107 Louisville & Nashville | |
| 69 Durham & Southern | |
| 71 East Carolina | |
| 72 East Tennessee & Western North Carolina | |
| 75 Graham County | |
| 78 High Point, Thomasville & Denton | |
| 81 Laurinburg & Southern | |

ATLANTIC OCEAN

PAMLICO SOUND

ALBEMARLE SOUND

RALEIGH BAY

ONSLOW BAY

SOUTH CAROLINA

TENN.

GEORGIA

**WESTERN PART OF NORTH CAROLINA**
Same scale as main map.

SCALE OF MILES

Copyright by C. S. Hammond & Co., N. Y.

Longitude West of Greenwich

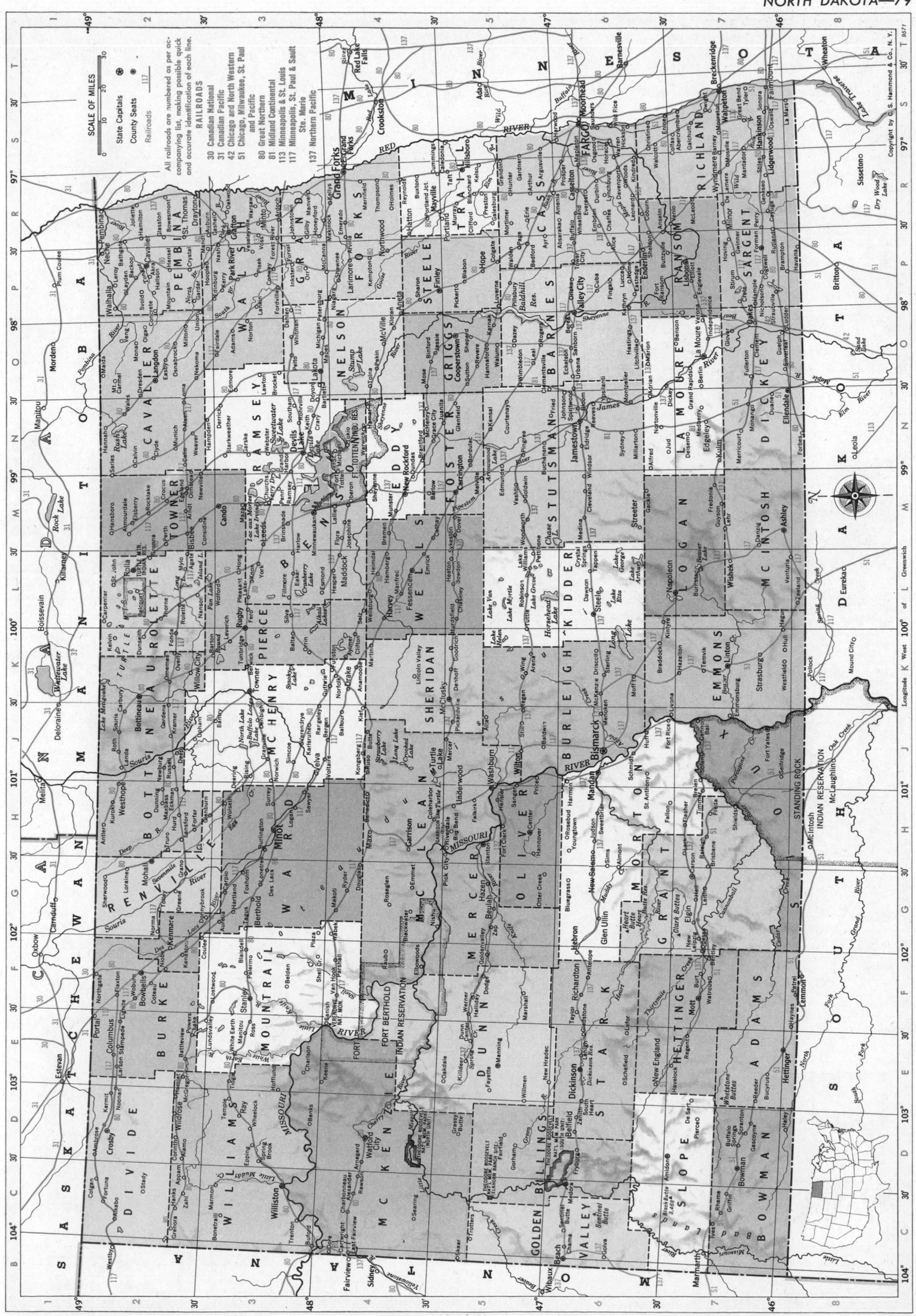

RAILROADS

2 Akron & Barberton Belt
3 Akron, Canton & Youngstown
4 Ann Arbor
18 Baltimore & Ohio
23 Bessemer & Lake Erie
25 Canadian National
30 Canadian Pacific
36 Chesapeake & Ohio
75 Detroit, Toledo & Ironton
76 Erie
77 Fairport, Painesville & Eastern
78 Federal Valley

82 Lakeside & Marblehead
107 Louisville & Nashville
130 New York Central
131 New York, Chicago & St. Louis
133 Norfolk & Western
142 Pennsylvania
152 Pittsburgh & West Virginia
168 Southern
169 Toledo, Angola & Western
171 Toledo Terminal
185 Wabash
189 New York, Chicago & St. Louis
200 Youngstown & Southern

SCALE OF MILES
0  5  10    20    30    40

⊛ State Capitals
◉ County Seats
130 Railroads

Copyright by C. S. HAMMOND & Co., N.Y.

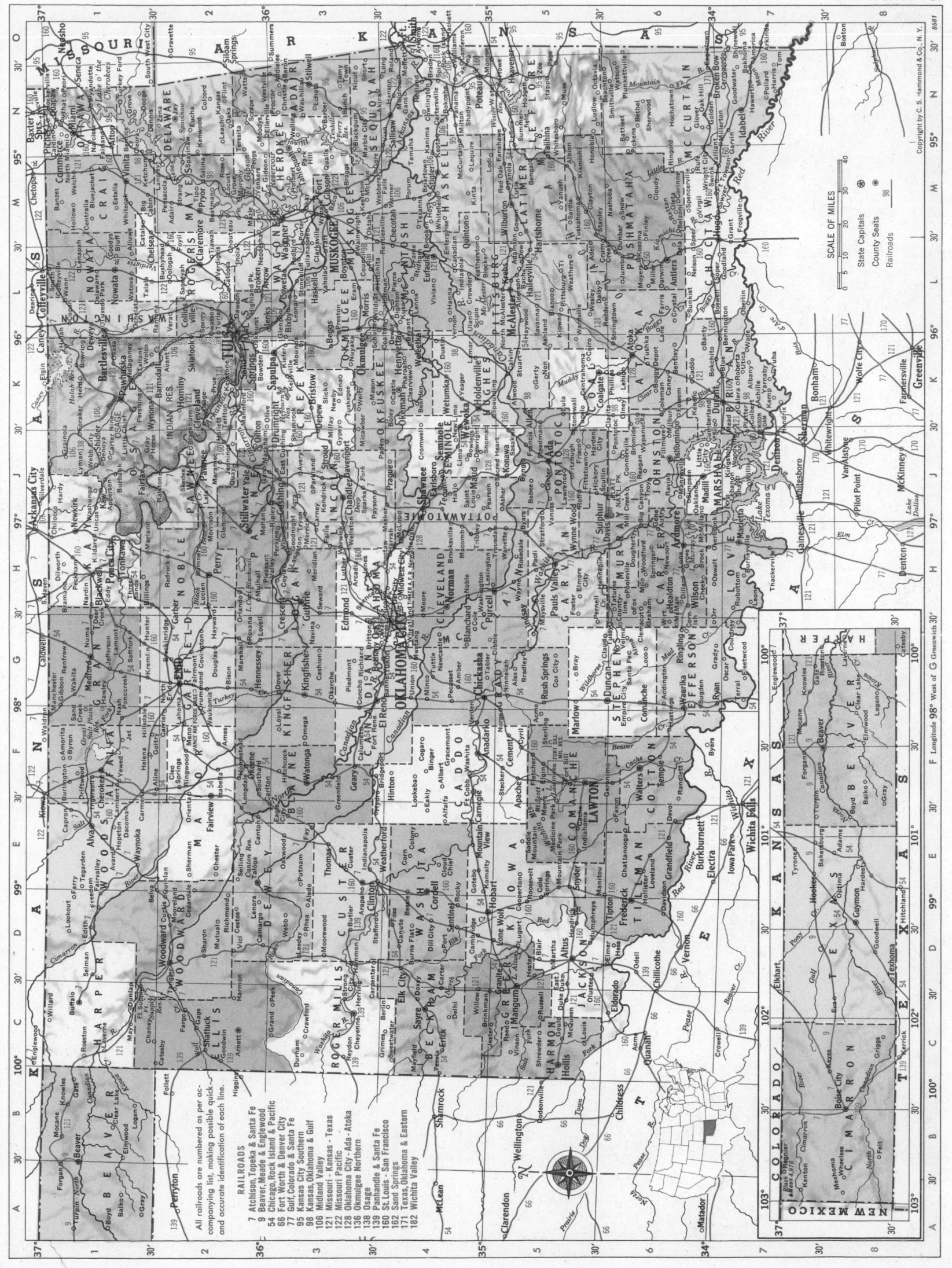

SCALE OF MILES

⊛ State Capitals
◉ County Seats
Railroads

RAILROADS

All railroads are numbered as per accompanying list, making possible quick and accurate identification of each line.

7 Atchison, Topeka & Santa Fe
7 Beaver, Meade & Englewood
54 Chicago, Rock Island & Pacific
66 Fort Worth & Denver City
77 Gulf, Colorado & Santa Fe
95 Kansas City Southern
98 Kansas, Oklahoma & Gulf
106 Midland Valley
121 Missouri - Kansas - Texas
122 Missouri Pacific
128 Oklahoma City - Ada - Atoka
136 Okmulgee Northern
138 Osage
139 Panhandle & Santa Fe
160 St. Louis - San Francisco
161 Sand Springs
171 Texas, Oklahoma & Eastern
182 Wichita Valley

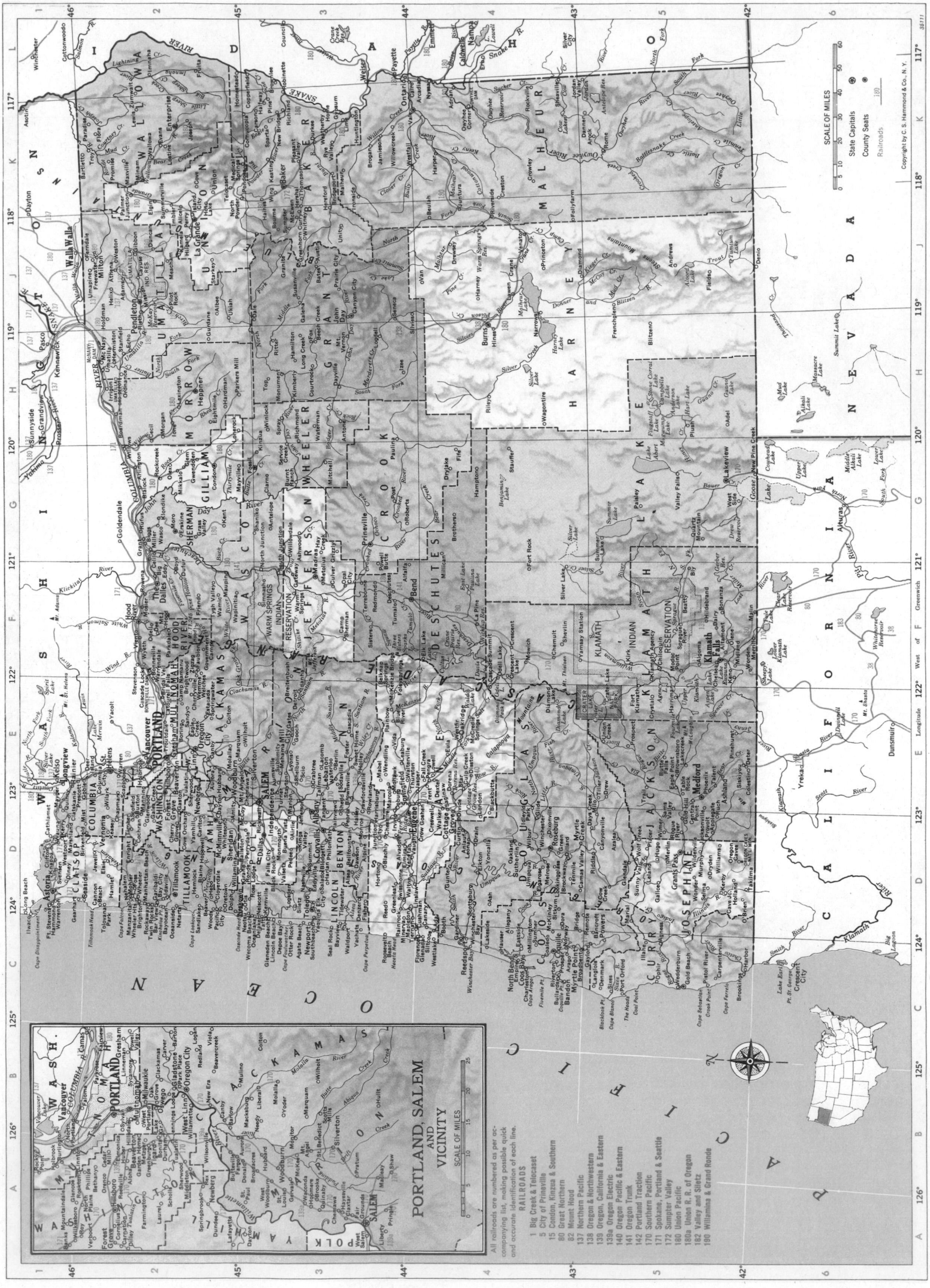
OREGON
PACIFIC OCEAN
WASHINGTON
IDAHO
NEVADA
CALIFORNIA
PORTLAND, SALEM AND VICINITY
SCALE OF MILES
All railroads are numbered as per accompanying list, making possible quick and accurate identification of each line.
RAILROADS
1 Big Creek & Telocaset
5 City of Prineville
15 Condon, Kinzua & Southern
80 Great Northern
82 Mount Hood
137 Northern Pacific
138 Oregon & Northwestern
139 Oregon, California & Eastern
139a Oregon Electric
140 Oregon Pacific & Eastern
141 Oregon Trunk
142 Portland Traction
170 Southern Pacific
171 Spokane, Portland & Seattle
172 Sumpter Valley
180 Union Pacific
180a Union R. R. of Oregon
182 Valley and Siletz
190 Willamina & Grand Ronde
SCALE OF MILES
State Capitals
County Seats
Railroads
Copyright by C. S. Hammond & Co., N. Y.

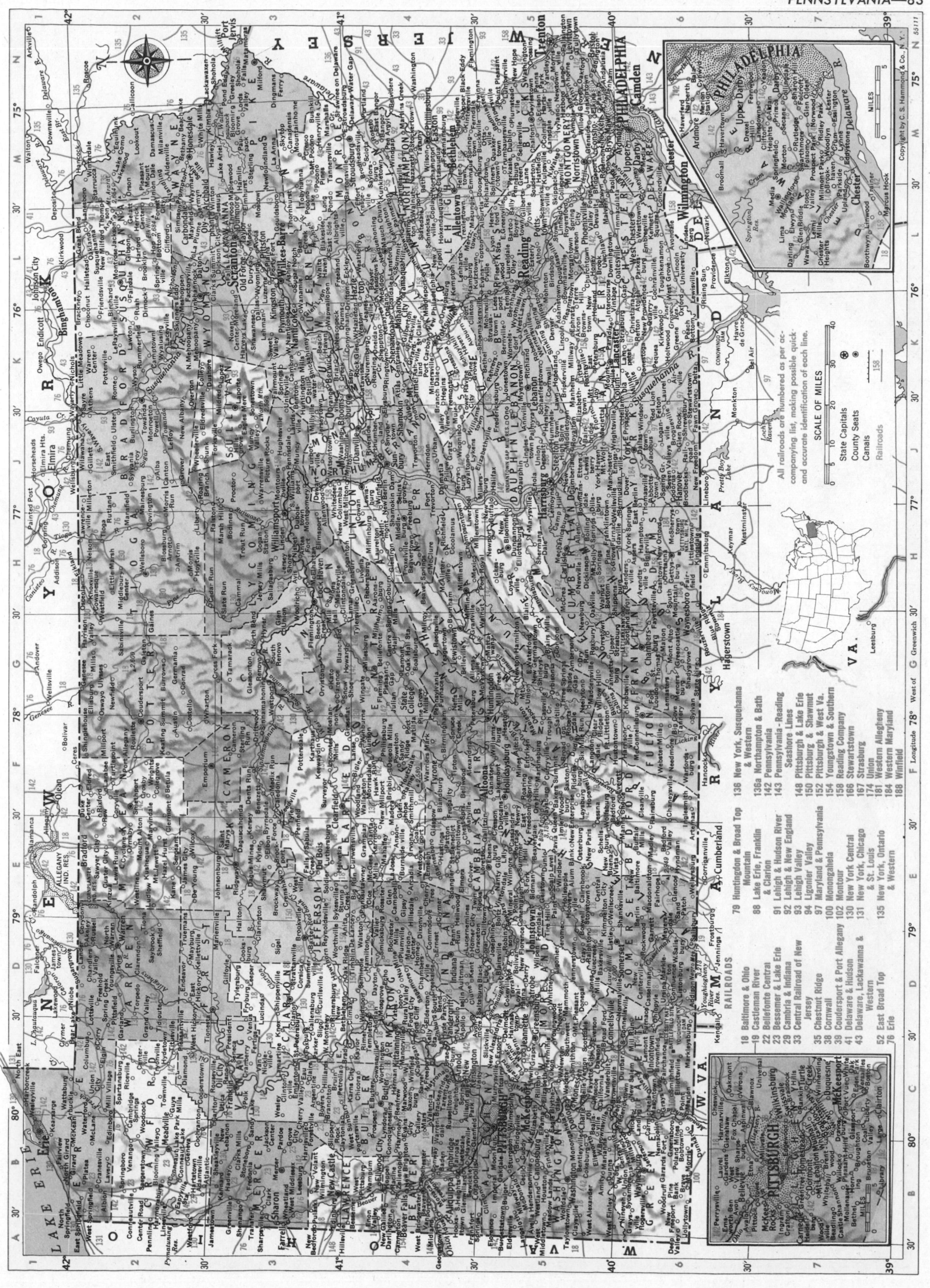

**RAILROADS**

| | |
|---|---|
| 18 | Baltimore & Ohio |
| 19 | Castleman River |
| 22 | Bellefonte Central |
| 23 | Bessemer & Lake Erie |
| 29 | Cambria & Indiana |
| 33 | Central Railroad of New Jersey |
| 35 | Chestnut Ridge |
| 38 | Cornwall |
| 39 | Coudersport & Port Allegany |
| 41 | Delaware & Hudson |
| 43 | Delaware, Lackawanna & Western |
| 52 | East Broad Top |
| 76 | Erie |

| | |
|---|---|
| 79 | Huntingdon & Broad Top Mountain |
| 88 | Lake Erie, Franklin & Clarion |
| 91 | Lehigh & Hudson River |
| 92 | Lehigh & New England |
| 93 | Lehigh Valley |
| 94 | Ligonier Valley |
| 97 | Maryland & Pennsylvania |
| 100 | Monongahela |
| 102 | Montour |
| 130 | New York Central |
| 131 | New York, Chicago & St. Louis |
| 135 | New York, Ontario & Western |

| | |
|---|---|
| 136 | New York, Susquehanna & Western |
| 136a | Northampton & Bath |
| 142 | Pennsylvania |
| 143 | Pennsylvania—Reading Seashore Lines |
| 148 | Pittsburg & Lake Erie |
| 150 | Pittsburg & Shawmut |
| 152 | Pittsburg & West Va. |
| 154 | Youngstown & Southern |
| 158 | Reading Company |
| 166 | Stewartstown |
| 167 | Strasburg |
| 174 | Union |
| 181 | Western Allegheny |
| 184 | Western Maryland |
| 188 | Winfield |

**SCALE OF MILES**

All railroads are numbered as per accompanying list, making possible quick and accurate identification of each line.

State Capitals
County Seats
Canals
Railroads

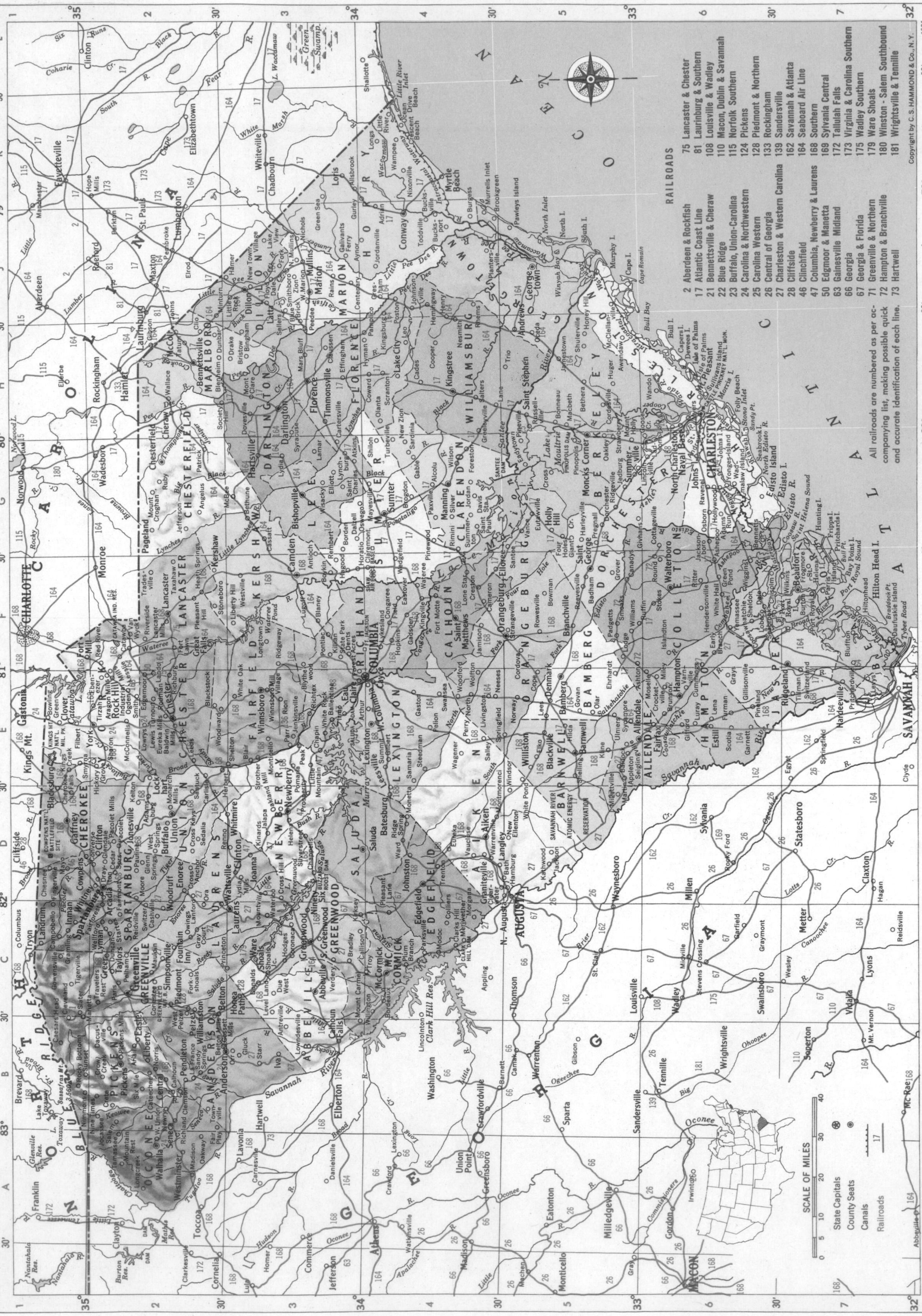
SOUTH CAROLINA
NORTH CAROLINA
GEORGIA
ATLANTIC OCEAN
RAILROADS
2 Aberdeen & Rockfish
17 Atlantic Coast Line
21 Bennettsville & Cheraw
22 Blue Ridge
23 Buffalo, Union-Carolina
24 Carolina & Northwestern
25 Carolina Western
26 Central of Georgia
27 Charleston & Western Carolina
28 Cliffside
46 Clinchfield
47 Columbia, Newberry & Laurens
50 Edgmoor & Manetta
63 Gainesville Midland
66 Georgia
67 Georgia & Florida
71 Greenville & Northern
72 Hampton & Branchville
73 Hartwell
75 Lancaster & Chester
81 Laurinburg & Southern
108 Louisville & Wadley
110 Macon, Dublin & Savannah
115 Norfolk Southern
124 Pickens
128 Piedmont & Northern
133 Rockingham
139 Sandersville
162 Savannah & Atlanta
164 Seaboard Air Line
168 Southern
169 Sylvania Central
172 Tallulah Falls
173 Virginia & Carolina Southern
175 Wadley Southern
179 Ware Shoals
180 Winston-Salem Southbound
181 Wrightsville & Tennille
All railroads are numbered as per accompanying list, making possible quick and accurate identification of each line.
SCALE OF MILES
0 5 10 20 30 40
State Capitals
County Seats
Canals
Railroads
Copyright by C.S. HAMMOND & Co., N.Y.
1681

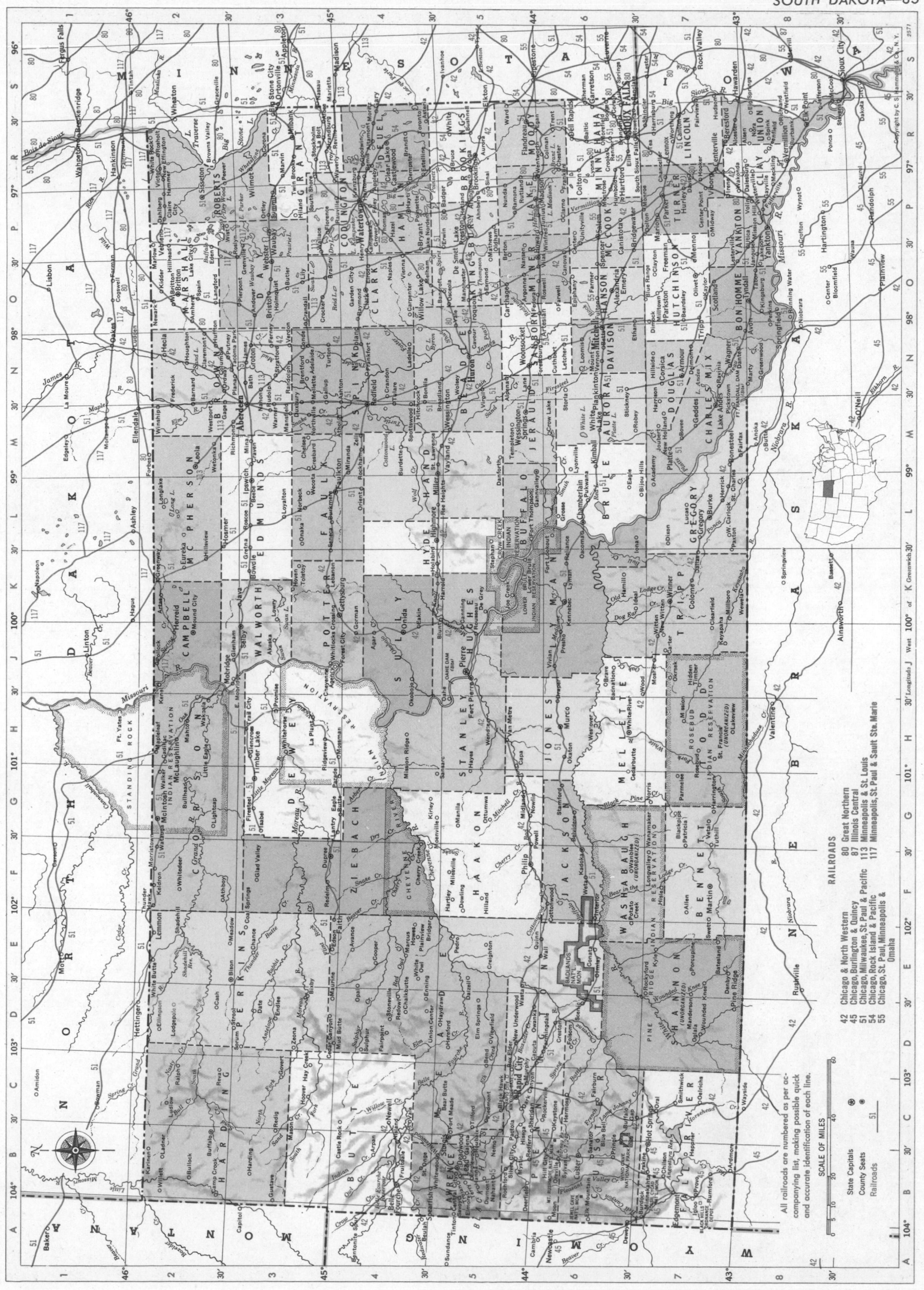

RAILROADS

| | |
|---|---|
| 42 Chicago & North Western | 80 Great Northern |
| 45 Chicago, Burlington & Quincy | 87 Illinois Central |
| 51 Chicago, Milwaukee, St. Paul & Pacific | 113 Minneapolis & St. Louis |
| 54 Chicago, Rock Island & Pacific | 117 Minneapolis, St. Paul & Sault Ste. Marie |
| 55 Chicago, St. Paul, Minneapolis & Omaha | |

All railroads are numbered as per accompanying list, making possible quick and accurate identification of each line.

State Capitals ⊛
County Seats ⊙
Railroads ————— 51

SCALE OF MILES

Copyright by C. S. Hammond & Co., N.Y.

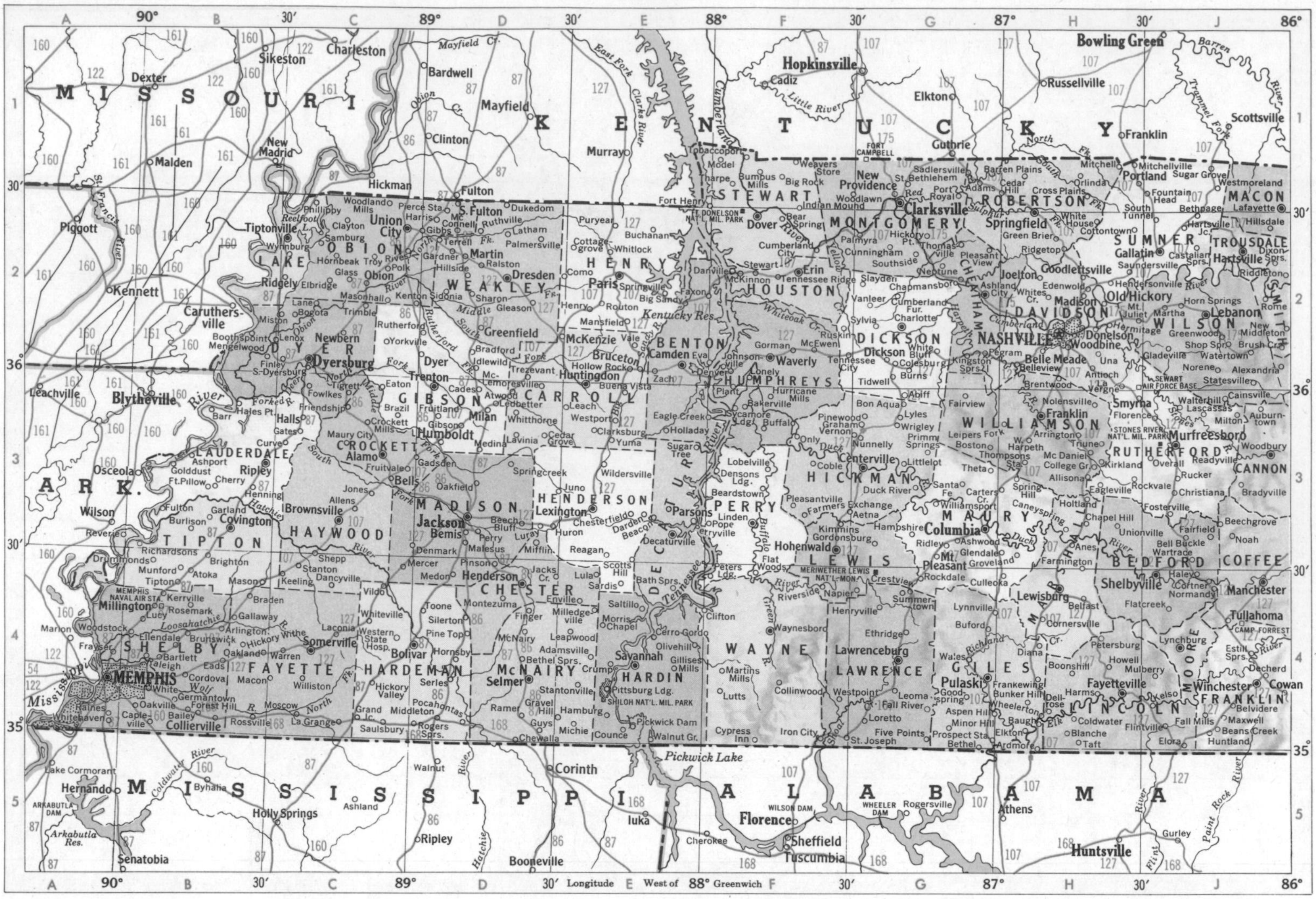

## RAILROADS

| | | | |
|---|---|---|---|
| 9 | Brimstone | 127 | Nashville, Chattanooga & St. Louis |
| 22 | Carolina & Northwestern | 133 | Norfolk & Western |
| 24 | Central of Georgia | 134 | Oneida & Western |
| 54 | Chicago, Rock Island & Pacific | 160 | St. Louis - San Francisco |
| 66 | Clinchfield | 161 | St. Louis Southwestern |
| 72 | East Tennessee & Western North Carolina | 165 | Smoky Mountain |
| 73 | Emory River | 168 | Southern |
| 86 | Gulf, Mobile & Ohio | 168a | Tallulah Falls |
| 87 | Illinois Central | 169 | Tennessee |
| 107 | Louisville & Nashville | 173 | Tennessee, Alabama & Georgia |
| 122 | Missouri Pacific | 175 | Tennessee Central |

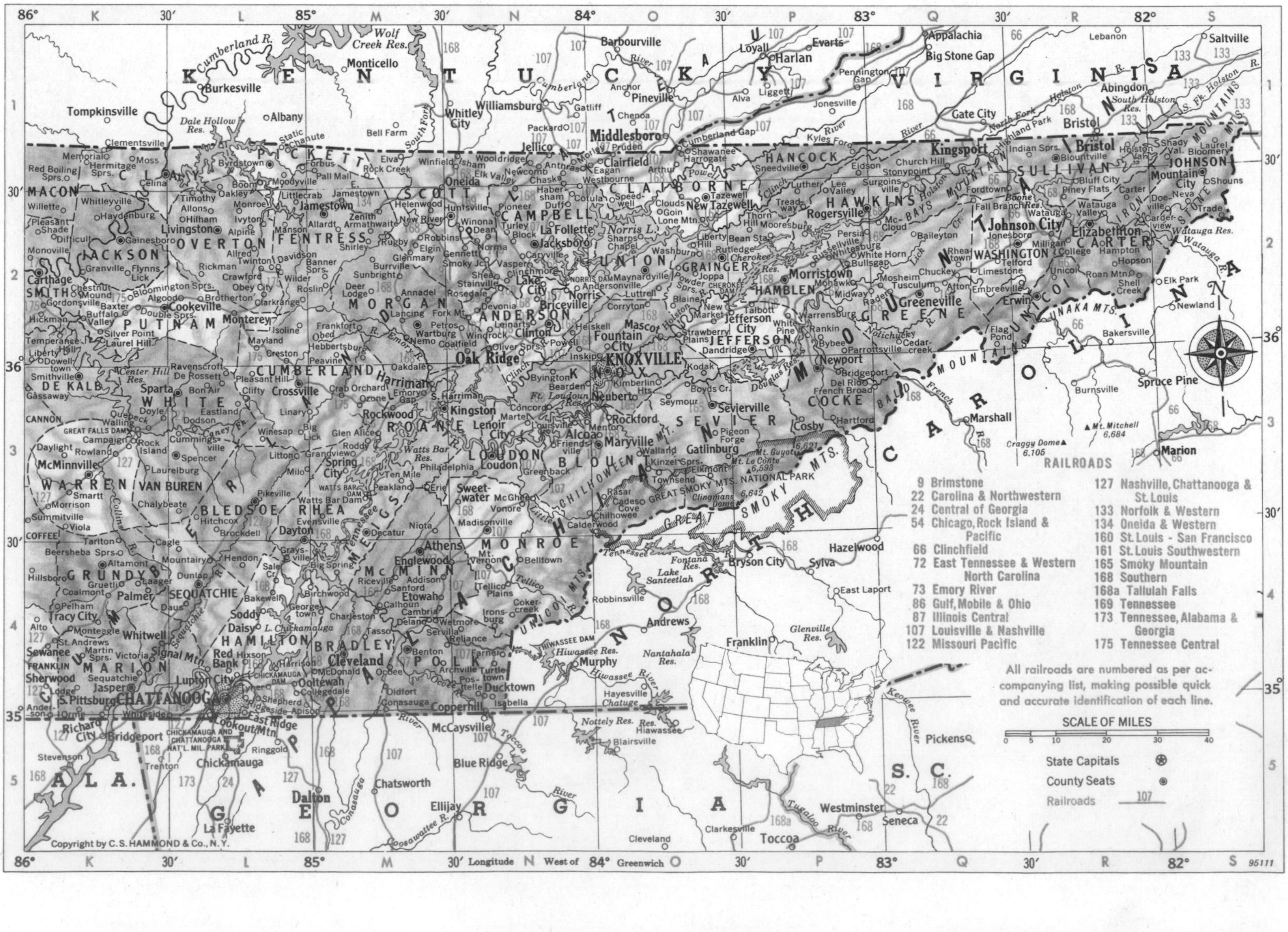

All railroads are numbered as per accompanying list, making possible quick and accurate identification of each line.

SCALE OF MILES

⊛ State Capitals

• County Seats

Railroads ——— 107

Copyright by C. S. Hammond & Co., N.Y.

95111

WESTERN PART OF
TEXAS

*Same scale as main map*

MEXICO

GULF
OF
MEXICO

All railroads are numbered as per accompanying list, making possible quick and accurate identification of each line.

3 Angelina & Neches River
7 Atchison, Topeka & Santa Fe
12 Burlington-Rock Island
54 Chicago, Rock Island & Pacific
56 Colorado & Southern
57 De Queen & Eastern
66 Fort Worth & Denver City
70 Galveston, Houston & Henderson
77 Gulf, Colorado & Santa Fe
94 Kansas City, Mexico & Orient
95 Kansas City Southern
98 Kansas, Oklahoma & Gulf
101 Louisiana & Arkansas
109 Mexico North-Western
121 Missouri-Kansas-Texas
122 Missouri Pacific
123 Moscow, Camden & San Augustine

125 Nacogdoches & Southeastern
126 National of Mexico
127 Panhandle & Santa Fe
128 Paris & Mt. Pleasant
129 Pecos Valley Southern
134 Quanah, Acme & Pacific
139 Rockdale, Sandow & Southern
140 Roscoe, Snyder & Pacific
160 St. Louis-San Francisco
161 St. Louis Southwestern
170 Southern Pacific
174 Texas & Pacific
176 Texas Mexican
177 Texas-New Mexico
179 Texas South-Eastern
188 Waco, Beaumont, Trinity & Sabine
190 Wichita Falls & Southern
192 Wichita Valley

SCALE OF MILES
0    20   40   60   80   100

⊛ State Capitals
◉ County Seats
170 Railroads

Copyright by C. S. Hammond & Co., N.Y.

F Longitude 98° West of G Greenwich 97°

1581 94°

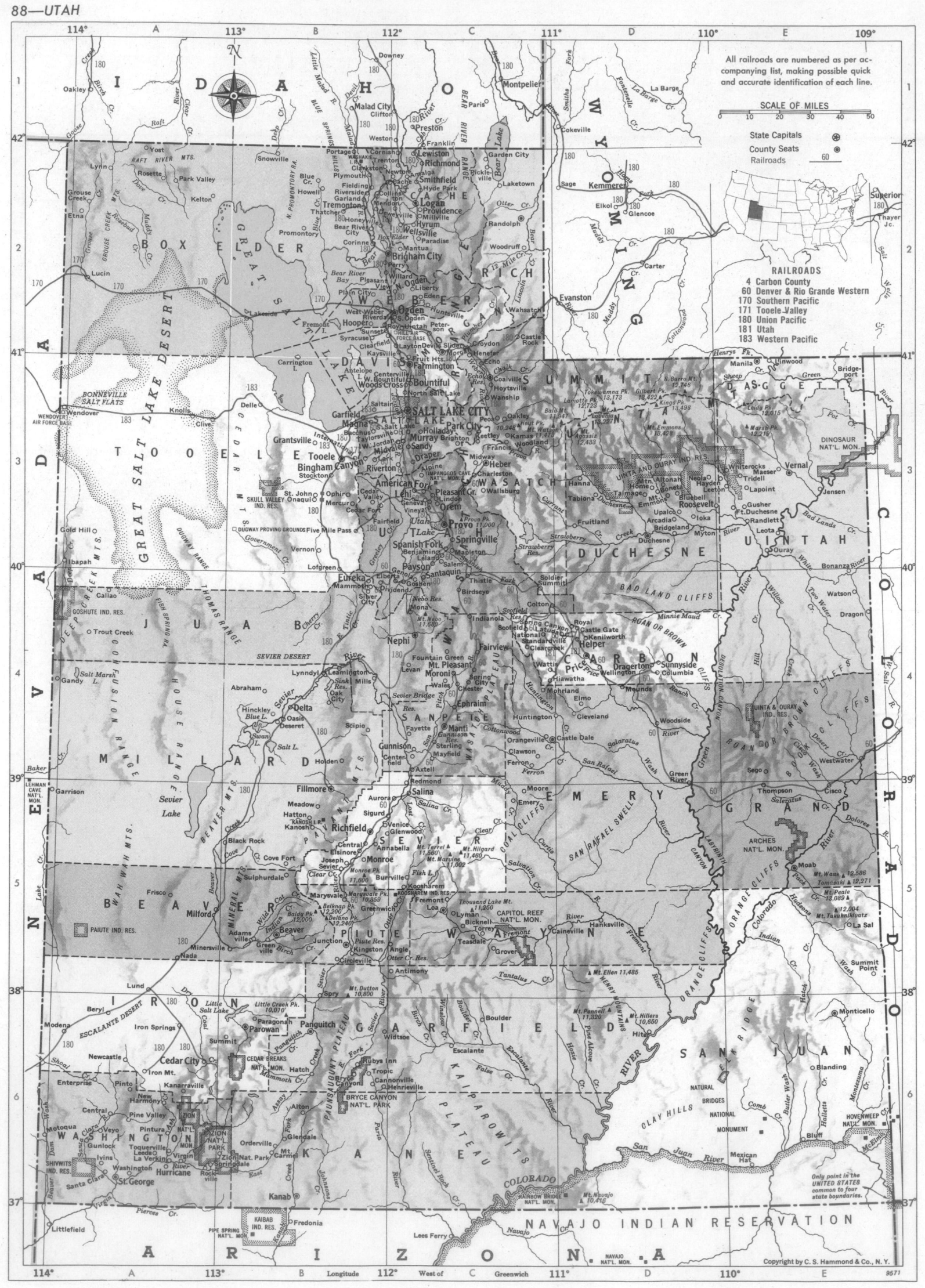

IDAHO

WYOMING

All railroads are numbered as per accompanying list, making possible quick and accurate identification of each line.

SCALE OF MILES
0  10  20  30  40  50

State Capitals ⊛
County Seats ◉
Railroads —— 60

RAILROADS
4  Carbon County
60  Denver & Rio Grande Western
170  Southern Pacific
171  Tooele Valley
180  Union Pacific
181  Utah
183  Western Pacific

BOX ELDER

CACHE

RICH

GREAT SALT LAKE DESERT

TOOELE

WEBER

DAVIS

MORGAN

SUMMIT

DAGGETT

SALT LAKE CITY

SALT LAKE

UINTA

DUCHESNE

UINTAH

JUAB

UTAH

WASATCH

MILLARD

SANPETE

CARBON

EMERY

GRAND

SEVIER

BEAVER

PIUTE

WAYNE

IRON

GARFIELD

KANE

SAN JUAN

WASHINGTON

COLORADO

ARIZONA

NAVAJO INDIAN RESERVATION

Only point in the UNITED STATES common to four state boundaries.

Copyright by C. S. Hammond & Co., N.Y.

9571

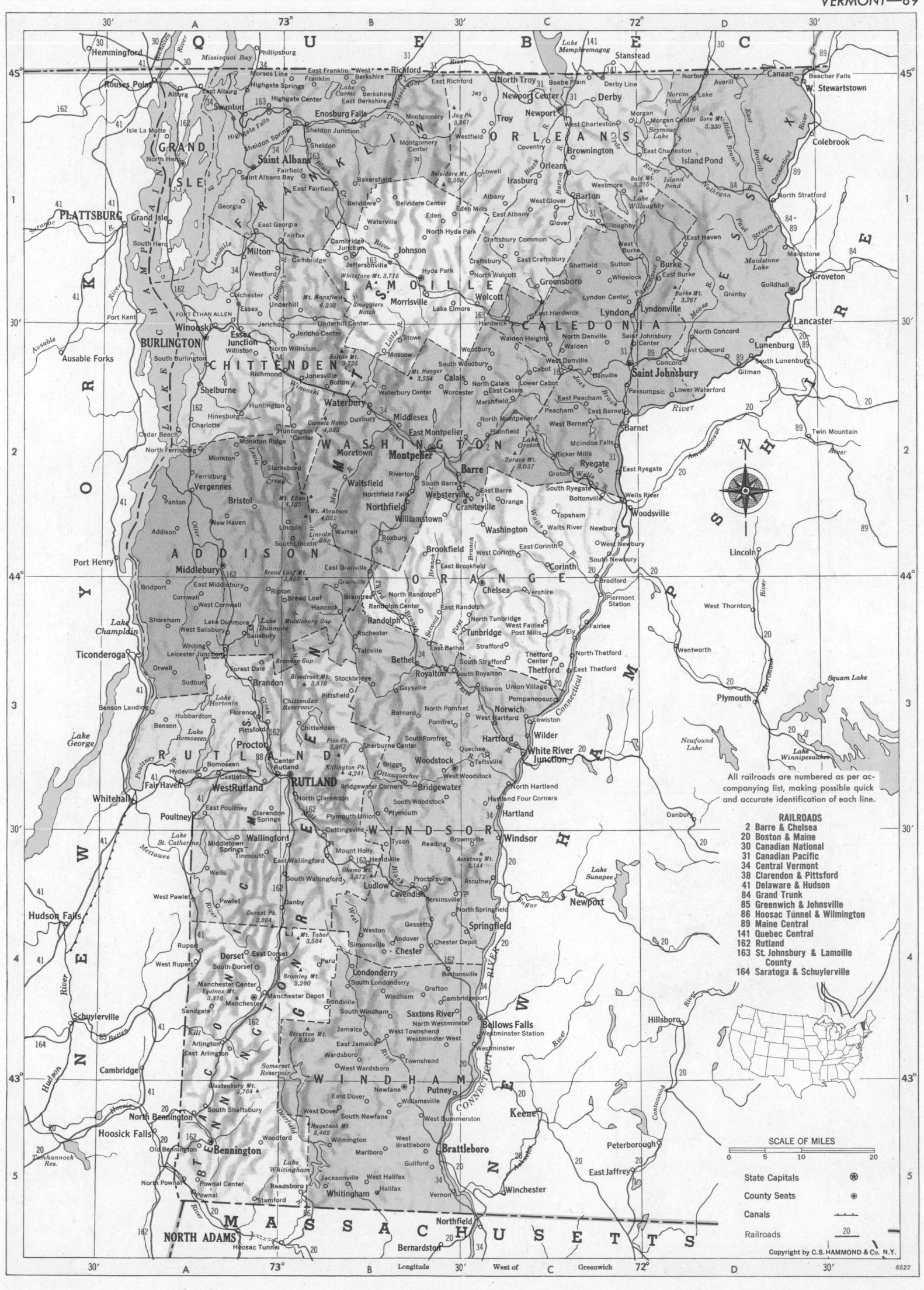

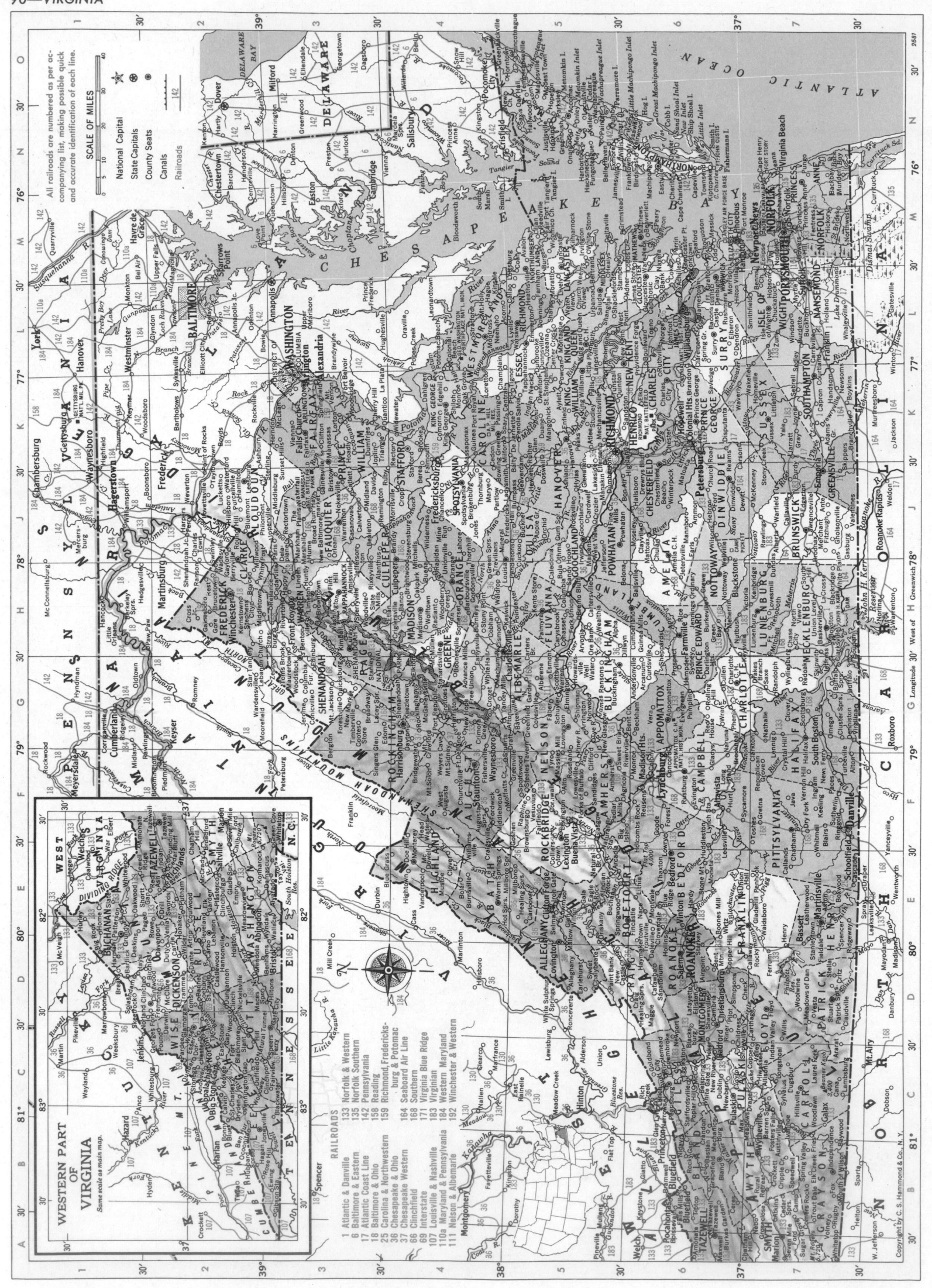

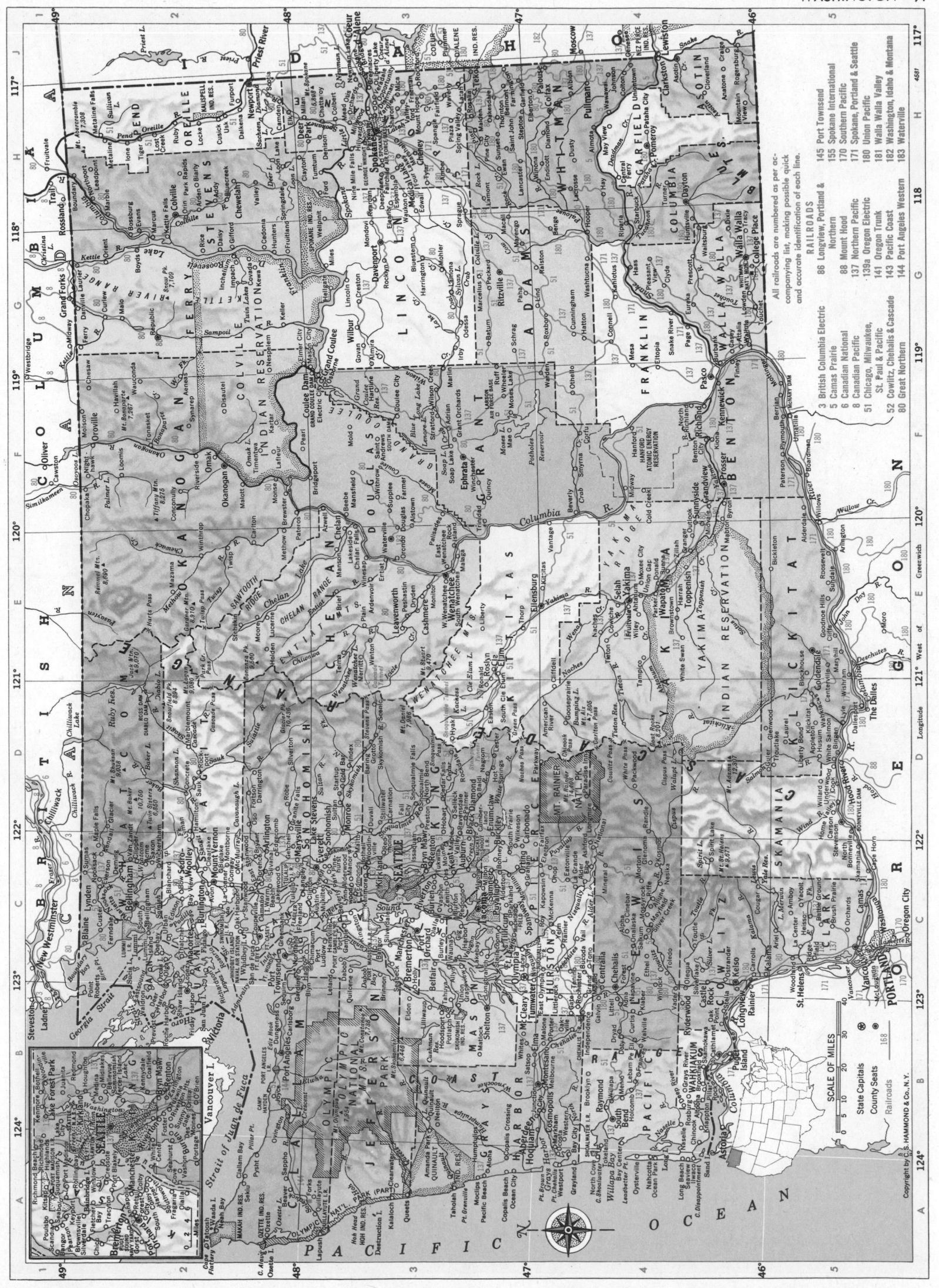

SCALE OF MILES

State Capitals ⊛
County Seats ⊙
Railroads ____ 168

RAILROADS

All railroads are numbered as per accompanying list, making possible quick and accurate identification of each line.

| | | |
|---|---|---|
| 3 | British Columbia Electric | |
| 5 | Camas Prairie | |
| 6 | Canadian National | |
| 8 | Canadian Pacific | |
| 51 | Chicago, Milwaukee, | |
| | St. Paul & Pacific | |
| 52 | Cowlitz, Chehalis & Cascade | |
| 80 | Great Northern | |
| 86 | Longview, Portland & | |
| | Northern | |
| 88 | Mount Hood | |
| 137 | Northern Pacific | |
| 139a | Oregon Electric | |
| 141 | Oregon Trunk | |
| 143 | Pacific Coast | |
| 144 | Port Angeles Western | |
| 145 | Port Townsend | |
| 155 | Spokane International | |
| 170 | Southern Pacific | |
| 171 | Spokane, Portland & Seattle | |
| 180 | Union Pacific | |
| 181 | Walla Walla Valley | |
| 182 | Washington, Idaho & Montana | |
| 183 | Waterville | |

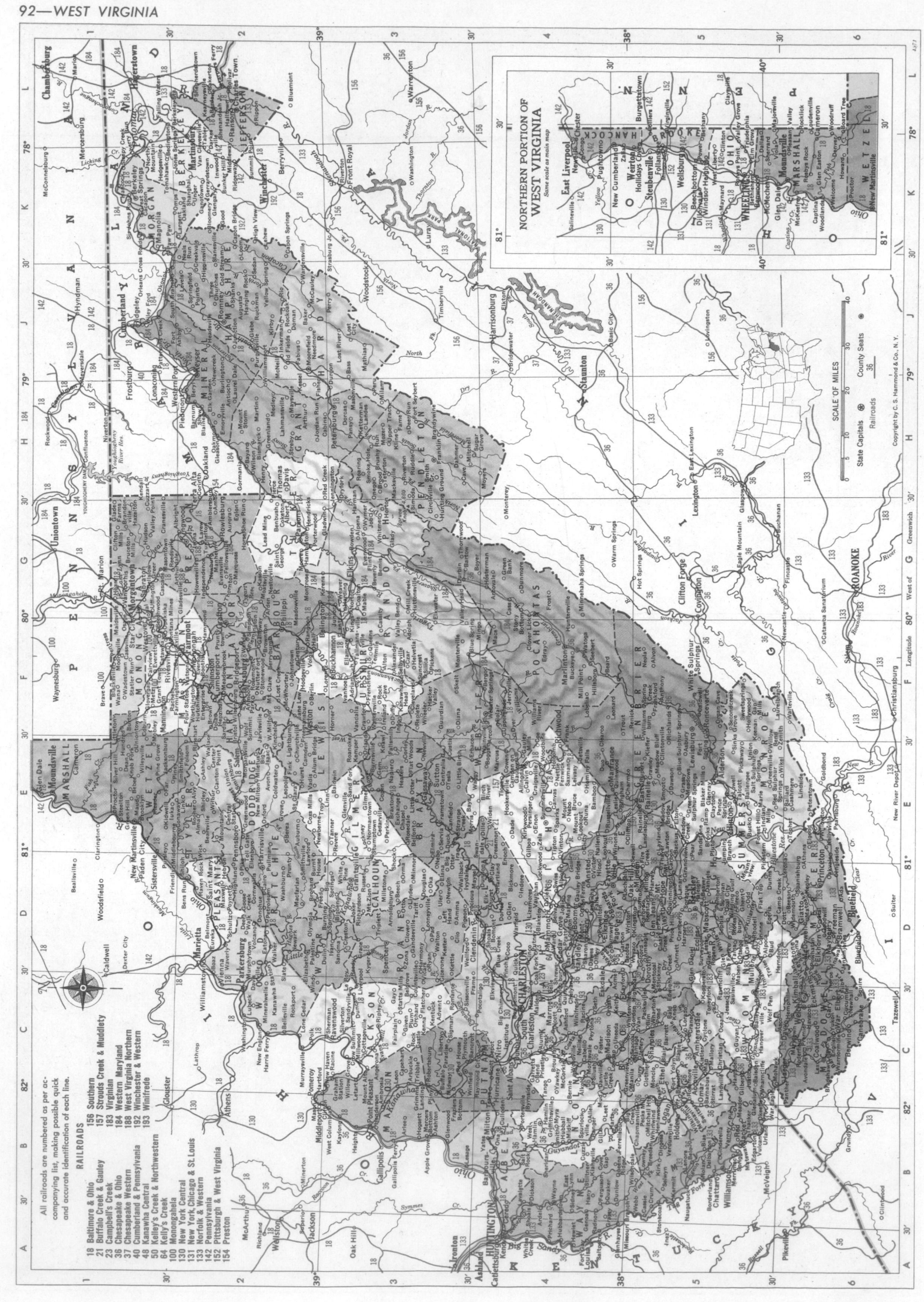

NORTHERN PORTION OF
WEST VIRGINIA
*Some scale as main map*

Copyright by C. S. Hammond & Co., N.Y.

SCALE OF MILES

State Capitals ⊛  County Seats ⊙
Railroads ___ 36

RAILROADS

All railroads are numbered as per accompanying list, making possible quick and accurate identification of each line.

| | |
|---|---|
| 18 Baltimore & Ohio | 155 Southern |
| 21 Buffalo Creek & Gauley | 157 Strouds Creek & Muddlety |
| 23 Campbell's Creek | 183 Virginian |
| 36 Chesapeake & Ohio | 184 Western Maryland |
| 37 Chesapeake Western | 188 West Virginia Northern |
| 40 Cumberland & Pennsylvania | 192 Winchester & Western |
| 48 Kanawha Central | 193 Winifrede |
| 50 Kelley's Creek & Northwestern | |
| 64 Kelly's Creek | |
| 100 Monongahela | |
| 130 New York Central | |
| 131 New York, Chicago & St. Louis | |
| 133 Norfolk & Western | |
| 142 Pennsylvania | |
| 152 Pittsburgh & West Virginia | |
| 154 Preston | |

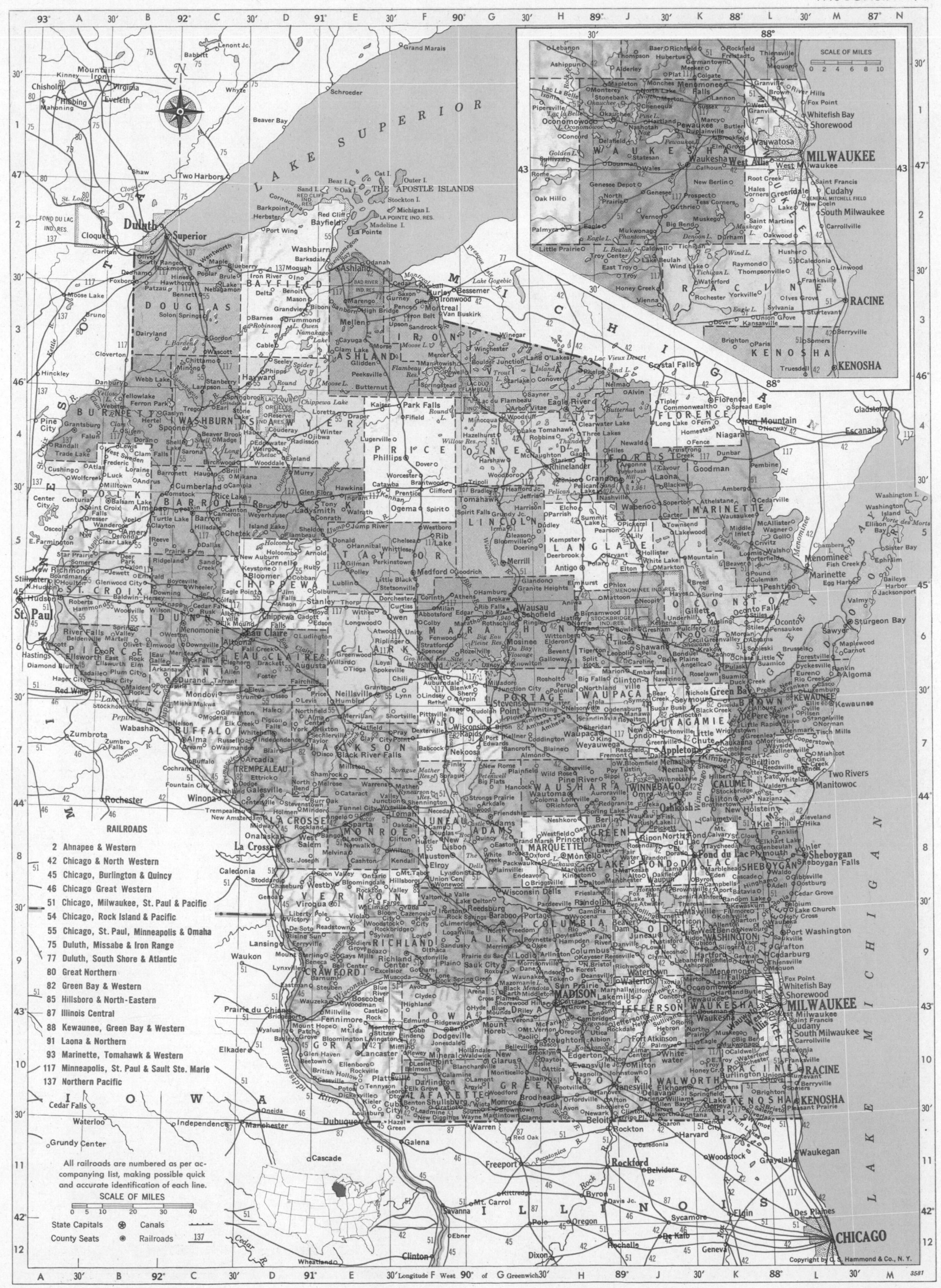

## RAILROADS

2   Ahnapee & Western
42  Chicago & North Western
45  Chicago, Burlington & Quincy
46  Chicago Great Western
51  Chicago, Milwaukee, St. Paul & Pacific
54  Chicago, Rock Island & Pacific
55  Chicago, St. Paul, Minneapolis & Omaha
75  Duluth, Missabe & Iron Range
77  Duluth, South Shore & Atlantic
80  Great Northern
82  Green Bay & Western
85  Hillsboro & North-Eastern
87  Illinois Central
88  Kewaunee, Green Bay & Western
91  Laona & Northern
93  Marinette, Tomahawk & Western
117 Minneapolis, St. Paul & Sault Ste. Marie
137 Northern Pacific

All railroads are numbered as per accompanying list, making possible quick and accurate identification of each line.

SCALE OF MILES
0  5  10  20  30  40

State Capitals
County Seats
Canals
Railroads        137

Copyright by C. S. Hammond & Co., N. Y.

3581

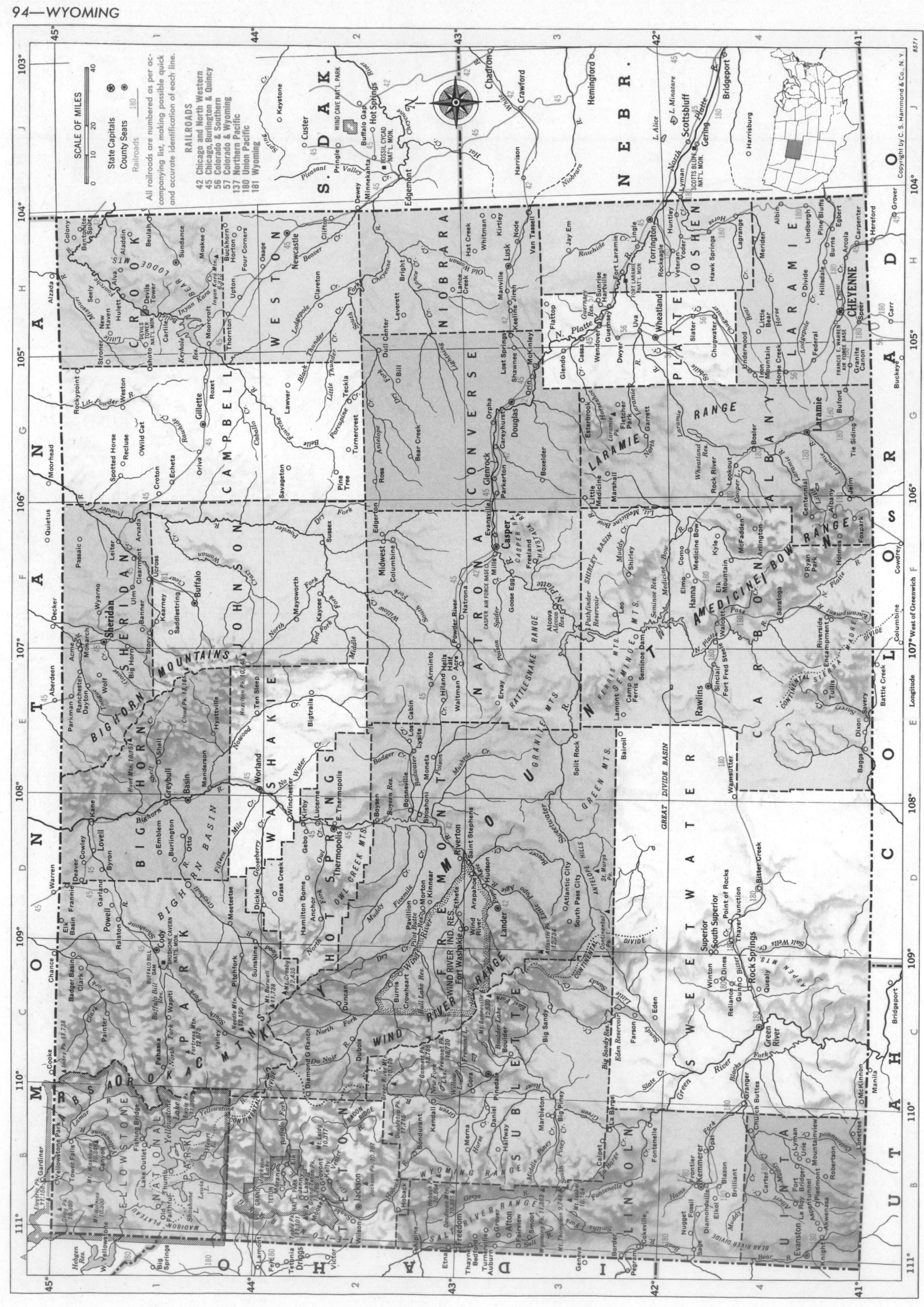

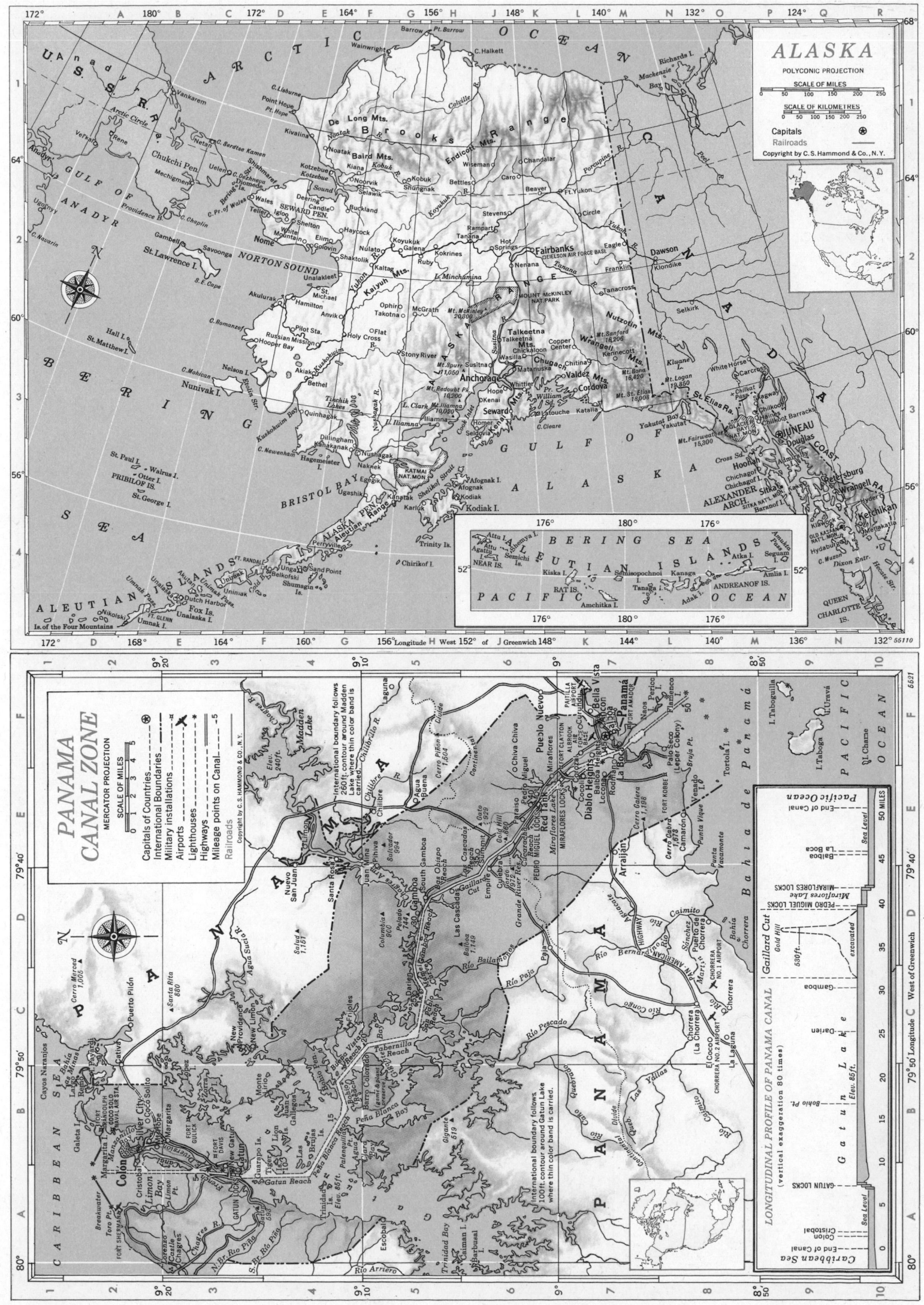

ALASKA
POLYCONIC PROJECTION
SCALE OF MILES
0 50 100 150 200 250
SCALE OF KILOMETRES
0 50 100 150 200 250
Capitals ⊛
Railroads
Copyright by C. S. Hammond & Co., N.Y.

PANAMA
CANAL ZONE
MERCATOR PROJECTION
SCALE OF MILES
0 1 2 3 4 5
Capitals of Countries ⊛
International Boundaries
Military installations
Airports
Lighthouses
Highways
Mileage points on Canal
Railroads
Copyright by C. S. Hammond & Co., N.Y.

LONGITUDINAL PROFILE OF PANAMA CANAL
(vertical exaggeration 80 times)

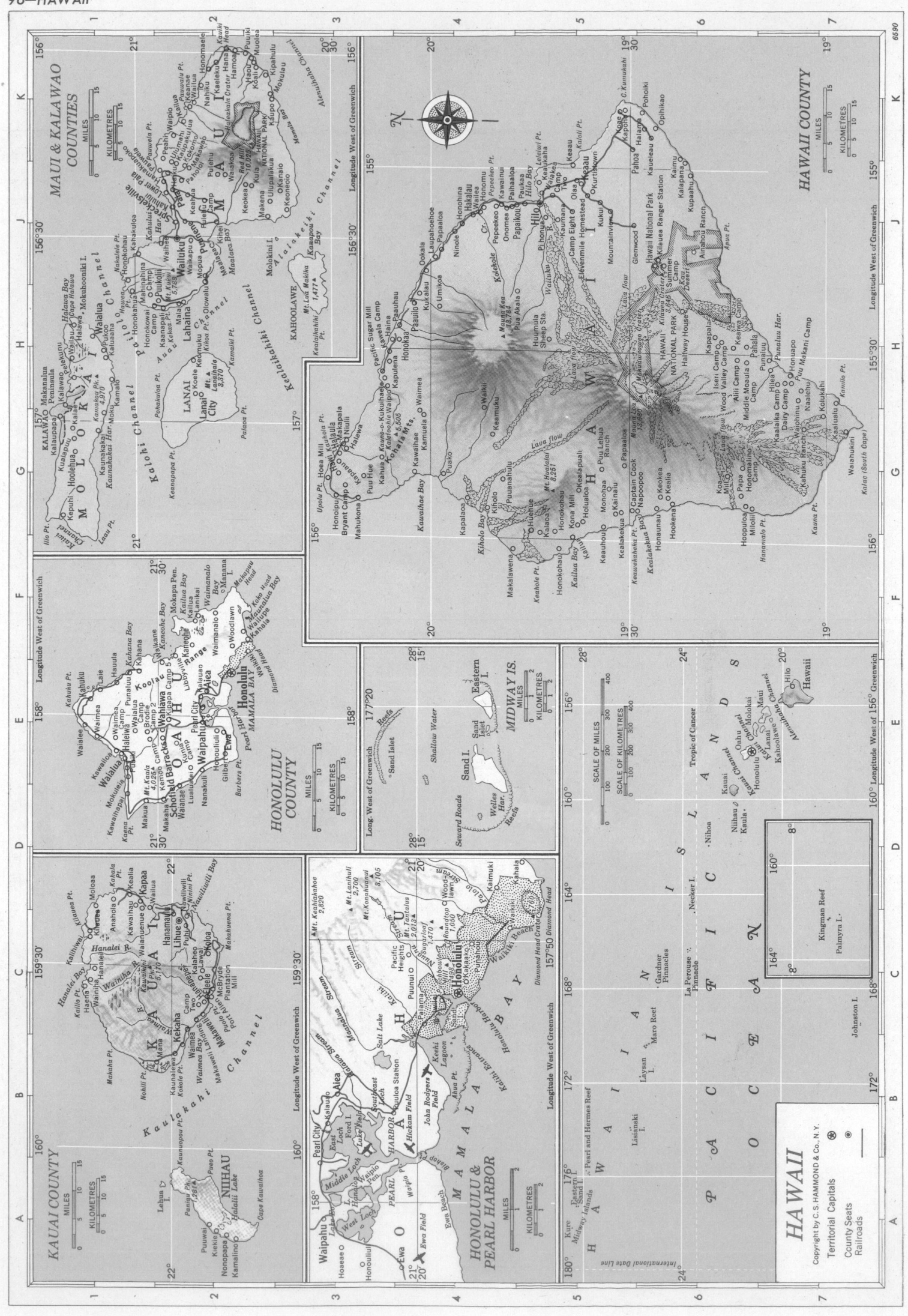

MAUI & KALAWAO COUNTIES

HAWAII COUNTY

KAUAI COUNTY

HONOLULU COUNTY

MIDWAY IS.

HAWAIIAN ISLANDS

Honolulu & Pearl Harbor

HAWAII

Copyright by C. S. HAMMOND & Co., N.Y.

Territorial Capitals

County Seats

Railroads

# Index of the
# UNITED STATES

## *Introduction*

THE INDEX OF CITIES AND TOWNS OF THE UNITED STATES gives the location and population statistics of all cities and towns appearing on the state maps in your atlas. The index entries are arranged alphabetically by states for easy reference and the proper state map page is given at the top of each state index. Each line begins with the name of the city or town, followed by the index reference and the population. The index reference gives the location of the city or town on the state map. The name is found within the square formed by the two lines of latitude and the two lines of longitude which enclose each of the index reference coordinates — i.e., the marginal letters and numbers.

The population figures are the most up-to-date statistics to be found in any reference work. The figures for all incorporated cities and villages are taken from the latest final Federal (1950) Census. The results of a special survey taken by the publishers are given for the population of unincorporated places which are not separately enumerated by the Census. This survey was taken at the same time as the Federal Census and constitutes a major population compilation in itself. Over 25,000 questionnaires were sent to the appropriate local township, county, state or federal authorities. The resulting answers provided the most reliable population statistics available today on unincorporated communities not covered by the Federal Census.

Places listed in the index without a population figure are largely points on the map without permanent inhabitants but which may be locally important as railroad shipping points, crossroad trading centers, or even post offices. In some cases they are communities with fluctuating populations such as resorts or military installations, as for example March Field Air Force Base in California.

A feature of the index especially valuable to the business man, sales manager and advertiser is the inclusion of "urban area" populations for the larger cities according to the 1950 Federal Census. The "urban areas" are defined as consisting of most central cities of over 50,000 inhabitants plus their surrounding built-up suburbs and urban fringes. In many cases the urban area figure gives a truer picture of the relative importance of a city than does the figure for the central municipality. This has become increasingly important with the accelerating movement of population to suburban areas. An example of this is Boston, Massachusetts, with 801,444 persons in the city itself and 2,218,893 in the urban area.

The photographs used throughout this index were used through the courtesy of the various state highway, conservation and publicity bureaus and the Standard Oil Company (N. J.).

# 160 YEARS OF URBAN AND RURAL POPULATIONS

| State | POPULATION IN 1950 Urban | Rural | PER CENT URBAN 1950 | 1940 | 1890 | 1840 | 1790 |
|---|---|---|---|---|---|---|---|
| Alabama | 1,228,209 | 1,833,534 | 40.1 | 30.2 | 10.1 | 2.1 | ...... |
| Arizona | 273,794 | 475,793 | 36.5 | 34.8 | 9.4 | ...... | ...... |
| Arkansas | 617,153 | 1,292,358 | 32.3 | 22.2 | 6.5 | * | ...... |
| California | 7,099,166 | 3,487,057 | 67.1 | 71.0 | 48.6 | ...... | ...... |
| Colorado | 759,939 | 565,150 | 57.4 | 52.6 | 45.0 | ...... | ...... |
| Connecticut | 1,286,817 | 720,463 | 64.1 | 67.8 | 50.9 | 12.6 | 3.0 |
| Delaware | 147,890 | 170,195 | 46.5 | 52.3 | 42.2 | 10.7 | * |
| Florida | 1,566,788 | 1,204,517 | 56.5 | 55.1 | 19.8 | * | ...... |
| Georgia | 1,381,868 | 2,062,710 | 40.1 | 34.4 | 14.0 | 3.6 | * |
| Idaho | 234,138 | 354,499 | 39.8 | 33.7 | * | ...... | ...... |
| Illinois | 6,486,673 | 2,225,503 | 74.5 | 73.6 | 44.9 | 2.0 | ...... |
| Indiana | 2,217,468 | 1,716,756 | 56.4 | 55.1 | 26.9 | 1.6 | ...... |
| Iowa | 1,229,433 | 1,391,640 | 46.9 | 42.7 | 21.2 | * | ...... |
| Kansas | 903,468 | 1,001,831 | 47.4 | 41.9 | 18.9 | ...... | ...... |
| Kentucky | 985,739 | 1,959,067 | 33.5 | 29.8 | 19.2 | 4.0 | * |
| Louisiana | 1,363,789 | 1,319,727 | 50.8 | 41.5 | 25.4 | 29.9 | ...... |
| Maine | 374,507 | 539,267 | 41.0 | 40.5 | 28.1 | 7.8 | * |
| Maryland | 1,274,618 | 1,068,383 | 54.4 | 59.3 | 47.6 | 24.2 | 4.2 |
| Massachusetts | 4,122,138 | 568,376 | 87.9 | 89.4 | 82.0 | 37.9 | 13.5 |
| Michigan | 4,099,007 | 2,272,759 | 64.3 | 65.7 | 34.9 | 4.3 | ...... |
| Minnesota | 1,607,446 | 1,375,037 | 53.9 | 49.8 | 33.8 | ...... | ...... |
| Mississippi | 601,772 | 1,577,142 | 27.6 | 19.8 | 5.4 | 1.0 | ...... |
| Missouri | 2,290,149 | 1,664,504 | 57.9 | 51.8 | 32.0 | 4.3 | ...... |
| Montana | 252,906 | 338,118 | 42.8 | 37.8 | 27.1 | ...... | ...... |
| Nebraska | 606,530 | 718,980 | 45.8 | 39.1 | 27.4 | ...... | ...... |

* — 100% Rural

| State | POPULATION IN 1950 Urban | Rural | PER CENT URBAN 1950 | 1940 | 1890 | 1840 | 1790 |
|---|---|---|---|---|---|---|---|
| Nevada | 84,079 | 76,004 | 52.5 | 39.3 | 33.8 | ...... | ...... |
| New Hampshire | 301,249 | 231,993 | 56.5 | 57.6 | 39.3 | 10.0 | 3.3 |
| New Jersey | 3,847,771 | 987,558 | 79.6 | 81.6 | 62.6 | 10.6 | * |
| New Mexico | 314,636 | 366,551 | 46.2 | 33.2 | 6.2 | ...... | ...... |
| New York | 11,889,008 | 2,941,184 | 80.2 | 82.8 | 65.1 | 19.4 | 11.5 |
| North Carolina | 1,238,193 | 2,823,736 | 30.5 | 27.3 | 7.2 | 1.8 | * |
| North Dakota | 164,817 | 454,819 | 26.6 | 20.6 | 5.6 | ...... | ...... |
| Ohio | 5,273,206 | 2,673,421 | 66.4 | 66.8 | 41.1 | 5.5 | ...... |
| Oklahoma | 1,107,252 | 1,126,099 | 49.6 | 37.6 | 3.7 | ...... | ...... |
| Oregon | 732,247 | 789,094 | 48.1 | 48.8 | 27.9 | ...... | ...... |
| Pennsylvania | 6,906,993 | 3,591,019 | 65.8 | 66.5 | 48.6 | 17.9 | 10.2 |
| Rhode Island | 700,410 | 91,486 | 88.4 | 91.6 | 85.3 | 43.8 | 19.0 |
| South Carolina | 609,225 | 1,507,802 | 28.8 | 24.5 | 10.1 | 5.7 | 6.6 |
| South Dakota | 216,157 | 436,583 | 33.1 | 24.6 | 8.2 | ...... | ...... |
| Tennessee | 1,264,159 | 2,027,559 | 38.4 | 35.2 | 13.5 | 0.8 | * |
| Texas | 4,612,666 | 3,098,528 | 59.8 | 45.4 | 15.6 | ...... | ...... |
| Utah | 412,518 | 276,344 | 59.9 | 55.5 | 35.7 | ...... | ...... |
| Vermont | 137,612 | 240,135 | 36.4 | 34.3 | 15.2 | * | * |
| Virginia | 1,335,944 | 1,982,736 | 40.3 | 35.3 | 17.1 | 5.7 | 1.6 |
| Washington | 1,274,152 | 1,104,811 | 53.6 | 53.1 | 35.6 | ...... | ...... |
| West Virginia | 640,606 | 1,364,946 | 31.9 | 28.1 | 10.7 | ...... | ...... |
| Wisconsin | 1,906,363 | 1,528,212 | 55.5 | 53.5 | 33.2 | * | ...... |
| Wyoming | 144,618 | 145,911 | 49.8 | 37.3 | 34.3 | ...... | ...... |
| U. S. A. | 88,927,464 | 61,769,897 | 59.0 | 56.5 | 35.1 | 10.8 | 5.1 |

# POPULATION OF AMERICA'S LEADING CITIES*

| City | 1950 | 1940 | 1890 | 1840 | 1790 |
|---|---|---|---|---|---|
| New York, N. Y. | 7,891,957 | 7,454,995 | 2,507,414 | 391,114 | 49,401 |
| Chicago, Ill. | 3,620,962 | 3,396,808 | 1,099,850 | 4,470 | ...... |
| Philadelphia, Pa. | 2,071,605 | 1,931,334 | 1,046,964 | 93,665 | 28,522 |
| Los Angeles, Calif. | 1,970,358 | 1,504,277 | 50,395 | ...... | ...... |
| Detroit, Mich. | 1,849,568 | 1,623,452 | 205,876 | 9,012 | ...... |
| Baltimore, Md. | 949,708 | 859,100 | 434,439 | 102,313 | 13,503 |
| Cleveland, Ohio | 914,808 | 878,336 | 261,353 | 6,071 | ...... |
| St. Louis, Mo. | 856,796 | 816,048 | 451,770 | 16,469 | ...... |
| Washington, D. C. | 802,178 | 663,091 | 188,932 | 23,364 | ...... |
| Boston, Mass. | 801,444 | 770,816 | 448,477 | 93,383 | 18,320 |
| San Francisco, Calif. | 775,357 | 634,536 | 298,997 | ...... | ...... |
| Pittsburgh, Pa. | 676,806 | 671,659 | 343,904 | 31,204 | ...... |
| Milwaukee, Wis. | 637,392 | 587,472 | 204,468 | 1,712 | ...... |
| Houston, Texas | 596,163 | 384,514 | 27,557 | ...... | ...... |
| Buffalo, N. Y. | 580,132 | 575,901 | 255,664 | 18,213 | ...... |
| New Orleans, La. | 570,445 | 494,537 | 242,039 | 102,193 | ...... |
| Minneapolis, Minn. | 521,718 | 492,370 | 164,738 | ...... | ...... |
| Cincinnati, Ohio | 503,998 | 455,610 | 296,908 | 46,338 | ...... |
| Seattle, Wash. | 467,591 | 368,302 | 42,837 | ...... | ...... |
| Kansas City, Mo. | 456,622 | 399,178 | 132,716 | ...... | ...... |
| Newark, N. J. | 438,776 | 429,760 | 181,830 | 17,290 | ...... |
| Dallas, Texas | 434,462 | 294,734 | 38,067 | ...... | ...... |
| Indianapolis, Ind. | 427,173 | 386,972 | 105,436 | 2,692 | ...... |
| Denver, Colo. | 415,786 | 322,412 | 106,713 | ...... | ...... |
| San Antonio, Texas | 408,442 | 253,854 | 37,673 | ...... | ...... |
| Memphis, Tenn. | 396,000 | 292,942 | 64,495 | ...... | ...... |
| Oakland, Calif. | 384,575 | 302,163 | 48,682 | ...... | ...... |
| Columbus, Ohio | 375,901 | 306,087 | 88,150 | 6,048 | ...... |
| Portland, Oreg. | 373,628 | 305,394 | 46,385 | ...... | ...... |
| Louisville, Ky. | 369,129 | 319,077 | 161,129 | 21,210 | 200 |
| San Diego, Calif. | 334,387 | 203,341 | 16,159 | ...... | ...... |
| Rochester, N. Y. | 332,488 | 324,975 | 133,896 | 20,191 | ...... |
| Atlanta, Ga. | 331,314 | 302,288 | 65,533 | ...... | ...... |
| Birmingham, Ala. | 326,037 | 267,583 | 26,178 | ...... | ...... |
| St. Paul, Minn. | 311,349 | 287,736 | 133,156 | ...... | ...... |
| Toledo, Ohio | 303,616 | 282,349 | 81,434 | 1,222 | ...... |
| Jersey City, N. J. | 299,017 | 301,173 | 163,003 | 3,072 | ...... |
| Fort Worth, Texas | 278,778 | 177,662 | 23,076 | ...... | ...... |
| Akron, Ohio | 274,605 | 244,791 | 27,601 | ...... | ...... |
| Omaha, Nebr. | 251,117 | 223,844 | 140,452 | ...... | ...... |
| Long Beach, Calif. | 250,767 | 164,271 | 564 | ...... | ...... |
| Miami, Fla. | 249,276 | 172,172 | ...... | ...... | ...... |
| Providence, R. I. | 248,674 | 253,504 | 132,146 | 23,171 | 6,380 |
| Dayton, Ohio | 243,872 | 210,718 | 61,220 | 6,067 | ...... |
| Oklahoma City, Okla. | 243,504 | 204,424 | 4,151 | ...... | ...... |
| Richmond, Va. | 230,310 | 193,042 | 81,388 | 20,153 | 3,761 |
| Syracuse, N. Y. | 220,583 | 205,967 | 88,143 | ...... | ...... |
| Norfolk, Va. | 213,513 | 144,332 | 34,871 | 10,920 | 2,959 |
| Jacksonville, Fla. | 204,517 | 173,065 | 17,201 | ...... | ...... |
| Worcester, Mass. | 203,486 | 193,694 | 84,655 | 7,497 | 2,095 |
| Tulsa, Okla. | 182,740 | 142,157 | ...... | ...... | ...... |
| Salt Lake City, Utah | 182,121 | 149,934 | 44,843 | ...... | ...... |
| Des Moines, Iowa | 177,965 | 159,819 | 50,093 | ...... | ...... |
| Hartford, Conn. | 177,397 | 166,267 | 53,230 | 9,468 | 2,683 |
| Grand Rapids, Mich. | 176,515 | 164,292 | 60,278 | ...... | ...... |
| Nashville, Tenn. | 174,307 | 167,402 | 76,168 | 6,929 | ...... |
| Youngstown, Ohio | 168,330 | 167,720 | 33,220 | ...... | ...... |
| Wichita, Kans. | 168,279 | 114,966 | 23,853 | ...... | ...... |
| New Haven, Conn. | 164,443 | 160,605 | 86,045 | 12,960 | 4,487 |
| Flint, Mich. | 163,143 | 151,543 | 9,803 | ...... | ...... |
| Springfield, Mass. | 162,399 | 149,554 | 44,179 | 10,985 | 1,574 |
| Spokane, Wash. | 161,721 | 122,001 | 19,922 | ...... | ...... |
| Bridgeport, Conn. | 158,709 | 147,121 | 48,866 | 3,294 | ...... |
| Yonkers, N. Y. | 152,798 | 142,598 | 32,033 | ...... | ...... |
| Tacoma, Wash. | 143,673 | 109,408 | 36,006 | ...... | ...... |
| Paterson, N. J. | 139,336 | 139,656 | 78,347 | ...... | ...... |
| Sacramento, Calif. | 137,572 | 105,958 | 26,386 | ...... | ...... |
| Albany, N. Y. | 134,995 | 130,577 | 94,923 | 33,721 | 3,498 |
| Charlotte, N. C. | 134,042 | 100,899 | 11,557 | ...... | ...... |
| Gary, Ind. | 133,911 | 111,719 | ...... | ...... | ...... |
| Fort Wayne, Ind. | 133,607 | 118,410 | 35,393 | ...... | ...... |
| Austin, Texas | 132,459 | 87,930 | 14,575 | ...... | ...... |
| Chattanooga, Tenn. | 131,041 | 128,163 | 29,100 | ...... | ...... |
| Erie, Pa. | 130,803 | 116,955 | 40,634 | 3,412 | ...... |
| El Paso, Texas | 130,485 | 96,810 | 10,338 | ...... | ...... |
| Kansas City, Kans. | 129,583 | 121,458 | 38,316 | ...... | ...... |
| Mobile, Ala. | 129,009 | 78,720 | 31,076 | 12,672 | ...... |
| Evansville, Ind. | 128,636 | 97,062 | 50,756 | ...... | ...... |
| Trenton, N. J. | 128,009 | 124,697 | 57,458 | 4,035 | ...... |
| Shreveport, La. | 127,206 | 98,167 | 11,979 | ...... | ...... |
| Baton Rouge, La. | 125,629 | 34,719 | 10,478 | 2,269 | ...... |
| Scranton, Pa. | 125,536 | 140,404 | 75,215 | ...... | ...... |
| Camden, N. J. | 124,555 | 117,536 | 58,313 | 3,371 | ...... |
| Knoxville, Tenn. | 124,769 | 111,580 | 22,535 | ...... | ...... |
| Tampa, Fla. | 124,681 | 108,391 | 5,532 | ...... | ...... |
| Cambridge, Mass. | 120,740 | 110,879 | 70,028 | 8,409 | 2,115 |
| Savannah, Ga. | 119,638 | 95,996 | 43,139 | 18,214 | ...... |
| Canton, Ohio | 116,912 | 108,401 | 26,189 | ...... | ...... |
| South Bend, Ind. | 115,911 | 101,268 | 21,819 | ...... | ...... |
| Berkeley, Calif. | 113,805 | 85,547 | 5,101 | ...... | ...... |
| Elizabeth, N. J. | 112,817 | 109,912 | 37,764 | 4,184 | ...... |
| Fall River, Mass. | 111,963 | 115,428 | 74,398 | 6,738 | ...... |
| Peoria, Ill. | 111,856 | 105,087 | 41,024 | 1,467 | ...... |
| Wilmington, Del. | 110,356 | 112,504 | 61,431 | 8,367 | ...... |
| Reading, Pa. | 109,320 | 110,568 | 58,661 | 8,410 | ...... |
| New Bedford, Mass. | 109,189 | 110,341 | 40,733 | 12,087 | 3,313 |
| Corpus Christi, Texas | 108,287 | 57,301 | ...... | ...... | ...... |
| Phoenix, Arizona | 106,818 | 65,414 | 3,152 | ...... | ...... |
| Allentown, Pa. | 106,756 | 96,904 | 25,228 | ...... | ...... |
| Montgomery, Ala. | 106,525 | 78,084 | 21,883 | 2,179 | ...... |
| Pasadena, Calif. | 104,577 | 81,864 | 4,882 | ...... | ...... |
| Duluth, Minn. | 104,511 | 101,065 | 33,115 | ...... | ...... |
| Waterbury, Conn. | 104,477 | 99,314 | 28,646 | ...... | ...... |
| Somerville, Mass. | 102,351 | 102,177 | 40,152 | ...... | ...... |
| Little Rock, Ark. | 102,213 | 88,039 | 28,874 | ...... | ...... |
| Utica, N. Y. | 101,531 | 100,518 | 44,007 | 12,782 | ...... |

★ U. S. Census

A closer study of the geography of the United States does much to explain the growth of the nation. For example, the stony soil of New England discouraged farming and caused the early settlers to turn to manufacturing and commerce. The swift streams furnished water power and the jagged coastline provided bays for harboring the ships from Europe. Farther south, the coastal plains widen out into broad stretches of fertile land, and the rivers are short and deep. This led to the development of the large plantations in the deep south, where the climate is favorable to crops that require long hot summers. Here the coastal plain includes half of Georgia, all of Florida, and extends along the Gulf of Mexico. It reaches into the interior as far north as southern Illinois.

The lake and prairie region of the upper Mississippi Valley is one of the most fertile in the world, and is linked by waterways with the East and South through the Great Lakes and the Mississippi River system. The Great Plains region, depending upon the nature of the topsoil and amount of rainfall, is either grain or grazing country, with valuable deposits of oil in Texas and Oklahoma.

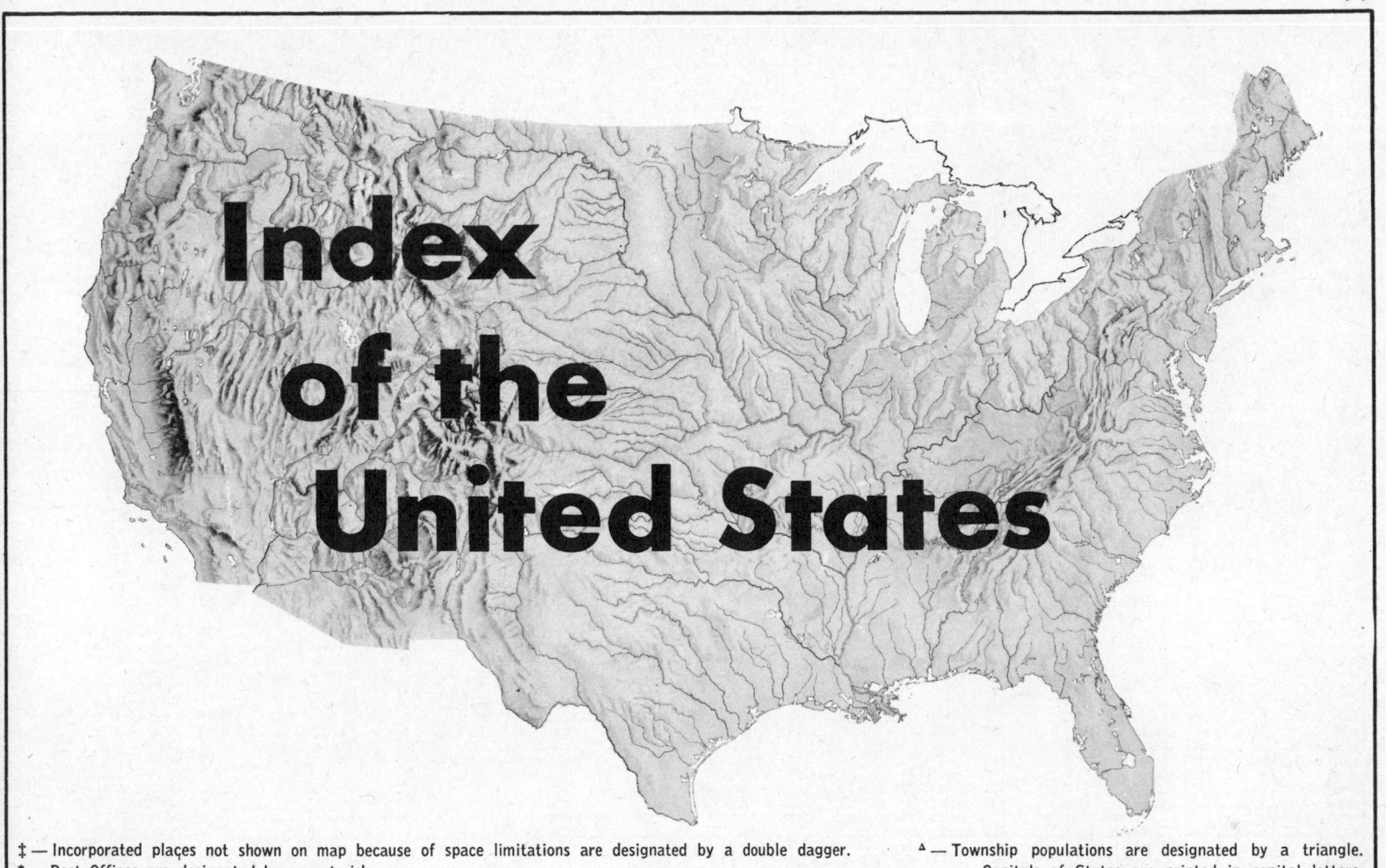

# Index of the United States

‡ — Incorporated places not shown on map because of space limitations are designated by a double dagger.  
* — Post Offices are designated by an asterisk.

△ — Township populations are designated by a triangle.  
Capitals of States are printed in capital letters.

*Map on Page 49*     **ALABAMA**     *Total Population 3,061,743*

**67 COUNTIES**

| | |
|---|---|
| Autauga (E5) | 18,186 |
| Baldwin (C9) | 40,997 |
| Barbour (H7) | 28,892 |
| Bibb (D5) | 17,987 |
| Blount (E2) | 28,975 |
| Bullock (G6) | 16,054 |
| Butler (E7) | 29,228 |
| Calhoun (G3) | 79,539 |
| Chambers (H5) | 39,528 |
| Cherokee (G2) | 17,634 |
| Chilton (E5) | 26,922 |
| Choctaw (B6) | 19,152 |
| Clarke (C7) | 26,548 |
| Clay (G4) | 13,929 |
| Cleburne (G3) | 11,904 |
| Coffee (G8) | 30,720 |
| Colbert (C1) | 39,561 |
| Conecuh (E8) | 21,776 |
| Coosa (F5) | 11,766 |
| Covington (F8) | 40,373 |
| Crenshaw (F7) | 18,981 |
| Cullman (E2) | 49,046 |
| Dale (G8) | 20,828 |
| Dallas (D6) | 56,270 |
| De Kalb (G2) | 45,048 |
| Elmore (G5) | 31,649 |
| Escambia (D8) | 31,443 |
| Etowah (F2) | 93,892 |
| Fayette (C3) | 19,388 |
| Franklin (C2) | 25,705 |
| Geneva (G8) | 25,899 |
| Greene (C5) | 16,482 |
| Hale (C5) | 20,832 |
| Henry (H8) | 18,674 |
| Houston (H8) | 46,522 |
| Jackson (F1) | 38,998 |
| Jefferson (E3) | 558,928 |
| Lamar (B3) | 16,441 |
| Lauderdale (C1) | 54,179 |
| Lawrence (D1) | 27,128 |
| Lee (H5) | 45,073 |
| Limestone (E1) | 35,766 |
| Lowndes (E6) | 18,018 |
| Macon (G6) | 30,561 |
| Madison (E1) | 72,903 |
| Marengo (C6) | 29,494 |
| Marion (C2) | 27,264 |
| Marshall (F2) | 45,090 |
| Mobile (B9) | 231,105 |
| Monroe (D7) | 25,732 |
| Montgomery (F6) | 138,965 |
| Morgan (E2) | 52,924 |
| Perry (D5) | 20,439 |
| Pickens (B4) | 24,349 |
| Pike (G7) | 30,608 |
| Randolph (H4) | 22,513 |
| Russell (H6) | 40,364 |
| Saint Clair (F3) | 26,687 |
| Shelby (E4) | 30,362 |
| Sumter (B5) | 23,610 |
| Talladega (F4) | 63,639 |
| Tallapoosa (G5) | 35,074 |
| Tuscaloosa (C4) | 94,092 |
| Walker (D3) | 63,769 |
| Washington (B8) | 15,612 |
| Wilcox (D7) | 23,476 |
| Winston (D2) | 18,250 |

**CITIES and TOWNS**

| | |
|---|---|
| Abanda (H4)* | 125 |
| Abbeville (H7)* | 2,162 |
| Abernant (D4)* | |
| Ackerville (E6) | 100 |
| Acmar (E3)* | 900 |
| Adamsville (D3)* | 1,531 |
| Addison (D2)* | 590 |
| Adger (D4)* | 500 |
| Aimwell (C6)* | 150 |
| Akron (C5)* | 684 |
| Alabama City (F2)* | |
| Alberta (D6)* | 200 |
| Albertville (F2)* | 5,397 |
| Aldrich (E4)* | 1,000 |
| Alexander City (G5)* | 6,430 |
| Alexandria (G3)* | 300 |
| Aliceville (B4)* | 3,170 |
| Allen (C7)* | 200 |
| Allenton (E7)* | 75 |
| Allenville (C6) | |
| Allgood (F3)* | 350 |
| Allison (C5) | |
| Allsboro (B1)* | 150 |
| Alma (C8)* | 50 |
| Alpine (F4)* | |
| Alton (E3)* | 500 |
| Altoona (F2)* | 860 |
| America (D3)* | |
| Andalusia (E8)* | 9,162 |
| Anderson (D1)* | 450 |
| Angel (G3) | 15 |
| Annemanie (D6)* | 100 |
| Anniston (G3)* | 31,066 |
| Ansley (F7)* | |
| Arab (E2)* | 1,592 |
| Ararat (B7) | 100 |
| Ardmore (E1) | 408 |
| Argo (E3)* | 197 |
| Ariton (G7)* | 620 |
| Arkadelphia (E3)* | |
| Arley (D2)* | 300 |
| Arlington (C6)* | 200 |
| Asahel (D7) | |
| Ashby (E4) | 75 |
| Ashford (H8)* | 1,400 |
| Ashland (G4)* | 1,593 |
| Ashville (F3)* | 494 |
| Athens (E1)* | 6,309 |
| Atmore (C8)* | 5,720 |
| Attalla (F2)* | 7,537 |
| Atwood (C2)* | 250 |
| Auburn (H5)* | 12,939 |
| Austinville (D1)* | 1,110 |
| Autaugaville (E6)* | 459 |
| Axis (B9)* | 130 |
| Baileyton (E2)* | 200 |
| Bakerhill (H7)* | |
| Bamford (E4) | 12 |
| Bangor (E3)* | |
| Banks (G7)* | 222 |
| Bankston (C3)* | 350 |
| Barlow Bend (C8)* | 364 |
| Barnwell (C10) | |
| Barton (C1)* | 250 |
| Bashi (C7)* | |
| Bass Station (G1) | 125 |
| Batesville (H6) | |
| Battles Wharf (C10)* | 300 |
| Bay Minette (C9)* | 3,732 |
| Bayou la Batre (B10)* | 2,196 |
| Bear Creek (C2)* | 223 |
| Beatrice (D7)* | 375 |
| Beaverton (B3)* | 192 |
| Bedford (B3) | |
| Belgreen (C2)* | 255 |
| Belk (C3)* | 152 |
| Bellamy (B6)* | |
| Belle Ellen (D4)* | 400 |
| Belle Mina (E1)* | |
| Belleville (D8)* | 300 |
| Bellview (D7) | 50 |
| Bellwood (G8)* | 263 |
| Belmont (C5) | 153 |
| Beloit (D6)* | 250 |
| Benson (G5) | |
| Benton (E6)* | |
| Bermuda (D8)* | 240 |
| Berry (C3)* | 715 |
| Bessemer (D4)* | 28,445 |
| Beulah (H5) | |
| Bevelle (G5) | |
| Bexar (B2)* | |
| Bigbee (B7)* | 30 |
| Billingsley (E5)* | 158 |
| Birmingham (D3)* | 326,037 |
| Birmingham (urban area) | 438,726 |
| Bishop (B1) | 75 |
| Black (G8)* | 239 |
| Blacksher (C8) | |
| Bladon Springs (B7)* | 375 |
| Blalock (D6) | 15 |
| Blanche (E2)* | 104 |
| Blanton (H5)* | |
| Bleecker (H5)* | 250 |
| Blocton (D4)* | 1,500 |
| Blount Springs (E3)* | |
| Blountsville (E2)* | 695 |
| Blue Mountain (G3)* | 529 |
| Blue Springs (G7)* | 111 |
| Bluffton (G2) | |
| Boaz (F2)* | 3,078 |
| Boligee (C5)* | 168 |
| Bolinger (B7)* | 200 |
| Bolling (E7)* | 300 |
| Bon Air (F4)* | 360 |
| Bon Secour (C10)* | 180 |
| Booth (E6)* | |
| Boothton (E4)* | 814 |
| Borden Springs (H3)* | 100 |
| Boston (C2)* | 700 |
| Boyd (B5) | 300 |
| Boylston (F6)* | 500 |
| Bradleyton (F7)* | 107 |
| Braggs (E6)* | 300 |
| Branchville (F3)* | |
| Brantley (F7)* | 1,102 |
| Bremen (E3)* | |
| Brent (D5)* | 1,100 |
| Brewton (D8)* | 5,146 |
| Brickyard (H6) | 150 |
| Bridgeport (G1)* | 2,386 |
| Bridgeton (E4) | |
| Brierfield (E4)* | 200 |
| Brighton (E4)* | 1,689 |
| Brilliant (C2)* | 600 |
| Bromley (C9) | 248 |
| Brompton (F3) | |
| Brooklyn (E8)* | 150 |
| Brookside (E3)* | 733 |
| Brooksville (F2)* | |
| Brookwood (D4)* | 500 |
| Browns (D6)* | 100 |
| Brownsboro (F1)* | 100 |
| Brownville (C4)* | 350 |
| Brundidge (G7)* | 2,605 |
| Bucks (B8)* | 60 |
| Buena Vista (D7)* | 200 |
| Buffalo (H5)* | 188 |
| Buhl (C4)* | |
| Burbank (H8)* | |
| Burkville (E6)* | 200 |
| Burl (D7)* | 100 |
| Burnett (G2) | |
| Burnsville (E6)* | 200 |
| Burnt Corn (D7)* | 250 |
| Butler (B6)* | 659 |
| Butler Springs (E7)* | |
| Calcis (E4)* | |
| Caldwell (F3)* | 25 |
| Caledonia (D7) | 150 |
| Calera (E4)* | 1,361 |
| Calhoun (F6)* | 150 |
| Calvert (B8)* | 500 |
| Camden (D7)* | 931 |
| Cameronsville (G1)* | 120 |
| Camp Hill (G5)* | 1,296 |
| Campbell (C7)* | 126 |
| Canoe (D8)* | |
| Canton Bend (D6)* | 300 |
| Capps (H8)* | 110 |
| Capshaw (E1)* | 275 |
| Carbon Hill (D3)* | 2,179 |
| Cardiff (E3)* | 204 |
| Carey (E1) | 25 |
| Carlowville (D6)* | 400 |
| Carlton (C8)* | |
| Carrollton (B4)* | 710 |
| Carrville (G5) | 760 |
| Carson (C8)* | 200 |
| Castleberry (D8)* | 667 |
| Caswell (D10)* | 33 |
| Catherine (D6)* | 200 |
| Cecil (F6)* | 150 |
| Cedar Bluff (G2)* | 563 |
| Cedar Cove (D4)* | 100 |
| Central (F5)* | 175 |
| Central Mills (D6) | 75 |
| Centre (G2)* | 1,672 |
| Centreville (D5)* | 1,160 |
| Champion (F3) | |
| Chance (C7)* | |
| Chancellor (G8)* | 125 |
| Chandler Springs (F4) | |
| Chapman (E7)* | 943 |
| Chase (E1)* | 750 |
| Chastang (B8)* | |
| Chatom (B8)* | 609 |
| Chavies (G2)* | 250 |
| Chelsea (E4)* | 300 |
| Cherokee (C1)* | 748 |
| Chesson (G6)* | |
| Chestnut (D7)* | 250 |
| Chickasaw (B9)* | 4,920 |
| Childersburg (F4)* | 4,023 |
| China Grove (G7) | |
| Choccolocco (G3)* | 267 |
| Choctaw (B6)* | 500 |
| Choctaw Bluff (C8)* | 500 |
| Chrysler (C8)* | |
| Chunchula (B9)* | 300 |
| Citronelle (B8)* | 1,350 |
| Claiborne (D7)* | 175 |
| Clairmont Spgs. (G4)* | 50 |
| Clanton (E5)* | 4,640 |
| Clarence (F2) | 100 |
| Claud (F5) | 80 |
| Clayton (G7)* | 1,583 |
| Cleveland (E3)* | 400 |
| Clinton (C5)* | 200 |
| Clio (G7)* | 840 |
| Clopton (G7) | 140 |
| Cloverdale (C1)* | 250 |
| Coal Bluff (D7) | 100 |
| Coal Valley (D3)* | 140 |
| Coaling (D4)* | |
| Cobb City (G3) | 20 |
| Cochrane (B4)* | 200 |
| Coden (B10)* | |
| Coffee Springs (G8)* | 173 |
| Coffeeville (B7)* | 211 |
| Cohasset (E8) | |
| Coker (C4)* | 325 |
| Coleanor (E4) | 25 |
| Collbran (G2)* | 109 |
| Collinsville (G2)* | 1,023 |
| Collirene (E6) | |
| Columbia (H8)* | 849 |
| Columbiana (E4)* | 1,761 |
| Columbus City (F2) | 75 |
| Comer (H6)* | 150 |
| Consul (C6) | |
| Cooks Springs (F3)* | 300 |
| Cooper (E5)* | 300 |
| Coosada (F5)* | 207 |
| Copeland (B7)* | |
| Cordova (D3)* | 3,156 |
| Corona (C3)* | 225 |
| Cortelyou (B8)* | |
| Cottage Grove (F5)* | 400 |
| Cotton Hill (H7) | |
| Cottondale (D4)* | |
| Cottonton (H6)* | 125 |
| Cottonville (F2) | 60 |
| Cottonwood (H8)* | 864 |
| Courtland (D1)* | 507 |
| Covin (C3)* | 110 |
| Cowarts (H8)* | 300 |
| Coy (D7)* | |
| Cragford (G4)* | 200 |
| Crane Hill (D2)* | |
| Crawford (H6) | 100 |
| Creek Stand (G6) | 50 |
| Creola (B9)* | 25 |
| Crews (B3)* | |
| Crichton (B9)* | |
| Cromwell (B6)* | 200 |
| Cropwell (F3)* | 125 |
| Crosby (H8) | 50 |
| Crossville (G2)* | 609 |
| Cuba (B6)* | 525 |
| Cullman (E2)* | 7,523 |
| Cullomburg (B7)* | 350 |
| Cusseta (H5)* | 350 |
| Cypress (C5)* | 165 |
| Dadeville (E5)* | 2,354 |
| Daleville (G8)* | 300 |
| Dallas Mills (E1)* | 2,200 |
| Dancy (B4)* | 200 |
| Danville (D2)* | 350 |
| Daphne (C9)* | 1,041 |
| Darlington (D7)* | 150 |
| Dauphin Island (B10)* | |
| Daviston (G4)* | 110 |
| Dawes (B9) | |
| Dawson (G2)* | |
| Dayton (C6)* | 85 |
| De Armanville (G3)* | 260 |
| Deatsville (F5)* | 200 |
| Decatur (D1)* | 19,974 |
| Deer Park (B8)* | 200 |
| Delmar (C2)* | 350 |
| Delta (G4)* | 150 |
| Demopolis (C6)* | 5,004 |
| Detroit (B2)* | 250 |
| Devenport (F6) | 150 |
| Dickinson (C7)* | 250 |
| Dixie (E8) | 50 |
| Dixons Mills (C6)* | 350 |
| Dixonville (E8) | |
| Dolomite (D4)* | 4,500 |
| Dora (D3)* | 984 |
| Dothan (H8)* | 21,584 |
| Double Springs (D2)* | 524 |
| Douglas (F2)* | 200 |
| Downing (F6) | 47 |
| Downs (G6) | |
| Dozier (F7)* | 362 |
| Drewry (D8)* | |
| Duke (G3)* | 175 |
| Dunavant (F4)* | 300 |
| Duncanville (D4)* | 10 |
| Dutton (G1)* | |
| Dyas (C9) | 30 |
| Easonville (F3)* | 400 |
| East Brewton (E8)* | 2,173 |
| East Florence (C1)* | |
| East Tallassee (G5)* | |
| Eastaboga (F3)* | 700 |
| Echo (G8) | 100 |
| Echola (C4)* | 120 |
| Eclectic (F5)* | 715 |
| Eden (F3)* | 621 |
| Edna (B6)* | 500 |
| Edwardsville (H3)* | 179 |
| Edwin (H7) | 170 |
| Eiler (B7) | 25 |
| Elamville (G7)* | 155 |
| Elba (F8)* | 2,936 |
| Elberta (C10)* | 350 |
| Eldridge (C3)* | 500 |
| Eleanor (D6) | 20 |
| Eliska (C8) | 75 |
| Elkmont (E1)* | 179 |
| Elkwood (E1) | 50 |
| Ellawhite (D6) | |
| Elmore (F5)* | 350 |
| Elon (F1) | 42 |
| Elrod (C4)* | 500 |
| Emelle (B5)* | |
| Empire (D3)* | |
| Enterprise (G8)* | 7,288 |
| Eoline (D4)* | 250 |
| Epes (B5)* | 342 |
| Equality (F5)* | 176 |
| Erin (G4) | 50 |
| Escatawpa (B8)* | 90 |
| Estillfork (F1)* | 121 |
| Ethelsville (B4)* | 135 |
| Eufaula (H7)* | 6,906 |
| Eunola (G8) | 112 |
| Eutaw (C5)* | 2,348 |
| Eva (E2)* | 200 |

## ALASKA

*Map on Page 95* — *Total Population 128,643*


Adak (isl.) (L4)
Admiralty (isl.) (N3)
Afognak (J3)* 158
Afognak (isl.) (J3)
Aggattu (isl.) (J3)
Akiak (F2)* 168
Akulurak (E2) 197
Akutan (E4)* 86
Alaska (gulf) (JM3)
Alaska (mt. range) (HJ2)
Alaska (peninsula) (G3)
Aleution (isls.) (JN3) 5,600
Aleution (mt. range) (G3)
Alexander (arch.) (M3)
Amchitka (isl.) (K4)
Amlia (isl.) (M4)
Amukta (passage) (N4)
Anchorage (J2)* 11,254
Andreanof (isls.) (M4)
Anvik (F2)* 99
Atka (isl.) (M4)*
Attu (J3)
Attu (isl.) (J3)
Baird (mts.) (F1)
Baranof (isl.) (N3)
Barrow (G1)* 951
Barrow (point) (H1)
Beaver (K1)* 101
Belkofsky (F4)* 119
Bering (strait) (D1)
Bering (sea) (BE3)
Bethel (F2)* 651
Bettles (H1)* 47
Bona (mt.) (L2)
Bristol (bay) (FG3)
Brooks(mt. range)(GK1)
Buckland (G1)
Candle (F1)* 105
Cape Halkett (J1)
Caro (J1)
Chandalar (K1)
Chichagof (M3)*
Chichagof (isl.) (M3)
Chickaloon (J2)
Chilkoot Barracks (N3)
Chirikof (isl.) (H4)
Chitina (K2)* 92
Chugach (mts.) (K2)
Circle (L1)* 83
Clark (lake) (H2)
Cleare (cape) (K3)
Coast (mt. range) (N3)
Cold (bay) (F4)
Coleville (river) (H1)
Cook (inlet) (H3)
Copper Center (K2)* 90
Cordova (K2)* 6,165
Cross (sound) (M3)
De Long (mts.) (F1)
Deering (F1)* 174
Dillingham (G3)* 577
Diomede (isls.) (D1)
Dixon Entrance (channel) (N4)
Douglas (N3)* 699
Dutch Harbor (E4)
Eagle (L1)* 55
Egegik (G3)* 119
Eielson Air Force Base (K1)
Elim (F1)* 154
Endicott (mts.) (H1)
Etolin (strait) (E2)
Fairbanks (K1)* 5,771
Fairweather (mt.) (M3)
Flat (G2)* 95
Fort Glenn (E4)
Fort Randall (F4)
Fort Yukon (K1)* 446
Four Mountains (isls.) (D4)
Fox (isls.) (E4)
Franklin (L1)
Galena (G1)* 176
Gambell (C2)* 309
Glacier Bay Nat'l Mon. (M3)
Golovin (F1)* 94
Hagemeister (isl.) (F3)
Haines (N3)* 338
Hall (isl.) (C2)
Hamilton (F2)* 43
Haycock (F1)*
Holy Cross (G2) 157
Homer (J3)* 307
Hoonah (M3)* 563
Hooper Bay (E2)* 307
Hope (J2)* 63
Hope (point) (E1)
Hot Springs (J1)* 29
Hydaburg (N4)* 353
Hyder (O4)* 30
Igloo (E1)* 64
Iliamna (H3)* 44
Iliamna (lake) (H3)
Iliamna (mt.) (H2)
JUNEAU (N3)* 5,956
Kaiyuh (mts.) (G2)
Kake (N3)* 376
Kaltag (G1)* 121
Kanaga (isl.) (L4)
Kanakanak (G3) 54
Kanatak (H3)*
Karluk (H3)* 144
Katalla (K2)
Katmai Nat'l Mon. (H3)
Kenai (J2)* 321
Kenai (mts.) (J2)
Kennecott (L2)
Ketchikan (O4)* 5,305
Kiana (F1)* 181
Kiska (isl.) (K4)
Kivalina (E1)* 117
Klawock (N4)* 404
Kobuk (H1)* 38
Kobuk (river) (G1)
Kodiak (J3)* 1,710
Kodiak (isl.) (J3)
Kokrines (H1)* 68
Kotzebue (sound) (F1)
Kotzebue (F1)* 623
Koyukuk (G1)* 79
Koyukuk (river) (H1)
Kuskokwim (river) (F2)
Kuskokwim (bay) (F3)
Latouche (K2)*
Lisburne (cape) (E1)
Matanuska (K2) 41
Mc Grath (H2)* 175
Mc Kinley (mt.) (H2)
Metlakatla (O4)* 817
Minchumina (lake) (H1)
Mohican (cape) (D2)
Mount McKinley Nat'l Park (K2) 59
Muzon (cape) (N4)
Naknek (G3)* 174
Near (isls.) (J4)
Nelson (isl.) (E2)
Nenana (J1)* 242
Newenham (cape) (F3)
Nikolski (D4)* 64
Noatak (F1)* 326
Noatak (river) (F1)
Nome (E1)* 1,876
Noorvik (G1)* 248
Norton (sound) (E2)
Nulato (G1)* 176
Nunivak (isl.) (E3)
Nushagak (G3)
Nushagak (river) (G3)
Nutzotin (mts.) (L2)
Old Kasaan Nat'l Mon. (N4)
Ophir (G2)* 68
Otter (isl.) (D3)
Perryville (G3)
Petersburg (O3)* 1,619
Pilot Station (F2)* 52
Point Hope (D1)*
Porcupine (river) (L1)
Pribilof (isls.) (D3)
Prince of Wales (cape) (D1)
Prince William (sound) (K2)
Quinhagak (F3)* 194
Rampart (J1)* 94
Rat (isls.) (K4)
Redoubt (mt.) (H2)
Romanzof (cape) (E2)
Ruby (H1)* 132
Russian Mission (F2)* 55
St. Elias (mt.) (L2)
St. Elias (mt. range) (M3)
St. George (isl.) (D3)
St. Lawrence (isl.) (D2)
St. Matthew (isl.) (C2)
St. Michael (F2)* 157
St. Paul (isl.) (D3)*
Sand Point (G4)* 107
Sanford (mt.) (L2)
Savoonga (D2)* 249
Seguam (isl.) (M4)
Selawik (G1)* 273
Seldovia (J3)* 437
Semichi (isls.) (J4)
Semisopochnoi(isl.)(L4)
Seward (J2)* 2,114
Seward (peninsula)(E1)
Shaktoolik (F1)* 127
Shelikof (strait) (H3)
Shelton (F1)
Shemya (isl.) (J3)
Shishmaref (E1)* 194
Shumagin (isls.) (F4)
Shungnak (H1)* 141
Sitka (N3)* 1,985
Sitka Nat'l Mon. (M3)
Skagway (N3)* 758
South East (cape) (D2)
Spurr (mt.) (H2)
Stevens Village (J1)* 84
Stony River (H2)*
Susitna (J2)
Susitna (river) (J2)
Takotna (G2)* 42
Talkeetna (J2)* 106
Talkeetna (mts.) (J2)
Tanacross (L2)* 137
Tanaga (L4)
Tanana (H1)* 228
Tanana (river) (K1)
Teller (E1)* 269
Tikchik (lakes) (G2)
Trinity (isls.) (H3)
Ugashik (G3)* 48
Umnak (isl.) (E4)
Umnak (passage) (D4)
Unalakleet (F2)* 469
Unalaska (E4)* 173
Unalaska (isl.) (E4)
Unga (F4)* 107
Unimak (E4)
Unimak (isl.) (E4)
Unimak (passage) (E4)
Valdez (K2)* 554
Wainwright (F1)* 227
Wales (E1)* 141
Walrus (isl.) (D3)
Wasilla (J2)* 97
White Mountain (E1)* 129
Whittier (J2)* 627
Wiseman (J1)*
Wrangell (O3)* 1,263
Wrangell (mts.) (L2)
Yakutat (L3)* 298
Yakutat (bay) (L3)
Yukon (river) (G2)


## ARIZONA

*Map on Page 50* — *Total Population 749,587*

### 14 COUNTIES


Apache (F3) 27,767
Cochise (F7) 31,488
Coconino (C3) 23,910
Gila (E5) 24,158
Graham (E6) 12,985
Greenlee (F5) 12,805
Maricopa (C5) 331,770
Mohave (A3) 8,510
Navajo (E3) 29,446
Pima (D6) 141,216
Pinal (D6) 43,191
Santa Cruz (E7) 9,344
Yavapai (C4) 24,991
Yuma (A5) 28,006


### CITIES and TOWNS


Adamana (F4)* 60
Agua Caliente (B6)* 75
Aguila (B5)* 180
Ajo (C6)* 5,817
Alpine (F5)*
Amado (D7)*
Apache (F7) 36
Apache Junction (D5)* 50
Aripine (E4)* 45
Arivaca (D7)* 120
Arlington (C5)* 500
Ash Fork (C3)* 800
Ashurst (F5)* 135
Avondale (C5)* 2,505
Aztec (B6)* 49
Bagdad (B4)*
Bannon (F4) 14
Bapchule (D5)* 50
Bellemont (D3)* 100
Benson (E7)* 1,440
Betatakin (Shonto) (E2)
Bisbee (F7)* 3,801
Blue (F5)* 50
Blue Bell (C4)
Bonita (E6)* 100
Bouse (A5)* 150
Bowie (F6)* 300
Buckeye (C5)* 1,932
Bullhead City (A3)*
Bumble Bee (C4)* 36
Bylas (E5)* 750
Cactus (D5)* 125
Calva (E5) 25
Cameron (D3)* 25
Camp Verde (D4)* 550
Camp Wood (C4)* 35
Cane Beds (B2) 30
Casa Grande (D6)* 4,181
Cashion (C5)* 700
Castle Butte (E3)*
Castle Hot Springs (C5)* 30
Cavecreek (D5)* 250
Central (F6)* 300
Chambers (F3)* 106
Chandler (D5)* 3,799
Cherry (C4)
Chinle (F2)* 150
Chino Valley (C4)* 500
Chloride (A3)* 250
Christmas (E5) 60
Chrysotile (E5)
Cibecue (E4)* 35
Clarkdale (C4)* 1,609
Clay Springs (E4)* 199
Claypool (E5)* 1,200
Cleator (C4)* 60
Clemenceau (C4)* 300
Clifton (F5)* 3,466
Cochise (F6)* 90
Concho (F4)* 175
Congress (C4)* 30
Congress Jct. (B4) 95
Continental (D7) 12
Coolidge (D6)* 4,306
Coolidge Dam (E5)* 35
Cordes (C4)
Cornfields (F3) 204
Cornville (D4)* 21
Cortaro (D6)* 360
Cottonwood (D4)* 1,326
Courtland (F7) 25
Crown King (C4)* 100
Dateland (B6)*
Davis Dam (A3) 1,000
Dewey (C4)* 25
Dilkon (E3) 15
Dome (A6)* 35
Dos Cabezas (F6)* 80
Douglas (F7)* 9,442
Dragoon (F6)* 44
Drake (C4) 5
Duncan (F6)* 941
Eagar (F4)* 637
Eden (F6)* 200
Elfrida (F7)* 277
Elgin (E7)* 143
Eloy (D6)* 3,580
Emery Park (E6)* 600
Escuela (D6) 10
Estrella (C6) 21
Fairbank (E7)* 50
Flagstaff (D3)* 6,771
Florence (D5)* 1,776
Florence Jct. (D5)* 32
Fort Apache (F5)* 500
Fort Defiance (F3)* 500
Fort Grant (E6)*
Fort Huachuca (E7)* 100
Fort Thomas (E5)*
Franklin (F6)* 300
Fredonia (C2)* 350
Fry (E7)* 150
Gadsden (A6)* 250
Ganado (F3)* 450
Geronimo (F5)* 23
Gila Bend (C6)* 873
Gilbert (D5)* 1,114
Gleeson (F7) 30
Glenbar (F6)* 170
Glendale (C5)* 8,179
Globe (E5)* 6,419
Goldroad (A3) 14
Goodwin (C4) 15
Goodyear (C5)* 1,254
Grand Canyon (C2)* 1,001
Greasewood Sprs. (F2)
Greaterville (E7)
Greer (F4)* 30
Hackberry (B3)* 250
Hassayampa (C5)
Hayden (E5)* 1,494
Hayden Junction (E6)* 71
Heber (E4)* 250
Hereford (E7)* 90
Higley (D5)* 150
Hillside (B4)* 40
Hilltop (F6) 34
Holbrook (E4)* 2,336
Hotevilla (E3)* 572
Houck (F3)*
Humboldt (C4)* 350
Indian Wells (E3)* 2
Inspiration (D5)* 500
Iron Springs (C4)* 3
Jacob Lake (C2)* 10
Jeddito (E3) 6
Jerome (C4)* 1,233
Joseph City (E4)* 500
Kayenta (E2)* 100
Keams Canyon (E3)* 500
Kelvin (E5)* 35
Kingman (A3)* 3,342
Kirkland (C4)* 96
Klagetoh (F3)
Klondyke (E6)* 150
Komatke (C5) 200
Lakeside (E4)*
Laveen (C5)* 300
Leupp (E3)*
Liberty (C5)
Linden (E4)* 105
Litchfield (C5) 1,000
Litchfield Park (C5)* 450
Littlefield (B2)* 100
Lowell (F7)* 1,136
Lukachukai (F2)*
Lupton (F3)* 115
Madera Canyon (E7) 40
Mammoth (E6)* 275
Marana (D6)* 1,000
Marble Canyon (D2) 5
Maricopa (C5)* 150
Marinette (C5)* 500
Maverick (F5)* 450
Mayer (C4)* 500
Mc Nary (F4)* 1,902
McNeal (F7)* 101
Mesa (D5)* 16,790
Miami (E5)* 4,329
Miller Valley (C4) 2,953
Mobile (C5)* 120
Moccasin (C2)* 55
Mohawk (B6)* 18
Morenci (F5)* 6,541
Mormon Lake (D4)*
Morristown (C5)* 185
Mount Trumbull (B2)* 57
Naco (E7)* 400
Navajo (F3)* 50
Nelson (B3)* 155
Nogales (E7)* 6,153
North Rim (C2)* 2
Nutrioso (F5)* 100
Oatman (A3)* 600
Olberg (D5) 51
Oracle (E6)*
Oraibi (E3)*
Palo Verde (C5)*
Pantano (E7)* 40
Paradise (F7) 14
Parker (A4)* 1,201
Parks (C3)* 50
Patagonia (E7)* 700
Paul Spur (F7)* 300
Paulden (C4)* 25
Payson (D4)* 350
Peach Springs (B3)* 575
Pearce (F7)* 150
Peoria (C5)* 2,000
Perkinsville (C4) 15
PHOENIX (C5)* 106,818
Phoenix (urban area) 214,335
Picacho (D6)* 150
Pima (F6)* 824
Pine (D4)*
Pinedale (E4)* 87
Pinetop (F4)* 300
Pirtleville (F7)* 1,246
Polacca (E3)*
Pomerene (E6)* 100
Portal (F7)* 65
Poston (A3)*
Prescott (C4)* 6,764
Quartzsite (A5)* 153
Queen Creek (D5)* 1,200
Quijotoa (C6) 50
Randolph (D6)*
Ray (E5)* 2,000
Red Rock (D6)* 50
Redington (E6) 51
Rillito (D6)* 200
Rimrock (D4)* 20
Rock Springs (C3)*
Roll (A6)* 66
Roosevelt (D5)*
Rowood (C6)* 50
Ruby (D7)
Sacaton (D5)* 600
Safford (F6)* 3,756
Sahuarita (E7)* 500
Saint David (E7)* 750
St. Johns (F4)* 1,469
St. Michaels (F3)* 120
Salome (B5)* 300
San Carlos (E5)* 3,000
San Luis (A6)*
San Simon (F6)* 175
Sanders (F3)*
Sasabe (D7)* 75
Scottsdale (D5)* 2,032
Sedona (D4)* 350
Seligman (B3)* 1,000
Sells (D7)* 650
Sentinel (B6)* 60
Shonto (E2)
Short Creek (B2)* 200
Show Low (F4)* 1,000
Shumway (E4)* 88
Shungopavy (E3)
Skull Valley (C4)* 250
Snowflake (E4)* 929
Solomon (F6)* 700
Sombrero Butte (E6) 10
Somerton (A6)* 1,825
Sonoita (E7)* 150
Sonora (D5)* 1,821
South Tucson (D6) 2,364
Springerville (F4)* 689
Steamboat (F3)
Stoneman Lake (D4)
Supai (C2)* 16
Supai (C3)
Superior (D5)* 4,500
Tacna (B6)* 18
Taylor (E4)* 500
Tempe (D5)* 7,684
Thatcher (F6)* 1,284
Tiger (E6)* 1,800
Tolleson (C5)* 3,042
Toltec (D6) 30
Tombstone (F7)* 910
Tonalea (E2)*
Tonopah (B5)* 4
Tonto Basin (D5)* 111
Topawa (D7)* 342
Topock (A4)* 50
Toreva (E3)
Tortilla Flat (D5)* 65
Tuba City (D2)* 250
Tubac (E7) 25
Tucson (D6)* 45,454
Tuweep (B2) 10
Vail (E6)*
Valentine (B3)* 127
Valley Farms (D6)* 212
Vernon (F4)* 155
Vicksburg (B5)* 33
Waddell (C5)*
Wagoner (C4)* 55
Walker (C4) 20
Warren (F7)* 2,610
Wellton (A6)*
Wenden (B5)* 100
Whipple (C4)* 650
Whiteriver (E5)* 950
Wickenburg (C5)* 1,736
Wide Ruins (F3) 9
Wikieup (B4)* 6
Wilhoit (C4) 12
Willcox (F6)* 1,266
Williams (C3)* 2,152
Window Rock (F3)*
Winkelman (E6)* 548
Winona (D3) 30
Winslow (E3)* 6,518
Wintersburg (B5) 50
Wittmann (C5)* 170
Wolf Hole (B2) 12
Woodruff (E4)* 164
Yarnell (C4)* 450
Yava (C4)* 35
Young (D4)* 242
Yucca (A4)* 40
Yuma (A6)* 9,145

## ARKANSAS

*Map on Page 51* — *Total Population 1,909,511*

### 75 COUNTIES


Arkansas (H5) 23,665
Ashley (G7) 25,660
Baxter (F1) 11,683
Benton (B1) 38,076
Boone (D1) 16,260
Bradley (F7) 15,987
Calhoun (E6) 7,132
Carroll (C1) 13,244
Chicot (H7) 22,306
Clark (D5) 22,998
Clay (K1) 26,674
Cleburne (F2) 11,487
Cleveland (F6) 8,956
Columbia (D7) 28,770
Conway (E3) 18,137
Craighead (J2) 50,613
Crawford (B2) 22,727
Crittenden (K3) 47,184
Cross (J3) 24,757
Dallas (E6) 12,416
Desha (H6) 25,155
Drew (G6) 17,959
Faulkner (F3) 25,289
Franklin (C2) 12,358
Fulton (G1) 9,187
Garland (D4) 47,102
Grant (F5) 9,024
Greene (J1) 29,149
Hempstead (C6) 25,080
Hot Spring (E5) 22,181
Howard (C5) 13,342
Independence (G2) 23,488
Izard (G1) 9,953
Jackson (H2) 25,912
Jefferson (G5) 76,075
Johnson (C2) 16,138
Lafayette (C7) 13,203
Lawrence (H1) 21,303
Lee (J4) 24,322
Lincoln (G6) 17,079
Little River (B6) 11,690
Logan (C3) 20,260
Lonoke (G4) 27,278
Madison (C1) 11,734
Marion (E1) 8,609
Miller (C7) 32,614
Mississippi (K2) 82,375
Monroe (H4) 19,540
Montgomery (C4) 6,680
Nevada (D6) 14,781
Newton (D2) 8,685
Ouachita (E6) 33,051
Perry (E4) 5,978
Phillips (J5) 46,254
Pike (C5) 10,032
Poinsett (J2) 39,311
Polk (B5) 14,182
Pope (D3) 23,291
Prairie (G4) 13,768
Pulaski (F4) 196,685
Randolph (H1) 15,982
Saint Francis (J3) 36,841
Saline (E4) 23,816
Scott (B4) 10,057
Searcy (E2) 10,424
Sebastian (B3) 64,202
Sevier (B6) 12,293
Sharp (G1) 8,999
Stone (F2) 7,662
Union (E7) 49,686
Van Buren (E2) 9,687
Washington (B2) 49,979
White (G3) 38,040
Woodruff (H3) 18,957
Yell (D3) 14,057


### CITIES and TOWNS


Abbott (B3)* 200
Adona (E3)* 194
Agnos (G1)* 80
Alabam (C1)* 37
Albert (C5) 5
Alco (F2)*
Alexander (F4)* 194
Algoa (H2)* 73
Alicia (H2)* 299
Alix (C3)*
Alleene (B6)*
Alma (B3)* 1,228
Almond (G2)* 150
Almyra (H5)* 235
Alpena (D1)* 304
Alpine (D5)* 100
Altheimer (G5)* 680
Altus (C3)* 431
Aly (D4)* 122
Amagon (H2)* 181
Amity (D5)* 591
Antoine (D5)* 209
Aplin (E4)* 125
Appleton (E3)* 265

## Map on Page 52    CALIFORNIA    Total Population 10,586,223

Map on Page 53

## COLORADO

Total Population 1,325,089

**Map on Page 54**

## CONNECTICUT

**Total Population 2,007,280**

Canton Center (D1)*... 300
Centerbrook (F3)*...... 487
Central Village (H2)*.. 800
Chaplin (G1)*..............△ 712
Cheshire (D2)*............△6,295
Chester (F3)*..............△1,920
Chesterfield (G3)........ 120
Chestnut Hill (G2)*.....
Clarks Corner (G1)...... 78
Clarks Falls (H3)........ 200
Clinton (E3)*..............△2,466
Clintonville (D3)*........ 850
Cobalt (E2)*............... 500
Colchester (F2)*......... 1,522
Colebrook (C1)*..........△ 592
Collinsville (D1)............2,078
Columbia (F2)*...........△1,327
Cooper (B3)................
Cornwall (B1)*............△ 896
Cornwall Bridge (B1)*
Cos Cob (A4)*............. 6,800
Coventry (F1)..............△4,043
Cranbury (B4)............. 3,000
Crescent Beach (G3)*..
Cromwell (E2)*...........△4,286
Crystal Lake (F1)....... 350
Danbury (B3)*.............22,067
Danielson (H1)*.......... 4,554
Darien (B4)*..............△11,767
Dayville (Killingly) (H1)* ...................... 1,105
Deep River (F3)*.........△2,570
Derby (C3)*................10,259
Devon (C4)*...............
Durham (E3)*.............△1,804
Durham Center (E3)*.
Eagleville (F1)*........... 265
East Berlin (E2)*....... 1,000
E. Brooklyn (H1)......... 1,062

E. Canaan (B1)*......... 800
E. Glastonbury (E2)* ...................... 450
E. Granby (E1)*..........△1,327
E. Haddam (F3)*........△2,554
E. Hampton (E2)*.......△4,000
E. Hartford (E1)*......△29,933
E. Hartland (D1)*....... 400
E. Haven (D3)*..........△12,212
E. Kent (B2)................
E. Killingly (H1)*........ 800
E. Litchfield (C1)........ 60
E. Lyme (G3)*............△3,870
E. Morris (C2)............
E. Norwalk (B4).......... 5,000
E. River (E3)*............ 450
E. Thompson (H1)....... 200
E. Wallingford (D3).....
E. Willington (F1)....... 50
E. Windsor (E1)..........△4,859
E. Windsor Hill (E1)* 671
E. Woodstock (H1)*.... 275
Eastford (G1)*...........△ 598
Easton (B4)*..............△2,165
Ellington (F1)*...........△3,099
Elliott (G1)................
Elmwood (D2)*.......... 6,000
Enfield (E1)*............△15,464
Essex (F3)*...............△3,491
Fabyan (H1)*............ 425
Fairfield (B4)*.........△30,489
Falls Village (B1)*...... 640
Farmington (D2)*......△7,026
Farmington Station (D2)
Fenwick (F3).............. 16
Fitchville (G2)*.......... 300
Flanders (B1).............
Florida (B3)...............
Forestville (D2)*......... 6,000

Franklin (G2)..............△ 727
Gales Ferry (G3)*........ 300
Gardner Lake (G2).....
Gaylordsville (B2)*...... 200
Georgetown (B4)*.......
Gildersleeve (E2)*.......
Gilead (F2)................ 70
Gilman (G2)............... 400
Glasgo (H2)*..............
Glastonbury (E2)*.......△8,818
Glenbrook (A4)*..........
Glenville (A4)*........... 976
Goodyear (H1)*.......... 1,000
Goshen (C1)*.............△ 940
Granby (D1)*.............△2,693
Greenfield Hill (B4)....
Greens Farms (B4)*.... 500
Greenville (G2)*..........
Greenwich (A4)*........△40,835
Greystone (C2)........... 150
Griffins (E1)...............
Grosvenor Dale (H1)*.. 800
Groton (G3)*............. 7,036
Groton Long Point (G3)*
Grove Beach (E3)........
Guilford (E3)*............△5,092
Gurleyville (G1)........... 120
Haddam (E3)*.............△2,636
Haddam Neck (E2)...... 50
Hadlyme (F3)*........... 300
Hallville (G2)..............
Hamburg (F3)*...........
Hamden (D3)*...........△29,715
Hampton (G1)*...........△ 672
Hancock (C2).............. 25
Hanover (G2)*........... 300
HARTFORD (E1)*......177,397
Hartford (urban area) 299,676
Harwinton (C1)...........△1,858

Hawleyville (B3)*........
Hazardville (E1)*....... 1,272
Hebron (F2)*.............△1,320
Higganum (E2)*..........
High Ridge (A4)..........
Highland Park (F1).....
Highwood (D3)...........
Hockanum (E2)..........
Hop River (F2)...........
Hotchkissville (C2)...... 300
Huntington (C3)..........
Hurlbutt (B4).............
Ivoryton (F3)*........... 885
Jewett City (H2)*...... 3,702
Jordan Village (Waterford*) (G3)...△9,100
Judds Bridge (B2)...... 30
Kensington (D2)*........ 4,700
Kent (B2)*..................△1,392
Kent Furnace (B2)......
Killingly (H1)............. 1,105
Killingworth (E3).......△ 677
Lakeside (B2)*...........
Lakeville (B1)*...........
Lebanon (G2)*............△1,654
Lebanon Station (G2)..
Ledyard (G3)..............△1,749
Leetes Island (E3)......
Lime Rock (B1)*......... 186
Litchfield (C2)*.......... 1,174
Long Hill (C3)............
Long Ridge (A4).........
Lords Point (H3)......... 400
Lyman Viaduct (F2).... 4
Lyme (F3)..................△ 857
Madison (E3)*............△3,078
Manchester (E1)*......△34,116
Manchester Green (E1)
Mansfield (F1)*.........△10,008
Mansfield Center (G1)* 600
Mansfield Depot (F1)*
Marble Dale (B2)*...... 150
Marion (D2)*.............. 366
Marlborough (F2).......△ 901
Massapeag (G3)..........
Mechanicsville (H1)*...
Melrose (E1)*............
Meriden (D2)*............44,088
Merrow (F1)*............. 125
Mianus (A4)...............
Middle Haddam (E2)*
Middlebury (C2)*........△3,318
Middlefield (E2)*........△1,983
Middletown (E2)*.......29,711
Milford (C4)*............△26,870
Mill Plain (A3)........... 125
Milldale (D2)*........... 1,200
Millstone (G3)...........
Milton (C1)................ 200
Minortown (C2).......... 100
Mohegan (G3)............
Monroe (C3)...............△2,892
Montowese (D3)..........
Montville (G3)*...........△4,766
Moodus (F2)*..............1,400
Moosup (H2)*............ 2,909
Morris (C2)*...............△ 799
Mount Carmel (D3)*...
Mount Hope (G1)........ 50
Mystic (H3)*............. 2,266
Naugatuck (C3)*.........17,455
New Britain (E2)*......73,726
New Britain-Bristol (urban area) ..........122,618
New Canaan (B4)*......△8,001
New Fairfield (B3)......△1,236
New Hartford (C1)*....△2,395
New Haven (D3)*.......164,443
New Haven (urban area) .....................242,589

New London (G3)*......30,551
New Milford (B2)*......△5,799
New Preston (B2)*..... 500
Newington (E2)*........△9,110
Newtown (B3)*............ 782
Niantic (G3)*............. 1,746
Nichols (C4)............... 1,171
Noank (G3)*............... 1,149
Norfolk (C1)*..............△1,572
Noroton (B4)*............ 3,000
Noroton Heights (B4)* 3,918
North Ashford (G1)....
N. Branford (E3).........△2,017
N. Canton (D1)*.......... 250
N. Franklin (G2)*....... 735
N. Granby (D1)*.......... 650
N. Grosvenor Dale (H1)* ...................... 2,232
N. Guilford (E3).......... 1,000
N. Haven (D3)*...........△9,444
N. Kent (B1)...............
N. Madison (E3).........
N. Newington (D2)......
N. Plain (F3)..............
N. Stamford (A4)........
N. Sterling (H1).........
N. Stonington (H3)*...△1,367
N. Westchester (F2)*.. 100
N. Wilton (B4)............
N. Windham (G1)*...... 300
N. Woodbury (C2)*......
N. Woodstock (G1)*....
Northfield (C2)*..........
Northford (D3)*.......... 800
Northville (B2)............ 150
Norwalk (B4)*.............49,460
Norwalk-Stamford (urban area) ..........172,197
Norwich (G2)*.............23,429
Norwichtown (G2)*..... 2,916
Oakdale (G3)*............. 150
Oakville (C2)*............ 5,100
Occum (G2)................
Old Greenwich (A4)*....5,348
Old Lyme (F3)*..........△2,141
Old Mystic (H3)*........ 600
Old Saybrook (F3)*.....△2,499
Oneco (H2)*............... 450
Orange (C3)*.............△3,032
Orcutts (F1)............... 150
Oronoque (C4)*.......... 650
Oxford (C3)................△2,037
Pachaug (H2)............. 75
Packer (H2)*.............. 65
Pawcatuck (H3).......... 5,269
Pequabuck (C2)*......... 600
Phoenixville (G1).........
Pine Meadow (D1)*.... 425
Pine Orchard (D3)*.... 5,100
Plainfield (H2)*..........△8,071
Plainville (D2)*..........△9,994
Plantsville (D2)*......... 1,536
Pleasant Valley (C1)*.. 325
Plymouth (C2)*...........△6,771
Pomfret (H1)*............△2,018
Pomfret Center (H1)*. 675
Poquetanuck (G3)........
Poquonock (E1)*........ 1,200
Poquonock Bridge (G3) ........................ 4,050
Portland (E2)*............△5,186
Preston (H2)*.............△1,775
Prospect (D2).............△1,896
Putnam (H1)*............ 8,181
Quaker Hill (G3)*........ 1,260
Quinebaug (H1)*......... 400
Rainbow (E1)..............
Redding (B3)*.............△2,037
Redding Ridge (B3)*...
Reynolds Bridge (C2).. 600

Ridgefield (A3)*.........△4,356
Riverside (A4)*.......... 2,000
Riverton (D1)*............ 220
Robertsville (C1)......... 130
Rockfall (E2)*............ 2,000
Rockville (F1)*............ 8,016
Rocky Hill (E2)*.........△5,108
Romford (B2)............. 30
Round Hill (A4).......... 600
Rowayton (B4)*.......... 3,200
Roxbury (B2)*............△ 740
Roxbury Falls (B2)......
Roxbury Station (B2)..
Sachem Head (E3)*....
Salem (F3)................△ 618
Salisbury (B1)*..........△3,132
Sandy Hook (B3)*...... 1,600
Saugatuck (B4)*......... 1,500
Saybrook Point (F3)*. 250
Scitico (E1)............... 125
Scotland (G2)*...........△ 513
Seymour (C3)*...........△7,832
Sharon (B1)*.............△1,889
Sharon Valley (B1)...... 174
Shelton (C3)*.............12,694
Sherman (B2)*...........△ 549
Short Beach (D3)*......
Silver Lane (E1).........
Simsbury (D1)*..........△4,822
Somers (F1)*.............△2,631
Somersville (F1)*........ 750
Sound View (F3)......... 100
South Britain (B3)*.... 400
S. Coventry (F1)*........ 1,617
S. Glastonbury (E2)*..
S. Kent (B2)*............. 108
S. Killingly (H1).......... 250
S. Lyme (F3)*............. 150
S. Manchester (E1).....
S. Meriden (D2)*......... 1,600
S. Norwalk (B4)*........18,000
S. Wethersfield (E2)... 200
S. Willington (F1)*....
S. Wilton (B4)............
S. Windham (G2)*....... 450
S. Windsor (E1)*........△4,066
S. Woodstock (G1)*.....
Southbury (C3)*.........△3,828
Southford (C3)...........
Southington (D2)*.....△13,061
Southport (B4)*.......... 3,000
Springdale (A4)*........ 5,280
Stafford (F1)*............△6,471
Stafford Sprs. (F1)*.. 3,396
Staffordville (G1)*...... 1,000
Stamford (A4)*...........74,293
Stamford-Norwalk (urban area) .........172,197
Stepney (B3)...............
Stepney Depot (B3)*.. 3,000
Sterling (H2)*............△1,298
Stevenson (C3)*.......... 200
Still River (B2)........... 200
Stonington (H3)*........ 1,739
Stony Creek (E3)*....... 1,800
Storrs (F1)*...............
Stratford (C4)*..........△33,428
Suffield (E1)*.............△4,895
Taconic (B1)*............. 150
Taftville (G2)*............ 3,598
Talcottville (F1)*........ 568
Talmadge Hill (A4)....
Tariffville (D1)*.......... 800
Terryville (C2)*.......... 6,500
Thamesville (G2)......... 5,518
Thomaston (C2)*.........△4,896
Thompson (H1)*..........△5,585
Thompsonville (E1)*.... 9,633
Tolland (F1)*.............△1,659
Topstone (B3)............

Torrington (C1)*.........27,820
Tracy (D2)..................
Trumbull (C4)............△8,641
Twin Lakes (B1).........
Tyler City (D3)...........
Tylerville (F3)............
Uncasville (G3)*.........
Union (G1)..................△ 261
Union City (C2)*......... 5,000
Unionville (D1)*.......... 2,197
Vernon (F1)*.............△10,115
Versailles (G2)*..........
Voluntown (H2)*.........△ 825
Wallingford (D3)*.......11,994
Wapping (E1)*........... 1,000
Warehouse Point (E1)*1,283
Warren (B2)................△ 437
Warrenville (G1)*........
Washington (B2)*.......△2,227
Washington Depot (B2)* ...................... 700
Waterbury (C2)*........104,477
Waterbury (urban area) ....................131,442
Waterford (Jordan Village) (G3)*.........△9,100
Watertown (C2)*.......△10,699
Waterville (C2)*..........
Wauregan (H2)*......... 1,002
Weatogue (D1)*.......... 800
West Ashford (G1).....
W. Avon (D1).............
W. Cheshire (D2)*....... 1,000
W. Cornwall (B1)*.......
W. Goshen (B1)*.........
W. Granby (D1)*.........
W. Hartford (D1)*.....△44,402
W. Hartland (D1)*...... 196
W. Haven (D3)*.........△32,010
W. Mystic (H3)*.......... 2,362
W. Norwalk (B4)......... 724
W. Redding (B3)*........ 1,000
W. Simsbury (D1)*...... 300
W. Stafford (F1)......... 312
W. Suffield (E1)*........ 1,800
W. Thompson (H1)......
W. Torrington (C1)..... 240
W. Willington (F1)*.... 100
W. Woodstock (G1)..... 100
Westbrook (F3)*.........△1,549
Westfield (E2)............ 1,250
Westford (G1).............
Weston (B4)...............△1,988
Westport (B4)*..........△11,667
Westway (F1).............
Wethersfield (E2)*....△12,533
Whitneyville (D3)........
Wildermere Beach (C4)
Willimantic (G2)*.......13,586
Wilson (E1)*.............. 3,500
Wilson Point (B4)....... 200
Wilsonville (H1)*......... 385
Wilton (B4)*...............△4,558
Winchester Center (C1)*
Windermere (F1)........ 95
Windham (G2)*.........△15,884
Windsor (E1)*...........△11,833
Windsor Locks (E1)*..△5,221
Windsorville (E1)*.......
Winnipauk (B4)........... 3,600
Winsted (C1)*............ 8,781
Wolcott (D2).............△3,553
Woodbridge (D3)........△2,822
Woodbury (C2)*..........△2,564
Woodmont (C4)*......... 5,000
Woodstock (H1)*........△2,271
Woodstock Valley (G1)*
Woodville (B2)............
Yalesville (D3)*.......... 1,122
Yantic (G2)*.............. 800

## DELAWARE

*Total Population 318,085*

*Map on Page 65*

### 3 COUNTIES

Kent (M4)...................37,870
New Castle (M2)........218,879
Sussex (N6)................61,336

### CITIES and TOWNS

Angola (O6)................. 22
Arden (M1)*............... 842
Bacons (M6)................ 28
Bayard (O6).................
Bear (M2)*.................. 150
Bellefonte (N1)............1,472
Bethany Beach (O6)*.... 190
Bethel (M6)*............... 271
Blackbird (M3)............ 50
Blades (M6)................. 789
Bowers (N4)*............... 284
Bridgeville (M6)*.........1,468
Camden (M4)*............. 606
Cannon (M6)*............. 150
Canterbury (M4).......... 50
Centerville (M1)........... 225
Cheswold (M4)*.......... 292
Christiana (M2)*.......... 500
Clarksville (O6)*.......... 150
Claymont (N1)*............5,370
Clayton (M3)*............. 825
Concord (M6).............. 100
Cooch (M2).................. 12
Cool Spring (O6).......... 25
Dagsboro (N6)*........... 474
Delaware City (M2)*....1,363
Delmar (M7)*...............1,015
DOVER (M4)*...............6,223
Edge Moor (N1).......... 25
Ellendale (N5)*........... 321
Elsmere (M2)...............5,314
Farmington (M5)*........ 113
Farnhurst (M2)*.......... 150
Felton (M4)*............... 455
Frankford (N6)*.......... 615
Frederica (N4)*........... 675
Georgetown (N6)*........1,923
Glasgow (M2).............
Glasgow Station (M2)...
Greenville (M1)*...........
Greenwood (M5)*......... 746
Harbeson (N6)*........... 142
Harrington (M5)*.........2,241
Hartly (M4)*............... 139
Hazlettville (M4).......... 20
Hickman (M5).............. 200
Hockessin (M1)*..........1,200
Hollyoak (N1)...............1,450
Hollyville (O6)............. 20
Houston (N5)*............. 332
Kenton (M4)*.............. 211
Kirkwood (M2)*............
Laurel (M6)*................2,700
Lebanon (N4)............... 150
Leipsic (N4)................. 253
Lewes (O5)*.................2,904
Lincoln (N5)*............... 400
Little Creek (N4)*........ 266
Magnolia (M4)*........... 207
Marshallton (M2)*.......1,600
Masten's Corner (M5).. 30
McDonough (M3).........
Middletown (M3)*........1,755
Midway (O6)................ 45
Milford (N5)*...............5,179
Millsboro (N6)*........... 470
Millville (O6)*............. 270
Milton (N5)*.................1,321
Mount Cuba (M1)......... 300
Mount Pleasant (M2)*.. 87
Nassau (O6)*............... 120
New Castle (M2)*........5,396
Newark (M2)*..............6,731
Newport (M2)*.............1,171
Oak Grove (M6)........... 50
Oak Orchards (O6)........
Oakley (M5)................
Ocean View (O6)*......... 450
Odessa (M3)*.............. 467
Port Penn (M2)*.........
Red Lion (M2)............. 50
Redden (N5)...............
Rehoboth Beach (O6)*.1,794
Rockland (M1)*........... 350
Roxana (O6)................ 100
Saint Georges (M2)*....
Seaford (M6)*.............3,087
Selbyville (N7)*...........1,086
Slaughter Beach (N5)... 85
Smyrna (M3)*...............2,346
Stanton (M2)*.............
Stockley (N6)*.............
Summit Bridge (M2)....
Townsend (M3)*.......... 441
Viola (M4)*................. 134
Williamsville (O7)........
Willowgrove (M4)......... 65
Wilmington (M2)*....110,356
Wilmington (urban area) ....................186,265
Woodside (M4)*........... 157
Wyoming (M4)*........... 911
Yorklyn (M1)*............. 500

## FLORIDA

*Total Population 2,771,305*

*Map on Page 55*

### 67 COUNTIES

Alachua (D2)..............57,026
Baker (D1)....................6,313
Bay (C6).....................42,689
Bradford (D2).............11,457
Brevard (F3)...............23,653
Broward (F5)...............83,933
Calhoun (D6).................7,922
Charlotte (E5)...............4,286
Citrus (D3)....................6,111
Clay (E2)....................14,323
Collier (E5)...................6,488
Columbia (D1).............18,216
Dade (F6)..................495,084
De Soto (E4)..................9,242
Dixie (C2).....................3,928
Duval (E1).................304,029
Escambia (B6)...........112,706
Flagler (E2)...................3,367
Franklin (B2).................5,814
Gadsden (B1)...............36,457
Gilchrist (D2).................3,499
Glades (E5)....................2,199
Gulf (D7).......................7,460
Hamilton (D1)................8,981
Hardee (E4).................10,073
Hendry (E5)...................6,051
Hernando (D3)...............6,693
Highlands (E4).............13,636
Hillsborough (D4)......249,894
Holmes (C5).................13,988
Indian River (F4)........11,872
Jackson (D5)................34,645
Jefferson (C1)..............10,413
Lafayette (C2)................3,440
Lake (E3)....................36,340
Lee (E5).......................23,404
Leon (B1)....................51,590
Levy (D2).....................10,637
Liberty (B1)...................3,182
Madison (C1)...............14,197
Manatee (D4)...............34,704
Marion (D2)..................38,187
Martin (F4).....................7,807
Monroe (E7)..................29,957
Nassau (E1)..................12,811
Okaloosa (C6)...............27,533
Okeechobee (F4).............3,454
Orange (E3).................114,950
Osceola (E3)..................11,406
Palm Beach (F5).......114,688
Pasco (D3)....................20,529
Pinellas (D4)..............159,249
Polk (E4)....................123,997
Putnam (E2)..................23,615
St. Johns (E2)...............24,998
St. Lucie (F4)................20,180
Santa Rosa (B6)............18,554
Sarasota (D4)................28,827
Seminole (E3)................26,883
Sumter (D3)...................11,330
Suwannee (C1)..............16,986
Taylor (C1)....................10,416
Union (D1).......................8,906
Volusia (E2)...................74,229
Wakulla (B1)....................5,258
Walton (C6)....................14,725
Washington (C6)............11,888

### CITIES and TOWNS

Alachua (D2)*...............1,116
Alford (D6)*................. 375
Allenhurst (F3)............ 60
Alliance (A1)............... 250
Altamonte Spgs. (E3)*. 858
Altha (A1)*................. 434
Altoona (E3)*.............. 500
Alturas (E4)*.............. 350
Alva (E5)*................... 300
Amelia City (E1)*........ 150
Anastasia (E2)*........... 500
Ankona (F4)*............... 75
Anna Maria (D4)*........ 345
Anthony (D2)*............. 400
Apalachicola (A2)*.......3,222
Apopka (E3)*...............2,254
Arcadia (E4)*...............4,764
Archer (D2)*............... 586
Argyle (C6)*...............
Aripeka (D3)*............. 75
Arlington (E1)*............3,200
Arran (B1)*.................
Artesia (F3)*...............
Astatula (E3)*............ 255
Astor (E2)*.................
Atlantic Beach (E1)*....1,604
Auburndale (E3)*.........3,763
Aucilla (C1)*...............
Avon Park (E4)*..........4,612
Babson Park (E4)*.......1,000
Bagdad (B6)*...............1,500
Baker (C5)*.................
Bal Harbour ‡(F6)........ 224
Baldwin (E1)*..............1,048
Barberville (E2)*......... 350
Barrineau Park (B6)*... 200
Barth (B6)*................. 300
Bartow (E4)*................8,694
Bascom (A1)*.............. 150
Basinger (F4)*............ 150
Bay Harbor (D6)*.........1,676
Bay Harbor Isls. ‡(F6).. 296
Bay Springs (B6)*........
Bayard (E1)*............... 300
Bayport (D3)*.............. 45
Bayshore (E5).............. 15
Bean City (F5)*........... 268
Bee Ridge (D4)*.......... 500
Bell (D2)*.................... 108
Belle Glade (F5)*.........7,219
Belleair (D4)............... 961
Belleview (D2)*............ 595
Belleville (C1).............. 20
Benhaden (B1)............. 25
Bennett (D6)............... 100
Beresford (E2)*........... 100
Biscayne Park ‡(F6)....2,009
Bithlo (E3)*................. 50
Blanton (D3)*.............. 75
Blountstown (A1)*........2,118
Bluffsprings (B5)*........ 100
Boca Ciega ‡(D4)......... 159
Boca Grande (D5)*...... 400
Boca Raton (F5)*........ 992
Bokeelia (D5)*............. 100
Bonifay (C5)*................2,252
Bonita Springs (E5)*....
Bostwick (E2)*............ 500
Bowling Green (E4)*.... 884
Boyd (C1)*.................. 200
Boynton Beach (F5)*....2,542
Bradenton (D4)*.........13,604
Bradenton Beach(D4)*. 500
Bradley (D4)*.............. 422
Brandon (D4)*.............1,250
Branford (D2)*............ 753
Brewster (E4)*............ 800
Brighton (E4)*............ 175
Bristol (B1)*.................1,800
Bronson (D2)*............. 624
Brooker ‡(D2)*............ 277
Brooksville (D3)*.........1,818
Broscan (C2)............... 10
Brownville (E4)*.......... 200
Bruce (C6)*................. 200
Bryant (F5)*................ 400
Bryceville (D1)*........... 150
Bulow (E2).................. 25
Bunnell (E2)*...............1,341
Burbank (E2)............... 80
Bushnell (D3)*............ 536
Callahan (E1)*............ 722
Campbellton (D5)*....... 307
Campville (D2)*........... 250
Canal Point (F5)*.......1,022
Canaveral (F3).............
Candler (E2)*.............. 150
Cantonment (B6)*.......
Capitola (B1)*............. 150
Captiva (D5)*.............. 50
Carrabelle (B2)*.......... 970
Caryville (C6)*............ 525

Cassadaga (E3)* ... 200
Casselberry ‡(E3) ... 407
Cedar Key (C2)* ... 900
Center Hill (D3)* ... 522
Century (B5)* ... 1,350
Chaires (B1)* ...
Charlotte Harbor (E5)*. 330
Chattahoochee (B1)* ... 8,473
Cherry Lake Farms (C1) ... 600
Chiefland (D2)* ... 843
Chipley (D6)* ... 2,959
Chokoloskee (E6)* ... 148
Chosen (F5)* ... 1,873
Christmas (E3)* ... 250
Citra (D2)* ... 500
Citrus Center (E5) ... 15
City Point (F3)* ... 250
Clarksville (D6)* ...
Clearwater (D4)* ... 15,581
Clermont (E3)* ... 2,168
Cleveland (E5)* ... 104
Clewiston (E5)* ... 2,499
Cloud Lake ‡(F5) ... 132
Cocoa (F3)* ... 4,245
Cocoa Beach (F3)* ... 246
Coleman (D3)* ... 849
Collier City (Goodland*) (E6) ... 337
Columbia (D1) ... 75
Compass Lake (D6)* ...
Concord (B1)* ...
Conner (E2) ... 100
Coral Gables (F6)* ... 19,837
Coreytown ‡(D4) ... 23
Cornwell (E4)* ... 10
Coronado (F2) ...
Cortez (D4)* ... 600
Cottagehill (B6)* ... 500
Cottondale (D6)* ... 737
Craig (F7)* ... 10
Crawfordville (B1)* ... 525
Crescent City (E2)* ... 1,393
Crestview (C6)* ... 5,003
Cross City (C2)* ... 1,522
Crystal Lake (D6)* ... 250
Crystal River (D3)* ... 1,026
Crystal Springs (D3)* ... 250
Curtis (D2) ... 50
Cypress (A1)* ... 262
Dade City (D3)* ... 3,806
Dania (F5)* ... 4,540
Darlington (C5)* ...
Davenport (E3)* ... 760
Davie (F5) ... 728
Day (C1)* ... 300
Daytona Beach (F2)* .. 30,187
De Funiak Springs (C6)* ... 3,077
De Land (E2)* ... 8,652
De Leon Springs (E2)* .. 900
De Soto City (E4)* ... 220
Deer Park (F3)* ...
Deerfield Beach (F5)* .. 2,088
Delray Beach (F5)* ... 6,312
Denaud (E5) ... 100
Destin (C6)* ...
Dinsmore (E1)* ... 1,010
Doctors Inlet (E1)* ... 490

Dover (D4)* ... 1,000
Dowling Park (C1) ... 35
Drifton (C1)* ... 200
Dundee (E3)* ... 1,152
Dunedin (D3)* ... 3,202
Dunnellon (D2)* ... 1,110
Eagle Lake (E4)* ... 1,060
Earleton (D2)* ... 100
East Palatka (E2)* ... 1,367
Eastpoint (B2)* ... 600
Eastport (E1) ...
Eau Gallie (F3)* ... 1,554
Ebb (C1)* ... 100
Ebro (C6)* ... 200
Edgewater (F3)* ... 837
Edgewood ‡(E3) ... 217
El Jobean (D5)* ... 60
El Portal ‡(F6) ... 1,371
Elfers (D3)* ... 560
Elkton (E2)* ...
Ellaville (C1) ... 5
Ellenton (D4)* ... 700
Ellzey (D2) ... 150
Emporia (E2)* ... 420
Englewood (D5)* ... 1,206
Enterprise (E3)* ... 300
Espanola (E2)* ... 125
Estero (E5)* ... 250
Esto (C5)* ... 217
Eureka (E2)* ... 300
Eustis (E3)* ... 4,005
Everglades (E6)* ... 625
Fairbanks (D2) ... 35
Fairfield (D2)* ... 135
Fairvilla (E3) ... 1,000
Falmouth (C1)* ...
Felda (E5)* ... 300
Fellsmere (F4)* ... 649
Fernandina (E1)* ... 4,420
Fernandina Beach ‡(E1) ... 554
Flagler Beach (E2)* ... 374
Fletcher (C2) ... 100
Florahome (E2)* ... 400
Floral City (D3)* ... 700
Florence Villa (E3)* ... 2,500
Florida City (F6)* ... 1,547
Floridatown (B6) ... 1,200
Florosa (B6) ...
Foley (C1)* ... 1,014
Ft. Barrancas (B6) ... 300
Ft. Drum (F4) ... 50
Ft. George (E1)* ... 150
Ft. Green (E4)* ...
Ft. Lauderdale (F5)* .. 36,328
Ft. Mc Coy (E2)* ... 500
Ft. Meade (E4)* ... 2,803
Ft. Myers (E5)* ... 13,195
Ft. Ogden (E4)* ... 750
Ft. Pierce (F4)* ... 13,502
Ft. Walton (C6)* ... 2,463
Ft. White (D2)* ... 329
Fountain (D6)* ... 150
Freeport (C6)* ...
Frink (D6)* ... 300
Frostproof (E4)* ... 2,329
Fruitland Park (D3)* ... 551
Fruitville (D4) ... 900
Gainer (D6) ... 25

Gainesville (D2)* ... 26,861
Garden City (E1)* ... 500
Gardner (E4)* ... 110
Gasparilla (D5)* ... 250
Geneva (E3)* ... 600
Genoa (D1) ... 100
Georgetown (E2)* ... 300
Gibsonton (D4)* ...
Gifford (F4)* ... 1,459
Glen Ridge ‡(F5) ... 126
Glen Saint Mary (D1)*.
Glendale (C5) ... 250
Glenwood (E2)* ... 155
Golden Beach ‡(F6)* ... 156
Golfview ‡(F5) ... 84
Gomez (F4) ... 65
Gonzalez (B6)* ... 700
Goodland (E6)* ... 337
Gotha (E3)* ... 275
Goulding (B6) ... 300
Goulds (F6)* ... 1,000
Graceville (D5)* ... 1,638
Graham (D2)* ... 50
Grand Ridge (A1)* ... 300
Grandin (E2)* ... 200
Grant (F4)* ...
Green Cove Spgs. (E2)*. 3,291
Greenacres City (F5)* ... 531
Greensboro (B1)* ... 565
Greenville (C1)* ... 1,163
Greenwood (A1)* ...
Gretna (B1)* ... 385
Groveland (E3)* ... 1,028
Gulf Breeze (B6)* ... 287
Gulf Hammock (D2)* ... 250
Gulf Stream ‡(F5) ... 163
Gulfport (D4)* ... 3,702
Gull Point (B6)* ... 65
Hague (D2) ... 150
Haines City (E3)* ... 5,630
Hallandale (F6)* ... 3,886
Hampton (D2)* ... 386
Hampton Spgs. (C1) ... 15
Hardee Town (D2) ...
Harold (B6)* ... 75
Hastings (E2)* ... 577
Havana (B1)* ... 1,634
Hawthorne (D2)* ... 1,058
Hernando (D3)* ... 304
Hesperides (E4) ... 70
Hialeah (F6)* ... 19,676
Hicora (E4) ...
High Springs (D2)* ... 2,088
Highland (E1)* ... 350
Highland Beach ‡(F5) ... 52
Highland City (E4)* ... 1,600
Highland Park ‡(E4) ... 52
Hildreth (D2)* ... 22
Hillcrest Hts. ‡(E4) ... 91
Hilliard (E1)* ... 607
Hillsboro Beach ‡(F5) .. 84
Hines (C2) ... 400
Hinson (B1)* ... 500
Hobe Sound (F5)* ... 950
Holder (D3)* ... 75
Hollister (E2)* ...
Holly Hill (E2) ... 3,232
Hollywood (F5)* ... 14,351
Holmes Beach ‡(D4) ... 137

Holopaw (E3)* ...
Holt (C6)* ...
Homestead (F6)* ... 4,573
Homosassa (D3)* ... 500
Homosassa Spgs. (D3)*. 100
Horseshoe Beach (C2)*. 150
Hosford (B1)* ...
Houston (D1)* ... 140
Howey in the Hills, (E3)* ... 188
Hudson (D3)* ... 350
Hull (E4)* ...
Immokalee (E5)* ... 1,200
Indian Creek ‡(F6) ... 44
Indian Pass (D7) ... 60
Indian River City (F3)*. 450
Indian Rocks Beach (D4)* ... 198
Indian Town (F4)* ...
Inglis (D2)* ... 200
Intercession City (E3)*.
Interlachen (E2)* ... 297
Inverness (D3)* ... 1,471
Inwood (A1) ... 100
Islamorada (F7)* ... 600
Island Grove (D2)* ... 400
Jacksonville (E1)* ... 204,517
Jacksonville (urban area) ... 241,579
Jacksonville Beach (E1)* 6,430
Jamieson (B1)* ... 120
Jasper (D1)* ... 2,327
Jay (B5)* ... 547
Jennings (C1)* ... 549
Jensen Beach (F4)* ...
Johnson (E2)* ...
Jupiter (F5)* ... 313
Kathleen (D3)* ... 750
Kenansville (F4)* ... 250
Kendall (F6)* ... 2,100
Kendrick (D2)* ... 600
Key Largo (F6) ... 60
Key West (E7)* ... 26,433
Keystone Heights (E2)* 307
Keysville (D4)* ... 500
Kinard (D6)* ... 300
Kissimmee (E3)* ... 4,310
Korona (E2)* ...
Kynesville (D6) ... 400
La Belle (E5)* ... 945
La Crosse (D2)* ... 146
Lacoochee (D3)* ... 1,792
Lady Lake (E3)* ... 331
Lake Alfred (E3)* ... 1,270
Lake Butler (D1)* ... 1,040
Lake City (D1)* ... 7,571
Lake City Jct. (D2) ... 11
Lake Como (E2)* ... 200
Lake Hamilton (E3)* ... 604
Lake Harbor (F5)* ... 800
Lake Helen (E3)* ... 926
Lake Jem (E3)* ... 300
Lake Maitland ‡(E3) ... 889
Lake Mary (E3)* ... 500
Lake Monroe (E3)* ... 300
Lake Park (F5)* ... 489
Lake Placid (E4)* ... 417
Lake Wales (E4)* ... 6,821
Lake Worth (G5)* ... 11,777
Lakeland (D3)* ... 30,851
Lakeport (E5) ... 70
Lakewood (C5)* ...
Lamont (C1)* ...
Land O'Lakes (D3)* ... 75
Lantana (F5)* ... 773
Largo (D4)* ... 1,547
Laurel (D4)* ... 500
Lauderdale-by-the-Sea ‡(F5) ... 234
Laurel Hill (C5)* ... 327
Lawtey (D1)* ... 576
Lebanon (D2) ... 75
Lecanto (D3)* ... 182
Lee (C1)* ... 228
Leesburg (E3)* ... 7,395
Leonia (C5)* ... 105
Limestone (E4)* ... 150
Linden (D3)* ... 250
Live Oak (D1)* ... 4,064
Lloyd (C1)* ... 325
Lochloosa (E2)* ... 200
Lockhart (E3)* ... 1,200
Longwood (E3)* ... 717
Lorida (E4)* ... 225
Loughman (E3)* ... 350
Lovett (C1)* ... 18
Lowell (D2)* ... 150
Loxahatchee (F5)* ... 200
Lulu (D1)* ... 100
Lumberton (D3) ... 25
Luraville (C1) ... 20
Lutz (D3)* ... 1,800
Lynn Haven (C6)* ... 1,787
Lynne (E2)* ... 125
Macclenny (D1)* ... 1,177
Madeira Beach ‡(D4)* .. 916
Madison (C1)* ... 3,150
Maitland (E3)* ...
Malabar (F3)* ... 375
Malone (A1)* ... 521
Manalapan ‡(F5) ... 54

Manatee (D4) ...
Mandarin (E1)* ... 800
Mango (D4)* ... 350
Mangonia Park ‡(F5) ... 348
Mannville (E2)* ... 70
Marathon (E2)* ... 1,200
Marco (E6)* ... 250
Marianna (A1)* ... 5,845
Marineland (E2) ... 40
Martin (D2)* ... 100
Mary Esther (B6)* ... 332
Masaryktown (D3) ... 190
Mascotte (E3)* ... 440
Mason (D1) ... 20
Maxville (E1)* ...
Mayo (C1)* ... 679
Mayport (E1)* ... 1,300
Maytown (F3) ... 25
Mc Alpin (D1)* ... 100
Mc David (B5)* ... 700
Mc Intosh (D2)* ... 247
Mc Neal (A1) ... 500
Medley ‡(F6) ... 106
Melbourne (F3)* ... 4,223
Melbourne Beach (F3)*. 230
Melrose (D2)* ... 750
Merritt Island (F3)* ...
Miami (F6)* ... 249,276
Miami (urban area) .. 453,004
Miami Beach (F6)* ... 46,282
Miami Shores (F6)* ... 5,086
Miami Springs (F6)* ... 5,108
Micanopy (D2)* ... 612
Micco (F4)* ... 250
Miccosukee (B1)* ... 160
Middleburg (E1)* ... 500
Midway (B1)* ... 500
Millers Ferry (C6)* ... 40
Milligan (C6)* ... 600
Millview (B6) ... 150
Milton (B6)* ... 2,040
Mims (F3)* ... 1,500
Minneola (E3)* ... 399
Molino (B6)* ... 600
Montbrook (D2)* ... 200
Monticello (C1)* ... 2,264
Montverde (E3)* ... 293
Moore Haven (E5)* ... 636
Morriston (D2)* ... 150
Mossy Head (C6)* ... 125
Moultrie (E2) ... 50
Mt. Dora (E3)* ... 3,028
Mt. Pleasant (B1)* ... 300
Mulat (B6)* ... 80
Mulberry (E4)* ... 2,024
Munson (B5)* ... 300
Murdock (D4)* ... 100
Muscogee (B6)* ... 165
Myakka City (D4)* ... 450
Myrtle Grove (B6)* ...
Naples (E5)* ... 1,465
Naranja (F6)* ... 500
Narcoossee (E3)* ... 120
National Gardens (E2)*. 125
Neptune Beach (E1)* ... 1,767
New Berlin (E1) ... 100
New Port Richey (D3)*. 1,512
New River (D2)* ... 150
New Smyrna Beach (F2)* ... 5,775
Newberry (D2)* ... 873
Newburn (C1) ... 10
Niceville (C6)* ... 2,497
Nichols (E4)* ... 550
Nobleton (D3)* ... 72
Nocatee (E4)* ... 1,200
Nokomis (D4)* ... 800
Noma (C5)* ...
North Bay ‡(F6) ... 198
North Miami (F6)* ... 10,734
N. Miami Beach (F6)* .. 2,129
O'Brien (D1)* ... 300
Oak Hill (F3)* ... 683
Oakland (E3)* ... 548
Oakland Park (F5)* ... 1,295
Ocala (D2)* ... 11,741
Ocean Ridge ‡(F5) ... 67
Ochopee (E6)* ... 300
Ocoee (E3)* ... 1,370
Odessa (D3)* ...
Ojus (F6)* ... 3,791
Okahumpka (D3)* ... 450
Okeechobee (F4)* ... 1,849
Oklawaha (E2)* ... 500
Old Town (C2)* ... 300
Oldsmar (D3)* ... 345
Olive (B6) ... 200
Olustee (D1)* ...
Ona (E4)* ... 89
Oneco (D4)* ... 650
Opa-Locka (F6)* ... 5,271
Orange (B1)* ...
Orange City (E3)* ... 797
Orange Lake (D2)* ... 500
Orange Park (E1)* ... 1,502
Orange Springs (E2)* ... 275
Orlando (E3)* ... 52,367
Orlando (urban area) .. 72,572
Ormond (E2)* ... 3,418
Ormond Beach (F2)* ... 900
Orsino (F3)* ... 55

Osceola (E3) ...
Osprey (D4)* ... 350
Osteen (E3)* ... 300
Otter Creek (D2)* ... 1,050
Overstreet (D6)* ... 100
Oviedo (E3)* ... 1,601
Oxford (D3)* ... 304
Ozona (D3)* ... 600
Pahokee (F5)* ... 4,472
Palatka (E2)* ... 9,176
Palm Bay (F3)* ... 300
Palm Beach (G5)* ... 3,886
Palm City (F4)* ...
Palm Harbor (D3)* ... 750
Palma Sola (D4)* ... 300
Palmdale (E5)* ... 82
Palmetto (D4)* ... 4,103
Panacea (B1)* ...
Panama City (C6)* ... 25,814
Panama City Beach (C6)*
Paola (E3)* ... 400
Parrish (D4)* ... 1,200
Parker (D6)* ...
Pass-a-Grille Beach (D4)* ... 1,000
Paxton (C5) ... 300
Pelican Lake (F5)* ...
Pembroke (E4)* ... 50
Penney Farms (E2)* ... 445
Pennsuco ‡(F6) ... 133
Pensacola (B6)* ... 43,479
Perrine (F6)* ... 2,859
Perry (C1)* ... 2,797
Pierce (E4)* ... 975
Pierson (E2)* ... 657
Pine Castle (E3)* ... 2,000
Pineland (D5)* ... 50
Pinellas Park (D4)* ... 2,924
Pinetta (C1)* ... 250
Pirates Cove (E7) ...
Plant City (D3)* ... 9,230
Plymouth (E3)* ... 300
Point Washington (C6)*
Polk City (E3)* ... 171
Pomona Park (E2)* ... 443
Pompano Beach (F5)* ... 5,682
Ponce de Leon (C6)* ... 600
Ponce Park (F2) ... 39
Ponte Vedra Beach (E1)* ... 1,000
Port Boca Grande (D5). 75
Port Everglades (F5)* ... 100
Port Mayaca (F5)* ... 155
Port Orange (F2)* ... 1,201
Port Richey (D3)* ... 376
Port Saint Joe (D6)* ... 2,752
Port Sewall (F4) ... 210
Port Tampa (D4)* ... 1,497
Portland (C6)* ... 350
Princeton (F6)* ... 1,300
Providence (D2) ... 16
Punta Gorda (E5)* ... 1,915
Punta Rassa (E5) ... 25
Quincy (B1)* ... 6,505
Raiford (D1)* ... 40
Raleigh (D2)* ... 156
Ramrod Key (E7)* ... 3
Redbay (C6)* ... 250
Reddick (D2)* ... 433
Redington Beach ‡(D4). 384
Richland (D3) ... 100
Richloam (D3) ... 10
River Junction (B1)* ...
Riverdale (E2) ... 100
Riverview (D4)* ...
Riviera Beach (F5)* ... 4,065
Rock Bluff (B1)* ... 250
Rock Harbor (F6)* ... 185
Rockledge (F3)* ... 1,347
Romeo (D2)* ... 300
Roseland (F4)* ... 100
Round Lake (D6)* ... 250
Ruskin (D4)* ...
Safety Harbor (D4)* ... 894
St. Augustine (E2)* ... 13,555
St. Catherine (D3)* ... 250
St. Cloud (E3)* ... 3,001
St. James City (E5)* ... 35
St. Leo (D3)* ... 261
St. Lucie (F4)* ... 300
St. Marks (B1)* ... 391
St. Petersburg (D4)* ... 96,738
St. Petersburg (urban area) ... 113,378
St. Petersburg Beach ‡(D4) ... 722
Salem (C2)* ... [illegible]
Salerno (F4)* ... 789
Samoset (D4)* ... 1,617
Sampson (D2)* ... 125
Samsula (E2) ... 500
San Antonio (D3)* ... 286
San Carlos (E5) ...
San Mateo (E2)* ... 750
Sanderson (D1)* ... 100
Sanford (E3)* ... 11,935
Sanibel (D5)* ... 125
Santa Fe (D2)* ... 100
Santa Rosa (C6)* ... 300
Santos (D2) ... 100
Sarasota (D4)* ... 18,896

Satsuma (E2)* ... 250
Scottsmoore (F3)* ... 150
Sears (E5) ...
Sebastian (F4)* ... 376
Sebring (E4)* ... 5,006
Seffner (D4)* ... 850
Seville (E2)* ... 427
Shady Grove (C1)* ... 50
Shalimar ‡(C6)* ... 694
Shamrock (C2)* ... 700
Sharpes (F3)* ... 300
Shiloh (F3)* ... 150
Silver Springs (D2)* ... 350
Slater (E5) ... 25
Sneads (B1)* ... 1,074
Sopchoppy (B1)* ...
Sorrento (E3)* ... 300
South Bay (F5)* ... 1,050
South Daytona (E2) ... 692
South Flomatin ‡(B5) ... 395
South Miami (F6)* ... 4,809
Southport (C6)* ... 825
Sparr (D2)* ... 450
Springfield (D6) ... 1,084
Starke (D2)* ... 2,944
Steinhatchee (C2)* ... 900
Stuart (F4)* ... 2,912
Sumatra (B1)* ...
Summerfield (D2)* ... 400
Sumner (D2) ... 25
Sun City (D4)* ... 325
Sunnyside (C6)* ... 85
Sunshine Beach ‡(D4) .. 469
Surfside ‡(F6) ... 1,852
Suwannee (C2)* ... 125
Sweetwater ‡(F6) ... 230
Switzerland (E1)* ... 350
Taft (E3)* ... 800
TALLAHASSEE (B1)*. 27,237
Tampa (D4)* ... 124,681
Tampa (urban area) .. 178,398
Tarpon Springs (D3)* .. 4,323
Tavares (E3)* ... 1,763
Tavernier (F6)* ... 480
Telogia (B1)* ...
Temple Terrace (D3)* ... 433
Terra Ceia (D4)* ... 1,500
Thonotosassa (D3)* ...
Tice (E5)* ... 1,133
Titusville (F3)* ... 2,604
Treasure Island ‡(D4) ... 75
Trenton (D2)* ... 904
Trilby (D3)* ... 500
Uleta (F6)* ...
Umatilla (E3)* ... 1,312
Useppa Island (D5) ... 25
Valparaiso (C6)* ... 1,047
Venice (D4)* ... 727
Venus (E4)* ... 35
Vernon (C6)* ... 610
Vero Beach (F4)* ... 4,746
Virginia Gardens ‡(F6) 235
Villa Tasso (C6) ... 75
Wabasso (F4)* ... 300
Wacissa (B1)* ... 450
Wakulla (B1)* ...
Waldo (D2)* ... 647
Walnut Hill (B5)* ...
Walton (F4) ... 175
Ward (B1) ... 30
Warrington (B6)* ... 13,570
Watertown (D1)* ... 1,473
Wauchula (E4)* ... 2,872
Waukeenah (C1)* ... 200
Wausau (D6)* ... 350
Waverly (E4)* ... 1,000
Webster (D3)* ... 569
Weirsdale (D3)* ... 800
Welaka (E2)* ... 459
Wellborn (D1)* ... 450
West Miami (F6) ... 4,043
W. Palm Beach (F5)* .. 43,162
Westbay (C6)* ... 400
Westgate (F6) ... 3,303
Westville (C6)* ... 428
Wewahitchka (D6)* ... 1,289
White City (F4) ... 750
White Springs (D1)* ... 700
Whitehouse (E1)* ... 175
Wilcox (D2)* ... 125
Wildwood (D3)* ... 2,019
Williston (D2)* ... 1,323
Wilma (B1)* ... 50
Wilton Manor ‡(F5) ... 883
Wimauma (D4)* ... 440
Windermere (E3)* ... 317
Winfield (D1) ... 100
Winter Beach (F4)* ... 350
Winter Garden (E3)* ... 3,503
Winter Haven (E3)* ... 8,605
Winter Park (E3)* ... 8,250
Woodville (B1)* ...
Worthington (D2)* ... 30
Yalaha (E3)* ... 600
Yankeetown (D2)* ... 322
Youngstown (D6)* ... 500
Yukon (E1)* ... 2,000
Yulee (E1)* ... 500
Zellwood (E3)* ... 1,500
Zephyrhills (D3)* ... 1,826
Zolfo Springs (E4)* ... 334

## GEORGIA

*Map on Page 56*

*Total Population 3,444,578*

**159 COUNTIES**

Appling (H7) ... 14,003
Atkinson (G8) ... 7,362
Bacon (G7) ... 8,940
Baker (D8) ... 5,952
Baldwin (F4) ... 29,706
Banks (E2) ... 6,935
Barrow (E2) ... 13,115
Bartow (C2) ... 27,370
Ben Hill (F7) ... 14,879
Berrien (F8) ... 13,966
Bibb (E5) ... 114,079
Bleckley (F6) ... 9,218
Brantley (J8) ... 6,387
Brooks (E9) ... 18,169
Bryan (K6) ... 5,965
Bulloch (J6) ... 24,740
Burke (J4) ... 23,458
Butts (E4) ... 9,079
Calhoun (C7) ... 8,578
Camden (J9) ... 7,322
Candler (H6) ... 8,063
Carroll (B3) ... 34,112
Catoosa (B1) ... 15,146
Charlton (H9) ... 4,821
Chatham (K6) ... 151,481
Chattahoochee (C6) ... 12,149
Chattooga (B1) ... 21,197
Cherokee (D2) ... 20,750
Clarke (F3) ... 36,550
Clay (B7) ... 5,844
Clayton (D3) ... 22,872
Clinch (G9) ... 6,007
Cobb (C3) ... 61,830
Coffee (G8) ... 23,961
Colquitt (E8) ... 33,999
Columbia (H3) ... 9,525
Cook (F8) ... 12,201
Coweta (C4) ... 27,796
Crawford (E5) ... 6,080
Crisp (E7) ... 17,663
Dade (A1) ... 7,364
Dawson (D2) ... 3,712
De Kalb (D3) ... 136,395
Decatur (C9) ... 23,620
Dodge (F6) ... 17,865
Dooly (E6) ... 14,159
Dougherty (D7) ... 43,617
Douglas (C3) ... 12,173
Early (C8) ... 17,413
Echols (G9) ... 2,494
Effingham (K6) ... 9,133
Elbert (G2) ... 18,585
Emanuel (H5) ... 19,789
Evans (J6) ... 6,653
Fannin (D1) ... 15,192
Fayette (C4) ... 7,978
Floyd (B2) ... 62,899
Forsyth (D2) ... 11,005
Franklin (F2) ... 14,446
Fulton (D3) ... 473,572
Gilmer (D1) ... 9,963
Glascock (G4) ... 3,579
Glynn (J8) ... 29,046
Gordon (C2) ... 18,922
Grady (D9) ... 18,928
Greene (F3) ... 12,843
Gwinnett (D2) ... 32,320
Habersham (E1) ... 16,553
Hall (E2) ... 40,113
Hancock (G4) ... 11,052
Haralson (B3) ... 14,663
Harris (C5) ... 11,265
Hart (G2) ... 14,495
Heard (B4) ... 6,975
Henry (D4) ... 15,857
Houston (E6) ... 20,964
Irwin (F7) ... 11,973
Jackson (E2) ... 18,997
Jasper (E4) ... 7,473
Jeff Davis (G7) ... 9,299
Jefferson (H4) ... 18,855
Jenkins (J5) ... 10,264
Johnson (G5) ... 9,893
Jones (E5) ... 7,538
Lamar (D4) ... 10,242
Lanier (F8) ... 5,151
Laurens (G6) ... 33,123
Lee (D7) ... 6,674
Liberty (J7) ... 8,444
Lincoln (H3) ... 6,462
Long (J7) ... 3,598
Lowndes (F9) ... 35,211
Lumpkin (D1) ... 6,574
Macon (D6) ... 14,213
Madison (F2) ... 12,238
Marion (C6) ... 6,521
Mc Duffie (H4) ... 11,443
Mc Intosh (K7) ... 6,008
Meriwether (C4) ... 21,055
Miller (C8) ... 9,023
Mitchell (D8) ... 22,528
Monroe (E4) ... 10,523
Montgomery (G6) ... 7,901

Morgan (F3)........11,899
Murray (C1)........10,676
Muscogee (C6)........118,028
Newton (E3)........20,185
Oconee (F3)........7,009
Oglethorpe (F3)........9,958
Paulding (C3)........11,752
Peach (E5)........11,705
Pickens (D2)........8,855
Pierce (H8)........11,112
Pike (D4)........8,459
Polk (B3)........30,976
Pulaski (E6)........8,808
Putnam (F4)........7,731
Quitman (B7)........3,015
Rabun (F1)........7,424
Randolph (C7)........13,804
Richmond (H4)........108,876
Rockdale (D3)........8,464
Schley (D6)........4,036
Screven (J5)........18,000
Seminole (C9)........7,904
Spalding (D4)........31,045
Stephens (F1)........16,647
Stewart (C6)........9,194
Sumter (D6)........24,208
Talbot (C5)........7,687
Taliaferro (G3)........4,515
Tattnall (J6)........15,939
Taylor (D5)........9,113
Telfair (G7)........13,221
Terrell (D7)........14,314
Thomas (E9)........33,932
Tift (E8)........22,645
Toombs (H6)........17,382
Towns (E1)........4,803
Treutlen (G6)........6,522
Troup (B4)........49,841
Turner (E7)........10,479
Twiggs (F5)........8,308
Union (E1)........7,318
Upson (D5)........25,078
Walker (B1)........38,198
Walton (E3)........20,230
Ware (H8)........30,289
Warren (G4)........8,779
Washington (G4)........21,012
Wayne (J7)........14,248
Webster (C6)........4,081
Wheeler (G6)........6,712
White (E1)........5,751
Whitfield (B1)........34,432
Wilcox (F7)........10,167
Wilkes (G3)........12,388
Wilkinson (F5)........9,781
Worth (E8)........19,357

**CITIES and TOWNS**

Aaron (J5)........50
Abac (E8)........
Abba (F7)*........
Abbeville (F7)*........890
Abbottsford (B4)........40
Acree (D7)*........225
Acworth (C2)*........1,466
Adairsville (C2)*........916
Adel (F8)*........2,776
Adgateville (E4)........75
Adrian (G5)*........503
Afton (D2)........7
Agnes (H3)*........30
Agricola (G4)........45
Aikenton (E4)........
Ailey (G6)*........508
Akes (B3)........400
Alamo (G6)*........800
Alapaha (F8)*........505
Albany (D7)*........31,155
Aldora (D4)........591
Alexander (J4)*........90
Aline (H6)........100
Allenhurst (J7)*........150
Allentown (F5)*........450
Allenville (F8)........15
Alma (G7)*........2,588
Almon (E3)........135
Alpharetta (D2)*........917
Alston (H6)*........147
Altamaha (H7)........
Alto (E2)*........302
Alvaton (C4)*........95
Amboy (E7)........50
Ambrose (G7)*........470
Americus (D6)*........11,389
Amity (H3)*........
Amsterdam (D9)*........700
Andersonville (D6)*........281
Apalachee (E3)*........178
Apollo (F4)........25
Appling (H3)*........250
Arabi (E7)*........376
Aragon (B2)*........1,272
Arcade (E2)........114
Arcola (J6)........78
Argyle (G8)*........244
Arlington (C8)*........1,382
Armuchee (B2)*........
Arnoldsville (F3)*........150
Arp (F7)........50
Ashburn (E7)*........2,918
Ashland (F2)*........250
Aska (D1)*........35
Atco (C2)*........1,443
Athens (F3)*........28,180
Atkinson (J8)*........500
ATLANTA (D3)*........331,314
Atlanta (urban area)........502,204
Attapulgus (D9)*........457
Auburn (E2)*........301
Augusta (J4)*........71,508
Augusta (urban area)........87,823
Auraria (E1)........200
Austell (C3)*........1,413
Autreyville (E8)........100
Avalon (F1)*........151
Avans (A1)*........
Avera (H4)*........230
Avondale Estates (D3)*........1,070
Axson (G8)*........200
Babcock (C8)........
Baconton (D8)*........500
Bainbridge (C9)*........7,562
Bairdstown (F3)*........75
Baldwin (E2)*........490
Ball Ground (D2)*........700
Banning (C3)........225
Bannockburn (F8)........15
Barnesville (D4)*........4,185
Barnett (G3)*........60
Barnett Shoals (F3)........
Barney (E8)*........157
Barretts (F8)*........150
Bartow (G5)*........347
Barwick (E9)*........436
Bascom (J5)........30
Baxley (H7)*........3,409
Baxter (D1)*........
Beach (G8)........62
Beachton (D9)........50
Belair (H4)........
Bellton (E2)*........266
Bellville (H6)*........300
Belmont (E2)........100
Bemiss (F9)........50
Benevolence (C7)*........157
Berlin (E8)*........309
Berner (E4)*........175
Berryton (B2)*........520
Bethlehem (E3)*........240
Between (E3)........120
Beverly (G2)........
Bibb City (B5)*........1,452
Big Springs (C5)........25
Bingen (C9)........4
Bishop (F3)*........253
Blackshear (H8)*........2,271
Bladen (J8)........8
Blaine (C1)........95
Blairsville (E1)*........430
Blakely (C8)*........3,234
Blalock (E1)........50
Blitchton (J6)*........50
Bloomingdale (K6)*........350
Blue Ridge (D1)*........1,718
Bluffton (C7)*........244
Blun (H5)........150
Blundale (H5)*........116
Blythe (H4)*........268
Bogart (E3)*........459
Bolen (G8)........90
Bolingbroke (E5)*........87
Bolton (D3)*........
Boneville (G4)*........100
Boston (E9)*........1,035
Bostwick (E3)*........287
Bowdon (B3)*........1,155
Bowdon Junction (B3)*........450
Bowens Mill (F7)........
Bowersville (G2)*........303
Bowman (G2)*........714
Box Springs (C5)*........100
Boykin (C8)........120
Bradley (E4)*........100
Braselton (E2)*........165
Braswell (C3)........25
Bremen (B3)*........2,299
Brentwood (H7)........50
Brest (D8)........
Brewton (G5)*........
Bridgeboro (E8)........
Briggston (F9)........35
Bright (D2)........150
Brighton (E7)........35
Brinson (C9)*........248
Bristol (H8)*........137
Broadhurst (J8)........225
Brobston (K8)........8
Bronwood (D7)*........337
Brooker (G7)........50
Brookfield (F8)*........350
Brooklet (J6)*........536
Brooklyn (C6)*........300
Brooks (D4)*........136
Brookton (E2)........200
Browns Crossing (F4)........50
Broxton (G7)*........890
Brunswick (K8)*........17,954
Buchanan (B3)*........651
Buckhead (F3)*........220
Buena Vista (C6)*........1,428
Buford (D2)*........3,812
Bullard (F5)........
Burnt Fort (J9)........75
Burtsboro (D1)........25
Burwell (B3)*........60
Bushnell (G7)........27
Butler (D5)*........1,182
Butts (J5)........10
Byromville (E6)*........288
Byron (E5)*........379
Cadwell (G6)*........310
Cairo (D9)*........5,577
Calhoun (B1)*........3,231
Calvary (D9)*........600
Calvin (F6)........50
Camak (G4)*........379
Camilla (D8)*........3,745
Camp Creek (D1)........
Campania (H4)........350
Campton (E3)*........163
Canon (F2)*........596
Canoochee (H5)*........62
Canton (C2)*........2,716
Carbondale (B1)........75
Carl (E3)*........214
Carlton (F2)*........249
Carnegie (C7)*........197
Carnesville (F2)*........349
Carrollton (C3)*........7,753
Carrs Station (F4)........50
Cartecay (D1)*........
Carters (C1)*........35
Cartersville (C2)*........7,270
Cass (C2)*........
Cassandra (B1)........125
Cassville (C2)*........
Cataula (C5)*........500
Cave (C2)........8
Cave Spring (B2)*........959
Cecil (F8)*........254
Cedar Grove (A1)*........75
Cedar Springs (C8)*........
Cedartown (B2)*........9,470
Center (F2)*........112
Centralhatchee (B4)........239
Chalybeate Spgs. (C5)........255
Chamblee (D3)*........3,445
Charing (D6)*........
Charles ‡(H6)........20
Chatsworth (C1)*........1,214
Chattahoochee (C3)*........
Chauncey (F6)*........348
Cherrylog (D1)*........
Chester (F6)*........315
Chickamauga (B1)*........1,747
Chipley (C5)*........817
Choestoe (E1)........
Chula (E7)*........210
Cisco (C1)*........100
Clarkdale (C3)*........750
Clarkesville (F1)*........1,106
Clarkston (D3)*........1,165
Claxton (J6)*........1,923
Clay Hill (H3)*........17
Clayton (F1)*........1,302
Clem (B3)*........400
Clermont (E2)*........323
Cleveland (E1)*........589
Climax (D9)*........373
Clinchfield (E6)*........200
Clito (J5)........25
Cloudland (A1)*........100
Clyattville (F9)*........75
Clyo (K6)*........600
Cobb (E7)*........150
Cobbtown (H6)*........288
Cobbville (G7)........126
Cobert (F2)........
Cochran (F6)*........3,357
Coffee (H7)*........200
Coffinton (C6)........
Cogdell (G8)*........
Cohutta (C1)*........450
Colbert (F2)*........407
Coleman (C7)*........295
Coleman (G4)........35
Colesburg (J9)........100
College Park (C3)*........14,535
Collegeboro (J6)*........1,000
Collins (H6)*........638
Colon (G9)........25
Colquitt (C8)*........1,664
Columbus (C6)*........79,611
Columbus (urban area)........118,122
Comer (F2)*........882
Commerce (E2)*........3,351
Concord (D4)*........360
Conyers (D3)*........2,003
Coolidge (E8)*........764
Coosa (B2)*........125
Cordele (E7)*........9,462
Corinth (B4)........135
Cork (E4)........50
Cornelia (E1)*........2,424
Cotton (D8)*........146
Council (G9)*........125
Covena (H6)*........
Coverdale (E7)........50
Covington (E3)*........5,192
Covington Mills (E3)........
Crandall (C1)*........202
Crawford (F3)*........555
Crawfordville (G3)*........966
Crest (D5)........96
Crosland (E8)*........127
Crystal Springs (B2)........
Culloden (D5)*........261
Culverton (G4)*........250
Cumming (D2)*........1,264
Curryville (B2)*........54
Cusseta (C6)*........571
Cuthbert (C7)*........4,025
Cutting (G8)........100
Cyrene (C9)........35
Dacula (E3)*........369
Dahlonega (D1)*........2,152
Daisy (J6)*........195
Dakota (E7)........40
Dallas (C3)*........1,817
Dalton (B1)*........15,968
Damascus (C8)*........402
Dames Ferry (E4)*........225
Danburg (G3)*........181
Danielsville (F2)*........298
Danville (F5)*........461
Darien (K8)*........1,380
Dasher (F9)*........100
Davisboro (G5)*........469
Dawson (D7)*........4,411
Dawsonville (D2)*........318
De Soto (D7)*........309
Dearing (H4)*........325
Decatur (D3)*........21,635
Deepstep (G4)*........159
Demorest (F1)*........1,166
Dennis (F4)........50
Denton (G7)*........273
Devereux (F4)*........170
Dewey Rose (G2)*........375
Dewitt (D8)........
Dexter (G6)*........264
Dial (D1)*........89
Dickey (C7)........135
Dillard (F1)*........186
Dixie (E9)*........261
Doctortown (J7)*........350
Doerun (E8)*........902
Doles (E7)*........125
Donalsonville (C8)*........2,569
Donovan (G5)*........225
Doogan (C1)........30
Dooling (E6)*........300
Doraville (D3)*........472
Dorchester (K7)*........150
Double Branches (H3)........100
Doublerun (E7)........
Douglas (G7)*........7,428
Douglasville (C3)*........3,400
Dover (J5)*........150
Doverel (D7)........25
Doyle (D6)*........
Draketown (B3)........200
Dry Branch (F5)*........250
Du Pont (G9)*........285
Dublin (G5)*........10,232
Ducktown (D2)........58
Dudley (F5)*........272
Due (D1)........50
Duluth (D2)*........842
Dunwoody (D3)*........240
Durand (C5)*........186
Dyas (E5)........12
Early (B2)........100
East Ellijay (C1)*........549
East Juliette (E4)........303
East Point (C3)*........21,080
East Thomaston (D5)........3,082
Eastanollee (F1)*........225
Eastman (F6)*........3,597
Eastville (F3)........96
Eatonton (F4)*........2,749
Echeconnee (E5)........56
Eden (K6)*........300
Edison (C7)*........1,247
Edith (G9)........150
Egypt (K6)*........
Elberton (G2)*........6,772
Eldora (J6)........50
Eldorendo (C8)*........250
Elko (E6)*........188
Ella Gap (C1)........
Ellabell (K6)*........100
Ellaville (D6)*........886
Ellenton (E8)*........429
Ellenwood (D3)*........250
Ellerslie (C5)*........650
Ellijay (C1)*........1,527
Elmodel (D8)*........125
Emerson (C2)*........508
Emma (D1)*........135
Emmalane (H5)........10
Empire (F6)*........157
Enigma (F8)*........499
Epworth (D1)*........100
Erick (G6)........20
Esom Hill (B3)*........175
Eton (C1)*........297
Eulonia (K7)*........
Evans (H3)*........
Everett (J8)*........200
Experiment (D4)*........4,265
Faceville (C9)*........700
Fairburn (C3)*........1,889
Fairfax (G8)........
Fairmount (C2)*........573
Fargo (G9)*........
Farmdale (J5)........
Farmington (F3)*........121
Farrar (E4)*........30
Fayetteville (C4)*........1,032
Felton (B3)*........250
Fender (E8)*........150
Ficklin (G3)*........100
Findlay (E6)........50
Finleyson (F6)*........79
Fish (B2)........200
Fitzgerald (F7)*........8,130
Fitzpatrick (F5)........150
Fleming (K7)*........200
Flemington (J7)*........90
Flint (D8)........
Flintstone (B1)*........200
Flippen (D3)*........500
Florence (C6)........
Flovilla (E4)*........315
Flowery Branch (E2)*........610
Folkston (H9)*........1,515
Forest Glen (F7)........
Forest Park (D3)*........2,653
Forsyth (E4)*........3,125
Fort Gaines (C7)*........1,339
Fort Lamar (F2)........15
Fort Mudge (H8)........25
Fort Oglethorpe ‡(B1)*........692
Fort Screven (L6)*........300
Fort Valley (E5)*........6,820
Fortson (C5)*........300
Fowlstown (D9)*........300
Franklin (B4)*........425
Franklin Spgs. (F2)*........182
Frolona (B4)*........123
Fry (D1)*........250
Fullerville (C3)........529
Funston (E8)*........233
Gabbettville (B5)*........275
Gaddistown (D1)*........175
Gaillard (D5)*........80
Gainesville (E2)*........11,936
Garden City (K6)*........1,557
Gardi (J7)*........225
Gardners (G5)*........150
Garfield (H5)*........213
Gay (C4)*........241
Geneva (C5)*........209
Georgetown (B7)*........550
Gibson (G4)*........460
Gillsville (E2)*........152
Girard (J4)*........244
Glenmore (H8)........30
Glenn (B4)*........
Glennville (J7)*........2,327
Glenwood (G6)*........684
Gloster (D3)........100
Godfrey (F4)*........168
Godwinsville (F6)........100
Goggins (D4)*........130
Good Hope (E3)*........189
Gordon (F5)*........1,761
Gore (B2)*........65
Gough (H4)*........450
Gracewood (H4)*........
Graham (H7)*........160
Grangerville (J8)........25
Grantville (C4)*........1,359
Gratis (E3)........70
Graves (C7)*........200
Gray (F4)*........866
Graymont (Twin City) (H5)*........1,018
Grayson (E3)*........227
Graysville (B1)*........120
Greenbush (B1)........150
Greenough (D8)........
Greensboro (F3)*........2,688
Greenville (C4)*........733
Greggs (F8)........4
Greshamville (F3)*........100
Gresston (F6)*........200
Griffin (D4)*........13,982
Griswoldville (F5)........
Grovania (E6)*........225
Groveland (J6)*........140
Grovetown (H4)*........500
Guyton (K6)*........633
Habersham (F1)*........750
Haddock (F4)*........475
Hagan (J6)*........525
Hahira (F9)*........1,010
Halcyon Dale (J5)*........330
Hamilton (C5)*........449
Hammett (D5)........15
Hampton (D4)*........864
Hanlin (C3)........50
Hapeville (D3)*........8,560
Haralson (C4)*........142
Hardwick (F4)*........3,000
Harlem (H4)*........1,033
Harris (C5)........250
Harrison (G5)*........261
Hartsfield (E8)*........113
Hartwell (G2)*........2,964
Hatcher (B7)*........90
Hatley (E7)........100
Hawkinsville (E6)*........3,342
Haylow (G9)*........
Hayner (J8)........20
Haywood (H8)........20
Hazlehurst (G7)*........2,687
Headlight (G9)........4
Heardmont (G2)*........65
Hebardville (H8)........1,113
Helen (E1)*........191
Helena (G6)*........1,027
Hephzibah (H4)*........525
Hermitage (B2)........25
Herndon (H5)*........300
Herod (D7)........126
Hiawassee (E1)*........375
Hickox (H8)*........139
Higgston (G6)*........155
High Shoals (F3)*........
High Tower (D2)........75
Hill City (C1)*........100
Hillsboro (E4)*........300
Hilltonia (J5)*........318
Hilton (C8)*........
Hinesville (J7)*........1,217
Hinsonton (D8)*........
Hiram (C3)*........299
Hoboken (H8)*........492
Hogansville (C4)*........3,769
Holland (B2)*........300
Holly Springs (D2)*........386
Hollywood (E1)*........100
Homeland (H9)........276
Homer (F2)*........340
Homerville (G8)*........1,787
Homestead (H8)........13
Hortense (J8)*........175
Hoschton (E2)*........378
Howard (D5)*........
Howell (F9)*........169
Huching (F3)........145
Hull (F2)*........153
Hunters (K5)........60
Huntington (D6)........100
Hurst (D1)*........195
Ideal (D6)*........318
Ila ((F2)*........225
Inaha (E7)........100
Indian Springs (E4)*........200
Inman (D4)*........300
Iron City (C8)*........293
Irwinton (F5)*........700
Irwinville (F7)*........275
Isle of Hope (K7)........800
Ivey (F5)........46
Jackson (E4)*........2,053
Jacksonville (G7)*........300
Jakin (B8)*........264
James (E5)*........150
Jasper (D2)*........1,380
Jefferson (F2)*........2,040
Jeffersonville (F5)*........787
Jenkinsburg (E4)*........166
Jersey (E3)*........182
Jesup (J7)*........4,605
Jewell (G4)*........200
Jimps (J6)........25
Johntown (D1)........8
Jonesboro (D4)*........1,741
Julia (C6)........
Juliette (E4)*........283
Junction City (C5)*........259
Juniper (C6)*........150
Juno (D2)*........30
Kathleen (E6)*........100
Keithsburg (C2)........150
Kelly (E4)*........100
Kennesaw (C2)*........564
Kenwood (D3)*........300
Keysville (H4)*........304
Kibbee (H6)*........100
Kildare (K5)........75
Killen (C7)........40
Kimbrough (C7)........100
Kingsland (J9)*........1,169
Kingston (C2)*........675
Kinlaw (J9)........35
Kirkland (G8)*........100
Kite (G5)*........447
Knoxville (E5)*........400
La Cross (D6)........
La Grange (B4)*........25,025
Ladds (C2)........75
LaFayette (B1)*........4,884
Lake Park (F9)*........334
Lake Tara ‡(D3)........224
Lakeland (F8)*........1,551
Lakemont (F1)*........500
Lanier (J6)*........100
Lavonia (F2)*........1,766
Lawrenceville (D3)*........2,932
Lax (F8)........100
Leaf (E1)*........251
Leah (H3)........200
Leary (C8)*........721
Leathersville (H3)*........
Lebanon (D2)*........200
Lee Pope (E5)*........75
Leesburg (D7)*........659
Lenox (F8)*........789
Leslie (D7)*........417
Lewiston (F5)........
Lexington (F3)*........514
Lexsy (H6)*........75
Lilburn (D3)*........567
Lilly (E6)*........177
Lincolnton (H3)*........1,315
Lindale (B2)*........2,834
Linton (F4)*........150
Linwood (B1)........858
Linwood (B2)........100
Lisbon (G3)*........95
Lithia Springs (C3)*........
Lithonia (D3)*........1,538
Little River (G3)........80
Lizella (E5)*........350
Loco (G3)........
Locust Grove (D4)*........405
Loganville (E3)*........699
Lollie (Minter) (G6)*........143
Lone Oak (C4)........120
Lookout (B1)........
Lorane (E5)........
Louisville (H4)*........2,231
Louvale (C6)*........
Lovejoy (D4)*........204
Lovett (G5)*........80
Lucile (C8)........50
Lucius (D1)........
Ludowici (J7)*........1,332
Ludville (C2)........
Luella (D4)*........200
Lula (E2)*........378
Lumber City (G7)*........1,232
Lumpkin (C6)*........1,209
Luthersville (C4)*........312
Lyerly (B2)*........524
Lynn (J7)........
Lynn Station (C8)........25
Lyons (H6)*........2,799
Machen (E4)*........40
Macon (E5)*........70,252
Macon (urban area)........93,305
Madison (F3)*........2,489
Madras (C4)*........185
Manassas (H6)*........128
Manchester (C5)*........4,036
Manor (G8)*........
Mansfield (E4)*........446
Marblehill (D2)*........
Margret (D1)*........145
Marietta (D3)*........20,687
Marion (D1)*........
Marlow (K6)*........250
Marshallville (D6)*........1,121
Martin (F2)*........207
Martinez (H3)*........2,500
Matthews (H4)*........100
Mauk (D6)*........100
Maxeys (F3)*........204
Maxim (H3)........25
Mayfield (G4)*........250
Maysville (E2)*........533
Mc Bean (J4)*........200
Mc Caysville (D1)*........2,067
Mc Collum (C4)........100
Mc Donough (D4)*........1,635
Mc Intosh (K7)*........
Mc Intyre (F5)*........194
Mc Kinnon (J8)*........65
Mc Rae (G6)*........1,904
Mc Whorter (C3)........45
Meansville (D4)*........224
Meda (F4)........20
Meeks (G5)*........100
Meigs (D8)*........1,125
Meinhard (K6)........160
Meldrim (K6)*........250
Mendes (H7)*........300
Menlo (B2)*........453
Meridian (K8)*........
Merrillville (E9)........109
Mershon (H8)*........
Mesena (G4)*........150
Metasville (G3)........82
Metcalf (E9)*........206
Metter (H6)*........2,091
Middleton (G2)*........144
Midland (C5)*........200
Midville (H5)*........682
Midway (K7)*........228
Milan (G6)*........750
Milford (C8)*........
Milledgeville (F4)*........8,835
Millen (J5)*........3,449
Millhaven (J5)*........50
Millwood (G8)*........
Milner (D4)*........345
Milstead (D3)*........1,075
Mineral Bluff (D1)*........209
Minter (Lollie*) (G6)........143
Minter (G6)*........143
Mitchell (G4)*........240
Mize (F2)........75
Molena (D4)*........307
Moniac (H9)*........200
Monroe (E3)*........4,542
Modoc ‡(A5)........32
Montezuma (E6)*........2,921
Monticello (E4)*........1,918
Montrose (F5)*........242
Moran (E5)*........250
Moreland (C4)*........306
Morgan (C7)*........304
Morganton (D1)*........244
Morris (C7)*........
Morrow ‡(D3)*........326
Morven (E9)*........474
Moultrie (E8)*........11,639
Mount Airy (F1)*........416
Mount Berry (B2)*........1,500
Mount Pleasant (J8)........50
Mount Vernon (H6)*........990
Mount Zion (B3)*........141
Mountain City (F1)*........524
Mountain Park ‡(D3)........15
Mountville (C4)*........142

## Map on Page 95    HAWAII    Total Population 499,794

Moanalua (stream) (C3)
Mokapu (peninsula) (F2)
Mokolii (isl.) (F1)
Moku (G1)
Mokuaweoweo (crater) (H6)
Mokuhooniki (isl.) (J1)
Mokulau (K3)
Mokuleia (D1) 150
Moloaa (D1)
Molokai (isl.) (G1) 5,280
Molokini (isl.) (J2)
Monohaa (G5) 2
Mopua (J2) 600
Mountainview (J5)* 747
Muolea (K2)
Naalehu (H7)* 1,004
Nahiku (K2)
Nakalele (point) (J1)
Nanakuli (D2)* 2,002
Napoopoo (G6)* 103
Nawiliwili (D2)
Nawiliwili (bay) (D2)
Necker (isl.) (D6)
Nihoa (isl.) (D6)
Niihau (isl.) (A2) 222
Ninini (point) (D2)
Ninole (J4)* 112
Niulii (G3)
Nohili (point) (B1)
Nonopapa (A2)
Nuuanu (stream) (C4)
Oahu (isl.) (E2) 353,020
Olaa-Keaau (J5)* 1,620
Olowalu (H2) 100
Onomea (J4) 300
Ookala (J4)* 662
Opihikao (K6)
Paauhau (H4)* 400
Paauilo (H4)*
Pacific Heights (C4)
Pacific Ocean (B6)
Pacific Sugar Mill (H3)
Pahala (H6)* 1,602
Pahoa (J5)* 990
Paholoi (J2) 50
Paia (J2)* 3,195
Paihaaloa (J4) 98
Pailolo (channel) (H1)
Palama (C4)
Palaoa (point) (G2)
Palmyra (isl.) (C7)
Palolo (stream) (D4)
Paniau (mt.) (A2)
Papa (G6)
Papaaloa (G5)
Papaaloa (J4)* 597
Papaikou (J5)* 1,427
Paukaa (J5) 200
Pauwalu (point) (K2)
Pauwela (K1)* 618
Pauwela (point) (K1)
Peahi (K2)
Pearl (harbor) (A3)
Pearl and Hermes (reef) (B5)
Pearl City (B3)* 2,663
Pelekunu (H1)
Pepeekeo (J4)* 1,002
Pepeekeo (point) (J4)
Piihonua (J5) 600
Pohakuloa (point) (H2)
Pohoiki (K6) 3
Port Allen (C2) 450
Pua Akala (H5)
Puako (G4)
Pueo (point) (A2)
Puhi (C2)* 765
Pukoo (H1)* 42
Pulehu (J2) 200
Pulehu Camp (J2)
Punahou (C4)
Punaluu (E1)
Punaluu (H7) 30
Punaluu (harbor) (H7)
Punchbowl (hill) (C4)
Puolo (point) (C2)
Puu Hue (G3)
Puu Lehua Ranch (G5)
Puu Makani Camp (H7)
Puuanahulu (G4) 62
Puuiki (E1) 170
Puuiki (K2)
Puukolii (J2) 689
Puuloa Station (B4)
Puunene (J2)* 5,000
Puunui (C4)
Puuwai (A2) 185
Red Hill (mt.) (K2)
Roundtop (hill) (C4)
Salt (lake) (B3)
Sand (isl.) (E4)
Sand (isl.) (C4)
Sand (isl.) (E4)
Schofield Barracks (E2)
Seward Roads (channel) (D4)
South (Kalae) (cape) (G7)
Southeast Loch (inlet) (B3)
Spreckelsville (J1)*
Sugarloaf (hill) (C4)
Summer Camp (J6) 400
Tantalus (mt.) (D4)
Ulumahi (K2)
Ulupalakua (J2)
Umikoa (J4)
Upolu (point) (G3)
Wahiawa (E2)* 8,369
Waiahukini (G7) 175
Waiakea (J5) 5,000
Waiakoa (J2)* 517
Waialee (E1) 72
Waialua (E1)* 2,602
Waialua (H1)
Waialua Camp (E1)
Waianae (D2)* 1,000
Waianuenue (C1)
Waihee (J2) 600
Waikane (F2) 85
Waikapu (J2) 549
Waikii (H4)
Waikiki (C4)* 50
Waikiki (beach) (C4)
Wailau (H1) 300
Wailea (J4) 341
Wailua (D2)
Wailua (K2)
Wailuku (J2)* 7,424
Wailuku (river) (J5)
Wailupe (F2)
Waimanalo (F2)* 868
Waimanalo (bay) (F2)
Waimea (B2)* 1,648
Waimea (E1)
Waimea-Kamuela (H4)
Waimea (bay) (B2)
Waimea (river) (C2)
Waimea Camp (E1)
Wainiha (C1) 60
Wainiha (river) (C1)
Waiohinu (G7) 163
Waipahu (A3)* 7,169
Waipio (K2)
Waipio (H3) 95
Waipio (peninsula) (A3)
Waipio (point) (A4)
Welles (harbor) (D4)
West Loch (inlet) (A3)
Wood Valley Camp (H6)
Woodlawn (D4)

*Map on Page 57*

## IDAHO

*Total Population 588,637*

### 45 COUNTIES

Ada (B6) 70,649
Adams (B5) 3,347
Bannock (F7) 41,745
Bear Lake (G7) 6,834
Benewah (B2) 6,173
Bingham (F6) 23,271
Blaine (D6) 5,384
Boise (C6) 1,776
Bonner (B1) 14,853
Bonneville (G6) 30,210
Boundary (B1) 5,908
Butte (E6) 2,722
Camas (D6) 1,079
Canyon (B6) 53,597
Caribou (G7) 5,576
Cassia (E7) 14,629
Clark (F5) 918
Clearwater (C3) 8,217
Custer (D5) 3,318
Elmore (C6) 6,687
Franklin (G7) 9,867
Fremont (G5) 9,351
Gem (B6) 8,730
Gooding (D6) 11,101
Idaho (C4) 11,423
Jefferson (F6) 10,495
Jerome (D7) 12,080
Kootenai (B2) 24,947
Latah (B3) 20,971
Lemhi (D4) 6,278
Lewis (B3) 4,208
Lincoln (D6) 4,256
Madison (G6) 9,156
Minidoka (E7) 9,785
Nez Perce (B3) 22,658
Oneida (F7) 4,387
Owyhee (B7) 6,307
Payette (B5) 11,921
Power (F7) 3,988
Shoshone (B2) 22,806
Teton (G6) 3,204
Twin Falls (D7) 40,979
Valley (C5) 4,270
Washington (B5) 8,576
Yellowstone Nat'l. Park† (G5)

† Part. See also Wyoming and Montana.

### CITIES and TOWNS

Aberdeen (F7)* 1,486
Acequia (E7)* 125
Addie (B1)* 15
Ahsahka (B3)*
Alameda (F7)* 4,694
Albion (E7)* 610
Alexander (G7)*
Almo (E7)*
Alpha (C5)*
Alpine (G6)* 172
Alridge (G6)
American Falls (E7)* 1,874
Ammon (G6) 447
Amsterdam (D7)* 100
Arbon (F7)
Archer (G6) 400
Arco (E6)* 961
Arimo (F7)* 337
Ashton (G5)* 1,256
Athol (B2)* 226
Atlanta (C6)* 300
Atomic City (F6)* 500
Avery (C2)* 350
Avon (B3)* 6
Baker (E4)* 150
Bancroft (G7)* 495
Banida (G7)* 140
Banks (B5)*
Basalt (F6)* 227
Bayview (B2)* 150
Bear (B4)*
Bellevue (D6)* 528
Benewah (B2) 50
Bennett (C6) 10
Bennington (G7)* 200
Berger (D7)
Bern (G7)* 140
Big Creek (C4)* 24
Big Springs (G5)* 5
Blackfoot (F6)* 5,180
Blanchard (A1)* 200
Bliss (D7)* 126
Bloomington (G7)* 302
BOISE (B6)* 34,393
Boles (B4) 25
Bone (G6) 50
Bonners Ferry (B1)* 1,776
Bovill (B3)* 437
Bowmont (B6)*
Bridge (E7)*
Broten (B1)* 30
Bruneau (C7)* 100
Buhl (D7)* 2,870
Burgdorf (B4)
Burke (C2)* 800
Burley (E7)* 5,924
Burmah (D6)
Cabinet (B1)* 60
Calder (B2)* 65
Caldwell (B6)* 10,487
Camas (F5)* 40
Cambridge (B5)* 354
Cameron (B3)* 83
Canfield (B4)* 50
Carey (E6)* 1,100
Careywood (B1)* 50
Carmen (E4)*
Cascade (C5)* 943
Castleford (C7)* 500
Cavendish (B3)
Centerville (C6)* 25
Central (G7)* 120
Challis (D5)* 728
Chatcolet (B2) 92
Chester (G5)* 247
Chesterfield (F7)*
Chilco (B2)* 45
Chilly (E5)* 84
Chubbuck ‡(F7)* 120
Churchill (D7)
Clagstone (B1) 15
Clark Fork (B1)* 387
Clarkia (B2)* 150
Clarkville ‡(B2) 19
Clawson (G6) 34
Clayton (D5)* 75
Clearwater (C3)* 53
Clementsville (G6) 38
Cleveland (G7)* 135
Cliffs (B7) 32
Clifton (F7)* 201
Coeur D'Alene (B2)* 12,198
Colburn (B1)*
Conda (G7)* 330
Coolin (B1)*
Copeland (B1)* 11
Corral (D6)* 157
Cottonwood (B3)* 689
Council (B5)* 748
Craigmont (B3)* 594
Crouch (B5)* 60
Crystal (F7)
Culdesac (B3)* 175
Cuprum (B4)* 20
Dalby ‡(G6) 13
Darlington (E6)* 200
Dayton (F7)* 287
De Lamar (B6)
Deary (B3)* 320
Declo (E7)* 219
Dent (B3)*
Denver (B4) 29
Desmet (B2)*
Dietrich (D7)* 160
Dingle (G7)*
Dixie (C4)* 56
Donnelly (C5)* 595
Dover (B1)* 385
Downey (F7)* 748
Driggs (G6)* 941
Drummond (G5)* 59
Dubois (F5)* 430
Dudley (B2)*
Eagle (B6)* 500
East Hope (B1) 149
Eastport (B1)* 108
Eddiville‡ (B2) 10
Eden (D7)* 456
Edgemere (B1)* 96
Elba (E7)* 180
Elk City (C4)* 300
Elk River (B3)* 312
Ellis (D5)*
Elmira (B1)* 128
Emida (B2)* 125
Emmett (B6)* 3,067
Enaville (B2)* 60
Fairfield (D6)* 502
Fairview (G7) 398
Felt (G6)* 120
Fenn (B4)* 57
Ferdinand (B3)* 206
Fernwood (B2)* 200
Filer (D7)* 1,425
Firth (F6)* 293
Fish Haven (G7)*
Forest (B3)
Forney (D4)*
Fort Hall (F6)*
Franklin (G7)* 467
French Creek (B4) 65
Fruitland (B6)* 573
Fruitvale (B5)* 125
Gannett (D6)* 43
Garden City (B6) 764
Garden Valley (C5)* 210
Gardena (B5)*
Gardner (F6)
Gem (C2)* 500
Genesee (B3)* 552
Geneva (G7)*
Georgetown (G7)* 404
Gibbonsville (E4)* 200
Gibbs (B2)* 35
Gifford (B3)* 51
Gilmore (E5)* 50
Glengary (B1)
Glenns Ferry (C7)* 1,515
Goldburg (E5)
Golden (C4)* 100
Gooding (D7)* 3,099
Goodrich (B5)* 16
Grace (G7)* 761
Grainville (G5) 30
Grand View (B7)*
Grangemont (C3)* 130
Grangeville (B4)* 2,544
Granite (B1)* 150
Gray (G6)*
Greencreek (B3)* 51
Greenleaf (B6)*
Greer (B3)* 127
Grimes Pass (C5)
Grouse (E6)* 43
Hagerman (D7)* 520
Hailey (D6)* 1,464
Hamer (F6)*
Hammett (C7)* 350
Hansen (D7)* 463
Harpster (C4)*
Harrison (B2)* 322
Harvard (B3)* 102
Hauser (B2) 70
Hayden Lake (B2)* 39
Hazelton (E7)* 429
Headquarters (C3)* 300
Heath (B5) 15
Heglar (E7) 10
Heise (G6) 87
Henry (G7)*
Heyburn (E7)* 539
Hibbard (G6) 400
Hill City (D6)* 15
Holbrook (F7)*
Hollister (D7)* 80
Homedale (A6)* 1,411
Hope (B1)* 111
Horse Shoe Bend (B6)* 401
Howe (F6)* 200
Huetter (B2)* 84
Humphrey (F5)* 36
Idaho City (C6)* 246
Idaho Falls (F6)* 19,218
Indian Valley (B5)* 50
Inkom (F7)* 434
Iona (G6)* 502
Irwin (G6)* 147
Island Park (G5)*
Jerome (D7)* 4,523
Joseph (B4)* 23
Juliaetta (B3)* 365
Juniper (F7)
Kamiah (B3)* 812
Kellogg (B2)* 4,913
Kendrick (B3)* 409
Ketchum (D6)* 757
Keuterville (B3)* 25
Kilgore (G5)* 160
Kimberly (D7)* 1,347
King Hill (C6)*
Kingston (B2)*
Kooskia (C3)* 629
Kootenai (B1)* 199
Kuna (B6)* 534
Laclede (B1)* 200
Lago (G7)* 250
Lake (G5) 8
Lake Fork (B5)* 11
Lakeview (B2)
Lamont (G6)* 50
Lane (B2)*
Lapwai (B3)* 480
Lava Hot Springs (F7)* 591
Leadore (E5)* 159
Leesburg (D4)
Lemhi (E5)* 150
Leonia (B1)*
Leslie (E6)* 40
Letha (B6)* 376
Lewiston (A3)* 12,985
Lewisville (F6)*
Liberty (G7)
Lincoln (F6)
Lorenzo (G6)* 250
Lost River (E6) 37
Lowell (C3)
Lowman (C5)* 30
Lucile (B4)* 13
Lund (G7)* 103
Mackay (E6)* 760
Macks Inn (G5)* 100
Maland City (F7)* 2,715
Malta (E7)* 518
Marble Creek (C2) 6
Marsing (B6)* 643
Marysville (G5) 190
May (E5)* 75
Mayfield (B6)
Mc Call (C5)* 1,173
Mc Cammon (F7)* 578
Meadow Creek (B1) 15
Meadows (B5)* 190
Melba (B6)* 203
Melrose (B3) 5
Menan (F6)* 430
Meridian (B6)* 1,810
Mesa (B5)* 179
Middleton (B6)* 496
Midvale (B5)* 231
Milner (D7)
Minidoka (E7)* 113
Minkcreek (G7)* 124
Monteview (F6)*
Montour (B6)* 155
Montpelier (G7)* 2,682
Moore (E6)* 256
Moravia (B1)
Moreland (F6)* 250
Moscow (B3)* 10,593
Mountain Home (C6)* 1,887
Moyie Springs (B1)* 109
Muldoon (E6)*
Mullan (C2)* 2,036
Murphy (B6)* 37
Murray (C2)* 158
Murtaugh (D7)* 239
Myrtle (B3)* 20
Naf (E7)*
Nampa (B6)* 16,185
Naples (B1) 300
New Meadows (B4)* 621
New Plymouth (B6)* 942
Newdale (G6)* 312
Nezperce (B3)* 543
Nordman (B1)* 18
North Fork (D4)* 100
N. Pocatello (F7) 575
Norwood (C5)
Notus (B6)* 313
Nounan (G7)*
Oakley (D7)* 684
Obsidian (D6)* 11
Ola (B5)* 300
Oldtown (A1) 358
Onaway (B3) 81
Orchard (B6)*
Orchards (A3) 4,494
Oreana (B6)* 100
Orofino (B3)* 1,656
Orogrande (C4)* 12
Ovid (G7)* 200
Oxford (F7)* 110
Pardee (B3)
Paris (G7)* 774
Parker (G6)* 306
Parma (B6)* 1,369
Patterson (E5)* 112
Paul (E7)* 560
Payette (B5)* 4,032
Pearl (B6) 38
Peck (B3)* 170
Pegram (G7)* 75
Picabo (D6)* 100
Pierce (C3)* 544
Pine (C6)*
Pingree (F6)* 102
Pioneerville (C6) 8
Placerville (C6)* 17
Plano (G6) 403
Plummer (B2)* 395
Pocatello (F7)* 26,131
Polaris (B2)* 214
Pollock (B4)*
Ponderay (B1)* 248
Porthill (B1)* 68
Portneuf (F7) 65
Post Falls (A2)* 1,069
Potlatch (A3)* 1,024
Prairie (C6)* 150
Preston (G7)* 4,045
Prichard (B2) 40
Priest River (A1)* 1,592
Princeton (B3)* 84
Rathdrum (A2)* 610
Raymond (G7)* 88
Red River Hot Springs (C4) 12
Regena (C6)
Reno (F5)
Reubens (B3)* 116
Rexburg (G6)* 4,253
Richfield (D6)* 429
Riddle (B7)* 35
Rigby (G6)* 1,826
Riggins (B4)* 287
Ririe (G6)* 527
Riverside (F6)
Roberts (F6)* 341
Robin (F7)* 165
Rockford (F6)
Rockford Bay (B2)* 27
Rockland (F7)* 277
Rocky Bar (C6)
Rogerson (D7)* 75
Roseberry (C5)
Roselake (B2)* 212
Roswell (A6)* 92
Roy (F7)* 25
Rupert (E7)* 3,098
Sagle (B1)* 75
Saint Anthony (G6)* 2,695
St. Charles (G7)* 363
St. Joe (B2) 75
St. Maries (B2)* 2,220
Salmon (D4)* 2,648
Samaria (F7)*
Samuels (B1)*
Sanders (B2)* 25
Sandpoint (B1)* 4,265
Santa (B2)*
Shelley (F6)* 1,856
Shoshone (D7)* 1,420
Shoup (D4)*
Silver City (B6)
Small (F5)*
Smelterville (B2)* 76
Smiths Ferry (C5)*
Soda Springs (G7)* 1,329
Southwick (B3)* 200
Spencer (F5)* 70
Spirit Lake (A2)* 823
Springfield (F6)* 435
Springston (B2)* 57
Squirrel (G5)*
Stanley (D5)* 33
Star (B6)* 525
Starkey (B5) 3
State Line ‡(B2) 52
Sterling (F6)*
Stibnite (C5)* 717
Stites (C3)* 227
Stone (F7)* 170
Strevell (E7) 25
Sugar City (G6)* 684
Sun Valley (D6)* 428
Sunbeam (D5)* 6
Swan Valley (G6)* 203
Swanlake (F7)* 250
Sweet (B6)* 200
Sweetwater (B3)* 80
Taber (F6)
Tamarack (B5)*
Tendoy (E5)*
Tensed (B2)* 189
Terreton (F6)* 35
Teton (G6)* 463
Tetonia (G6)* 232
Thatcher (G7)* 50
Thornton (G6)* 300
Three Creek (C7) 65
Tindall (C7) 5
Treasureton (G7)
Triangle (B7)* 35
Triumph (D6)* 97
Troy (B3)* 531
Tuttle (D7)* 15
Twin Falls (D7)* 17,600
Twin Lakes (B2) 225
Twin Springs (C6)*
Tyhee (F7) 350
Ucon (F6)* 356
Ustick (B6)* 200
Vay (B1)* 80
Victor (G6)* 431
Viola (B3)* 150
Virginia (F7)* 245
Wallace (C2)* 3,140
Wapello (F6)
Wardner (B2)* 772
Warm Lake (C5)* 500
Warren (C4)* 30
Wayan (G7)*
Weippe (C3)* 1,000
Weiser (B5)* 3,961
Wendell (D7)* 1,483
Westlake (B3)* 35
Weston (F7)* 382
White Bird (B4)*
Wilder (A6)* 555
Wildhorse (B5)* 18
Winchester (B3)* 488
Winona (B3)
Winsper (F5) 62
Woodland (C3)*
Worley (B2)* 233
Yellow Pine (C4)* 35

*Map on Page 58*

## ILLINOIS

*Total Population 8,712,176*

### 102 COUNTIES

Adams (B4) 64,690
Alexander (D6) 20,316
Bond (D5) 14,157
Boone (E1) 17,070
Brown (C4) 7,132
Bureau (D2) 37,711
Calhoun (C4) 6,898
Carroll (D1) 18,976
Cass (C4) 15,097
Champaign (E3) 106,100
Christian (D4) 38,816
Clark (F4) 17,362
Clay (E5) 17,445
Clinton (D5) 22,594
Coles (E4) 40,328
Cook (F2) 4,508,792
Crawford (F4) 21,137
Cumberland (E4) 10,496
De Kalb (E2) 40,781
De Witt (E3) 16,894
Douglas (E4) 16,706
Du Page (E2) 154,599
Edgar (F4) 23,407
Edwards (E5) 9,056
Effingham (E4) 21,675
Fayette (D4) 24,582
Ford (E3) 15,901
Franklin (E5) 48,685
Fulton (C3) 43,716
Gallatin (E6) 9,818
Greene (C4) 18,852
Grundy (E2) 19,217
Hamilton (E5) 12,256
Hancock (B3) 25,790
Hardin (E6) 7,530
Henderson (C3) 8,416
Henry (C2) 46,492
Iroquois (F3) 32,348
Jackson (D6) 38,124
Jasper (E4) 12,266
Jefferson (E5) 35,892
Jersey (C4) 15,264
Jo Daviess (C1) 21,459
Johnson (E6) 8,729
Kane (E2) 150,388
Kankakee (F2) 73,524
Kendall (E2) 12,115
Knox (C3) 54,366
La Salle (E2) 100,610
Lake (E1) 179,097
Lawrence (F5) 20,539
Lee (D2) 36,451
Livingston (E3) 37,809
Logan (D3) 30,671
Macon (E4) 98,853
Macoupin (D4) 44,210
Madison (D5) 182,307
Marion (E5) 41,700
Marshall (D2) 13,025
Mason (D3) 15,326
Massac (E6) 13,594
Mc Donough (C3) 28,199
Mc Henry (E1) 50,656
Mc Lean (E3) 76,577
Menard (D3) 9,639
Mercer (C2) 17,374
Monroe (C5) 13,282
Montgomery (D4) 32,460
Morgan (C4) 35,568
Moultrie (E4) 13,171
Ogle (D1) 33,429
Peoria (D3) 174,347
Perry (D5) 21,684
Piatt (E4) 13,970
Pike (C4) 22,155
Pope (E6) 5,779
Pulaski (D6) 13,639
Putnam (D2) 4,746
Randolph (D5) 31,673
Richland (E5) 16,889
Rock Island (C2) 133,558
Saint Clair (D5) 205,995
Saline (E6) 33,420
Sangamon (D4) 131,484
Schuyler (C3) 9,613
Scott (C4) 7,245
Shelby (E4) 24,434
Stark (D2) 8,721
Stephenson (D1) 41,595
Tazewell (D3) 76,165
Union (D6) 20,500
Vermilion (F3) 87,079
Wabash (F5) 14,651
Warren (C3) 21,981
Washington (D5) 14,460
Wayne (E5) 20,933
White (E5) 20,935
Whiteside (D2) 49,336
Will (F2) 134,336
Williamson (E6) 48,621
Winnebago (D1) 152,385
Woodford (D3) 21,335

### CITIES and TOWNS

Abingdon (C3)* 3,300
Adair (C3)* 400
Addieville (D5)* 271
Addison (A2)* 813
Adeline (D1) 1,135
Adrian (B3)* 63
Akin (E6)*
Albany (C2)* 544
Albers (D5)* 365
Albion (E5)* 2,287
Alden (E1)* 200
Aledo (C2)* 2,919
Alexander (D4)* 350
Alexis (C2)* 821
Algonquin (E1)* 1,223
Alhambra (D5)* 476
Allendale (F5)* 442
Allenville (E4)* 253
Allerton (F4)* 244
Alma (E5)* 404
Alorton (B6) 2,547
Alpha (C2)* 630
Alsey (C4)* 294
Alsip (B2) 1,228
Altamont (E4)* 1,580
Alto Pass (D6)* 462
Alton (A6)* 32,550
Altona (C2)* 462
Alvin (F3)* 287
Amboy (D2)* 2,128
America (D6)
Anchor (E3)* 175
Ancona (E2)*
Andalusia (C2)* 510
Andover (C2)* 216
Anna (D6)* 4,380
Annapolis (F4)* 147
Annawan (D2)* 592
Antioch (E1)* 1,307
Apple River (C1)* 431
Arcola (E4)* 1,700
Arenzville (C4)* 513
Argenta (E4)* 575
Argo (B2)* 9,000
Arlington (D2)* 247
Arlington Hts. (A1)* 8,768
Armington (D3)* 314
Armstrong (F3)* 325
Aroma Park (F2)* 544
Arrowsmith (E3)* 316
Arthur (E4)* 1,573
Ashkum (E3)* 420
Ashland (C4)* 1,039

## Map on Page 59

## INDIANA

## Total Population 3,934,224

Vermillion (C5)..........19,723
Vigo (C6)..........105,160
Wabash (F3)..........29,047
Warren (C4)..........8,535
Warrick (C8)..........21,527
Washington (E7)..........16,520
Wayne (G5)..........68,566
Wells (G3)..........19,564
White (D3)..........18,042
Whitley (F2)..........18,828

**CITIES and TOWNS**

Abington (H5).......... 200
Aboite (G3).......... 50
Acton (E5)*..........
Adams (F6)*.......... 350
Adamsboro (E3).......... 150
Ade (C3).......... 90
Advance (D5)*.......... 413
Aix (C2)..........
Akron (E2)*.......... 946
Aladdin ‡(F4).......... 19
Alamo (C5)*.......... 163
Albany (G4)*..........1,846
Albion (G2)*..........1,341
Aldine (D2).......... 75
Alert (F6).......... 110
Alexandria (F4)*..........5,147
Alfordsville (C7)*.......... 101
Algiers (C7)*.......... 102
Alpine (G5)*.......... 55
Alquina (G5).......... 114
Alton (E8)*.......... 71
Altona (G2).......... 344
Alvarado (H1)..........
Ambia (C4)*.......... 356
Amboy (F3)*.......... 414
Americus (D3).......... 105
Amity (E6).......... 150
Amo (D5)*.......... 354
Anderson (F4)*..........46,820
Andersonville (G5).......... 250
Andrews (F3)*..........1,083
Angola (G1)*..........5,081
Anthony (G4).......... 50
Antiville (G3).......... 14
Apalona (D8)*.......... 14
Arba (H4).......... 84
Arcadia (E4)*..........1,073
Arcola (G2)*.......... 272
Ardmore (E1)..........
Argos (E2)*..........1,284
Ari (G2).......... 29
Arlington (F5)*.......... 430
Armstrong (B8)*.......... 155
Aroma (F4).......... 30
Arthur (C8).......... 225
Artic (H2).......... 50
Ash Grove (D3).......... 14
Ashboro (C6).......... 100
Asherville (C6)..........
Ashley (G1)*.......... 680
Athens (E2)*.......... 105
Atlanta (E4)*.......... 613
Attica (C4)*..........3,862
Atwood (F2)*.......... 300
Auburn (G2)*..........5,879
Augusta (C8).......... 117
Aurora (H6)*..........4,780
Austin (F7)*..........2,906
Avilla (G2)*.......... 660
Avoca (D7)*.......... 400
Azalia (F6).......... 100
Bacon (E8)..........
Bainbridge (D5)*.......... 455
Bakers Corner (E4).......... 75
Ballstown (G6).......... 3
Bandon (D8)*..........
Banquo (F3).......... 105
Bargersville (E5)*.......... 413
Bartonia (H4).......... 26
Bass (D2).......... 40
Batesville (G6)*..........3,194
Bath (H5)*.......... 95
Battle Ground (D3)*.......... 634
Bean Blossom (E6).......... 74
Bear Branch (G7).......... 120
Beard (E4).......... 20
Beardstown (D2).......... 50
Bedford (E7)*..........12,562
Beech Grove (E5)*..........5,685
Belle Union (D5).......... 75
Belleville (E5)..........
Bellmore (C5)*.......... 120
Belshaw (C2).......... 100
Bengal (F6).......... 35
Bennetts Switch (E3).......... 120
Bennington (G7)*.......... 50
Benton (F2)*.......... 225
Bentonville (G5)*.......... 77
Berne (H3)*..........2,277
Bethlehem (G7)*.......... 200
Beverly Shores (C1)*.......... 488
Bicknell (C7)*..........4,572
Billingsville (H5).......... 35
Bippus (F3)*.......... 200
Birdseye (D8)*.......... 354
Blackhawk (C6).......... 100
Blackoak (C1)..........
Blaine (G4).......... 25
Blairville (B8)..........
Blanford (B5)*.......... 750
Blocher (F7)*.......... 250
Bloomfield (D6)*..........2,086
Blooming Grove (G5).......... 105
Bloomingdale (C5)*.......... 434
Bloomingport (G5).......... 60
Bloomington (D6)*..........28,163
Blountsville (G4)*.......... 229
Blue Ridge (F5).......... 100
Bluegrass (E3).......... 50
Bluffton (G3)*..........6,076
Boggstown (F5)*.......... 149
Bono (E7).......... 25
Boone Grove (C2)*.......... 170
Boonville (C8)*..........5,092
Borden (F8)*.......... 426
Boston (H5)*.......... 257
Boswell (C3)*.......... 963
Boundary (H4).......... 35
Bourbon (E2)*..........1,404
Bowers (D4).......... 25
Bowling Green (D6)*.......... 235
Boyleston (E4).......... 100
Bracken (F3).......... 9
Bradford (E8)*.......... 119
Branchville (D8)*.......... 75
Brazil (C5)*..........8,434
Bremen (E2)*..........2,664
Brems (D2).......... 112
Brewersville (F6).......... 62
Brice (H4).......... 12
Bridgeport (E5)*.......... 500
Bridgeton (C5)*.......... 350
Bright (H6).......... 275
Brighton (G1).......... 100
Brimfield (G2)*.......... 210
Brinckley (G4)..........
Bringhurst (E3)*.......... 253
Bristol (F1)*.......... 738
Bristow (D8)*..........
Bromer (E7).......... 75
Bronson (Losantville*) (G4).......... 247
Brook (C3)*.......... 915
Brooklyn (E5)*.......... 592
Brooksburg (G7)*.......... 132
Brookston (D3)*..........1,014
Brookville (G6)*..........2,538
Browns Corner (F3).......... 35
Browns Valley (D5).......... 125
Brownsburg (E5)*..........1,578
Brownstown (F7)*..........1,998
Brownsville (H5)*.......... 275
Bruceville (C7)*.......... 800
Brunswick (B2).......... 150
Brushy Prairie (G1).......... 100
Bryant (G3)*.......... 339
Bryantsburg (G7).......... 35
Buck Creek (D4)*.......... 279
Buckeye (G3).......... 25
Buckskin (C8)*.......... 250
Bud (E6)*.......... 10
Buena Vista (G6)..........
Buffalo (D3)*.......... 135
Buffaloville (D8)*..........
Bullock (C9).......... 39
Bunker Hill (B7).......... 25
Bunker Hill (E3)*.......... 659
Burdick (D1)..........
Burket (F2)*.......... 217
Burlington (E4)*.......... 600
Burnettsville (D3)*.......... 457
Burney (F6)*.......... 232
Burns City (D7)*.......... 242
Burnsville (F6)..........
Burr Oak (E2)*.......... 120
Burrows (E3)*.......... 350
Butler (H2)*..........1,914
Butlerville (F6)*.......... 306
Byron (C5).......... 50
Caborn (B9).......... 50
Cadiz (G5).......... 222
Cale (D7).......... 60
Calvertsville (D6).......... 20
Cambria (D4).......... 70
Cambridge City (G5)*..........2,559
Camden (D3)*.......... 600
Cammack (G4).......... 200
Campbellsburg (E7)*.......... 637
Canaan (G7)*.......... 270
Cannelburg (C7)*.......... 128
Cannelton (D9)*..........2,027
Canton (E7).......... 125
Cape Sandy (E8)*..........
Carbon (C5)*.......... 480
Carlisle (C7)*.......... 767
Carlos (G4)*.......... 120
Carmel (E5)*..........1,009
Carp (D6).......... 30
Carpentersville (D5).......... 80
Cartersburg (E5)*.......... 260
Carthage (F5)*..........1,065
Cass (C6)*..........
Cassville (E3).......... 100
Castleton (E5)*.......... 268
Cataract (D6).......... 46
Cates (C4)*.......... 150
Catlin (C5)*..........
Cato (C8)..........
Cayuga (C5)*..........1,022
Cedar Grove (H6)*.......... 193
Cedar Lake (C2)*..........3,907
Cedarville (G2).......... 220
Celestine (D8)*.......... 200
Centenary (B5).......... 200
Center (E4)*.......... 275
Center Square (H7).......... 55
Centerpoint (C6)*.......... 297
Centerton (E5)*.......... 125
Centerville (H5)*..........1,386
Central (E8)*.......... 40
Chalmers (D3)*.......... 508
Chambersburg (E7).......... 200
Chandler (C8)*..........1,050
Chapel Hill (E6).......... 6
Charlestown (F8)*..........4,785
Charlottesville (F5)*.......... 400
Chase (C3).......... 40
Chelsea (F7).......... 35
Cherry Grove (D4).......... 15
Chester (H5).......... 102
Chesterfield (F4)*..........1,086
Chesterton (D1)*..........3,175
Chili (F3)*.......... 115
Chrisney (C8)*.......... 439
Churubusco (G2)*..........1,232
Cicero (E4)*..........1,021
Clare (F4).......... 75
Clarks Hill (D4)*.......... 493
Clarksburg (G6)*.......... 325
Clarksville (F5).......... 117
Clarksville (F8)*..........5,905
Clay City (C6)*..........1,068
Claypool (F2)*.......... 416
Claysburg (F8)..........
Clayton (D5)*.......... 598
Clear Creek (E6)*.......... 450
Clear Lake (H1).......... 151
Clear Springs (E7).......... 205
Clermont (E5)*.......... 824
Clifford (F6)*.......... 232
Clifty (F6)*.......... 175
Clinton (C5)*..........6,462
Cloverdale (D5)*.......... 649
Cloverland (C6).......... 150
Clymers (E3).......... 150
Coal Bluff (C5)*.......... 128
Coal City (D6)*.......... 300
Coal Creek (C4).......... 75
Coalmont (C6)*.......... 595
Coatesville (D5)*.......... 444
Coe (C8)..........
Coesse (G2)*.......... 150
Colburn (D3)*.......... 234
Colfax (D4)*.......... 75
Collamer (F2).......... 50
Collegeville (C3)*.......... 600
Collett (H4).......... 30
Collins (G2)..........
Columbia City (G2)*..........4,745
Columbus (E6)*..........18,370
Commiskey (F7)*.......... 100
Concord (H2)..........
Connersville (G5)*..........15,550
Conroe (D4)..........
Converse (F3)*.......... 979
Cook (C2).......... 350
Cope (E6).......... 50
Corning (D7).......... 49
Correct (G7).......... 150
Cortland (F7)*.......... 102
Corunna (G2)*.......... 338
Cory (C6)*.......... 250
Corydon (E8)*..........1,944
Cosperville (F1).......... 45
Cottage Grove (H5)*.......... 100
Covington (C4)*..........2,235
Cowan (G4)*.......... 400
Coxville (C5).......... 56
Craigville (G3)*..........
Crandall (E8)*.......... 149
Crane (D4).......... 21
Crane (D7)*..........2,000
Crawfordsville (D4)*..........12,851
Cresco (F2)..........
Creston (C2)*.......... 110
Crete (H4).......... 25
Crisman (C1).......... 300
Crocker (C1).......... 150
Cromwell (F2)*.......... 449
Crooked Creek (G1)..........
Cross Plains (G7)*.......... 150
Crothersville (F7)*..........1,276
Crown Center (D5)..........
Crown Point (C2)*..........5,839
Crows Nest ‡(E5).......... 86
Crumstown (E1).......... 200
Crystal (D8).......... 61
Cuba (D6).......... 17
Culver (E2)*..........1,563
Cumback (C7).......... 50
Cumberland (F5)*.......... 550
Curtisville (F4)*.......... 122
Cutler (D4)*.......... 165
Cuzco (D8)*.......... 55
Cyclone (E4).......... 70
Cynthiana (B8)*.......... 591
Cypress (B9)..........
Dabney (G6).......... 50
Dale (D8)*.......... 850
Daleville (F4)*..........
Dana (C5)*.......... 854
Danville (D5)*..........2,802
Darlington (D4)*.......... 711
Daylight (B8)..........
Dayton (D4)*.......... 650
Decatur (H3)*..........7,271
Decker (B7)*.......... 386
Deedsville (E3)*.......... 150
Deer Creek (E3).......... 120
Deerfield (H4).......... 100
Delaware (G6).......... 229
Delong (E2)*.......... 150
Delphi (D3)*..........2,530
Demotte (C2)*.......... 700
Denham (D2)*.......... 150
Denver (E3)*.......... 528
Depauw (E8)*.......... 155
Deputy (F7)*.......... 250
Derby (D8)*.......... 73
Desoto (G4)*.......... 205
Dexter (E8).......... 1
Diamond (C5)..........
Dillman (G3).......... 30
Dillsboro (G6)*.......... 681
Disko (E2)*.......... 150
Doans (D7)*.......... 30
Dolan (E6).......... 24
Domestic (G3).......... 26
Donaldson (E2)*..........
Doolittle Mills (D8)*..........
Dora (F3).......... 80
Dover (H6).......... 100
Dover Hill (D7).......... 150
Downey's Corner (H7).......... 25
Dublin (G5)*.......... 993
Dubois (D8)*.......... 451
Dudleytown (F7).......... 65
Duff (C8).......... 68
Dugger (C6)*..........1,204
Dundee (F4).......... 56
Dune Acres (C1).......... 86
Dunfee (G2).......... 45
Dunkirk (G4)*..........3,048
Dunlap (F1)..........1,154
Dunnington (C3).......... 20
Dunreith (G5)*.......... 196
Dupont (G7)*..........
Durbin (F4).......... 24
Dyer (C1)*..........1,556
Eagletown (E4).......... 100
Earl Park (C3)*.......... 488
East Chicago (C1)*..........54,263
East Columbus (F6)..........
East Enterprise (H7)*.......... 125
East Gary (C1)*..........5,635
East Germantown (Pershing*) (G5).......... 389
Eaton (G4)*..........1,598
Eby (C8).......... 26
Eckerty (D8)*.......... 180
Economy (G5)*.......... 285
Eden (F5).......... 94
Edgerton (H2)*.......... 112
Edgewood (F4).......... 796
Edinburg (E6)*..........3,283
Edwardsport (C7)*.......... 850
Edwardsville (F8).......... 120
Effner (C3).......... 50
Ege (G2).......... 50
Ekin (E4).......... 50
Elberfeld (C8)*.......... 499
Elizabeth (F8)*.......... 211
Elizabethtown (F6)*.......... 323
Elizaville (E4).......... 51
Elkhart (F1)*..........35,556
Elkinsville (E6).......... 25
Ellettsville (D6)*.......... 855
Elmdale (D4).......... 75
Elnora (C7)*.......... 849
Elon (D8)..........
Elrod (G6).......... 66
Elston (D4).......... 40
Elwood (F4)*..........11,362
Eminence (D5)*.......... 175
Emison (C7)*.......... 90
Emma (F1).......... 50
Emporia (F5).......... 65
English (E8)*.......... 839
English Lake (D2)*.......... 148
Enochsburg (G6).......... 40
Enos (C2).......... 25
Epsom (C7).......... 125
Ethel (E8).......... 10
Etna (F2)..........
Etna Green (E2)*.......... 444
Eugene (B5).......... 350
Eureka (C9).......... 75
Evans Landing (F8)..........
Evanston (D8)*.......... 39
Evansville (C9)*..........128,636
Evansville (urban area)..........133,200
Everton (G5)..........
Fair Oaks (C2)*.......... 200
Fairbanks (B6)*..........
Fairland (F5)*.......... 750
Fairmount (F4)*..........2,646
Fairview (G4).......... 52
Fairview (G7).......... 54
Fairview Park (C5).......... 902
Falmouth (G5)*.......... 200
Farlen (D7).......... 7
Farmers Retreat (G7).......... 70
Farmersburg (C6)*..........1,024
Farmland (C4)*.......... 943
Fayette (E5).......... 98
Fayetteville (D7).......... 50
Fenns (F6).......... 40
Ferdinand (D8)*..........1,252
Ferndale (C5).......... 15
Fiat (G3).......... 50
Fickle (D4).......... 10
Fillmore (D5)*.......... 375
Fincastle (D5).......... 75
Finly (F5)*..........
Fishers (E5)*.......... 219
Fishersburg (F4).......... 130
Flat Rock (F6)*.......... 196
Flint (G1).......... 100
Flora (E3)*..........1,657
Florence (H7)*..........
Florida (F4).......... 100
Floyds Knobs (F8)*.......... 455
Folsomville (C8)*..........
Fontanet (C5)*..........
Foraker (F1)*.......... 144
Foresman (C3).......... 90
Forest (E4)*.......... 400
Forest Hill (F6).......... 75
Fort Branch (B8)*..........1,944
Fort Ritner (E7)*.......... 150
Fort Wayne (G2)*..........133,607
Fort Wayne (urban area)..........139,529
Fortville (F5)*..........1,786
Foster (C4).......... 25
Fountain (C4).......... 50
Fountain City (H5)*.......... 588
Fountaintown (F5)*.......... 250
Fowler (C3)*..........2,117
Fowlerton (F4)*.......... 292
Francesville (D3)*.......... 856
Francisco (B8)*.......... 606
Frankfort (E4)*..........15,028
Franklin (E6)*..........7,316
Frankton (F4)*..........1,047
Fredericksburg (E8)*.......... 211
Fredonia (E8)*..........
Free (C3).......... 4
Freedom (D6)*.......... 175
Freeland Park (C3)*.......... 94
Freelandville (C7)*.......... 789
Freeman (D6).......... 28
Freeport (F5).......... 60
Freetown (E7)*.......... 500
Fremont (H1)*.......... 947
French (H6).......... 75
French Lick (D7)*..........1,946
Friendship (G7)*.......... 130
Friendswood (E5).......... 115
Fritchton (C7).......... 125
Fulda (D8)*.......... 100
Fulton (E3)*.......... 366
Galena (F8).......... 207
Galveston (E3)*.......... 905
Garrett (G2)*..........4,291
Gary (C1)*..........133,911
Gas City (F4)*..........3,787
Gaston (G4)*.......... 729
Gatchel (D8).......... 20
Geetingsville (D4).......... 25
Gem (F5)..........
Geneva (H3)*.......... 999
Gentryville (C8)*.......... 234
Georgetown (F8)*.......... 449
Georgia (D7).......... 10
Gerald (D9)*..........
Gessie (C4)*.......... 115
Gifford (D2).......... 43
Gilead (E3).......... 75
Gilman (F4).......... 12
Gimco City ‡(F4).......... 13
Gings (G5).......... 45
Glendale (C7).......... 150
Glenn (C6).......... 75
Glenwood (G5)*.......... 412
Glezen (C8)*.......... 400
Glidas (E8).......... 10
Gnaw Bone (E6).......... 2
Goblesville (G3).......... 57
Goldsmith (E4)*.......... 242
Goodland (C3)*..........1,218
Goshen (F1)*..........13,003
Gosport (D6)*.......... 672
Grabill (H2)*.......... 370
Grafton (B9).......... 50
Grammer (F6)*.......... 125
Grand View (C9)*.......... 664
Granger (E1)*.......... 160
Grantsburg (E8)*.......... 90
Grasscreek (E3)*.......... 105
Gravelton (F2).......... 40
Graysville (B6)*.......... 100
Green Center (G2).......... 20
Green Hill (C4).......... 50
Green Oak (E2).......... 4
Greencastle (D5)*..........6,888
Greendale (H6)*..........2,018
Greenfield (F5)*..........6,159
Greenfield Mills (G1).......... 25
Greens Fork (H5)*.......... 413
Greensboro (G5)*.......... 241
Greensburg (G6)*..........6,599
Greentown (E4)*..........1,160
Greenville (F8)*.......... 298
Greenwood (E5)*..........3,066
Griffin (B8)*.......... 249
Griffith (C1)*..........4,470
Groveland (D5).......... 30
Grovertown (D2)*.......... 200
Groves (G5)..........
Guilford (H6)*.......... 300
Guion (C5).......... 14
Guthrie (D7)..........
Gwynneville (F5)*.......... 244
Hackleman (F4).......... 30
Hadley (D5).......... 50
Hagerstown (G5)*..........1,694
Hall (E5)*.......... 125
Hamilton (H1)*.......... 376
Hamlet (D2)*.......... 659
Hammond (B1)*..........87,594
Hancock (E8).......... 50
Hanna (D2)*.......... 450
Hanover (F7)*..........1,060
Hardinsburg (E8)*.......... 247
Harlan (H2)*.......... 500
Harmony (C5)*.......... 650
Harrisburg (G5)..........
Harrisville (H4).......... 83
Harrodsburg (D6)*.......... 400
Hartford City (G4)*..........7,253
Hartsville (F6)*.......... 340
Hastings (F2).......... 35
Hatfield (C9)*..........
Haubstadt (B8)*.......... 894
Hayden (F7)*.......... 200
Haymond (G6).......... 20
Haysville (D8).......... 352
Hazelrigg (D4).......... 45
Hazelwood (D5)..........
Hazleton (B8)*.......... 498
Headlee (D3).......... 69
Heath (D4).......... 12
Hebron (C2)*..........1,010
Hedrick (C4)*.......... 68
Heilman (C8).......... 100
Helmer (G1)*.......... 110
Helmsburg (E6)*.......... 150
Heltonville (E7)*.......... 500
Hemlock (F4)*.......... 177
Henderson (F5).......... 68
Henryville (F7)*..........
Herbst (F3)*.......... 250
Hibbard (E2)*.......... 100
Highland (B1)*..........5,878
Highwoods ‡(F5).......... 40
Hillham (D7)..........
Hillisburg (E4)*.......... 225
Hillsboro (C4)*.......... 526
Hillsdale (C5)*.......... 250
Hoagland (H3)*.......... 375
Hobart (C1)*..........10,244
Hobbieville (D6).......... 125
Hobbs (F4)*.......... 185
Holland (C8)*.......... 501
Hollandsburg (C5).......... 25
Holton (G6)*.......... 400
Home Corner (Vet's Adm. Hosp.*) (F3)..........3,950
Homer (F5)*.......... 105
Homestead (H6)..........
Honey Creek (F4)*.......... 125
Hoover (E3).......... 75
Hope (F6)*..........1,215
Hortonville (E4).......... 125
Houston (E6).......... 75
Howe (G1)*.......... 576
Howesville (C6).......... 75
Hudson (G1)*.......... 420
Hudsonville (C7).......... 76
Huntertown (G2)*.......... 500
Huntingburg (D8)*..........4,056
Huntington (G3)*..........15,079
Huntsville (G4).......... 50
Huntsville (F4).......... 265
Hurlburt (C2).......... 18
Huron (D7)*..........
Hymera (C6)*..........1,069
Idaville (D3)*.......... 500
Independence (C4).......... 200
Indian Springs (D7)*.......... 115
Indian Village (E1).......... 57
INDIANAPOLIS (E5)*..........427,173
Indianapolis (urban area)..........499,799
Ingalls (F5)*.......... 666
Inglefield (B8)*.......... 100
Inwood (E2)*.......... 178
Ireland (C8)*.......... 325
Jacksonburg (G5).......... 94
Jalapa (F3).......... 150
Jamestown (D5)*.......... 718
Jasonville (C6)*..........2,937
Jasper (D8)*..........5,215
Jefferson (D4).......... 90
Jeffersonville (F8)*..........14,685
Jessup (C5).......... 67
Jimtown (E1).......... 200
Johnson (B8).......... 250
Jolietville (E4).......... 125
Jonesboro (F4)*..........1,973
Jonesville (F6)*.......... 225
Judson (C5)*.......... 96
Judyville (C4)*.......... 90
Keller (C6).......... 25
Kempton (E4)*.......... 438
Kendallville (G2)*..........6,119
Kennard (G5)*.......... 485
Kenneth (E3).......... 40
Kent (F7)*.......... 123
Kentland (C3)*..........1,633
Kersey (C2)*.......... 100
Kewanna (E2)*.......... 680
Keystone (G3)*.......... 225
Kimmell (F2)*.......... 300
Kingman (C5)*.......... 509
Kingsbury (D1)*.......... 281
Kingsford Heights (D2)*..........1,104
Kingston (G6).......... 50
Kirklin (E4)*.......... 734
Kirkpatrick (D4).......... 60
Kirksville (D6)..........
Kitchel (H5)*.......... 60
Knightstown (F5)*..........2,486
Knightsville (C5)*.......... 768
Kniman (C2).......... 150
Knox (D2)*..........3,034
Kokomo (E4)*..........38,672
Koleen (D7)*..........
Kountz Lake (D2)..........1,200
Kossuth (E7).......... 50
Kouts (C2)*.......... 718
Kramer (C4)*..........
Kurtz (E7)*.......... 225
Kyana (D8)*..........
La Crosse (D2)*.......... 618
La Fontaine (F3)*.......... 627
La Porte (D1)*..........20,414
Laconia (E8)*.......... 82
Ladoga (D5)*.......... 912
Lafayette (D4)*..........35,568
Lagrange (F1)*..........1,892
Lagro (F3)*.......... 545
Lake Bruce (E2).......... 100
Lake Cicott (D3)*.......... 128
Lake James (H1)*..........
Lake Village (C2)*..........
Lakeland (D1)..........2,172
Lakeside (D3).......... 10
Laketon (F3)*..........
Lakeville (E1)*.......... 736
Lamar (D8)*.......... 99
Lamb (G7).......... 35
Lancaster (F7).......... 50
Landess (F3)*.......... 135
Lanesville (E8)*.......... 314
Laotto (G2)*.......... 264
Lapaz (E2)*.......... 512
Lapel (F4)*..........1,389
Larwill (F2)*.......... 316
Laud (G2)..........
Lauer (D9)..........
Laughery (H7)..........
Laurel (G6)*.......... 680
Lawrence (E5)..........1,951
Lawrenceburg (H6)*..........4,806
Lawrenceport (D7).......... 125
Lawrenceville (H6).......... 50
Lawton (D2).......... 20
Leavenworth (E8)*.......... 358
Lebanon (D4)*..........7,631
Lee (D3)..........
Leesburg (F2)*.......... 428
Leesville (E7).......... 75
Leipsic (E7)*.......... 150
Leisure (F4).......... 20
Leiters Ford (E2)*.......... 250
Lena (C5).......... 75
Leo (G2).......... 385
Leopold (D8)*.......... 101
Leota (F7).......... 35
Leroy (C2)*.......... 350
Letts (F6)*.......... 208
Lewis (C6)*.......... 600
Lewis Creek (F6).......... 62
Lewisville (G5)*.......... 591
Lexington (F7)*.......... 350
Liberty (H5)*..........1,730
Liberty Center (G3)*.......... 300
Liberty Mills (F2)*.......... 200
Ligonier (F2)*..........2,375
Limedale (D5)..........
Lincoln (E3)*.......... 130
Lincoln City (C8)*..........
Lincolnville (F3).......... 200
Linden (D4)*.......... 590
Linngrove (H3)*..........
Linnsburg (D5).......... 75
Linton (C6)*..........5,973
Linwood (F4).......... 72
Lisbon (G2).......... 67
Little York (F7)*.......... 146
Livonia (E7).......... 185
Lizton (D5)*.......... 276
Lochiel (C3).......... 38
Locust Point (F8)*.......... 18
Logan (H6).......... 125
Logansport (E3)*..........21,031
London (F5)*.......... 135
Long Beach (D1)..........1,103
Loogootee (D7)*..........2,424
Lookout (G6).......... 16
Losantville (G4)*.......... 247
Lovett (F7).......... 52
Lowell (C2)*..........1,621
Lucerne (E3)*.......... 200
Luther (F2).......... 6
Lydick (E1)..........1,175
Lyford (C5).......... 368
Lynhurst ‡(E5).......... 160
Lynn (H4)*..........1,149
Lynnville (C8)*.......... 404
Lyons (C7)*.......... 695
Mace (D4).......... 90
Mackey (C8)*.......... 170
Macy (E3)*.......... 288
Madison (G7)*..........7,506
Magley (G3).......... 50
Magnet (D8)*.......... 73
Mahalasville (E6).......... 75
Majenica (F3.......... 97
Malden (C2).......... 50
Manchester (H6).......... 3

Manhattan (D5)..........
Manilla (F5)*.......... 400
Mansfield (C5).......... 35
Manson (D4).......... 65
Maples (H2).......... 110
Marco (C7)*.......... 195
Marengo (E8)*.......... 801
Mariah Hill (D8)*..........
Marietta (F6).......... 150
Marion (F3)*..........30,081
Markland (G7).......... 200
Markle (G3)*.......... 733
Markleville (F5)*.......... 314
Marshall (C5)*.......... 326
Marshfield (C4)*.......... 100
Martinsburg (E8).......... 125
Martinsville (D6)*..........5,991
Marysville (F7)*.......... 98
Matthews (F4)*.......... 501
Mauckport (E8)*.......... 154
Maumee (E6).......... 25
Maxinkuckee (E2).......... 75
Maxwell (F5)*.......... 285
Mays (G5)*.......... 200
Maywood (E5)*.......... 525
Mc Cool (C1)*.......... 250
Mc Cordsville (F5)*.......... 735
Mc Coysburg (C3)..........
Mc Grawsville (E3).......... 50
Mc Natts (G3).......... 25
Mecca (C5)*..........
Mechanicsburg (G5).......... 250
Medaryville (D2)*.......... 833
Medora (E7)*.......... 627
Mellott (C4)*.......... 266
Memphis (F8)*.......... 380
Mentone (E2)*.......... 798
Merom (B6)*.......... 374
Merriam (G2).......... 110
Merrillville (C2)..........1,400
Metamora (G6)*.......... 400
Metea (E3).......... 45
Metz (H1)*.......... 175
Mexico (E3)*.......... 521
Miami (E3)*..........
Michigan City (C1)*..........28,395
Michigantown (E4)*.......... 443
Middlebury (F1)*.......... 839
Middlefork (E4).......... 62
Middletown (F4)*..........1,731
Midland (C6)*..........
Midway (C8).......... 20
Mier (F3).......... 63
Milan (G6)*..........1,014
Milford (F2)*.......... 952
Milford (Clifty*) (F6).......... 175
Mill Creek (D1)*.......... 162
Millersburg (C8)..........
Millersburg (F1)*.......... 437
Millgrove (G4)*.......... 160
Millhousen (G6)*.......... 184
Milligan (C5)*.......... 100
Milltown (E8)*.......... 760
Millville (G5).......... 120
Milo (G3)..........
Milroy (G6)*.......... 800
Milton (G5)*.......... 752
Mineral (D7).......... 55
Mishawaka (E1)*..........32,913
Mitchell (E7)*..........3,245
Modoc (G4)*.......... 275
Mohawk (F5)*.......... 150
Mongo (G1)*.......... 225
Monitor (D4).......... 50
Monmouth (H3).......... 100
Monon (D3)*..........1,439
Monroe (H3)*.......... 428
Monroe City (C7)*.......... 453
Monroeville (H3)*..........1,150
Monrovia (E5)*.......... 375
Monterey (D2)*.......... 250
Montezuma (C5)*..........1,220
Montgomery (C7)*.......... 538
Monticello (D3)*..........3,467
Montmorenci (D4)*.......... 235
Montpelier (G3)*..........1,826
Moody (C3)..........
Moore (H2).......... 30
Moorefield (G7)..........
Mooreland (G5)*.......... 497
Moores Hill (G6)*.......... 445
Mooresville (E5)*..........2,264
Moran (D4)*.......... 140
Morgantown (E6)*.......... 838
Morocco (C3)*..........1,141
Morris (G6)*.......... 500
Morristown (F5)*.......... 679
Morton (D5)..........
Moscow (F6)..........
Mount Auburn ‡(G5).......... 164
Mt. Ayr (C3)*.......... 222
Mt. Carmel (H6).......... 134
Mt. Comfort (F5)*.......... 115
Mt. Etna (F3).......... 171
Mt. Meridian (D5)..........
Mt. Pisgah (G1).......... 54
Mt. Pleasant (D8)*.......... 24
Mt. Sterling (G7).......... 40
Mt. Summit (G4)*.......... 295
Mt. Vernon (B9)*..........6,150
Mt. Zion (G3).......... 30
Mulberry (D4)*.......... 950
Muncie (G4)*..........58,479
Munster (B1)*..........4,753
Murray (G3).......... 94
Nabb (F7)*.......... 110
Napoleon (G6)*.......... 350
Nappanee (F2)*..........3,393
Nashville (E6)*.......... 526
Nead (E3).......... 48
Nebraska (F6)*.......... 104
Needham (E5)*.......... 110
Needmore (E7).......... 150
Nevada (F4).......... 45
Nevada Mills (G1).......... 75
New Albany (F8)*..........29,436
New Amsterdam (E8).......... 76
New Augusta (E5)*.......... 225
New Bellsville (E6).......... 20
New Burlington (G4).......... 100
New Carlisle (E1)*.......... 983
New Castle (G5)*..........18,271
New Chicago (C1).......... 921
New Corydon (H3)*.......... 105
New Goshen (B5)*.......... 600
New Harmony (B8)*..........1,360
New Haven (H2)*..........2,336
New Holland (F3).......... 20
New Hope (D6).......... 11
New Lebanon (C6)*.......... 125
New Lisbon (G5)*.......... 290
New London (E4).......... 210
New Marion (G6).......... 150
New Market (D5)*.......... 370
New Middletown (E8)*.......... 153
New Mt. Pleasant (G4).......... 100
New Palestine (F5)*.......... 504
New Paris (F2)*.......... 985
New Pekin (F7).......... 543
New Philadelphia (F7)*
New Point (G6)*.......... 322
New Providence (Borden*) (F8).......... 426
New Richmond (D4)*.......... 391
New Ross (D5)*.......... 336
New Salem (G5).......... 206
New Salisbury (E8)*.......... 215
New Trenton (H6)*.......... 150
New Washington (F7)*.......... 750
New Waverly (E3)*.......... 190
New Winchester (D5).......... 75
Newbern (F6)..........
Newberry (C7)*.......... 340
Newburgh (C9)*..........1,324
Newland (C2)..........
Newport (C5)*.......... 660
Newton Stewart (D8)*.......... 40
Newtonville (D8)*.......... 123
Newtown (C4)*.......... 287
Newville (H2).......... 75
Nineveh (E6)*.......... 300
Noblesville (F4)*..........6,567
Norman (E7)*.......... 110
Norristown (F6).......... 75
North Grove (F3).......... 126
N. Hayden (B2).......... 150
N. Judson (D2)*..........1,705
N. Liberty (E1)*..........1,165
N. Madison (G7)*.......... 715
N. Manchester (F3)*..........3,977
N. Salem (D5)*.......... 544
N. Terre Haute (C5)*..........
N. Vernon (F6)*..........3,488
N. Webster (F2)*.......... 487
Norway (D3)..........
Notre Dame (E1)*..........5,000
Nulltown (G5)..........
Oak (D3)*.......... 150
Oak Forest (G6).......... 120
Oakford (E4)*.......... 230
Oakland City (C8)*..........3,539
Oaklandon (E5)*.......... 346
Oaktown (C7)*.......... 763
Oakville (G4)*.......... 224
Oatsville (C8).......... 100
Obed (D2)*.......... 100
Ockley (D4)*.......... 140
Odell (C4).......... 210
Odon (C7)*..........1,177
Ogden Dunes (C1).......... 429
Oldenburg (G6)*.......... 591
Olean (G7).......... 225
Oliver (B8)..........
Omega (F4).......... 50
Ontario (G1).......... 150
Onward (E3)*.......... 140
Oolitic (E7)*..........1,125
Ora (D2)*.......... 140
Orange (G5).......... 200
Orangeville (D7).......... 85
Orestes (F4)*.......... 482
Orland (G1)*.......... 386
Orleans (D7)*..........1,531
Osceola (E1)*..........1,091
Osgood (G6)*..........1,228
Ossian (G3)*.......... 761
Oswego (F2)..........
Otis (D1)*..........
Otisco (F7)*.......... 250
Otterbein (C4)*.......... 641
Otto (G7)..........
Otwell (C8)*.......... 400
Owensburg (D7)*.......... 400
Owensville (B8)*..........1,110
Oxford (C3)*.......... 888
Packertown (F2).......... 72
Palestine (F2).......... 90
Palmer (C2).......... 200
Palmyra (E8)*.......... 327
Paoli (E7)*..........2,575
Paragon (D6)*.......... 463
Paris Crossing (F7)*.......... 132
Parker (G4)*.......... 915
Parkersburg (D5).......... 100
Parr (C2)*.......... 132
Patoka (B8)*.......... 626
Patricksburg (D6)*.......... 450
Patriot (H7)*.......... 315
Patronville (C9).......... 30
Paxton (C6)*.......... 275
Paynesville (F7).......... 50
Peabody (G2)..........
Pekin (E7)*.......... 553
Pelzer (C8).......... 49
Pence (C4)*.......... 122
Pendleton (F5)*..........2,082
Pennville (G4)*.......... 626
Peoga (E6).......... 48
Percy Junction (C3).......... 4
Perkinsville (F4).......... 250
Perrysburg (E3).......... 50
Perrysville (C4)*.......... 462
Pershing (G5)*.......... 389
Pershing (E2).......... 50
Peru (E3)*..........13,308
Petersburg (C7)*..........3,035
Peterson (G3).......... 50
Petersville (F6)..........
Petroleum (G3)*..........
Phenix (G3)..........
Pickard (E4)..........
Pierceton (F2)*.......... 973
Pierceville (G6)*..........
Pikes Peak (E6)..........
Pikeville (C8).......... 50
Pilot Knob (E8)*.......... 200
Pimento (C6)*.......... 125
Pine Village (C4)*.......... 311
Pinelake (D1)*.......... 250
Pinola (D1).......... 50
Pittsboro (D5)*.......... 599
Pittsburg (D3).......... 350
Plainfield (E5)*..........2,585
Plainville (C7)*.......... 568
Plato (G1).......... 40
Pleasant (G7).......... 15
Pleasant Lake (H1)*.......... 500
Pleasant Mills (H3)*.......... 175
Pleasant Ridge (C3)..........
Pleasant View (F5).......... 11
Pleasantville (C7)*.......... 200
Plevna (E3).......... 72
Plum Tree (G3).......... 40
Plummer (C7).......... 10
Plymouth (E2)*..........6,704
Poe (G3).......... 80
Point Isabel (F4).......... 75
Poland (C6)*.......... 150
Poneto (G3)*.......... 244
Porter (C1)*..........1,458
Portersville (C8).......... 75
Portland (H4)*..........7,064
Poseyville (B8)*..........1,005
Pottawattomie Park(D1) 35
Powers (G4).......... 50
Prairie Creek (C6)*.......... 225
Prairieton (B6)*..........
Preble (H3)*.......... 150
Prescott (F6).......... 30
Priam (G4)..........
Princeton (B8)*..........7,673
Providence (E6).......... 100
Pulaski (D3).......... 100
Putnamville (D5)*.......... 165
Pyrmont (D4).......... 100
Queensville (F6).......... 70
Quincy (D6)*.......... 320
Raber (G2)..........
Raccoon (D5).......... 100
Radley (F4).......... 150
Radnor (D3)*.......... 110
Ragsdale (C7)*.......... 230
Rainsville (C4).......... 130
Raleigh (G5).......... 150
Ramsey (E8)*.......... 106
Ranger (D8)*..........
Raub (C3)*.......... 110
Ravenswood (E5)*.......... 498
Ray (H1)*.......... 175
Raymond (H6).......... 62
Rays Crossing (F5).......... 75
Reagan (D4).......... 2
Red Key (G4)*..........1,639
Redbridge (F3).......... 75
Reddington (F6).......... 220
Reelsville (D5)*.......... 90
Reese Mill (D4).......... 130
Reiffsburg (G3).......... 43
Remington (C3)*..........1,053
Rensselaer (C3)*..........4,072
Rexville (G7).......... 60
Reynolds (D3)*.......... 499
Riceville (D8).......... 4
Richland (C9)*.......... 530
Richland Center (E2).......... 10
Richmond (H5)*..........39,539
Richvalley (F3)*.......... 111
Ridgeview (E3)..........
Ridgeville (G4)*.......... 950
Rigdon (F4).......... 80
Riley (C6)*.......... 251
Rileysburg (B4).......... 40
Rising Sun (H7)*..........1,930
River (G3).......... 75
Riverside (C4).......... 120
Riverton (B6).......... 54
Roachdale (D5)*.......... 918
Roann (F3)*.......... 492
Roanoke (G3)*.......... 905
Rob Roy (C4).......... 54
Rochester (E2)*..........4,673
Rock Creek (G3)..........
Rockfield (D3)*.......... 325
Rocklane (E5)..........
Rockport (C9)*..........2,493
Rockville (C5)*..........2,467
Rocky Ripple (E5).......... 528
Roll (G3)*.......... 150
Rolling Prairie (D1)*.......... 625
Rome (D9)*..........
Rome City (G1)*..........1,303
Romney (D4)*.......... 500
Rosedale (C5)*.......... 673
Roseland (E1).......... 984
Roselawn (C2)*..........
Rosston (E4).......... 35
Rossville (D4)*.......... 739
Royal Center (E3)*.......... 876
Royalton (E5).......... 50
Royerton (G4).......... 400
Rumble (C8).......... 21
Rushville (G5)*..........6,761
Rusk (D7)*..........
Russellville (D5)*.......... 361
Russiaville (E4)*..........1,025
Saint Anthony (D8)*.......... 152
St. Bernice (C5)*..........1,200
St. Croix (D8)*.......... 100
St. Henry (D8).......... 183
St. Joe (H2)*.......... 479
St. John (C2)*.......... 684
St. Joseph Hill (F8).......... 200
St. Leon (H6)*.......... 288
St. Louis Crossing(F6)* 150
St. Mary of the Woods (B6)*..........1,300
St. Mary's (E1)*..........
St. Maurice (G6).......... 60
St. Meinrad (D8)*.......... 720
St. Omer (F6).......... 75
St. Paul (F6)*.......... 669
St. Peters (H6).......... 130
St. Philip (B9).......... 200
St. Wendells (B8)..........
Salamonia (H4)*.......... 181
Salem (E7)*..........3,271
Salem Center (G1).......... 50
Saline City (C6)*.......... 115
Saltillo (E7)*.......... 122
Samaria (E6).......... 88
San Pierre (D2)*.......... 350
Sandborn (C7)*.......... 572
Sanders (E6).......... 200
Sandford (B5)*.......... 195
Sandusky (G6).......... 200
Santa Claus (D8)*.......... 45
Santa Fe (E3).......... 92
Saratoga (H4)*.......... 333
Sardinia (F6)*.......... 150
Savah (B8).......... 100
Schererville (C2)*..........1,457
Schneider (C2)*.......... 356
Schnellville (D8)*.......... 300
Scipio (H6).......... 75
Scipio (F6)*.......... 200
Scircleville (E4)*.......... 181
Scotland (D7)*.......... 100
Scott (F1).......... 100
Scottsburg (F7)*..........2,953
Sedalia (E4)*.......... 180
Sedan (G2).......... 30
Seelyville (C6)*.......... 898
Sellersburg (F8)*..........1,664
Selma (G4)*.......... 499
Selvin (C8)*..........
Servia (F3)*.......... 143
Sevastopol (F2).......... 50
Sexton (G5).......... 80
Seybert (F1).......... 30
Seymour (F7)*..........9,629
Shadeland (C4).......... 78
Shannondale (D4).......... 20
Sharpsville (E4)*.......... 508
Shelburn (C6)*..........1,412
Shelby (C2)*.......... 519
Shelbyville (F6)*..........11,734
Shepardsville (B5)*.......... 300
Sheridan (E4)*..........1,965
Shideler (G4)..........
Shipshewana (F1)*.......... 277
Shirley (F5)*..........1,087
Shirley City (Woodburn*) (H2).......... 540
Shoals (D7)*..........1,039
Shooters Hill ‡(E5).......... 13
Shrock (F1)..........
Siberia (D8)*.......... 50
Sidney (F2)*.......... 168
Silver Lake (F2)*.......... 472
Silverville (D7).......... 60
Silverwood (C5).......... 75
Simpson (G3).......... 9
Sims (F3)*.......... 231
Skelton (B8).......... 50
Smartsburg (D4).......... 55
Smith Valley (E5).......... 150
Smithville (D6)*.......... 425
Snow Hill (H4).......... 15
Solon (F7).......... 137
Solsberry (D6)*.......... 500
Somerset (F3)*.......... 255
Somerville (C8)*.......... 353
South Bend (E1)*..........115,911
South Bend (urban area)..........167,879
S. Boston (F7).......... 125
S. Milford (G1)*.......... 350
S. Raub (D4).......... 30
S. Wanatah (D2).......... 95
S. Whitley (F2)*..........1,299
Southport (E5)*.......... 730
Spades (G6)..........
Sparksville (E7)*.......... 136
Spartanburg (H4).......... 200
Spearsville (E6).......... 38
Speed (F8)*..........1,000
Speedway (E5)*..........5,498
Speicher (F3).......... 60
Spelterville (C5).......... 150
Spencer (D6)*..........2,394
Spencerville (G2)*.......... 450
Spiceland (F5)*.......... 739
Spraytown (E6).......... 63
Spring Grove (H5).......... 333
Spring Hills ‡(E5).......... 27
Spring Lake Park (F5). 156
Springfield (B8)..........
Springport (G4)*.......... 217
Springville (D7)*.......... 500
Spurgeon (C8)*.......... 327
Stacer (B8)..........
Stanford (D6)*.......... 100
Star City (D3)*.......... 600
Starlight (F8).......... 50
State Line (C4)*.......... 152
Staunton (C6)*.......... 487
Steele (H3).......... 26
Stendal (C8)*.......... 175
Stewartsville (B8)*.......... 240
Stilesville (D5)*.......... 330
Stillwell (D1)*..........
Stinesville (D6)*.......... 355
Stockwell (D4)*.......... 632
Stone (G4).......... 10
Stonebluff (C4)*.......... 172
Stones Crossing (E5).......... 75
Story (E6)..........
Straughn (G5)*.......... 345
Stroh (G1)*.......... 475
Strouse (G2)..........
Sullivan (C6)*..........5,423
Sulphur (E8)*.......... 43
Sulphur Springs (G4)*. 351
Sumava Resorts (C2)*.......... 125
Summit (G1).......... 2
Summitville (F4)*..........1,061
Sunman (G6)*.......... 358
Surprise (E7).......... 55
Swanington (C3).......... 125
Swayzee (F4)*.......... 690
Sweetsers (F3)*.......... 535
Switz City (C6)*.......... 328
Sycamore (F4).......... 76
Sylvania (C5).......... 35
Syracuse (F2)*..........1,453
Tab (C4)*..........
Talbot (C3)*..........
Talma (E2).......... 150
Tampico (F7).......... 150
Tangier (C5)*.......... 100
Taswell (D8)*.......... 110
Taylorsville (F6)*.......... 290
Tecumseh (C8)..........
Teegarden (E2)*..........
Tefft (D2)*.......... 140
Tell City (D9)*..........5,735
Templeton (C3)*.......... 143
Tennyson (C8)*.......... 409
Terhune (E4).......... 100
Terre Haute (C6)*..........64,214
Terre Haute (urban area)..........77,845
Thayer (C2)*.......... 250
Thorntown (D4)*..........1,380
Tiosa (E2).......... 125
Tippecanoe (E2)*.......... 400
Tipton (E4)*..........5,633
Tobinsport (D9)*.......... 205
Tocsin (G3)*.......... 175
Topeka (F1)*.......... 557
Toto (D2).......... 275
Tower (E8)..........
Trafalgar (E6)*.......... 439
Trail Creek (D1).......... 817
Treaty (F3).......... 90
Trevlac (E6)*.......... 48
Trinity Springs (D7).......... 150
Troy (D9)*.......... 537
Tulip (D6).......... 20
Tunker (F2).......... 40
Tunnelton (E7)*.......... 300
Twelve Mile (E3)*.......... 247
Tyner (E2)*.......... 250
Ulen (E4).......... 83
Underwood (F7)*.......... 328
Union (C8)*.......... 209
Union City (H4)*..........3,572
Union Mills (D2)*.......... 450
Uniondale (G3)*.......... 293
Unionport (G4).......... 50
Uniontown (D8)*..........
Unionville (E6)*.......... 475
Universal (C5)*.......... 479
Upland (F4)*..........1,565
Urbana (F3)*.......... 400
Utica (F8).......... 250
Valeene (E8)*.......... 94
Valentine (G1).......... 110
Vallonia (E7)*.......... 510
Valparaiso (C2)*..........12,028
Van Buren (F3)*.......... 815
Veedersburg (C4)*..........1,719
Velpen (C8)*.......... 197
Vera Cruz (G3).......... 143
Verne (C7).......... 50
Vernon (F7)*.......... 480
Versailles (G6)*.......... 886
Veterans Adm. Hospital (F3)*..........3,950
Vevay (G7)*..........1,309
Vicksburg (C6).......... 390
Vienna (F7).......... 80
Vincennes (C7)*..........18,831
Vine (C4).......... 15
Virgie (C2)..........
Vistula (F1).......... 100
Wabash (F3)*..........10,621
Wadena (C3).......... 65
Wadesville (B8)*..........
Wakarusa (F1)*..........1,143
Wakefield (F7).......... 45
Waldron (F6)*.......... 700
Walesboro (F6)..........
Walkerton (E2)*..........2,102
Wallace (C5)*.......... 123
Wallace Junction (D6)..
Wallen (G2).......... 120
Walton (E3)*.......... 837
Wanamaker (E5)*.......... 325
Wanatah (D2)*.......... 750
Warren (G3)*..........1,247
Warren Park (F5).......... 336
Warrenton (B8).......... 100
Warrington (F5).......... 95
Warsaw (F2)*..........6,625
Washington (C7)*..........10,987
Waterloo (G2)*..........1,414
Waterman (C5).......... 100
Watson (F8).......... 200
Waveland (D5)*.......... 553
Waverly (E5).......... 150
Wawaka (F2)*.......... 300
Wawasee (F2)*.......... 400
Wawpecong (F3).......... 84
Waymansville (E6).......... 250
Waynedale (G3)..........
Waynesville (F6)..........
Waynetown (C4)*.......... 658
Webster (H5)*.......... 175
Weisburg (H6)*.......... 148
Wellsboro (D1)*.......... 170
West Baden Springs (D7)*..........1,047
W. College Corner(H5). 513
W. Fork (D8)*.......... 58
W. Franklin (B9).......... 100
W. Harrison (H6).......... 308
W. Lafayette (D4)*..........11,873
W. Lebanon (C4)*.......... 642
W. Middleton (E4)*.......... 250
W. Newton (E5)*..........
W. Terre Haute (B6)*..3,357
Westchester (H4).......... 8
Westfield (E4)*.......... 849
Westphalia (C7)*.......... 250
Westpoint (C4)*.......... 315
Westport (F6)*.......... 658
Westville (D1)*.......... 624
Wheatfield (C2)*.......... 496
Wheatland (C7)*.......... 735
Wheeler (C1)*.......... 400
Wheeling (G4)..........
Wheeling (C8).......... 50
Whitaker (D6).......... 25
Whitcomb (H6).......... 150
White Cloud (E8).......... 50
White Lick (E5)..........
Whitehall (D6).......... 80
Whiteland (E5)*.......... 465
Whitestown (E5)*.......... 550
Whitesville (D5).......... 75
Whitewater (H5).......... 104
Whiting (C1)*..........9,669
Wickliffe (D8)*.......... 9
Wilbur (D5).......... 75
Wilfred (C6).......... 50
Wilkinson (F5)*.......... 365
Williams (D7)*.......... 400
Williams (H3).......... 75
Williams Creek (E5).......... 288
Williamsport (C4)*..........1,241
Willow Branch (F5)*..........
Wilmington (H6).......... 200
Wilmot (F2).......... 100
Wilson (F6).......... 25
Winamac (D2)*..........2,166
Winchester (G4)*..........5,467
Windfall (F4)*.......... 963
Windom (D7).......... 8
Windsor (G4)..........
Wingate (C4)*.......... 400
Winona Lake (F2)*..........1,366
Winslow (C8)*..........1,322
Wirt (G7)..........
Wolcott (C3)*.......... 778
Wolcottville (G1)*.......... 672
Wolflake (F2)*.......... 250
Woodburn (H2)*.......... 540
Woodland (E1).......... 115
Woodlawn Heights(F4)
Woodruff Place (E5)..........1,557
Woodstock ‡(E5).......... 29
Worthington (C6)*..........1,627
Wyandotte (E8)*.......... 50
Wyatt (E1)*.......... 250
Wynnedale ‡(E5).......... 75
Yankeetown (C9).......... 323
Yeddo (C4)*.......... 115
Yeoman (D3)*.......... 180
Yoder (G3)*.......... 200
Yorktown (G4)*..........1,109
Yorkville (H6)*.......... 87
Young America (E3)*.......... 250
Youngs Creek (D8)*.......... 79
Youngstown (C6).......... 72
Zanesville (G3)*.......... 300
Zenas (G6).......... 44
Zionsville (E5)*..........1,536
Zipp (B8)..........
Zoar (C8).......... 5
Zulu (H2).......... 175

*Map on Page 60*

## IOWA

*Total Population 2,621,073*

**99 COUNTIES**

Adair (E6)..........12,292
Adams (D6)..........8,753
Allamakee (L2)..........16,351
Appanoose (H7)..........19,683
Audubon ([illegible])..........11,[illegible]
Benton (J4)..........22,656
Black Hawk (J4)..........100,448
Boone (F5)..........28,139
Bremer (J3)..........18,884
Buchanan (K4)..........21,927
Buena Vista (C3)..........21,113
Butler (H3)..........17,394
Calhoun (D4)..........16,925
Carroll (D4)..........23,065
[illegible]
Cedar (L5)..........16,910
Cerro Gordo (G2)..........46,053
Cherokee (B3)..........19,052
Chickasaw (J2)..........15,228
Clarke (F6)..........9,369
Clay (C2)..........18,103
Clayton (L3)..........22,522
Clinton (M5)..........49,664
Crawford (C4)..........19,741
Dallas ([illegible])..........23,661
Davis (J7)..........9,995
Decatur (F7)..........12,601
Delaware (L4)..........17,734
Des Moines (L7)..........42,056
Dickinson (C2)..........12,756
Dubuque (M4)..........71,337
Emmet (D2)..........14,102
Fayette (K3)..........28,294
Floyd (H2)..........21,505
Franklin ([illegible])..........16,268
Fremont (B7)..........12,323
Greene (E5)..........15,544
Grundy (H4)..........13,722
Guthrie (D5)..........15,197
Hamilton (F4)..........19,660
Hancock (F2)..........15,077
Hardin (G4)..........22,218
Harrison (B5)..........19,560
Henry (K6)..........18,708
Howard ([illegible])..........13,105
Humboldt (E3)..........13,117
Ida (C4)..........10,697
Iowa (J5)..........15,835
Jackson (M4)..........18,622
Jasper (G5)..........32,305
Jefferson (K6)..........15,696
Johnson (K5)..........45,756
Jones (L4)..........19,401
Keokuk (J6)..........16,797
Kossuth (F2)..........26,241
Lee (L7)..........43,102
Linn (K4)..........104,274
Louisa (L6)..........11,101
Lucas (G6)..........12,069
Lyon (A2)..........14,697
Madison (E6)..........13,131
Mahaska (H6)..........24,672
Marion (G6)..........25,930
Marshall (G4)..........35,611
Mills (B6)..........14,064
Mitchell (H2)..........13,945
Monona (B4)..........16,303
Monroe (H7)..........11,814

Ossian (K2)* 804
Osterdock (L3)* 51
Otho (E4)* 403
Otley (G6)* 177
Oto (B4)* 302
Otranto (H2)* 75
Otterville (K3)
Ottosen (E3)* 127
Ottumwa (J6)* 33,631
Owasa (G4)* 100
Oxford (K5)* 543
Oxford Junction (M4)* 663
Oxford Mills (L5) 103
Oyens (A3)* 95
Pacific Junction (B6)* 550
Packwood (J6)* 211
Page (C7) 9
Palmer (D3)* 296
Palo (K4)* 285
Panama (B5)* 230
Panora (E5)* 1,062
Paris (K4) 75
Parkersburg (H3)* 1,300
Parnell (J5)* 206
Paton (E4)* 404
Patterson (F6)* 133
Paullina (B3)* 1,289
Payne (B7)* 14
Pekin (J6) 75
Pella (H6)* 4,427
Peoria (H6) 150
Peosta (M4)* 60
Percival (B7)* 250
Percy (G6)*
Perkins (A2) 50
Perlee (K6) 22
Perry (E5)* 6,174
Pershing (G6)* 300
Persia (B5)* 373
Peru (F6)* 250
Peterson (C3)* 589
Pierson (B3)* 453
Pilot Grove (L7)* 50
Pilot Mound (F4)* 246
Pioneer (E3)* 83
Pisgah (B5)* 327
Plain View (M5) 42
Plainfield (J3)* 387
Plano (G7)* 106
Pleasant Plain (K6)* 148
Pleasant Valley (N5)* 500
Pleasanton (F7)* 130
Pleasantville (G6)* 893
Plover (D3)* 243
Plymouth (G2)* 395
Pocahontas (D3)* 1,949
Polk City (F5)* 336
Pomeroy (D3)* 868
Popejoy (G3)* 201
Portsmouth (C5)* 299
Postville (K2)* 1,343
Powersville (H3) 25
Prairie City (G5)* 834
Prairieburg (L4)* 210
Prescott (D6)* 372
Preston (N4)* 684
Primghar (B2)* 1,152
Primrose (K7)* 65
Princeton (N5)* 495
Prole (F6)*
Promise City (G7)* 218
Protivin (J2)* 283
Pulaski (J7)* 381
Purdy (G6)
Quarry (H4) 204
Quasqueton (K4)* 374
Quimby (B3)* 398
Quincy (D6)
Radcliffe (G4)* 638
Rake (F2)* 351
Ralston (D4)* 166
Randalia (K3)* 132
Randall (F4)* 202
Randolph (B7)* 295
Rathbun (H7)* 229
Raymond (J4)* 260
Read (L3)
Readlyn (J3)* 468
Reasnor (G5)* 227
Red Oak (C6)* 6,526
Redding (E7)* 200
Redfield (E5)* 892
Reinbeck (H4)* 1,460
Rembrandt (C3)* 296
Remsen (B3)* 1,280
Renwick (E3)* 474
Rhodes (G5)* 369
Riceville (H2)* 962
Richards (D4)* 48
Richland (K6)* 591
Richmond (K6)* 140
Rickardsville (M3) 75
Ricketts (B4)* 166
Ridgeway (K2)* 307
Rinard (D4)* 115
Ringsted (D2)* 578
Rippey (E5)* 354
River Junction (L5) 36
River Sioux (B5)* 135
Riverside (K6)* 631
Riverton (B7)* 472
Robertson (G3) 30
Robins (K4)* 272
Robinson (K4) 50
Rochester (L5) 67
Rock Falls (G2)* 139
Rock Rapids (A2)* 2,640
Rock Valley (A2)* 1,581
Rockdale (M4) 132
Rockford (H2)* 979
Rockwell (G3)* 753
Rockwell City (D4)* 2,333
Rodman (D2)* 123
Rodney (A4)* 127
Roland (F4)* 687
Rolfe (D3)* 997
Rome (K7)* 134
Roscoe (L6) 2
Rose Hill (J6)* 243
Roselle (D5) 82
Ross (D5) 50
Rossie (C2)* 112
Rossville (L2)
Rowan (F3)* 304
Rowley (K4)* 249
Royal (C2)* 495
Rubio (K6)* 70
Rudd (H2)* 398
Runnells (G5)* 307
Russell (G7)* 566
Ruthven (D2)* 868
Rutland (E3)* 225
Ryan (K4)* 362
Sabula (N4)* 888
Sac City (C4)* 3,170
Sageville (M3) 118
Saint Ansgar (H2)* 981
St. Anthony (G4)* 175
St. Benedict (E2)* 135
St. Charles (F6)* 319
St. Donatus (M4)* 100
St. Lucas (K2)* 158
St. Marys (F6)* 89
St. Olaf (L3)* 158
St. Paul (L7) 113
Salem (K7)* 473
Salina (K6) 50
Salix (A4)* 337
Sanborn (B2)* 1,337
Sand Springs (L4) 50
Sandyville (G6) 92
Saratoga (J2)* 85
Saylor (F5) 100
Scarville (F2)* 105
Schaller (C4)* 841
Schleswig (B4)* 751
Scotch Grove (L4)* 55
Scranton (D4)* 891
Searsboro (H5)* 183
Sedan (H7) 80
Selma (J7)* 175
Seney (A3) 82
Sergeant Bluff (A4)* 569
Sewal (G7)* 100
Sexton (E2)*
Seymour (G7)* 1,223
Shambaugh (D7)* 251
Shannon City (E7)* 171
Sharpsburg (D7)* 147
Sheffield (G3)* 1,163
Shelby (C5)* 592
Sheldahl (F5)* 211
Sheldon (B2)* 4,001
Shell Rock (H3)* 1,013
Shellsburg (K4)* 632
Shenandoah (C7)* 6,938
Sherrill (M3) 162
Sherwood (D4) 21
Shueyville (K5) 75
Sibley (B2)* 2,559
Sidney (B7)* 1,132
Sigourney (J6)* 2,343
Silver City (B6)* 311
Sioux Center (A2)* 1,860
Sioux City (A3)* 83,991
Sioux City (urban area) 90,144
Sioux Rapids (C3)* 1,010
Slater (F5)* 583
Sloan (A4)* 654
Smithland (B4)* 373
Soldier (B5)* 323
Solon (L5)* 527
Somers (E4)* 217
South Amana (J5)* 185
S. English (J6)* 248
Spechts Ferry (M3) 10
Spencer (C2)* 7,446
Sperry (L7)* 65
Spillville (J2)* 363
Spirit Lake (D2)* 2,467
Spragueville (N4)* 115
Spring Hill (F6)* 86
Springbrook (N4)* 109
Springdale (L5) 72
Springville (L4)* 680
Stacyville (H2)* 544
Stanhope (F4)* 420
Stanley (K3)* 158
Stanton (C7)* 570
Stanwood (L5)* 547
Stanzel (E6)* 25
State Center (G5)* 1,040
Steamboat Rock (G4)* 395
Stennett (C6) 28
Stiles (J7) 50
Stockport (K7)* 346
Stockton (M5)* 165
Stone City (L4)* 200
Storm Lake (C3)* 6,954
Story City (F4)* 1,545
Stout (H3)* 135
Strahan (B7)* 100
Stratford (F4)* 673
Strawberry Point (K3)* 1,247
Struble (A3)* 91
Stuart (E6)* 1,500
Sully (H5)* 452
Sulphur Springs (C3)* 90
Summerset (F6)
Summitville (K8)
Sumner (J3)* 1,911
Sunbury (M5)* 100
Superior (D2)* 240
Sutherland (B3)* 835
Swaledale (G3)* 205
Swan (G6)* 194
Swea City (E2)* 869
Swedesburg (L6)* 104
Swisher (K5)* 205
Tabor (B7)* 869
Taintor (H6)* 78
Talleyrand (J6) 24
Talmage (E6) 44
Tama (H5)* 2,930
Tara (E4) 70
Teeds Grove (N4)*
Templeton (D5)* 385
Tennant (C5)* 95
Terril (C2)* 425
Thayer (E6)* 152
The Inn (C2)
Thompson (F2)* 698
Thor (E3)* 271
Thornburg (J6)* 138
Thornton (G3)* 441
Thurman (B7)* 284
Ticonic (B4) 35
Tiffin (K5)* 256
Tingley (E7)* 333
Tipton (L5)* 2,633
Titonka (E2)* 589
Toddville (K4)* 200
Toeterville (H2)* 75
Toledo (H4)* 2,106
Toronto (M5)* 165
Tracy (H6)*
Traer (J4)* 1,627
Trenton (K6) 104
Treynor (B6)* 247
Tripoli (J3)* 1,124
Troy (J7)* 103
Troy Mills (K4)*
Truax (H6) 60
Truesdale (C3)* 158
Truro (F6)* 354
Turin (B4)* 160
Turkey River (L3) 9
Udell (H7)* 96
Ulmer (D4)*
Underwood (B6)* 278
Union (G4)* 490
Unionville (H7)* 204
University Heights (K5) 446
University Park (H6)* 457
Urbana (K4)* 414
Urbandale (F5)* 1,777
Ute (B4)* 563
Vail (C4)* 532
Valeria (G5)* 57
Van Cleve (G5) 25
Van Horne (J4)* 511
Van Meter (E5)* 364
Van Wert (F7)* 318
Vandalia (G5) 55
Varina (D3)* 144
Ventura (F2)* 300
Victor (J5)* 741
Villisca (C7)* 1,838
Vincennes (K7)* 72
Vincent (E3)* 193
Vining (J5)* 112
Vinton (J4)* 4,307
Viola (L4)*
Volga (L3)* 423
Voorhies (J4)* 56
Wadena (K3)* 316
Wahpeton ‡(C2) 127
Walcott (M5)* 480
Walford (K5)* 165
Walker (K4)* 549
Wall Lake (C4)* 753
Wallingford (D2)* 229
Walnut (C6)* 888
Wapello (L6)* 1,755
Ware (D3)*
Washburn (J4)* 132
Washington (K6)* 5,902
Washta (B3)* 403
Waterloo (J4)* 65,198
Waterloo (urban area) 83,551
Waterville (L2)* 199
Watkins (J5)* 130
Waubeek (K4)* 120
Waucoma (J2)* 385
Waukee (F5)* 501
Waukon (L2)* 3,158
Waukon Junction (L2)* 40
Waupeton (M3)* 11
Waverly (J3)* 5,124
Wayland (K6)* 600
Webb (D3)* 235
Webster (J6)* 136
Webster City (F4)* 7,611
Weldon (F7)* 229
Wellman (K6)* 1,071
Wellsburg (H4)* 744
Welton (M5)* 93
Wesley (E2)* 509
West (J5)*
West Bend (D3)* 772
W. Branch (L5)* 769
W. Burlington (L7)* 1,614
W. Chester (K6)* 218
W. Des Moines (F5)* 5,615
W. Grove (J7)* 90
W. Liberty (L5)* 1,866
W. Mitchell (H2) 112
W. Okoboji (C2) 158
W. Point (K7)* 662
W. Union (K3)* 2,141
Western College (K5)
Westfield (A3)* 172
Westgate (K3)* 226
Weston (B6) 75
Westphalia (C5)* 160
Westside (C4)* 393
Wever (L7)* 100
What Cheer (J6)* 1,119
Wheatland (M5)* 568
Whiting (A4)* 663
Whittemore (E2)* 678
Whitten (H4)* 174
Whittier (K4)* 134
Wick (F6)* 58
Willey (D5) 94
Williams (F3)* 519
Williamsburg (J5)* 1,183
Williamson (G6)* 294
Wilton Junction (M5)* 1,446
Winfield (L6)* 888
Windsor Heights (F5) 1,414
Winterset (E6)* 3,570
Winthrop (K4)* 604
Wiota (D6)* 227
Woden (F2)* 272
Woodbine (B5)* 1,304
Woodburn (F7)* 255
Woodland (F7)
Woodward (F5)* 908
Woolstock (F3)* 255
Worthington (L4)* 337
Wright (J6)* 125
Wyman (L6)* 100
Wyoming (L4)* 724
Yale (E5)* 293
Yarmouth (L6)* 160
Yetter (D4)* 121
Yorkshire (B5)
Yorktown (C7)* 146
Zearing (G4)* 514
Zook Spur (F5) 20
Zwingle (M4)* 132

*Map on Page 61*

## KANSAS

*Total Population 1,905,299*

### 105 COUNTIES

Allen (G4) 18,187
Anderson (G3) 10,267
Atchison (G2) 21,496
Barber (D4) 8,521
Barton (D3) 29,909
Bourbon (H4) 19,153
Brown (G2) 14,651
Butler (F4) 31,001
Chase (F3) 4,831
Chautauqua (F4) 7,376
Cherokee (H4) 25,144
Cheyenne (A2) 5,668
Clark (C4) 3,946
Clay (E2) 11,697
Cloud (E2) 16,104
Coffey (G3) 10,408
Comanche (C4) 3,888
Cowley (F4) 36,905
Crawford (H4) 40,231
Decatur (B2) 6,185
Dickinson (E3) 21,190
Doniphan (G2) 10,499
Douglas (G3) 34,086
Edwards (C4) 5,936
Elk (F4) 6,679
Ellis (C3) 19,043
Ellsworth (D3) 8,465
Finney (B3) 15,092
Ford (C4) 19,670
Franklin (G3) 19,928
Geary (F3) 21,671
Gove (B3) 4,447
Graham (C2) 5,020
Grant (A4) 4,638
Gray (B4) 4,894
Greeley (A3) 2,010
Greenwood (F4) 13,574
Hamilton (A3) 3,696
Harper (D4) 10,263
Harvey (E3) 21,698
Haskell (B4) 2,606
Hodgeman (C3) 3,310
Jackson (G2) 11,098
Jefferson (G2) 11,084
Jewell (D2) 9,698
Johnson (H3) 62,783
Kearny (A3) 3,492
Kingman (D4) 10,324
Kiowa (C4) 4,743
Labette (G4) 29,285
Lane (B3) 2,808
Leavenworth (G2) 42,361
Lincoln (D2) 6,643
Linn (H3) 10,053
Logan (A3) 4,206
Lyon (F3) 26,576
Marion (E3) 16,307
Marshall (F2) 17,927
Mc Pherson (E3) 23,670
Meade (B4) 5,710
Miami (H3) 19,698
Mitchell (D2) 10,320
Montgomery (G4) 46,487
Morris (F3) 8,485
Morton (A4) 2,610
Nemaha (F2) 14,341
Neosho (G4) 20,348
Ness (C3) 6,322
Norton (C2) 8,808
Osage (G3) 12,811
Osborne (D2) 8,558
Ottawa (E2) 7,265
Pawnee (C3) 11,041
Phillips (C2) 9,273
Pottawatomie (F2) 12,344
Pratt (D4) 12,156
Rawlins (A2) 5,728
Reno (D4) 54,058
Republic (E2) 11,478
Rice (D3) 15,635
Riley (F2) 33,405
Rooks (C2) 9,043
Rush (C3) 7,231
Russell (D3) 13,406
Saline (E3) 33,409
Scott (B3) 4,921
Sedgwick (E4) 222,290
Seward (B4) 9,972
Shawnee (G2) 105,418
Sheridan (B2) 4,607
Sherman (A2) 7,373
Smith (D2) 8,846
Stafford (D3) 8,816
Stanton (A4) 2,263
Stevens (A4) 4,516
Sumner (E4) 23,646
Thomas (A2) 7,572
Trego (C3) 5,868
Wabaunsee (F3) 7,212
Wallace (A3) 2,508
Washington (E2) 12,977
Wichita (A3) 2,640
Wilson (G4) 14,815
Woodson (G4) 6,711
Wyandotte (H2) 165,318

### CITIES and TOWNS

Abbyville (D4)* 99
Abilene (E3)* 5,775
Achilles (B2)* 18
Acres (C4)* 2
Ada (E2)* 175
Adams (E4)* 45
Admire (F3)* 184
Aetna (D4) 40
Agenda (E2)* 159
Agra (C2)* 354
Agricola (G3)* 30
Alamota (B3)* 39
Albert (C3)* 218
Alden (D3)* 286
Alexander (C3)* 188
Aliceville (G3)* 100
Alida (F2) 81
Alki (F3) 10
Allen (F3)* 241
Alma (F2)* 716
Almena (C2)* 616
Alta Vista (F3)* 420
Altamont (G4)* 652
Alton (D2)* 317
Altoona (G4)* 582
America City (F2) 10
Americus (F3)* 339
Ames (E2)* 67
Amiot (G3)* 200
Amy (B3)* 35
Andale (E4)* 316
Andover (E4)* 250
Angola (G4)* 50
Anness (E4)* 11
Anson (E4)* 50
Antelope (F3)* 40
Anthony (D4)* 2,792
Antonino (C3)* 75
Arcadia (H4)* 572
Argonia (E4)* 562
Arkansas City (E4)* 12,903
Arlington (D4)* 405
Arma (H4)* 1,334
Arnold (B3)* 108
Arrington (G2)* 50
Ash Grove (D2) 55
Ash Valley (C3)
Asherville (D2)* 105
Ashland (C4)* 1,493
Ashton (E4)* 45
Assaria (E3)* 221
Atchison (G2)* 12,792
Athol (D2)* 203
Atlanta (F4)* 309
Attica (D4)* 622
Atwood (B2)* 1,613
Auburn (G3)* 110
Augusta (F4)* 4,483
Aulne (E3)* 182
Aurora (E2)* 221
Axtell (F2)* 510
Baileyville (F2)* 150
Bala (F2)* 50
Baldwin City (G3)* 1,741
Bancroft (G2) 26
Barclay (G3)* 47
Barker (H2) 735
Barnard (D2)* 242
Barnes (F2)* 308
Bartlett (G4)* 143
Basehor (G2)* 275
Bassett (G4) 117
Bavaria (E3)* 90
Baxter Springs (H4)* 4,647
Bazaar (F3) 64
Bazine (C3)* 456
Beagle (G3)* 150
Beardsley (A2)* 30
Beattie (F2)* 321
Beaumont (F4)* 150
Beaver (D3)* 118
Beeler (B3)* 100
Bellaire (D2)* 55
Belle Plaine (E4)* 971
Bellefont (C4)* 35
Belleville (E2)* 2,858
Belmont (D4)* 48
Beloit (D2)* 4,035
Belpre (C4)* 231
Belvidere (C4)* 52
Belvue (F2)* 193
Bendena (G2)* 94
Benedict (G4)* 176
Bennington (E2)* 325
Bentley (E4)* 200
Benton (E4)* 269
Bern (F2)* 216
Berryton (G3)* 213
Berwick (G2) 14
Beverly (E2)* 255
Big Bow (A4)* 100
Bigelow (F2)* 170
Bird City (A2)* 784
Bison (C3)* 326
Black Wolf (D3)* 23
Blaine (F2)* 45
Blair (H2)* 100
Blakeman (A2)* 10
Block (H3) 21
Bloom (C4)* 125
Bloomington (D2)* 50
Blue Mound (H3)* 424
Blue Rapids (F2)* 1,430
Bluff City (E4)* 172
Bogue (C2)* 211
Boicourt (H3)* 30
Bonner Springs (H2)* 2,277
Bradford (F3) 25
Brantford (E2) 23
Brazilton (H4)* 75
Bremen (F2)* 80
Brenham (C4) 21
Brewster (A2)* 467
Bridgeport (E3)* 53
Bronson (H4)* 415
Brookville (E3)* 213
Broughton (E2)* 96
Brownell (C3)* 211
Buckeye (E2) 15
Bucklin (C4)* 824
Bucyrus (H3)* 131
Buffalo (G4)* 437
Buffville (G4) 50
Buhler (E3)* 750
Bunker Hill (D3)* 271
Burden (F4)* 541
Burdett (C3)* 355
Burdick (F3)* 110
Burlingame (G3)* 1,065
Burlington (G3)* 2,304
Burns (F3)* 294
Burr Oak (D2)* 505
Burrton (E3)* 749
Burt (G4) 35
Busby (F4) 42
Bush City (G3)* 65
Bushong (F3)* 93
Bushton (D3)* 532
Byers (D4)* 83
Cairo (D4) 40
Caldwell (E4)* 2,000
Calista (D4)* 12
Calvert (C2)* 22
Cambridge (F4)* 221
Canada (E3)* 38
Caney (G4)* 2,876
Canton (E3)* 771
Carbondale (G3)* 453
Carlton (E3)* 76
Carlyle (G4)* 45
Carneiro (D3)* 55
Carona (H4)* 175
Cassoday (F3)* 150
Castleton (E4)* 64
Catharine (C3)* 218
Cawker City (D2)* 691
Cedar (D2)* 86
Cedar Bluffs (B2)* 45
Cedar Point (F3)* 107
Cedar Vale (F4)* 1,010
Centerview (C4)* 30
Centerville (H3)* 155
Centralia (F2)* 574
Chanute (G4)* 10,109
Chapman (E3)* 990
Chardon (A2)
Charleston (B4) 12
Chase (D3)* 961
Chautauqua (F4)* 215
Cheney (E4)* 777
Cherokee (H4)* 849
Cherryvale (G4)* 2,952
Chetopa (G4)* 1,671
Chicopee (H4) 250
Chiles (H3) 20
Cimarron (B4)* 1,189
Circleville (G2)* 169
Claflin (D3)* 921
Claudell (C2)* 25
Clay Center (E2)* 4,528
Clayton (B2)* 157
Clearwater (E4)* 647
Cleburne (F2)* 150
Clements (F3)* 75
Clifton (E2)* 743
Climax (F4)* 91
Clonmel (E4) 25
Cloverdale (F4)
Clyde (E2)* 1,067
Coats (D4)* 255
Codell (C2)* 100
Coffeyville (G4)* 17,113
Colby (A2)* 3,859
Coldwater (C4)* 1,208
Collano (B4) 25
Collyer (B2)* 282
Colony (G3)* 387
Columbus (H4)* 3,490
Colwich (E4)* 339
Como (E2) 17
Concordia (E2)* 7,175
Conway (E3)* 101
Conway Springs (E4)* 816
Coolidge (A3)* 168
Copeland (B4)* 242
Corbin (E4)* 100
Corinth (D2) 3
Corning (F2)* 254
Corwin (D4)* 60
Cottonwood Falls (F3)* 957
Council Grove (F3)* 2,722
Courtland (E2)* 367
Covert (D2)* 75
Coyville (G4)* 106
Crawford (E3)* 50
Crestline (H4)* 150
Crisfield (D4)* 11
Croft (D4)* 6
Crystalsprings (D4)* 73
Cuba (E2)* 345
Cullison (D4)* 174
Culver (E3)* 153
Cummings (G2)* 52
Cunningham (D4)* 510
Damar (C2)* 305
Danville (E4)* 122
Day (E2) 6
De Graff (F4) 30
De Soto (H3)* 518
Dearing (G4)* 261
Deerfield (A4)* 440
Delavan (F3)* 75
Delia (G2)* 164
Dellvale (B2)* 12
Delphos (E2)* 676
Denison (G2)* 166
Denmark (D3)* 50
Dennis (G4)* 200
Densmore (C2)* 61
Denton (G2)* 157
Derby (E4)* 432
Detroit (E3)* 124
Devon (H4)* 124
Dexter (F4)* 354
Dighton (B3)* 1,246
Dillon (E3) 35
Dillwyn (D4) 10
Dispatch (D2) 17
Dodge City (B4)* 11,262
Doniphan (G2) 50
Dorrance (D3)* 365
Douglass (F4)* 729
Dover (G3)* 50
Downs (D2)* 1,221
Dresden (B2)* 162
Dubuque (D3) 12
Duluth (F2)* 70
Dundee (D3)
Dunlap (F3)* 134
Duquoin (D4)* 15
Durham (E3)* 229
Dwight (F3)* 281
Earlton (G4)* 141
Eastborough (E4) 708
Easton (G2)* 255
Edgerton (H3)* 266
Edmond (C2)* 110
Edna (G4)* 422
Edson (A2)* 70
Edwardsville ‡(H2)* 274
Effingham (G2)* 525
El Dorado (F4)* 11,037
Elbing (E3)* 98
Elgin (F4)* 212
Elk City (G4)* 524
Elk Falls (F4)* 276
Elkader (B3) 5
Elkhart (A4)* 1,132
Ellinwood (D3)* 2,569
Ellis (C3)* 2,649
Ellsworth (D3)* 2,193
Elmdale (F3)* 180
Elmo (E3)* 50
Elmont (G2)* 65
Elsmore (G4)* 152
Elwood (H2)* 1,020
Elyria (E3)* 65
Emmett (F2)* 143
Emporia (F3)* 15,669
Englevale (H4)* 150
Englewood (C4)* 341
Enosdale (E2) 11
Ensign (B4)* 227
Enterprise (E3)* 795
Erie (G4)* 1,296
Esbon (D2)* 278
Eskridge (F3)* 601
Eudora (G3)* 929
Eureka (F4)* 3,958
Everest (G2)* 368
Fact (E2) 15
Fairport (C2)* 35
Fairview (G2)* 336
Fairway ‡(H2) 1,816
Fall River (G4)* 261
Falun (E3)* 92
Farlington (H4)* 96
Farlinville (H3) 15
Faulkner (H4) 36
Fellsburg (C4)* 43
Feterita (A4) 10
Florence (E3)* 1,009
Flush (F2) 304
Fontana (H3)* 168
Ford (C4)* 244
Formoso (D2)* 271
Fort Dodge (C4)* 500
Ft. Leavenworth (H2)*
Ft. Riley (F2)* 2,531
Ft. Scott (H4)* 10,335
Fostoria (F2)* 100
Fowler (B4)* 778
Frankfort (F2)* 1,237
Franklin (H4)* 600
Frederick (D3)* 53
Fredonia (G4)* 3,257
Freeport (E4)* 30
Friend (B3)* 44
Frontenac (H4)* 1,569
Fulton (H4)* 243
Furley (E4)* 75
Galatia (D3)* 89
Galena (H4)* 4,029
Galesburg (G4)* 189
Galva (E3)* 426
Garden City (B4)* 10,905
Garden Plain (E4)* 323
Gardner (H3)* 676
Garfield (C3)* 297
Garfield Center (E2)
Garland (H4)* 280

Garnett (G3)*....2,693
Garrison (F2)*....80
Gas (G4)*....294
Gaylord (D2)*....231
Gem (B2)*....118
Geneseo (D3)*....660
Gerlane (D4)....2
Geuda Springs (E4)*....245
Girard (H4)*....2,426
Glade (C2)*....107
Glasco (E2)*....803
Glen Elder (D2)*....582
Glendale (E3)....35
Glenloch (G3)....
Goddard (E4)*....274
Goessel (E3)*....270
Goff (G3)*....315
Goodland (A2)*....4,690
Goodrich (G3)....50
Gordon (F4)....75
Gorham (D3)*....375
Gove (B3)*....206
Grainfield (B2)*....371
Grantville (G2)*....100
Gray (C3)....12
Great Bend (D3)*....12,665
Greeley (G3)*....436
Green (E2)*....219
Greenleaf (E2)*....614
Greensburg (C4)*....1,723
Greenwich (E4)*....50
Grenola (F4)*....380
Gretna (C2)....12
Gridley (G3)*....360
Grigston (B3)*....35
Grinnell (B2)*....364
Groveland (E3)....10
Gypsum (E3)*....523
Haddam (D2)*....375
Haggard (B4)....42
Hale (F4)....8
Halford (B2)*....6
Hallowell (H4)*....223
Halls Summit (G3)....62
Hallville (E3)....5
Halstead (E4)*....1,328
Hamilton (F4)*....456
Hamlin (G2)....118
Hammond (H4)*....62
Hanover (F2)*....854
Hanston (C3)*....286
Hardtner (D4)*....373
Hargrave (C3)....8
Harlan (D2)*....125
Harper (D4)*....1,672
Harris (G3)....84
Hartford (F3)*....395
Harveyville (F3)*....236
Havana (G4)*....215
Haven (E4)*....720
Havensville (F2)*....208
Haviland (C4)*....606
Hawk (E4)....
Hayne (B4)....6
Hays (C3)*....8,625
Haysville (E4)*....
Hazelton (D4)*....250
Healy (B3)*....200
Hedville (E3)....39
Heizer (D3)*....100
Hepler (H4)*....224
Herington (E3)*....3,775
Herkimer (F2)....120
Herndon (B2)*....321
Hesston (E3)*....686
Hewins (G4)....200
Hiattville (H4)*....150
Hiawatha (G2)*....3,294
Hickok (A4)....37
Highland (G2)*....717
Hill City (C2)*....1,432
Hillsboro (E3)*....2,150
Hillsdale (H3)*....
Hilltop (F3)*....15
Hoisington (D3)*....4,012
Holcomb (B3)*....206
Holland (E3)....50
Hollenberg (F2)*....97
Hollis (E2)*....49
Holton (G2)*....2,705
Holyrood (D3)*....748
Home (E3)....200
Homewood (G3)*....60
Hooser (F4)....6
Hope (E3)*....480
Hopewell (D4)*....26
Horace (A3)*....258
Horton (G2)*....2,354
Howard (F4)*....1,149
Hoxie (B2)*....1,157
Hoyt (G2)*....246
Hudson (D3)*....194
Hugoton (A4)*....2,781
Humboldt (G4)*....2,308
Hunnewell (E4)*....103
Huron (G2)*....128
Hunter (D2)*....236
Hutchinson (D3)*....33,575
Hymer (F3)....10
Idana (E2)*....115
Independence (G4)*....11,335
Industry (E2)....100
Ingalls (B4)*....173
Inman (E3)*....615

Iola (G4)*....7,094
Ionia (D2)*....160
Iowa Point (G2)....110
Irving (F2)*....279
Isabel (D4)*....205
Iuka (D4)*....129
Jamestown (E2)*....494
Jarbalo (G2)*....75
Jefferson (G4)*....50
Jennings (B2)*....330
Jetmore (B3)*....988
Jewell (D2)*....593
Jingo (H3)....12
Johnson (A4)*....994
Junction City (E2)*....13,462
Juniata (D3)....
Kackley (E2)*....60
Kalvesta (B3)*....49
Kanona (B2)*....25
Kanopolis (D3)*....743
Kanorado (A2)*....285
Kansas City (H2)*....129,553
Keats (E4)*....105
Kechi (E4)*....160
Keighley (F4)....21
Kelly (G2)*....150
Kenbro (F3)....50
Kendall (A4)*....125
Kensington (C2)*....635
Kimball (F4)....67
Kincaid (G3)*....309
Kingman (D4)*....3,200
Kingsdown (C4)*....125
Kinsley (C4)*....2,479
Kiowa (D4)*....1,561
Kipp (E3)*....50
Kirwin (C2)*....374
Kismet (B4)*....180
La Crosse (C3)*....1,769
La Cygne (H3)*....794
La Harpe (G4)*....511
Labette (G4)....145
Lafontaine (G4)*....125
Lake City (D4)*....185
Lakin (A4)*....1,618
Lamar (E2)*....100
Lamont (F3)*....100
Lancaster (G2)*....200
Lane (G3)*....200
Langdon (D4)*....128
Langley (D3)*....75
Lansing (H2)*....1,100
Larkinburg (G2)*....99
Larned (C3)*....4,447
Latham (F4)*....218
Latimer (F3)*....34
Lawrence (G3)*....23,351
Lawton (H4)*....85
Le Loup (G3)*....110
Le Roy (G3)*....695
Leavenworth (H2)*....20,579
Leawood (H3)*....1,167
Lebanon (D2)*....610
Lebo (G3)*....575
Lecompton (G2)*....263
Lehigh (E3)*....240
Lenexa ‡(H3)*....803
Lenora (C2)*....511
Leon (F4)*....518
Leona (G2)*....130
Leonardville (F2)*....320
Leoti (A3)*....1,250
Leoville (B2)*....100
Levant (A2)*....130
Lewis (C4)*....475
Liberal (B4)*....7,134
Liberty (G4)*....185
Liebenthal (C3)*....211
Lillis (F2)*....50
Lincoln (D2)*....1,636
Lincolnville (F3)*....228
Lindsborg (E3)*....2,383
Linn (E2)*....395
Linwood (G2)*....261
Little River (E3)*....635
Logan (C2)*....859
Lone Elm (G3)*....82
Lone Star (G3)*....50
Long Island (C2)*....247
Longford (E3)*....178
Longton (F4)*....478
Loretta (F2)....30
Lorraine (D3)*....195
Lost Springs (E3)*....184
Louisburg (H3)*....677
Louisville (F2)*....190
Lovewell (D2)*....76
Lucas (D2)*....631
Lucerne (B2)....2
Ludell (B2)*....120
Luray (D2)*....351
Lyle (B2)....2
Lyndon (G3)*....729
Lyons (D3)*....4,545
Macksville (D4)*....624
Madison (F3)*....1,212
Mahaska (E2)*....179
Maize (E4)*....266
Manchester (E2)*....151
Manhattan (F2)*....19,056
Mankato (D2)*....1,462
Manning (B3)*....22
Manter (A4)*....200
Maple City (F4)*....50

Maple Hill (F2)*....176
Mapleton (H3)*....213
Marienthal (A3)*....110
Marietta (F2)*....49
Marion (F3)*....2,050
Marquette (E3)*....666
Marysville (F2)*....3,866
Matfield Green (F3)*....119
May Day (F2)....27
Mayetta (G2)*....247
Mayfield (E4)....134
Mc Allaster (A3)*....35
Mc Cracken (C3)*....553
Mc Cune (G4)*....532
Mc Donald (A2)*....426
Mc Farland (F2)*....279
Mc Louth (G2)*....477
Mc Pherson (E3)*....8,689
Meade (B4)*....1,763
Medicine Lodge (D4)*....2,288
Medora (E3)*....125
Melrose (G4)....100
Melvern (E3)*....389
Menlo (B2)*....113
Mentor (E3)*....44
Mercier (G2)*....70
Meriden (G2)*....378
Merriam (H3)*....1,649
Michigan Valley (G3)*....105
Middletown (G4)*....22
Midian (F4)....50
Milan (E4)*....165
Milberger (D3)*....40
Mildred (G3)*....79
Milford (F3)*....284
Miller (F3)*....87
Milton (E4)*....100
Miltonvale (E2)*....911
Mingo (B2)....12
Minneapolis (E2)*....1,801
Minneola (C4)*....660
Mission (H3)*....13,000
Mission Hills ‡(H2)*....1,275
Mission Woods ‡(H2)....205
Mitchell (D3)*....85
Modoc (A3)*....56
Moline (F4)*....871
Monrovia (G2)*....20
Mont Ida (G3)....50
Montezuma (B4)*....509
Montrose (D2)*....106
Monument (A2)*....160
Moran (G4)*....616
Morehead (G4)*....70
Morganville (E2)*....278
Morland (B2)*....287
Morrill (G2)*....362
Morrowville (F2)*....229
Morse (H3)*....80
Moscow (A4)*....222
Mound City (H3)*....707
Mound Valley (G4)*....566
Moundridge (E3)*....942
Mount Hope (E4)*....473
Mulberry (H4)*....779
Mullinville (C4)*....410
Mulvane (E4)*....1,387
Muncie (H2)*....60
Munden (E2)*....169
Munjor (C3)....150
Murdock (E4)*....120
Muscotah (G2)*....248
Narka (E2)*....220
Nashville (D4)*....159
Natoma (C3)*....775
Navarre (E3)*....80
Neal (F4)*....102
Nekoma (C3)*....96
Neodesha (G4)*....3,723
Neola (D4)....15
Neosho Falls (G3)*....355
Neosho Rapids (F3)*....204
Ness City (C3)*....1,612
Netawaka (F2)*....213
Neutral (H4)....23
New Albany (G4)*....152
New Almelo (B2)*....78
New Cambria (E3)*....160
New Lancaster (H3)....15
New Salem (F4)*....63
Newton (E3)*....11,590
Nickerson (D3)*....1,013
Nicodemus (C2)*....
Niles (E2)*....100
Niotaze (G4)*....162
Norcatur (B2)*....368
North Newton (E3)*....566
Northbranch (D2)*....60
Norton (C2)*....3,060
Nortonville (G2)*....568
Norway (E2)....100
Norwich (E4)*....378
Nye (B4)....
Oak Valley (G4)*....60
Oakhill (E2)*....100
Oakley (B2)*....1,915
Oberlin (B2)*....2,019
Odin (D3)....115
Offerle (C4)*....269
Ogallah (C3)*....100
Ogden (F2)*....845
Oil Hill (F4)*....450
Oketo (F2)*....169
Olathe (H3)*....5,593

Olivet (G3)*....127
Olmitz (D3)*....125
Olpe (F3)*....293
Olsburg (F2)*....140
Onaga (F2)*....882
Oneida (G2)*....138
Opolis (H4)*....160
Oronoque (C2)....26
Osage City (G3)*....1,919
Osawatomie (H3)*....4,347
Osborne (D2)*....2,068
Oskaloosa (G2)*....721
Oswego (G4)*....1,997
Otego (G2)*....10
Otis (C3)*....410
Ottawa (G3)*....10,081
Ottumwa (G3)....26
Overbrook (G3)*....387
Overland Park (H3)*....10,000
Oxford (E4)*....798
Ozawkie (G2)*....204
Page City (A2)*....100
Palco (C2)*....405
Palmer (E2)*....150
Paola (H3)*....3,972
Paradise (D2)*....145
Parallel (F2)....15
Park (B2)*....223
Parker (H3)*....251
Parkerville (F3)*....78
Parsons (G4)*....14,750
Partridge (D4)*....221
Pauline (G3)*....131
Pawnee Rock (D3)*....359
Paxico (F2)*....196
Peabody (E3)*....1,194
Pearl (E3)....4
Peck (E4)*....89
Penalosa (D4)*....71
Pendennis (B3)*....10
Penokee (C2)*....90
Peoria (G3)....40
Perry (G2)*....399
Perth (E4)*....75
Peru (F4)*....368
Petrolia (G4)*....125
Pfeifer (C3)*....156
Phillipsburg (C2)*....2,589
Piedmont (F4)*....130
Pierceville (B4)*....175
Pilsen (E3)*....52
Piqua (G4)*....200
Pittsburg (H4)*....19,341
Plains (B4)*....718
Plainville (C2)*....2,082
Pleasanton (H3)*....1,178
Plevna (D4)*....200
Plymouth (F3)....80
Pomona (G3)*....453
Portis (D2)*....286
Potter (G2)*....120
Potwin (F4)*....465
Powhattan (G2)*....150
Prairie View (C2)*....192
Prescott (H3)*....283
Preston (D4)*....307
Pretty Prairie (D4)*....484
Princeton (G3)*....177
Protection (C4)*....814
Purcell (G2)*....50
Quenemo (G3)*....391
Quincy (F4)*....100
Quinter (B2)*....741
Radium (D3)*....64
Rago (D4)*....100
Ramona (E3)*....190
Randall (D2)*....240
Randolph (F2)*....391
Ransom (C3)*....405
Rantoul (G3)*....197
Raymond (D3)*....275
Reading (F3)*....289
Reager (B2)*....8
Reamsville (C2)....10
Redfield (H4)*....173
Redwing (D3)*....50
Reece (F4)*....250
Reno (G2)....50
Republic (E2)*....360
Reserve (G2)*....169
Rest (G2)....10
Rexford (B2)*....304
Rice (E2)*....27
Richfield (A4)*....105
Richland (G3)*....141
Richmond (G3)*....433
Richter (E2)*....25
Riga (C3)....21
Riley (F2)*....414
Riverdale (E4)*....65
Riverton (H4)*....250
Robinson (G2)*....381
Rock (F4)*....124
Rock Creek (G2)*....100
Rolla (A4)*....433
Rosalia (F4)*....100
Rose (G4)*....50
Rose Hill (E4)*....200
Roseland ‡(H4)*....118
Rossville (G2)*....577
Roxbury (E3)*....145
Rozel (C3)*....233
Ruella (D4)....10

Ruleton (A2)*....52
Runnymede (E4)....5
Rush Center (C3)*....350
Russell (D3)*....6,483
Russell Springs (A3)*....161
Rydal (E2)*....42
Sabetha (G2)*....2,173
Saffordville (F3)*....110
Saint Benedict (F2)*....150
St. Clere (F2)....7
St. Francis (A2)*....1,892
St. George (F2)*....251
St. John (D3)*....1,735
St. Joseph (E2)....28
St. Marys (G2)*....1,201
St. Paul (G4)*....783
St. Peter (B2)....100
Salina (E3)*....26,176
Sanford (C3)*....50
Satanta (B4)*....667
Savonburg (G4)*....155
Sawyer (D4)*....223
Saxman (D3)*....33
Scammon (H4)*....561
Scandia (E2)*....611
Schoenchen (C3)*....170
Scott City (B3)*....3,204
Scottsville (D2)*....108
Scranton (G3)*....487
Sedan (F4)*....1,640
Sedgwick (E4)*....732
Seguin (B2)....12
Selden (B2)*....438
Selkirk (A3)*....100
Selma (G2)....45
Seneca (F2)*....1,911
Severance (G2)*....197
Severy (F4)*....477
Seward (D3)*....130
Shady Bend (D2)*....25
Shaffer (C3)....15
Shallow Water (B3)*....105
Sharon (D4)*....278
Sharon Springs (A3)*....994
Sharpe (E3)....31
Shaw (G4)....35
Shawnee (H3)*....845
Sherman (H4)*....100
Shields (D3)....75
Silica (D3)*....10
Silver Lake (G2)*....331
Silverdale (F4)*....150
Simpson (E2)*....234
Sitka (C4)*....150
Skiddy (F3)*....70
Smith Center (D2)*....2,026
Smolan (E3)*....180
Soldier (G2)*....193
Solomon (E3)*....834
Solomon Rapids (D2)*....100
South Haven (E4)*....358
S. Hutchinson (D3)*....1,045
S. Mound (G4)*....50
Sparks (G2)*....129
Spearville (C4)*....610
Speed (C2)*....70
Spivey (D4)*....109
Spring Hill (H3)*....619
Stafford (D4)*....2,005
Stanley (H3)*....300
Stark (G4)*....157
Sterling (D3)*....2,243
Stilwell (H3)*....209
Stockdale (F2)....80

Stockton (C2)*....1,867
Strawberry (E2)....11
Strawn (E3)*....150
Strong City (F3)*....680
Studley (B2)*....73
Stull (G3)....100
Stuttgart (C2)*....100
Sublette (B4)*....838
Summerfield (F2)*....305
Sun City (D4)*....231
Sunflower (G3)*....3,834
Susank (D3)*....100
Sycamore (G4)*....350
Sylvan Grove (D2)*....506
Sylvia (E3)*....496
Syracuse (A3)*....2,075
Talmage (E2)*....250
Talmo (E2)*....40
Tampa (E3)*....216
Tasco (B2)*....16
Tecumseh (G2)*....200
Tescott (E2)*....412
Teterville (F3)*....100
Thayer (G4)*....423
Thornburg (D2)....
Thrall (F3)*....38
Timken (C3)*....138
Tipton (D2)*....268
Tonganoxie (G2)*....1,138
TOPEKA (E2)*....78,791
Topeka (urban area)....88,100
Toronto (G4)*....600
Towanda (E4)*....417
Trading Post (H3)....
Traer (B2)*....69
Treece (H4)*....378
Tribune (A3)*....1,010
Trousdale (C4)*....110
Troy (G2)*....977
Turner (H2)*....1,500
Turon (D4)*....632
Tyro (G4)*....279
Udall (E4)*....410
Ulysses (A4)*....2,243
Uniontown (G4)*....232
Upland (E2)....25
Urbana (G4)*....70
Utica (B3)*....365
Valeda (G4)*....125
Valley Center (E4)*....854
Valley Falls (G2)*....1,139
Varner (D4)*....54
Vassar (G3)*....80
Vermillion (F2)*....283
Vernon (G4)*....45
Vesper (D2)*....100
Victor (D2)....6
Victoria (C3)*....988
Vilas (G4)*....34
Vine Creek (E2)....13
Vining (F2)*....168
Vinland (G3)*....68
Viola (E4)*....132
Virgil (F4)*....354
Vliets (F2)*....79
Voda (C2)....30
Volland (F3)*....20
Wabaunsee (F2)....110
Waconda Springs (D2)*....20
Wakarusa (G3)....72
Wakeeney (C2)*....2,446
Wakefield (E2)*....591
Waldo (D2)*....216
Waldron (D4)*....83

Walker (C3)*....103
Wallace (A3)*....111
Walnut (G4)*....534
Walton (E3)*....220
Wamego (F2)*....1,869
Washington (E2)*....1,527
Waterloo (E4)....45
Waterville (F2)*....676
Wathena (H2)*....797
Wauneta (F4)*....75
Waverly (G4)*....487
Wayne (E2)*....60
Wayside (G4)*....90
Webber (D2)*....96
Webster (C2)*....130
Weir (H4)*....819
Welborn (H2)*....3,425
Welda (G3)*....214
Wellington (E4)*....7,747
Wells (E2)*....75
Wellsford (C4)*....59
Wellsville (H3)*....729
Weskan (A3)*....200
West Mineral (H4)*....349
West Plains (Plains*) (B4)....718
Westfall (D3)*....75
Westmoreland (F2)*....416
Westphalia (G3)*....254
Westwood (H2)*....1,581
Westwood Hills ‡(H2)....431
Wetmore (G2)*....397
Wheaton (F2)*....134
Wheeler (A2)*....35
White City (F3)*....540
White Cloud (G2)*....308
Whitewater (E4)*....453
Whiting (G2)*....267
Wichita (E4)*....168,279
Wichita (urban area)....192,009
Wilburton (A4)*....22
Willard (G2)*....95
Williamsburg (G3)*....297
Williamstown (G2)*....60
Willis (G2)*....140
Wilmore (C4)*....172
Wilmot (W4)*....25
Wilsey (F3)*....251
Wilson (D3)*....1,039
Winchester (G2)*....355
Windom (E3)*....193
Winfield (F4)*....10,264
Winifred (F2)*....53
Winkler (F2)*....6
Winona (A2)*....382
Wolcott (H2)....
Wolf (A3)....2
Womer (D2)....15
Woodbine (E3)*....195
Woodruff (C2)*....46
Woodston (C2)*....296
Worden (G3)....50
Wright (C4)*....350
Xenia (G4)....24
Yates Center (G4)*....2,178
Yocemento (C3)....
Yoder (E4)*....100
Zeandale (F2)....40
Zenda (D4)*....226
Zenith (D4)*....100
Zimmerdale (E3)....25
Zook (C2)*....30
Zurich (C2)*....186

**Map on Page 62**

**120 COUNTIES**

## KENTUCKY

Total Population 2,944,806

Adair (G6)....17,603
Allen (E7)....13,787
Anderson (H5)....8,984
Ballard (C3)....8,545
Barren (F7)....28,461
Bath (K4)....10,410
Bell (K7)....47,602
Boone (H3)....13,015

Bourbon (J4)....17,752
Boyd (M4)....49,949
Boyle (H5)....20,532
Bracken (J3)....8,424
Breathitt (L5)....19,964
Breckinridge (E5)....15,528
Bullitt (F5)....11,349
Butler (D6)....11,309
Caldwell (E3)....13,199
Calloway (D4)....20,147

Campbell (L2)....76,196
Carlisle (C3)....6,206
Carroll (G3)....8,517
Carter (L4)....22,559
Casey (H6)....17,446
Christian (C7)....42,359
Clark (J5)....18,898
Clay (K6)....23,116
Clinton (G7)....10,605
Crittenden (E2)....10,818

Cumberland (G7)....9,309
Daviess (C5)....57,241
Edmonson (E6)....9,376
Elliott (L4)....7,085
Estill (K5)....14,677
Fayette (J4)....100,746
Fleming (K4)....11,962
Floyd (M5)....53,500
Franklin (H4)....25,933
Fulton (C4)....13,668

Gallatin (H3)....3,969
Garrard (M5)....11,029
Grant (H3)....9,809
Graves (D3)....31,364
Grayson (E5)....17,063
Green (F6)....11,261
Greenup (M3)....24,887
Hancock (D5)....6,009
Hardin (F5)....50,312
Harlan (L7)....71,751

Harrison (J4)....13,736
Hart (F6)....15,321
Henderson (B5)....30,715
Henry (G4)....11,394
Hickman (C3)....7,778
Hopkins (B6)....38,815
Jackson (J6)....13,101
Jefferson (F4)....484,615
Jessamine (H5)....12,458
Johnson (M5)....23,846

Kenton (K2)....104,254
Knott (M6)....20,320
Knox (K7)....30,409
Larue (F5)....9,956
Laurel (J6)....25,797
Lawrence (M4)....14,418
Lee (K5)....8,739
Leslie (L6)....15,537
Letcher (M6)....39,522
Lewis (L3)....13,520

Lincoln (H6).....18,668
Livingston (D2).....7,184
Logan (D7).....22,335
Lyon (E5).....6,853
Madison (J5).....31,179
Magoffin (L5).....13,839
Marion (G5).....17,212
Marshall (D3).....13,387
Martin (M5).....11,677
Mason (K3).....18,486
McCracken (D3).....49,137
McCreary (J7).....16,660
McLean (C5).....10,021
Meade (E5).....9,422
Menifee (K5).....4,798
Mercer (H5).....14,643
Metcalfe (F7).....9,851
Monroe (F7).....13,770
Montgomery (K4).....13,025
Morgan (L5).....13,624
Muhlenberg (C6).....32,501
Nelson (F5).....19,521
Nicholas (J4).....7,532
Ohio (D6).....20,840
Oldham (G4).....11,018
Owen (H3).....9,755
Owsley (K6).....7,324
Pendleton (J3).....9,610
Perry (L6).....46,566
Pike (N6).....81,154
Powell (K5).....6,812
Pulaski (H6).....38,452
Robertson (J3).....2,881
Rockcastle (J6).....13,925
Rowan (L4).....12,708
Russell (G7).....13,717
Scott (H4).....15,141
Shelby (G4).....17,912
Simpson (D7).....11,678
Spencer (G4).....6,157
Taylor (G6).....14,403
Todd (C7).....12,890
Trigg (E3).....9,683
Trimble (G3).....5,148
Union (E2).....14,893
Warren (E6).....42,758
Washington (G5).....12,777
Wayne (H7).....16,475
Webster (E2).....15,555
Whitley (J7).....31,940
Wolfe (K5).....7,615
Woodford (H4).....11,212

## CITIES and TOWNS

Aberdeen (D6)*..... 50
Adair (D5)*..... 100
Adairville (D7)*..... 800
Adams (M4)*..... 300
Adolphus (E7)*..... 500
Aflex (N5)*..... 250
Akersville (F7)*..... 152
Albany (G7)*.....1,920
Alcalde (J6)*.....
Alcorn (K5)*..... 100
Alexandria (J3)*..... 536
Allais (L6)*..... 600
Allegre (C7)*..... 125
Allen (M5)*..... 421
Allen Springs (E7)*.....
Allensville (C7)*..... 337
Allock (L6)*..... 608
Almo (D3)*..... 150
Alpha (G7)*..... 75
Alpine (H7)*..... 150
Alton Station (H4)*..... 75
Altro (L6)*..... 75
Alva (L7)*.....1,341
Alvaton (E7)*..... 250
Amburgey (M6)*.....
Ammie (K6)*.....
Anchorage (F4)*..... 883
Anco (L6)*..... 400
Anna (E6)*.....
Anneta (E6)*..... 100
Annville (K6)*..... 350
Ansel (H6)*..... 195
Arabia (H6)*..... 229
Arjay (K7)*.....1,000
Arlington (C3)*..... 584
Artemus (K7)*.....1,000
Arvel (K5)*.....
Ashbyburg (C5)*.....
Ashcamp (N6)*.....
Ashland (M4)*.....31,131
Ashland, Ky.—Huntington, W. Va. (urban area).....156,136
Athertonville (F5)*..... 166
Auburn (D7)*..... 994
Audubon Park (F4).....1,790
Augusta (J3)*.....1,599
Austin (F7)*..... 150
Auxier (M5)*.....1,000
Avenstoke (H4)..... 125
Bagdad (G4)*..... 400
Baizetown (D6)*..... 127
Bakerton (G7)*.....
Balkan (K7)*.....
Bandana (C2)*..... 300
Bangor (L4)*..... 155
Banner (M5)*.....
Barbourville (K7)*.....2,926
Bardstown (G5)*.....4,154
Bardstown Jct. (F5)*. 75
Bardwell (C3)*.....1,033
Barlow (C3)*..... 657
Barnrock (M5)*.....
Barretts Ferry (D5)*..... 10
Barterville (J4)*..... 100
Baskett (B5)*..... 275
Battletown (E4)*..... 125
Bayou (D2)..... 125
Bays (L5)*.....
Beals (C5)*..... 150
Beattyville (K5)*.....1,042
Beauty (N5)*..... 577
Beaver Dam (D6)*.....1,349
Bedford (G3)*..... 533
Bee Spring (E6)*.....
Beech Creek (C6)*.....
Beech Grove (C5)*..... 162
Belcher (N6)*.....
Belfry (N5)*.....1,315
Bell Farm (H7)*.....
Bellevue (L1)*.....9,040
Belmont (F5)*..... 75
Belton (D6)*.....
Benham (M7)*.....3,982
Benton (D3)*.....1,980
Berea (J5)*.....3,372
Bernstadt (J6)*..... 300
Berry (J3)*..... 312
Berrys Lick (D6)*..... 50
Bertis (K4)*..... 97
Bethel (K4)*..... 225
Bethelridge (H6)*..... 190
Bethlehem (G4)*..... 188
Betsy Layne (M5)*.....1,500
Beverly (L7)*..... 500
Bevier (C6)*..... 175
Big Branch (M6)*.....
Big Clifty (E5)*..... 500
Big Creek (K6)*..... 560
Big Rock (L6)*..... 430
Big Spring (E5)*..... 250
Billows (J6)..... 50
Birdsville (D2)*..... 113
Black Rock (E6)*..... 25
Blackey (M6)*..... 393
Blackford (B6)*..... 165
Blacks Ferry (G7)*.....
Blaine (M4)*.....
Blairs Mills (L4)*.....
Blanche (K7)*..... 455
Blandville (C3)*..... 124
Bloomfield (G5)*..... 666
Blue Diamond (L6)*.....1,968
Bluestone (L4)*..... 60
Boaz (D3)*..... 100
Boldman (M5)*..... 300
Bolyn (M6)*..... 150
Bond (J6)*.....
Bondville (H5)*..... 91
Bonnieville (F6)*..... 300
Bonnyman (L6)*..... 900
Boone (J5)*..... 137
Booneville (K6)*..... 165
Boreing (J6)*..... 250
Boston (F5)*..... 300
Botto (K6)*..... 60
Bowen (K5)*..... 150
Bowling Green (D7)*...18,347
Boyd (J3)*..... 55
Bradford (J3)*..... 45
Bradfordsville (G6)*..... 450
Brandenburg (E4)*..... 755
Brazil (J5)*.....
Breeding (G7)*..... 100
Bremen (C6)*..... 410
Brent (L2).....
Brewers (D3)*..... 57
Brightshade (K7)*..... 200
Bristow (E6)*..... 73
Brodhead (J6)*..... 808
Bromley (K1)*..... 980
Bronston (H7)*..... 300
Brooklyn (D6)*..... 50
Brooks (F4)*..... 150
Brookside (L7)*..... 600
Brooksville (J3)*..... 622
Browder (D6)*..... 350
Brownsville (E6)*..... 447
Bruin (L4)*..... 125
Brushart (L3)*..... 50
Bryan (G7)*..... 137
Bryantsville (H5)*..... 126
Buchanan (M4)*..... 160
Buckner (G4)*..... 250
Buechel (F4)*.....1,500
Buffalo (F6)*..... 495
Buford (D5)..... 100
Bulan (L6)*.....1,446
Bunch (J6)*.....
Burgin (H5)*..... 777
Burkesville (G7)*.....1,278
Burkley (C3)*..... 340
Burlington (J2)*..... 400
Burna (D2)*..... 300
Burning Springs (K6)*.. 350
Burnside (H6)*..... 615
Burton (Bypro*) ‡(M6) 257
Burtonville (L4)*..... 200
Bush (K6)*..... 200
Buskirk (L5)*.....
Busseyville (M4)*..... 100
Butler (J3)*..... 404
Cadiz (B7)*.....1,280
Cains Store (H6)*.....
Calhoun (C5)*..... 746
California (J3)*..... 117
Calvary (G6)..... 250
Calvert City (D3)*..... 900
Calvin (K7)*.....
Camp Dix (L3)*..... 75
Camp Taylor (F4)*.....
Campbellsburg (G3)*..... 361
Campbellsville (G6)*.....3,477
Campton (K5)*..... 431
Canada (N5)*.....1,500
Cane Valley (G6)*..... 150
Caney (L5)*..... 400
Caneyville (E6)*..... 377
Canmer (F6)*.....
Cannel City (L5)*..... 400
Canton (B7)*..... 250
Carbon Glow (M6)*..... 300
Carlisle (J4)*.....1,524
Carntown (J3)..... 100
Carpenter (K7)*.....
Carrollton (G3)*..... 226
Carrsville (D2)*..... 205
Carter (L4)*..... 84
Cartwright (G7)*..... 110
Casey Creek (G6)*..... 117
Caseyville (B5)*..... 73
Cash (F6)*..... 75
Catlettsburg (M4)*.....4,750
Cave City (F6)*.....1,119
Cawood (L7)*.....1,232
Cayce (C4)*..... 200
Cecilia (F5)*..... 400
Center (F6)*..... 175
Centertown (C6)*..... 370
Central City (C6)*.....4,110
Cerulean (B7)*..... 218
Chance (G7)*..... 350
Chaplin (G5)*..... 200
Chappell (L7)*.....

Charley (M5)*.....
Charters (L3)*..... 20
Chavies (L6)*..... 300
Chenoa (K7)*.....
Cherokee (M4)*.....
Chevrolet (L7)*..... 500
Chilesburg (J4)*..... 50
Christianburg (G4)*..... 100
Clark Hill (L4)*..... 400
Clarkson (E6)*..... 489
Claxton (B6)*..... 72
Clay (B6)*.....1,291
Clay City (K5)*..... 636
Claymour (C7)..... 150
Claypool (E7)*..... 50
Clearfield (L4)*.....
Cleaton (C6)*..... 450
Clermont (F5)*..... 40
Cliff (M5)*..... 500
Clifford (N4)*..... 50
Clifty (C7)*..... 200
Climax (J6)*..... 75
Clinton (C3)*.....1,593
Clintonville (J4)*..... 100
Closplint (L7)*..... 600
Clover Bottom (J5)*..... 600
Cloverport (D5)*.....1,357
Co-Operative (H7)*..... 400
Coakley (F6)*..... 150
Cobb (B6)*..... 200
Cold Spring (L2)*..... 518
Coleman (N6)*..... 200
Colesburg (F5)*..... 73
College Hill (J5)*..... 400
Collista (M5)*..... 175
Colmar (K7)*..... 500
Colson (M6)*..... 200
Columbia (G6)*.....2,167
Columbus (C3)*..... 482
Combs (L6)*..... 800
Concord (L3)*..... 142
Concordia (D4)*..... 75
Confluence (L6)*..... 285
Constance (J1)*..... 150
Conway (J6)*..... 75
Cooper (H7)*..... 275
Coopersville (H7)*..... 250
Coral Ridge (F4)*.....3,010
Corbin (J7)*.....7,744
Corinth (H3)*..... 283
Cork (F6)*..... 83
Cornishville (H5)*..... 230
Corydon (B5)*..... 742
Cottle (L5)*.....
Cottonburg (J5)*..... 122
Covington (K1)*.....64,452
Cowan (K4)*..... 200
Cowcreek (K6)*..... 250
Coxton (L7)*..... 700
Crab Orchard (H6)*..... 757
Crailhope (F6)*..... 50
Crane Nest (K7)*..... 200
Crayne (A6)*..... 300
Creal (F6)*..... 30
Creekville (L6)*..... 67
Creelsboro (G7)*..... 50
Crescent Springs (K1)...
Creston (G6)*..... 25
Crestwood (G4)*..... 450
Crider (B6)*..... 125
Crittenden (H3)*..... 287
Crofton (C6)*..... 500
Cromwell (D6)*..... 200
Cropper (G4)*..... 175
Crummies (L7)*..... 400
Crutchfield (C4)*..... 170
Cub Run (E6)*..... 250
Cubage (K7)*..... 325
Cumberland (M6)*.....4,249
Cundiff (G7)*..... 125
Cunningham (C3)*..... 275
Curdsville (C5)*..... 169
Custer (E5)*..... 200
Cutshin (L6)*.....
Cynthiana (J4)*.....4,847
Dabney (H6)*.....
Daisy (L6)*..... 300
Dalton (B6)*..... 75
Daniel Boone (C6).....
Danville (H5)*.....8,686
David (M5)*..... 800
Dawson Springs (B6)*..2,374
Daysville (C7)..... 50
Dayton (L1)*.....8,977
De Coursey (L2).....
De Mossville (J3)*..... 104
Decoy (L5)*..... 250
Defoe (G4)*..... 142
Dekoven (B5)*.....
Delaware (C5)*..... 28
Delphia (L6)*..... 395
Denton (M4)*..... 200
Depoy (C6)*.....
Dewitt (K7)*..... 250
Dexter (D3)*..... 277
Dixon (B5)*..... 624
Donansburg (F6)*..... 200
Donerail (J4)*..... 91
Dorton (M6)*..... 500
Dover (K3)*..... 334
Drakesboro (D6)*.....1,102
Dreyfus (J5)*..... 150
Dry Ridge (H3)*..... 640
Dublin (C3)..... 100
Duckers (H4)*..... 50
Duncan (H5)..... 125
Dundee (D5)*..... 150
Dunham (M6)*.....1,200
Dunmor (C6)*..... 156
Dunnville (H6)*..... 140
Dwale (M5)*..... 495
Dycusburg (E3)*..... 147
Dyer (E5)*..... 39
Eadsville (H7)..... 300
Eagle Station (G3)*..... 35
Earlington (B6)*.....2,753
East Bernstadt (J6)*..... 900
East Point (M5)*..... 200
Eby (L4)*..... 50
Echols (D6)*..... 50
Eddyville (B6)*.....1,840
Edmonton (F7)*..... 519
Edo (N6)*..... 200
Edsel (M4)*..... 50
Eighty Eight (F7)*..... 75
Ekron (E5)*..... 188
Elamton (L5)*.....
Eli (H6)*..... 250
Elias (K6)*.....
Elihu (H6)*.....
Elizabethtown (F5)*.....5,807
Elizaville (K4)*..... 150
Elk Creek (G4)..... 90
Elk Horn (G6)*.....
Elkatawa (K5)*..... 250
Elkfork (L5)*.....
Elkhorn City (Praise*) (N6).....1,349
Elkton (C7)*.....1,312
Elliottville (L4)*..... 100
Elmrock (L6)*..... 276
Elrod (J6)*..... 75
Elsmere (K2).....3,483
Elva (D3)*..... 95
Eminence (G4)*.....1,462
Emlyn (J7)*..... 700
Emma (M5)*..... 600
English (G3)*..... 150
Ennis (D6)*..... 612
Eolia (M6)*..... 100
Erlanger (K2)*.....3,694
Essie (L6)*.....
Estill (M6)*.....
Etoile (F7)*..... 40
Etty (M6)*..... 200
Eubank (H6)*..... 322
Evarts (L7)*.....1,937
Evelyn (K5)*.....
Ewing (K4)*..... 400
Ezel (L5)*.....
Fagan (K5)*..... 50
Fairfield ‡(G5)*..... 202
Fairplay (G7)*..... 78
Fairview (C7)*.....
Falcon (L5)*..... 300
Falls of Rough (D5)*..... 195
Fallsburg (M4)*..... 200
Falmouth (J3)*.....2,186
Fancy Farm (C3)*..... 419
Fariston (J6)*..... 290
Farler (L6)*..... 200
Farmers (L4)*.....
Farmington (D4)*..... 221
Faubush (H6)*..... 300
Fedscreek (N6)*.....
Felty (K6)*..... 200
Ferguson (D7)..... 50
Ferguson (H6)*..... 550
Field (K7)*..... 300
Finchville (G4)*..... 75
Finley (G6)*..... 105
Finney (E7)*..... 75
Firebrick (L3)*..... 150
Fishtrap (N6)*.....1,000
Fitchburg (K5)*..... 200
Flat (K5)*..... 200
Flat Fork (L5)*.....
Flat Lick (K7)*.....1,000
Flat Rock (H7)*.....
Flatgap (M5)*..... 130
Fleming (M6)*..... 943
Flemingsburg (K4)*.....1,502
Flint (M6)*..... 100
Flippin (F7)*..... 150
Florence (J2)*.....1,325
Fonde (K7)*.....1,300
Fonthill (H6)*..... 50
Ford (J5)*..... 250
Fordsville (D5)*..... 533
Forks of Elkhorn (H4)* 400
Fort Knox (F5)*.....10,000
Fort Mitchell (K1)..... 312
Fort Thomas (L1)*.....10,870
Fort Wright ‡(K2)..... 594
Foster (J3)*..... 108
Fountain Run (F7)*..... 218
Francisville (J1)..... 25
FRANKFORT (H4)*.....11,916
Franklin (D7)*.....4,343
Fredonia (B6)*..... 395
Freeburn (N5)*.....2,200
Freedom (F7)*..... 75
Frenchburk (K5)*..... 268
Frew (L6)*..... 162
Frogue (G7)*..... 300
Fry (G6)*..... 50
Frymire (E5)*..... 25
Fullerton (L3)*.....1,501
Fulton (C4)*.....3,224
Furnace (K5)*..... 75
Gabbard (K6).....
Gallup (M4)*.....
Gamaliel (F7)*..... 500
Gapcreek (H7)*..... 300
Garfield (E5)*..... 150
Garlin (G6)*..... 75
Garrett (M6)*.....
Garrison (L3)*..... 300
Gatliff (K7)*..... 500
Gatton (F6)*..... 101
Gausdale (J7)*.....
Geneva (B5)*..... 195
Georges Creek (M5)*..... 300
Georgetown (H4)*.....5,516
Germantown (K3)*..... 260
Gesling (L4)*..... 100
Gest (H4)*..... 47
Ghent (G3)*..... 368
Gilbertsville (D3)*..... 700
Gimlet (L4)*..... 100
Girdler (K7)*..... 500
Glasgow (E6)*.....7,025
Glen Dean (E5)*..... 100
Glen Springs (K3)*..... 50
Glencoe (H3)*..... 500
Glendale (F5)*..... 300
Glens Fork (G6)*..... 213
Glenwood (M4).....
Glo (M6)*..... 500
Glomawr (L6)*..... 800
Golden Pond (B7)*..... 125
Goodloe (M5)*.....
Gooserock (K6)*.....
Goshen (F4)*..... 100
Gracey (B7)*.....
Gradyville (G6)*..... 200
Graham (C6)*.....1,100
Grahn (L4)*..... 600
Grand Rivers (E3)*..... 234
Grange City (K4)*..... 225
Grant (H3)*..... 100
Grassland (E6)*..... 79
Gratz (H4)*..... 150
Gravel Switch (G5)*..... 200
Gray (K7)*..... 300
Gray Hawk (J6)*..... 300
Graysbranch (M3)*..... 156
Grayson (M4)*.....1,383
Green Hall (K6)*..... 120
Greenmount (J6)*..... 119
Greensburg (F6)*.....1,032
Greenup (M3)*.....1,276
Greenville (C6)*.....2,661
Greenwood (J7)*..... 100
Grove Center (B5)*..... 200
Guage (L5)*..... 50
Gulnare (M5)*..... 150
Gus (D6)*.....
Guston (E5)*..... 108
Guthrie (C7)*.....1,253
Guy (D6)*.....
Haddix (L6)*..... 500
Hadensville (C7)..... 85
Hadley (D6)*..... 675
Haldeman (L4)*.....
Haleys Mill (C6)*.....
Halfway (E7)*..... 200
Hall (M6)*.....
Hamilton (H3)..... 25
Hamlin (E4)*..... 20
Hammond (K7)*..... 400
Hampton (D2)*..... 120
Hanson (C6)*..... 393
Happy (L6)*..... 800
Hardburly (L6)*..... 800
Hardin (D3)*..... 324
Hardin Springs (E5)*..... 112
Hardinsburg (D5)*..... 902
Hardshell (L6)*..... 50
Hardy (N5)*.....
Hardyville (F6)*..... 300
Harlan (L7)*.....4,786
Harned (E5)*..... 140
Harold (M5)*..... 500
Harrods Creek (F4)*.....
Harrodsburg (H5)*.....5,262
Hartford (D6)*.....1,564
Harveyton (L6)*..... 368
Hatcher (G6)*.....
Hatfield (N5)*..... 250
Hawesville (D5)*.....925
Hazard (L6)*.....6,985
Hazel (D4)*..... 444
Hazel Green (K5)*..... 264
Hazle Patch (J6)*.....
Head of Grassy (L4)*..... 50
Hebbardsville (C5)*..... 238
Hebron (J1)*..... 250
Heidelberg (K5)*.....
Heidrick (K7)*..... 600
Heisey (N5)..... 150
Helechawa (L5)*..... 120
Hellier (N6)*..... 346
Helton (L7)*.....
Henderson (B5)*.....16,837
Hendricks (L5)*.....
Henshaw (B5)*..... 210
Herndon (C7)*..... 250
Hesler (H4).....
Hi Hat (M6)*..... 650
Hibernia (G6)*..... 100
Hickman (C4)*.....2,037
Hickory (D3)*..... 185
High Bridge (H5)*..... 350
Highland Heights (L1)..1,569
Highsplint (L7)*.....1,500
Highway (G7)*..... 100
Hillsboro (K4)*..... 141
Hima (K6)*..... 200
Himlerville (Beauty*) (N5)..... 577
Himyar (K7)*..... 400
Hindman (M6)*..... 521
Hinton (J4)*..... 125
Hiram (L7)*..... 300
Hiseville (F6)*.....
Hitchins (M4)*.....1,000
Hodgenville (F5)*.....1,695
Holland (E7)*..... 120
Homer (D7)*..... 58
Hope (K4)*.....
Hopewell (M4)*..... 158
Hopkinsville (B7)*.....12,526
Horse Branch (D6)*..... 225
Horse Cave (F6)*.....1,545
Horton (D6)*..... 30
Howardstown (F5)*..... 100
Howel (B7)*..... 50
Huddy (N5)*.....
Hudson (E5)*..... 133
Huntersville (G7)*..... 193
Huntsville (D6)*..... 140
Hustonville (H6)*..... 435
Hyden (L6)*..... 647
Ilsley (B6)*..... 400
Independence (H3)*..... 285
Indian Hills ‡(F4)..... 291
Inez (N5)*..... 622
Irad (M4)*.....
Irvine (K5)*.....3,259
Irvington (E5)*..... 831
Island (C6)*..... 566
Isonville (L4)*..... 150
Iuka (D3)*..... 21
Ivel (M5)*.....1,200
Ivis (M6)*.....
Ivyton (L5)*..... 300
Jackson (L5)*.....1,978
Jamestown (G7)*.....1,064
Jason (K6)*..... 250
Jeff (L6)*.....1,500
Jeffersontown (G4)*.....1,246
Jeffersonville (K5)*..... 479
Jellicocreek (J7)*.....
Jenkins (M6)*.....6,921
Jericho (G4)*..... 110
Jeriel (M4)*..... 175
Jett (H4)*..... 240
Jetts Creek (K6)*..... 75
Johnetta (J6)*..... 100
Jonesville (H3)*..... 158
Joy (D2)*..... 70
Junction City (H5)*..... 988
Kayjay (K7)*..... 350
Keaton (L5)*.....
Keavy (J6)*.....
Keene (H5)*..... 500
Kehoe (L4)*..... 175
Kelly (C7)..... 90
Keltner (F6)*.....
Kemp (F6)*.....
Kenton (J3)*..... 165
Kenvir (L7)*.....3,250
Kevil (C3)*..... 202
King (K7)..... 50
Kings Mountain (H6)*.. 350
Kingsley ‡(F4)..... 488
Kingswood (E5)*..... 225
Kirk (D5)*..... 75
Kirkmansville (C6)*..... 138
Kirksey (D3)*..... 182
Kirksville (J5)*.....1,500
Kite (M6)*.....
Kitts (L7)*.....1,431
Knifley (G6)*..... 225
Knob Lick (F6)*.....
Knottsville (D5)..... 250
Kona (M6)*..... 400
Kosmosdale (E4)*..... 375
Krypton (L6)*..... 88
Kuttawa (E3)*..... 794
Kyrock (E6)*.....
La Center (C3)*..... 593
La Fayette (B7)*..... 246
La Grange (G4)*.....1,558
Lackey ‡(M6)*..... 452
Lair (J4)..... 65
Lake (K6)*..... 250
Lakeside (K2)..... 988
Lamasco (B7)*..... 100
Lambric (L5)*..... 75
Lancaster (H5)*.....2,402
Latonia (K2).....
Laurel Creek (K6)*..... 300
Lawrenceburg (H4)*.....2,369
Lawton (L4)*..... 375
Lebanon (G5)*.....4,640
Lebanon Junction(F5)*.1,243
Lecta (F6)*..... 50
Lee (E6)*..... 25
Lee City (L5)*..... 120
Leeco (K5)*..... 200
Leighton (K5)*..... 500
Leitchfield (E6)*.....1,312
Lejunior (L7)*.....
Leon (M4)*..... 125
Levee (K5)*.....
Level Green (J6)*..... 75
Lewisburg (C6)*..... 496
Lewisport (D5)*..... 656
Lexington (J4)*.....55,534
Liberty (H6)*.....1,291
Lida (K6)*..... 200
Liggett (L7)*..... 450
Ligon (M6)*..... 396
Lily (J6)*.....
Limaburg (J2)..... 45
Linton (E3)..... 200
Linwood (F6)*.....
Lisman (B6)*..... 175
Littcarr (M6)*.....
Livermore (C5)*.....1,441
Livia (C5)*..... 75
Livingston (J6)*..... 378
Lockport (H4)*.....
Locust Branch (J5)*..... 300
Locust Hill (E5)*..... 50
Logansport (D6)*..... 125
Lola (D2)*..... 150
London (J6)*.....3,426
Loneoak (D3).....1,250
Lookout (N6)*.....1,300
Lookout Heights (K1)... 603
Loretto (G5)*..... 600
Lost Creek (L6)*..... 250
Lothair (L6)*.....1,313
Louellen (L7)*.....1,600
Louisa (M4)*.....2,015
Louisville (F4)*.....369,129
Louisville (urban area).....470,394
Lovelaceville (C3)*..... 275
Lovely (N5)*..... 500
Lowes (C3)*..... 150
Lomansville (M5)*..... 500
Loyall (L7)*.....1,548
Lucas (F7)*..... 150
Lucile (L4)..... 75
Ludlow (K1)*.....6,374
Lynch (M7)*.....3,970
Lynn Grove (D4)*..... 75
Lynnville (D4)*..... 100
Lyons (F5)*.....
Mac (G6)*.....
Maceo (D5)*..... 350
Mackville (G5)*..... 250
Macon (E6)*.....
Madisonville (B6)*.....11,132
Majestic (N5)*.....1,140
Malone (L5)*..... 260
Maloneton (M3)*..... 100
Manchester (K6)*.....1,706
Manitou (B6)*..... 100
Mannington (C6)*..... 300
Mannsville (G6)*..... 200
Mariba (K5)*..... 75
Marion (A6)*.....2,375
Marrowbone (F7)*..... 250
Marshes Siding (H7)*... 500

Map on Page 63    **LOUISIANA**    Total Population 2,683,516

## 64 PARISHES

### CITIES and TOWNS

Warnerton (K5)*
Washington (G5)* 1,291
Water Proof (H3)* 1,180
Watson (L1)* 400
Waverly (H2)*
Waxia (G5)* 567
Weeks (G7)* 1,499
Weiss (L1)
Welcome (L3)* 300
Weldon (E1) 35
Welsh (E6)* 2,416
West Monroe (F1)* 10,302
Westlake (D6)* 1,871
Westwego (O4)* 8,281
Weyanoke (H5)*
White Castle (J3)* 1,839
White Sulphur Springs (F3) 50
Whitehall (M2)* 450
Whiteville (F5)*
Wilda (E4)*
Wildsville (G3)*
Willetts (G3)* 12
Wills Point (L7)
Wilmer (K5)* 75
Wilson (H5)* 375
Winnfield (E3)* 5,629
Winnsboro (G2)* 3,655
Wisner (G3)* 738
Woodland (J5)*
Woodlawn (E6) 210
Woodside (G5)*
Woodworth (E4)* 392
Wright (F6)* 36
Wyatt (E2)* 40
Yellow Pine (D2) 90
Youngsville (G6)* 769
Zachary (K1)* 1,542
Zenoria (F3)* 100
Zimmerman (E4)* 500
Zwolle (C3)* 1,555

*Map on Page 64*

## MAINE

*Total Population 913,774*

### 16 COUNTIES

Androscoggin (C7) 83,594
Aroostook (F2) 96,039
Cumberland (C8) 169,201
Franklin (B5) 20,682
Hancock (G6) 32,105
Kennebec (D7) 83,881
Knox (E7) 28,121
Lincoln (D7) 18,004
Oxford (B6) 44,221
Penobscot (F5) 108,198
Piscataquis (E4) 18,617
Sagadahoc (D7) 20,911
Somerset (C4) 39,785
Waldo (E6) 21,687
Washington (H6) 35,187
York (B9) 93,541

### CITIES and TOWNS

Abbot Village (E5)* △462
Acton (B8)* △473
Addison (H6)* △846
Albion (E6)* △992
Alexander (H5) △282
Alfred (B9)* △1,112
Allagash (F1) △680
Allens Mills (C6) 175
Alna (D7)* △350
Alton (F5) △314
Amherst (G6)* △151
Andover (B6)* △756
Anson (D6)* △2,199
Appleton (E7)* △671
Argyle (F5) △133
Ashdale (D8) 60
Ashland (G2)* △2,370
Ashville (G7)* 100
Athens (D6)* △725
Atkinson (E5) △400
Atlantic (G7)*
Auburn (C7)* 23,134
AUGUSTA (D7)* 20,913
Aurora (G6)* △91
Ayers (J6)*
Bailey Island (D8)* 175
Bancroft (H4)* △165
Bangor (F6)* 31,558
Bar Harbor (G7)* △3,864
Bar Mills (C8)* 800
Baring (J5)* △157
Bath (D8)* 10,644
Bay Point (D8)
Bayside (F7)*
Beals (H7)* △590
Beddington (H6) △26
Belfast (F7)* 5,960
Belgrade (D7)* △1,099
Belgrade Lakes (D6)* 450
Belmont (E7) △258
Bemis (B6)
Benedicta (G4)* △225
Benton (D6)* △1,421
Berry Mills (C6) 100
Berwick (B9)* △2,166
Bethel (B7)* △2,367
Biddeford (C9)* 20,836
Biddeford Pool (C9)*
Bingham (D5)* △1,354
Birch Harbor (H7)*
Birches (B6)
Blaine (H2)* △1,118
Blanchard (D5)* △75
Blue Hill (F7)* △1,308
Bolsters Mills (B7)* 115
Boothbay (D8)* △1,559
Boothbay Harbor (D8)* △2,290
Boundary (H3) 100
Bowdoinham (D7)* △1,039
Bowerbank (E5)* △20
Boyd Lake (F5)
Bradford (F5)* △793
Bradford Center (F5)* 150
Bradley (F6)* △786
Bremen (E8) △409
Brewer (F6)* 6,862
Bridgewater (H3)* △1,279
Bridgton (B7)* △2,950
Brighton (D5)* △106
Bristol (E8)* △1,476
Brooklin (F7)* △546
Brooks (E6)* △747
Brooksville (F7)* △751
Brookton (H4)* △206
Brownfield (B8)* △612
Brownville (E5)* △1,964
Brownville Jct. (E5)* 1,086
Brunswick (C8)* △10,996
Bryant Pond (B7)* 500
Buckfield (C7)* △899
Bucks Harbor (J6)* 160
Bucksport (F6)* △3,120
Burkettville (E7)* 100
Burlington (G5)* △425
Burnham (E6)* △706
Buxton (C8) △2,009
Buxton Center (B8)
Byron (B6) △96
Calais (J5)* 4,589
Cambridge (E5)* △326
Camden (F7)* △3,670
Canaan (D6)* △785
Canton (C7)* △746
Cape Neddick (B9)*
Cape Porpoise (C9)* 400
Capens (D4) 1
Caratunk (C5)* △96
Cardville (F5)* 200
Caribou (G2)* △9,923
Carmel (E6)* △996
Carrabassett (C5) 10
Carroll (G5)* △288
Carry Pond (C5)
Carthage (C6) △339
Cary (H4) △278
Casco (B7)* △881
Castine (F7)* △793
Cedar (J5)
Center Belmont (E7)
Center Lovell (B7)*
Center Montville (E7) 175
Centerville (H6)* △63
Chapman (G2) △381
Charleston (F5)* △771
Charlotte (J5) △252
Chebeague Island (C8)* 300
Chelsea (D7) △2,169
Cherryfield (H6)* △904
Chester (F5) △256
Chesterville (C6) △588
Chesuncook (D3)* 18
China (E7)* △1,375
Chisholm (C7)* 1,135
Citypoint (E7)
Clark Island (E8)* 175
Clarks Mill (B8)
Clayton Lake (E2)* 6
Cleveland (G1) 200
Cliff Island (C8)*
Clifton (G6) △193
Clinton (D6)* △1,623
Columbia (H6) △352
Columbia Falls (H6)* △550
Cooper (H6) △128
Coopers Mills (E7)* 239
Corea (H7)* 156
Corinna (E6)* △1,752
Cornish (B8)* △795
Cornville (D6) △563
Costigan (F5)* 158
Cranberry Isles (G7)* △228
Crawford (H5)* △83
Crescent Lake (C7)*
Criehaven (F8)* 60
Crouseville (G2)* 400
Crystal (G4) △373
Cumberland Ctr. (C8)* △2,030
Cumberland Mills (C8)*
Cundys Harbor (D8)* 80
Curtis Corner (C7)*
Cushing (E7) △376
Cutler (J6)* △483
Daigle (G1)
Damariscotta (E7)* △1,113
Danforth (H4)* △1,174
Danville (C7)*
Darkharbor (F7)*
Davidson (F4) 45
Dayton (B8) △502
Deblois (H6) △59
Dedham (F6) △374
Deer Isle (F7)* △1,234
Denmark (B8)* △447
Dennistown (C4) △24
Dennysville (J6)* △345
Derby (E5)* 500
Detroit (E6)* △492
Dexter (E5)* △4,126
Dixfield (C6)* △2,022
Dixmont (E6)* △631
Dorman (H6)
Dover-Foxcroft (E5)* △4,218
Dover South Mills (E5)
Dresden Mills (D7)* 100
Dry Mills (C8)* 220
Dryden (C6)* 800
Dyer Brook (G3) △219
Eagle Lake (F1)* △1,516
East Andover (B6)* 150
E. Baldwin (B8)*
E. Blue Hill (G7)* 200
E. Boothbay (D8)* 500
E. Brownfield (B8)* 130
E. Corinth (F5)* 450
E. Dixfield (C6)* 242
E. Dixmont (E6)
E. Dover (E5)* 67
E. Eddington (F6)* 300
E. Franklin (G6)* 78
E. Hampden (F6)
E. Hiram (B8)* 350
E. Holden (F6)*
E. Jackson (E6)
E. Knox (E7)
E. Lebanon (B9)*
E. Limington (B8) 150
E. Livermore (C7)* 500
E. Lowell (G5)
E. Machias (J6)* △1,101
E. Madison (D6) 692
E. Millinocket (F4)* △1,358
E. New Portland (D6)* 43
E. Orland (F6)*
E. Otisfield (B7) 50
E. Parsonfield (B8)* 175
E. Peru (C7)
E. Pittston (D7) 1,050
E. Poland (C7)* 490
E. Sebago (B8)*
E. Stoneham (B7)* 300
E. Sullivan (G6)* 250
E. Sumner (C7)* 114
E. Union (E7)* 190
E. Vassalboro (D7)* 200
E. Waterboro (B8)* 175
E. Waterford (B7)* 175
E. Wilton (C6)* 450
E. Winn (G5) 75
Easton (H2)* △1,664
Eastport (K6)* 3,123
Eaton (H4)* 120
Eddington (F6) △664
Edgecomb (D8)* △447
Edmunds (J6) △288
Eliot (B9)* △2,509
Ellsworth (F6)* 3,936
Ellsworth Falls (G6)* 500
Elms (B9)
Emery Mills (B9)* 150
Enfield (F5)* △1,196
Etna (E6)* △458
Eustis (B5)* △763
Exeter (E6)* △734
Fairbanks (C6) 200
Fairfield (D6)* △5,811
Fairfield Center (D6) 150
Falmouth (C8) △4,342
Farmington (C6)* △4,677
Farmington Falls (D6)*
Fayette (C7)* △397
Five Islands (D8)* 200
Forest City (H4)* 27
Forest Station (H4)* 30
Fort Fairfield (H2)* △5,791
Fort Kent (F1)* △5,343
Fort Kent Mills (F1)* 175
Fortunes Rocks (C9) 82
Frankfort (F6)* △578
Franklin (G6)* △709
Freedom (E7)* △466
Freeport (C8)* △3,280
Frenchboro (G7)* 104
Frenchville (G1)* △1,528
Friendship (E7)* △772
Frye (B6)* 150
Fryeburg (A7)* △1,926
Gardiner (D7)* 6,649
Garland (E5)* △581
Georgetown (D8)* △510
Gerard (C5) 20
Gilbertville (C7) 100
Gilead (B7)* △140
Glen Cove (E7)* 200
Glenburn (F6) △694
Goodrich (H2)
Goodwins Mills (B8) 200
Goose Rocks Beach (C9) 135
Gorham (C8)* △4,742
Gouldsboro (H7)* 1,168
Grand Isle (G1)* △1,230
Grand Lake Stream (H5)* △294
Grants (B5)* △9
Gray (C8)* △1,631
Great Pond (G6) 40
Great Works (F6)*
Green Lake (F6)* 40
Greene (C7)* △974
Greenville (D5)* △1,889
Greenville Jct. (D5)* 780
Grindstone (F4)* 60
Grove (J5)* 125
Guerette (G1)
Guilford (E5)* △1,842
Haines Landing (B6)
Hale (B6) 60
Hallowell (D7)* 3,404
Hamlin (H1) △430
Hampden (F6)* △3,608
Hampden Highlands (F6)*
Hancock (G6)* △755
Hanover (B7)* △211
Harmony (D6)* △709
Harpswell Center (D8) 100
Harrington (H6)* △853
Harrison (B7)* △1,026
Hartford (C7) △381
Hartland (D6)* △1,310
Haynesville (G4)* △185
Hebron (C7)* △829
Hermon (F6) 1,728
Highland Lake (C8)
Highpine (B9)* 125
Hinckley (D6)* 250
Hiram (B8)* △804
Hodgdon (H3)* △1,162
Holeb (C4)* 54
Hollis Center (B8)* 230
Hope (E7)* △504
Houghton (B6)
Houlton (H3)* △8,377
Howland (F5)* △1,441
Hudson (F5)* △455
Hulls Cove (G7)* 450
Indian River (H6)
Intervale (C8)*
Island Falls (G3)* △1,237
Isle au Haut (F7)* △82
Islesboro (F7)* △529
Islesford (G7)* 150
Jackman (C4)* △964
Jackman Station (C4)* 980
Jacksonville (J6)* 300
Jay (C7)* △3,102
Jefferson (D7)* △1,215
Jemtland (G1) 100
Jimpond (B5) 8
Jonesboro (J6)* △459
Jonesport (H6)* △1,727
Katahdin Iron Works (E5) 15
Keegan (G1)* 1,100
Kellyland (H5) 23
Kenduskeag (E6)* △387
Kennebago Lake (B5)*
Kennebunk (B9)* △4,273
Kennebunk Beach (C9)* 125
Kennebunk Port (C9)* △1,522
Kents Hill (D7)* 170
Kezar Falls (B8)* 1,400
Kineo (D4) △40
Kingfield (C6)* △963
Kingman (G4)* △358
Kingsbury (D5)* △35
Kittery (B9)* △8,380
Kittery Depot (B9) 1,220
Kittery Point (B9)* 1,137
Knox (E6) △445
Kokadjo (E4)*
La Grange (F5)* △511
Lake Moxie (D5)
Lake View (F5) △23
Lambert Lake (H4)*
Lamoine (G7) △443
Lebanon (B9) △1,499
Lee (G5)* △610
Leeds (C7) △797
Leeds Junction (C7)* 54
Levant (F6)* △706
Lewiston (C7)* 40,974
Liberty (E7)* △497
Lille (G1)*
Limerick (B8)* △961
Limestone (H2)* △2,427
Limington (B8)* △851
Lincoln (G5)* △4,030
Lincoln Center (G5)*
Lincolnville (E7)* 881
Lincolnville Ctr. (E7)*
Linneus (H3)* △777
Lisbon (C7)* △4,318
Lisbon Center (C7)* 300
Lisbon Falls (D7)* 2,155
Litchfield (D7)* △953
Little Deer Isle (F7)* 350
Littleton (H3) △1,001
Livermore (C7)* △1,313
Livermore Falls (C7)* △3,359
Locke Mills (B7)* 380
Long Island (C8)* 350
Long Pond (C4)* 84
Longcove (E8)
Loon Lake (B5) 10
Lovell (B7)* △640
Lowell (F5)* △192
Lubec (K6) △2,973
Ludlow (G3) △361
Machias (J6)* △2,063
Machiasport (H6)* △781
Macwahoc (G4) △131
Madawaska (G1)* △4,900
Madison (D6)* △3,639
Madrid (B6) △162
Mainstream (D6)
Manchester (D7)* 664
Mapleton (G2)* △1,367
Mariner (C8)
Mars Hill (H2)* △2,060
Masardis (G3)* △523
Matagamon (F3) 3
Matinicus (F8)* △188
Mattawamkeag (G4)* △803
Maysville (G2) 135
McKinley (G7)*
Mechanic Falls (C7)* △2,061
Meddybemps (J5)* △109
Medford (F5) △191
Medford Center (F5) 25
Medway (G4)* △725
Mercer (D6)* △348
Mexico (B6)* △4,762
Michaud (F1)
Middledam (B6) 25
Milbridge (H6)* △1,199
Milford (F6)* △1,435
Millinocket (F4)* △5,890
Milltown (J5)*
Milo (F5)* △2,898
Minot (C7)* △750
Minturn (G7)* 134
Monarda (G4)* 250
Monhegan (E8)* △75
Monmouth (D7)* △1,683
Monroe (E6)* △593
Monson (E5)* △855
Monticello (H3)* △1,284
Montville (E7) △466
Moody (B9)*
Moose River (C4)* △203
Moosehead (D4) 17
Morrill (E7)* △306
Mount Desert (G7)* △1,776
Mount Vernon (D7)* △653
Naples (B8)* △747
New Gloucester (C8)* △2,628
New Harbor (E8)* 500
New Limerick (G3)* △543
New Portland (C6)* △733
New Sharon (C6)* △755
New Sweden (G2)* △827
New Vineyard (C6)* △447
Newagen (D8)*
Newburgh (F6) △599
Newcastle (D7)* △1,021
Newfield (B8)* △355
Newport (E6)* △2,190
Nobleboro (D7)* △654
Norcross (F4) 46
Norridgewock (D6)* △1,784
North Amity (H4)* 250
N. Anson (D6)* 1,000
N. Bancroft (G4)* 71
N. Belgrade (D7)* 200
N. Berwick (B9)* △1,655
N. Bradford (F5) 25
N. Bridgton (B7)*
N. Brooksville (F7)* 190
N. Buckfield (C7)
N. Cutler (J6)
N. Dexter (E5) 60
N. Dixmont (E6)
N. East Carry (D4)* 13
N. Ellsworth (G6)
N. Fryeburg (B7)* 200
N. Gorham (C8) 500
N. Haven (F7)* △410
N. Islesboro (F7)
N. Jay (C6)* 550
N. Lebanon (B9)
N. Leeds (C7)* 47
N. Limington (B8) 150
N. Livermore (C7)* 145
N. Lovell (B7)* 85
N. Lubec (J6)* 150
N. Lyndon (G2) 200
N. New Portland (C6)* 350
N. Newry (B6)* 100
N. Parsonfield (A8) 67
N. Penobscot (F7)* 150
N. Perry (J5)
N. Raymond (C8) 50
N. Searsmont (E7) 150
N. Shapleigh (B8)* 90
N. Sullivan (G6)* 850
N. Turner (C7)* 232
N. Vassalboro (D7)* 1,000
N. Waldoboro (E7)*
N. Waterboro (B8)* 500
N. Waterford (B7)* 450
N. Wayne (C7)*
N. Whitefield (D7)* 200
N. Windham (C8)* 500
N. Yarmouth (C8) △942
Northeast Harbor (G7)* 700
Northfield (H6) △75
Northport (E7)* △574
Norway (B7)* △3,811
Norway Lake (B7) 150
Oakfield (G3)* △1,009
Oakland (D6)* △2,679
Ocean Park (C9)*
Ogunquit (B9)* 800
Olamon (F5)* 600
Old Orchard Beach (C9)* △4,707
Old Town (F6)* 8,261
Onawa (E5)* 25
Oquossoc (B6)*
Orient (H4)* △176
Orland (F6)* △1,155
Orono (F6)* △7,504
Orrington (F6)* △1,895
Orrs Island (D8)* 450
Otisfield (B7) △599
Otter Creek (G7)* 1,000
Ouellette (G1)
Owls Head (F7)* △784
Oxbow (G3)* △189
Oxford (C7)* △1,569
Palermo (E7)* △511
Palmyra (E6)* △965
Paris (B7)* △4,358
Parkman (D5)* △590
Passadumkeag (F5)* △331
Patten (F4)* △1,536
Pejepscot (D8)*
Pemaquid (E8)*
Pemaquid Beach (E8)*
Pembroke (J6)* △998
Penobscot (F7)* △699
Perham (G2)* △572
Perkins (F4) △5
Perry (J6)* △613
Peru (C6)* △1,080
Phair (G2) 150
Phillips (C6)* △1,088
Phippsburg (D8)* △1,134
Pine Point (C8) 650
Pittsfield (E6)* △3,909
Pittston (D7) △1,258
Plaisted (F1)* 300
Pleasant Island (B5)*
Pleasant Pond (D5) 11
Plymouth (E6)* △496
Poland (C7)* △1,503
Poland Spring (C7)* 500
Popham Beach (D8)*
Port Clyde (E8)* 350
Portage (G2)* △542
Porter (B8)* △1,052
Portland (C8)* 77,634
Portland (urban area) 112,659
Pownal (C8)* △752
Prentiss (G5)* △315
Presque Isle (H2)* △9,954
Princeton (H5)* △865
Prospect (F6) △392
Prospect Harbor (H7)* 270
Prouts Neck (C9)* 2,000
Pulpit Harbor (F7) 25
Quimby (F2)*
Randolph (D7) △1,733
Rangeley (B6)* △1,228
Raymond (B8) △620
Readfield (D7)* △1,022
Red Beach (J5)*
Redding (B7) 11
Richmond (D7)* △2,217
Richmond Corner (D7)* 43
Ridlonville (C6)* 2,000
Riley (C6)* 175
Ripley (E5)* △389
Robbinston (J5)* △554
Robinsons (H3)* 350
Rockland (E7)* 9,234
Rockport (F7)* △1,656
Rockville (E7) 265
Rockwood (D4)* 300
Rome (D6) △420
Roque Bluffs (H6)* △80
Round Mountain (B5) 3
Round Pond (E8)* 500
Roxbury (B6)* △348
Rumford (B6)* △9,954
Rumford Center (B7)* 300
Rumford Point (B6)* 200
Sabattus (C7)* 1,216
Saco (C9)* 10,324
Saint Agatha (G1)* △1,512
St. Albans (E6)* △1,035
St. David (G1)* 1,000
St. Francis (E1)* △1384
St. George (E7)* △1,482
St. John (F1) △569
Salem (C6) △67
Sandy Creek (B7)
Sandy Point (F7)* 250
Sanford (B9)* △15.177
Sangerville (E5)* △1,161
Saponac (G5)* 25
Scarboro (C8)* △4,600
Seal Cove (G7)*
Seal Harbor (G7)* 400
Searsmont (E7)* △558
Searsport (F7)* △1,457
Sebago (B8) △577
Sebago Lake (B8)* 346
Sebec (E5)* △442
Sebec Lake (E5)* 7
Sebec Station (E5)* 23
Seboeis (F5)* △70
Seboomook (D4) △18
Sedgwick (F7)* △614
Selden (H4)* 25
Shapleigh (B8)* △531
Shawmut (D6)* 1,200
Sheepscott (D7)* 100
Sheridan (F2)* 310
Sherman (G4)* △1,029
Sherman Mills (G4)* 1,030
Sherman Station (F4)* 400
Shin Pond (F3)* 17
Shirley Mills (D5)* 250
Sidney (D7) △918
Silvers Mills (E5)* 55
Sinclair (G1)* 800
Skinner (B4)
Skowhegan (D6)* △7,422
Small Point Beach (D8)*
Smithfield (D6)* △354
Smyrna Mills (G3)* 650
Soldier Pond (F1)*
Solon (D6)* △746
Somerville (D7) △227
Sorrento (G7)* △201
South Acton (B9) 200
S. Addison (H6) 170
S. Bancroft (G4)
S. Berwick (B9)* △2,646
S. Blue Hill (F7) 141
S. Brewer (F6)*
S. Bridgton (B8)* 125
S. Bristol (D8)* △631
S. Brooksville (F7)* 140
S. Casco (B8)* 150
S. China (D7)* 310
S. Deer Isle (F7) 85
S. Eliot (B4) 1,331
S. Exeter (E6) 25
S. Harpswell (C8)* 300
S. Hiram (B8)* 250
S. Hollis (B8) 30
S. Hope (E7)* 125
S. Jefferson (D7)
S. La Grange (F5) 150
S. Lebanon (A9)
S. Levant (E6) 110
S. Liberty (E7) 47
S. Lincoln (G5) 164
S. Monmouth (D7)
S. Orrington (F6)* 300
S. Paris (C7)* 2,067
S. Penobscot (F7)*
S. Portland (C8)* 21,866
S. Robbinston (J5)
S. Sanford (B9) 600
S. Thomaston (E7)* △654
S. Union (E7)*
S. Waldoboro (E7)
S. Warren (E7)
S. Waterford (B7)*
S. Windham (C8)* 1,569
Southport (D8)* △435
Southwest Harbor (G7)* △1,534
Spencer (C5)
Springfield (G5)* △414
Springvale (B9)* 2,745
Squa Pan (G2) 75
Stacyville (F4)* △679
Standish (B8)* △1,786
Starks (D6)* △421
Steep Falls (B8)* 480
Stetson (E6)* △434
Steuben (H6)* △784
Stillwater (F6)* 800
Stockholm (G1)* △641
Stockton Springs (F7)* △949
Stonington (F7)* △1,660
Stow, (A7)* △147
Stratton (B5)* 560
Strong (C6)* △1,036
Sugar Island (D4) 4
Sullivan (G6)* △762
Sumner (C7) △526
Sunset (F7)*
Sunshine (G7) 120
Surry (F7)* △448
Swans Island (G7)* △468
Swanville (E6) △437
Sweden (B7) △212
Sweden (G2)*
Tarratine (D4) 8
Temple (C6)* △284
Tenants Harbor (E8)* 400
The Forks (D5)* △45
Thomaston (E7)* △2,810
Thorndike (E6)* △534
Topsfield (H5)* △231
Topsham (D8)* △2,626
Tremont (G7) △1,115
Trenton (G7) △358
Trescott (J6) △362
Trevett (D8)* 350
Troutdale (D5) 25
Troy (E6)* △553
Turner (C7)* △1,712
Turner Center (C7)*
Union (E7)* △1,085
Unionville (H6) 150
Unity (E6)* △1,014
Upper Dam (B6)
Upper Frenchville (G1)* 500
Upper Gloucester (C8)* 150
Upton (B6)* △105
Van Buren (G1)* △5,094
Vanceboro (H4)* △497
Vassalboro (D7)* △2,261
Veazie (F6) △776
Vienna (D6)* △231
Vinalhaven (F7)* △1,427
Waite (H5)* △117
Waldo (E7) △324
Waldoboro (E7)* △2,536
Walnut Hill (C8) 250
Waltham (G6) △154
Warren (E7)* △1,576
Washburn (G2)* △1,913
Washington (E7)* △722
Waterboro (B8)* △1,071
Waterford (B7)* △828
Waterville (E6)* 18,287
Wayne (D7)* △459
Webhannet (C9)*
Weeks Mills (E7)* 100
Welchville (C7)*
Weld (C6)* △361
Wellington (D5)* △252
Wells (B9)* △2,321
Wells Beach (C9)
Wesley (H6)* △149
West Athens (D6) 175
W. Baldwin (B8)*
W. Bath (D8) △578
W. Bethel (B7)* 250
W. Boothbay Harbor (D8)*
W. Brooksville (F7)* 140
W. Buxton (B8)* 350
W. Enfield (F5)*
W. Falmouth (C8) 1,500
W. Farmington (C6)* 500
W. Franklin (G6)* 115
W. Gardiner (D7) △946
W. Garland (E5) 50
W. Gorham (C8)
W. Gouldsboro (G7)* 105
W. Hampden (E6)
W. Harpswell (C8) 100
W. Jonesport (H6) 850
W. Kennebunk (B9)*
W. Lebanon (B9)* 150
W. Lubec (J6)*
W. Mills (C6) 50
W. Minot (C7)* 300
W. Newfield (B8)* 175
W. Old Town (F6) 35
W. Paris (B7)* 800
W. Pembroke (J6)* 500
W. Penobscot (F7)
W. Peru (C7)* 300
W. Poland (C7)*
W. Ripley (E6)
W. Rockport (E7)* 200
W. Scarboro (C8)* 1,500
W. Seboois (F4)*
W. Sumner (C7)* 101
W. Tremont (G7)* 250
W. Winterport (E6) 30
Westbrook (C8)* 12,284
Westfield (G2)* △557
Weston (H4)* △248
Wheelock (F1)
Whitefield (D7)* △1,030
Whiting (J6)* △354
Whitneyville (H6)* △227
Willimantic (E5) △189
Wilsons Mills (B6)* 80
Wilton (C6)* △3,455
Windsor (D7)* △740
Winn (G5)* △497
Winnecook (E6) 35
Winslow (D6) △4,413
Winslows Mills (E7)* 200
Winter Harbor (G7)* △568
Winterport (F6)* △1,694
Winterville (F2)* △373
Winthrop (C7)* △3,026
Wiscasset (D7)* △1,584
Woodland (H5)* △1,292
Wollwich (D8)* △1,344
Wyman Dam (D5)* 451
Wytopitlock (G4)* 352
Yarmouth (C8)* △2,669
York (B9) 2,000
York Beach (B9)* 500
York Corners (B9) 100
York Harbor (B9)* 750

*Map on Page 65*

## MARYLAND

*Total Population 2,343,001*

**24 COUNTIES**

Allegany (A2) 89,556
Anne Arundel (H4) 117,392
Baltimore (H3) 270,273
Baltimore City (H3) 949,708
Calvert (H6) 12,100
Caroline (L5) 18,234
Carroll (F2) 44,907
Cecil (L2) 33,356
Charles (F6) 23,415
Dorchester (K7) 27,815
Frederick (E3) 62,287
Garrett (A7) 21,259
Harford (J2) 51,782
Howard (G4) 23,119
Kent (K3) 13,667
Montgomery (E4) 164,401
Prince Georges (G5) 194,182
Queen Annes (L4) 14,579
Saint Marys (H7) 29,111
Somerset (M8) 20,745
Talbot (K5) 19,428
Washington (C2) 78,886
Wicomico (M7) 39,641
Worcester (N8) 23,148

**CITIES and TOWNS**

Abell (H8)* 400
Aberdeen (K2)* 2,944
Abingdon (J3)* 650
Accident (A7)* 242
Accokeek (G6)*
Adamstown (D3)* 265
Aikin (K2)
Aireys (K6)* 110
Allen (M7)* 350
Alta Vista (A4) 3,000
American Corner (L5) 15
Andrews (K7)*
ANNAPOLIS (H5)* 10,047
Annapolis Jct. (H4)* 322
Antietam (D3) 250
Antietam Station (D3) 50
Aquasco (G6)
Arbutus (H3) 4,000
Ardmore (C4) 500
Arlington (H3)* 71,750
Baden (H6) 150
Baldwin (J3)* 350
Balnew (H4) 1,500
Baltmiore (H3)* 949,708
Baltimore (urban area) 1,151,050
Barclay (L4)* 108
Barnesville (E4)* 130
Barstow (H6)* 151
Bartholows (F3) 100
Barton (C7)* 695
Bayview (L2)
Beane (A4) 50
Beaver Creek (D2) 50
Bel Air (J2)* 2,578
Bel Alton (G7)* 250
Bellevue (K6)* 300
Beltsville (C3)* 800
Benedict (H6)* 250
Bengies (J3) 500
Bentley Springs (H2)* 130
Berlin (O7)* 2,001
Berwyn (B4)*
Berwyn Heights (C4) 674
Bethesda (A4)* 36,000
Bethlehem (L6)*
Betterton (K3)* 314
Big Spring (C2)* 125
Bigpool (C2)* 175
Bishop (N7)* 25
Bishops Head (K7)* 300
Bishopville (O7)* 375
Bivalve (L7)* 270
Bladensburg (C4)* 2,899
Bloomington (B8)* 400
Blythedale (K2) 100
Boonsboro (D2)* 1,071
Borden Shaft (C7) 419
Boring (G2)* 130
Boulevard Heights (B5)
Bowens (H6)* 220
Bowie (G4)* 860
Boyds (E4)* 250
Bozman (J5)*
Bradbury Heights (C5) 1,800
Bradbury Park (C5) 500
Bradshaw (J3)* 500
Branchville (B4)* 500
Brandywine (G6)* 1,000
Breathedsville (C2)* 150
Brentwood (B4)* 3,523
Bridgetown (L4) 16
Bristol (H5)* 300
Broad Creek (B6) 50
Brookeville (F4)* 117
Brookview (L6) 150
Brown (C5) 200
Brownsville (D3)* 202
Brunswick (D3)* 3,752
Buck Lodge (E4) 100
Buckeystown (E3)*
Burkittsville (D3)* 190
Burnt Mills (B3) 100
Burrsville (L5) 200
Burtonsville (G4)*
Bushwood (G7)* 300
Butler (H2)* 57
Cabin Creek (L6)
Cabin John (A4)* 2,000
California (H7)* 250
Calvert (K2) 150
Cambridge (K6)* 10,351
Camp Springs (C6) 315
Capitol Heights (C5)* 2,729
Cardiff (J2)* 325
Carney (H3) 1,523
Carrollton (G2)* 180
Castleton (J2)* 343
Catoctin (E2) 300
Catonsville (H3)* 29,638
Cavetown (D2)* 300
Cecilton (L3)* 510
Cedar Grove (F4) 200
Cedar Heights (C5) 788
Cedartown (N8) 50
Cedarville (G6) 200
Centreville (K4)* 1,804
Chance (L8)* 400
Chaptico (H7)* 350
Charlestown (L2)* 551
Charlotte Hall (H7)* 150
Chase (J3)* 900
Cheltenham (G6)* 500
Cherry Hill (L2) 300
Chesapeake Beach (J6)* 504
Chesapeake City (L2)* 1,154
Chester (J5)* 1,100
Chestertown (K4)* 3,143
Chesterville (L3) 36
Cheverly (C4)* 3,318
Chevy Chase (A4)* 1,971
Chewsville (D2)* 180
Childs (L2)* 90
Chillum (B4)* 15,000
Choptank (L6)*
Church Creek (K6)* 187
Church Hill (K4)* 271
Churchton (J5)*
Churchville (J2)*
Claiborne (J5)* 150
Clara (L7) 200
Clarksburg (E4)* 367
Clarksville (G4)* 200
Clear Spring (C2)* 558
Clements (G7)* 300
Clinton (C6)* 500
Cockeysville (H3)* 3,000
College Park (C4)* 11,170
Collington (G5)
Colmar Manor (B4) 1,732
Colora (K2)* 190
Compton (H7)* 500
Conowingo (K2)* 500
Cooksville (F3)* 150
Cordova (K5)* 500
Cornersville (K6) 100
Corriganville (D7)*
Cottage City (B4) 1,249
Crapo (K7)*
Creagerstown (E2) 325
Crellin (A8)* 500
Cresaptown (C7)* 2,000
Crisfield (L9)* 3,688
Crocheron (K8)*
Crownsville (H4)* 350
Crumpton (L4)*
Cumberland (D7)* 37,679
Damascus (F3)* 1,000
Dameron (J8)* 250
Dames Quarter (L8)* 450
Daniels (G3)* 800
Daniels Park (C4) 750
Dargan (D3) 300
Darlington (J2)* 500
Darnestown (E4) 200
Davidsonville (H5)* 900
Day (F3)
Deal Island (L8)* 1,200
Deer Park (A8)* 320
Delmar (M7) 1,328
Denton (L5)* 1,806
Derwood (F4)* 300
Dickerson (E4)* 300
District Heights (C5) 1,735
Doncaster (F7)*
Doubs (E3)* 250
Downsville (C2) 210
Drayden (J8)* 300
Dublin (J2) 250
Dundalk (J3)* 40,182
Eagle Harbor ‡(F6) 7
Earleigh Heights (H4) 400
Earleville (L3)* 42
East New Market (L6)* 264
East Riverdale (C4) 1,200
Easton (K5)* 4,836
Eastport (J5)*
Eckhart Mines (C7)* 2,350
Eden (M7)* 150
Edgemere (J3) 6,000
Edmonston (C4)* 1,190
Eldersburg (G3) 300
Eldorado (L6) 79
Elk Mills (L2)* 300
Elkneck (L2)
Elkridge (H4)* 3,000
Elkton (L2)* 5,245
Ellerslie (D7)* 850
Ellerton (D2) 41
Ellicott City (G3)* 1,500
Elliott (L7)* 130
Emmitsburg (E2)* 1,261
Essex (J3)* 35,000
Ewell (K9)* 400
Fair Hill (L2) 150
Fairbank (J6) 300
Fairland (G4)
Fairlee (K4) 240
Fairmount (L8)* 600
Fairmount Heights (C5) 2,097
Fallston (J2)* 300
Farmington (K2) 50
Fearer (A7) 50
Federalsburg (L6)* 1,878
Ferndale (H4)* 2,500
Finchville (M6) 3
Finksburg (G3)* 500
Fishing Creek (J7)* 700
Flint Stone (A2)* 170
Forest Glen (B4) 1,500
Forest Heights (B5) 1,125
Forest Hill (J2)* 300
Forestville (C5) 1,500
Fort Foote (B6) 75
Ft. Howard (J4)* 1,000
Ft. Washington (G6) 210
Foxville (E2) 150
Frederick (E3)* 18,142
Freeland (H2)* 200
Friendship (H6)* 300
Friendship Heights (A4) 315
Friendsville (A7)* 607
Frizellburg (F2) 193
Frostburg (C7)* 6,876
Fruitland (M7)* 1,028
Fullerton (J3)* 2,500
Funkstown (D2)* 879
Gaithersburg (F4)* 1,755
Galena (L3)* 259
Galestown (L6) 100
Galesville (H5)* 900
Gamber (G3) 600
Gambrills (H4)* 500
Garrett Park (A3)* 524
Garrison (G3)* 1,000
Germantown (E4)* 200
Girdletree (N8)* 200
Glen Burnie (H4)* 8,000
Glen Echo (A4)* 356
Glen Echo Heights (A4) 600
Glenarden (C4)* 492
Glenarm (J3)* 350
Glenelg (G3)* 40
Glenn Dale (C4)* 625
Glyndon (G3)* 500
Golden Hill (K7)
Goldsboro (L4)* 198
Golts (L3)* 100
Graceham (E2)* 225
Granite (G3)* 600
Grantsville (B7)* 461
Grasonville (K5)* 1,200
Greenbelt (C4)* 7,074
Greenmount (G2)* 200
Greensboro (L5)* 1,181
Hagerstown (C2)* 36,260
Halethorpe (H4)* 5,000
Hall (G5)* 195
Hampstead (G2)* 677
Hancock (B2)* 963
Hanover (G4)* 1,000
Harmans (H4)* 200
Harney (F2) 142
Havre de Grace (K2)* 7,809
Hebbville (G3) 150
Hebron (M7)* 723
Helen (H7)* 125
Henderson (L4)* 106
Henryton (G3)* 600
Hereford (E2)* 310
Highfield (E2)* 1,000
Highland Beach ‡(J6)* 5
Hillsboro (L5)* 179
Hillside (C5) 3,000
Hobbs (L5)* 95
Hollywood (H7)* 800
Hood (B2) 11
Hoopersville (K7)* 300
Hopewell (L8) 200
Howardville (G3)
Hudson (J6) 200
Hughsville (G6)* 550
Huntingtown (H6)* 438
Hurlock (L6)* 944
Hutton (A8)* 350
Hyattstown (E3)* 135
Hyattsville (B4)* 12,308
Ijamsville (E3)*
Ilchester (G4)* 200
Indian Head (F6)* 491
Ingleside (L4)* 150
Ironshire (O7) 100
Ironshire Station (N7) 25
Island Creek (H7)* 250
Issue (G7)* 160
Jacksonville (H2) 75
Jarrettsville (H2)* 250
Jefferson (E3)* 275
Jennings (B7)* 300
Jesterville (L7)* 175
Johnsonville (F2) 200
Keedysville (D3)* 417
Kempton (A9)* 260
Kemptown (E3)* 200
Kennedyville (L3)* 180
Kensington (A4)* 1,611
Keymar (F2)*
Kingston (M8)* 50
Kingsville (J3)*
Kitzmiller (B8)* 652
Knoxville (D3)* 750
Koontz (B7)
La Plata (G6)* 780
Ladiesburg (E2)* 126
Lakesville (K7)* 37
Landover (C4)* 1,175
Landover Hills (C4)* 1,661
Lanham (C4)* 1,133
Lansdowne (H3)* 7,500
Lantz (E2)* 75
Largo (C5) 100
Lauraville (H3)
Laurel (G4)* 4,482
Lawsonia (L9) 800
Laytonsville (F4)* 132
Le Gore (E2)* 400
Leeds (L2) 40
Leitersburg (D2) 250
Leonardtown (H7)* 1,017
Leslie (L2)
Level (K2) 450
Lewistown (E2)* 350
Lexington Park (J7)* 6,000
Liberty Grove (K2)* 210
Libertytown (E3)* 600
Lime Kiln (E3)* 185
Linden (A4) 1,000
Lineboro (G2)* 200
Linkwood (L6)* 125
Linthicum Heights (H4)* 3,500
Linwood (F2)*
Lisbon (F3)* 150
Little Orleans (A2)* 300
Loch Lynn Heights (A8) 415
Lonaconing (C7)* 2,289
Long Green (H3)* 500
Lothian (H5)*
Love Point (J4) 120
Loveville (H7)* 500
Lower Marlboro (H6)* 135
Luke (B8)* 820
Lusby (J7)* 225
Lutherville (H3)* 2,800
Lynch (K3)* 97
Mackall (H7)*
Madison (K6)*
Madonna (H2) 25
Magnolia (J3)* 500
Manchester (G2)* 1,027
Manokin (L8)* 400
Mapleville (D2)* 175
Marbury (F6)*
Mardela Springs (L7)* 428
Marion Station (M8)* 475
Marshall Hall (F6) 50
Marydel (L4)* 110
Maryland Line (H2)* 202
Maryland Park (C5) 1,500
Mason Springs (F6) 50
Massey (L3)* 125
Maugansville (D2)* 725
Mayberry (F2) 108
Mayo (H5)* 583
Mc Daniel (J5)* 197
Meadows (C5) 350
Mechanicsville (H7)* 500
Medford (F2)* 125
Melitota (K4) 100
Melrose (G2) 150
Middle River (J3)* 27,500
Middleburg (F2)* 150
Middletown (E3)* 936
Midland (C7)* 889
Milestown (H7) 400
Millers (G2)* 225
Millersville (H4)* 250
Millington (L3)* 356
Monie (L8)* 250
Monkton (H2)* 105
Monrovia (E3)* 112
Montrose (A3) 200
Morningside (C5) 1,520
Moscow Mills (B7) 300
Mount Airy (F3)* 1,061
Mt. Lena (D2) 150
Mt. Pleasant (E3)
Mt. Rainier (B4)* 10,989
Mt. Savage (C7)* 2,094
Mt. Vernon (L8) 400
Mt. Washington (H3)* 4,153
Mountain Lake Park (A8)*
Mountaindale (E2) 175
Muirkirk (G4)* 400
Mullinix Mill (F3) 25
Myersville (D3)* 250
Nanjemoy (F7)* 264
Nanticoke (L7)* 650
National (C7) 348
Neavitt (J6)*
New Glatz (B6) 50
New Market (E3)* 301
New Windsor (F2)* 707
Newark (N7)* 500
Newport (G7)*
Nikep (C7)* 275
Norbeck (F4) 500
Norrisville (J2) 100
North Beach (J6)* 314
N. Branch (D7) 280
N. Brentwood (B4) 833
N. East (L2)* 1,517
Oakland (A8)* 1,640
Ocean City (O7)* 1,234
Odenton (H4)* 1,059
Oella (G3)* 1,500
Oldtown (D7)* 500
Olivet (J7)* 250
Olney (F4)* 1,000
Orangeville (H3) 300
Oraville (H7)* 300
Oriole (L8)* 268
Owings (H6)* 230
Owings Mills (G3)* 1,500
Oxford (K6)* 757
Oxon Hill (B6) 280
Palmers (H8)* 300
Park Hall (J8)* 400
Parkton (H2)* 500
Parkville (H3)* 6,500
Parole (H5)* 1,032
Parran (H6)*
Parsonsburg (M7)* 350
Pasadena (H4)* 1,500
Patapsco (G2)*
Perry Hall (H3) 1,000
Perryman (K3)* 300
Perryville (K2)* 679
Petersville (D3) 250
Phoenix (H2)* 150
Pikesville (G3)* 15,000
Piney Point (H8)* 1,000
Pinto (C7)* 275
Piscataway (G6) 77
Pisgah (F6)* 450
Pittsville (N7)* 497
Pleasant Valley (G2) 170
Plum Point (J6)*
Pocomoke City (M8)* 3,191
Point of Rocks (E3)* 361
Pomfret (G6)* 500
Pomona (K4) 35
Pomonkey (F6) 200
Poolesville (E4)* 161
Popes Creek (G7)* 75
Port Deposit (K2)* 1,139
Port Republic (J6)* 50
Port Tobacco (F6)* 125
Port Tobacco Station (Springhill*) (G7) 150
Potomac (F4) 250
Powellville (N7)* 350
Preston (L6)* 353
Price (L4)* 245
Prince Frederick (H6)* 500
Princess Anne (L8)* 1,407
Principio Furnace (L2)* 250
Providence (L2) 300
Purdum (E3) 175
Quantico (M7)* 250
Queen Anne (K5)* 396
Queenstown (K5)* 316
Randallstown (G3)* 1,550
Rawlings (C7)* 500
Reid (D2) 50
Reids Grove (L6) 45
Reisterstown (G3)* 1,500
Relay (H4)* 1,000
Reliance (L6) 30
Revell (J4) 100
Rhodes Point (K9)* 150
Riderwood (H3)*
Ridge (J8)* 400
Ridgely (L5)* 834
Ridgeville (F3) 150
Ringgold (D2) 212
Rising Sun (K2)* 668
Ritchie (C5) 200
River Springs (G8) 300
Riverdale (B4)* 5,530
Riverside (F7) 150
Rock Hall (K4)* 786
Rock Point (G7)* 200
Rocks (J2)*
Rockville (F4)* 6,934
Rogers Heights (C4) 2,000
Rohrersville (D3)* 165
Roland Park (H3)* 12,000
Rosaryville (G5) 100
Rosedale (H3) 3,000
Rowlandsville (K2)
Royal Oak (K6)*
Rumbley (L8)* 113
Ruthsberg (L4) 25
Rutland (H5) 300
Ruxton (H3)*
Sabillasville (E2)* 300
Saint Augustine (L3) 50
St. Inigoes (J8)* 400
St. James (C2)* 100
St. Leonard (J7)*
St. Martin's (O7)
St. Michaels (J5)* 1,470
Salem (L7)* 42
Salisbury (M7)* 15,141
Sandy Spring (F4)* 650
Sassafras (L3) 100
Savage (G4)* 1,238
Savage Station (G4) 25
Scotland (J8)* 300
Seabrook (C4)* 2,500
Seat Pleasant (C5)* 2,255
Secretary (L6)* 344
Security (D2)* 300
Severn (H4)* 250
Severna Park (H4)* 1,000
Sharpsburg (C3)* 866
Sharptown (M6)* 680
Shawsville (H2) 50
Shelltown (M9)* 28
Shipley (H4) 1,500
Showell (O7)* 100
Silver Hill (B5) 1,000
Silver Run (F2) 325
Silver Spring (B4)* 75,000
Smallwood (F2) 160
Smithsburg (D2)* 641
Snow Hill (N8)* 2,091
Solomons (J7)* 270
Somerset (A4) 430
Sparrows Point (J4)* 12,000
Spickler (C2) 85
Spielman (C2) 202
Springhill (G7)* 150
Stemmers Run (H3) 1,260
Stevensville (J5)* 350
Steyer (A8)* 55
Still Pond (K3)* 290
Still Pond Station (K3) 4
Stockton (N8)* 500
Street (J2)* 200
Sudlersville (L4)* 500
Sudley (H5)
Suitland (C5)* 2,500
Swanton (A8)* 242
Sweetair (H2) 35
Sykesville (F3)* 941
T. B. (G6) 100
Takoma Park (B4) 13,341
Taneytown (F2)* 1,420
Taylors Island (J7)* 300
Taylorsville (F3) 125
Templeville (L4)* 82
Texas (H3)*
Thomas (J6) 200
Thurmont (E2)* 1,676
Tilghman (J6)* 1,250
Timonium (H3)* 1,300
Toddville (K7)* 330
Tolchester Beach (J4) 4
Tompkinsville (G7)* 510
Town Creek (A2) 50
Town Point (L3) 25
Towson (H3)* 11,000
Trappe (K6)* 325
Trappe Station (K6) 35
Trenton (G2) 100
Tunis Mills (K5) 100
Tuxedo (C5)* 1,000
Tyaskin (L7)* 150
Union Bridge (F2)* 840
Union Mills (F2)* 300
Uniontown (F2)* 265
Unionville (F3)* 150
Unity (F4) 82
University Park (B4) 2,205
Upper Fairmount (L8)* 824
Upper Falls (J3)* 200
Upper Marlboro (H5)* 702
Upperco (G2)* 150
Urbana (E3)
Vale Summit (C7) 450
Valley Lee (H8)* 300
Venton (M8)* 100
Vienna (L7)* 414
Vindex (B8)* 175
Waldorf (G6)* 1,100
Walkersville (E3)* 761
Warwick (L3)*
Washington Grove (F4)* 400
Waterview (L8) 50
Welcome (F7)* 200
Wenona (L8)* 300
West Annapolis (H4)*
W. Lanham Hills (C4)* 1,200
W. River (H5)*
Western Port (B8)* 3,431
Westminster (G2)* 6,140
Westover (M8)* 400
Wetipquin (L7) 500
Weverton (D3)* 150
Whaleysville (N7)* 350
Wheaton (A3)* 20,000
White Hall (H2)* 300
White Marsh (J3)* 500
White Oak (B3) 50
White Plains (G6) 700
Whiteford (J2)* 300
Whitehaven (L7)* 95
Wicomico (G7)* 225
Willards (N7)* 464
Williamsburg (L6)* 150
Williamsport (C2)* 1,890
Williston (L5) 100
Willows (H6)*
Winfield (F3)
Wingate (K7)*
Wittman (J5)*
Wolfsville (D2) 96
Woodbine (F3)*
Woodlawn (H3) 5,000
Woodmoor (B4)* 500
Woodsboro (E2)* 427
Woodside (B4) 3,500
Woodstock (G3)* 100
Woolford (K7)* 150
Worton (K3)* 150
Wye Mills (K5)* 125
Wye Mills Station (K5) 100
Wynne (J8) 300
Yellow Springs (D3)
Zion (L2)

**DISTRICT OF COLUMBIA**

Anacostia (B5)*
Benning (B5)*
Brightwood (B4)*
Brookland (B4)*
Cleveland Park (A4)*
Congress Heights (B5)*
Georgetown (A5)*
Petworth (B4)*
Tenleytown (A4)
WASHINGTON, D. C. (B5)* 802,178
Washington (urban area) 1,281,572

*Map on Page 66*

# MASSACHUSETTS

*Total Population 4,690,514*

**14 COUNTIES**

Barnstable (N6)...46,805
Berkshire (B3)...132,966
Bristol (K5)...381,569
Dukes (M7)...5,633
Essex (L2)...522,384
Franklin (D2)...52,747
Hampden (D4)...367,971
Hampshire (D3)...87,594
Middlesex (J3)...1,064,569
Nantucket (O7)...3,484
Norfolk (K4)...392,308
Plymouth (L5)...189,468
Suffolk (K3)...896,615
Worcester (G3)...546,401

**CITIES and TOWNS**

Abington (L4)*...▲7,152
Accord (E8)*...150
Acoaxet (K7)*...130
Acton (J3)*...▲3,510
Acushnet (L6)*...▲4,401
Adams (B2)*...▲12,034
Agawam (D4)*...▲10,166
Allerton (E7)*...500
Amesbury (L1)*...▲10,851
Amherst (E3)*...▲10,856
Andover (K2)*...▲12,437
Annisquam (M2)*...
Arlington (C6)*...▲44,353
Ashburnham (G2)*...▲2,603
Ashby (G2)*...▲1,464
Ashfield (C2)*...▲ 977
Ashland (J3)*...▲3,500
Ashley Falls (A4)*...500
Assinippi (E8)*...500
Assonet (K5)*...1,002
Athol (F2)*...▲11,554
Attleboro (J5)*...23,809
Attleboro Falls (J5)*.. 2,500
Auburn (G4)*...▲8,840
Auburndale (B7)*...6,218
Avon (K4)*...▲2,666
Ayer (H2)*...▲5,740
Baldwinville (F2)*...1,407
Ballard Vale (K2)*...1,200
Barnstable (N6)*...▲10,480
Barre (F3)*...▲3,406
Barre Plains (F3)*...144
Barrowsville (K5)*...700
Becket (B3)*...▲ 755
Bedford (B6)*...▲5,234
Beechwood (F8)*...200
Belchertown (E3)*...▲4,487
Bellingham (J4)*...▲4,100
Belmont (C6)*...▲27,381
Berkley (K5)...▲1,284
Berlin (H3)*...▲1,349
Bernardston (D2)*...▲1,117
Beverly (E5)*...28,884
Beverly Farms (E5)*.. 2,500
Billerica (J2)*...▲11,101
Blackinton (B2)*...440
Blackstone (H4)*...▲4,968
Blandford (C4)*...▲ 597
Bolton (H3)*...▲ 956
Bondsville (E4)*...1,200
BOSTON (D7)*...801,444
Boston (urban area)...2,218,893
Bourne (M6)*...▲4,720
Bournedale (M5)...
Boxford (K2)*...▲ 926
Boylston Center (H3)*...
Braintree (D8)*...▲23,161
Brant Rock (M4)*...350
Brewster (O5)*...▲ 987
Bridgewater (K5)*...▲9,512
Brimfield (F4)*...▲1,182
Brockton (K4)*...62,860
Brockton (urban area) 92,086
Brookfield (F4)*...▲1,567
Brookline (C7)*...▲57,589
Brookville (K4)*...1,300
Bryantville (L4)*...
Buckland (C2)*...▲1,605
Burlington (C5)...▲3,250
Buzzards Bay (M5)*.. 1,459
Byfield (L1)*...950
Cambridge (C6)*...120,740
Canton (C8)*...▲7,465
Canton Jct. (C8)...
Carlisle (J2)*...▲ 846
Carver (M5)*...▲1,530
Caryville (J4)*...300
Cataumet (M6)*...100
Centerville (N6)*...1,100
Central Village (K6)*.. 350
Charlemont (C2)*...▲ 855
Charlton (F4)*...▲3,136
Charlton City (F4)*... 1,200
Charlton Depot (F4)*. 150
Chartley (K5)*...600
Chatham (P6)*...▲2,457
Chathamport (P6)...150
Chelmsford (J2)*...▲9,407
Chelsea (D6)*...38,912
Cherry Valley (G3)*... 1,300
Cheshire (B2)*...▲2,022
Chester (C3)*...▲1,292
Chesterfield (C3)*...▲ 496
Chicopee (D4)*...49,211
Chicopee Falls (D4)*..12,915
Chilmark (M7)*...▲ 183
Chiltonville (M5)...
City Mills (J4)*...500
Clifton (E6)*...5,000
Clinton (H3)*...▲12,287
Cochituate (A7)*...2,500
Cohasset (F7)*...▲3,731
Collinsville (J2)*...1,500
Colrain (D2)*...▲1,546
Concord (A6)*...▲8,623
Conway (D2)*...▲ 873
Cordaville (H3)*...250
Cotuit (N6)*...700
Crescent Beach (M6)*
Cummaquid (N6)*...200
Cummington (C3)*...▲ 620
Cushing (L1)*...398
Cushman (D3)*...250
Cuttyhunk (L7)*...40
Dalton (B3)*...▲4,772
Danvers (D5)*...▲15,720
Danversport (E5)...2,500
Dartmouth (K6)*...▲11,115
Dedham (C7)*...▲18,487
Deerfield (D2)*...▲3,086
Dennis (O5)*...▲2,499
Dennis Port (O6)*...1,200
Dighton (K5)*...▲2,950
Dodge (G4)*...835
Dodgeville (K5)*...1,500
Dorchester (D7)*...
Douglas (H4)...▲2,624
Dover (B7)*...▲1,722
Dracut (J2)...▲8,666
Dudley (G4)*...▲5,261
Dunstable (J2)*...▲ 522
Duxbury (M4)*...▲3,167
E. Blackstone (H4)...
E. Braintree (D8)...7,000
E. Brewster (O5)*...500
E. Bridgewater (L4)*..▲4,412
E. Brookfield (G4)*...▲1,243
E. Dedham (C8)*...5,000
E. Dennis (O5)*...275
E. Douglas (G4)*...1,846
E. Falmouth (M6)*...1,405
E. Foxboro (K4)*...500
E. Freetown (L5)*...1,200
E. Harwich (O6)*...500
E. Lee (B3)*...350
E. Longmeadow (E4)*.▲4,881
E. Milton (D7)...7,500
E. Northfield (E2)*...950
E. Norton (K5)...800
E. Orleans (P5)*...383
E. Otis (B4)*...95
E. Pembroke (M4)*...200
E. Pepperell (H2)*...2,500
E. Sandwich (N6)*...325
E. Saugus (D6)...
E. Taunton (K5)*...5,000
E. Templeton (G2)*...1,200
E. Village (G4)...
E. Walpole (C8)*...2,000
E. Wareham (M5)*...500
E. Weymouth (E8)*...10,000
E. Whately (D3)...
Eastham (O5)*...▲ 860
Easthampton (D3)*...▲10,694
Easton (K4)*...▲6,244
Eastondale (K4)*...600
Edgartown (M7)*...▲1,508
Egypt (F8)*...600
Elmwood (L4)*...350
Erving (E2)*...▲1,322
Essex (L2)*...▲1,794
Everett (D6)*...45,982
Fairhaven (L6)*...12,764
Fairview (D4)*...2,108
Fall River (K6)*...111,963
Fall River (urban area)...117,881
Falmouth (M6)*...▲8,662
Farnams (B2)*...200
Farnumsville (H4)*...1,427
Fayville (H3)*...1,000
Feeding Hills (D4)*...3,500
Fisherville (H4)*...1,167
Fiskdale (F4)*...
Fitchburg (G2)*...42,691
Florence (D3)*...4,500
Forest Hills (C7)...10,000
Forge Village (H2)*...1,115
Foxboro (J4)*...▲7,030
Framingham (A7)*...▲28,086
Framingham Center (J3)*...4,500
Franklin (J4)*...▲8,037
Furnace (F3)*...150
Gardner (G2)*...19,581
Gay Head (L7)...▲ 88
Georgetown (L2)*...▲2,411
Gilbertville (F3)*...1,039
Gill (D2)...▲1,070
Gleasondale (J3)*...
Glendale (A3)*...350
Gloucester (M2)*...25,167
Goshen (C3)*...▲ 321
Grafton (H4)*...▲8,281
Granby (E3)*...▲1,861
Graniteville (J2)*...1,000
Granville (C4)*...▲ 740
Great Barrington (A4)*...▲6,712
Green Harbor (M4)*...300
Greenbush (F8)*...650
Greenfield (D2)*...▲17,349
Greenwood (D6)*...5,500
Griswoldville (D2)*...590
Groton (H2)*...▲2,889
Groveland (L1)*...▲2,340
Hadley (D3)*...▲2,639
Halifax (L5)*...▲ 944
Hamilton (L2)*...▲2,764
Hampden (E4)*...▲1,322
Hancock (A2)*...▲ 445
Hanover (L4)*...▲3,389
Hanson (L4)*...▲3,264
Hardwick (F3)*...▲2,348
Hartsville (B4)...
Harvard (H2)*...▲3,983
Harwich (O6)*...▲2,649
Harwich Port (O6)*...1,350
Hatfield (D3)*...▲2,179
Haverhill (K1)*...47,280
Haydenville (C3)*...1,009
Heath (C2)*...▲ 305
Hebronville (J5)*...754
Hingham (E8)*...▲10,665
Hingham Center (E8)..
Hinsdale (B3)*...▲1,560
Holbrook (D8)*...▲4,004
Holden (G3)*...▲5,975
Holland (F4)...▲ 377
Holliston (A8)*...▲3,753
Holyoke (D4)*...54,661
Holyoke-Springfield (urban area)...356,471
Hoosac Tunnel (C2)*.. 150
Hopedale (H4)*...▲3,479
Hopkinton (J4)*...▲3,486
Hortonville (K5)...
Housatonic (A3)*...1,601
Hubbardston (F3)*...▲1,134
Hubbardston Station (F3)...120
Hudson (H3)*...▲8,211
Hull (E7)*...▲3,379
Humarock (M4)*...50
Huntington (C4)*...▲1,257
Hyannis (N6)*...4,235
Hyannis Port (N6)*...300
Hyde Park (C7)*...
Indian Orchard (E4)*.10,000
Interlaken (A3)*...60
Ipswich (L2)*...▲6,985
Islington (C8)*...2,300
Jamaica Plain (C7)*...
Jefferson (G3)*...
Kendal Green (B6)...
Kingston (M5)*...▲3,461
Lakeville (L5)...▲2,066
Lancaster (H3)*...▲3,601
Lanesboro (A2)*...▲2,069
Lanesville (M2)*...1,046
Lawrence (K2)*...80,536
Lawrence (urban area)...111,937
Lee (B3)*...▲4,820
Leeds (D3)*...1,700
Leicester (G4)*...▲6,029
Lenox (A3)*...▲3,627
Lenox Dale (B3)*...500
Leominster (G2)*...24,075
Leverett (E3)*...▲ 791
Lexington (B6)*...▲17,335
Leyden (D2)...▲ 306
Lincoln (B6)*...▲2,427
Linwood (H4)*...981
Littleton (H2)*...▲2,349
Littleton Common (J2)*...1,017
Longmeadow (D4)*...▲6,508
Lowell (J2)*...97,249
Lowell (urban area)..105,783
Ludlow (E4)*...▲8,660
Ludlow Center (E4)...500
Lunenburg (H2)*...▲3,906
Lynn (D6)*...99,738
Lynnfield (D5)*...▲3,927
Lynnfield Center (C5)* 2,600
Magnolia (M2)*...
Malden (D6)*...59,804
Manchaug (G4)*...790
Manchester (F5)*...▲2,868
Manomet (M5)*...350
Mansfield (J4)*...▲7,184
Marblehead (E5)*...▲13,765
Marion (L6)*...▲2,250
Marlboro (H3)*...15,756
Marshfield (M4)*...▲3,267
Marshfield Hills (M4)*. 500
Marstons Mills (N6)*. 600
Mashpee (M6)*...▲ 438
Mattapan (C7)*...
Mattapoisett (L6)*...▲2,265
Maynard (J3)*...▲6,978
Medfield (B8)*...▲4,549
Medfield Jct. (B8)...500
Medford (C6)*...66,113
Medway (J4)*...▲3,744
Melrose (D6)*...26,988
Melrose Highlds. (D6)*..7,713
Mendon (H4)*...▲1,619
Menemsha (L7)*
Merrimac (L1)*...▲2,804
Merrimacport (L1)...210
Methuen (K2)*...▲24,477
Middleboro (L5)*...▲10,164
Middlefield (B3)*...▲ 295
Middleton (K2)*...▲2,916
Milford (H4)*...▲15,442
Mill River (A4)...▲ 300
Millbrook (M4)*...200
Millbury (H4)*...▲8,347
Millers Falls (E2)*...1,134
Millis (A8)*...▲2,551
Millville (H4)*...▲1,692
Milton (D7)*...▲22,395
Minot (F8)*...150
Monroe Bridge (C2)*...150
Monson (E4)*...▲6,125
Montague (E2)*...▲7,812
Montague City (D2)*...668
Monterey (B4)*...▲ 367
Montvale (C6)...
Montville (B4)*...
Monument Beach (M6)*...650
Moores Corner (E2)*..
Mt. Hermon (D2)*...750
Mt. Hope (C7)...5,000
Mt. Tom (D3)*...230
Mt. Washington (A4)▲ 34
Myricks (K5)...210
Nabnasset (J2)*...500
Nahant (E6)*...▲2,679
Nantasket Beach (E7)*...1,900
Nantucket (O7)*...▲3,484
Natick (A7)*...▲19,838
Needham (B7)*...▲16,313
Needham Hts. (B7)*.. 5,500
Neponset (D7)...

New Bedford (K6)*...109,185
New Bedford (urban area)...125,354
New Boston (B4)*...
New Braintree (F3)*..▲ 478
New Lenox (B3)...
New Marlboro (B4)*..▲ 989
New Salem (E2)...▲ 392
Newbury (L1)...▲1,994
Newburyport (L1)*...14,111
Newton (C7)*...81,994
Newton Center (C7)*.15,214
Newton Highlands (C7)*...11,480
Newton Lower Falls (B7)*...1,215
Newton Upper Falls (C7)*...3,451
Newtonville (C7)*...13,689
Nonquitt (L6)*...18
Norfolk (J4)*...▲2,704
N. Abington (L4)*...3,906
N. Acton (J2)...300
N. Adams (B2)*...21,567
N. Amherst (E3)*...750
N. Andover (K2)*...▲8,485
N. Attleboro (J5)*...▲12,146
N. Bellingham (J4)*...300
N. Billerica (J2)*...3,300
N. Brewster (O5)...
N. Brookfield (F3)*...▲3,444
N. Carver (L5)*...
N. Chatham (O6)*...200
N. Chelmsford (J2)*...3,249
N. Cohasset (F7)*...
N. Dartmouth (K6)*...
N. Dighton (K5)*...1,000
N. Eastham (O5)*...270
N. Easton (K4)*...4,000
N. Egremont (A4)*...215
N. Falmouth (M6)*...800
N. Grafton (H4)*...2,000
N. Hadley (D3)*...1,000
N. Hanover (L4)*...800
N. Harwich (O6)*...210
N. Hatfield (D3)*...300
N. Leominster (G2)...
N. Marshfield (M4)*...450
N. Middleboro (L5)...500
N. Oxford (G4)*...1,250
N. Pembroke (M4)*...400
N. Plymouth (L5)*...4,000
N. Reading (C5)*...▲4,402
N. Rutland (G3)...125
N. Scituate (F8)*...1,100
N. Swansea (K5)...
N. Truro (O4)*...250
N. Uxbridge (H4)*...2,100
N. Westport (K6)*...3,000
N. Weymouth (D8)*...700
N. Wilbraham (E4)*...
Northampton (D3)*...29,063
Northboro (H3)*...▲3,122
Northbridge (H4)*...▲10,476
Northfield (E2)*...▲2,246
Northfield Farms (E2) 500
Norton (K5)*...▲4,401
Norwell (F8)*...▲2,515
Norwood (B8)*...▲16,636
Oak Bluffs (M7)*...▲1,521
Oakdale (G3)*...
Oakham (F3)*...▲ 455
Ocean Bluff (M4)*...600
Ocean Grove (K6)*...1,000
Old Sturbridge Village (F4)...
Onset (M6)*...1,674
Onset Station (M5)...
Orange (E2)*...▲5,894
Orleans (O5)*...▲1,759
Osterville (N6)*...1,003
Otis (B4)*...▲ 359
Otter River (F2)...
Oxford (G4)*...▲5,841
Palmer (E4)*...▲9,533
Paxton (G3)*...▲1,066
Peabody (E5)*...22,645
Pembroke (L4)*...▲2,579
Pepperell (H2)*...▲3,460
Petersham (F3)*...▲ 814
Phillipston (F2)...▲ 638
Pigeon Cove (M2)*...1,011
Pinehurst (B5)*...2,905
Pittsfield (A3)*...55,348
Plainfield (C2)*...▲ 228
Plainville (J4)*...▲2,088
Pleasant Lake (O6)*...125
Plymouth (M5)*...▲13,608
Plympton (L5)*...▲ 697
Pocasset (M6)*...500
Pottersville (K6)...2,700
Prides Crossing (E5)*.. 450
Princeton (G3)*...▲1,032
Princeton Depot (G3).
Provincetown (O4)*...▲3,795
Quincy (D7)*...83,835
Quissett (M6)...300
Randolph (D8)*...▲9,982
Raynham (K5)*...▲2,426
Raynham Center (K5)* 1,800
Reading (C5)*...▲14,006
Readville (C8)*...6,000
Rehoboth (K5)*...▲3,700
Renfrew (B2)...
Revere (D6)*...36,763
Richmond (A3)*...▲ 737
Richmond Furnace (A3)...250
Riverside (D2)...
Riverside (B7)...400
Rochdale (G4)*...1,800
Rochester (L6)*...▲1,328
Rock (L5)...600
Rockland (L4)*...▲8,960
Rockport (M2)*...▲4,231
Rockville (A8)...500
Rowe (C2)*...▲ 199
Rowley (L2)*...▲1,768
Roxbury (C7)*...
Royalston (F2)*...▲ 838
Russell (C4)*...▲1,298
Rutland (G3)*...▲3,056
Sagamore (M5)*...1,500
Salem (E5)*...41,880
Salisbury (L1)*...▲2,695
Sandwich (N5)*...▲2,418
Santuit (N6)*...400
Saugus (D6)*...▲17,162
Saundersville (G4)*...380
Savoy (B2)*...▲ 291
Saxonville (A7)*...3,200
Scituate (F8)*...▲5,993
Scotland (L5)...
Seekonk (J5)*...▲6,104
Segreganset (K5)*...300
Sharon (K4)*...▲4,847
Shattuckville (D2)*...225
Shawsheen Village (K2)*...2,100
Sheffield (A4)*...▲2,150
Shelburne Falls (D2)*. 2,364
Sheldonville (J4)*...300
Sherborn (A8)*...▲1,245
Shirley (H2)*...▲4,271
Shirley Center (H2)*.. 1,082
Shrewsbury (H3)*...▲10,594
Shutesbury (E3)*...▲ 213
Siasconset (P7)*...225
Silver Lake (L5)*...2,024
Somerset (K5)*...▲8,566
Somerville (C6)*...102,351
S. Acton (J3)*...1,200
S. Amherst (E3)...750
S. Ashburnham (G2)*.. 1,000
S. Athol (F2)*...100
S. Attleboro (J5)*...
S. Barre (F3)*...1,800
S. Berlin (H3)*...200
S. Braintree (D8)*...5,600
S. Bridgewater (L5)*..
S. Carver (M5)*...300
S. Chatham (O6)*...450
S. Dartmouth (L6)*...6,300
S. Deerfield (D3)*...1,418
S. Dennis (O6)*...300
S. Duxbury (M4)*...800
S. Easton (K4)*...1,500
S. Egremont (A4)*...415
S. Essex (L2)*...
S. Groveland (L2)...900
S. Hadley (D4)*...▲10,145
S. Hadley Falls (D4)* 4,000
S. Hanover (L4)*...600
S. Harwich (O6)*...400
S. Hingham (E8)...650
S. Lancaster (H3)*...1,462
S. Lawrence (K2)...25,000
S. Lee (A3)*...325
S. Lincoln (J3)*...
S. Middleboro (L5)...600
S. Middleton (D5)...
S. Natick (A7)*...1,500
S. Orleans (O5)*...89
S. Royalston (F2)*...415
S. Sandisfield (B4)*...
S. Sudbury (J3)*...900
S. Vernon (D2)*...225
S. Walpole (K4)*...750
S. Wareham (L5)...
S. Wellfleet (P5)*...450
S. Westport (K6)*...200
S. Weymouth (E8)*...8,500
S. Worthington (C3)...50
S. Yarmouth (O6)*...1,185
Southampton (C4)*...▲1,387
Southboro (H3)*...▲2,760
Southbridge (G4)*...▲17,519
Southfield (B4)...100
Southville (H3)*...300
Southwick (C4)*...▲2,850
Spencer (F3)*...▲7,027
Springfield (D4)*...162,399
Springfield-Holyoke (urban area)...356,471
State Line (A3)*...200
Sterling (G3)*...▲2,166
Still River (H3)*...150
Stockbridge (A3)*...▲2,311
Stoneham (C6)*...▲13,229
Stoughton (K4)*...▲11,146
Stow (H3)*...▲1,700
Straits Pond (F7)*...250
Sturbridge (F4)*...▲2,805
Sudbury (A6)*...▲2,596
Sunderland (D3)*...▲ 905
Sutton (G4)...▲3,102
Swampscott (E6)*...▲11,580
Swansea (K5)*...▲6,121
Swansea Center (K5)..
Taunton (K5)*...40,109
Teaticket (M6)*...600
Templeton (F2)*...▲4,757
Tewkesbury (K2)*...▲7,505
Thorndike (E4)*...1,650
Three Rivers (E4)*...2,359
Tolland (B4)...▲ 107
Topsfield (L2)*...▲1,412
Townsend (H2)*...▲2,817
Townsend Harbor (G2)*...197
Truro (O5)*...▲ 661
Tully (E2)...
Turners Falls (D2)*...5,179
Tyngsboro (J2)*...▲2,059
Tyringham (A4)*...▲ 235
Unionville (J4)...150
Upton (H4)*...▲2,656
Uxbridge (H4)*...▲7,007
Vineyard Haven (M7)* 1,864
Waban (B7)*...6,000
Wakefield (C5)*...▲19,633
Wales (F4)*...▲ 497
Walpole (B8)*...▲9,109
Waltham (B6)*...47,187
Waquoit (M6)*...400
Ward Hill (K2)*...580
Ware (E3)*...▲7,517
Wareham (L5)*...▲7,569
Warren (F4)*...▲3,406
Warwick (E2)*...▲ 429
Washington (B3)...▲ 281
Watertown (C6)*...▲37,329
Waterville (F2)*...450
Waverly (B6)*...10,000
Wayland (A7)*...▲4,407
Webster (G4)*...▲13,194
Wellesley (B7)*...▲20,549
Wellesley Hills (B7)*..18,000
Wellfleet (O5)*...▲1,123
Wendell (E2)*...▲ 342
Wendell Depot (E2)*..
Wenham (L2)*...▲1,644
W. Acton (H3)*...1,300
W. Auburn (G4)...
W. Barnstable (N6)*...750
W. Berlin (H3)*...325
W. Boxford (K2)*...400
W. Boylston (G3)*...▲2,570
W. Brewster (O5)...
W. Bridgewater (K4)*...▲4,059
W. Brookfield (F4)*...▲1,674
W. Chatham (O6)*...300
W. Chelmsford (J2)*...300
W. Chesterfield (C3)*. 200
W. Concord (A6)*...1,285
W. Cummington (B3)* 180
W. Dennis (O6)*...600
W. Dudley (F4)...200
W. Falmouth (M6)*...700
W. Granville (C4)...200
W. Groton (H2)*...
W. Hanover (L4)*...1,200
W. Harwich (O6)*...400
W. Hawley (C2)*...56
W. Mansfield (K5)*...900
W. Medway (J4)*...1,625
W. Millbury (G4)*...300
W. Newbury (L1)*...▲1,598
W. Newton (B7)*...15,000
W. Peabody (D5)*...1,100
W. Pittsfield (A3)...2,000
W. Rutland (F3)...
W. Springfield (D4)*.▲20,438
W. Stockbridge (A3)*▲ 1,165
W. Tisbury (M7)*...▲ 347
W. Townsend (H2)*...900
W. Upton (H4)*...1,400
W. Wareham (L5)*...800
W. Warren (F4)*...1,244
W. Yarmouth (N6)*...1,355
Westboro (H3)*...▲7,378
Westfield (D4)*...20,962
Westford (J2)*...▲4,262
Westford Station (J2). 300

Westhampton (C3).....△ 452
Westminster (G2)*......△2,768
Weston (B6)*.............△5,026
Westport (K6)*..........△4,989
Westport Point (K6)*. 500
Westwood (B8)*..........△5,837
Weymouth (D8)*.......△32,690
Whately (D3)*...........△ 939
Wheelwright (F3)*..... 270
Whitinsville (H4)*....... 5,662
Whitman (L4)*...........△8,413
Wilbraham (E4)*........△4,003
Wilkinsonville (G4)*....
Williamsburg (C3)*.....△2,056
Williamstown (B2)*....△6,194
Williamstown Station (B2) ...................... 5,000
Willimansett (D4)*..... 9,474
Wilmington (C5)*.......△7,039
Winchendon (F2)*......△6,585
Winchendon Spgs.(G2)* 500
Winchester (C6)*......△15,509
Windsor (B2)*............△ 372
Winthrop (D6)*........△19,496
Woburn (C6)*.............20,492
Woods Hole (M6)*...... 750
Woodville (H4)*.......... 350
Worcester (H3)*.......203,486
Worcester (urban area) ....................217,705
Woronoco (C4)*.......... 501
Worthington (C3)*.....△ 462
Wrentham (J4)*..........△5,341
Yarmouth (O6)*..........△3,297
Yarmouth Port (N6)*. 330


## MICHIGAN

Map on Page 67

Total Population 6,371,766

### 83 COUNTIES


Alcona (F4)...................5,856
Alger (C2)...................10,007
Allegan (D6)..............47,493
Alpena (F4)................22,189
Antrim (D3)................10,721
Arenac (F4)...................9,644
Baraga (A2)..................8,037
Barry (D6)...................26,183
Bay (E5).....................88,461
Benzie (C4)...................8,306
Berrien (C7)..............115,702
Branch (D7).................30,202
Calhoun (D6)............120,813
Cass (C7)....................28,185
Charlevoix (D3)...........13,475
Cheboygan (E3)..........13,731
Chippewa (E2)............29,206
Clare (E5)...................10,253
Clinton (E6)................31,195
Crawford (E4)...............4,151
Delta (C2)...................32,913
Dickinson (B2)............24,844
Eaton (E6)..................40,023
Emmet (E3).................16,534
Genesee (F5).............270,963
Gladwin (E4)..................9,451
Gogebic (F2)...............27,053
Grand Traverse (D4)....28,598
Gratiot (E5).................33,429
Hillsdale (E7)..............31,916
Houghton (G1)............39,771
Huron (F5)...................33,149
Ingham (E6)..............172,941
Ionia (D6)....................38,158
Iosco (F4)....................10,906
Iron (G2).....................17,692
Isabella (E5)...............28,964
Jackson (E6)..............107,925
Kalamazoo (D6)........126,707
Kalkaska (D4)...............4,597
Kent (D5)..................288,292
Keweenaw (A1).............2,918
Lake (D5).......................5,257
Lapeer (F5)..................35,794
Leelanau (D4)................8,647
Lenawee (E7)...............64,629
Livingston (F6).............26,725
Luce (D2).......................8,147
Mackinac (D2)................9,287
Macomb (G6)............184,961
Manistee (C4)..............18,524
Marquette (B2)............47,654
Mason (C4)...................20,474
Mecosta (D5)...............18,968
Menominee (B3)...........25,299
Midland (E5)................35,662
Missaukee (D4)...............7,458
Monroe (F7)..................75,666
Montcalm (D5)..............31,013
Montmorency (E3)..........4,125
Muskegon (C5)...........121,545
Newaygo (D5)...............21,567
Oakland (F6)..............396,001
Oceana (C5).................16,105
Ogemaw (E4)..................9,345
Ontonagon (F1)............10,282
Osceola (D5)................13,797
Oscoda (E4)....................3,134
Otsego (E3)....................6,435
Ottawa (C6)..................73,751
Presque Isle (F3)..........11,996
Roscommon (E4)............5,916
Saginaw (E5)..............153,515
Saint Clair (G6)............91,591
St. Joseph (D7).............35,071
Sanilac (G5).................30,837
Schoolcraft (C2).............9,148
Shiawassee (E6)...........45,967
Tuscola (F5)................38,258
Van Buren (C6)............39,184
Washtenaw (F6)........134,606
Wayne (F6)............2,435,235
Wexford (D4)..............18,628


### CITIES and TOWNS


Acme (D4).................... 300
Ada (D6)*..................... 500
Addison (E7)*.............. 488
Adrian (F7)*..............18,393
Advance (D3)............... 50
Afton (E3)*.................. 450
Ahmeek (A1)*............... 360
Akron (F5)*.................. 431
Alabaster (F4)*............ 125
Alanson (E3)*.............. 319
Alaska (D6)................. 335
Alba (E4)*................... 500
Albion (E6)*...............10,406
Alden (D4)*................. 350
Alger (E4)*.................. 445
Algonac (G6)*..............2,639
Allegan (D6)*..............4,801
Allen (E7)*.................. 340
Allen Park (B7)*........12,329
Allenville (E3)*............ 200
Allouez (A1)*............... 310
Alma (E5)*....................8,341
Almont (F6)*.................1,035
Alpena (F3)*..............13,135
Alpha (A2)*................. 378
Alpine (D5).................. 100
Alston (G1)*................ 150
Alto (D6)*.................... 400
Altona (D5).................. 85
Amasa (G2)*................ 700
Amble (D5)*................. 51
Amelith (F5)................ 150
Anchorville (G6)*.......... 950
Ann Arbor (F6)*.........48,251
Antrim (D4)................. 300
Applegate (G5)*........... 244
Arcadia (C4)*............... 450
Argyle (G5)*................ 400
Arlene (D4).................. 86
Armada (G6)*............... 961
Arnheim (G1)*............. 50
Arnold (B2)*................
Ashley (E5)*................ 449
Ashton (D5)*................ 178
Assyria (D6)................. 200
Athens (D6)*................ 768
Atlanta (E3)*................ 350
Atlantic Mine (G1)*..... 800
Attica (F5)*.................
Atwood (D3)................. 60
Au Gres (F4)*............... 442
Au Sable (F4)............... 300
Au Train (C2)*.............. 106
Auburn (F5)*................ 869
Auburn Heights (F6)*...2,500
Augusta (D6)*.............. 898
Aura (A2)*................... 295
Averill (E5).................. 100
Avoca (G5)*................. 300
Avondale (D4).............. 50
Azalia (F6)*................. 100
Bach (F5) ..................... 125
Bad Axe (G5)*.............2,973
Bagley (B3).................. 60
Baie de Wasai (E2)...... 100
Bailey (D5)*................. 300
Baldwin (D5)*............... 835
Baltic (G1)*.................. 500
Bancroft (E6)*.............. 615
Bangor (C6)*................1,694
Bannister (E5)*............ 300
Baraga (G1)*............... 942
Barbeau (E2)*.............. 50
Bark River (B3)*.......... 500
Baroda (C7)*................ 344
Barryton (D5)*.............. 445
Barton City (F4)*.......... 100
Batavia (D7)*............... 124
Bates (D4).................... 75
Bath (E6)*.................... 600
Battle Creek (D6)*......48,666
Bay City (F5)*............52,523
Bay Port (F5)*.............. 557
Bay View (E3)*............. 25
Bayshore (D3)*............. 200
Beacon (B2)*............... 300
Beal City (D5).............. 338
Bear Lake (C4)*............ 364
Beaverton (E5)*........... 794
Bedford (D6)*..............
Belding (D5)*................4,436
Bellaire (D4)*............... 693
Belleville (F6)*.............1,722
Bellevue (E6)*..............1,168
Belmont (D5)*.............. 200
Bendon (D4)*............... 79
Benson (D4)................. 22
Bentley (E5)*............... 150
Benton Harbor (C6)*...18,769
Benton Heights (C6).....6,160
Benzonia (D4)*............ 407
Bergland (F1)*............ 800
Berkley (B6)*.............17,931
Berrien Springs (C7)*...1,761
Bessemer (F2)*............3,509
Beulah (C4)*................ 458
Big Bay (B2)*............... 670
Big Rapids (D5)*..........6,736
Birch (B2).................... 8
Birch Run (F5)*............ 800
Birmingham (B6)*......15,467
Bishop (D5).................. 100
Bitely (D5)*................. 200
Blackriver (F4)*........... 259
Blaine (G5)*................ 108
Blanchard (D5)*........... 300
Blaney Park (D2)*........ 30
Bliss (E3)..................... 75
Blissfield (F7)*............2,365
Bloomfield Hills (B6)*.1,468
Bloomingdale (C6)*....... 465
Bolton (F3)*................. 25
Boon (D4)*.................. 260
Boyne City (E3)*..........3,028
Boyne Falls (E3)*......... 236
Brampton (B3)*............ 300
Branch (D5)*................ 150
Brant (E5)*.................. 95
Brassar (E2)................ 75
Breckenridge (E5)*...... 985
Breedsville (C6)*......... 239
Brethren (D4)*............. 500
Brevort (E2)*............... 80
Bridgeport (F5)*..........1,200
Bridgeton (D5)............. 100
Bridgman (C7)*............ 977
Brighton (F6)*..............1,861
Brimley (E2)*............... 500
Bristol (D4).................. 40
Britton (F6)*................ 517
Brohman (D5)*............. 150
Bronson (D7) ...............2,106
Brooklyn (E6)*............. 862
Brown City (G5)*......... 878
Bruce Crossing (G2)*.... 200
Brutus (E3)*................ 200
Buchanan (C7)*............5,224
Buckley (D4)*.............. 194
Burlington (D6)*.......... 329
Burnips (D6)*.............. 170
Burr Oak (D7)*............ 814
Burt (F5)*.................... 200
Burt Lake (E3)*............ 60
Butternut (E5)*............ 128
Byron (E6)*.................. 439
Byron Center (D6)*....... 650
Cadillac (D4)*.............10,425
Caledonia (D6)*............ 619
Calumet (A1)*...............1,256
Cambria (E7)................ 210
Camden (E7)*.............. 380
Capac (G5)*..................1,104
Carleton (F6)*..............1,039
Carlshend (B2)*............ 100
Carney (B3)*................ 325
Caro (F5)*.....................3,464
Carp Lake (E3)*............ 200
Carrollton (E5)*............2,000
Carson City (E5)*..........1,168
Carsonville (G5)*.......... 487
Caseville (F5)*............. 482
Casnovia (D5)*............ 312
Caspian (G2)*...............1,608
Cass City (F5)*.............1,762
Cassopolis (C7)*...........1,527
Castle Park (C6)*......... 9
Cathro (F3)*................. 100
Cedar (D4)*................. 249
Cedar River (B3)*........ 75
Cedar Springs (D5)*....1,378
Cedarville (E2)*........... 250
Cement City (E6)*........ 500
Center Line (B6)*........7,659
Central Lake (D3)*....... 692
Centreville (D7)*.......... 879
Ceresco (D6)*..............
Champion (B2)*........... 567
Channing (B2)*............ 497
Charleston (G5)........... 85
Charlevoix (D3)*...........2,695
Charlotte (E6)*.............6,606
Chase (D5)*................. 300
Chatham (B2)*............. 650
Cheboygan (E3)*..........5,687
Chelsea (E6)*...............2,580
Chesaning (E5)*............2,264
Chester (D6)................ 50
Chippewa Lake (D5)*.... 125
Clare (E5)*...................2,440
Clarion (E3)................. 84
Clarklake (E6)*............ 500
Clarkston (F6)*............ 722
Clarksville (D6)*.......... 339
Clawson (B6)*...............5,196
Clayton (E7)*............... 467
Clifford (F5)*............... 330
Climax (D6)*................ 524
Clinton (F6)*.................1,344
Clio (F5)*......................1,963
Cohoctah (F6)*............. 150
Coldwater (D7)*............8,594
Coleman (E5)*...............1,024
Coloma (C6)*.................1,041
Colon (D7)*...................1,000
Columbiaville (F5)*....... 789
Comins (E4)*................ 87
Comstock (D6)*............8,314
Concord (E6)*.............. 730
Conklin (D5)*............... 350
Connorville (F1)........... 50
Constantine (D7)*........1,514
Conway (E3)*............... 100
Cooks (C3)*................. 300
Coopersville (C5)*........1,371
Copemish (D4)*............ 255
Copper City (A1)*......... 336
Copper Harbor (B1)*.... 30
Coral (D5)*................... 300
Cornell (B3)*................ 20
Corunna (E6)*...............2,358
Covert (C6)*................. 450
Covington (G2)*........... 260
Cross Village (D3)*...... 200
Croswell (G5)*..............1,775
Crump (E5)*................. 75
Crystal (E5)*................ 450
Crystal Falls (A2)*........2,316
Crystal Valley (C5)*...... 250
Curran (F4)*................. 50
Curtis (D2)*.................. 300
Curtisville (F4)*............ 25
Cusino (C2).................. 50
Custer (C5)*................. 260
Dafter (E2)*.................. 125
Daggett (B3)*............... 341
Dalton (C5).................. 500
Dansville (E6)*............. 433
Darragh (E4)................ 20
Davison (F5)*...............1,745
Dayton (C7)*................ 125
De Witt (E6)*................ 824
Dearborn (B7)*............94,994
Decatur (C6)*................1,664
Decker (F5)*................. 100
Deckerville (G5)*.......... 719
Deerfield (F7)*............. 725
Deerton (B2)*............... 225
Deford (F5)*................. 200
Delton (D6)*................. 700
Delwin (E5).................. 100
Detour (F3)*................. 611
Detroit (B7)*..............1,849,568
Detroit(urban area)2,644,476
Dewings (D4)............... 6
Dexter (F6)*..................1,307
Dighton (D4)*.............. 100
Dimondale (E6)*.......... 774
Dollar Bay (G1)*.......... 600
Dollarville (D2)............ 100
Dorr (D6)*.................... 428
Douglas (C6)*.............. 447
Dover (E5).................... 20
Dowagiac (D6)*............6,542
Dowling (D6)*.............. 126
Drayton Plains (F6)*....3,500
Drummond (F3)*.......... 443
Dryden (F6)*................ 476
Dublin (D4).................. 25
Dukes (B2)*................. 150
Dundee (F7)*................1,975
Durand (E6)*................3,194
Dutton (D6)*................ 150
Eagle (E6)*.................. 145
Eagle Harbor (A1)*...... 75
Eagle River (A1)*........ 65
East Ann Arbor (F6)....1,826
E. Detroit (B6)*..........21,461
E. Grand Rapids (D6)....6,403
E. Jordan (D3)*.............1,779
E. Lansing (E6)*........20,325
E. Tawas (F4)*..............2,040
Eastlake (C4)*............. 376
Eastport (D3)*............. 125
Eaton Rapids (E6)*......3,509
Eau Claire (C6)*.......... 480
Eben Junction (B2)*..... 400
Eckerman (E2)*............ 300
Ecorse (B7)*...............17,948
Edenville (E5)*............ 140
Edgerton (D5).............. 200
Edgewood (E5)............. 50
Edmore (E5)*............... 971
Edwardsburg (C7)........ 616
Elba (F5).....................
Elberta (C4)*............... 597
Eldorado (E4)*............. 31
Elk Rapids (D4)*.......... 889
Elkton (F5)*................. 854
Ellsworth (D3)*............ 369
Elmira (E3)*................ 230
Elmwood (F5).............. 100
Elo (G1)*..................... 35
Eloise (F6)*..................5,000
Elsie (E5)*................... 911
Elwell (E5)*................. 150
Emerson (F3)...............
Emmett (G6)*.............. 230
Empire (C4)*............... 251
Engadine (D2)*............ 500
Ensign (C3)*................ 446
Epoufette (D2)*........... 50
Erie (F7)*..................... 800
Escanaba (C3)*...........15,170
Essexville (F5)*............3,167
Estey (E5).................... 50
Estral Beach (F7)......... 188
Eureka (E5)*................
Evart (D5)*...................1,578
Ewen (F2)*................... 817
Fair Haven (G6)*..........1,200
Fairgrove (F5)*............ 570
Fairview (F4)*.............. 300
Faithorn (B3)*.............. 233
Falmouth (E4)*............. 300
Fargo (G5)*.................. 110
Farmington (F6)*..........2,325
Farwell (E5)*................ 694
Felch (B3)*................... 200
Fennville (C6)*............. 639
Fenton (F6)*..................4,226
Fenwick (D5)*.............. 150
Ferndale (B6)*............29,675
Ferry (C5)*................... 200
Ferrysburg (C5)*...........1,454
Fife Lake (D4)*............. 347
Filer City (C4)*............. 340
Filion (G5)*.................. 200
Flat Rock (F6)*..............1,931
Flint (F6)*..................163,143
Flint (urban area)....197,151
Flushing (F5)*...............2,226
Forest Lake (C2)*......... 110
Forester (G5)............... 100
Forestville (G5)*........... 124
Forsyth (B2)*............... 400
Foster City (B3)*.......... 300
Fosters (F5)*................ 130
Fostoria (F5)*............... 275
Fountain (C4)*.............. 247
Fowler (E5)*................. 675
Fowlerville (F6)*...........1,466
Fox (B3)*..................... 20
Frankenmuth (F5)*.......1,208
Frankfort (C4)*.............1,858
Franklin Mine (G1)*..... 90
Fraser (B6)*..................1,379
Frederic (E4)*............... 250
Free Soil (C4)*............. 208
Freeland (E5)*...............1,000
Freeport (D6)*.............. 452
Fremont (D5)*...............3,056
Frontier (E7)*............... 265
Fruitport (C5)*.............. 638
Fulton (D6)*.................. 200
Gaastra (G2)*............... 575
Gagetown (F5)*............ 401
Gaines (F6)*................. 352
Galesburg (D6)*............1,200
Galien (C7)*................. 610
Ganges (C6)*................ 150
Garden (C3)*................ 399
Garden City (B7)*..........9,012
Garnet (D2)*................ 75
Gay (A1)*..................... 156
Gaylord (E3)*................2,271
Genesee (F5)*.............. 600
Germfask (C2)*............. 300
Gibbs City (G2)*........... 200
Gilford (F5)*................. 200
Gilmore (E5)................
Girard (E6)................... 275
Gladstone (C3)*............4,831
Gladwin (E5)*................1,878
Glen Arbor (C4)*.......... 100
Glen Haven (C4)........... 25
Glenn (C6)*.................. 180
Glennie (F4)*................ 250
Glenwood (C6)*............ 110
Gobles (D6)*................. 622
Goetzville (E2)*............ 150
Good Hart (D3)*........... 50
Goodells (G5)*.............. 600
Goodrich (F6)*.............. 525
Gotts (F5).................... 50
Gould City (D2)*........... 350
Gowen (D5)*................ 200
Grace (E3).................... 50
Grand Beach (C7)*........ 105
Grand Blanc (F6)*........ 998
Grand Haven (C5)*........9,536
Grand Junction (C6)*.... 350
Grand Ledge (E6)*........4,506
Grand Marais (D2)*...... 600
Grand Rapids (D5)*..176,515
Grand Rapids (urban area) .....................225,427
Grandville (D6)*............2,022
Grant (D5)*................... 646
Grass Lake (E6)*.......... 878
Grawn (D4)*................. 175
Grayling (E4)*...............2,066
Green (F1)....................
Greenbush (F4)*........... 100
Greenland (G1)*........... 600
Greenville (D5)*............6,668
Gregory (E6)*............... 300
Grind Stone City (G4)*.
Grosse Ile (B7)*............2,500
Grosse Pointe (B7)*......6,283
Grosse Pointe Farms (B6) .........................9,410
Grosse Pointe Park (B7) .......................13,075
Grosse Pointe Shores (B6) ........................1,032
Grosse Pointe Woods (B6) ......................10,381
Gulliver (D2)*.............. 300
Gwinn (B2)*................. 900
Hadley (F6)*................ 275
Hagensville (F3)........... 100
Hale (F4)*.................... 500
Hamburg (F6)*............. 350
Hamilton (C6)*............. 600
Hamtramck (B6)*........43,355
Hancock (G1)*...............5,223
Hanover (E6)*.............. 377
Harbor Beach (G5)*.....2,349
Harbor Springs (D3)*....1,626
Harper Woods (B6)......9,148
Harrietta (D4)*............. 152
Harris (B3)*................. 150
Harrison (E4)*.............. 884
Harrisville (F4)*........... 485
Hart (C5)*.................. 2,172
Hartford (C6)*...............1,838
Hartland (F6)*..............
Haslett (E6)*..................1,000
Hastings (D6)*...............6,096
Hawkins (D5)................ 50
Hawks (F3)*................. 250
Hazel Park (B6)*........17,770
Helena (G5)................. 75
Helmer (D2)................. 35
Hemlock (E5)*.............. 700
Henderson (E5)*........... 200
Herman (A2)*............... 155
Hermansville (B3)*....... 800
Herron (F3)*................
Hersey (D5)*................ 239
Hesperia (D5)*............. 760
Hessel (E2)*................. 200
Hiawatha (C2).............. 150
Hickory Corners (D6)* ...................... 180
Highland Park (B6)*...46,393
Hillman (F3)*............... 442
Hillsdale (E7)*..............7,297
Hockaday (E4)............. 5
Holland (C6)*..............15,858
Holly (F6)*....................2,663
Holt (E6)*......................6,500
Holton (C5)*................. 350
Home Acres (D6).......20,000
Homer (E6)*..................1,301
Honor (D4)*................. 269
Hope (E5)*................... 100
Hopkins (D6)*.............. 531
Horton (E6)*................ 350
Horton Bay (D3)........... 50
Houghton (G1)*............3,829
Houghton Lake (E4)*....
Houghton Point (E4)*..
Howard City (D5)*....... 791
Howell (E6)*..................4,353
Hoxeyville (D4)*.......... 128
Hubbard Lake (F4)*..... 150
Hubbardston (E5)*....... 335
Hubbell (A1)*.................1,690
Hudson (E7)*.................2,773
Hudsonville (D6)*..........1,101
Hulbert (D2)*................ 400
Huntington Woods (F6)* ........................4,949
Huron City (G4)........... 55
Huron Mountain (B2)*.. 20
Ida (F7)*...................... 950
Idlewild (D5)*.............. 450
Imlay City (F5)*............1,654
Ina (D4)....................... 30
Indian River (E3)*........ 600
Ingalls (B3)*................ 150
Ingallston (B3)*........... 50
Inkster (B7)*...............16,728
Interlochen (D4)*......... 150
Ionia (D6)*....................6,412
Iron Mountain (B3)* ....................9,679
Iron River (G2)*............4,048
Irons (D4)*.................. 30
Ironwood (F2)*............11,466
Isabella (C3)................ 2
Ishpeming (B2)*............8,962
Ithaca (E5)*..................2,377
Ivanhoe (F5)................
Jackson (E6)*..............51,088
Jacobsville (A1)*.......... 145
Jamestown (D6)*.......... 300
Jasper (E7)*................ 300
Jeddo (G5)*................. 150
Jenison (D6)*............... 300
Jennings (D4)*............. 250
Johannesburg (E4)*...... 250
Jones (D7)*.................. 300
Jonesville (E6)*.............1,594
Kalamazoo (D6)*........57,704
Kalamazoo (urban area) ......................82,859
Kalamo (D6)................ 135
Kaleva (C4)*................ 346
Kalkaska (D4)*..............1,250
Kawkawlin (F5)*........... 500
Keego Harbor (F6)*.....7,700
Kent City (D5)*............ 506
Kenton (G2)*................ 400
Keweenaw Bay (G1)*.... 300
Kilmanagh (F5)...........
Kinde (G5)*.................. 571
Kingsford (A3)*.............5,038
Kingsley (D4)*.............. 425
Kingston (F5)*.............. 371
Kipling (B3).................. 335
Kneeland (E4).............. 60
La Salle (F7)*............... 74
Labranche (B3)............ 25
Lachine (F3)*............... 90
Laingsburg (E6)*.......... 942
Lake (E5)*.................... 300
Lake Angelus ‡(F6)...... 123
Lake Ann (D4)*............ 99
Lake City (D4)*............ 719
Lake George (E5)*....... 145
Lake Leelanau (D4)*.... 400
Lake Linden (A1)*........1,462
Lake Odessa (D6)*.......1,596
Lake Orion (F6)*...........2,385
Lakeland (F6)*............. 300
Lakeview (D5)*............. 975
Lamont (D6)*................ 350
L'Anse (G1)*.................2,376
LANSING (E6)*..........92,129
Lansing (urban area) .....................133,625
Lapeer (F5)*.................6,143
Laporte (E5)................. 300
Larkin (E5).................. 50
Lathrop (B2)................ 46
Laurium (A1)*...............3,211
Lawrence (C6)*............ 679
Lawton (D6)*.................1,206
Le Roy (D4)*................ 243
Leer (F3)..................... 20
Leetsville (D4)*............ 35
Leland (D3)*................. 536
Lenox (G6)*.................. 975
Leonard (F6)*............... 391
Leonidas (D6)*............. 225
Leslie (E6)*...................1,543
Levering (E3)*.............. 387
Lewiston (E4)*.............. 700
Lexington (G5)*............ 594
Lincoln (F4)*................ 409
Lincoln Park (B7)*......29,310
Linden (F6)*................. 933
Linkville (F5)...............
Livonia (F6)................17,534
Linwood (F5)*.............. 425
Lisbon ‡(D5)...............
Liske (F3).................... 6
Litchfield (E6)*............ 882
Long Lake (F4)*........... 100
Long Rapids (F3)......... 50
Loretto (B3)*................ 350
Lovells (E4)................. 100
Lowell (D6)*..................2,191
Lucas (D4)*.................. 120
Ludington (C5)*.............9,506
Lum (F5)*.................... 300
Lupton (E4)*................ 200
Luther (D4)*................. 314
Luzerne (E4)*............... 150
Lyon Manor (E4)*........ 87
Lyons (E6)*.................. 683
Mackinac Island (E3)*.. 572
Mackinaw City (E3)*.... 970
Mancelona (E4)*............1,000
Manchester (E6)*..........1,388
Manistee (C4)*..............8,642
Manistique (C3)*...........5,086
Manton (D4)*................1,085
Maple City (D4)*.......... 190
Maple Rapids (E5)*...... 645
Maple Ridge (F4)......... 75
Mapleton (D4)............. 60
Marcellus (D6)*.............1,014
Marenisco (F2)*.............1,300
Marilla (D4).................. 80
Marine City (G6)*..........4,270
Marion (D4)*................. 879
Marlette (G5)*...............1,489
Marne (D5)*.................. 600

Marquette (B2)*.....17,202
Marshall (E6)*.....5,777
Martin (D6)*..... 407
Marysville (G6)*.....2,534
Mason (E6)*.....3,514
Mass (G1)*.....
Matchwood (F1)*..... 100
Maybee (F6)*..... 428
Mayville (F5)*..... 888
Mc Bain (D4)*..... 506
Mc Brides (D5)*..... 223
Mc Ivor (F4)*..... 50
Mc Millan (D2)*..... 336
Mears (C5)*..... 262
Mecosta (D5)*..... 305
Melvin (G5)*..... 204
Melvindale (B7)*.....9,483
Memphis (G6)*..... 800
Mendon (D7)*..... 844
Menominee (B3)*.....11,151
Merrill (E5)*..... 809
Merritt (D4)*..... 61
Merriweather (F1)*..... 100
Mesick (D4)*..... 359
Metamora (F6)*..... 390
Metropolitan (A3)*..... 250
Metz (F3)*..... 35
Michiana (C7)..... 102
Michigamme (A2)*..... 600
Michigan Center (E6)*..3,012
Michillinda (C5)*..... 50
Middleton (E5)..... 450
Middleville (D6)*.....1,047
Midland (E5)*.....14,285
Mikado (F4)*..... 204
Milan (F6)*.....2,768
Milford (F6)*.....1,924
Millbrook (D5)*..... 200
Millersburg ....(F3)*..... 281
Millington (F5)*.....1,043
Minden City (G5)*..... 359
Mineral Hills (G2)..... 333
Mio (E4)*..... 975
Missaukee Park (D4).... 30
Mohawk (A1)*..... 900
Moline (D6)*..... 300
Monroe (F7)*.....21,467
Montague (C5)*.....1,530
Montgomery (E7)*..... 397
Montrose (F5)*..... 937
Moorestown (D4)*..... 53
Moran (E2)*..... 310
Morenci (E7)*.....1,983
Morley (D5)*..... 413
Morrice (E6)*..... 401
Mount Clemens (G6)*..17,027
Mt. Morris (F5)*.....2,890
Mt. Pleasant (E5)*.....11,393
Mountforest (F5)*..... 50
Muir (D5)*..... 466
Mullett Lake (E3)*..... 75
Mulliken (E6)*..... 411
Munger (F5)*..... 250
Munising (C2)*.....4,339
Munith (E6)*..... 500
Muskegon (C5)*.....48,429
Muskegon (urban area).....84,775
Muskegon Heights (C5)*.....18,828
Nadeau (B3)*..... 400
Nahma (C3)*..... 750
Napoleon (E6)*..... 530
Nashville (D6)*.....1,374
Nathan (B3)..... 76
National City (F4)*..... 100
National Mine (B2)*..... 250
Naubinway (D2)*..... 200
Nazareth (D6)*..... 500
Negaunee (B2)*.....6,472
Nestoria (A2)*..... 32
New Baltimore (G6)*...2,043
New Boston (F6)*..... 800
New Buffalo (C7)*.....1,565
New Era (C5)*..... 247
New Haven (G6)*.....1,082
New Lothrop (F5)*..... 459
New Troy (C7)*..... 300
Newaygo (D5)*.....1,385
Newberry (D2)*.....2,802
Newland (C4)..... 100
Niles (C7)*.....13,145
Nirvana (D5)*..... 40
North Adams (E7)*..... 499
N. Bradley (E5)*..... 300
N. Branch (F5)*..... 832
N. Lake (B2)..... 200
N. Manitou Island (C3) 15
N. Muskegon (C5)*.....2,424
Northland (B2)*..... 100
Northport (D3)*..... 582
Northstar (E5)*..... 285
Northville (F6)*.....3,240
Norwalk (C4)*..... 25
Norway (B3)*.....3,258
Novi (F6)*.....1,000
Oak Grove (F6)*..... 125
Oak Park (B6).....5,267
Oakley (E5)*..... 333
Oberlin (E4)..... 5
Ocqueoc (F3)*..... 90
Okemos (E6)*..... 950
Old Mission (D4).....
Olivet (E6)*..... 887
Omena (D3)*..... 80
Omer (F4)*..... 321
Onaway (E3)*.....1,421
Onekama (C4)*..... 435
Onondaga (E6)*..... 423
Onsted (E6)*..... 486
Ontonagon (F1)*.....2,307
Orangeville (D6)..... 900
Orchard Lake (F6)*..... 696
Ortonville (F6)*..... 702
Oscoda (F4)*.....1,800
Oshtemo (D6)*..... 300
Osseo (E7)*..... 300
Ossineke (F4)*..... 150
Otisville (F5)*..... 592
Otsego (D6)*.....3,990
Otsego Lake (E4)*.....
Ottawa Beach (C6)..... 40
Ottawa Lake (F7)*..... 200
Otter Lake (F5)*..... 523
Overisel (C6)..... 350
Ovid (E5)*.....1,410
Owendale (F5)*..... 307
Owosso (E5)*.....15,948
Oxford (F6)*.....2,305
Ozark (E2)*..... 70
Painesdale (G1)*.....1,100
Palmer (B2)*..... 825
Palms (G5)*..... 100
Palmyra (E7)*..... 250
Palo (E5)*..... 300
Parchment (D6)*.....1,179
Paris (D5)*..... 225
Parisville (G5)..... 150
Parma (E6)*..... 680
Paw Paw (D6)*.....2,382
Payment (E2)..... 100
Paynesville (G2)*..... 250
Peacock (D4)..... 25
Pearl Beach (G6)*.....
Peck (G5)*..... 471
Pelkie (G1)*..... 25
Pellston (E3)*..... 442
Pentoga (G2)..... 50
Pentwater (C5)*.....1,097
Pequaming (A2)..... 21
Perkins (B3)*..... 500
Perrinton (E5)*..... 383
Perronville (B3)*..... 100
Perry (E6)*.....1,203
Petersburg (F7)*.....1,001
Petoskey (E3)*.....6,468
Pewamo (E5)*..... 432
Pickford (E2)*..... 600
Pierson (D5)*..... 169
Pigeon (F5)*.....1,015
Pinckney (F6)*..... 695
Pinconning (F5)*.....1,223
Pine River (F5)..... 24
Pinnebog (F5)..... 100
Pioneer (D4)..... 10
Pittsford (E7)*..... 600
Plainwell (D6)*.....2,767
Pleasant Ridge (B6)*....3,594
Plymouth (F6)*.....6,637
Pointe Aux Barques (G4)* 9
Pointe Aux Pins (E3)*.. 42
Pompeii (E5)*..... 171
Pontiac (F6)*.....73,681
Pontiac (urban area)..91,799
Port Austin (F4)*..... 724
Port Hope (G5)*..... 353
Port Huron (G6)*.....35,725
Port Sanilac (G5)*..... 247
Portage (D6)*.....1,677
Portland (E6)*.....2,807
Posen (F3)*..... 274
Potterville (E6)*..... 624
Powers (B3)*..... 510
Prescott (F4)*..... 281
Presque Isle (F3)*..... 75
Princeton (B2)*..... 330
Prosper (E4)..... 150
Prudenville (E4)*..... 800
Pullman (C6)*..... 300
Puritan (F2)*..... 150
Quincy (E7)*.....1,527
Quinnesec (A3)*..... 600
Raco (E2)*..... 100
Ralph (B2)*..... 55
Ramsay (F2)*.....1,200
Rapid City (D4)*..... 250
Rapid River (C3)*..... 700
Rapson (G5).....
Rasmus (E4)..... 40
Ravenna (D5)*..... 551
Reading (E7)*.....1,125
Red Oak (E4)..... 51
Redman (G5)..... 40
Redridge (G1)*..... 94
Reed City (D5)*.....2,241
Reeman (D5)*..... 150
Reese (F5)*..... 632
Remus (D5)*..... 600
Republic (B2)*.....1,092
Rexton (D2)*..... 200
Rhodes (E5)*..... 107
Richland (D6)*..... 389
Richmond (G6)*.....2,025
Richville (F5)*..... 400
River Rouge (B7)*.....20,549
Riverdale (E5)*..... 304
Riverside (C6)*..... 500
Riverview (B7)*.....1,432
Rives Junction (E6)*..... 350
Rochester (F6)*.....4,279
Rock (B2)*..... 550
Rock Harbor (E1)*..... 50
Rockford (D5)*.....1,937
Rockland (G1)*..... 500
Rockwood (F6)*.....1,044
Rodney (D5)*..... 75
Rogers City (F3)*.....3,873
Romeo (F6)*.....2,985
Romulus (F6)*.....1,300
Roosevelt Park (C5).....1,254
Roscommon (E4)*..... 877
Rose City (E4)*..... 446
Rosebush (E5)*..... 507
Roseville (G6)*.....15,816
Rothbury (C5)*..... 350
Rousseau (G1).....
Royal Oak (B6)*.....46,898
Rudyard (E2)*..... 800
Ruth (G5)*..... 222
Saganing (F5)..... 67
Saginaw (F5)*.....92,918
Saginaw (urban area)105,358
Sagola (B2)*..... 300
Saint Charles (E5)*.....1,469
St. Clair (G6)*.....4,098
St. Clair Shores (G6)*19,823
St. Helen (E4)*.....
St. Ignace (E3)*.....2,946
St. Jacques (C3)*.....
St. James (D3)*..... 400
St. Johns (E6)*.....4,954
St. Joseph (C6)*.....10,223
St. Louis (E5)*.....3,347
Salem (F6)*..... 350
Saline (F6)*.....1,533
Samaria (F7)*..... 315
Sand Lake (D5)*..... 394
Sands (B2)*..... 125
Sandusky (G5)*.....1,819
Sanford (E5)*..... 550
Sans Souci (G6)*..... 100
Saranac (D6)*..... 885
Saugatuck (C6)*..... 770
Sault Sainte Marie (E2)*.....17,912
Sawyer (C7)*..... 800
Schaffer (B3)*..... 200
Schoolcraft (D6)*.....1,078
Scotts (D6)*..... 375
Scottville (C5)*.....1,142
Sears (D5)*..... 76
Sebewaing (F5)*.....1,911
Selkirk (F4)*..... 50
Seney (C2)*..... 300
Shabbona (G5)..... 100
Shelby (C5)*.....1,500
Shepherd (E5)*..... 899
Sheridan (D5)*..... 535
Sherman (D4)..... 100
Sherman City (D5)..... 25
Sherwood (D6)*..... 362
Shingleton (C2)*..... 400
Shoreham (C6)..... 391
Sidnaw (G2)*..... 400
Sidney (D5)*..... 100
Silverwood (F5)*..... 75
Sister Lakes (C6)*..... 175
Sixlakes (D5)*..... 221
Skanee (A2)*..... 190
Skeels (E4)..... 7
Smiths Creek (G6)*..... 400
Smyrna (D5)*..... 350
Snover (G5)*..... 350
Sodus (C6)*..... 300
South Boardman (D4)* 125
S. Haven (C6)*.....5,629
S. Lyon (F6)*.....1,312
S. Manitou Island (C3).. 24
S. Range (G1)*..... 712
S. Rockwood (F7)*.....1,100
Southbranch (E4)..... 70
Spalding (B3)*..... 600
Sparr (E3)..... 85
Sparta (D5)*.....2,327
Spencer (D4)*..... 49
Spratt (F3)..... 52
Spring Arbor (E6)*..... 650
Spring Lake (C5)*.....1,824
Springport (E6)*..... 598
Spruce (F4)*..... 50
Stalwart (E2)*.....
Stambaugh (G2)*.....1,969
Standish (F5)*.....1,186
Stanton (D5)*.....1,123
Stanwood (D5)*..... 189
Stephenson (B3)*..... 791
Sterling (E4)*..... 444
Steuben (C2)*..... 39
Stevensville (C6)*..... 480
Stirlingville (E2)..... 100
Stittsville (D4)..... 10
Stockbridge (E6)*.....1,098
Stonington (C3)*..... 408
Stony Lake (C5)*..... 38
Stronach (C4)*..... 350
Strongs (E2)*..... 250
Sturgis (D7)*.....7,786
Sullivan (C5)..... 250
Summit City (D4)*..... 75
Sumner (E5)*..... 150
Sunfield (D6)*..... 400
Suttons Bay (D3)*..... 485
Swartz Creek (F6)*.....1,000
Sylvan Lake (F6).....1,165
Tawas City (F4)*.....1,441
Taylor Center (B7)*....20,000
Tecumseh (E7)*.....4,020
Tekonsha (E6)*..... 647
Temperance (F7)*.....1,062
Temple (E4)*..... 150
The Heights (E4)*..... 100
Thompson (C3)*..... 250
Thompsonville (C4)*..... 313
Three Oaks (C7)*.....1,572
Three Rivers (D7)*.....6,785
Topinabee (E3)*..... 390
Tower (E3)*..... 400
Traverse City (D4)*.....16,974
Trenary (C2)*..... 150
Trenton (B7)*.....6,222
Trout Creek (G2)*.....
Trout Lake (E2)*..... 350
Trufant (D5)*..... 215
Turin (B2)*..... 236
Turner (F4)*..... 193
Tuscola (F5)*..... 150
Tustin (D4)*..... 229
Twin Lake (C5)*..... 550
Twining (F4)*..... 196
Ubly (G5)*..... 743
Union City (D6)*.....1,564
Union Pier (C7)*..... 700
Unionville (F5)*..... 531
Utica (F6)*.....1,196
Van Dyke (B6)*.....21,000
Vandalia (D7)*..... 360
Vanderbilt (E3)*..... 410
Vassar (F5)*.....2,530
Vermontville (E6)*..... 707
Vernon (F6)*..... 678
Vestaburg (E5)*..... 450
Vicksburg (D6)*.....2,171
Vogel Center (E4)..... 70
Volney (D5)..... 50
Vulcan (B3)*..... 650
Wabaningo (C5)*..... 12
Wahjamega (F5).....1,613
Wakefield (F2)*.....3,344
Waldenburg (G6)..... 350
Waldron (E7)*..... 427
Walhalla (C5)*..... 210
Walkerville (C5)*..... 233
Wallace (B3)*..... 200
Walled Lake (F6)*.....2,788
Walloon Lake (E3)*..... 214
Waltz (F6)*..... 350
Warren (B6)*..... 727
Waters (E4)*..... 40
Watersmeet (F2)*..... 600
Watervliet (C6)*.....1,327
Watton (G2)*..... 400
Waucedah (B3)..... 260
Wayland (D6)*.....1,591
Wayne (F6)*.....9,409
Webberville (E6)*..... 600
Weidman (D5)*..... 410
Wells (B3)*..... 600
Wellston (D4)*..... 150
West Branch (E4)*.....2,098
W. Olive (C6)*..... 81
Weston (E7)*..... 270
Westphalia (E6)*..... 459
Wetmore (C2)*..... 150
Wexford (D4)..... 50
Wheeler (E5)*..... 300
White Cloud (D5)*..... 977
White Pigeon (D7)*.....1,113
Whitefish Point (E2)*.. 75
Whitehall (C5)*.....1,819
Whitmore Lake (F6)*....1,500
Whittaker (F6)*..... 300
Whittemore (F4)*..... 452
Willard (E5)..... 100
Williamsburg (D4)*..... 200
Williamston (E6)*.....2,051
Willis (F6)*..... 200
Willow Run (F6).....11,365
Wilson (B3)*..... 450
Winegars (E5)*..... 125
Winn (E5)*..... 350
Winona (G1)*..... 125
Wisner (F5)..... 98
Wolverine (E3)*..... 318
Woodland (D6)*..... 410
Wyandotte (B7)*.....36,846
Yale (G5)*.....1,641
Yalmer (B2)..... 200
Ypsilanti (F6)*.....18,302
Yuma (D4)*..... 93
Zeeland (D6)*.....3,075
Zilwaukee (F5).....1,219

*Map on Page 68*

## MINNESOTA

*Total Population 2,982,483*

**87 COUNTIES**

Aitkin (E4).....14,327
Anoka (E5).....35,579
Becker (C4).....24,836
Beltrami (C2).....24,962
Benton (D5).....15,911
Big Stone (B5).....9,607
Blue Earth (D6).....38,327
Brown (D6).....25,895
Carlton (F4).....24,584
Carver (E6).....18,155
Cass (D4).....19,468
Chippewa (C5).....16,739
Chisago (F5).....12,669
Clay (B4).....30,363
Clearwater (C3).....10,204
Cook (H3).....2,900
Cottonwood (C6).....15,763
Crow Wing (D4).....30,875
Dakota (E6).....49,019
Dodge (F7).....12,624
Douglas (C5).....21,304
Faribault (D7).....23,879
Fillmore (F7).....24,465
Freeborn (E7).....34,517
Goodhue (F6).....32,118
Grant (B5).....9,542
Hennepin (E5).....676,579
Houston (G7).....14,435
Hubbard (D3).....11,085
Isanti (E5).....12,123
Itasca (E3).....38,321
Jackson (C7).....16,306
Kanabec (E5).....9,192
Kandiyohi (C5).....28,644
Kittson (B2).....9,649
Koochiching (E2).....16,910
Lac qui Parle (B6).....14,545
Lake (G3).....7,781
Lake of the Woods (D2).....4,955
Le Sueur (E6).....19,088
Lincoln (B6).....10,150
Lyon (C6).....22,253
Mahnomen (C3).....7,059
Marshall (B2).....16,125
Martin (D7).....25,655
McLeod (D6).....22,198
Meeker (D5).....18,966
Mille Lacs (E5).....15,165
Morrison (D4).....25,832
Mower (F7).....42,277
Murray (C6).....14,801
Nicollet (D6).....20,929
Nobles (C7).....22,435
Norman (B3).....12,909
Olmsted (F7).....48,228
Otter Tail (C4).....51,320
Pennington (B2).....12,965
Pine (F4).....18,223
Pipestone (B6).....14,003
Polk (B3).....35,900
Pope (C5).....12,862
Ramsey (E5).....355,332
Red Lake (B3).....6,806
Redwood (C6).....22,127
Renville (C6).....23,954
Rice (E6).....36,235
Rock (B7).....11,278
Roseau (C2).....14,505
Saint Louis (F3).....206,062
Scott (E6).....16,486
Sherburne (E5).....10,661
Sibley (D6).....15,816
Stearns (D5).....70,681
Steele (E7).....21,155
Stevens (B5).....11,106
Swift (C5).....15,837
Todd (D4).....25,420
Traverse (B5).....8,053
Wabasha (F6).....16,878
Wadena (D4).....12,806
Waseca (E6).....14,957
Washington (F5).....34,544
Watonwan (D7).....13,881
Wilkin (B4).....10,567
Winona (G6).....39,841
Wright (D5).....27,716
Yellow Medicine (B6).....16,279

**CITIES and TOWNS**

Acton (D5)..... 2
Ada (B3*.....2,121
Adams (F7)*..... 663
Adolph (F4)*..... 53
Adrian (C7)*.....1,115
Afton (F6)*..... 142
Ah-gwah-ching (D3)*... 360
Aitkin (E4)*.....2,079
Akeley (D3)*..... 525
Albany (D5)*.....1,196
Albert Lea (E7)*.....13,545
Alberta (B5)*..... 139
Albertville (E5)*..... 238
Alborn (F4)*..... 30
Alden (E7)*..... 668
Aldrich (C4)*..... 131
Alexandria (C5)*.....6,319
Alida (C3)..... 6
Allen (F3)..... 21
Alma City (E6)*..... 150
Almelund (F5)*..... 175
Almora (C4)*..... 82
Alpha (D7)*..... 230
Altura (G6)*..... 269
Alvarado (B2)*..... 317
Alvwood (D3)*..... 25
Amboy (D7)*..... 585
Amiret (C6)*..... 90
Amor (C4)..... 20
Angle Inlet (C1)*..... 50
Angora (F3)*..... 65
Angus (B2)*..... 100
Annandale (D5)*..... 899
Anoka (E5)*.....7,396
Anthony (B3)..... 2
Appleton (C5)*.....2,256
Arago (C3)*..... 11
Arco (B6)*..... 178
Argyle (B2)*..... 846
Arlington (D6)*.....1,313
Armstrong (E7)*..... 25
Arnold (F4).....
Arthyde (E4)*..... 10
Asbury (C6)..... 2
Ash Creek (B7)..... 70
Ash Lake (F2)..... 15
Ashby (C4)*..... 443
Askov (F4)*..... 387
Aspelund (F6)..... 20
Atkinson (F4)*..... 20
Atwater (D5)*..... 880
Audubon (C4)*..... 275
Augusta (F6)..... 20
Aurora (F3)*.....1,371
Austin (F7)*.....23,100
Automba (F4)*..... 25
Averill (B4)*..... 46
Avoca (C7)*..... 281
Avon (D5)*..... 386
Axel (C4)..... 2
Babbitt (G3)*..... 35
Backus (D4)*..... 367
Badger (B2)*..... 448
Badoura (D4)..... 250
Bagley (C3)*.....1,554
Bain (E4)..... 15
Baker (B4)*..... 70
Balaton (C6)*..... 723
Bald Eagle (E5).....1,650
Ball Club (E3)*..... 100
Balmoral (C4)..... 10
Barnesville (B4)*.....1,593
Barnum (F4)*..... 344
Barrett (B5)*..... 402
Barry (B5)*..... 74
Basswood (C4)..... 22
Battle Lake (C4)*..... 714
Baudette (D2)*..... 929
Baxter (D4)..... 507
Bay Lake (E4)..... 50
Bayport (F5)*.....2,502
Bear River (E3)*..... 75
Beardsley (B5)*..... 435
Beauford (D7)..... 250
Beaulieu (C3)*..... 100
Beaver (F6)..... 13
Beaver Bay (G3)*..... 100
Beaver Creek (B7)*..... 245
Bechyn (C6)..... 32
Becida (C3)*..... 8
Becker (E5)*..... 264
Bee (G7)..... 11
Bejou (B3)*..... 173
Belgrade (C5)*..... 659
Belle Plaine (E6)*.....1,708
Belle River (C5).....
Bellechester (F6)*..... 225
Bellingham (B5)*..... 388
Beltrami (B3)*..... 199
Belvidere Mills (F6)..... 10
Belview (C6)*..... 381
Bemidji (D3)*.....10,001
Bena (D3)*..... 331
Benedict (D3)*..... 10
Bennettville (E4).....
Benson (C5)*.....3,398
Bergen (D7)..... 40
Bernadotte (D6)..... 19
Berner (C3)..... 20
Beroun (F5)*..... 120
Bertha (C4)*..... 577
Bethany (F6)..... 35
Bethel (E5)*..... 250
Big Bend City (C5)..... 650
Big Falls (E2)*..... 441
Big Lake (E5)*..... 480
Bigelow (C6)*..... 238
Bigfork (E3)*..... 463
Bingham Lake (C7)*..... 229
Birchdale (D2)*..... 20
Birchwood ‡(F5)..... 312
Bird Island (D6)*.....1,333
Biscay (D6)*..... 90
Biwabik (F3)*.....1,245
Bixby (E7)*..... 75
Blackberry (E3)..... 20
Blackduck (D3)*..... 732
Blakeley (E6)*..... 98
Blomkest (D6)*..... 150
Blooming Prairie (E7)*.....1,442
Bloomington (G6)*..... 500
Blue Earth (D7)*.....3,843
Blue Grass (C4)..... 50
Bluffton (C4)*..... 239
Bock (E5)*..... 96
Bodum (E5)..... 4
Bombay (F6)..... 28
Border (D2)*..... 5
Borup (B3)*..... 200
Bovey (E3)*.....1,320
Bowlus (D5)*..... 233
Bowstring (E3)*..... 300
Boy River (D3)*..... 82
Boyd (C6)*..... 496
Bradford (E5)*.....
Braham (E5)*..... 697
Brainerd (D4)*.....12,637
Brandon (C5)*..... 319
Breckenridge (B4)*.....3,623
Breezy Point (D4)*.....
Brevik (D3)*..... 50
Brewster (C7)*..... 478
Bricelyn (E7)*..... 639
Brimson (F3)*..... 40
Britt (F3)*..... 50
Brook Park (F5)*..... 148
Brooklyn Center (G5)...4,284
Brooks (B3)*..... 184
Brookston (F4)*..... 180
Booten (C5)*..... 669
Browerville (D4)*..... 735
Browns Valley (B5)*.....1,117
Brownsdale (F7)*..... 493
Brownsville (G7)*..... 330
Brownton (D6)*..... 696
Bruno (F4)*..... 193
Brunswick (E5)..... 100
Brush Creek (E7)..... 18
Brushvale (B4)*..... 16
Buckman (D5)*..... 173
Buffalo (E5)*.....1,914
Buffalo Lake (D6)*..... 724
Buhl (F3)*.....1,462
Burchard (C6)..... 25
Burnett (F4)*..... 68
Burr (B6)*..... 63
Burschville (E5)..... 16
Burtrum (D5)*..... 194
Butler (C4)*..... 72
Butterfield (D7)*..... 529
Butternut (D6)..... 22
Buyck (F2)*..... 98
Bygland (B3).....
Byron (F6)*..... 385
Cable (D5)..... 10
Caledonia (G7)*.....2,243
Callaway (C3)*..... 193
Calumet (E3)*..... 854
Cambria (D6)*..... 63
Cambridge (E5)*.....2,978
Campbell (B4)*..... 391
Canby (B6)*.....2,173
Cannon Falls (F6)*.....1,831
Canton (F7)*..... 459
Canyon (F3)*..... 115
Carlisle (B4)*..... 24
Carlos (C5)*..... 233
Carlton (F4)*..... 650
Carp (D2)..... 15
Carson Lake (E3)*..... 700
Carver (E6)*..... 548
Cass Lake (D3)*.....1,936
Castle Danger (G3)..... 75
Castle Rock (E6)*..... 100
Cazenovia (B6)..... 26
Cedar (E5)*..... 75
Cedar Lake (E4)..... 3
Cedar Mills (D6)*..... 99
Celina (E3).....
Center City (F5)*..... 311
Center Valley (E5).....
Centerville (E5)..... 209
Ceylon (D7)*..... 618
Champlin (E5)*..... 828
Chandler (C7)*..... 331
Chanhassen (F6)*..... 182
Chaska (E6)*.....2,008
Chatfield (F7)*.....1,605
Cherry Grove (F7)..... 100
Chester (F6)*..... 100
Chisago City (E5)*..... 703
Chisholm (E3)*.....6,861
Chokio (B5)*..... 541
Clara City (C6)*.....1,106
Claremont (F6)*..... 426
Clarissa (C4)*..... 650
Clarkfield (C6)*.....1,012
Clarks Grove (E7)*..... 254
Claybank (F6)..... 6
Clear Lake (E5)*..... 297
Clearbrook (C3)*..... 539
Clearwater (D5)*..... 224
Clements (D6)*..... 239
Clementson (D2)*..... 11
Cleveland (E6)*..... 325
Climax (B3)*..... 271
Clinton (B5)*..... 482
Clinton Falls (E6).....
Clitherall (C4)*..... 175
Clontarf (C5)*..... 206
Cloquet (F4)*.....7,685
Clotho (C4)..... 6
Cloverdale (F4)..... 25
Cloverton (F4)*..... 26
Cobden (D6)*..... 118
Cohassett (E3)*..... 484
Coin (E5)*..... 3
Cokato (D5)*.....1,403
Cold Spring (D5)*.....1,488
Coleraine (E3)*.....1,321
Collegeville (D5)*..... 480
Collis (B5)*..... 50
Cologne (E6)*..... 462
Columbia Heights(G5)*.8,175
Comfrey (D6)*..... 642
Comstock (B4)*..... 139
Conception (F6)..... 300
Concord (F6)..... 85
Conger (E7)*..... 161
Constance (E5)*..... 25
Cook (F3)*..... 482
Cooley (E3)*..... 113
Coon Creek (G5)..... 275
Corcoran (E5)..... 75
Cormorant (B4)..... 34
Correll (B5)*..... 130
Corvuso (D6)*..... 22
Cosmos (D6)*..... 382
Cottage Grove (F6)*..... 143
Cotton (F3)*..... 20
Cottonwood (C6)*..... 709
Courtland (D6)*..... 251
Cove (E4)..... 35
Craigville (E3)*..... 50
Crane Lake (F2)*..... 93
Cromwell (F4)*..... 197
Crookston (B3)*.....7,352
Crosby (D4)*.....2,777
Crosslake (E4)*..... 50
Crow Wing (D4)..... 18
Crown (E5)..... 30
Crowriver (D5)..... 10
Crystal (G5).....5,713
Crystal Bay (E6)*..... 250
Culver (F4)*..... 45
Current Lake (C6)..... 20
Currie (C6)*..... 551
Cushing (D4)*..... 71
Cusson (F2)..... 25
Cuyuna (E4)*..... 112
Cyrus (C5)*..... 363
Dakota (G7)*..... 300
Dalbo (E5)*..... 58
Dale (B4)*..... 54
Dalton (C4)*..... 279
Danube (C6)*..... 437
Danvers (C5)*..... 162
Darfur (D6)*..... 150
Darwin (D5)*..... 273
Dassel (D5)*..... 962
Dawson (B6)*.....1,834
Day (E5)..... 45
Dayton (E5)*..... 363
De Graff (C5)*..... 270
Debs (C3)..... 25
Deephaven (F5).....1,823
Deer Creek (C4)*..... 349
Deer River (E3)*.....1,033
Deerwood (E4)*..... 572
Delano (E5)*.....1,386
Delavan (D7)*..... 302
Delft (C7)*..... 125
Delhi (C6)*..... 152
Dell (E7)..... 15
Dellwood (F5)..... 245
Denham (F4)*..... 96
Dennison (E6)*.....163
Dent (C4)*..... 187
Detroit Lakes (C4)*.....5,787
Dexter (F7)*..... 316
Dilworth (B4)*.....1,429
Dodge Center (F6)*.....1,151
Donaldson (B2)*..... 128
Donnelly (B5)*..... 396
Doran (B4)*..... 126
Dorothy (B3)..... 46
Dorset (D4)*..... 55
Douglas (F6)*..... 102
Douglas Lodge (C3)*..... 2
Dover (F7)*..... 263
Dovray (C6)*..... 127
Downer (B4)*..... 135
Dresbach (G7)*..... 200
Duluth (F4)*.....104,511
Duluth, Minn.-Superior, Wis.(urban area)....142,344

## Map on Page 69

## MISSISSIPPI

Total Population 2,178,914

Kolola Springs (H3)* 81
Kosciusko (E4)* 6,753
Kossuth (G1)* 242
Kreole (H10)* 1,106
Lafayette Spgs. (F2)*
Lake (F6)* 345
Lake Como (F7)* 150
Lake Cormorant (D1)*
Lake View (D1) 100
Lakeshore (F10)* 107
Lamar (F1)*
Lambert (D2)* 1,023
Lamkin (D4)* 100
Lamont (B3)* 250
Landon (F10) 500
Laneheart (B8)*
Langford (E6)
Langsdale (G7)* 100
Lauderdale (G5)* 648
Laurel (F7)* 25,038
Lawrence (F6)* 300
La Flore (D3)* 75
Leaf (G8)*
Leakesville (G8)* 893
Learned (C6)* 126
Leedo (C7)*
Leedy (H1)
Leesburg (E6)
Leesdale (B7) 20
Leland (C4)* 4,736
Lemon (E6)
Lena (E5)* 353
Leota Landing (B4) 20
Lessley (B8)*
Lexie (D8)
Lexington (D4)* 3,198
Liberty (C8)* 683
Little Rock (F5)*
Lobdell (B3) 50
Lockhart (G6) 50
Lodi (E3)* 50
Logtown (E10)* 300
Lombardy (C3) 300
Long (C4) 100
Long Beach (F10)* 2,703
Longtown (D1) 82
Longview (G4)*
Longwood (C4)* 65
Looxahoma (E1)* 50
Lorena (F6)
Lorenzen (C5)*
Lorman (B7)*
Louin (F6)* 478
Louise (C5)* 479
Louisville (G4)* 5,282
Love (D1)* 75
Luce Farms (H9) 85
Lucedale (G9)* 1,631
Lucien (C7)*
Ludlow (E5)* 500
Lula (C2)* 488
Lumberton (E8)* 1,803
Lux (F8)
Lyman (F10)*
Lynn Creek (G4)
Lyon (D2)* 386
Maben (F3)* 616
Macel (D3)* 50
Macon (G4)* 2,241
Madden (F5)* 350
Madison (D6)* 540
Magee (E7)* 1,738
Magnolia (D8)* 1,984
Mahned (F8) 100
Malone (E1) 25
Malvina (C3)*
Mantachie (H2)* 178
Mantee (F3)* 189
Marietta (H2)* 125
Marion (G6)*
Marks (D2)* 2,209
Martinsville (D7)*
Marydell (F5) 200
Mashulaville (G4)* 150
Matagorda (D2)
Matherville (G7)*
Mathiston (F3)* 584
Mattson (C2)*
Maud (D1)* 102
Maxie (F9)* 80
Mayersville (B5)*
Mayhew (G4)*
Mc Adams (E4)*
Mc Bride (C7)* 35
Mc Call Creek (C7)* 300
Mc Carley (E3)* 300
Mc Comb (D8)* 10,401
Mc Condy (G3) 100
Mc Cool (F4)* 305
Mc Crary (H4) 10
Mc Donald (F5)*
Mc Henry (F9)*
Mc Lain (G8)*
Mc Laurin (F8)*
Mc Leod (H4)*
Mc Nair (C7)* 200
Mc Neill (E9)* 500
Mc Ville (E5)
Meadville (C8)* 524
Mechanicsburg (D5)* 15
Meehan (G6)* 107
Meltonia (C3)*
Mendenhall (E7)* 1,539
Meridian (G6)* 41,893
Merigold (C3)* 682
Merit (E7) 25
Merrill (G9)*
Mesa (D8)
Metcalfe (B4)* 100
Michigan City (F1)* 38
Midnight (C4)* 400
Mileston (D4)* 47
Millard (E9)
Miller (E1)* 200
Millville (E5)
Mineral Wells (E1)* 275
Minter City (D3)* 400
Mississippi City (F10)* 2,125
Misterton (E3)
Mize (E7)* 430
Money (D3)*
Monroe (C8)* 100
Monticello (D7)* 1,382
Montpelier (G3)*
Montrose (F6)* 222
Mooreville (G2)*
Moorhead (C4)* 1,749
Morgan City (D4)*
Morgantown (E8)* 300
Morton (E6)* 1,664
Moscow (G5)
Moselle (F8)* 500
Moss (F7)*
Moss Point (G10)* 3,782
Mound Bayou (C3)* 1,328
Mount Carmel (E7) 50
Mount Helena (C5)
Mount Olive (E7)* 827
Mount Pleasant (E1)* 300
Muldon (G3)* 60
Murphy (C4)* 200
Myles (C7) 50
Myrleville (D5)
Myrtle (F1)* 331
Nanachehaw (B6) 19
Natchez (B7)* 22,740
Neely (G8)* 300
Nesbit (D1)* 250
Neshoba (F5)* 300
Nettleton (G2)* 1,204
New Albany (G2)* 3,680
New Augusta (F8)* 500
New Site (H1)* 24
Newhebron (D7)* 303
Newman (C6) 12
Newton (F6)* 2,912
Nicholson (E10)* 500
Nitta Yuma (C4)*
Nod (D5) 20
Nola (D7) 120
Norfield (C8)* 123
Norris (F6)
Northcarrollton (E3)* 506
Noxapater (F5)* 615
Nugent (F10)
Oak Ridge (C6) 200
Oak Vale (E8)* 136
Oakland (E2)* 551
Oakley (D6) 205
Ocean Springs (G10)* 3,058
Ofahoma (E5)* 50
Okolona (G2)* 2,167
Oldenburg (C7)*
Olive Branch (E1)*
Oloh (E8) 50
Oma (D7)* 50
Onward (C5)*
Ora (E7)
Orange Grove (H10) 150
Orvisburg (E9)
Osborn (G3)
Osyka (D8)* 724
Ovett (F8)* 357
Owens Wells (E4)
Oxford (F2)* 3,956
Pace (C3)* 422
Pachuta (G6)* 273
Paden (H1)* 158
Palmers Crossing (F8)*
Panther Burn (C4)* 30
Parchman (D3)*
Paris (F2)* 84
Pascagoula (G10)* 10,805
Pass Christian (F10)* 3,383
Pattison (C7)* 300
Paulding (F6)* 400
Paulette (H4)* 126
Paynes (D3)*
Pearlington (E10)* 150
Pearson (D6)*
Pecan (H10) 100
Pelahatchie (E6)* 867
Penton (D1)
Peoria (C8)*
Percy (C4)*
Perkinston (F9)* 400
Perthshire (C3)*
Petal (F8)* 2,148
Pettit (C4)* 175
Peyton (C7)* 25
Pheba (G3)*
Philadelphia (F5)* 4,472
Philipp (D3)* 350
Phoenix (C5)*
Piave (G8)*
Picayune (E9)* 6,707
Pickens (E5)* 638
Pinckneyville (B8)*
Pine Ridge (B7)*
Pine Valley (E2)*
Pineville (F6)*
Piney Woods (D6)* 750
Pinola (E7)* 143
Pittsboro (F3)* 246
Plain (D6)* 409
Plantersville (G2) 479
Plattsburg (F5)
Pleasant Grove (D2)*
Pleasant Hill (E1) 200
Plumpoint (E1)
Pocahontas (D6)* 500
Polkville (E6)* 150
Pond (B8)*
Pontotoc (G2)* 1,596
Pope (E2)* 246
Poplar Creek (E4)* 350
Poplarville (E9)* 1,852
Port Gibson (B7)* 2,920
Porterville (G5)* 88
Potts Camp (F1)* 432
Powell (D2)* 80
Prairie (G3)* 654
Prairie Point (H4)*
Prentiss (E7)* 1,212
Preston (G5)* 375
Pricedale (D8)* 300
Prichard (D1)*
Priscilla (C3)* 75
Puckett (E6)* 300
Pulaski (E6)* 1,000
Purvis (F8)* 1,270
Pyland (F3) 125
Quentin (C8)* 300
Quincy (H3)*
Quitman (G6)* 1,817
Raleigh (F6)* 580
Randolph (F2)* 243
Rara Avis (H2)
Ratliff (H2) 60
Ravine (H4)
Raymond (D6)* 1,259
Red Banks (F1)* 450
Red Lick (B7)*
Redwood (C6)*
Reform (F4)* 400
Rena Lara (C2)* 50
Renfro (F5)
Renova (C3) 250
Riceville (F9) 40
Rich (D2)* 61
Richey (C4)* 86
Richton (G8)* 1,158
Ridgeland (D6)* 526
Rienzi (G1)* 468
Rio (G5)*
Ripley (G1)* 2,383
Roberts (F6)
Robinsonville (D1)* 100
Rockport (D7)*
Rodney (B7)* 209
Rolling Fork (C5)* 1,229
Rome (C3)* 189
Rose Hill (F6)* 500
Rosedale (B3)* 2,197
Rosetta (B8)*
Roundaway (C2) 150
Roundlake (C2)* 230
Rounsaville (G8) 19
Roxie (B7)* 521
Rudyard (C2)* 110
Ruleville (C3)* 1,521
Runnelstown (F8)
Rural Hill (F4) 3
Russell (G6)* 275
Russum (B7)* 350
Ruth (D8)*
Sabougla (F3) 100
Sallis (E4)* 228
Saltillo (G2)* 501
Sanatorium (E7)*
Sandersville (F7)* 681
Sandhill (E5)*
Sandy Hook (E8)*
Sanford (F8)*
Sapa (F3)
Sarah (D1)* 93
Saratoga (E7) 65
Sardis (E2)* 1,913
Sarepta (F2)* 90
Satartia (C5)* 105
Saucier (F9)*
Savage (D1)*
Schlater (D3)*
Scobey (E3)* 112
Scooba (G5)* 734
Scott (B3)* 2,000
Sebastopol (F5)* 330
Selma (B7) 2
Seminary (E7)* 345
Senatobia (E1)* 2,108
Seneca (F8) 12
Sessums (G4)*
Shannon (G2)* 520
Sharon (E5)*
Shaw (C3)* 1,892
Shelby (C3)* 2,148
Sherard (C2)* 75
Sherman (G2)* 386
Shipman (G9) 7
Shivers (E7)* 100
Shoccoe (E5)
Shubuta (G7)* 782
Shuqualak (G5)* 714
Sibley (D8)* 25
Sidon (D4)* 361
Signal (C6) 360
Silver City (C4)* 381
Silver Creek (D7)* 275
Skene (C3)* 250
Slate Spring (F3)* 134
Slayden (F1) 45
Sledge (D2)* 383
Smedes (C5)
Smithdale (C8)*
Smiths (C6)
Smithville (H2)* 419
Soegaard (D7)
Sontag (D7)*
Soso (F7)* 171
Spanish Fort (C5)* 120
Springville (F2)* 400
Stafford Springs (F7)* 200
Stallo (F5)* 500
Stampley (B7)* 23
Stanton (B7)*
Star (D6)* 300
Starkville (G4)* 7,107
State College (G4)* 4,000
State Line (G8)* 492
Steel (F6)
Steens (H3)* 95
Stewart (F4)* 311
Stokes (D5)
Stoneville (C4)* 1,015
Stonewall (G6)*
Stovall (C2)*
Stover (D2)*
Stratton (F6)*
Strayhorn (D1) 125
Street (C8) 50
Stringer (F7)* 150
Stringtown (C3)* 500
Strong (G3)* 500
Sturgis (G4)* 402
Sucarnochee (H5)*
Summerland (F7)* 112
Summit (D8)* 1,558
Sumner (D3)* 550
Sumrall (E8)* 853
Sun (F6)
Sunflower (C3)* 639
Swan Lake (D3)* 50
Sweatman (E3)*
Swiftown (D4)*
Swiftwater (B4) 10
Sylvarena (F6)* 112
Symonds (C3)*
Tallula (B5)*
Tamola (G5) 55
Taylor (E2)* 125
Taylorsville (F7)* 1,116
Tchula (D4)* 927
Terry (D6)* 497
Thaxton (F2)* 300
Theadville (G7) 75
Thomastown (E5)* 250
Thomasville (E6) 25
Thorn (F3)* 60
Thornton (D4)* 50
Thrasher (G1)* 200
Thyatira (E1)*
Tibbee Station (G3) 35
Tie Plant (E3)* 400
Tilden (H2) 150
Tillatoba (E3)* 127
Tillman (C7)* 150
Tiplersville (G1)* 110
Tippo (D3)* 80
Tishomingo (H1)* 335
Toccopola (F2)* 262
Tomnolen (F4)* 150
Toomsuba (G6)* 500
Topton (G6) 15
Tougaloo (D6)*
Tralake (C4)* 250
Traxler (E6) 75
Trebloc (G3)* 300
Tremont (H2)*
Trenton (E6)*
Tribbett (C4)* 100
Troy (G2)*
Tula (F2)*
Tunica (D1)* 1,354
Tupelo (G2)* 11,527
Turnbull (B8)*
Tuscola (E5)* 250
Tutwiler (D2)* 939
Tylertown (D8)* 1,331
Tyro (E1)* 750
Union (F5)* 1,559
Union Church (C7)* 275
University (E2)* 1,200
Utica (C6)* 824
Utica Institute (C6)*
Vaiden (E4)* 583
Valley (D5)* 125
Valley Park (C5)*
Value (D6)* 300
Van Vleet (G3)* 300
Vance (D2)*
Vancleave (G9)*
Vardaman (F3)* 686
Vaughan (D5)* 350
Velma (E2)
Verba (F6)
Verna (D8) 12
Vernal (G8)*
Verona (G2)* 589
Vicksburg (C6)* 27,948
Victoria (E1)*
Vidalia (F10) 25
Vimville (H6)*
Vossburg (F7)* 500
Wade (G9)* 300
Wahalak (G5)*
Waldrup (F7)*
Wallerville (G2)* 100
Wallfield (F2)
Walls (D1)* 318
Walnut (G1)* 481
Walnut Grove (F5)* 517
Waltersville (C6) 250
Walthall (F3)* 149
Wanilla (D7)*
Washington (B7)*
Water Valley (E2)* 3,113
Waterford (E1)* 125
Waveland (F10)* 793
Waxhaw (C3)*
Way (E5)*
Waynesboro (G7)* 3,442
Wayside (C4)*
Weathersby (E7)* 145
Webb (D3)* 680
Weir (F4)* 570
Wanasoga (G1)* 150
Wesson (D7)* 1,235
West (E4)* 354
West Enterprise (G6)*
West Point (G3)* 6,432
Whaley (D3) 15
Wheeler (G1)* 300
White Apple (B8) 25
White Bluff (E8) 25
Whitfield (E6)*
Whitfield (D3)
Whiteoak (E6) 50
Whynot (G6) 60
Wicker (E6)
Wiggins (F9)* 1,436
Wilkinson (B8)* 300
Williamsville (F4)
Willows (C6) 30
Winborn (F1)*
Winchester (G7)*
Wingate (G8) 150
Winona (E4)* 3,441
Winstonville (C3)* 322
Winterville (B4)*
Woodland (F3)* 133
Woodville (B8)* 1,609
Wren (G3) 250
Wyatte (E1)* 100
Yazoo City (D5)* 9,746
Yokena (C6)* 25
Youngs (E3) 25
Zama (F5)*
Zion Hill (C8) 50

*Map on Page 70*

## MISSOURI

*Total Population 3,954,653*

### 115 COUNTIES

Adair (G2) 19,689
Andrew (C3) 11,727
Atchison (B2) 11,127
Audrain (J4) 23,829
Barry (E9) 21,755
Barton (D7) 12,678
Bates (D6) 17,534
Benton (F6) 9,080
Bollinger (M8) 11,019
Boone (H4) 48,432
Buchanan (C3) 96,826
Butler (M9) 37,707
Caldwell (E3) 9,929
Callaway (J5) 23,316
Camden (G6) 7,861
Cape Girardeau (N8) 38,397
Carroll (F4) 15,589
Carter (L9) 4,777
Cass (D5) 19,325
Cedar (E7) 10,663
Chariton (G3) 14,944
Christian (F9) 12,412
Clark (J2) 9,003
Clay (D4) 45,221
Clinton (D3) 11,726
Cole (H6) 35,464
Cooper (G5) 16,608
Crawford (K7) 11,615
Dade (E8) 9,324
Dallas (F7) 10,392
Daviess (E3) 11,180
De Kalb (D3) 8,047
Dent (J7) 10,936
Douglas (G9) 12,638
Dunklin (M10) 45,329
Franklin (K6) 36,046
Gasconade (J6) 12,342
Gentry (D2) 11,036
Greene (F8) 104,823
Grundy (E2) 13,220
Harrison (E2) 14,107
Henry (E6) 20,043
Hickory (F7) 5,387
Holt (B2) 9,833
Howard (G4) 11,857
Howell (J9) 22,725
Iron (L7) 9,458
Jackson (D5) 541,035
Jasper (D8) 79,106
Jefferson (L6) 38,007
Johnson (E5) 20,716
Knox (H2) 7,617
Laclede (G7) 19,010
Lafayette (E4) 25,272
Lawrence (E8) 23,420
Lewis (J2) 10,733
Lincoln (L4) 13,478
Linn (F3) 18,865
Livingston (E3) 16,532
Macon (G3) 18,332
Madison (M8) 10,380
Maries (J6) 7,423
Marion (J3) 29,765
Mc Donald (D9) 14,144
Mercer (E2) 7,235
Miller (H6) 13,734
Mississippi (O9) 22,551
Moniteau (G5) 10,840
Monroe (H3) 11,314
Montgomery (K5) 11,555
Morgan (G6) 10,207
New Madrid (N9) 39,444
Newton (D9) 28,240
Nodaway (C2) 24,033
Oregon (K9) 11,978
Osage (J6) 11,301
Ozark (H9) 8,856
Pemiscot (N10) 45,624
Perry (N7) 14,890
Pettis (F5) 31,577
Phelps (J7) 21,504
Pike (K4) 16,844
Platte (C4) 14,973
Polk (F7) 16,062
Pulaski (H7) 10,392
Putnam (F2) 9,166
Ralls (J3) 8,686
Randolph (G3) 22,918
Ray (E4) 15,932
Reynolds (L8) 6,918
Ripley (L9) 11,414
St. Charles (L5) 29,834
St. Clair (E6) 10,482
St. Francois (M7) 35,276
St. Louis (M5) 406,349
St. Louis City (M5) 856,796
Ste. Genevieve (M7) 11,237
Saline (F4) 26,694
Schuyler (G2) 5,760
Scotland (H2) 7,332
Scott (N8) 32,842
Shannon (K8) 8,377
Shelby (H3) 9,730
Stoddard (N9) 33,463
Stone (F9) 9,748
Sullivan (F2) 11,299
Taney (F9) 9,863
Texas (J8) 18,992
Vernon (D7) 22,685
Warren (K5) 7,666
Washington (L7) 14,689
Wayne (L8) 10,514
Webster (G8) 15,072
Worth (D2) 5,120
Wright (H8) 15,834

### CITIES and TOWNS

Aaron (D6) 15
Abo (H7)
Acorn (K9)
Adrian (D6)* 905
Advance (N8)* 733
Affton (P3)* 5,000
Agency (C3)* 234
Aholt (G4)
Aid (M9) 55
Airport Drive ‡(D8) 225
Alanthus Grove (D2) 45
Alba (D8)* 352
Albany (D2)* 1,850
Aldrich (F7)* 198
Alexandria (K2)* 465
Allbright (M8)
Allendale (D2)* 142
Allenton (N3)*
Allenville (N8)* 125
Alley Spring (K8)*
Alma (E4)* 357
Almartha (H9)*
Alpha (F3) 25
Altamont (D3)* 178
Altenburg (O7)* 272
Alton (K9)* 571
Altona (D6) 13
Amazonia (C3)* 308
Americus (J5)*
Amity (D3)* 128
Amoret (C6)* 255
Amsterdam (C6)*
Anabel (H3)* 25
Ancell (N8)* 295
Anderson (D9)* 1,073
Andover (E1) 18
Annada (L4)* 93
Annapolis (L8)* 490
Anniston (O9)* 377
Anthonies Mill (K6)*
Anutt (J7)* 250
Apex (L4)
Appleton (Old Appleton*) (N7) 120
Appleton City (E6)* 1,150
Aquilla (N9) 50
Arab (M8)*
Arbela (H2)* 87
Arbor Terrace ‡(P3) 1,150
Arbyrd (M10)* 679
Arcadia (L7)* 414
Archie (D5)* 300
Arcola (E7)* 125
Ardmore (H3) 25
Argyle (J6)* 162
Arkoe (C2)* 48
Arlington (H7)*
Armstrong (G4)* 424
Arnica (E7) 4
Arno (G9)
Arrow Rock (F4)* 170
Asbury (C8)* 210
Ash Grove (E8)* 970
Ashburn (K3)* 153
Ashland (H5)* 416
Ashley (K4)* 205
Ashton (J2)*
Atherton (R5)* 375
Atlanta (H3)* 438
Augusta (M3)* 218
Aullville (E4)* 123
Aurora (E9)* 4,153
Austin (D5) 40
Auxvasse (J4)* 507
Ava (G9)* 1,611
Avalon (F3)* 200
Avert (N9) 45
Avilla (D8)* 142
Avondale (P5)* 532
Azen (H1)
Bachelor (J5)* 20
Bado (H8)* 15
Bagnell (G6) 74
Bakersfield (H9)*
Ballard (D6) 49
Ballwin (O3)* 600
Banner (L7)*
Bardley (K9)* 75
Baring (H2)* 274
Barnard (C2)* 275
Barnesville (G3) 12
Barnett (G6)* 200
Barry (P5) 30
Bartlett (K8) 15
Bates City (E5)* 87
Battlefield (F8)
Bay (J5)*
Beaman (F5)* 45
Bearcreek (E7)* 41
Beaufort (K6)* 250
Beck (P4)
Bedford (F3) 50
Bedison (C2) 13
Bel-Nor ‡(P3)* 1,290
Bel-Ridge ‡(P3) 1,116
Belgique (N7)* 66
Belgrade (L7)*
Bell City (N8)* 482
Bella Villa ‡(P3) 557
Bellamy (D7) 25
Belle (J6)* 906
Bellefontaine (O3)
Bellerive ‡(P3) 180
Belleview (L7)*
Bellflower (K4)* 226
Belton (C5)* 1,233
Bem (K6) 18
Bennett (L9)* 3
Benton (O8)* 546
Benton City (J4)* 141
Bentonville (F6)* 11
Berdell Hills ‡(P3) 583
Berger (K5)* 210
Berkeley (P2)* 5,268
Bernie (M9)* 1,308
Bertha (H9)* 80
Bertrand (O9)* 390
Bessville (N8)*
Bethany (E2)* 2,714
Bethel (J3)* 194
Beulah (J7)* 110
Beverly (O4)* 29
Beverly Hills ‡(P3) 938
Bevier (G3)* 838
Big Piney (H7)* 80
Bigelow (B2)* 132
Billings (F8)* 597
Billingsville (G5) 10
Billmore (K9)
Birch Tree (K9)* 409
Birdspoint (O9)
Birmingham (P5)* 236
Bismarck (L7)* 1,244
Bixby (K7)* 20
Black (L7)*
Black Jack (P2) 700
Blackburn (F4)* 306
Black Walnut (P2) 20
Blackwater (G5)* 313
Blairstown (E5)* 199
Bland (J6)* 596
Bliss (L6) 20
Blodgett (O8)* 218
Bloomfield (M9)* 1,382
Bloomington (H3) 18
Bloomsdale (M6)*
Blue Lick (F4)
Blue Ridge (D2) 27
Blue Springs (R6)* 1,068
Blythedale (E2)* 238
Boaz (F8) 26
Bogard (E4)* 285
Bois D'Arc (F8)*
Bolckow (C2)* 250
Boles (M3)
Bolivar (F7)* 3,482
Bona (E7) 12
Bonfils (O2) 125
Bonne Terre (L7)* 3,533
Bonnots Mill (J5)* 150
Boomer (F3)* 30
Boonesboro (G4)* 46
Boonville (G5)* 6,686
Boss (K7)* 108
Boston (D8)* 52
Bosworth (F4)* 503
Bourbon (K6)* 543
Bowen (E5) 30
Bowers Mill (E8) 29
Bowling Green (K4)* 2,396
Bradleyville (F9)* 69
Bragg City (N10)* 294
Braggadocio (N10)* 350
Branch (G7)* 29
Brandsville (J9)* 204
Branson (F9)* 1,314
Brashear (H2)* 119
Brasher (N10) 152
Braymer (E3)* 955
Brays (H6)
Brazil (K7)* 25
Brazito (H6) 25
Breckenridge (E3)* 617
Breckenridge Hills‡(P3) 4,063
Brentwood (P3)* 7,504
Brewer (N7)
Brickeys (M6)*
Bridgeton (P8)* 202
Bridgeton Terrace‡(P3) 578
Brighton (F8)* 84
Brimson (E2)* 139
Brinktown (J6)* 48
Bronaugh (C7)* 214
Brookfield (F3)* 5,810
Brooklyn (D2) 30
Brookline (F8)*
Broseley (M9)* 177
Brownbranch (G9)* 13
Browning (F2)* 492
Brownington (E6)* 179
Browns Spring (F9)
Browns Station (H4)* 75
Brumley (H6)* 78
Bruner (F8)* 85
Brunot (M8)* 31
Brunswick (F4)* 1,653
Brush Creek (G7)* 91
Brushy (H8) 14
Brushyknob (G9)*
Bryant (G8) 6
Bryson (F5) 25
Buckhart (H9)* 18
Buckhorn (M8)*
Bucklin (G3)* 783
Buckner (R5)* 556
Bucoda (M10) 20
Bucyrus (H8)* 25
Buell (K4)* 69
Buffalo (F7)* 1,213
Buick (K7)* 101
Bunceton (G5)* 556
Bunker (K8)*
Burch (M8)
Burfordville (N8)* 88
Burgess (C7) 123
Burlington Jct. (B2)* 746
Burnham (J9) 74
Burton (G4) 11
Burtville (E5) 75
Busch (K3) 3
Bute (G2)
Butler (D6)* 3,333
Butterfield (E9)* 116

Burnham (G2) 26
Burns (M3) 8
Busby (J5)* 20
Butte (D5)* 33,251
Butte Creek (J3)
Bynum (D3)* 52
Cabin Creek (M4) 6
Calkins (F4)
Calvert (E3)
Camas (B3)* 125
Camas Prairie (B3) 5
Cameron (E5)* 138
Camps Pass (L5)*
Campsite (E3) 3
Canton (E4) 10
Canyon Creek (D4)* 76
Canyon Ferry (E4)* 150
Capitol (M5)* 4
Carbella (F5) 5
Carbert (L2)
Cardwell (E5)* 98
Carlyle (M4)*
Carter (E3)* 100
Cartersville (K4)*
Cascade (E3)* 447
Cat Creek (H3)* 65
Ceekay (H3)
Centerville (D4) 1,800
Central Park (E5)
Chadbourn (F5) 7
Chalk Buttes (M5) 41
Chance (H5) 7
Chapman (J2)* 35
Charlo (B3)* 260
Chester (E2)* 733
Chestnut (F5) 12
Chico (F5) 20
Chinook (G2)* 2,307
Choteau (D3)* 1,618
Christina (G3)* 20
Circle (L3)* 856
Clancey (E4)* 161
Clarkston (E4)* 20
Clasoil (E4) 8
Cleiv (E3)
Cleveland (G2)* 17
Cliff Lake (E6)* 21
Clinton (C4)* 150
Clyde Park (F5)* 280
Coalridge (M2)* 49
Coalwood (L5)* 2
Coburg (H2)
Coffee Creek (F3)* 50
Cohagen (K3)* 36
Cole (J2)
Collins (E3)* 26
Colony Bay (F2)
Colstrip (K5)* 300
Columbia Falls (B2)* 1,232
Columbus (G5)* 1,097
Comanche (H4) 12
Comertown (M2)* 50
Conner (B5)* 150
Conrad (D2)* 1,865
Content (J3)
Cooke (G5)* 45
Coolidge (C5) 2
Coram (C2)* 500
Corbin (D4) 50
Cordova (E3) 175
Corinth (J5)* 16
Corvallis (C4)* 350
Corwin Springs (F5)* 2
Corwine Center (J2)
Cottonwood (G2) 40
Cottonwood (C3)
Craig (D3)* 80
Crane (M3)* 50
Creston (C2)* 200
Crow Agency (J5)* 500
Crow Rock (L4)
Culbertson (M2)* 779
Cushman (H4)* 17
Custer (J4)* 300
Cut Bank (D2)* 3,721
Dagmar (M2)* 46
Dailey (F5)
Daleview (M2)
Danvers (G3)* 32
Darby (B4)* 415
Dayton (B3)* 95
De Smet (C4) 10
Dean (G5)* 92
Deborgia (A3)* 75
Decker (K5)* 21
Deer Lodge (D4)* 3,779
Dell (D6)* 150
Delphia (H4)* 14
Delphine (F4)
Dempsey (D4) 10
Denton (G3)* 435
Devon (E2)* 50
Dillon (D5)* 3,268
Divide (D5)* 116
Dixon (B3)* 350
Dodson (H2)* 330
Dooley (M2)* 17
Dover (F3) 20
Dovetail (H3) 35
Dowd (M2)
Drexel (A3)* 9
Drummond (D4)* 531
Dryhead (H5) 4
Duderanch (F5) 3
Dunkirk (E2)* 13
Dupuyer (D2)* 125
Dutton (E3)* 431
Eagle Butte (F3) 72
Eagleton (G3)
East Glacier Park (C2)* 300
Eddy (A3)* 25
Eden (E3)* 5
Edgar (H5)* 160
Ekalaka (M5)* 904
Electric (F5) 20
Elgin (M5) 15
Elk Park (D4) 80
Elliston (D4)*
Elmdale (M3) 25
Elmer (J4) 10
Elmo (B3)* 104
Emigrant (F5)* 25
Emory (G4)
Enid (M3)* 8
Ennis (E5)* 600
Epsie (L5)* 65
Essex (C2)* 75
Ethridge (D2)* 45
Eureka (B2)* 929
Evans (E3)
Evaro (C3)* 92
Fairchild (F2) 20
Fairfield (D3)* 693
Fairview (M3)* 942
Fallon (L4)* 251
Family (D2) 150
Farmington (D3) 30
Ferdig (E2)* 15
Fergus (H3)* 4
Finch (K4)
Findon (F4)
Finn (D4) 50
First Creek (J3)
Fishtail (G5)* 50
Fishtrap (C5) 10
Flaxville (L2)* 220
Florence (B4)* 350
Floweree (E3)* 60
Forestgrove (H3)* 25
Forks (J2)* 3
Forsyth (K4)* 1,906
Fort Belknap (H2)
Ft. Benton (F3)* 1,522
Ft. Browning (D2) 1,674
Ft. Logan (E4)
Ft. Maginnis (H3) 4
Ft. Peck (K2)* 1,214
Ft. Shaw (E3)* 180
Ft. Union (M2)
Fortine (A2)* 100
Foundation (L4)
Four Buttes (L2)* 50
Fourchette (H3)
Fowler (E2)
Fox (G5) 15
Francis (F4)* 10
Franklin (G4)* 7
Frazer (K2)* 575
Frenchtown (B3)* 100
Fresno (G2) 10
Froid (M2)* 555
Fromberg (H5)* 442
Gage (H4) 8
Galata (E2)* 63
Galen (D4) 220
Gallatin Gateway (E5)* 200
Gardiner (F5)*
Garland (L4) 3
Garneill (G4)* 33
Garnet (C4) 20
Garrison (D4)* 150
Garryowen (J5)* 28
Gateway (A2) 50
Genou (E2)* 25
Geraldine (F3)* 374
Geyser (F3)* 150
Gibson (G4)
Giffen (E3) 12
Gildford (F2)* 340
Gilman (D3) 15
Giltedge (G3) 8
Girard (M3) 7
Glasgow (K2)* 3,821
Glen (D5)* 100
Glendive (M3)* 5,254
Glengarry (G3) 7
Glentana (K2)* 65
Gold Stone (F2)* 9
Goldbutte (E2)
Goldcreek (D4)* 190
Golden (G5)
Grant (C5)* 25
Grantsdale (B4)* 50
Grass Valley (B4)
Grassrange (H3)* 234
Grayling (E6)* 20
Great Falls (E3)* 39,214
Greenough (C4)* 50
Gregson (D4) 35
Greycliff (G5)* 125
Grisdella (J3) 2
Gunsight (D2)
Hall (C4)* 100
Hamilton (B4)* 2,678
Hammond (M5)* 10
Hanover (G3)* 100
Hardin (J5)* 2,306
Hardy (E3)
Harlem (H2)* 1,107
Harlowton (F4)* 1,733
Harrison (E5)* 305
Hathaway (K4)* 25
Haugan (A3)* 70
Havre (G2)* 8,086
Haxby (K3)* 25
Hay Coulee (F2) 12
Hays (H2)* 150
Hazel (L3)
Heart Butte (C2)* 50
Heath (G3)* 16
Hedgesville (G4)* 25
HELENA (E4)* 17,581
Helmville (C4)* 50
Henderson (A3)
Heron (A2)* 200
Hesper (H5) 27
Hibbard (J4)
Highwood (F3)* 272
Hilger (G3)* 42
Hill (E2)*
Hillsboro (H5) 4
Hillside (K4)
Hingham (F2)* 214
Hinsdale (K2)* 350
Hobson (G4)* 205
Hodges (M4)* 40
Hogeland (H2)* 75
Holland (E5)
Homestake (D5)* 15
Homestead (M2)* 87
Hoosac (G3) 4
Horton (L4)
Hot Springs (B3)* 733
Howard (K4)
Hughesville (F3) 18
Hungry Horse (B2)*
Hunters Hotsprings (F5) 7
Huntley (H5)* 268
Huson (B3)* 75
Hysham (J4)* 410
Inga (F2)
Ingomar (J4)* 100
Intake (M3)* 8
Inverness (F2)* 360
Iron Mountain (A3) 3
Ismay (M4)* 182
Ivanell (J4)
Jackson (C5)* 82
Jardine (F5)* 40
Jeffers (E5)* 60
Jefferson City (E4)* 100
Jefferson Island (E5)* 50
Jennings (A2)* 10
Jens (D4)* 25
Joliet (G5)* 410
Joplin (F2)* 368
Jordan (J3)* 800
Judith Gap (G4)* 175
Kalispell (B2)* 9,737
Kenilworth (F2)
Kevin (D2)* 351
Kila (B2)* 100
Kinsey (L4)* 8
Kintla (B2)
Kirby (J5)* 14
Klein (H4)* 400
Knobs (M5) 33
Knowlton (L4)
Kolin (G3)* 12
Korner (D2) 50
Koyl (D3)
Kremlin (F2)* 160
Lake Mc Donald (B2)* 1
Lakeview (E6) 18
Lambert (M3)* 359
Lame Deer (K5)* 400
Lanark (M2) 3
Landusky (H3)* 65
Lane (M3) 25
Laredo (G2)* 38
Larslan (K2)* 159
Laurel (H5)* 3,663
Laurin (D5)* 110
Lavina (H4)* 195
Lebo (F4)
Ledger (E2)* 20
Lee (K5)
Legg (J3)
Lehigh (F3) 5
Lennep (F4)* 25
Leroy (G3)* 10
Lewistown (G3)* 6,573
Libby (A2)* 2,401
Lima (D6)* 483
Limestone (F5)* 43
Lincoln (D4)* 250
Lindsay (L3)* 57
Lingshire (E4)
Little Crooked (H3) 3
Living Springs (G4)* 7
Livingston (F5)* 7,683
Lloyd (G2)* 5
Locate (L4)* 4
Lockwood (H5) 200
Lodge Grass (J5)* 536
Lodgepole (H2) 50
Loesch (L5) 10
Logan (E5)* 172
Lohman (G2)*
Lolo (B4)* 210
Lolo Hot Springs (B4) 25
Loma (F3) 200
Lombard (E4)* 26
Lonepine (B3)* 9
Loring (J2)* 50
Lost Lake (H2) 25
Lothair (E2)* 72
Lothrop (B4)
Loweth (F4) 20
Lowry (D3)
Lozeau (B3)* 12
Lupfer (B2) 8
Lustre (K2)* 4
Luther (G5)* 22
Madoc (L2)* 33
Malta (J2)* 2,095
Manhattan (E5)* 716
Manicke (A2) 30
Manson (E2)
Marias (E2) 10
Marion (B2)* 47
Marsh (M4)* 100
Martinsdale (F4)* 130
Marysville (D4)*
Maschetah (J5) 25
Maudlow (E4)* 50
Maxville (C4)* 40
Mc Allister (E5)* 21
Mc Cabe (M2)* 55
Mc Elroy (M2) 2
Mc Leod (G5)* 10
Mc Rae (J5)* 5
Meaderville (D4) 250
Mecaha (J3)
Medicine Lake (M2)* 454
Meharry (J2) 4
Melrose (D5)* 130
Melstone (H4)* 195
Melville (F4)* 29
Menard (E5)
Merino (F3)* 5
Midby (M2) 7
Mike Horse (D4)* 200
Mildred (M4)* 75
Miles City (L4)* 9,243
Mill Iron (M5)* 75
Millegan (E3)
Milltown (C4)* 750
Miner (E5)* 53
Mink (L3) 30
Mission (F5)
Missoula (C4)* 22,485
Mizpah (L4)
Moccasin (F3)* 300
Mock (Radnor) (B2) 8
Moiese (B3)* 8
Molt (H5)* 25
Mona (M3) 25
Monarch (F3)* 53
Monida (D6)* 50
Montague (F3)* 20
Moon Creek (L4)
Moore (G4)* 224
Moorhead (K5)* 15
Mosby (J4)* 3
Mossmain (H5) 12
Moulton (G3)* 50
Musselshell (H4)* 250
Myers (J4)* 37
Nashua (K2)* 691
Natal (G4) 3
Navajo (M2)* 7
Neihart (F4)* 289
Nelson (E4)
New Chicago (C4) 20
Niarada (B3)* 4
Nibbe (H4)* 20
Nickwall (L2)
Nihill (G4) 2
Nimrod (C4)* 45
Ninemile (B4)*
Nohly (M3)* 57
Norris (E5)* 100
Noxon (A3)* 113
Nyack (C2) 40
Nye (G5)* 3
Oilmont (E2)* 250
Oka (G4)
Olanda (L3)
Olive (L5)* 6
Ollie (M4)*
Olney (B2)* 147
Oneill (L4)
Opheim (K2)* 383
Osborn (H5)
Ossette (L2)
Oswego (L2)* 100
Otter (K5)* 57
Outlook (M2)* 235
Ovando (D3)* 100
Oxford (G4) 10
Pablo (B3)* 150
Paola (C2)
Paradise (B3)* 300
Paragon (K4)
Park City (H5)* 450
Paxton (L3) 20
Peerless (L2)* 125
Pendroy (D2)* 80
Perma (B3)* 60
Philipsburg (C4)* 1,048
Phillips (H2)
Piedmont (D5) 21
Pineview (J4)
Piniele (M5) 10
Pioneer (D4)
Piper (G4) 6
Pipestone Hot Springs (D5) 12
Placer (E4)
Plains (B3)* 714
Plentywood (M2)* 1,862
Plevna (M4)* 247
Polaris (C5)* 25
Polebridge (B2)* 56
Polson (B3)* 2,280
Polytechnic (H5)* 250
Pompeys Pillar (J5)* 200
Pony (E5)* 185
Poplar (L2)* 1,169
Portage (E3) 22
Post Creek (C3)
Potomac (C4)* 65
Powderville (L5)* 4
Power (E3)* 75
Pray (F5)* 14
Proctor (B3)* 125
Pryor (H5)* 70
Quartz (B3) 4
Quietus (K5)* 3
Race Track (D4) 20
Radersburg (E4)*
Radio (B3)
Radnor (Mock) (B2) 8
Ramsay (D5)* 131
Ranchcreek (L5)*
Rapelje (G5)* 150
Rapids (G5)
Ravalli (B3)* 190
Rayfield (G4) 11
Raymond (M2)* 50
Raymond (M2)* 50
Raynesford (F3)* 45
Red Lodge (G5)* 2,730
Redstone (M2)* 105
Redwater (L3)
Reedpoint (G5)* 150
Regina (J3)*
Renova (D5) 6
Reserve (M2)* 215
Rexford (A2)* 200
Richey (L3)* 595
Richland (K2)*
Ridge (M5)* 50
Ridgway (M5)* 3
Riebeling (D3)
Rimini (D4)
Rimroad (L3) 20
Rimrock (H5)
Ringling (F4)* 135
Riverdale (E3) 50
Rivulet (B4)* 47
Roanwood (K2) 3
Roberts (G5)* 200
Rock Springs (K4)* 1
Rockvale (H5) 10
Rocky Boy (G2) 50
Rollins (B3)* 200
Ronan (C3)* 1,251
Roscoe (G5)* 75
Rosebud (K4)* 125
Ross Fork (G3)*
Rothiemay (G4)* 55
Round Butte (B3)*
Roundup (H4)* 2,856
Roy (H3)* 175
Rudyard (F2)* 521
Rumble Creek (C3) 30
Ryegate (G4)* 339
Saco (J2)* 539
Saint Ignatius (C3)* 781
St. Pauls (H3) 70
St. Peter (E3)
St. Phillips (M4) 6
St. Regis (A3)* 500
St. Xavier (J5)* 150
Salem (E3)
Saltese (A3)* 95
Sand Creek (L3)
Sand Springs (J3)* 12
Sandcoulee (E3)* 500
Sanders (J4)* 40
Santa Rita (D2)* 145
Sappington (E5)* 34
Sarpy (J5) 5
Savage (M3)* 300
Savoy (H2)* 15
Sayle (L5)* 10
Scobey (L2)* 1,628
Sedan (F4) 6
Seeley Lake (C3)* 250
Selma (E2) 7
Selmes (G5) 6
Selway (K5) 4
Shambo (G2)*
Shawmut (G4)* 122
Sheffield (K4)
Shelby (E2)* 3,058
Shepherd (H5)* 100
Sheridan (D5)* 572
Shirley (L4)
Shonkin (F3)* 6
Shriver (H5) 10
Sidney (M3)* 3,987
Silesia (H5)* 50
Silver Star (D5)* 55
Silverbow (D5)* 50
Simms (E3)* 250
Simpson (F2)*
Sioux Pass (M3)* 40
Sipple (G4)
Sixteen (F4) 10
Sloan (B3)
Snowden (M2) 16
Somers (B2)* 750
Sonnette (L5)* 5
Soo (L2)
Southern Cross (C4) 50
Spion Kop (F3) 10
Springdale (F5)* 75
Springhill (F5)
Square Butte (F3)* 75
Stacey (L5)* 7
Stanford (F3)* 542
Stark (B3)* 25
Stevensville (C4)* 772
Stipek (M3) 50
Stockett (E3)* 300
Stone (C4)
Stonehill (A2) 5
Strater (J2)
Straw (G4)* 25
Stryker (B2)* 60
Suffolk (G3)* 14
Sula (B5)* 112
Sumatra (J4)*
Sun Prairie (J3)
Sun River (E3)* 115
Sunburst (E2)* 845
Superior (B3)* 626
Sutherland (L4)
Swan Lake (C3)* 100
Sweetgrass (E2)*
Swingley (F5)
Taft (A3) 2
Tampico (K2)* 80
Tarkio (B4)* 75
Teigen (H3)*
Telegraph Creek (J3)* 5
Terry (L4)* 1,191
Teton (F3)
Thoeny (K2)* 10
Thompson Falls (A3)* 851
Three Forks (E5)* 1,114
Thurlow (K4)
Tonquin (M4)
Toston (E4)* 100
Townsend (E4)* 1,316
Trailcreek (B2)* 10
Trego (B2)* 48
Trident (E5)* 150
Trine (H3)
Trout Creek (A3)* 52
Troy (A2)* 770
Tunis (F3) 6
Turner (H2)* 200
Tuscor (A3)* 4
Twin Bridges (D5)* 497
Twodot (F4)* 150
Tyler (H4) 3
Ulm (E3)* 150
Union (L3) 50
Ural (A2)* 37
Utical (F4)* 60
Valentine (H3) 3
Valier (D2)* 710
Van Norman (K3)* 4
Vananda (K4)* 100
Vandalia (J2)* 25
Vanstel (K4)
Varney (E5) 12
Vaughn (E3)* 190
Verona (F2)
Victor (B4)* 350
Vida (L3)* 58
Virgelle (F2)* 20
Virginia City (E5)* 323
Volborg (L5)* 7
Volt (L2)
Wagner (H2)*
Waleston (J2)
Walkerville (D4)* 1,631
Wallum (G4)
Waltham (E3)* 25
Ware (G3)* 4
Warland (A2)* 90
Warmsprings (D4)* 2,000
Warren (H5)* 40
Warrick (G2)* 3
Washoe (G5)*
Waterloo (D5)* 95
Watkins (K3)* 10
Webster (M4)* 2
Weldon (K3)* 2
West Fork (L2)
W. Gallatin (E5)
W. Glacier (C2)* 440
W. Yellowstone (E6)* 500
Westby (M2)* 396
Westmore (M4) 16
Wheat Basin (G5) 10
Wheeler (K2)*
White Sulphur Springs (E4)* 1,025
Whitefish (B2)* 3,268
Whitehall (D5)* 929
Whitepine (A3)* 175
Whitetail (L2)* 240
Whitewater (J2)* 85
Whitlash (E2)* 18
Wibaux (M3)* 739
Wickes (D4)* 70
Wickett (H5)
Wilborn (D4)
Willard (M4)* 3
Williams (D2)* 10
Willow Creek (E5)* 300
Wilsall (F5)* 300
Windham (F3)* 116
Winifred (G3)* 217
Winnett (H4)* 407
Winston (E4)* 53
Wisdom (C5)* 125
Wise River (C5)* 50
Wolf Creek (D3)* 156
Wolf Point (L2)* 2,557
Woodside (B4) 100
Woodworth (C3) 45
Worden (H5)* 375
Wyola (J5)* 110
Yaak (A2)*
Yakt (B2) 28
Yates (M4)
Yegen (H5) 10
Youngs Point (G5)
Zero (L4)* 22
Zortman (H3)*
Zurich (G2)* 85

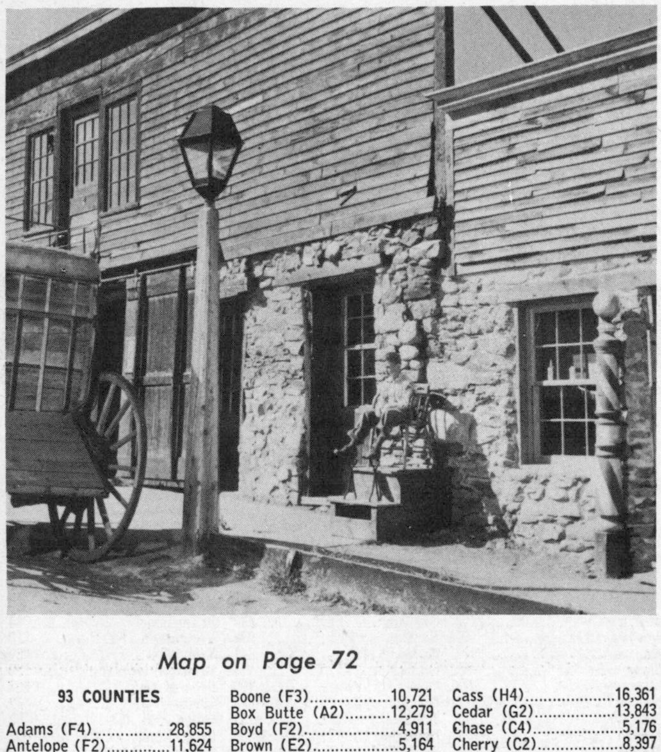

*Map on Page 72*

## NEBRASKA

*Total Population 1,325,510*

**93 COUNTIES**

Adams (F4) 28,855
Antelope (F2) 11,624
Arthur (C3) 803
Banner (A3) 1,325
Blaine (E3) 1,203
Boone (F3) 10,721
Box Butte (A2) 12,279
Boyd (F2) 4,911
Brown (E2) 5,164
Buffalo (E4) 25,134
Burt (H3) 11,536
Butler (G3) 11,432
Cass (H4) 16,361
Cedar (G2) 13,843
Chase (C4) 5,176
Cherry (C2) 8,397
Cheyenne (A3) 12,081
Clay (F4) 8,700
Colfax (G3) 10,010
Cuming (H3) 12,994
Custer (E3) 19,170
Dakota (H2) 10,401
Dawes (A2) 9,708
Dawson (E4) 19,393
Deuel (B3) 3,330
Dixon (H2) 9,129
Dodge (H3) 26,265
Douglas (H3) 281,020
Dundy (C4) 4,354
Fillmore (G4) 9,610
Franklin (F4) 7,096
Frontier (D4) 5,282
Furnas (E4) 9,385
Gage (H4) 28,052
Garden (B3) 4,114
Garfield (F3) 2,912
Gosper (E4) 2,734
Grant (C3) 1,057
Greeley (F3) 5,575
Hall (F4) 32,186
Hamilton (F4) 8,778
Harlan (E4) 7,189
Hayes (C4) 2,404
Hitchcock (C4) 5,867
Holt (F2) 14,859
Hooker (C3) 1,061
Howard (F3) 7,226

## NEVADA

*Map on Page 73* — *Total Population 160,083*

### 17 COUNTIES

Churchill (C3).... 6,161
Clark (F6).... 48,289
Douglas (B4).... 2,029
Elco (F1).... 11,654
Esmeralda (D5).... 614
Eureka (E3).... 896
Humboldt (C1).... 4,838
Lander (D3).... 1,850
Lincoln (F5).... 3,837
Lyon (B3).... 3,679
Mineral (C4).... 5,560
Nye (E5).... 3,101
Ormsby (B3).... 4,172
Pershing (C2).... 3,103
Storey (B3).... 671
Washoe (B2).... 50,205
White Pine (F3).... 9,424

### CITIES and TOWNS

Adaven (F4)*.... 25
Alamo (F5)*.... 384
Arden (F6)*.... 43
Arthur (F2)*.... 3
Austin (E3)*.... 300
Babbitt (C4)*.... 2,464
Baker (G3)*.... 50
Battle Mountain (E2)*. 850
Beatty (E6)*.... 485
Beowawe (E2)*.... 175
Black Springs (B3)*.... 100
Blue Diamonds (F6).... 210
Bonne Springs (G2).... 12
Boulder City (G7)*.... 3,903
Bristol Silver (G4).... 25
Bunkerville (G6)*.... 180
Caliente (G5)*.... 970
Carlin (E2)*.... 1,203
Carp (G5)*.... 120
CARSON CITY (B3)*.... 3,082
Charleston (F1)*....
Cherry Creek (G3)*.... 75
Coaldale (D4).... 16
Cobre (G1)*.... 51
Contact (G1)*.... 20
Cortez (E2).... 7
Crystal Bay (A3)*.... 150
Currant (F4)....
Currie (G2)*.... 52
Dayton (B3).... 300
Deeth (F1)*.... 75
Denio (C1)....
Dry Lake (G6)*.... 48
Duckwater (F4)*.... 5
Dunphy (E2).... 6
Dyer (C5)*.... 87
East Ely (G3)*.... 1,000
East Gate (D3).... 10
Elgin (G5)*.... 50
Elko (F2)*.... 5,393
Ely (G3)*.... 3,558
Eureka (E3)*.... 500
Fallon (C3)*.... 2,400
Fernley (B3)*.... 650
Flanigan (B2)*.... 44
Gabbs (D4)*.... 278
Gardnerville (B4)*.... 600
Genoa (B4)*.... 75
Gerlach (B2)*.... 200
Glenbrook (B3)*.... 30
Glendale (G6).... 20
Golconda (D2)*.... 350
Gold Hill (B3).... 68
Gold Point (D5)*.... 100
Goldfield (D5)*.... 275
Goodsprings (F7)*.... 175
Halleck (F2)*....
Hawthorne (C4)*.... 1,861
Hazen (C3)*.... 70
Henderson (G6)*.... 3,643
Hiko (F5)*.... 23
Hudson (B4).... 2
Humboldt (C2).... 30
Imlay (C2)*.... 250
Indian Springs (F6).... 50
Ione (D4)*....
Jarbidge (F1)*.... 46
Jean (F7)*.... 52
Jiggs (F2)*.... 100
Jungo (C2)*.... 30
Kimberly (F3)*.... 300
Lamoille (F2)*.... 200
Las Vegas (F6)*.... 24,624
Lee (F2)*.... 135
Logandale (G6)*.... 300
Lovelock (C2)*.... 1,604
Lower Rochester (C2).... 5
Lund (F4)*.... 365
Luning (C4)*.... 52
Manhattan (E4)*.... 125
Mason (B4)*.... 89
Mc Dermitt (D1)*.... 100
Mc Gill (G3)*.... 2,297
Mesquite (G6)*.... 540
Metropolis (G1).... 15
Midas (E1).... 100
Mill City (D2).... 35
Mina (C4)*.... 274
Minden (B4)*.... 250
Moapa (G6)*.... 18
Montello (G1)*.... 350
Mt. Montgomery (C5).... 19
Mountain City (F1)*.... 180
Nelson (G7).... 67
Nivloc (D5).... 4
Nixon (B3)*.... 450
North Fork (F1).... 31
North Las Vegas (F6)*.... 3,875
Oasis (G1).... 25
Oreana (C2).... 24
Orovada (D1)*.... 150
Overton (G6)*.... 750
Owyhee (F1)....
Pahrump (E6)*.... 120
Palisade (E2)*.... 53
Panaca (G5)*.... 499
Paradise Valley (D1)*.. 95
Pioche (G5)*.... 1,392
Pittman (F6)*.... 150
Potts (E3).... 35
Preston (G4)*.... 45
Pyramid (B2)*.... 27
Rawhide (C4).... 10
Rebel Creek (D1).... 10
Red House (D2)*....
Reese River (D4)*.... 184
Reno (B3)*.... 32,497
Rio Tinto (E1).... 1
Riverside (G6).... 25
Round Mountain (E4)*. 305
Rowland (F1).... 11
Rox (G6).... 20
Ruby Valley (F2)*.... 200
Ruth (F3)*.... 1,244
San Jacinto (G1).... 6
Schurz (C4)*.... 150
Searchlight (F7)*.... 229
Shafter (G2)*.... 91
Shoshone (G4)*.... 25
Silver City (B3)*.... 200
Silverpeak (D5)*.... 63
Sloan (F7)*.... 200
Smith (B4)*.... 28
Sparks (B3)*.... 8,203
Steamboat (B3)*.... 94
Stillwater (C3)*.... 9
Sulphur (C2)*.... 33
Tippett (G3).... 50
Tobar (G2).... 10
Tonopah (D4)*.... 1,375
Tungsten (C2)*.... 300

Tuscarora (E1)*.... 30
Unionville (C2)*.... 15
Ursine (G5)*.... 60
Valmy (D2)*.... 75
Verdi (B3)*.... 350
Virginia City (B3)*.... 800
Vya (B1).... 30
Wabuska (B3)*.... 50
Wadsworth (B3)*.... 275
Weeks (B3).... 200
Wellington (B4)*.... 60
Wells (G1)*.... 947
White Rock (E1).... 26
Whitney (F6)*.... 200
Wilkins (G1)*.... 60
Winnemucca (D2)*.... 2,847
Yerington (B4)*.... 1,157
Zephyr Cove (A3)*.... 50

## NEW HAMPSHIRE

*Map on Page 74* — *Total Population 533,242*

### 10 COUNTIES

Belknap (D4).... 26,632
Carroll (D4).... 15,868
Cheshire (B6).... 38,811
Coos (D2).... 35,932
Grafton (C4).... 47,923
Hillsboro (C6).... 156,987
Merrimack (C5).... 63,022
Rockingham (D5).... 70,059
Strafford (D5).... 51,567
Sullivan (B5).... 26,441

### CITIES and TOWNS

Acworth (B5)*.... △418
Alexandria (C4)*.... △402
Allenstown (D5).... △1,540
Alstead (B5)*.... △851
Alton (D5)*.... △1,189
Alton Bay (D5)*.... 200
Amherst (C6)*.... △1,461
Andover (C5)*.... △1,057
Antrim (C5)*.... △1,030
Apthorp (C3)....
Ashland (C4)*.... △1,599
Ashuelot (B6)*.... 500
Atkinson (D6).... △492
Atkinson Depot (D6)*.
Auburn (D5)*.... △1,158
Barnstead (D5)*.... △846
Barrington (E5).... △1,052
Bartlett (D3)*.... △1,074
Bath (C3)*.... △706
Bear Island (D4)*....
Bedford (C6).... △2,176
Beebe River (C4)*.... 275
Belmont (D5)*.... △1,611
Bennington (C5)*.... △593
Benton (C3).... △247
Berlin (D3)*.... 16,615
Berlin Mills (D3)....
Bethlehem (C3)*.... △882
Blodgett (D5)....
Blodgett Landing (C5)*
Boscawen (C5)*.... △1,857
Bow (C5).... △1,062
Bradford (C5)*.... △606
Brentwood (D6).... △819
Bretton Woods (D3)*.. 14
Bridgewater (C4).... △222
Bristol (C4)*.... △1,586
Brookfield (D4).... △159
Brookline (C6)*.... △671
Campton (C4)*.... △1,149
Canaan (B4)*.... △14,065
Canaan Center (B4)*.. 179
Candia (D5)*.... △1,243
Canobie Lake (D6)*.... 778
Canterbury (C5)*.... △627
Carroll (D3).... △359
Cascade (D3)*.... 1,000
CenterBarnstead (D5)* 550
Ctr. Conway (D4)*.... 400
Ctr. Harbor (D4)*.... △451
Ctr. Ossipee (D4)*.... 750
Ctr. Sandwich (C4)*... 725
Ctr. Strafford (D5)*...
Ctr. Tuftonboro (D4)*. 500
Charlestown (B5)*.... △2,077
Chatham (D3).... △177
Chesham (B6)*....
Chester (D6)*.... △807
Chesterfield (B6)*.... △970
Chichester (D5).... △735
Chocorua (D4)*.... 375
Claremont (B5)*.... 12,811
Colebrook (D2)*.... △2,116
CONCORD (C5)*.... 27,988
Contoocook (C5)*.... 1,000
Conway (D4)*.... △4,109
Coos Junction (C2)....
Cornish Flat (B5)*.... 200
Crawford House (D3)* 6
Croydon (B5)*.... △349
Crystal (D2).... 50
Dalton (C3).... △557
Danbury (C4)*.... △496
Danville (D6)*.... △508
Deerfield (D5)*.... △706
Deering (C5).... △392
Derry (D6)*.... △5,826
Dixville Notch (D2)*.. △13
Dorchester (C4).... △133
Dover (E5)*.... 15,874
Drewsville (B5)*.... 150
Dublin (B6)*.... △675
Dummer (D2).... △229
Dunbarton (C5)*.... △533
Durham (E5)*.... △4,770
East Andover (C5)*....
E. Barrington (E5)*....
E. Candia (D5)*.... 250
E. Canterbury (D5)....
E. Concord (D5)*....
E. Derry (D6)*.... 300
E. Grafton (C4).... 100
E. Hampstead (D6)*.... 920
E. Haverhill (C3)*.... 150
E. Hebron (C4)*....
E. Jaffrey (B6)*.... 1,866
E. Kingston (E6)*.... △449
E. Lempster (B5)*....
E. Madison (D4)*.... 80
E. Milford (C6)....
E. Rochester (E5)*.... 1,100
E. Rindge (C6)*.... 200
E. Sullivan (B6)*.... 150
E. Swanzey (B6)*.... 700
E. Tilton (D5)....
E. Wakefield (E4)*....
E. Weare (C5)*.... 260
E. Westmoreland (B6)* 200
E. Wolfeboro (D4)*.... 301
Easton (C3).... △94
Eaton Center (D4)*.... △221
Effingham Falls (D4).. △341
Elkins (C5)*.... 200
Ellsworth (C4).... △24
Elmwood (C6)*....
Emerson (West
 Henniker) (C5)....
Enfield (B4)*.... △1,612
Enfield Center (B4)*....
Epping (D5)*.... △1,796
Epsom (D5)*.... △756
Errol (D2)*.... △224
Etna (B4)*....
Exeter (E6)*.... △5,664
Fabyan House (D3)*.... 300
Fairview (C3)....
Farmington (D5)*.... △3,454
Fitzwilliam (B6)*.... △872
Fitzwilliam Depot
 (B6)*.... 250
Francestown (C6)*.... △405
Franconia (C3)*.... 549
Franklin (C5)*.... 6,552
Freedom (E4)*.... △315
Fremont (D6)*.... △698
Gaza (C4)....
Georges Mills (B5)*.... 170
Gerrish (C5)*.... 275
Gilford (D4).... △1,251
Gilmanton (D5)*.... △754
Gilmanton Iron
 Works (D5)*....
Gilsum (B5)*.... △578
Glen (D3)*....
Glencliff (C4)*.... 200
Glendale (D4)....
Goffs Falls (D6)*.... 800
Goffstown (C5)*.... △5,638
Gonic (E5)*.... 1,000
Gorham (D3)*.... △2,639
Goshen (B5)*.... △356
Gossville (D5)*....
Grafton (C4)*.... △442
Grafton Center (C4)*.. 93
Grange (D3).... 80
Grantham (B5)*.... △359
Grasmere (D5)*.... 1,545
Greenfield (C6)*.... △430
Greenland (E5)*.... △719
Greenville (C6)*.... △1,280
Groton (C4).... △105
Groveton (C2)*.... 1,918
Guild (B5)*.... 200
Hampstead (D6)*.... △902
Hampton (E6)*.... △2,847
Hampton Beach (E6)*....
Hampton Falls (E6)*.. △629
Hancock (B6)*.... △612
Hanover (B4)*.... △6,259
Harrisville (B6)*.... △519
Haverhill (B3)*.... △3,357
Hedding (E5)*....
Henniker (C5)*.... △1,675
Hill (C4)*.... △310
Hillsboro (C5)*.... △2,179
Hillsboro Lower
 Village (C5).... 400
Hillsboro Upper
 Village (C5)....
Hinsdale (A6)*.... △1,950
Holderness (C4)*.... △731
Hollis (C6)*.... △1,196
Hollis Depot (C6)*.... 380
Hooksett (D5)*.... △2,792
Hopkinton (C5)*.... △1,831
Hudson (D6)*.... △4,183
Intervale (D3)*.... 600
Jackson (D3)*.... △344
Jaffrey (B6)*.... △2,911
Jefferson (C3)*.... △728
Kearsarge (D3)*....
Keene (B6)*.... 15,638
Kingston (D6)*.... △1,283
Laconia (D4)*.... 14,745
Lakeport (C4)*.... 3,600
Lancaster (C3)*.... △3,113
Landaff (C3).... △342
Langdon (B5).... 378
Leavitts Hill (D5)*....
Lebanon (B4)*.... △8,495
Lee (E5).... △575
Lempster (B5)*.... △309
Lincoln (C3)*.... △1,415
Lisbon (C3)*.... △2,009
Litchfield (D6).... △427
Little Boars Head (E6)
Littleton (C3)*.... △4,817
Livermore Falls (C4)...
Londonderry (D6)*.... △1,640
Loudon (D5)*.... △1,012
Lyme (B4)*.... △924
Lyme Center (B4)*.... 350
Lyndeboro (C6).... △552
Madbury (E5)*.... △489
Madison (D4)*.... △486
Manchester (C6)*.... 82,732
Manchester (urban
 area).... 84,768
Maplewood (C3)*....
Marlboro (B6)*.... △1,561
Marlow (B5)*.... △330
Martins (D5)....
Mascoma (B4)*.... 100
Meadows (C3)*.... 89
Melvin Mills (C5)*.... 65
Melvin Village (D4)*..
Meredith (C4)*.... △2,222
Meredith Ctr. (C4)*.... 150
Meriden (B4)*.... 500
Merrimack (C6)*.... △1,908
Middleton (D5).... △255
Milan (D2)*.... △743
Milford (C6)*.... △4,159
Milton (E5)*.... 1,510
Milton Mills (E5)*.... 280
Mirror Lake (D4)*.... 135
Monroe (B3)*.... △410
Mont Vernon (C6)*.... △405
Moultonboro (D4)*.... △880
Moultonville (D4)*.... 200
Mount Sunapee (B5)*. 125
Munsonville (B5)*....
Nashua (C6)*.... 34,669
Nelson (B5).... △231
New Boston (C6)*.... △865
New Castle (E5)*.... △583
New Durham (D5)*.... △463
New Hampton (C4)*.... △723
New Ipswich (C6)*.... △1,147
New London (C5)*.... △1,484
Newbury (C5)*.... △320
Newfields (E5)*.... △469
Newington (E5).... △494
Newmarket (D5)*.... △2,709
Newport (B5)*.... △5,131
Newton (E6)*.... △1,173
Newton Jct. (D6)*....
North Branch (C5)....
N. Charlestown (B5)*.. 200
N. Chatham (D3)*.... 177
N. Chichester (D5)*.... 740
N. Conway (D3)*.... 1,200
N. End (C4)*....
N. Groton (C4).... 30
N. Hampton (E6)*.... △1,104
N. Haverhill (C3)*.... 500
N. Holderness (C4)....
N. Monroe (C3).... 160
N. Newport (B5)*.... 200
N. Rochester (E5)*....
N. Salem (D6)*.... 400
N. Sandwich (D4)*....
N. Stratford (C2)*....
N. Sutton (C5)*....
N. Wakefield (D4)....
N. Walpole (B5).... 1,000
N. Weare (C5)*....
N. Woodstock (C3)*.... 675
Northfield (C5).... △1,561
Northumberland
 (D2)*.... △2,779
Northwood (D5)*.... △966
Northwood Ctr. (D5)* 120
Northwood
 Narrows (D5)*.... 325
Nottingham (D5)*.... △566
Orange (C4).... △82
Orford (B4)*.... △726
Orfordville (B4)*....
Ossipee (D4)*.... △1,412
Parkhill (B6).... 45
Pelham (D6)*.... △1,317
Pembroke (D5).... △3,094
Penacook (C5)*.... 3,100
Percy (D2)*.... 48
Peterborough (C6)*.... △2,556
Piermont (B4)*.... △511
Pike (B3)*.... 175
Pittsburg (D1)*.... △697
Pittsfield (D5)*.... △2,321
Plainfield (B4)*.... △1,011
Plaistow (D6)*.... △2,082
Plymouth (C4)*.... △3,039
Ponemah (C6)....
Portsmouth (E5)*.... 18,830
Powwow River (D6).... 75
Province Lake (E4)....
Quincy (C4)*.... 125
Randolph (D3)*.... △158
Raymond (D5)*.... △1,428
Redstone (D3)*.... 250
Reeds Ferry (C6)*.... 500
Richmond (B6).... △259
Rindge (B6)*.... △707
Riverdale (C5)....
Rochester (D5)*.... 13,776
Rockingham (E5)....
Roxbury (B6).... △117
Rumney (C4)*.... △859
Rumney Depot (C4)*... 165
Rye (E5)*.... △1,982
Rye Beach (E6)*.... 1,000
Rye North Beach (E5)
Saint Paul's School (C5)*
Salem (D6)*.... △4,805
Salem Depot (D6)*.... 1,637
Salisbury (C5)*.... △423
Salmon Falls (E5)*.... 1,290
Sanbornton (C5)*.... △755
Sanbornville (E4)*.... 460
Sandown (D6)*.... △315
Sandwich (D4)*.... △615
Seabrook (E6)*.... △1,788
Sharon (C6).... △62
Shelburne (D3)*.... △184
Short Falls (D5)*.... 100
Silver Lake (D4)*.... 500
Smithtown (E6)*.... 100
Somersworth (E5)*.... 6,927
Snowville (D4)*.... 100
Soo Nipi (C5).... 25
South Acworth (B5)*..
S. Alexandria (C4).... 100
S. Chatham (E3)*.... 54
S. Danbury (C5)*....
S. Danville (D6)*.... 125
S. Deerfield (D5)*....
S. Effingham (E4)*....
S. Hampton (E6).... △314
S. Keene (B6).... 200
S. Lee (D5).... 70
S. Lyndeboro (C6)*.... 552
S. Merrimack (C6)*.... 250
S. Newbury (C5)*.... 88
S. Pittsfield (D5)....
S. Seabrook (E6).... 1,000
S. Stoddard (B5)....
S. Sutton (C5)*.... 139
S. Tamworth (D4)*....
S. Wolfeboro (D4).... 248
S. Weare (C5)....
Spofford (B6)*.... 350
Springfield (B4)*.... △324
Stark (D2).... △373
State Line (B6)*.... 125
Stewartstown (D2).... △970
Stinson Lake (C4)*....
Stoddard (B5)*.... △200
Strafford (D5)*.... △770
Stratford (C2)*.... △973
Stratham (E5)*.... △759
Sugar Hill (C3)*.... 250
Sullivan (B5)*.... △272
Sunapee (B5)*.... △1,108
Suncook (C5)*....
Surry (B5)*.... △291
Sutton (C5)*.... △554
Swanzey (B6).... △2,806
Swiftwater (C3)....
Tamworth (D4)*.... △1,025
Temple (C6)*.... △330
The Weirs (D4)*....
Thornton (C4).... △460
Tilton (C5)*.... △2,085
Troy (B6)*.... △1,360
Tuftonboro (D4).... △697
Twin Mountain (C3)*. 352
Union (D5)*.... 550
Unity (B5)*.... △653
Village (D6)*....
Wakefield (E4)*.... △1,267
Walpole (B5)*.... △2,536
Warner (C5)*.... △1,080
Warren (C4)*.... △581
Washington (B5)*.... △168
Waterville Valley
 (C4).... △11
Weare (C4).... △1,345
Webster (C5).... △386
Wendell (B5)*.... 200
Wentworth (C4)*.... △413
Wentworth Location
 (D2)*.... △48
West Alton (D4)*....
W. Andover (C5)*....
W. Brentwood (D6)....
W. Campton (C4)*.... 125
W. Canaan (B4)*....
W. Chesterfield
 (A6)*.... 250
W. Claremont (B5)*... 100
W. Epping (D5)....
W. Hampstead (D6)*...
W. Henniker (Emerson)
 (C5)
W. Hopkinton (C5)*.... 100
W. Lebanon (B4)*.... 1,737
W. Manchester (C6)....
W. Milan (D2)*.... 250
W. Nottingham
 (D5)*.... 80
W. Ossipee (D4)*.... 175
W. Peterborough (B6)* 350
W. Rindge (C6)*.... 230
W. Rumney (C4)*.... 200
W. Rye (E6)*.... 55
W. Springfield (B5)*.. 100
W. Stewartstown (C2)* 385
W. Swanzey (B6)*.... 1,400
W. Thornton (C4)*.... 450
W. Windham (D6)....
Westmoreland (B6)*△ 789
Westmoreland Depot
 (A6)*....
Westport (B6).... 328
Westville (D6)*.... 300
Whiteface (D4)....
Whitefield (C3)*.... △1,677
Willey House (D3)*.... 10
Wilmot (C5)*.... △370
Wilmot Flat (C5)*....
Wilton (C6)*.... △1,952
Winchester (B6)*.... △2,388
Windham (D6).... △964
Windham Depot (D6)*.
Winnipesaukee (D4)*..
Winnisquam (D5)*.... 400
Wolfeboro (D4)*.... △2,581
Wolfeboro Falls
 (D4)*.... 600
Wonalancet (D4)*.... 36
Woodstock (C4)*.... 894
Woodsville (B3)*.... 1,542

## NEW JERSEY

*Map on Page 75* — *Total Population 4,835,329*

### 21 COUNTIES

Atlantic (D5).... 132,399
Bergen (E2).... 539,139
Burlington (D4).... 135,910
Camden (D4).... 300,743
Cape May (D5).... 37,131
Cumberland (C5).... 88,597
Essex (E2).... 905,949
Gloucester (C4).... 91,727
Hudson (E2).... 647,437
Hunterdon (D2).... 42,736
Mercer (D3).... 229,781
Middlesex (E3).... 264,872
Monmouth (E3).... 225,327
Morris (D2).... 164,371
Ocean (E4).... 56,622
Passaic (E1).... 337,093
Salem (C4).... 49,508
Somerset (D2).... 99,052
Sussex (D1).... 34,423
Union (E2).... 398,138
Warren (C2).... 54,374

### CITIES and TOWNS

Absecon (D5)*.... 2,355
Adamston (E3)*.... 450
Adelphia (E3)*.... 300
Allamuchy (D2)*.... 600
Allendale (B1)*.... 2,409
Allenhurst (F3)*.... 758
Allentown (D3)*.... 931
Allenwood (E3)*....
Alloway (C4)*.... 700
Almonesson (B4)*....
Alpha (C2)*.... 2,117
Alpine (C1)*.... 644
Ampere (B2)*.... 10,000
Andover (D2)*.... 560
Annandale (D2)*....
Arlington (B2)*.... 16,000
Asbury (C2)*.... 300
Asbury Park (F3)*.... 17,094
Ashland (D4)*.... 1,240
Atco (D4)*.... 2,500
Atlantic City (E5)*.... 61,657
Atlantic City (urban
 area).... 105,326
Atlantic Highlands
 (F3)*.... 3,083
Audubon (C4)*.... 9,531
Audubon Park (B3).... 1,859
Augusta (D1)*.... 80
Aura (C4).... 100
Avalon (D5)*.... 428
Avenel (E2)*.... 8,700
Avon by the Sea (F3)*.... 1,650
Awosting (E1)....
Baptistown (D2)*.... 350
Barber (E2)*....
Barnegat (E4)*.... 1,150
Barnegat Light (E4)*.... 227
Barrington (B3)*.... 2,651
Bartley (D2)*.... 500
Basking Ridge (D2)*.... 1,899
Bay Head (E3)*.... 808
Bayonne (B2)*.... 77,203
Bayville (E4)*.... 2,000
Beach Haven (E4)*.... 1,050
Beach Haven Crest
 (E4)*
Beach Haven Terrace
 (E4)*.... 350
Beachwood (E4)*.... 1,251
Beaver Lake (D1)*.... 175

## NEW MEXICO

Map on Page 76

Total Population 681,187

### 32 COUNTIES

Bernalillo (C3) 145,673
Catron (A4) 3,533
Chaves (E5) 40,605
Colfax (E2) 16,761
Curry (F4) 23,351
De Baca (E4) 3,464
Dona Ana (C6) 39,557
Eddy (E6) 40,640
Grant (A5) 21,649
Guadalupe (E4) 6,772
Harding (F3) 3,013
Hidalgo (A7) 5,095
Lea (F6) 30,717
Lincoln (D5) 7,409
Los Alamos (C3) 10,476
Luna (B6) 8,753
Mc Kinley (A3) 27,451
Mora (E3) 8,720
Otero (D6) 14,909
Quay (F3) 13,971
Rio Arriba (B2) 24,997
Roosevelt (F4) 16,409
San Juan (A2) 18,292
San Miguel (D3) 26,512
Sandoval (C3) 12,438
Santa Fe (C3) 38,153
Sierra (B5) 7,186
Socorro (C5) 9,670
Taos (D2) 17,146
Torrance (D4) 8,012
Union (F2) 7,372
Valencia (A4) 22,481

### CITIES and TOWNS

Abbott (E2)*
Abeytas (C4)
Abiquiu (C2)*
Abo (C4)
Acme (E5)
Acomita (B3)*
Adams Diggings (A4)
Afton (B6) 15
Agua Fria (D2)
Akela (B6) 40
Alameda (C3)* 1,792
Alamogordo (C6)* 6,783
Albert (F3)* 35
Albuquerque (C3)* 96,815
Alcalde (C2)*
Algodones (C3)* 250
Alma (A5) 50
Alto (D5)* 50
Amalia (D2)*
Amistad (F3)* 33
Anapra (C7)
Ancho (D5)* 100
Animas (A7)*
Anthony (C6)* 800
Anton Chico (D3)* 600
Apache Creek (A5)* 85
Arabela (D5) 60
Aragon (A5)* 89
Arch (F4)* 35
Arrey (B6)* 350
Arroyo Hondo (D2)* 500
Arroyoseco (D2)* 400
Artesia (E6)* 8,244
Atarque (A4)* 100
Atoka (E6) 64
Augustine (B4)*
Aztec (B2)* 885
Bard (F3)* 45
Bayard (A6)* 2,119
Beaverhead (A5)
Belen (C4)* 4,495
Bell Ranch (E3)* 20
Bellview (F4)* 150
Bent (D5)* 250
Berino (C6)* 300
Bernalillo (C3)* 1,922
Bernardo (C4) 30
Bibo (B3)
Bingham (C5)* 7
Blanco (B2)* 135
Bloomfield (A2)* 500
Bluewater (A3)* 350
Bluit (F5)
Boaz (F5)* 30
Bosque (C4)* 400
Brilliant (E2)* 225
Broadview (F4)* 80
Buchanan (E4)*
Buckeye (F6)* 227
Buckhorn (A5)* 500
Buena Vista (D3)* 265
Bueyeros (F3)* 38
Caballo (B6)*
Cabezon (B3)
Cambray (B6)* 8
Cameron (F4)* 18
Canjilon (C2)* 900
Canones (C2)* 140
Canoncito (C3)
Capitan (D5)* 575
Caprock (F5)* 12
Capulin (F2)* 200
Carlsbad (E6)* 17,975
Carrizozo (D5)* 1,389
Carson (D2)* 25
Carthage (C5)
Casa Blanca (B4)* 493
Causey (F5)* 50
Cebolla (C2)* 1,000
Cedar Crest (C3)* 1,000
Cedar Hill (B2)* 130
Cedarvale (D4)* 50
Central (A6)* 1,511
Cerrillos (D3)*
Cerro (D2)* 600
Chacon (D2)*
Chama (C2)* 1,300
Chama (C6)* 1,000
Chamberino (C6)* 1,000
Chamisal (D2)* 500
Chapelle (D3) 25
Chaperito (E3)* 125
Chico (E2)* 6
Chilili (C4)
Chimayo (D3)* 1,550
Chloride (B5)* 56
Cienega (D6) 2
Cimarron (E2)* 855
Clapham (F2)*
Claunch (C4)*
Clayton (F2)* 3,515
Cleveland (D2)* 700
Cliff (A6)* 250
Closson (A3)
Cloudcroft (D6)* 251
Cloverdale (A7)
Clovis (F4)* 17,318
Cochiti (C3) 250
Colfax (E2)
Colmor (E2)* 80
Colonias (E3)* 150
Columbus (B7)* 251
Conchas Dam (E3)* 100
Contreras (C4)
Coolidge (A3)* 8
Cooper (F6) 6
Cordova (D2)*
Corona (D4)* 530
Correo (B4)* 8
Costilla (D2)* 300
Cowles (D3)* 200
Coyote (C2)*
Coyote Canyon (A3)
Crossroads (F5)* 60
Crownpoint (A3)* 125
Crystal (A2) 125
Cuba (B2)* 850
Cubero (B3)*
Cuchillo (B5)* 105
Cuervo (E3)* 100
Cundiyo (D3)* 160
Cunico (E2) 60
Cutter (B5)* 55
Dahlia (D3)* 100
Datil (B4)* 80
Dawson (E2)* 1,206
Dayton (E6)
Delphos (F4) 2
Deming (B6)* 5,672
Derry (B6)* 300
Des Moines (F2)* 282
Dexter (E5)* 784
Dilia (D3)* 250
Dixon (D2)* 1,250
Domingo (C3) 120
Dona Ana (C6)* 400
Dora (F5)* 120
Dulce (B2)* 500
Dunlap (E4)* 90
Duoro (D4)
Duran (D4)* 300
Dusty (B5)* 15
Dwyer (B6)
Eagle Nest (D2)* 200
East Vaughn (D4)* 1,800
Edgewood (C3)* 45
El Morro (A3)* 300
El Paso Gap (E6) 12
El Porvenir (D3)* 350
El Prado (D2)*
El Pueblo (D3) 175
El Rito (C2)* 1,200
El Vado Dam (C2) 18
Elephant Butte (B5)* 150
Elida (F5)* 430
Elizabethtown (D2)
Elk (D6)* 35
Elkins (E5)* 26
Embudo (C2)*
Encino (D4)* 408
Endee (F3)* 50
Engle (B5)* 65
Ensenada (C2)* 400
Escabosa (C4)
Espanola (C3)* 1,446
Espuella (E6) 50
Estancia (D4)* 916
Eunice (F6)* 2,352
Fairacres (C6)* 350
Farley (E2)* 111
Farmington (A2)* 3,637
Faywood (B6)*
Fence Lake (A4)* 250
Field (B4) 300
Fierro (A6)* 500
Fillmore (C6)
Flora Vista (A2)* 150
Florida (B6) 15
Florida (C4)* 350
Floyd (F4)* 50
Flying H (E5)* 55
Folsom (F2)* 206
Forrest (F4)* 130
Fort Bayard (A6)* 483
Fort Stanton (D5)* 500
Ft. Sumner (E4)* 1,978
Ft. Wingate (A3)* 250
Frazier (E5)* 12
French (E2) 10
Frisco (A5)
Fruitland (A2)* 200
Gage (A6)* 100
Galisteo (D3)* 150
Gallegos (F3)*
Gallina (C2)* 31
Gallup (A3)* 9,133
Gamerco (A3)* 200
Gardiner (E2) 50
Garfield (B6)* 300
Garita (E3)* 200
Gila (A6)* 700
Gilman (C3) 300
Gladiola (F5)* 99
Gladstone (F2)* 61
Glencoe (D5)* 200
Glenrio (F3)* 60
Glenwood (A5)* 300
Glorieta (D3)* 500
Golden (C3) 75
Governador (B2) 45
Grady (F4)* 130
Gran Quivira (D4)* 50
Grants (B3)* 2,251
Green Tree (D5)* 363
Greens Gap (A4) 25
Grenville (F2)* 102
Grier (F4)* 200
Guadalupita (D2)* 475
Guy (F2)
Hachita (A7)* 200
Hagerman (E5)* 1,024
Hanover (A6)* 1,200
Hatch (B6)* 1,064
Hayden (F3)*
Heck Canyon (D2)
Hernandez (C2)* 400
Hickman (B4)* 17
High Rolls (D5)* 175
Hill (C6) 100
Hillsboro (B6)* 300
Hilton Lodge (D3) 2
Hobbs (F6)* 13,875
Hollene (F4)* 20
Hollywood (D5)*
Holman (D2)*
Hondo (D5)* 250
Hope (E6)* 186
Horse Springs (A5)* 100
House (F4)* 295
Humble City (F6)* 42
Hurley (A6)* 2,079
Ilfeld (D3)*
Ima (E4)* 4
Ione (F3)* 3
Isleta (C4)* 1,400
Jal (F6)* 2,047
Jarales (C4)* 1,199
Jemez Pueblo (C3)* 878
Jemez Springs (C3)* 135
Jicarilla (D5) 20
Jordan (F4)* 93
Kelly (B4)* 55
Kenna (F5)* 100
Kingston (B6)* 50
Kirtland (A2)* 200
Knowles (F6) 10
Koehler (E2)* 385
La Cueva (D3)
La Jara (B2)* 2,500
La Lande (E4)* 35
La Liendre (E3) 12
La Luz (C6)* 200
La Madera (C2)*
La Mesa (C6)* 650
La Puente (C2) 300
La Union (C7) 475
La Ventana (B3)
Laguna (B3)* 3,004
Lajoya (C4)*
Lake Arthur (E5)* 380
Lake Valley (B6)* 9
Lakewood (E6)*
Lamy (D3)* 105
Laplata (A2)*
Las Cruces (C6)* 12,325
Las Padillas (C3) 487
Las Palomas (B5)* 60
Las Tablas (C2)* 100
Las Vegas (city) (D3)* 7,494
Las Vegas (town) (D3) 6,269
Ledoux (D3)* 800
Lemitar (B4)* 500
Levy (E2)* 15
Leyba (D3)*
Lincoln (D5)* 80
Lindrith (C2)* 300
Lingo (F5)* 20
Llano (D2)* 550
Loco Hills (F6)* 300
Logan (F3)* 500
Lon (D4)
Lordsburg (A6)* 3,525
Los Alamos (C3)* 9,934
Los Griegos (C3) 3,025
Los Lunas (C4)* 889
Lourdes (D3)*
Loving (E6)* 1,487
Lovington (F6)* 3,134
Lucy (D4) 10
Lumberton (C2)*
Luna (A5)* 300
Lyden (C2)*
Madrid (C3)* 477
Maes (E3)* 50
Magdalena (B4)* 1,297
Malaga (E6)* 250
Mangas (A4) 25
Manuelito (A3)*
Manzano (C4)* 250
Marquez (B3)* 60
Maxwell (E2)* 404
Mayhill (D6)*
Mc Alister (F4)*
Mc Donald (F5)* 100
Mc Gaffey (A3) 50
Mc Intosh (D4)* 25
Melrose (F4)* 936
Mentmore (A3)* 100
Mescalero (D5)*
Mesilla (C6)* 1,264
Mesilla Park (C6)* 2,000
Mesquite (C6)* 400
Mexican Springs (A3)*
Miami (E2)*
Mills (E2)*
Milnesand (F5)*
Mimbres (B6)* 36
Mogollon (A5)* 26
Monero (C2)* 207
Montezuma (D3)* 1,200
Monticello (B5) 400
Montoya (F3)* 75
Monument (F6)*
Mora (D3)* 1,750
Moriarty (D4)*
Moses (F2)* 70
Mosquero (F3)* 583
Mount Dora (F2)* 100
Mountain Park (D6)* 60
Mountainair (C4)* 1,418
Mule Creek (A5)* 16
Nambe (D3) 500
Nara Visa (F3)* 350
New Laguna (B3)* 150
Newcomb (A2) 200
Newkirk (E3)* 250
Nogal (D5)* 25
Nolan (E2) 11
Norton (F4) 7
Obar (F3)* 5
Ocate (E2)* 105
Oil Center (F6)* 70
Ojo Caliente (D2)*
Ojo Feliz (E2)* 365
Ojo Sarco (D2)* 150
Old Albuquerque (C3)*
Old Tapicitoes (C2)
Olive (E5)* 12
Omega (A4)* 30
Onava (D3)
Optimo (E3)
Organ (C6)* 50
Orogrande (D6)* 45
Oscura (C5) 50
Otis (E6) 150
Paguate (B3)* 500
Palma (D4)*
Park View (C2)* 300
Pasamonte (F2) 12
Pastura (E4)* 120
Pecos (D3)* 1,241
Pedernal (D4)* 30
Penablanca (C3)* 350
Penasco (D2)* 700
Penistaja (B3)
Pep (F5)* 30
Peralta (C4)* 300
Perea (A3)
Petaca (C2)*
Picacho (D5)* 175
Pie Town (A4)* 135
Pinehaven (A3)
Pinon (D6)* 100
Pinos Altos (A6)* 250
Pintada (D4)*
Placitas (C3)* 350
Pleasanton (A5) 48
Pojoaque (C3) 200
Polvadera (B4)*
Ponderosa (C3)* 100
Portales (F4)* 8,112
Prewitt (B3)* 65
Puerto de Luna (E4)* 600
Quarai (C4) 55
Quay (F4)* 120
Quemado (A4)* 400
Questa (D2)* 1,400
Radium Springs (B6)*
Ragland (F4) 12
Rainsville (D2)* 350
Ramah (A3)* 300
Ramon (D4)
Ranches of Taos (D2)* 1,386
Raton (E2)* 8,241
Rayo (C4)
Red Hill (A4)*
Red River (D2)* 150
Redrock (A6)* 17
Regina (B2)* 100
Rehoboth (A3)* 90
Rencona (D3)* 32
Reserve (A5)*
Ribera (D3)* 400
Ricardo (E4)* 25
Rincon (C6)* 500
Riverside (C2)
Rociada (D3)* 40
Rodarte (D2)* 750
Rodeo (A7)* 250
Rodey (B6) 250
Rogers (F5)* 71
Romeroville (D3) 18
Rosa (B2) 100
Rosebud (F3)
Roswell (E5)* 25,738
Rowe (D3)* 365
Roy (E3)* 1,074
Ruidoso (D5)* 806
Rutheron (C2)* 25
Sabinoso (E3)* 125
Sacramenta (D6)*
Saint Vrain (F4)* 48
Sais (C4)
Salem (B6)* 350
San Acacia (B4)* 200
San Antonio (B5)* 900
San Cristobal (D2)* 215
San Felipe (C3) 500
San Fidel (B3)* 89
San Ignacio (D4)
San Ildefonzo (C3) 400
San Jon (F3)* 362
San Jose (D3)*
San Juan (B6)
San Juan Pueblo (C2)* 1,200
San Lorenzo (B6)* 350
San Marcial (C5)
San Mateo (B3)* 150
San Miguel (C6) 300
San Patricio (D5)* 300
San Rafael (A3)* 500
San Ysidro (C3)*
Sandia Park (C3)* 100
Sandoval (C3)*
Santa Clara (C3)
Santa Cruz (D3)*
SANTA FE (C3)* 27,998
Santa Rita (B6)* 2,135
Santa Rosa (E4)* 2,199
Sapello (D3)* 80
Scholle (C4)*
Seboyeta (B3)*
Sedan (F2)* 100
Sena (D3)* 190
Seneca (F2)* 20
Separ (A6)* 50
Serafina (D3)* 100
Servilleta (D2) 15
Sherman (B6)*
Shiprock (A2)* 250
Shoemaker (E3)* 200
Silver City (A6)* 7,022
Skarda (D2) 25
Socorro (C4)* 4,334
Soham (D3)* 250
Solano (E3)* 40
Springer (E2)* 1,558
Spur Lake (A5)* 3
Stanley (D3)* 75
State College (C6)* 1,200
Stead (F2)* 11
Steins (A6)
Stong (D2)
Strauss (C7)*
Sugarite (E2) 10
Sunshine Valley (D2) 20
Tafoya (E2)* 325
Taiban (F4)*
Tajique (C4)* 250
Talpa (D2)
Taos (D2)* 1,815
Tapicitoes (B2)*
Tatum (F5)* 688
Taylor Springs (E2) 25
Tecolotenos (D3) 95
Tererro (D3)* 40
Tesuque (C3)*
Texico (F4)* 691
Thoreau (A3)* 150
Three Rivers (C5)* 350
Tierra Amarilla (C2)* 800
Tijeras (C3)*
Tinnie (D5)* 80
Toadlena (A2)* 500
Tohatchi (A3)* 350
Tolar (F4)
Tome (C4)* 400
Torrance (D4) 10
Torreon (C4)* 100
Trampas (D2)*
Trementina (E3)*
Tres Lagunas (B4)* 14
Tres Piedras (D2)* 75
Tres Ritos (D2) 50
Truchas (D2)* 750
Trujillo (E3)* 500
Truth or Consequences (B5)* 4,563
Tsaya (A2) 50
Tucumcari (F3)* 8,419
Tularosa (C5)* 1,642
Turley (B2)
Two Wells (A3)
Tyrone (A6)*
Ute Park (D2)*
Vadito (D2)* 500
Vado (C6)* 350
Valdez (D2)* 360
Valencia (C4) 818
Vallecitos (C2)* 400
Valley Ranch (D3)
Valmora (D3)* 100
Van Houten (E2)*
Vanadium (A6)* 450
Vaughn (D4)* 1,356
Veguita (C4)*
Velarde (C2)* 600
Vermejo Park (D2)* 300
Villanueva (D3)*
Virden (A6) 146
Wagon Mound (E2)* 1,120
Waterflow (A2)* 150
Watrous (D3)* 250
Weed (D6)* 100
White Oaks (D5)* 61
White Signal (A6)
Whitewater (A6)* 40
Willard (D4)* 296
Wilna (A6) 8
Winston (B5)* 150
Witt (D4) 12
Yeso (E4)* 500
Youngsville (C2)* 120
Zamora (C3)
Zuni (A3)* 2,563

## NEW YORK

Map on Page 77

Total Population 14,830,192

### 62 COUNTIES

Albany (M5) 239,386
Allegany (D6) 43,784
Bronx (C2) 1,451,277
Broome (J6) 184,698
Cattaraugus (C6) 77,901
Cayuga (G4) 70,136
Chautauqua (B6) 135,189
Chemung (G6) 86,827
Chenango (J6) 39,138
Clinton (N1) 53,622
Columbia (N6) 43,182
Cortland (H5) 37,158
Delaware (K6) 44,420
Dutchess (N7) 136,781
Erie (C5) 899,238
Essex (N2) 35,086
Franklin (M1) 44,830
Fulton (M4) 51,021
Genesee (D4) 47,584
Greene (M6) 28,745
Hamilton (L3) 4,105
Herkimer (L4) 61,407
Jefferson (J2) 85,521
Kings (C3) 2,738,175
Lewis (K3) 22,521
Livingston (E5) 40,257
Madison (J5) 46,214
Monroe (E4) 487,632
Montgomery (M5) 59,594
Nassau (D2) 672,765
New York (C2) 1,960,101
Niagara (C4) 189,992
Oneida (J4) 222,855
Onondaga (H5) 341,719
Ontario (F5) 60,172
Orange (C1) 152,255
Orleans (D4) 29,832
Oswego (H4) 77,181
Otsego (K5) 50,763
Putnam (D1) 20,307
Queens (D2) 1,550,849
Rensselaer (O5) 132,607
Richmond (C3) 191,555
Rockland (C1) 89,276
St. Lawrence (K2) 98,897
Saratoga (N4) 74,869
Schenectady (M5) 142,497
Schoharie (M5) 22,703
Schuyler (G6) 14,182
Seneca (G5) 29,253
Steuben (F6) 91,439
Suffolk (F2) 276,129
Sullivan (L7) 40,731
Tioga (H6) 30,166
Tompkins (H6) 59,122
Ulster (M7) 92,621
Warren (N3) 39,205
Washington (O4) 47,144
Wayne (F4) 57,323
Westchester (D1) 625,816
Wyoming (D5) 32,822
Yates (F5) 17,615

### CITIES and TOWNS

Accord (M7)* 500
Adams (J3)* 1,762
Adams Center (H3)* 850
Addison (F6)* 1,920
Adirondack (N3)* 150
Afton (J6)* 875
Akron (C4)* 2,481
ALBANY (N5)* 134,995
Albany-Troy (urban area) 290,209
Albion (D4)* 4,850
Alden (C5)* 1,252
Alder Creek (K4)* 50
Alexander (D5)* 304
Alexandria Bay (J2)* 1,688
Alfred (E6)* 2,053
Allegany (C6)* 1,738
Allentown (E6)* 500
Almond (E6)* 659
Alpine (G6)* 194
Altamont (M5)* 1,127
Altmar (J3)* 299
Alton (G4)* 350
Altona (N1)* 500
Amagansett (G2)* 1,000
Amber (H5) 130
Amenia (N7)* 1,300
Ames (L5)* 193
Amityville (E3)* 6,164
Amsterdam (M5)* 32,240
Ancram (N6)* 200
Andes (L6)* 430
Andover (E6)* 1,351
Angelica (E6)* 928
Angola (C5)* 1,936
Annandale-on-Hudson (N6)* 405
Antwerp (J2)* 846
Apalachin (H6)* 900
Appleton (C4)* 100
Apulia Station (H5)* 220
Arcade (D5)* 1,818
Ardsley (H1)* 1,744
Argyle (O4)* 351
Arkport (E6)* 701
Arkville (L6)* 600
Arlington (N7) 5,374
Asharoken ‡(E2) 116
Ashland (M6)* 275
Ashokan (M7)*
Ashwood (D4) 110
Athens (N6)* 1,545
Athol (N4)* 60
Atlanta (F5)* 500
Atlantic Beach (D3)* 2,000
Attica (D5)* 2,676
Au Sable Forks (N2)* 1,643
Auburn (G5)* 36,722
Aurora (G5)* 711
Ava (K4)*
Averill Park (O5)*
Avoca (F6)* 952
Avon (E5)* 2,412
Babylon (D2)* 6,015
Bainbridge (J6)* 1,505
Baldwin (B3)* 22,000
Baldwinsville (H4)* 4,495
Ballston Spa (N5)* 4,937
Bangor (M1)* 300
Barker (C4)* 523
Barnes Corners (J3)* 105
Barneveld (K4)* 331

## NORTH CAROLINA

Map on Page 78          Total Population 4,061,929

E. Lake (N3)* 100
E. Laport (D8)* 240
E. Laurinburg (G5)* 745
E. Lumberton (H5)* 1,106
E. Spencer (E3)* 2,444
Edenton (M2)* 4,468
Edgemont (D7)* 85
Edneyville (F8)* 500
Edward (M4)* 155
Efland (G2)* 500
Elams (K1)* 10
Elberon (J2)* 75
Eldorado (F4)*
Eldreth (D5) 50
Eleazer (F3)* 60
Elizabeth City (N2)* 12,685
Elizabethtown (H5)* 1,611
Elk Park (C7)* 545
Elkin (D2)* 2,842
Elkton (H6)*
Ellenboro (B4)* 537
Ellerbe (F4)* 773
Elliott (J5) 25
Elm City (K3)* 839
Elmwood (D3)* 300
Elon College (G2)* 1,109
Elrod (G5)* 135
Emerson (H6)* 85
Enfield (K2)* 2,361
Engelhard (O3)* 500
Enka (E8)* 1,792
Ernul (L4)* 150
Erwin (H4)* 3,344
Essex (J2)* 35
Estatoe (C7) 300
Ether (F4)* 50
Etowah (E8)* 400
Eufola (D3) 150
Eure (M2)* 200
Eureka (K3)* 192
Everetts (L3)* 244
Evergreen (H6)* 245
Ewart (B7)*
Fair Bluff (H6)* 1,056
Fairfield (N3)* 250
Fairmount (G6)* 2,319
Fairview (E8)* 300
Faison (J4)* 768
Faith (E3)* 490
Falcon (H4)* 245
Falkland (K3)* 174
Fallston (B4)* 500
Farmer (F3)* 125
Farmington (D3)* 300
Farmville (K3)* 2,942
Faro (K4) 140
Faust (E7) 100
Fayetteville (H4)* 34,715
Ferguson (C2)* 50
Fig (D6)* 75
Finley (D7) 100
Flat Rock (E9)* 1,000
Flats (C8)* 150
Fleetwood (D6)* 50
Fletcher (E8)* 500
Florence (M4)* 500
Folkstone (K5)* 100
Forbes (B7)* 253
Forest City (B4)* 4,971
Fork (E3)* 300
Fort Bragg (H4)* 16,000
Fountain (K3)* 451
Four Oaks (H4)* 942
Francisco (E2)*
Frank (C7)* 25
Franklin (C9)* 1,975
Franklinton (J2)* 1,414
Franklinville (F3)* 778
Freeland (J6)* 300
Fremont (J3)* 1,395
Frisco (O4)* 100
Fuquay Springs (H3)* 1,992
Furches (E6)* 150
Garland (J5)* 539
Garner (H3)* 1,180
Garysburg (K2)* 344
Gaston (K1)* 1,218
Gastonia (C4)* 23,069
Gates (M2)* 150
Gatesville (M2)* 323
Germanton (E2)* 118
Ghio (F5)* 104
Gibson (F5)* 609
Gibsonville (F2)* 1,866
Gilkey (B4)*
Glade Valley (C2)* 75
Glen Alpine (B3)* 695
Glen Raven (G2) 750
Glendale Springs (D6)* 200
Glendon (G4)* 110
Glenola (F3) 100
Glenville (D9)* 200
Glenwood (A3)*
Globe (D7)* 200
Gloucester (N5)* 130
Gneiss (D9)* 250
Godwin (H4)* 145
Gold Hill (E3)*
Gold Point (L3) 132
Goldsboro (K4)* 21,454
Goldston (G3)* 372
Graham (G2)* 5,026
Grainger (K4) 168
Grandview (B9) 75
Grandy (O2)* 500
Granite Falls (C3)* 2,286
Granite Quarry (D3) 591
Grantsboro (M4)* 1,500
Grassy Creek (E5)* 500
Greenmountain (B7)* 600
Greensboro (F2)* 74,389
Greensboro, (urban area) 82,719
Greenville (L3)* 16,724
Grifton (L4)* 510
Grimesland (L3)* 414
Grover (C4)* 535
Guilford (F2)* 500
Guilford College (F2)* 500
Gulf (G3)* 300
Gulrock (O4)* 51
Gupton (J2) 75
Halifax (K2)* 346
Halls Mills (E6) 300
Hallsboro (H6)* 300
Hamilton (L3)* 514
Hamilton Lakes ‡(F2) 882
Hamlet (F5)* 5,061
Hampstead (K6)*
Hamptonville (D2)* 150
Hanes (E2)* 1,000
Harbinger (O2)* 250
Harkers Island (M5)* 1,244
Harmony (D3)* 374
Harrellsville (M2)* 167
Harrell Store ‡(J5) 147
Harris (G9)* 110
Harrisburg (D4)* 300
Hassell (L3)* 137
Hasty (G5) 125
Hatteras (O4)* 700
Havelock (M5)* 4,500
Haw River (G2)* 1,175
Hawk (C7)*
Hayesville (C9)* 356
Hayne (H5) 40
Hays (C2)* 400
Haywood (G3) 169
Hazelwood (D8)* 1,769
Heathsville (K2) 150
Heaton (C6)* 50
Helton (D5)* 192
Hemlock (D5) 750
Henderson (J2)* 10,996
Hendersonville (F8)* 6,103
Hendrix (E7)* 150
Henrietta (B4)* 1,013
Hertford (N2)* 2,096
Hester (H2) 110
Hickory (C3)* 14,755
Hiddenite (C3)* 600
Higgins (B7)*
High Point (E3)* 39,973
High Rock (E3) 75
Highfalls (F4)* 310
Highlands (D9)* 515
Highshoals (C4)* 875
Hildebran ‡(B3)* 529
Hillsboro (G2)* 1,329
Hobbsville (M2)* 75
Hobgood (L2)* 603
Hobucken (N4)*
Hoffman (F4)* 398
Hollifield (A3) 200
Hollis (B4)* 65
Hollister (K2)* 200
Holly Springs (H3)* 406
Hollyridge (L6)* 1,082
Hookerton (K4)* 253
Hope Mills (H5)* 1,077
Hot Springs (E7)* 721
Houstonville (D2)* 150
Hubert (L5)* 40
Hudson (C3)* 922
Huntdale (B7)*
Huntersville (D4)* 916
Hurdle Mills (G2)* 200
Husk (D5)* 78
Icard (C3)* 1,100
Icemorler (D5)
Idlewild (E6)* 175
Indian Trail (D4)* 308
Inez (J2)* 40
Ingalls (C7)* 75
Ingold (J5)* 350
Iron Station (C4)* 232
Ivanhoe (J5)* 200
Jackson (L2)* 843
Jackson Springs (F4)* 246
Jacksons Creek (F3)* 100
Jacksonville (K5)* 3,960
James City (M4)* 750
Jamestown (F3)* 748
Jamesville (M3)* 529
Jarvisburg (O2)*
Jefferson (E6)* 359
Joe (E7)* 200
Johns (F5)* 300
Jonas Ridge (C7)*
Jonesville (D2)* 1,768
Joynes (C2)* 240
Julian (F3)* 300
Jupiter (E8) 136
Kannapolis (D4)* 28,448
Kelford (L2)* 405
Kelly (J6)* 100
Kenansville (K5)* 674
Kenly (J3)* 1,129
Kernersville (E2)* 2,396
Kerr (J5)* 40
Kill Devil Hills (O3)* 125
Kimesville (G3) 100
King (E2)* 1,000
Kings Creek (C3)* 300
Kings Mountain (C4)* 7,206
Kinston (K4)* 18,336
Kipling (H4)* 101
Kittrell (H2)* 189
Kitty Hawk (O2)* 300
Knightdale (J3)* 461
Knotts Island (O2)* 400
Kure Beach (K6)* 228
La Grange (K4) 1,852
Lagoon (J5)* 233
Lake Landing (O4)*
Lake Lure (A4)* 174
Lake Toxaway (E9)* 270
Lake Waccamaw (J6)* 575
Lakedale (H4) 4,000
Lakeview (G4)* 300
Landis (D3)* 1,827
Lansing (D5)*
Lasker (L2)* 177
Lassiter (J3) 35
Lattimore ‡(B4)* 286
Laurel Hill (F5)* 400
Laurel Park (E8) 302
Laurel Springs (E6)* 25
Laurinburg (F5)* 7,134
Lawndale (B4)* 964
Lawsonville (E2)* 200
Laxon (D6)* 61
Leaksville (F2)* 4,045
Leaman (F4)* 21
Leasburg (G2)* 400
Leechville (M3)* 200
Legerwood (B2)* 85
Leggett (K3) 200
Leicester (E7)* 750
Leland (J6)*
Lemon Springs (G4)* 200
Lenoir (C3)* 7,888
Letitia (B9)* 35
Lewarae (F5) 479
Lewiston (L2)* 339
Lexington (E3)* 13,571
Liberty (F3)* 1,342
Lilesville (F5)* 605
Lillington (H4)* 1,061
Lincolnton (C4)* 5,423
Linden (H4)* 194
Linville (C7)* 500
Linville Falls (A3)*
Linwood (E3)* 350
Little Switzerland (A3)* 400
Littleton (K2)* 1,173
Locust (E4) 216
Lola (N5)* 150
Longhurst (G2)* 1,539
Longisland (D3)* 350
Longview (C3)* 2,291
Longwood (J6)* 800
Loray (C3)* 115
Louisburg (J2)* 2,545
Lovill (D6)
Lowe (G5) 75
Lowell (C4)* 2,313
Lowgap (D1)* 500
Lowland (N4)* 200
Lucama (J3)* 405
Lumber Bridge (G5)* 154
Lumberton (G5)* 9,186
Lynn (F9)* 600
Mabel (C6)* 200
Macclesfield (K3)* 370
Mackeys (M3)* 250
Macon (J2)* 238
Madison (F2)* 1,789
Maggie (D8)*
Magnolia (K5)* 585
Maiden (C3)* 1,952
Mamers (G4)* 200
Mamie (O2)* 250
Manly (G4)* 280
Manns Harbor (O3)* 325
Manson (J2)* 40
Manteo (O3)* 635
Maple Hill (K5)* 75
Mapleton (L2)
Mapleville (J2) 50
Marble (C9)*
Margarettsville (L1)* 113
Marietta (G6)* 94
Marion (A3)* 2,740
Mars Hill (E7) 1,404
Marshall (E8)* 983
Marshallberg (N5)* 784
Marshville ‡(E4)* 1,258
Marston (F5)* 159
Mashoes (O3)*
Matthews (D4)* 589
Maury (K4)* 251
Maxton (G5)* 1,974
Mayodan (F2)* 2,246
Maysville (L5)* 818
Mc Adenville (D4)* 1,060
Mc Cain (G4)* 900
Mc Cullers (H3) 89
Mc Donalds (G5)* 78
Mc Farlan (E5)* 136
Mc Grady (E6)* 175
Mebane (G2)* 2,068
Melvin Hill (A4)* 150
Merrimon (M5)* 250
Merry Hill (M2)* 250
Merry Oaks (G3)* 160
Mesic (M4)* 425
Method (H3)* 350
Micaville (B7)* 200
Micro (J3)* 310
Middleburg (J2)* 217
Middlesex (J3)* 446
Middletown (O4)* 200
Midland (E4)* 250
Midway Park (L5)* 3,703
Milam (D6)* 50
Mill Spring (A4)*
Millbrook (H3)* 100
Millers Creek (E6)* 500
Milton (G1)* 317
Milwaukee (L2)* 302
Mineral Springs (D5)* 135
Minneapolis (C7)* 100
Mint Hill (D4)
Mocksville (D3)* 1,909
Momeyer (J3) 200
Moncure (G3)* 500
Monroe (E5)* 10,140
Montague (K6) 100
Montezuma (C7)* 75
Mooresboro (B4)*
Mooresville (D3)* 7,121
Moravian Falls (C2)* 375
Morehead City (M5)* 5,144
Morganton (B3)* 8,311
Morrisville (H3)* 221
Mortimer (B2)* 13
Morven (E5)* 601
Mount Airy (D1)* 7,192
Mt. Gilead (F4)* 1,201
Mt. Holly (D4)* 2,241
Mt. Mourne (D3)* 232
Mt. Olive (K4)* 3,732
Mt. Pleasant (E4)* 1,019
Mt. Vernon Springs (G3)* 90
Mount Zion (D7)* 100
Moyock (N1)*
Murfreesboro (M2)* 2,140
Murphy (C9)* 2,433
Nags Head (O3)*
Nakina (H6)* 350
Nantahala (C8)* 125
Nashville (K3)* 1,302
Nathans Creek (E6)* 75
Navassa (J6)* 500
Nebo (B3)*
Needmore (C8)* 200
Neuse (H3)*
New Bern (L4)* 15,812
New Holland (N4)* 50
New London (E4)* 285
Newhill (H3)* 232
Newhope (C2)* 25
Newland (C7)* 425
Newport (M5)* 676
Newsom (E3)
Newton (C3)* 6,039
Newton Grove (J4)* 374
Norlina (J2)* 874
Norman (F4)* 300
North Cove (B3)* 500
N. Harlowe (M5)* 300
N. Lumberton (H5) 423
N. Wilkesboro (C2)* 4,379
Northside (H2)* 100
Norwood (E4)* 1,735
Oak City (L3)* 518
Oak Ridge (F2)* 500
Oakboro (E4)* 631
Oakland (E9)* 200
Oakley (L3) 58
Ocracoke (O4)* 600
Old Dock (H6) 300
Old Fort (A3)* 771
Old Trap (O2)* 380
Olin (D3)* 60
Olivia (G4)* 450
Olyphic (H7) 50
Orange (H4) 50
Oriental (M4)* 590
Orrum (G6)* 162
Oteen (E8) 1,000
Otto (C9)* 100
Overhills (G4)* 50
Oxford (H2)* 6,685
Pactolus (L3)* 265
Paint Gap (B7)* 200
Palmyra (L2)* 67
Pantego (M3)* 275
Parker (D6)* 50
Parkersburg (J5)* 114
Parkton (H5)* 527
Parmele (L3)* 406
Parsonville (E6)* 250
Paschall (J1) 75
Passion (F9) 196
Patterson (B3)* 195
Peachland (E5)* 485
Pee Dee (F5)* 200
Peletier (L5)*
Pelham (G1)* 200
Pembroke (G5)* 1,212
Pendleton (L2)* 88
Penrose (E8)* 350
Pensacola (B8)* 150
Peoria (C6) 300
Phoenix (J6)
Pike Road (M3)* 250
Pikeville (J4)* 464
Pilot Mountain (D2)* 1,092
Pine Hall (F2)* 575
Pine Level (J4)* 602
Pinebluff (F4) 575
Pinehurst (F4) 1,016
Pineola (C7)* 350
Pinetops (K3)* 1,031
Pinetown (M3)* 301
Pineview (G4) 175
Pineville (D4)* 1,373
Piney Creek (E5)* 35
Pink Hill (K4)* 386
Pinnacle (E2)* 450
Pisgah (F3)* 60
Pisgah Forest (E9)* 900
Pittsboro (G3)* 1,094
Pleasant Hill (K1)* 200
Plumtree (C7)* 300
Plymouth (M3)* 4,486
Point Harbor (O2)* 110
Polkton (E4)* 459
Pollocksville (L5)* 420
Pomona (F2)* 1,500
Ponzer (N3)* 110
Poplar (B7)* 575
Poplar Branch (O2)* 325
Pores Knob (C2)* 150
Portsmouth (N4)* 15
Postell (B9) 120
Powells Point (O2)* 375
Powellsville (M2)* 250
Prentiss (D9)* 100
Price (F1)* 175
Princeton (J4)* 608
Princeville (L3) 919
Proctorville (H6)* 232
Prospect Hill (G2)* 110
Pungo (M3)* 200
Purlear (E6)* 60
Purvis (G5)*
Quitsna (L3) 210
Radical (E6) 50
Raeford (G5)* 2,030
RALEIGH (H3)* 65,679
Raleigh (urban area) 68,190
Ramsaytown (B7)* 100
Ramseur (F3)* 1,134
Randleman (F3)* 2,066
Ranger (B9)* 150
Ransomville (M4)* 170
Raynham (G5) 30
Red Oak (J2)* 250
Red Springs (G5)* 2,245
Reddies River (E6) 175
Reese (C6)* 1,450
Reidsville (F2)* 11,708
Relief (B7)* 129
Rennert (G5)*
Rex (H5)* 180
Reynolda (E2)* 300
Rhodhiss ‡(B3)* 923
Rich Square (L2)* 971
Richfield (E4)* 237
Richlands (K5)* 877
Ridgeville (G2) 45
Ridgeway (J2)* 250
Ringwood (K2) 60
Roanoke Rapids (K2)* 8,156
Roaring Gap (D2)*
Roaring River (C2)* 350
Robbins (F4)* 1,158
Robbinsville (C8)* 515
Roberdell (F5)* 451
Robersonville (L3)* 1,414
Rockfish (G5)* 150
Rockford (D2)* 225
Rockingham (F5)* 3,356
Rockwell (E3)* 852
Rocky Mount (K3)* 27,697
Rocky Point (K6)*
Rodanthe (P3)* 86
Roe (N5)* 215
Rolesville (J3)* 288
Rominger (C6)* 200
Ronda (D2)* 545
Roper (M3)* 793
Roseboro (J5)* 1,241
Rosehill (K5)* 896
Rosindale (J6) 35
Rosman (E9)* 535
Rougemont (G2)* 300
Rowland (G5)* 1,293
Roxboro (H2)* 4,321
Roxobel (L2)* 394
Royal (M4)* 250
Royall Cotton Mills (H2) 250
Ruffin (F2)* 530
Rufus (B3) 80
Rural Hall (E2)* 1,200
Ruth (A4)* 324
Rutherford College (B3)* 750
Rutherfordton (A4)* 3,146
Ryland (H2)* 50
Saint Pauls (H5)* 2,251
Salemburg (J4)* 435
Salisbury (D3)* 20,102
Salter Path (M5)* 300
Saluda (F9)* 547
Salvo (P3)* 77
Sandy Ridge (E1)* 200
Sanford (G4)* 10,013
Sapphire (E9)* 50
Saratoga ‡(K3)* 366
Saxapahaw (G3)* 660
Scaly (D9)* 200
Scotland Neck (L2)* 2,730
Scotts (D3)* 50
Scotts Hill (K6) 150
Scottville (E5)* 180
Scranton (N4)* 125
Seaboard (K1)* 745
Seagrove (F3)* 319
Sealevel (N5)*
Selma (J3)* 2,639
Semora (G3)* 250
Senia (C7)* 25
Seven Springs (K4)* 197
Severn (L2)* 340
Sevier (A3) 130
Shallotte (J7)* 493
Shannon (G5)* 150
Sharpsburg (K3)* 415
Shawboro (N2)* 150
Shelby (C4)* 15,508
Shelmerdine (L4) 32
Sherwood (D6)* 350
Shoals (E2) 250
Shooting Creek (C9)* 260
Shulls Mills (D7)* 175
Siler City (G3)* 2,501
Siloam (D2)* 250
Silverdale (L5)*
Simpson (Chicod*) (L3) 278
Sims (J3)* 207
Skyland (E8)* 1,200
Sly (D6)*
Smithfield (J3)* 5,574
Smithtown (E2) 182
Smyrna (M5)* 200
Sneads Ferry (L5)* 125
Snow Camp (G3)* 90
Snow Hill (K4)* 946
Snowden (N2)* 85
Sophia (F3)* 200
South Creek (M4)* 108
S. Mills (N2)*
S. Wadesboro (E5) 390
S. Pines (G4)* 4,272
Southmont (E3)* 500
Southport (J7)* 1,748
Southside (C4)* 250
Sparta (C1)* 820
Spear (C7)* 445
Speed (L3)* 103
Spencer (D3)* 3,242
Spies (F4)* 100
Spindale (B4)* 3,891
Spray (F1)* 5,542
Spring Hope (K3)* 1,275
Spring Lake (H4)* 3,500
Springfield (E6)* 50
Spruce Pine (C7)* 2,280
Stacy (N5)* 302
Staley (F3)* 236
Stanfield (E4)* 350
Stanley (C4)* 1,644
Stantonsburg (K3)* 627
Star (F4)* 677
State Road (D2)* 475
Statesville (D3)* 16,901
Stecoah (C8)* 160
Stedman (H4)* 424
Steeds (F4)* 50
Stella (L5)* 100
Stem (H2)* 217
Stokes (L3)* 217
Stokesdale (F2)* 400
Stoneville (F2)* 786
Stonewall (M4)* 272
Stony Point (C3)* 1,020
Stovall (H2)* 410
Straits (M5)* 100
Stratford (E5)* 16
Stumpy Point (O3)* 300
Sturgills (D5)*
Sugar Grove (C6)* 225
Suit (B9)* 150
Summerfield (F2)* 923
Summit (E6)* 50
Sunbury (M2)* 350
Supply (J6)* 207
Surf City (L6)
Swannanoa (F8)* 1,800
Swanns (G4) 30
Swanquarter (N4)* 212
Swansboro (L5)* 559
Sylva (D8)* 1,382
Tabor City (H6)* 2,033
Tamarack (D6)* 150
Tapoco (B8)* 100
Tarboro (K3)* 8,120
Tarheel (H5)* 200
Taylorsville (C3)* 1,310
Teacheys (J5)* 226
Terrell (C3)* 200
Thomasville (E3)* 11,154
Thurmond (D2)* 77
Tillery (K2)* 250
Timberlake (H2)* 200
Timberland (G4) 11
Toast (D2)* 1,401
Todd (D6)* 89
Toecane (B7)* 250
Toliver (D6)*
Tomahawk (J5)* 30
Topia (E5)* 69
Topton (C9)* 125
Townsville (J1)* 219
Traphill (D2)* 150
Trenton (L4)* 469
Trinity (F3)* 764
Triplett (D6)* 120
Troutmans (D3)* 613
Troy (F4)* 2,213
Tryon (A4)* 1,985
Tunis (M2) 200
Turkey (J4)* 223
Turnersburg (D3)* 75
Tyner (M2)* 150
Ulah (F3)*
Unaka (B9)*
Union (L2)
Union Grove (D2)* 125
Union Mills (B3)* 200
Unionville (E4) 124
University (G2)*
Upton (D7)* 93
Uree (A4) 100
Vade Mecum (E2)*
Valdese (B3)* 2,730
Vale (C3)* 200
Valle Crucis (C6)* 200
Vanceboro (L4)* 753
Vandemere (M4)* 475
Vannoy (E6)* 25
Varina (H3)* 593
Vass (G4)* 757
Vaughan (J2)* 181
Vein Mountain (A3) 75
Verona (K5)* 125
Vilas (C6)* 60
Waco ‡(C4)* 310
Wade (H4)*
Wadesboro (E5)* 3,408
Wadeville (E4)*
Wagoner (E6)* 200
Wagram (G5)* 397
Wake Forest (H3)* 3,704
Walkertown (E2)* 1,000
Wallace (J5)* 1,622
Wallburg (E3)* 165
Walnut (E7)* 450
Walnut Cove (E2)* 1,132
Walstonburg (K3)* 177
Wanchese (O3)* 1,000
Warne (C9)* 200
Warren Plains (J2)* 100
Warrensville (E6)* 120
Warrenton (J2)* 1,166
Warsaw (J4)* 1,598
Washington (M3)* 9,698
Washington Park (M3) 421
Watha (J5)* 222
Waves (P3)* 65
Waxhaw (D5)* 818
Waynesville (E8)* 5,295
Weaverville (E8)* 1,111
Webster (D8)* 142
Weeksville (N2)*
Welcome (E3)* 600
Weldon (K2)* 2,295
Wendell (J3)* 1,253
Wenona (M3)*
Wentworth (F2)* 100
West End (F4)* 850
W. Jefferson (D6)* 871
Westfield (D2)* 300
Wests Mill (D9)* 50
Whitakers (K2)* 962
White Lake (H5)* 400
White Oak (H5)* 125
White Plains (D2)* 500
Whitehall (Seven Springs*) (K4) 197
Whitehead (E6)* 250
Whiterock (E7) 100
Whiteville (H6)* 4,238
Whitnel (B3)* 1,405
Whittier (D8)* 400
Wilkesboro (C2)* 1,370
Willard (J5)*
Williamston (M3)* 4,975
Wilmington (J6)* 45,043
Wilson (K3)* 23,010
Wilsons Mills (H3)* 349
Windom (B7)* 100
Windsor (L2)* 1,781
Winfall (N2)* 421
Wingate (E5)* 793
Winnabow (J6)* 250
Winston-Salem (E2)* 87,811
Winston-Salem, (urban area) 91,493
Winterville (L3) 870
Winton (L2)* 834
Wise (J2)* 300
Wolf Mountain (D9)* 25
Wood (J2)* 128
Woodard (M3)* 325
Woodland (L2)* 590
Woodleaf (D3)* 500
Woodsdale (H2)* 200
Woodville (L2)* 387
Worthville (F3)* 550
Wrightsville Beach (K6)* 711
Wrightsville Sound (K6)* 500
Yadkin College (E3)* 82
Yadkin Valley (C2)* 12
Yadkinville (D2)* 820
Yanceyville (G2)* 1,391
Yellowcreek (B8)* 4
Youngsville (J2)* 619
Zebulon (J3)* 1,378
Zionville (D6)* 250
Zirconia (E9)*

*Map on Page 79*

## NORTH DAKOTA

*Total Population 619,636*

### 53 COUNTIES

Adams (F7) 4,910
Barnes (O5) 16,884
Benson (M3) 10,675
Billings (D5) 1,777
Bottineau (J2) 12,140
Bowman (C7) 4,001
Burke (E2) 6,621
Burleigh (J6) 25,673
Cass (R5) 58,877
Cavalier (N2) 11,840
Dickey (N7) 9,121
Divide (C2) 5,967
Dunn (E5) 7,212
Eddy (N4) 5,372
Emmons (K7) 9,715
Foster (N5) 5,337
Golden Valley (C5) 3,499
Grand Forks (P3) 39,443
Grant (G6) 7,114
Griggs (O5) 5,460
Hettinger (E7) 7,100
Kidder (L6) 6,168
La Moure (N7) 9,498
Logan (L7) 6,357
Mc Henry (J3) 12,556
Mc Intosh (L7) 7,590
Mc Kenzie (D4) 6,849
Mc Lean (G4) 18,824
Mercer (G5) 8,686
Morton (H6) 19,295
Mountrail (E3) 9,418
Nelson (O4) 8,090
Oliver (H5) 3,091
Pembina (P2) 13,990
Pierce (K3) 8,326
Ramsey (N3) 14,373
Ransom (P7) 8,876
Renville (G2) 5,405
Richland (R7) 19,865
Rolette (L2) 11,102
Sargent (P7) 7,616
Sheridan (K4) 5,253
Sioux (H7) 3,696
Slope (C7) 2,315
Stark (E6) 16,137
Steele (P4) 5,145
Stutsman (M5) 24,158
Towner (M2) 6,360
Traill (R5) 11,359
Walsh (P3) 18,859
Ward (G3) 34,782
Wells (L4) 10,417
Williams (C3) 16,442

### CITIES and TOWNS

Abercrombie (S7)* 244
Absaraka (P6)* 45
Adams (O3)* 411
Adrain (O6)* 55
Agate (L2)* 14
Akra (P2)* 25
Alamo (D2)* 192
Alexander (C4)* 302
Alfred (N6)* 150
Alice (P6)* 162
Alkabo (C2)* 70
Almont (H6)* 190
Alsen (N2)* 114
Alta (J5) 6
Ambrose (D2)* 286
Amenia (R6)* 127
Amidon (D7)* 82
Anamoose (K4)* 542
Aneta (P4)* 469
Anselm (R6) 22
Antelope (F6)* 23

Map on Page 80

## OHIO

**Total Population 7,946,627**

### 88 COUNTIES

**CITIES and TOWNS**

Aberdeen (C8)*........... 551
Ada (C4)*....................3,640
Adams Mills (G5)*........ 150
Adamsville (G5)*......... 164
Addison (F8)*............. 120
Addyston (B9)*............1,651
Adelphi (E7)*.............. 392
Adena (J5)*................1,517
Adrian (D3)*............... 65
Ai (C2)......................... 50
Aid (F8)*...................... 96
Akron (G3)*...........274,605
Akron (urban area)....365,130
Albany (F7)*............... 525
Alcony (B5)................. 106
Alexandria (E5)*......... 464
Alger (C4)*................. 943
Allensville (E7)*......... 105
Allentown (B4)............ 150
Alliance (H4)*.........26,161
Alpha (B6)*................ 300
Alvada (D3)*............... 89
Alvordton (A2)*.......... 335
Amanda (E6)*.............. 587
Amberley (C9)............. 885
Amboy (J2).................. 300
Amelia (D10)*............. 601
Amesville (F7)*........... 269
Amherst (F3)*............3,542
Amity (F5)................... 100
Amsden (D3)*.............. 151
Amsterdam (J5)*.........1,048
Andover (J2)*.............1,102
Anna (B5)*.................. 554
Ansonia (A5)*.............. 877
Antioch (H6)*.............. 112
Antiquity (G8)............ 100
Antrim (H5)*............... 85
Antwerp (A3)*............1,162
Apple Creek (G4)*....... 548
Apple Grove (G8)........ 125
Appleton (E5).............. 75
Aquilla (H2)................ 386
Arabia (F8)................. 75
Arcadia (D3)*.............. 529
Arcanum (A6)*............1,530
Archbold (B2)*............1,486
Arlington (C4)*........... 825
Arlington Hts. (C9)......1,312
Armstrong Mills (J6)*.. 135
Arnheim (C8)............... 33
Ash Ridge (C8)............ 64
Ashland (F4)*...........14,287
Ashley (E5)*............... 798
Ashtabula (J2)*.........23,696
Ashville (E6)*.............1,303
Assumption (B2)......... 75
Athalia (F8)*.............. 307
Athens (F7)*............11,660
Atlanta (D6)*.............. 180
Attica (E3)*................ 858
Attica Jct. (E3)........... 100
Atwater (H3)*.............. 750
Auburn (H3)................ 100
Augusta (J4)*.............. 300
Aultman (H4)............... 200
Aurora (H3)*............... 571
Austinburg (J2)*.........1,375
Austintown (J3)*......... 350
Ava (G6)*.................... 300
Avery (E3)*................. 50
Avon (F3)*..................2,773
Avon Lake (F2)*..........4,342
Ayersville (B3)............ 105
Bainbridge (D7)*......... 964
Bairdstown (C3).......... 188
Bakersville (G5)*......... 119
Baltic (G5)*................ 493
Baltimore (E6)*...........1,843
Bangs (F5)*................. 125
Bantam (B7)................. 100
Barberton (G4)*.........27,820
Barlow (G7)*............... 152
Barnesville (H6)*.........4,665
Barnhill (H5)............... 392
Bartlett (G7)*.............. 183
Barton (J5)*................1,300
Bascom (D3)*.............. 400
Basil (E6)*.................
Batavia (B7)*..............1,445
Batesville (H6)*........... 149
Bay Village (G9)*.........6,917
Beach City (G4)*.......... 940
Beachwood ‡(G3).........1,073
Beallsville (J6)*........... 410
Beaver (E7)*............... 285
Beaverdam (C4)*......... 450
Bedford (J9)*..............9,105
Belden (F3)................. 45
Belfast (D7)................. 100
Bellaire (J5)*............12,573
Bellbrook (C6)*........... 425
Belle Center (C4)*....... 889
Belle Valley (G6)*........ 458
Bellefontaine (C5)*....10,232
Bellevue (E3)*.............6,906
Bellville (E4)*.............1,355
Belmont (J5)*.............. 638
Belmore (B3)*.............. 216
Beloit (J4)*................. 778
Belpre (G7)*...............2,451
Bennetts Corners (G10) 500
Bentleyville ‡(H3)........ 152
Benton (G4)*............... 150
Benton (D4)................. 150
Benton Ridge (C4)*..... 337
Bentonville (C8)*......... 175
Berea (G10)*.............12,051
Bergholz (J4)*............1,035
Berkey (C2)*............... 239
Berlin (G4)*................ 310
Berlin Center (J3)*...... 193
Berlin Cross Roads (E7) 100
Berlin Heights (F3)*.... 613
Berne (H6)*................. 40
Berwick (D3)*.............. 100
Bethany (B7)*.............. 160
Bethel (B8)*................1,932
Bethesda (H5)*............1,158
Bettsville (D3)*........... 687
Beverly (G6)*.............. 723
Bexley (E6)*..............12,378
Bidwell (F8)*.............. 340
Big Plain (D6).............. 146
Big Prairie (G4)*......... 250
Birmingham (F3)*....... 300
Birmingham (H5)........ 55
Blachleyville (F4)........ 85
Blackfork (E8)*........... 420
Blacklick (E6)*............ 325
Bladen (F8)*............... 200
Bladensburg (F5)*....... 230
Blaine (J5)*................. 400
Blakeslee (A2)*........... 142
Blanchester (B7)*........2,109
Blissfield (G5)*........... 102
Bloomdale (D3)*.......... 592
Bloomfield (G5)........... 70
Bloomfield
(Bloomingdale*) (J5) 324
Bloomingburg (D6)*..... 623
Bloomingdale (J5)*...... 324
Bloomington (C6)........ 88
Bloomville (D3)*.......... 759
Blue Ash (C9)*............1,420
Blue Creek (D8)*......... 100
Blue Rock (G6)*........... 70
Bluffton (C4)*.............2,423
Bogart (E3)..................
Bolivar (G4)*.............. 776
Bono (D2)*..................
Boston (H10)*............. 350
Boston Heights (H3).... 646
Botkins (B5)*.............. 608
Bourneville (D7)*........ 195
Bowerston (H5)*.......... 522
Bowersville (C6)*......... 362
Bowling Green (C3)*..12,005
Bradford (B5)*............2,055
Bradley (J5)*............... 300
Bradner (C3)*.............. 924
Brady Lake ‡(H3)*....... 444
Branch Hill (B7)*......... 500
Brandon (F5)*..............
Brandt (B6)................. 200
Bratenahl (H9)............1,240
Brecksville (H10)*.......2,664
Bremen (F6)*...............1,187
Brewster (G4)*............1,618
Brice (E6)*.................. 182
Bridgeport (J5)*..........4,309
Bridgetown (B9)..........1,500
Brighton (F3).............. 107
Brilliant (J5)*.............2,066
Brimfield (H3)............. 500
Brinkhaven (F5)*......... 150
Bristolville (J3)*.......... 250
Broadview Hts. (H10)...2,279
Broadway (C5)*........... 210
Broadwell (G7)............ 90
Brokensword (E4)....... 100
Brook Park (G9)..........2,606
Brookfield (J3)*...........1,000
Brooklyn (H9)*............6,317
Brooklyn Hts. (H9)...... 931
Brookside (J5)............. 845
Brookville (B6)*...........1,908
Broughton (B3)........... 128
Brownhelm (F3)........... 107
Brunswick (G3)*..........
Bryan (A3)*.................6,365
Buchtel (F7)*.............. 569
Buckeye Lake (F6)*.....1,401
Buckland (B4)*............ 274
Bucyrus (E4)*............10,327
Buena Vista (C7)......... 89
Buena Vista (D8)*....... 200
Buffalo (G6)*.............. 700
Buford (C7)*............... 250
Burbank (F4)*.............. 393
Burghill (J3)*.............. 150
Burgoon (D3)*............. 223
Burkettsville (A5)*...... 211
Burlington (F9)............ 325
Burton (H3)*............... 932
Bushnell (J2)................ 170
Butler (F4)*................. 833
Butlerville ‡(B7).......... 152
Byer (E7)*................... 250
Byesville (G6)*...........2,236
Cable (C5)*................. 125
Cadiz (J5)*.................3,020
Cairo (B4)*................. 505
Calcutta (J4)................ 200
Caldwell (G6)*.............1,767
Caledonia (D4)*........... 655
Cambridge (G5)*........14,739
Camden (A6)*..............1,084
Cameron (J6)*............. 124
Camp Dennison (D9)*.. 350
Campbell (J3)*...........12,882
Campbellstown (A6)*... 98
Canal Fulton (H4)*......1,258
Canal Winchester (E6)*1,194
Canfield (J3)*..............1,465
Cannelville (G6).......... 250
Canton (H4)*............116,912
Canton (urban area)..173,215
Carbon Hill (F7)*......... 400
Carbondale (F7)*......... 400
Cardington (E5)*.........1,465
Carey (D4)*.................3,260
Carlisle (B6)*.............. 325
Carmel (D7)................. 40
Carpenter (F7)*........... 45
Carroll (E6)*............... 416
Carrollton (J4)*...........2,658
Carrothers (D3)*.......... 110
Casstown (B5)*............ 368
Castalia (E3)*.............. 736
Castine (A6)*............... 146
Catawba (C6)*.............. 313
Catawba Island (E2).... 200
Cebee (F8)..................
Cecil (A3)*.................. 266
Cedarville (C6)*..........1,292
Celina (A4)*.................5,703
Center Belpre (G7)*.... 150
Center Village (E5)..... 120
Centerburg (E5)*......... 887
Centerfield (C7)........... 69
Centerville (B6)*.......... 827
Centerville (Thurman*)
(F8) ......................... 142
Chagrin Falls (J9)*......3,085
Chambersburg
(F8) ......................... 225
Chandlersville (G6)*.... 140
Chardon (H2)*.............2,478
Charlestown (H3)........ 225
Chatfield (E4)*............ 204
Chatham (G3).............. 250
Chattanooga (A4)........ 150
Chauncey (F7)*...........1,016
Cherry Fork (C8)*........ 197
Cherry Grove (C10)...... 250
Chesapeake (E9)*........1,285
Cheshire (F8)*............. 300
Cheshire (E5)............... 99
Chester (G7)*.............. 184
Chesterhill (G6)*......... 426
Chesterland (H2)*........ 300
Chesterville (E5)*........ 208
Cheviot (B9)................9,944
Chickasaw (A5)*.......... 166
Chillicothe (E7)*........20,133
Chilo (B8)*.................. 250
Chippewa Lake (G3)*... 107
Christiansburg (C5)*.... 666
Churchill (J3).............. 100
Cincinnati (B9)*........503,998
Cincinnati (urban
area) ......................808,021
Circleville (D6)*...........8,723
Claiborne (D5)............. 112
Clarington (J6)*.......... 478
Clark (G5)*................. 250
Clarksburg (D7)*......... 391
Clarkson (J4).............. 68
Clarksville (C7)*.......... 510
Clay Center (D2)*....... 590
Claysville (G6)*........... 55
Clayton (B6)*.............. 466
Cleveland (H9)*........914,808
Cleveland (urban
area) .................1,372,274
Cleveland Hts. (J9)*...59,141
Cleves (B9)*................1,981
Clifton (C6)*................ 220
Clinton (G4)*............... 397
Cloverdale (B3)*.......... 200
Clyde (E3)*..................4,083
Coal Grove (E9)*..........2,492
Coalton (E7)*............... 628
Coldwater (A5)*...........2,217
Colebrook (J2)*............ 70
College Corner (A6)*.... 468
Collins (E3)*................ 250
Collinsville (A6)*......... 176
Colton (C3)*................ 135
Columbia Station
(G10)* ....................... 58
Columbiana (J4)*.........3,369
COLUMBUS (E6)*.......375,901
Columbus (urban
area) .......................436,257
Columbus Grove (B4)*..1,936
Commercial Point(E6)* 238
Condit (E5)*................ 200
Conesville (G5)*........... 466
Congo (F6)*................ 300
Congress (F4).............. 186
Conneaut (J2)*...........10,230
Conover (B5)*.............. 130
Constitution (G7)*....... 100
Continental (B3)*.........1,023
Convoy (A4)*............... 910
Coolville (G7)*............. 469
Cooperdale (F5)*......... 100
Copley (G3)*............... 600
Corning (F6)*..............1,215
Cortland (J3)*.............1,259
Corwin‡ (B6)............... 326
Coshocton (G5)*.........11,675
Cove (E8)*.................. 25
Covington (B5)*...........2,172
Cozaddale (B7)*.......... 180
Craig Beach ‡(J3)........ 569
Creola (E7)*................ 75
Crescentville (C9)........ 100
Crestline (E4)*.............4,614
Creston (G3)*..............1,300
Cridersville (B4)*......... 684
Cromers (D3)*.............. 50
Crooksville (F6)*..........2,960
Croton (E5)*................ 356
Crown City (F8)*.......... 301
Cuba (C7)*................... 150
Cumberland (G6)*........ 537
Curtice (D2)*............... 500
Custar (C3)*................ 263
Cutler (G7)*................. 500
Cuyahoga Falls (G3)*..29,195
Cuyahoga Hts. (H9)..... 413
Cygnet (C3)*................ 527
Cynthiana (D7)*........... 110
Dalton (G4)*................ 938
Damascus (J4)*............ 700
Danville (F5)*.............. 853
Darbyville (D6)............ 203
Darrtown (A7).............. 215
Dawn (A5).................... 85
Dayton (B6)*...........243,872
Dayton (urban area)..343,781
Deavertown (G6)*........
Decatur (C8)*............... 170
Deer Park (C9).............7,241
Deerfield (H3)*............ 450
Deersville ‡(H5)*......... 149
Defiance (B3)*............11,265
Degraff (C5)*............... 972
Delaware (E5)*...........11,804
Delisle (A5)................. 55
Dellroy (H4)*............... 358
Delphos (B4)*..............6,220
Delta (B2)*..................2,120
Dennison (H5)*............4,432
Dent (B9)..................... 640
Derby (D6)*................. 300
Deshler (C3)*...............1,623
Deunquat (D4).............. 97
Dexter City (G6)*......... 170
Diamond (H3)*............. 300
Dillonvale (J5)*............1,407
Dixon (A4)*.................. 160
Dodgeville (J2)............ 100
Dola (C4)*................... 175
Donnelsville ‡(B6)....... 285
Dorset (J2)*................ 400
Dover (G4)*.................9,852
Dowling (C3)............... 100
Doylestown (G4)*.........1,358
Dresden (G5)*.............1,310
Dry Run (D8)............... 300
Dublin (D5)*................ 289
Dunbridge (C3)*........... 250
Duncan Falls (G6)*....... 575
Dundas (E7)*............... 300
Dunkinsville (C8)......... 75
Dunkirk (C4)*.............. 972
Dupont (B3)*............... 225
E. Canton (H4)*............1,001
E. Claridon (H2)*......... 350
E. Cleveland (J9)*.......40,047
E. Fultonham (F6)*....... 565
E. Greenville (G4)........ 450
E. Liberty (C5)*............ 425
E. Liverpool (J4)*........24,217
E. Orwell (J2)*............. 168
E. Palestine (J4)*.........5,195
E. Ringgold (E6)........... 120
E. Rochester (H4)*........ 250
E. Sparta (H4)*............ 811
Eastlake (J8)...............7,486
Eaton (A6)*.................4,242
Edenton (C7)*.............. 200
Edgerton (A3)*............1,246
Edison (E4)*................ 471
Edon (A2)*.................. 645
Eifort (E8)*................. 134
Elba (H6)*................... 150
Eldorado (A6)*............. 364
Elery (B3)................... 50
Elgin (A4)*.................. 126
Elida (B4)*.................. 607
Elizabethtown (A9)...... 100
Ellerton (B6)................ 160
Elliston (D2)*............... 130
Ellsworth (J3)*............. 200
Elmira (B2)*................ 125
Elmore (D3)*...............1,215
Elmwood Place (B9)*....4,113
Elyria (F3)*................30,307
Empire (J5)*................ 610
Englewood (B6)*.......... 678
Enon (C6)*.................. 462
Enterprise (F6)*........... 100
Era (D6)...................... 80
Erhart (G3).................. 90
Etna (E6)*................... 325
Euclid (J9)*...............41,396
Evansport (B3)*............ 250
Ewington (F8)*............. 64
Excello (B7)*................ 575
Fairborn (B6)*..............7,847
Fairhaven (A6)............. 290
Fairpoint (J5)*.............. 500
Fairport Harbor
(Fairport) (H2)*.........4,519
Fairview (G9)...............9,311
Fairview (H5)*.............. 192
Farmdale (J3)*.............. 202
Farmer (A3)*................ 200
Farmersville (A6)*........ 587
Fayette (B2)*...............1,003
Fayetteville (C7)*......... 401
Feesburg (B6)*............. 150
Felicity (B8)*................ 716
Findlay (C3)*..............23,845
Fitchville (E3).............. 157
Five Points (D6).........
Flat Rock (E3)*............ 325
Fletcher (B5)*.............. 515
Florida (B3)................. 227
Flushing (J5)*..............1,158
Fly (H6)*..................... 200
Footville (J2)................ 75
Foraker (C4)................ 110
Forest (C4)*................1,114
Forestville (C10)..........1,500
Fort Jennings (B4)*...... 330
Fort Loramie (B5)*....... 508
Fort Recovery (A5)*.....1,231
Fort Seneca (D3)*......... 155
Foster (C9)*................ 200
Fostoria (D3)*............14,351
Frank (E3)................... 100
Frankfort (D7)*............ 869
Franklin (B6)*..............5,388
Franklin Furnace (E8)* 450
Franklin Square (J4).... 110
Frazeysburg (F5)*........ 689
Fredericksburg (G4)*.... 517
Fredericktown (F5)*.....1,467
Freedom Station (H3)* 500
Freeport (H5)*............. 566
Fremont (D3)*............16,537
Fresno (G5)*................ 225
Friendship (D8)*.......... 500
Frost (G7)*.................. 29
Fruit Hill (C10)............ 300
Fryburg (B4)................ 45
Fulda (H6)................... 60
Fullertown (H2)........... 100
Fulton (E5)*................ 269
Fultonham (F6)*........... 232
Gahanna (E5)*.............. 596
Galena (E5)*................ 424
Galion (E4)*.................9,952
Gallipolis (F8)*.............7,871
Galloway (D6)*............. 300
Gambier (F5)*..............1,037
Ganges (E4)................. 120
Gann ‡(F5).................. 177
Garfield Hts. (J9)*......21,662
Garrettsville (H3)*.......1,504
Gates Mills (J9)*..........1,056
Geauga Lake (J10)*.....1,300
Geneva (J2)*................4,718
Geneva-on-the-Lake
(H2)* ........................ 388
Genoa (D2)*.................1,723
Georgesville (D6)......... 150
Georgetown (C8)*.........2,200
Germano (J5)*.............. 180
Germantown (B6)*........2,478
Getaway (F9)............... 100
Gettysburg (A5)*.......... 451
Ghent (B3)................... 75
Gibsonburg (D3)*.........2,281
Gilboa (C3)*................. 181
Gilmore (H5)*.............. 65
Girard (J3)*................10,113
Glandorf (B3)*.............. 479
Glen Roy (E7)............... 100
Glencoe (J6)*............... 500
Glendale (C9)*.............2,402
Glenford (F6)*.............. 180
Glenmont (F4)*............. 242
Glenwillow (J10)*.......... 257
Gloria Glens Park
‡(G3) ......................... 98
Glouster (F6)*..............2,327
Gnadenhutten (G5)*...... 895
Golf Manor (C9)...........3,603
Gomer (B4)*................ 300
Good Hope (D7)*.......... 300
Gordon (B6)*................ 197
Gore (F6)*................... 250
Grafton (F3)*...............1,194
Grand Rapids (C3)*...... 657
Grand River (H2)*......... 448
Grandview (H7)*........... 125
Grandview Hts. (D6).....7,659
Granville (E5)*.............2,653
Gratiot (F6)*................ 187
Gratis (A6)*................. 575
Graysville (H6)*........... 138
Graytown (D2)*............ 125
Green Camp (D4)*........ 388
Green Springs (E3)*.....1,082
Greenfield (D7)*...........4,862
Greenford (J4)*............ 245
Greenhills (B9)*............3,005
Greensburg (G4)*......... 550
Greentown (H4)*.......... 750
Greenville (A5)*...........8,859
Greenwich (E3)*...........1,204
Greer (F4).................... 95
Grelton (C3)*............... 145
Groesbeck (B9)............ 700
Grove City (D6)*...........2,339
Groveport (E6)*............1,165
Grover Hill (B3)*.......... 463
Gustavus (J3)............... 150
Guysville (G7)*............. 250
Gypsum (E2)*............... 650
Halls Corners ‡(J3)...... 254
Hallsville (E7)*............. 182
Hamden (F7)*............... 951
Hamersville (C8)*......... 380
Hamilton (A7)*...........57,951
Hamilton (urban
area) ........................63,021
Hamler (B3)*................ 490
Hamlet (B8).................. 200
Hammansburg (C3)....... 81
Hammondsville (J4)*.... 475
Hanford ‡(E6).............. 922
Hanging Rock (E8)*...... 465
Hannibal (J6)*.............. 500
Hanover (F5)*.............. 308
Hanoverton (J4)*.......... 344
Harbor View (D2)*....... 392
Hardin (B5).................. 50
Harlem Spgs. (J4)*....... 275
Harpersfield (J2)..........
Harpster (D4)*............. 236
Harriettsville (H6)*...... 175
Harrisburg (D6)*.......... 344
Harrison (A9)*.............1,943
Harrisonville (F7)*....... 100
Harrisville (J5)*........... 420
Harrod (C4)*............... 482
Hartford (J3)*.............. 225
Hartford (Croton*)
(E5) .......................... 356
Hartsgrove (J2)............ 575
Hartville (H4)*.............1,200
Harveysburg (C7)*........ 477
Haskins (C3)*.............. 469
Hatton (C3).................. 72
Havana (E3)*................ 93
Haverhill (E8)*............. 150
Haviland (A3)*............. 235
Haydenville (F7)*......... 800
Hayesville (F4)*........... 381
Hazelwood (C9)............ 500
Hebbardsville (F7)........ 75
Hebron (E6)*................ 864
Helena (D3)*................ 314
Hemlock (F6)*.............. 253
Hemlock Grove (F7)*.... 75
Hendrysburg (H5)*....... 300
Hepburn (D4)............... 120
Hicksville (A3)*............2,629
Higginsport (C8)*......... 385
Highland (C7)*............. 280
Highland Hts. ‡(H2)..... 762
Hill Grove (A5)............. 85
Hilliards (D5)*............. 610
Hills and Dales ‡(G4).. 125
Hillsboro (C7)*.............5,126
Hinckley (G3)..............1,796
Hiram (H3)*................. 986
Hockingport (G7)*........ 100
Holgate (B3)*...............1,092
Holland (C2)*............... 714
Hollansburg (A5)*........ 295
Holloway (H5)*............ 654
Holmesville (G4)*......... 392
Homer (E5)*.................
Homerville (F3)*.......... 110
Homeworth (J4)*.......... 600
Hooven (A9)*............... 550
Hopedale (J5)*............. 888
Hopewell (F6)*............. 225
Houcktown (C4)........... 110
Houston (B5)*.............. 150
Howard (F5)*............... 350
Hoytville (C3)*............. 340
Hubbard (J3)*..............4,560
Hudson (H3)*...............1,538
Hume (B4)*.................. 92
Hunting Valley ‡(H3).. 477
Huntsburg (H2)*.......... 112
Huntsville (C5)*........... 408
Huron (E3)*.................2,515
Iberia (E4)*................. 250
Idaho (D7)*................. 50
Independence (H9)*.....3,105
Indian Hill (C9)...........2,090
Irondale (J4)*.............. 775
Ironton (E8)*..............16,333
Irwin (D5)*.................. 183
Ithaca (A6)*................. 146
Ivorydale (B9)*............
Jackson (E7)*...............6,504
Jackson Center (B5)*... 698
Jacksonburgh ‡(A6)...... 114
Jacksontown (F6)*........ 257
Jacksonville (F7)*........ 657
Jaite (H10)*................. 71
Jamestown (C6)*..........1,345
Jasper (D7)*................ 150
Jefferson (J2)*.............1,844
Jeffersonville (C6)*...... 865
Jelloway (F4)............... 100
Jenera (C4)*................ 316
Jeromesville (F4)*........ 513
Jerry City (C3)*............ 360
Jersey (E5).................. 140
Jerusalem (H6)*........... 175
Jewell (B3)*................. 225
Jewett (H5)*................1,019
Johnstown (E5)*...........1,220
Junction (A3)............... 75
Junction City (F6)*...... 805
Justus (G4)*................. 325
Kalida (B4)*................. 533
Kanauga (F8)*.............. 275
Kansas (D3)*................ 350
Keene (G5)*................. 150
Kelleys Island (E2)*...... 324
Kelloggsville (J2)......... 200
Kennard (C5)................ 75
Kensington (J4)*........... 500
Kent (H3)*..................12,418
Kenton (C4)*.................8,475
Kettlersville (B5)*........ 172
Kidron (G4)*................. 150
Kilgore (H5)*................ 116
Killbuck (G5)*.............. 767
Kimball (E3)*................ 75
Kimbolton (G5)*........... 228
Kings Creek (C5)........... 150
Kings Mills (B7)*.......... 650
Kingston (E7)*.............. 958
Kingsville (J2)*.............1,000
Kinsman (J3)*.............. 750
Kipton (F3)*................. 300
Kirby (D4)*.................. 164
Kirkersville (E6)*.......... 299
Kirkpatrick (D4)........... 55
Kirtland Hills (H2)....... 235
Kitts Hill (E8)*............. 90
Kossuth (B4)................ 75
Kunkle (A2)*................ 260
Kyger (F8)*.................. 110
La Fayette (C4)*.......... 444
La Rue (D4)*................ 793
Ladd (D8)*................... 80
Lafferty (H5)*............... 630
Lagrange (F3)*.............. 712
Laings (J6)*.................. 65
Lakeline (J8)................. 183
Lakemore (H3)*.............2,463
Lakeside Park (E2)*......1,034
Lakeview (C4)*............. 966
Lakeville (F4)*.............. 190
Lakeville (J2)................3,432
Lakewood (G9)*...........68,071
Lamartine (H5)*...........
Lancaster (E6)*............24,180
Landeck (B4)................ 119
Langsville (F7)*............ 50
Lansing (J5)*.................2,000
Latham (D7)*................ 100
Latty (A3)*................... 272
Laura (B6)*.................. 380
Laurel (B8)................... 100
Laurelville (E7)*........... 482
Lawrenceville (C6)........ 191
Lawshe (D8)*............... 180
Leavittsburg (J3)*.........2,533
Lebanon (B7)*...............4,618
Lees Creek (C7)*........... 150
Leesburg (D7)*............. 841
Leesville (H5)*.............. 297
Leesville Cross Roads
(E4) ........................... 214
Leetonia (J4)*................2,565
Leipsic (C3)*..................1,706
Lemert (D4)*................. 50
Lemoyne (D3)*.............. 155
Lena (B5)..................... 202
Leonardsburg (D5)*...... 63
Leroy (G3)*................... 320
Letart Falls (F8)*........... 400
Levering (E4)................ 75
Lewis Center (D5)*........ 200
Lewisburg (A6)*.............1,230
Lewistown (C5)*............ 250
Lewisville (H6)*............. 217
Lexington (E4)*............. 739
Liberty (B6).................. 175
Liberty Center (B3)*...... 816
Lightsville (A5)............. 50
Lilly Chapel (D6)*......... 250
Lima (B4)*...................50,246
Limaville (H4)*.............. 209
Lincoln Hts. (C9)...........5,531
Lindsey (D3)*................ 512
Linndale ‡(G3).............. 399
Lisbon (J4)*...................3,293
Litchfield (F3)*.............. 350
Lithopolis (E6)*............. 350
Little Hocking (G7)*.....
Little Sandusky (D4)...... 70
Little York (B6)............. 150
Lockbourne (E6)*.......... 376
Lockington (B5)............ 245
Lockland (C9)*..............5,736
Lockwood (J3)*............. 61
Locust Grove (D8)......... 118
Lodi (F3)*.....................1,523
Logan (F6)*...................5,972
London (C6)*.................5,222
Londonderry (H5).......... 46
Londonderry (E7)*......... 210
Long Bottom (G7)*........ 200
Lorain (F3)*..................51,202
Lore City (H6)*.............. 495
Loudonville (F4)*...........2,523
Louisville (H4)*..............3,801
Loveland (D9)*...............2,149
Lowell (H6)*.................. 638
Lowellville (J3)*.............2,227
Lower Salem (H6)*......... 126
Lucas (F4)*................... 573
Lucasville (E8)*............
Luckey (D3)*................. 764
Ludlow Falls (B6)*......... 277
Lynchburg (C7)*............ 972
Lyndhurst (J9)*..............7,359
Lyndon (D7)*................ 50
Lyons (B2)*................... 511
Lytle (B6).................... 200
Macedonia (J10)*........... 600
Mack (B9)..................... 870
Macksburg (G6)*........... 272
Macon (C8)*.................. 75
Madeira (C9)*................2,689
Madison (H2)*................1,127
Madison Mills (D6)........
Madisonburg (G4).......... 135
Magnetic Spgs. (D5)*..... 321
Magnolia (H4)*.............. 901
Maineville (B7).............. 182

## Map on Page 81

# OKLAHOMA

**Total Population 2,233,351**

### 77 COUNTIES

### CITIES and TOWNS

Spiro (N4)*....1,365
Springer (H6)*.... 325
Stafford (D3)*.... 60
Stanley (M5)*.... 50
Stapp (N5)....
Stecker (F5)*.... 60
Steedman (J5).... 75
Sterling (F5)*.... 447
Stidham (L4)*.... 46
Stigler (M4)*....2,125
Stillwater (J2)*....20,238
Stilwell (N3)*....1,813
Stonebluff (L3)*.... 300
Stonewall (K5)*.... 634
Strang (M2)*.... 201
Stratford (H5)*....1,065
Stringtown (L6)*.... 499
Strong City (C3)*.... 107
Stroud (J3)*....2,450
Stuart (K5)*.... 303
Sugden (G6)*.... 105
Sulphur (J5)*....4,389
Summerfield (N5)*.... 300
Sumner (H2)*.... 46
Sunkist (L6)*.... 15
Sweetwater (C4)*.... 60
Swink (M6)*.... 96
Tabler (G4)*....
Taft (M3)*.... 541
Tahlequah (M3)*....4,750
Tahona (N4)*.... 45
Talala (L1)*.... 210
Talihina (N5)*.... 965
Tallant (K1)*.... 130
Taloga (E2)*.... 430
Tamaha (N4)*.... 117
Tangier (C2).... 25
Tatums (H6)*.... 210
Tecumseh (J4)*....2,275
Tegarden (E1)*.... 14
Temple (F6)*....1,442
Teresita (N2)*.... 50
Terlton (K2)*.... 122
Terral (G7)*.... 616
Texanna (M4).... 25
Texhoma (D8)*....1,464
Texola (C4)*.... 265
Thackerville (H7)*.... 178
Thomas (E3)*....1,171
Three Sands (H1)*.... 50
Ti (L5)*.... 23
Tiawah (L2).... 100
Tip (M2)*.... 25
Tipton (D6)*....1,172
Tishomingo (J6)*....2,325
Tom (N7)*....
Tomy Town (N3).... 75
Tonkawa (H1)*....3,643
Tribbey (H4)*.... 100
Trousdale (H4)*.... 50
Troy (J6)*....
Tryon (J3)*.... 285
Tullahassee (L3)*.... 209
Tulsa (K2)*....182,740
Tulsa (urban area)....203,968
Tupelo (K5)*.... 376
Turkey Ford (N1)*.... 100
Turley (L2)*.... 200
Turpin (A1)*.... 175
Tushka (K6)*....
Tuskahoma (M5)*.... 325
Tuskegee (K3)*.... 84
Tussy (G6)*.... 96
Tuttle (G4)*.... 715
Tuxedo Park (L1)....1,179
Tyrone (E7)*.... 261
Ulan (L4)*.... 30
Uncas (H1)*.... 100
Union (G4)*.... 301
Utica (K7)*.... 100
Valliant (M6)*.... 661
Vanoss (J5)*.... 118
Velma (G6)*....1,034
Vera (L2)*.... 164
Verden (F4)*.... 508
Verdigris (L2)*.... 150
Vernon (L4)*.... 450
Veterans Village ‡(H2) 3,355
Vian (N4)*.... 927
Vici (D2)*.... 620
Vinco (H3).... 25
Vinita (M1)*....5,518
Vinson (C5)*.... 125
Virgil (M6).... 55
Vivian (L4).... 75
Wade (K7)*.... 150
Wagoner (M3)*.... 4,395
Wainwright (M3)*.... 138
Wakita (G1)*.... 440
Walters (F6)*....2,743
Wanette (H5)*.... 594
Wann (L1)*.... 99
Wapanucka (J6)*.... 592
Wardville (L5)*.... 89
Warner (M4)*.... 382
Warr Acres (G3)*....2,378
Warwick (H3)*.... 132
Washington (H4)*.... 292
Washita (F4)*.... 45
Washunga (J1).... 91
Watonga (F3)*....3,249
Watova (L1)*.... 250
Watson (N6)*.... 100
Watts (N2)*.... 267
Wauhillau (N3).... 48
Waukomis (F2)*.... 537
Waurika (G6)*....2,327
Wayne (H5)*.... 501
Waynoka (E1)*....2,018
Weatherford (E4)*....3,529
Weathers (L5).... 200
Webb (D3)*.... 33
Webb City (J1)*.... 284
Webbers Falls (M3)*.... 489
Welch (M1)*.... 483
Weleetka (K4)*....1,548
Welling (N3)*.... 77
Wellston (H3)*.... 643
Welty (K3)*.... 50
Wesley (L5)*.... 35
Westville (N2)*.... 781
Wetumka (K4)*....2,025
Wewoka (K4)*....6,747
Wheatland (G4)*.... 300
Wheeless (B8)*.... 15
Whitefield (M4)*.... 350
Whiteoak (M1)*.... 100
Whitesboro (N5)*....
Wilburton (M5)*....1,939
Wildcat (L3).... 147
Willard (C1).... 2
Williams (O4)*.... 200
Willis (J7)*.... 115
Willow (C4)*.... 223
Wilson (H6)*....1,832
Wirt (G6)*.... 700
Wister (N5)*.... 729
Wolco (K1)*.... 100
Woodford (H6)*.... 105
Woodville (J7)*.... 78
Woodward (D2)*....5,915
Wright City (M6)*....1,121
Wyandotte (N1)*.... 242
Wybark (M3).... 50
Wynne Wood (H5)*....2,423
Wynona (K1)*.... 678
Yahola (L3).... 65
Yale (J2)*....1,359
Yanush (M5).... 156
Yarnaby (K7)*.... 200
Yeager (K4)*.... 180
Yewed (F1)*.... 100
Yonkers (M2)*.... 20
Yuba (K7)*.... 108
Yukon (G3)*....1,990
Zena (N2)*.... 25
Zincville (N1)*....
Zoe (N5)*.... 80

*Map on Page 82*

## OREGON

*Total Population 1,521,341*

### 36 COUNTIES

Baker (K3)....16,175
Benton (D3)....31,570
Clackamas (E2)....86,716
Clatsop (D1)....30,776
Columbia (D2)....22,967
Coos (C4)....42,265
Crook (G3)....8,991
Curry (C5)....6,048
Deschutes (F4)....21,812
Douglas (E4)....54,549
Gilliam (G2)....2,817
Grant (J3)....8,329
Harney (H4)....6,113
Hood River (F2)....12,740
Jackson (E5)....58,510
Jefferson (F3)....5,536
Josephine (D5)....26,542
Klamath (F5)....42,150
Lake (G5)....6,649
Lane (E4)....125,776
Lincoln (D3)....21,308
Linn (E3)....54,317
Malheur (K4)....23,223
Marion (E3)....101,401
Morrow (H2)....4,783
Multnomah (E2)....471,537
Polk (D3)....26,317
Sherman (G2)....2,271
Tillamook (D2)....18,606
Umatilla (J2)....41,703
Union (J2)....17,962
Wallowa (K2)....7,264
Wasco (F2)....15,552
Washington (D2)....61,269
Wheeler (G3)....3,313
Yamhill (D2)....33,484

### CITIES and TOWNS

Ada (D4)*.... 100
Adams (J2)*.... 154
Adel (H5)*.... 83
Adrian (K4)*.... 170
Agate Beach (C3)*.... 379
Agness (D5)*.... 48
Airlie (D3).... 30
Albany (D3)*....10,115
Albee (J2).... 7
Alfalfa (F3).... 25
Algoma (F5).... 50
Alicel (J2)*.... 30
Allegany (D4)*.... 220
Aloha (A2)*.... 50
Alpine (D3)*.... 325
Alsea (D3)*.... 130
Altamont (F5)....9,419
Alvadore (D3)*.... 130
Amity (D2)*.... 672
Andrews (J5)*.... 8
Anlauf (D4).... 50
Antelope (G3)*.... 60
Antone (H3)....
Applegate (D5)*.... 75
Arago (C4)*.... 117
Arcadia (K4)....
Arlington (G2)*.... 686
Arock (K5)*.... 100
Ash (D4).... 120
Ashland (E5)*....7,739
Ashwood (G3)*.... 50
Astoria (D1)*....12,331
Athena (J2)*.... 750
Aumsville (E3)*.... 281
Aurora (A2)*.... 242
Austin (J3).... 39
Azalea (D5)*.... 50
Baker (K3)*....9,471
Ballston (D2)*.... 100
Bancroft (D5).... 75
Bandon (C4)*....1,251
Banks (A1)*.... 376
Bar View (C2)*.... 200
Barlow (B2)*.... 75
Bartlett (K2)....
Barton (B2)....
Bates (J3)*.... 500
Bay City (D2)*.... 761
Bayocean (C2)*.... 75
Bayview (C3).... 15
Beatty (F5)*.... 50
Beaver (D2)*.... 567
Beavercreek (B2)*.... 60
Beaverton (A2)*....2,512
Beech Creek (H3)*.... 2
Belknap Springs (F3)*.. 12
Bellfountain (D3).... 50
Bend (F3)*....11,409
Berlin (E3)....
Bethany (A2).... 20
Beulah (J4).... 10
Big Eddy (F2).... 36
Biggs (G2)*.... 15
Birkenfeld (D1)*.... 100
Blachly (D3)*.... 24
Black Rock (D3).... 17
Blackbutte (E4)*.... 50
Blaine (D2)*.... 75
Blalock (G2)*.... 21
Blitzen (H5).... 7
Blodgett (D3)*.... 200
Blue River (E3)*.... 200
Bly (F5)*.... 800
Boardman (H2)*.... 120
Bonanza (F5)*.... 259
Bonita (A2).... 50
Bonneville (F2)*.... 250
Booth (C4)....
Boring (E2)*....
Bourne (J3)....
Boyd (F2)*.... 38
Breitenbush (F3)*.... 6
Bridal Veil (E2)*.... 120
Bridge (D4).... 200
Bridgeport (K3)*.... 63
Brighton (C2)*.... 107
Brightwood (E2)*.... 150
Broadacres (A3).... 30
Broadbent (C4)*.... 50
Brockway (D4)*.... 61
Brogan (K3)*.... 75
Brookings (C5)*....1,000
Brooks (A3)*.... 350
Brothers (G4).... 15
Brownlee (L3)....
Brownsboro (E5)*.... 100
Brownsville (E3)*....1,175
Buena Vista (D3).... 160
Bullards (C4)*.... 25
Burlington (A1).... 200
Burns (H4)*....3,093
Burnt Ranch (G3)....
Butte Falls (E5)*.... 372
Butteville (A2).... 50
Buxton (D2)*.... 150
Cairo (K4).... 50
Camas Valley (D4)*.... 60
Camp Namanu (E2)*.... 2
Camp Sherman (F3)*.... 50
Canary (D4).... 50
Canby (B2)*....1,671
Cannon Beach (D2)*....
Canyon City (J3)*.... 508
Canyonville (D5)*.... 861
Carlton (D2)*....1,081
Carnation (A2).... 100
Carpenterville (C5).... 30
Carson (K3)*.... 100
Carver (B2).... 200
Cascade Locks (F2)*.... 733
Cascade Summit (F4)*.. 50
Cascadia (E3)*.... 200
Cave Junction (D5)*.... 283
Cayuse (J2)*.... 48
Cecil (H2)*.... 20
Cedar Mill (A2).... 300
Celilo (G2).... 300
Central Point (D5)*....1,667
Chapman (D2).... 100
Charleston (C4)*.... 576
Chelsea (F5).... 300
Chemawa (A3)*.... 850
Chemult (F4)*.... 115
Cherry Grove (D2)*.... 375
Cherryville (E2)*.... 160
Cheshire (D3)*.... 73
Chiloquin (F5)*.... 668
Clackamas (B2)*.... 550
Clarno (G3)....
Clatskanie (D1)*.... 901
Claxtar (A3).... 100
Clem (G2).... 12
Clifton (D1)*.... 68
Cloverdale (D2)*.... 280
Coaledo (C4).... 125
Coburg (D3)*.... 693
Cochran (D2).... 50
Colestin (E5).... 7
Colton (B3)*.... 167
Columbia City (E2)*.... 405
Condon (G2)*.... 968
Coos Bay (C4)*....6,223
Copperfield (K3).... 13
Coquille (C4)*....3,523
Cornelius (A2)*.... 998
Cornucopia (K3)....
Corvallis (D3)*....16,207
Cottage Grove (D4)*....3,536
Courtrock (H3)*.... 60
Cove (K2)*.... 282
Cove Orchard (D2)*.... 140
Cow Creek (D5)....
Crabtree (E3)*.... 350
Crane (J4)*.... 99
Crater Lake (E5)*.... 47
Crawfordsville (E3)*.... 250
Crescent (F4)*.... 300
Crescent Lake (F4)*.... 50
Creston (K4).... 4
Creswell (D4)*.... 662
Crow (D4).... 100
Crowley (K4).... 5
Crystal (E5).... 15
Culp Creek (E4)*.... 260
Culver (F3)*.... 301
Curry (J3).... 4
Curtin (D4)*.... 70
Cushman (D4)*.... 150
Dairy (F5)*.... 50
Dale (J3)*.... 10
Dallas (D3)*....4,793
Danner (K5).... 20
Dawson (D3).... 40
Days Creek (D5)*.... 40
Dayton (A3)*.... 719
Dayville (H3)*.... 286
Dee (F2)*.... 250
Deer Island (E2)*.... 79
Delake (C3).... 644
Denmark (C5)*.... 13
Denzer (D3)....
Depoe Bay (C3)*.... 750
Deschutes (F3).... 20
Deter (E5).... 15
Detroit (E3)*....
Dexter (E4)*.... 400
Diamond (J4)*.... 8
Diamond Lake (E4)*....
Dillard (D4)*.... 300
Dilley (A2)*.... 200
Disston (E4)*.... 300
Divide (D4)....
Dixonville (D4).... 30
Dolph (D2).... 50
Donald (A3)*.... 187
Dora (D4).... 80
Dorena (E4)*.... 300
Drain (D4)*....1,150
Draperville (D3).... 201
Drew (E5)*.... 265
Drewsey (J4)*.... 50
Dryden (D5)*.... 25
Drylake (G4).... 18
Dufur (F2)*.... 422
Duncan (J2)*.... 18
Dundee (A2)*.... 308
Durham (A2).... 250
Durkee (K3)*.... 100
Eagle Creek (E2)*.... 75
Eagle Point (E5)*.... 607
Eastside (C4)*.... 890
Echo (H2)*.... 457
Eddyville (D3)*....
Eightmile (H2)....
Elgarose (D4).... 12
Elgin (K2)*....1,223
Elk City (D3)*.... 50
Elk Lake (F4)*....
Elkton (D4)*.... 201
Elmira (D3)*.... 500
Elmonica (A2).... 50
Elsie (D2)....
Empire (C4)*....2,261
Enright (D2).... 5
Enterprise (K2)*....1,718
Erskine (G2).... 7
Estacada (E2)*.... 950
Eugene (D3)*....35,879
Eula (E4).... 20
Evans (K2).... 47
Fair Grounds (A3)....
Fairview (B2)*.... 438
Fall Creek (E4)*.... 144
Falls City (D3)*.... 853
Faloma (B2).... 600
Fargo (A3).... 18
Farmington (A2).... 20
Faubion (F2).... 30
Ferndale (J2).... 225
Fields (J5)*.... 12
Fife (G4)....
Fisher (D3)....
Flora (K2)*.... 190
Florence (C4)*....1,026
Foleysprings (E3).... 4
Follyfarm (J4).... 5
Forest Grove (A2)*....4,343
Fort Klamath (E5)*.... 350
Ft. Rock (G4)*.... 18
Ft. Stevens (C1).... 60
Foss (D2).... 50
Fossil (G2)*.... 645
Foster (E3)*.... 350
Fox (H3)*.... 65
Freewater (J2)*....1,489
Frenchglen (H5)*.... 46
Friend (F2)*.... 15
Fruita (L2)....
Galena (J3).... 1
Gales Creek (D2)*.... 200
Galice (D5).... 40
Garden Home (A2)*.... 750
Gardiner (C4)*.... 600
Garibaldi (D2)*....1,249
Gaston (D2)*.... 368
Gates (E3)*.... 445
Gateway (F3)*.... 75
Gaylord (C5)*.... 135
Gearhart (C1)*.... 568
Gervais (A3)*.... 457
Gibbon (J2)*.... 52
Gladstone (B2)*....2,434
Glenada (C4).... 110
Glencoe (A1).... 10
Glendale (D5)*.... 871
Gleneden Beach (C3)*.. 185
Glenwood (D2)*.... 250
Glide (D4)*.... 100
Goble (E1)*.... 73
Gold Beach (C5)*.... 677
Gold Hill (D5)*.... 619
Gooch (E3).... 25
Goshen (D4)*.... 250
Government Camp (F2)* 100
Grand Ronde (D2)*.... 800
Granite (J3)*.... 40
Grant (G2).... 25
Grants Pass (D5)*....8,116
Grass Valley (G2)*.... 195
Green (D4).... 60
Greenburg (A2).... 20
Greenhorn (J3)....
Greenleaf (D3)*.... 111
Gresham (B2)*....3,049
Grizzly (G3).... 25
Gunter (D4).... 25
Gurdane (J2).... 18
Gwendolen (G2).... 6
Gypsum (K3)....
Haines (J3)*.... 321
Halfway (K3)*.... 312
Halsey (D3)*.... 388
Hamilton (H3)*.... 58
Hamlet (D2)*.... 20
Hammond (C1)*.... 522
Hampton (G4)*.... 22
Harbor (C5)*.... 600
Hardman (H2)*.... 58
Harlan (D3)*.... 240
Harney (J4).... 6
Harper (K4)*.... 200
Harriman (E5)*.... 42
Harrisburg (D3)*.... 862
Hauser (C4)*.... 158
Hay Creek (G3).... 15
Hayesville (A3)....2,697
Hebo (D2)*.... 250
Helix (J2)*.... 182
Hemlock (D2).... 20
Heppner (H2)*....1,648
Hereford (K3)*.... 66
Hermiston (H2)*....3,804
Hershal (K3).... 4
Hildebrand (F5)....
Hilgard (J2).... 40
Hillsboro (A2)*....5,142
Hillsdale (B2)*....
Hines (H4)*.... 918
Holbrook (A1).... 100
Holdman (J2).... 30
Holland (D5)*.... 100
Holley (E3)*.... 225
Home (K3)*.... 10
Homestead (L2).... 25
Hood River (F2)*....3,701
Hopewell (D2).... 125
Hopmere (A3).... 75
Horton (D3)*.... 168
Hot Lake (K2).... 25
Hubbard (A3)*.... 493
Huber (A2)*.... 250
Hugo (D5)*.... 100
Hullt (B3)....
Huntington (K3)*.... 733
Idanha (E3)*.... 442
Idaville (D2).... 150
Idleyld Park (D4)*.... 100
Illahe (C5)....
Imbler (J2)*.... 149
Imnaha (L2)*.... 30
Independence (D3)*....1,987
Ione (H2)*.... 262

Ironside (K3)*.... 150
Irrigon (H2)*.... 75
Irving (D3).... 300
Island City (K2)*.... 138
Izee (H3)*.... 4
Jacksonville (D5)*....1,193
Jamieson (K3)*.... 300
Jasper (E3)*.... 200
Jefferson (D3)*.... 636
Jennings Lodge (B2)*..3,500
Jewell (D2)*....
John Day (J3)*....1,597
Jordan Valley (K5)*.... 236
Joseph (K2)*.... 666
Junction City (D3)*....1,475
Juntura (K4)*.... 107
Kamela (J2).... 25
Keasey (D2)*.... 8
Keating (K3)*.... 10
Keno (F5)*.... 300
Kent (G2)*.... 60
Kerby (D5)*.... 150
Kernville (D3)*.... 105
Kerry (D1).... 30
Kimberly (H3)*.... 60
Kings Valley (D3)*.... 210
Kinzua (H3)*.... 900
Kirk (F5).... 25
Klamath Agency (F5)*.. 150
Klamath Falls (F5)*..15,875
Klondike (G2)*.... 6
Knappa (D1).... 100
La Grande (J2)*....8,635
La Pine (F4)*.... 250
Lacomb (E3)*.... 100
Lafayette (A2)*.... 662
Lake Grove (B2)*....4,000
Lakecreek (E5)*.... 30
Lakeside (C4)*....
Lakeview (G5)*....2,831
Langlois (C5)*.... 65
Latourell Falls (E2)*.... 72
Laurel (A2).... 30
Lawen (J4)*.... 15
Leaburg (E3)*.... 106
Lebanon (E3)*....5,873
Leland (D5).... 71
Leona (D4).... 50
Lewis (K2).... 2
Lexington (H2)*.... 237
Liberal (B3).... 40
Liberty (A3)....
Lime (K3)*.... 100
Lincoln Beach (C3)*.... 100
Linneman (B2).... 550
Linnton (A2)....
Linslaw (D4)*.... 75
Logan (B2).... 50
Logdell (H3).... 4
Logsden (D3)*.... 340
London (D4)....
Lonerock (H2)*.... 38
Long Creek (H3)*.... 288
Lookingglass (D4).... 100
Lostine (K2)*.... 178
Lowell (E4)*.... 700
Lyons (E3)*.... 600
Mabel (E3)*.... 85
Macksburg (B3).... 50
Macleay (A3).... 25
Madras (F3)*....1,258
Malheur (K3).... 25
Malin (F5)*.... 592
Manhattan Beach (D2)*
Manning (D2)*.... 100
Manzanita (C2)*.... 339
Mapleton (C3)*....1,016
Marcola (E3)*.... 800
Marial (D5)*.... 45
Marion (D3)*.... 200
Marquam (B3)*.... 70
Marshland (D1)*.... 120
Maupin (F2)*.... 312
Maxville (K2)....
Mayger (D1)*.... 95
Mayville (G2)*.... 102
Mc Coy (D2)*.... 75
Mc Credie Springs (E4)* 87
Mc Ewen (J3).... 25
Mc Kee (A3).... 75
Mc Kenzie Bridge (E3)* 195
Mc Kinley (D4)*.... 155
Mc Minnville (D2)*....6,635
Mc Nary (H2)*....
Meacham (J2)*....
Medford (E5)*....17,305
Medical Springs (K2)*.. 15
Mehama (E3)*.... 200
Melrose (D4).... 150
Merlin (D5)*.... 225
Merrill (F5)*.... 835
Metolius (F3)*.... 157
Metzger (A2)*....2,000
Middleton (A2).... 150
Midland (F5)*.... 85
Mikkalo (G2)*.... 125
Mill City (E3)*....1,792
Miller (G2)*.... 75
Millican (F4)*.... 5
Millington (C4).... 300
Milo (E5)*.... 300
Milton (J2)*....2,362
Milwaukie (B2)*....5,253
Minam (K2)....
Minerva (C3).... 25
Mission (J2).... 200
Mist (D1)*.... 269
Mitchell (G3)*.... 415
Modoc Point (F5)*.... 100
Mohawk (E3)*.... 20
Mohler (D2)*.... 100
Molalla (B3)*....1,497
Monitor (B3)*.... 50
Monmouth (D3)*....1,956
Monroe (D3)*.... 362
Monument (H3)*.... 228
Morgan (H2)*.... 10
Moro (G2)*.... 359
Mosier (F2)*.... 259
Mount Angel (B3)*....1,315
Mt. Hood (F2)*.... 59
Mt. Vernon (H3)*.... 451
Mountaindale (A1).... 50
Mowich (F4).... 20
Mulino (B2)*.... 275
Multnomah (B2)*....5,000
Murphy (D5)*.... 50
Myrtle Creek (D4)*....1,781
Myrtle Point (C4)*....2,033
Narrows (H4).... 7
Nashville (D3)*.... 25
Needy (B3).... 50
Nehalem (D2)*.... 270
Nelscott (D3)*.... 400
Neotsu (C2)*.... 300
Neskowin (D2)*.... 120
Netarts (C2)*.... 500
New Bridge (K3)*.... 51
New Era (B2).... 100
New Pine Creek (G5)*.. 200
Newberg (A2)*....3,946
Newport (C3)*....3,241
North Bend (C4)*....6,099
N. Junction (G3).... 2
N. Plains (A2)*.... 600
N. Portland (B1)*.... 340
N. Powder (K2)*.... 403
Norway (C4)*.... 250
Nyssa (K4)*....2,525
Oak Grove (B2)*....2,000
Oakland (D4)*.... 829
Oakridge (E4)*....1,562
O'Brien (D5)*.... 265
Oceanlake (C3)*.... 700
Oceanside (C2)*.... 150
Odell (F2)*.... 350
Odell Lake (F4).... 50
Olene (F5)*.... 35
Olex (G2)*.... 168
Olney (D1)....
Ontario (K3)*....4,465
Opal City (F3)....
Ophir (C5)*....
Ordnance (H2)*....
Oregon Caves (D5)*.... 2
Oregon City (B2)*....7,682
Orenco (A2)*.... 313
Oretown (D2)*.... 60
Oswego (B2)*....3,316
Otis (D2)*.... 200
Otter Rock (C3)*.... 100
Owyhee Corner (K4)....
Pacific City (C2)*.... 200
Paisley (G5)*.... 214
Palmer Junction (K2).... 3
Paradise (K2).... 42
Park Place (B2)*.... 500
Parkdale (F2)*.... 300
Parkers Mill (H2)....
Parkrose (B2)*....3,800
Paulina (G3)*....
Pedee (D3)....
Pendleton (J2)*....11,774
Pengra (E4)....
Peoria (D3).... 76
Perry (J2).... 125
Perrydale (D2)*.... 75
Phillips (A2).... 3
Philomath (D3)*....1,289
Phoenix (E5)*.... 746
Pilot Rock (J2)*.... 847
Pine (K3)*.... 73
Pinehurst (E5).... 6
Pistol River (C5)*.... 100
Placer (D5).... 48
Plainview (D3).... 20
Pleasant Valley (K3)*.. 30
Plush (H5)*.... 110
Pondosa (K2)*.... 150
Port Orford (C5)*.... 674
Portland (B2)*....373,628
Portland (urban area)....509,120
Post (G3)*....
Powell Butte (G3)*.... 661
Powell Valley (B2).... 725
Powers (D5)*.... 895
Prairie City (J3)*.... 822
Pratum (A3)*.... 44
Prescott (D1).... 119
Princeton (J4)*.... 6
Prineville (G3)*....3,233
Pringle (A3).... 250
Promise (K2)....
Prospect (E5)*.... 500
Prosper (C4).... 55
Provolt (D5)*.... 200
Quartz Mountain (G5).. 12
Quinaby (A3).... 100
Quincy (D1)*.... 400
Rainbow (E3).... 65
Rainier (E1)*....1,285
Rainrock (C3)....
Redland (B2).... 50

Redmond (F3)*............2,956
Reed (D3)....................
Reedsport (C4)*...........2,288
Reedville (A2)*............ 250
Remote (D5)*............... 60
Rex (A2)....................... 5
Richland (K3)*............ 220
Richmond (H3)*...........
Rickreall (D3)*............ 150
Riddle (D5)*................ 634
Rieth (J2)*.................. 325
Riley (H4)*.................. 5
Ritter (H3)*................. 107
Riverside (J4)*............ 38
Riverton (C4)*............. 125
Roberts (G3)................
Robinette (L3)*............ 20
Rockaway (C2)*...........1,027
Rockcreek (G2)............ 19
Rockton (A2)............... 150
Rockville (K4)............. 31
Rocky Point (A1)........
Rogue River (D5)*...... 590
Rome (K5).................. 50
Roosevelt Beach (C3)...
Rose Lodge (D3)*........ 150
Roseburg (D4)*...........8,390
Rowena (F2)............... 75
Rowland (D3).............. 15
Roy (A2)*.................... 48
Ruch (E5).................... 50
Rufus (G2)*................. 50
Rye Valley (K3)............ 25
Saginaw (E4)*.............
Saint Benedict (B3)*.... 230
St. Helens (E2)*..........4,711
St. Louis (A3)............. 30
Saint Paul (A3)*.......... 226
Saloda (D3)................. 12
SALEM (A3)*..............43,140
Sams Valley (E5)*........
Sandlake (C2)*............ 300
Sandy (E2)*................1,003
Scappoose (E2)*.......... 654
Scholls (A2)................ 70
Scio (E3)*.................. 448
Scofield (D2)............... 75
Scotts Mills (B3)*........ 217
Scottsburg (D4)*......... 100
Seal Rock (C3)*........... 330
Seaside (D2)*..............3,886
Selma (D5)*................ 125
Seneca (J3)*............... 760
Service Creek (G3)*..... 13
Shaniko (G3)*.............. 61
Shaw (A3)................... 150
Sheaville (K4)*............ 64
Shedd (D3)*................ 165
Shelburn (E3).............. 20
Sheridan (D2)*............1,922
Sherwood (A2)*........... 575
Shevlin (F4)................ 600
Siletz (D3)*................. 570
Siltcoos (C4)*.............. 28
Silver Lake (F4)*.........
Silverton (A3)*............3,146
Silvies (H3)*................
Simnasho (F3)*............ 40
Siskiyou (E5)............... 50
Sisters (F3)*................ 723
Sitkum (D4)*............... 50
Sixes (C5)*.................. 250
Sodaville (E3).............. 157
South Junction (G3)*.... 10
Southbeach (C3)*......... 300
Sparta (K3)*................ 25
Sprague River (F5)*..... 350
Spray (H3)*................. 375
Springbrook (A2)*........ 500
Springfield (E3)*........10,807
Springwater (E2).......... 300
Stanfield (H2)*............ 845
Star (E4).....................
Starkey (J2)................ 30
Stauffer (G4)............... 2
Stayton (E3)*..............1,507
Sublimity (E3)*............ 367
Summer Lake (G5)*..... 3
Summerville (K2)*....... 73
Summit (D3)*.............. 250
Sumner (C4)*.............. 141
Sumpter (J3)*............. 146
Sunny Valley (D5)*...... 79
Susanville (J3)*............ 9
Sutherlin (D4)*............2,230
Svensen (D1)............... 100
Sweet Home (E3)*........3,603
Swisshome (D3)*......... 500
Sycamore (B2).............
Sylvan (B2).................1,500
Table Rock (E5)........... 200
Taft (C3)*.................... 450
Takilma (D5)*............. 50
Talent (E5)*................ 739
Tallman (E3)................ 25
Tangent (D3)*............. 200
Telocaset (K2)*........... 80
Tenmile (D4)*.............. 40
Terrebonne (F3)*......... 198
The Dalles (F2)*...........7,676
Thompson (K3)............ 3
Thurston (E3)*............ 66
Tidewater (D3)*.......... 100
Tiernan (C3)*.............. 200
Tigard (A2)*................ 800
Tillamook (D2)*............3,685
Tiller (E5)*.................. 150
Timber (D2)*............... 300
Toledo (D3)*................2,323
Tolovana Park (C2)*.....
Top (H3)*.................... 27
Trail (E5)*................... 45
Trent (E4)*.................. 300
Troutdale (E2)*........... 541
Troy (K2)*.................... 150
Tualatin (A2)*.............. 248
Tumalo (F3).................. 50
Turner (E3)*................. 610
Twin Rocks (C2)*.......... 300
Tygh Valley (F2)*......... 449
Ukiah (J2)*................... 300
Umapine (J2)*.............. 50
Umatilla (H2)*.............. 883
Umpqua (D4)*.............. 20
Union (K2)*..................1,307
Union Creek (E5).......... 100
Unity (J3)*................... 212
Vale (K4)*....................1,518
Valley Falls (G5).......... 14
Valsetz (D3)*............... 60
Van (J4)*...................... 5
Vaughn (D3)................. 200
Venator (J4)................. 28
Veneta (D3)*................ 750
Verboort (A2)............... 125
Vernonia (D2)*.............1,521
Vida (E3)*..................... 250
Viento (F2).................... 50
Viola (B2)...................... 50
Waconda (A3)............... 50
Wagontire (H4)............. 3
Waldport (C3)*............. 689
Walker (D4)................... 100
Wallowa (K2)*...............1,055
Walterville (E3)*.......... 100
Walton (D3)*................ 70
Wamic (F2)*................. 125
Wapinitia (F2)............. 20
Warm Springs (F3)*.... 350
Warren (E2)*................ 81
Warrendale (F2)........... 50
Warrenton (C1)*..........1,896
Wasco (G2)*................. 305
Waterloo (E3)*............ 180
Waterman (H3)............
Wauna (D1)*................ 325
Weatherby (K3)............ 25
Wecoma Beach (C3)*.... 350
Wedderburn (C5)*........ 250
Welches (E2)*.............. 119
Wemme (E2)*.............. 109
Wendling (E3)*............ 124
West Linn (B2)*...........2,945
West Portland (B2)......3,000
W. Salem (A3).............
W. Side (G5)................ 16
W. Woodburn (A3)....... 150
Westfall (K3)*.............. 3
Westfir (E4)*................1,200
Westlake (C4)*............ 180
Weston (J2)*............... 679
Westport (D1)*............ 600
Wheeler (D2)*............. 291
Wheeler Heights (C2)... 125
Whiteson (D2)*............ 200
Whitney (J3)................ 3
Wilark (D2).................. 10
Wilbur (D4)*................ 150
Wilderville (D5)*.......... 300
Wilhoit (B3).................. 5
Wilkesboro (A2)............ 45
Willamette (B2)*..........
Willamina (D2)*............1,082
Williams (D5)*.............. 100
Willowcreek (K3)*........ 300
Willowdale (G3)............ 35
Willows (G2)................ 100
Wilsonville (A2)*.......... 162
Wimer (D5).................. 100
Winchester (D4)*......... 300
Winchester Bay (C4)*... 500
Wing (K3)....................
Winlock (H3)................ 12
Wolf Creek (D5)*.......... 250
Wonder (D5)*............... 300
Woodburn (A3)*............2,395
Woods (C2).................. 110
Worden (F5)*...............
Wyeth (F2)................... 15
Yachats (C3)*............... 300
Yamhill (D2)*................ 539
Yamsay Station (F4)....
Yaquina (C3)*............... 76
Yoder (B3).................... 150
Yoncalla (D4)*.............. 626
Zigzag (F2)*................. 150
Zumwalt (L2)................ 2

*Map on Page 83*

## PENNSYLVANIA

*Total Population 10,498,012*

### 67 COUNTIES

Adams (H6)................44,197
Allegheny (B5)........1,515,237
Armstrong (D4)..........80,842
Beaver (B4)..............175,192
Bedford (E6)..............40,775
Berks (K5)...............255,740
Blair (F4).................139,514
Bradford (J2).............51,722
Bucks (M5)...............144,620
Butler (C4).................97,320
Cambria (E4)............209,541
Cameron (F3)...............7,023
Carbon (L4)................57,558
Centre (G4)................65,922
Chester (L6)..............159,141
Clarion (D3)................38,344
Clearfield (F3)............85,957
Clinton (G3)................36,532
Columbia (K3)............53,460
Crawford (B2)............78,948
Cumberland (H5).........94,457
Dauphin (J5)..............197,784
Delaware (M6)...........414,234
Elk (E3).......................34,503
Erie (B2)....................219,388
Fayette (C6)..............189,899
Forest (D2)....................4,944
Franklin (G6)...............75,927
Fulton (F6)...................10,387
Greene (B6)..................45,394
Huntingdon (F5)............40,872
Indiana (D4)..................77,106
Jefferson (D3)...............49,147
Juniata (H4)..................15,243
Lackawanna (L3).........257,396
Lancaster (K5)............234,717
Lawrence (B4).............105,120
Lebanon (K5).................81,683
Lehigh (L4)..................198,207
Luzerne (L3)................392,241
Lycoming (H3).............101,249
Mc Kean (E2)................56,607
Mercer (B3)..................111,954
Mifflin (G4)....................43,691
Monroe (M3)..................33,773
Montgomery (M5)....353,068
Montour (J3)................16,001
Northampton (M4)....185,243
Northumberland
(J4) ........................117,115
Perry (H5)....................24,782
Philadelphia (M6)...2,071,605
Pike (M3).......................8,425
Potter (G2)....................16,810
Schuylkill (K4)...........200,577
Snyder (H4)..................22,912
Somerset (D6)..............81,813
Sullivan (J3)...................6,745
Susquehanna (L2)........31,970
Tioga (H2).....................35,474
Union (H4)....................23,150
Venango (C3)................65,328
Warren (D2)..................42,698
Washington (B5)........209,628
Wayne (M2)..................28,478
Westmoreland (D5)....313,179
Wyoming (K2)..............16,766
York (J6)....................202,737

### CITIES and TOWNS

Aaronsburg (H4)*......... 350
Abbottstown (J6)*........ 538
Adamsburg ‡(C5)*........ 238
Adamstown (K5)*.........1,020
Adamsville (B2)*.......... 200
Addison (D6)*.............. 237
Adrian (D4)*................ 130
Airville (K6)*................ 125
Aitch (F5)*................... 219
Akeley (D2)*................ 50
Akron (K5)*..................1,028
Alba (J2)*.................... 190
Albion (B2)*.................1,729
Albrightsville (L3)*...... 150
Alburtis (L5)*.............. 979
Aldan (M7)*..................3,430
Aldenville (M2)*........... 100
Alexandria (F4)*.......... 443
Aliquippa (B4)*...........26,132
Allen (H5)*.................. 395
Allenport ‡(C5)* ......... 923
Allensville (G4)*.......... 300
Allentown (L4)*.........106,756
Allentown-Bethlehem
(urban area)...........225,155
Allenwood (H3)*.......... 367
Allison Park (C4)*........2,000
Altoona (F4)*..............77,177
Altoona (urban area)..86,249
Alum Bank (E5)*.......... 342
Amberson (G5)*...........
Ambler (M5)*...............4,565
Ambridge (B4)*...........16,429
Amity (B5)*.................. 240
Andalusia (N5)*...........1,800
Anita (D3)*.................. 350
Annville (J5)*...............3,564
Ansonville (E4)*........... 158
Antes Fort (H3)*.......... 300
Antrim (H2)*................ 300
Apollo (D4)*.................3,015
Applewold ‡(C4)*......... 500
Ararat (L2)*................. 72
Arbuckle (C1).............. 25
Arcadia (E4)*.............. 500
Archbald (M2)*............6,304
Ardmore (M6)*...........20,000
Arendtsville (H6)*........ 409
Argentine (C3)*........... 150
Armagh ‡(E4)*............ 176
Arnold (C4)*................10,263
Arnot (H2)*.................. 300
Arona ‡(C5)*............... 482
Artemas (E6)*.............. 19
Ashland (K4)*...............6,192
Ashley (L3)*..................5,243
Ashville (F4)*............... 441
Aspers (H6)*................ 220
Aspinwall (C6)*............4,084
Atglen (K6)*................ 668
Athens (K2)*.................4,430
Athol (L5)*................... 200
Atlantic ....(B3)*......... 157
Atlas (K4)*....................3,090
Atwood ‡(D4)............... 110
Auburn (K4)*................ 994
Aultman (D4)*.............. 600
Austin (F2)*................. 804
Avalon (B6)*.................6,463
Avella (B5)*..................1,356
Avis (H3)*.....................1,193
Avoca (L3)*...................4,040
Avondale (L6)*.............. 941
Avonmore (C4)*............1,367
Baden (B4)*...................3,732
Bainbridge (J5)*........... 500
Bakers Summit (F5)*... 70
Bakersville (D5)............ 170
Bala-Cynwyd (N6)*......
Bally (L5)*.................... 753
Bangor (M4)*................6,050
Barnesboro (E4)*.........3,442
Barto (L5)*................... 151
Bartonsville (M4)*........ 150
Bath (M4)*....................1,824
Baxter (D3)*................. 87
Beach Haven (K3)*....... 500
Beachlake (M2)*.......... 250
Beadling (B7)*.............. 500
Beallsville (C5)*........... 598
Bear Creek (L3)*.......... 150
Bear Lake (C1)*........... 239
Beaver (B4)*.................6,360
Beaver Falls (B4)*......17,375
Beaver Meadows (L4)*.1,723
Beaver Spgs. (H4)*....... 750
Beaverdale (E5)*..........2,200
Beavertown (H4)*........ 700
Bechtelsville ‡(L5)*...... 603
Bedford (F5)*................3,521
Bedford Valley (E6)..... 300
Bedminster (M5)*......... 500
Beech Creek (G3)*....... 574
Belle Vernon (C5)*.......2,271
Bellefonte (G4)*...........5,651
Belleville (G4)*.............1,304
Bellevue (B6)*.............11,604
Bellwood (F4)*.............2,559
Ben Avon (B6)*.............2,465
Ben Avon Hts. ‡(B5).... 394
Bendersville (H6)*........ 409
Benezett (F3)*............. 400
Benson (Hollsopple*)
(E5) ......................... 377
Bentleyville (B5)*........3,295
Benton (K3)*................ 890
Berlin (E6)*..................1,507
Bermudian (J5)............ 50
Bernharts (K5)............. 760
Bernville (K5)*............. 363
Berrysburg (J4)*.......... 386
Berwick (K3)*.............14,010
Berwyn (L5)*................3,000
Bessemer (B4)*............1,461
Bethany (M2)............... 148
Bethel (K5)*................. 500
Bethel (B7).................11,324
Bethlehem (M4)*.........66,340
Bethlehem-Allentown
(urban area)...........225,155
Betula (F2)*.................. 90
Big Cove Tannery (F6)* 25
Big Run (E4)*............... 896
Bigler (F4)*.................. 500
Biglerville (H6)*........... 870
Birchardville (L2)*........ 35
Birdsboro (L5)*............3,158
Birmingham (F4)*........ 178
Black Lick (D4)*..........1,000
Blain (H5)*................... 315
Blairs Mills (G5)*......... 150
Blairsville (D5)*...........5,000
Blakely ‡(L3)................6,828
Blakeslee (L3)*............ 50
Blanchard (G3)*.......... 550
Blandburg (F4)*............1,200
Blawnox (C6)*...............2,165
Bloomfield (New
Bloomfield*) (H5).....1,098
Blooming Grove (M3)*.. 113
Blooming Valley (B2)... 256
Bloomsburg (J3)*........10,633
Blossburg (H2)*............1,954
Blue Ridge Summit
(G6)* ........................ 650
Blythedale (C5)*........... 890
Boalsburg (G4)*............ 500
Bobtown (B6)*..............1,553
Bodines (H3)*............... 110
Boiling Spgs. (H5)*...... 900
Bolivar (D5)*................ 828
Boltz (E5)*................... 250
Boothwyn (L7)*............4,500
Boston (C7)*.................1,700
Boswell (E5)*................1,679
Bowmansdale (J5)*...... 200
Bowmanstown (L4)*..... 878
Bowmansville (L5)*...... 350
Boyers (C3)*................ 800
Boyertown (L5)*...........4,074
Brackenridge (C4)*.......6,178
Brackney (K2)*............ 75
Braddock (C7)*............16,488
Braddock Hills (C7)......1,965
Bradford (E2)*.............17,354
Bradfordwoods ‡(B4)*.. 458
Braeburn (C4)*............ 800
Branch Dale (K4)*........1,500
Branchton (C3)*.......... 130
Brave (B6)*.................. 200
Brentwood (B7)*.........12,535
Briar Creek (K3)*........ 348
Brickerville (K5).......... 150
Bridgeport (M5)*..........5,827
Bridgeville (B5)*...........5,650
Bridgewater (W.
Bridgewater*) (B4)....1,316
Brisbin (F4)*................ 463
Bristol (N5)*...............12,710
Broad Ford (C5)*......... 112
Broad Top (F5)*.......... 483
Brockport (E3)*........... 450
Brockway (E3)*............2,650
Brodbecks (J6)*............ 50
Brodheadsville (M4)*.... 550
Brogueville (J6)*.......... 55
Brookhaven (M7)..........1,042
Brooklyn (L2)*.............. 500
Brookville (D3)*............4,274
Broomall (M6)*.............6,000
Broughton (B7)*...........2,500
Brownfield (C6)*..........
Brownstown (K5).......... 700
Brownstown ‡(E5)........1,508
Brownsville (C5)*..........7,643
Bruceton (B7)*............. 250
Bruin (C3)*................... 717
Bryn Athyn (M5)*........ 913
Bryn Mawr (M5)*.......12,000
Bucksville (M5)*.......... 200
Buffalo Mills (E6)*....... 105
Bulger (B5)*................. 800
Burgettstown (A5)*......2,379
Burlington (J2)*.......... 148
Burnham (H4)*.............2,954
Burnside (E4)*............. 400
Burnt Cabins (G5)*...... 125
Burrows (G2)............... 15
Bushkill (M3)*............. 500
Butler (C4)*................23,482
Byrnedale (E3)*........... 500
Cadogan (C4)*.............. 727
Cairnbrook (E5)*..........1,504
Caledonia (F3)............. 300
California (C5)*...........2,831
Callensburg (D3)*........ 261
Callery (C4)*................ 407
Cambra (K3)*............... 100
Cambridge Spgs. (C2)*.2,246
Cameron (F3)*............. 114
Cammal (H3)*.............. 120
Camp Hill (H5)*............5,934
Camptown (K2)*........... 300
Canadensis (M3)*........ 400
Cannelton (A4)*........... 100
Canonsburg (B5)*........12,072
Canton (J2)*..................2,118
Carbondale (L2)*.........16,296
Carlisle (H5)*...............16,812
Carlton (C3)*................ 50
Carmichaels (C6)*........ 895
Carnegie (B7)*............12,105
Carrolltown (E4)*.........1,452
Cashtown (H6)*............ 270
Cassandra (E5)*........... 381
Casselman (D6)............ 130
Cassville (G5)*............. 158
Castle Shannon (B7)*..5,459
Catasauqua (M4)*........4,923
Catawissa (K4)*............2,000
Cecil (B5)*....................1,200
Cedar Run (H2)*.......... 62
Center Moreland (K3)*.. 100
Center Road (A2)......... 35
Centerport ‡(K5)*........ 226
Centerville (C2)*.......... 245
Centerville (B6)............5,845
Central City (E5)*........1,935
Centralia (K4)*.............1,986
Centre Hall (G4)*......... 834
Cessna (F5)................. 50
Chalfant ‡(C7).............1,381
Chalfont (M5)*............. 828
Chambersburg (G6)*...17,212
Chambersville (D4)*...... 300
Chandlers Valley (D2)* 170
Chaneysville (F6).......... 80
Chapman ‡(M4)............ 285
Charleroi (C5)*..............9,872
Cheltenham (M5)*....△22,854
Cherry Tree (E4)*........ 517
Cherry Valley (C3)........ 94
Chest Springs (E4)*..... 232
Chester (L7)*...............66,039
Chester Hts. (L7)*........ 474
Chester Hill ‡(F4)......... 954
Cheswick (C6)*.............1,534
Cheyney (M6)*............. 289
Chicora (C4)*................1,172
Choconut (K2).............. 50
Christiana (K6)*............1,043
Churchill ‡(C7)..............1,733
Churchtown (L5)*......... 250
Clairton (C7)*...............19,652
Clarence (G3)*..............1,700
Clarendon (D2)*........... 748
Clarington (D3)*.......... 125
Clarion (D3)*.................4,409
Clark (B3)*................... 345
Clarks Green ‡(L3)*...... 824
Clarks Mills (B3)*........ 100
Clarks Summit (L3)......2,940
Clarksville (B6)*........... 428
Clarksville (Clark*)
(B3) ......................... 345
Claysburg (F5)*............1,355
Claysville (B5)*............ 963
Claytonia (B3).............. 50
Clear Ridge (F5)*........ 31
Clearfield (F3)*.............9,357
Clearville (F6)*............ 200
Cleona ‡(K5)*...............1,483
Clermont (E2)*............ 175
Clifford (L2)*................ 300
Clifton Heights (M7)*..7,549
Climax (D4)*................ 300
Clinton (B5)*................ 575
Clintondale (H3)........... 120
Clintonville (C3)*......... 307
Cloe (E4)*.................... 275
Clune (D4)*.................. 500
Clymer (E4)*.................2,500
Coal Center ‡(C5)*....... 584
Coal Valley (C7)*......... 700
Coaldale (L4)*...............5,318
Coaldale ‡(F5)............. 231
Coalmont ‡(F5)*.......... 207
Coalport (E4)*...............1,052
Coatesville (L5)*.........13,826
Coburn (H4)*................ 280
Cochranton (B2)*..........1,092
Cochranville (L6)*........ 350
Cocolamus (H4)*..........
Codorus (J6)*............... 449
Cogan Station (H3)*..... 39
Cokeburg (B5)*.............1,170
Cokeville (D5)*............. 600
Colegrove (F2)*............ 50
Collegeville (M5)*.........1,900
Colley (K2)*.................. 100
Collingdale (N7)*..........8,443
Colmar (M5)................. 600
Columbia (K5)*............11,993
Columbus (C2)*............
Colver (E4)*..................1,708
Colwyn ‡(M7)................2,143
Commodore (D4)*......... 450
Concord (G5)*.............. 190
Concordville (M6)*........ 126
Conemaugh (E5)*.........5,000
Conestoga (K6)*........... 480
Confluence (D6)*..........1,037
Conneaut Lake (B2)*.... 676
Conneaut Lake Park
(B2) ......................... 225
Conneautville (A2)*......1,177
Connellsville (D5)*.......13,293
Conoquenessing (B4)*... 441
Conrad (G2)................. 15
Conshohocken (M5)*....10,922
Conway (B4)*................1,570
Conyngham (K3)*......... 935
Cooksburg (D3)*.......... 50
Coopersburg (M5)*........1,462
Cooperstown (C2)......... 271
Coplay (L4)*..................2,994
Coral (D5)*................... 675
Coraopolis (B4)*..........10,498
Cornwall (K5)*..............1,760
Corry (C2)*....................7,911
Corsica (D3)*................ 421
Corydon (D2)*............... 250
Coryville (F2)*.............. 320
Costello (G2)................ 100
Coudersport (G2)*.........3,210
Courtdale ‡(L3)............ 982
Covington (J2)*............ 725
Cowan (H4).................. 105
Cowanesque (H2)*........ 200
Cowansville (C4)*......... 306
Crafton (B7)*.................8,066
Cranberry (C3)*............ 450
Cranesville (B2)*.......... 602
Creekside (D4)*............ 525
Creighton (C4)*............
Crenshaw (E3)*............
Cresco (M3)*................ 150
Cresson (E5)*................2,569
Cressona (K4)*..............1,758
Crosby (F2)*................. 400
Cross Fork (G3)*.......... 85
Cross Roads ‡(J6)......... 178
Crum Lynne (M7)*.........3,500
Cuddy (B5)*...................2,500
Curllsville (D3)*............ 156
Curryville (F5)*............. 150
Curwensville (E4)*.........3,332
Custer City (E2)*.......... 500
Cyclone (E2)*............... 700
Dagus Mines (E3)*....... 500
Daguscahonda (E3)*.... 190
Daisytown ‡(E5)........... 442
Dale ‡(E5).....................3,310
Dallas (K3)*...................1,674
Dallastown (J6)*............3,304
Dalmatia (J4)*.............. 517

Dalton (L2)*.....1,109
Damascus (M2)*.....300
Danielsville (M4)*.....
Danville (J4)*.....6,994
Darby (N7)*.....13,154
Darling (L7)*.....50
Darlington (A4)*.....354
Dauphin (J5)*.....667
Dawson (C5)*.....723
Dayton (D4)*.....828
De Lancey (D4)*.....300
De Young (E2)*.....85
Deemston ‡(B5).....775
Deep Valley (A6)*.....95
Deer Lake ‡(L4).....174
Delano (K4)*.....950
Delaware Water Gap (N4)*.....734
Delmont (D5)*.....695
Delta (K6)*.....840
Denbo (C6)*.....1,300
Dents Run (F3).....30
Denver (K5)*.....1,658
Derry (D5)*.....3,752
Devault (L5)*.....300
Dewart (J3)*.....350
Diamond (C2)*.....100
Dickinson (H5)*.....250
Dickson City (L3)*.....8,948
Dillsburg (J5)*.....1,146
Dilltown (E5)*.....200
Dimock (L2)*.....100
Dingmans Ferry (N3)*.....525
Dixonville (D4)*.....1,050
Donegal (D5)*.....198
Donora (C5)*.....12,186
Dormont (B7)*.....13,405
Douglassville (L5)*.....800
Dover (J6)*.....809
Downingtown (L5)*.....4,948
Doylestown (M5)*.....5,262
Dravosburg (C7)*.....3,786
Drexel Hill (M6)*.....40,000
Drifton (L3)*.....950
Driftwood (F3)*.....289
Drums (K3)*.....450
Dry Run (G5)*.....200
Du Bois (E3)*.....11,497
Dublin (M5)*.....400
Duboistown (H3).....1,140
Dudley (F5)*.....350
Duke Center (F2)*.....1,200
Dunbar (C6)*.....1,363
Duncannon (H5)*.....1,852
Duncansville (F5)*.....1,391
Dunkard (B6)*.....
Dunlevy ‡(C5)*.....379
Dunlo (E5)*.....2,200
Dunmore (L3)*.....20,305
Dunns Station (B5)*.....45
Dupont ‡(L3)*.....4,107
Duquesne (C7)*.....17,620
Duryea (L3)*.....6,655
Dushore (K2)*.....759
Eagles Mere (J3)*.....157
E. Bangor (M4)*.....988
E. Berlin (J6)*.....913
E. Brady (C3)*.....1,400
E. Butler (C4)*.....758
E. Conemaugh ‡(E5).....4,101
E. Freedom (E5)*.....325
E. Greenville (L5)*.....1,945
E. Hickory (D2)*.....232
E. Lansdowne ‡(M7).....3,527
E. Mauch Chunk ‡(L4)*.....3,132
E. McKeesport ‡(C5)*.....3,171
E. Petersburg (K5)*.....1,268
E. Pittsburgh (C7)*.....5,259
E. Prospect (J6)*.....500
E. Rochester ‡(B4).....985
E. Side (L3)*.....286
E. Smithfield (J2)*.....250
E. Springfield (A2)*.....499
E. Stroudsburg (M4)*.....7,274
E. Vandergrift ‡(C4)*.....1,665
E. Washington ‡(B5).....2,304
E. Waterford (G5)*.....185
Easton (M4)*.....35,632
Eastvale ‡(B4).....533
Eau Claire (C3)*.....403
Ebensburg (E5)*.....4,086
Echo (D4).....200
Eckley (L3)*.....650
Eddington (N5)*.....2,000
Eddystone (M7)*.....3,014
Eden Park (C7).....1,531
Edgewood (B7)*.....5,292
Edgeworth ‡(B4).....1,466
Edinboro (B2)*.....1,567
Edinburg (B3)*.....500
Edison (M5)*.....450
Edwardsville ‡(L3).....6,686
Effort (M4)*.....300
Elbon (E3)*.....150
Elco ‡(C5)*.....596
Eldersville (A5)*.....250
Elderton (D4)*.....336
Eldred (F2)*.....1,199
Eldredsville (J2)*.....20
Elgin (C2)*.....202
Elimsport (H3)*.....75
Elizabeth (C5)*.....2,615
Elizabethtown (J5)*.....5,083
Elizabethville (J5)*.....1,506
Elkins Park (M5)*.....12,000
Elkland (H1)*.....2,326
Elliottsburg (H5)*.....100
Elliottsville (C6).....120
Ellisburg (G2)*.....100
Ellport ‡(B4).....1,122
Ellsworth (B5)*.....1,670
Ellwood City (B4)*.....12,945
Elmhurst (M3)*.....800
Elmora (E4)*.....1,850
Elrama (C5)*.....1,675
Elverson (L5)*.....370
Elwyn (L7)*.....1,800
Elysburg (K4)*.....700
Embreeville (L6)*.....48
Emeigh (E4)*.....
Emigsville (J5)*.....650
Emlenton (C3)*.....945
Emmaus (M4)*.....7,780
Emporium (F2)*.....3,646
Emsworth (B6)*.....3,128
Endeavor (D2)*.....400
Enola (J5)*.....2,500
Enon Valley (B4)*.....392
Entriken (F5)*.....101
Ephrata (K5)*.....7,027
Equinunk (M2)*.....300
Erie (B1)*.....130,803
Erie (urban area).....151,282
Ernest (D4)*.....1,170
Erwinna (N5)*.....150
Espy (K4)*.....700
Espyville Station (B2)*.....75
Essington (M7)*.....3,700
Esterly (L5)*.....900
Etna (B6)*.....6,750
Etters (J5)*.....558
Evans City (B4)*.....1,637
Evansburg (Evans City) (B4).....1,637
Evansville (L5)*.....100
Everett (F5)*....., 97
Everson (C5)*.....1,520
Exeter ‡(L3)*.....5,130
Export (C5)*.....1,690
Factoryville (L2)*.....1,005
Fairchance (C6)*.....2,091
Fairdale (L2)*.....300
Fairfield (H6)*.....451
Fairhope (E6)*.....166
Fairmount Spgs. (K3).....50
Fairoaks (B4)*.....1,600
Fairview (B1)*.....697
Fairview ‡(C4).....259
Falls (L3)*.....315
Falls Creek (E3)*.....1,191
Fallsington (N5)*.....830
Fallston ‡(B4).....511
Fannettsburg (G5)*.....290
Farrell (A3)*.....13,644
Fawn Grove (J6)*.....397
Fayette City (C5)*.....1,404
Fayetteville (H6)*.....956
Felton (J6)*.....429
Ferndale (M4)*.....194
Ferndale (D5).....2,619
Fernwood (M7)*.....400
Fertigs (C3)*.....108
Finleyville (B5)*.....684
Fleetwood (L5)*.....2,338
Fleming (G4)*.....320
Flemington (G3)*.....1,446
Florence (A5)*.....150
Florin (J5)*.....1,319
Folcroft (M7)*.....1,909
Folsom (M7)*.....2,500
Force (E3)*.....500
Ford City (D4)*.....5,352
Ford Cliff (D4)*.....597
Forest City (L2)*.....3,122
Forest Hills ‡(C5)*.....6,301
Fort Littleton (F5)*.....117
Forestville (B3)*.....150
Forksville (J3)*.....145
Fort Loudon (G6)*.....500
Forty Fort (L3)*.....6,173
Fountain Hill ‡(M4).....5,456
Fox Chapel (C6).....1,721
Foxburg (C3)*.....422
Frackville (K4)*.....6,541
Frankfort Spgs. (A4).....149
Franklin (C3)*.....10,006
Franklin ‡(E5).....1,833
Franklintown (H5)*.....328
Fredericksburg (J5)*.....850
Fredericktown (C6)*.....1,000
Fredonia (B3)*.....588
Freeburg (H4)*.....506
Freedom (B4)*.....3,000
Freehold (D2).....120
Freeland (L3)*.....5,909
Freemansburg (M4)*.....1,739
Freeport (C4)*.....2,685
Friendsville (L2)*.....65
Frugality (F4).....63
Fryburg (D3)*.....300
Gaines (G2)*.....125
Galeton (G2)*.....1,646
Gallitzin (E4)*.....3,102
Ganister (F5)*.....253
Gap (L6)*.....850
Garards Fort (B6)*.....200
Garland (C2)*.....450
Garrett (D6)*.....761
Geistown (E5)*.....2,148
Gelatt (L2)*.....110
Genesee (G2)*.....600
Geneva (B2)*.....335
Georgetown (A4)*.....246
Germania (G2)*.....200
Gettysburg (H6)*.....7,046
Gibson (L2)*.....100
Gilberton (K4)*.....2,641
Gilbertsville (L5)*.....500
Gilfoyle (D3).....25
Gillett (J2)*.....200
Gipsy (E4)*.....300
Girard (B2)*.....2,141
Girardville (K4)*.....3,864
Glasgow (E4)*.....214
Glassport (C7)*.....8,707
Gleasonton (G3).....150
Glen Campbell (E4)*.....510
Glen Lyon (K3)*.....3,921
Glen Olden (M7)*.....6,450
Glen Riddle (L7)*.....300
Glen Rock (J6)*.....1,477
Glen Union (G3)*.....19
Glencoe (E6)*.....80
Glendon ‡(M4).....601
Glenfield (B6)*.....870
Glenhope (F4)*.....199
Gleniron (H4)*.....250
Glenshaw (C6)*.....8,000
Glenside (M5)*.....8,000
Glenwillard (B4)*.....1,200
Goldsboro (Etters*) (J5).....558
Gordon ‡(K4)*.....1,039
Gouldsboro (L3)*.....462
Graceton (D4)*.....500
Grampian (E4)*.....589
Grand Valley (D2)*.....
Granville (G4)*.....2,157
Grapeville (C5)*.....1,563
Grassflat (F3)*.....1,000
Gratz (J4)*.....653
Gray (D5)*.....600
Grays Landing (C6)*.....450
Graysville (B6)*.....300
Great Bend (L2)*.....751
Greeley (N3)*.....590
Green Lane (M5)*.....550
Greenburr (H4)*.....125
Greencastle (G6).....2,661
Greene (K6)*.....75
Greensboro (B6)*.....651
Greensburg (D5)*.....16,923
Greentree (B7).....2,818
Greenville (B3)*.....9,210
Grove City (B3)*.....7,411
Grover (J2)*.....200
Guys Mills (C2)*.....300
Hadley (B3)*.....350
Halifax (J5)*.....822
Hallstead (L2)*.....1,445
Hallton (E3)*.....75
Hamburg (L4)*.....3,805
Hamilton (D4)*.....100
Hamlin (M3)*.....250
Hampton (H6)*.....200
Hannastown (D5)*.....800
Hanover (J6)*.....14,048
Harborcreek (C1)*.....500
Harford (L2)*.....185
Harmarville (C6)*.....3,000
Harmonsburg (B2)*.....350
Harmony (B4)*.....912
HARRISBURG (J5)*.....89,544
Harrisburg (urban area).....168,933
Harrison Valley (G2)*.....400
Harrisonville (F6)*.....23
Harrisville (B3)*.....780
Hartleton ‡(H4).....240
Hartstown (B2)*.....160
Hartsville (M5)*.....
Harveys Lake (L3)*.....1,500
Hastings (E4)*.....1,846
Hatboro (M5)*.....4,788
Hatfield (M5)*.....1,624
Haverford (M6)*.....△39,641
Havertown (M6)*.....22,000
Hawk Run (F4)*.....
Hawley (M3)*.....1,602
Hawthorn (D3)*.....666
Haysville (B4).....177
Hazel Hurst (E1)*.....600
Hazleton (L4)*.....35,491
Hegins (K4)*.....
Heidelberg (B7).....2,250
Heilwood (E4)*.....1,000
Hellam (J6)*.....976
Hellertown (M4)*.....5,435
Helvetia (E3).....500
Hendersonville (B5)*.....600
Henryville (M3)*.....100
Hereford (L5)*.....225
Herman (C4)*.....700
Herminie (C5)*.....2,072
Herndon (J4)*.....677
Herrick Center (L2)*.....190
Hershey (J5)*.....4,500
Hesston (F5)*.....137
High Spire (J5)*.....2,799
Hilliards (C3)*.....230
Hillsdale (E4)*.....200
Hillsgrove (J3)*.....337
Hillsville (A4)*.....
Hokendauqua (L4)*.....1,460
Hollidaysburg (F5)*.....6,483
Hollsopple (E5)*.....377
Holtwood (K6)*.....500
Home (D4)*.....82
Homer City (D4)*.....2,372
Homestead (B7)*.....10,046
Homewood ‡(B4)*.....316
Honesdale (M2)*.....5,662
Honey Brook (L5)*.....864
Hookstown (B4)*.....247
Hooversville (E5)*.....1,240
Hop Bottom (L2)*.....375
Hopeland (K5)*.....400
Hopewell (F5)*.....360
Horning (B7).....500
Houston (B5)*.....1,957
Houtzdale (F4)*.....1,306
Howard (G3)*.....754
Hoytville (H2).....13
Hughestown ‡(L3).....1,888
Hughesville (J3)*.....2,095
Hummelstown (J5)*.....3,789
Hunkers ‡(C5)*.....404
Huntingdon (G5)*.....7,330
Huntington Mills (K3)*.....300
Hustontown (F5)*.....200
Hyde Park (D4)*.....758
Hydetown (C2)*.....530
Hyndman (E6)*.....1,322
Hyner (G3)*.....300
Ickesburg (H5)*.....250
Idaville (H5)*.....325
Imler (E5)*.....175
Immaculata (L6)*.....400
Imperial (B5)*.....1,895
Indiana (D4)*.....11,743
Industry (B4).....468
Inglesmith (F6).....14
Ingram (B7)*.....4,236
Intercourse (K5)*.....550
Irvine (D2)*.....300
Irvona (E4)*.....915
Irwin (C5)*.....4,228
Iselin (D4)*.....
Ivyland (M5)*.....358
Jackson (L2)*.....100
Jackson Center (B3)*.....266
Jacksonville ‡(D4).....204
Jacobus (J6)*.....706
James City (E2)*.....500
Jamestown (A3)*.....931
Jeanesville (K4)*.....500
Jeannette (C5)*.....16,172
Jeddo ‡(L3)*.....262
Jefferson (B6)*.....575
Jefferson (Codorus*) (J6).....449
Jenkintown (M5)*.....5,130
Jennerstown (D5)*.....376
Jermyn (L2)*.....2,535
Jerome (D5)*.....1,960
Jersey Mills (H3)*.....90
Jersey Shore (H3)*.....5,595
Jerseytown (J3)*.....165
Jessup (L3)*.....6,650
Johnsonburg (E3)*.....4,567
Johnstown (D5)*.....63,232
Johnstown (urban area).....92,780
Jollytown (B6)*.....100
Jones Mills (D5)*.....150
Jonestown (K5)*.....853
Josephine (D5)*.....675
Julian (G4)*.....196
Kane (E2)*.....5,706
Karns City (C4)*.....508
Karthaus (F3)*.....575
Kato (G3).....
Kaylor (C4)*.....300
Kearsarge (B1).....375
Keating Summit (F2)*.....70
Keewaydin (F3).....121
Kelayres (K4)*.....1,059
Kellettville (D2)*.....80
Kelly Station (C4)*.....81
Kempton (L4)*.....
Kenhorst ‡(L5).....2,551
Kennard (B3)*.....175
Kennett Square (L6)*.....3,699
Kent (D4)*.....175
Kerrmoor (E4)*.....120
Kersey (E3)*.....500
Kimble (M3).....72
Kimmelton (E5)*.....156
Kinsdale (H6).....103
Kingston (K3)*.....21,096
Kintnersville (M4)*.....77
Kinzua (E2)*.....475
Kirkwood (K6)*.....102
Kistler ‡(G5).....468
Kittanning (C4)*.....7,731
Knobsville (G6)*.....117
Knox (C3)*.....1,213
Knoxville (H2)*.....656
Koppel (B4)*.....1,137
Kresgeville (L4)*.....250
Kulpmont (J4)*.....5,199
Kulpsville (M5)*.....
Kunkletown (M4)*.....300
Kushequa (E2)*.....100
Kutztown (L4)*.....3,110
Kyler (E3).....
La Anna (M3).....120
La Jose (E4)*.....180
La Plume (L2)*.....50
Laceyville (K2)*.....505
Lackawaxen (N3)*.....450
Laflin ‡(L3).....256
Lairdsville (J3)*.....150
Lake Ariel (M3)*.....400
Lake Como (M2)*.....102
Lakemont (F5)*.....1,600
Lakewood (M2)*.....200
Lamar (H4)*.....225
Lamartine (C3)*.....250
Lampeter (K6)*.....443
Lancaster (K5)*.....63,774
Lancaster (urban area).....76,087
Landenberg (L6)*.....225
Lander (D2).....131
Landingville ‡(K4)*.....230
Landisburg (H5)*.....279
Lanesboro (M2)*.....591
Langdondale (F5)*.....300
Langeloth (A5)*.....1,068
Langhorne (N5)*.....1,579
Langhorne Manor ‡(N5).....781
Lansdale (M5)*.....9,762
Lansdowne (M7)*.....12,169
Lane (F4)*.....300
Lansford (L4)*.....7,487
Laporte (K3)*.....199
Larabee (F2).....50
Large (C7)*.....500
Larimer (C8)*.....1,057
Larksville ‡(L3).....6,360
Latrobe (D5)*.....11,811
Laurel (K6)*.....159
Laurel Gardens (B6)*.....1,200
Laurel Run ‡(L3).....858
Laureldale (L5)*.....3,585
Laurelton (H4)*.....375
Lavery (B2).....
Lawn (J5)*.....200
Lawrenceville (H2)*.....479
Lawton (K2)*.....140
Le Raysville (K2)*.....310
Le Roy (J2)*.....125
Lebanon (K5)*.....28,156
Lebanon Independent ‡(K5).....2,778
Lecontes Mills (F3)*.....200
Leechburg (C4)*.....4,042
Leeper (D3)*.....275
Leesburg (B3).....1,059
Leesport (K5)*.....700
Leetsdale (B4)*.....2,411
Lehighton (L4)*.....6,565
Lehman (K3)*.....580
Lemasters (G6)*.....325
Lemont (G4)*.....1,100
Lemont Furnace (C6)*.....
Lemoyne (J5)*.....4,605
Lenhartsville (L4)*.....229
Lenni Mills (L7)*.....200
Lester (M7)*.....2,100
Levittown (N5)*.....
Lewis Run (E2)*.....694
Lewisberry (J5)*.....299
Lewisburg (J4)*.....5,268
Lewistown (G4)*.....13,894
Lewisville (Ulysses*)(G2).....495
Lewisville (L6)*.....200
Liberty (H2)*.....271
Liberty (C7).....1,900
Library (B7)*.....2,124
Ligonier (D5)*.....2,160
Lilly (E5)*.....1,898
Lima (L7)*.....580
Lincoln (K5)*.....930
Lincoln University (L6).....
Linden (H3)*.....262
Linesville (A2)*.....1,246
Linfield (L5)*.....1,025
Linglestown (J5)*.....400
Linwood (L7)*.....5,000
Listie (D5)*.....700
Listonburg (D6)*.....145
Lititz (K5)*.....5,568
Little Marsh (H2)*.....100
Little Meadows (K2)*.....196
Littlestown (H6)*.....2,635
Livermore ‡(D5).....57
Liverpool (H4)*.....654
Livonia (H4)*.....32
Lock Haven (H3)*.....11,381
Loganton (H3)*.....346
Loganville (J6)*.....569
Long Branch ‡(C5).....450
Long Pond (L3)*.....50
Lookout (M2)*.....300
Lopez (K3)*.....800
Lorain ‡(E5).....1,406
Lords Valley (N3)*.....
Loretto (E4)*.....863
Lottsville (D2).....150
Loyalhanna (D5)*.....500
Loyalton (J4)*.....200
Loysburg (F5)*.....175
Loysville (H5)*.....500
Lucernemines (D4)*.....1,075
Lucinda (D3)*.....350
Ludlow (E2)*.....500
Lumber City ‡(E4).....262
Lumberville (N5)*.....225
Luthersburg (E3)*.....240
Luzerne (L3)*.....6,176
Lykens (J4)*.....2,735
Lyndora (B4)*.....4,800
Lyon Station (Lyons) (L5)*.....545
Macdonaldton (E6)*.....400
Mackeyville (H3)*.....200
Macungie (L4)*.....983
Maddensville (G5)*.....34
Madera (F4)*.....
Madison ‡(C5)*.....386
Madley (E6).....45
Mahaffey (E4)*.....646
Mahanoy City (K4)*.....10,934
Mainesburg (J2)*.....300
Malvern (L5)*.....1,764
Mammoth (D5)*.....500
Manchester (J5)*.....1,264
Manheim (K5)*.....4,246
Manns Choice (F6)*.....313
Manor (C5)*.....1,230
Manorville (C4)*.....662
Mansfield (J2)*.....2,657
Mapleton Depot (Mapleton) (F5)*.....742
Maplewood (M3)*.....130
Marcus Hook (L7)*.....3,843
Marianna (B5)*.....1,269
Marienville (D3)*.....1,000
Marietta (J5)*.....2,442
Marion (G6)*.....650
Marion Center (D4)*.....433
Marion Heights ‡(K4).....1,551
Marklesburg (Aitch*) (F5).....219
Markleton (D6)*.....92
Markleysburg (C6)*.....291
Mars (C4)*.....1,385
Marsh Hill (H3).....100
Marshalls Creek (M3)*.....
Martins Creek (M4)*.....1,000
Martinsburg (F5)*.....1,562
Marvindale (E2).....50
Marwood (C4)*.....125
Marysville (H5)*.....2,158
Masontown (C6)*.....4,550
Matamoras (N3)*.....1,761
Mattawana (G5)*.....253
Mauch Chunk (L4)*.....2,959
Mayburg (D2).....39
Mayfield (L2)*.....2,373
Mc Adoo (L4)*.....4,260
Mc Alisterville (H4)*.....515
Mc Clure (H4)*.....1,000
Mc Connellsburg (F6)*.....1,126
Mc Crea (H5)*.....150
Mc Donald (B5)*.....3,543
Mc Elhattan (H3)*.....175
Mc Ewensville ‡(J3)*.....297
Mc Gees Mills (E4)*.....112
Mc Kean (B2)*.....379
Mc Kees Rocks (B7)*.....16,241
Mc Keesport (C7)*.....51,502
Mc Lane (B2).....212
Mc Sherrystown (H6)*.....2,510
Mc Veytown (G4)*.....546
Meadow Lands (B5)*.....1,059
Meadville (B2)*.....18,972
Mechanicsburg (H5)*.....6,786
Mechanicsville ‡(K4).....540
Media (L7)*.....5,726
Medix Run (F3).....100
Mehoopany (K2)*.....250
Mercer (B3)*.....2,397
Mercersburg (G6)*.....1,613
Merion Station (M6)*.....2,000
Mertztown (L4)*.....200
Meshoppen (L2)*.....574
Mexico (H4)*.....275
Meyersdale (E6)*.....3,137
Middleboro (Mc Kean*) (B2).....379
Middleburg (H4)*.....1,283
Middlebury Center (H2)*.....90
Middleport (L4)*.....942
Middletown (J5)*.....9,184
Midland (A4)*.....6,491
Midway (B5)*.....993
Mifflin (H4)*.....835
Mifflinburg (H4)*.....2,259
Mifflintown (H4)*.....1,013
Milanville (M2)*.....200
Mildred (K3)*.....1,000
Milesburg (G4)*.....733
Milford (N3)*.....1,111
Mill Creek (G5)*.....417
Mill Hall (G3)*.....1,677
Mill Run (C6)*.....300
Mill Village (C2)*.....324
Millbourne ‡(M6).....901
Millersburg (J4)*.....2,861
Millerstown (H4)*.....682
Millerstown (Chicora*) (C4).....1,172
Millersville (K6)*.....2,551
Millerton (J2)*.....250
Millheim (G4)*.....750
Millmont (H4)*.....250
Millport (F2)*.....250
Millrift (N3)*.....206
Mills (G2)*.....150
Millsboro (B6)*.....1,100
Millvale (B7)*.....7,287
Millville (J3)*.....878
Millway (K5)*.....200
Milmont Park (M7)*.....2,200
Milroy (G4)*.....1,443
Milton (J3)*.....8,578
Mineral Point (E5)*.....350
Minersville (K4)*.....7,783
Mines (F5).....160
Modena ‡(L6).....824
Mohnton (L5)*.....2,004
Mohrsville (K5)*.....600
Mollenauer (B7)*.....700
Monaca (B4)*.....7,415
Monessen (C5)*.....17,896
Monongahela (B5)*.....8,922
Monroeton (Monroe) (J2)*.....466
Mont Alto (G6)*.....984
Montgomery (H3)*.....2,166
Montoursville (J3)*.....3,293
Montrose (L2)*.....2,075
Moon Run (B5)*.....1,143
Moosic (L3)*.....3,965
Morgantown (L5)*.....415
Morris (H2)*.....257
Morris Run (J2)*.....600
Morrisdale (F4)*.....1,000
Morrisville (N5)*.....6,787
Morton (M7)*.....1,352
Moscow (L3)*.....1,050
Mosgrove (D4).....
Moshannon (F3)*.....500
Mount Alton (E2)*.....105
Mt. Carbon ‡(K4).....302
Mt. Carmel (K4)*.....14,222
Mt. Gretna ‡(J5)*.....83
Mt. Holly Springs (H5)*.....1,701
Mt. Jewett (E2)*.....1,415
Mt. Joy (K5)*.....3,006
Mt. Lebanon (B7)*.....△26,604
Mt. Morris (B6)*.....
Mt. Oliver ‡(B7)*.....6,646
Mt. Penn ‡(L5).....3,635
Mt. Pleasant (D5)*.....5,883
Mt. Pocono (M3)*.....619
Mt. Union (G5)*.....4,690
Mt. Wolf (J5)*.....1,164
Mountainhome (M3)*.....750
Mountville (K5)*.....1,064
Moylan (L7)*.....300
Muir (J4)*.....950
Muncy (J3)*.....2,756
Muncy Valley (J3)*.....310
Munhall (C7)*.....16,437
Munson (F4)*.....460
Murrysville (C5)*.....800
Myerstown (K5)*.....3,050
Nanticoke (K3)*.....20,160
Nanty Glo (E5)*.....5,425
Narberth (M6)*.....5,407
Natrona (C4)*.....
Nazareth (M4)*.....5,830
Needmore (F6)*.....104
Neelyton (G5)*.....100
Neffs Mills (G4).....55
Nelson (H2)*.....
Nemacolin (B6)*.....1,800
Nescopeck (K3)*.....1,907
Nesquehoning (L4)*.....
New Albany (J2)*.....365
New Alexandria (C5)*.....523
New Baltimore (E6)*.....221
New Bedford (A3)*.....550
New Berlin (J4)*.....589
New Bethlehem (D3)*.....1,604
New Bloomfield (H5)*.....1,098
New Brighton (B4)*.....9,535
New Britain ‡(M5)*.....581
New Buena Vista (E5).....300
New Buffalo (H5)*.....155
New Castle (B3)*.....48,834
New Centerville (D6).....145
New Columbia (H3)*.....500
New Columbus ‡(L3).....152
New Cumberland (J5)*.....6,204
New Eagle (B5)*.....2,316
New Enterprise (F5)*.....317
New Florence (D5)*.....924
New Freedom (J6)*.....1,271
New Freeport (B6)*.....150
New Galilee (A4)*.....507
New Germantown (G5)*.....140
New Holland (K5)*.....2,602
New Hope (N5)*.....1,066
New Kensington (C4)*.....25,146
New Lebanon (B3).....179
New Milford (L2)*.....880
New Millport (F4)*.....200
New Oxford (H6)*.....1,366
New Paris (E5)*.....202
New Philadelphia (K4)*.....2,200
New Providence (K6)*.....220
New Ringgold ‡(K4)*.....302
New Salem (C6)*.....1,000
New Salem ‡(York New (D5).....695
New Salem ‡(York New Salem*) (J6).....333
New Tripoli (L4)*.....258
New Washington ‡(E4).....65
New Wilmington (B3)*.....1,943
Newburg (G5)*.....182
Newburg ‡(E4).....289
Newfield (G2).....100
Newfoundland (M3)*.....650
Newport (H5)*.....1,893
Newry (F5)*.....412
Newton Hamilton (G5).....397
Newtown (N5)*.....2,095
Newville (H5)*.....1,788
Nicholson (L2)*.....979
Nickleville (C3)*.....100
Nineveh (B6)*.....76
Nisbet (H3)*.....396
Normalville (D5)*.....250
Norristown (M5)*.....38,126
North Apollo (D4)*.....1,502
N. Belle Vernon ‡(C5).....3,147
N. Bend (G3)*.....100
N. Braddock ‡(C7).....14,724
N. Catasauqua ‡(M4).....2,629
N. Charleroi ‡(C5).....2,554
N. East (C1)*.....4,247
N. Girard (B1)*.....1,369
N. Irwin ‡(C5).....1,076
N. Mehoopany (K2)*.....120
N. Springfield (A1)*.....
N. Wales (M5)*.....2,998
N. Warren (D2)*.....900
N. York ‡(J5).....2,445
Northampton (M4)*.....9,332
Northumberland (J4)*.....4,207
Norvelt (D5)*.....
Norwood (M7)*.....5,246
Noxen (K3)*.....400
Nu Mine (D4)*.....2,000
Nuangola ‡(C4)*.....295
Nuremberg (K4)*.....1,200
Oak Hall Station (G4)*.....225
Oak Ridge (D3)*.....800
Oakdale (B5)*.....1,572
Oakford (N5)*.....1,900
Oakland (L2).....871
Oakmont (C6)*.....7,264
Oakville (H5)*.....116
Ohiopyle (D6)*.....345
Oil City (C3)*.....19,581
Oklahoma ‡(C4).....930
Olanta (E4)*.....125
Old Forge (L3)*.....9,749
Oley (L5)*.....498
Oliver (C6)*.....2,180
Olyphant (L3)*.....7,047
Oneida (K4)*.....800
Ono (J5)*.....220
Orangeville (K3)*.....424
Orbisonia (G5)*.....648
Ore Hill (F5).....150
Ormsby (E2)*.....169
Orrstown (G5)*.....295
Orrtanna (H6)*.....300
Orson (M2)*.....250
Orviston (G3)*.....340
Orwigsburg (K4)*.....3,029
Osborne ‡(B5).....496
Osceola (H2)*.....300
Osceola Mills (F4)*.....1,992
Osterburg (E5)*.....200
Oswayo (G2)*.....167
Ottsville (M5)*.....817
Overton (K2)*.....
Oxford (K6)*.....3,091
Paint (E5).....1,547
Palmerton (L4)*.....6,646
Palmyra (J5)*.....5,910
Palo Alto ‡(K4).....1,767
Paoli (M5)*.....2,039
Paradise (K5)*.....600
Pardoe (B3)*.....200
Parker (C3)*.....979
Parkesburg (L6)*.....2,611
Parkside (M7).....1,637
Parryville ‡(L4)*.....598
Patterson Heights ‡(B4).....678
Patton (E4)*.....3,148
Paupack (M3)*.....250
Pavia (E5).....100
Paxtang ‡(J5).....1,857
Peach Bottom (K6)*.....80
Pen Argyl (M4)*.....3,878
Penbrook ‡(J5).....3,691
Penfield (E3)*.....831
Penn (C5)*.....987
Penndel ‡(N5)*.....1,100
Penn Run (D4)*.....232
Pennline (A2).....25
Penns Park (N5)*.....160
Pennsburg (M5)*.....1,625
Pennsdale (J3)*.....200
Pennsylvania Furnace (G4)*.....100
Pequea (K6)*.....121
Perkasie (M5)*.....4,358
Perrysville (B6)*.....1,500
Petersburg (G4)*.....621
Petrolia (C3)*.....571

Philadelphia (N6)* 2,071,605
Philadelphia (urban area) 2,913,516
Philipsburg (F4)* 3,988
Phoenixville (L5)* 12,932
Picture Rocks (J3)* 569
Pillow (J4)* 369
Pine Bank (B6)* 25
Pine Grove (K4)* 2,237
Pine Grove Furnace (H5) 40
Pine Grove Mills (G4)* 1,200
Pipersville (M5)* 125
Pitcairn (C5)* 5,857
Pittock (B7)* 2,600
Pittsburgh (B7)* 676,806
Pittsburgh (urban area) 1,525,966
Pittsfield (D2)*
Pittston (L3)* 15,012
Plains (L3)* ▲12,541
Platea (B2)* 290
Pleasant Gap (G4)* 1,312
Pleasant Hills (B7) 3,808
Pleasant Mount (M2)* 438
Pleasantville (C2)* 704
Pleasantville ‡(E5) 242
Plumsteadville (M5)* 312
Plumville (D4)* 452
Plymouth (K3)* 13,021
Pocono Lake (L3)* 225
Pocono Pines (M3)* 475
Point Marion (C6)* 2,197
Point Pleasant (N5)* 400
Poland Mines (B6)*
Polk (C3)* 4,004
Pond Eddy (N3)*
Port Allegany (F2)* 2,519
Port Carbon (K4)* 3,024
Port Clinton (K4)* 451
Port Matilda (F4)* 685
Port Royal (H4)* 800
Port Trevorton (J4)* 280
Port Vue (C7) 4,756
Portage (E5)* 4,371
Portersville (B4)* 294
Portland (M4)* 551
Pottersdale (F3)* 325
Potterville (K2) 63
Pottstown (L5)* 22,589
Pottsville (K4)* 23,640
Powell (J2)* 300
Powelton (F4)* 315
President (C3) 100
Primos (M7)* 500
Pringle ‡(L3) 1,727
Proctor (J3)* 100
Prompton (M2)* 197
Prospect (B4)* 726
Prospect Park (M7)* 5,834
Pulaski (B3)* 350
Punxsutawney (E4)* 8,969
Quakertown (M5)* 5,673
Quarryville (K6)* 1,187
Quecreek (D5)* 550
Queen (E5)* 200
Racine (B4)* 500
Railroad (J6)* 300
Rainsburg (F6) 189
Ralphton (D5)* 225
Ralston (H2)* 700
Ramey (F4)* 696
Rankin (C7)* 6,941
Ravine (K4)* 250
Reading (L5)* 109,320
Reading (urban area) 154,571
Reamstown (K5)* 950
Rebersburg (H4)* 600
Red Hill ‡(M5)* 914
Red Lion (J6)* 5,119
Reedsville (G4)* 1,238
Refton (K6)* 235
Rehrersburg (K5)* 365
Renfrew (C4)* 400
Reno (C3)* 1,000
Renovo (G3)* 3,751
Rew (F2)* 500
Reynoldsville (D3)* 3,569
Rices Landing (C6)* 796
Riceville (C2)* 200
Richfield (H4)* 350
Richland (K5)* 1,090
Richlandtown (M5)* 762
Riddlesburg (F5)* 700
Ridgway (E3)* 6,244
Ridley Park (M7)* 4,921
Riegelsville (M4)* 871
Rillton (C5)* 875
Rimer (C4)* 80
Rimersburg (D3)* 1,398
Ringtown (K4)* 835
Riverside (J4)* 524
Rixford (F2)* 650
Roaring Branch (J2)* 375
Roaring Creek (K4) 40
Roaring Spring (F5)* 2,771
Robertsdale (F5)*
Robesonia (K5)* 1,590
Robinson (D5)*
Rochester (B4)* 7,197
Rochester Mills (D4)* 230
Rock Glen (K4)* 250
Rockhill ‡(G5) 567
Rockledge ‡(M5) 2,261
Rockwood (D6)* 1,237
Rogersville (B6)* 300
Rome (K2)* 257
Roscoe (C5)* 1,396
Rose Valley (L7) 498
Rosemont (M5)* 2,000
Roseto (M4)* 1,676
Roseville (Rutland*) (J2) 126
Rossiter (E4)* 1,078
Rosslyn Farms ‡(B7) 448
Rothsville (K5)* 1,000
Roulette (F2)* 800
Rouseville (C3)* 1,009
Rouzerville (G6)* 1,000
Roxbury (G5)* 400
Royalton (J5)* 1,175
Royersford (L5)* 3,862
Rummerfield (K2)* 100
Rural Valley (D4)* 857
Rush (K2)*
Russell (D2)* 800
Russellton (C4)* 1,670
Rutland (J2)* 126
Rutledge (M7)* 919
Sabinsville (G2)* 300
Sabula (E3) 275
Saegerstown (B2)* 836
Sagamore (D4)* 1,128
Saint Benedict (E4)* 500
St. Clair (K4)* 5,856
St. Clairsville ‡(E5)* 127
St. Lawrence ‡(E4)* 810
St. Marys (E3)* 7,846
St. Petersburg (C3)* 451
St. Thomas (G6)* 534
Salisbury (D6)* 865
Salladasburg (H3)* 250
Salona (H3)* 500
Saltillo (G5)* 435
Saltsburg (D4)* 1,156
Sand Patch (E6)* 56
Sandy Lake (B3)* 767
Sandy Ridge (F4)* 700
Sankertown ‡(E5) 865
Sarver (C4)* 410
Sawyer City (E2) 500
Saxonburg (C4)* 602
Saxton (F5)* 1,093
Saybrook (D2)* 137
Saylorsburg (M4)* 513
Sayre (K2)* 7,735
Scalp Level (E5)* 1,756
Schaefferstown (K5)* 1,000
Schellsburg (E5)* 305
Schnecksville (L4)* 375
Schuylkill Haven (K4)* 6,597
Schwenksville (L5)* 563
Sciota (M4)* 300
Scotland (G6)* 500
Scottdale (C5)* 6,249
Scranton (L3)* 125,536
Scranton (urban area) 235,122
Secane (M7)* 1,500
Seelyville (M2)* 600
Selinsgrove (J4)* 3,514
Sellersville (M5)* 2,373
Seminole (D4)* 250
Seneca (C3)* 700
Sergeant (E2)* 150
Seven Valleys (J6)* 437
Seward (E5)* 852
Sewickley (B4)* 5,836
Sewickley Heights ‡(B4) 679
Shade Gap (G5)* 157
Shadygrove (G6)* 500
Shamokin (J4)* 16,879
Shamokin Dam (J4)* 730
Shanksville (E5)* 342
Sharon (B3)* 26,454
Sharon Hill (N7)* 5,464
Sharpsburg (B6)* 7,296
Sharpsville (A3)* 5,414
Shawanese (K3)* 200
Shawmut (E3)
Shawnee on Delaware (N3)* 200
Sheakleyville (B3)* 141
Sheffield (D2)* 2,087
Shelocta ‡(D4)* 105
Shenandoah (K4)* 15,704
Shenango (A3)* 200
Sheppton (K4)*
Shermans Dale (H5)* 83
Shickshinny (K3)* 2,156
Shillington (K5)* 5,059
Shinglehouse (F2)* 1,201
Shippensburg (H5)* 5,722
Shippenville (D3)* 522
Shippingport ‡(B4)* 408
Shiremanstown ‡(H5)* 887
Shirleysburg (G5)* 241
Shoemakersville (K4)* 1,066
Shohola (N3)* 600
Shohola Falls (N3)* 70
Shrewsbury (J6)* 787
Shunk (J2)* 60
Sidman (E5)* 490
Sigel (D3)* 600
Silverdale ‡(M5)* 384
Simpson (M2)* 2,800
Sinking Spring (K5)* 1,982
Sinnamahoning (G3)* 450
Six Mile Run (F5)* 400
Skinners Eddy (K2)* 225
Skippack (M5)* 425
Skytop (M3)* 25
Slate Run (H3)*
Slatedale (L4)* 800
Slatington (L4)* 4,343
Slickville (C5)* 1,266
Sligo (C3)* 913
Slippery Rock (B3)* 2,294
Smethport (F2)* 1,797
Smicksburg (D4)* 92
Smithfield (C6)* 1,066
Smithmill (F4)* 1,500
Smithton (C5)* 690
Snow Shoe (G3)* 670
Snydertown (J4)* 314
Soldier (E3) 300
Somerfield ‡(D6)
Somerset (D6)* 5,936
Sonestown (K3)* 275
Souderton (M5)* 4,521
South Bend (D4)* 100
S. Bethlehem ‡(D4) 489
S. Coatesville ‡(L6) 1,996
S. Connellsville (D6)* 2,610
S. Fork (E5)* 2,616
S. Greensburg ‡(C5) 2,980
S. Heights (B4)* 691
S. Mountain (H6)* 1,300
S. New Castle ‡(B4) 993
S. Philipsburg ‡(F4) 512
S. Renovo (G3) 862
S. Waverly (J2) 1,298
S. Williamsport (J3) 6,364
Southmont ‡(E5) 2,278
Southwest (C5)* 800
Southwest Greensburg ‡(C5) 3,144
Spangler (E4)* 3,013
Spartansburg (C2)* 482
Speers ‡(C5) 1,089
Spinnerstown (M5)* 400
Spring City (L5)* 3,258
Spring Creek (D2)* 160
Spring Grove (J6)* 1,238
Spring Mills (G4)* 720
Springboro (B2)* 611
Springdale (C4)* 4,939
Springfield (M7)* 8,000
Springtown (M4)* 600
Springville (L2)* 250
Spruce Creek (F4)* 150
Starrucca (M2)* 326
State College (G4)* 17,227
State Line (G6)* 375
Steelton (J5)* 12,574
Sterling (M3)* 40
Sterling Run (F3)* 225
Stewartstown (K6)* 1,133
Stillwater (K3)* 189
Stockdale ‡(C5)* 870
Stockertown (M4)* 757
Stoneboro (B3)* 1,294
Stowe (L5)* 2,524
Stowe (B7) ▲12,210
Stoystown (E5)* 517
Strasburg (K6)* 1,109
Strattanville (D3)* 562
Strausstown (K5)* 368
Stroudsburg (M4)* 6,361
Stump Creek (E3)* 675
Sturgeon (B5)* 1,150
Sugar Notch (L3)* 2,002
Sugargrove (D1)* 520
Summer Hill (E5)* 849
Summerville (D3)* 933
Summit Hill (L4)* 4,294
Sunbury (J4)* 15,570
Surveyor (F3)* 53
Susquehanna (L2)* 2,646
Sutersville ‡(C5)* 854
Swarthmore (M7)* 4,825
Sweet Valley (K3)* 200
Swissvale (C7)* 16,488
Swoyersville ‡(L3) 7,795
Sycamore (B6)* 69
Sykesville (E3)* 1,652
Sylvan (G6)* 22
Sylvania (J2)* 211
Tamaqua (L4)* 11,508
Tamarack (G3) 60
Tannersville (M3)* 500
Tarentum (C4)* 9,540
Tatamy (M4)* 681
Taylor (L3)* 7,176
Taylorstown (A5)* 400
Telford ‡(M5)* 2,042
Temple (L5)* 1,460
Templeton (C4)* 1,000
Terre Hill (L5)* 1,000
Thomasville (J6)* 320
Thompson (L2)* 320
Thompsontown (H4)* 486
Thornburg ‡(B7) 335
Thornhurst (L3)* 100
Three Springs (G5)* 417
Throop (L3)* 5,861
Tidioute (D2)* 998
Timblin (D4)* 327
Tioga (H2)* 544
Tiona (D2)* 350
Tionesta (C2)* 728
Tipton (F4)* 425
Tire Hill (E5)* 700
Titusville (C2)* 8,923
Tobyhanna (M3)* 825
Topton (L5)* 1,572
Torpedo (D2)* 65
Torrance (D5)* 500
Toughkenamon (L6)* 500
Towanda (J2)* 4,069
Tower City (J4)* 2,054
Townville (C2)* 351
Trafford (C5)* 3,965
Trainer (L7) 2,001
Transfer (A3)* 400
Trappe ‡(M5) 773
Tremont (K4)* 2,102
Trevorton (J4)* 2,545
Trexlertown (L4*) 500
Trough Creek (F5) 60
Trout Run (H3)* 325
Troutville ‡(E3)* 223
Troxelville (H4)* 130
Troy (J2)* 1,371
Truemans (D2)* 80
Trumbauersville (M5)* 838
Tryonville (C2)* 134
Tullytown (N5)* 648
Tunkhannock (L2)* 2,170
Tunnelhill ‡(E5) 535
Turbotville (J3)* 518
Turtle Creek (C7)* 12,363
Turtlepoint (F2)* 150
Twilight ‡(C5) 318
Twin Rocks (E4)* 1,850
Tyler (F3)* 250
Tylersburg (D3)* 215
Tylersville (G4)* 200
Tyrone (F4)* 8,214
Ulster (J2)* 400
Ulysses (G2)* 495
Union City (C2)* 3,911
Union Dale (M2)* 350
Union Deposit (J5)* 550
Uniontown (C6)* 20,471
Uniontown ‡(J4) 1,280
Unionville ‡(H4)* 341
Unity (C4)* 700
Unityville (K3)* 55
Universal (C7)* 3,200
Upland (L7)* 4,081
Upper Black Eddy (N4)* 550
Upper Darby (M6)* ▲84,951
Upper Strasburg (G5)* 262
Urban (J4)* 100
Ursina (D6)* 334
Utica (C3)* 264
Uwchland (L5)* 300
Valencia (C4)* 298
Valier (D4)* 600
Valley Forge (L5)* 475
Valley View (J4)* 1,618
Van (C3)* 75
Vanderbilt (C5)* 937
Vandergrift (D4)* 9,524
Vandling (M2)* 722
Vanport (B4)* 2,500
Venango (B2)* 359
Venus (C3)* 150
Verona (C6)* 4,235
Versailles (C7) 2,484
Villanova (M6)* 1,500
Vintage (K5) 150
Vintondale (E5)* 1,185
Volant (B3)* 229
Wall (C5)* 1,850
Wallaceton (F4)* 440
Wallingford (L7)* 6,000
Walnut (G4)* 85
Walnut Bottom (H5)* 325
Walnutport (L4)* 1,427
Walston (D4)* 330
Wampum (B4)* 1,090
Wanamie (L3)* 1,092
Wapwallopen (K3)* 377
Warfordsburg (F6)* 105
Warren (D2)* 14,849
Warren Center (K2)* 275
Warrendale (B4)* 600
Warrensville (J3)* 175
Warrior Run ‡(L3) 1,056
Warriors Mark (F4)* 225
Washington (B5)* 26,280
Washington Boro ‡(K6)* 483
Washington Crossing (N5)* 300
Washingtonville (J3)* 194
Waterford (B2)* 1,195
Watsontown (J3)* 2,327
Wattsburg (C1)* 343
Wawa (L7)* 600
Waymart (M2) 1,068
Wayne (M6)* 6,000
Waynesboro (G6)* 10,334
Waynesburg (B6)* 5,514
Weatherly (L4)* 2,622
Webster (C5)*
Webster Mills (F6)* 95
Weedville (F3)* 700
Weissport ‡(L4)* 674
Wellersburg (E6)* 369
Wellsboro (H2)* 4,215
Wellscreek (E5) 100
Wellsville (J5)* 309
Wernersville (K5)* 1,280
Wesley (C3) 80
Wesleyville (C1)* 3,411
West Alexander (B5)* 466
W. Bridgewater (B4)* 1,316
W. Brownsville (C5)* 1,610
W. Chester (L6)* 15,168
W. Conshohocken ‡(M5)* 2,482
W. Easton ‡(M4) 1,368
W. Elizabeth (C5)* 1,137
W. Fairview ‡(J5)* 1,896
West Finley (B5)* 93
W. Grove (L6)* 1,521
W. Hazleton (K4)* 6,988
W. Hickory (C2)* 400
W. Homestead ‡(B7) 3,257
W. Kittanning ‡(C4) 910
W. Lawn (K5)* 2,144
W. Leechburg ‡(C4) 1,113
W. Leesport ‡(L5)* 535
W. Liberty ‡(C5) 245
W. Mayfield ‡(B4) 1,768
W. Middlesex (B3)* 1,217
W. Middletown (A5)* 268
W. Mifflin (C7)* 17,985
W. Milton (J3)* 700
W. Monterey (C3)* 125
W. Nanticoke (K3)* 1,780
W. Newton (C5)* 3,619
W. Pittsburg (B4)* 900
W. Pittston ‡(L3)* 7,230
W. Reading ‡(L5) 5,072
W. Salisbury (D6)* 300
W. Springfield (B2)*
W. Sunbury (B4)* 262
W. Union (B6) 25
W. View (B6)* 7,581
W. Winfield (C4)* 600
W. Wyoming ‡(L3) 2,863
W. York ‡(J6) 5,756
Westfield (H2)* 1,357
Westford (A2)* 47
Westland (B5)* 1,025
Westline (E2)* 150
Westmont ‡(C5) 4,410
Weston (K4)* 602
Westover (E4)* 605
Westport (G3)* 221
Westtown (L6)* 258
Westville (E3)* 250
Wharton (G2) 50
Wheatland (B3)* 1,402
Wheelerville (J2)* 34
Whitaker (C7)* 2,149
White Haven (L3)* 1,461
White Mills (M2)* 600
White Oak (C7) 6,159
Whitedeer (J3)* 300
Whitehall (B7) 7,342
Whitney (D5)* 875
Wiconisco (J4)* 1,549
Widnoon (D4)* 350
Wilawana (J2)* 100
Wilcox (E2)* 1,000
Wilkes-Barre (L3)* 76,826
Wilkes-Barre (urban area) 270,978
Wilkinsburg (C7)* 31,418
Williamsburg (F5)* 1,792
Williamsport (H3)* 45,047
Williamstown (J4)* 2,332
Willock (B7)* 275
Willow Grove (M5)* 7,000
Willow Hill (G5)* 440
Wilmerding (C7)* 5,325
Wilmore (E5)* 390
Wilpen (D5)*
Wilson (M4)* 8,159
Winburne (F4)* 785
Windber (E5)* 8,010
Windgap (M4)* 1,577
Windsor (J6)* 1,126
Winfield (J4)* 300
Wingate (G4)* 216
Winterdale (M2) 50
Winterstown ‡(J6) 298
Winton (M3) 6,280
Wolfdale (B5)* 800
Wolfsburg (F5) 125
Womelsdorf (K5)* 1,549
Woodbury (F5)* 254
Woodcock (C2) 130
Woodland (F4)* 1,000
Woodlyn (M7)* 5,000
Woodruff (B6) 25
Woodville (B7)* 3,775
Woolrich (H3)* 450
Wormleysburg ‡(J5)* 1,511
Worthington (C4)* 800
Worthville (D3)* 73
Wrights (F2)* 250
Wrightsville (J5)* 2,104
Wyalusing (K2)* 612
Wyoming (L3)* 4,511
Wyomissing (K5)* 4,187
Wyomissing Hills ‡(K5) 646
Wysox (K2)* 250
Yardley (N5)* 1,916
Yatesboro (D4)* 1,264
Yatesville ‡(L3) 565
Yeadon (N7)* 11,068
Yeagertown (G4)* 1,628
Yoe ‡(J6)* 681
York (J6)* 59,953
York (urban area) 78,495
York Haven (J5)* 743
York Springs (H6)* 413
Yorkana ‡(J6)* 229
Youngstown (D5)* 577
Youngsville (D2)* 1,944
Youngwood (D5)* 2,720
Yukon (C5)* 1,099
Zelienople (B4)* 2,981

*Map on Page 66*

## RHODE ISLAND

*Total Population 791,896*

### 5 COUNTIES

Bristol (J6) 29,079
Kent (H6) 77,763
Newport (K6) 61,539
Providence (H5) 574,973
Washington (H7) 48,542

### CITIES and TOWNS

Adamsville (K6)* 250
Albion (H5)* 800
Allenton (H6)* 250
Alton (G7)* 300
Anthony (H6)* 2,000
Arcadia (H6) 100
Arctic (J6) 3,000
Arnold Mills (J5) 300
Ashaway (G7)* 1,022
Ashton (J5)* 1,000
Barrington (J6)* ▲8,246
Block Island (H8)* 848
Bradford (H7)* 1,024
Bridgeton (G5) 661
Bristol (J6)* ▲12,320
Canonchet (H7) 150
Carolina (H7)* 200
Centerdale (H5)* 2,500
Central Falls (J5)* 23,550
Charlestown (H7)* ▲1,598
Chepachet (H5)* 1,200
Clayville (H5)* 300
Conimicut (J6)*
Coventry (H6)* ▲9,869
Cranston (J5)* 55,060
Crompton (J6) 1,500
Davisville (H6) 1,400
East Greenwich (H6)* ▲4,923
E. Providence (J5)* ▲35,871
Esmond (H5)* 2,000
Exeter (H6)* ▲1,870
Farmingdale (H5)
Fiskeville (H6)*
Foster (H5) ▲1,630
Foster Center (H5)* 225
Georgiaville (H5)* 1,247
Glendale (H5)* 243
Greene (G6)* 71
Greenville (H5)* 2,000
Hamilton (J6)* 950
Harmony (H5)* 500
Harrisville (H5)* 1,055
Hillsgrove (J6)*
Hope (H6)* 800
Hope Valley (H6)* 1,000
Hopkinton (H7)* ▲3,676
Howard (J5)* 6,000
Jamestown (J6)* ▲2,068
Kenyon (H7)* 100
Kingston (J7)* 2,156
La Fayette (H6)* 550
Little Compton (K6)* ▲1,556
Lonsdale (J5)* 2,500
Lymansville (J5)
Manton (J5) 2,500
Manville (H5)* 3,429
Mapleville (H5)* 1,015
Middletown (J6) ▲7,382
Narragansett (J7)* ▲2,288
Nasonville (H5) 677
Natick (H6)* 2,000
Newport (J7)* 37,564
North Scituate (H5)* 1,000
N. Tiverton (K6) 4,000
Norwood (J5) 2,300
Oak Lawn (H5)* 600
Oakland (H5)* 226
Oakland Beach (J6)* 10,000
Pascoag (H5)* 1,760
Pawtucket (J5)* 81,436
Peace Dale (J7)* 2,177
Phenix (H6)* 1,500
Phillipsdale (J5) 1,500
Pontiac (J6)*
Portsmouth (J6)* ▲6,578
Potter Hill (H7)* 400
PROVIDENCE (H5)* 248,674
Providence (urban area) 581,607
Prudence (J6)
Prudence Island (J6)* 80
River Point (H6) 1,000
Riverside (J5)* 10,000
Rockville (G6)* 175
Rumford (J5)* 10,000
Saunderstown (J6)* 450
Saylesville (J5)* 3,500
Shannock (H7)* 300
Shawomet (J6) 1,500
Slatersville (H4)* 1,780
Slocum (H6)* 100
South Foster (H5)
Stillwater (H5)
Summit (H6) 110
Tarkiln (H5) 191
Thornton (H5)
Tiverton (K6)* ▲5,659
Tiverton Four Corners (K6) 12
Usquepaug (H6) 142
Valley Falls (J5)* 2,500
Wakefield (H7)* 3,047
Warren (J6) ▲8,513
Warwick (J6)* 43,028
Warwick Neck (J6)*
Washington (H6)* 2,800
Watch Hill (G7)* 750
Weekapaug (G7)* 200
West Barrington (J5)* 4,250
W. Glocester (G5) 100
W. Greenwich (H6) ▲847
W. Kingston (H7)* 500
Westerly (G7)* ▲12,380
Wickford (J6)* 2,437
Wood River Jct. (H7)* 103
Woonsocket (J4)* 50,211
Wyoming (H6)* 315

Map on Page 84

## SOUTH CAROLINA

Total Population 2,117,027

### 46 COUNTIES

Abbeville (B3)....22,456
Aiken (D4)....53,137
Allendale (E6)....11,773
Anderson (B2)....90,664
Bamberg (F5)....17,533
Barnwell (E5)....17,266
Beaufort (F7)....26,993
Berkeley (G5)....30,251
Calhoun (F4)....14,753
Charleston (H6)....164,856
Cherokee (D1)....34,992
Chester (E2)....32,597
Chesterfield (G2)....36,236
Clarendon (G4)....32,215
Colleton (F6)....28,242
Darlington (H3)....50,016
Dillon (J3)....30,930
Dorchester (G5)....22,601
Edgefield (D4)....16,591
Fairfield (E3)....21,780
Florence (H3)....79,710
Georgetown (J5)....31,762
Greenville (C2)....168,152
Greenwood (C3)....41,628
Hampton (E6)....18,027
Horry (J4)....59,820
Jasper (E6)....10,995
Kershaw (F3)....32,287
Lancaster (F2)....37,071
Laurens (D2)....46,974
Lee (G3)....23,173
Lexington (E4)....44,297
Marion (J3)....33,110
Marlboro (H2)....31,766
McCormick (C4)....9,577
Newberry (D3)....31,771
Oconee (A2)....39,050
Orangeburg (F5)....68,726
Pickens (B2)....40,058
Richland (F3)....142,565
Saluda (D3)....15,924
Spartanburg (D2)....150,349
Sumter (G4)....57,634
Union (D2)....31,334
Williamsburg (H4)....43,807
York (E2)....71,596

### CITIES and TOWNS

Abbeville (C3)*....5,395
Adams Run (G6)*....250
Adamsburg (D2)*....150
Adrian (J4)*....150
Aiken (D4)*....7,083
Alcolu (G4)*....800
Allendale (E5)*....2,474
Allsbrook (K3)....200
Anderson (B2)*....19,770
Andrews (H5)*....2,702
Angelus (G2)*....50
Antioch (F3)....350
Antreville (B3)....300
Appleton (E5)*....
Aragon Mills (E2)....
Arcadia (C2)*....2,554
Ariail (B2)*....1,098
Arthur (E3)....50
Ashepoo (G6)*....150
Ashton (E5)*....
Atkins (G3)*....50
Awendaw (H5)*....75
Aynor (J3)*....551
Badham (F5)....118
Baldock (E5)*....80
Baldwin Mills (E2)*....1,440
Ballentine (E3)*....150
Bamberg (E5)*....2,954
Barnwell (E5)*....2,005
Batesburg (D4)*....3,169
Bath (D5)*....1,232
Beaufort (F7)*....5,081
Belton (C2)*....3,371
Belton Mills (B2)....1,500
Bennetts Point (G6)*....73
Bennettsville (H2)*....5,140
Bethera (H5)*....
Bethune (G3)*....639
Bingham (H3)....169
Bishopville (G3)*....3,076
Blacksburg (D1)*....2,056
Blackstock (E2)*....
Blackville (E5)*....1,294
Blair (E3)*....74
Blaney (F3)*....183
Blenheim (H2)*....153
Blue Brick (J3)*....
Bluffton (F7)*....474
Blythewood (E3)*....400
Bonneau (H5)*....408
Bordeaux (B4)....75
Borden (G3)*....50
Bowling Green (E1)*....
Bowman (F5)*....857
Boykin (F3)*....13
Bradley (C3)*....100
Branchville (F5)*....1,353
Bristow (H3)....50
Brogdon (G4)....25
Brookgreen (K4)....
Brunson (E6)*....607
Bucksport (J4)*....800
Bucksville (J4)*....
Buffalo (D2)*....1,580
Burgess (J4)*....200
Burnettown ‡(D5)....578
Burton (F7)*....275
Cades (H4)*....150
Caesars Head (B1)*....16
Calhoun (B2)*....
Calhoun Falls (B3)*....2,396
Callison (C3)*....50
Camden (F3)*....6,986
Cameron (F4)*....630
Campobello (C1)*....394
Canadys (F5)*....150
Carlisle (D2)*....405
Cartersville (H3)*....96
Cashville (C2)....58
Cassatt (G3)*....125
Catawba (F2)*....150
Cateechee (B2)*....650
Cayce (E4)*....3,294
Cedar Springs (D2)*....1,500
Centenary (J3)*....
Central (B2)*....1,263
Chapin (E3)*....327
Chappells (D3)*....199
Charleston (G6)*....70,174
Charleston (urban area)....116,441
Cheraw (H2)*....4,836
Cherokee Falls (D1)*....
Chesnee (D1)*....1,051
Chester (E2)*....6,893
Chesterfield (G2)*....1,530
Chisolm (F6)....5
Claremont (G4)....
Clarks Hill (C4)*....
Claussen (H3)*....
Clearwater (D4)*....800
Clemson (B2)*....1,204
Cleveland (C1)*....250
Clifton (D2)*....1,707
Clinton (D3)*....7,168
Clio (H2)*....837
Clover (E1)*....3,276
Colliers (C4)....175
COLUMBIA (F4)*....86,914
Columbia (urban area)....119,747
Conestee (C2)*....750
Congaree Field (F4)....50
Converse (D2)*....1,200
Conway (J4)*....6,073
Cooper (H4)*....200
Coosawhatchie (F6)*....
Cope (E5)*....209
Cordesville (H5)*....450
Cordova (F5)*....175
Coronaca (C3)*....
Cottageville (G6)*....553
Coward (H4)*....500
Cowpens (D1)*....1,879
Crescent Beach (K4)*....540
Creston (F4)....75
Crete (B2)....
Crocketville (E6)*....120
Cross (G5)*....85
Cross Anchor (D2)*....350
Cross Hill (D3)*....543
Cross Keys (D2)....250
Crow Creek (B2)....40
Cummings (E6)....
Dacusville (B2)*....95
Dale (F6)*....300
Dalzell (G3)*....209
Darlington (H3)*....6,619
Daufuskie Island (F7)*....270
Davis Station (G4)*....200
Denmark (E5)*....2,814
Dents (F3)....200
Dillon (J3)*....5,171
Donalds (C3)*....332
Dorchester (G5)*....350
Dovesville (H3)*....250
Drake (H3)*....50
Drayton (D2)*....1,228
Due West (C3)*....1,033
Dunbar (H2)*....200
Duncan (C2)*....599
Eadytown (G5)....87
Early Branch (F6)*....250
Easley (B2)*....6,316
Eastover (F4)*....564
Eau Claire (E3)*....9,238
Ebenezer (E2)....680
Edgefield (C4)*....2,518
Edgemoor (E2)*....258
Edisto Island (G6)*....2,500
Effingham (H3)*....200
Ehrhardt (E5)*....510
Elko (E5)*....142
Elliott (G3)*....
Elloree (F4)*....1,127
Enoree (D2)*....1,045
Estill (E6)*....1,659
Eureka (D4)....50
Eureka Mills (E2)....1,990
Eutawville (G5)*....478
Fair Play (A2)*....250
Fairfax (E6)*....1,567
Fairforest (C2)*....800
Fairmont (D2)*....250
Filbert (E1)*....200
Fingerville (D1)*....400
Florence (H3)*....22,513
Floyd Dale (J3)*....100
Folly Beach (H6)*....800
Forest Acres (F3)....3,240
Foreston (G4)*....
Fork (J3)*....115
Fork Shoals (C2)....250
Fort Lawn (F2)*....216
Fort Mill (F1)*....3,204
Fort Motte (F4)*....350
Fountain Inn (C2)*....1,325
Four Holes (G5)*....200
Frogmore (F7)*....200
Furman (E6)*....293
Gable (G4)*....90
Gadsden (F4)*....
Gaffney (D1)*....8,123
Galivants Ferry (J3)*....150
Garnett (E6)*....100
Gaston (E4)*....250
Georgetown (J5)*....6,004
Giant (G5)....
Gifford (E6)*....
Gilbert (E4)*....172
Gillisonville (E6)....25
Givhans (G5)....100
Glendale (D2)*....1,244
Glenn Springs (D2)*....
Gluck (B3)*....1,634
Goldville (Joanna*) (D3)....1,730
Goose Creek (H6)*....600
Gossett Mills (B2)....
Govan (E5)*....109
Gowensville (C1)....100
Gramling (C1)*....200
Graniteville (D4)*....3,362
Gray Court (C2)*....479
Grays (E6)....50
Great Falls (F2)*....3,533
Greeleyville (H4)*....600
Green Pond (F6)*....
Green Sea (J3)*....500
Greenville (C2)*....58,161
Greenwood (C3)*....13,806
Greer (C2)*....5,050
Gresham (J4)*....150
Grover (F5)*....145
Gurley (J3)*....300
Hagood (F3)*....4
Hamburg (D5)....
Hamer (J3)*....500
Hampton (E6)*....2,007
Hardeeville (E7)*....546
Harleyville (G5)*....483
Hartsville (G3)*....5,658
Heath Springs (F2)*....694
Helena (D3)*....
Hemingway (J4)*....821
Hendersonville (F6)....
Henry (J4)....100
Herbert (E2)....25
Hickory Grove (E2)*....275
Hilda (E5)*....304
Hiltonhead (F7)*....1,600
Hodges (C3)*....275
Holly Hill (G5)*....1,116
Hollywood (G6)*....246
Honea Path (C3)*....2,840
Honey Hill (H5)*....69
Hopkins (F4)*....125
Horatio (G3)*....50
Huger (H5)*....500
Hyman (H4)*....150
Industrial Mills (E2)....1,868
Inman (C1)*....1,514
Irmo (E3)*....281
Islandton (F6)*....25
Isle of Palms (H6)*....1,379
Iva (B3)*....1,164
Jackson (D5)*....500
Jacksonboro (G6)*....150
Jalapa (D3)....50
Jamestown (H5)*....1,100
Jamison (F4)....75
Jedburg (G5)*....500
Jefferson (G2)*....556
Jenkinsville (E3)*....
Joanna (D3)*....1,730
Jocassee (A2)....25
Johns Island (G6)*....5,000
Johnsonville (J4)*....616
Johnston (D4)*....1,426
Jonesville (D2)*....1,345
Jordan (G4)....15
Jordanville (J4)....150
Kathwood (D5)*....30
Kelton (D2)*....90
Kershaw (G2)*....1,376
Killian (F3)....50
Kinards (D3)*....
Kings Creek (E1)*....140
Kingsburg (H4)....50
Kingstree (H4)*....3,621
Kingville (F4)....100
Kirksey (C3)....
Kline (E5)*....230
La France (B2)*....
Ladson (G6)*....500
Lake City (H4)*....5,112
Lake View (J3)*....653
Lamar (G3)*....958
Lancaster (F2)*....7,159
Lancaster Mills (F2)....4,313
Lando (E2)*....500
Landrum (C1)*....1,333
Lane (H5)*....580
Lanford (C2)*....250
Langley (D4)*....3,000
Latta (J3)*....1,602
Laurens (C3)*....8,658
Leeds (E2)*....150
Lees (E5)....25
Leesville (E4)*....1,453
Lena (E6)*....71
Leo (H4)*....350
Leslie (E2)*....275
Level Land (C3)....230
Levys (E7)*....50
Lewis Turnout (E2)....
Lexington (E4)*....1,081
Liberty (B2)*....2,291
Liberty Hill (F3)*....200
Lincolnville (G6)....278
Little Mountain (E3)*....213
Little River (K4)*....108
Little Rock (J3)*....150
Livingston (E4)*....210
Lobeco (F6)*....137
Lockhart (D2)*....1,685
Lodge (F5)*....316
Lone Star (F4)*....50
Long Creek (A2)*....35
Longs (K4)*....300
Longtown (F3)....
Loris (K3)*....1,614
Lowndesville (B3)*....252
Lowrys (E2)*....368
Lugoff (F3)*....
Luray (E6)*....102
Lydia (G3)*....
Lydia Mills (D3)*....1,212
Lykesland (F4)*....300
Lyman (C2)*....1,365
Lynchburg (G3)*....506
Macbeth (H5)*....100
Madison (A2)*....450
Manning (G4)*....2,775
Marietta (C1)*....1,000
Marion (J3)*....6,834
Mars Bluff (H3)*....
Martin (D5)*....
Mauldin (C2)*....300
Mayesville (G4)*....706
Mayo (D1)*....500
McBee (G3)*....420
McClellanville (H5)*....417
McColl (H2)*....2,688
McConnells (E2)*....255
McCormick (C4)*....1,744
Meggett (G6)*....224
Meriwether (C4)....
Miley (E6)*....300
Millettville (D5)*....
Minturn (J2)*....47
Modoc (C4)*....150
Monarch Mills (D2)....2,158
Moncks Corner (G5)*....1,818
Monetta (D4)*....
Mont Clare (H3)*....150
Monticello (E3)*....100
Montmorenci (D4)*....425
Moore (D2)*....300
Morgana (D4)....50
Moselle (E6)....30
Mount Carmel (B3)*....84
Mount Croghan (G2)*....209
Mount Holly (H5)*....
Mount Pleasant (H6)*....1,857
Mountain Rest (A2)*....
Mountville (C3)*....
Mullins (J3)*....4,916
Murrells Inlet (K4)*....50
Myers (H6)*....
Myrtle Beach (K4)*....3,345
Naval Base (G6)*....
Neeses (E4)*....328
Nesmith (H4)*....72
New Ellenton (D5)....
New Town Village (J3)....650
New Zion (H4)*....140
Newberry (D3)*....7,546
Newry (B2)*....1,000
Nichols (J3)*....380
Nimmons (B1)*....130
Nine Times (B2)....
Ninety Six (D3)*....1,556
Nixonville (K4)*....
Norris (B2)*....325
North (E4)*....954
North Augusta (C5)*....3,659
North Charleston (G6)*....18,000
North Mullins (J3)....297
Norway (E5)*....476
Oakland Mill (D3)....621
Oakley (G5)*....150
Oakway (A2)....99
Ocean Drive Beach (K4)*....255
Oceda (H5)....300
Ogden (E2)....12
Olanta (H4)*....586
Olar (E5)*....414
Ora (D2)*....185
Orangeburg (F4)*....15,322
Orr (B3)*....2,625
Osborn (G6)*....100
Oswego (G3)*....300
Owings (C2)*....200
Pacolet (D2)*....455
Pacolet Mills (D2)*....2,170
Padgetts (F5)....35
Pageland (G2)*....1,925
Pamplico (H4)*....728
Paris (C2)*....200
Parksville (C4)*....198
Parr (E3)*....100
Paris Island (F7)*....
Patrick (G2)*....310
Pauline (D2)*....200
Pawleys Island (J5)*....2,000
Paxville (G4)*....208
Peak (E3)*....134
Peedee (H3)*....150
Pelham (C2)*....750
Pelion (E4)*....196
Pelzer (B2)*....2,692
Pendleton (B2)*....1,432
Perry (E4)*....133
Pickens (B2)*....1,961
Pickens Mill (B2)....1,000
Piedmont (C2)*....2,673
Pineland (E6)*....
Pineville (H5)*....500
Pinewood (G4)*....578
Pinopolis (G5)*....300
Plantersville (J4)*....100
Pleasant Hill (F2)....200
Pleasant Lane (D4)....102
Plum Branch (C4)*....158
Pomaria (E3)*....251
Pontiac (F3)....45
Port Royal (F7)*....793
Poston (J4)*....100
Pregnall (G5)....200
Princeton (C2)*....
Pritchardville (E7)*....200
Prosperity (D3)*....699
Rains (J3)*....50
Ravenel (G6)*....337
Red River (F2)....346
Reevesville (F5)*....285
Reidville (C2)*....236
Rembert (G3)*....300
Renno (D2)*....100
Rhems (H4)....
Richburg (E2)*....238
Richland (A2)*....75
Richtex (E3)*....85
Ridge Spring (D4)*....598
Ridgeland (E7)*....1,078
Ridgeville (G5)*....507
Ridgeway (F3)*....414
Rimini (G4)*....250
Rion (E3)*....500
Ritter (F6)*....
Riverside (F2)....30
Rock Hill (E2)*....24,502
Rocky Bottom (B1)....100
Rodman (E2)*....750
Round O (F6)*....103
Rowesville (F5)*....363
Ruby (G2)*....315
Ruffin (F6)*....500
Russellville (H5)*....300
Saint Andrews (G6)*....20,000
Saint Charles (G3)*....100
Saint George (F5)*....1,938
Saint Matthews (F4)*....2,351
Saint Paul (G4)....125
Saint Stephen (H5)*....1,341
Salem (A2)*....504
Salley (E4)*....407
Salters (H4)*....
Saluda (D4)*....1,594
Samaria (E4)*....100
Sandy Springs (B2)*....500
Santee (F5)*....107
Santuck (D2)*....300
Sardinia (G4)*....150
Scotia (E6)*....226
Scranton (H4)*....602
Seabrook (F6)*....500
Sedalia (D2)*....300
Seiglingville (E5)....
Sellers (H3)*....530
Seneca (A2)*....3,649
Sharon (E2)*....365
Sheldon (F6)*....300
Shelton (E3)*....50
Shiloh (G4)....
Shoals Junction (C3)*....85
Shulerville (H5)*....400
Silver (G4)....15
Silverstreet (D3)*....201
Simpsonville (C2)*....1,529
Six Mile (B2)*....157
Slater (C1)*....1,000
Smith (E2)*....55
Smithboro (J3)....53
Smoaks (F5)*....130
Smyrna (E1)*....105
Snelling (E5)....34
Society Hill (H2)*....645
South Greenwood (C3)*....3,712
Spartanburg (C1)*....36,795
Springfield (E4)*....782
Starr (B3)*....282
Startex (C2)*....1,638
State Park (F3)*....
Steedman (E4)....50
Stokes (F6)....80
Stoneboro (F2)....100
Strangeville (F5)....626
Strawberry (G5)....
Strother (E3)*....25
Sullivans Island (H6)*....898
Summerton (G4)*....1,419
Summerville (G5)*....3,312
Summit (E4)*....105
Sumter (G4)*....20,185
Sunset (B1)*....40
Swansea (E4)*....762
Switzer (C2)*....64
Switzerland (E7)*....74
Sycamore (E5)*....383
Syracuse (G3)....50
Tamassee (A2)*....300
Tatum (H2)*....119
Taxahaw (F2)....40
Taylors (C2)*....1,518
Tigerville (C1)*....
Tillman (E7)*....500
Timmonsville (H3)*....2,001
Tirzah (E2)....75
Toddville (J4)*....200
Townville (B2)*....250
Tradesville (F2)....125
Travelers Rest (C2)*....1,200
Trenton (D4)*....296
Trio (H5)*....187
Troy (C3)*....242
Turbeville (G4)*....271
Ulmers (E5)*....139
Union (D2)*....9,730
Van Wyck (F2)*....100
Vance (G5)*....106
Varnville (E6)*....1,180
Vaucluse (D4)*....750
Verdery (C3)*....119
Wadmalaw Island (G6)*....2,500
Wagener (E4)*....584
Walhalla (A2)*....3,104
Wallace (H2)*....
Walterboro (F6)*....4,616
Wampee (K4)*....162
Wando (H6)*....114
Ward (D4)*....122
Ware Shoals (C3)*....3,032
Warrenville (D4)*....1,604
Wateree (F4)*....100
Waterloo (C3)*....162
Wattsville (D3)*....1,649
Wedgefield (F4)*....450
Wellford (C2)*....721
West Columbia (E4)*....4,373
West Marion (J3)....175
West Pelzer (B2)....578
West Springs (D2)....300
West Union (B2)*....429
Westminster (A2)*....2,219
Westville (F3)*....350
White Hall (F6)*....
White Oak (E3)*....200
White Pond (D5)*....275
White Rock (E3)*....250
Whitmire (D3)*....3,006
Whitney (D1)*....1,611
Wiggins (F6)*....50
Wilkins (F7)*....150
Williams (F5)*....254
Williamston (B2)*....2,782
Willington (B4)*....75
Williston (E5)*....896
Wilson (G4)*....300
Windsor (D5)*....
Winnsboro (E3)*....3,267
Winnsboro Mills (E3)....2,936
Wisacky (G3)*....135
Wolfton (E4)*....40
Woodford (E4)*....179
Woodruff (D2)*....3,831
Woodward (E2)*....150
Yemassee (F6)*....712
Yonges Island (G6)*....
York (E1)*....4,181
Zion (J3)....

Map on Page 85

## SOUTH DAKOTA

Total Population 652,740

### 67 COUNTIES

Aurora (M6)....5,020
Beadle (N5)....21,082
Bennett (F7)....3,396
Bon Homme (O7)....9,440
Brookings (R5)....17,851
Brown (N2)....32,617
Brule (L6)....6,076
Buffalo (L5)....1,615
Butte (B4)....8,161
Campbell (J2)....4,046
Charles Mix (M7)....15,558
Clark (O4)....8,369
Clay (P8)....10,993
Codington (P4)....18,944
Corson (G2)....6,168
Custer (B6)....5,517
Davison (N6)....16,522
Day (O3)....12,294
Deuel (R4)....7,689
Dewey (G3)....4,968
Douglas (N7)....5,636
Edmunds (L3)....7,275
Fall River (B7)....10,439
Faulk (L3)....4,752
Grant (R3)....10,233
Gregory (L7)....8,556
Haakon (F5)....3,167
Hamlin (P4)....7,058
Hand (L4)....7,149
Hanson (O6)....4,896
Harding (B2)....2,289
Hughes (J5)....8,111
Hutchinson (O7)....11,423
Hyde (K4)....2,811
Jackson (F6)....1,768
Jerauld (M5)....4,476
Jones (H6)....2,281
Kingsbury (O5)....9,962
Lake (P5)....11,792
Lawrence (B5)....16,648
Lincoln (R7)....12,767
Lyman (J6)....4,572
Marshall (O2)....7,835
McCook (P6)....8,828
McPherson (L2)....7,071
Meade (D5)....11,516
Mellette (H6)....3,046
Miner (O5)....6,268
Minnehaha (R6)....70,910
Moody (R5)....9,252
Pennington (C6)....34,053
Perkins (D3)....6,776
Potter (J3)....4,688
Roberts (P2)....14,929
Sanborn (N5)....5,142
Shannon (D7)....5,669
Spink (N4)....12,204
Stanley (H5)....2,055
Sully (J4)....2,713
Todd (H7)....4,758
Tripp (K7)....9,139
Turner (P7)....12,100
Union (R8)....10,792
Walworth (J3)....7,648
Washabaugh (F6)....1,551
Yankton (P7)....16,804
Ziebach (F4)....2,606

**CITIES and TOWNS**

Aberdeen (M3)* 21,051
Academy (M7)* 20
Adelaide (N3)
Agar (J4)* 141
Ahnberg (P5) 3
Akaska (J3)* 84
Albee (S3)* 75
Alcester (R7)* 585
Alexandria (O6)* 714
Allen (F7)* 130
Alpena (N5)* 426
Alsen (R8) 22
Altamont (R4)* 76
Amherst (O2)* 70
Andover (O3)* 277
Appleby (R4) 8
Ardmore (B7)* 107
Argonne (O5)* 25
Arlington (P5)* 1,096
Armour (N7)* 900
Arpan (B4) 50
Artas (K2)* 172
Artesian (O6)* 429
Ashton (N3)* 222
Astoria (S4)* 206
Athboy (F2) 2
Athol (M3)* 120
Aurora (R5)* 202
Avance (E4)* 10
Avon (N8)* 692
Badger (P5)* 180
Badnation (J6) 3
Baltic (R6)* 255
Bancroft (O4)* 100
Barnard (N2)* 108
Batesland (E7)* 88
Bath (N3)* 90
Bear Butte (C5)* 50
Beardsley (O7) 4
Beebe (L3) 4
Belle Fourche (B4)* 3,540
Belvidere (G6)* 172
Bemis (R4)* 51
Benclare (R6) 15
Bend (D5) 5
Beresford (R7)* 1,686
Berton (P5) 9
Betts (N6) 5
Big Springs (S8) 21
Big Stone City (S3)* 829
Bijou Hills (L6)* 35
Bison (E2)* 457
Bixby (D3)* 1
Black Hawk (C5)* 91
Blackpipe (G7)*
Blue Bell (C6) 4
Blue Range (O7)
Blunt (J4)* 423
Bonesteel (M7)* 485
Bonilla (N4)* 90
Booge (R6) 10
Bovee (M7)* 25
Bowdle (K3)* 788
Box Elder (D5)* 33
Bradley (O3)* 226
Brandon (R6)* 250
Brandt (R4)* 211
Brave (J6) 2
Brentford (N3)* 132
Bridger (E4) 5
Bridgewater (P6)* 748
Bristol (O3)* 647
Britton (O2)* 1,430
Broadland (N4)* 74
Brookings (R5)* 7,764
Bruce (R5)* 305
Bryant (P4)* 624
Buffalo (B2)* 380
Buffalo Gap (C6)* 186
Bullhead (G2)* 250
Bullock (B2)* 5
Burbank (R8)* 125
Burdette (M4) 6
Burdock (B7)* 7
Burke (L7)* 829
Burkmere (L3)* 10
Bushnell (R5)* 96
Butler (O3)* 109
Cadillac (H2) 6
Camp Crook (B2)* 122
Canistota (P6)* 687
Canning (K5)*
Canova (O6)* 340
Canton (R7)* 2,530
Capa (H5)* 49
Caputa (D5)* 30
Carpenter (O4)* 75
Carter (J7)* 16
Carthage (O5)* 458
Cash (D2) 2
Castle Rock (B4)* 11
Castlewood (R4)* 498
Cavour (N5)* 154
Cedar Canyon (D3) 3
Cedarbutte (H6)* 5
Center (P6) 18
Center Point (P7) 10
Centerville (R7)* 1,053
Central City (B5)* 218
Chalkbutte (D4)* 4
Chamberlain (L6)* 1,912
Chance (E3)* 16
Chancellor (R7)* 193
Chelsea (M3)* 41
Cherry Creek (F4)* 140
Chester (R6)* 200
Cheyenne Agency (J3)* 450
Cilson (B7)
Claire City (P2)* 109
Claremont (N2)* 236
Clark (O4)* 1,471
Clarno (P6) 2
Clayton (O7) 10
Clearfield (K7)* 31
Clear Lake (R4)* 1,105
Coal Springs (F3)* 2
Colman (R6)* 509
Colome (K7)* 451
Colton (P6)* 521
Columbia (N2)* 270
Conata (E6) 50
Conde (N3)* 409
Cooper (E4)* 3
Corona (R3)* 191
Corsica (N7)* 551
Corson (R6)* 49
Cottonwood (F6)* 102
Crandall (O3)* 35
Crandon (N4) 10
Craven (M3) 1
Creighton (E5)* 5
Cresbard (M3)* 235
Creston (D6) 10
Crocker (O3)* 72
Crooks (R6)* 120
Crow Lake (M6) 10
Custer (B6)* 2,017
Cuthbert (N6)* 14
Dahlberg (P2) 8
Dalesburg (P8) 35
Dallas (K7)* 244
Dalzell (E5)* 62
Danforth (M5) 10
Dante (N7)* 140
Dark Canyon (C5) 50
Date (D3)* 4
Davis (P7)* 153
De Grey (K5)* 6
De Smet (O5)* 1,180
Deadwood (B5)* 3,288
Deerfield (B5)* 38
Dell Rapids (R6)* 1,650
Delmont (N7)* 405
Dempster (R4)* 99
Denby (E7)* 5
Dewey (A6)* 40
Dimock (O7)* 120
Dixon (L7)* 25
Doland (N4)* 535
Dolton (P7)* 93
Dowling (F5)* 9
Draper (J6)* 252
Dumont (B5) 6
Dupree (F3)* 438
Duxbury (M3) 5
Eagle (L6) 11
Eagle Butte (G3)* 375
Eakin (K4)
East Mobridge (J2) 51
Eden (P2)* 149
Edgemont (B7)* 1,158
Edson (E3) 10
Egan (R6)* 347
Elk Mountain (B6)
Elk Point (R8)* 1,367
Elkton (S5)* 657
Ellingson (D2)* 4
Ellis (R6) 21
Elm Springs (D5)* 7
Elmore (B5) 8
Elrod (O4)* 37
Emery (O6)* 480
Endlee (D3) 3
Englewood (B5) 16
Enning (E4)* 20
Epiphany (O6) 40
Erskine (B7) 5
Erwin (P5)* 153
Esmond (O5)* 49
Estelline (R4)* 760
Ethan (N6)* 319
Eureka (K2)* 1,576
Fairburn (C6)* 80
Fairfax (M7)* 301
Fairpoint (D4)*
Fairview (R7)* 155
Faith (E4)* 599
Farmer (O6)* 114
Farmingdale (D6)* 19
Farwell (O6) 13
Faulkton (M3)* 837
Fedora (O5)* 125
Ferney (N3)* 100
Firesteel (G3)* 110
Flandreau (R5)* 2,193
Florence (P3)* 226
Foley (P4) 5
Folsom (D6) 2
Forest City (J4) 12
Forestburg (N5)* 144
Fort Lookout (K6)
Fort Meade (C5)* 860
Fort Pierre (H5)* 951
Fort Thompson (L5)* 225
Frankfort (N4)* 331
Franklin (P6) 27
Frederick (N2)* 408
Freeman (O7)* 944
Fruitdale (B4)* 70
Fullerville (P8)
Fulton (O6)* 139
Gage (M2) 2
Galena (B5) 10
Gallup (N3) 6
Gannvalley (L5)* 101
Garden City (O4)* 282
Garretson (S6)* 745
Gary (S4)* 558
Gayville (P8)* 271
Geddes (M7)* 502
Gettysburg (K3)* 1,555
Glad Valley (F3)* 20
Glencross (H3)* 30
Glenham (J2)* 168
Goodwin (R4)* 141
Gorman (K4) 6
Govert (C3)* 10
Greenfield (R8) 22
Greenway (K2)*
Greenwood (N8)* 44
Gregory (L7)* 1,375
Grenville (O3)* 207
Gretna (L3) 2
Grosse (L6) 4
Groton (N3)* 1,084
Grover (P4)* 30
Gustave (B3)* 2
Hamill (K6)* 48
Hammer (R2)* 77
Hanna (B5) 12
Hanton (P4)
Harding (B3)*
Harrington (G7)* 3
Harrisburg (R7)* 274
Harrison (M7)* 88
Harrold (K4)* 263
Hartford (R6)* 592
Hartley (F5) 1
Hay Creek (C3)
Haydraw (D5)* 5
Hayes (H4)* 30
Hayti (P4)* 413
Hazel (P4)* 161
Hecla (N2)* 500
Henry (P4)* 323
Heppner (B7)* 3
Hereford (D5)* 4
Hermosa (C6)* 123
Herreid (K2)* 633
Herrick (L7)* 169
Hetland (P5)* 123
Hidden Timber (J7)* 12
Highmore (L4)* 1,158
Hiland (P3)* 5
Hill City (B6)* 361
Hilland (F5)* 5
Hillhead (O2)* 100
Hillside (N7) 14
Hillsview (L2)* 68
Hisega (C5) 15
Hisle (F7)* 29
Hitchcock (M4)* 227
Holabird (K4)* 30
Holmquist (O3)* 35
Hooker (R7)* 30
Hoover (C3)* 4
Hosmer (L2)* 533
Hot Springs (C7)* 5,030
Houghton (N2)* 90
Hoven (K3)* 552
Howard (P5)* 1,251
Howes (E4)*
Hudson (R7)* 500
Huffton (N2)* 17
Humboldt (P6)* 450
Hurley (P7)* 474
Huron (N5)* 12,788
Ideal (K6)* 10
Igloo (B7)* 1,920
Imlay (E6)* 3
Interior (F6)* 126
Iona (L6)* 17
Ipswich (L3)* 1,058
Irene (P7)* 374
Iroquois (O5)* 413
Isabel (G3)* 511
James (N3) 8
Janousek (O8)
Java (K3)* 433
Jefferson (S8)* 466
Joe Creek (K5)* 56
Joubert (M7) 20
Junius (P6)* 30
Kadoka (F6)* 584
Kampeska (P4) 16
Karinen (B2)* 1
Kaylor (O7)* 175
Keldron (F2)* 10
Kenel (H2)* 129
Kennebec (K6)* 374
Keyapaha (J7)* 19
Keystone (C6)* 600
Kidder (O2)* 146
Kimball (M6)* 952
Kingsburg (O8) 11
Kirley (G4)* 5
Kranzburg (R4)* 135
Kyle (E7)* 89
La Bolt (R3)* 164
La Plant (H3)* 100
Ladelle (N4) 5
Ladner (B2)* 10
Lake Andes (M7)* 1,851
Lake City (O2)* 110
Lake Norden (P4)* 373
Lake Preston (P5)* 957
Lakeport (O8)
Lakeview (H7)* 16
Lane (N5)* 145
Langford (O2)* 456
Lantry (G3)* 26
Lead (B5)* 6,422
Lebanon (K3)* 215
Lemmon (E2)* 2,760
Lennox (R7)* 1,218
Leola (M2)* 772
Lesterville (O7)* 192
Letcher (N6)* 291
Lightcap (G2) 2
Lily (O3)* 139
Little Eagle (H2)* 575
Lodgepole (D2)* 30
Longlake (L2)* 175
Longvalley (F7)* 10
Loomis (N6)* 67
Lower Brule (K5)* 162
Lowry (K3)* 70
Loyalton (L3)* 57
Lucas (L7)* 25
Ludlow (C2)* 6
Lyman (K6)* 16
Lyons (R6)* 77
Lyonville (M6)
Madison (P6)* 5,153
Mahto (H2)* 55
Manchester (O5)* 40
Manderson (D7)* 110
Manila (G5) 5
Mansfield (M3)* 200
Mapleleaf (H2)
Marcus (E4)* 11
Marion (P7)* 794
Marlow (P2) 8
Martin (F7)* 989
Marty (N8)* 600
Marvin (R3)* 110
Mason (B3) 1
Mathews (P5)
Maurine (E3)* 11
McCook (S8) 300
McIntosh (G2)* 628
McLaughlin (H2)* 713
Meadow (E2)* 37
Meckling (R8)* 111
Melham (O4)
Mellette (N3)* 250
Menno (P7)* 868
Midland (G5)* 387
Midway (P7) 15
Milbank (R3)* 2,982
Milesville (F5)* 19
Millboro (K7)* 33
Miller (L4)* 1,916
Milltown (O7)* 39
Mina (M3)* 46
Minnekahta (B7) 6
Miranda (M4)* 79
Mission (H7)* 388
Mission Hill (P8)* 169
Mission Ridge (H4)* 2
Mitchell (N6)* 12,123
Mobridge (J2)* 3,753
Moenville (G4)* 4
Monroe (P7)* 160
Montrose (P6)* 448
Moon (B6)* 4
Morefield (R6) 7
Moritz (S4) 16
Morristown (F2)* 190
Mosher (J7)* 18
Mossman (H3) 7
Mound City (K2)* 177
Mount Vernon (N6)* 387
Mud Butte (D4)* 16
Murdo (H6)* 739
Murphy (C5) 10
Mystic (B5)* 40
Nahant (B5)
Nahon (N3) 4
Nansen (O5) 2
Naples (O4)* 62
Nemo (B5)* 100
New Effington (R2)* 367
New Holland (M7)* 125
New Underwood (D5)* 268
New Witten (K7) 198
Newark (O2)* 80
Newell (C4)* 784
Nisland (C4)* 216
Nora (R8) 10
Norbeck (L3)* 16
Norris (G7)* 111
Northville (M3)* 220
Nowlin (G5)* 20
Nunda (P5)* 102
Oacoma (L6)* 231
Oahe (J5) 32
Oelrichs (C7)* 168
Oglala (D7)*
Okaton (H6)* 137
Okobojo (J4) 2
Okreek (J7)* 260
Oldham (P5)* 349
Olivet (O7)* 202
Onaka (L3)* 158
Onida (K4)* 822
Opal (D4)* 50
Oral (C7)* 100
Ordway (N2) 6
Oreville (B6)
Orient (L4)* 206
Ortley (P3)* 144
Osceola (O5)* 37
Ottumwa (G5)* 4
Owanka (D5)* 50
Pactola (C5)* 85
Parade (G3)* 8
Parker (P7)* 1,148
Parkston (O7)* 1,354
Parmelee (G7)* 116
Patricia (G7)* 10
Paxton (L7) 11
Pedro (E5)* 19
Peever (R2)* 221
Perkins (O8) 14
Philip (F5)* 810
Pickstown (M7)* 2,217
Piedmont (C5)* 200
Pierpont (O3)* 326
PIERRE (J5)* 5,715
Pine Ridge ((E7)* 2,000
Plainview (E4)* 7
Plana (N2) 15
Plankinton (N6)* 754
Platte (M7)* 1,069
Poinsette (P4) 50
Pollock (J2)* 395
Porcupine (E7)* 25
Potato Creek (F6)* 8
Powell (G5)* 15
Presho (J6)* 712
Pringle (B6)* 193
Promise (H3)* 7
Provo (B7)* 100
Pukwana (L6)* 302
Putney (N2)* 14
Quinn (E5)* 214
Ralph (C2)* 2
Ramona (P5)* 278
Randolph (N3)* 29
Rapid City (C5)* 25,310
Rauville (P3) 8
Ravinia (N7)* 200
Raymond (O4)* 174
Redelm (F3)* 6
Redfern (B5)
Redfield (N4)* 2,655
Redig (C3)* 10
Redowl (D4)* 11
Ree Heights (L4)* 254
Reliance (K6)* 215
Renner (R6)* 99
Reva (C2)* 6
Revillo (R3)* 249
Richland (R8) 30
Richmond (M2) 7
Ridgeview (H3)* 60
Robey (M6) 100
Rochford (B5)* 50
Rockerville (C6) 30
Rockham (M4)* 113
Rockyford (E7)* 11
Roscoe (L3)* 726
Rosebud (H7)*
Rosholt (R2)* 387
Roslyn (P2)* 222
Roswell (O6)* 69
Roubaix (B5)
Rouseau (K5) 41
Rowena (R6)* 70
Rudolph (N3) 4
Rumford (B7)* 8
Running Water (O8) 23
Rutland (P5)* 100
Saint Charles (L7)* 50
St. Francis (H7)* 241
St. Lawrence (M4)* 261
St. Onge (B4)* 104
Salem (P6)* 1,119
Sanator (B6)* 251
Sansarc (H5)* 4
Savoy (B5) 16
Scenic (D6)* 75
Scotland (O7)* 1,188
Selby (J3)* 706
Seneca (L3)* 204
Shadehill (E2)* 21
Sheridan (C5) 8
Sherman (S6)* 120
Shindler (R7)* 50
Silver City (B5)* 35
Sinai (P5)* 181
Sioux Falls (R6)* 52,696
Sisseton (R2)* 2,871
Smithwick (C7)* 100
Sorum (D3)* 3
South Shore (P3)* 269
So. Sioux Falls (R6) 1,586
Spain (O2)
Spearfish (B5)* 2,755
Spencer (O6)* 552
Spink (R8) 41
Spottswood (M4)
Springfield (N8)* 801
Stamford (G6)* 10
Stephan (K5)* 150
Stevens (R8)* 300
Stickney (M6)* 388
Stockholm (R3)* 114
Stoneville (D4)* 5
Storla (M6) 36
Strandburg (R3)* 144
Stratford (N3)* 164
Strool (D3)* 75
Sturgis (B5)* 3,471
Sulphur (D4)* 3
Summit (P3)* 431
Swett (E7) 12
Sylvan Lake (B6)*
Tabor (O8)* 373
Tacoma Park (N2)* 15
Tea (R7)* 151
Templeton (M5) 5
Terry (B5) 70
Thomas (P4)* 37
Thunder Hawk (F2)* 82
Tilford (C5)* 85
Timber Lake (H3)* 552
Tinton (A5)* 10
Tolstoy (K3)* 180
Toronto (R4)* 322
Trail City (H3)* 200
Trent (R6)* 213
Tripp (N7)* 913
Trojan (B5)* 200
Troy (R3)* 44
Tulare (N4)* 212
Turton (N3)* 201
Tuthill (G7)* 50
Twin Brooks (R3)* 113
Tyndall (O8)* 1,292
Union Center (D4)* 10
Unityville (P6)* 85
Utica (P8)* 84
Vale (C4)* 152
Valley Springs (S6)* 389
Van Metre (H5)* 10
Vayland (M5)* 24
Veblen (P2)* 476
Verdon (N3)* 34
Vermillion (R8)* 5,337
Vetal (G7)* 38
Viborg (P7)* 644
Victor (R2)* 35
Vienna (O4)* 306
Viewfield (D5)* 3
Vilas (O6)* 71
Virgil (N5)* 124
Vivian (J6)* 250
Volga (R5)* 578
Volin (P8)* 197
Wagner (N7)* 1,528
Wakonda (P7)* 454
Wakpala (H2)* 350
Walker (G2)* 27
Wall (E6)* 556
Wallace (P3)* 188
Wanamaker (G7)* 5
Wanblee (F6)* 325
Ward (R5)* 96
Warner (M3)* 115
Wasta (D5)* 144
Watauga (G2)* 96
Watertown (P4)* 12,699
Waubay (P3)* 879
Waverly (R3)* 50
Webster (P3)* 2,503
Wecota (L3)* 40
Wendte (H5)* 40
Wentworth (R6)* 270
Wessington (M5)* 467
Wessington Spgs. (M5)* 1,453
West Britton (O2)
West Carlock (L7) 3
Westerville (P8) 17
Westover (H6)* 2
Westport (M2)* 116
Weta (F6)
Wetonka (M2)* 115
Wewela (K7)* 29
White (R5)* 525
White Butte (E2)* 154
White Lake (M6)* 395
White Owl (E4)* 19
White River (H6)* 465
White Rock (R2)* 113
Whitedeer (F2)
Whitehorse (H3)* 67
Whitewood (B5)* 304
Whitlocks Cross'g (J3)* 23
Willett (B2)*
Willow Lake (O4)* 484
Wilmot (R3)* 590
Winfred (P6)* 171
Winner (K7)* 3,252
Winship (M2) 6
Wist (P2) 8
Witten (J7)*
Wolsey (N5)* 391
Wood (J6)* 260
Woonsocket (N5)* 1,051
Worthing (R7)* 272
Wounded Knee (D7)* 150
Yale (O5)* 164
Yankton (P8)* 7,709
Zell (M4)* 95
Zeona (D3)* 2

## TENNESSEE

Map on Page 86

*Total Population 3,291,718*

**95 COUNTIES**

Anderson (N2) 59,407
Bedford (J3) 23,627
Benton (E2) 11,495
Bledsoe (L3) 8,561
Blount (O3) 54,691
Bradley (M4) 32,338
Campbell (N2) 34,369
Cannon (J3) 9,174
Carroll (E3) 26,553
Carter (R2) 42,432
Cheatham (G2) 9,167
Chester (D4) 11,149
Claiborne (O2) 24,788
Clay (K1) 8,701
Cocke (P3) 22,991
Coffee (J3) 23,049
Crockett (C3) 16,624
Cumberland (M3) 18,877
Davidson (H2) 321,758
De Kalb (K3) 11,680
Decatur (F3) 9,442
Dickson (G2) 18,805
Dyer (C2) 33,473
Fayette (C4) 27,535
Fentress (M2) 14,917
Franklin (J4) 25,431
Gibson (D3) 48,132
Giles (G4) 26,961
Grainger (O2) 13,086
Greene (Q2) 41,048
Grundy (K4) 12,558
Hamblen (P2) 23,976
Hamilton (L4) 208,255
Hancock (P1) 9,116
Hardeman (C4) 23,311
Hardin (E4) 16,908
Hawkins (P2) 30,494
Haywood (C3) 26,212
Henderson (E3) 17,173
Henry (E2) 23,828
Hickman (G3) 13,353
Houston (F2) 5,318
Humphreys (F2) 11,030
Jackson (K2) 12,348
Jefferson (P2) 19,667
Johnson (S2) 12,278
Knox (O3) 223,007
Lake (B2) 11,655
Lauderdale (B3) 25,047
Lawrence (G4) 28,818
Lewis (F3) 6,078
Lincoln (H4) 25,624
Loudon (N3) 23,182
Macon (J1) 13,599

Madison (D3) 60,128
Marion (K4) 20,520
Marshall (H4) 17,768
Maury (G3) 40,368
Mc Minn (M4) 32,024
Mc Nairy (D4) 20,390
Meigs (M3) 6,080
Monroe (N4) 24,513
Montgomery (G2) 44,186
Moore (J4) 3,948
Morgan (M2) 15,727
Obion (C2) 29,056
Overton (L2) 17,566
Perry (F3) 6,462
Pickett (M1) 5,093
Polk (N4) 14,074
Putnam (K2) 29,869
Rhea (M3) 16,041
Roane (M3) 31,665
Robertson (H1) 27,024
Rutherford (J3) 40,696
Scott (M2) 17,362
Sequatchie (L4) 5,685
Sevier (O3) 23,375
Shelby (B4) 482,393
Smith (K2) 14,098
Stewart (F1) 9,175
Sullivan (R1) 95,063
Sumner (J2) 33,533
Tipton (B3) 29,782
Trousdale (J2) 5,520
Unicoi (R2) 15,886
Union (O2) 8,670
Van Buren (L3) 3,985
Warren (K3) 22,271
Washington (Q2) 59,971
Wayne (F4) 13,864
Weakley (D2) 27,962
White (L3) 16,204
Williamson (H3) 24,307
Wilson (J2) 26,318

**CITIES and TOWNS**

Abiff (G3) 12
Adams (G1)* 525
Adamsville (E4)* 927
Addison (M4) 40
Aetna (G3)* 100
Afton (Q2)* 150
Alamo (C3)* 1,501
Alcoa (N3)* 6,355
Alexandria (J2)* 372
Algood (K2)* 729
Allardt (M2)* 800
Allens (C3)
Allisona (H3)* 75
Allons (L2)* 270
Allred (L2)* 300
Alpine (L2)* 200
Altamont (K4)* 296
Alto (K4) 125
Anderson (K4)* 375
Andersonville (O2)* 525
Anes (H3) 35
Annadel (M2) 25
Anthras (N1) 100
Antioch (H2)* 298
Apison (L5)*
Archville (N4)* 150
Ardmore (H4)* 157
Arlington (B4)* 463
Armathwaite (M2)* 350
Arrington (H3)* 250
Arthur (O1)* 450
Ashland City (G2)* 1,024
Ashport (B3)*
Ashwood (G3)* 80
Aspen Hill (G4)* 225
Athens (M4)* 8,618
Atoka (B4)* 334
Atwood (D3)* 1,000
Auburntown (J3)* 273
Bailey (B4)* 207
Baileyton (Q2)* 224
Bakerville (F3)* 68
Bakewell (L4)* 250
Banner Springs (M2)* 406
Barr (B3)* 100
Barren Plains (H1) 100
Bartlett (B4)* 489
Bath Springs (E4)* 50
Baugh (H4) 25
Baxter (K2)* 861
Beacon (E3)* 200
Bean Station (P2)*
Beans Creek (J4)* 50
Bear Spring (F2) 100
Bearden (N3) 1,600
Beardstown (F3)* 100
Beech Bluff (D3)* 180
Beechgrove (J3)* 250
Beersheba Springs (K4)* 300
Belfast (H4)* 150
Bell Buckle (J3)* 341
Belle Meade (H2) 2,831
Belleview (H2)* 250
Bells (C3)* 1,225
Belltown (N4) 100
Belvidere (J4)* 250
Bemis (D3)* 3,248
Benton (M4)* 650
Berry Hill ‡(H2)* 1,248
Bethel (G4)* 150
Bethel Springs (D4)* 623
Bethpage (J1)* 280
Big Lick (L3)* 150
Big Rock (F1)* 250
Big Sandy (E2)* 621
Big Spring (M4)* 68
Birchwood (M4)* 800
Blaine (O2)* 300
Blanche (H4)* 250
Block (N2)* 160
Bloomington Springs (K2)* 200
Blountville (R1)* 500
Bluff City (R2)* 1,074
Bogota (C2)* 300
Bolivar (C4)* 2,429
Bon Air (L3)* 300
Bon Aqua (G3)* 120
Boom (L1)* 121
Boonshill (H4) 35
Boothspoint (B2)* 200
Boston (G3) 100
Boyds Creek (O3)* 485
Braden (B4)* 250
Bradford (D2)* 599
Bradyville (J3)* 98
Brazil (C3) 140
Brentwood (H2)*
Briceville (N2)* 2,500
Bridgeport (P3)*
Brighton (B4)* 306
Bristol (R1)* 16,771
Brockdell (L3)*
Brotherton (L2)* 600
Brownsville (C3)* 4,711
Bruceton (E2)* 1,204
Brunswick (B4)* 500
Brush Creek (J2)* 200
Buchanan (E2)* 100
Buena Vista (E3)* 60
Buffalo (F3)* 25
Buffalo Valley (K2)* 300
Buford (G4)
Bullsgap (P2)* 558
Bumpus Mills (F1)* 225
Bunker Hill (H4) 100
Burlison (B3)* 75
Burns (G2)*
Burrville (M2)* 230
Bybee (P2)* 250
Byington (N3)* 125
Byrdstown (L1)* 379
Cades (D3)* 68
Cades Cove (O3) 40
Cagle (L4) 165
Cainsville (J3)
Calderwood (N3)* 245
Calhoun (M4)* 450
Cambria (M4) 100
Camden (E2)* 2,029
Campaign (K3)* 100
Caneyspring (H3) 55
Capleville (B4)* 950
Carderview (S2)*
Carter (R2) 600
Carters Creek (G3)* 250
Carthage (K2)* 1,604
Caryville (N2)* 1,234
Castalian Springs (J2)* 129
Cedar Grove (D3)* 25
Cedar Hill (H1)* 872
Cedarcreek (Q2)* 175
Celina (K1)* 1,136
Centerville (G3)* 1,532
Cerro Gordo (E4)* 10
Chalybeate (K3)
Chanute (L1) 450
Chapel Hill (H3)* 603
Chapmansboro (G2)* 26
Charleston (M4)*
Charlotte (G2)* 478
Chaska (N1)* 121
Chattanooga (K4)* 131,041
Chattanooga (urban area) 167,031
Cherry (B3)
Chesterfield (E3)* 150
Chestnut Mound (K2)* 150
Chewalla (D4)* 150
Chilhowee (O3)* 150
Christiana (J3)* 300
Chuckey (Q2)* 300
Church Hill (Q1)* 1,741
Clairfield (O1)* 2,000
Clarkrange (L2)*
Clarksburg (E3)* 350
Clarksville (G1)* 16,246
Clayton (C2) 30
Clementsville (K1) 25
Cleveland (M4)* 12,605
Clifton (F4)* 818
Clifty (L3)* 51
Clinchmore (N2)*
Clinton (N2)* 3,712
Clouds (O2)* 50
Coalfield (M2)*
Coalmont (K4)* 800
Coble (F3) 100
Cokercreek (N4)* 366
Coldwater (H4) 85
Colesburg (G2) 100
College Grove (H3)* 300
Collegedale (M4)* 1,200
Collierville (B4)* 1,153
Collinwood (F4)* 589
Columbia (G3)* 10,911
Como (E2)* 175
Conasauga (M4)* 475
Concord (N3)* 294
Cookeville (L2)* 6,924
Copperhill (N4)* 924
Cordova (B4)* 250
Cornersville (H4)* 358
Corryton (O2)* 1,275
Cortner (J4) 63
Cosby (P3)*
Cottagegrove (E2)* 126
Cottontown (H2)* 250
Cotula (O2) 250
Counce (E4)*
Covington (B3)* 4,379
Cowan (J4)* 1,835
Crab Orchard (M3)* 315
Crawford (L2)* 100
Creston (L2) 125
Crestview (G4) 356
Crockett Mills (C3)* 148
Cross Plains (H1)* 200
Crossville (L3)* 2,291
Crump (E4)* 500
Culleoka (G4)* 500
Cumberland City (F2)* 500
Cumberland Furnace (G2)* 350
Cumberland Gap (O1)* 403
Cummingsville (L3) 50
Cunningham (G2)* 250
Curve (B3)
Cypress Inn (F4)* 1,000
Daisy (L4)* 1,336
Dale Hollow ‡(K1) 5
Dancyville (C4) 80
Dandridge (O2)* 690
Danville (F2)
Darden (E3)* 250
Daus (L4)*
Davidson (L2)
Daylight (K8)* 250
Dayton (L3)* 3,191
De Rossett (L3)* 250
Dean (N2)* 130
Decatur (M3)* 235
Decaturville (E3)* 514
Decherd (J4)* 1,435
Deer Lodge (M2)* 275
Del Rio (P3)* 300
Delano (M4)* 350
Dellrose (H4)* 350
Denmark (D3)* 69
Densons Landing (F3)
Denver (F2)* 130
Devonia (N2)* 250
Diana (H4)*
Dickson (G2)* 3,348
Difficult (K2)* 500
Dixon Springs (J2)* 200
Dodson (L3) 98
Doeville (S2)* 125
Donelson (H2)* 1,765
Double Springs (K2)* 200
Dover (F2)* 800
Dowelltown (K2)* 262
Doyle (K3)* 500
Dresden (D2)* 1,509
Drummonds (A4)* 160
Duck River (G3)*
Ducktown (N4)* 1,064
Duff (N2)*
Dukedom (D2)* 115
Dunlap (L4)* 873
Dyer (D2)* 1,864
Dyersburg (C2)* 10,885
Eads (B4)* 250
Eagan (O1)* 300
Eagle Creek (E3)*
Eagleville (H3)* 378
East Jamestown (M2)* 100
East Ridge (L5)* 9,645
Eastland (L3)*
Eaton (C3)*
Edenwold (H2)* 500
Eidson (P1)* 300
Elbridge (C2)* 89
Elgin (M2)* 350
Elizabethton (R2)* 10,754
Elk Valley (N1)* 300
Elkmont (O3) 35
Elkton (H4)* 168
Ellendale (B4)* 700
Elora (J4)* 225
Elva (M1) 15
Embreeville (Q2)* 1,273
Emory Gap (M3)* 350
Englewood (M4)* 1,545
Enville (E4)* 350
Erie (M3)* 25
Erin (F2)* 858
Erwin (R2)* 3,387
Estill Springs (J4)* 496
Ethridge (G4)* 500
Etowah (M4)* 3,261
Eva (E2)* 250
Evensville (M3)* 450
Fairfield (J3) 100
Fairview (G3)*
Fall Branch (Q2)* 300
Fall Mills (J4) 34
Fall River (G4) 50
Farmers Exchange (F3)* 134
Farmington (H3) 200
Farner (N4)* 200
Faxon (E2)* 120
Fayetteville (H4)* 5,447
Finger (D4)* 130
Finley (B2)* 1,000
Five Points (G4)* 125
Flag Pond (Q2)* 300
Flat Woods (F4)* 275
Flatcreek (J4)
Flintville (J4)* 300
Florence (H3) 125
Flynns Lick (K2) 50
Forbus (M1)* 200
Fordtown (Q2)*
Forest Hill (B4)* 200
Fork Mountain (N2)* 900
Fort Henry (E1)* 100
Fort Pillow (B3)* 150
Fosterville (J3)* 100
Fountain City (O2)* 15,000
Fountain Head (J1)* 252
Fowlkes (C3)* 150
Frankewing (H4)* 90
Frankfort (M2)
Franklin (H3)* 5,475
Frayser (A4)*
French Broad (P3)* 154
Friendship (C3)* 452
Friendsville (N3)* 625
Fruitland (D3)*
Fruitvale (C3)* 50
Fulton (B3)* 150
Gadsden (D3)* 255
Gainesboro (K2)* 992
Gallatin (H2)* 5,107
Gallaway (B4)* 200
Gardner (D2)
Garland (B3) 157
Gassaway (K3)* 80
Gates (C3)* 234
Gatlinburg (O3)* 1,301
Gennett (N2) 25
Georgetown (L4)* 100
Germantown (B4)* 408
Gibbs (D2) 100
Gibson (D3)* 308
Gillises Mills (E4)
Gladeville (J2)* 114
Glass (C2) 75
Gleason (D2)* 1,063
Glen Alice (M3) 300
Glendale (G3) 130
Glenmary (M2)* 300
Goin (O2)* 300
Golddust (B3)* 50
Goodlettsville (H2)* 1,590
Goodspring (G4)* 31
Gordonsburg (F3)
Gordonsville (K2)* 304
Gorman (F2) 80
Graham (G3)* 25
Grand Junction (C4)* 477
Grandview (M3)* 250
Granville (K2)* 130
Gravel Hill (D4) 42
Graysville (L4)* 820
Green Brier (H2)* 890
Greenback (N3)* 1,200
Greeneville (Q2)* 8,721
Greenfield (D2)* 1,706
Greenwood (J2) 200
Groveland (G3) 25
Gruetli (K4)* 600
Guys (D4)* 100
Habersham (N2)* 500
Hales Point (B3) 25
Haley (J4)* 150
Halls (C3)* 1,808
Hamburg (E4) 350
Hampshire (G3)* 200
Hampton (R2)* 1,164
Harms (H4) 75
Harriman (M3)* 6,389
Harris (C2) 75
Harrison (L4)* 500
Harrogate (O1)*
Hartford (P3)* 200
Hartsville (J2)* 1,130
Hartsville Junction (J2) 40
Haydenburg (K2)* 100
Hebbertsburg (M2) 110
Heiskell (O2)* 130
Helenwood (M2)* 500
Henderson (D4)* 2,532
Hendersonville (J2)* 1,000
Hendon (L4)* 125
Henning (B3)* 493
Henry (E2)* 200
Henryville (G4)* 150
Hermitage (H2)* 800
Hermitage Springs (K1) 200
Hickman (K2)* 175
Hickory Point (G2)* 100
Hickory Valley (C4)* 400
Hickory Withe (C4)* 50
Highland Park (R1) 3,500
Hilham (L2)* 177
Hillsboro (K4)* 200
Hillsdale (J2)*
Hillside (D2) 160
Hitchcox (L3)* 98
Hixon (L4)* 2,100
Hohenwald (F3)* 1,703
Holladay (E3)* 200
Hollow Rock (E2)* 397
Holston Valley (R1) 125
Holtland (H3)* 400
Hopson (R2) 300
Horn Springs (J2) 200
Hornbeak (C2)* 309
Hornsby (D4)* 280
Howell (H4)* 100
Humboldt (D3)* 7,426
Huntingdon (E2)* 2,043
Huntland (J4)* 285
Huntsville (N2)* 1,400
Huron (E3)* 70
Hurricane Mills (F3)* 35
Idlewild (D2)* 200
Indian Mound (F1)* 375
Indian Springs (R1)* 300
Inskip (N2) 5,000
Iron City (F4)* 750
Ironsburg (N4) 100
Isabella (N4)* 400
Isham (N1) 75
Isoline (L2) 275
Ivyton (L2)*
Jacks Creek (D4)* 75
Jacksboro (N2)* 1,500
Jackson (D3)* 30,207
Jamestown (M2)* 2,115
Jasper (K4)* 1,198
Jefferson City (P2)* 3,633
Jellico (N1)* 1,556
Joelton (H2)* 2,500
Johnson City (R2)* 27,864
Johnsonville (F2)* 100
Jones (C3)* 140
Jonesboro (Q2)* 1,126
Joppa (O2) 85
Juno (E3)* 80
Keeling (C4) 100
Kelso (J4)* 85
Kenton (C2)* 899
Kerrville (B4)* 300
Kimberlin Heights (O3) 120
Kimmins (F3)* 78
Kingsport (Q1)* 19,571
Kingston (N3)* 1,627
Kingston Springs (G2)* 390
Kinzel Springs (O3) 100
Kirkland (H3) 225
Knoxville (O3)* 124,769
Knoxville (urban area) 148,174
Kodak (O3)* 1,670
Kyles Ford (P1)* 75
La Follette (N2)* 5,797
La Grange (C4)* 241
La Vergne (H2)* 500
Laager (K4)* 650
Laconia (C4)* 75
Lafayette (J1)* 1,195
Lake City (N2)* 1,827
Lancing (M2)* 250
Lane (C2)* 150
Lascassas (J3)* 250
Latham (D2) 85
Laurel Bloomery (S1)* 208
Laurel Hill (K2)*
Laurelburg (L3)*
Lavinia (D3)* 88
Lawrenceburg (G4)* 5,442
Leach (E3)* 15
Leapwood (E4)* 110
Lebanon (J2)* 7,913
Ledbetter (D3) 25
Lee Valley (P2)* 200
Leinarts (N2)* 32
Leipers Fork (G3) 325
Lenoir City (N3)* 5,159
Lenox (C2)* 500
Leoma (G4)* 398
Lewisburg (H4)* 5,164
Lexington (E3)* 3,566
Liberty (K2)* 314
Liberty Hill (O2)*
Limestone (Q2)* 450
Linary (L3)* 160
Linden (F3)* 854
Littlecrab (L2)* 100
Littlelot (G3)* 150
Litton (L3)* 25
Livingston (L2)* 2,082
Lobelville (F3)* 600
Lodge (K4)*
Lone Mountain (O2)* 175
Lonely (F2) 76
Lookout Mountain (L5)* 1,675
Loretto (G4)* 706
Loudon (N3)* 3,567
Louisville (N3)* 130
Lucy (B4)* 600
Lula (E4)*
Lupton City (L4)* 1,250
Luray (D3)* 300
Luther (P2)*
Luttrell (O2)* 382
Lutts (F4)* 250
Lyles (G3)* 500
Lynchburg (J4)* 401
Lynnville (G4)* 356
Macon (B4)* 215
Madison (H2)* 7,000
Madisonville (N3)* 1,487
Malesus (D3)* 500
Manchester (J4)* 2,341
Mansfield (E2)* 110
Manson (L2)*
Martel (N3)* 95
Martha (J2)* 25
Martin (D2)* 4,082
Martin Springs (K4) 200
Martins Mills (F4) 33
Maryville (O3)* 7,742
Mascot (O2)* 2,500
Mason (B4)* 414
Masonhall (C2) 175
Maury City (C3)* 553
Maxwell (J4)* 85
Mayland (L2)* 175
Maynardville (O2)*
Mc Cloud (Q2)* 100
Mc Connell (D2)
Mc Daniel (H3) 100
Mc Donald (M4)* 150
Mc Ewen (F2)* 710
Mc Ghee (N3) 75
Mc Kenzie (E2)* 3,774
Mc Kinnon (F2)* 250
Mc Lemoresville (D3)* 242
Mc Minnville (K3)* 7,577
Mc Nairy (D4)* 90
Medina (D3)* 690
Medon (D4)* 115
Memorial (K1)* 300
Memphis (B4)* 396,000
Memphis (urban area) 404,033
Mengelwood (B2) 200
Mentor (O3)* 425
Mercer (D4)* 400
Michie (E4)*
Middleton (D4)* 362
Midway (P2)* 200
Mifflin (D3) 250
Milan (D3)* 4,938
Milledgeville (E4)* 300
Milligan College (R2)* 213
Millington (B4)* 4,696
Milo (L3)* 300
Milton (J3)* 75
Minor Hill (G4)* 292
Miston (B2)* 350
Mitchell (H1)
Mitchellville (J1)* 202
Model (F1)* 140
Mohawk (P2)* 200
Monoville (K2)* 75
Monroe (L2)*
Monteagle (K4)* 865
Monterey (L2)* 2,043
Montezuma (D4)* 130
Moodyville (L1)* 400
Mooresburg (P2)* 500
Morley (O1)* 300
Morris Chapel (E4)*
Morrison (K3)* 301
Morristown (P2)* 13,019
Moscow (C4)* 394
Mosheim (Q2)* 350
Moss (K1)* 200
Mount Juliet (H2)*
Mount Pleasant (G3)* 2,931
Mount Vernon (M4)* 250
Mountain City (S2)* 1,405
Mountainy (L4)* 140
Mulberry (H4)* 220
Munford (B4)* 976
Murfreesboro (J3)* 13,052
Napier (F4) 75
NASHVILLE (H2)* 174,307
Nashville (urban area) 257,898
Nemo (M2) 8
Neptune (G2)* 125
Neubert (O3)* 2,800
Neva (S2)* 50
New Market (O2)* 600
New Middleton (J2)* 150
New Providence (G1) 1,825
New River (M2)* 650
New Tazewell (O2)* 1,400
Newbern (C2)* 1,734
Newcomb (N1)*
Newport (P3)* 3,892
Niota (M3)* 956
Noah (J3) 100
Nolensville (H3)*
Norene (J2)* 250
Norma (N2)*
Normandy (J4)* 159
Norris (N2)* 1,134
Nunnelly (G3)*
Oak Ridge (N2)* 30,229
Oakdale (M3)* 718
Oakfield (D3)* 125
Oakland (B4)* 236
Oakley (L2) 50
Oakville (A4) 1,500
Obey City (L2)
Obion (C2)* 1,212
Ocoee (M4)* 225
Old Hickory (H2)* 10,000
Oldfort (M4)* 133
Olivehill (E4)* 140
Olive Springs (N2)* 1,089
Oneida (N1)* 1,304
Only (F3)*
Ooltewah (M4)* 900
Orlinda (H1)* 275
Orme (K4)* 230
Overall (J3)* 135
Ozone (M3)* 140
Pall Mall (M1)* 100
Palmer (K4)* 871
Palmersville (D2)* 100
Palmyra (G2)* 200
Paris (E2)* 8,826
Parrottsville (P2)* 115
Parsons (E3)* 1,640
Peakland (M3)*
Peavine (M2) 35
Pegram (H2)* 325
Pelham (K4)*
Perry (D3) 100
Perryville (F3)* 150
Persia (P2)* 50
Peters Landing (F4)* 40
Petersburg (H4)* 497
Petros (M2)* 800
Philadelphia (M3)* 600
Phillippy (C2)* 375
Pickwick Dam (E4)* 250
Pierce Station (C2)* 50
Pigeon Forge (O3)* 1,500
Pikeville (L3)* 882
Pine Top (D4) 15
Pinewood (F3) 5
Piney Flats (R2)* 300
Pinson (D4)* 300
Pioneer (N2)*
Pittsburg Landing (E4)* 114
Plant (F3) 250
Pleasant Hill (L3)* 152
Pleasant Shade (K2)* 125
Pleasant View (G2)* 300
Pleasantville (F3)*
Pocahontas (D4)* 250
Polk (C2)* 50
Pope (F3)* 30
Port Royal (G1)
Portland (H1)* 1,660
Postelle (N4)* 232
Powder Springs (O2)* 110
Powell (N2)* 400
Primm Springs (G3)* 4
Prospect Station (G4)* 350
Pruden (O1)* 250
Pulaski (G4)* 5,762
Puryear (E2)* 430

*Map on Page 87*    **TEXAS**    *Total Population 7,711,194*

Shallowater (B4)* 500
Shamrock (D2)* 3,322
Sheffield (B7)* 350
Shelbyville (L6)*
Sheldon (K1)* 200
Shepherd (K7)*
Sherman (H4)* 20,150
Sherwood (D6)* 247
Shiner (G8)* 1,778
Shiro (J7)* 300
Shore Acres ‡(J8) 783
Sierra Blanca (B11)* 900
Silsbee (K7)* 3,179
Silverton (C3)* 857
Sinton (G9)* 4,254
Skellytown (C2)* 700
Skidmore (G9)* 800
Slaton (C4)* 5,036
Slocum (J6)* 200
Smeltertown (A10)* 3,500
Smiley (G8)* 503
Smithfield (F1)* 500
Smithville (G7)* 3,379
Snyder (D5)* 12,010
Socorro (A10)*
Somerset (F8)* 920
Somerville (H7)* 1,425
Sonoma ‡(H5) 210
Sonora (D7)* 2,633
Sourlake (K7)* 1,630
South Bend (F5)* 325
South Groveton (J7)
South Houston (J2)* 4,126
South Plains (C3) 100
Southland (C4)* 210
Southside Place (J2) 1,436
South Texarkana ‡(K4) 317
Spanish Fort (G4)* 203
Sparenberg (B5)*
Spearman (C1)* 1,852
Spicewood (F7)*
Spofford (D8)* 246
Spring (J7)* 500
Springlake (B3)*
Springtown (G5)* 650
Spur (D4)* 2,183
Stamford (E5)* 5,819
Stanton (C5)* 1,603
Star (F6)*
Stephenville (F5)* 7,155
Sterley (C3)* 96
Sterling City (D6)* 846
Stinnett (C2)* 1,170
Stockdale (G8)* 1,105
Stonewall (F7)* 135
Stratford (C1)* 1,385
Strawn (F5)* 922
Streeter (E7)* 26
Streetman (H6)* 419
Sudan (B3)* 1,348
Sugar Land (J8)* 2,285
Surphur Spgs. (J4)* 8,991
Summerfield (B3)*
Sundown (B4)* 1,492
Sunray (C1)* 1,530
Sunset (G4)*
Swearingen (D3)* 45
Sweeny (J8)* 1,393
Sweet Home (H8)* 500
Sweetwater (D5)* 13,619
Swenson (D4)* 175
Sylvester (D5)*
Taft (G9)* 2,978
Tahoka (C4)* 2,848
Talco (K4)* 917
Talpa (E6)* 234
Tarzan (B5)* 79
Tascosa (B2)* 125
Tatum (K5)* 599
Taylor (G7)* 9,071
Teague (H6)* 2,925
Tehuacana ‡(H6)* 389
Telegraph (E7)* 17
Telephone (J4)* 275
Tell (D3)* 100
Temple (G6)* 25,467
Tenaha (K6)* 715
Tennyson (D6)*
Terlingua (D12)* 20
Terrell (H5)* 11,544
Terrell Hills ‡(F8) 2,708
Tesnus (B7)* 8
Texarkana (L4)* 24,753
Texas City (K3)* 16,620
Texhoma (C1) 299
Texline (B1)* 437
Texon (C6)* 500
Thalia (E4)* 223
Thomas (J5)* 200
Thorndale (G7)* 855
Thornton (H6)* 623
Thorp Spring (F5)* 200
Thrall ‡(G7)* 585
Three Rivers (F9)* 2,026
Throckmorton (F4)* 1,320
Tilden (F9)* 425
Timpson (K6)* 1,455
Tioga (H4)* 529
Tivoli (H9)* 300
Tokio ((B4)* 200
Tolar (G5)* 338
Tom Bean ‡(H4)* 286
Tomball (J7)* 1,065
Tornillo (A10)* 400
Toyah (D11)* 409
Toyahvale (D11)* 16
Trent (D5)* 296
Trenton (H4)* 603
Trinidad (J5)* 950
Trinity (J7)* 2,054
Troup (J5)* 1,539
Truscott (E4)* 255
Tulia (C3)* 3,222
Turkey (D3)* 1,005
Turnersville (G6)* 150
Tuscola (E5)* 497
Twin Sisters (F7) 50
Tyler (J5)* 38,968
Tynan (G9)* 70
Umbarger (B3)* 465
University Park (H2)* 24,275
Utopia (E8)* 350
Uvalde (E8)* 8,674
Valentine (C11)* 510
Valera (E6)* 300
Valley Mills (G6)* 1,037
Valley Spg. (F7)*
Valley View (H4)* 500
Van (J5)* 610
Van Alstyne (H4)* 1,649
Van Horn (C11)* 1,161
Vance (E8)* 100
Vancourt (D6)* 11
Vanderbilt (H9)* 400
Vanderpool (E8)* 150
Vealmoor (C5)* 35
Vega (B2)* 620
Velasco (J9)* 2,260
Venus ‡(H5)* 357
Vera (E4)* 270
Veribest (D6)* 33
Vernon (E3)* 12,651
Victoria (H9)* 16,126
Vigo Park (C3)*
Village Mills (K7)* 267
Voca (E7)* 100
Voth (K7)* 1,200
Waco (G6)* 84,706
Waco (urban area) 92,299
Wadsworth (J9)* 250
Waelder (G8)* 1,275
Waka (D1)* 100
Wake ‡(K4)* 1,066
Wall (D6)* 200
Waller (J7)* 715
Wallis (H8)* 1,500
Wallisville (L1)* 300
Walnut Spgs. (G5)* 626
Waring (F8)* 176
Washington (J7)* 300
Waskom (L5)* 719
Watauga (F1) 150
Water Valley (C6)* 300
Waxahachie (H5)* 11,204
Wayside (C3)* 43
Weatherford (G5)* 8,093
Webb (E10)* 17
Webb (F2) 45
Webster (K2)*
Weesatche (G9)* 250
Weimar (H8)* 1,663
Weinert (E4)* 288
Welch (B5)*
Weldon (J6)* 250
Wellington (D3)* 3,676
Wellman (B5)* 165
Wells (J6)* 718
Weslaco (G11)* 7,514
West (G6)* 2,130
W. Columbia (J8)* 2,100
W. University Pl. (J2) 17,074
W. Vernon (E3)
W. Worth (E2) 529
Westbrook (C5)* 220
Westhoff (G8)* 610
Westminster ‡(H4)* 192
Westover Hills (E2) 266
Wharton (J8)* 4,450
Wheeler (D2)* 904
White Deer (C2)* 629
White Settlement (E2) 10,827
Whiteface (B4)* 579
Whiteflat (D3)* 100
Whitesboro (H4)* 1,854
Whitewright (H4)* 1,372
Whitharral (B4)* 275
Whitney (G6)* 1,383
Whitsett (F9)* 100
Whitt (G5)* 150
Wichita Falls (F4)* 68,042
Wickett (B6)*
Wiergate (L6)* 1,000
Wildorado (B2)* 150
Willis (J7)* 1,164
Willow City (F7)* 75
Wills Point (J5)* 2,030
Wilmer (H2)* 465
Wilson (C4)* 300
Winchell (E6)* 100
Winchester (H7)* 275
Windom ‡(H4)* 297
Windthorst (F4)* 400
Winfield (K4)* 319
Winfree (L1) 50
Wingate (D5)* 262
Wink (A6)* 1,521
Winnie (K8)* 800
Winnsboro (J5)* 2,512
Winona (J5)* 450
Winters (E6)* 2,676
Wolfe City (J4)* 1,345
Wolfforth (C4)* 383
Woodsboro (G9)* 1,836
Woodson (E5)* 483
Woodville (K7)* 1,863
Wooster (K2) 2,500
Wortham (H6)* 1,170
Wylie (H5)* 1,295
Yantis (J5)* 300
Yoakum (G8)* 5,231
Yorktown (G9)* 2,596
Ysleta (A10)* 4,782
Zapata (E11)* 1,409
Zavalla (K6)* 956
Zephyr (F6)*

*Map on Page 88*

## UTAH

*Total Population 688,862*

**29 COUNTIES**

Beaver (A5) 4,856
Box Elder (A2) 19,734
Cache (C2) 33,536
Carbon (D4) 24,901
Daggett (E3) 364
Davis (B3) 30,867
Duchesne (D3) 8,134
Emery (D4) 6,304
Garfield (C6) 4,151
Grand (E5) 1,903
Iron (A6) 9,642
Juab (A4) 5,981
Kane (B6) 2,299
Millard (A4) 9,387
Morgan (C2) 2,519
Piute (B5) 1,911
Rich (C2) 1,673
Salt Lake (B3) 274,895
San Juan (E6) 5,315
Sanpete (C4) 13,891
Sevier (C5) 12,072
Summit (D3) 6,745
Tooele (A3) 14,636
Uintah (E3) 10,300
Utah (C3) 81,912
Wasatch (C3) 5,574
Washington (A6) 9,836
Wayne (C5) 2,205
Weber (B2) 83,319

**CITIES and TOWNS**

Abraham (B4)* 100
Adamsville (B5)* 50
Alpine (C3) 571
Alton (B6)* 154
Altonah (D3)* 363
Amalga (C2) 225
American Fork (C3)* 5,126
Angle (C5) 30
Annabella (C5)* 263
Antimony (C5)* 187
Arcadia (D3)* 168
Aurora (B5)* 614
Axtell (C4)* 155
Bacchus (B3)* 94
Bear River City (B2)* 438
Beaver (B5)* 1,685
Benjamin (C3) 450
Beryl (A6)* 26
Bicknell (C5)* 373
Bingham Canyon (B3)* 2,569
Birdseye (C4)* 75
Black Rock (B5)* 19
Blanding (E6)* 1,177
Blue Creek (B2) 43
Bluebell (D3)* 218
Bluff (E6)* 100
Bonanza (E4)*
Boneta (D3)* 134
Bothwell‡ (B2) 317
Boulder (C6)* 185
Bountiful (C3)* 6,004
Bridgeland (D3)* 240
Bridgeport (E3) 6
Brigham City (C2)* 6,790
Brighton (C3)*
Bryce Canyon (B6)* 200
Burrville (C5) 35
Cache Junction (C2)* 80
Caineville (D5) 12
Callao (A4)* 65
Cannonville (C6)* 205
Castle Dale (D4)* 715
Castle Gate (D4)* 701
Castle Rock (C2) 20
Cedar City (A6)* 6,106
Cedar Fort (B3) 213
Cedar Valley (B3)* 82
Centerfield (C4)* 601
Centerville (C3)* 1,262
Central (A6)* 49
Central (B5) 100
Charleston (C3) 201
Chester (C4)* 153
Circleville (B5)* 603
Cisco (E5)* 41
Clarkston (B2)* 526
Clawson (C4)* 136
Clearcreek (C4)* 168
Clearfield (B2)* 4,723
Cleveland (D4)* 343
Clinton ‡(B2) 670
Clive (A3) 10
Clover (B3) 110
Coalville (C3)* 850
Collinston (B2)* 145
Colton (C4) 21
Columbia (D4)* 412
Corinne (B2)* 427
Cornish (B2)* 181
Cove Fort (B5) 10
Croydon (C2)* 90
Delle (B3)* 35
Delta (B4)* 1,703
Deseret (B4)* 332
Devils Slide (C2)* 200
Deweyville (B2)* 233
Dividend (C4)* 30
Dragerton (D4)* 3,453
Dragon (E4)
Draper (C3)* 2,000
Duchesne (D3)* 804
East Layton‡ (C2) 217
Echo (C3)* 175
Eden (C2)* 235
Elberta (B4)* 138
Elmo (D4)* 170
Elsinore (B5)* 657
Elwood ‡(B2) 393
Emery (C5)* 488
Enterprise (A6)* 790
Ephraim (C4)* 1,987
Escalante (C6)* 773
Etna (A2) 22
Eureka (B4)* 1,318
Fairfield (B3) 37
Fairview (C4)* 974
Farmington (C3)* 1,468
Fayette (C4)* 200
Ferron (C4)* 478
Fielding (B2)* 249
Fillmore (B5)* 1,890
Five Mile Pass (B3)
Fort Duchesne (E3)* 200
Fountain Green (C4)* 767
Francis (C3) 276
Fremont (C5)* 224
Frisco (A5)
Fruit Heights (C2) 124
Fruitland (D3)* 127
Gandy (A4) 48
Garden City (C2)* 164
Garfield (B3)* 2,079
Garland (B2)* 1,008
Garrison (A5)* 34
Geneva (C3)
Genola (C4) 314
Glendale (B6)* 226
Glenwood (C5)* 338
Gold Hill (A3) 4
Goshen (C4)* 525
Grantsville (B3)* 1,537
Green River (D4)* 583
Greenville (B5)* 128
Greenwich (B5)* 50
Grouse Creek (A2)* 167
Grover (C5)* 53
Gunlock (A6)* 89
Gunnison (C4)* 1,144
Gusher (E3)* 125
Hanksville (D5)* 100
Hanna (D3)* 175
Hatch (B6)* 244
Hatton (B5) 9
Hayden (D3)* 185
Heber (C3)* 2,936
Helper (D4)* 2,850
Henefer (C2)* 346
Henrieville (C6)* 114
Hiawatha (D4)* 1,421
Hinckley (B4)* 589
Hite (D6)
Holden (B4)* 476
Holladay (C3) 3,100
Honeyville (B2)* 599
Hooper (B2)* 1,243
Howell (B2)* 176
Hoytsville (C3) 330
Huntington (C4)* 1,029
Huntsville (C2)* 494
Hurricane (A6)* 1,271
Hyde Park (C2)* 644
Hyrum (C2)* 1,704
Ibapah (A3)* 150
Indianola (C4) 50
International (B3)
Ioka (D3) 238
Iron Mountain (A6)
Iron Springs (A6) 20
Ivins (A6)* 95
Jensen (E3)*
Joseph (B5)* 208
Junction (B5)* 285
Kamas (C3)* 721
Kanab (B6)* 1,287
Kanarraville (A6)* 263
Kanosh (B5)* 476
Kaysville (B2)* 1,898
Keetley (C3)*
Kelton (A2)
Kenilworth (D4)* 932
Kingston (B5)* 138
Knolls (A3) 12
Koosharem (C5)* 300
La Sal (E5)* 75
La Verkin (A6)* 387
Lakeside (B2) 25
Laketown (C2)* 217
Lapoint (E3)* 400
Lark (B3)* 750
Latuda (C4)* 200
Layton (C2)* 3,456
Laytona ‡(C2) 405
Leamington (B4)* 214
Leeds (A6)* 160
Leeton (D3) 50
Lehi (C3)* 3,627
Leland (C3) 175
Leota (E3) 124
Levan (C4)* 521
Lewiston (C2)* 1,533
Liberty (C2) 196
Lindon (C3) 801
Linwood (E3)* 22
Loa (C5)* 437
Lofgreen (B3)* 20
Logan (C2)* 16,832
Lucin (A2)* 51
Lund (A5)* 42
Lyman (C5)* 276
Lynn (A2)* 50
Lynndyl (B4)* 241
Maeser (E3) 643
Magna (B3)* 3,502
Mammoth (B4)* 137
Manila (E3)* 147
Manti (C4)* 2,051
Mantua (C2) 271
Mapleton (C3) 1,175
Marysvale (B5)* 520
Mayfield (C4)* 390
Meadow (B5)* 378
Mendon (B2)* 369
Mercur (B3) 2
Mexican Hat (E6)
Midvale (B3)* 3,996
Midway (C3)* 711
Milford (A5)* 1,673
Mills, (B4) 42
Millville (C2)* 401
Minersville (A5)* 593
Moab (E5)* 1,274
Modena (A6)* 130
Mohrland (D4)
Mona (C4)* 328
Monroe (B5)* 1,214
Monticello (E6)* 1,172
Moore (C5)* 41
Morgan (C2)* 1,064
Moroni (C4)* 1,076
Motoqua (A6) 25
Mounds (D4) 15
Mount Carmel (B6)* 158
Mount Emmons (D3)* 276
Mount Pleasant (C4)* 2,030
Mountain Home (D3)* 300
Murray (C3)* 9,006
Myton (D3)* 435
Nada (A5)
National (C4)*
Neola (D3)* 400
Nephi (C4)* 2,990
New Harmony (A6)* 126
Newcastle (A6)* 229
Newton (C2)* 497
Nibley (C2) 304
North Logan (C2) 535
North Ogden (C2) 1,105
North Salt Lake (C3)* 255
Oak City (B4)* 334
Oakley (C3)* 264
Oasis (B4)* 190
Ogden (C2)* 57,112
Onaqui ‡(B3) 333
Ophir (B3)* 199
Orangeville (C4)* 589
Orderville (B6)* 371
Orem (C3)* 8,351
Ouray (E3)* 111
Panguitch (B6)* 1,501
Paradise (C2)* 401
Paragonah (B6) 404
Park City (C3)* 2,254
Park Valley (A2)* 142
Parowan (B6)* 1,455
Payson (C3)* 3,998
Peoa (C3)* 210
Perry (C2) 449
Peterson (C2) 275
Pickleville (C2) 96
Pine Valley (A6) 16
Pinto (A6)
Pintura (A6)* 40
Plain City (B2) 899
Pleasant Grove (C3)* 3,195
Pleasant View (B2) 420
Plymouth (B2)* 228
Portage (B2)* 254
Price (D4)* 6,010
Promontory (B2) 72
Providence (C2)* 1,055
Provo (C3)* 28,937
Randlett (E3)* 400
Randolph (C2)* 562
Redmond (C4)* 600
Richfield (B5)* 4,212
Richmond (C2)* 1,091
River Heights ‡(C2) 468
Riverdale (C2) 871
Riverside (B2)* 281
Riverton (B3)* 1,666
Rockville (A6)* 180
Roosevelt (D3)* 1,628
Rosette (A2) 68
Roy (B2)* 3,723
Royal (D4)* 195
Rubys Inn (B6)*
Saint George (A6)* 4,562
St. John (B3)* 130
Salem (C3)* 781
Salina (C5)* 1,789
SALT LAKE CITY (C3)* 182,121
Salt Lake City (urban area) 226,880
Saltair (B3)* 75
Sandy (C3)* 2,095
Santa Clara (A6)* 319
Santaquin (C4)* 1,214
Scipio (B4)* 491
Scofield (C4)* 236
Sego (E4)* 50
Sevier (B5)* 104
Sigurd (B5)* 431
Silver City (B4)* 30
Smithfield (C2)* 2,383
Snowville (B2)* 199
Soldier Summit (C4)* 93
South Jordan (C3) 1,048
S. Ogden (C2) 3,763
S. Salt Lake (C3)* 7,704
S. Weber (C2) 244
Spanish Fork (C3)* 5,230
Spring Canyon (C4)* 458
Spring City (C4)* 703
Springdale (B6)* 174
Springville (C3)* 6,475
Spry (B5)* 56
Standardville (C4)* 307
Sterling (C4)* 188
Stockton (B3)* 414
Sulphurdale (B5) 2
Summit (B6)* 145
Summit Point (E5)* 42
Sunnyside (D4)* 1,881
Sunset (B2) 993
Syracuse (B2) 837
Tabiona (D3)* 160
Talmage (D3)* 174
Taylorsville (B3)
Teasdale (C5)* 237
Thatcher (B2) 268
Thistle (C4)* 200
Thompson (E5)* 100
Tooele (B3)* 7,269
Toquerville (A6)* 219
Torrey (C5)* 241
Tremonton (B2)* 1,662
Trenton (B2)* 451
Tridell (E3)* 347
Tropic (B6)* 483
Trout Creek (A4)* 65
Uintah (C2) 317
Upalco, (D3)* 175
Venice (C5)* 238
Vernal (E3)* 2,845
Vernon (B3)* 175
Veyo (A6)* 84
Vineyard (C3) 113
Virgin (A6)* 147
Wahsatch (C2)* 35
Wales (C4)* 179
Wallsburg (C3)* 207
Wanship (C3) 173
Washington (A6)* 435
Watson (E4)
Wattis (C4)* 283
Wellington (D4)* 845
Wellsville (C2)* 1,241
Wendover (A3)* 250
West Bountiful (C3) 682
W. Jordan (C3)* 2,107
W. Point ‡(B2) 433
W. Weber (B2) 276
Westwater (E4)* 50
Whiterocks (E3)* 395
Widtsoe (C6) 25
Willard (C2)* 548
Woodland (C3) 200
Woodruff (C2)* 175
Woods Cross (B3)* 273
Woodside (D4)* 14
Yost (A2)* 107
Zion Nat'l. Park (B6)* 63

*Map on Page 89*

## VERMONT

*Total Population 377,747*

**14 COUNTIES**

Addison (A2) 19,442
Bennington (A4) 24,115
Caledonia (C1) 24,049
Chittenden (A2) 62,570
Essex (D1) 6,257
Franklin (B1) 29,894
Grand Isle (A1) 3,406
Lamoille (B1) 11,388
Orange (C3) 17,027
Orleans (C1) 21,190
Rutland (A3) 45,905
Washington (B2) 42,870
Windham (B5) 28,749
Windsor (B4) 40,885

**CITIES and TOWNS**

Addison (A2) △628
Albany (C1)* 196
Alburg (A1)* 563
Andover (B4) △185
Arlington (A4)* △1,163
Ascutney (C4)* 200
Averill (D1)* △20
Bakersfield (B1)* △779
Barnard (B3)* △439
Barnet (D2)* △1,425
Barre (C2)* 10,922
Barton (C1)* 1,267
Bartonsville (B4)* 200
Beebe Plain (C1)* 173
Beecher Falls (D1)* 500
Bellows Falls (C4)* 3,881
Belvidere (B1) 207
Belvidere Center (B1)* 50
Bennington (A5)* 8,002
Benson (A3)* △573
Benson Landing (A3) 2
Berkshire (B1)* △1,063
Bethel (B3)* △1,534
Bolton (B2) △301
Boltonville (C2)* 50
Bomoseen (A3)* 275
Bondville (B4)* 229
Bradford (C3)* 725
Braintree (B3)* △626
Brandon (A3)* △3,304
Brattleboro (C5)* △11,522
Bread Loaf (B3)* 11
Bridgewater (B4)* △903
Bridgewater Corners* (B3) 173
Bridport (A3)* △663
Briggs (B3) 125
Bristol (A2)* 1,308

Brookfield (B2)* ... △ 762
Brownington (C1) ... △ 673
Brownsville (C4)* ... △ 125
Burke (D1) ... △1,042
Burlington (A2)* ... 33,155
Cabot (C2)* ... △ 219
Calais (B2)* ... △ 778
Cambridge (B1)* ... 244
Cambridge Jct. (B1)* 80
Cambridgeport (C4)* .. 48
Canaan (D1)* ... △ 969
Castleton (A3)* ... △1,748
Cavendish (B4)* ... △1,374
Cedar Beach (A2)* ...
Center Rutland (A3)* .. 540
Charlotte (A2)* ... △1,215
Chelsea (C2)* ... △1,025
Chester (C4)* ... 796
Chester Depot (C4)* .. 600
Chittenden (B3)* ... △ 424
Clarendon Springs (A3) 75
Colchester (A1)* ... △3,897
Concord (D2)* ... 348
Corinth (C2)* ... △ 786
Cornwall (A3) ... △ 728
Coventry (C1)* ... △ 497
Craftsbury (C1)* ... △ 709
Craftsbury Common* (C1) ... 225
Cuttingsville (B3)* ... 164
Danby (B4)* ... △ 990
Danville (C2)* ... △1,312
Derby (Derby Center) (C1)* ... 383
Derby Line (C1)* ... 767
Dorset (A4)* ... △1,150
Duxbury (B2) ... △ 489
East Albany (C1) ... 148
E. Alburg (A1) ... 20
E. Arlington (A4)* ... 500
E. Barnet (D2)* ... 166
E. Barre (C2)* ... 600
E. Berkshire (B1)* ... 225
E. Bethel (B3)* ... 64
E. Brookfield (C2)* ... 175
E. Burke (D1)* ... 330
E. Calais (C2)* ... 140
E. Charleston (D1)* ... 350
E. Concord (D2)* ... 220
E. Corinth (C2)* ... 185
E. Craftsbury (C1)* ... 43
E. Dorset (A4)* ... 350
E. Dover (B5)* ... 150
E. Fairfield (B1)* ... 500
E. Franklin (B1)* ... 80
E. Georgia (B1)* ... 60
E. Granville (B2)* ... 65
E. Hardwick (C1)* ... 267
E. Haven (D1)* ... △ 85
E. Jamaica (B4)* ... 100
E. Middlebury (A3)* ... 300
E. Montpelier (B2)* ... △1,128
E. Peacham (C2) ... 70
E. Poultney (A3)* ... 500
E. Randolph (C3)* ... 175
E. Richford (C1)* ... 160
E. Ryegate (D2)* ... 225
E. Thetford (C3)* ... 50
E. Wallingford (B4)* ... 300
Eden (B1)* ... △ 496
Eden Mills (C1)* ... 225
Ely (C3)* ... 51
Enosburg Falls (B1)* .. 1,289
Essex (A1)* ... △3,931
Essex Junction (A2)* .. 2,741
Fair Haven (A3)* ... 2,058
Fairfax (B1)* ... △1,129
Fairfield (B1)* ... △1,428
Fairlee (C3)* ... 571
Ferrisburg (A2)* ... △1,387
Florence (A3)* ... 300
Forest Dale (A3)* ... 400
Franklin (B1)* ... △ 878
Gassetts (B4)* ... 50
Gaysville (B3)* ... 172
Georgia (A1) ... △1,055
Gilman (D2)* ... 900
Glover (C1)* ... 228
Grafton (B4)* ... △ 422
Granby (D1)* ... △ 74
Grand Isle (A1)* ... △ 735
Graniteville (C2)* ... 1,500
Granville (B3)* ... △ 213
Greensboro (C1)* ... △ 737
Groton (C2)* ... 435
Guildhall (D1)* ... △ 270
Guilford (B5) ... △ 796
Halifax (B5)* ... △ 343
Hancock (B3)* ... △ 391
Hardwick (C2)* ... 1,696
Hartford (C3)* ... △5,827
Hartland (C3)* ... △1,559
Hartland Four Corners (C3)* ... 300
Healdville (B4)* ... 124
Highgate Center (B1)* 350
Highgate Falls (A1)* .. 218
Highgate Springs (A1)* 300
Hinesburg (A2)* ... △1,120
Hubbardton (A3)* ... △ 332
Huntington (A2)* ... △ 601
Huntington Ctr. (B2)* 150
Hyde Park (B1)* ... 440
Hydeville (A3)* ... 400
Irasburg (C1)* ... △ 711
Island Pond (D1)* ... 1,252
Isle La Motte (A1)* ... △ 295
Jacksonville (B5)* ... 220
Jamaica (B4)* ... △ 597
Jay (C1) ... △ 243
Jeffersonville (B1)* ... 387
Jericho (A2)* ... △1,135
Jericho Center (B2)* .. 125
Johnson (B1)* ... 900
Jonesville (B2)* ... 156
Lake (D1) ... 6
Lake Dunmore (A3)* ... 35
Lake Elmore (B1)* ... 75
Leicester Jct. (A3)* ... 97
Lewiston (C3)* ... 55
Lincoln (B2)* ... △ 577
Londonderry (B4)* ... △ 953
Lowell (C1)* ... △ 643
Lower Cabot (C2) ... 120
Lower Waterford (D2)* 550
Ludlow (B4)* ... 1,678
Lunenburg (D2)* ... △1,299
Lyndon (C1)* ... △3,360
Lyndon Center (C1)* ... 321
Lyndonville (D1)* ... 1,506
Maidstone (D1) ... △ 81
Manchester (A4)* ... 454
Manchester Center (A4)* 900
Manchester Depot (B4)* 561
Marlboro (B5)* ... △ 311
Marshfield (C2)* ... 274
Mc Indoe Falls (C2)* .. 200
Middlebury (A2)* ... 3,614
Middlesex (B2)* ... △ 887
Middletown Springs (A4)* ... △ 496
Milton (A1)* ... 739
Monkton (A2)* ... △ 520
Monkton Ridge (A2) ... 150
Montgomery (B1)* ... △1,091
Montgomery Center (B1)* ...
MONTPELIER (B2)* ... 8,599
Moretown (B2)* ... △ 883
Morgan (D1)* ... △ 296
Morgan Center (D1)* .. 130
Morrisville (B1)* ... 1,995
Morses Line (B1) ... 25
Moscow (B2)* ... 245
Mount Holly (B4)* ... △ 567
New Haven (A2)* ... △ 932
Newbury (C2)* ... △1,667
Newfane (B4)* ... 156
Newport (C1)* ... 5,217
Newport Center (C1)* 235
North Bennington (A5)* 1,327
N. Calais (C2)* ... 20
N. Clarendon (B3)* ... 226
N. Concord (D2)* ... 108
N. Danville (C2) ... 250
N. Ferrisburg (A2)* ... 500
N. Hartland (C3)* ... 268
N. Hero (A1)* ... △ 407
N. Hyde Park (B1)* ... 250
N. Montpelier (C2)* ... 136
N. Pomfret (B3)* ... 200
N. Pownal (A5)* ... 650
N. Randolph (C3) ... 36
N. Springfield (C4)* ... 450
N. Thetford (C3)* ... 110
N. Troy (C1)* ... 1,057
N. Tunbridge (C3) ... 50
N. Westminster (C4) ... 404
N. Williston (B2) ... 75
N. Wolcott (C1) ... 100
Northfield (B2)* ... 2,262
Northfield Falls (B2) .. 340
Norton (C1)* ... △ 279
Norwich (C3)* ... △1,532
Old Bennington (A5) ... 198
Orange (C2) ... △ 410
Orleans (C1)* ... 1,261
Orwell (A3)* ... △ 902
Panton (A2) ... △ 332
Passumpsic (C2)* ... 180
Pawlet (A4)* ... △1,156
Peacham (C2)* ... △ 501
Perkinsville (B4)* ... 142
Peru (B4)* ... △ 197
Piermont Station (C3). 75
Pittsfield (B3)* ... △ 225
Pittsford (A3)* ... 622
Plainfield (C2)* ... 604
Plymouth (B3)* ... △ 348
Plymouth Union (B3)* 130
Pomfret (B3)* ... △ 586
Pompanoosuc (C3) ... 50
Post Mills (C3)* ... 200
Poultney (A3)* ... 1,685
Pownal (A5)* ... △1,453
Pownal Center (A5) ... 300
Proctor (A3)* ... 1,813
Proctorsville (B4)* ... 349
Putney (B4)* ... △1,019
Quechee (C3)* ... 330
Randolph (B3)* ... 2,223
Randolph Center (B3)* 141
Reading (B4)* ... △ 470
Readsboro (A5)* ... 654
Richford (B1)* ... 1,916
Richmond (A2)* ... 731
Ricker Mills (C2) ... 10
Ripton (B3)* ... △ 207
Riverton (B2)* ... 125
Rochester (B3)* ... △ 937
Roxbury (B2)* ... △ 465
Royalton (B3)* ... △1,331
Rupert (A4)* ... △ 713
Rutland (B3)* ... 17,659
Ryegate (C2)* ... △ 996
Saint Albans (A1)* ... 8,552
St. Albans Bay (A1)* .. 335
St. Johnsbury (D2)* ... 7,370
St. Johnsbury Ctr. (D2) 350
Salisbury (A3)* ... △ 573
Saxtons River (B4)* ... 715
Sharon (C3)* ... △ 470
Sheffield (C1)* ... △ 451
Shelburne (A2)* ... △1,365
Sheldon (B1)* ... △1,352
Sheldon Junction (B1)* 70
Sheldon Springs (A1)* 325
Sherburne Center (B3)* 70
Shoreham (A3)* ... △ 829
Simonsville (B4)* ... 100
South Barre (B2)* ... 675
S. Burlington (A2) ... △3,279
S. Dorset (A4)* ... 173
S. Hero (A1)* ... △ 567
S. Lincoln (B2)* ... 80
S. Londonderry (B4)* .. 400
S. Lunenburg (D2)* ... 78
S. Newbury (D2)* ... 105
S. Newfane (B5)* ... 119
S. Pomfret (B3)* ... 100
S. Royalton (C3)* ... 700
S. Ryegate (C2)* ... 340
S. Shaftsbury (A5)* ... 480
S. Strafford (C3)* ... 300
S. Wallingford (B4)* .. 350
S. Windham (B4)* ... 40
S. Woodbury (B2)* ... 62
S. Woodstock (B3)* ... 250
Springfield (C4)* ... 4,940
Stamford (A5) ... △ 514
Starksboro (A2)* ... △ 576
Stockbridge (B3)* ... △ 427
Stowe (B2)* ... 556
Strafford (C3)* ... △ 680
Sudbury (A3)* ... △ 263
Sutton (C1)* ... △ 528
Swanton (A1)* ... 2,275
Taftsville (C3)* ... 125
Talcville (B3) ... 70
Thetford (C3)* ... △1,046
Thetford Center (C3)* 125
Tinmouth (B4) ... △ 248
Topsham (C2)* ... △ 733
Townshend (B4)* ... 178

Troy (C1)* ... △1,786
Tunbridge (C3)* ... △ 774
Tyson (B4) ... 175
Underhill (B1)* ... △ 698
Underhill Center (B2)*
Union Village (C3)* ... 45
Vergennes (A2)* ... 1,736
Vernon (B5)* ... △ 712
Vershire (C3)* ... △ 284
Waits River (C2)* ... 76
Waitsfield (B2)* ... △ 661
Walden (C2)* ... △ 481
Walden Heights (C2)* 60
Wallingford (A4)* ... △1,482
Wardsboro (B4)* ... △ 377
Warren (B2)* ... △ 498
Washington (C2)* ... △ 650
Waterbury (B2)* ... 3,153
Waterbury Center (B2)* ... 650
Waterville (B1)* ... △ 409
Websterville (C2)* ... 975
Wells (A4)* ... △ 487
Wells River (D2)* ... 570
West Barnet (C2)* ... 88
W. Berkshire (B1)* ... 70
W. Brattleboro (B5)* ..
W. Burke (C1)* ... 414
W. Charleston (C1)* ... 185
W. Corinth (C2)* ... 52
W. Cornwall (A3) ... 50
W. Danville (C2)* ... 131
W. Dover (B5)* ... 45
W. Dummerston (C5)* ... 200
W. Fairlee (C3)* ... △ 363
W. Glover (C1)* ... 58
W. Halifax (B5)* ... 200
W. Hartford (C3)* ... 225
W. Newbury (C2)* ... 100
W. Pawlet (A4)* ... 500
W. Rupert (A4)* ... 300
W. Rutland (A3)* ... △2,487
W. Salisbury (A3) ... 145
W. Townshend (B4)* ... 200
W. Wardsboro (B4)* ... 82
W. Woodstock (B3)* ... 80
Westfield (C1)* ... △ 358
Westford (A1)* ... △ 685
Westminster (C4)* ... 298
Westminster Sta. (C4)* 70
Westminster West (B4)* 150
Westmore (C1) ... △ 210
Weston (B4)* ... △ 468
Wheelock (C1)* ... △ 287
White River Jct. (C3)* 2,365
Whiting (A3)* ... △ 282
Whitingham (B5)* ... △ 816
Wilder (C3)* ... 1,097
Williamstown (B2)* ... △1,600
Williamsville (B5)* ... 150
Williston (A2)* ... △1,182
Willoughby (C1) ... 150
Wilmington (B5)* ... 571
Windham (B4)* ... △ 146
Windsor (C4)* ... 3,467
Winooski (A2)* ... 6,734
Wolcott (C1)* ... △ 766
Woodbury (C2)* ... △ 449
Woodford (A5)* ... △ 198
Woodstock (B3)* ... 1,326
Worcester (B2)* ... △ 445

*Map on Page 90*

## VIRGINIA

*Total Population 3,318,680*

### 100 COUNTIES

Accomack (N5) ... 33,832
Albemarle (G5) ... 26,662
Alleghany (D5) ... 23,139
Amelia (H6) ... 7,908
Amherst (F5) ... 20,332
Appomattox (G6) ... 8,764
Arlington (K3) ... 135,449
Augusta (F4) ... 34,154
Bath (E4) ... 6,296
Bedford (E6) ... 29,627
Bland (B6) ... 6,436
Botetourt (E5) ... 15,766
Brunswick (J7) ... 20,136
Buchanan (D1) ... 35,748
Buckingham (G5) ... 12,288
Campbell (F6) ... 28,877
Caroline (K4) ... 12,471
Carroll (C7) ... 26,695
Charles City (K6) ... 4,676
Charlotte (G6) ... 14,057
Chesterfield (J6) ... 40,400
Clarke (H2) ... 7,074
Craig (D6) ... 3,452
Culpeper (H3) ... 13,242
Cumberland (H6) ... 7,252
Dickenson (D2) ... 23,393
Dinwiddie (J6) ... 18,839
Essex (L5) ... 6,530
Fairfax (K3) ... 98,557
Fauquier (J3) ... 21,248
Floyd (D7) ... 11,351
Fluvanna (H5) ... 7,121
Franklin (E6) ... 24,560
Frederick (H2) ... 17,537
Giles (C6) ... 18,956
Gloucester (L6) ... 10,343
Goochland (J5) ... 8,934
Grayson (B7) ... 21,379
Greene (H4) ... 4,745
Greensville (J7) ... 16,319
Halifax (G7) ... 41,442
Hanover (J5) ... 21,985
Henrico (K6) ... 57,340
Henry (E7) ... 31,219
Highland (E4) ... 4,069
Isle of Wight (L7) ... 14,906
James City (L6) ... 6,317
King and Queen (L5) ... 6,299
King George (K4) ... 6,710
King William (K5) ... 7,589
Lancaster (M5) ... 8,640
Lee (B2) ... 36,106
Loudoun (J2) ... 21,147
Louisa (J5) ... 12,826
Lunenburg (H7) ... 14,116
Madison (H4) ... 8,273
Mathews (M6) ... 7,148
Mecklenburg (H7) ... 33,497
Middlesex (M5) ... 6,715
Montgomery (D6) ... 29,780
Nansemond (L7) ... 25,238
Nelson (G5) ... 14,042
New Kent (L5) ... 3,995
Norfolk (M7) ... 99,937
Northampton (N6) ... 17,300
Northumberland (M5) ... 10,012
Nottoway (H6) ... 15,479
Orange (H4) ... 12,755
Page (H3) ... 15,152
Patrick (D7) ... 15,642
Pittsylvania (F7) ... 66,096
Powhatan (J5) ... 5,556
Prince Edward (H6) ... 15,398
Prince George (K6) ... 19,679
Prince William (K3) ... 22,612
Princess Anne (M7) ... 42,277
Pulaski (C6) ... 27,758
Rappahannock (H3) ... 6,112
Richmond (L5) ... 6,189
Roanoke (D6) ... 41,486
Rockbridge (F5) ... 23,359
Rockingham (G4) ... 35,079
Russell (E2) ... 26,818
Scott (D2) ... 27,640
Shenandoah (G3) ... 21,169
Smyth (E2) ... 30,187
Southampton (K7) ... 26,522
Spotsylvania (J4) ... 11,920
Stafford (K4) ... 11,902
Surry (L6) ... 6,220
Sussex (K7) ... 12,785
Tazewell (B6) ... 47,512
Warren (H3) ... 14,801
Washington (E2) ... 37,536
Westmoreland (L4) ... 10,148
Wise (C2) ... 56,336
Wythe (B7) ... 23,327
York (L6) ... 11,750

### CITIES and TOWNS

Abingdon (E2)* ... 4,709
Accomac (N5)* ... 500
Achilles (M6)* ...
Acorn (L4)* ... 100
Adams Grove (K7)* ... 75
Adner (L5)* ... 71
Advance Mills (G4) ... 25
Afton (G4)* ... 370
Agricola (F5)* ... 65
Airpoint (D6)* ... 150
Alanthus (H3)
Alberene (G5)* ... 500
Alberta (J7)* ... 430
Alexandria (L3)* ... 61,787
Allegheny (D5)* ...
Allisonia (C7)* ... 400
Alpha (H5)* ...
Altavista (F6)* ... 3,332
Alto (F5) ... 75
Alton (F7)* ... 53
Alvarado (E2)* ... 50
Amelia Court House (J6)* ... 800
Amherst (F5)* ... 1,038
Amissville (H3)* ... 100
Ammon (J6)* ... 50
Amonate (A6)* ... 1,800
Andersonville (G6)* ... 50
Andover (C2)* ...
Ante (J7)* ...
Appalachia (C2)* ... 2,915
Apple Grove (J5) ... 50
Appomattox (G6)* ... 1,094
Ararat (C7)* ...
Arcadia (E5)* ... 125
Arcanum (G6)* ...
Arlington (L3)* ... 135,449
Arrington (G5)* ... 200
Artrip (D2)* ... 350
Arvonia (H5)* ...
Ashburn (K2)* ... 210
Ashland (J5)* ... 2,610
Atkins (B7)* ... 500
Atlee (K5) ... 207
Augusta Springs (F4)* ... 300
Austinville (B7)* ...
Avalon (M5)* ... 25
Axton (E7)* ... 166
Aylett (K5)* ... 100
Backbay (M7)* ... 150
Bacons Castle (L6)* ... 75
Ballsville (H6)* ... 95
Balty (K5)* ... 50
Banco (H4)* ... 90
Banner (D2)* ... 700
Barboursville (H4)* ... 250
Barren Springs (C7) ... 300
Bartlick (D1)* ... 275
Baskerville (H7)* ... 51
Bassett (E7)* ... 3,421
Bastian (B6)* ... 1,200
Batesville (G5)* ... 150
Baywood (C7)* ... 91
Beach (J6)* ... 40
Bealeton (J3)* ... 350
Beaverdam (J5)* ... 500
Beaverlett (M6)* ... 188
Beckham (G6)* ... 35
Bedford (E6)* ... 4,061
Belle Haven (N5)* ... 453
Belona (H5)* ... 80
Belspring (C6)* ... 300
Ben Hur (B2)* ... 200
Benhams (D2)* ... 148
Benns Church (L7)* ... 100
Bent Creek (G5)* ... 60
Bent Mountain (D6)* ... 88
Bentonville (H3)* ... 600
Berea (J4)* ... 22
Bergton (G3)* ... 100
Berryville (J2)* ... 1,401
Bertrand (L5)* ... 27
Big Island (F5)* ... 500
Big Rock (D1)* ... 250
Big Stone Gap (C2)* ... 5,173
Birchleaf (D1)* ... 500
Birdsnest (N6)* ... 200
Blackridge (H7)* ... 10
Blacksburg (D6)* ... 3,358
Blackstone (J6)* ... 3,536
Blackwater (B2)* ... 500
Blairs (F7)* ... 300
Bland (B6)* ... 600
Bloxom (N5)* ... 400
Blue Grass (E3)* ... 105
Blue Ridge (E6)* ... 765
Bluefield (B6)* ... 4,212
Bluemont (J2)* ... 180
Bluff City (C6)* ... 225
Bohannon (M6)* ... 250
Boissevain (B6)* ... 1,197
Bolar (E4)* ... 111
Bon Air (J5)* ... 1,500
Bondtown (C2)* ... 240
Bonny Blue (B2)* ... 930
Boones Mill (E6)* ... 335
Boonesville (H4)* ... 400
Boulevard (L6)* ... 100
Bowers Hill (M7)* ... 400
Bowling Green (K4)* ... 616
Boxwood (E7) ... 18
Boyce (H2) ... 372
Boydton (H7)* ... 501
Boykins (K7)* ... 811
Branchville (K7)* ... 169
Brandon (K6)* ... 100
Brandy (J4)* ... 350
Breaks (D1)* ... 300
Bremo Bluff (H5)* ... 300
Bridgewater (F4)* ... 1,537
Brightwood (H4)* ... 250
Bristol (D3)* ... 15,954
Bristow (J3)* ... 75
Broad Run (J3)* ... 30
Broadford (E2)* ... 800
Broadway (G3)* ... 561
Brodnax (J7)* ... 499
Brokenburg (J4)* ... 100
Brooke (K4)* ... 450
Brookneal (G6)* ... 883
Brownsburg (F5)* ... 360
Browntown (H3)* ... 150
Brucetown (H2)* ... 265
Buchanan (E5)* ... 1,300
Buckhorn (L7)* ... 100
Buckingham (G5)* ... 264
Buckner (J5)* ... 100
Buena (H4) ...
Buena Vista (F5)* ... 5,214
Buffalo Junction (G7)* 15
Buffalo Springs (G7)* ... 55
Bula (H5)* ...
Bumpass (J5)* ... 75
Burdette (L7)* ... 250
Burgess (M5)* ...
Burkes Garden (B6)* ...
Burkeville (H6)* ... 695
Burnleys (H4)* ... 125
Burnsville (E4)* ... 20
Caledonia (H5)* ... 100
Callands (E7)* ... 35
Callao (L5)* ... 400
Callaville (J7)* ...
Callaway (D7)* ...
Calverton (J3)* ... 200
Calvin (C2)* ... 800
Cambria (D6)* ... 853
Camp (B7)* ... 100
Cana (C7)* ...
Capahosic (L6)* ...
Cape Charles (M6)* ... 2,427
Cape Henry (N7)
Capeville (M6)* ... 300
Capron (K7)* ... 281
Carbo (D2)* ... 50
Cardwell (J5)* ... 130
Carloover (E5)* ... 65
Carrie (D1)* ... 500
Carrsville (L7)* ... 200
Carson (K6)* ... 105
Carters Bridge (H5)* ... 8
Cartersville (H5)* ... 109
Carthage (D6)* ... 25
Carysbrook (H5)* ... 70
Casanova (J3)* ... 105
Cascade (E7)* ... 275
Castlewood (D2)* ... 250
Catawba Sanatorium (D6)* ... 500
Catlett (J3)* ... 250
Cedar Bluff (E2)* ... 1,083
Cedar Springs (B7) ... 97
Cedarville (H3)* ...
Cedon (K4)* ... 45
Center Cross (L5)* ... 100
Central Point (K4)* ...
Ceres (B6)* ... 200
Champlain (L4)* ... 65
Chancellor (J4)* ... 150
Charles City (K6)* ...
Charlotte Court House (G6)* ... 397
Charlottesville (H4)* ... 25,969
Chase City (H7)* ... 2,519
Chatham (F7)* ... 1,456
Chatham Hill (A7)* ...
Check (D6)* ... 40
Cheriton (M6)* ... 1,000
Cherry Hill (K3) ... 250
Chester (K6)* ... 1,168
Chesterfield (J6)* ... 200
Childress (D6)* ... 73
Chilhowie (E2)* ... 1,022
Chincoteague (O5)* ... 2,724
Christiansburg (D6)* ... 2,967
Chuckatuck (L7)* ... 500
Chula (J6)* ... 200
Church Road (J6)* ... 150
Church View (L5)* ...
Churchville (F4)* ...
Cismont (H4)* ... 250
Claremont (L6)* ... 374
Clarksville (H7)* ... 1,035
Clarkton (G7)* ... 50
Claudville (D7)* ...
Clay Bank (L6)* ... 100
Clayville (J6)* ... 50
Cleveland (D2)* ... 388
Clifford (F5)* ... 175
Clifton (K3)* ... 262
Clifton Forge (E5)* ... 5,795
Clinch (D2)* ... 166
Clinchburg (E2)* ... 250
Clinchco (D1)* ... 1,390
Clinchport (C2)* ... 359
Clintwood (D2)* ... 1,366
Clover (G7)* ... 274
Clover Creek (E4) ... 50
Cloverdale (E6)* ... 350
Cluster Springs (G7)* ... 100
Coan (M5) ... 10
Cobbs Creek (M6)* ... 200
Cobham (H4)* ... 400
Coeburn (D2)* ... 760
Cohasset (H5)* ... 100
Coke (L6)* ...
Collierstown (E5)* ... 300
Colonial Beach (L4)* ... 1,464
Colonial Heights (K6) .. 6,077
Colony (F6)* ... 250
Columbia (H5)* ... 119
Columbia Furnace (G3)* 100
Comers Rock (B7)* ... 50
Comorn (K4)* ...
Concord (F6)* ... 600
Conicville (G3)* ... 82
Cootes Store (G3) ... 50
Copper Hill (D6)* ... 153
Copper Valley (C7)* ... 86
Cornwall (F5)* ... 20
Coulwood (E2)* ... 100
Courtland (K7)* ... 443
Covesville (G5)* ... 300
Covington (D5)* ... 5,860
Craig Healing Springs (D6)* ... 50
Craigsville (E4)* ... 1,200
Crandon (C6)* ... 135
Crewe (H6)* ... 2,030
Criglersville (H4)* ... 50
Crimora (G4)* ... 250
Cripple Creek (B7)* ... 200
Critz (D7)* ... 150
Crockett (B7)* ... 150
Cropp (J4)
Cross Junction (H2)* ... 50
Crozet (G4)* ... 1,000
Crozier (J5)* ... 200
Crystal Hill (G7)* ... 50
Cuckoo (J5)* ... 200
Cullen (G6)* ... 160
Culpeper (H4)* ... 2,527
Cumberland (H6)* ... 300
Curdsville (G6)* ...
Dahlgren (K4)* ... 500
Daleville (E6)* ... 200

Damascus (E2)*............1,726
Dante (D2)*...................2,405
Danville (F7)*............35,066
Darlington Heights
(G6)* ........................ 50
Darwin (C1)*................ 500
Davenport (D1)*...........
David (J3).................... 100
Dayton (G4)*................ 788
De Jarnette (K5)..........
Delaplane (J3)*............ 75
Deltaville (M5)*..........1,000
Denbigh (L6)*.............1,500
Dendron (L6)*.............. 476
Denniston (G7)*........... 100
Deskins (D1)*.............. 225
Dewitt (J6)*................ 80
Dillwyn (H5)*.............. 556
Dinwiddie (J6)*........... 200
Disputanta (K6)*......... 500
Doe Hill (F4)*.............. 40
Dorchester (C2)*.........1,129
Doswell (J5)*............... 500
Downings (L5)*............ 84
Drakes Branch (G7)*.... 410
Draper (C7)*............... 258
Drewrys Bluff (J6)*..... 160
Drewryville (K7)*......... 185
Drill (E1)*.................. 200
Dry Fork (F7)*............ 250
Dryden (B2)*............... 350
Duane (K5)*................
Dublin (C6)*...............1,313
Duffield (C2)*............. 176
Dugspur (C7)*............. 26
Dumbarton (J5)............ 400
Dumfries (K3)*...........1,300
Dunbar (C2)*...............
Dunbrooke (L5)*.......... 25
Dundas (H7)*............... 139
Dungannon (D2)*.......... 431
Dunnsville (L5)*.......... 100
Duty (D1)*.................. 104
Eagle Rock (E5)*.......... 700
Earlehurst (D5)............
Earls (J6)*.................. 150
Earlysville (H4)*.......... 91
East Lexington (F5)*.... 300
East Stone Gap (C2)*...
Eastville (N6)*............. 311
Eclipse (M7)*.............. 300
Edgehill (K4)*............. 150
Edgerton (J7)*............ 112
Edinburg (H3)*............ 533
Edom (G3)*................. 90
Eggleston (C6)*........... 350
Elberon (L6)*..............
Elk Creek (B7)*........... 150
Elk Garden (E2)*.......... 150
Elko (K6)*...................
Elkton (G4)*...............1,361
Ellerson (K5)*............. 140
Elliston (D6)*.............. 600
Elmington (G5)*.......... 100
Emmerton (L5)*............ 30
Emory (E2)*................ 300
Emporia (J7)*.............5,664
Enfield (K5)*...............
Esmont (G5)*............... 750
Esserville (C2)*..........1,000
Etlan (H3)*................. 300
Ettrick (K6)*..............3,030
Evergreen (G6)*.......... 100
Evington (F6)*............ 145
Ewing (B2)*...............1,000
Exmore (N5)*.............1,362
Faber (G5)*................ 100
Fair Port (M5)*........... 100
Fairfax (K3)*..............1,946
Fairfield (F5)*............ 265
Fairview (C2)*............ 200
Falls Church (K3)*........7,535
Falls Mills (B6)*.......... 300
Falmouth (K4)*...........1,176
Farmville (H6)*...........4,375
Farnham (L5)*............ 100
Fentress (M7)*............ 500

Ferrum (D7)*............... 350
Fieldale (D7)*.............1,295
Fincastle (E6)*............ 405
Fine Creek Mills (J5)*.. 10
Fishersville (F4)*......... 500
Fitzhugh (J7)*............. 30
Flint Hill (H3)*............ 250
Floyd (D7)*................. 493
Ford (J6)*................... 75
Fordwick (F4)*............
Forest (F6)*................ 300
Forestville (G3)*.......... 63
Fork Union (H5)*......... 800
Forks of Buffalo (F5)*. 25
Fort Belvoir (K3)*........
Fort Blackmore (C2)*.... 250
Fort Defiance (G4)*......
Fort Mitchell (H7)*...... 25
Fort Monroe (M6)*.......2,500
Fort Myer (K3)*...........
Fosters Falls (C7)*....... 160
Fox (B7)*.................... 200
Franklin (L7)*.............4,670
Franktown (N6)*.......... 100
Fredericksburg (J4)*...12,158
Fredericks Hall (J4)*.... 102
Free Union (G4)*.......... 80
Fremont (D1)*............. 150
Fries (B7)*.................1,442
Front Royal (H3)*........8,115
Gainesboro (H2)*.......... 110
Gainesville (J3)*.......... 200
Gala (E5)*...................
Galax (C7)*.................5,248
Gasburg (J7)*.............. 200
Gate City (C3)*............2,126
Gaylord (H2)*.............. 25
Georges Fork (C1)........ 500
Gholsonville (J7)*.........
Gibson Station (A2)*.... 250
Glade Spring (E2)*....... 827
Gladehill (E7)*............. 50
Gladys (F6)*................ 220
Glamorgan (C1)............
Glasgow (F5)*.............. 810
Glen Lyn (C6)*............. 240
Glen Wilton (E5)*......... 350
Glenallen (J5)*............ 600
Gloucester (L6)*........... 600
Gloucester Point (M6)*
Goldbond (C6)*............
Goochland (J5)*........... 125
Goode (F6)*................ 150
Gordonsville (H4)*........1,118
Gore (H2)*.................. 150
Goshen (F5)*............... 125
Grafton (L6)*.............. 100
Grapefield (B6)*........... 75
Gray (K7)*.................. 50
Green Bay (H6)*........... 200
Green Cove (E2)*.......... 585
Green Springs (H4)*.....
Greenbackville (O5)*..... 400
Greenbush (N5)*........... 300
Greenfield (G5)*........... 200
Greenville (F5)*...........
Greenwood (G4)*.......... 500
Gretna (F7)*............... 803
Grimsted (M5)*............
Groseclose (B7)*.......... 25
Grottoes (G4)*............. 908
Grundy (D1)*...............1,947
Guinea (K4)*............... 325
Guinea Mills (H6)*....... 40
Gum Spring (J5)*......... 200
Hacksneck (N5)*.......... 200
Hagan (B2)*................ 125
Hague (L4)*................ 100
Halifax (G7)*............... 791
Hallsboro (J6)*............ 100
Hallwood (N5)*............ 500
Hamilton (J2)*............. 351
Hampden Sydney (G6)* 500
Hampton (M6)*............5,966
Handsom (K7)*............. 200
Hanover (K5)*.............. 500
Hansonville (D2)*.......... 350

Happy Creek (H3)*.......
Harborton (N5)*........... 300
Hardy (E6)*.................
Harman (D1)*...............
Harrisonburg (F4)*.....10,810
Harriston (G4)*........... 98
Haymakertown (D6)*....
Haymarket (J3)*.......... 213
Haysi (D1)*................. 476
Head Waters (F4)*... .... 34
Healing Springs (E5)*.. 400
Healys (M5)*............... 30
Heathsville (L5)*.......... 350
Hebron (J6)*............... 40
Henry (E7)*................. 200
Herndon (K3)*.............1,461
Hewlett (J5)*............... 200
Hickory (M7)*.............. 170
Highland Springs(K5)*.3,171
Hightown (E4)*............ 25
Hill (C2).....................
Hillsboro (J2)*............ 129
Hillsville (C7)*............ 764
Hilton Village (L6)*.....4,486
Hiltons (D2)*...............
Hiwassee (C7)*............ 300
Hoadly K3)*................ 200
Hobson (L7)*............... 200
Holcombs Rock (F6)*... 82
Holland (L7)*.............. 289
Hollins (E6)*............... 800
Holston (D2)*.............. 80
Home Creek (D1)*........ 150
Homeville (K7)*........... 85
Honaker (D1)*............. 847
Hopeton (N5)*............. 324
Hopewell (K6)*..........10,219
Hopkins (N5)*.............. 80
Horntown (O5)*........... 400
Hot Springs (E4)*........1,500
Howardsville (G5)*....... 50
Hubbard Springs (B2)*
Huddleston (F6)*.........
Hume (J3)*.................. 300
Huntley (H3)*..............
Hurley (D1)*............... 225
Hurt (F6)*................... 500
Hylas (J5)*.................. 95
Independence (B7)*...... 486
Indian (E1)*................ 750
Indian Neck (K5)*........ 203
Indian Rock (E5)*........ 98
Indian Valley (C7)*....... 20
Ingram (F7)*............... 30
Iron Gate (E5)*............ 725
Irvington (M5)*............ 800
Irwin (J5)*.................. 50
Isle of Wight (L7)*...... 100
Ivanhoe (C7)*..............
Ivor (L7)*................... 377
James Store (L6)*........
Jamestown (L6)*.......... 10
Jamesville (N5)*..........
Jarratt (K7)*............... 574
Java (F7)*.................. 100
Jefferson (J5)*............ 40
Jeffersonton (J3)*........ 300
Jeffress (G7)*.............. 65
Jennings Ordinary(H6)* 50
Jerome (G3)*............... 225
Jetersville (H6)*.......... 150
Jewel Ridge (E1)*........ 465
Jones (J4)*.................. 150
Jonesville (B3)*........... 597
Joplin (K3)..................
Joyner (K7)*............... 75
Justisville (N5)*.......... 100
Keeling (F7)*...............
Keezletown (G4)*......... 150
Keller (N5)*................ 500
Kenbridge (H7)*..........1,176
Kents Store (H5)*........ 50
Keokee (C2)*............... 700
Kernstown (H2)*.......... 300
Keswick (H4)*............. 200
Keysville (H6)*............ 690
Kilmarnock (M5)*......... 689

Kimball (H3)*.............. 20
King and Queen Court
House (L5)*.............. 150
King George (K4)*....... 246
King William (K5)*...... 125
Kinsale (L4)*............... 350
Kiptopeke (M6)............ 25
Konnarock (E2)*.......... 500
La Crosse (H7)*........... 675
Lacey Spring (G3)*...... 300
Ladysmith (J4)*..........
Lafayette (D6)*........... 150
Lahore (J4)*...............
Lakeside (J5)*.............9,000
Lambsburg (C7)*.........
Lancaster (M5)*.......... 100
Lanesville (L5)*........... 36
Laurel Fork (C7)*......... 31
Lawrenceville (J7)*......2,239
Leatherwood (E7)*....... 60
Lebanon (D2)*............. 672
Lebanon Church (G2)*.. 107
Leesburg (J2)*.............1,703
Leesville (F6)*............. 50
Lennig (G7)*................ 50
Lexington (F5)*............5,976
Lightfoot (L6)*............
Lilian (M5)*................ 40
Limeton (H3)*............. 250
Linden (H3)*...............
Lithia (E6)*.................
Little Plymouth (L5)*.. 110
Littleton (K7)*............ 67
Lively (L5)*................ 275
Locustville (N5)*......... 200
Long Island (F6)*........ 100
Longshoal (C7)*.......... 75
Loretto (K4)*............... 10
Lorton (K3)*............... 132
Lottsburg (M5)*.......... 350
Louisa (H4)*............... 344
Lovesmill (H7)*........... 10
Lovettsville (J2)*......... 341
Lovingston (G5)*......... 350
Lowesville (F5)*.......... 200
Lowmoor (E5)*............ 750
Lowry (F6)*................ 125
Lucketts (J2)*............. 35
Lunenburg (H7)*......... 100
Luray (H3)*.................2,731
Lurich (C6).................. 150
Lyells (L5)*................. 15
Lynch Station (F6)*..... 300
Lynchburg (F6)*.........47,727
Lynnhaven (M7)*......... 300
Maces Spring (D2)*...... 50
Machipongo (N6)*........
Madison (H4)*............. 308
Madison Heights (F6)*.2,830
Maggie (D6)*............... 100
Maidens (J5)*.............. 26
Mallow (E5)*...............
Manakin (J5)*............. 382
Manassas (K3)*...........1,804
Mangohick (K5)*......... 250
Mannboro (J6)*........... 75
Mappsville (O5)*......... 175
Marion (A7)*...............6,982
Markham (J3)*............ 50
Marshall (J3)*............. 500
Martinsville (E7)*......17,251
Marye (J4).................. 150
Massaponax (K4).......... 40
Massies Mill (F5)*....... 175
Mathews (M6)*...........1,500
Matoaca (J6)*.............1,027
Mattoax (J6)*............. 150
Maurertown (G3)*........ 150
Max Meadows (C6)*....1,000
Maxwell (A6)*............. 150
McClure (D2)*.............1,000
McCoy (C6)*............... 125
McCrady (E2).............. 350
McDowell (E4)*........... 107
McGaheysville (G4)*..... 450
McKenney (J7)*........... 476
McLean (K3)*..............1,094
McMullen (H4)*........... 100
Meadows of Dan (D7)*. 450
Meadowview (E2)*........ 722
Mechanicsburg (C6)*....
Mechanicsville (K5)*.....1,500
Mechum River (G4)*..... 50
Meherrin (H6)*............ 250
Melfa (N5)*................ 300
Mendota (D2)*............
Merchant (J7)*............
Messick (M6)*.............2,000
Middlebrook (F4)*........ 175
Middleburg (J3)*.......... 663
Middletown (H2)*......... 386
Midland (J3)*.............. 145
Milford (K4)*.............. 300
Millboro (E5)*............. 500
Millboro Spring (E4)*... 300
Millwood (H2)*............ 700
Mine Run (J4)*............ 80
Mineral (J4)*.............. 414
Mitchells (J4)*............ 83
Modest Town (O5)*...... 150
Moffatts Creek (F4)*.... 60
Moneta (E6)*............... 200
Monroe (F6)*............... 800
Monroe Hall (K4)*........ 200
Montague (L5)*............ 50
Monterey (F4)*............ 262
Montross (L4)*............ 331
Montvale (E6)*............ 400
Morattico (L5)*............ 250
Morrison (L6)*.............2,357
Morrisville (J4)*.......... 120
Moseley (J6)*.............. 100
Mount Crawford (G4)*.. 303
Mount Holly (L4)*........ 238
Mount Jackson (G3)*.... 732
Mount Sidney (G4)*...... 500
Mount Solon (F4)*........ 115
Mount Vernon (K3)*.....
Mouth of Wilson (B7)*. 100
Munden (M7)*............. 65

Mustoe (E4)*............... 12
Myrtle (L7).................. 100
Nace (E6)*.................. 50
Narrows (C6)*.............2,520
Naruna (G6)*............... 200
Nassawadox (N6)*........
Nathalie (G7)*............. 200
Natural Bridge (E5)*....
Natural Bridge Station
(F5)* ........................ 950
Natural Tunnel (C2)*.... 300
Naxera (M6)*.............. 207
Nebo (B7)*.................. 216
Neenah (L4)*............... 125
New Baltimore (J3)...... 60
New Castle (D5)*.......... 239
New Church (N5)*........ 379
New Glasgow (G5)*...... 110
New Hope (G4)*........... 200
New Kent (L5)*............ 50
New Market (G3)*........ 701
New River (C6)*........... 400
Newbern (C6)*............. 175
Newport (D6)*............. 247
Newport News (M7)*..42,358
News Ferry (F7)*......... 21
Newsoms (K7)*............ 392
Nickelsville (D2)*......... 268
Niday (B6)*................. 150
Nokesville (J3)*........... 300
Norfolk (M7)*...........213,513
Norfolk-Portsmouth
(urban area)...........351,342
Norge (L6)*................. 100
Norland (C1)................ 500
North Garden (G5)*...... 500
North Tazewell (B6)*... 816
North View (H7)*......... 5
Northwest (M7)*.......... 145
Norton (C2)*...............4,315
Norwood (G5)*............. 200
Nottoway (H6)*............ 100
Nutbush (H6)*............. 100
Oak Grove (K4)*........... 80
Oak Hall (N5)*............. 160
Oakpark (H4)*............. 150
Oakwood (E1)*.............
Occoquan (K3)*............ 317
Oceana (N7)*...............1,500
Ocoonita (B2)*.............
Odd (M6)*................... 300
Omega (G7)................. 30
Onancock (N5)*...........1,353
Onley (N5)*................ 650
Orange (H4)*...............2,571
Orchid (J5)*................ 35
Ore Bank (H5)*............
Oriskany (E5)*............ 240
Orlean (J3)*................ 200
Othma (J5)*................
Owenton (K5)*............. 190
Oyster (N6)*................ 250
Ozeana (L5)*............... 10
Paces (F7)*................. 70
Page (D1)*..................
Paint Bank (D5)*......... 75
Painter (N5)*.............. 250
Palls (K5)*.................. 150
Palmyra (H5)*............. 300
Pamplin (G6)*............. 370
Pardee (C1)*............... 300
Paris (J3)* ................ 110
Parksley (N5)*............ 883
Partlow (J4)*.............. 37
Passing (K4)*..............
Patrick Springs (D7)*... 300
Patterson (D1)*........... 500
Peaks (K5)*................ 200
Pearisburg (C6)*.........2,005
Peary (M6)*................ 225
Pedlar Mills (F5)*........ 150
Pembroke (C6)*...........1,010
Pendletons (J5)*.......... 150
Penhook (E7)*............. 55
Pennington Gap (C2)*...2,090
Penola (K5)*...............
Perrin (M6)*................ 200
Petersburg (J6)*.........35,054
Phenix (G6)*............... 290
Philomont (J2)*........... 157
Phoebus (M6)*.............3,694
Pilot (D6)*.................. 100
Piney River (G5)*......... 325
Plasterco (E2)*............ 350
Pocahontas (B6)*.........2,410
Poindexter (H5)*.......... 25
Poplar Hill (C6)*.......... 28
Poquoson (M6)*........... 300
Port Republic (G4)*...... 340
Port Richmond (L5)*.... 900
Port Royal (K4)*.......... 139
Portlock (M7)...............3,809
Portsmouth (M7)*.......80,039
Portsmouth-Norfolk
(urban area)...........351,342
Potomac Beach (L4)*... 125
Pound (C1)*.................1,193
Pounding Mill (E1)*..... 350
Powcan (L5)................ 80
Powhatan (J5)*............ 275
Prince George (K6)*..... 50
Princess Anne (M7)*.... 500
Prospect (G6)*............ 300
Providence Forge (L6)* 250
Pulaski (C6)*...............9,202
Pungo (N7)*................ 175
Pungoteague (N5)*....... 250
Purcellville (J2)*......... 945
Purdy (J7)*................. 250
Putnam (E1)*............... 75
Quantico (K3)*............1,240
Quicksburg (G3)*......... 170
Quinby (N5)*............... 450
Quinton (K5)*.............. 34
Radford (C6)*..............9,026
Radiant (H4)*.............. 224
Randolph (G7)*............ 200
Ransons (G5)*............. 200
Raphine (F5)*.............. 325
Rapidan (H4)...............

Raven (E1)*................. 750
Rawlings (J7)*............. 500
Reams (K6)................. 18
Rectortown (J3)*.......... 300
Rectory (K4)............... 100
Red Ash (E2)*............. 750
Red House (G6)*.......... 50
Redoak (G7)*............... 125
Reedville (M5)*........... 400
Rehoboth (H7)*............ 16
Reliance (H3)*............. 150
Remington (J3)*........... 309
Republican Grove (F7)* 100
Rest (H2)..................... 60
Reusens (F6)*.............. 450
Rice (H6)*................... 215
Rich Creek (C6)*.......... 740
Richlands (E1)*............4,648
RICHMOND (K5)*....230,310
Richmond (urban
area) .....................257,423
Ridgeway (E7)*............ 440
Riner (D6)*.................. 180
Ringgold (F7)*.............
Ripplemead (C6)*......... 450
Riverton (H3)*............. 500
Riverville (G5)*............ 75
Rixeyville (H3)*...........
Roanoke (D6)*............91,921
Roanoke (urban
area) .....................105,883
Rockingham (G4)*........ 150
Rockville (J5)*............. 100
Rocky Gap (B6)*.......... 350
Rockymount (E7)*........1,432
Rolling Hill (G6)*......... 32
Rose Hill (B3)*............ 750
Roseland (F5)*............ 60
Round Hill (J2)*........... 403
Rowe (D1)*..................
Ruby (J3)*................... 50
Rugby (B7)*................ 150
Rural Retreat (B7)*..... 478
Rushmere (L6)*............ 150
Rustburg (F6)*............ 650
Ruther Glen (K5)*........ 50
Ruthville (L6)*............. 122
Saint Brides (M7)*....... 400
St. Charles (C2)*......... 550
St. Paul (D2)*..............1,014
St. Stephens Church
(K5)* ........................ 50
Salem (D6)*.................6,823
Saltville (E2)*..............2,678
Saluda (L5)*................ 300
Salvia (K5)*................ 75
Sandidges (F5)*........... 200
Sandston (K5)*............3,500
Sandy Hook (J5)*......... 75
Savedge (K6)*............. 45
Saxe (G7)*.................. 100
Saxis (N5)*................. 600
Schoolfield (E7)*..........
Schuyler (G5)*............. 900
Scottsburg (G7)*.......... 222
Scottsville (G5)*........... 396
Seaford (M6)*.............1,500
Sebrell (K7)*............... 175
Sedley (L7)*................ 225
Selma (E5)*.................1,200
Seven Mile Ford (A7)*.. 150
Shacklefords (L5)*........ 150
Shanghai (L5)*............. 60
Sharps (L5)*................ 300
Shawsville (D6)*........... 500
Shenandoah (G4)*.........1,903
Sheppards (H6)*........... 60
Shiloh (K4)*................
Shipman (G5)*............. 500
Shortt Gap (E1)*..........
Simpsons (D6)*............ 102
Singers Glen (F3)*........ 126
Skeetrock (D1)*........... 300
Skippers (K7)*............ 400
Skipworth (G7)*........... 35
Slant (C2)*.................. 75
Slate (E1)*..................
Slate Mills (H3)*..........
Smithfield (L7)*...........1,180
Snowville (C6)*............ 200
Somerset (H4)*............
Soudan (H7)*............... 50
South Boston (G7)*......6,057
South Hill (H7)*...........2,153
South Norfolk (M7)*...10,434
Sparta (K4)*................ 200
Speedwell (B7)*........... 700
Speers Ferry (C2)*........
Spencer (E7)*.............. 500
Sperryville (H3)*.......... 800
Splashdam (D1)*.......... 200
Spotsylvania (J4)*........ 75
Spottswood (F5)*......... 111
Spring Grove (L6)*....... 28
Spring Valley (B7)........ 300
Springfield (K3)*.........
Springwood (E5)*......... 300
Stafford (K4)*.............
Staffordsville (C6)*...... 200
Stampers (L5)*............
Stanardsville (G4)*....... 182
Stanley (G3)*............... 399
Stanleytown (E7)*........
Star Tannery (G2)*....... 175
Starkey (E6)*.............. 750
Staunton (F4)*...........19,927
Steeles Tavern (F5)*.... 146
Stella (D7)...................
Stephens City (H2)*...... 676
Sterling (K2)*.............. 100
Stevensburg (J4)*......... 80
Stone Mountain (E6)*..
Stonega (C2)*..............1,400
Stony Creek (J7)*......... 482
Stony Point (H4)*.........
Strasburg (H3)*............2,022
Stratford (L4)*............. 150
Stuart (D7)*................ 849
Stuarts Draft (G4)*..... 600
Studley (K5)*............... 125

Suffolk (L7)*.............12,339
Sugar Grove (B7)*........ 500
Sunset Hills (K3)*........ 100
Surry (L6)*................. 248
Sussex (K7)*............... 40
Sutherlin (F7)*............ 50
Sweet Briar (F5)*......... 200
Sweet Chalybeate (D5)* 150
Swimley (J2)*.............. 10
Swords Creek (E1)*...... 400
Sycamore (F6)*............ 120
Sylvatus (C7)*............. 500
Tacoma (C2)*............... 500
Tangier (M5)*.............. 915
Tappahannock (K5)*.....1,011
Taylors Valley (E2)*..... 100
Taylorstown (J2).......... 90
Tazewell (B6)*.............1,347
Temperanceville (O5)*... 300
Tetotum (K4)*.............
Thaxton (E6)*.............. 500
The Plains (J3)*.......... 405
Thornburg (J4)*........... 100
Thornhill (J4)*............ 7
Tignor (K5)*............... 106
Timberville (G3)*......... 271
Tiptop (B6)*................ 200
Toano (L6)*................. 250
Toms Brook (G3)*........ 256
Toms Creek (D2)*........ 650
Toshes (F7)*................ 100
Townsend (M6)*........... 200
Trammel (D1)*.............
Trevilians (H4)*........... 30
Triangle (K3)*............. 285
Trout Dale (B7)*.......... 250
Troutville (E6)*............ 600
Troy (H5)*................... 35
Tunstall (K5)*.............. 30
Turbeville (F7)*........... 65
Tye River (G5)*........... 100
Tyro (F5)*................... 35
Union Hall (E6)*........... 60
Union Level (H7)*......... 194
Unionville (J4)*............ 250
Upperville (J2)*........... 400
Urbanna (L5)*.............. 505
Valentines (J7)*........... 200
Vanderpool (E4)*.......... 9
Venia (D1)*................. 200
Vera (G6)*................... 44
Vernon Hill (G6)*......... 150
Vesta (D7)*.................. 150
Vesuvius (F5)*............. 300
Vicker (C6)*................. 75
Victoria (H6)*..............1,607
Vienna (K3)*................2,029
Vinton (E6)*................3,629
Virgilina (G7)*............. 323
Virginia Beach (N7)*....5,390
Volney (B7)*................ 100
Wachapreague (N5)*.... 551
Wadesville (H2)*.......... 15
Waidsboro (E7)*..........
Wakefield (K7)*........... 949
Waldrop (H4)*............. 80
Wallace (D2)*.............. 125
Ware Neck (M6)*......... 500
Warfield (J7)*.............. 86
Warm Springs (E4)*..... 300
Warren (G5)*............... 300
Warrenton (J3)*...........1,797
Warsaw (L5)*............... 435
Warwick (L6)*............39,875
Washington (H3)*........ 249
Water View (L5)*......... 154
Waterfall (J3)*............ 25
Waverly (K6)*..............1,502
Waynesboro (F4)*.......12,357
Wealthia (H5)*............ 75
Weems (L5)*................ 250
Weirwood (N6)*............ 50
Well Water (G5)........... 50
Wellville (J6)*.............. 25
West Augusta (F4)*...... 8
West Norfolk (M7)*...... 800
West Point (L5)*..........1,919
West View (J5)*........... 25
Weyers Cave (G4)*....... 500
Whaleyville (L7)*.......... 500
White Gate (C6)*.......... 241
White Hall (G4)*.......... 52
White Plains (J7)*........
White Post (H2)*.......... 150
White Stone (M5)*....... 800
Whitetop (A7)*............ 300
Whitewood (E1)*..........
Whitmell (F7)*............. 150
Wicomico Church (M5)* 100
Widewater (K4)*.......... 50
Wilder (D1)*................ 137
Wilderness (J4)............ 100
Williamsburg (L6)*......6,735
Williamsville (E4)*....... 133
Willis (D7)*................. 60
Willis Wharf (N5)*....... 525
Wilsons (J6)*.............. 250
Winchester (H2)*........13,841
Windsor (L7)*.............. 451
Winterpock (J6)*.......... 200
Wirtz (E6)*.................. 100
Wise (C2)*...................1,574
Wolftown (H4)*............ 75
Wood (C2)*..................
Woodberry Forest(H4)* 40
Woodbridge (K3)*......... 600
Woodlawn (C7)*........... 375
Woodstock (G3)*..........1,816
Woodville (H3)*............ 73
Woodway (C2)*............ 500
Woolwine (D7)*............ 60
Wren (G6)*.................. 25
Wylliesburg (G7)*........ 100
Wyndale (D2)*............. 300
Wytheville (C7)*...........5,513
Yale (K7)*................... 30
Yancey Mills (G4)*....... 178
Yorktown (M6)*........... 384
Zepp (G3)*.................. 110
Zuni (L7)*................... 150

Map on Page 91

# WASHINGTON

Total Population 2,378,963

## 39 COUNTIES

Adams (G3) 6,584
Asotin (H4) 10,878
Benton (F4) 51,370
Chelan (E3) 39,301
Clallam (B2) 26,396
Clark (C5) 85,307
Columbia (H4) 4,860
Cowlitz (C4) 53,369
Douglas (F3) 10,817
Ferry (G2) 4,096
Franklin (G4) 13,563
Garfield (H4) 3,204
Grant (F3) 24,346
Grays Harbor (B3) 53,644
Island (C2) 11,079
Jefferson (B3) 11,618
King (D3) 732,992
Kitsap (C3) 75,724
Kittitas (E3) 22,235
Klickitat (E5) 12,049
Lewis (C4) 43,755
Lincoln (G3) 10,970
Mason (B3) 15,022
Okanogan (F2) 29,131
Pacific (B4) 16,558
Pend Oreille (H2) 7,413
Pierce (C3) 275,876
San Juan (C2) 3,245
Skagit (D2) 43,273
Skamania (D5) 4,788
Snohomish (D2) 111,580
Spokane (H3) 221,561
Stevens (H2) 18,580
Thurston (C4) 44,884
Wahkiakum (B4) 3,835
Walla Walla (G4) 40,135
Whatcom (D2) 66,733
Whitman (H4) 32,469
Yakima (E4) 135,723

## CITIES and TOWNS

Aberdeen (B3)* 19,653
Acme (C2)* 300
Addy (H2)* 387
Adna (B4)* 110
Adrian (F3)* 33
Aeneas (F2)* 5
Ahtanum (E4) 45
Ajlune (C4)* 6
Albion (H4)* 256
Alder (C4)*
Alderdale (E5)* 20
Alderton (C3)* 300
Alderwood Manor (C3)* 250
Algona (C3)* 1,400
Allyn (C3)* 275
Almira (G3)* 395
Almota (H4)* 33
Aloha (A3)* 150
Alpha (C4)*
Alstown (F3)
Altoona (B4)* 81
Amanda Park (A3)* 150
Amber (H3)* 20
Amboy (C5)* 225
American River (D4) 10
Anacortes (C2)* 6,919
Anatone (H4)* 60
Annapolis (A2) 800
Appleton (D5)* 50
Appleyard (South Wenatchee*) (E3) 1,479
Arden (H2) 25
Ardenvoir (E3)* 350
Ariel (C5)* 95
Arlington (C2)* 1,635
Ashford (C4)* 350
Asotin (H4)* 740
Attalia (G4)* 75
Auburn (C3)* 6,497
Austin (C3) 12
Avon (C2) 150
Azwell (F3)* 105
Baldi (D3) 5
Bangor (A1) 124
Baring (D3)* 150
Battle Ground (C5)* 750
Batum (G3)
Bay Center (A4)* 200
Bay City (B4)
Bay View (C2)* 200
Beaver (A2)* 125
Beebe (F3)
Belfair (C3)* 450
Bellevue (B2)* 14,182
Bellingham (C2)* 34,112
Belmont (H3)* 72
Benge (G4)* 50
Benton City (F4)* 863
Berrian (F5)
Beverly (F4)* 75
Beverly Park (C3)*
Biarly (H2) 5
Bickleton (E5)* 125
Biglake (C2) 120
Bingen (D5)* 736
Black Diamond (D3)* 1,500
Blaine (C2)* 1,693
Blanchard (C2)* 150
Blockhouse (E5) 8
Bluecreek (H2)* 62
Bluestem (G3)* 23
Blyn (B3) 200
Bonney Lake (C3) 275
Bossburg (H2)
Bothell (B1)* 1,019
Boundary (H2)* 3
Bow (C2)* 100
Boyds (G2)* 61
Bremerton (A2)* 27,678
Brewster (F2)* 851
Bridgeport (F3)* 802
Brief (E3) 20
Brinnon (B3)* 150
Brookfield (B4)* 13
Brooklyn (B4)* 85
Brownstown (E4)* 80
Brownsville (A2) 75
Brush Prairie (C5)* 60
Bryant (C2)*
Bryn Mawr (B2)* 4,781
Buckley (D3)* 2,705
Bucoda (C4)* 473
Buena (E4)* 600
Burbank (G4)* 150
Burien (A2)* 4,387
Burley (C3)* 350
Burlington (C2)* 2,350
Burton (C3)* 1,400
Byron (F4)* 50
Camas (C5)* 4,725
Camden (H2)* 12
Cape Horn (C5)
Carbonado (D3)* 412
Carlsborg (B2)* 350
Carlton (F2)* 200
Carnation (D3)* 446
Carrolls (C4)* 400
Carson (D5)* 450
Casey (G4)* 75
Cashmere (E3)* 1,768
Castle Rock (B4)* 1,255
Cathlamet (B4)* 501
Cedar Falls (D3)* 300
Cedonia (G2)* 26
Centerville (D5)* 125
Central Ferry (H4) 10
Centralia (C4)* 8,657
Chattaroy (H3)* 141
Chehalis (C4)* 5,639
Chelan (E3)* 2,157
Chelan Falls (E3)* 350
Cheney (H3)* 2,797
Chesaw (G2)* 45
Chewelah (H2)* 1,683
Chico (A2) 1,151
Chimacum (C3)*
Chinook (B4)* 390
Chopaka (F2)
Cinebar (C4)* 160
Clallam Bay (A2)* 350
Clarkston (H4)* 5,617
Clayton (H3)* 280
Cle Elum (E3)* 2,206
Clearlake (C2)* 400
Clearwater (A3)* 100
Cliffdell (E4) 10
Cliffs (E5) 16
Clinton (C3)* 1,623
Clipper (C2)* 70
Cloverland (H4) 10
Clyde (G4) 10
Coalfield (B2) 150
Colbert (H3)* 52
Colby (A2)* 200
Cold Creek (F4)
Colfax (H4)* 3,057
College Place (G4)* 3,174
Colton (H4)* 207
Colville (H2)* 3,033
Conconully (F2)* 141
Concrete (D2)* 760
Connell (G4)* 465
Conway (C2)* 150
Cook (D5)* 20
Copalis Beach (A3)* 500
Copalis Crossing (B3)* 100
Corfu (F4) 11
Cosmopolis (B4)* 1,164
Cougar (C4)* 70
Coulee City (F3)* 977
Coulee Dam (F2)*
Coupeville (C2)* 379
Covada (G2)* 31
Cove (A2)* 150
Cowiche (E4)* 200
Craige (H4) 40
Creosote (A2)* 225
Creston (G3)* 268
Cumberland (D3)* 175
Cunningham (G4)* 23
Curlew (G2)* 100
Curtis (B4)* 46
Cusick (H2)* 360
Custer (C2)* 250
Dabob (C3)* 102
Daisey (G2)* 180
Dalkena (H2) 25
Dallesport (D5)* 25
Danville (G2)* 155
Darrington (D2)* 921
Davenport (G3)* 1,417
Dayton (H4)* 2,979
Deep Creek (H3)* 95
Deep River (B4)* 45
Deer Harbor (B2)* 145
Deer Park (H3)* 1,167
Deming (C2)* 500
Denison (H3)* 26
Des Moines (B2)* 2,694
Diamond (H4)* 98
Disautel (F2)* 121
Dishman (H3)* 1,500
Dixie (G4)* 250
Doebay (C2)* 60
Donald (E4) 100
Doty (B4)* 350
Douglas (F3)* 50
Dryad (B4)* 400
Dryden (E3)* 300
Dungeness (B2) 300
Dusty (H4) 65
Duvall (D3)* 236
Duwamish (B2) 900
Earlington (B2) 175
East Olympia (B4)* 300
E. Stanwood (C2)* 378
E. Wenatchee (E3)* 389
Easton (D3)* 300
Eastsound (B2)* 125
Eatonville (C4)* 1,048
Edgecomb (C2)* 75
Edison (C2)* 150
Edmonds (C3)* 2,057
Edwall (H3)* 143
Elbe (C4)* 250
Elberton (H4)* 145
Eldon (B3) 50
Eleanor (G3)
Electric City (F3)* 1,484
Electron (C4)
Elk (H2)* 97
Ellensburg (E3)* 8,430
Elma (B4)* 1,543
Elmer City (G2)* 513
Eltopia (G4)* 61
Endicott (H4)* 397
Entiat (E3)* 420
Enumclaw (D3)* 2,789
Ephrata (F3)* 4,589
Espanola (H3)* 35
Ethel (C4)*
Eureka (G4)* 25
Evans (H2)* 326
Everett (C3)* 33,849
Everson (C2)* 345
Ewan (H3)* 100
Fairchild (H3) 10,000
Fairfax (C4) 70
Fairfield (H3)* 369
Fall City (D3)* 850
Farmer (F3)* 125
Farmington (H3)* 239
Ferndale (C2)* 979
Ferry (G2)
Finley (F4) 25
Fircrest ‡(C3) 1,459
Fletcher Bay (A2)
Florence (C2) 20
Ford (H3)* 20
Forest (C4) 62
Forest City (A2)* 300
Forks (A3)* 1,120
Fort Lewis (C3)* 35,000
Fortson (D2)*
Foster (B2) 400
Four Lakes (H3)* 200
Fragaria (A2)* 20
Frances (B4)* 250
Freeland (C2)*
Freeman (H3)* 100
Friday Harbor (B2)* 783
Fruitland (G2)* 75
Fruitvale (E4) 3,654
Furport (H2) 40
Galvin (B4)* 250
Gardiner (B2)* 150
Garfield (H3)* 674
Gate (B4)*
Getchell (C2) 35
Gifford (G2)* 74
Gig Harbor (C3)* 803
Glacier (D2)* 114
Glenoma (C4)*
Glenwood (D4)*
Gold Bar (D3)* 305
Goldendale (E5)* 1,907
Goodnoe Hills (E5)* 114
Gooseprairie (D4)* 20
Gorst (A2)* 550
Govan (G3)* 22
Graham (C3)* 95
Grand Coulee (G3)* 2,741
Grand Mound (C4)* 55
Grandview (F4)* 2,503
Granger (E4)* 1,164
Granite Falls (D2)* 635
Grant Orchards (F3)* 102
Grapeview (C3)* 150
Grayland (A4)* 600
Grays River (B4)* 300
Greenacres (J3)* 1,287
Greenbank (C2)* 200
Grotto (D3)* 90
Guler (D4) 87
Haas (G4)*
Hadlock (C2)* 250
Hamilton (D2)* 294
Hanford (F4)
Hansville (C3)* 127
Harper (A2)* 478
Harrah (E4)* 297
Harrington (G3)* 620
Hartline (F3)* 205
Hatton (G4)* 42
Havillah (F2) 20
Hay (H4)* 130
Heisson (C5)* 50
Hellgate (G3) 15
Hillyard (H3)*
Hobart (D3)* 350
Holcomb (B4) 150
Holden (E2)* 601
Holly (C3) 60
Home Valley (D5)* 175
Hoodsport (B3)* 500
Hooper (G4)* 200
Hoquiam (A3)* 11,123
Hot Springs (D3)
Houghton (B2)* 1,005
Humptulips (A3)* 100
Hunters (G2)* 350
Huntsville (G4)* 113
Husum (D5)* 75
Hyak (D3)* 20
Ilwaco (A4)* 628
Impach (G2)* 30
Inchelium (G2)* 97
Independence (B4)
Index (D3)* 211
Ione (H2)* 714
Irby (G3)* 30
Issaquah (C3)* 955
Johnson (H4)* 200
Joyce (B2)* 350
Juanita (B1) 900
Junction City (B4)* 176
Kahlotus (G4)* 151
Kalaloch (A3)* 24
Kalama (C4)* 1,121
Kapowsin (C4)*
Kartar (F2)
Keller (G2)* 75
Kelso (C4)* 7,345
Kendall (C2) 72
Kenmore (B1)* 2,500
Kennewick (F4)* 10,106
Kennydale (B2)* 2,200
Kent (C3)* 3,278
Kettle Falls (H2)* 714
Kewa (G2)* 5
Keyport (A2)* 500
Kingston (C3)* 500
Kiona (F4)* 102
Kirkland (B2)* 4,713
Kitsap (A1)* 200
Kittitas (E4)* 586
Klaber (B4)*
Klickitat (D5)* 800
Knappton (B4) 20
Kosmos (C4)
Krupp (Marlin*) (F3) 98
La Center (C5)* 204
La Conner (C2)* 594
La Grande (C4)* 102
Lacey (C3)* 1,952
Lacrosse (H4)* 457
Lafleur (F2) 28
Lake City (B1)* 2,800
Lake Forest Park (B1) 3,500
Lake Stevens (D3)* 2,586
Lakebay (C3)* 250
Lakeside (E3)* 288
Lakewood (C2)* 40
Lamona (G3)* 44
Lamont (H3)* 101
Lancaster (H3)* 65
Langley (C2)* 427
Lapush (A3)* 248
Latah (H3)* 244
Laurel (D5)* 200
Laurier (G2)* 29
Leadpoint (H2) 10
Leavenworth (E3)* 1,503
Lebam (B4)* 400
Leland (C3)* 115
Lester (D3)* 150
Liberty (E3) 30
Liberty Bond (D5) 6
Liberty Lake (J3)* 600
Lilliwaup (B3)* 200
Lincoln (G3)* 200
Lind (G4)* 796
Littell (B4) 68
Littlerock (B4)* 250
Locke (H2)* 6
Long Beach (A4)* 783
Longbranch (C3)* 495
Longmire (D4)* 85
Longview (B4)* 20,385
Loomis (F2)* 210
Loon Lake (H2)* 300
Lopez (C2)* 33
Lost Creek (H2) 20
Lowden (G4)* 30
Lowell (C3)* 1,754
Lucerne (E2)* 142
Lummi Island (C2)* 232
Lyle (D5)* 250
Lyman (D2)* 378
Lynden (C2)* 2,161
Lynnwood (C3)* 650
Mabton (E4)* 831
Macall (G3)
Mae (F3)* 14
Malaga (E3)* 70
Malden (H3)* 332
Malo (G2)* 27
Malone (B4)* 340
Malott (F2)* 250
Maltby (C3)* 385
Manchester (A2)* 500
Mansfield (F3)* 414
Manson (E3)* 2,000
Maple Falls (D2)* 105
Maple Valley (C3)* 1,800
Marble (H2) 25
Marblemount (D2)* 80
Marcellus (G3) 15
Marcus (H2)* 149
Marengo (G3)* 35
Marietta (C2)* 200
Markham (B4)
Marlin (F3)* 98
Marshall (H3)* 115
Maryhill (E5)* 120
Marysville (C2)* 2,259
Mason City (G3) 2,606
Matlock (B3)* 100
May View (H4)* 16
Mayfield (C4)* 70
Mazama (E2)* 4
Mc Cleary (B3)* 1,175
Mc Kenna (C4)* 95
Mc Loughlin Heights (C5)* 14,500
Mc Millin (C3)* 100
Mc Murray (C2) 70
Mead (H3)* 520
Medical Lake (H3)* 4,488
Medina (B2)* 500
Melbourne (B4) 100
Menlo (B4)*
Mercer Island (B2)* 6,000
Merritt (E3) 25
Mesa (G4)* 105
Metaline (H2)* 547
Metaline Falls (H2)*
Methow (E2)*
Mica (H3)* 155

Midlakes (B2) 20
Midvale (E4)
Midway (F4)* 500
Milan (H3)* 95
Miles (G3)* 25
Millwood (H3)* 1,240
Milton (C3)* 1,374
Mineral (C4)* 600
Moclips (A3)* 425
Mohler (G3)* 30
Mold (F3)* 6
Molson (F2)*
Mondovi (G3)* 150
Monitor (E3)* 308
Monroe (D3)* 1,556
Monse (F2)* 62
Montborne (C2) 66
Montesano (B4)* 2,328
Moore (E2)* 40
Morton (C4)* 1,140
Moses Lake (F3)* 2,679
Mossyrock (C4)* 356
Mottinger (F5) 28
Mount Hope (H3)* 20
Mt. Vernon (C2)* 5,230
Mountain View (H4)* 31
Moxee City (E4)* 543
Mukilteo (C3)* 826
Naches (E4)* 633
Nagrom (D3)
Nahcotta (A4)* 250
Napavine (C4)* 242
Naselle (B4)* 750
National (D4)* 350
Neah Bay (A2)* 1,000
Neilton (B3)* 100
Nesika (C4)
Nespelem (G2)* 425
Newman Lake (J3)* 64
Newport (H2)* 1,385
Nighthawk (F2)* 36
Nine Mile Falls (H3)* 130
Nisqually (C3)* 250
Nooksack (C2)* 323
Nordland (C2)* 500
North Bend (D3)* 787
N. Bonneville (C5)* 564
N. Cove (A4)
N. Richland (F4)* 3,067
Northport (H2)* 487
Oak Harbor (C2)* 1,193
Oak Point (B4)
Oakesdale (H3)* 576
Oakville (B4)* 372
O'Brien (B2) 350
Ocean City (A3)*
Ocean Park (A4)* 550
Ocosta (B4)
Odessa (G3)* 1,127
Ohop (C4)*
Okanogan (F2)* 2,013
Olalla (A2)* 800
Olequa (C4)
Olga (C2)* 100
OLYMPIA (C3)* 15,819
Omak (F2)* 3,791
Onalaska (C4)* 280
Opportunity (H3)* 10,000
Orchards (C5)* 600
Orient (G2)* 200
Orillia (B2)* 135
Orin (H2) 37
Orondo (E3)* 250
Oroville (F2)* 1,500
Orting (C3)* 1,299
Osborne (G3) 100
Oso (D2)* 250
Ostrander (C4)
Othello (F4)* 526
Otis Orchards (H3)* 1,500
Outlook (F4)* 308
Ovington (B2) 10
Oysterville (A4)* 140
Ozette (A2) 21
Pacific ‡(C3)* 755
Pacific Beach (A3)* 600
Packard (G3)
Packwood (D4)* 650
Page (G4)* 31
Paha (G3) 12
Palisades (E3)* 120
Palmer (D3)* 80
Palouse (H4)* 1,036
Paradise Inn (D4)*
Park Rapids (H2) 11
Parker (E4)* 200
Parkland (C3)* 3,000
Parkwater (H3)* 1,000
Parkway (D3) 25
Pasco (F4)* 10,288
Pataha City (H4) 60
Pateros (E2)* 866
Paterson (F5)* 100
Pe Ell (B4)* 787
Pearl (F2)
Pearson (A2) 50
Peshastin (E3)* 675
Pillar Rock (B4) 31
Pine City (H3)* 75
Pinehurst (C3)* 4,260
Plain (E3) 30
Plaza (H3)* 55
Plymouth (F5)* 325
Point Roberts (B2)* 230
Pomeroy (H4)* 1,775
Port Angeles (B2)* 11,233
Port Blakely (A2)* 250
Port Gamble (C3)* 500
Port Ludlow (C3)* 275
Port Madison (A1)
Port Orchard (A2)* 2,320
Port Townsend (C2)* 6,888
Portage (A2)* 200
Porter (B4)* 200
Potlatch (B3)* 150
Poulsbo (A1)* 1,014
Prescott (G4)* 244
Preston (D3)* 500
Prevost (B2)* 8
Prosser (F4)* 2,636
Puget Island (B4) 735
Pullman (H4)* 12,022
Puyallup (C3)* 10,010
Pysht (A2) 15
Queets (A3) 250
Quilcene (B3)* 600
Quillayute (A3) 10
Quinault (B3)* 450
Quincy (F3)* 804
Rainier (C4)* 331
Ralston (G4)* 27
Randle (D4)* 500
Ravensdale (D3)* 300
Raymond (B4)* 4,110
Reardan (H3)* 410
Redmond (B1)* 573
Redondo (C3)* 540
Renton (B2)* 16,039
Republic (G2)* 895
Retsil (A2)* 738
Rice (G2)* 40
Richardson (B2)* 10
Richland (F4)* 21,809
Richmond Beach (A1)* 1,900
Richmond Highlands (A1)* 11,081
Ridgefield (C5)* 762
Riffe (C4)* 750
Riparia (G4)* 37
Ritzville (G3)* 2,145
Riverside (F2)* 149
Riverton (A2)* 2,000
Riverton Heights (B2) 3,060
Robe (D2)* 55
Roche Harbor (B2)* 98
Rochester (C4)* 325
Rock Island (E3)* 152
Rockdale (D3) 12
Rockford (H3)* 360
Rocklyn (G3)* 24
Rockport (D2)* 100
Rogersburg (H4) 3
Rollingbay (A2)* 800
Ronald (E3)*
Roosevelt (E5)* 75
Rosalia (H3)* 660
Rosburg (B4)* 300
Roslyn (E3)* 1,537
Roxboro (G4)* 9
Roy (C4)* 263
Ruby (H2) 10
Ruff (F3)* 75
Ruston ‡(C3) 838
Ryderwood (B4)*
Saint Andrews (F3)* 120
St. John (H3)* 542
Salkum (C4)* 360
San de Fuca (C2)* 90
Sappho (A2)* 250
Satsop (B3)* 125
Sauk (D2) 75
Saxon (C2) 149
Scandia (A1) 50
Scenic (D3) 25
Schrag (G3) 5
Scotia (H2) 2
Seabeck (C3)* 300
Seabold (A1) 250
Seahurst (A2)* 2,305
Seattle (A2)* 467,591
Seattle (urban area) 616,047
Seaview (A4)* 600
Sedro Woolley (C2)* 3,299
Sekiu (A2)* 211
Selah (E4)* 2,489
Selleck (D3)* 250
Sequim (B2)* 1,044
Sharon (H3) 95
Shaw Island (B2)* 80
Shelton (B3)* 5,045
Silvana (C2)* 300
Silver Creek (C4)* 312
Silverdale (A2)* 750
Silverlake (C4)* 1,500
Silverton (D2) 16
Skamania (C5)*
Skamokawa (B4)* 562
Skykomish (D3)* 497
Smyrna (F4)* 21
Snake River (G4)* 35
Snohomish (D3)* 3,094
Snoqualmie (D3)* 806
Snoqualmie Falls (D3)*
Soap Lake (F3)* 2,091
South Bellingham (C2)*
S. Bend (B4)* 1,857
S. Cle Elum (D3)* 442
S. Colby (A2)* 280
S. Prairie (D3)* 207
S. Wenatchee (E3)* 1,479
Southworth (A2)* 250
Spanaway (C3)* 600
Spangle (H3)* 242
Spirit Lake (C4) 20
Spokane (H3)* 161,721
Spokane (urban area) 174,853
Spokane Bridge (J3)* 50
Sprague (G3)* 598
Spring Valley (H3)
Springdale (H2)* 268
Stanwood (C2)* 710
Starbuck (G4)* 194
Startup (D3)* 386

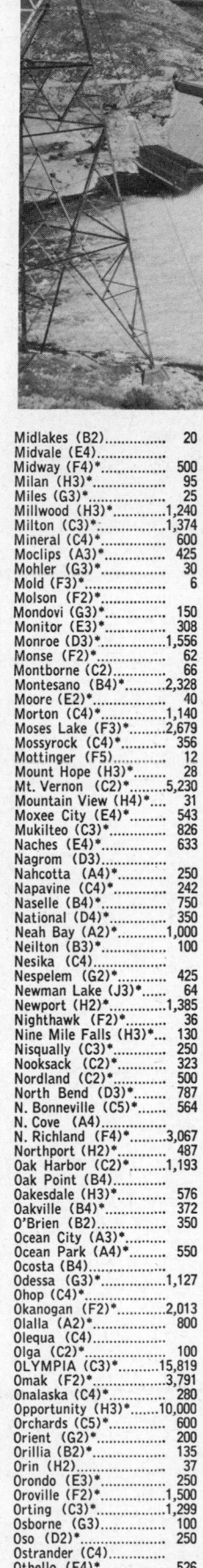

Stehekin (E2)* 37
Steilacoom (C3)* 1,233
Stella (B4)
Steptoe (H3)* 110
Stevenson (C5)* 584
Stillwater (D3)
Stratford (F3)* 112
Sultan (D3)* 814
Sumas (C2)* 658
Sumner (C3)* 2,816
Sundale (E5) 72
Sunnydale (B2) 1,296
Sunnyside (F4)* 4,194
Sunset (H3)* 65
Supplee (F3)
Suquamish (A1)* 1,000
Synarep (F2)* 3
Tacoma (C3)* 143,673
Tacoma (urban area) 166,910
Tahola (A3)* 380
Tahuya (B3)* 60
Tampico (E4) 50
Tatoosh (A2) 30
Tekoa (H3)* 1,189
Telma (E3) 12
Tenino (C4)* 969
Thatcher (C2) 4
Thornton (H3)* 225
Thorp (E3)* 350
Tieton (E4)* 620
Tiger (H2)* 79
Tillicum (C3)* 3,000
Timentwa (F2)
Tokeland (A4)* 150
Toledo (C4)* 602
Tolt (Carnation*) (D3) 446
Tonasket (F2)* 957
Tono (C4) 1
Toppenish (E4)* 5,265
Touchet (G4)* 350
Toutle (C4)*
Tracy (G4)
Tracyton (A2)* 500
Trinidad (F3)* 25
Troutlake (D5)* 350
Tukwila (B2)* 800
Tulalip (C2)*
Tumtum (H3)* 100
Tumwater (B3)* 2,725
Turner (H4) 25
Twisp (E2)* 776
Tyler (H3)* 25
Underwood (D5)* 370
Union (B3)* 350
Union Gap (E4)* 1,766
Uniontown (H4)* 254
Urban (C2)* 11
Usk (H2)* 300
Vader (B4)* 426
Vail (C4)* 175
Valley (H2)* 250
Valleyford (H3)* 213
Van Zandt (C2)* 62
Vancouver (C5)* 41,664
Vantage (E4)* 67
Vashon (A2)* 550
Vaughn (C3)* 280
Veradale (H3)* 1,700
Wahkiacus (D5)* 40
Waitsburg (G4)* 1,015
Waldron (B2)* 40
Walla Walla (G4)* 24,102
Wallula (G4)* 400
Walville (B4) 15
Wapato (E4)* 3,185
Warden (F4)* 322
Warm Beach (C2)*
Washougal (C5)* 1,577
Washtucna (G4)* 316
Waterville (E3)* 1,013
Wauconda (F2)* 3
Waukon (H3)* 40
Wauna (C3)* 100
Waverly (H3)* 120
Wawawai (H4)* 6
Wellpinit (G3)* 60
Wenatchee (E3)* 13,072
West Wenatchee (E3) 2,690
Western (B4)
Westport (A4)* 731
Wheeler (F3)* 30
White Center (A2)* 30,000
White Salmon (D5)* 1,353
White Swan (E4)* 200
Whites (B3) 75
Wickersham (C2)* 135
Wilbur (G3)* 1,043
Wiley (E4) 450
Wilkeson (D3)* 386
Willapa (B4)* 230
Willard (D5) 245
Wilson Creek (F3)* 337
Winchester (F3)* 30
Winesap (E3)
Winlock (C4)* 878
Winona (H4)* 75
Winslow (A2)* 637
Winthrop (E2)* 396
Winton (E3) 23
Wishram (D5)* 678
Withrow (F3)* 53
Woodinville (B1)* 1,500
Woodland (C5)* 1,292
Yacolt (C5)* 411
Yakima (E4)* 38,486
Yardley (H3)* 500
Yelm (C4)* 470
Zenith (C3)* 600
Zillah (E4)* 911

*Map on Page 92*

## WEST VIRGINIA

*Total Population 2,005,552*

**55 COUNTIES**

Barbour (F2) 19,745
Berkeley (K2) 30,359
Boone (C4) 33,173
Braxton (E3) 18,082
Brooke (K5) 26,904
Cabell (B4) 108,035
Calhoun (D3) 10,259
Clay (D4) 14,961
Doddridge (E2) 9,026
Fayette (D4) 82,443
Gilmer (E3) 9,746
Grant (H2) 8,756
Greenbrier (F5) 39,295
Hampshire (J2) 12,577
Hancock (K4) 34,388
Hardy (J2) 10,032
Harrison (F2) 85,296
Jackson (C3) 15,299
Jefferson (L2) 17,184
Kanawha (C4) 239,629
Lewis (E2) 21,074
Lincoln (B4) 22,466
Logan (C5) 77,391
Marion (F2) 71,521
Marshall (K6) 36,893
Mason (B3) 23,537
Mc Dowell (C6) 98,887
Mercer (D6) 75,013
Mineral (J2) 22,333
Mingo (B5) 47,409
Monongalia (F1) 60,797
Monroe (E5) 13,123
Morgan (K1) 8,276
Nicholas (E4) 27,696
Ohio (K5) 71,672
Pendleton (H3) 9,313
Pleasants (D2) 6,369
Pocahontas (F4) 12,480
Preston (G1) 31,399
Putnam (C4) 21,021
Raleigh (D5) 96,273
Randolph (G3) 30,558
Ritchie (D2) 12,535
Roane (D3) 18,408
Summers (E5) 19,183
Taylor (F2) 18,422
Tucker (G2) 10,600
Tyler (E2) 10,535
Upshur (F3) 19,242
Wayne (B4) 38,696
Webster (F4) 17,888
Wetzel (E1) 20,154
Wirt (D2) 5,119
Wood (C2) 66,540
Wyoming (C5) 37,540

**CITIES and TOWNS**

Accoville (C5)* 1,400
Acme (D4)* 200
Ada (D6)* 300
Addison (Webster Springs*) (F4) 1,313
Adolph (F3)* 85
Adrian (F3)* 400
Advent (C3)* 100
Albert (G2)*
Albion (D4)
Albright (G1) 396
Alderson (E5)* 1,489
Alexander (F3)* 250
Algoma (D6)*
Alkol (C4)* 125
Allen (B4)*
Allingdale (E4)
Alma (E2)*
Alpena (G3)* 125
Alpoca (D5)* 550
Alton (F3)* 156
Alum Bridge (E2) 125
Alum Creek (C4)* 249
Alvon (F5)* 100
Alvy (E2)* 155
Amblersburg (G2) 4
Amboy (G2)* 75
Ambrosia (C3) 100
Ameagle (D5)*
Amherstdale (C5)
Amma (D3)* 500
Anawalt (D6)* 1,383
Angerona (C3) 10
Anmoore (F2)* 1,388
Ansted (D4)* 1,543
Anthony (F5)* 82
Antioch (H2)* 50
Apple Grove (B3)* 22
Arbovale (G4)* 80
Arbuckle (C3)* 50
Arcola (F4)* 125
Ardel (A4) 200
Arden (G2)* 250
Arlee (B3)* 100
Arnett (D5)*
Arnoldsburg (D3)* 130
Arthur (H2)* 30
Arthurdale (G1)* 900
Asbury (E5)* 320
Asco (C6)* 200
Ashford (C4)* 350
Ashley (E2)* 90
Ashton (B3)* 66
Athens (E6)* 935
Auburn (E2)* 149
Augusta (J2)* 250
Aurora (G2)* 337
Avon (E2) 50
Avondale (C6)* 975
Backus (E5) 200
Baileysville (C5)* 1,127
Baisden (C5)*
Baker (J2)* 75
Bakerton (L2)* 300
Bald Knob (C5)* 500
Baldwin (E3)* 95
Ballard (E6)* 300
Ballengee (E5)*
Bamboo (E4) 25
Bancroft (C3)* 700
Barboursville (B4)* 1,943
Bardane (L2) 120
Barnabus (C5) 1,500
Barnum (H2)* 95
Barrackville (F1)* 2,500
Barrett (C5)*
Bartley (C6)* 1,275
Bartow (G3)* 200
Bass (J3) 25
Bath (Berkeley Sprs.*) (K1) 1,213
Bayard (H2)* 589
Bays (E3)*
Beard (F4)* 50
Beards Fork (D4)* 750
Bearsville (E2) 30
Beaver (Glen Hedrick) (D5)* 1,484
Bebee (E1)* 200
Beckley (D5)* 19,397
Bedington (L1)* 150
Beech (D3)* 41
Beechbottom (K5)* 1,100
Beechwood (G1)
Beeson (D6)*
Belfont (E3) 25
Belgrove (C3)*
Belington (F2)* 1,699
Belle (C4)* 2,350
Belleville (C2)* 101
Belmont (D2)* 215
Belo (B5) 150
Belva (D4)* 301
Bemis (G3)* 75
Benbush (G2)* 135
Bens Run (D2)* 135
Benwood (K5)* 3,485
Berea (E2)* 66
Bergoo (F4)* 800
Berkeley Springs (K1)* 1,213
Berkeley Station (L2) 75
Berlin (F2) 66
Bernie (C4)*
Berryburg (F2) 200
Berwind (C6)* 1,354
Beryl (H2)* 150
Bethany (L5)* 1,063
Bethlehem (K5) 1,146
Beverly (G3)* 515
Bias (B5)
Bickmore (D4)*
Big Chimney (C4)* 500
Big Creek (B5)* 500
Big Four (C6) 200
Big Isaac (E2)* 30
Big Otter (D3)* 200
Big Springs (D3)* 150
Bigbend (D3)* 100
Bim (C5)* 750
Bingham (E4) 90
Birch River (E4)* 200
Bismarck (H2)*
Blacksville (F1)* 241
Blaine (H2) 300
Blair (C5)* 624
Blakeley (D4)*
Blaker Mills (E5)* 115
Bloomery (K2)*
Blue Creek (D4)* 140
Blue Spring (F3)
Blue Sulphur Springs (E5)* 400
Bluefield (D6)* 21,506
Board Tree (L6) 25
Boaz (D2) 50
Boggs (E4)* 211
Bolair (F4)* 300
Bomont (D4)* 206
Booher (E2)
Boomer (D4)*
Boothsville (F2) 200
Borderland (B5)* 270
Bowden (G3)* 150
Bower (E3) 35
Bownemont (C4) 400
Boyer (G3)* 150
Bradshaw (C6)* 1,062
Bramwell (D6)* 1,587
Brandonville (G1)* 100
Brandywine (H3)* 150
Braxton (E3)* 67
Breeden (B5)* 300
Bridgeport (F2)* 2,414
Bristol (F2)* 300
Brohard (D2)* 400
Brood (H3)
Brooklyn (E1)* 500
Brooks (E5)*
Brounland (C4)* 50
Brown (F2)* 250
Brownton (F2)* 928
Bruce (E4)* 175
Bruceton Mills (G1)* 165
Brushy Run (H3)* 300
Buck (E5) 50
Buckeye (F4)* 40
Buckhannon (F3)* 6,016
Bud (D5)* 500
Buffalo (C3)* 333
Bunker Hill (K2)* 350
Burlington (J2)* 300
Burning Springs (D3)*
Burnsville (E3)* 731
Burnt House (D2)* 40
Burnwell (D4)* 1,000
Burton (F1)* 219
Byrnside (C4)
Cabell (C4)
Cabins (H2)* 120
Cairo (D2)* 500
Caldwell (F5)* 600
Caloric (D5) 320
Calvin (E4)*
Camden (E2)* 150
Camden on Gauley (E4)* 373
Cameron (L6)* 1,736
Camp Creek (D5)* 150
Canebrake (C6)* 568
Canfield (E3)* 65
Canton (E2)
Canvas (E4)* 500
Capehart (C3) 15
Capon Bridge (K2)* 223
Capon Springs (K2)* 220
Captina (K6)* 200
Carbon (D4)* 500
Cascade (G1)* 200
Cashmere (E6)* 100
Cass (G4)* 417
Cassie (B5)* 350
Cassity (G3)* 250
Cassville (F1)*
Catawba (F1)*
Cave (H3)* 50
Cedar Grove (D4)* 1,738
Cedarville (E3)* 103
Center Point (E2)* 200
Central Station (E2)* 350
Centralia (E3)*
Century (F2)* 500
Ceredo (B4)* 1,399
Chapel (E3)* 50
Chapmanville (B5)* 1,349
Charles Town (L2)* 3,035
CHARLESTON (D4)* 73,501
Charleston (urban area) 130,122
Charmco (E4)* 700
Chattaroy (B5)* 1,484
Chelyan (C4)*
Cherry Run (L1)* 150
Chesapeake (D4)* 2,566
Chester (L4)* 3,758
Christian (C5)*
Churchville (E2) 125
Cicerone (D3)*
Cinco (D4)*
Cinderella (B5)* 600
Circleville (H3)* 250
Clarksburg (F2)* 32,014
Clay (D4)* 500
Clayton (E5) 135
Clear Creek (D5)*
Clearco (F4)* 120
Clendenin (D3)* 1,475
Cleveland (F3)* 150
Clifftop (E4)* 400
Clifton (B3)* 355
Clifton Mills (G1)* 51
Clifty (E4)*
Clinton (K5)
Clintonville (E5)*
Clio (D3)*
Clothier (C5)* 636
Clover (D3)*
Clover Lick (F4)* 324
Coal City (D5)* 1,000
Coal Fork (D4)* 1,185
Coalton (G3)* 407
Coalwood (C6)* 1,310
Coburn (F1)*
Coco (D4)* 200
Coe (F4)
Coketon (G2)* 200
Colcord (D5)* 1,800
Cold Stream (J2)* 50
Coldwater (E2)* 27
Colliers (L5)* 425
Conaway (E2) 10
Congo (K4) 100
Copen (E3)* 309
Corinne (D5)*
Corinth (H2)* 175
Corley (E3)* 15
Cornwallis (D2)* 124
Costa (C4)* 168
Cottageville (C3)* 250
Countsville (C3)* 6
Cove Gap (B4)* 125
Cowen (E4)* 632
Coxs Mills (E2)* 50
Craigsville (E4)*
Cranberry (D5)* 750
Craneco (C5) 596
Cranesville (G1) 25
Crawford (F3)* 100
Crawley (E5)* 150
Creekvale (K2) 30
Cressmont (E4)
Creston (D3)*
Crow Summit (C3) 25
Crum (B5)* 350
Crystal (D6)* 400
Cucumber (C6)* 350
Culloden (B4)* 250
Curry (C5)*
Custis (E3)
Cuzzart (H1)* 75
Cuzzie (B4)* 100
Cyclone (C5)* 265
Czar (F3)*
Dahmer (H3) 125
Dallas (K5)* 110
Daniels (D5)* 800
Danville (C4)* 544
Darkesville (L2) 275
Davis (H2)* 1,271
Davisville (C2)* 45
Davy (C6)* 1,650
Dawes (D4)* 700
Dawson (E5)* 100
Dean (E1) 15
Decota (D4)* 1,300
Deer Run (H3)*
Deer Walk (D2) 75
Delbarton (B5)* 1,353
Dellslow (G1)*
Denver (K6) 50
Diamond (C4)*
Diana (F3)*
Dickson (B4)
Dille (E4)* 500
Dingess (B5)* 400
Dixie (D4)* 50
Dola (F2)* 110
Doman (J2) 50
Donohue (D2) 75
Dorcas (H3)* 60
Dorfee (D4) 19
Dorothy (D5)* 3,000
Dott (D6)* 400
Douglas (D3) 25
Dry Creek (D5)* 489
Dryfork (H3)* 200
Duck (E3)*
Duffy (F3)* 40
Dulin (D2) 3
Dunbar (C4)* 8,032
Duncan (C3)* 50
Dundon (D4)* 125
Dunlow (B4)* 125
Dunmore (G4)* 65
Dunns (D5)* 35
Duo (E4)*
Durbin (G3)* 540
Durgon (J3) 50
Dyer (F4) 25
East Lynn (B4)* 300
E. Rainelle (E5)* 1,695
Eastbank (D4)* 735
Eatons (D2)*
Eccles (D5)* 1,885
Eckman (C6)* 1,574
Edgarton (B5)* 500
Edray (F4) 32
Edwight (C5)*
Egeria (D5)* 300
Eglon (G2)* 110
Elana (D3)* 145
Elbert (C6)* 1,565
Elgood (E6)* 75
Elizabeth (D2)* 755
Elk Garden (H2)* 318
Elkhorn (D6)* 1,035
Elkhurst (D4)* 66
Elkins (G3)* 9,121
Elkridge (D4)* 475
Elkview (C4)* 400
Elkwater (G3)* 75
Ellamore (F3)* 600
Ellenboro (D2)* 307
Elm Grove (K5)* 8,000
Elmira (E3)* 200
Elton (E5)* 200
Emoryville (H2)* 100
English (C6)* 890
Enoch (E4)* 282
Enon (E4)
Enterprise (F2)* 1,200
Erbacon (E3)* 210
Eskdale (C4)*
Ethel (C5)* 1,032
Eureka (D2)* 125
Evans (C3)* 150
Evansville (G2) 45
Evenwood (G3) 25
Everettville (F1)* 750
Everson (F2) 50
Exchange (E3)* 25
Fabius (J2)* 30
Fairmont (F2)* 29,346
Fairplain (C3)*
Fairview (F1)* 775
Falling Springs (Renick*) (F4) 307
Failing Waters (L1)* 75
Fallsmill (E3)* 50
Fame (H3) 15
Far (E1) 20
Farmington (F1)* 824
Farmington (F1)* 824
Fayetteville (D4)* 1,952
Fellowsville (G2) 120
Fenwick (E4)* 500
Ferguson (B4)*
Ferrellsburg (B4)* 275
Fink (E2) 8
Fire Creek (E5) 30
Fireco (D5)*
Fisher (H2)* 20
Flat Top (D5)* 150
Flat Woods (E3)* 288
Flemington (F2)* 572
Fletcher (C3)
Flint (G3)
Follansbee (K5)* 4,435
Folsom (E2)* 485
Forest Hill (E5)* 45
Fort Ashby (J2)* 800
Ft. Branch (C5)
Ft. Gay (A4)* 714
Ft. Seybert (H3)* 200
Ft. Spring (E5)* 225
Foster (C4)*
Four States (F2)* 470
Frame (C3)* 98
Frametown (E3)* 500
Frankford (F5)* 185
Franklin (H3)* 777
Fraziers Bottom (B3)* 75
Freed (D2)*
Freeman (D6)* 400
Freemansburg (F2) 21
French Creek (F3)* 175
Frenchton (F3)* 221
Friendly (D1)* 216
Frost (G4)* 99
Gallipolis Ferry (B3)* 100
Galloway (F2)* 1,000
Gandeeville (D3)* 328
Ganotown (K2) 75
Gap Mills (F5)*
Garretts Bend (C4)* 125
Gary (C6)* 1,600
Gassaway (E3)* 1,306
Gauley Bridge (D4)* 1,134
Gauley Mills (E4)* 200
Gay (C3)*
Gem (E3)* 22
Genoa (B4)*
Gerrardstown (K2)* 205
Ghent (D5)* 488
Giatto (D6)* 550
Gilbert (C5)* 722
Gilboa (E4)* 275
Gill (B4)* 300
Gilmer (E3)* 250
Given (C3)* 250
Glade Farms (G1)
Gladesville (G2) 100
Gladwin (G2) 30
Glady (G3)* 300
Glasgow ‡(D4)* 881
Gleason (H2) 40
Glebe (J2) 50
Glen (D4)* 200
Glen Dale (K5)* 1,467
Glen Daniel (D5)*
Glen Easton (K6)* 200
Glen Ferris (D4)* 500
Glen Jean (D5)* 1,800
Glen Hedrick (Beaver*) (D5) 1,484
Glen Rodgers (D5)* 1,593
Glen White (D5)* 300
Glenalum (C5)* 600
Glengary (K2)* 50
Glenhayes (A4)* 300
Glenray (E5) 75
Glenville (E3)* 1,789
Glenwood (B3)* 150
Glovergap (F1)* 150
Good (K2) 100
Goodwill (D6)* 800
Goose Creek (D2) 100
Gordon (C5)* 800
Gormania (H2)* 185
Grace (D3) 3
Grafton (G2)* 7,365
Grandview (D5)* 175
Grant Town (F1)* 1,273
Grantsville (D3)* 959
Granville (Mona*) (G3) 1,004
Grassy (B4)*
Grassy Meadows (E5)* 100
Great Cacapon (K1)* 550
Green Bank (G4)* 200
Green Hill (E1) 175
Green Sulphur Springs (E5)*
Greenland (H2)* 14
Greenview (C4)* 400
Greenville (E5)* 65
Greenwood (E2)* 366
Greer (G1)*
Griffithsville (B4)* 500
Grimms Landing (B3)* 420
Grove (E2)
Guardian (F3)* 600
Guyan (C5)* 300
Hacker Valley (F3)* 150
Hall (F2)* 43
Halltown (L2)* 250
Hambleton (G2)* 283
Hamlin (B4)* 841
Hammond (F2)* 102
Hampden (C5)* 50
Hancock (K1)* 131
Handley (D4)* 1,007
Hanging Rock (J2)* 75
Hanover (C5)* 500
Hany (B4) 350
Harding (G3)* 250
Harman (G3)* 146
Harmony (D3)* 13
Harper (D5)* 1,700
Harpers Ferry (L2)* 822
Harris Ferry (C2) 25
Harrisville (E2)* 1,387
Hartford (C2)* 366
Hartland (D4) 50
Harts (B4)* 160
Harvey (D5)* 503
Havaco (C6)*
Hazelton (G1)* 80
Headsville (J2)* 240
Heaters (E3)*
Hebron (D2)* 50
Hedgesville (K1)* 419
Heights (B3)* 300
Helvetia (F3)* 94
Hemphill (C6)* 2,300
Henderson (B3)* 483
Hendricks (G2)* 492
Henlawson (B5)* 1,750
Henry (H2) 5
Hepzibah (F2)* 1,800
Herndon (D5)* 500
Hewlet (A4) 75
Higginsville (J2) 150
Hico (D4)* 300
High View (K2)* 50
Highcoal (C5)* 500
Highland (D2)* 100
Hillsboro (F4)* 241
Hilltop (D5)* 615
Hinton (E5)* 5,780
Hoard (G1) 6
Hodgeville (F2) 100
Hogsett (B3)* 25
Holcomb (E4)* 50
Holden (B5)*
Hollidays Cove (K5)
Hollywood (F5)* 75
Hominy Falls (E4)* 310
Hookersville (E4)*
Horner (F3)* 97
Horse Shoe Run (G2)* 125
Horton (G3)
Hosterman (G4) 25
Howard (K6) 25
Howesville (G2)* 250
Hubball (B4) 200
Hubbardstown (A4) 400
Hudson (G1) 40
Hundred (E1)* 587
Huntersville (G4)* 80
Hunting Ground (H3) 75

## Map on Page 93    WISCONSIN    Total Population 3,434,575

### 71 COUNTIES

### CITIES and TOWNS

## WYOMING

**Map on Page 94**     **W Y O M I N G**     *Total Population 290,529*

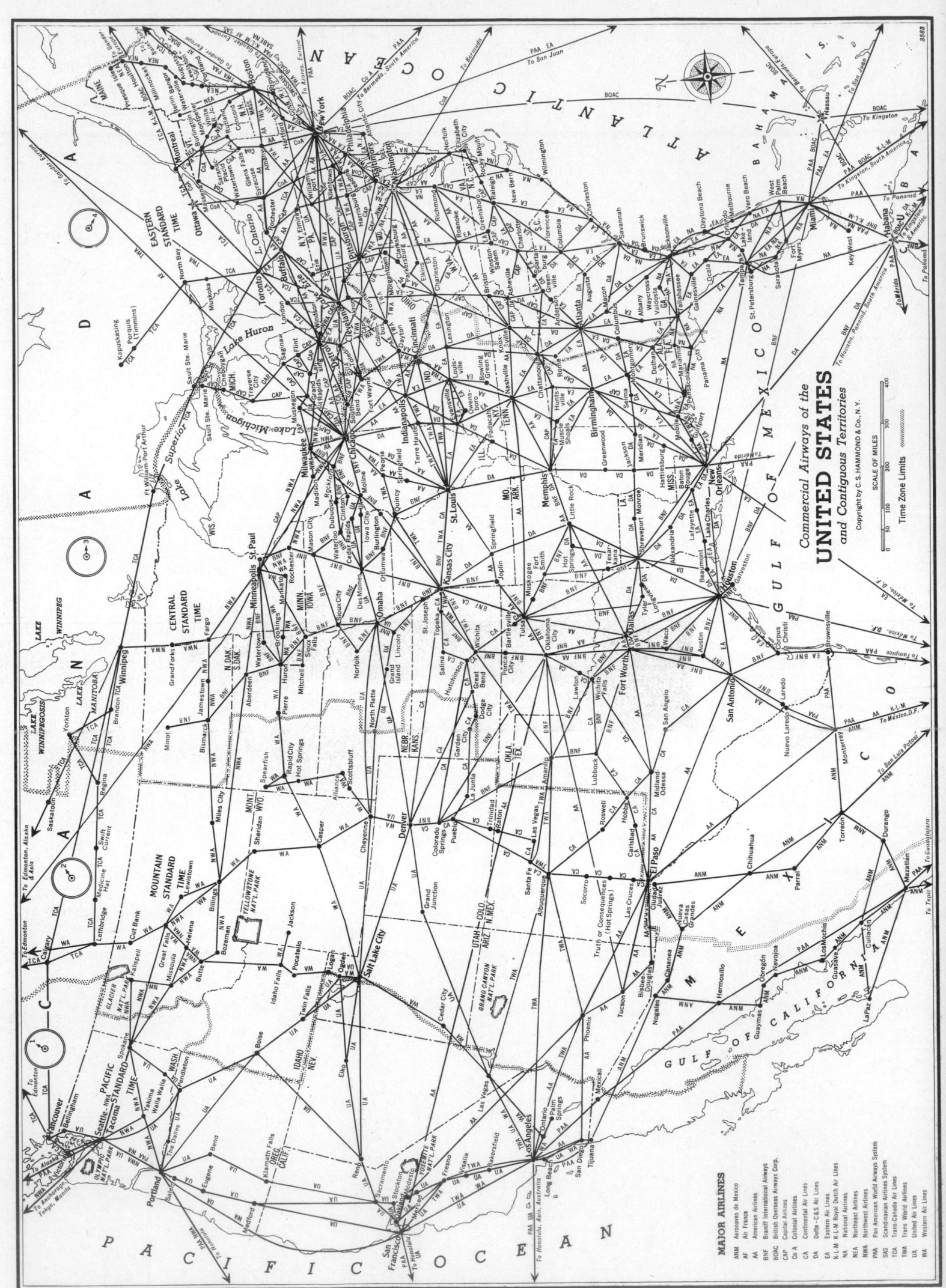

Commercial Airways of the
**UNITED STATES**
and Contiguous Territories

Copyright by C. S. HAMMOND & Co., N.Y.

SCALE OF MILES

Time Zone Limits

**MAJOR AIRLINES**
ANM  Aeronaves de Mexico
AF   Air France
AA   American Airlines
BNF  Braniff International Airways
BOAC British Overseas Airways Corp.
CAP  Capital Airlines
Co A  Colonial Airlines
CA   Continental Air Lines
DA   Delta–C&S Air Lines
EA   Eastern Air Lines
K-L-M K-L-M Royal Dutch Air Lines
NA   National Airlines
NEA  Northeast Airlines
NWA  Northwest Airlines
PAA  Pan American World Airways System
SAS  Scandinavian Airlines System
TCA  Trans-Canada Air Lines
TWA  Trans World Airlines
UA   United Air Lines
WA   Western Air Lines

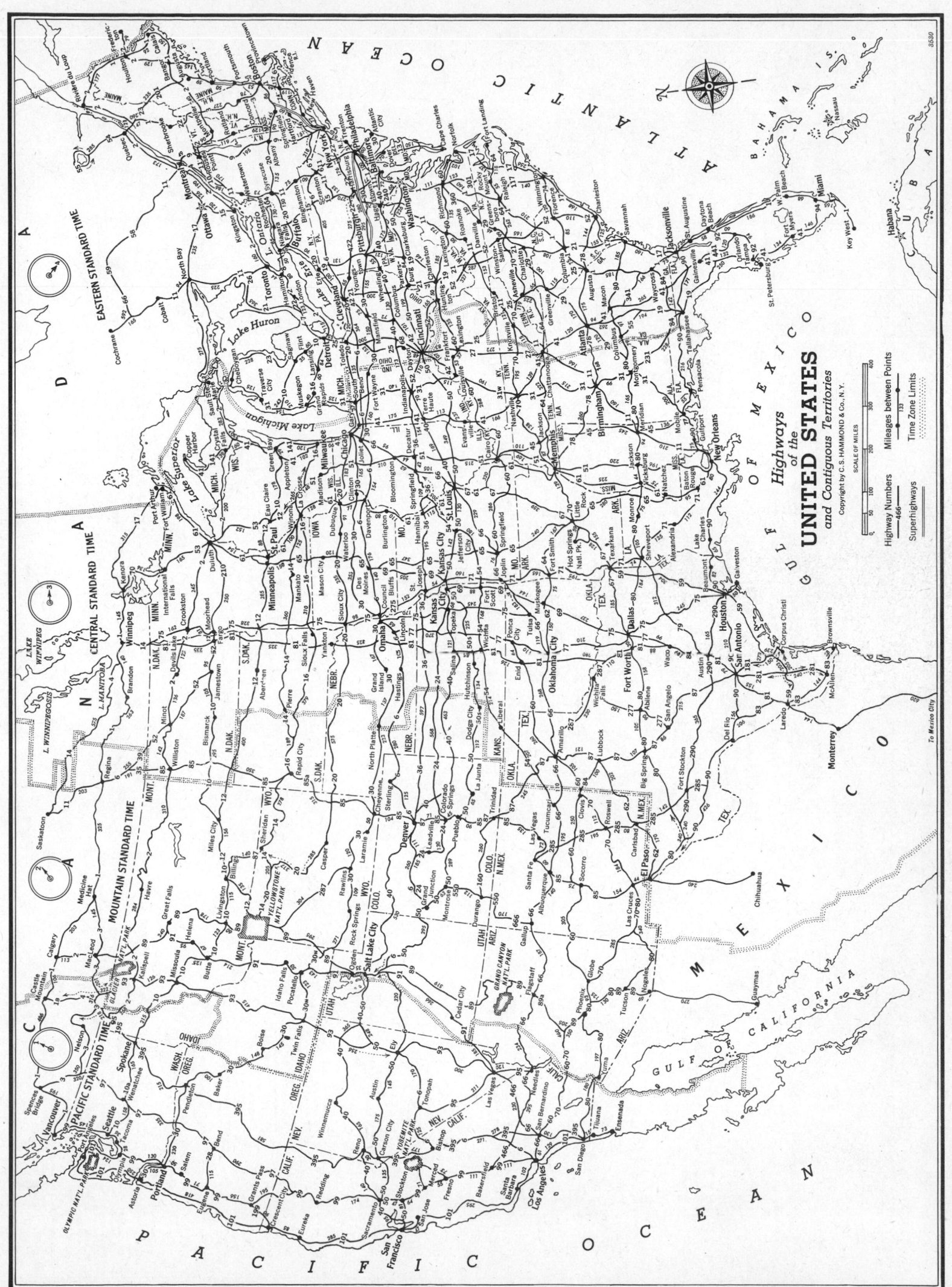

Highways of the
**UNITED STATES**
and Contiguous Territories

Copyright by C.S. HAMMOND & Co., N.Y.

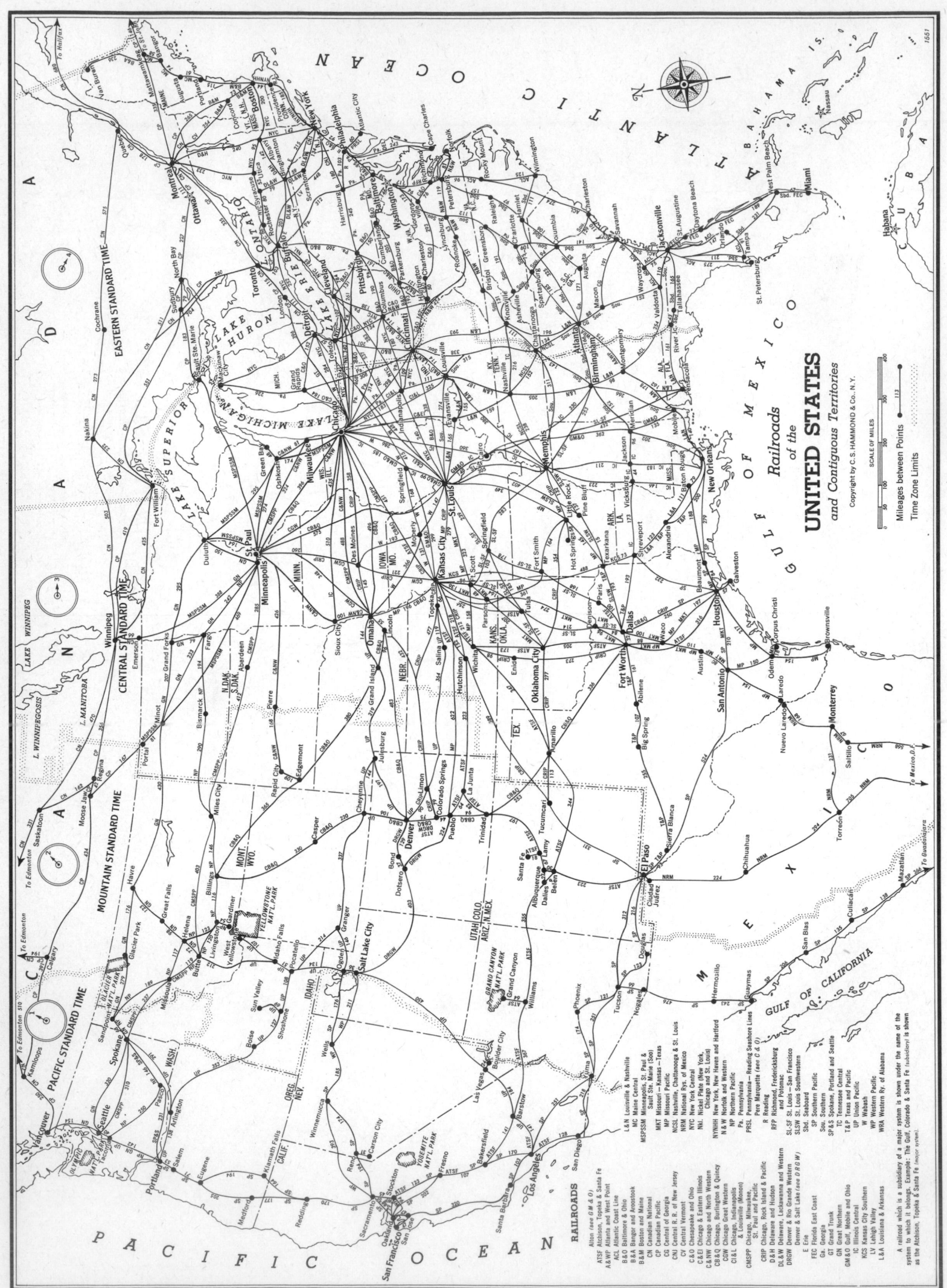

### Railroads of the
# UNITED STATES
*and Contiguous Territories*

Copyright by C.S. HAMMOND & Co., N.Y.

SCALE OF MILES

Mileages between Points ●———113———●

Time Zone Limits ·········

# Illustrated Gazetteer of the
# UNITED STATES
## and Possessions

## *Introduction*

THE AMERICAN PEOPLE are blessed with the richest and most productive homeland on the globe. Nowhere else in the world do *all* the important factors of favorable climate, level terrain, plentiful mineral resources and rich soil interract so favorably. Because of its huge size, America enjoys a climatic range that permits the growth of citrus fruit in Florida and California, wheat on the Great Plains and potatoes along the northern frontier — all within the same borders. The nation's mineral storehouse is a repository containing a vast variety of the metals and fuels so vital to an industrial economy.

This treasure house would have been worthless, however, without the brain and brawn that the American people have given with such vitality to its exploitation. The epic labors of the pioneers in transforming our homeland from an undeveloped wilderness to its present magnificent stature among the nations are familiar to all. As important as the actual physical conquest of the continent, however, is the story of the vast increase in the productivity of agriculture, mining and industry through the ever-growing use of machinery. Each person in the United States has at his command the resources of many mechanical slaves — a situation unequalled elsewhere. This has been brought about through American initiative and inventiveness which derives from the basic enterprise of our people and the unmatched productivity of our economic system.

On the following pages you will find a graphic summary of the American achievement in map, picture and text. The state resource and product maps give a vivid picture of the state's economic life, while carefully chosen illustrations present scenes of human interest. Short descriptions of the states' histories present the background to the present economic and social development of the area.

Copyright MCMLIV by

C. S. HAMMOND & CO.

Maplewood, N. J.          New York, N. Y.

Printed in U. S. A.

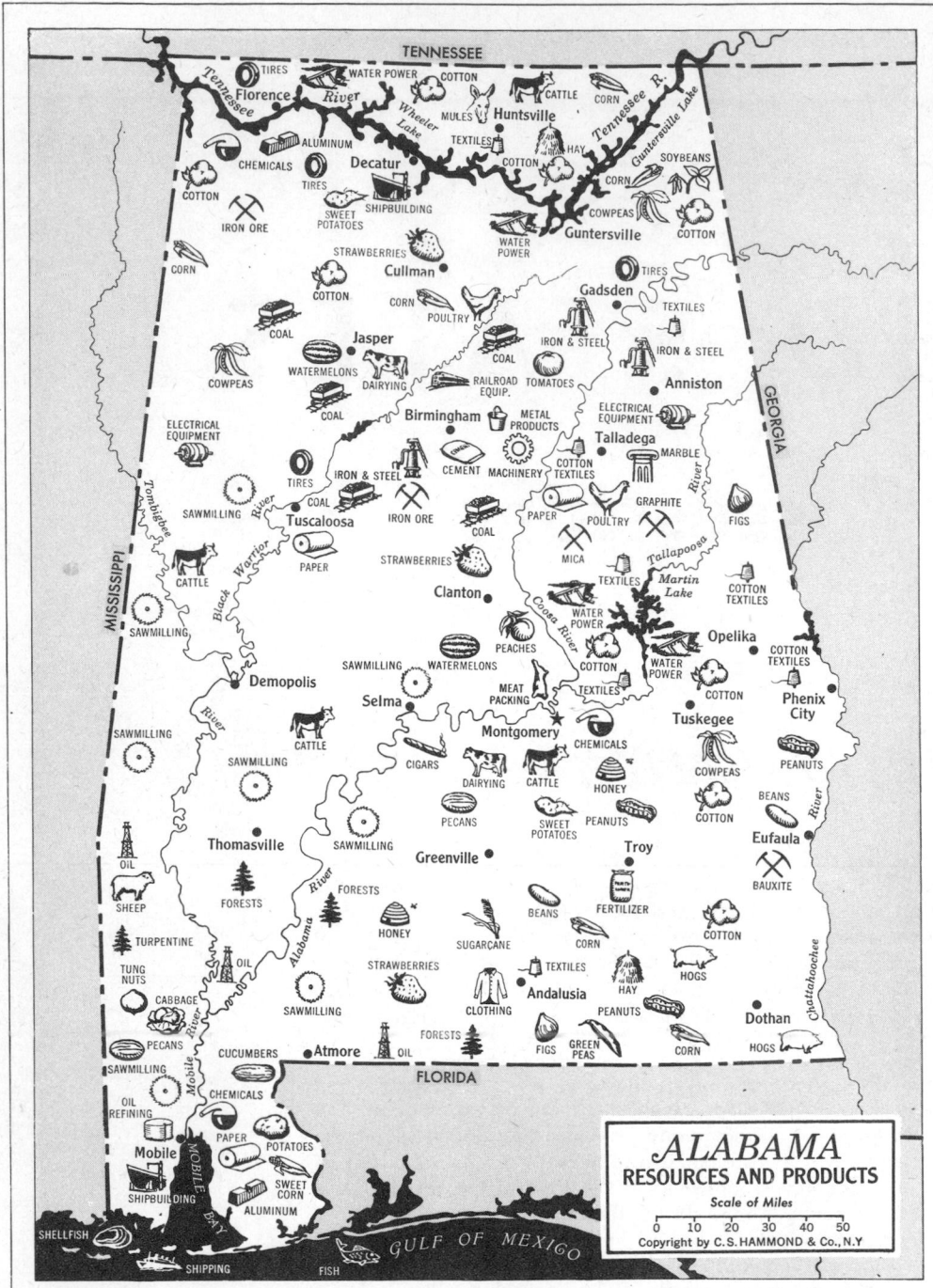

ALABAMA
RESOURCES AND PRODUCTS
Scale of Miles
0   10   20   30   40   50
Copyright by C.S. HAMMOND & Co., N.Y

## ALABAMA

Alabama was settled by the French in 1702. Mobile, the first important town, was founded by them in 1711 as the base of operations in tapping the rich fur-bearing region of the Tombigbee and Alabama Rivers. As English traders and trappers moved in from the east, they displaced the French by offering guns and other valuable implements to the Indians. The region was ceded to the United States in 1783. The Mobile Bay area was added in 1817 by the purchase of Spanish Florida, and Alabama became a territory in the same year. It was admitted to the Union in 1819. Encroachment of the settlers and the violation of Indian rights led to the Bloody Creek wars in which Andrew Jackson gained further fame. The defeated Indians were settled in Oklahoma Territory. The state seceded from the Union on January 11, 1861, but Northwest Alabama attempted to secede from Alabama and set up the state of Nickajack. Though defeated, the "Free Winstons" sent 2,500 white and 10,000 negro soldiers to the Union Army. Of 120,000 troops mobilized in Alabama, 75,000 were lost. The defeated state was readmitted in July 1868.

Standard Oil Co. (N. J.)

▲ COTTON PICKER. Cotton is still the chief crop of Alabama.

◄ WHEELER DAM. The value of flood-control projects was dramatically shown soon after Wheeler Dam was completed in 1937. Floods of that winter swelled the Tennessee River into a mighty instrument of destruction, but Wheeler and Norris Dams held back the flood by storing millions of gallons and regulated runoff. Though agriculture is still the chief industry of Alabama, TVA is affording rapid gains in manufacturing, especially since the failure of a one-crop (cotton) system threatened the economy of the state.

Tennessee Valley Authority

## ARIZONA

Pueblo ruins and aboriginal remains are found in the river basins of Arizona, notably in those of the Colorado, Little Colorado, and Gila. Arizona was explored by Spaniards from Mexico in the 16th Century. Jesuit and Franciscan missionaries labored among the Indians from the days of the early explorers until about 1820, when they finally abandoned the country because of Indian wars, and there was little attempt on the part of the Spaniards to settle the country for the same reason. American traders and explorers began to visit Arizona about 1820. As a result of the Mexican War, New Mexico, which then included all of Arizona north of the Gila, was ceded to the United States. The strip of territory known as the Gadsden Purchase was added to New Mexico in 1854. The progress of American settlement was slow and the removal of troops during the Civil War, led to the outbreak of Indian hostilities and prolonged wars. In 1861, Arizona was occupied by a Texan force and joined the Confederacy. In 1862, the Texans were driven out. In 1863, Congress organized Arizona as a territory, with the meridian of 109° W. longitude as its eastern boundary. It was admitted as a state on February 14, 1912.

HOOVER DAM. Though the largest, ▲ Hoover Dam is only one of many extensive power and irrigation projects in Arizona. In no other state is water so vitally important. Nearly all agriculture is on irrigated land.

▼ A TEEN-AGE COWBOY. The Arizona cowboy shuns the ornate regalia of California "Vaqueros" and adopts the simple habit of Texas cowhands. His riding skill is amply demonstrated in numerous rodeos, such as the annual powwow at Flagstaff.

Arizona State Highway Dep't

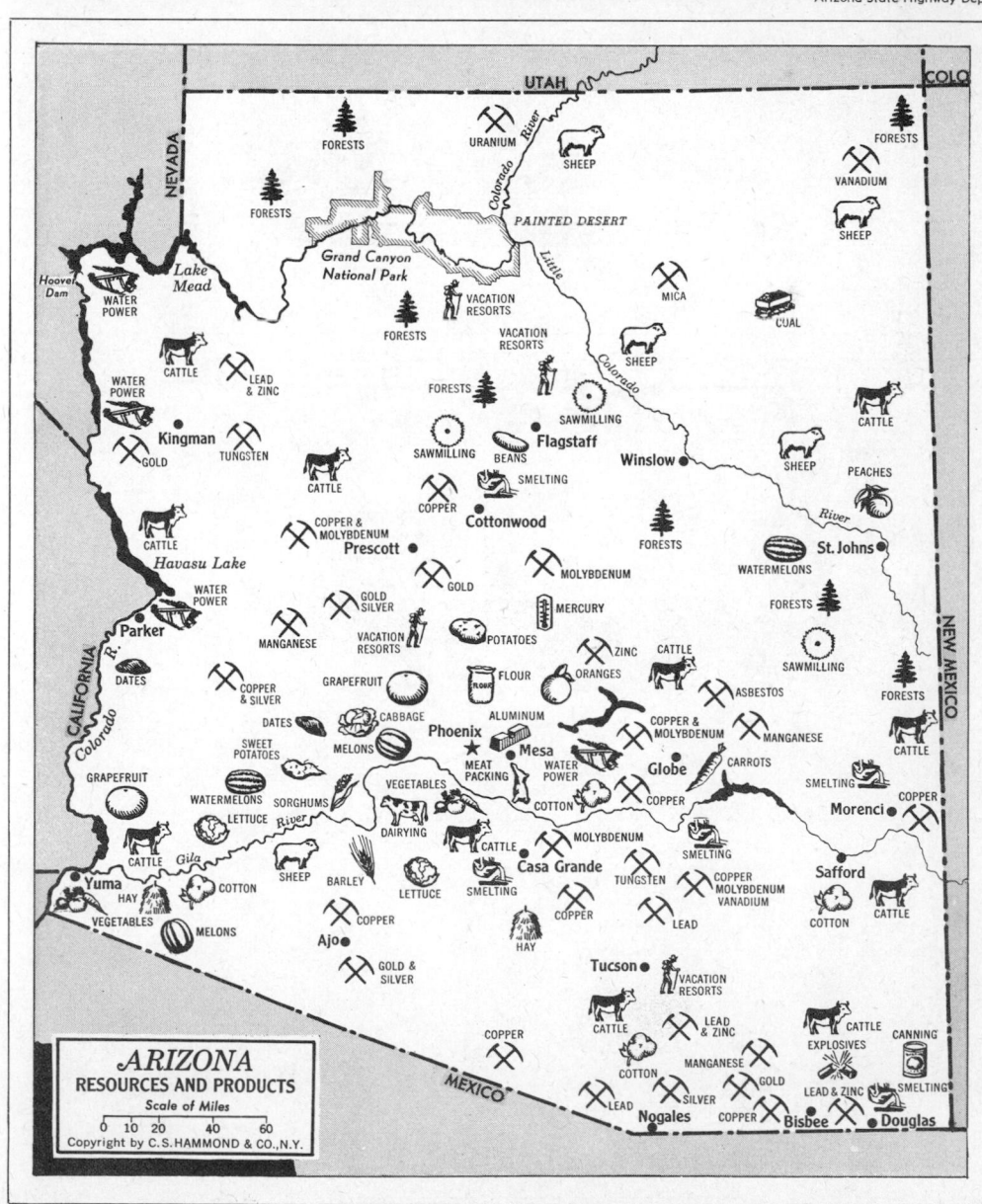

ARIZONA
RESOURCES AND PRODUCTS
Scale of Miles
0  10  20      40        60
Copyright by C.S. HAMMOND & CO., N.Y.

Arkansas Resources and Development Comm.

## ARKANSAS

The first settlement of Europeans in what is now Arkansas was made by the French (1686) at Arkansas Post, important as a trading post in the earlier days of the American occupation, and the first territorial capital, 1819-20. In 1717, a grant on the Arkansas was made to John Law as a part of what turned out to be the "Mississippi Bubble"; in 1763, the territory passed to Spain; in 1800, it reverted to France, and formed a part of the French Colony of Louisiana which was purchased by the United States in 1803. It was organized as a territory in 1819, became a state in 1836, seceded in 1861, and was readmitted in 1868.

◄HOT SPRINGS, ARKANSAS. Famed Central Avenue, winding its way through the foothills of the Ouachita Mountains, is the mecca for tourists and visitors to the spa and park area in America's oldest National Park. Its sidewalks are lined with gift and curio shops, luxurious hotels and bathhouses. Hot Springs boasts that it bathes the world, recording more than 1,000,000 baths in its hot, thermal waters annually.

▼SACRAMENTO VALLEY ORANGE GROVES. Oranges were introduced into California in 1804, and are now the most intensively developed crop-culture in the world. The present giant industry dates from the coming of the navel orange in 1873. Today 47 million crates of oranges from 20 million trees are produced annually in California. Pest control, frost protection, irrigation and wind protection are only some of the problems accounting for the intensiveness of the industry.

United Air Lines

UNITED AIR LINES PHOTO

## CALIFORNIA

California was formerly a part of Mexico, and the Franciscan Fathers made several settlements here between 1769 and 1776. In 1846, during the war between the United States and Mexico, it was occupied by the former country and annexed by it in 1848. The gold discoveries later in 1848, caused a rush of immigrants to the territory, which in 1850 was admitted to the Union. The prosperity of the state was greatly stimulated by the opening of the Union Pacific Railway in 1869. In April, 1906, a disastrous earthquake and the resultant fires destroyed a great part of San Francisco and injured many other towns. Visitors to the Panama-Pacific Exposition, held in San Francisco in 1915, found a new and more beautiful city built upon the ruins of the old town.

➡ GOLDEN GATE BRIDGE. Golden Gate Channel, entrance to San Francisco Bay, the world's largest landlocked harbor, is spanned by the world's longest single-span bridge (6,450 ft.). It typifies one of America's most dramatic cities.

TWA-Trans World Airlines

⬇ HOLLYWOOD NIGHT VIEW. Hollywood Boulevard mirrors the splendor and wealth of the world's movie capital. The city was annexed to Los Angeles in 1910 and now forms a district in the latter metropolis. Other large industries connected with the movies and also major broadcasting companies have moved to Hollywood. California's natural grandeur in mountains, canyons, deserts and valleys is fully exploited by the movie industry.

TWA-Trans World Airline

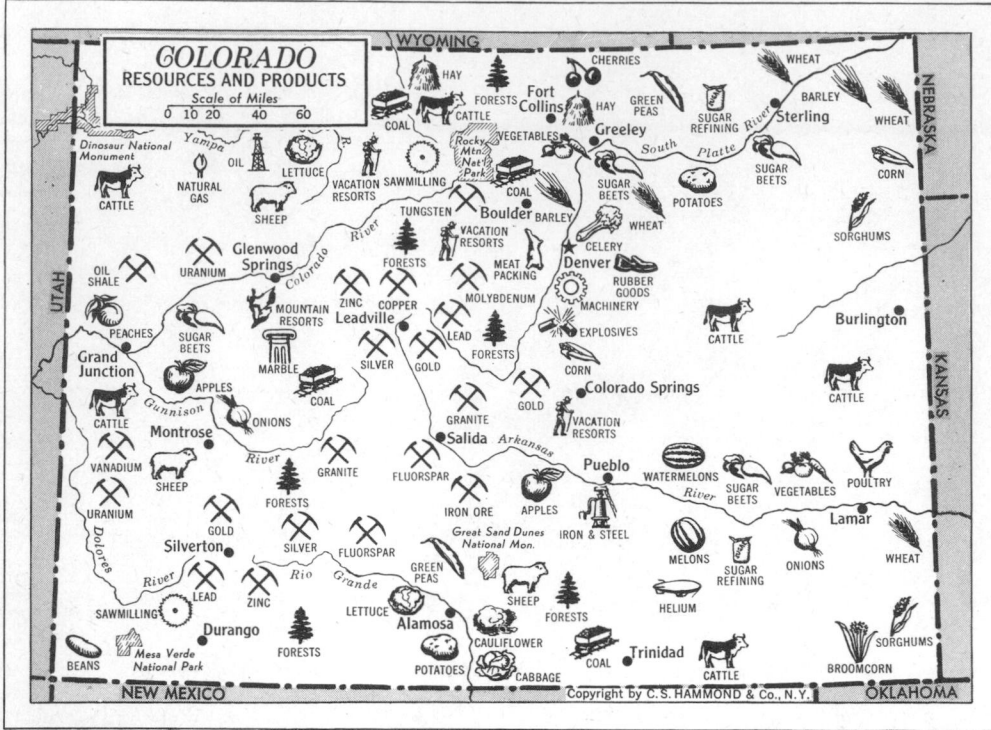

Denver Rio Grande Railroad

## COLORADO

Within Colorado are pueblos and cave dwellings which are survivals of the Indian period and culture of the southwest. Coronado may have entered Colorado in 1540. There are records of Spanish exploration in the south in the latter half of the 18th century. In 1806, while exploring for the Federal government, Zebulon M. Pike discovered the famous peak that bears his name. From 1804 to 1854, the whole or parts of Colorado were included nominally under some half dozen territories carved successively out of the trans-Mississippi country. It was practically an unknown region when, in 1858, gold was discovered on the tributaries of the South Platte near Denver. During 1860, '61 and '62, it received a continuous stream of immigration. The territory was organized in 1861, and was admitted as a state in 1876.

◄ ROYAL GORGE. Perhaps the best known of Colorado's scenic and engineering wonders is Royal Gorge of the Arkansas River, spanned by the world's highest suspension bridge, 1,053 feet above the floor of the gorge. Here a colorful, violent chapter in Colorado history was written by steel rails. The Denver Rio Grande Western fought bitterly with the "Sante Fe" for control of this passage. Both lines laid rails for half the day and spent the other half ripping up their opponent's tracks. The history of settlement in Colorado is, indeed, largely the history of Colorado's railroads. Today the state is exploiting its mineral wealth, its land and great scenic beauty vigorously and progressively. Colorado looks forward to a prosperous future.

## CONNECTICUT

The first settlement in Connecticut was made by English colonists on the site of Hartford in 1633. Trading and exploring parties from Massachusetts soon opened the way for the immigration into the Connecticut Valley of Puritan colonists from Dorchester, Watertown, and New Town (now Cambridge). This colony may be said to date from the secession in 1634 of the more democratic element from Massachusetts. Its constitution of 1639 was "the first written democratic constitution on record." The Royal Charter of 1662, mainly a confirmation of the older one, was superseded only in 1818 when the present state constitution was framed and adopted. Prominent events in Connecticut history were the bloody war with the Pequot Indians, 1637; the governorship of Sir Edmond Andros (during a part of which, 1687-88, the colonial charter was in abeyance), and the abolition of slavery in 1818.

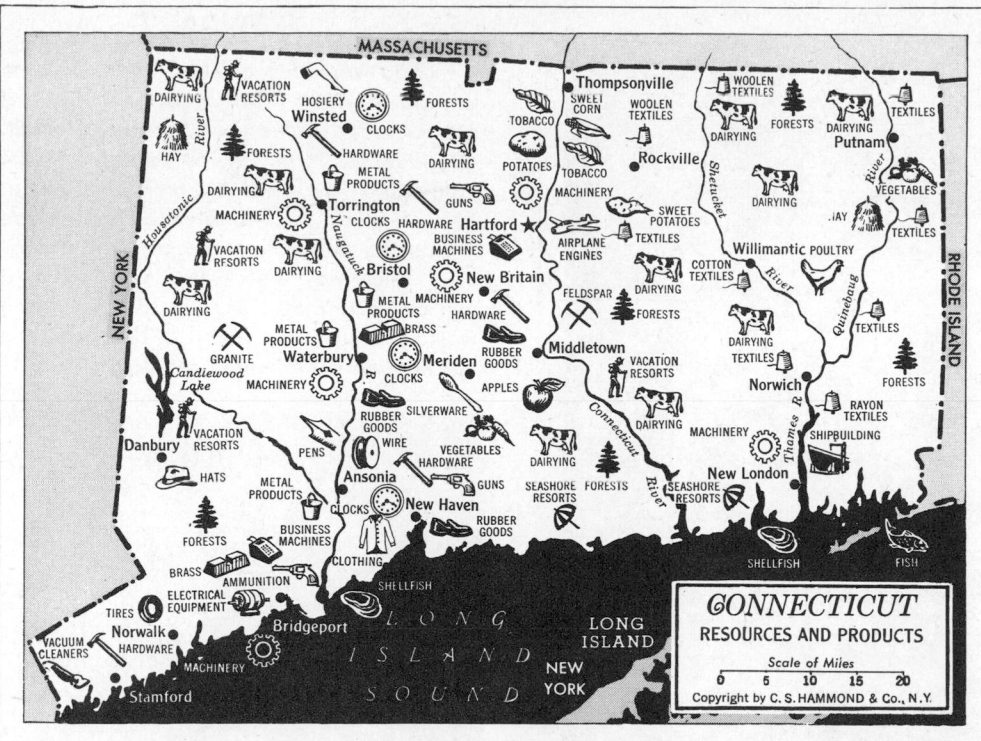

CONNECTICUT
RESOURCES AND PRODUCTS
Scale of Miles
0   5   10   15   20
Copyright by C. S. HAMMOND & Co., N.Y.

**PIGMENTS FOR PAINTS.** Delaware is dotted with chemical factories manufacturing a multitude of chemical products for industrial use throughout the country. This picture shows a hill of Ilmenite, widely used in the preparation of quality white paint. Wilmington, Delaware, is one of the chief chemical centers of the world. For such a small state, Delaware has a great diversity of important industries, including textiles, leather, canning, machinery, shipbuilding, iron and steel, buttons, paper, dental supplies and rubber hose. Of great importance to the State's commerce is the Chesapeake and Delaware Canal, built in 1829 and enlarged to accommodate ocean liners in 1919.

E. I. du Pont de Nemours & Co.

**SILVERCRAFT.** The skilled workmanship which goes into the making of metal ware has long been traditional in Connecticut, dating back to Revolutionary days. Supplied with a great quantity of mineral resources, Connecticut is a leader in metal products. Waterbury's clocks and Danbury's hats are nationally known. Astonishing growth has been realized in the aircraft industry, and shipbuilding continues to break records.

Connecticut Development Comm.

Connecticut Development Comm.

**↑ SPLITTING ROLLED BRASS.** Rolled metal is split into narrow strips from which many coins and small articles are stamped by machines. Waterbury is the U. S. center for the brass industry. Many Latin American coins, the majority of shell-casings and thousands of smaller brass or copper articles are made here. Leadership in metal working, skill and design accounts for Connecticut's industrial success.

## DELAWARE

Delaware River and Bay was explored by Henry Hudson in 1609. As a result of that voyage, the territory was claimed by the Dutch who planted a settlement near the present town of Lewes in 1631. The Dutch settlement was soon destroyed by the Indians, and the first permanent white settlements were made by Swedes and Finns in 1638; Dutch and Swedes contended for this region until 1655 when it passed under Dutch sway. After the transfer of New Netherland (New York) to the English in 1664, Delaware became English also. Though a slave state until the Civil War, Delaware took no part in the secession movement. During the Reconstruction Period Delaware entered a phase of general prosperity which resulted in the expansion of industry and transportation. Throughout its history "The First State" has contributed many outstanding figures to the national scene.

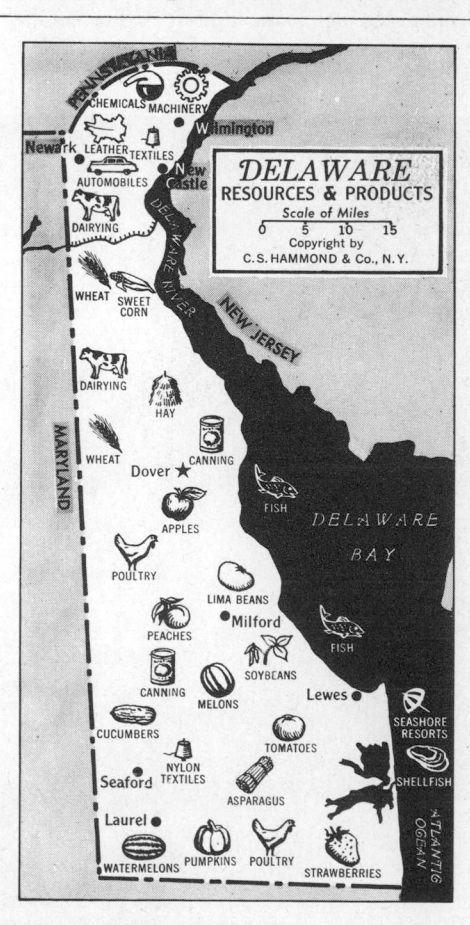

DELAWARE
RESOURCES & PRODUCTS
Scale of Miles
0   5   10   15
Copyright by
C. S. HAMMOND & Co., N.Y.

FLORIDA
RESOURCES AND PRODUCTS
Scale of Miles
0   20   40   60   80   100
Copyright by C. S. HAMMOND & Co., N.Y.

## FLORIDA

Florida was discovered by Ponce de Leon in 1513, settled by Huguenots in 1562, and permanently settled by Spaniards in St. Augustine in 1565. It was ceded to Great Britain in 1763 and to Spain in 1783. In 1818, General Jackson invaded Florida, attacked the Seminoles, and captured Pensacola which was then restored to Spain. It was ceded to the U. S. A. in 1819. The state was admitted to the Union in 1845; seceded in 1861; was readmitted in 1868.

Florida State News Bureau

⬇ **FLORIDA PHOSPHATES.** The world's largest phosphate works is at Bartow, Florida, pictured below. Phosphate production in Florida has been the highest in the country for over forty years, amounting to 79% of the national volume. Phosphate rock yields bone phosphate of lime for fertilizers; phosphoric acid, used in preserves and jellies, soft drinks, and rust-proof metals; and compound derivatives.

⬆ **SHRIMPING.** Shrimp fishermen quickly toss back to the sea all the crabs, fish, seashells and even octopuses from their nets. Of 700 species of fish in Florida over 100 are edible.

⬇ **BEACH SCENE.** Known as the foremost vacation spot in the eastern half of the United States, Miami Beach yearly receives thousands of tourists who stream to her health-giving shore line.

Florida State News Bureau

Florida State News Bureau

## GEORGIA

Georgia, named in honor of George the Second, was settled by a chartered company of English colonists under Oglethorpe in 1733, as a refuge for poor whites and persons seeking religious freedom. Georgia became a Royal Province in 1763, and was the fourth state to ratify the Federal Constitution (January 2, 1788). It seceded in January, 1861, and was readmitted to the Union in 1870. It has experienced a rapid industrial growth.

Georgia Dept. of Commerce

▲ GRANITE QUARRY AT ELBERTON. Georgia is noted for her granite and marble quarries. At Stone Mountain is the largest exposed mass of granite in North America. This huge mountain, over a mile long and about 800 feet high, is the site of a massive Confederate memorial which is being carved into its face. Granite and marble are shipped all over the world from Georgia's quarries. One seventy-six ton block of marble was shipped from Tate to be used in the Buckingham Fountain in Chicago. Georgia also produces vast amounts of fuller's earth and commercial quantities of talc, manganese, bauxite, iron and coal. Her steady industrial growth has been made possible because of the state's diversity of raw materials.

Standard Oil Co. (N. J.)

▲ PAPER ON DRYING MACHINE. Georgia's huge yellow and slash pine forests provide raw material for an expanding paper and pulp industry.

GEORGIA
RESOURCES AND PRODUCTS
Scale of Miles
0   10   20     40      60
Copyright by C. S. HAMMOND & Co., N.Y.

Georgia Dept. of Commerce

▲ UNLOADING SUGAR CANE. Sugar, another of Georgia's many products, is important to her canning and preserving industries.

Standard Oil Co. (N. J.)

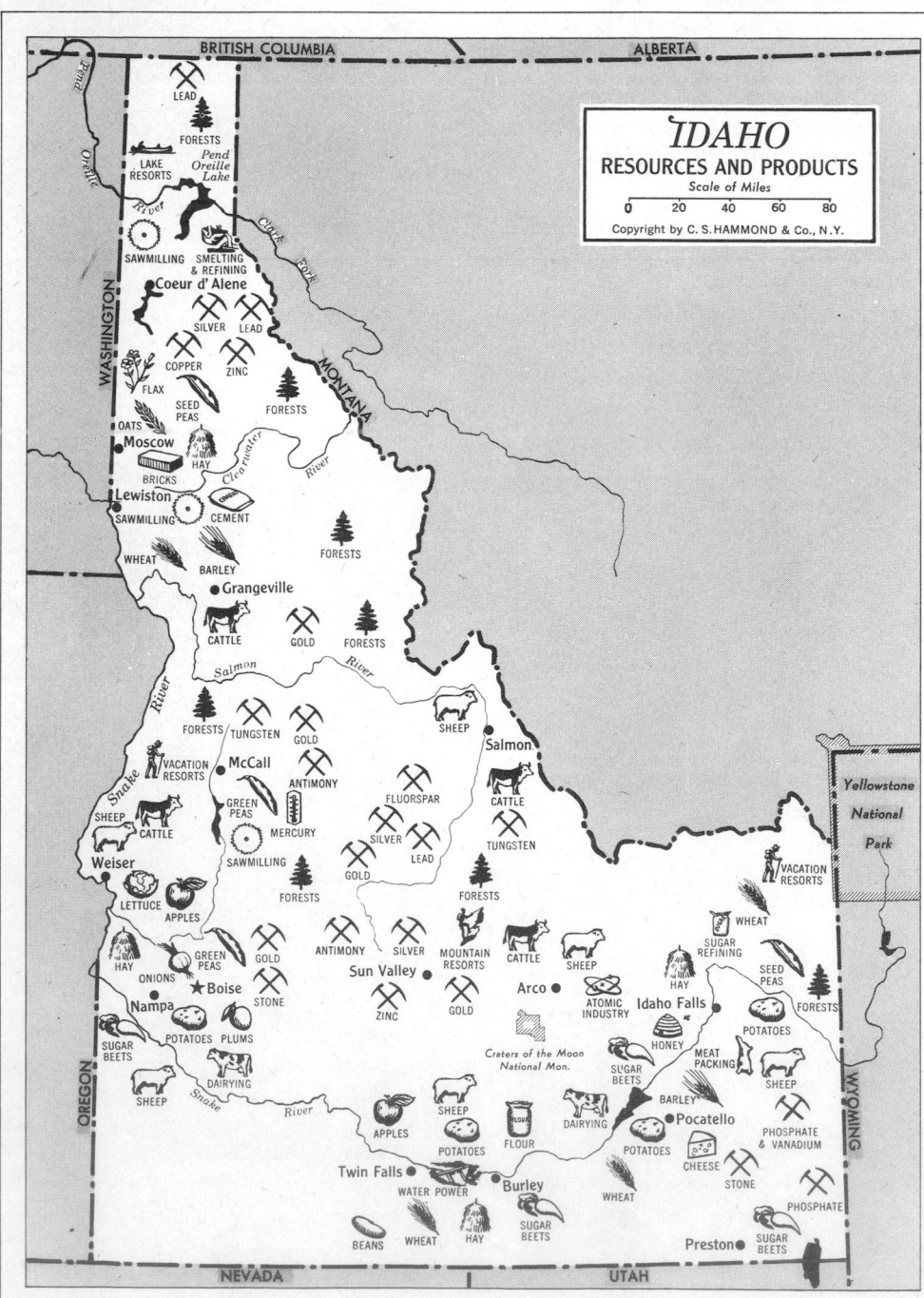

▲ PEAK IN THE LOST RIVER RANGE. The Lost River Mountains lie in a primitive area, a 1,000,000 acre tract of wilderness which is entered only by pack and by foot. This vast undeveloped playground is heavily forested with 50 lakes, countless canyons, buttes, glaciers, water falls and snow-capped peaks.

➡ SHEEP HERDER AND HIS FLOCK. Idaho provides grazing for a million sheep and four million head of cattle. Although rich in agricultural products, the state's greatest asset is in its beautiful recreational areas. Containing more lakes than have been counted or explored and high peaks perennially crowned with snow, Idaho has few scenic rivals.

## IDAHO

The first recorded exploration of Idaho was made by Lewis and Clark in 1805. In 1810, Ft. Henry on the Snake River was established by the Missouri Fur Company. In 1834, Ft. Hall in east Idaho was founded. Missions for the Indians were established by both Catholics and Protestants about the same time. The territory now constituting Idaho was comprised in the territory of Oregon from 1848-53; from 1854-59, the southern portion of the present state was a part of Oregon, and the northern portion, a part of Washington Territory; from 1859-63, the territory was within the bounds of Washington Territory. Idaho was organized as a territory on March 3rd, 1863, but at that time included both Montana and Wyoming. In May, 1864, a part was set aside as Montana and in 1868, Wyoming was organized, and Idaho assumed its present boundaries. Gold was discovered in 1860, and the population of the territory rapidly increased. From 1857 to 1877 there were many serious Indian outbreaks. Later there were frequent conflicts among the miners. Idaho became a state in 1890.

## ILLINOIS

The first Europeans to explore the country were French traders and missionaries. In 1675 Father Marquette founded a mission at the Indian town of Kaskaskia near the present Utica. In 1679 La Salle built Creve Coeur, a fort, not far from Lake Peoria. After 1682 the French made a number of permanent settlements which had originated in missions, or in trading posts. By the Treaty of Paris of 1763, France ceded to Great Britain her claims to the country between the Ohio and Mississippi Rivers. Owing to Indian resistance, the English were unable to take possession until 1765. The Northwest Territory, of which Illinois was a part, was secured to the United States by the Treaty of Paris of 1783. Illinois was a part of Indiana Territory in 1800; was made a separate territory in 1809; and became a state in 1818. Black Hawk's War occurred in 1832, and the Mormon troubles culminated in 1844. Slavery existed in the state until 1848. Illinois bore a notable part in the Civil War.

Standard Oil Co. (N. J.)

▼ CATTLE FEEDING. Two-thirds of farm income in Illinois is derived from livestock and three-fourths of the land is in feed crops.

### ILLINOIS
RESOURCES AND PRODUCTS

Scale of Miles

0 5 10    20    30    40    50    60

Copyright by C. S. HAMMOND & Co., N. Y.

Standard Oil Co. (N. J.)

## INDIANA

Extensive remains (mounds and fortifications) of the prehistoric inhabitants of Indiana are numerous in Knox and Sullivan Counties. The first Europeans to enter the state found it occupied chiefly by the tribes of the Miami Confederacy, a league of Algonquin Indians formed to oppose the advance of the Iroquois. La Salle undoubtedly passed through Indiana during his journeys of 1669 and succeeding years. Vincennes, founded in 1731, was the first permanent white settlement; no other was made until after the War of Independence. Indiana was a part of the Northwest Territory which passed under the control of the United States in 1779, and an American settlement was made at Clarksville in 1784. The Northwest Territory was governed under the Ordinance of 1787. Indiana assumed its present limits in 1809 when it was organized as a territory. Indian wars were frequent. In 1810 began the last great Indian war in Indiana, which ended in November, 1811, with the battle of Tippecanoe when Gen. Harrison defeated the confederated Indians under Tecumseh. The territory was admitted to statehood in 1816. Slavery existed until 1830. Indiana took the Union side in the Civil War.

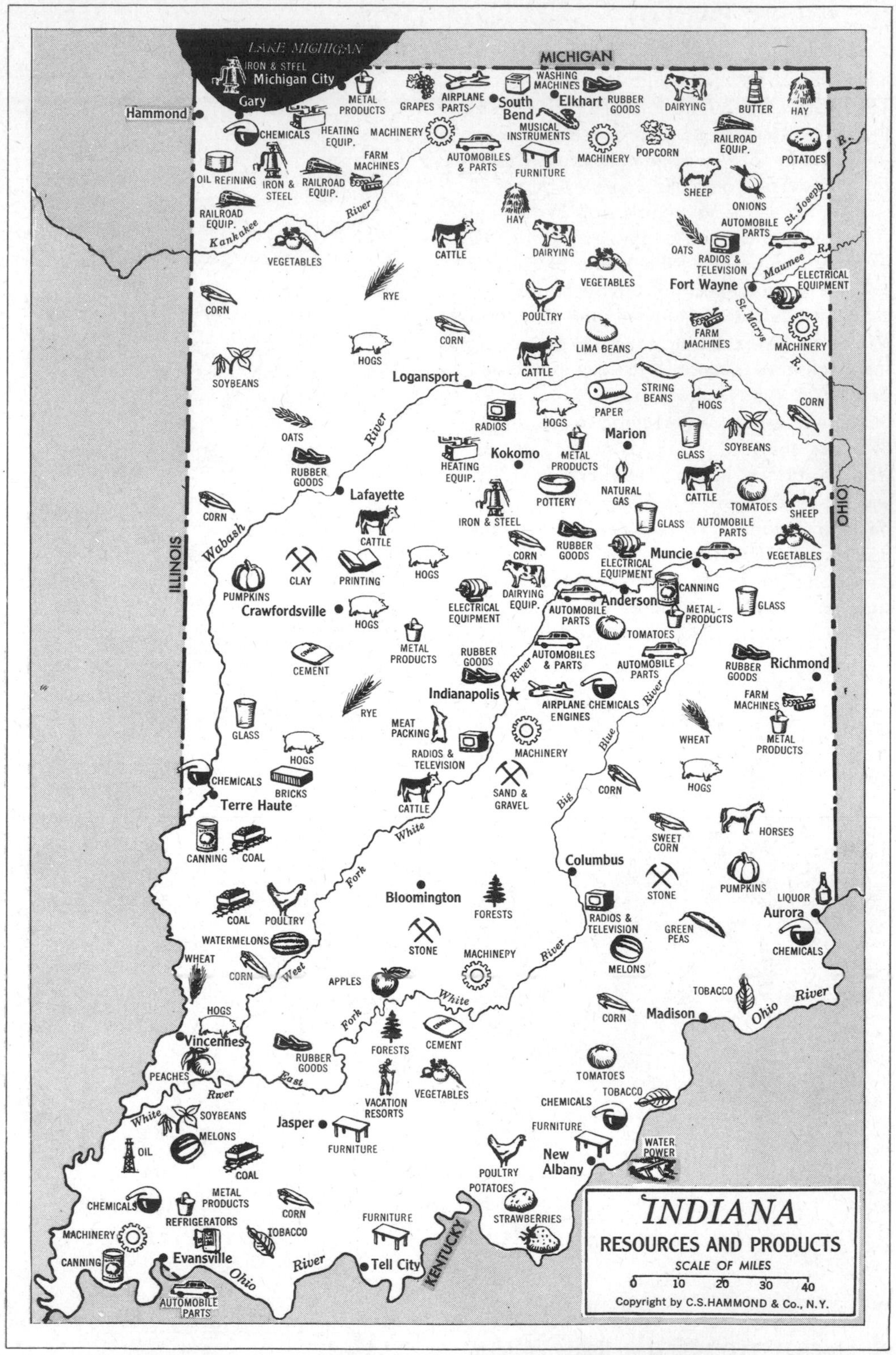

TWA-Trans World Airline

▲ WRIGLEY BUILDING. Overlooking Lake Michigan, the Wrigley Building is a familiar landmark of the "Windy City", Chicago, Ill.

Indiana Dept. of Comm. & Public Rel.

INDIANA
RESOURCES AND PRODUCTS
SCALE OF MILES
0   10   20   30   40
Copyright by C.S. HAMMOND & Co., N.Y.

◄WEEDING PEPPERMINT. Indiana produces more peppermint oil than any other state. Much hand labor is required to keep the fields free of obnoxious weeds.

► PREPARING TILE FOR THE KILN. The State's almost unlimited deposits of clay, sand and gravel are used in the making of cement, glass, pottery and brick. The topography of Indiana is marked by definite contrasts. The roll of the western prairie begins in "The Hoosier State," while the northern and central portions are fertile farm regions. Lakes and sloping hills grace the northeastern area. Such physical diversity creates a happy balance between agriculture and industry.

Indiana Dept. of Comm. & Public Rel.

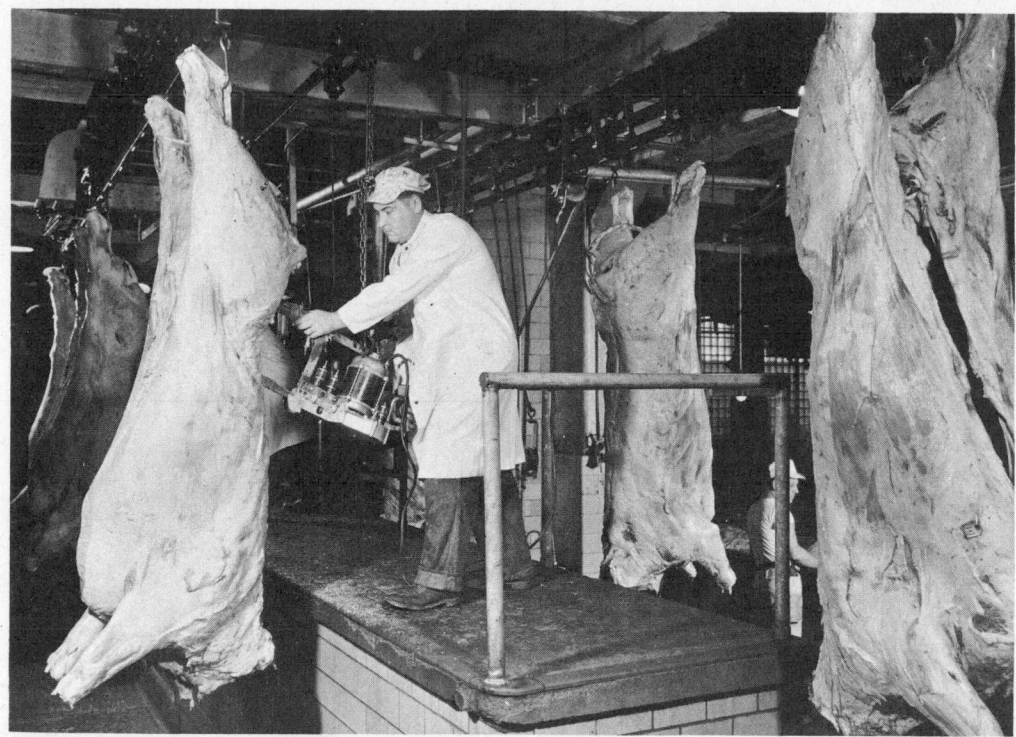

Iowa Development Comm.

Iowa Development Comm.

Iowa Development Comm.

▲ SPLITTING BEEF INTO SIDES. Excepting general farming and livestock raising, meat packing is Iowa's largest industry with thirty-eight packing plants employing over 15,000 workers. The annual income of the industry is over $500,000,000.

◄ IOWA CORN. Iowa produces 20% of the nation's total corn yield. In 1952 Iowa farmers realized their biggest corn crop in history, over 680 million bushels or their first billion dollar crop.

▲ GYPSUM MINING. The United States is the world's leading producer of gypsum. Plentiful natural deposits, in Iowa and elsewhere, make it the least expensive of raw materials. Its uses are chiefly confined to the manufacture of plaster and other building materials. Iowa's mineral resources and fertile soil provide the basis for a continually growing economy. In recent years an attempt to stem the injurious effects of erosion has resulted in the reclamation of much unarable land.

## IOWA

The first white men to visit Iowa were the Frenchmen, Marquette and Joliet, in 1673, and Hennepin in 1680. They found the country occupied by a tribe of Sioux Indians from which came the name of the state, "Iowa." With the Louisiana Purchase, 1803, the territory became the property of the United States. From 1804-05, as part of the District of Louisiana, it was under the government of Indiana Territory; from 1805-12, it was part of Louisiana Territory; from 1812-21, part of Missouri Territory; from 1821-34, part of the unorganized territory of the United States; from 1834-36, part of Michigan Territory; and from 1836-38, part of Wisconsin Territory. In 1838, the western portion of Wisconsin Territory was named "Iowa" and out of this, the state, with its present boundaries, was carved in 1846.

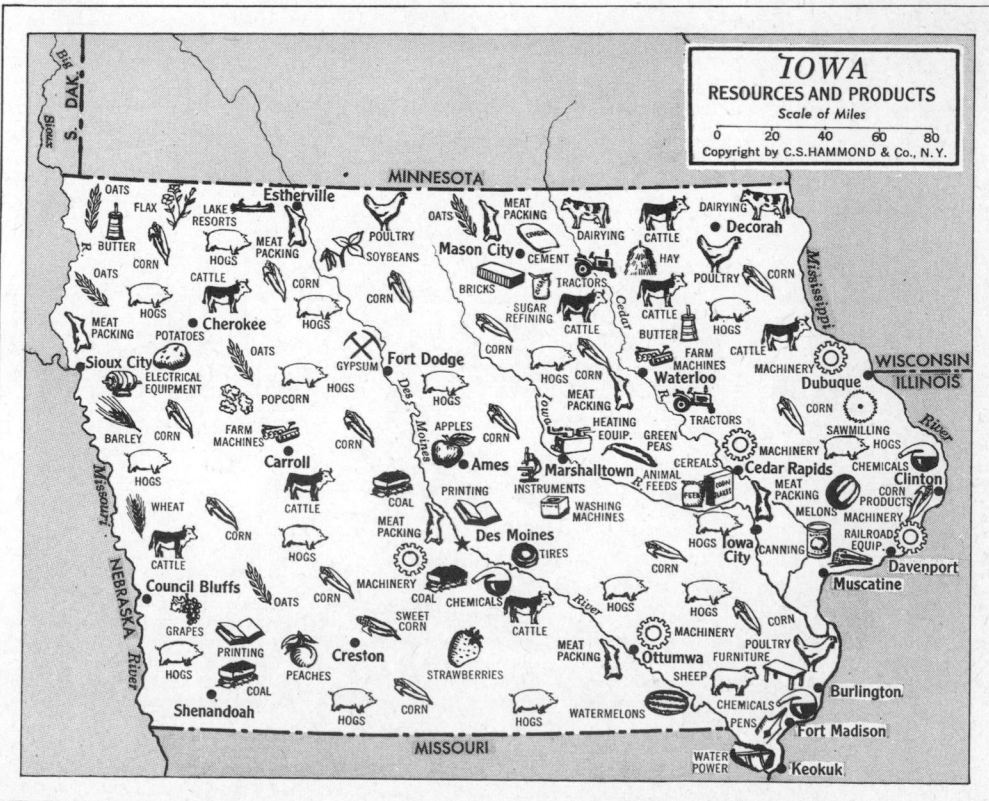

IOWA
RESOURCES AND PRODUCTS
Scale of Miles
0    20    40    60    80
Copyright by C.S. HAMMOND & Co., N.Y.

Standard Oil Co. (N. J.)

## KANSAS

Kansas was a part of the Louisiana Purchase (1803), and was colonized by both free and slave state settlers. It was made a territory in 1854, and at once became the battleground between the partisans of slavery and freedom. A bloody civil war broke out, in which many almost-battles took place. One of the most ardent of the anti-slavery partisans was John Brown. The Topeka Constitution, prohibiting slavery, was framed in 1855 and the Lecompton Constitution, sanctioning slavery, in 1857. The Wyandotte Constitution, forbidding slavery, was adopted in 1859, and Kansas was admitted as a free state in 1861. It took a prominent part in the Civil War.

◄ AERIAL VIEW OF KANSAS CITY. Railroad freight cars wait alongside filled grain elevators. Kansas, after the first decade of immigration, was settled by means of a railroad expansion plan. Because of this, the State has always had adequate transportation from farm to market. Grain elevators form the point of convergence for the scattered wheat-growing areas. The grain is stored in the elevators until freight cars carry it to the mills.

▼ PORTABLE DRILLING RIG. The state of Kansas is fourth in the output of oil and great industries have arisen near its source. The land is equally rich in deposits of zinc, coal, salt and building stone. Such raw materials are converted into a thousand commercial items by over three thousand manufacturing plants.

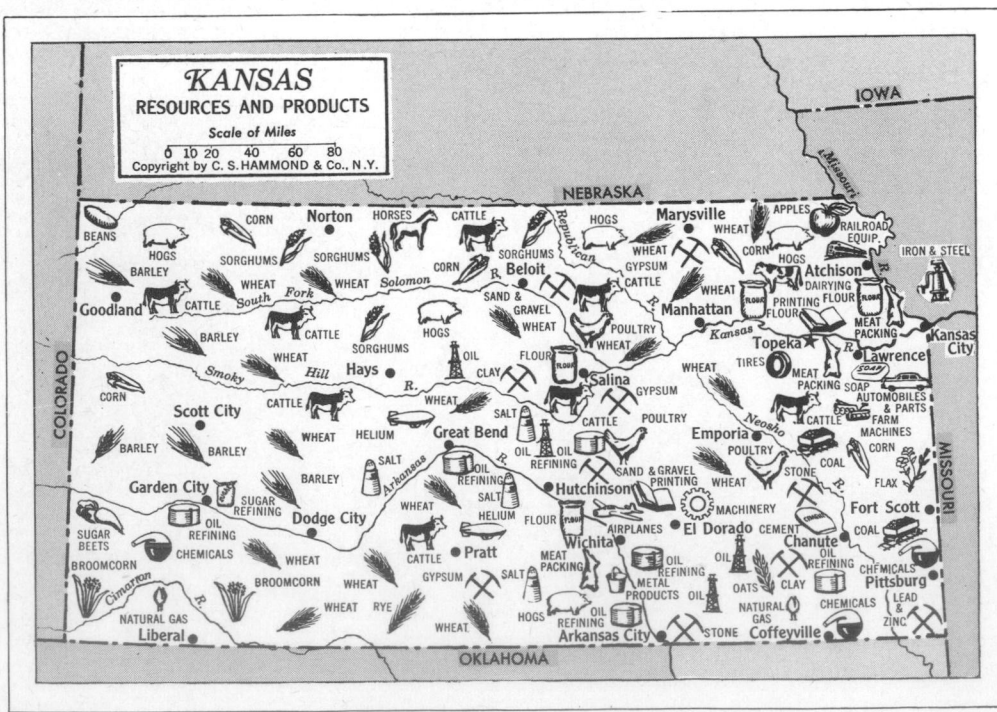

KANSAS
RESOURCES AND PRODUCTS
Scale of Miles
0  10  20    40    60    80
Copyright by C. S. HAMMOND & Co., N.Y.

Standard Oil Co. (N. J.)

## KENTUCKY

Numerous historic remains indicate that the mound-builders once lived in this territory. The name Kentucky, meaning "dark and blooay ground," commemorates the conflicts between various tribes of Indians. Kentucky was explored by Dr. Thomas Walker in 1750, by John Finley in 1767, and by Daniel Boone in 1769; was settled at Harrodsburg in 1774; was formed into a county of Virginia in 1776; was admitted to the Union in 1792; was distinguished in the War of 1812 and in the Mexican War; was a slave state, but did not secede; was occupied by Federals and Confederates in 1861; was the scene of campaigns and raids.

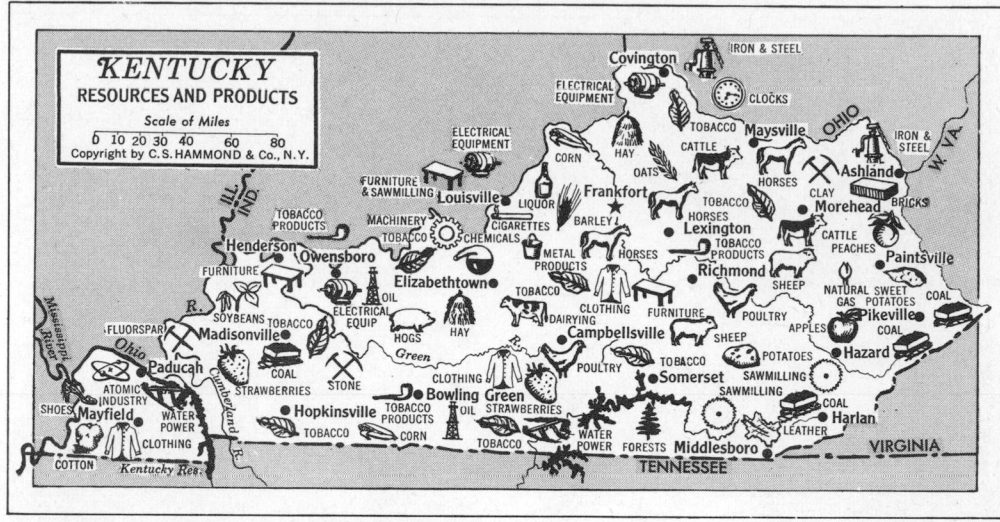

E. L. du Pont de Nemours & Co.

◄ SYNTHETIC RUBBER. Neoprene (man-made rubber) is processed in Louisville, Kentucky. Other world-famous Kentucky products are tobacco products, hemp and cotton.

▼ RAW SUGAR. The raw sugar shown here is a product of Louisiana's cane fields. Ninety per cent of the nation's cane sugar is from the "sugar bowl" of southeastern Louisiana.

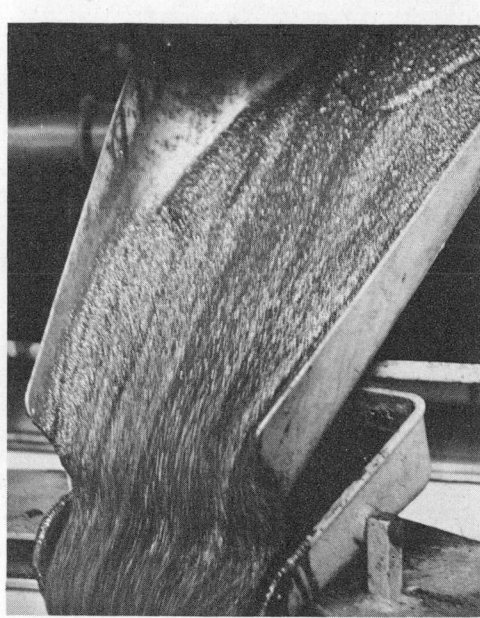

Standard Oil Co. (N. )

## LOUISIANA

Louisiana was explored by De Soto in 1541, and by La Salle in 1682; was settled by the French under Iberville and Bienville about 1700. The latter founded the city of New Orleans on its present site in 1718. In 1717, Louisiana was granted to a company, of which John Law was the head, but in 1731, reverted to the crown; was ceded by France to Spain in 1763, but in 1800 again became French territory. It was purchased by the United States in 1803 and was created the Territory of Orleans in 1804; had the portion east of the Mississippi annexed in 1810; was admitted to the Union in 1812; seceded in January, 1861; occupied by the Federals 1862-63; readmitted in 1868.

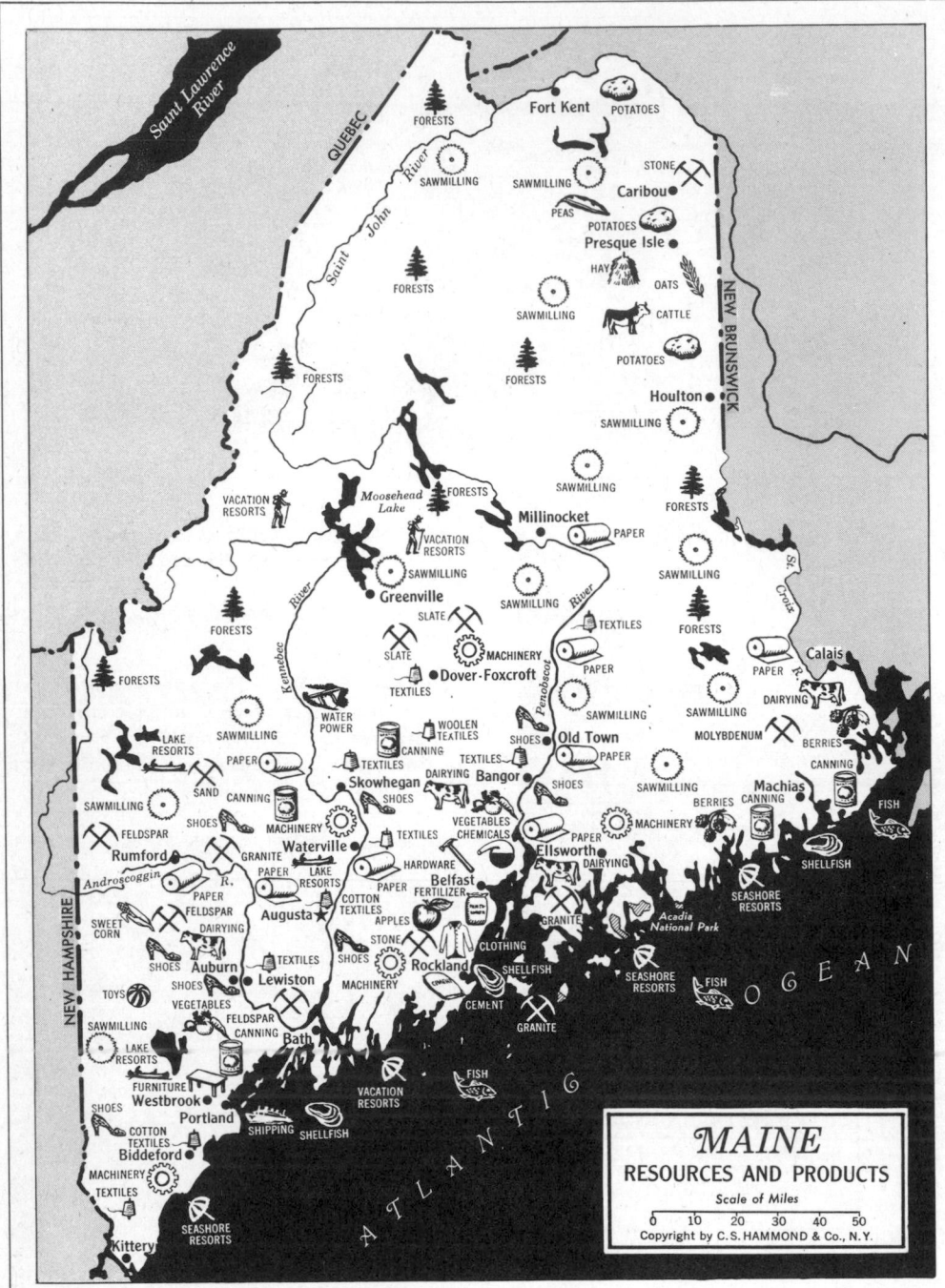

MAINE
RESOURCES AND PRODUCTS
Scale of Miles
0   10   20   30   40   50
Copyright by C. S. HAMMOND & Co., N.Y.

▲ TURTLES. Familiar natives of Louisiana are these small turtles commonly sold as household pets. Their eggs are deposited and hatched beneath the earth which makes discovery of the nests difficult. Each year thousands are shipped to different parts of the U. S.

## MARYLAND

Maryland, through the grant made by Charles I to George Calvert, first Lord Baltimore, became a proprietary colony, and its settlement was begun at St. Mary's, in 1634. During colonial times, it was involved in the Claiborne rebellion and in boundary and other disputes. In 1649, religious toleration was enacted for all sects and churches which acknowledged a belief in the Trinity. For many years, the colony was torn by quarrels between the proprietary party and Puritan settlers. There was a time when Roman Catholics were denied the privileges which Lord Baltimore had granted to Protestants. The city of Baltimore was founded in 1729. The boundary with Pennsylvania was finally settled, 1763-69, by Charles Mason and Jeremiah Dixon, who established the line named after them, which runs along the parallel 39° 43' 26.3" N. lat.

## MAINE

Maine was visited by many of the early explorers, including the Cabots, Verrazano, Gomez, Gosnold, Pring, du Guast, De Monts, and others. The first permanent settlement, at Bristol, dates from 1624. The eastern part of the state was a part of Acadia or Nova Scotia until 1691, at which time the whole region was merged in the "province of Massachusetts Bay." Maine became a separate state in 1820. A dispute with Great Britain over the northern boundary of the state was settled by the Webster-Ashburton Treaty in 1842. The Maine liquor law, the first state law on the subject, was passed in 1851. In World War I, Maine contributed a larger proportion of men (on a population basis) than any other state.

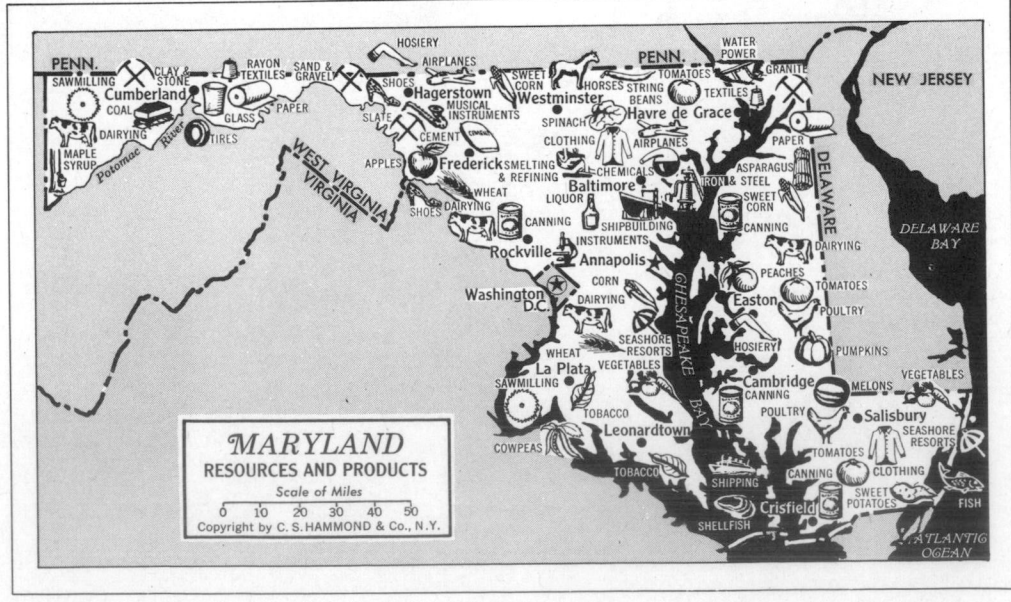

MARYLAND
RESOURCES AND PRODUCTS
Scale of Miles
0   10   20   30   40   50
Copyright by C. S. HAMMOND & Co., N.Y.

↑ MAINE HARBOR. The rocky coast of Maine, with its various vacation spots, is provided with many natural harbors. Known for its invigorating climate, the State offers ideal facilities for the sportsman and tourist.

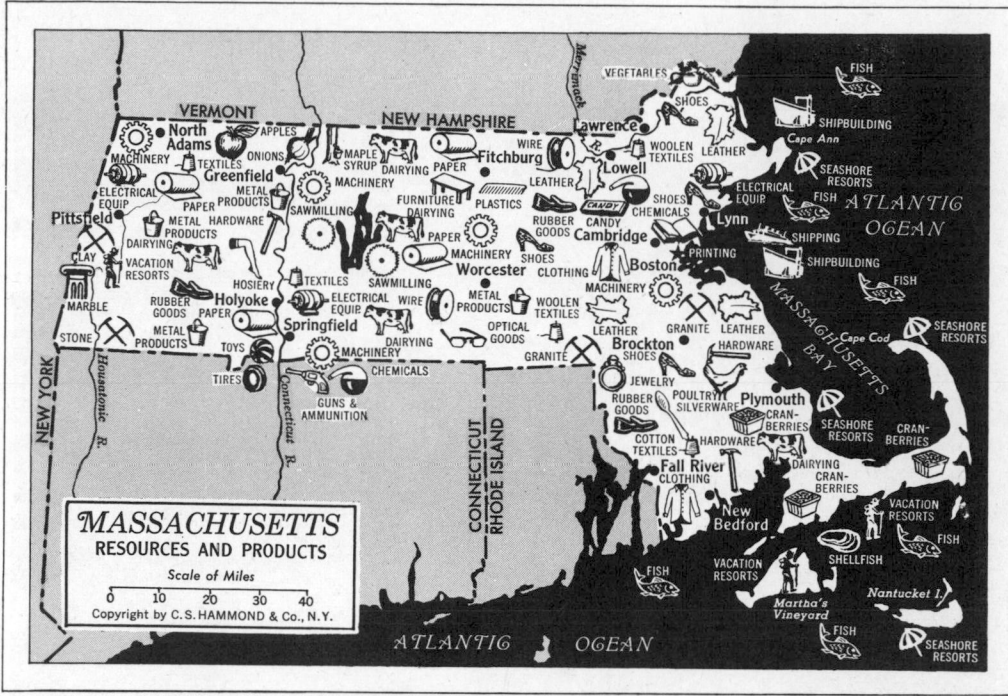

## MASSACHUSETTS

The coast of Massachusetts is supposed to have been visited by the Norsemen about 1000 A.D.; but the first permanent white settlement was made by the Pilgrim Fathers at Plymouth, on the coast north of Cape Cod, in December, 1620. This was known as the Plymouth Colony. In 1628, a company of Puritans settled at Salem, and from that beginning was formed the Massachusetts Bay Colony which included the settlements of Boston, Lynn, and other towns. In 1692, the two colonies were united.

The early history of Massachusetts is the inspiring heritage of much of America. The state was settled by men seeking liberty for their own form of religious worship and intolerant of all other forms. However, they were far ahead of their European contemporaries; gradually that bigotry diminished and religious tolerance grew; the state became a leader in all that stood for liberty. The War of Independence began in Massachusetts in 1775, with the battles of Lexington and Bunker Hill.

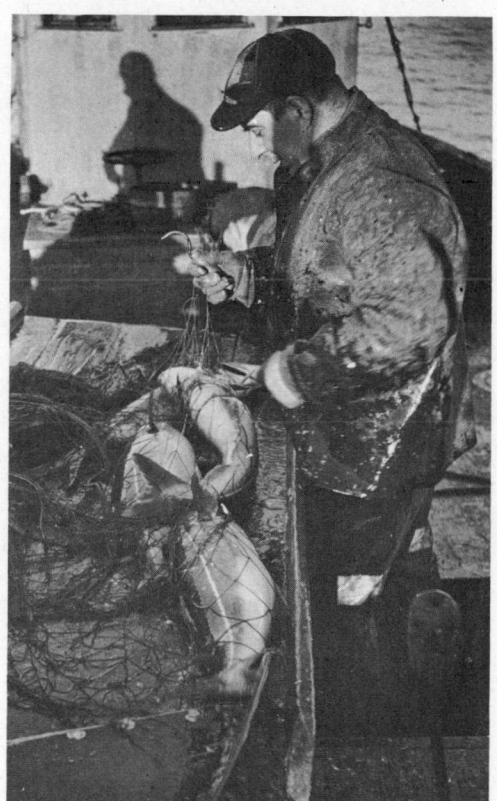

Standard Oil Co. (N. J.)

↑ FISHING IN GLOUCESTER. The fishermen above are busy freeing fish from the nets. Their boats, battered by the stormy seas of the iceberg-infested Grand Banks, bring in codfish for food, fertilizer, glue and isinglass. Once the leading industry of Massachusetts, fishing has left the foreground to be supplanted by a wide variety of other industries.

➤ OIL REFINERY. Not a Martian city, but the propane section of a Baltimore oil refinery. Oil refining, like other huge industries, has come to Baltimore because it is a key transportation center. Chesapeake Bay, in turn, provides the international outlet.

Standard Oil Co. (N. J.)

## MICHIGAN

What is now the state of Michigan was probably visited by Jean Nicolet in 1634 at Sault Ste. Marie where the first permanent white settlement was made by Father Marquette in 1668. In 1701 Detroit was founded as a fur trading center by the French. The country was ceded to Great Britain in 1763; later was the scene of Pontiac's War; was surrendered to the United States in 1796; formed part of the Northwest Territory and later of Indiana Territory; and was constituted Michigan Territory in 1805. Detroit was taken by the British during the War of 1812, Michigan was recovered by the United States in 1813, and was admitted to the Union in 1837.

The Kellogg Co.

◄CEREAL PLANT. Much of Michigan's cereal grain is converted into the nation's traditional breakfast foods. The commercial need for cereal grain by such a company as Kellogg has accounted for an ever-increasing rise in the State's agricultural output. Other staple foods like corn, oats and beans form the mainstay of the State's agrarian economy. Additional crops of celery, onions and an abundant yield of strawberries and cantaloupes place Michigan among the leading farm areas of the United States.

▼ STEEL MILLS. A view of the steel mills in Dearborn, Michigan. Michigan, surrounded by the greatest inland waterway in the world and containing large mineral and timber resources, has become one of the most highly industrialized regions in the world. Michigan has created more manufacturing industries than could be named here. Probably the best known is that of the automobile. Of approximately 60 other industries, furniture, paper, chemicals, cereals, stoves and machinery are the largest.

### MICHIGAN
### RESOURCES AND PRODUCTS
Scale of Miles
0  20  40  60  80
Copyright by C.S. HAMMOND & Co., N.Y.

Standard Oil Co. (N. J.)

## MINNESOTA

Before the coming of Europeans, Minnesota was occupied by two powerful Indian tribes, the Ojibways (or Chippewas) in the north and along the Mississippi River, and the Sioux (or Dakotas) in the south and west. The region was first explored by the French near the end of the 17th century. That part of Minnesota which lies east of the Mississippi River belonged to the Northwest Territory, acquired by the United States in 1783. West of the Mississippi, it was a part of the Louisiana Purchase of 1803. In 1838, the Chippewa Indians surrendered the land east of the Mississippi. Immigration began: Minnesota became a territory in 1849, and a state in 1858. In 1862 occurred a terrible massacre by the Sioux Indians, finally defeated in 1864.

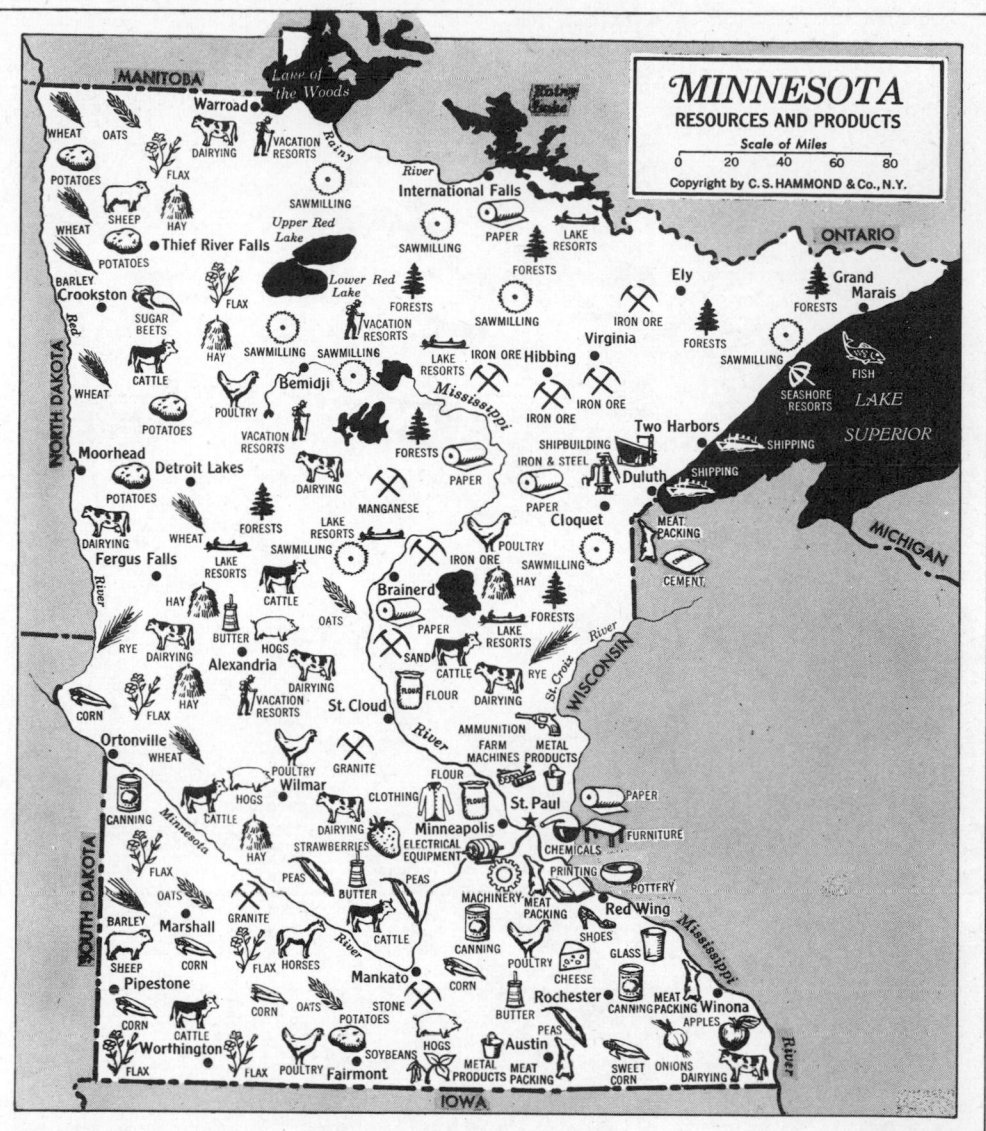

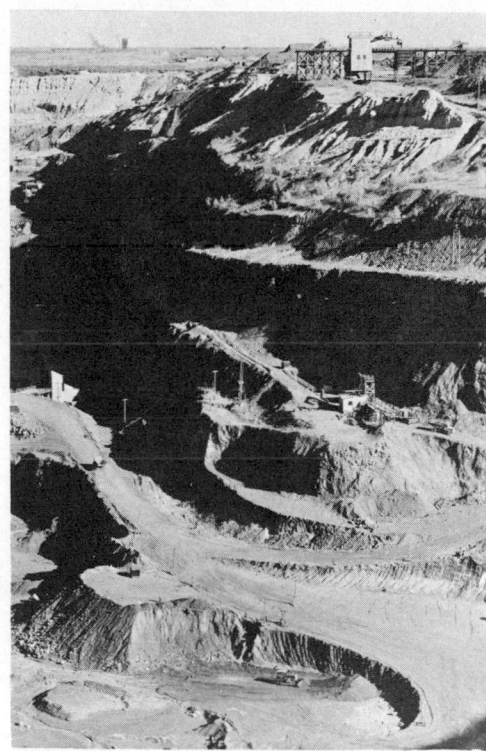

Standard Oil Co. (N. J.)

▲ IRON ORE MINE. The Susquehanna mine near Hibbing, Minnesota is the largest in the world. It is a mile wide and has 55 miles of track. Minnesota supplies nearly three-quarters of the total production of iron ore of the United States. The State also has millions of acres of forest and 10,000 lakes which makes it one of the nation's major vacation areas.

➤ LOADING GRAIN. Grain-loading from elevators in the Duluth-Superior harbor. Minnesota is a world center for flour-milling. The State is also famous for its meat, butter and cheese. With much tillable land, it is one of the world's great agricultural regions. Strangely enough, coffee roasting is a large industry in Minnesota. Other products include paper, machinery, cement and glass.

Standard Oil Company (N. J.)

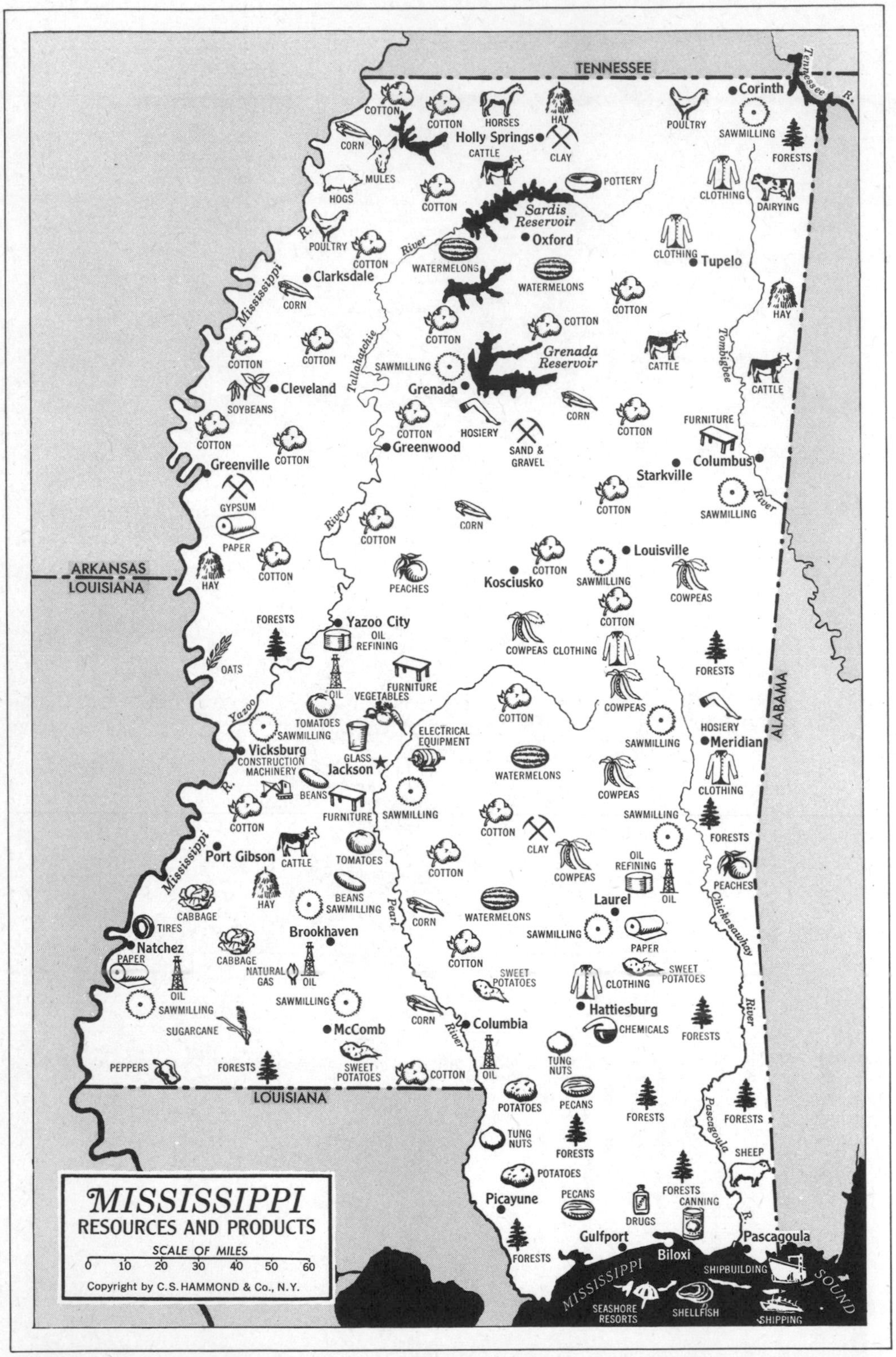

**MISSISSIPPI**
**RESOURCES AND PRODUCTS**
SCALE OF MILES
0  10  20  30  40  50  60
Copyright by C.S. HAMMOND & Co., N.Y.

Standard Oil Company (N. J.)

## MISSISSIPPI

Mississippi was visited by De Soto in 1540. The Mississippi River was explored by Marquette and La Salle in 1681. An attempt was made at settlement by the French at Iberville in 1699, and a settlement was made on the site of Natchez in 1716. It was ceded by France to Great Britain in 1763; part was ceded to the United States in 1783; the remainder was acquired in 1811. Mississippi was organized as a territory in 1798, and was admitted to the Union as a state in 1817. It seceded in 1861; was the scene of various conflicts during the Civil War; was readmitted to the Union in 1870. In the Mississippi River flood of 1927 more than $45,000,000 worth of property and crops was destroyed.

Mississippi A. & I. Board

▲ THE GULF COAST. Few areas of the South have a more colorful and varied history than the Gulf Coast. Seven flags have flown over the territory since 1699. The influence of the French, Spanish and English is still evident in architecture, customs and Old World symbols of its two and a half centuries of history. Early Spanish and Civil War forts, presidential homes, legendary pirate hide-outs and Indian myths are all part of the highly interesting Gulf Coast story. Today, Biloxi, a major city on the Gulf Coast, is the scene of an annual regatta in which many outstanding yachtsmen participate to vie for its coveted trophies.

◄ MECHANICAL PICKER. The mechanical cotton-pickers, shown operating in Delta County, Mississippi, have set off the spark of much dispute among the hand-pickers of cotton. The machine requires an evenly-grown crop and dry fields. Because of its high cost, it can only be used on large plantations. Recent improvement may bring about its wider use.

## MISSOURI

The territory included in the present state of Missouri formed part of the French colony of Louisiana. Ste. Genevieve was settled in 1735, and Ft. Orleans on the Missouri River, had been temporarily established in 1720, but few others were made before the transfer of Louisiana to Spain in 1763. St. Louis was founded in 1764. It was ceded back to France in 1800; formed part of the Louisiana Purchase of 1803; and was included in Louisiana Territory in 1805. Missouri Territory was formed in 1812, and admitted to the Union as a slave state in 1821. The state did not receive its present limits until 1835. In the Kansas troubles of 1855, the citizens of the western border took an active part against the free state movement. At the outbreak of the Civil War in 1861, the people of Missouri were divided with regard to secession, but the unionists finally prevailed. A world's fair was held in St. Louis in 1904 to commemorate the Louisiana Purchase.

Standard Oil Company (N. J.)

▲ FARMLANDS. The undulating upland region of Missouri rises to the west and forms a level land which is devoted to the raising of wheat and livestock. Winding rivers from the highlands cut across the fertile plains.

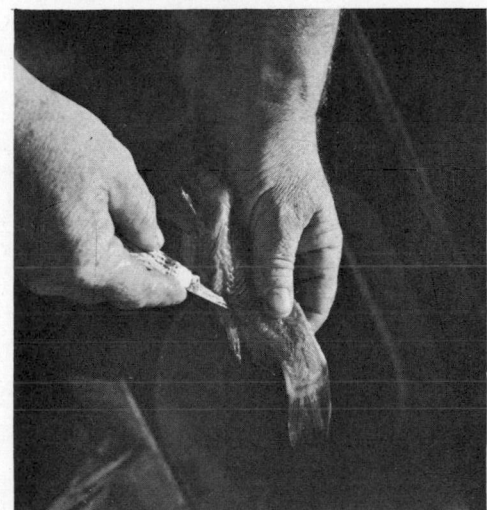

Standard Oil Co. (N. J.)

▲ CAT FISH. Quiet waters of Missouri's Ozark Hills provide a catch for an old-fashioned fish-fry.

▼ MISSOURI MULE. The Missouri mule is known for its exceptional quality and fine breeding.

Standard Oil Co. (N. J.)

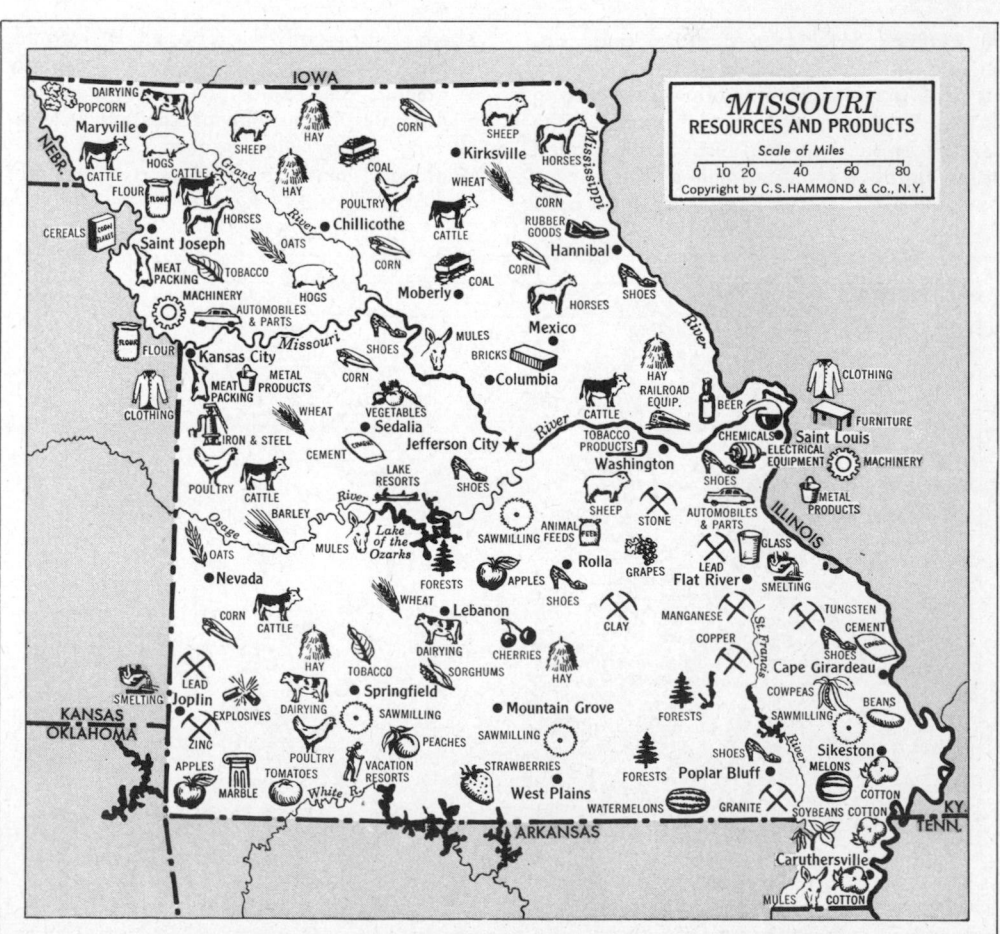

## MONTANA

The portion of Montana east of the Rocky Mountains was part of the Louisiana Purchase (1803); that to the west was part of Oregon and Washington. It was first visited by the French in 1742, and by Lewis and Clark in 1804-06; these explorers were followed by fur traders, trappers and Jesuit missionaries. The part of Montana which was included in the Louisiana Purchase became successively a part of Missouri Territory (1812), of Nebraska Territory (1854), of Dakota Territory (1861), and of Idaho Territory (1863); that which lies west of the mountains became successively a part of Oregon (1848), of Washington Territory (1853), and of Idaho Territory (1863). Gold was discovered in 1861. In 1864, the territory was organized and in 1889 Montana became a state of the Union.

Montana Highway Dept.

▲ LEWIS AND CLARK CAVERN. The beautiful Lewis and Clark Cavern, near Bozeman, was discovered when a prospector decided to find out how an eagle disappeared into a mountainside. The Paradise Room is shown above. Montana's varied topography ranges from emerald-like meadows in the east to raging cascades and towering mountains in the west.

➤ WHITEFACED STEERS. Western Nebraska is a cattleman's country. Cattle is the State's leading product. Often livestock are grazed in the west but later sent east to the Omaha area for fattening.

Montana Highway Dept.

▲ COPPER SMELTER. Montana and copper are so closely associated that often injustice is done to all the other vast wealth of the "Treasure State." One-sixth of the world's copper and one-third of the United States' supply is Montana-mined. The smelter shown above is in the Butte-Anaconda area where nearly all the copper is located. Montana yields half of the nation's supply of arsenic, and ranks next to the continent of Australia in sapphire production. It leads all other states in manganese. Of the latter, Montana's mines produce forty-three per cent of the nation's supply.

## NEBRASKA

French explorers followed the Platte River (or the Nebraska) to the Forks, in 1739. Nebraska passed to the United States in 1803 as part of the Louisiana Purchase, and was explored by several American expeditions. Several trading posts were probably established between 1795 and 1812. In 1823 Bellevue became an Indian agency, and later was the first postoffice in the state. Nebraska was one of the two territories created by the Kansas-Nebraska Bill of 1854. Slaves were within its borders from the beginning, but a territorial law of 1861 excluded slavery. As organized in 1854, Nebraska extended from 40° N. latitude to British America, and from the Missouri and White Earth Rivers to the summit of the Rockies; it was reduced to its present boundaries in 1861 and 1863. The state was torn by bitter factional quarrels over the location of the capital and admission to statehood, and during part of 1866 and 1867, there were two de facto governments—the territorial and the state. It was admitted to the Union in 1867.

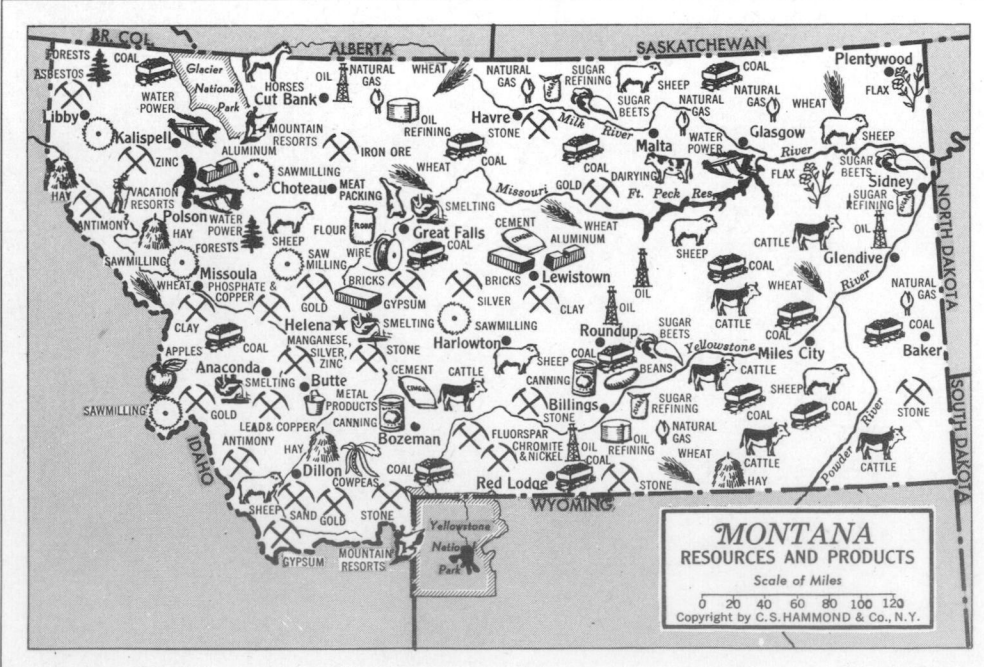

Montana Highway Dept.

MONTANA
RESOURCES AND PRODUCTS
Scale of Miles
0  20  40  60  80  100  120
Copyright by C.S. HAMMOND & Co., N.Y.

## NEVADA

Francisco Garces, a Franciscan monk, passed through the state on his way to California in 1775. Some fifty years later, American and Canadian trappers worked along the Humboldt River. Many overland immigrants, on their way to California, crossed Nevada in the early '40's. In 1843-45, Fremont made a series of explorations in this region. In 1848, by the Treaty of Guadalupe-Hidalgo which concluded the war with Mexico, Nevada became United States territory. It was known as the Washoe Country, California, until September, 1850, when most of the present state was included in the territory of Utah. The first settlement in what is now the state of Nevada was made at Genoa in the valley of the Carson River in 1849. In 1859 the discovery of the fabulous "Comstock Lode" brought thousands of people into the territory. In March, 1861, the territory of Utah was divided at 39° west of Washington, and the western portion called Nevada was admitted as a state in 1864. In 1931, the legislature passed a bill permitting divorces to those establishing a six-weeks residence, and another bill legalizing gambling. The famous Hoover Dam was built across the Colorado River in 1936.

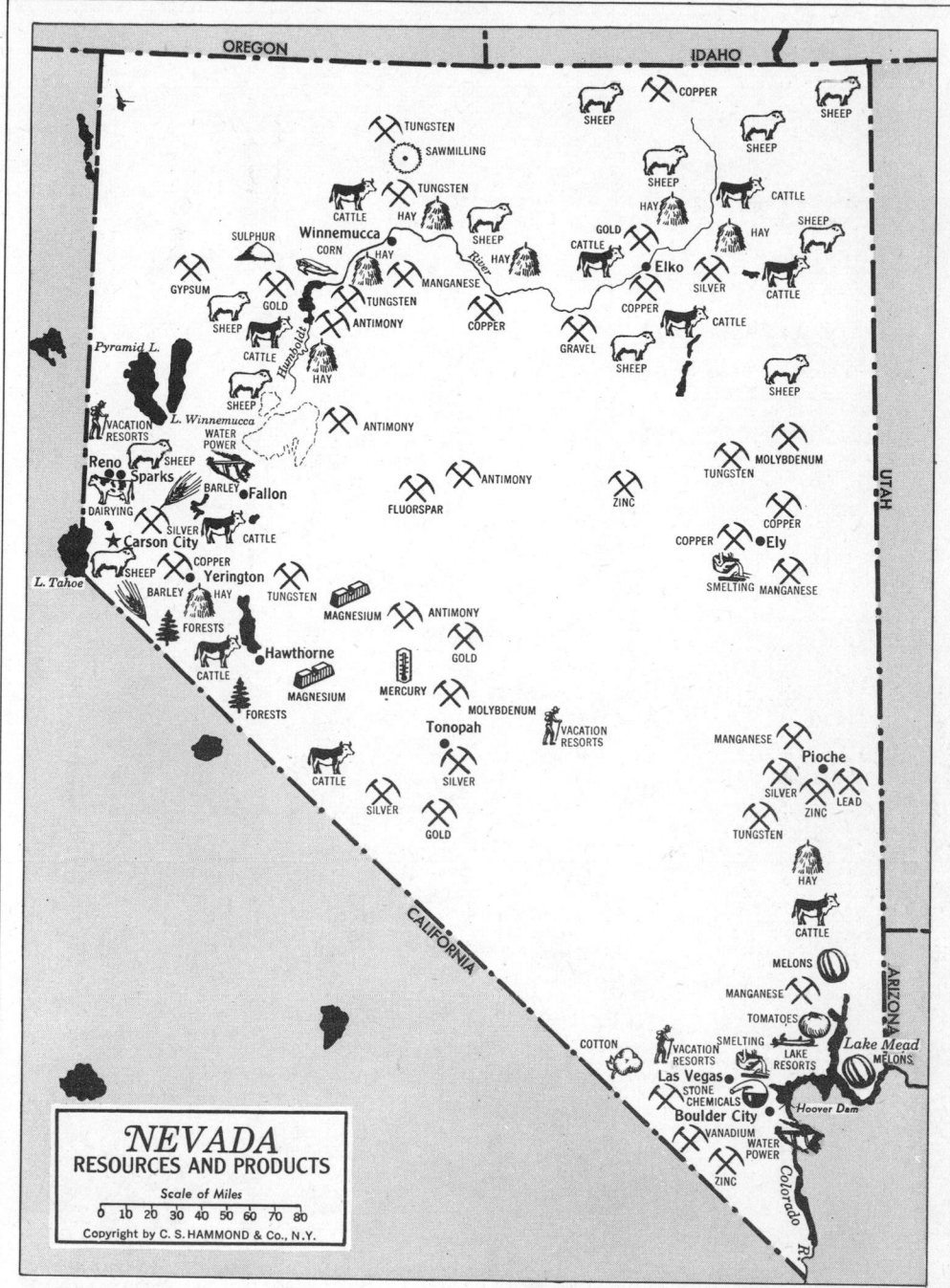

NEVADA
RESOURCES AND PRODUCTS
Scale of Miles
0 10 20 30 40 50 60 70 80
Copyright by C. S. HAMMOND & Co., N.Y.

Standard Oil Co. (N. J.)

► INDUSTRIAL SCENE at Henderson, Nev.

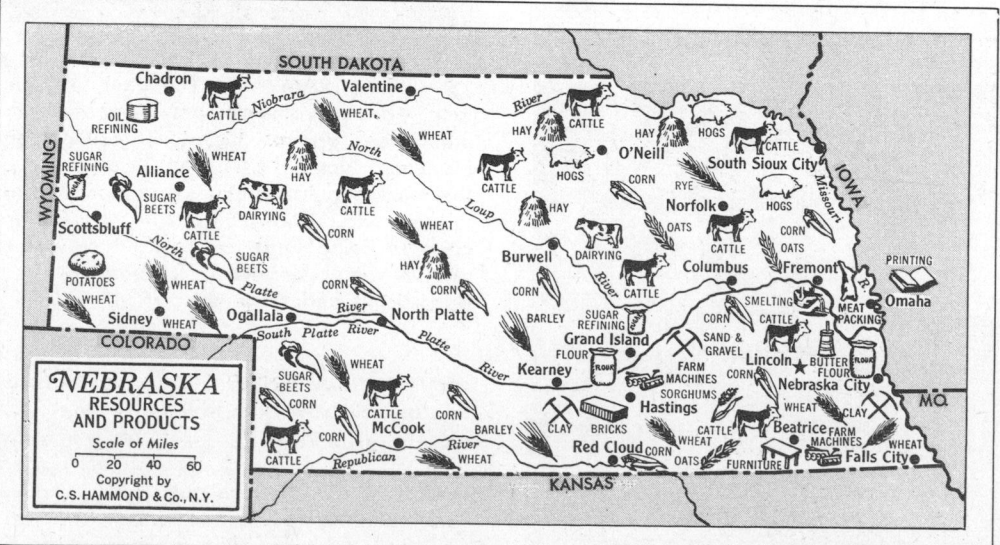

NEBRASKA
RESOURCES AND PRODUCTS
Scale of Miles
0 20 40 60
Copyright by
C. S. HAMMOND & Co., N.Y.

Nevada Dept. of Highways

## NEW HAMPSHIRE

Among the early explorers who visited New Hampshire were Martin Pring (1603), Samuel de Champlain (1605), and Captain John Smith (1614). The first settlement, of which there is positive evidence, was made in 1623 by David Thomson at Little Harbor, now in the town of Rye. In 1641-79, 1689-92, and 1699-1741, New Hampshire was joined to the Massachusetts Colony; but during the intervening dates and until 1775, it was under royal governors of its own. A provisional government was formed in 1776, a state constitution adopted in 1784, and New Hampshire was the ninth state to ratify the National Constitution in 1788. During the 19th century the state became involved in the Northeastern Boundary Dispute with Great Britain, which was finally settled by Daniel Webster in the famous Webster-Ashburton Treaty of 1842. New Hampshire gained national attention in 1852, when Franklin Pierce was elected president, the first and only chief executive to come from New Hampshire.

White Mts. Region Ass'n

▲ AERIAL TRAMWAY. The Cannon Mountain Aerial Tramway carries passengers 2,000 feet up for high-level skiing near Franconia Notch, N. H. The State is one of the most popular winter recreational areas in the world. "Snowtrains" run from Eastern cities to bring huge out-of-state crowds to attend winter carnivals, ice-boating, sleddog racing and ski meets.

◄ NEW HAMPSHIRE COWS. Rich pasturage affords New Hampshire with ideal facilities for raising dairy cows. Milk and by-products are shipped by rail to eastern markets where they are purchased in wholesale quantities. Hay, too, is an important crop and is harvested in large amounts.

### NEW HAMPSHIRE — RESOURCES AND PRODUCTS

Scale of Miles

0 5 10 15 20 25

Copyright by C.S. HAMMOND & CO., N.Y.

Standard Oil Company (N. J.)

► CHEMICAL PLANT. Typical of New Jersey's expanding industry is this chemical plant at Deepwater which manufactures organic compounds for the many other industrial companies of the state.

▼ AERONAUTICAL PRODUCTION. New Jersey is among the nation's foremost producers of aircraft engines. Factories in northern New Jersey, such as this one at Wood-Ridge, turn out some of the country's finest precision-built aeronautical parts and equipment.

E. I. du Pont de Nemours & Co.

Curtiss-Wright Corp.

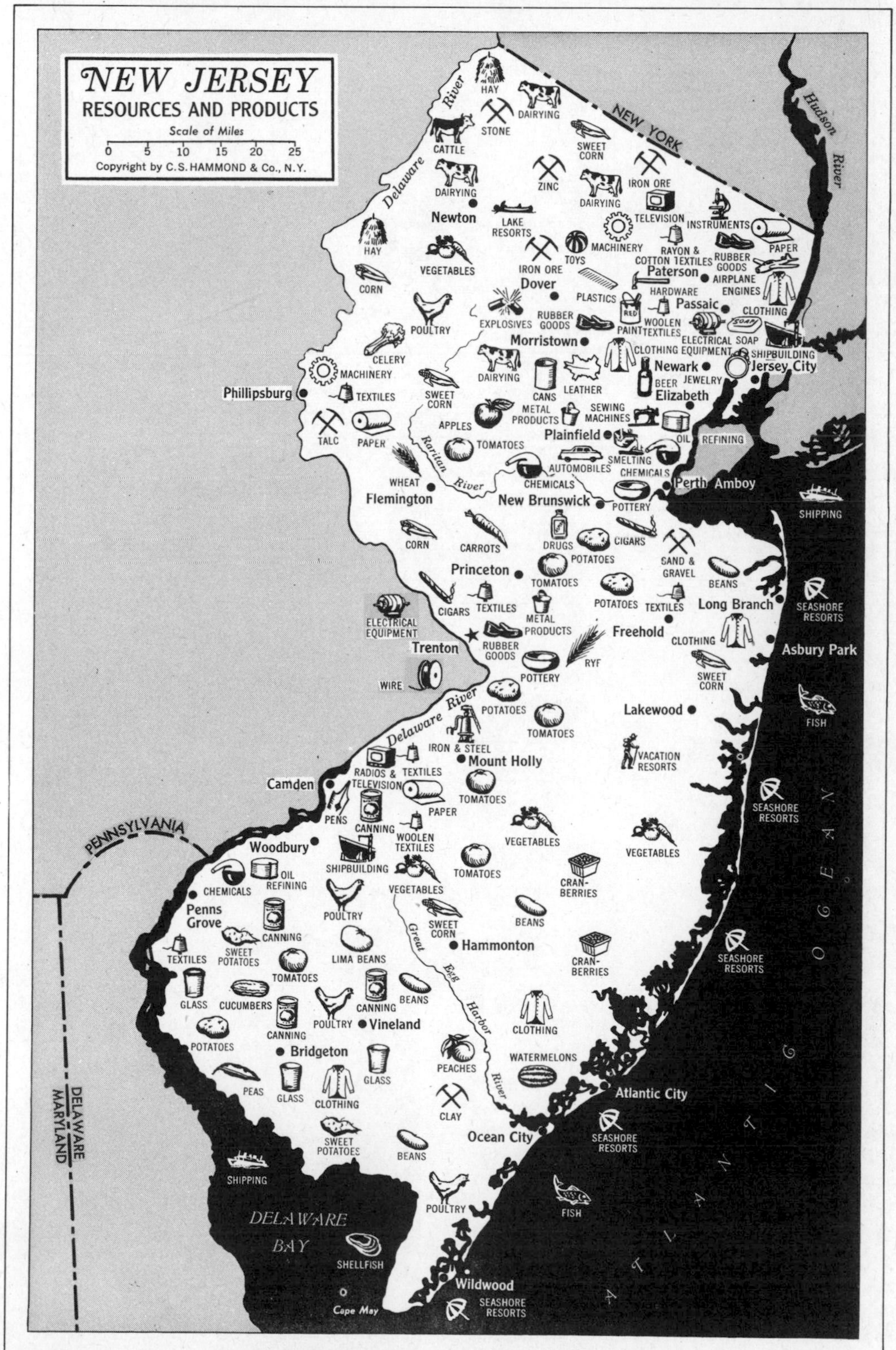

## NEW JERSEY

Voyages made with a view to exploration and settlement of the region now called New Jersey may be said to have begun with the voyage of Henry Hudson in 1609. The English claim to the territory was founded on the voyage of Cabot in 1498. The Dutch settled at Bergen in 1617. Soon after, some Swedes settled on the lower Delaware but were expelled by the Dutch in 1655. In 1664, New Netherland passed to the English, and the Duke of York gave the portion included in the present New Jersey to Lord Berkeley and Sir George Carteret. The latter had been administrator of the Island of Jersey, so the American province was named New Jersey. In 1676 the province was divided into West and East New Jersey, the former being under a Quaker proprietorship and the latter under Carteret. West New Jersey soon passed to William Penn who, in 1682, purchased East New Jersey also. In 1702 the government of both colonies passed to the Crown and the two were united. Until 1736, New Jersey was under the governor of New York, but had a separate assembly. New Jersey was one of the original thirteen states and was the scene of stirring events in the struggle for independence. The Morristown National Historical Park, established by Congress in 1933, commemorates some of these events.

### NEW JERSEY
RESOURCES AND PRODUCTS

Scale of Miles

0   5   10   15   20   25

Copyright by C.S. HAMMOND & Co., N.Y.

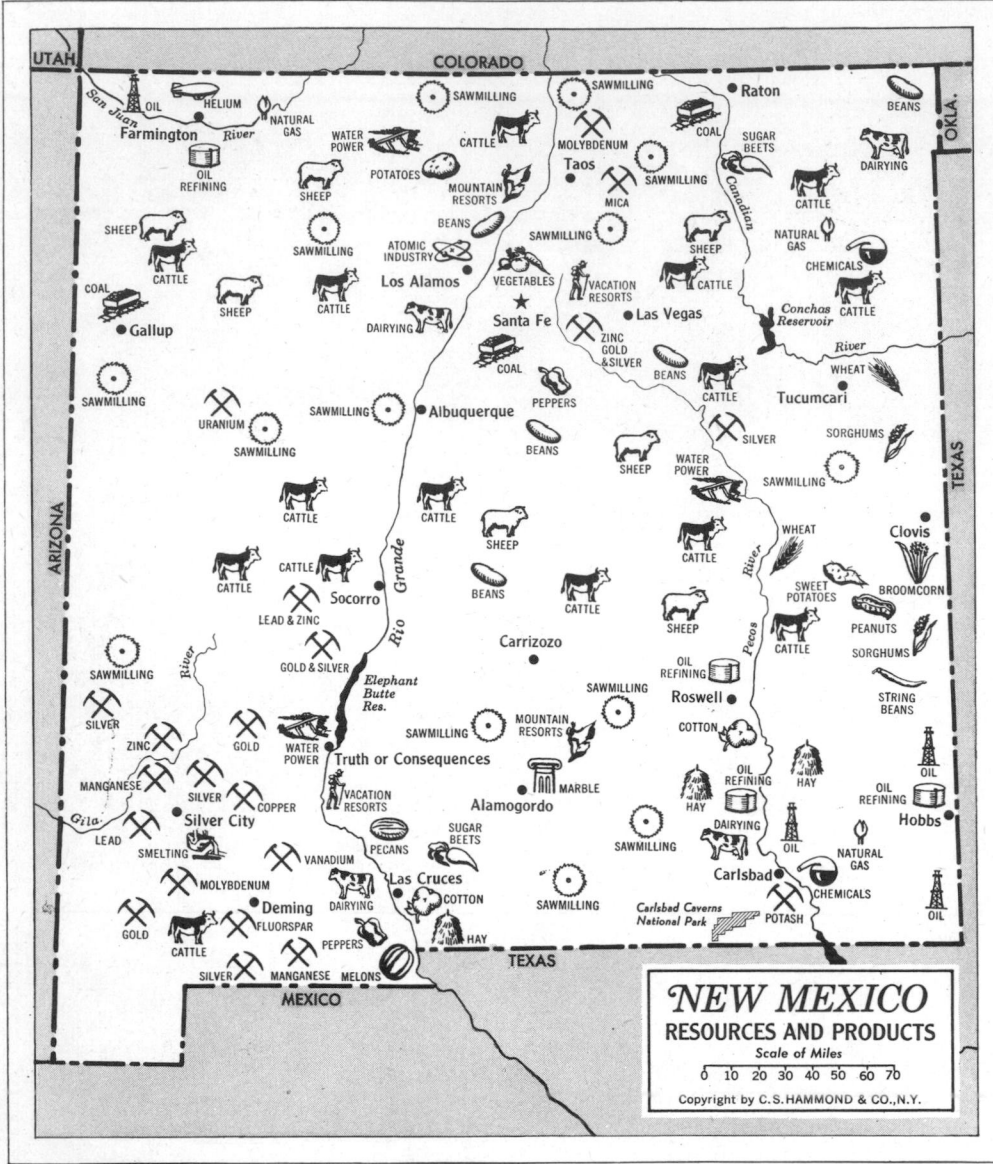

NEW MEXICO
RESOURCES AND PRODUCTS
Scale of Miles
0 10 20 30 40 50 60 70
Copyright by C.S.HAMMOND & CO.,N.Y.

## NEW MEXICO

New Mexico was explored by Spaniards from Mexico at various times between 1536 and 1581. Between 1583 and 1595, several attempts at the conquest and occupation of New Mexico were made but were unsuccessful. Santa Fe, which occupies a site nearly 7,000 ft. in elevation, is, after St. Augustine, Florida, the oldest town in the United States, dating from 1605. An Indian revolt in 1680 resulted in the massacre of over 400 Spanish settlers and the capture of Santa Fe but in 1692 the Spaniards regained their hold on the territory, and European occupation was assured. The history of New Mexico, during the 18th century, was uneventful. After the achievement of Mexican independence in 1821, New Mexico became successively a province, a territory, and a department of that country. It was ceded to the United States by the Treaty of Guadalupe-Hidalgo in 1848. Previous to that time, American traders had been active in the territory and after that date, the settlement of the region by Americans progressed steadily. The territorial form of government was provided by Congress in 1850 and was inaugurated on the 3rd of March, 1851. Its area was increased by the Gadsden Purchase from Mexico and by the Texan cession of the country lying east of the Rio Grande. New Mexico assumed its present boundaries in 1863. It was admitted to the Union as a state in January, 1912. In 1915 and 1916, frequent raids of New Mexico villages by Mexican bandits caused strained relations between Mexico and the United States.

New Mexico State Tourist Bur.

▲ COPPER MINE. The Santa Rita, one of New Mexico's most productive copper mines, was worked as far back as 1800 by the Spaniards. The State's mineral deposits are abundant, and include zinc, silver and some iron ore.

➤ WHITE SANDS. A wide desert area of 270 square miles, White Sands has become the site of our national rocket experimentation program. The Sands, situated west of Alamagordo, is one of New Mexico's numerous natural wonders.

New Mexico State Tourist Bur.

## NEW YORK

Before the coming of Europeans, the territory now known as New York was occupied by the Iroquois Indians (Five Nations). New York Bay was entered by Verrazano in 1524. In 1609, Samuel de Champlain, the French explorer, penetrated the northeastern part of the state, and Henry Hudson, an Englishman in the service of the Netherlands, explored the Hudson River as far as the present site of Albany. A few years later (1613-14) settlements were made by the Dutch on Manhattan Island, and the region was called New Netherlands. Among the early Dutch governors were Minuit, Wouter van Twiller, Kieft, and Stuyvesant. New Amsterdam (New York City) was founded in 1623. The Dutch colony was devastated by an Indian war in 1641. England, basing her demands on the Cabot voyages, claimed New Netherlands, forced its surrender and renamed it New York. New York, New Jersey, and New England were consolidated under Andros in 1686-89. New York was the scene of many events in the French and Indian Wars, and of Burgoyne's surrender (1777) and other events in the Revolutionary War and the War of 1812. The completion of the Erie Canal in 1825 led to a rapid development of western New York and all of the states carved from the old Northwest Territory. New York City was the capital of the United States from 1785-90, and the state capital from 1784-97.

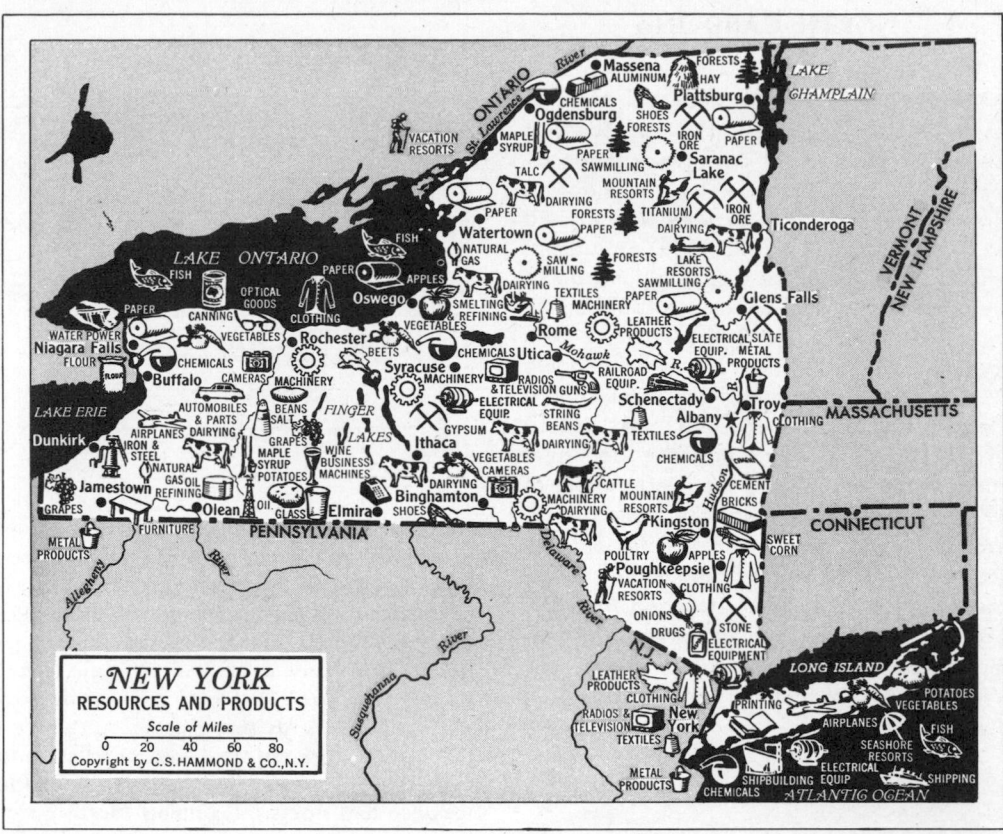

**NEW YORK RESOURCES AND PRODUCTS**
Scale of Miles
0   20   40   60   80
Copyright by C.S. HAMMOND & CO., N.Y.

▼ NEW YORK SKYLINE. Truly an American mecca, New York City, cultural and commercial focal point of the nation, is an example of the dynamism which is expressive of American civilization. With a population of almost eight million, it counts among its inhabitants the most diversified elements of any American city. Both artisan and artist find the great metropolis the logical center for the full employment and appreciation of their respective talents.

Standard Oil Co. (N. J.)

▲ BROOKLYN BRIDGE. Familiar landmark for New Yorkers is Brooklyn's famous bridge. At one time the longest suspension bridge in the world, it has been superseded by the more modern structures of which it was a forerunner.

TWA-Trans World Airline

## NORTH CAROLINA

Unsuccessful attempts were made to colonize the Carolina region under the auspices of Sir Walter Raleigh in 1584-87. The first permanent English settlement was made by Virginians at Albemarle on the Chowan River, about 1660. The territory was granted to proprietors in 1663 and 1665. An attempt was made to introduce a constitution framed by Shaftsbury and Locke in 1669 but it ended in failure. A Royal Province was formed in 1728 when North and South Carolina were separated. The "Mecklenburg Declaration of Independence" was passed in 1775; it is claimed that this document formed the model for the Declaration of 1776. North Carolina was the scene of several battles in the Revolution (1780-81); rejected the United States Constitution in 1788, but adopted it in 1789; seceded May 20, 1861. It was the scene of various engagements and military operations in the Civil War. It was readmitted to the Union in July, 1868.

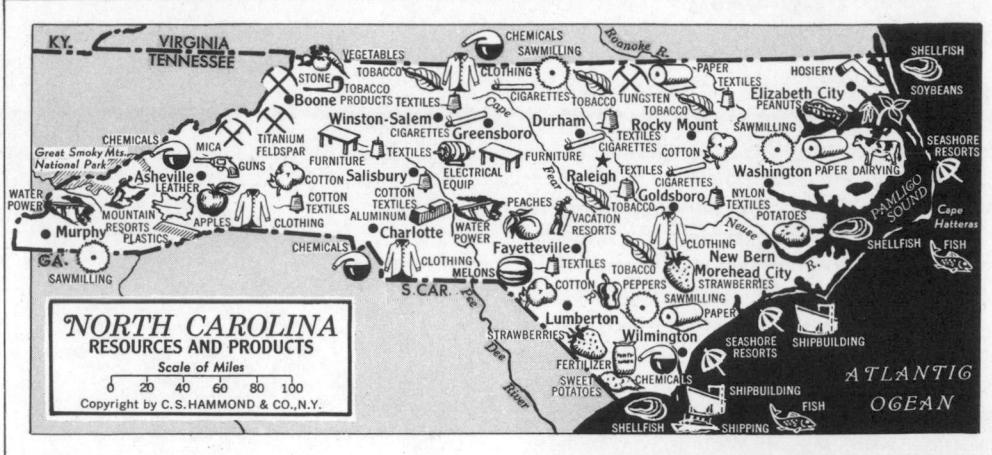

NORTH CAROLINA RESOURCES AND PRODUCTS
Scale of Miles
0 20 40 60 80 100
Copyright by C.S. HAMMOND & CO., N.Y.

► HANGING TOBACCO. As one of the principal commercial crops, tobacco has long been one of North Carolina's agricultural assets. Contributing greatly to the South's tobacco monopoly, the local producers are proud of their "bright leaf" variety. The flue-cured tobacco is taken from the curing barn as shown in the picture on the right, is graded, tied into bundles, and then sold at auction. The buyer re-dries the tobacco and stores it for aging. North Carolina is the world's largest producer of tobacco.

◄ PULP MILL. Among North Carolina's other industries lumber-processing is notable. Through a well-planned forestry program, the State has managed to develop an adequate lumber supply; and takes special precautions to replace and cultivate all trees which are essential to proper soil conservation. Forests cover fifty per cent of North Carolina and furnish many different wood types. Oak, poplar, ash and hickory grow in the mountain region, while pine predominates on the coastal plain.

Standard Oil Co. (N. J.)

Standard Oil Co. (N. J.)

## NORTH DAKOTA

North Dakota was visited by traders of the Hudson Bay Company late in the 18th Century. It was part of the region ceded by France in the Louisiana Purchase of 1803. It was successively a part of the District of Louisiana, of the Louisiana Territory, the Missouri Territory, the Territory of Michigan, Wisconsin Territory, Iowa Territory, and Minnesota Territory. The first permanent settlement was made by Scottish Highlanders at Pembina in 1812. They had formerly been located at Winnipeg and thought their new settlement was in British territory. The Territory of Dakota was created in 1861 and included the present Dakotas and portions of Wyoming and Montana. In 1863, the boundaries of the Dakotas were fixed at practically their present limits. The settlement of the territory was impeded by the Civil War and by Indian hostilities. Rapid development began in 1872; the territory was divided into North and South Dakota, and both entered the Union as states in 1889. Many advanced social and economic experiments have been made in North Dakota, since the organization in 1915 of the Non-Partisan League. Among these are a state-owned grain elevator and mill, and a state bank at the capital.

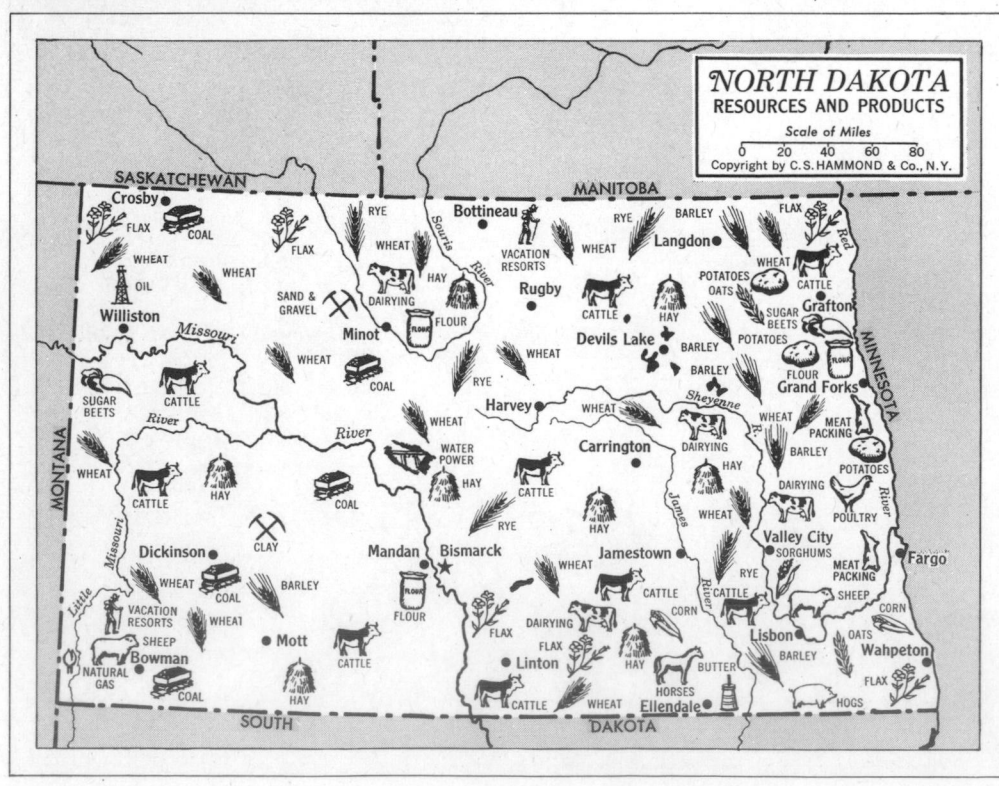

NORTH DAKOTA RESOURCES AND PRODUCTS
Scale of Miles
0 20 40 60 80
Copyright by C.S. HAMMOND & Co., N.Y.

WHEAT FIELD. North Dakota is second only to Kansas in total wheat production. Other crops include potatoes and a large yield of barley.

## OHIO

Ohio was part of the Northwest Territory which, besides Ohio, included the present states of Michigan, Indiana, Illinois, Wisconsin, and the NE. part of Minnesota. Discovered late in the first half of the 17th Century, it was claimed by both France and England. France founded her claim on exploration and occupation covering the period between the middle and the close of the 17th Century; England based her claim to the same territory on the discovery of the Atlantic coast by the Cabots, and upon the Virginia, Massachusetts, and Connecticut charters, under which these grants extended westward to the Pacific Ocean. New York also had a claim to the territory. The contest between France and England, known as the Seven Years' War, ended in the cession of the entire Northwest to Great Britain. After winning the Northwest Territory, however, Great Britain no longer recognized those claims of her colonies to this territory, which she had asserted against France, and finally annexed the region to the Province of Quebec. This embittered the colonies and was one of the grievances which brought on the War of Independence and during that war, the Northwest was won for the Americans by George Rogers Clark. Marietta (founded in 1788) at the mouth of the Muskingum, is regarded as the oldest permanent settlement of the state, and the first territorial government was established there. The state was admitted to the Union in 1803. Ohio was the scene of many important actions during the War of 1812, among them Commodore Perry's victory on Lake Erie, in 1813. In no other state have been found so many antique implements of stone, copper, bone, and clay, and such extensive systems of earthworks.

SNOW FENCES. The expansive land of North Dakota, which is bordered on the north by Canada, is exposed to cold and blustering winters. The fences above are constructed to serve as barriers against snowdrifts.

### OHIO
RESOURCES AND PRODUCTS
Scale of Miles
0  10  20  30  40
Copyright by C. S. HAMMOND & Co., N.Y.

## OKLAHOMA

With the exception of the strip comprising the Counties of Beaver, Texas, and Cimarron, the territory included in the present state of Oklahoma was set apart by Congress in 1834 under the name of Indian Territory, for the possession of certain Indian tribes. Oklahoma, the western part of Indian Territory, was ceded by the Indians to the United States in 1866. The treaties under which these lands were transferred stipulated that they were to be used by the government for the settlement of other Indian tribes or freedmen, but not for whites. Many parties of "Boomers" entered the territory, and military forces were required to eject them. In 1889 arrangements were made with certain Indian tribes by which, in consideration of the payment by the government of several million dollars, the clause forbidding settlement by white citizens on this land was cancelled, and it was thrown open for settlement at noon on April 22, 1889. In 1890, this portion of Indian Territory, together with the narrow strip north of Texas, became Oklahoma Territory. In 1893, Congress opened negotiations with the Indians, which led to the passage of the Curtis Act in 1898. That act provided for individual allotment of land to the Indians of Indian Territory, and for a government administered from Washington. When the allotments were nearly all made, Congress, in 1906, authorized Oklahoma and Indian Territories to qualify for admission to the Union as one state, and the state was admitted on the 16th of November, 1907.

Toledo Scale Co.

▲ SCALES. Synonymous with the city of Toledo is its famous scales. Cleveland, Cincinnati and Youngstown combine with the "scale city" to form the chain of industrial centers which lie along the periphery of the state.

Ohio Development and Pub. Comm.

◄ OHIO FARM. Favored by its advantageous position, the farms that are scattered along western Ohio are assured a profitable market.

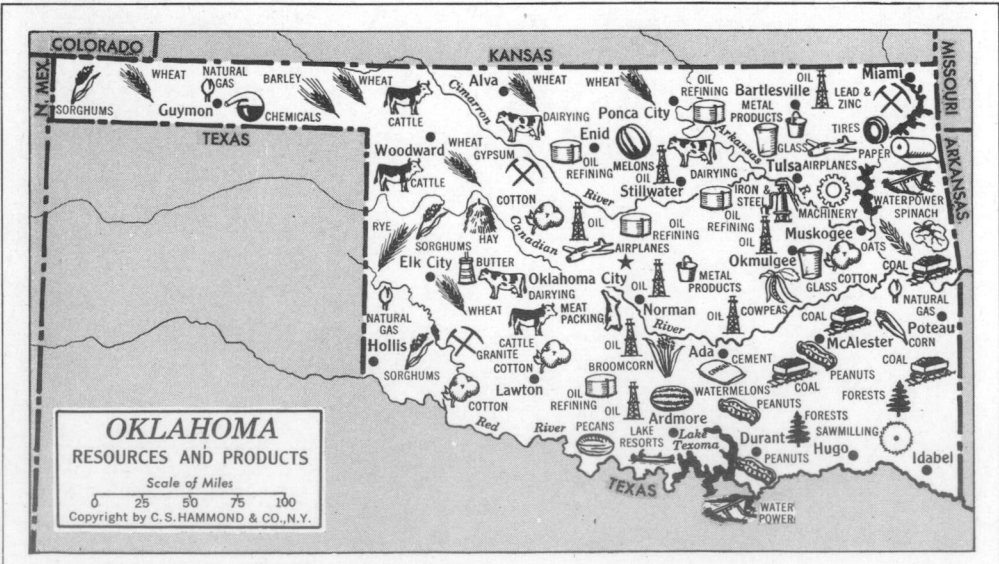

OKLAHOMA
RESOURCES AND PRODUCTS
Scale of Miles
0   25   50   75   100
Copyright by C. S. HAMMOND & CO., N.Y.

Libbey-Owens-Ford Glass Co.

▲ GLASS CUTTER. Lured in the '80s by the inexpensive fuel provided by large gas fields, the glass industry, among others, came to the growing state of Ohio. Since then glass-making has been a prominent industry and manufactures some of the finest plate-glass in the world.

➤ HOPPER CARS. The transportation of Oklahoma's principal crop, wheat, is the job of its efficient railway system. The rich soil of the State is highly adaptable to most grain crops. The climate is consistently mild so that no shelter is required for livestock. The state's various soils are cultivated to raise many staple crops among which cotton, wheat, potatoes, corn, oats and alfalfa figure predominantly. Cotton, once Oklahoma's leading crop, has been replaced in recent years by wheat. Diversified farming has added considerably to the state's agricultural production.

Rock Island Lines

## OREGON

In 1579, Francis Drake sailed along the Pacific coast of the United States as far as 43° N. latitude. He took possession of the country in the name of Queen Elizabeth and called it New Albion. Between the date of Drake's voyage and 1774, the coast was visited by a number of Spanish explorers, the most successful of all being Juan Perez. Among others who sailed along the coast was Bruno Heceta who landed off what is called Point Granville and took formal possession of the country, and later, in latitude 46° 9', discovered a bay whose swift currents indicated that he was in the mouth of a large river or strait. The Spaniards made no effort to colonize North America or to develop trade with the Indians. In 1778, the English Captain James Cook sighted the coast of Oregon in the latitude 44°, and explored it between 47° and 48°, in the hope of finding the Straits of Juan de Fuca of Spanish accounts. The mouth of the Columbia River was discovered by the American Captain Gray in 1792. It was partly explored by Lewis and Clark in 1804-05. A trading post was founded in Astoria in 1811. The territory between latitudes 42° and 54° 40' N. was long in dispute between Great Britain and the United States. The claims were finally settled by treaty in 1846. Oregon Territory was organized in 1849, and admitted to statehood in 1859.

Oregon State Highway Comm.

▲ PORTLAND, OREGON. Different from many Eastern centers, Portland, largest city in Oregon, is noticeably free of smoke. Most factories are operated by electric power.

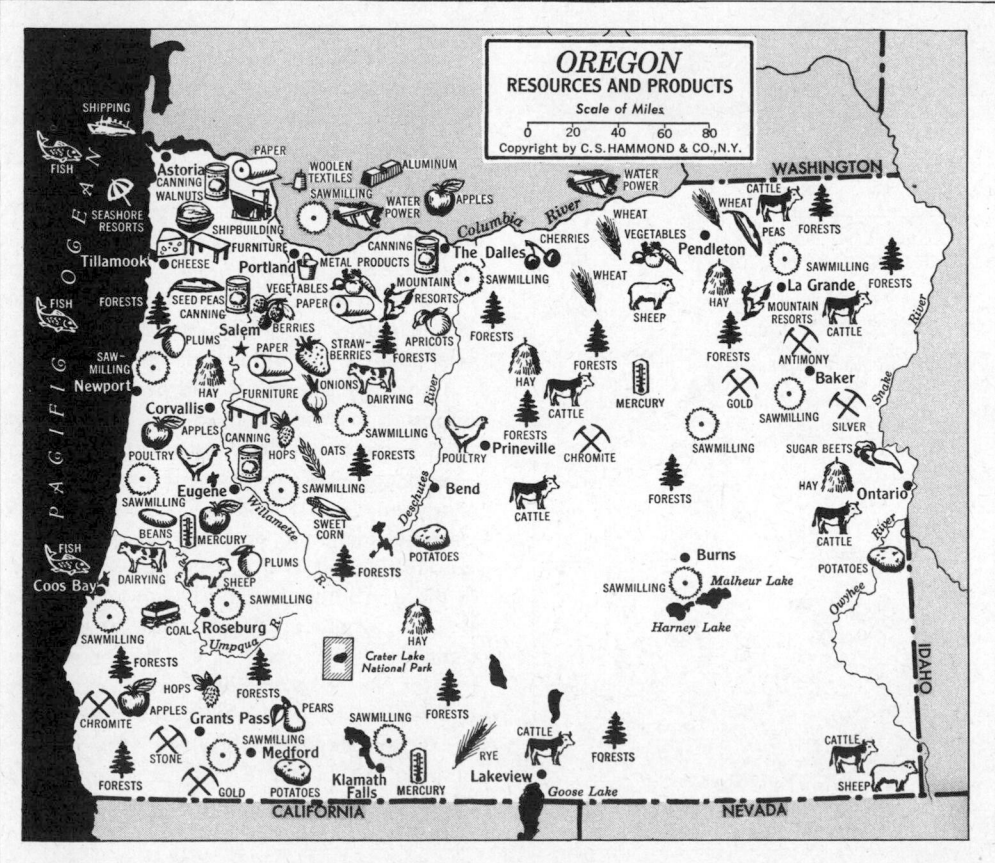

Oregon State Highway Comm.

▲ ALPINE FORESTS. Vast source of the country's timber supply, almost 30 million acres of forests constitute one-fourth of the United States lumber resources. Mount Hood stands in the distance.

► PITTSBURGH. Foremost producer of the life-blood of American industry, the steady flow of Pittsburgh steel surges through the nation's commercial arteries to be transformed into everything from tools to railway cars. This great steel center ranks among the highest producers in the world.

Standard Oil Company (N. J.)

Standard Oil Company (N. J.)

▲ THE BETSY ROSS HOUSE. Philadelphia, "cradle of the Revolution," is filled with historic landmarks. Notable among them is the alleged birthplace of Betsy Ross, reputed designer of the first American flag.

► COAL STRIP MINE. Large coal deposits are found throughout Pennsylvania. Veins of coal near the surface are extracted by means of "strip mining." Deposits which are deep in the earth are mined by shaft.

Standard Oil Company (N. J.)

## PENNSYLVANIA

The earliest European settlements (1643-81) within the present limits of Pennsylvania were made by Swedish and Dutch traders in the lower valley of the Delaware River. In 1664, the English obtained possession of the territory and in 1681, it was granted by Charles the Second to William Penn, a prominent member of the Society of Friends. In colonial days, Quaker influence was very strong, but religious freedom was given to all. The colony had serious boundary disputes with Maryland, Virginia, and New York, and a dispute with Connecticut over the Wyoming Valley, which was settled in favor of Pennsylvania in 1782. A strong antiproprietary sentiment grew among the people after the death of William Penn, the great leaders of the movement being Joseph Galloway and Benjamin Franklin. The people of the colony were not united in sentiment over the War of Independence. There were not only many loyalists and many who were opposed to war on religious grounds, but the people generally were satisfied with the liberal and free government which they already enjoyed. The liberty party, however, became dominant, and Pennsylvania bore a creditable part in the struggle which ended in the establishment of independence. Philadelphia, where the Declaration of Independence was adopted in 1776, became the seat of the Federal Government, except for a brief period in 1789-90, until the removal to Washington in 1800. The state bore a notable part in the Civil War. Many of the miners and ironworkers are of foreign birth, and serious industrial disturbances have occured at intervals since 1865.

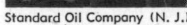

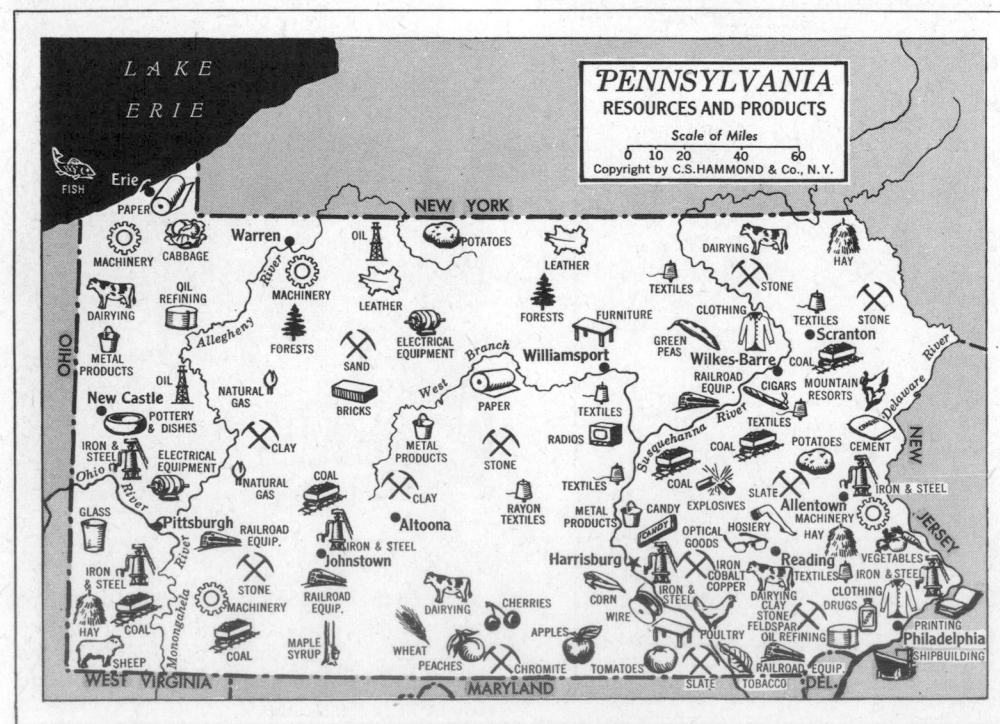

PENNSYLVANIA
RESOURCES AND PRODUCTS
Scale of Miles
0   10   20    40     60
Copyright by C.S. HAMMOND & Co., N.Y.

## RHODE ISLAND

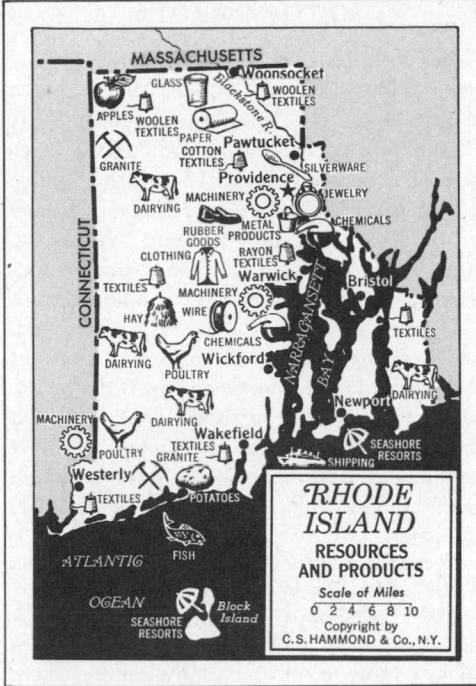

Rhode Island was founded by religious and political exiles from Massachusetts. Roger Williams planted the first settlement at Providence in 1636 .William Coddington and others settled on Aquidneck or Rhode Island in 1638. Newport was founded in 1639. The Royal Charter for Rhode Island and Providence Plantations was issued in 1663. The government of Rhode Island permitted complete freedom in religious matters. Rhode Island did not ratify the federal constitution until 1790. The first successful cotton mill in the country was established at Pawtucket in 1790. In 1842 occurred the Dorr Rebellion, a revolt against conditions which were the outgrowth of the charter of 1663, which served in place of a constitution, gave undue power to country towns, and restricted suffrage. As a result of this revolt, a constitution was adopted. There were two centers of government until 1900.

Standard Oil Company (N. J.)

▲ PAPER MILL. South Carolina uses some of its timber supply for the processing of paper. The wood is first converted into pulp and then filtered through screens. The pulp is then chemically bleached, and later the thin, fibrous mass is rolled smooth. Pictured above is the filtering stage where the paper is drained of excess moisture.

Rhode Island Dept. of Agr. and Conservation

◄ RHODE ISLAND TURKEYS. Comparatively small but known for quality is Rhode Island's poultry. The State's name has become associated with the type of fowl produced. At the left, is a typical Rhode Island turkey farm.

## SOUTH CAROLINA

An unsuccessful attempt was made by the French to colonize what is now South Carolina in 1562. The first permanent English settlement was made in 1670. Charleston was founded in 1680. The territory remained under a proprietary government with North Carolina until 1729, when it became a separate colony. Many of the early colonists were French Huguenots, Scotch, Irish, Swiss, and Germans. South Carolina was the scene of many battles during the Revolution, those of Ft. Moultrie, Charleston, Camden, King's Mountain, Cowpens, and Eutaw Springs being among the most notable. It was held by the British 1780-1781. Its advocacy of nullification nearly led to civil war in 1832-33. It was foremost among the southern states in the advocacy of the states' rights doctrine, and was the first state to secede (Dec. 20, 1860). It opened the Civil War by the bombardment of Fort Sumter (April 12, 1861), suffered severely by the blockade attacks at Charleston Harbor and near the close of the war (in 1865) by the march of Sherman's army. It was readmitted to the Union in 1868. The state was visited by a severe earthquake in 1886.

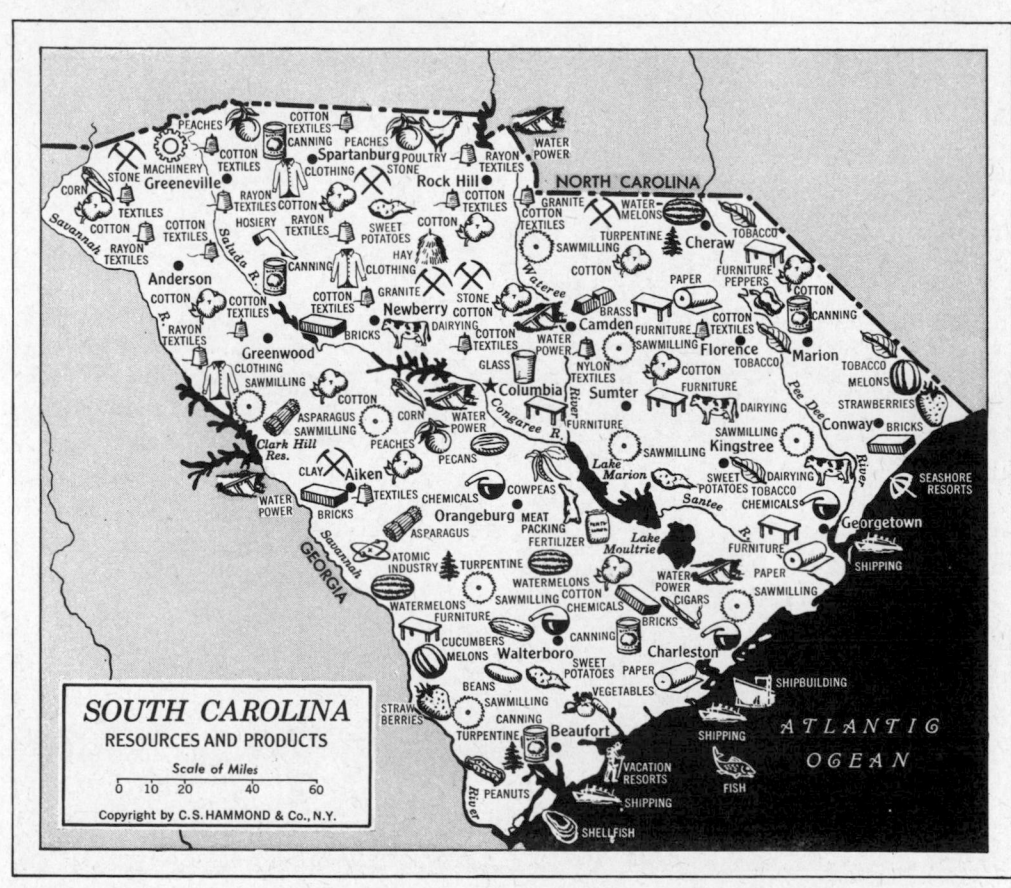

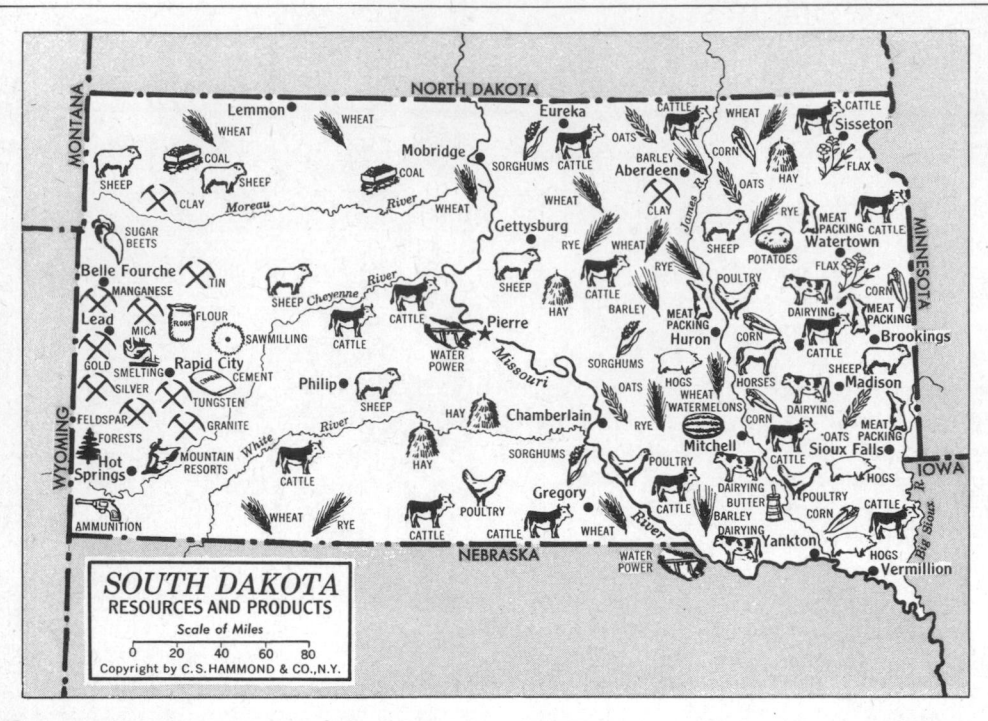

SOUTH DAKOTA
RESOURCES AND PRODUCTS
Scale of Miles
0    20    40    60    80
Copyright by C.S. HAMMOND & CO., N.Y.

## SOUTH DAKOTA

The territory included within the present limits of the state was a part of the District of Louisiana from 1803-05; of the Territory of Louisiana from 1805-20, and of the Territory of Missouri from 1812-20. The section east of the Missouri was successively a part of the Territories of Louisiana, Wisconsin, Iowa, and Minnesota; and the western section a part of the Territory of Nebraska. In 1861, the Territory of Dakota was created, including the present Dakotas and portions of Wyoming and Montana. The Dakotas acquired their present territorial limits in 1882. The territory was divided into two states in November, 1887, and both were admitted to the Union on November 2, 1889. After admission, South Dakota underwent a period of Indian resistance which culminated in the so-called Wounded Knee Massacre. In 1905, after much debate, Pierre was selected as the state's capital. The state contains a national shrine at Mount Rushmore where the likenesses of four presidents have been carved from the natural rock.

▼ GRAZING SHEEP. In some parts of South Dakota sheep-raising is carried on in addition to farming. Such flocks are known as "farm flocks." Sheep that are raised as a sole occupation are known as "range flocks." South Dakota possesses many miles of natural range country for grazing. The rich natural grasses and a facilitative soil for growing alfalfa and other feeds make South Dakota important in stock-raising.

➤ HAY STACK. South Dakota's agricultural wealth undoubtedly resides in its fertile soil, half of which still remains to be cultivated by tractor and plow. The land is equally divided into grazing and farm areas, thus offering facilities for both farmer and cattleman alike. An irrigation program has been put into operation so that increased productivity may be obtained in the drier sections of the State.

U. S. Bureau of Reclamation

South Dakota State Highway Comm.

➤ TEXTILES. Textile mills have long been a prominent industry in Tennessee. During the Civil War, the manufacture of cotton thread was seriously affected, but throughout the Reconstruction Period new possibilities were discovered for textile production. Synthetic yarn is one of the State's more recent developments.

➤ SMOKY MOUNTAINS. Rising more than 6,000 feet, "The Smokies" form one of the landmarks of Tennessee. Because of varied climatic conditions, this mountain area possesses a wide variety of flora and therefore furnishes a playground for the explorer, amateur or professional.

➤ BAD LANDS. First named by aboriginal Indians, the Bad Lands are an isolated and barren region devoid of any great amount of vegetation. Close by lie the Black Hills of South Dakota which hold a magnetic attraction for the archaeologist who finds himself amidst a superabundance of fossil-bearing rock. It is also a haven for writers, artists and engineers whose presence adds a note of urbanity to an otherwise primitive setting. These hills were formally the site of a gold rush in 1875. Weather-beaten prospectors arrived in swarms to claim a portion of the rich earth. Such activity soon transformed a hitherto unknown locality into a familiar mining town with its traditionally colorful characters. Even today the State's mining is concentrated in the Black Hills, gold being a principal source of South Dakota's wealth.

Standard Oil Company (N. J.)

E. I. du Pont de Nemours Co.

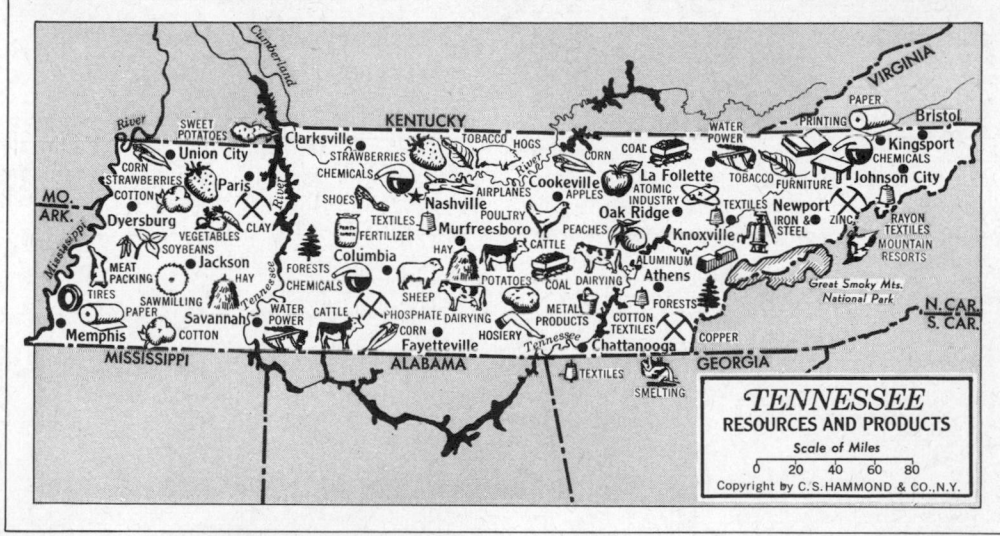

TENNESSEE
RESOURCES AND PRODUCTS
Scale of Miles
0  20  40  60  80
Copyright by C. S. HAMMOND & CO., N.Y.

## TENNESSEE

Tennessee was included in the English grant to Sir Walter Raleigh in 1584, and in the later Stuart grants including that of North Carolina in 1663. The region was claimed in early times by North Carolina and by the French and Spanish. The leading settlement was made from Virginia and North Carolina in 1769. North Carolina ceded its claim to the United States, and the territory was formed in 1790. It was admitted to the Union as a state in 1796. It seceded June 8, 1861 and next to Virginia, was the chief battleground during the Civil War. Among the stirring events of that period were the capture of Fort Henry and Fort Donelson and of Island No. 10; the battles of Shiloh, Memphis, Murfreesboro, Lookout Mountain, and Chickamauga; the relief of Chattanooga and Knoxville; and the battles of Franklin and Nashville. The state was re-admitted to the Union in 1866.

Standard Oil Company (N. J.)

Standard Oil Company (N. J.)

▼ OIL WELL. Mineral wealth, above all oil, is part of the foundation upon which the reputation of Texas rests. Great reserves of natural gas, including those in the well-known Panhandle, make up the largest single supply that is found in any area in the United States. Underdeveloped though potential deposits of iron ore exist in the northeast, while in other sections a good supply of marble, asphalt and granite is present. Texas has attained undoubted superiority in the extent of its mineral assets as well as in its quality of beef cattle.

▲ CANTALOUPES. Over 100 crops are grown in "The Lone Star State" varying from almonds to avocados. Citrus fruit production constantly maintains its leadership in the State's agricultural market. Recent steps have been taken to insure a greater horticultural yield than has been previously possible. The amount of rainfall is sufficient to guarantee the growing of all important crops.

Standard Oil Company (N. J.)

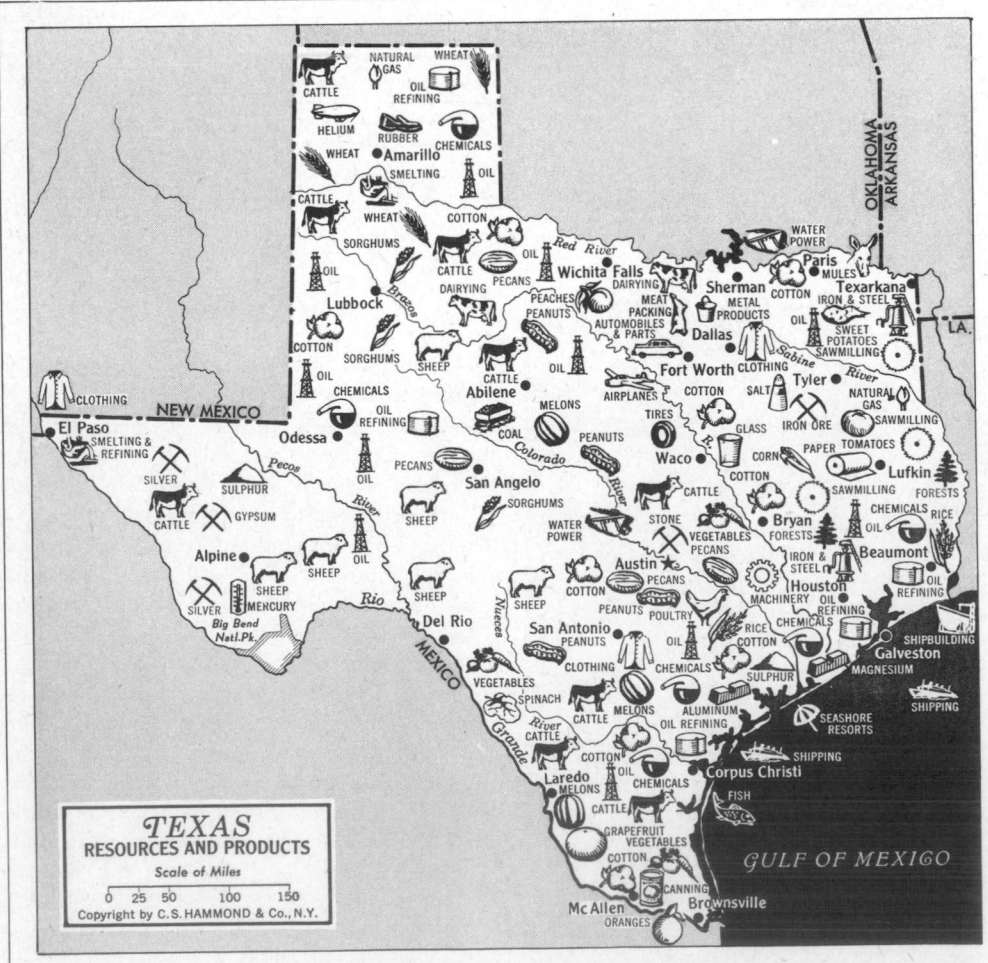

## TEXAS

An attempt at settlement was made by Sieur de la Salle about 1685 and several missions were established by the Spaniards in the 18th Century. The region was invaded by various adventurers early in the 19th century. It formed, with Coahuila, a state of Mexico, and was settled rapidly about 1820-30 by American colonists. Most of these colonists came from the southern states of the Union and brought their slaves with them. A rebellion against Mexico broke out in 1835; the garrisons at Alamo and Goliad were massacred by the Mexicans in 1836; and the Mexicans were finally defeated by Houston at San Jacinto, April 21, 1836. Texas was a republic from 1836-45 when it was annexed to the United States. It was largely the cause of the Mexican War of 1846 and the scene of many of the conflicts in that struggle. By the terms of the treaty which terminated the conflict, the Rio Grande River became the boundary between Texas and Mexico. Texas seceded in 1861. Because of its isolated position, there was little military action in the state during the Civil War. However, the last battle of that conflict was fought on its soil at Palmito, more than a month after the surrender at Appomatox. Texas was readmitted to the Union in 1870.

## UTAH

This arid desert country, part of the area ceded by Mexico in 1848, was colonized by Mormons in the first large-scale use of irrigation in this country. Driven from Missouri and Illinois by mobs because of their religious beliefs, the Mormons, under the direction of Brigham Young, sought refuge in the Salt Lake Valley. They were without federal government until organized as a territory in 1850. Until then the Church acted as the only authority. Now only three-fifths of Utah is Mormon. It was admitted as a state in 1896.

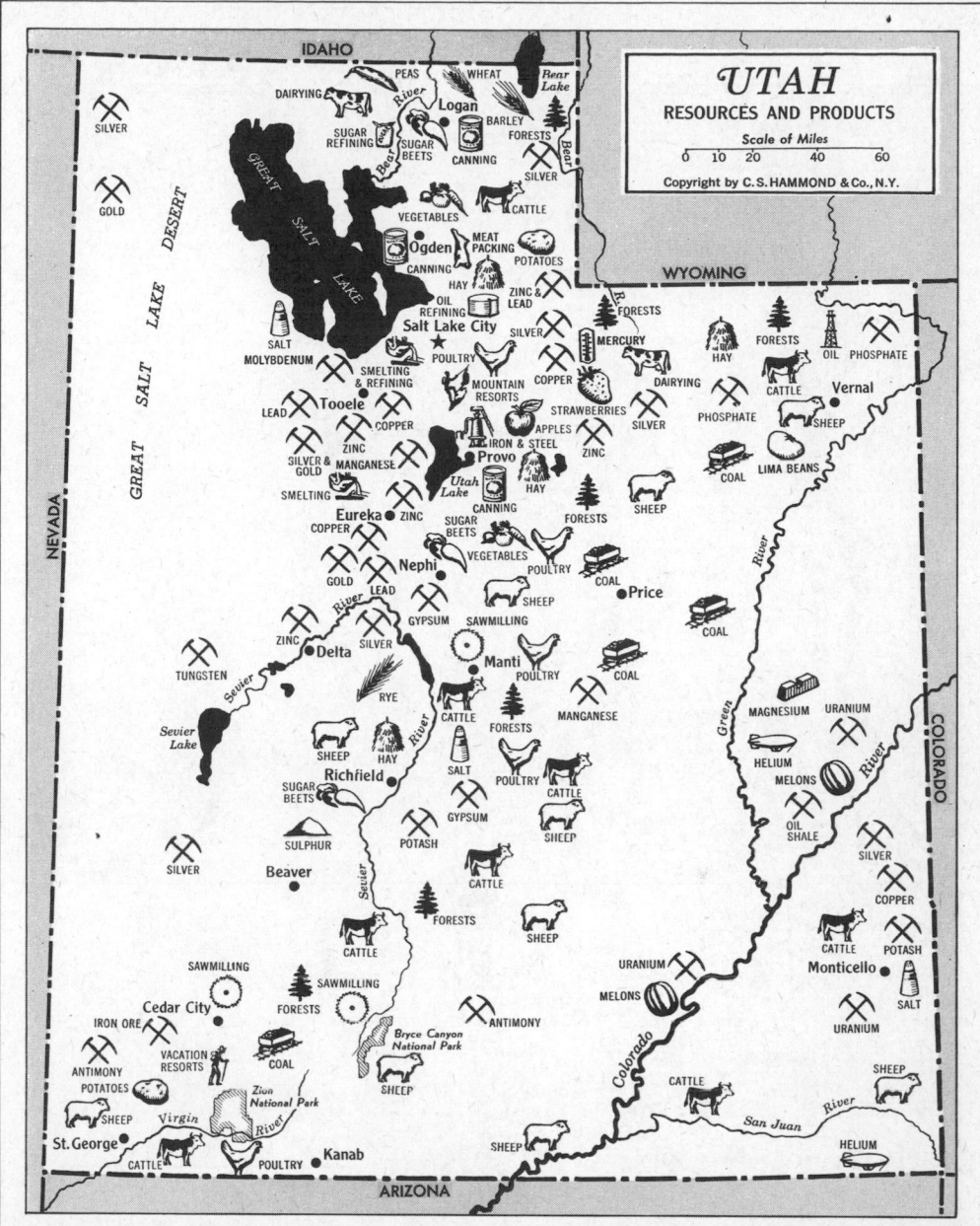

UTAH
RESOURCES AND PRODUCTS
Scale of Miles
0  10  20    40    60
Copyright by C. S. HAMMOND & Co., N.Y.

Dow Chemical Co.

▲ CHEMICAL MANUFACTURE. Texas' soil offers itself to the exploitation of many chemical deposits.

Salt Lake City C. of C.

▲ SALT. Endowed by nature with an almost inexhaustible supply of salt, the Salt Lake City vicinity is the location for many refining companies.

▶ COPPER MINE. Mining the great untapped mineral reservoirs of Utah accounts for at least fifty per cent of the State's livelihood.

Salt Lake City C. of C.

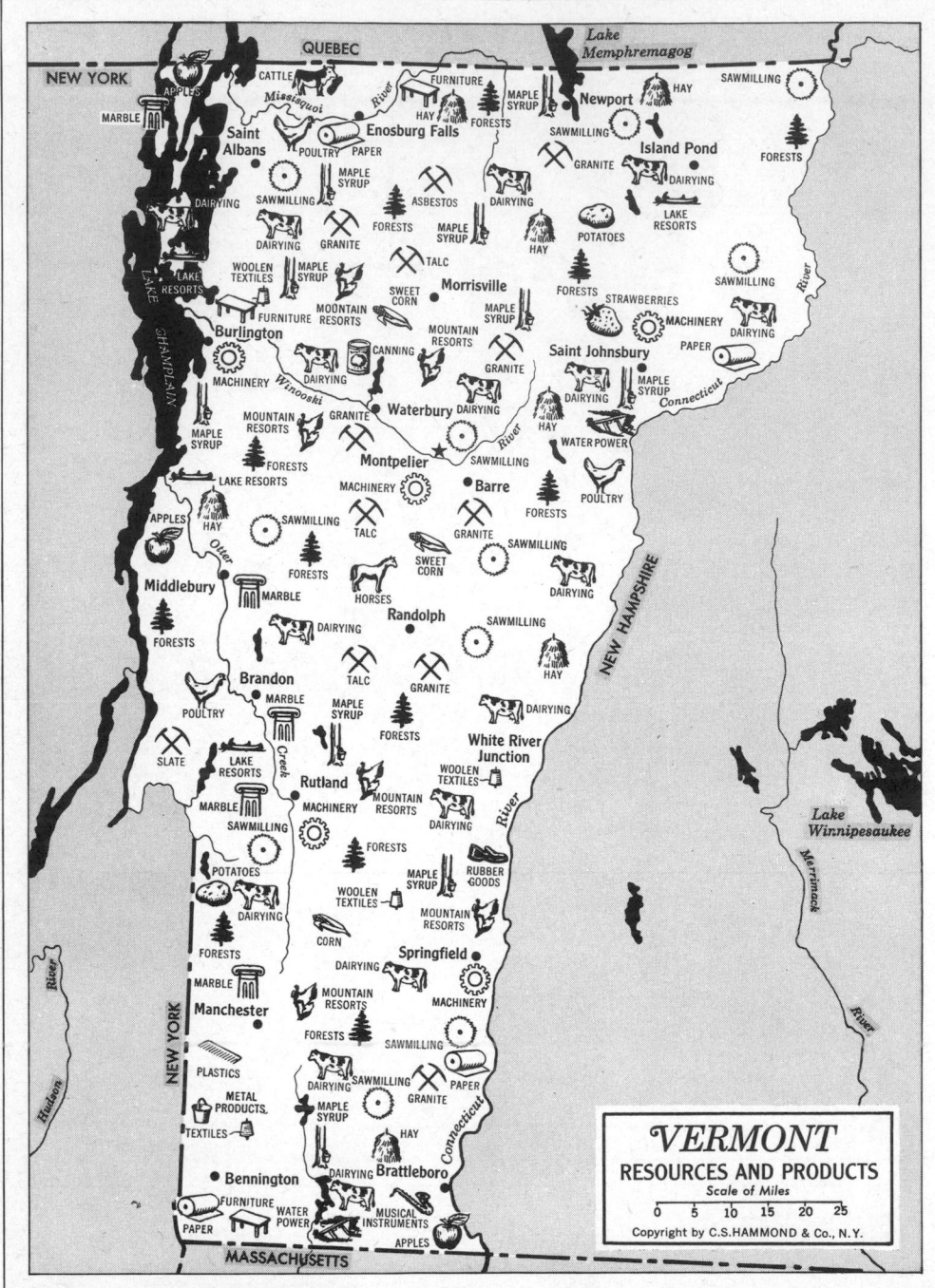

VERMONT
RESOURCES AND PRODUCTS
Scale of Miles
0   5   10   15   20   25
Copyright by C.S. HAMMOND & Co., N.Y.

# VERMONT

Samuel de Champlain, the French governor of Quebec, discovered the lake which bears his name in 1609, and thus laid the basis for the French claim to the region. The French built a fort on Isle La Motte in 1665. Part of the country was claimed by Massachusetts which planted the first permanent white settlement (1724) at Fort Dummer in the present town of Brattleboro. Soon after 1750, numerous settlements were made under the auspices of New Hampshire which also claimed jurisdiction in the region. New York laid claim to the country as far east as the Connecticut River, by virtue of the charter granted to the Duke of York. George the Third decided in favor of New York in 1764, and discord continued until 1771 when the people declared themselves independent and drew up a state constitution. In 1791, Vermont was admitted into the Union, the first state added to the original thirteen. The "Green Mountain Boys" bore a notable part in the War of the Revolution; and in the War of 1812, and again in the Civil War, the sons of Vermont distinguished themselves by their bravery and devotion to the Union.

Standard Oil Company (N. J.)

▲ SNOW SCENE. Vermont is a blend of the rural and the modern. Its farm and mountain regions serve to breed a thrifty individualism which is so typical of the Vermonter. Like most of the northern states its climate is varied with deep snows in the central section during the winter.

◄ WILLIAM AND MARY COLLEGE. Many of the famous figures of American history were from Virginia and the state has many historic shrines. The homes of Jefferson, Washington and Lee, as well as the easily recollected names of Williamsburg and Yorktown, are a reminder to the state of its great historic past. The picture shows the Wren building at William and Mary College. The college, founded in 1693, is the second oldest one in the United States.

Virginia Conservation Comm.

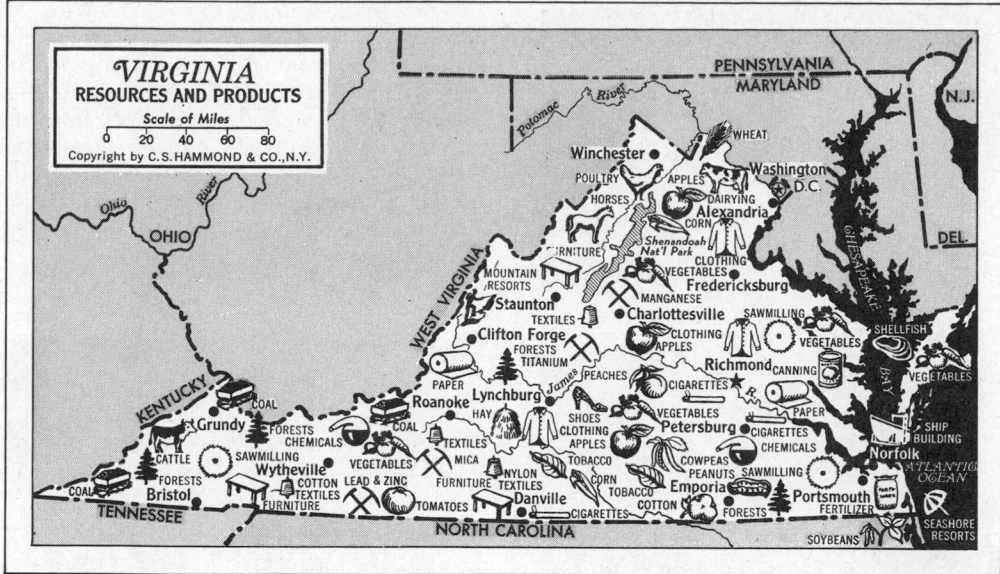

## VIRGINIA

At Jamestown, in Virginia, in 1607, was planted the first permanent English settlement in North America. Capt. John Smith became the head of the government there, established law and order and laid the foundations of industrial life. Slavery in America had its beginnings in the Virginia colony in 1619. At the close of the colonial period, Virginia was the most populous and the wealthiest of the thirteen colonies. In the protest against the Stamp Act and the encroachment of Great Britain, Virginia took the lead, and in the Revolutionary struggle furnished such noted sons as Washington, Jefferson, Patrick Henry, the Lees, and Madison. At Yorktown, Cornwallis's surrender put an end to the contest. In the Civil War, Virginia furnished the great commander, Rob-

PLYWOOD. Lumbering in Washington is a thriving industry. The production of plywood, made by compressing several thin layers of wood together to form a strong panel, has greatly stimulated the lumber output. The cultivation of tree farms safeguards against possible depletion of forest reserves. Douglas fir, birch, maple, spruce and hemlock constitute the State's timber resources.

ert E. Lee. Of the first twenty-one presidents of the United States, seven were Virginians, as was also President Woodrow Wilson. The part played by Virginia in the history of the country has endeared it to all Americans, and the national shrines at Mt. Vernon, Monticello, and the Arlington National Cemetery are visited by hundreds of thousands annually.

## WASHINGTON

The Strait of Juan de Fuca was discovered in 1592, and explored in 1789. The mouth of the Columbia River was explored by the American Captain Gray in 1792, and further explorations were conducted by Lewis and Clark in 1805. A settlement at the mouth of the Columbia was founded by John Jacob Astor in 1811. The boundary question was settled with Great Britain in 1846. Washington formed part of the territory of Oregon; was organized as a territory in 1853; and was admitted to the Union in 1889.

CRAB BOAT. To the west of Washington is the open expanse of the North Pacific. It is these waters and those of the Columbia River which offer up to the fishing and canning industry the catches of salmon, halibut and tuna.

Washington State Adv. Comm.

◄ MOUNT SHUKSAN. Washington abounds in facilities for winter sports. For the less active, the lakes, coast and forests provide unusual scenic beauty. Innumerable streams attract fishing enthusiasts from all sections of the country, and for the hunter the uplands and mountains afford a wide variety of game. Such natural accommodations make Washington the vacation spot of the West.

## WEST VIRGINIA

West Virginia was a part of Virginia until the beginning of the secession movement in 1861. The separation of these states had, however, been agitated before the adoption of the Federal Constitution. West Virginia was settled largely by immigrants who entered by way of Pennsylvania, and the population included Germans, Protestant Irish, and people from the states farther north.

Slavery was rendered unprofitable by the difficulties in agriculture, caused by the rugged nature of the country and the climate. Social conditions were, therefore, entirely unlike those of the eastern part of the state, and little sympathy existed between the two sections. At the outbreak of the Civil War, the inhabitants of the northern and western counties remained loyal to the United States and in 1863 West Virginia was admitted to the Union.

West Virginia Ind. & Pub. Comm.

▲ WHITE SULPHUR SPRINGS. A nationally-known spa, these springs are visited by people from all over the country. Consequently, hotel accommodations are offered to the many visitors seeking the curative possibilities of the springs. This hotel, built in Georgian style, is situated near by.

▼ COAL CARS. The great binder of industries, coal is one of the most important elements in West Virginia's earth. Iron, one of the principal needs of steel-making, follows a close second. The prosperity of industry depends in large amount on the railroads.

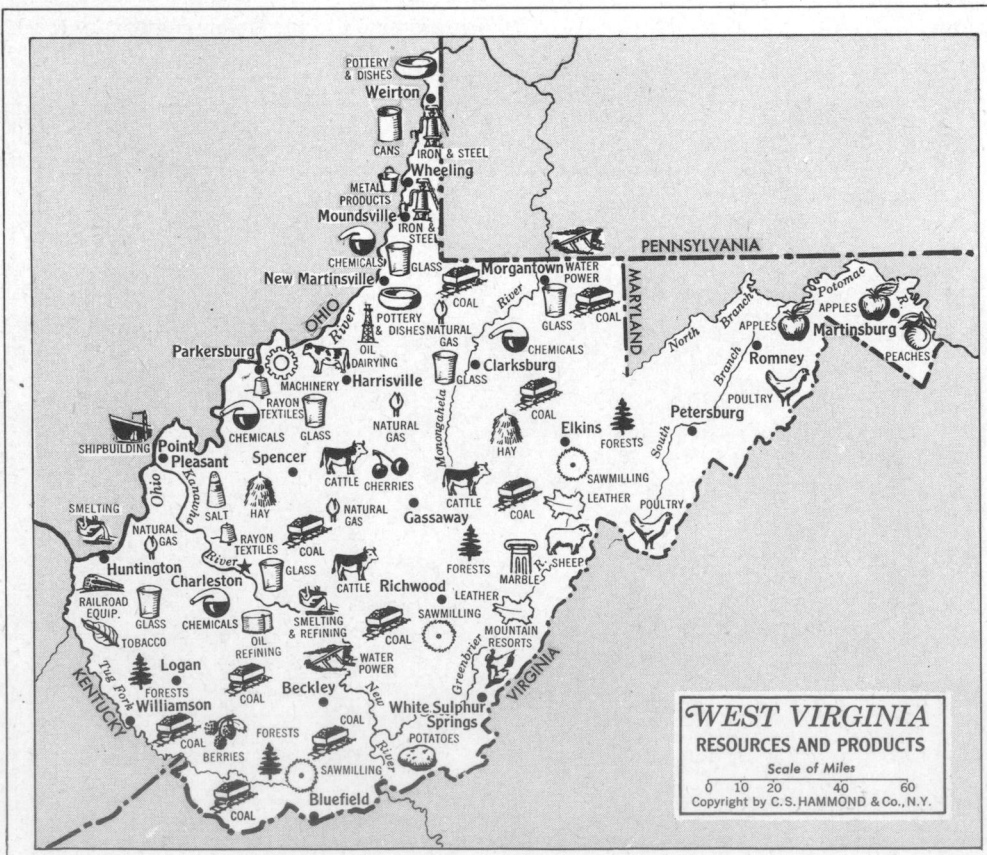

WEST VIRGINIA
RESOURCES AND PRODUCTS
Scale of Miles
0  10  20    40    60
Copyright by C.S. HAMMOND & Co., N.Y.

Standard Oil Co. (N. J.)

## WISCONSIN

Wisconsin was opened to wide settlement by French explorers, missionaries, and traders. Among the Frenchmen whose names are associated with its early history are those of Jean Nicollet, Sieur de Radisson, Sieur des Groseilliers, Jacques Marquette, Louis Joliet, Rene Menard, Claude Allouez, La Salle, Henri de Tonty, Duluth, and Louis Hennepin. The French claimed, and to a greater or less extent, occupied the territory from 1634 until the close of the Seven Years' War in 1760 when it passed to Great Britain. British occupation was brief and in 1783, it became a part of the United States, and was included in 1787 in the Northwest Territory; afterward in Indiana Territory; in 1809 in Illinois Territory; and in 1818 in Michigan Territory. Wisconsin Territory was organized in 1836 and was admitted as a state in 1848.

▼ WISCONSIN'S WOODS. Wisconsin's many rivers, lakes and forests enhance the state's scenic value, making it a beautiful vacation spot as well as a lucrative area for valuable lumber resources. A land covered by forests, it furnishes a large amount of timber yearly. The typical beauty of Wisconsin's forest lakes—and there are many—is the natural result of prehistoric glaciers which imperceptibly gouged out large indentations in the earth's surface. Geologically, Wisconsin's boundaries encompass some of the oldest land to be found anywhere in the world.

Philip Gendreau, N. Y.

▲ INLAND SHIPPING. Unusual facilities are supplied by the waters of Lake Superior for commercial shipping. This waterway is of prime importance in providing an ideal means of transportation for Wisconsin's natural and manufactured products. The picture shows a freighter being loaded with ore cargo.

Philip Gendreau, N. Y.

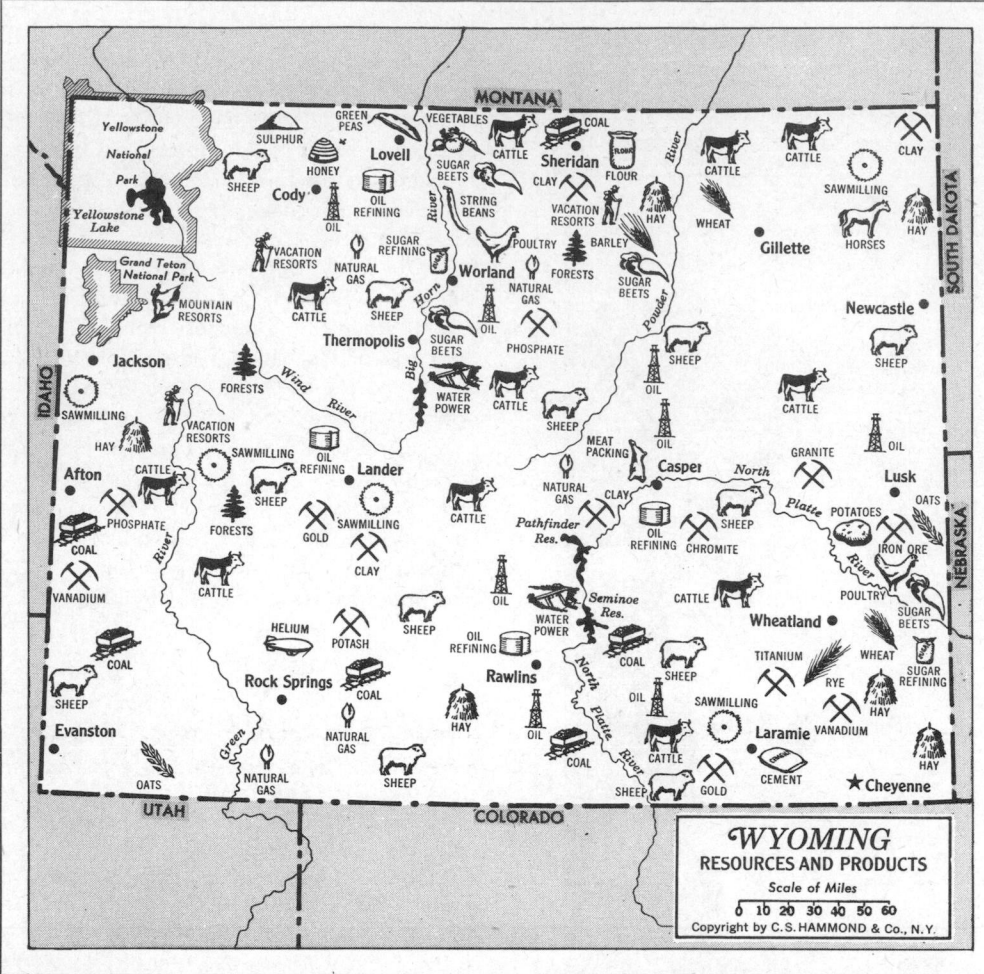

WYOMING
RESOURCES AND PRODUCTS
Scale of Miles
0  10  20  30  40  50  60
Copyright by C.S. HAMMOND & Co., N.Y.

Standard Oil Co. (N. J.)

▲ THE WIND RIVER MOUNTAINS. The Wind River Mountains are one of many ranges that form the Continental Divide. Three large rivers have their origins in Wyoming; the Columbia, Colorado and Missouri. In the northwest of the State is Yellowstone National Park. The mountains, serried with timber, make a natural storage place for the winter's snows which, in summer, drain off into the adjacent streams or lakes.

## WYOMING

Fort Laramie, near the mouth of the Laramie River, was established in 1834 to control the fur trade of the Arapahoes, Cheyennes, and Sioux. The United States exploring expedition, commanded by John C. Fremont, explored the Wind River Mountains and the South Pass in 1842. From this time, the favorite route to the Pacific led through Wyoming, but the aridity of the land and the pronounced hostility of the Indians were not conducive to settlement. For the protection of immigrant trains, the United States government built Fort Kearney in 1848, and purchased Fort Laramie in 1849. A Mormon settlement was made on the Green River in 1853. These Mormons afterwards retired to Salt Lake City. Indian hostilities were active from 1851 to 1868. Gold was discovered on the Sweetwater River in 1867, and population increased rapidly. The Territory of Wyoming, with its present boundaries, was organized in 1868. The state was admitted to the Union in 1890.

Wyoming Comm. & Ind. Comm.

◄ DUDE RANCH. Ranching has changed from what it used to be at one time. Most large ranches, many of which were converted into "dude ranches," have been reduced in size. This has been so because the cattleman is no longer able to compete merely on the basis of spacious lands. Cattle must be raised in strict proportion to the amount of feed which the land furnishes.

## ALASKA

Alaska, formerly called Russian-America, was first visited by Vitus Bering in 1742. In 1799, the whole country passed under the control of the Russian-American Company. In 1867, the United States purchased the entire territory from Russia for $7,200,000 in gold. When Mr. Seward, our Secretary of State, concluded the negotiations for the purchase of Alaska, there were many critics who felt that the country was paying a great price for comparatively valueless territory. It is interesting in this connection to note that as a return for the $7,200,000 purchase money, the United States received untold wealth in mineral resources, farming lands, furs and fisheries.

➡ ALASKAN VOLCANO. Alaska's thick snows coat mountainsides and form glaciers which slowly descend into the fiords below and break up into icebergs. But Alaska is not all frozen waste. In the valleys of the Yukon thousands of acres of fertile soil await proper cultivation.

U. S. Navy Photo

Philip Gendreau, N. Y.

⬆ SALMON LOADING. The center of the salmon industry in Alaska is located at Bristol Bay. After the fish are caught, they are brought in to the canning plants where they are prepared for shipment.

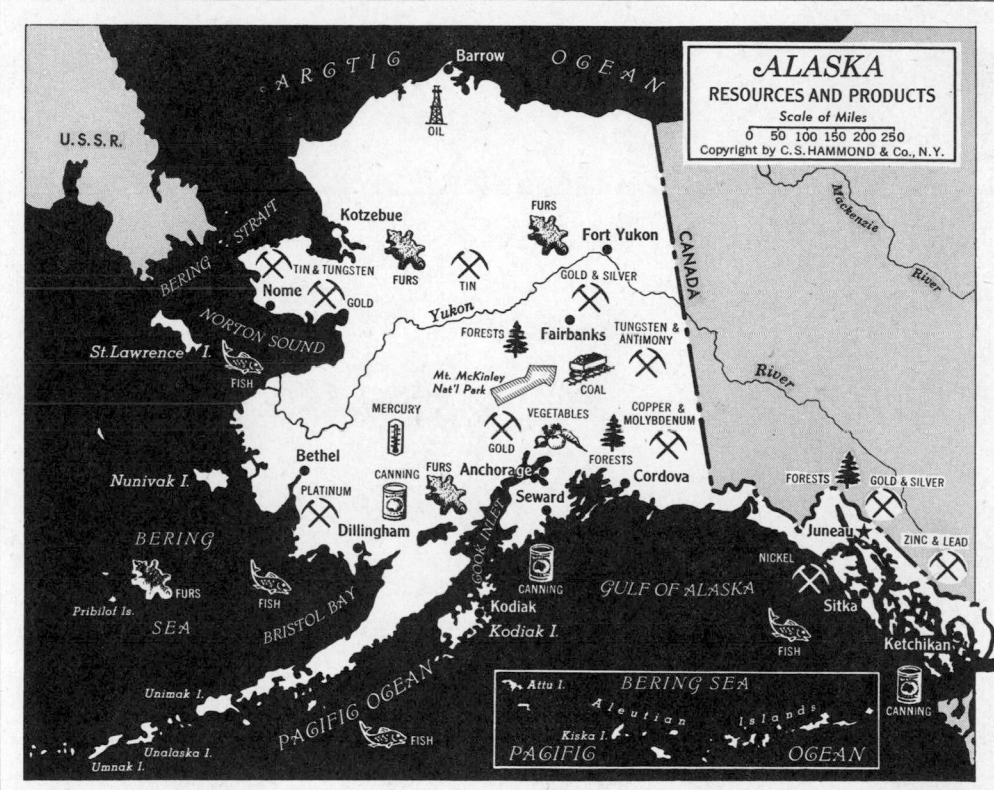

ALASKA
RESOURCES AND PRODUCTS
Scale of Miles
0 50 100 150 200 250
Copyright by C. S. HAMMOND & Co., N.Y.

Hawaiian Pineapple Co.

⬅ PLANTING PINEAPPLES. Pineapples do not usually bear seeds. In Hawaii they are sometimes planted from "slips"—tufts of leaves from the base of the fruit. Because the planting of pineapples is not mechanized, the operation must be carried on by hand. From 15,000 to 20,000 plants are cultivated per acre.

➡ CATTLE LOADING AT KAILUA. About half of the land of Hawaii is used as pasturage for livestock. Cattle are raised on the larger sections and tended by *Paniolas* (Hawaiian cowboys). At Kailua the waters of the bay are so shallow the *Paniolas* must swim out with the steers to the freighter to load the stock aboard.

Hawaii Visitors Bureau

## HAWAII

The islands are said to have been discovered in 1542 by Gaetano, and rediscovered in 1778 by Captain Cook who lost his life in a conflict with natives the following year. In 1790, Kamehameha formed the islands into one kingdom. Missionaries came from America in 1820 and in less than forty years, they gave to the whole Hawaiian people the rudiments of a common school education and taught them something of domestic science. In 1843, the independence of the kingdom was guaranteed by the French and English governments. Kalakaua, elected king in 1874, died in 1891 and was succeeded by his eldest sister, Liliuokalani who was dethroned in January, 1893, and a provisional republican government set up. The islands were finally annexed by the United States in 1898, and in 1900 were organized as one of the Territories of the United States.

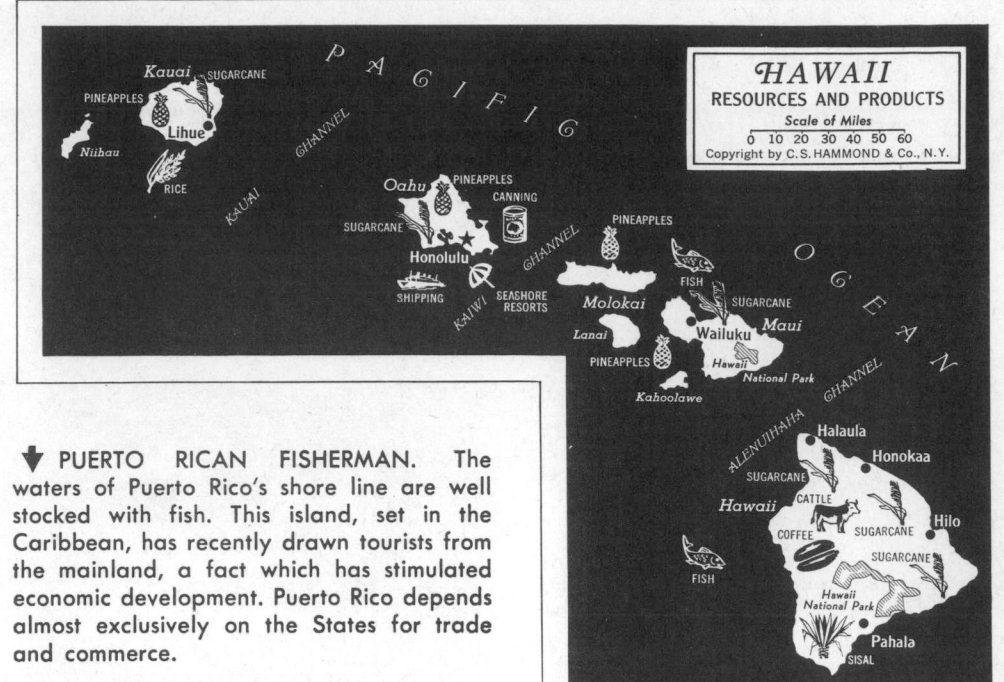

**▼ PUERTO RICAN FISHERMAN.** The waters of Puerto Rico's shore line are well stocked with fish. This island, set in the Caribbean, has recently drawn tourists from the mainland, a fact which has stimulated economic development. Puerto Rico depends almost exclusively on the States for trade and commerce.

Hamilton Wright

**▼ JIBARO ON HORSEBACK.** From the 16th century on, the export of sugar has been the most valuable source of revenue for the island of Puerto Rico. Other cash crops on which the internal economy is based are tobacco, coffee and citrus fruits.

Hamilton Wright

## PUERTO RICO

Puerto Rico was discovered by Columbus in 1493, and Ponce de Leon founded a settlement there in 1510. The island was ceded by Spain to the United States after the war of 1898 and in 1900, civil government was given to the Territory. Since then, the island has prospered greatly, except in 1928, when a terrific hurricane left 245 people dead and 400,000 homeless, and destroyed property worth $30,000,000 and crops worth $20,000,000.

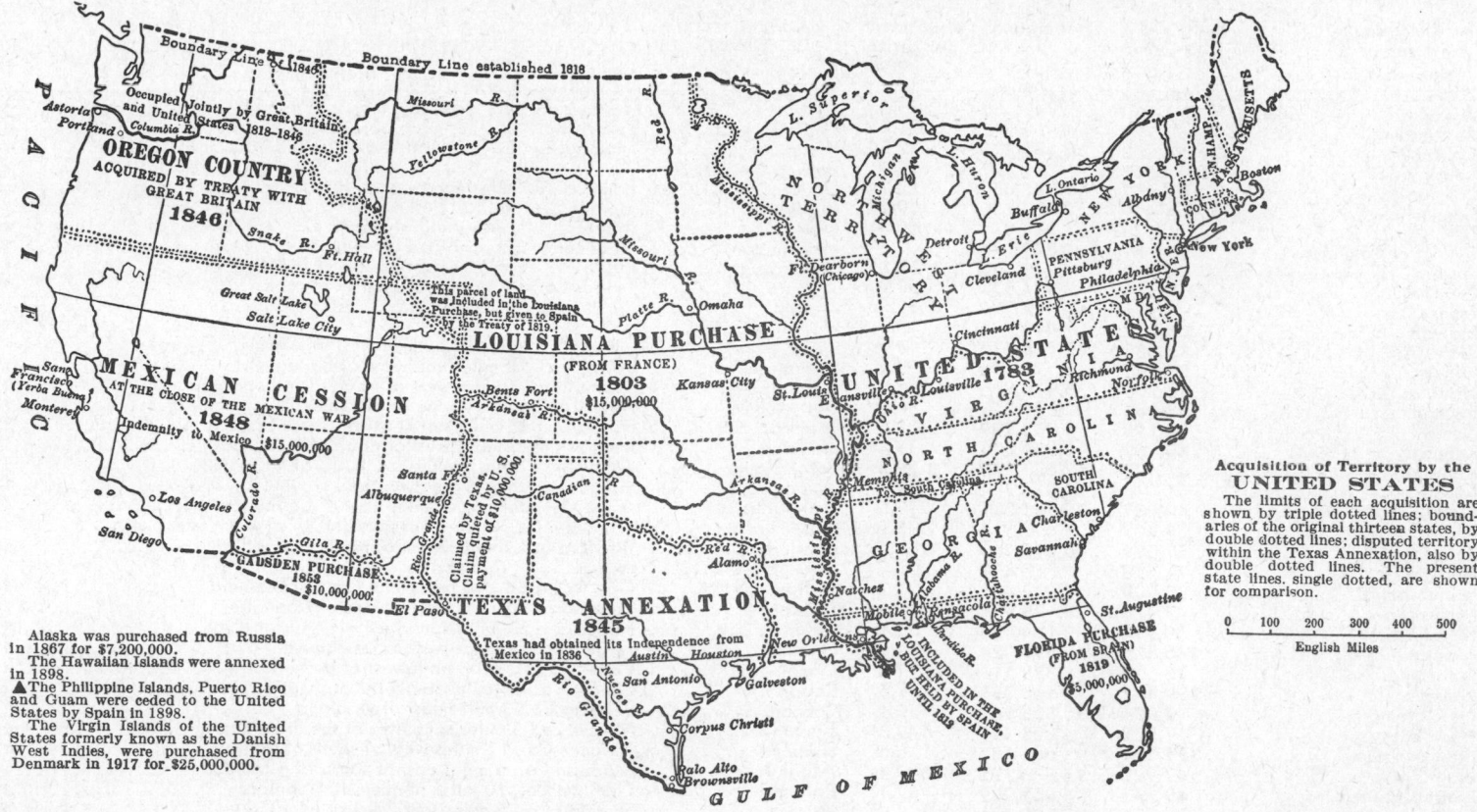

**Acquisition of Territory by the UNITED STATES**

The limits of each acquisition are shown by triple dotted lines; boundaries of the original thirteen states, by double dotted lines; disputed territory within the Texas Annexation, also by double dotted lines. The present state lines, single dotted, are shown for comparison.

Alaska was purchased from Russia in 1867 for $7,200,000.
The Hawaiian Islands were annexed in 1898.
▲The Philippine Islands, Puerto Rico and Guam were ceded to the United States by Spain in 1898.
The Virgin Islands of the United States formerly known as the Danish West Indies, were purchased from Denmark in 1917 for $25,000,000.

| State or Territory | Admitted to the Union | Settled at | Date | State Nickname | State Flower |
|---|---|---|---|---|---|
| Alabama | Dec. 14, 1819 | Mobile | 1702 | Cotton State | Golden Rod |
| Alaska Territory | *Aug. 24, 1912 | Sitka | 1801 | | |
| Arizona | Feb. 14, 1912 | Tucson | 1580 | Baby State | Saguaro Cactus |
| Arkansas | June 15, 1836 | Arkansas Post | 1685 | Wonder State | Apple Blossom |
| California | Sept. 9, 1850 | San Diego | 1769 | Golden State | Golden Poppy |
| Colorado | Aug. 1, 1876 | Near Denver | 1858 | Centennial State | Columbine |
| Connecticut | †Jan. 9, 1788 | Windsor | 1635 | Nutmeg State | Mountain Laurel |
| Delaware | †Dec. 7, 1787 | Cape Henlopen | 1627 | Diamond State | Peach Blossom |
| District of Columbia | ** 1790-1791 | | 1790 | | American Beauty Rose |
| Florida | Mar. 3, 1845 | St. Augustine | 1565 | Peninsula State | Orange Blossom |
| Georgia | †Jan. 2, 1788 | Savannah | 1733 | Cracker State | Cherokee Rose |
| Guam | ‡Dec. 10, 1898 | Agana | .... | | |
| Hawaii | *June 14, 1900 | | .... | | |
| Idaho | July 3, 1890 | Coeur d'Alene | 1842 | Gem of the Mt. State | Syringa |
| Illinois | Dec. 3, 1818 | Kaskaskia | 1720 | Sucker State | Violet |
| Indiana | Dec. 11, 1816 | Vincennes | 1730 | Hoosier | Zinnia |
| Iowa | Dec. 28, 1846 | Burlington | 1788 | Hawkeye State | Wild Rose |
| Kansas | Jan. 29, 1861 | | 1831 | Sunflower State | Sunflower |
| Kentucky | June 1, 1792 | Harrodsburg | 1774 | Blue Grass State | Goldenrod |
| Louisiana | April 30, 1812 | Iberville | 1699 | Pelican State | Magnolia |
| Maine | Mar. 15, 1820 | Bristol | 1624 | Pine Tree State | Pine Cone |
| Maryland | †April 28, 1788 | St. Mary's | 1634 | Free State | Blackeyed Susan |
| Massachusetts | †Feb. 6, 1788 | Plymouth | 1620 | Bay State | Mayflower |
| Michigan | Jan. 26, 1837 | Near Detroit | 1650 | Wolverine State | Apple Blossom |
| Minnesota | May 11, 1858 | St. Peter's River | 1805 | North Star State | Lady Slipper |
| Mississippi | Dec. 10, 1817 | Natchez | 1716 | Magnolia State | Magnolia |
| Missouri | Aug. 10, 1821 | St. Louis | 1764 | Show Me State | Hawthorn |
| Montana | Nov. 8, 1889 | | 1809 | Treasure State | Bitter Root |
| Nebraska | Mar. 1, 1867 | Bellevue | 1847 | Tree Planter's State | Goldenrod |
| Nevada | Oct. 31, 1864 | Genoa | 1850 | Battle Born State | Sage Brush |
| New Hampshire | †June 21, 1788 | Dover and Portsmouth | 1623 | Granite State | Purple Lilac |
| New Jersey | †Dec. 18, 1787 | Bergen | 1617 | Garden State | Violet |
| New Mexico | Jan. 6, 1912 | Santa Fe | 1605 | Sunshine State | Yucca |
| New York | †July 26, 1788 | Manhattan Island | 1614 | Empire State | Rose |
| North Carolina | †Nov. 21, 1789 | Albemarle | 1650 | Tar Heel State | Dogwood |
| North Dakota | Nov. 2, 1889 | Pembina | 1780 | Sioux State | Wild Prairie Rose |
| Ohio | Nov. 29, 1802 | Marietta | 1788 | Buckeye State | Scarlet Carnation |
| Oklahoma | Nov. 16, 1907 | | 1889 | Sooner State | Mistletoe |
| Oregon | Feb. 14, 1859 | Astoria | 1810 | Beaver State | Oregon Grape |
| Pennsylvania | †Dec. 12, 1787 | Delaware River | 1682 | Keystone State | Mountain Laurel |
| Puerto Rico | †Dec. 10, 1898 | Caparra | 1510 | | |
| Rhode Island | †May 29, 1790 | Providence | 1636 | Little Rhody | Violet |
| South Carolina | †May 23, 1788 | Port Royal | 1670 | Palmetto State | Yellow Jessamine |
| South Dakota | Nov. 2, 1889 | Sioux Falls | 1856 | Coyote State | The Pasque |
| Tennessee | June 1, 1796 | Ft. Loudon | 1757 | Volunteer State | Iris |
| Texas | Dec. 29, 1845 | Matagorda Bay | 1686 | Lone Star State | Bluebonnet |
| Utah | Jan. 4, 1896 | Salt Lake City | 1847 | Beehive State | Sego Lily |
| Vermont | Mar. 4, 1791 | Ft. Dummer | 1764 | Green Mountain State | Red Clover |
| Virgin Islands | ***Mar. 31, 1917 | | .... | | |
| Virginia | †June 26, 1788 | Jamestown | 1607 | Old Dominion State | American Dogwood |
| Washington | Nov. 11, 1889 | Astoria | 1811 | Evergreen State | Rhododendron |
| West Virginia | June 19, 1863 | Wheeling | 1774 | Mountain State | Rhododendron |
| Wisconsin | May 29, 1848 | Green Bay | 1670 | Badger State | Violet |
| Wyoming | July 10, 1890 | Ft. Laramie | 1834 | Equality State | Indian Paintbrush |

* Organized as Territory.    † Ratified the Constitution.    ‡ Treaty of Peace with Spain.    ** Established under Acts of Congress.    ***See Virgin Is. note above, left.

△ U. S. Geological Survey—World Almanac.    ▲ Philippines became independent in 1946.

| State or Territory | Land Area (Sq. Mi.) | Population | Inhabitants per Sq. Mi. | Capital or Chief Town | Geographic Centers | Page |
|---|---|---|---|---|---|---|
| Alabama | 51,078 | 3,061,743 | 59.9 | Montgomery | Chilton Co., 12 miles southwest of Clanton | 164 |
| Alaska | 586,400 | 128,643 | .... | Juneau | 95 miles south of Fort Gibbon | 205 |
| Arizona | 113,580 | 749,587 | 6.6 | Phoenix | Yavapai Co., 55 miles southeast of Prescott | 165 |
| Arkansas | 52,725 | 1,909,511 | 36.2 | Little Rock | Pulaski Co., 12 miles north of west of Little Rock | 166 |
| California | 156,803 | 10,586,223 | 67.5 | Sacramento | Madera Co., 35 miles northeast of Madera | 167 |
| Canal Zone | 362 | 51,827 | .... | Balboa Heights | | ... |
| Colorado | 103,967 | 1,325,089 | 12.7 | Denver | Park Co., 30 miles northwest of Pikes Peak | 168 |
| Connecticut | 4,899 | 2,007,280 | 409.7 | Hartford | Hartford Co., at East Berlin | 168 |
| Delaware | 1,978 | 318,085 | 160.8 | Dover | Kent Co., 11 miles south of Dover | 169 |
| District of Columbia | 61 | 802,178 | | Washington | Near corner of Fourth and L streets, NW | 178 |
| Florida | 54,262 | 2,771,305 | 51.1 | Tallahassee | Citrus Co., 12 miles west of north of Brooksville | 170 |
| Georgia | 58,518 | 3,444,578 | 58.9 | Atlanta | Twiggs Co., 18 miles southeast of Macon | 171 |
| Guam | 206 | 22,295 | .... | Agana | | 206 |
| Hawaii | 6,407 | 499,794 | .... | Honolulu | | |
| Idaho | 82,808 | 588,637 | 7.1 | Boise | Custer Co., 24 miles south of west of Challis | 172 |
| Illinois | 55,947 | 8,712,176 | 155.7 | Springfield | Logan Co., 28 miles northeast of Springfield | 173 |
| Indiana | 36,205 | 3,934,224 | 108.7 | Indianapolis | Boone Co., 14 miles west of north of Indianapolis | 173 |
| Iowa | 55,986 | 2,621,073 | 46.8 | Des Moines | Story Co., 5 miles northeast of Ames | 175 |
| Kansas | 82,113 | 1,905,299 | 23.2 | Topeka | Barton Co., 15 miles northeast of Great Bend | 176 |
| Kentucky | 40,109 | 2,944,806 | 73.4 | Frankfort | Marion Co., 3 miles west of north of Lebanon | 177 |
| Louisiana | 45,177 | 2,683,516 | 59.4 | Baton Rouge | Avoyelles Parish, 3 miles southeast of Marksville | 177 |
| Maine | 31,040 | 913,774 | 29.4 | Augusta | Piscataquis Co., 18 miles north of Dover | 178 |
| Maryland | 9,887 | 2,343,001 | 237.0 | Annapolis | Anne Arundel Co., 3 miles east of Collington | 178 |
| Massachusetts | 7,907 | 4,690,514 | 593.2 | Boston | Worcester Co., in northern part of City of Worcester | 179 |
| Michigan | 57,022 | 6,371,766 | 111.7 | Lansing | Wexford Co., 5 miles west of north of Cadillac | 180 |
| Midway Is. | 28 | 437 | | | | ... |
| Minnesota | 80,009 | 2,982,483 | 37.3 | St. Paul | Crow Wing Co., 10 miles southwest of Brainerd | 181 |
| Mississippi | 47,420 | 2,178,914 | 45.9 | Jackson | Leake Co., 9 miles north of west of Carthage | 182 |
| Missouri | 69,270 | 3,954,653 | 57.1 | Jefferson City | Miller Co., 20 miles southwest of Jefferson City | 183 |
| Montana | 146,316 | 591,024 | 4.0 | Helena | Fergus Co., 12 miles west of Lewistown | 184 |
| Nebraska | 76,653 | 1,325,510 | 17.3 | Lincoln | Custer Co., 10 miles northwest of Broken Bow | 184 |
| Nevada | 109,802 | 160,083 | 1.5 | Carson City | Lander Co., 23 miles southeast of Austin | 185 |
| New Hampshire | 9,024 | 533,242 | 59.1 | Concord | Belknap Co., 3 miles east of Ashland | 186 |
| New Jersey | 7,522 | 4,835,329 | 642.8 | Trenton | Mercer Co., 5 miles southeast of the State Capital | 187 |
| New Mexico | 121,511 | 681,187 | 5.6 | Santa Fe | Torrance Co., 12 miles west of south of Willard | 188 |
| New York | 47,929 | 14,830,192 | 309.4 | Albany | Madison Co., 6 miles east of south of Oneida | 189 |
| North Carolina | 49,142 | 4,061,929 | 82.7 | Raleigh | Chatham Co., 10 miles northwest of Sanford | 190 |
| North Dakota | 70,054 | 619,636 | 8.8 | Bismarck | Sheridan Co., 5 miles southwest of McClusky | 190 |
| Ohio | 41,122 | 7,946,627 | 193.2 | Columbus | Delaware Co., 25 miles east of north of Columbus | 191 |
| Oklahoma | 69,283 | 2,233,351 | 32.2 | Oklahoma City | Oklahoma Co., 8 miles north of Oklahoma City | 192 |
| Oregon | 96,350 | 1,521,341 | 15.8 | Salem | Crook Co., 25 miles east of south of Prineville | 193 |
| Pennsylvania | 45,045 | 10,498,012 | 233.1 | Harrisburg | Center Co., 2.5 miles southwest of Bellefonte | 194 |
| Puerto Rico | 3,435 | 2,210,703 | | San Juan | | 206 |
| Rhode Island | 1,058 | 791,896 | 748.5 | Providence | Kent Co., 1 mile west of south of Crompton | 195 |
| St. Croix, Virgin Is. | 82 | 12,096 | .... | Christiansted | | 206 |
| St. John, Virgin Is. | 19 | 747 | | | | 206 |
| St. Thomas, Virgin Is. | 32 | 13,811 | .... | Charlotte Amalie | | 206 |
| Samoa | 76 | 13,273 | .... | Pago-Pago | | ... |
| South Carolina | 30,594 | 2,117,027 | 69.2 | Columbia | Richland Co., 13 miles southeast of Columbia | 195 |
| South Dakota | 76,536 | 652,740 | 8.5 | Pierre | Hughes Co., 8 miles northeast of Pierre | 196 |
| Tennessee | 41,961 | 3,291,718 | 78.4 | Nashville | Rutherford Co., 5 miles northeast of Murfreesboro | 197 |
| Texas | 263,644 | 7,711,194 | 29.2 | Austin | McCulloch Co., 15 miles northeast of Brady | 198 |
| United States | 3,022,387 | 150,697,361 | .... | Washington | Smith Co., Kansas, 11 miles northeast of Smith Center | ... |
| Utah | 82,346 | 688,862 | 8.4 | Salt Lake City | Sanpete Co., 3 miles north of Manti | 199 |
| Vermont | 9,278 | 377,747 | 40.7 | Montpelier | Washington Co., 3 miles east of Roxbury | 200 |
| Virgin Islands | 133 | 26,654 | .... | Charlotte Amalie | | 206 |
| Virginia | 39,899 | 3,318,680 | 83.2 | Richmond | Appomattox Co., 11 miles south of east of Amherst | 201 |
| Wake Island | | | | | | ... |
| Washington | 66,977 | 2,378,963 | 35.5 | Olympia | Chelan Co., 10 miles south of west of Wenatchee | 201 |
| West Virginia | 24,090 | 2,005,552 | 83.3 | Charleston | Braxton Co., 4 miles east of Sutton | 202 |
| Wisconsin | 54,715 | 3,434,575 | 62.8 | Madison | Wood Co., 9 miles southeast of Marshfield | 203 |
| Wyoming | 97,506 | 290,529 | 3.0 | Cheyenne | Fremont Co., 58 miles north of east of Lander | 204 |

## TEMPERATURES AND PRECIPITATION OF PRINCIPAL CITIES

| States | Cities | Jan. Aver. | July Aver. | Max. | Min. | Annual Precip. | States | Cities | Jan. Aver. | July Aver. | Max. | Min. | Annual Precip. |
|---|---|---|---|---|---|---|---|---|---|---|---|---|---|
| Ala. | Mobile | 53 | 82 | 103 | −1 | 60.67 | Nebr. | Omaha | 24 | 78 | 114 | −32 | 25.49 |
| Ariz. | Phoenix | 52 | 90 | 118 | 16 | 7.62 | Nev. | Winnemucca | 28 | 72 | 108 | −36 | 8.20 |
| Ark. | Little Rock | 43 | 81 | 110 | −12 | 46.12 | N. H. | Concord | 22 | 70 | 102 | −37 | 36.24 |
| Calif. | San Francisco | 50 | 59 | 101 | 27 | 20.23 | N. J. | Atlantic City | 35 | 73 | 104 | −9 | 40.91 |
| Colo. | Denver | 32 | 73 | 105 | −29 | 13.99 | N. Mex. | Santa Fe | 29 | 69 | 97 | −13 | 14.19 |
| Conn. | New Haven | 30 | 73 | 101 | −15 | 44.96 | New York | New York | 32 | 74 | 102 | −14 | 41.63 |
| Del. | Wilmington | 33 | 76 | 107 | −15 | 44.58 | N. C. | Charlotte | 41 | 78 | 103 | −5 | 44.22 |
| Fla. | Miami | 68 | 82 | 96 | 27 | 59.18 | N. Dak. | Bismarck | 9 | 71 | 114 | −45 | 15.43 |
| Ga. | Atlanta | 44 | 79 | 103 | −8 | 47.58 | Ohio | Cincinnati | 33 | 77 | 108 | −17 | 37.21 |
| Idaho | Boise | 30 | 74 | 121 | −28 | 12.47 | Okla. | Oklahoma City | 38 | 82 | 113 | −17 | 31.15 |
| Ill. | Chicago | 26 | 74 | 105 | −23 | 31.85 | Oreg. | Portland | 39 | 67 | 107 | −2 | 39.43 |
| Ind. | Indianapolis | 30 | 76 | 106 | −25 | 38.26 | Pa. | Philadelphia | 34 | 77 | 106 | −11 | 41.86 |
| Iowa | Dubuque | 20 | 75 | 110 | −32 | 31.32 | R. I. | Block Island | 32 | 69 | 92 | −10 | 38.81 |
| Kans. | Wichita | 32 | 80 | 114 | −22 | 29.64 | S. C. | Charleston | 50 | 81 | 104 | 7 | 40.26 |
| Ky. | Louisville | 35 | 79 | 107 | −20 | 40.58 | S. Dak. | Pierre | 18 | 76 | 115 | −40 | 16.21 |
| La. | New Orleans | 54 | 80 | 102 | 7 | 59.72 | Tenn. | Nashville | 40 | 79 | 106 | −13 | 44.77 |
| Me. | Portland | 23 | 68 | 103 | −39 | 42.05 | Texas | Galveston | 55 | 83 | 101 | 8 | 44.36 |
| Md. | Baltimore | 36 | 78 | 107 | −7 | 41.94 | Utah | Salt Lake City | 30 | 77 | 105 | −20 | 15.79 |
| Mass. | Boston | 30 | 72 | 104 | −18 | 38.94 | Vt. | Burlington | 19 | 69 | 100 | −29 | 31.87 |
| Mich. | Detroit | 26 | 73 | 105 | −24 | 31.04 | Va. | Norfolk | 42 | 78 | 105 | 2 | 40.45 |
| Minn. | Minneapolis | 13 | 73 | 108 | −34 | 27.31 | Wash. | Seattle | 40 | 63 | 98 | 3 | 31.80 |
| Miss. | Vicksburg | 50 | 81 | 104 | −1 | 49.40 | W. Va. | Parkersburg | 33 | 75 | 106 | −27 | 37.89 |
| Mo. | St. Louis | 33 | 80 | 110 | −22 | 36.67 | Wis. | Milwaukee | 21 | 70 | 105 | −25 | 29.64 |
| Mont. | Helena | 20 | 66 | 103 | −42 | 12.54 | Wyo. | Cheyenne | 27 | 67 | 100 | −38 | 15.82 |

*U. S. Weather Bureau.

# Illustrated Geography and Gazetteer

# of

# THE WORLD

## *Introduction*

THE HEADLINE EVENTS of the last half-century have made the average American acutely curious of the vast world beyond the national borders of the American homeland. Constant repetition has tended to make this thought a cliché, yet it is one of the most significant truths of our times. This new national concern for the external world and its problems is one of the hopeful signs pointing to a better future for mankind. However, no matter how well-intentioned our concern for international relations may be it is of no value unless it is grounded on an intelligent appreciation of the great diversity of social, economic and political forms extant throughout the globe.

One of the main roads to a better knowledge of this fascinating planet is a thorough indoctrination in the golden lore of geography. This science is not a narrow and limited scholarly discipline but a universal department of knowledge drawing on the sum total of man's explorations in the field of thought. The very pervasiveness of earth science makes it intriguing reading for the average non-specialist. At the same time that it entertains, it also builds a permanent edifice of information for the general reader. As more individuals discover this golden key to understanding the tumultuous happenings of the day, our collective actions in the field of enlightened citizenship will gain immeasurably in effectiveness.

On the following pages the editors have presented a treasure-trove of information on the world's nations, resources, peoples and governments. Salient facts regarding the many countries of our Mother Earth have been arranged in easily-found tabular form. This arrangement by tables makes comparison between political units a simple task. Striking photographs lend a sense of immediacy to the equally engaging text descriptions of countries and continents. Highlighting the gazetteer and geography are the colorful Resource-Relief maps which locate at a glance the major relief and resource features of the continental land masses.

Alaska Development Board

Salmon fishing is the chief enterprise in Alaska. These small fleets play a vital part in providing tons of fish for the industry.

Canadian National Railroads

Ragged peaks and stoney crags form the watercourse for Emperor Falls in British Columbia.

**NORTH AMERICA** — Lying across the wide expanse of the Atlantic Ocean, was a new World waiting discovery and recognition. Europe was completely unaware of its existence for many centuries. Its discovery was destined to change the whole course of history and affect the fortunes of men and nations the world over. More than that, its discovery ushered in a whole new era of civilization, and marked the first faltering step towards the exploration and charting of all lands and waters of the world.

No discovery, before or since, has added more to man's opportunities and the wealth of the world; or played a more important part in shaping a world's destiny. Yet, its discoverer died in ignorance of his epoch-making contribution to the world. It remained for those who followed to prove the existence of a New World.

Landing on one of the Bahamas, how was Columbus to know that his quest for a new route to the East Indies had led him to an island outpost of two fabulous empires ? ... now but a bare few hours by air travel from the sister continents of North and South America. In his wildest dreams Columbus could not have conceived of a land extending virtually from the North Pole to the South Pole, for a distance of some nine thousand miles.

We can imagine Balboa's thrill twenty-one years later, when he fought his way across the rocky Ithmus of Panama to gaze upon the Pacific. But, how was he to know that this narrow ribbon of tapering land joined two vast domains ? That, from where he stood, an unbroken expanse of land reached

northward for forty-five hundred miles, and actually spread out into a gigantic fan three thousand miles wide ? Also, that, to the south a similar, though lesser triangle of land, reached thousands of miles below the equator to the icy waters of the Antarctic ?

Today these are historical incidents of common knowledge, thanks to the intrepid discoverers, explorers and map-makers. We take their hard won glories for granted, and even forget the adventure and romance that has gone into the making of our geographical maps.

We must be constantly reminded that, of all the continents of the world, North America is the most favored for natural wealth, climate and position on the earth. Being situated between the two largest oceans has protected the people of North America from enemy invasion, and also enabled them to develop an extensive commerce. The millions of square miles of fertile soil and untold mineral wealth has provided a standard of living unknown elsewhere in the world. Hence, composed of peoples from all over the world, its inhabitants have enjoyed peace and plenty, without fear of their independent ways of life being encroached upon, or destroyed by jealous and covetous neighbors. We can be assured that such a fortunate people will not easily relinquish what they have come to hold so dear.

The principal geographical features of North America are its two mountain ranges and the intervening central plains. The high and rugged mountains to the westward extend from the tip of Alaska to the base of the Isthmus of Panama, or from the northern

to the southern extremity of the continent. These mountain ranges include the Coastal system that hugs the Pacific Coast, and the Rocky Mountains that branch out eastward and southward across the United States to become, in Mexico and Central America, the Sierra Madres. The Cascade Mountains, which farther south become the Sierra Nevada, are separate ranges that work inland from the coastal mountains. These diverging mountain chains in the east and west, form the bulwark for a number of high plateaus that lie between. The land adjoining the Cascade Mountains is the Columbia Plateau, while farther south lies the Colorado Plateau. In between is the arid region of the Great Basin. The Great Salt Lake is all that remains to reveal that this vast area was once a geologic lake.

In the east, extending from the Gulf of Saint Lawrence to the Gulf of Mexico is the Appalachian Range. These mountains are older and less rugged than the Rockies. Time has worn them down and rounded their peaks. On the side toward the Atlantic Ocean, they merge with the Piedmont Plateau, which slopes off into a coastal plain.

The great central plains that slope towards the center, and lie between the Rocky Mountain and Appalachian Highlands describe a giant "V" which extends from the Arctic Ocean to the Gulf of Mexico.

More varieties of climate prevail in North America than in any other land in the world. The greater part of the continent, however, enjoys a temperate and invigorating climate. The inhabitants of the far north must adjust themselves to the rigors of Arctic weather,

Spacious fields of wheat stacked for harvest are a frequent sight in the Prairie regions of Canada.

Canadian National Railroads

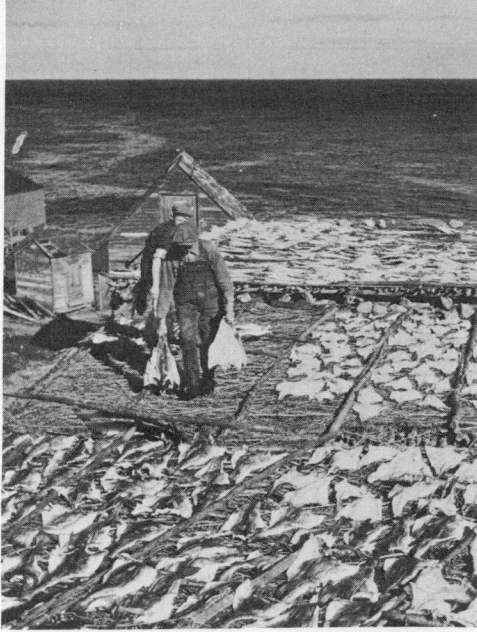

National Film Board of Canada

Fishing is the chief occupation in the Maritime Provinces of Canada.

Mexico endures sub-tropical temperatures, and Central America a tropical heat. Even from the east to west there is a wide variety of climate due to difference in altitude, and other conditions not affected by latitude.

To an airman soaring above the shifting panorama of North America, the realization must come that this is indeed a rich land of fertile soils, spreading forests, rolling plains, inland lakes, and mighty rivers. There is hardly an area of any size on the entire continent but contains, on the surface or beneath it, a species of natural wealth. On the western coast, the great Pacific Ocean, generally a protective barrier, separating most of North America from the shores of Asia, offers little promise of isolation at its far northwest corner. While eight thousand miles separate the peoples of China from the United States, Russia and Alaska almost meet at the Bering Strait, which is only fifty-seven miles wide.

**ALASKA**—Purchased from Russia in 1867 for a pittance of $7,200,000 and is still today the United States' most valued possession strategically. Although partially in the Arctic Circle, it is by no means the frozen and inhospitable land its latitude would suggest. Alaska has a wide area of equable climate. Along its mountainous and island-fringed coast, the warm Japanese Current keeps the temperature at all times above zero. This rises in the summer to a seasonal heat of 80°. These sections endure drenching rain, caused

by the condensation of warm winds striking the snow-capped peaks of the mountains. In the center of Alaska is a broad upland where grasses, flowers and mosses grow.

The Yukon River, rising in Canada, swings across Alaska for fifteen hundred miles, twelve hundred of which are navigable. Although frozen for two-thirds of the year, this river is a main artery of travel. Dog sled teams replace the large steamers during the months when it is ice-bound. A half million acres of land is cultivated in the Yukon Valley, and even though the growing season is short, the Arctic days provide long hours of sunshine.

First known as "Seward's Folly," Alaska justified its purchase within a few short years and has proved a veritable storehouse of treasure. Each year it produces more than twice its purchase price, in minerals alone.

The popular conception of the Arctic does, however, exist in the northern regions. Here the ground thaws only a few inches at the surface during the summer. Except for a few Eskimo and reindeer, there is comparatively no life or vegetation able to survive the rigors of the frigid climate.

While at one time Alaska·was a remote and unexplored country, today with ever increasing population and extensive building and improvement of roads, development is steadily expanding.

The Aleutian islands are strung out in a broad arc off the tip of Alaska for a thousand miles and separate the Bering Sea

from the North Pacific. Numbering about one hundred and fifty islands, they are the tops of submerged mountains. Included in the purchase of Alaska, they have great strategic value as air bases and weather observing stations for the United States.

**CANADA**—The three thousand mile boundary between the United States and Canada is convincing proof that two great nations may live side by side in peace and harmony. For over a hundred years this boundary line —the longest in the world—has been free from fortification of any kind by either nation. In a world that has been repeatedly torn by war during the past century here is lasting evidence that national progress, pride and ambition can exist without adjoining countries being tempted to encroach on the other's domain.

Canada is the largest domain of the British Commonwealth. It extends from the icy waters of the Arctic to the borders of the United States, and from east to west its greatest distance is 3,700 miles. Its area is greater than that of the United States and nearly as large as the continent of Europe.

Canada is a vast diversified land of fertile plains, of mountains and rivers, and countless lakes. Over 6 per cent of the total is water area, affording ready power for her ever increasing industrial development. Like the United States it can be roughly divided into three sections; the eastern highlands, a great level central plain, and mountain ranges extending from the Rockies to the Pacific.

In the east the Appalachian region is a beautiful land of hilly or mountainous terrain with very heavily forested sections and fertile farm lands. Just west of the highlands lies the St. Lawrence Valley including the Ontario peninsula, the hub of Canada's in-

TWA Trans World Airline

A leading city of the Pacific Coast, Los Angeles has drawn its inhabitants from all parts of the United States.

North Carolina News Bureau

The American South contains unusually picturesque mountain scenery.

dustry. In this area, rich in minerals, forests, water power and fertile land, is the highest concentration of population. Moderate climate combined with valuable accessible resources have made this section of the greatest economic importance. Northwest of the Valley is the Canadian Shield, an area characterized by low hills, countless lakes connected by streams and rapids. Here is Canada's greatest store of resources, minerals, forests, furs and water power. In the interior Plains is the great wheat belt. In the west, parallel to the Pacific, is the magnificent mountain country formed by the Cordilleran Mountain System. In addition to minerals and valuable forests, this area, in the fertile valleys, produces much of Canada's fruit and vegetable crops.

Although primarily an agricultural country, Canada has developed rapidly in recent years as an industrial country. Lumbering is of great importance, which is to be expected, for the forests of Canada are among the largest in the world. Furs have been an important source of wealth since the early days of the Hudson's Bay Company, and the fishing grounds of Canada are the largest and most productive on earth. Wheat is the principal crop of the prairie provinces, and Canada is one of the biggest producers and exporters of this grain.

The provinces in the southern sections of Canada enjoy much the same climate as exists in the Great Lakes regions of the United States. The southern parts of Ontario and Quebec have less severe winters, but the northern sections of these provinces have very severe winters, with short, hot summers. The prairies experience great extremes in temperature, while moderate rainfall in this region favors wheat production.

About half of the population is of British origin and one quarter is French. The remaining fourth is principally Russian, German, Austrian and Scandinavian. Some hundred thousand Indians live mostly on reservations.

**UNITED STATES**—In a little over one hundred and fifty years the United States of America has written an amazing chapter in history. In that brief period a wilderness has been tamed, and a powerful nation has arisen to take its place among the foremost countries of the world. A land populated by every race, creed and color, and a haven of refuge for the oppressed, its phenomenal growth has never been equalled. Far removed from the traditions and hampering fetters of the Old World, it has charted a new course in government. Its freedom loving people have devoted their energies to developing the riches that Nature has so lavishly supplied.

The United States has reached its present position of greatness because of a number of reasons. It is blessed with a climate that cannot be surpassed elsewhere in the world, and is rich in mineral wealth beyond that of any other country. With a coastline on three sides well supplied with harbors, it is ideally situated for trade with the rest of the world. Its rivers and lakes are navigable and give easy access into the interior of the country. The variety of climate and the fertility of the soil make a great diversity of crops possible.

Climate has made the people of the United States energetic, and Nature has endowed the land with more than enough to meet their needs. This country's way of life has provided the incentive for continually bettering the standards of living of its people. All this has brought continued economic, cultural and scientific progress.

The United States is the greatest manufacturing nation in the world, with half the population depending upon industry for a living. It has the finest systems of transportation and communication, including the great majority of the automobiles in the world. More than half the coal, and a quarter of the iron in the world, as well as large deposits of almost all important minerals are found here.

The three principal geographical features are a continuation of those in Canada. They are the eastern highlands, comprising the Appalachian Range, the broad central plains, and the Rockies and Coastal ranges in the Far West.

A closer study of the geography of the United States does much to explain the growth of the nation. For example, the stony

Gendreau

The favorite sport of the Mexicans is the "corrida" or bullfight. Physical dexterity and fluid grace are requisites for this profession.

Publishers' Photo Service

The raising and export of indigenous fruit is an important activity in Central America.

An attraction for all visitors to Mexico is Xochimilco's floating gardens.

Gendreau

soil of New England discouraged farming and caused the early settlers to turn to manufacturing and commerce. The swift streams furnished water power and the jagged coastline provided bays for harboring the ships from Europe. Farther south, the coastal plains widen out into broad stretches of fertile land, and the rivers are short and deep. This led to the development of the large plantations in the deep South, where the climate is favorable to crops that require long hot summers. Here the coastal plain includes half of Georgia, all of Florida, and extends along the Gulf of Mexico. It reaches into the interior as far north as southern Illinois.

The lake and prairie region of the upper Mississippi Valley is one of the most fertile in the world, and is linked by waterways with the East and South through the Great Lakes and the Mississippi River system. The Great Plains region, depending upon the nature of the topsoil and the amount of rainfall, is either grain or grazing country, with valuable deposits of oil in Texas and Oklahoma.

The great size of the country and the seemingly endless store of natural wealth, both above and below the surface of the earth, have been responsible for great waste in the past. Fortunately, strict conservation measures are now in force to protect the resources of the earth for future generations and to assure them an equal place in this "Land of Opportunity".

**MEXICO**—Beyond the southern border of the United States and across the Rio Grande, where North America begins to taper sharply to a point, lies Latin America. It is difficult to conceive of the contrast to be found beyond this man-made boundary with the rest of the continent. It is another world, with a totally different culture, another language, and traditions and customs which set it apart from its northern neighbors.

About one-fourth the area of the United States, Mexico swings south for about eleven hundred miles, ending in the narrow hook of the peninsula of Yucatan.

While half of Mexico lies in the torrid zone, its climate is determined more by elevation than latitude. Along the coast the weather is hot and humid, with luxuriant tropical vegetation. As the land rises the climate changes to temperate and the mountain peaks are snow-clad. Two mountain chains, that are a continuation of those in the United States, converge and meet at the southern tip, leaving a flat tableland between. The average altitude of this plateau is about 6,500 feet. Mexico's highest concentration of population is here where the fertile land, ideal climate and favorable rainfall afford excellent conditions for agricultural crops. Although industrial development has increased rapidly in recent years and most of Mexico's wealth is derived from her mines and petroleum, the great majority of the people are still employed in agricultural pursuits. Except for the coastal plain bordering the Gulf of Mexico, mountains and plateaus occupy the greater part of Mexico. Lying in both the temperate and torrid zones allows the country to produce a greater

Bermuda News Bureau
The islands of the Caribbean depend largely on the tourist trade to support their economy.

Jamaica Development Board
Jamaica is the largest of the British West Indies possessions.

variety of crops than is possible in most other countries.

Mexico is a beautiful and picturesque country with ancient ruins of pyramids and temples still standing as mute evidence of a flourishing civilization that existed before the coming of the Spanish invaders in the early fifteenth century.

## CENTRAL AMERICA—As North America
decreases in size from a land of magnificent distance to a slender neck of land where the Isthmus of Panama joins South America, the sizes of its nations shrink to even greater extent. In Central America a string of six small countries, Guatemala, Honduras, El Salvador, Nicaragua, Costa Rica and Panama, is confined to an area less than that of the State of Texas. Their total population does not equal that of New York City.

The Cordilleras, a continuation of the mountain chains starting far north in Alaska, extend the entire length of the land. Many of the peaks are volcanic and frequent eruptions occur. These mountains have formed many high and fertile plateaus which provide fine pasturage for livestock and rich soil for a diversity of crops. As in Mexico, the tropical climate of the lower regions is tempered by the elevation of the high plateaus. There are a number of harbors on both coasts, with the principal seaports on the Caribbean Sea. Most of the

rivers that flow into the Caribbean are navigable.

These agricultural nations have become increasingly important in the past few years. With the organizing of the Pan-American Union, the growth of air travel, and the fostering of a new spirit of co-operation between the republics of North and South America, Central America's future became one of promise. When global war shut off supplies of many important crops to the Western world from the East, it was found that here in the Americas could be grown many necessities that formerly had been imported from afar. Great variation in soils, rainfall, and terrain afford an enormous variety of tropical, semi-tropical and temperate crops. Experiments have successfully produced important quantities of spices, fibres, and essential oils for medicinal and industrial purposes that were introduced from the East. Among the important crops exported almost exclusively to the United States are bananas, natural rubber, coffee, rope fibres, cacao and sugar.

Although there is potential mineral wealth in most of the countries of Central America this resource, for the most part, has been unexploited. Much of the land is heavily forested and some of the world's most valuable woods such as mahogany, rosewood, teak and ebony are found here. However, only a very small part of the for-

ests have been as yet cut for commercial purposes.

## ISLANDS OF THE CARIBBEAN—The
Caribbean Sea is a vital water link between the Americas and the West Indies. With the opening of the Panama Canal it took on added importance as a trade route for the ships of the world.

The island republics and colonies lying in the Caribbean have likewise become increasingly important with the passing years, both for their economic and strategic value.

The West Indies, numbering hundreds of islands, extend in a sweeping arc beginning near southern Florida and ending off the coast of Venezuela. Columbus named the islands, in the belief that he had reached India. Most of the islands, forming two main groups, the Greater and the Lesser Antilles, are mountainous. However, there is sufficient fertile land to afford a variety of tropical products. In general the climate is hot but is tempered by the sea breezes. All the islands are subject to tropical hurricanes and in many regions there are occasional volcanic eruptions.

With the greater part of the West Indies under the control of the United States and Great Britain, the islands enjoy advantages not usually possessed by small independent countries. Nearness to markets and the great manufacturing centers, and cheap ocean transportation are added advantages. As with the Central American republics, the West Indies have enjoyed increased production and trade with the importation of new crops from the East that are now grown throughout Middle America.

| POLITICAL DIVISION | GOVERNMENT | MONETARY UNIT | PRINCIPAL LANGUAGES | PRINCIPAL RELIGIONS | MAJOR PRODUCTS |
|---|---|---|---|---|---|
| ALASKA | Territory of the U. S. ruled by Congress and a territorial legislature jointly with a governor appointed by the President. | dollar | English | Protestant | Vegetables, hay and other forage crops; salmon, halibut, herring; lumber; gold, copper, coal, tin, silver, lead, zinc, antimony, mercury, platinum and petroleum; canned fish, paper and wood products. |
| ALBERTA PROVINCE | Province of Canada with a lieutenant-governor, cabinet and unicameral legislature. | Canadian dollar | English French | Protestant Roman Catholic | Wheat, oats, barley, rye, flax, hay, clover, fodder-corn; cattle, swine, sheep, poultry; lumber; fish; furs, wool, eggs; petroleum, gas, coal, gypsum, bituminous sands, clay, sulphur; meat packing; flour milling, oatmeal, biscuits and macaroni, dairy products; textiles, oil refineries, linseed oil. |
| BAHAMAS | British colony with governor, executive and legislative council and house of assembly. | B.W.I. pound | English | Roman Catholic Protestant | Tomatoes, pineapples, okra, vegetables, citrus fruits, bananas, sisal; crawfish, shells; lumber; salt; handicraft products. |
| BARBADOS | British colony with governor, executive committee, executive and legislative council and house of assembly. | B. W. I. dollar | English | Protestant | Sugar cane, cotton; flying fish; manjak (asphalt); sugar, molasses, rum, edible oil, margarine. |
| BERMUDA | British colony with governor, executive and legislative council and house of assembly. | pound | English | Protestant | Lily bulbs, onions, bananas, cabbage, tomatoes, beans; coral; fish; perfume. |
| BRITISH COLUMBIA PROVINCE | Province of Canada with a lieutenant-governor, cabinet and unicameral legislature. | Canadian dollar | English French | Protestant Roman Catholic | Wheat, oats, barley, potatoes, clover, apples, pears, cherries, peaches, grapes, other fruits, tobacco; cattle, sheep, swine, horses, poultry; furs; salmon, halibut, herring, cod, whaling; lead, copper, coal, zinc, gold, uranium, cadmium, silver, tungsten, aluminum; shipbuilding, saw mills, fish curing and packing, pulp, paper; slaughtering and meat packing, petroleum products; machinery; fruit and vegetable preparations. |
| BRITISH HONDURAS | British colony with governor, executive council and legislative assembly. | Br. Honduras dollar | English and Spanish | Protestant and Roman Catholic | Rice, maize, beans, bananas, coconuts, citrus fruits, sugar cane; mahogany, chicle, pine, cedar; fish; rum, food products. |
| CANADA | Member of the British Commonwealth with a governor-general, prime minister and cabinet. Parliament consists of a senate and house of commons. | Canadian dollar | English French | Protestant Roman Catholic | (See individual provinces) |
| COSTA RICA | Republic with president, cabinet and one-house legislature. | colon | Spanish | Roman Catholic | Coffee, bananas, cocoa, abaca, sugar cane, maize, rice, tobacco; cattle; tuna; gold, silver; cigars and cigarettes, textiles, furniture and woodwork, sugar. |
| CUBA | Republic with president, vice-president, cabinet and a two-house legislature. | Cuban peso | Spanish | Roman Catholic | Sugar cane, tobacco, coffee, pineapples, citrus fruits, bananas, henequen; cattle; cedar, mahogany and other woods; fish; chromite, iron, manganese, copper, nickel, asphalt; sugar, textiles, alcohol, molasses, chemicals, tobacco products, electrical goods, clothing. |
| CURACAO (NETH. ANTILLES) | Self-governing part of Netherlands Union with governor, executive council and one-house legislature. | Antillian guilder | Dutch and Papiamento | Protestant | Fish; dividivi (tannin), crude salt, phosphates; refined petroleum. |
| DOMINICAN REPUBLIC | Republic with president, cabinet and a two-house legislature. | peso | Spanish | Roman Catholic | Sugar cane, cacao, coffee, tobacco, bananas, rice, corn; cattle; lumber; gold; starch, alcohol, molasses, sugar, chocolate, meats, cigars, cigarettes, leather. |
| GREENLAND | An integral part of the Danish kingdom, with representation in Parliament. | krone | Danish and Greenlandic | Protestant | Grass for fodder; cod and other fish; sheep, furs; cryolite; processed fish, hides. |
| GUADELOUPE | Overseas department of France with a prefect and elective general council. | French franc | French, French Patois | Roman Catholic | Sugar cane, bananas, coffee, cocoa, vanilla, cassava; fish; alcohol, rum. |
| GUATEMALA | Republic with a president, cabinet and one-house legislature. | quetzal | Spanish | Roman Catholic | Coffee, bananas, sugar cane, rubber, chicle, cacao, abaca, cattle; mahogany and dye woods; essential oils; gold; textiles. |
| HAITI | Republic with a president, cabinet and a two-house legislature. | gourde | Creole, French | Roman Catholic | Coffee; sugar, fig bananas, sisal, cotton, rice, cocoa; logwood; molasses, sisal products. |
| HONDURAS | Republic with a president, council of ministers and a one-house legislature. | lempira | Spanish | Roman Catholic | Bananas, coffee, coconuts, tobacco, grapefruit, rice, henequen; mahogany; cattle; gold, silver. |
| JAMAICA | British colony with a governor, executive and legislative councils and house of representatives. | pound | English | Protestant Roman Catholic | Sugar cane, bananas, tobacco, coconuts, cacao, pimentos, coffee, ginger; bauxite; honey; logwood; rum, textiles, cigars. |
| LEEWARD ISLANDS | Four separate British colonies under a single governor but with separate executive and legislative councils. | B. W. I. dollar | English | Protestant Roman Catholic | Sugar cane, cotton, vegetables, limes, fruits; fish; barites; sugar, molasses, rum, lime products, cotton lint, charcoal. |
| MANITOBA PROVINCE | Province of Canada with a lieutenant-governor, cabinet and unicameral legislature. | Canadian dollar | English French | Protestant Roman Catholic | Wheat, oats, barley, hay, clover, potatoes, sugar beets, honey; cattle, swine, poultry, fish; furs; lumber, pulp-wood; gold, copper, coal, zinc, silver, selenium, tellurium, cadmium, nickel, cobalt; meat packing, dairy products, railway shops, flour and feed mills, chemicals, clothing, cotton and jute bags. |
| MARTINIQUE | Overseas department of France with a prefect and elective general council. | French franc | Creole, French | Roman Catholic | Sugar cane, cocoa, pineapples, bananas, coffee; rum, sugar. |
| MEXICO | Federative republic with a president, council of ministers and a two-house legislature. | peso | Spanish | Roman Catholic | Corn, wheat, beans, chick-peas, sugar, bananas, barley, cotton, coffee, vegetables; cattle; henequen; fish; silver, petroleum, lead, gold, zinc, copper; textiles, sugar, alcohol, foundry products. |
| NEW BRUNSWICK PROVINCE | Province of Canada with a lieutenant-governor, cabinet and unicameral legislature. | Canadian dollar | English French | Roman Catholic Protestant | Potatoes, oats, mixed grains, hay, clover; cattle, swine, sheep, horses, poultry; limestone, granite, coal, gypsum; fish curing and packing; lumber, pulp, paper; shipbuilding and repairs, meat packing, wood working, furniture. |

# GAZETTEER OF THE WORLD
## NORTH AMERICA

| POLITICAL DIVISION | GOVERNMENT | MONETARY UNIT | PRINCIPAL LANGUAGES | PRINCIPAL RELIGIONS | MAJOR PRODUCTS |
|---|---|---|---|---|---|
| NEWFOUNDLAND PROVINCE | Province of Canada which includes Labrador, with a lieutenant-governor, cabinet and unicameral legislature. | Canadian dollar | English French | Roman Catholic Protestant | Sheep, cattle, dairying; furs; fish: cod, salmon, halibut, lobsters, herring, caplin, seals, whales; cod liver oil; newsprint, pulp, lumber; iron ore, lead, zinc, copper, limestone; fluorspar, cement, gold, gypsum, silveró fish processing, woodwork, furniture, shipbuilding, marine engines, fishing equipment, hydroelectric power. |
| NICARAGUA | Republic with a president, cabinet and a two-house legislature. | córdoba | Spanish | Roman Catholic | Coffee, sugar cane, sesame, corn, bananas, rice, cacao, cotton, beans; cattle; hardwoods; gold, silver; sugar, wood products. |
| NORTHWEST TERRITORIES | Canadian territory under administration by a commissioner advised by the governor in council or the Minister of Northern Affairs and Natural Resources. | Canadian dollar | English French | Protestant Roman Catholic | Gold, copper, silver, pitchblende, lead, salt, gypsum, uranium, cobalt, petroleum, cadmium; furs; fish; reindeer. |
| NOVA SCOTIA PROVINCE | Province of Canada with a lieutenant-governor, cabinet and unicameral legislature. | Canadian dollar | English French | Protestant Roman Catholic | Fruit, apples, cherries, plums, berries; hay, clover, oats, wheat, potatoes, turnips, alfalfa, barley, beets; cattle, sheep, dairying, poultry, horses, swine; lumber, wood-pulp, paper, Christmas trees; fish: lobsters, cod, haddock, mackerel, herring, halibut; coal, gypsum, iron, gold, manganese, barite, salt, silica, quartz, limestone, dolomite; fruits and vegetables, fish canning, shipbuilding, marine engines, steel. |
| ONTARIO PROVINCE | Province of Canada with a lieutenant-governor, cabinet and unicameral legislature. | Canadian dollar | English French | Protestant Roman Catholic | Oats, wheat, barley, mixed grains, rye, flax, potatoes, soy beans, hay, clover, fodder corn, alfalfa, vegetables, fruits, tobacco, sugar beets; swine, cattle, sheep, horses, poultry, dairy products, eggs; furs; fish; gold, silver, nickel, copper, cobalt, iron ore, zinc, petroleum, gas, asbestos, fluorspar, timber, pulp, paper, sawn lumber; automobiles, iron and steel, electrical apparatus, machinery, meat packing, textiles, leather, rubber goods, hydroelectric power, flour and feed; chemicals, smelting, refining. |
| PANAMA | Republic with a president, two vice-presidents, and a one-house legislature. | balboa | Spanish | Roman Catholic | Bananas, cacao, abaca, coconuts, rice, sugar cane, coffee, pineapples; cattle; hardwoods; gold; hides, sugar, wood products. |
| PRINCE EDWARD ISLAND PROVINCE | Province of Canada with a lieutenant-governor, cabinet and unicameral legislature. | Canadian dollar | English French | Protestant Roman Catholic | Oats, mixed grains, barley, wheat, potatoes, hay, clover, fruits, turnips, beets; swine, sheep, cattle, horses, poultry; lumber; fish: lobsters, smelts, herring, cod, mackerel, oysters; furs (silver fox); wood products, printing and publishing, fish processing; castings, forgings, meat products, dairy products. |
| PUERTO RICO | A constitutional self-governing Commonwealth of the U. S., with a governor, an advisory council and a two-house legislature. | dollar | Spanish English | Roman Catholic | Sugar cane, tobacco, fruits, pineapples, grapefruit, coconuts, coffee, cotton, livestock, vegetables; molasses, embroideries, rum, canned fruit and juice, alcohol, cordials, tobacco products. |
| QUÉBEC PROVINCE | Province of Canada with a lieutenant-governor, cabinet and a bicameral legislature. | Canadian dollar | French English | Roman Catholic Protestant | Oats, barley, wheat, buckwheat, rye, flax, mixed grains, peas, beans, potatoes, turnips, beets, hay, clover, corn, alfalfa, fruits, maple products, cattle, swine, sheep, horses, poultry; butter, cheese; lumber, pulp, paper; fur farms; fish (cod, herring, mackerel, lobsters, salmon); gold, iron, titanium, asbestos, lime, dolomite, brucite, quartz, pyrite, copper, zinc, silver, chrome, molybdenum, cement, sand and gravel, limestone, clay, granite, non-ferrous metals; tobacco, clothing, chemicals, meat packing, petroleum products, cotton yarn and cloth, railroad rolling stock, shipbuilding, brass and copper products, electrical goods, hydroelectric power. |
| ST. PIERRE AND MIQUELON | French territory with a governor, privy council and elective general council. | French franc | French | Roman Catholic | Fish; silver fox; dried cod and cod liver oil; sienna earth, yellow ocher. |
| SALVADOR, EL | Republic with a president, a cabinet and a one-house legislature. | colon | Spanish | Roman Catholic | Coffee, cotton, corn, tobacco, henequen, sugar cane, rice; balsam and other woods; gold, silver; cotton textiles, henequen bags, sugar. |
| SASKATCHEWAN PROVINCE | Province of Canada with a lieutenant-governor, cabinet and unicameral legislature. | Canadian dollar | English French | Protestant Roman Catholic | Wheat, oats, barley, rye, flax, potatoes, hay, clover, alfalfa; cattle, swine, sheep, horses, poultry; fish; furs; gold, copper, lead, zinc, lignite, petroleum, gas, cadmium, silver, uranium, salt, sodium sulphate, selenium, tellurium, coal; flour, feed, meats, butter, cheese, eggs; beer; machinery, hydroelectric power, printing and publishing, aerated mineral water. |
| TRINIDAD AND TOBAGO | British colony with a governor and executive and legislative councils. | B. W. I. dollar | English | Roman Catholic Protestant Hindu | Coffee, cocoa, sugar cane, citrus fruits; cattle; petroleum, asphalt; rum, canned grapefruit juice, sugar. |
| UNITED STATES | Federal republic with a president, vice-president and two-house legislature. | dollar | English | Protestant Roman Catholic Jewish | Corr., hay, tobacco, wheat, cotton, oats, soy beans, potatoes, barley, sorghum, peanuts, rye, rice, citrus fruits, fruits, sugar beets, sugar cane, vegetables, tree nuts, feed grains and hay; livestock; fish; lumber; petroleum, coal, cement, iron, natural gas, copper, sand and gravel, zinc, lead, stone, gold, silver, molybdenum, bauxite, phosphates, mica, sulphur; foods, transportation equipment, machinery, primary metal products, electrical machinery, textiles, chemicals, paper and wood products, beverages, dairy products. |
| VIRGIN ISLANDS (U. S.) | Territory of the U. S. with an appointed governor. | dollar | English Creole | Roman Catholic Protestant | Sugar cane, vegetables, citrus fruits, coconuts; cattle; fish; rum, bay rum, bay oil, molasses, handicrafts, sugar, lime juice, hides, bitters. |
| WINDWARD ISLANDS | Four British colonies under a governor. Each of the four islands has its own separate governing councils. | B. W. I. dollar | English | Roman Catholic Protestant | Cocoa, sugar cane, nutmeg, sea island cotton, limes and other citrus fruits, coconuts, bananas, cassava; cattle; fish; sugar, bay rum, bay oil, bitters, hides, rum, molasses, copra, arrowroot starch, charcoal, spices, lime products. |
| YUKON TERRITORY | Canadian territory administered by a commissioner and an elective legislative council. | Canadian dollar | English | Protestant Roman Catholic | Gold, silver, lead, copper, coal; furs; timber; grains and vegetables. |

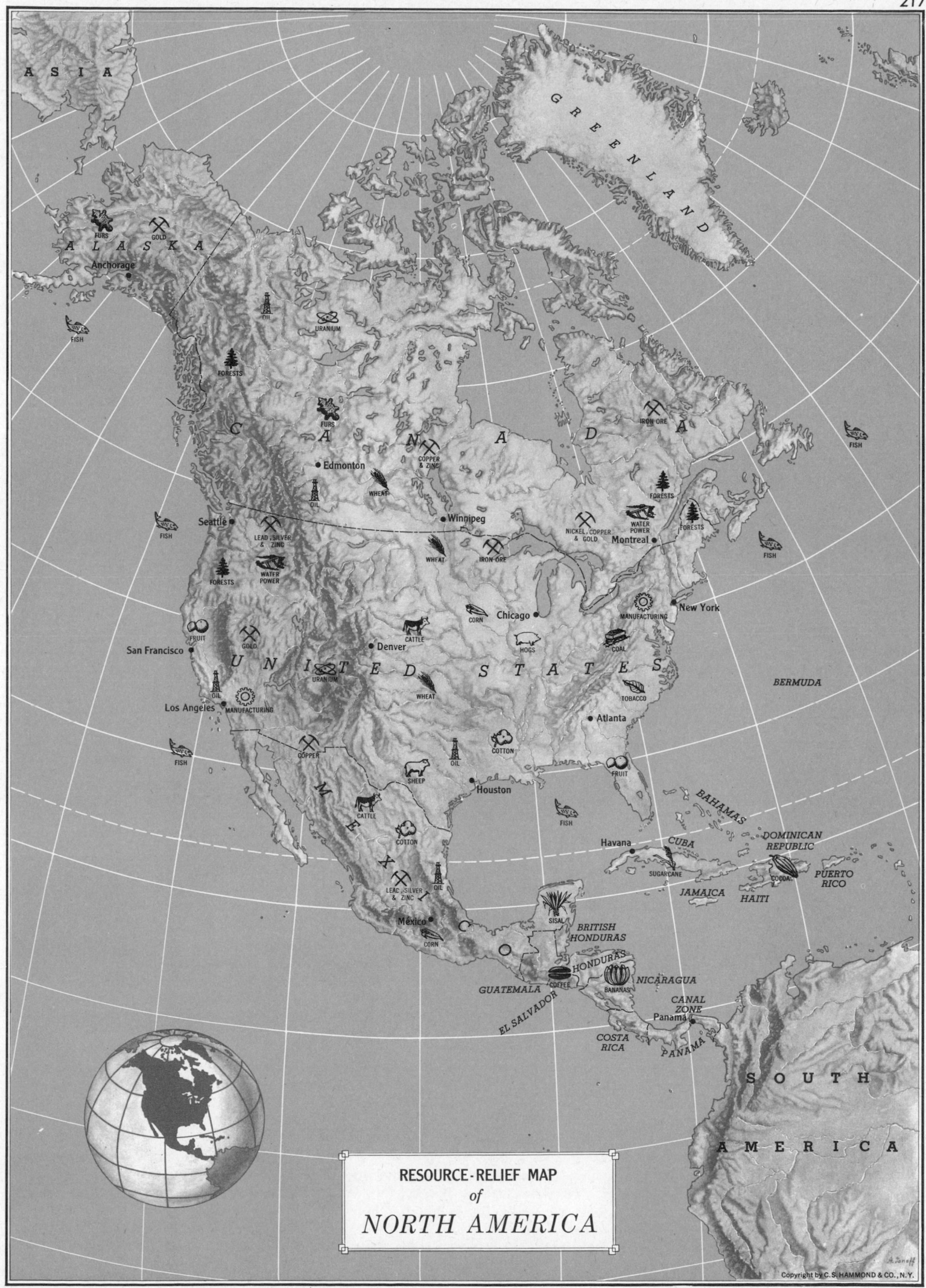

RESOURCE-RELIEF MAP
*of*
NORTH AMERICA

Hamilton Wright

South America's roads undergo constant improvement.

Hamilton Wright

Chile's coastal region extends for more than 2,500 miles along the Pacific. The country has many ports but its harbors cannot accommodate large ships.

**SOUTH AMERICA**—It is a common error to think of South America as being directly south of the United States. A glance at the globe will show that this is far from the truth. Except for the bulge to the west and the southern tip, all of South America is east of the Atlantic coast boundary of the United States. This places South America much closer to Africa than North America is to Europe. A theory has been advanced, though never proved, that at one time Africa and South America were joined.

Smaller than North America by nearly two million square miles, and representing one-seventh of the world's total land area, South America is the fourth largest continent.

With the equator crossing South America on a line with the Amazon River, two-thirds of this southern neighbor is in the tropics and the balance in the temperate zone. In common with other lands situated in the Southern Hemisphere, it has the further disadvantage of being far removed from the principal world markets. These factors, together with the history of the continent, explain why it has not developed as rapidly as the United States, although discovered at the same time. But in spite of the handicaps of climate, position and history, South America has an extensive trade with the United States and Europe. And, although for centuries the Spaniards robbed it of its buried treasures, South America still possesses great mineral wealth.

South of the Isthmus of Panama, the great line of mountains which extends the entire length of North America becomes the mighty Andes. Second only to the Himalayas, they follow the western coast to Cape Horn, rising steeply from the Pacific in long ranges of snow-capped peaks and wide plateaus. Mount Aconcagua is the highest peak in the Americas and rises to a height of twenty-three thousand feet. Several lesser peaks are active volcanos. To the south the range begins to narrow and the coast is bordered by a tattered fringe of islands clothed with pines and swept by fierce northwesterly winds.

On the east are two broad plateaus, the Guiana and Brazilian highlands, which might be compared with the Laurentian highlands and the Appalachian chain of North America. Between the eastern slope of the Andes and these plateaus lie broad lowlands. The grassy, tree dotted plains, or *llanos*, of the Orinoco Basin in Venezuela and Colombia, provide fine pasturage between the dry and rainy seasons. In the dry season they practically revert to desert. To the south are the dry plains, or *pampas*, of Northern Argentina, which is the great cattle country of the continent.

The Amazon—largest river system in the world—drains over one-third of the continent. This area is equal to two-thirds that of the United States. This mighty river is thirty-five hundred miles long and in places is over fifty miles wide. It flows through the densest tropical forest in the world and much of it is unexplored.

The La Plata River is actually the estuary for three rivers, the Parana, with a drainage area almost as large as that of the Mississippi, the Uruguay and the Paraguay. Buenos Aires, metropolis of the Southern Hemisphere is situated on the south bank of the La Plata 175 miles from the Atlantic. Buenos Aires is one of the world's most beautiful cities and important seaports. The above mentioned rivers drain Northern Argentina, Uruguay and Paraguay.

Other rivers of less importance are the São Francisco of Brazil, the Magdalena of Colombia, the Orinoco of Venezuela, and the Río Colorado of Argentina.

Lying in the Andes at an altitude of over twelve thousand feet is Lake Titicaca. With an area over half that of Lake Erie, it is the highest navigable lake in the world.

Much of Argentina and Chile are in southern latitudes that compare with the northern latitudes of the United States, but there are only sections where the climate is similar. Parts of Chile have a climate that compares with the Pacific coast states, and sections of Argentina and Uruguay are comparable to the east coast of the United States.

The heat is insufferable and the rainfall extremely heavy in the low Orinoco and Amazon Valleys. In the northern countries, while hot, the climate is tempered by the highlands. At the extreme southern tip the seasons are exactly the opposite of those in North America, but there is not the vari-

Snowy mountain slopes provide ideal ski runs for winter vacationists in Argentina.

Peru's cultural past is evident to all who visit her attractive cities.

ation in temperature. This is due to the influence of oceans and mountains.

The only important indentations on the Pacific are found along the rugged coast of southern Chile and the Gulf of Guayaquil in Ecuador.

The high temperature and humidity of the tropical regions, together with many insects and diseases, discourage the activity of white people and even sap the strength of the natives. Large areas of swamp and rugged mountains have made the development of transportation difficult and expensive. Only with the growth of air travel has it been possible for the Andean countries to contact one another with relative ease.

In the main, South America is sparsely settled, with the greatest density of population along the coasts. The original inhabitants were Indians, but, due to the early colonization by the Spanish and Portuguese, many of the present inhabitants are *mestizos,* a mixture of Indian and Spanish or Portuguese blood. The remainder is largely composed of Italian and German immigrants. Except in Brazil, where the official language is Portuguese, Spanish is spoken in all the other independent countries.

The three countries of Chile, Argentina and Uruguay, where there has been the largest European immigration, are making rapid industrial progress. The rest of South America is still largely agricultural. Most of the countries produce only one or two major products and there is little diversity of crops. Practically all exports are raw materials, while imports are manufactured goods.

With the exception of the three col-onies of British, French and Dutch Guiana, all of South America is composed of independent republics. In spite of a common language and form of government there is little interchange between countries. In general they are more concerned with world trade than dealing with each other.

Since the early coming of the Spaniards, South America has continued to yield great stores of precious metals. The Andes are rich in minerals, and the eastern highlands contain iron, gold, and diamonds. Some coal is found in Brazil, Chile and Colombia, but not in great quantity. Water-power and oil are being utilized to make up for this lack.

Ecuador, Peru and Chile are all west coast countries, which, until the opening of the Panama Canal, were practically isolated from the rest of the world. Bolivia, having no outlet to the sea, moves nearly all of her exports through the seaports of Chile and Peru.

**CHILE**—Sometimes called the "Shoestring Republic," Chile stretches along the west coast for twenty-six hundred miles, from the borders of Peru to Cape Horn. It has a variety of climate ranging from frigid to torrid. This long, narrow and mountainous country is one of the most progressvie in South American. It is one of the three republics where there are more white people than natives. The other two are Argentina and Uruguay.

From north to south Chile is divided into three regions: the desert, a dry sub-tropical region which includes the coast, and a section that is forested. The greatest mineral region lies between Santiago and the Peru-vian border. In the northern half of this area are the nitrate fields which have produced almost the entire world's supply of this important fertilizer. The nitrate beds located in the Pacific coastal desert (Atacama) were wrested from Peru during the War of the Pacific (1879-83) from which Chile emerged victorious. Chile's fame as a nitrate region has waned with the introduction of synthetic nitrate into world industry. The country is now seeking to stimulate the export of wine, honey and livestock. In the southern half there are deposits of copper, iron, gold and silver. Chile ranks next to the United States in the mining of copper and supplies about 20 per cent of the world's output.

**PERU**—This country is an extension of the narrow and arid coastal plain in northern Chile, with the Andes occupying fully half of the land. A densely wooded tropical region drops down in the east to meet the low plains of Brazil.

About a fourth of the population is white, most of whom are Spanish. The balance are *mestizos* (mixed) or Indians. Descendants of the ancient Incas, the Indians of Peru, are found principally living on the high mountain slopes of the Andes, and sailing their strange fiber craft on Lake Titicaca. These Indians have domesticated the llama and the alpaca, two animals which are native to this region, and which have never been raised successfully elsewhere. The llama is a sure-footed animal upon which the Indians depend for food, clothing and transportation. Used as a beast of burden in this lofty arid country, the llama, like the camel, can

One of the most beautiful cities of South America, Rio is a fine example of urban planning.

Fish abounds in South American rivers and coasts.

Although in the torrid zone, Brazil's climate is tempered by rainfall, favorable winds and altitude.

go several days without water. The alpaca is too small to carry loads and is raised for its very long wool.

**ECUADOR**—Peru and Ecuador have a similar climate and topography except for the northern part of the coastal plain of Ecuador. This plain is as fertile as any area in South America and is the principal agricultural section of Ecuador. The principal crops are cacao and coffee, the former heading the articles of export. Ecuador's coffee has been increasing in importance since its cacao, blighted by witches'-broom, has suffered an appreciable decrease in export. Tagua, a substitute for ivory, is produced in

limited quantities. Ecuador is world-famous for its amazing variety of wild birds. The country contains one-fourth of all recorded species in South America.

**BOLIVIA**—Shut off from the sea by Chile and Peru, Bolivia is one of the most sparsely populated countries in the world. It consists of a high plateau in the southwest that is cold and dry, and wet tropical lowlands in the north and east. Though Bolivia's surface is three-fifths lowlands, the country includes one of the highest inhabitable regions in the world. The Andes spread out into two great chains of mountains which enclose a plateau nearly as high as the peaks themselves. Lake Titicaca, one of the highest of the larger lakes in the world, is situated on this plateau.

Bolivia ranks next to the Malay Peninsula and the Indonesian islands in its tin deposits, and is well supplied with nearly all the known metals. Strangely enough, although having local supplies of coal, necessary in smelting, it is usually cheaper to import coal.

Lack of capital, the high cost of transportation, and the scarcity of labor, have retarded mining in all the countries of the Andes. Only the natives can do manual labor in the high altitudes and the people are not inclined toward mining. However, mining is the chief industry. Aside from tin, there is abundant amounts of gold, copper, bismuth, antimony, lead, zinc, wolfram and oil. Tobacco, wine and vanilla, together with quinine and rubber, are exported.

**BRAZIL**—Covering nearly half the continent and with half the population, Brazil lies almost entirely in the tropics. This re-

public is 10 per cent larger than the United States, and has three times the area of Argentina.

The Amazon and its tributaries have a total length of over nineteen thousand miles, of which thirteen thousand are navigable. This huge system extends through more than half the country's area.

The great plateau country, known as the Brazilian Highlands, lies in the south and east. It is composed of numerous mountain ranges and river valleys. Rio de Janeiro, the second largest city on the continent, is located in this region. Hemmed in by mountains and a wide bay, it has one of the finest and most beautiful harbors in the world.

Brazil at one time was the greatest rubber-producing country. Brazil has embarked on a program of intensified manufacturing. Silk, cotton and woolen mills have sprung up all over the eastern seaboard. Shoes and hats are becoming major products. Many paper mills are being built to utilize some of the billion acres of forests that cover half the land area. Its greatest mineral wealth has yet to be exploited, though one of the largest estimated deposits of iron ore in the world is now being developed. The country produces nearly fifty percent of the world's coffee. Efforts to do away with the one-crop system are gaining success and coffee is no longer the economic tyrant that it was. A growing cacao industry now ranks second in the world, while tobacco, rice, cotton and sugar are attaining commercial significance.

**URUGUAY**—This is the smallest republic in South America. It has a fine climate with

Inland lakes and quiet forests offer their charm to the natural serenity of the rural areas of South America.

the winds of the ocean modifying the temperature.

Since the Spanish brought sheep and cattle to the grassy plains of Uruguay in the 17th century, it has been a stock raising country. Today it is one of the leading meat producers of the world. Only a small percentage of the arable land is devoted to the raising of crops and it is limited in both minerals and manufacturing.

**PARAGUAY**—One of the two republics of South Amercia that is completely surrounded by other nations. Little has been done to develop its natural resources.

Most of the surface of western Paraguay is a low, swampy and unhealthy plain. The climate in the north is hot and unsuited to the white man. Most of the people live in the southern area east of the Paraguay River. It is a country of small villages, grazing, and farm lands, which depends upon the rivers for means of transportation.

Extending from Bolivia, across the western third of Paraguay, and south into Argentina, is the Gran Chaco, a great plain.

**THE ARGENTINE REPUBLIC**—The early colonists' anticipation of finding silver and gold in Argentina prompted them to name the country for the Latin word meaning silver. Although the colonists' search for great mineral wealth was in vain, the fertile soil and temperate climate have fostered the country's great economic progress. The Republic is the second largest of the South American countries.

The Gran Chaco, in the northern part, is a land of forests, lakes and swamps, which is largely unexplored. The grassy plains of the *Pampas* occupy a large area of Argentina. This cattle country and farm land extends from the Atlantic coast to the Andes in the west, and northwest to the highlands which reach into Brazil. The rich grazing lands, which have led to Argentina becoming a large exporter of meat and wool are in the center of the *Pampas*; the largest meat refrigerating plant in the world is at Buenos Aires.

Only about 10 per cent of the land is under cultivation, although it has been said that 80 per cent is capable of producing crops, grass or forests. An idea may be gained from this of the great possibilities for future development that lie ahead.

Argentina is an agricultural and commercial, rather than an industrial country. It has been hindered in the development of manufacture by a shortage of coal, the lack of water power, and an inadequate supply of minerals.

Descendants of the Spanish settlers are the leaders of the country, with most of the farm population consisting of Italians. Immigrants from the British Isles have taken to sheep raising, and many Germans have migrated to Argentina. Today half of the population is foreign-born or are descendants of immigrants.

**NORTH COAST COUNTRIES**—Colombia, Venezuela, and the British, French and Dutch Guianas, are all on the north coast.

**COLOMBIA**—The only South American country having a coastline along both the Atlantic and Pacific oceans. Half the country is high in the rugged Andes; the other half

Gendreau

Stockraising forms an important part of the economic life of South America.

Gendreau

Native handicraft display in Venezuela.

The most cosmopolitan city of South America, Buenos Aires has been strongly influenced by Europe.

Pan-American-Grace Airways

lies in unhealthy tropical plains. Three cordilleras of the Andes traverse in a parallel line from north and south which forms a barrier between the seacoast and the rich inland valleys. The chief source of welath is coffee. Colombian coffee is the finest in the world and the bean is jealously guarded. Ninety percent of the exported coffee is shipped to the United States. A type from the area around Medellin commands the highest price per pound in the world. Surpassed by Brazil in quantity, Colombia's coffee yields to none in quality. Next to coffee in export value is oil. The fields are to a large extent a continuation of those in Venezuela. Production has been over twenty million barrels since World War II. Other resources include platinum, emeralds and coal.

**VENEZUELA**—One of the most productive oil regions in the world, is on the coast of the Caribbean. Easy access to this coast from the interior affords great possibilities for commercial and industrial development. Venezuela's land area is distinguished by its llanos or wide lowlands along the Orinoco River. The river is navigable for a course of 700 miles and is connected to the Amazon system by a canal. Coffee, chiefly from the basin of the Maracaibo, is second only to that of Colombia. A ranking producer of petroleum, Venezuela's exploitation of oil is fraught with difficulties which have never been successfully surmounted. Virgin forests cover the country and include about 600 species of wood. At Margarita is located a profitable pearl industry. Salt, asphalt, coal and gold figure as the main mineral resources.

**THE GUIANAS**—On the north coast of South America are the only European possessions on the continent. Their combined area is 178,000 square miles. The surface is composed of an alluvial plain at sea-level and another plain farther south which is distinguished by hills and forested mountains. The climate is tolerable except in the south where the northeast trade winds do not prevail. Though their topography is similar their economic importance varies greatly from east to west. British Guiana, about the size of Great Britain, is the most highly developed. Dutch Guiana (Surinam) has no important industries except the mining of bauxite. French Guiana, the easternmost colony, is of little importance economically. Its sparse population and the excessive emphasis placed on the mining of gold has led to the neglect of its fertile soil. Mineral resources in the form of gold and diamonds are about equally divided among the three Guianas.

## SOUTH AMERICA

| POLITICAL DIVISION | GOVERNMENT | MONETARY UNIT | PRINCIPAL LANGUAGES | PRINCIPAL RELIGIONS | MAJOR PRODUCTS |
|---|---|---|---|---|---|
| ARGENTINA | A republic with a president, vice-president, appointive cabinet, elective senate and house of deputies. | peso | Spanish | Roman Catholic | Wheat, corn, oats, barley, linseed, rye, grapes and other fruit, tobacco, vegetables; yerba maté; cattle, sheep; quebracho, lumber; petroleum, natural gas, gold, lead, silver, tungsten; vegetable oils, wines, hides, wool, meats, textiles, metal products, vehicles and machinery, chemicals, wood and paper products, leather, clothing and shoes. |
| BOLIVIA | A republic with a president, vice-president, appointive ministers of state, and an elective senate and chamber of deputies. | boliviano | Spanish Indian | Roman Catholic | Potatoes, corn, barley, quinoa, nuts, cocoa, vanilla, rubber, quinine; tin, zinc, lead, copper, silver, antimony, tungsten, sulphur, petroleum; cattle; textiles, flour, cement, tobacco products, hides, beer, earthenware. |
| BRAZIL | Federal republic with a president, vice-president, appointive secretaries of state and a bicameral legislature. | cruzeiro | Portuguese | Roman Catholic | Coffee, corn, rice, cotton, cacao, sugar cane, cassava, beans, carnauba wax, medicinal plants, oranges, balata, tobacco, fibers, castor oil; livestock; timbo, brazil nuts; iron, manganese, gold, rutile, zirconium, diamonds, mica, bauxite, quartz, beryllium, chrome, tungsten, silver; foods, textiles, chemicals, pharmaceuticals, metallurgical products, paper and wood products, hides, vegetable oils, machinery. |
| CHILE | A republic with a president, appointive cabinet of ministers of state, elective senate and chamber of deputies. | peso | Spanish | Roman Catholic | Wheat, potatoes, oats, rice, barley, corn, kidney beans, lentils, fruits; fish; livestock; copper, silver, nitrates, iodine, iron, sulphur, gold, manganese, coal; foods, textiles, leather, wood products, cement, chemicals and pharmaceuticals, wines and beer, wool. |
| COLOMBIA | A centralized federal republic with a president, vice-president, appointive cabinet, elective senate and house of representatives. | peso | Spanish | Roman Catholic | Coffee, sugar cane, corn, rice, root crops, cotton, bananas, cacao, wheat, tobacco, cinchona; cattle; rubber, fibers; petroleum, gold, silver, platinum, emeralds, salt; textiles, beer, sugar, cement, flour, tobacco products. |
| ECUADOR | A centralized republic with a president, a cabinet and an elective bicameral legislature, the senate including representatives of various social, economic and governmental groups. | sucré | Spanish Indian | Roman Catholic | Rice, cacao, coffee, bananas, rubber, kapok, cotton, tagua (ivory) nuts, cinchona; livestock; gold, petroleum, salt, balsa wood; textiles, toquilla (Panama) hats, buttons, sugar, flour, shoes, beer and liquors, chemicals, pharmaceuticals, cement, soap, candles. |
| FALKLAND ISLANDS | British colony with a governor and an executive and a legislative council. | pound | English | Protestant Roman Catholic | Forage crops, sheep; wool, skins, tallow, whale oil, whale-meat meal. |
| GUIANA, BRITISH | A British colony with an interim constitution providing for a governor, nominated executive and appointed legislative councils. | B. W. I. dollar | English | Protestant | Sugar cane, rice, coconuts, coffee, citrus fruits, cacao; balata, rubber, green heart and other timber; livestock; bauxite, diamonds, gold; textiles, milled rice, beer and rum, lime rum and oil, sugar, woods, molasses, charcoal, matches. |
| GUIANA, FRENCH | Overseas department of France governed by a prefect, with an elective council-general. | French franc | French | Roman Catholic | Rice, cacao, bananas, sugar cane, corn, cassava, woods; gold; hides, rosewood essence, shoes, rum, fish glue. |
| GUIANA, NETH. (SURINAM) | Self-governing part of the Netherlands Union with an appointed governor, an appointive council of ministers, an advisory council and an elective legislative body. | Surinam florin | Dutch | Christian Moslem Hindu | Rice, citrus fruits, coconuts, coffee, bananas, sugar cane, cacao, balata, corn, tobacco; lumber; gold, bauxite; sugar, rum, plywood, molasses. |
| PARAGUAY | A centralized republic with a president, an appointed cabinet and a one-house legislature. The constitution of 1940 greatly increased the president's powers. | guarani | Spanish Indian | Roman Catholic | Cotton, tobacco, sugar cane, rice, cassava, yerba maté, corn, citrus fruits; cattle, hides; lumber, quebracho; iron, manganese, copper; canned meats, vegetable oils, petit-grain oil, tobacco products. |
| PERU | A republic with a president, two vice-presidents, appointive cabinet and a two-house legislature. | sol | Spanish Indian | Roman Catholic | Cotton, sugar, potatoes, barley, corn, rice, wheat, coca, quinoa, cacao, tobacco, coffee, quinine, flax, rubber, balata, guano; fish; livestock; petroleum, lead, zinc, copper, silver, gold, vanadium; textiles, foodstuffs, cement, leather, wool, hides, pharmaceuticals, paper products, clothing, metal products. |
| URUGUAY | A republic governed (as of March, 1955) by a national council, an appointive cabinet and a two-house elective legislature. | peso | Spanish | Roman Catholic | Wheat, corn, linseed, oats, sunflower seeds, peanuts, barley, rice, citrus fruits, peaches, grapes, vegetables, tobacco; sheep, cattle; gold; meat, hides, wool, textiles, leather, boots and shoes, wines. |
| VENEZUELA | A republic, with a president, appointive cabinet and elective, two-house legislature. | bolivar | Spanish | Roman Catholic | Coffee, cacao, sugar cane, cotton, tobacco, coconuts, tonka beans; balata, dividivi, rubber; livestock; fish and pearls; petroleum, iron, gold, coal, copper, phosphates, magnesite, asphalt, salt, diamonds; textiles, leather, sugar, cement, wood products, foodstuffs, beverages, soap, tobacco products, meats, milk; refined petroleum. |

224

RESOURCE-RELIEF MAP
*of*
SOUTH AMERICA

VENEZUELA

COLOMBIA

BRITISH GUIANA

SURINAM

FRENCH GUIANA

ECUADOR

P E R U

BOLIVIA

B R A Z I L

PARAGUAY

A R G E N T I N A

URUGUAY

C H I L E

FALKLAND ISLANDS

Bogotá

Manaus

Belém

Lima

Salvador

São Paulo

Rio de Janeiro

Santiago

Buenos Aires

OIL

OIL

OIL

GOLD

IRON ORE

BAUXITE

COFFEE

COCOA

FORESTS

RUBBER

BANANAS

COTTON

FISH

SUGARCANE

SUGARCANE

LEAD, ZINC & COPPER

COTTON

COCOA

TIN, SILVER & TUNGSTEN

IRON ORE

TOBACCO

COFFEE

COPPER, NITRATE & SULPHUR

LEAD & ZINC

CORN

FISH

IRON ORE

SUGARCANE

COTTON

YERBA MATÉ

FORESTS

CATTLE

FLAX

GRAPES

CORN

SHEEP

FISH

CATTLE

WHEAT

FISH

SHEEP

OIL

SHEEP

Copyright by C. S. HAMMOND & CO., N. Y.

The British Isles retain many landmarks of a by-gone age which bear mute testimony to its historical heritage.

*TWA—Trans World Airline*

*British Travel Association*

England's rolling countryside is specked with tiny cottages which augment the natural beauty of the landscape.

**EUROPE**—Eurasia is the world's largest land mass and includes both Europe and Asia. Europe occupies about a third of the western end of Eurasia, and, with the exception of Australia, is the smallest continent. It is the most densely populated for its size and no other continent has so many separate nations. Nearly all of these countries have distinctive customs and speak different languages. This does much to explain Europe's turbulent history.

Actually Europe is a huge peninsula, subdivided into a number of lesser peninsulas, caused by the oceans and inland seas which encroach upon it. Its irregular form, together with the mountain barriers, and the presence of important islands near the continent, have contributed to the growth of individual nations. Differences in language and customs have a natural tendency to arouse a strong nationalistic spirit. This keeps people apart and makes them suspicious of those with different customs, and who speak alien tongues. Among mountain people an independent spirit and love of freedom is even more pronounced.

In the northwest, two peninsulas are formed by the Baltic Sea. The countries of Norway and Sweden occupy the Scandinavian Peninsula. Denmark is on the Jutland Peninsula between the Baltic and North Seas. To the south, Portugal and Spain comprise the Iberian Peninsula. The peninsular boot of Italy thrusts out into the Mediterranean, and the Balkan Peninsula is surrounded by the Black Sea and the Adriatic, Ionian and Aegean Seas of the Mediterranean.

Great Britain is prevented from being a peninsula only by the narrow English Channel, and was once a part of the mainland. The entire course of history has been changed by this strip of water which made England an island. The same may be said for the Straits of Gibraltar separating Europe from Africa. But for this nine-mile passage, the Mediterranean would have had no outlet to the Atlantic.

Europe may be divided into five natural regions: (1) the Northwest Highlands, (2) the Central Plains, (3) the Central Highlands, (4) the Southern Mountains and Plateaus, and (5) the Southern Lowlands.

Most of the British Isles, a section of France, and a good part of the Scandinavian Peninsula are included in the Northwest Highlands. This is the coastal region with excellent harbors where men have made their living by the sea, and commerce has become most important. In those places where coal and iron are found it has led to an industrial life. This highland region enjoys a cool, temperate climate and people are energetic.

The great Central Plains extend from the British Isles to the Ural Mountains that separate Europe from Asia. These plains range from the tundra regions of the Far North to the Caspian Sea, the Caucasus Mountains, and the Black Sea of the Southeast. In the Southwest they reach into southern France. Within such an extensive area there are naturally great differences in climate. There is also great diversity of vegetation and the occupations of the people.

South of the Arctic tundra belt are exten-sive evergreen forests that reach westward to the Scandinavian Peninsula. In the grasslands to the south of the forests are large areas used for the growing of grain, and stock grazing is the chief occupation in the drier southeastern sections. This is the region of the dry and treeless steppes.

The Central Highlands include the plateau in central France and take in parts of Belgium, southern Germany, Austria, and the Czecho-Slovakian area. It is the region of forest, water-power, and varied mineral resources. The industrial districts of Central Europe are the outgrowth of the great deposits of coal and iron found here.

The impressive peaks of the Alps rise south of the Central Highlands, forming one of the many ranges of Southern Europe. The Apennines extend the length of Italy, and other ranges follow the eastern coast of the Adriatic through Yugoslavia and Albania to the southern tip of Greece. Spreading out to the east they include most of the Balkan Peninsula. To the north the Carpathian Mountains swing east and north around the valley of the Danube and then run northeast to almost circle the Plain of Hungary. Farther to the east, the Caucasus Mountains reach from the Black to the Caspian Sea. Separating France and Spain are the Pyrenees, and the Sierra Nevadas are in southern Spain bordering the Mediterranean.

The Alps are particularly famous for their scenic grandeur. The Sierra Nevadas and Carpathian Mountains are rich in mineral resources, and some of the world's greatest oil fields are in the Caucasus. The mountains of Italy lack valuable ores and have been largely stripped of their forests.

The Southern Lowlands of the Danube

British Travel Association

Scotland's lakes and hills are offset by the curious charm of her historical cities.

Danish Information Office

The sea-washed land of Denmark lies at the entrance of the Baltic endowing Danish seaports with excellent facilities for maritime commerce.

Valley and the Plain of Hungary represent some of the finest farming and grazing land in the world.

The extreme irregularity of the European coastline has been of great importance to the life of the people. With the North and Baltic Seas, the Mediterranean and Black Seas, penetrating far into the interior, only Central Europe and Eastern Russia are very far from the coast. Although the combined areas of South America and Africa are nearly five times that of Europe, the coastline of Europe is longer.

A majority of the great seaports of the world are in Western Europe. Its people have led the world in sea-faring.

Europe has a generally mild, temperate climate, particularly in the western areas, which are warmed by ocean currents and the winds blowing over these waters. Even the British Isles have a mild climate in spite of being in the same latitude as Labrador. Greater extremes of temperature exist in eastern Europe where these winds lose their moderating effect.

Due to the Alps blocking the cold north winds, and the influence of the warm waters of the Mediterranean, the southern shores of Europe enjoy a mild year-round climate. Excepting in eastern Europe, where the rainfall is light, there is generally sufficient moisture for agriculture.

An abundance of mineral resources, fine forests, rich farmlands, water-power, and the seas plentifully supplied with fish, have encouraged Europe's growth. An invigorating climate, waterways, harbors and access to

the oceans of the world, have contributed to its commercial importance.

The climate and natural resources of each country have largely determined their individual occupations and prosperity.

## GREAT BRITAIN AND NORTHERN IRELAND

—The British Isles and the British Commonwealth of Nations owe much of their commercial and industrial growth to the daring and initiative of their early mariners. Although we usually think of the British Isles as comprising Great Britain and Ireland, it actually consists of nearly five thousand islands. Within the small compass of the islands there is a considerable variety of topography.

In Northern Ireland there are many lakes, including the largest one of the island, Lough Neagh, as well as a range known as the Mourne Mountains. A large portion of the country consists of the basalt plateau of Antrim.

Northern Ireland, or Ulster, as the six counties are sometimes called, is the seat of a very extensive lace and linen industry. In County Down and County Antrim there are highgrade deposits of granite and bauxite which are being exploited. Shipbuilding is a major industry centered in the capital, Belfast.

In Scotland the three well-marked divisions stand out, the highlands, the southern uplands, and between these two, the central lowlands, into which four-fifths of the population is crowded. The lowlands contain the richest agricultural land, as well as the coal

fields. They are penetrated by three great estuaries, the Firths of Tay and Forth on the east, and of Clyde on the west, so that communication coastwise or overseas is everywhere easy.

Scotland has some of the largest shipbuilding yards in the world on the Firth of Clyde. Sheep and cattle are raised in large numbers since the land is not well suited to agriculture.

The Welsh cliffy upland is flanked to the north and east by small coal fields, but the greatest field lies to the south. A belt of limestone running from Bill of Portland to Tees Bay, and bearing at many points valuable iron ores, serves as a rough boundary of industrial England, for to the south and east of it, apart from the metropolis, agricultural interests predominate. Lying to the west of the limestone band is the Devon-Cornwall peninsula, where great bosses of granite and slate form the famous moors.

Wales, after 700 years as a part of the English kingdom, retains its individuality and is nationalistic in speech, dress and customs. The Welsh language is Celtic akin to the Gaelic of Ireland. It is the only speech of nearly one-tenth of the people.

Channel Islands, lying across the English Channel off the coast of Normandy, and Scilly Islands, lying southwest of Land's End, enjoy an almost complete freedom from frost and severe weather.

Because of the density of population Great Britain is far from self-sustaining and must depend upon the raw materials and products of other countries. This has led to the development of her world-wide commerce, a large part of which is carried on with her far-flung and numerous colonies. Agriculture is intensive with much importance placed on livestock. Many of the world's most valuable breeds of farm animals have been de-

The snow-encrusted northlands of Scandinavia force its northernmost inhabitants to lead nomadic existences.

veloped on English farms. This is exemplified by such names as Guernsey, Shropshire, Jersey, Hereford, Hampshire and Plymouth.

**IRELAND**—Except for coastal hills and mountains, the country is largely an ill-drained plain dotted with lakes and peat-bogs, and crossed by the sluggish Shannon. In the southwest is the beautiful Killarney Lakes region which attracts many tourists each year. Although little of the land is suitable for large scale agriculture, grass and fodder crops are abundant and provide stockraising needs which is the major industry of the country. The Shannon River, Royal Canal, and the Grand Canal provide an excellent inland waterway system of transportation. Shannon airport, near Limerick, is a major international airway terminal. Horse-breeding is the most famous of Irish farm industries. A prosperous tourist trade is developing.

**NORWAY AND SWEDEN**—With its saw-toothed coast, great fiords, and neighboring islands, it is natural that Norway, occupying the western part of the Scandanavian peninsula, would be a maritime country. Norway's long coast line, facing the Atlantic, is edged with lofty cliffs and seamed with deep fiords. Islands, countless in number, fringe the coast. Most of the country is a rocky, rugged and barren land, about 20 per cent of which is forested. The rivers are short and torrential, but provide the finest salmon fishing in Europe. The Kjolen Mountains which form the backbone of the peninsula separate Norway from Sweden. These mountains rise in many parts to over 6,000 feet, the highest peaks being over 8,000 feet.

Norway is the land of the "midnight sun". From Trondheim northward at least a part of the disk of the sun is visible from May through July. But the winter nights are 17 hours long and midday seems like twilight during the winter months. Another striking

Norway, with its deep fiords and high cliffs, contain many placid scenes of captivating grace.

feature is that much of the area above the Arctic Circle is warmer than some regions further south. Northeast Norway is the warmest part of the country in the summer.

Sweden consists primarily of a tableland sloping from the Kjolen Range to the Baltic. No less than 8 per cent of the surface of Sweden is water, the immense number of lakes covering almost 15,000 square miles. The two largest, Vanern and Vattern, in the southern portion of the country, are connected by a system of canals. Besides the large number of small islands which fringe the coast, Sweden includes the two large Baltic islands of Gotland and Oland. Most of the people live in the southern part of their country while the Norwegians have settled chiefly near the fiords. Hydro-electric development is in an advanced stage in both countries.

In Sweden, iron deposits are among the richest in the world. Swedish steel is universally famous for its fine qualities. The making of machinery for export is a major industry. Swedish agriculture is in a very high state of development, and exports wheat, bacon and butter in large quantities. In forestry and sawmilling the nation has evolved such advanced methods that foreign technicians in the industry often go to Sweden to study logging and forestry. Nearly half of her exports are in pulp and paper products.

**DENMARK**—Denmark occupies a peninsula and numerous islands lying at the entrance to the Baltic. It is a lowland country characterized by many lakes, ponds and short rivers. Its sandy shores are shallow, with

lagoons shut in by shifting sand bars. Most of Denmark is farm land, about half of which is used for grazing. The Faeroe Islands produce fish, mutton and wool for the homeland.

Dairy farming is the country's chief industry, the products of which comprise nearly all her exports. Greenland, the largest island in the world, is Denmark's only possession.

**ICELAND**—The republic is an island in the north Atlantic consisting of a great tableland averaging 2,000 feet above sea level. Of its whole area barely a quarter is habitable. The surface is dotted by over 100 volcanic peaks. There are many boiling springs and the geysers are world-famous. It is too cold for agriculture but has rich grazing land for sheep and cattle.

**FINLAND**—Finland consists of a great plateau, ranging from 400 to 600 feet in elevation. The southern half of the plateau has about 25 per cent of its area occupied by thousands of shallow lakes, many of them linked by short natural or artificial channels, providing many miles of navigable waterways. Forests cover the greater part of the country which has led to lumbering, paper-making and the manufacture of woodenware. Over half the population is engaged in agricultural pursuits which are carried on under great difficulties.

**THE NETHERLANDS**—The tiny kingdom of the Netherlands, lacking natural resources has been largely a nation of seafarers for centuries. Along the canals, the meadows are often ten or twelve feet below the water line, and between the land and the sea at

The European peasant has long been a factor in the economic development of the Old World.

high tide there may be a difference of twenty-five feet or more. The land is protected by embankments and dikes, and it may be pictured as a great trough, the floor of which slopes down from east and southeast toward the North Sea. The rivers which flow across the country from the higher continent beyond, are at their mouths, frequently below the level of the sea, into which they have to be lifted by canals and locks across the dams or dikes. A large part of the land has been reclaimed from the sea and little by little it has become a fertile country.

**BELGIUM**—Smaller than Holland, Belgium is the most densely populated country in Europe. Situated between England, Holland, France and Germany, it is in the very center of industrial Europe. The country is well watered, and has two principal rivers, the Scheldt and the Maas. Four-fifths of the land is under cultivation, and although over half the people are engaged in either farming or stock raising the country still does not raise sufficient food to feed her people. Belgium's intensive industrialization has been at the expense of its agriculture, for the valley of the Sambre-Meuse, the chief industrial center, is also the richest farming land. Metals from the Katanga region of the Belgian Congo are intensifying industrial activities, and Belgium is regaining her pre-war level of output. The textile industry is reviving also. The nation furnishes a great variety of farm products and is known for its world-famous breed of horses.

**LUXEMBURG**—The Grand Duchy of Luxemburg, smaller than the state of Rhode Island, is one of Europe's oldest states. An abundant store of iron ore has encouraged mining, smelting and some manufacturing. International trade of the duchy has been carried on through a customs union with Belgium.

Symbol of the "City of Light", the Eiffel Tower represents a capital that has known splendor, wealth and a long cultural tradition.

**LIECHTENSTEIN**—Only 27 square miles larger than San Marino, Liechtenstein is separated from Switzerland by the Rhine river and is bounded by Austria in the east. The population is largely German but Switzerland administers its postal and telegraph facilities, and its currency is Swiss. It also belongs to the Swiss customs union. The tillable soil, a long strip along the Rhine river, yields grapes, grains and pasturage for a small cattle industry.

**FRANCE**—France is largely an agricultural country where the farmers, instead of living on their farms, usually live in nearby villages. Although rich in minerals, it has lagged behind both England and Germany as an industrial country. The surface is diversified, but much of it is lowland, with a few level plains. In the center is a triangular plateau called the Auvergne Mountains, with a height of something over 3,000 feet. The Cevennes form the eastern edge of this plateau, and from them to the Vosges, the tableland continues. There is a mountainous area in Brittany, but the greatest heights are on the frontiers, the Jura, the Pyrenees, and the Alps separating it respectively from Switzerland, Spain and Italy. The Ardennes in the northeast are less lofty. The Seine drains the

north, the Loire and the Garonne the west, and the Rhone the east and south. France enjoys a delightful climate. Only in the region of the Alps is real winter encountered. Protected by the mountains to the north, the balmy area along the Mediterranean is a magnet that has drawn countless vacationers. Many semi-tropical plants and fruits are grown in this section. Indeed, France's greatest resource is her soil. Grape culture is by far the leading agricultural pursuit, for France produces a billion gallons of wine in a vintage year. Yet, the country imports millions of gallons. Textile production, particularly the silk industry centered around Lyons, is a valuable undertaking in the country; cotton mills are the leading producers of goods.

**MONACO**—The Principality of Monaco is one of the smallest states in the world. It possesses the administrative organs and institutions of larger nations in miniature. It has no taxes for it is supported by the gambling casino of Monte Carlo from which its own citizens are barred. The most striking feature of this 370 acre state is the Monagasque Acropolis on a headland 200 feet above the water. The Prince's Palace, a magnificent structure, is located on it. On the

Switzerland is a country whose imposing mountains and dense forests are a lure to tourists who come for relaxation and sport.

Austria's small villages are nestled among the deep valleys of its mountainous countryside.

Mediterranean coast, surrounded by the Riviera of France, Monaco offers to the tourist auto-racing, skiing, bathing, sailing, and of course, gambling. There is also an oceanographic museum.

**SWITZERLAND**—This rugged little country is a completely land-locked republic nestling among the beautiful Alps. It has succeeded in maintaining its neutrality and independence while the rest of Europe engaged in costly and devastating wars. Between Lake Constance on the Rhine and Lake Geneve on the Rhone are Lakes Neuchatel, Zurich, Lucerne, Brienz, Thun, all of which drain to the Aar. Lake Geneve and Lake Constance each exceed 200 square miles in area. Many of Switzerland's mountains are permanently covered with snow. Capitalizing upon its wonderful mountain and lake scenery, and making the most of its limited resources, Switzerland has become one of the most prosperous of the smaller nations. With its snow-capped peaks rising from ten to fifteen thousand feet, it has been the playground of Europe for many years.

**GERMANY**—There are two natural regions in Germany, the northern plain and southern highlands. The former is the most extensive

agricultural region. The land which borders Denmark is favorable to the grazing of cattle, and, in the northeast, large numbers of sheep and goats are raised. The minerals found in the central highlands have had the greatest influence upon the development of Germany in the last fifty years.

Except for ample supplies of coal and potash, Germany is deficient in natural resources. During the glacial period, sand was deposited over the plains region and as a result the soil is not naturally fertile. Only by intensive cultivation and the heavy use of fertilizers, made from potash, is much of the soil made productive. Germany's great scientific development has been largely the result of solving agricultural problems, and of searching for new uses to utilize the coal reserves.

Germany's only access to the ocean, and world trade, is through the Baltic and North Seas. To make the most of this she has developed a remarkable system of waterways. The Rhine rises in the Alps and flows through the fertile lowlands of western Germany to the border of Holland, and thence to the sea. The Elbe, Weser, and the Oder flow north across the low plain of Germany. The Oder empties into the Baltic. The Elbe and Weser flow into the North Sea. All three

are navigable far inland for ocean-going vessels. The rivers, together with fifteen hundred miles of canals, form a network of waterways which provide cheap transportation.

**AUSTRIA AND HUNGARY**—Austria is characterized by its beautiful mountain scenery, over 90 percent of the land is classified as mountainous, which has contributed to development of one of its largest industries—tourist and resort trade. However, over 80 per cent of the land is productive and half of this is under cultivation. In contrast, Hungary is largely comprised of a low fertile plain. The country is primarily agricultural and is a great grain and wine producer.

**CZECHOSLOVAKIA**—This land-locked country contains strategic routes between north and south Europe of economic and political value. The country has two large mountain ranges, the Carpathian in the east and the Sudeten in the west. Czechoslovakia is famous for its subterranean caverns and its spas and mineral springs. The people are energetic and progressive and there are valuable forest resources, fertile soil and varied mineral deposits.

**THE BALKANS**—They include Rumania, Yugoslavia, Bulgaria, Albania, Greece and European Turkey. Located at the gateway to Asia, and on a natural route connecting the two continents, this region has been a battleground for centuries. Repeated invasions from various directions have resulted in a number of racial groups and religious beliefs. The rugged nature of the country has isolated the people into many rival factions with intense racial and national spirit.

**YUGOSLAVIA** consists essentially of a mountainous core, which stretches from the

The Italian peninsula possesses many fine harbors whose importance rivals those of the rest of Europe.

Both nature and time have combined to produce the bizarre interior of this cave in Yugoslavia.

Dinaric Alps in the northwest to the Balkan Mountains on the Bulgarian frontier. The only valley which cuts the mountains and forms a passageway is that of the Marava River, which with that of the Vardar, leads from Beograd to Thessalonike. Beyond the Sava-Danube, as far as the northern boundary, the land is low and swampy near the rivers, with a few minor elevations. The chief concentrations of people are around Zagreb and Beograd. Yugoslavia has recently experienced a crisis resulting from a boycott by the Cominform countries and the Soviet Union. Forced to turn to the West, the nation has signed trade agreements with several Western European states. Its greatest problem is the lack of communications between its regions. The more highly developed coastal areas have access to outside markets, but the distribution of economic aid further inland is hampered by the mountains which impose a rugged barrier between the provinces.

**RUMANIA**—In western Rumania the Carpathian Mountains from the northwest and the Transylvanian Alps from the southwest meet in the center to form a crescent. To the north and west of this crescent is the Transylvanian plateau; to the south and east are the plains of Moldavia and Walachia. The principal rivers are the Danube in the south which enters the Black Sea at Sulina, and the Prut in the northeast and the Siret in the southeast—both of which connect with the Danube.

**BULGARIA**—The country is hilly and well watered by numerous streams, of which the Isker, Struma and Maritza are the most important. Although nearly one-third of the country's area is in forests, only a small part of the wood is used commercially since about one-fourth of the forest area is completely unproductive. Many of the forests consist of scrub timber and a sizeable portion of the good forests are inaccessible. Eighty percent of Bulgaria's population is employed in agriculture, the chief crops being tobacco and cereals. Attar of rose and silk are important products.

**ALBANIA**—Albania is a mountainous country on the western side of the Peninsula. In the center, part of the plateau is cultivable, and in the south there is fertile alluvial soil with grazing land on the slopes.

**GREECE**—With a very long coast line on the Aegean and Ionian Seas, and a large number of islands, including Crete, Mitylene, Dodecanese and Chios, the area is generally mountainous. The mountains, though not very high, divide the country into a number of small districts, between which communication is difficult. It is the sea which links the different regions of Greece.

**ITALY**—Once the hub of the known world, Italy's importance declined as the age of exploration and discovery opened up the ocean routes of the world. Taking no part in this period of conquest and empire building,

she did not acquire colonies. Lacking unity she was in no position to demand her share of the rich prizes of newly discovered land being acquired by other European nations.

With the opening of the Suez Canal and tunnels through the Alps, her trade somewhat improved, but the absence of the necessary minerals prevented her from keeping pace with industrial development elsewhere in Europe.

The south slope of the Alps belongs to Italy. At the point where the Alps reach the Mediterranean, the Apennines begin. These mountains follow the length of Italy and form a rugged backbone which extends through the island of Sicily. The southern and western parts of the peninsula have been subjected to volcanic eruptions, and Vesuvius, Etna, and Stromboli are still active volcanoes. The chief lowlands are in the Po Valley with narrow coastal plains east and west of the Apennines. The majority of the people, and most of the agriculture and manufacturing, are located in the Po Valley. Consequently Northern Italy does not experience the poverty to be found in Southern Italy. It is from the south that most of the immigrants to the United States have come.

Italy's colorful history, scenery and balmy climate have attracted many tourists which has in some measure offset an unfavorable balance of trade.

**SAN MARINO**—San Marino is one of the oldest republics in the world and is the smallest. It has always been on good terms with its big neighbor, Italy, by whom it is surrounded. The state was founded in the fourth century by Marinius of Dalmatia, a stonecutter. Except for a few invasions, its liberty has been respected, even by Napoleon. During World War II it declared war

The coastal cities of Portugal draw heavily on the sea for their principal commodity.

against Germany and was occupied by the Germans and subsequently liberated by the British. Much of its revenue is obtained through the sale of its postage stamps issued for the benefit of collectors.

**SPAIN AND PORTUGAL**—About three-fourths of the Iberian Peninsula is a granite plateau with a range of mountains dividing it in the center. The rivers that flow through this region through deep gorges block transportation and are unsuited for navigation, waterpower or irrigation. The dry climate, lack of water, a rugged land formation, poor soil and an absence of transportation have been great obstacles standing in the way of the economic development of both Spain and Portugal. A portion of the land in the valleys and plains has been made fertile through irrigation and farming is the main industry. Fishing is important along the Portugal coast, although a great part of the coast is too rugged for harbors. There are forests in most of the higher areas where half the world's supply of cork is produced.

**ANDORRA**—Tiny Andorra is in the Pyrenees Mountains between France and Spain. It is not a republic, as is often supposed, but a joint dependency of France and the Bishops of Urgel in Spain. Its mountains are high and arid, and its valleys contain poor soil so that the people are nearly all engaged in pastoral pursuits. The one product of the soil is tobacco. Sheep-herding is the main industry, and the need of hay for winter

A land of color and birthplace of Western culture, Greece still posesses the remnants of a once glorious past.

forage further limits the use of soil for any other crop.

**POLAND**—Poland was for many years a chiefly agricultural country but good supplies of coal, lead, iron and zinc have helped her industrial progress to such an extent that it is now almost equally industrial and agricultural. Most of the land is comprised of a plain, although there are low hills in the northeast in Pomerania. The lower regions of the Vistula have marshes, sand dunes and lakes. The central plain of Poland with an elevation of about 500 feet is traversed by great rivers, the most important being the Oder and the Vistula. Her strategic position near the Baltic Sea, and the lack of natural boundaries and barriers, have long made the people of this country, as well as those of the former Baltic States, the victims of stronger nations seeking an outlet to the sea.

**U. S. S. R.**—Almost three times the size of the United States and comprising more than one-seventh of the world's land surface, the Union of Soviet Socialist Republics sprawls across two continents. Most of Russia is a great plain reaching from the Pacific to its western boundaries. Its position in northern latitudes and the absence of protecting barriers result in an extreme climate with long, cold winters. Vladivostok, on the Pacific coast, and the ports on the Arctic Ocean and Baltic Sea are closed by ice during the long winter months. Vladivostok, however, is kept open the year round by ice-breakers. In no part of the land is the rainfall heavy, and there are frequent and widespread

droughts, which bring hunger and starvation to its people.

From the Black Sea in the south to the Arctic Ocean, and from the Baltic Sea to the Ural Mountains, which divide Asiatic Russia from European Russia, is a vast lowland. To the east of the Urals is Siberia, two-thirds of which is a flat, unbroken plain. In the far north the ground has been found to be frozen to a depth of over six hundred feet. This presents peculiar problems, if the government is to succeed with plans to mine the ores found there and industrialize this Arctic region. Here in the tundra country the moss, upon which the reindeer of the nomadic tribes feed, is often five feet thick.

South of the tundra belt is a great evergreen forest covering billions of acres, where lumbering and fur-trapping are the chief occupations.

Russia's supply of minerals is so great and widely scattered that the extent of many of the deposits is still unknown. There are immense reserves of coal in both European and Asiatic Russia. Copper, platinum, iron, gold, manganese and other minerals are found in the Urals. Some of the richest petroleum deposits in the world are located in the Baku region of the Caspian Sea.

Great strides have been made in industrial development, with the manufacture of iron and steel, machinery, textiles and leather goods in the lead.

In spite of climate, high cost of manufacture and difficulties of transportation, the U. S. S. R. is a country that is largely self-sustaining, and has become increasingly important industrially.

232

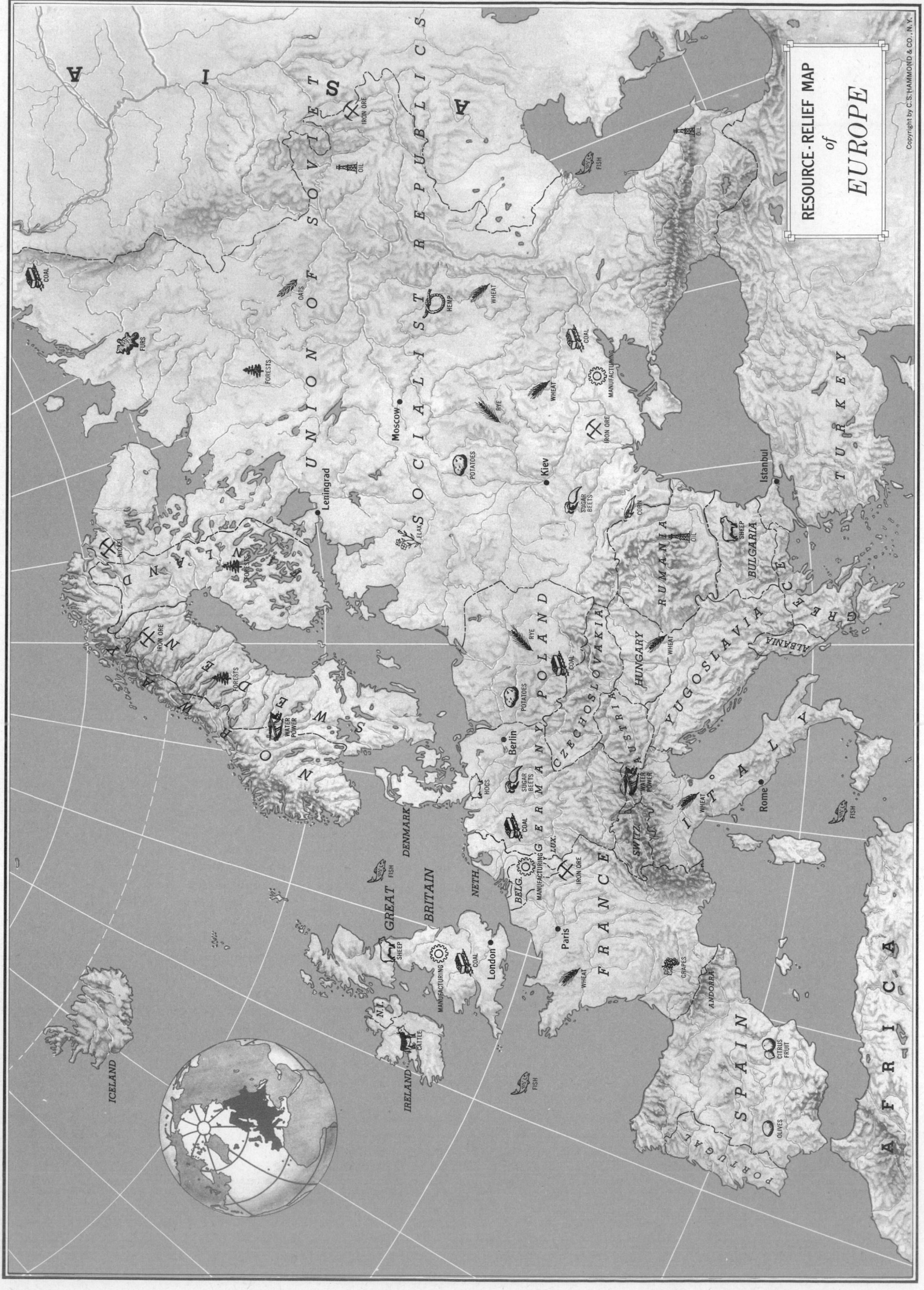

RESOURCE · RELIEF MAP
*of*
EUROPE

Copyright by C.S. HAMMOND & CO., N.Y.

| POLITICAL DIVISION | GOVERNMENT | MONETARY UNIT | PRINCIPAL LANGUAGES | PRINCIPAL RELIGIONS | MAJOR PRODUCTS |
|---|---|---|---|---|---|
| ALBANIA | A Soviet-type republic with president, cabinet and one-house legislature. Actually ruled by the politburo, supreme body of the Communist party. | lek | Albanian | Moslem Orthodox Roman Catholic | Corn, tobacco, wheat, flax, oats, barley, rye, rice, olives, fruit; cattle, sheep; fish; wool, hides; dairy products; furs; bitumen, salt, lignite, aluminum, petroleum, copper, chromite; flour, olive oil, cheese; cement, leather. |
| ANDORRA | A republic under the joint suzerainty of the French State and the Bishop of Urgel in Spain, with a council general of 24 elective members. Executive authority is vested in the First Syndic. | French franc and peseta | Catalan | Roman Catholic | Tobacco, potatoes, barley; sheep, cattle; lumber. |
| AUSTRIA | Republic with a president, chancellor and vice-chancellor, cabinet of ministers and a two-house assembly. | schilling | German | Roman Catholic | Rye, wheat, oats, barley, corn, potatoes, sugar beets, hops, grapes, rapeseed, flax, hemp, tobacco; iron, copper, lead, magnesite, graphite, coal, aluminum, petroleum, lignite, salt; timber; pulp, poultry and livestock; steel, machinery, machine tools, chemicals, textiles, paper, building materials, processed foods, leather. |
| BELGIUM | Constitutional, hereditary monarchy. King appoints a cabinet of ministers. Parliament consists of a senate and chamber of deputies. | Belgian franc | French and Flemish | Roman Catholic | Wheat, rye, oats, barley, potatoes, sugar beets, flax, tobacco, vegetables, fruit, hops, hemp, bulbs, livestock; fish; coal, iron, zinc, lead, copper, tin, silver; coke, steel, machinery, textiles, lace, glass, chemicals, uranium refining, sugar, margarine, cheese, vinegar, alcohol, beer, matches, paper, foods, beverages, wool, cut diamonds, dairy products. |
| BULGARIA | Soviet-type republic with a one-house legislature, which elects a presidium whose president is the nominal chief of state. Actual power resides in the politburo, highest body of communist party. | lev | Bulgarian | Eastern Orthodox | Wheat, corn, barley, oats, rye, tobacco, fruit, cotton, sugar beets, potatoes; livestock, silkworm cocoons; fish; coal, salt, bauxite, copper, iron, lead, manganese, silver, kaolin; tobacco products, attar of roses, sugar, flour, textiles, leather goods, shoes, lead concentrates, wines and spirits. |
| CZECHOSLOVAKIA | Soviet-type republic with a president, a cabinet and a one-house elective parliament. Actual power resides in the politburo, highest body of communist party. | koruna | Czech and Slovak | Roman Catholic | Wheat, rye, barley, oats, corn, hops, sugar beets, grapes, potatoes; poultry, livestock; timber; coal, lignite, iron, graphite, garnets, silver, copper, lead, salt, manganese, zinc; beer, spirits, malt, metals, munitions, machinery, iron and steel, porcelain, shoes, textiles, wood products, pulp and paper, sugar, leather, foods, chemicals, rubber products. |
| DENMARK | Constitutional, hereditary monarchy with a two-house, elective legislature and an appointive council of ministers. | krone | Danish | Protestant | Barley, mixed grains, oats, rye, wheat, potatoes, sugar beets; livestock; fish; clay; ships and transportation equipment; butter, bacon, eggs, cheese, milk, footwear, clothing, machines, chemicals, tobacco products, metal goods, leather goods, beverages; stone, earthenware and glassware, electrical goods. |
| FINLAND | A republic with a president, a one-house elective diet and an appointive council of state. | markka | Finnish and Swedish | Protestant | Hay, potatoes, wheat, oats, barley, rye, sugar beets, flax, hemp, vegetables; cattle, horses, sheep, pigs, poultry, reindeer; wood and timber; fish; copper; lumber, plywood, furniture, pulp and paper, cardboard, textiles, butter, eggs, cheese, flour, leather, chemicals, china and glass, foodstuffs. |
| FRANCE | A republic with a president, a two-house elective parliament and an appointive council of ministers. | French franc | French | Roman Catholic | Sugar beets, potatoes, wheat, oats, barley, rye, corn, turnips, fruits, nuts, wine grapes, buckwheat; cattle, sheep, pigs, horses; fish; coal, iron ore, lignite, salt, bauxite, pyrites, potash salts, glass, kaolin, natural gas, iron and steel, chemicals; silk, cotton, rayon, wool and linen, textiles, clothing, lace, perfumes and cosmetics, automobiles, machinery, dairy products, beet sugar, wines, porcelain, aluminium, foods, leather, spirits. |
| GERMANY | Country is divided between two governments — a democratic **Federal Republic of Germany** in the west and a Soviet-dominated **German "Democratic" Republic** in the east. **Federal Republic** has an elected federal diet and council who elect the president and chancellor. **German "Democratic" Republic** has a communist-controlled legislative branch which elects the president, cabinet and prime minister. | East German and West German Deutsche Mark | German | Protestant Roman Catholic | Wheat, rye, barley, oats, potatoes, sugar beets, fruits, hops; pigs, cattle, poultry, horses; fish; forest products; coal, lignite, iron, copper, potash, sulphur, salt, uranium, lead, zinc, fluorspar, gypsum, vanadium, aluminum; automobiles, steel, cement, diesel oil, gasoline, cotton yarn, woolen yarn, rayon fiber, beet sugar, beer, wines, optical instruments, sulphuric acid, sodium bicarbonate, chemicals. |
| GIBRALTAR | British Crown Colony administered by a governor, executive and legislative councils. | pound | English and Spanish | Roman Catholic | Fish for export and processing of commodities for local consumption. |
| GREAT BRITAIN: | | | | | |
| ENGLAND AND WALES | England is governed directly by the government of Great Britain and Northern Ireland. Executive power resides nominally in the Crown but actually in the prime minister and cabinet, appointed with consent of House of Commons. | pound | English and Welsh (Celtic) | Protestant | Potatoes, turnips, beets, oats, wheat, barley, rye, hay, beans, peas, cabbage, vetches, hops, fruits; sheep, cattle, pigs, horses, poultry; fish; coal, coke, gas, iron, copper, lead, nickel, tin, clay; dairy products, wool, cotton and linen textiles; electrical goods, vehicles, steel, scientific instruments, cutlery, foods and beverages, tobacco products, clothing and shoes, chemicals, pottery, china, machinery, locomotives, carpets, knitwear, lace, pharmaceuticals. |

| POLITICAL DIVISION | GOVERNMENT | MONETARY UNIT | PRINCIPAL LANGUAGES | PRINCIPAL RELIGIONS | MAJOR PRODUCTS |
|---|---|---|---|---|---|
| NORTHERN IRELAND | Executive power vested in appointed governor and cabinet responsible to legislative two-house parliament. | pound | English and Gaelic | Protestant Roman Catholic | Potatoes, oats, flax, turnips, hay; cattle, sheep, pigs, poultry; basalt and igneous rocks, sand and gravel, grit and conglomerate, chalk, clays; linen, rayon, woolen goods, carpets, hosiery, cotton goods, shirts, collars, underwear, shipbuilding, aircraft, marine machinery, rope, tobacco, whiskey. |
| SCOTLAND | A secretary of state for Scotland in the British cabinet has in his charge four departments for Scotland (agriculture, education, health and home). Authority in other matters is exercised by other members of the British cabinet. | pound | English and Gaelic | Protestant | Turnips, potatoes, wheat, barley, sugar beets, flax, vegetables, forage crops, fruits; sheep, cattle, pigs, horses; coal, iron ore, granite, sandstone, limestone, slate, lead, clay; steel, machinery, tools, locomotives, electronic equipment, linoleum, shipbuilding and repair, watches, clocks, jute bagging, burlap, textiles, hosiery, thread, lace, carpet, yarn, chemicals, whiskey, ale, paper, bricks and other clay products, preserves, boots and shoes, furniture. |
| GREECE | A constitutional hereditary monarchy with a prime minister, cabinet of ministers and an elective assembly. | drachma | Greek | Greek Orthodox | Wheat, barley, corn, oats, rye, tobacco, currants, sultana raisins, olives, figs, grapes, cottonseed, sesame seed; sheep, goats, cattle, pigs, horses, mules; fish; iron ore, sulphur, emery, magnesite, zinc, lead, lignite, marble, bauxite; textiles, olive oil, foods, wines, chemicals, leather, wood and paper, metal products, machinery. |
| HUNGARY | Soviet-type republic with a president and a presidential council selected by the national assembly. Actual power in hands of politburo, highest organ of communist party. | forint | Hungarian | Catholic Protestant | Wheat, corn, rye, barley, oats, potatoes, sugar beets, tobacco, grapes and other fruits, peppers, hemp, flax; pigs, cattle, sheep, horses, poultry; fish; coal, lignite, petroleum, natural gas, iron ore, bauxite, manganese; flour, sugar, distilling, brewing, iron and steel, wines, textiles, paprika, chemicals, leather, metal products, wood and paper products. |
| ICELAND | A republic with a president, an elective, two-house legislature and an appointive cabinet of ministers. | króna | Icelandic | Protestant | Hay, potatoes, turnips, hothouse fruits and vegetables; sheep, poultry, horses, cattle; fish; dairy products, meats, animal and vegetable oils, hides, skins, leather, clothing, textiles, frozen fish, herring oil, herring meal. |
| IRELAND | A republic with a president, premier and an elective, two-house parliament. | Irish pound | English and Gaelic | Roman Catholic | Hay, potatoes, turnips, fodder, beets, sugar beets, oats, wheat, barley, cabbage, rye, flax; cattle, sheep, pigs, horses, poultry; fish; coal, peat, gypsum; tobacco, dairy products, foodstuffs, beer, malt, clothing, meats, textiles, boots and shoes, wood and paper products. |
| ITALY | A republic with a president, a two-house, elective legislature and an appointive cabinet. | lira | Italian | Roman Catholic | Wheat, corn, oats, sugar beets, potatoes, tomatoes, rice, olives, grapes, lemons and other fruits, hemp, tobacco, nuts; fish; sheep and goats, cattle, pigs, horses, donkeys; iron ore, sulphur, zinc, bauxite, lead, mercury, barite, copper, marble, manganese, lignite; textiles, chemicals, wines, automobiles and machinery, electrical goods, beet sugar, olive oil, cheese, processed foods, clothing. |
| LIECHTENSTEIN | A principality headed by a prince and an elective, one-house legislature. | Swiss franc | German | Roman Catholic | Grain, fruit, grapes, wood; cattle, pigs, chickens; cotton textiles, wine, leather, false teeth, pottery, wood-carving. |
| LUXEMBOURG | A grand duchy and hereditary, constitutional monarchy with an elective chamber of deputies and appointive minister of state and cabinet. | Luxembourg franc | Mosel-frankisch (German dialect) | Roman Catholic | Oats, potatoes, wheat, rye, grapes; livestock; iron ore, slate, gypsum, sand and gravel; iron, steel and metal working; chemicals, non-metallic minerals, beverages, tobacco, leather, wines, dairy products, quarrying. |
| MALTA | A self-governing colony of Great Britain with a governor, lieutenant-governor, a prime minister, a cabinet and an elective legislative assembly. | pound | Maltese and English | Roman Catholic | Wheat, barley, potatoes, onions, grapes and other fruits, cumin seed, cotton; goats, sheep, pigs, cattle; fish; lace, filigree, wine, footwear, beer, cigarettes, buttons, pipes, gloves. |
| MONACO | A principality. The prince's authority exercised through a state ministry and 3 government counsellors. The one-house legislative body is elective. | French franc | French | Roman Catholic | Principal revenue derived from Monte Carlo gambling casino. Tobacco, postage stamps, perfume, liqueurs, olive oil, oranges. |
| NETHERLANDS | A constitutional hereditary monarchy governed by the queen, her ministers and a two-house legislature, partly elective and partly chosen by provincial councils. | guilder | Dutch | Roman Catholic Protestant | Potatoes, sugar beets, rye, wheat, oats, barley, flax, legumes, flower bulbs, seeds, vegetables, fruit; cattle, pigs, sheep, horses, poultry; fish; coal, petroleum, salt; leather, rubber, footwear, metal products, textiles, paper, building materials, chemicals, foods and beverages, clothing, shipbuilding, cheese and other dairy products, fertilizers, ceramics, cement, tobacco products. |
| NORWAY | A constitutional hereditary monarchy headed by the king, his council of state and a two-house, elective legislature. | Norwegian krone | Norwegian | Protestant | Hay, potatoes, oats, barley, wheat, rye, fruits, vegetables; dairy products, livestock; herring, cod and other fish; sulphur, iron, copper, zinc, silver, nickel, molybdenum; timber, pulp, cellulose, paper, canned foods, electro-chemical products, transportation equipment, salted, dried and canned fish, leather, basic metals, textiles, fertilizers, shipbuilding. |

| POLITICAL DIVISION | GOVERNMENT | MONETARY UNIT | PRINCIPAL LANGUAGES | PRINCIPAL RELIGIONS | MAJOR PRODUCTS |
|---|---|---|---|---|---|
| POLAND | A Soviet-type "People's Republic" headed by a one-party legislative Sejm which elects an executive council of ministers. The supreme de facto power is in the hands of the politburo, highest organ of communist party. | zloty | Polish | Roman Catholic | Potatoes, straw and hay, rye, sugar beets, mangolds, oats, barley, wheat, peas, beans, flax, hemp, rapeseed; livestock; fish; zinc, lead, coal, salt, iron ore, petroleum, natural gas, phosphates, lignite; iron and steel products, coke, foods and beverages, textiles, cement, lime, bricks, electrical goods, chemicals, wood, timber, paper, cellulose, leather and leather products, glass. |
| PORTUGAL | A "unitary corporative republic" with a president, premier, and a one-house, elective legislature. | escudo | Portuguese | Roman Catholic | Wheat, corn, oats, barley, rye, rice, French beans, potatoes, grapes, olives; livestock; cork, lumber, resin; sardines, tuna and other fish; copper pyrites, coal, copper, tin, kaolin, cement, wolfram, sulphur, tungsten, iron; wines, olive oil, canned sardines, textiles, porcelain, tiles, embroideries, lace. |
| RUMANIA | A Soviet-type "People's Republic" with a 17-member presidium, cabinet of ministers and a one-house legislature. Supreme power resides with politburo, highest organ of communist party. | leu | Rumanian | Rumanian Orthodox Mohammedan | Wheat, barley, rye, corn, oats, potatoes, sugar beets, hemp, flax, grapes, fruits, tobacco; lumber; sheep, cattle, pigs, horses; petroleum, natural gas, salt, coal, lignite, iron and copper ores, gold, silver, bauxite, lead, manganese, zinc; flour, brewing and distilling, iron and steel, metal products, textiles, wood and paper products. |
| SAN MARINO | A republic with two regents, a council of state and an elective, one-house legislature. | lira | Italian | Roman Catholic | Cattle, hides, wines, quarrying. |
| SPAIN | A nominal monarchy governed by a chief of state. The legislative Cortes prepares laws subject to the veto of the chief of state. A king is to be chosen by a regency council upon the death or incapacitation of the chief of state. | peseta | Spanish Catalan | Roman Catholic | Wheat, barley, potatoes, oranges, olives, oats, rye, rice, corn, peas, beans, grapes, onions, sugar beets, esparto, flax, hemp, pulse, cork, nuts; pigs, sheep, goats, donkeys, mules, horses, poultry; sardines, tuna, cod and other fish; coal, lignite, iron ore, lead, iron pyrites, potash, zinc, mercury, sulphur, copper; textiles, wines, olive oil, paper, cement, hides, preserved and canned fish and shellfish, paper products. |
| SWEDEN | A constitutional, hereditary monarchy with a prime minister, council of state and a two-house, elective legislature. | krona | Swedish | Protestant | Hay, sugar beets, potatoes, fodder crops, oats, wheat, rye, barley; forest products, cattle, pigs, sheep, horses, poultry; fish; iron ore, sulphur, arsenic, zinc, copper, silver, gold, lead, manganese; lumber and wood products, machinery, textiles, iron and steel and metal goods, chemicals, dairy products, electric power, tobacco products, brick, porcelain and glass, shipbuilding, matches. |
| SWITZERLAND | A republic with a president, vice-president, an executive federal council and a two-house, elective legislature. | Swiss franc | German French Italian Romansch | Protestant Roman Catholic | Wheat, potatoes, sugar beets, rye, oats, barley, fruits, tobacco; livestock; salt, iron, manganese; dairy products, textiles, watches and clocks, chemicals, foods, wines, dyes, instruments. |
| TURKEY | A republic with a president, a cabinet and a one-house, elective legislature. | Turkish pound | Turkish | Mohammedan | Tobacco, cereals, olives, cotton, figs, nuts, fruits; cattle, livestock; fish; chromium, iron ore, copper, coal, lignite, meerschaum, manganese; textiles, iron and steel, paper, rugs, olive oil. |
| U.S.S.R. | A federation of 15 socialist republics with a two-chamber legislative assembly (Supreme Soviet) which elects the executive presidium and council of ministers. The policy of the state is largely defined by the Central Committee of the communist party, the only legal party. | ruble | Russian, Ukrainian, White Russian, Uzbek, Tatar, Azerbaizhani, Georgian, Lithuanian, Armenian, Yiddish, Latvian, Mordvinian, Chuvash, Tadzhik, Esthonian, Kazakh. | Russian Orthodox Mohammedan | Wheat, rye, oats, barley, corn, sugar beets, sunflower seeds, cotton, forage crops, flax, hemp, potatoes, tobacco; cattle, sheep, goats, pigs, horses; lumber; furs; fish; coal, peat, petroleum, iron, lignite, copper, lead, zinc, nickel, aluminum, phosphates, manganese, gold, sulphur, potash, asbestos, platinum, salt, chromite; steel, machinery, textiles, sugar, flour, meats, automobiles, paper, synthetic rubber, foods, wines, chemicals. |
| VATICAN CITY | The Pope, who is elected for life by the cardinals of the Roman Catholic Church, exercises absolute legislative, executive and judicial power. He appoints a governor of the state and delegates diplomatic and judicial power. | lira | Italian Latin | Roman Catholic | |
| YUGOSLAVIA | A Soviet-type republic combining 6 republics under a central government with a president, a federal executive council and a two-house elective legislature. Actual power rests with the secretary-general of the communist league of Yugoslavia, the only legal party. | dinar | Serbo-Croatian Slovenian Macedonian | Eastern Orthodox Roman Catholic | Wheat, barley, rye, oats, corn, sugar beets, hemp, hops, opium, tobacco, flax, alfalfa, vegetables, fruits; sheep, cattle, pigs, goats, horses, poultry; coal, lignite, iron, copper, lead, salt, zinc, mercury, antimony, petroleum, bauxite, chrome, cement; lumber, textiles, foods, beverages, sugar, wood-distillates, wines. |

Africa's varied topography lends itself to all sorts of livlihoods ranging from the industrial to the pastoral.

Many natural phenomena, like these hot springs, are present in Africa's terrain.

**AFRICA**—The term "sleeping giant," which has often been used in referring to China, can best be applied to Africa. This second largest continent is three times the size of China, and is richer in natural resources, but it has only one-third the population. Although two of the world's oldest civilizations once flourished along its northern shores in Egypt and Carthage, the rest of Africa long remained shrouded in mystery.

Joined to Asia by a land bridge at the Isthmus of Suez, and only separated from Europe by the narrow Strait of Gibraltar, it was not until the nineteenth century that Europe finally set about the conquest of the "Dark Continent." For centuries an unfavorable climate and natural barriers combined to guard its secrets and hold back development.

Almost midway of its length Africa is crossed by the equator. Being triangular in shape, this places most of the continent in unhealthy torrid regions. Added to this its coastline is steep and regular, and offers few places for ships to anchor. The rivers as regards navigability cannot be considered in the same light as the great rivers of Europe, Asia and the Americas. None, except the Nile and the Congo, has unimpeded entrance to the sea.

The deltas of the Niger and the Zambesi are choked by silt and, on nearly all, navigation is impeded by shoal or cataract. Nevertheless the Congo and the Nile with their tributaries have many thousands of miles of navigable waterways, as have the Niger, the Benue and the Zambesi.

To the north, the Sahara Desert proved an effective barrier of sand and intense heat, which for hundreds of years prevented any important exchange of ideas or trade between the white man of the north and the black man in the south. Extending from the Atlantic to the River Nile, and reaching from the Mediterranean to the Sudan, the dry Sahara is a region of desolation. What trade existed between Asia, Europe and Africa followed caravan routes which led from oasis to oasis. The only life to be found there is at these scattered oases.

It was only following the explorations of Livingstone, Stanley and others in the last century, that Europe became aware of the possibilities existing in Africa. Then, suddenly awakened to the great wealth that had been overlooked, the European powers rushed in to carve out vast empires. When they had finished only two sections remained which were not possessions or dependencies of the white man. Only the Republic of Liberia and the Kingdom of Ethiopia remained, where the native African had a voice in the government of his affairs. Later Egypt became independent, and the Union of South Africa acquired a dominion status in the British Commonwealth. Following the second world war, Libya, Sudan, Morocco, Tunisia and Ghana (formerly Gold Coast) became independent.

Africa is a great plateau, over tour thousand miles long from north to south. The average height of the entire continent is over two thousand feet above sea level. Its loftiest peak is nearly twenty thousand feet high, while the Qattara Depression in the Libyan Desert sinks to four hundred feet below sea level.

The Atlas Mountains parallel the north coast of Africa, with their southern slopes dropping down to the Sahara. The Sudan Belt, which extends south from the Sahara to the Gold Coast and the Gulf of Guinea, is a lower region of hills, valleys and plains. To the southwest are the low Cameroon Mountains; and another chain in the eastern part follows the Red Sea.

In Eastern Africa, a ridge of highlands reaches below the equator to form a series of mountain ranges. It is here that the great lakes region is found. Only in North America are there lakes which compare to these in size. Unlike the mountain ranges of other continents, those of Africa do not follow a regular pattern. This, together with their location, provides an unusual drainage system. A mountain ridge separates the lakes that drain into the three great rivers, the Nile, the Congo and the Zambesi. This ridge dictates the direction of their courses, with the Nile flowing north toward the Mediterranean, the Congo twisting and turning to finally reach the Atlantic to the west, and the Zambesi flowing east to empty into the Indian Ocean. Each river follows a devious course through the mountains before finding a way over the edge of the plateau to reach the sea. This results in many falls and rapids which interrupt transportation. The Victoria Falls on the Zambesi, the rapids of the Congo, and the cataracts of the Nile are typical.

The Congo, winding through the gloomy depths of the fever-infested forests, is three thousand miles long. It is second only to the Amazon of South America in the volume of

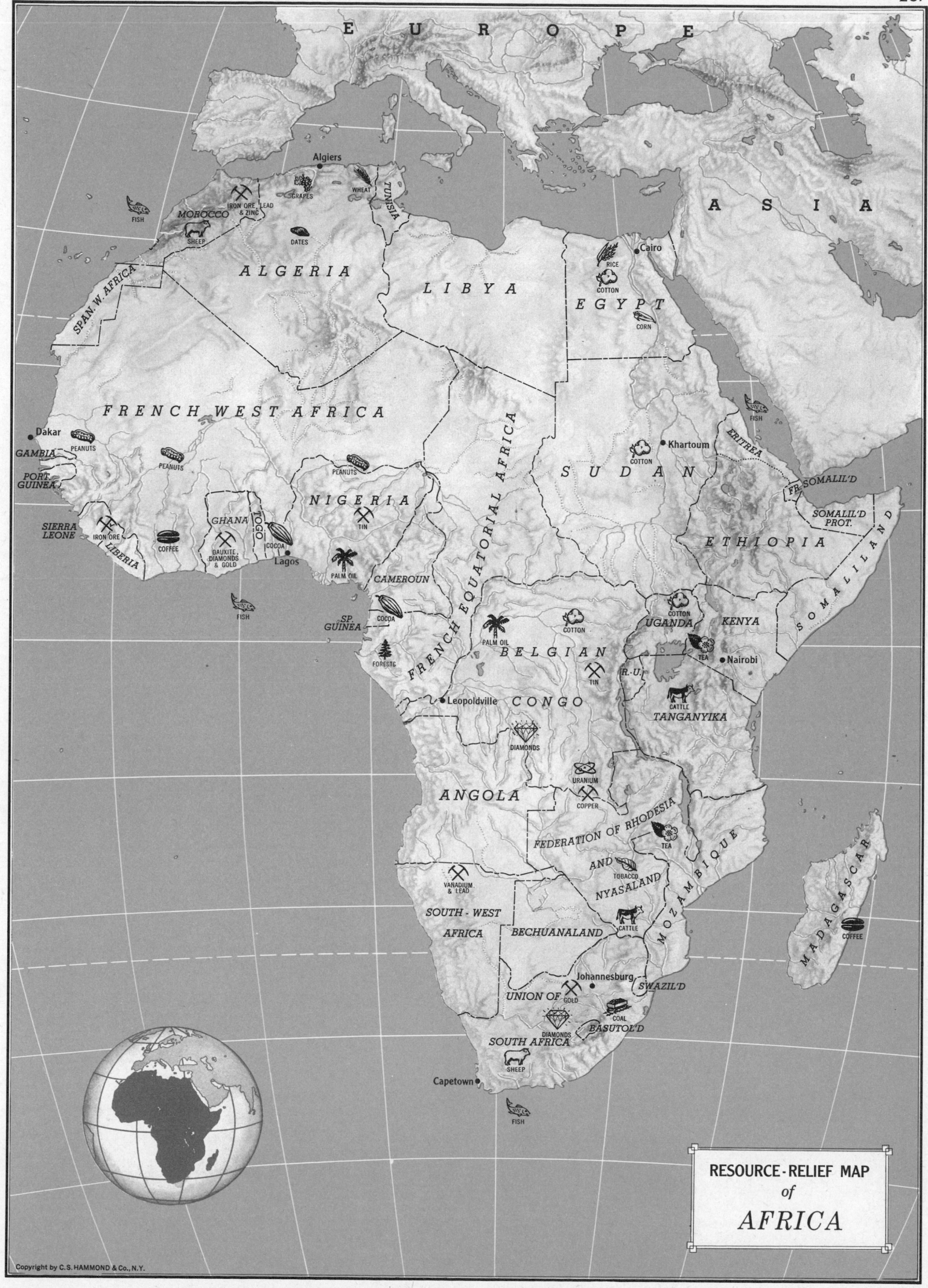

EUROPE

ASIA

FISH

Algiers
IRON ORE LEAD
MOROCCO
SHEEP
GRAPES
WHEAT
TUNISIA
DATES

SPAN. W. AFRICA

ALGERIA

LIBYA

EGYPT

Cairo
RICE
COTTON
CORN

FRENCH WEST AFRICA

Dakar
GAMBIA
PEANUTS
PORT.
GUINEA

PEANUTS

PEANUTS

NIGERIA

SUDAN

Khartoum
COTTON

ERITREA

FR. SOMALIL'D

SOMALIL'D
PROT.

FISH

SIERRA
LEONE
IRON ORE
LIBERIA

GHANA
COFFEE

TOGO

BAUXITE,
DIAMONDS
& GOLD

COCOA

Lagos

TIN

PALM OIL

CAMEROUN

COCOA

FRENCH EQUATORIAL AFRICA

ETHIOPIA

SOMALILAND

SP.
GUINEA

FISH

FORESTS

PALM OIL

COTTON

BELGIAN

COTTON
UGANDA

KENYA

TEA
Nairobi

Leopoldville

CONGO

TIN

R. U.

CATTLE

TANGANYIKA

DIAMONDS

ANGOLA

URANIUM

COPPER

FEDERATION OF RHODESIA

TEA

AND

TOBACCO

NYASALAND

MOZAMBIQUE

MADAGASCAR

COFFEE

VANADIUM
& LEAD

SOUTH - WEST
AFRICA

BECHUANALAND

CATTLE

Johannesburg
UNION OF
GOLD

SWAZIL'D

COAL
BASUTOL'D

DIAMONDS

SOUTH AFRICA

SHEEP

Capetown

FISH

RESOURCE-RELIEF MAP
*of*
AFRICA

| POLITICAL DIVISION | GOVERNMENT | MONETARY UNIT | PRINCIPAL LANGUAGES | PRINCIPAL RELIGIONS | MAJOR PRODUCTS |
|---|---|---|---|---|---|
| ALGERIA | Consists of 12 overseas departments and 4 territories with a governor-general, central elective assembly, and government council. | French franc | Arabic French Berber | Mohammedan Roman Catholic Jewish | Wheat, barley, oats, corn, grapes, olives, tobacco, dates, figs, flax, pomegranates, prunes, apricots, legumes, potatoes; sheep, goats, cattle, mules, horses, pigs, camels; sardines, anchovies, tuna; forestry products; iron phosphates, zinc, petroleum; wine, olive oil, distilling, flour, carpet weaving, alcohol, cotton weaving, tobacco products, wool, cork. |
| ANGOLA | Portuguese overseas province with a governor-general. | angolar | Bantu languages Portuguese | Tribal religions | Coffee, corn, sugar, palm oil and kernels, cotton, sisal, wax, tobacco; diamonds; whale oil, fish oil, sugar, palm oil, vegetables, fruit. |
| ASCENSION ISLAND | Possession of Great Britain, administered through the government of St. Helena by a resident magistrate and a Justice of the Peace. | pound | English | Protestant | |
| BASUTOLAND | British protectorate. Governed by a resident commissioner under High Commissioner for Basutoland Bechuanaland and Swaziland. | pound | Bantu languages Afrikaans English | Tribal religions Christian missions | Corn, wheat, sorghum, barley, oats, beans, peas; cattle, sheep, goats, horses, donkeys, pigs, mules; wool, mohair. |
| BECHUANALAND | British protectorate. Governed by a resident commissioner under High Commissioner for Basutoland, Bechuanaland and Swaziland. | pound | Bantu languages Bushman English | Tribal religions Protestant | Kaffir, wheat and wheatmeal; cattle, sheep, goats, pigs; hides, gold. |
| BELGIAN CONGO | Belgian colony administered by a governor-general. | franc | Bantu languages French Flemish | Tribal religions Roman Catholic | Palm oil and kernels, cotton, coffee, oil cakes, copal, rice, groundnuts; rubber, manioc, fibers; copper, cement, coal, silver, cassiterite (tin), diamonds, gold, cobalt, radium, uranium, tantalum, zinc. |
| CAMEROONS | Under United Nations trusteeship, administered by Great Britain. | pound | Bantu and Sudanese languages | Mohammedan Tribal religions Christian | Cocoa, coffee, rubber, bananas, palm oil and kernels; cattle, goats, sheep, horses. |
| CAMEROUN | Under United Nations trusteeship, administered by France as an associated territory. | French franc | Sudanese and Bantu languages Arabic French | Tribal religions Mohammedan Roman Catholic | Cocoa, palm kernels, bananas, caoutchouc, coffee, cacao, palm oil; timber; cattle, sheep, pigs, horses, asses; rubber, tobacco. |
| CANARY ISLANDS | Islands forming two provinces of Spain, each island governed by a Cabildo Insular. | peseta | Spanish | Roman Catholic | Bananas, cochineal, potatoes, sugar cane, onions, fruits; fish; wine, sugar. |
| CAPE VERDE ISLANDS | Portuguese overseas province, ruled by a governor. | escudo | Portuguese | Roman Catholic | Coffee, castor beans, corn, fruit, grains, tobacco; goats, oxen, pigs, asses; hides, skins; preserved fish, salt, lime, sugar. |
| COMORO ISLANDS | An overseas territory of the French Union with an administrator, privy council and an elective general council. | French franc | Arabic French | Mohammedan | Sugar cane, vanilla, rice, sweet potatoes, yams, copra, sisal, cacao, perfume plants; rum distilling. |
| DAHOMEY | Territory of the federation of Fr. West Africa with a governor, a government council and an elective territorial assembly. | French franc | Sudanese languages French | Tribal religions Mohammedan | Palm oil, shea nuts, groundnuts, cotton fiber, copra, castor oil, kapok, millet; gold, diamonds, bauxite, iron ore. |
| EGYPT | Republic with a president, prime minister and cabinet and a two-house parliament. | Egyptian pound | Arabic | Mohammedan Christian minorities | Cotton, barley, wheat, rice, sugar cane, onions, corn, millet, fruits, vegetables; sheep, goats, cattle, buffalo, donkeys, pigs, horses, mules; fish; petroleum, cement, phosphates, asbestos, chromite, cotton ginning, milling, pottery, perfume, soap. |
| ERITREA | Autonomous state federated with Ethiopia. Administered locally by a representative legislature. | Ethiopian dollar | Hamitic languages Arabic | Coptic Christian Mohammedan | Coffee, barley, sisal, bananas, legumes, gum arabic, wheat, tobacco, dates, dom nuts, senna; goats, sheep, camels; horses, mules, donkeys, cattle; hides, skins; fish-meal; pearls, mother-of-pearl; gold, salt, potassium salts, matting, matches, footwear. |
| ETHIOPIA | Constitutional monarchy with an emperor assisted by a council of ministers and a bicameral legislature. (See Eritrea). | Ethiopian dollar | Amharic Hamitic languages Arabic | Coptic Christian Mohammedan | Coffee, teff, barley, durra, wheat, cotton, sugar cane; cattle, sheep, goats, horses, mules; hides, skins; wax, gold, rocksalt. |
| FRENCH EQUATORIAL AFRICA | Federated overseas territory of France with a governor-general and an elective grand assembly representing the 4 constituent territories. | French franc | Bantu and Sudanese languages Arabic French | Mohammedan Tribal religions Roman Catholic | Palm oil and kernels, coconuts, cotton, coffee, cocoa, groundnuts, kapok, butter; hides; timber, rubber, copal gum, wax; ivory, gold, copper, lead, zinc, diamonds. |
| FRENCH SUDAN | Territory of the federation of Fr. W. Africa with a governor, a government council and an elective territorial assembly. | French franc | Sudanese languages Hamitic languages Arabic French | Mohammedan Tribal religions | Millet, rice, groundnuts, corn, sweet potatoes, cotton, manioc, tobacco, karite, shea nuts, yams, kapok, sisal; cattle, goats, sheep, horses, asses, camels; hides and skins; pottery, bricks, jewelry, weaving, leather, rice mills, soap. |
| FRENCH WEST AFRICA | Federation of 8 overseas territories of France with a governor-general and an elective grand assembly representing the constituent territories. | French franc | Sudanese and Hamitic languages Arabic French | Mohammedan Tribal religions Roman Catholic | Millet, rice, corn, cotton and fibers, nuts, oilseeds and oil, manioc, coffee, bananas, cocoa; cattle; gold, diamonds, iron ore, bauxite. |
| GAMBIA | Crown colony and protectorate of Great Britain administered by a governor, executive and legislative councils. | pound | Sudanese languages English | Mohammedan Tribal religions Christian | Groundnuts, palm kernels; hides and skins; beeswax. |

| POLITICAL DIVISION | GOVERNMENT | MONETARY UNIT | PRINCIPAL LANGUAGES | PRINCIPAL RELIGIONS | MAJOR PRODUCTS |
|---|---|---|---|---|---|
| GHANA (GOLD COAST) | Since March 1957 independent member of the British Commonwealth with an appointed governor-general and an elective parliament. | pound | Sudanese languages English | Mohammedan Tribal religions Christian | Cocoa, coffee, palm oil and kernels, sorghum, millet, corn, rice, yams, cassava, groundnuts, cotton; tobacco; mats, pottery. |
| GUINEA, FRENCH | Territory of the federation of Fr. West Africa with a governor, a government council and an elective territorial assembly. | franc | Sudanese languages French | Tribal religions Mohammedan | Rice, groundnuts, palm oil and nuts, wax, honey, bananas, indigo, kola, orange products, coffee; cattle, sheep, goats, pigs; hides and skins; bauxite, iron ore, gold. |
| GUINEA, PORTUGUESE | Portuguese overseas province ruled by a governor. | escudo | Sudanese languages Portuguese | Tribal religions Roman Catholic | Rice, palm kernels and oil, wax, groundnuts; hides. |
| GUINEA, SPANISH | Spanish colony ruled by a governor. | peseta | Bantu languages Spanish | Tribal religions Roman Catholic | Cocoa, coffee, vegetables and fruit; wood. |
| IFNI | Spanish territory ruled by a sub-governor. | peseta | Berber Arabic Spanish | Mohammedan | Barley, alfalfa, corn, tomatoes, argan oil, wheat; fish. |
| IVORY COAST | Territory of the federation of Fr. West Africa with a governor, a government council and an elective territorial assembly. | French franc | Sudanese languages French | Tribal religions Mohammedan | Coffee, cocoa, bananas, manioc, corn, rice, yams, kola, coconuts, palm oil, groundnuts, cotton, millet, tobacco; mahogany, caoutchouc; sheep, cattle, goats, pigs; gold, diamonds, manganese, iron ore, ilmenite. |
| KENYA | Colony and protectorate of Great Britain with a governor, a council of ministers, an appointive executive and a partly elective legislative council. | East African shilling | Swahili English Sudanese Hamitic Bantu | Tribal religions Mohammedan | Sisal, wheat, tea, coffee, pyrethrum, cotton, corn, sugar cane, sesame, groundnuts, wattle; hides and skins; sodium carbonate, gold, kyanite, salt, silver, lime, bags, butter, sugar, sisal products. |
| LIBERIA | Republic with president, cabinet, senate and house of representatives. | Liberian dollar | English Sudanese languages | Christian Tribal religions Mohammedan | Rubber, rice, coffee, cassava, sugar cane, cacao, palm oil and kernels, piassava, groundnuts; rum; iron ore. |
| LIBYA | A constitutional monarchy with a bicameral legislature. | Libyan pound | Arabic | Mohammedan | Barley, wheat, olives, grapes, dates, almonds, figs, tobacco, esparto; goats, sheep, camels, cattle, donkeys, mules and horses; sponge and tuna fishing; matting, carpets, leather articles, embroidered fabrics. |
| MADAGASCAR | Overseas territory of France with a high commissioner assisted by a government council and an elective assembly. | French franc | French Malagasy and Bantu languages | Tribal religions Roman Catholic Protestant | Cassava, rice, corn, potatoes, coffee, sugar cane, haricot beans, groundnuts, sisal, castor oil, tobacco, raffia; cattle, pigs, goats, sheep; graphite, mica, gold, rock crystal, corundum, phosphates, agate; textiles, sugar and rice factories, tapioca. |
| MAURITANIA | Territory of the federation of Fr. West Africa with a governor, a government council and an elective territorial assembly. | French franc | Arabic Hamitic and Sudanese languages French | Mohammedan | Millet, gum, dates, corn, watermelons, wheat, henna; sheep and goats, cattle, camels, asses, horses; hides and skins; salt. |
| MAURITIUS | British colony ruled by a governor, an executive council and a legislative council. | rupee | English Hindustani French | Roman Catholic | Sugar, aloe fiber, rice, vanilla beans, hemp, sisal, groundnuts, tea, yams, manioc, pineapples, tobacco, coconuts; alcohol, molasses, rum, copra. |
| MOROCCO | Independent sultanate with an interim representative government. A constitutional monarchy with a national assembly is planned. | Moroccan franc peseta | Arabic Berber French Spanish English | Mohammedan Roman Catholic Jewish | Wheat, barley, sorghum, corn, rye, rice, olives, almonds, citrus fruits, dates, beans, chickpeas, grapes, vegetables, linseed; cork, cedar; essential oils, sheep, goats, cattle, asses, camels, horses, mules, pigs; fish; soap, phosphate, iron ore, anthracite, manganese, lead, zinc, cobalt, copper, antimony; leather, carpets. |
| MOZAMBIQUE | Portuguese overseas province ruled by a governor and a government council. | escudo | Bantu languages Portuguese | Tribal religions Roman Catholic | Sugar, corn, cotton, copra, sisal, cashew nuts, bananas, coffee, kapok, sorghum, manioc, beeswax, tea, tobacco, vegetable oils; mangrove bark, timber; oxen, goats, pigs, sheep, cattle; gold, silver, asbestos, uranium, bauxite, samerskite. |
| NIGERIA | A federated colony and protectorate of Great Britain with a governor-general, a council of ministers and a federal house of representatives. | pound | Sudanese languages Arabic English | Mohammedan Christian | Palm oil and kernels, cacao, groundnuts, cotton, rubber, bananas, benni seeds, shea nuts, yams, cassava, corn, rice, fruits, millet, coffee; cattle, sheep, goats; hides and skins; timber; tin, coal, columbite, lead, gold, silver, zinc; cigarettes, soap, sugar. |
| NIGER | Territory of the federation of Fr. West Africa with a governor, a government council and an elective territorial assembly. | franc | Sudanese Hamitic Arabic French | Mohammedan Tribal religions | Millet, manioc, groundnuts, rice, wheat, cotton, gum arabic, kapok, kidney beans, corn, onions, sorghum, dates, sugar cane; goats, sheep, cattle, asses, camels, horses; hides and skins, leather; natron, sodium sulphate, salt. |
| NORTHERN RHODESIA | *British protectorate administered by a governor and executive and legislative council. | pound | Bantu languages English | Tribal religions | Corn, wheat, potatoes, tobacco, sorghum, millet, groundnuts, cassava, rice, beans, cowpeas, cotton; lumber; cattle and other livestock. |
| NYASALAND | *British protectorate administered by a governor and executive and legislative council. | pound | Bantu languages English | Tribal religions | Tobacco, tea, cotton, pulses, tung oil, sisal, corn, cassava, wheat, rice, millet, groundnuts, rubber, beeswax; timber; goats, cattle, pigs, sheep; hides, skins, meat, ghee, soap; gold, mica, corundum. |
| SÃO TOMÉ AND PRINCIPE | Portuguese overseas province administered by a governor. | escudo | Bantu languages Portuguese | Tribal religions Roman Catholic | Cacao, coffee, coconuts, copra, palm oil, cinchona, bananas. |
| RÉUNION | French overseas department administered by a prefect and a council-general. | French franc | French | Roman Catholic | Sugar, rum, vanilla, tapioca, essences, fruit and vegetable preserves. |

*Member of new Federation of Rhodesia and Nyasaland.

| POLITICAL DIVISION | GOVERNMENT | MONETARY UNIT | PRINCIPAL LANGUAGES | PRINCIPAL RELIGIONS | MAJOR PRODUCTS |
|---|---|---|---|---|---|
| RUANDA—URUNDI | Under United Nations trusteeship, administered by Belgium and governed by a vice governor-general. | franc | Bantu languages Flemish French | Tribal religions Roman Catholic | Food; cattle; hides. |
| ST. HELENA | British colony administered by a governor, an executive and an advisory council. | pound | English | Protestant | Hemp, lily bulbs, potatoes, tow, rope and twine, lace; sheep, goats, cattle, donkeys, poultry. |
| SENEGAL | Territory of the federation of Fr. West Africa with a governor, a government council and an elective territorial assembly. | French franc | Sudanese languages Arabic French | Mohammedan Tribal religions Roman Catholic | Millet, groundnuts, manioc, rice, corn, gum arabic, palm nuts, honey, sweet potatoes, sisal, indigo; sheep, goats, cattle, asses, horses; fish; titanium, zircon; brick, pottery, weaving, jewelry, oil cakes. |
| SEYCHELLES | A British colony ruled by a governor and a legislative and executive council. | rupee | English French | Roman Catholic | Coconuts, cinnamon, patchouli, copra, vanilla, corn; guano; salted fish, tortoise shell, calipee. |
| SIERRA LEONE | A British colony and protectorate ruled by a governor and a legislative and executive council. | pound | Sudanese languages English | Tribal religions Mohammedan Christian | Palm oil and kernels, kola nuts, ginger, piassava, groundnuts, cocoa; diamonds, iron ore, chrome ore. |
| SOMALILAND | Under United Nations trusteeship and administered by Italy with U. N. and local advisory councils. | somalo | Somali Arabic Italian | Mohammedan Roman Catholic | Sugar, cotton, tobacco, bananas, aromatic gums, resin, kapok, grains, beans; camels, goats, sheep, cattle; skins, hides; tunny, mother-of-pearl. |
| SOMALILAND, BRITISH | British protectorate ruled solely by a governor, assisted by advisory councils. | Indian rupee East African shilling | Somali Arabic | Mohammedan | Millet, sorghum, corn; sheep, goats, camels, cattle; skins, hides; gums, salt. |
| SOMALILAND, FRENCH | Overseas territory of France with a governor and an elective representative assembly. | Djibouti franc | Hamitic languages Arabic French | Mohammedan | Boats; sheep; salt. |
| SOUTHERN RHODESIA | *Member of British Commonwealth with governor and elective executive and legislative assembly. | pound | Bantu languages English | Tribal religions Protestant | Corn, tobacco, groundnuts, wheat, potatoes, citrus and other fruits; cattle, sheep, pigs, goats; meats, hides; gold, asbestos, chromite, coal; footwear, apparel, cigarettes, flour, groundnut oil, wood products. |
| SPANISH SAHARA | Spanish territory, consisting of Saguia el Hamra and Río de Oro, ruled by a sub-governor. | peseta | Arabic Spanish | Mohammedan | Barley, corn; goats, sheep, camels; fish. |
| SUDAN | A republic with a bicameral parliament and council of ministers. Executive power resides temporarily in a council of state. | Egyptian pound | Arabic Sudanese Hamitic languages English | Mohammedan Tribal religions | Cotton, cotton seed, gum arabic, senna leaves and pods, groundnuts, sesame, millet, dates, dom nuts (vegetable ivory), wheat, shea nuts; sheep, goats, cattle, camels, asses; mahogany; hides and skins, ivory, gold, salt, trochus shell, mother-of-pearl. |
| SWAZILAND | British protectorate governed by a resident commissioner under the High Commissioner for Basutoland, Bechuanaland and Swaziland. | pound | Bantu languages English | Tribal religions Christian missions | Tobacco, corn, groundnuts, kaffir corn, wheat, oats, rye, barley, fruits; cattle, goats, sheep, pigs; butter; hides, skins; asbestos, gold, tin. |
| TANGANYIKA TERRITORY | Under United Nations trusteeship and administered by Great Britain. Ruled by a governor and a legislative and executive council. | East African shilling | Bantu languages Swahili English | Tribal religions Mohammedan Christian missions | Sisal, cotton, coffee, bananas, tobacco, papain, beeswax, grains, sugar; cattle, goats, sheep; hides, skins; wood, timber, wax, gum arabic; diamonds, gold, tin, mica, salt, camphor, tungsten. |
| TOGO (FRENCH) | Under United Nations trusteeship administered by France as a republic within the French Union. | French franc | Sudanese languages French | Tribal religions Mohammedan Roman Catholic | Palm oil and kernels, tapioca, cocoa, yams, coffee, plantains, corn, groundnuts, cotton, copra, kola, cassava, rubber; sheep, goats, pigs, cattle, asses, horses. |
| TRISTAN DA CUNHA | Possession of Great Britain governed by an administrator and an island council responsible to St. Helena. | pound | English | Protestant | Potatoes, fruit; cattle, sheep; fish. |
| TUNISIA | A kingdom with a Bey (monarch), a prime minister, council of ministers and assembly. | French franc | Arabic French Berber | Mohammedan Roman Catholic | Wheat, barley, oats, corn, sorghum, beans, grapes, olives, citrus fruits, dates, alfa grass, almonds, oranges, shaddocks, pistachios, cork; sheep, goats, cattle, horses, asses, mules, camels, pigs; fish, sponges; flour milling, oil refining, wool spinning, pottery, leather, silk weaving; phosphates, iron ore, lignite, lead, zinc. |
| UGANDA | British protectorate controlled by a governor with an executive and a legislative council. Native kings and their assemblies rule locally. | East African shilling | Bantu and Sudanese languages English | Tribal religions Christian | Cotton, coffee, plantains, millet, cotton seed, tobacco, chilies, sugar cane, rubber; cattle, sheep, goats; hides, skins; tin; cigarettes. |
| UNION OF SOUTH AFRICA | Member of British Commonwealth with a governor-general, cabinet, elective senate and house of assembly. | pound | Afrikaans English Bantu languages Bushman | Protestant Roman Catholic Mohammedan Hindu Buddhist | Corn, wheat, potatoes, oats, kaffir corn, barley, tobacco, sugar cane, tea, citrus fruits, rye, groundnuts, grapes, pineapples; cattle, sheep, goats, pigs, horses, donkeys, mules; gold, coal, diamonds, copper, asbestos, manganese, lime, limestone, platinum, chrome, iron, silver, tungsten, mercury, vanadium, tin, antimony, silver, scheelite, talc; hides, chemicals, wool, footwear, rubber, machinery, clothing, textiles, food, vehicles, printing, furniture, building materials. |
| UPPER VOLTA | Territory of the federation of Fr. West Africa with a governor, a government council and an elective territorial assembly. | French franc | Sudanese languages French | Tribal religions Mohammedan | Millet, groundnuts, corn, karite nuts and butter (shea nut), vegetables, rice, tapes, cotton, kapok, sesame, sorghum, tea; sheep, goats, cattle, asses, pigs; gold, manganese, copper, silver, chrome, lignite, iron. |
| ZANZIBAR | British protectorate nominally ruled by a sultan but under the effective control of a governor and a legislative and executive council. | East African shilling | Bantu languages Swahili English | Tribal religions Mohammedan Christian missions | Sisal, cotton, coffee, bananas, tobacco, papain, beeswax, grains, sugar; cattle, goats, sheep; hides, skins; wood, gum arabic; diamonds, gold, tin, mica, salt, camphor, tungsten. |

*Member of new Federation of Rhodesia and Nyasaland.

TWA—Trans World Airline

TWA—Trans World Airline

The cities along the coast of North Africa are crowded with market places and their exotic wares.

Except for the fertile soil of the Nile valley, Egypt's land is arid and unproductive.

water it empties into the sea. The Nile travels four thousand miles before reaching the Mediterranean, and today, as in ancient times, makes Egypt a habitable country. As the Nile winds slowly through the Sahara, the evaporation is so great that the river would dry up before reaching the sea were it not fed by rivers from the high Abyssinian Mountains. It is these waters of the Blue Nile which bring the great Nile floods and supply the water for irrigation to make of Egypt a fertile strip of land hemmed in by cliffs and burning sands. Africa's fourth large river, the Niger, while rising only one hundred and fifty miles from the ocean, flows twenty-five hundred miles before reaching the Atlantic.

Africa is a land of climatic contradictions. At the equator the temperature ranges from typical jungle weather at the lower levels, to a climate similar to that found well over a thousand miles to the north. This occurs in the high altitudes of the mountains. Along the Mediterranean, the weather compares with that of southern Europe. The weather in the Congo Basin is always hot and humid, although to the east, in the mountain and lake region, it is tempered by the higher altitudes. In the far south, around Cape-town, the weather is mild and sunny like the climate of southern California. The same extremes exist in rainfall. At the equator it is excessive, with periods of torrential rains. Traveling north or south from this wet center there is less and less rain, with parts of the Sahara never getting a drop.

Plant life varies with the rainfall. The dense, matted tropical jungles, which are

exceeded only in size by the forests of the Amazon, give way to grassy plains and open forests. The only vegetation in the Sahara is around the springs that nourish the oases. Because the hot winds of the south are blocked by the Atlas Mountains, the entire coastal area of North Africa from the Atlantic to the Nile River is agriculturally productive.

Africa is a strange mixture of white and black races. The four original races of Hamites and Semites, Negroes and Hottentots have become so intermingled that it is no longer possible to draw clear lines between racial groups. The Hamites and Semites of North Africa are white and Mohammedans. The Negroes and Hottentots are the black people of Central and South Africa. While probably members of the Negro race, the Hottentots have distinctive characteristics which put them in a class by themselves. These native tribes have a barbaric form of worship. The Sudanese, blackest of the Negroes, were sought by the early slave traders. For over three hundred years millions of these poor blacks were seized and transported to strange lands.

The slave trade was started by the son of a man who accompanied Columbus to America. Needing labor in her New World colonies to replace the Indian slaves, who preferred death to captivity, Spain granted each Spanish colonist the right to import twelve African Negroes. A year later the king of Spain bestowed a grant upon the Dutch allowing them to take four thousand slaves a year. Soon the "black ivory trade"

had grown to huge proportions, and it has been estimated that as many as two million slaves were removed from Africa in a single year.

In recent years Africa has been undergoing tremendous changes. Railroads, motor roads and airlines continue to reach out and draw distant points closer together. Modern engineering genius is overcoming the obstacles imposed by climate and land formation, and Africa is rapidly taking its place among the more fortunate continents.

**TUNISIA**—Battleground of World War II, is the most productive land in North Africa. Its fertile valleys produce grain and tropical fruits. Seat of ancient Carthage, it was once the wealthiest city of its time until Rome destroyed it during the Punic Wars.

**LIBYA**— Is relatively unprotected from the scorching desert winds and, consequently, the least valuable of North African regions. However, the coastal areas are cultivated with the aid of shade and irrigation.

**EGYPT**—In the heart of the Nile valley, has been one of the most productive regions in the world since recorded time. Recent dam construction regulating the flow of the Nile has increased the productivity of the soil. Agricultural methods are the same today as they were 6,000 years ago.

**SUDAN** (former Anglo-Egyptian)—Embracing the upper Nile basin to the borders of Uganda and Ethiopia, produces gum arabic

TWA—Trans World Airline

Modern methods of travel have made additional roads and bridges necessary in modern Africa.

Gendreau

Many races and a variety of languages and religions are represented within the boundaries of South Africa.

for the entire world. Cotton is raised in the fertile areas between the Blue and the White Niles. Dates, ivory and meat are also exported.

**ETHIOPIA**—The first country to be liberated by the Allies in World War II, has many undeveloped resources. Gold and platinum are mined. The Djimmah Province produces a fine, robust coffee. There is, as yet, only one railroad which leads out of the country. The Italians, true to the Roman tradition, built 4,340 miles of roads while they were occupying the country.

**UGANDA**—The Source of the Nile River. Much of the country is situated in the lofty mountains of East Africa. The climate is usually mild because of the altitude of the land.

**KENYA**—Eastern gateway to Central Africa abounds in big game. The lowlands bordering the Indian Ocean are fertile, the climate bearable. Western Kenya is a high plateau with isolated towering peaks, snow-capped the year 'round.

**TANGANYIKA**—Within its borders is Kilimanjaro, Africa's highest known peak. Tanganyika is famous as the gorilla country of Africa. Its jungle brims with wildlife, there-

by making it a paradise for big-game hunters.

**NYASALAND**—A British protectorate, lies along the west shore of Lake Nyasa. Semi-autonomous and self-supporting, it has a good system of roads and railways.

**UNION OF SOUTH AFRICA** comprises the Transvaal, Orange Free State, Natal and the Cape of Good Hope. Its northern areas contain many valuable minerals, chief of which is gold and diamonds. Most of the world's diamonds and half the world's gold are exported from this country.

**NORTHERN RHODESIA**—Protectorate on the borders of the jungles of Central Africa and the wide plains of South Africa. Copper, lead and cattle comprise its principal forms of wealth. Victoria Falls, the world's highest, are on the Zambesi River in Northern Rhodesia.

**SOUTHERN RHODESIA**—Border region, is well suited to agriculture and European settlement. It possesses vast amounts of gold, asbestos and chrome.

**ANGOLA** or Portuguese West Africa, on Africa's west coast, is a huge treeless plain, arid in many places. Diamonds are mined, and recently coffee has been cultivated for export.

The grazing lands of Ruanda-Urundi have been added to the Belgian Congo, and a ten-year plan to develop the Congo region has been inaugurated. The Belgian Congo has the richest terrain in Africa. Metals, both common and rare, are imbedded in its soil.

The most important product of the Ghana is cacao. Some diamonds and gold are mined to a limited extent.

**LIBERIA**—Long unimportant economically, is presently producing rubber and coffee for export.

French colonies are located in most of West Africa. The areas from Dakar southward yield rubber, mahogany, ebony, cacao and coffee. The interior of West Africa merges with the Sahara Desert. A narrow savanna region stretches across the French lands to the headwaters of the Nile. This area contains some of Africa's large lakes and is the best suited for grazing. The great forests on its southern edge lead into the jungles of the Congo and Cameroons. The region is a habitat for a diversity of animal life including the leopard, lion and rhinoceros as well as some of the larger animals of the country.

**MADAGASCAR**—One of the world's largest islands, is located off the east coast of Africa. Graphite, copper and precious stones form a part of its mineral resources.

Rapid strides in industrial growth have been made by many of Australia's port cities.

Grendreau

New Zealand Consulate

Modified by ocean currents, New Zealand's climate remains moderate.

**AUSTRALIA**—This island continent of the South Seas is the smallest, and last to be discovered of all the continents.

The United States and Australia are nations of about the same age and size, and in other respects have much in common. The loss of America as a British Colony directly led to the settling of Australia. It was first claimed for the British Crown in 1788 as a settlement for British convicts who had previously been sent to America. Landing in a virgin country, the early pioneers of the two countries had to conquer the wilderness before creating a nation. In the process of so doing the people of both lands developed similar characteristics. In later years Australia even patterned its constitution after that of the United States.

But, whereas the United States became a melting pot for all the races and creeds in the world, Australia has been peopled almost entirely by British stock. Today 97 per cent of the population are descendants of British colonists, and 86 per cent are Australian born. Strict laws have confined immigration to the white race. Few of the natives who originally inhabited Australia remain. These aborigines are similar to the African Negro but not so intelligent, and are believed to be a separate race.

Almost half of Australia lies within the tropics, but being surrounded by great oceans, the continent has a mild climate throughout the year. Snow normally falls only in the high mountains in the winter.

Since the seasons are the reverse of those in the United States, this occurs in their winter months of June, July, and August.

Australia is said to be most level in surface and regular in outline of all the continents. There is an entire absence of towering mountains. The highest peak is only about seventy-three hundred feet above sea level. The mountains parallel the east coast, with, by far, the greater part of the continent a vast, irregular, and undulating plateau.

Australia can be regarded as falling into four well-defined regions: (1) The Great Plateau in the west extends over about half of the continent; (2) The Eastern Highlands follow along the whole of the eastern coastline, rarely exceeding a distance of a hundred miles inland; (3) The Central Basin is a lowland area much of which was once a sea-bed; and (4) the Coastal Plains, which form a rim surrounding most of the continent.

Despite rich coastal lands and an immense grazing area in the interior, much of this interior is unsuited for agriculture. It is a great arid region of desert and semi-desert which is sparsely settled and will never support a dense population. The heaviest rainfall is in the tropical regions of the north, and there is adequate moisture along the south coast and southern part of the highlands. Elsewhere there is insufficient rain. But for the presence of innumerable artesian wells scattered over wide areas, much more of the country would be without water. It is these wells that make stock-raising possible,

but because of its mineral content, the water is seldom used for agriculture or human use.

The major rivers of Australia are of two types—those which flow toward the coast and are similar to such rivers in other parts of the world; and the inland rivers which gradually lose their water as they flow away from the coastal regions. The headwaters of most of these inland rivers are in the Eastern Highlands.

The Murray River with its tributaries is the main river system and flows into the ocean on the south coast. The Gilbert, Norman and Flinders are the principal streams flowing into the Gulf of Carpentaria in the north. On the west the Murchison, Gascoyne, Ashburton and Fitzroy empty into the Indian Ocean.

The rivers which flow inland vary greatly in volume during the year. For long periods they are mere strings of waterholes, but during floods their waters spread out over the flat country for many miles. Most of their waters evaporate or soak into the ground before they flow very far. In the center of the continent the rivers flow into Lake Eyre when there is sufficient water in them, but generally they are merely beds of dry sand.

The lakes that appear to be scattered so liberally over the land are also a disappointment as they are little more than shallow basins that carry water only after rains.

Great Barrier Reef, the largest of all coral formations, follows the northeast coast for twelve hundred miles of Australia's twelve-thousand-mile coastline. Except in a few places this reef is impassable to ships, but it does provide an inner passage for coastal navigation. There are good harbors on the southeastern coast.

Wherever there is sufficient moisture for grass to grow, the land is especially adapted to grazing. This land has proved the most

Hawaiian Pineapple Co.

Hawaii's fertile soil facilitates the growing of tropical fruits and sugar cane. Its pineapple cultivation accounts for 90% of the world's production.

Gendreau

The vast expanse of the Pacific Ocean contains thousands of uninhabited coral isles.

suitable in the world for raising sheep. Merino sheep, which produce a very fine quality of wool, comprise most of the flocks. The heavy fleece from these sheep exceeds that of breeds raised elsewhere, so, although Australia produces less than one-sixth of the world's sheep, the wool yield is more than a quarter of the world's requirement.

Lacking navigable rivers, most of the transportation is by railways. These have been of first importance in developing the country, but one great drawback of railroad transportation is that there are several gauges. During the last twenty-five years there has been a steady expansion of motor roads, and air routes are rapidly increasing.

In addition to the mainland and the island of Tasmania, Australia has extensive territorial interests. These comprise the Trust Territory of New Guinea, Papua, Nauru and Norfolk Island.

The Trust Territory of New Guinea includes the northeastern section of New Guinea, the Bismarck Archipelago, and the northern islands of the Solomon group. Scattered over a sea area of more than one million square miles, these islands are mountainous with limited coastal areas suitable for cultivation.

**NEW ZEALAND**—Two large islands and several small ones make up New Zealand. Situated about twelve hundred miles southeast of Australia, New Zealand is a lonely member of the British Commonwealth.

The two principal islands, North and South Island are separated by Cook Strait which is ninety miles wide. Close as they are to each other, these islands have little in common except that they are both mountainous. North Island is of volcanic origin and consists chiefly of forested hills and plateaus. South Island is more rugged with glaciers and snow-clad peaks that rival the Alps of Switzerland.

**PACIFIC ISLANDS**—The Pacific Islands fall into three major regions: Polynesia, Micronesia and Melanesia.

Polynesia, or "Many islands," consists of widely scattered groups and a few isolated islands forming a rough triangle. The Hawaiian Islands are at the northern point, twenty degrees north of the Equator. The Fiji Islands, at the western point of the triangle, are the meeting place of Polynesian and Melanesian cultures, the people being of mixed stock. The easternmost point lies in the Gambier group of the Tuamota Archipelago, although isolated Pitcairn Island, inhabited by Anglo-Tahitian descendants of the mutinous crew of the "Bounty," is generally included geographically. Within this area lies the most highly developed group of Pacific peoples, a mixture of white, black and yellow racial stocks, the Polynesians. Famous as navigators, they crossed the Pacific from Asia hundreds of years ago, and sailed their canoes eastward to their

present homes. For the most part, the islands are mountainous, volcanic and covered with dense vegetation, often fringed by coral reefs. Along the equator and in the southeast, low coral atolls predominate, often only a few feet above sea level, and frequently torn by hurricanes.

The people, often easy-going to the point of idleness, are not always used in local production, some Chinese having been hired to do manual work. Famous for dancing and feasting, the generally happy Polynesians strive to maintain their early customs against the inroads of European traders, missionaries and government regulations.

In the western Pacific, for the most part north of the equator, lies Micronesia, or "little islands," confined to the Marianas, Carolines, Marshall Islands, and Gilbert and Ellice Islands. Except for the latter islands, they are mostly volcanic and coral-fringed, and are peopled by a light-skinned group—the latest arrivals in the Pacific. These inhabitants show more evidence of a recent black and yellow mixture.

The earliest inhabited area of the Pacific, New Guinea and the islands spreading to the southeast of it, is known as Melanesia, the "black islands." Of early Negroid stock, this area was generally by-passed by the later Polynesians and Micronesians, as settlement was already established. Melanesia is a rapidly developing area, rich in minerals as well as the usual coconuts. Today the people range from Europeanized workers in the plantations of New Caledonia and Fiji, and the missions of the New Guinea coast, to half-naked savages, often head-hunters and cannibals, in the higher regions of New Guinea.

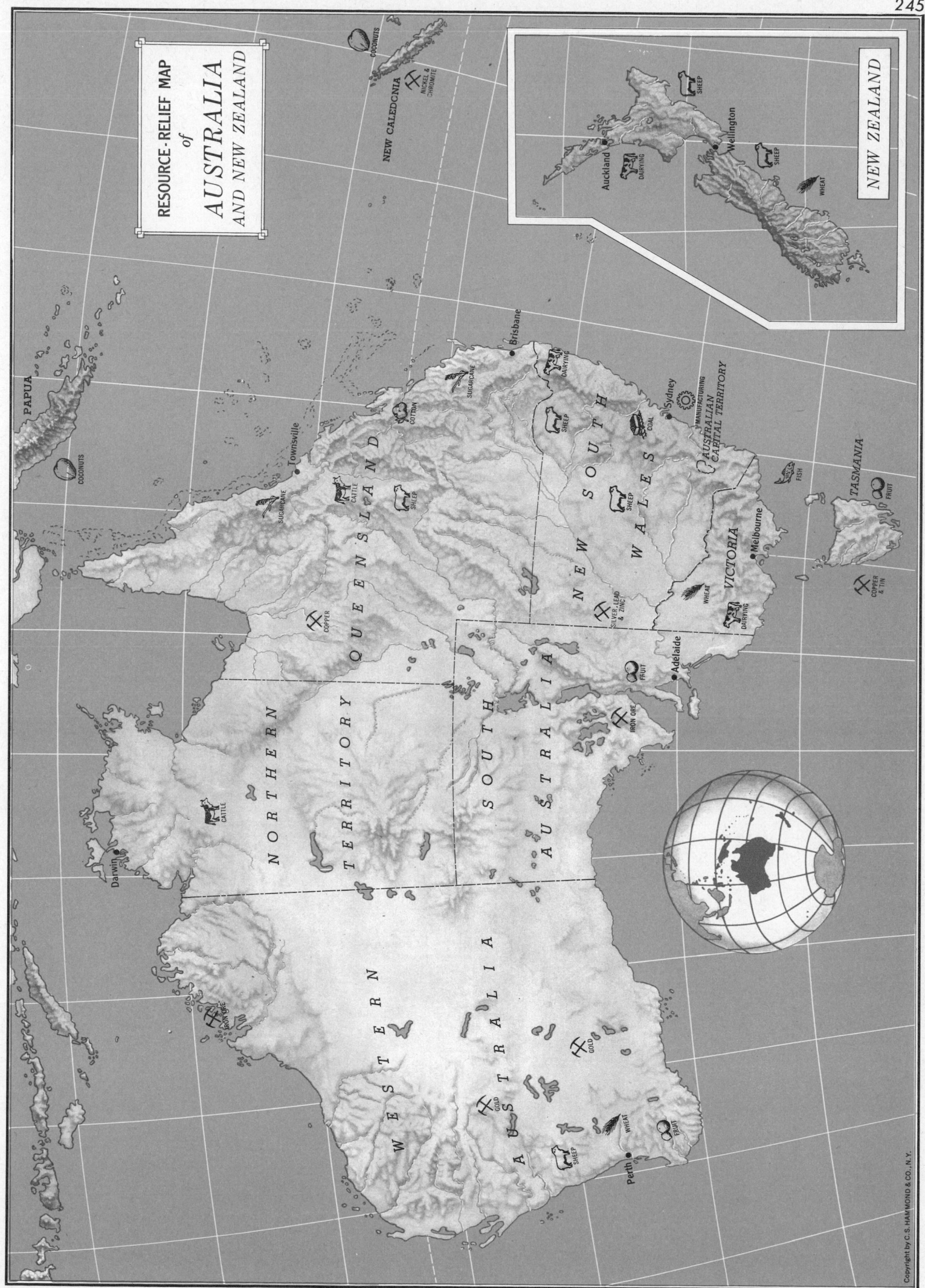

RESOURCE-RELIEF MAP
of
AUSTRALIA
AND NEW ZEALAND

NEW ZEALAND

SHEEP

SHEEP

DAIRYING

WHEAT

Auckland

Wellington

NEW CALEDONIA

NICKEL &
CHROMITE

COCONUTS

PAPUA

COCONUTS

Brisbane

DAIRYING

SUGARCANE

COTTON

Sydney

MANUFACTURING

SHEEP

COAL

AUSTRALIAN
CAPITAL TERRITORY

Townsville

SUGARCANE

CATTLE

SHEEP

N O R T H   S O U T H

FISH

TASMANIA

SHEEP

W A L E S

FRUIT

Q U E E N S L A N D

COPPER

Melbourne

VICTORIA

WHEAT

COPPER & TIN

DAIRYING

CATTLE

N O R T H E R N   T E R R I T O R Y

S O U T H   A U S T R A L I A

N E W

Adelaide

FRUIT

Darwin

IRON ORE

IRON ORE

W E S T E R N   A U S T R A L I A

GOLD

GOLD

SHEEP

WHEAT

FRUIT

Perth

Copyright by C.S. HAMMOND & CO., N.Y.

| POLITICAL DIVISION | GOVERNMENT | MONETARY UNIT | PRINCIPAL LANGUAGES | PRINCIPAL RELIGIONS | MAJOR PRODUCTS |
|---|---|---|---|---|---|
| AUSTRALIA | Member of the British Commonwealth of Nations with a governor-general, prime minister and cabinet. Parliament consists of a senate and house of representatives. | Australian pound | English | Protestant Roman Catholic | (See individual States) |
| BISMARCK ARCHIPELAGO | A part of the territory of New Guinea administered by Australia as a U.N. trust territory. | Australian pound | Papuan English Chinese | Tribal religions Roman Catholic Protestant | Coconuts, cocoa, coffee, kapok, rubber, grains; cattle, goats, pigs; fish. |
| BONIN ISLANDS | Administered by the United States. | dollar yen | Japanese | Shinto-Buddhist | Vegetables, sugar, cocoa; poultry, pigs, cattle; fish. |
| CAROLINE ISLANDS | A group in the United States trust territory of the Pacific Islands and administered by a high commissioner. | dollar | Micronesian dialects Malayo-Polynesian languages | Tribal religions Protestant Roman Catholic | Copra, breadfruit, cassava, taro, sweet potatoes; pigs, cattle, poultry, fish; phosphates. |
| COOK ISLANDS | Territory of New Zealand administered by a resident commissioner. | New Zealand pound | Polynesian dialects English | Protestant Tribal religions | Citrus fruits, coconuts, copra, tomatoes, arrowroot, pineapples, breadfruit, taro, kumaras, plantains, yams; mother-of-pearl. |
| EASTER ISLAND (RAPA NUI) | Administered as part of Valparaíso province in Chile. | peso | Polynesian dialect Spanish | Roman Catholic | Plantains, sweet potatoes; fish; cattle, sheep; wool. |
| FIJI | British colony ruled by a governor with an executive and legislative council. | Fiji pound | English Fijian Hindustani Chinese | Protestant Roman Catholic Moslem Hindu | Sugar cane, coconuts, bananas, pineapples, rice, root vegetables, citrus fruits, cotton, rubber, castor oil seeds, taro, yams, cassava, sweet potatoes, groundnuts, pulses, corn, fodder crops, tobacco; cattle, pigs; tuna, bêche-de-mer, trochus shell; gold, silver; sugar, copra, coconut oil, soap, biscuits, molasses, butter, ghee, candlenut oil. paint. |
| FRENCH OCEANIA | See Gambier, Marquesas, Tubuai Islands and Tuamotu Archipelago. | | | | |
| GAMBIER ISLANDS | A group of Islands in French Oceania governed from Tahiti. | franc | Polynesian dialects | Roman Catholic Tribal religions | Coconuts, copra, oranges, breadfruit; pearls, pearl shell, fish. |
| GILBERT AND ELLICE ISLANDS | British colony administered by a resident commissioner. | Australian pound | English Gilbertese Samoan | Tribal religions Protestant Roman Catholic | Coconuts, copra, phosphate of lime; pearl shell, fish; hats, mats. |
| GUAM | Territory of the United States administered by a governor and advisory and legislative bodies. | dollar | English Chamorro Spanish | Roman Catholic | Copra, coconut oil, corn, taro, bananas, citrus fruits, mangoes, papayas, breadfruit, sweet potatoes, cocoa, cassava, sugar cane, pineapples; cattle, pigs, poultry, buffalo. |
| HAWAII | Territory of the United States administered by a governor, a cabinet, a senate and a house of representatives. | dollar | English Japanese Hawaiian | Protestant Roman Catholic Buddhist | Sugar, pineapples, coffee, molasses, bananas, rice, flowers, cotton, tobacco; beef cattle, swine, sheep, poultry; hides, wood, stone, fish; printing, foodstuffs, ironworks, fertilizers, chemicals, clothing, fiber insulating board, handicrafts. |
| MARQUESAS ISLANDS | A group of islands in French Oceania administered from Tahiti. | French franc | Marquesan French | Tribal religions Roman Catholic | Bananas, breadfruit, yams, bamboo, coconuts, sugar cane. |
| MARIANA ISLANDS | A group of islands in the United States trust territory of the Pacific administered by a high commissioner. | dollar | Micronesian dialects Spanish | Tribal religions | Fruits, corn, sweet potatoes, vegetables, breadfruit, cacao; fish; phosphates. |
| MARSHALL ISLANDS | A group of islands in the United States trust territory of the Pacific administered by a high commissioner. | dollar | Micronesian dialects | Tribal religions Protestant | Arrowroot, breadfruit, coconuts, pandanus, taro, vegetables, copra, bananas; poultry, pigs; fish. |
| NAURU | Trust territory of Great Britain, Australia and New Zealand. Administered by Australia. | Australian pound | English Micronesian Chinese | Protestant Roman Catholic | Phosphates; fishing; mats. |
| NEW CALEDONIA | French overseas territory administered by a high commissioner assisted by an appointive executive council and an elective general council. | French franc | Melanesian dialects French | Roman Catholic Tribal religions | Coconuts, copra, coffee, cotton, manioc, corn, tobacco, bananas, pineapples, wheat, rice, kauri logs; cattle, pigs, horses, goats, sheep, hides; guano, trochus shell; nickel, chrome, manganese, iron, cobalt, copper, lead, platinum; canned meat. |
| NEW GUINEA, TERR. OF | United Nations trust territory administered by Australia under the administrator of Papua. | Australian pound | Papuan Pidgin English English | Tribal religions Roman Catholic Protestant | Coconuts, copra, cocoa, dairying; timber; gold, silver, platinum; boat making. |
| NEW HEBRIDES | British and French condominium administered by British and French resident commissioners. | Australian currency Bank of Indo-china Notes | Melanesian dialects Pidgin English English French | Tribal religions Protestant Roman Catholic | Coconuts, copra, cocoa, coffee, yams, taro, manioc, fruits; kauri pine; cattle, pigs; trochus shells. |
| NEW SOUTH WALES | Australian state with a governor, cabinet and a legislative council and assembly. | Australian pound | English | Protestant Roman Catholic | Wheat, rice, oats, corn, hay, potatoes, tobacco, sugar cane, grapes, bananas; sheep, cattle, horses, pigs, meats, dairy products, poultry, eggs; fish; timber; coal, silver, lead, zinc, sulphur, gold, tungsten, bismuth, antimony, cadmium, cobalt, titanium, zirconium, tin, platinum; steel, metal products, machinery; foods, beverages, tobacco, clothing; chemicals, paint, oil, grease, paper, printing, textiles, woodwork, baskets, bricks, pottery, glass, furniture, quarry products, skins, leather, rubber, precious metal, jewelry. |

| POLITICAL DIVISION | GOVERNMENT | MONETARY UNIT | PRINCIPAL LANGUAGES | PRINCIPAL RELIGIONS | MAJOR PRODUCTS |
|---|---|---|---|---|---|
| NEW ZEALAND | A member of the British Commonwealth with dominion status governed by a governor-general, cabinet and unicameral assembly. | New Zealand pound | English Maori | Protestant | Wheat, oats, barley, seeds, kauri, gum; sheep, cattle, pigs, horses; hides, skins; fish; gold, silver, coal, copper, limestone, manganese, iron, tungsten; dairy products, meats, wool, clothing, lumber, woodwork, furniture, electrical and radio goods, motor assembly, printing, publishing, biscuits, confections, footwear, rubber products, chemical fertilizers, tobacco products, brewing. |
| NIUE | Dependency of New Zealand administered by a resident commissioner. | New Zealand pound | Melanesian and Polynesian dialects English | Protestant | Copra, sweet potatoes, bananas; hats, baskets. |
| NORFOLK ISLAND | Administered by Australia. | Australian pound | English | Protestant | Citrus, passion fruits, bananas, cherry guavas; hides; fish |
| NORTHERN TERRITORY | Australian territory governed by appointed administrator. | Australian pound | English Aboriginal dialects | Protestant Roman Catholic Tribal religions | Grains, groundnuts, cotton, millet, coconuts, vegetables, fruits; cattle, horses, sheep, goats, swine, donkeys, mules, camels; hides, skins; gold, silver, lead, tin, copper, nitrates, mica, wolfram, ocher, uranium, pearl shell, trapang. |
| PACIFIC ISLANDS (TERR. OF THE) | See Caroline, Mariana, Marshall and Palau Islands. | | | | |
| PALAU ISLANDS | A civil administrative district in the Western Carolines and part of the United States Pacific trust territory. | dollar | Micronesian dialects | Tribal religions Christian | Coconuts, manioc, taro, pineapples, sweet potatoes, papayas; poultry, pigs, goats; fish; phosphate; handicrafts. |
| PAPUA TERRITORY | Australian territory governed by an administrator. | Australian pound | Papuan Pidgin English English | Tribal religions Protestant Roman Catholic | Coconuts, rubber, sweet potatoes, yams, taro, sago, rice, bananas, coffee, kapok, bamboo, sisal hemp, copra; shells; sponges; cattle, goats, poultry; gold, copper, manganese. |
| PITCAIRN ISLAND | British colony administered by a chief magistrate responsible to the governor of Fiji. | Fiji pound | English Tahitian | Protestant (Seventh Day Adventist) | Fruits, vegetables, goats, poultry; handicraft. |
| QUEENSLAND | Australian state with a governor, cabinet and a legislative assembly. | Australian pound | English | Protestant Roman Catholic | Sugar cane, wheat, sorghum, corn, barley, oats, potatoes, hay, pumpkins, tomatoes, peanuts, grapes, pineapples, citrus fruits, bananas, cotton, tobacco; sheep, cattle, pigs, horses, poultry, eggs, wool, meats, fish, dairy products; lead, zinc, coal, gold, silver, copper, tin, fluorspar, lumber, clothing, metal work, machinery, furniture, motor vehicles, paper, printing, sugar milling, wines, rum. |
| SAMOA, EASTERN | Possession of the United States with a governor and a bicameral legislature of an advisory nature. | dollar | English Samoan | Protestant | Copra, taro, breadfruit, yams, bananas, arrowroot, pineapples, oranges; mats. |
| SAMOA, WESTERN | Under United Nations trusteeship administered by New Zealand. | New Zealand pound | Samoan English | Protestant Tribal religions | Copra, cocoa beans, bananas, taro; fish; pigs, poultry. |
| SOCIETY ISLANDS | Part of French Oceania governed from Tahiti. | | | | |
| SOLOMON ISLANDS | A protectorate administered by a British resident commissioner. | Australian pound | Melanesian Pidgin English English | Tribal religions Protestant Roman Catholic | Copra, pigs, poultry; trochus shell, turtle shell, bêche-de-mer. |
| SOUTH AUSTRALIA | Australian state with a governor, cabinet and a legislative council and assembly. | Australian pound | English | Protestant Roman Catholic | Wheat, barley, oats, hay, grapes, fruits, vegetables, flax, gums, chicory, eucalyptus oil; sheep, cattle, horses, pigs, poultry, eggs, meats; hides, skins, wool, dairy products; iron, gypsum, salt, opals, talc, barite, clays, coal, uranium, pyrites, phosphates, gold, manganese, copper, steel, wines. |
| TASMANIA | Australian State with a governor, cabinet and a legislative council and assembly. | Australian pound | English | Protestant Roman Catholic | Oats, wheat, hay, peas, turnips, apples, barley, potatoes, hops; sheep, cattle, pigs, horses, poultry, eggs, meats, wool, dairy products; hides, skins; timber, paper, pulp; fish; zinc, lead, copper, tin, silver, limestone, gold, cadmium, osmiridium, phosphates, coal; refined metals, lumber, preserves, brick, tile, pottery, tanning, chemicals, cement, carbide, electrodes, furniture, agricultural tools, confections. |
| TOKELAU ISLANDS | An island territory of New Zealand administered by a high commissioner. | New Zealand pound | Samoan | Protestant Roman Catholic | Coconuts, fiber, taro, copra; pigs, chickens; fish; hats, mats. |
| TONGA | Constitutional monarchy under British protection ruled by queen with cabinet and legislative assembly. | Tongan pound | Tongan English | Protestant Roman Catholic | Copra, bananas, fungus, candlenuts; pigs, cattle, goats. |
| TUAMOTU ARCHIPELAGO | Part of French Oceania governed from Tahiti. | French franc | Polynesian dialects French | Tribal religions Roman Catholic | Copra, pearls, pearl shell. |
| TUBUAI ISLANDS | Part of French Oceania governed from Tahiti. | French franc | | | |
| VICTORIA | Australian state with a governor, cabinet and a legislative council and assembly. | Australian pound | English | Protestant Roman Catholic | Wheat, oats, barley, potatoes, hay, raisins, currants, oranges; sheep, cattle, pigs, horses, poultry, eggs, meats, wool, dairy products; timber; coal, gold, limestone, titanium, antimony, potash, tin, bauxite; textiles, clothing, food processing, metal products, wines, woodwork, machinery vehicles, printing. |
| VOLCANO ISLANDS | Administered by the United States. | dollar yen | Japanese | Shintoist Buddhist | Sugar cane; fish; sulphur. |
| WESTERN AUSTRALIA | Australian state with a governor, cabinet and a legislative council and assembly. | Australian pound | English | Protestant Roman Catholic | Wheat, oats, barley, hay, potatoes, fruits, tobacco, grapes, vegetables; sheep, cattle, pigs, horses, poultry, eggs; wool, hides, skins; meats, dairy products; gold, coal, pyrite, lead, asbestos, silver, manganese, tin; timber; fish; food processing, clothing, woodwork, machinery, vehicles, wines. |

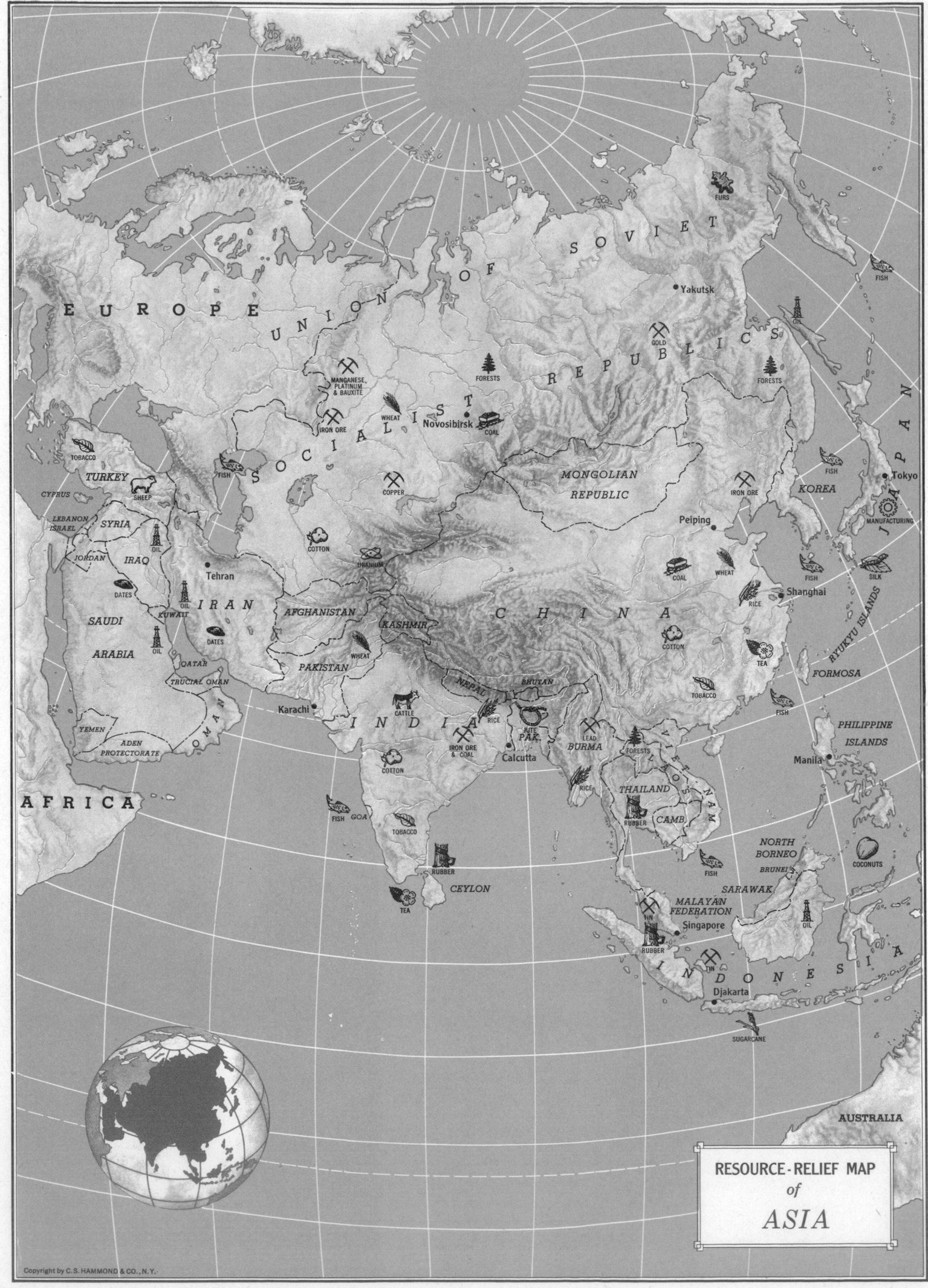

RESOURCE-RELIEF MAP
*of*
**ASIA**

TWA—Trans World Airline

For centuries fishing has been the chief occupation of the people who live along the Sea of Galilee.

TWA—Trans World Airline

A rapid development of industry and commerce is forseeable in Israel's economic future.

**ASIA**—To say that this is the largest continent in the world gives no idea of its immensity. Covering one-third of the land area of the world, Asia is more than a million square miles larger than the combined areas of North and South America. It extends from the ice-bound regions of the Arctic Circle to the sun-burnt islands of the Tropics. It claims the highest and lowest elevations, as well as the wettest and driest areas In the world. Mount Everest is the highest and the Dead Sea the lowest. Assam is the wettest, and Northern Siberia the driest. Asia is the cradle of the earliest civilization and is now the home of over half the population of the world.

Man has drawn a line separating Asia from Europe but the only natural division is the low Ural Mountains and a depression extending from the mountains to the Caspian Sea. Only a man-made canal at the Isthmus of Suez separates Asia from Africa.

Washed by three oceans and a number of seas, Asia has a coast line over thirty thousand miles in length. Deep indentations along the irregular coast form seas, such as the Bay of Bengal and the Arabian Sea. Twisting and pointed peninsulas reach far out into the oceans. The shores are dotted with archipelagos and island groups. Among the island groups are Japan, the Philippines, and Indonesia, all of which have become as important as mainland countries.

The mountain ranges that sweep across

Europe from west to east continue in long parallel lines through Asia. These mountain chains rise in height, first curving away from one another, and then closing in abruptly in a knot of massed mountains which has been referred to as "the roof of the world." Eastward, the awe-inspiring Himalayas reach to the plateau of Tibet, turn suddenly south through Indochina in long lines of deep, forested ravines, and disappear in a string of islands, drowned by the waters of the Indian Ocean. The Himalayas, covered with eternal snows and scored by mighty glaciers, are the highest mountains in the world. From Mount Everest, their loftiest peak, they drop steeply down to the low river plains below.

To the north of the mountains lies the great plain of Northern Asia, a continuation of the North European plain. Broken only by the Urals it sinks slowly to the frozen Arctic shore. To the south, in India and Arabia, are two low plateaus with steep sides, and the river lowlands of Mesopotamia and the Ganges plain.

This enormous continent is drained by many large rivers. Flowing toward the Arctic Ocean are the Ob, Yenisei and Lena Rivers. They are often blocked with ice for months and flood the surrounding country in thaw. In the east the silt carried down by the rivers has built the wide alluvial plains of China. The Hwang-ho, or Yellow River, flows into the Yellow Sea. Yellow is a sacred color, for this is the color of the silt deposited by the

great river on the fertile plain, where crowded millions of Chinese grow their crops and find their livelihood. The Yangtse Kiang, or Blue River, rises in Tibet and passes through deep walls before winding sluggishly across the lowlands of China. These rivers often overflow in disastrous floods and have changed their courses many times.

The Ganges, Indus and Brahmaputra have built up the fertile lowlands of North India and are slowly extending it in broad, swampy deltas, out to sea.

Covering so many degrees of latitude, the climate of Asia would naturally show great variation. There are great extremes of cold and heat in the Siberian lowlands and Northern China. Great areas in the center of the continent, far from the sea, are dry; with tropical conditions prevailing in the south. The heaviest rainfall anywhere in the world is in some localities of Southeastern Asia and everywhere in the eastern region there is sufficient moisture for agriculture. In Assam, India, the rainfall averages about thirty-five feet a year.

There is every type of vegetation, ranging from tundra mosses in the extreme north to tropical plant life in the south. There are great stores of mineral wealth, but much of this is still undeveloped. Asia has been slow to awaken to the possibilities of an industrialized civilization.

Southwestern Asia is that section of the continent lying between India and the

Altered only slightly by a few modern buildings, Nazareth still rests in its ancient setting.

Flocks of sheep and goats are the economic mainstay of the Arab's life.

Aegean Sea. It is a rugged, mountainous country which includes the two desert plateaus of Iran and Arabia, and the rich lowlands of the Tigris and Euphrates valley.

Great nations flourished in Southwestern Asia several thousand years before the birth of Christ. Composed almost entirely of the white race, their civilizations contributed much to the early nations along the Mediterranean. Mongolian hordes invaded these lands in the thirteenth century, almost destroying the civilizations which they found. Growing in power, a mighty nation which spread into Africa and Europe came into being. The Turks are descendants of these war-like people.

**TURKEY**—Surrounded by mountains on three sides is a high, dry plateau which slopes to the fertile shores of the Mediterranean. Among the chief mountains are the Taurus range, stretching from the southwestern shore of the Aegean to the north of Syria, their principal peaks rising from 7,000 to 10,000 feet; the Bulgar Mountains rising over 10,000 feet; and the Ala Mountains, north of Seyhan, rising 8,000 to 10,000 feet high. The highest peak in the country is Mt. Ararat, 16,145 feet. Flowing into the Black Sea are the Coruh, the Yesil Irmak, the Kizil Irmak and the Sakariya. Into the Mediterranean flow the Seyhan and Ceyhan. In the east of Asia Minor are the head-

waters of both the Euphrates and the Tigris as well as of the Araks.

**ISRAEL**—After 2,000 years the Jewish people realized their dream of an independent homeland with the establishment of the new state of Israel in 1948. Lying between Egypt and Jordan on the eastern shores of the Mediterranean, the country is a hot and arid land. The new nation's economy is based on the cultivation of citrus fruit for export made possible by extensive irrigation of the lands of Zionist sponsored settlements. Oil refining, chemical production and light industry are also important to the economy.

**SYRIA AND LEBANON**—The occupations of the people of these countries have not changed since Biblical times, and are similar to those of Turkey. Mostly agricultural, there is little mineral wealth, and manufacturing is largely for local markets. Lebanon is mainly mountainous with a fertile valley lying in the center between the Lebanon Mountains on the west coast and the Anti-Lebanon Mountains which form the eastern border between Lebanon and Syria. Syria consists largely of desert surrounded by mountains. In the northeast, the Euphrates flows across the desert and irrigates a valuable strip of agricultural land. Other fertile areas are found near Homs and Hama, both in the northwest, and Damascus and the Jebel Druze district in the southwest.

**IRAQ**—Once the site of the Babylonian Empire, the region of the Tigris and Euphrates is the "Fertile Crescent" of ancient times. The country is a great alluvial plain, bounded on the north by Kurdistan, on the east by Iran, on the south by the Persian Gulf, and on the west by the Syrian and Arabian Deserts. Northern Iraq has a valuable supply of oil which is piped to Haifa and Tripoli.

**IRAN (Persia)**—Most of the country is plateau, surrounded by mountain chains, except in the east where huge salt deserts are found. An extension of the mountain ranges, locally known as the Khorasan Mountains of the Hindu Kush, enters on the northeast from Afghanistan and merges into the Elburz Range south of the Caspian, the highest peak being Mt. Demavend. Except for narrow fertile areas along the Caspian Sea and Persian Gulf the land is too dry to sustain many people.

**ARABIA**—The Arabian Peninsula is a land composed almost entirely of desert, mostly of a barren and stony type, with an abundance of sand in the southeast. Besides scattered oases there are only a few small areas in Arabia with enough rainfall to permit the growing of crops. Saudi Arabia, which occupies the central two-thirds of the peninsula, has experimented with modern, mechanized methods of irrigation to improve farming conditions, and a modern railroad now reaches the interior from the Persian Gulf. The finest Arabian horses and camels are raised in the central highlands. Discovery of valuable oil reserves in the desert near the

TWA—Trans World Airline

One of the two chief ports of India, Bombay is a center for exported raw material and imported manufactures.

Representative of the fine architecture of India is the luxurious structure of the Taj Mahal.

TWA—Trans World Airline

Persian Gulf fostered new economic development, and many local sheikhs, or tribal rulers, have become suddenly rich. Pearling, once important in the Gulf, is now declining. In the mountain valleys of Yemen is the most fertile soil of the peninsula, and its Red Sea ports, such as Mocha and Hodeida handle its coffee and other exports, as well as pearls from nearby islands.

**AFGHANISTAN**—Barren tablelands, deep ravines and snow-covered mountains leave Afghanistan an unproductive land. Lying as a barrier between Siberia and India, it has been the scene of many invasions and conquests but the war-like Afghans have never

been completely vanquished. Cereals, fruits and vegetables are grown only in small areas under irrigation, and the fat-tailed sheep—a native of the country—furnishes meat and a butter substitute.

**PAKISTAN**—Pakistan is divided into two widely separated sections. The larger part, West Pakistan on the Arabian Sea, consists of the fertile Indus valley, the extremely rugged Northwest frontier and arid Baluchistan. Cereal raising and cotton production are concentrated in the Indus Valley which possesses one of the oldest and most efficient canal irrigation systems in the world. East Pakistan, on the Bay of Bengal, occupies the lower Ganges-Brahmaputra delta and the Assam highland foothills. This nation, while almost wholly Mohammedan in religion, is influenced politically and culturally not only by the Islamic world to the west but also the neighboring Hindu civilization of India.

**INDIA**—For over four thousand years, India has been at the mercy of marauding and conquering races. Unlike many lesser countries, who have successfully thrown off the yoke of oppression, India, until recently, has always been subject to foreign rule. As a result it is a confusion of races, castes, and religions, with a civilization ranging from the

highest type of culture to the most primitive. In 1947 India was granted independence and now takes her place among the important powers of the globe.

Except for the rocky slopes of the mountains, the soil is fertile and supports the largest agricultural population in the world. Like the farmers of France, a large majority of these people live in small villages surrounded by tilled fields. And, while primitive methods and equipment are used, surprisingly large crops are raised. Disastrous droughts, due to the vagaries of the weather, and the famines which followed, have been partially relieved by government sponsored irrigation works and the construction of railroads and motor roads.

**SIKKIM, NEPAL AND BHUTAN**—These three small independent states are shut off from the outside world by the Himalayas. Several of the world's highest mountains, including Mount Everest, are in southern Nepal. Their inhabitants are energetic people who raise cattle, wheat, rice, tobacco and spices which they export in exchange for necessary manufactured goods, sugar, oil, etc.

**CEYLON**—The island of Ceylon has been called the "Pearl of the Orient." Situated off the southern coast of India it is famous

The land surface of the Malay Peninsula is uneven and traversed by snow-capped peaks.

Much modernization in Indonesia has caused sharp contrasts between the old and new.

Indonesia Information Office

Indonesia Information Office

Asian art has been stimulated by many of the Eastern republics through the establishment of technical and cultural institutions.

for its tea, precious stones and tropical beauty. The broad coastal strip which surrounds the central mountains is, for the most part, fertile and produces a luxuriant vegetation. Although the climate is tropical, sea breezes temper the heat.

**INDOCHINA**—Included on this southeastern peninsula of Asia are a part of Burma, Thailand, Indochina and the Malayan Federation. Most of the peninsula is characterized by heavily forested valleys and mountain ridges of the Himalayas running the length of the land. This is the great rice-producing region, and most of the world's rubber comes from this area. The rainfall is heavy in the entire area and the land is very productive. In the dense forests are

valuable stands of prize woods, teak, ebony and other trees used for their wood or gum. Agriculture is the chief industry throughout the peninsula but there are many important deposits of valuable minerals. Modern methods of agriculture and mining have been introduced. Singapore, situated on an island at the extreme southern end of the peninsula, commands one of the most important sea routes in the world.

**THE MALAY ARCHIPELAGO** — The world's largest group of islands extends from Sumatra to the Philippine Islands off the coast of China, and includes many thousands of islands. With the exception of the Philippines, and parts of Timor, Borneo and New Guinea, the archipelago was ruled for

hundreds of years by the Netherlands.

**INDONESIA**—Colonization and development begun by the Dutch in the XVIIth century has resulted in the richest and most important island group in the world.

Most of the islands are mountainous and of volcanic origin. At one time they were a part of the mainland connecting Asia with Australia. Java is the most productive and highly developed of the East Indies. It is one of the most densely populated regions in the world. Much of the land is divided into native farms and large plantations. The plantation crops are chiefly for export.

Next to Greenland, New Guinea and Borneo are the largest islands in the world. Sumatra and Celebes are next in size in the East Indies. Much of the mineral wealth of these islands is yet untouched. Borneo is crossed almost in the middle by the equator and few white people occupy the island because of the humidity and heat. Petroleum is an important resource of Borneo, Sumatra and Java, and two small islands adjoining Sumatra have valuable deposits of tin. Bali, while one of the lesser islands, has been one of the most publicized, and is favored by tourists as a tropical paradise.

**PHILIPPINE ISLANDS**—Numbering over seven thousand islands, Philippines, like other islands of the Malay Archipelago, are the tops of drowned mountains protruding from the sea. There are well watered fertile plains between the mountains. Being near the equator the temperature is never very low. Although the days are warm, the nights are usually cool. Some of the many volcanoes in

The narrow streets of Peking are typical of China's crowded cities where the nation's trading and business are daily transacted.

Publishers' Photo Service

Publishers' Photo Service

Japan's development as a leading industrial nation has not effaced her customs and traditions.

the Philippines are still active and the islands are subject to earthquakes.

## CHINA

CHINA—Chinese civilization is of greater antiquity than any other existent world culture. It has shown great powers of survival and has possessed the ability to absorb all foreign influences without losing its own identity.

The Chinese people are patient, industrious, and have great physical endurance. They are among the world's best farmers, having grown more food for longer periods on the same land, without exhausting the soil, than any other people. They take naturally to mechanics and are fine traders and business men.

With the possible exception of Africa, China has the largest undeveloped natural resources in the world. There are rich deposits of coal, with China ranking second to the United States in total reserves. Iron ore reserves are large enough to meet its needs for many years to come. It is believed that China has one of the most valuable deposits of copper, and tin has been a leading mineral export.

China is a land of garden farmers and the soil is cultivated intensively. Few animals are raised, which conserves acreage for food crops. Hence the Chinese diet consists almost entirely of vegetable products. In a relatively mild climate people can subsist on less food than in a colder region. Rice is the most

important crop but almost every known crop is raised.

Inner Mongolia, Tibet and Sinkiang are outer provinces of China. Until the building of railroads and motor roads they were reached entirely by caravan routes. This region has extreme temperatures and is largely desert. The Great Wall was built to keep the Mongols out of China. Tibet, until recently opened up to British trade, excluded all foreigners. Sinkiang consists almost entirely of a desert basin.

## MONGOLIAN REPUBLIC

MONGOLIAN REPUBLIC—This almost entirely pastoral country consists largely of an arid plateau composed mainly of the Gobi Desert. In the northwest are high mountains whose streams flow into numerous sizable lakes. The Mongolian people are almost entirely a nomadic race who wander from place to place seeking new pastures for their herds of cattle.

## JAPAN

JAPAN—The chief feature of the country is its mountainous character, for each island has a mountainous backbone. Fujiyama, the highest mountain, reaches 12,395 feet. One of the most notable physical features is the Inland Sea or Japanese Mediterranean. It is almost entirely landlocked and surrounded by chains of volcanoes, of which few are now active. The climate is temperate and healthful, with abundant rainfall.

Only 20 per cent of the land can be cultivated and the balance is largely mountainous, with frequent destructive earthquakes and volcanic activity. While minerals have been a major factor in her industrial growth, Japan is not well supplied with them. The only large mineral deposits are coal and copper, with some gold, silver and lead. The petroleum produced falls far short of her needs.

The low standard of living and the small amount of land suitable for cultivation have made farming highly intensive. A large percentage of the farms are only an acre or two in size and most of the farmers are forced to carry on some other occupation to exist.

Manufacturing has risen rapidly in Japan with the production of textiles leading. Because of low wages and nearness to the Oriental market, Japan has been able to compete in cheaper goods to the disadvantage of other countries.

## KOREA

KOREA—Korea's strategic position between the Asiatic mainland and Japan has made it an historic pathway for invasion. Coveted at different times by China, Russia and Japan, she lost her independence early in the century to the Japanese Empire. During the second World War, Korea was promised her independence, but the end of the fighting brought her only division between the great powers and later renewed military conflict.

Physically and economically Korea is divided into two contrasting natural regions. The agricultural heart of the nation is south of the thirty-eighth parallel, producing chiefly rice and barley. North of the parallel, industry and mining of coal and iron predominate.

| POLITICAL DIVISION | GOVERNMENT | MONETARY UNIT | PRINCIPAL LANGUAGES | PRINCIPAL RELIGIONS | MAJOR PRODUCTS |
|---|---|---|---|---|---|
| ADEN | British colony administered by a governor and an executive and legislative council. | East African shilling | Arabic Hindu | Mohammedan | Salt, cigarettes, dhowbuilding, fish; cloth, dyeing, sesame oil, soap, sorghum, ship-bunkering. |
| ADEN PROTECTORATE | Ruled by native sultans and sheikhs advised by British political officers under a British agent. | East African shilling | Arabic | Mohammedan | Dates, gums, tobacco, fish oil, butter, wheat, barley, sesame, millet, sorghum, aloes, ghee; goats, sheep, camels, cattle. |
| AFGHANISTAN | A constitutional monarchy ruled by a king, a cabinet and a bicameral legislative assembly. | Afghani rupee | Afghan (Pushtu) Persian | Mohammedan | Wheat, barley, millet, corn, sorghum, lentils, vegetables, fruits, nuts, castor beans, madder, asafetida, cotton, tobacco; fat-tailed sheep (karakul), camels, zebus; wool, skins; sheepskin, textiles, leather, carpets, rugs; gold, iron, lapis lazuli, coal, copper, lead, silver. |
| BAHREIN | Arab sheikhdom protected by Great Britain and advised by British political agent. | rupee | Arabic | Mohammedan | Pearl fishing, petroleum, boatbuilding, fishing; reed mats, dates, lucerne; donkeys; textiles. |
| BHUTAN | Ruled by a maharaja and advised by India in foreign relations. | rupee | Bhutanese (Tibetan dialect) | Lamaist Hindu | Rice, corn, millet, lac, wax, musk; elephants, ponies, chowries; cloth, baskets, mats, metalwork, guns, swords. |
| BRUNEI | A sultanate under British protection administered by a British resident. | Malayan dollar | Malay English | Mohammedan | Rice, sago, rubber, jelutong, cutch, sugar cane, tapioca, bananas, pineapples; timber; domestic birds, buffalo, pigs, cattle; petroleum, natural gas; boatbuilding, cloth, brass and silverware. |
| BURMA, UNION OF | A republic with a president elected by a bicameral legislature. | kyat | Burmese Shan Karen Kachin | Buddhist Tribal religions | Rice, sesame, peanuts, corn, cotton, millet, tobacco, sugar, beans, fruit, vegetables, pulses, rubber; teakwood, lumber; cattle, buffalo, pigs, goats, sheep; petroleum, silver, lead, zinc, tin, copper, tungsten, rubies, sapphires, amber, jade, nickel, gold, antimony, cobalt, salt; textiles, hides, matches, lacquer ware. |
| CAMBODIA | Constitutional monarchy with a national assembly. | riel | Khmer Tao | Buddhist | Rice, tobacco, kapok, cotton, pepper, coin, sugar, rubber; timber; cattle; fish; silk, cotton, textiles, pottery, rush mats, precious stones, phosphates. |
| CEYLON | Member of the British Commonweath ruled by a governor-general, a prime minister, a cabinet and a bicameral legislature. | rupee | Singhalese Tamil | Buddhist Hindu | Tea, coconuts, rubber, rice, millet, tobacco, cacao, cinnamon, citronella, cloves, fruits, palmyra, fish; cattle, buffalo, goats, swine, sheep; graphite, plumbago, mica, ilmenite, monazite, iron ore; salt, pearls, zircon, glass sands, copra, plywood, leather, shoes, glass, steel, acetic acid, ceramics, quinine, strychnine, shark-liver oil, coconut oil, textiles. |
| CHINA: MAINLAND (COMMUNIST) | In theory, governmental power resides in the National People's Congress and the State Council. In practice, power resides in the communist party's Central Committee. | Chinese dollar | Chinese Mongol Turki | Confucianist Buddhist Taoist Mohammedan | Rice, wheat, sweet potatoes, corn, barley, millet, kaoliang, soybeans, cotton, tea, sugar cane, tobacco, peanuts, peas, beans, opium, tung, silk; pigs, oxen, sheep, goats, buffalo, donkeys, horses, mules, poultry; timber; fish; iron, coal, tungsten, tin, antimony, mercury, copper, lead, zinc, silver, salt, soda, gold, petroleum, bismuth, molybdenum; foodstuffs, textiles, chemicals, machinery, metal work, metallurgical products, bristles, cement, clothing, embroideries, ceramics. |
| CHINA: FORMOSA (NATIONALIST) | A republic whose supreme organ of government is the popularly elected National Assembly. The Assembly elects the president and vice-president. Legislative powers reside with the Legislative Yuan. | new Taiwan yuan | Chinese (Amoy dialect) Formosan | Confucianist Buddhist Taoist Christian Tribal religions | Rice, tea, sugar, sweet potatoes, ramie, jute, tumeric, pineapples, bananas, camphor; pigs, buffalo, cattle, goats, horses. |
| CHRISTMAS ISLAND | A part of Singapore colony administered by a district officer of the Malayan civil service. | Malayan dollar | Chinese Malay English | Confucianist Mohammedan | Phosphate of lime. |
| CYPRUS | British colony ruled by a governor with the assistance of an executive council. | Cyprus pound | Greek Turkish | Greek Orthodox Mohammedan | Wheat, barley, oats, grapes, raisins, olives, fodder crops, potatoes, carobs, cotton, tobacco, linseed, hemp, flax, citrus fruits, bread beans, corn, sesame, melons; sponges, fish; sheep, goats, donkeys, cattle, pigs, horses, mules; copper pyrites, asbestos, chromite, gypsum, amber, copper concentrates; tobacco products, buttons, wines, spirits, false teeth, lace, gum, boots and shoes, dried fruits, cheese. |
| DAMÃO | Portuguese overseas province subject to government at Gôa and ruled by lieutenant-governor. | rupia | Portuguese Marathi | Hindu Roman Catholic Mohammedan | Salt, fish, rice, wheat, tobacco; palm-mat weaving. |
| DIU | Portuguese overseas province subject to government at Gôa and ruled by lieutenant-governor. | rupia | Portuguese Marathi | Hindu Roman Catholic Mohammedan | Salt; fish. |
| GÔA | Portuguese overseas province ruled by a governor assisted by executive and legislative councils. | rupia | Portuguese Marathi | Hindu Roman Catholic Mohammedan | Rice, cashew nuts, betel nuts, grains, vegetables, coconuts, mangoes; teak, bamboo, blackwood; fish; salt, manganese, asbestos, asphalt, guano, silica, coal, petroleum; sugar, textiles, distilling, dessicated coconut, tobacco products, rice milling, cocoa, coconut oil, embroideries. |
| HONG KONG | A British colony ruled by governor assisted by executive and legislative councils. | Hong Kong dollar | Chinese English | Confucianist Buddhist Christian | Rice, sugar cane, peanuts, sweet potatoes; fish; poultry, pigs; kaolin, lead, iron, wolfram, granite, silver, cement; shipbuilding and repair; rape, rubber shoes, enameled hollow-ware, textiles, electric flashlights and batteries, preserved ginger. |

| POLITICAL DIVISION | GOVERNMENT | MONETARY UNIT | PRINCIPAL LANGUAGES | PRINCIPAL RELIGIONS | MAJOR PRODUCTS |
|---|---|---|---|---|---|
| INDIA | An independent republic within the British Commonwealth with a president, vice president, cabinet and a bicameral legislature. | rupee | Indo-Aryan (Hindi, Bengali, Gujarati, Punjabi, Urdu) and Dravidian (Tamil, Kanarese, Telugan) English | Hindu Mohammedan Buddhist Animist Christian Sikh Jain Parsi | Rice, wheat, legumes, groundnuts, oilseeds, tea, tobacco, jute, cotton, rubber, coffee, sugar cane, barley, millet, corn; cattle, goats, buffalo, sheep, pigs; fish; coal, manganese, gold, petroleum, salt, mica, iron, copper, chromite, ilmenite, diamonds, silver, bauxite; textiles, shawls, carpets, jute manufacturers, wood-carving and metalwork, leather, chemicals, shipbuilding, petroleum refining, sugar refining, cotton ginning, iron and steel mills, glass, soap, matches. |
| INDONESIA | Republic with president, cabinet and unicameral legislature. | rupiah | Indonesian (Malay, Javanese, etc.) | Mohammedan Tribal religions Christian Hindu | Rice, sugar cane, rubber, palm oil, tobacco, corn, coconuts, copra, cassava, sweet potatoes, groundnuts, soya beans, cotton, kapok, coffee, cinchona, cocoa, pepper, fruits, vegetables; cattle, buffalo; tin, coal, petroleum, bauxite, manganese; rubber goods, chemicals, shipyards, textiles, paper, breweries, glass, handicrafts. |
| IRAN | Constitutional monarchy governed by a shah, prime minister, cabinet and a bicameral legislature. | rial | Persian Arabic Kurdish | Mohammedan Parsi | Wheat, cotton, gums, opium, fruit, rice, barley, sugar beets, tobacco, tea, corn, millet, legumes, vegetables, nuts; sheep, goats, cattle, asses, horses, mules; fish; petroleum, red-oxide, copper, sulphur, arsenic, coal, salt, marble, nickel, manganese, lead, cobalt, turquoise, iron ore; carpets, rugs, textiles, leather, glass, matches, chemicals, jute, tobacco products, oil refining, casings, wood, oils. |
| IRAQ | Constitutional monarchy with prime minister, cabinet, appointive senate and elective chamber of deputies. | Iraqi dinar | Arabic Turkish Kurdish | Mohammedan | Dates, other fruits, barley, wheat, rice, tobacco, cotton, beans, corn, sorghum, sesame; sheep, goats, asses, camels, horses, buffalo; oil, salt, wool, textiles, cigarettes, distilling. |
| ISRAEL | Republic with president, prime minister, cabinet and elective unicameral legislature. | Israeli pound | Hebrew Arabic | Judaist Mohammedan | Dairy products, vegetables, eggs, fruit, green fodder, wheat, hay, barley, corn, durra; goats, sheep, cattle, camels, poultry; fish; textiles, clothing, foods, beverages, tobacco, diamond polishing, shoes, metal and woodwork, furniture, building materials, leather, dairy products, electrical products, paper, printing, false teeth, pharmaceuticals, chemicals, dyes, soap, radios, oil refining, wines. |
| JAPAN | Constitutional monarchy with the executive power vested in prime minister and cabinet, the legislative power residing in a two-house parliament. The duties of the emperor are merely ceremonial. | yen | Japanese | Buddhist Shinto | Rice, wheat, barley, mulberry trees, potatoes, sweet potatoes, fruits, rape, vegetables, oats, tobacco, soy beans, tea, flax, hemp, camphor; timber, bamboo; horses, cattle, sheep, goats, pigs, rabbits; fish, agar, pearl oysters; silk worms; coal, pyrites, gold, copper, pyrethrum, manganese, silver, sulphur, chromite, zinc, salt, tin, lead, iron, petroleum; textiles, steel, paper, porcelain, earthenware, lacquer ware, vegetable oil, toys, slippers, shoes, machinery. |
| JORDAN | Constitutional monarchy with cabinet and bicameral legislature. | Jordan dinar | Arabic | Mohammedan | Wheat, barley, legumes, vegetables, fruits, olives; sheep, goats, camels; salt, phosphate, potash; wool, tobacco products, flour milling, building materials, olive oil. |
| KOREA | Divided into two parts by Armistice Line of August, 1953, pending final decisions of peace treaty. Communist "People's Republic" in North Korea; South Korea headed by a president, a prime minister, a cabinet and a unicameral legislature. | hwan | Korean | Confucianist Buddhist Christian | Rice, barley, millet, wheat, soya beans, red beans, cotton, tobacco, hemp, ginseng, fruit, radishes; timber; draft cattle, pigs, horses, mules, donkeys, sheep, goats, rabbits; fish; gold, iron ore, coal, tungsten, copper, silver, graphite, salt, kaolin, talc, bismuth, fluorite, minerals. N. Korea: textiles, fertilizer, chemicals, cement, heavy industries. S. Korea: textiles, cement, tobacco, silkworms, chemicals, machinery, metal, rubber, wood and paper and tobacco products. |
| KUWAIT | Arab sheikdom protected by Great Britain and advised by British political agent. | Indian rupee | Arabic | Mohammedan | Petroleum, shipbuilding (dhows), pearls, skins wool. |
| LAOS | Constitutional monarchy with a cabinet and a national assembly. | kip | Khmer (Annamese) Lao | Buddhist | Rice, coffee, tea, citrus fruits, corn, cinchona, gum, benzoin, cardamom; stick-lac; teak; tin. |
| LEBANON | Independent republic governed by a president, cabinet and an elective legislature. | Lebanese pound | Arabic French | Christian Mohammedan | Wheat, barley, corn, potatoes, citrus and other fruits, onions, olives, tobacco (Latakia); goats, asses, cattle, buffalo, sheep, horses, mules; iron, lignite; textiles, cement, olive oil, tobacco products, soap, matches, petroleum refining, gasoline, leather. |
| MACAO | Portuguese overseas province ruled by a governor. | pataca | Chinese Portuguese | Confucianist Buddhist Taoist Christian | Fish; preserves, firecrackers, vegetable oil, cement, metal work, lumber, tobacco (processed), matches, wine. |
| MALAYAN FEDERATION | Federated protectorate of Great Britain whose rulers have delegated power and are assisted by executive and legislative councils. | Malayan dollar | Malay Chinese English | Mohammedan Confucianist | Rubber, rice, coconuts, pineapples, tapioca, pepper, spices, tobacco, fibers, gambier, vegetables, tea; buffalo, swine, oxen, goats, sheep; fish; guano, tin, coal, iron ore, bauxite, manganese, copra, palm oil, timber, gold, rubber products, gutta-percha, wood products, canned pineapples, textiles. |
| MALDIVE ISLANDS | An independent sultanate, under British protection, with a bicameral legislature. | rupee | Singhalese Arabic Dravidian | Mohammedan | Coconuts, copra, coir, fruit, nuts; fish; cowries; cloth, mats, boats. |
| MONGOLIAN REPUBLIC | Communist republic with a president, cabinet and people's assembly. Prime minister is also head of politburo, supreme body of the communist party, which is the actual ruler. | Tugrik | Mongolian Russian | Lamaist Tribal religions | Stock raising (sheep, goats, cattle, horses, camels); milk, butter, cheese; wool, hides, skins, horns, bricks, machinery; coal, lead, gold. |

| POLITICAL DIVISION | GOVERNMENT | MONETARY UNIT | PRINCIPAL LANGUAGES | PRINCIPAL RELIGIONS | MAJOR PRODUCTS |
|---|---|---|---|---|---|
| NEPAL | An independent kingdom governed by a maharaja, prime minister and an advisory and a constituent assembly. | Nepalese rupee | Indo-Aryan languages Tibetan | Hindu Buddhist Lamaist | Rice, grains, jute, sugar cane, tea, vegetables, tobacco, cotton, potatoes, medicinal herbs; timber; cattle, hides, skins, ghee; iron, coal, copper, lead, zinc; cotton cloth, pottery, paper. |
| NEW GUINEA, NETHERLANDS | Status undetermined pending negotiations between Dutch and Indonesian Governments. | guilder | Papuan Dutch Negrito | Tribal religions | Sago, coconuts, sweet potatoes, wild nutmeg, mace, copra; bird of paradise plumes; petroleum. |
| NORTH BORNEO | British colony ruled by a governor and assisted by executive and legislative councils. | Malayan dollar | Malay Indonesian languages English Chinese | Tribal religions Mohammedan | Rubber, coconuts, copra, tobacco, manila hemp, sago, rice, cutch, sugar, pepper, kapok, groundnuts, Derris root, vegetables; timber; fish. |
| OMAN AND MUSCAT | An independent sultanate. | rupee (official) Maria Theresa dollar | Arabic | Mohammedan | Dates, pomegranates, limes and other fruits, sugar cane; dried fish. |
| PAKISTAN | Self-governing republic of the British Commonwealth ruled by a president, cabinet and a unicameral legislature. | Pakistani rupee | Indo-Aryan languages (Urdu, Bengali, Hindi, Punjabi, etc.) | Mohammedan Hindu Christian Sikh | Jute, rice, wheat, corn, cotton, sugar cane, fruit, oilseeds, tobacco, tea, fibers; timber; cattle, goats, sheep, horses, camels, poultry; hides, skins, wool; fish; salt, copper, petroleum, chromite, gypsum, magnesite, sulphur, antimony; textiles, flour milling, cement, iron and steel foundries, sugar, leather, chemicals, glass, sportsgoods, handicrafts, surgical instruments. |
| PHILIPPINES | Republic governed by a president, cabinet and a bicameral legislature. | peso | Malayan languages (Tagalog, Visayan, etc.) English Spanish | Roman Catholic Mohammedan Tribal religions | Rice, sugar cane, copra, manila hemp (abacá), corn, tobacco, maguey, rubber, bananas, pineapples, mangoes, papaya, citrus fruits, other fruits; hogs, carabaos, cattle, horses, goats, sheep; fish; timber, gum resins, tan and dye barks, dye woods; gold, iron, copper, chromite, silver, manganese, asbestos, asphalt, guano, silica, coal, petroleum; sugar, textiles, distilling, dessicated coconuts, tobacco products, rice milling, cocoa, coconut oil, embroideries. |
| QATAR | Arab sheikhdom protected by Great Britain and advised by British political agent. | rupee riyal | Arabic | Mohammedan | Dates; pearl fishing, dried fish; camels; petroleum. |
| RYUKYU IS. | Administered by the United States. | yen | Luchuan Japanese English | Animistic Shinto | Sweet potatoes, sugar cane, rice, fruits, mulberries; swine, cattle, goats, horses, poultry; silkworms; fish; Panama hats, textiles, lacquer, pottery, china, glassware, tiles. |
| SARAWAK | British colony administered by a governor and an executive and legislative council. | Malayan dollar | Malay Indonesian languages Chinese English | Mohammedan Tribal religions | Rice, rubber, sago, pepper, coconuts, pineapples, tobacco, coffee, fruits, vegetables; timber, rattan cane, guttas; buffalo, cattle, pigs, goats; fish; petroleum, gold, antimony, phosphate, cutch. |
| SAUDI ARABIA | Absolute monarchy, with premier and cabinet responsible to the king, and advisory councils. | riyal | Arabic | Mohammedan | Dates, sorghum, wheat, rice, henna, coffee, fruits, nuts, vegetables, honey, gum, sesame oil; fish; camels, sheep, goats, cattle, donkeys, poultry, horses; hides, wool, clarified butter, charcoal, pottery, tile, salt, soap, weaving; petroleum, gold, pearls. |
| SIKKIM | A protectorate of India ruled by a maharaja and a council. | rupee | Nepali Tepcha Bhutia | Hindu Buddhist | Millet, corn, pulse, rice, fruits; cattle; woolen cloth. |
| SINGAPORE | British colony administered by a governor, council of ministers and legislative assembly. | Malayan dollar | Chinese Malay Hindi English | Confucianist Buddhist Taoist Mohammedan Hindu Christian | Rubber, coconuts, fruits, vegetables, rice, coffee, tapioca, tobacco, sweet potatoes, pepper, pineapples; pigs, poultry, cattle; fish; tin, tin smelting, rubber milling, coconut milling, soap, beer, pineapple canning, biscuits, brick making, shipping, textiles, palm oil, cigarettes, gasoline, kerosene. |
| SYRIA | Republic with a president, prime minister and legislative assembly. | Syrian pound | Arabic Turkish Kurdish | Mohammedan Christian | Wheat, barley, sorghum, corn, cotton, lentils, chickpeas, sesame, vegetables, olives, grapes, tobacco (Latakia); sheep, goats, cattle, donkeys, camels, horses, poultry; wool, hides, skins; gypsum; leather, textiles, food, tobacco, wine, flour. |
| THAILAND (SIAM) | Constitutional monarchy with a prime minister, a cabinet, and a partly elective legislative assembly. | baht | Thai Khmer | Buddhist Tribal religions | Rice, rubber, coconuts, tobacco, cotton, corn, beans; teak and other woods; bullocks, buffalo, horses, elephants; fish; tin, wolfram. |
| TIBET | Theocracy. Nominally independent but under effective Chinese Communist control. Religious affairs are directed by the Dalai Lama. | sang | Tibetan | Lamaist | Barley, wheat, pulse, corn, vegetables, rice; yaks, asses, sheep, goats, donkeys; hides, wool, furs, musk; borax, salt, gold; cult objects. |
| TIMOR, PORTUGUESE | Portuguese overseas province ruled by a governor. | escudo | Malay Portuguese | Mohammedan Tribal religions Roman Catholic | Coffee, copra, sandalwood, wax, cocoa; hides, shells. |
| TRUCIAL OMAN | Seven Arab sheikhdoms protected by Great Britain and advised by British political agent. | rupee riyal | Arabic | Mohammedan | Dates, grains, vegetables; fishing, pearl fishing. |
| VIETNAM | Divided into two parts by Armistice Line Sept. 1954. North of 17th parallel is communist controlled "republic". South is a republic with a president and an assembly. | piaster | Khmer (Annamese) Lao | Buddhist | Rice, corn, sugar, tobacco, coffee, fruits, manioc, betel nuts, arrowroot, tea, cotton, areca nut, medicinal plants, cardamom, soya, rubber, copra, groundnuts, haricots, sweet potatoes, cinnamon; mulberries, bamboo, silk; cattle, buffalo, pigs; lumber; gold, tin, copper, coal, zinc, iron, cement, limestone, calamine, tungsten, manganese, phosphate, lead, bauxite. |
| YEMEN | Independent kingdom ruled by an Imam. | riyal | Arabic | Mohammedan | Coffee, barley, wheat, millet, sesame; cattle, hides; fish. |

# THE RACES OF MANKIND

BY DR. HENRY FIELD FORMERLY CURATOR OF PHYSICAL ANTHROPOLOGY

Revised by DR. W. D. HAMBLY CURATOR OF AFRICAN ETHNOLOGY

CHICAGO NATURAL HISTORY MUSEUM

FORMERLY FIELD MUSEUM OF NATURAL HISTORY

MONGOLOID     WHITE     NEGRO

GROUP SYMBOLIZING UNITY OF MANKIND

SCULPTURE BY MALVINA HOFFMAN

TEXT AND ILLUSTRATIONS COPYRIGHTED MCMXLVI BY CHICAGO NATURAL HISTORY MUSEUM

PUBLISHED BY C. S. HAMMOND & CO., INC., NEW YORK

# DESCRIPTION OF RACES

FOR MANY YEARS THE WORD "RACE" WAS FREELY AND UNCRITICALLY USED BY ANTHROPOLOGISTS; IT HAS EVEN BEEN MADE TO INCLUDE PSYCHOLOGICAL AND SOCIAL QUALITIES, AND HAS OFTEN BEEN CONFUSED WITH NATIONALITY; ALSO, IT HAS BEEN ALLIED WITH IDEAS OF INHERENT SUPERIORITY OR INFERIORITY. LET IT BE CLEAR THAT BY "RACE" WE MEAN A CERTAIN COMBINATION OF HERITABLE PHYSICAL TRAITS, WITHOUT ANY IMPLICATION OF SOCIAL STATUS OR PSYCHOLOGICAL ATTRIBUTES.

## AFRICA

The continent of Africa covers an area of 12,000,000 square miles, almost four times the size of the United States. The total population has been estimated at 150,000,000, but this is a vague approximation. About two-thirds of the continent—the forest zone comprising a western coastal strip and a large central area—is the habitat of typical Negroes. These show many important local variations in physical appearance. The general physique of the African is well represented in the Negro's statue in the group symbolizing the unity of mankind.

### TYPICAL NEGROES OF THE WEST COAST

The Negro is characterized by a dark skin color varying from extremely dark brown to almost black, though perhaps the skin is never jet black, and the stature varies considerably according to locality. The Kru of Liberia, the Ibo of Nigeria, and the Ijaw of the Niger Delta are often mentioned as exemplary Negro types. The West African coastal Negro is long-headed, of medium stature, extremely well developed, with a heavy torso and massive limbs. The arms are long and the legs short in comparison with the length of the trunk. In all Negroes the face is usually broad and massive, sometimes with a projecting chin. The nose is broad, and the lips are thick and everted. Dark eyes and woolly hair likewise are constant Negro features. The problems as to the origin of Negro types are too complex to be discussed here, yet the main branches of Negro stock may be mentioned.

### NEGROES OF THE UPPER NILE

In order to account for this type, which is usually called Nilotic, a hypothesis regarding the intrusion of a foreign race is helpful. Anthropologists believe that migratory waves of people, called Hamites, have been penetrating northeast Africa from a remote time long before the period of recorded history. It is thought also that the crossing of these Hamitic intruders with the true Negro produced the Nilotic type. The Nilotic Negros, if compared with typical Negroes of West Africa, show greater stature, a far more slender build, and heads longer in relation to their breadth (more dolichocephalic).

### NEGROES OF NORTHEAST AFRICA

In Kenya Colony are tribes whose physical type has been affected by intrusive Hamites. Here, as among the Nilotic Negroes, the true Negro physique has been modified in the direction of greater stature, less massive build, and refinement of the nose and mouth. These "Hamiticized" Negroes, of whom the Suk, the Masai, and the Nandi are examples, are referred to by some anthropologists as Half-Hamites.

### HAMITES

The Hamites, who inhabit north and northeast Africa, belong to the Caucasian branch of mankind. They possess dark brown or black hair, which is either curly or wavy in form, and the skin varies in color from reddish brown to dark brown. Their average stature varies from very tall to medium and their build is slender. The typical Hamite possesses a long head, an oval, elongated face with no forward protrusion, thin lips, pointed chin, and a prominent, well-shaped, narrow nose. Two main divisions of Hamites must be recognized, northern and eastern. The principal northern Hamites are the Berbers and the Tuareg, who are confined to the Sahara region. The eastern group of Hamites comprises the Somali, Hadendoa, and Bisharin peoples.

**BERBER MAN**
**MOROCCO**
**NORTH AFRICA**
**WHITE STOCK**

SOME NOTES ON MALVINA HOFFMAN. *Malvina Hoffman may be called the leading portrayer, in plastic form, of the world's racial types. Before Miss Hoffman was commissioned to create her racial studies in bronze, she was a recognized sculptor. After having studied under Gutzon Borglum and Auguste Rodin, she was awarded first prize at the Paris Salon for "Russian Dancers." Her works may be seen in the Metropolitan Museum of Art, New York, the Luxembourg Musée, Paris, the Carnegie Institute, Pittsburgh, and the American Academy, Rome. In 1929 Miss Hoffman was commissioned by the Field Museum of Chicago to record in bronze certain selected racial types. In her journeys to the native habitats of these races, she travelled in all of the continents and visited many out-of-the-way tribes. Accompanying the articles on The Races of Mankind are photographs of the bronzes resulting from Miss Hoffman's work in the service of anthropology.*

## SEMITES

The words Semitic and Hamitic have a definite linguistic connotation in the minds of anthropologists. The two languages, of which there are many dialects, were long ago split off from the original Hamitico-Semitic stock. But in addition to a linguistic meaning the terms bring to mind physical types which differ greatly from Negroes. Some characteristics of Hamites were mentioned in the preceding paragraph, and in a measure the physical traits of Hamites resemble those of Semites. Members of the Semitic group now living chiefly in the extreme north of Africa migrated from Arabia at early dates. One great migration and conquest occurred in the seventh and another in the eleventh century of the Christian Era. The Arabs, who are typical Semites in both physique and language, are usually medium in stature, are dark-haired, and generally have oval faces with long, narrow, straight noses. There are two typical head-forms among the Arabs—one is long, the other broad. For centuries the Arabs enslaved and sometimes intermarried with Negroes, consequently many Arab-Negro types may be seen in the north and the northeast of Africa. The Jews, of whom there are many in North Africa, speak Semitic languages, and in physiognomy some of them are not unlike the Arabs. We must regard the Semites as a big ethnic family which anciently split up into physical and linguistic types such as Arabs, Jews, and many of the tribes and nations so often mentioned in the Old Testament.

## PYGMIES

It has not yet been determined what genetic relationship exists between typical Negroes, Pygmies (sometimes misnamed Negrillos), Bushmen, and Hottentots. It must be noted that many small Negroid tribes of the central forest region are referred to as Pygmies. But some of these, for example, the Batwa Pygmy boy represented in a bronze bust, have probably issued from a crossing of Pygmies with Negroes.

There are, however, groups of true Pygmies, the most typical of which are the Wambuti of the Ituri Forest in the Belgian Congo. Their dark brown hair is usually short. Their skin color varies from light brown with a yellow tinge to a very dark chocolate color. The average male stature is four feet six inches, and both body and legs are short. There is a peculiar development of the buttocks similar to that of the Kalahari Bushmen. In shape the head is typically round and there is some protrusion of the face. The lips are full, and the root of the nose is flat and broad.

## BUSHMEN AND HOTTENTOTS

From a racial standpoint the Bushmen are the most interesting people south of equatorial Africa. At present they are confined mainly to the Kalahari Desert. The Bushmen possess short, frizzly hair which grows in separate tufts coiled into balls and because of its appearance is known as "peppercorn" hair. There is very little hair on the face and body. The skin ranges in color from yellow to olive, and becomes markedly wrinkled at an early age. The head is extremely small, low in the crown, and in shape intermediate between long and round. The width of the cheekbones combined with the narrowness of the forehead gives the face a lozenge-shaped appearance. The forehead is slightly protruding, and the nose is broader and flatter than in any other race. The dark eyes are often narrow and slightly oblique. The average male is below five feet in stature. In both sexes there is excessive development of the buttocks, which is often extremely accentuated among the women. The racial mixture of the Bushmen with Negroes and possibly with early invading Hamites resulted in a slightly taller people called Hottentots, who possess a longer and narrower head and a more protruding face. The Hottentots formerly inhabited the western part of South Africa, but their tribal organization is preserved at present only in southwestern Africa.

ETHIOPIAN MAN
ETHIOPIA
NORTHEAST AFRICA
WHITE STOCK

ETHIOPIAN WOMAN
ETHIOPIA
NORTHEAST AFRICA
WHITE STOCK

NUER WARRIOR
NUER TRIBE
UPPER WHITE NILE
NORTHEAST AFRICA
NEGRO STOCK

BATWA
PYGMY BOY
BELGIAN CONGO
CENTRAL AFRICA
NEGRO STOCK

SOMALI MAN
SOMALI TRIBE
NORTHEAST AFRICA
WHITE STOCK

MANGBETU WOMAN
MANGBETU TRIBE
NORTHEASTERN
BELGIAN CONGO
NEGRO STOCK

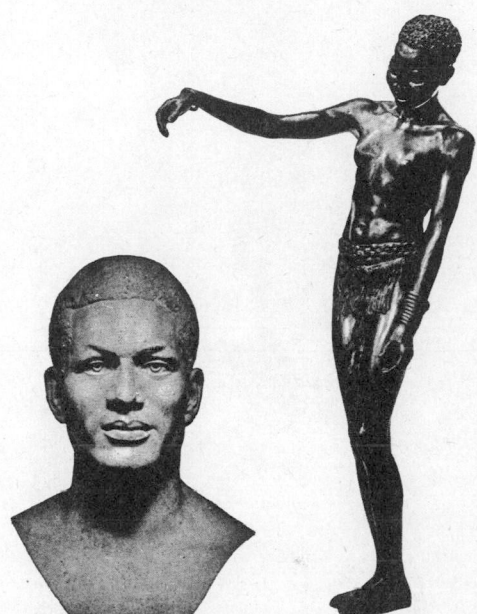

NUBIAN MAN
NUBIA
NILE VALLEY
EGYPT
WHITE STOCK

SARA GIRL
SARA TRIBE
LAKE CHAD DISTRICT
FRENCH EQUATORIAL
AFRICA
NEGRO STOCK

SENEGAL MAN
SENEGAL
FRENCH WEST
AFRICA
NEGRO STOCK

SUDANESE WOMAN
NORTHEAST AFRICA
NEGRO STOCK

ZULU WOMAN
ZULU TRIBE
SOUTHEAST AFRICA
NEGRO STOCK

We now proceed to a review of the sculptures pictured in this article, beginning two pages back. The Hamitic peoples from the north and northeast of Africa are represented by four examples. The bronze bust of a Hamite from Ethiopia shows the fine, delicate features characteristic of the group. There is also the head of an Ethiopian woman carved out of black Belgian marble. The regularity of the features and the peculiar method of dressing the hair are particularly well portrayed by the medium employed. The bust of a Somali also exhibits typical Hamitic features, while the Nubian shows a mixture of Hamitic and Negro blood. This man is from Luxor in Egypt, but the thickness of his lips differentiates him slightly from the typical Fellah of the Nile Valley.

The Negroes of the Upper Nile Valley are represented by a full-length statue—a dark-skinned Nuer warrior who is six feet eight inches in height. He is standing on one leg in the peculiar pose characteristic of these people. The Mangbetu of the northeastern Congo region are primarily a true Negro type; but the light brown skin of the aristocratic class suggests some Hamitic mixture. The bust of a Mangbetu woman is interesting for the peculiar mode of hairdressing and the deformation of the skull. The heads of some children are bound tightly with bandages which force them to grow both long and narrow. The resulting deformation is considered a mark of beauty and social distinction. The profile of this woman clearly shows the effects of this treatment.

The Negro type is illustrated by two full-length figures which are complementary: a Senegalese drummer and a dancing girl of the Sara tribe. These bronzes, patinated with a rich, black sheen, are shown in poses characteristic of the rhythmic movements associated with Negro music. The vivacious and graceful figure of the girl in dancing posture contrasts strikingly with the dreamy expression of the drummer.

In Dahomey, West Africa, there exists, as illustrated, a modified Negro type with features and hair suggesting Hamitic mixture. A Dahomey man is shown in a bust. The head of a woman from the Sudan illustrates the remarkable coiffure which is fashionable among her people. The head of a Ubangi duck-billed girl portrays one of the most remarkable artificial deformations in existence. A girl's lips are perforated, and small studs are inserted in order to broaden them. At intervals the size of the lip studs is increased. For many years, this custom has been prohibited by the French government. The central or equatorial peoples of Africa are represented by a life-size family group of Ituri Forest Pygmies. While the man beats rhythmically on the drum, his wife, carrying her small baby, listens attentively.

The realistic Bushman family group shows a woman carrying a baby strapped to her back. In addition, there is the head of an aged man. All three portray in detail the racial characters of this primitive desert dwelling people. The Zulu woman is a Negro type found in the far southeastern part of Africa.

DAHOMEY MAN
DAHOMEY
WEST AFRICA
NEGRO-WHITE
MIXTURE

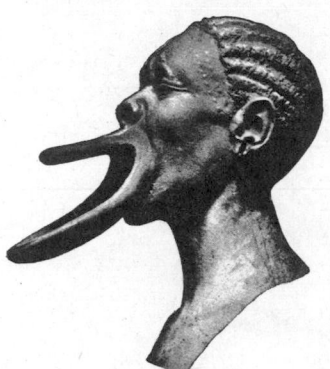

UBANGI WOMAN
UBANGI TRIBE
LAKE CHAD
FRENCH EQUATORIAL
AFRICA
NEGRO STOCK

BUSHMAN MAN
KALAHARI DESERT
SOUTH AFRICA
NEGRO-MONGOLOID
MIXTURE

WAMBUTI PYGMY
FAMILY
ITURI FOREST
NORTHEAST
BELGIAN CONGO
NEGRO STOCK

BUSHMAN WOMAN
AND BABY
KALAHARI DESERT
SOUTH AFRICA
NEGRO-MONGOLOID
MIXTURE

## EUROPE

The modern inhabitants of Europe can be divided into three groups—Mediterranean (southern European), Alpine (central European), and Nordic (northern European). While there has been untold interbreeding of these basic stocks since Paleolithic times, it is still possible to adopt this general classificatory system. Terminology tends toward change and elaboration. The Dinarics are broad-headed people of Alpine type; the Baltics are part of the Nordic or northern stock. Under "Mediterranean" stock are southern Europeans and north Africans (northern Hamites).

The Mediterranean race is exemplified by a Sicilian, who is short in stature and stocky in build, with an olive complexion, dark hair and eyes, long head, narrow oval face, and a small mouth. This group is now confined mainly to the Iberian Peninsula, western Mediterranean islands, southern France and Italy, and the western parts of Wales and Ireland.

The Alpine race comprises the majority of the round-headed peoples of Europe. They extend from the central plateau of France, Switzerland, and Czechoslovakia southward into the Balkans and eastward into the Soviet Union. A typical member of this group possesses a fairly dark complexion, brown wavy hair, thick eyebrows over brown eyes, heavy body hair, a broad face, sometimes a thick neck, and a medium to heavy build. The bust of an Austrian man is a good example of this group.

The Nordic peoples inhabit Scandinavia, northern Germany, and part of Holland and Belgium. There is also a strong Nordic element in Great Britain. A tall Swede, with light complexion and hair, blue eyes, long head, and a face with a prominent nose and chin, is a typical member of this group.

The racial divisions of Europe are represented by the full-length figures of a Sicilian fisherman, who is shown with his fishing net, and a Nordic man. In this section are also displayed busts of a Breton woman from Brittany, France, with her picturesque headdress, and of a Basque from northern Spain. There are also heads of an Englishman, a Frenchman, a Russian, a Turk and a Lapp.

SICILIAN MAN
SICILY
WHITE STOCK

LAPP MAN
LAPP TRIBE
EXTREME NORTHWEST
EUROPE
WHITE-MONGOLOID
MIXTURE

RUSSIAN MAN
GEORGIA U.S.S.R.
WHITE STOCK

ENGLISHMAN
GREAT BRITAIN
WHITE STOCK

FRENCHMAN
FRANCE
WHITE STOCK

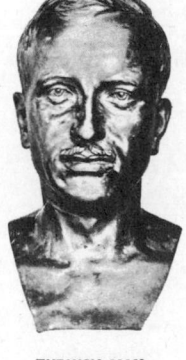

TURKISH MAN
TURKEY
WHITE STOCK

BRETON WOMAN
BRITTANY
NORTHWESTERN
FRANCE
WHITE STOCK

AUSTRIAN MAN
CENTRAL EUROPE
WHITE STOCK

ITALIAN MAN
NORTHERN ITALY
WHITE STOCK

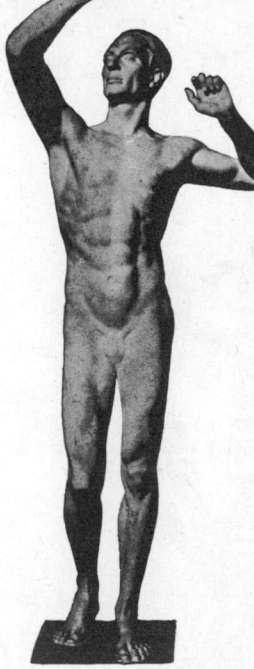

NORDIC MAN
NORTHERN EUROPE
WHITE STOCK

BASQUE MAN
NORTHERN SPAIN
WHITE STOCK

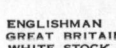

# ASIA

The study of the peoples of Asia is beset with numerous difficulties and presents many complex problems. In view of the evidence available it seems probable that man originated somewhere on this vast continent. A general survey of Asia is presented here, based on six large geographical divisions: southwest, south, southeast, east, central, and north.

## SOUTHWESTERN ASIA

This area was inhabited originally by early members of the Mediterranean stock, which forms the basic population at the present time. The northern and southern extremities of this section are inhabited by round-headed peoples. For example, in Armenia and Anatolia (Asiatic Turkey) the characteristic individual possesses dark hair, a tawny-white skin, medium stature, and a prominent aquiline nose with a depressed tip and large wings. Along the southern coast of Arabia the dominant type is round-headed, and there are also smaller brachycephalic (round-headed) groups, such as the Druze of Syria and part of the basic element in Iraq (Mesopotamia) on the east. As a representative of the great Arab group there was selected one of the workmen at Kish, in Iraq, where the Field Museum—Oxford University Joint Expedition conducted archaeological excavations from 1922 to 1933.

The Jewish people, who are a section of the larger Semitic group, form part of the great Mediterranean stock and are divided into two groups–the Ashkenazim and the Sephardim. The former includes the Jews of the U.S.S.R. and of central and western Europe, while the latter comprises those of Spain, Portugal, Asia Minor, Egypt, and Arabia. According to Haddon, the original Jews were racially akin to the modern Beduins of northern Arabia and blended at an early date with Amorites, Philistines, and Hittites, from whom they acquired the so-called "Jewish" nose. This entire region, with the exception of certain isolated zones, has been overrun in historic times by numerous invasions so that the modern population is extremely mixed.

In Iran (Persia) there are direct descendants of the ancient dwellers on the Iranian plateau together with Mediterranean elements on the west and Mongoloid traits on the northeast. There are also intrusive elements, such as the Kurds, Arabs, Armenians, and others who have settled in the country. Afghanistan is essentially the homeland of the Indo-Afghan stock, which is characterized by black, wavy hair, light, transparent brown complexion, long heads and faces, prominent, narrow noses, and dark eyes. An Afghan money lender pictured in the article, possesses the features typical of this group. The inhabitants of Baluchistan are closely related to the Afghans. Among the Baluchi, however, the head is rounder in shape; therefore they may be classified among Indo-Iranian peoples.

## SOUTHERN ASIA

There are three main geographical regions in India which appear to have influenced the principal racial groups. In the north lies the Himalayan chain of mountains; in the central northern portion are the sweeping plains of Hindustan; and to the south extends the great plateau, in many places jungle-covered, called the Deccan. With a varied population of about 350,000,000, racial origins in India are incapable of exact definition. In prehistoric times India was probably inhabited by a primitive Negroid population related to the aborigines of Ceylon, Sumatra, and possibly even Australia. It is believed also that at an early date Dravidian stocks entered India from the North-West Frontier region and Mongoloid races from the northeast territory. Dravidian is a general term used for the main population of the Deccan. The physical characters are a long head, abundant, wavy hair, brownish black skin, and medium stature.

The Veddas of Ceylon are one of the most interesting primitive groups in India. They belong to the pre-Dravidian division, and their physical characters comprise long, black hair which is coarse and wavy, dark brown skin, and short stature. The form of the head is long and narrow and the forehead slightly retreating, with prominent brow ridges, a relatively broad face and nose, thin lips, and pointed chin. The Veddas are modern survivors of the earliest inhabitants of India.

Among the photographic illustrations is shown a sculpture of a typical young Vedda with a bow by his side; also the full-length figure of a Tamil (linguistic term) and the head of a man from Kashmir, India. The Tamil occupy the northern half of the island of Ceylon and part of the mainland of southern India. In physique they belong to the Dravidian group. A Tamil is shown in the act of climbing a large palm tree—a feat which is performed with remarkable skill. The Kashmiri possess a light, transparent, brown skin, and are usually of relatively tall stature. The head is long with a well-developed forehead, a long, narrow face, regular features, and prominent, finely chiseled, narrow nose. Except for their skin color, many people of northern India closely resemble Europeans.

Other figures in this section represent a Singhalese from Kandy in Ceylon; a woman from Rajputana, belonging to the "untouchable" caste; a Brahman from

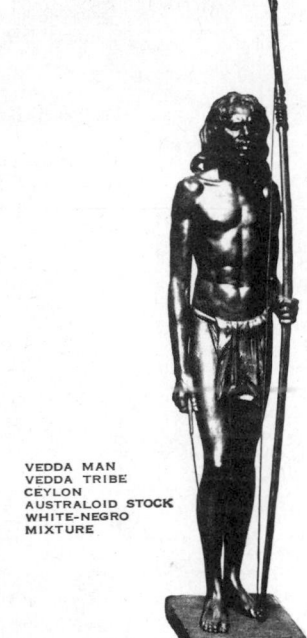

VEDDA MAN
VEDDA TRIBE
CEYLON
AUSTRALOID STOCK
WHITE-NEGRO
MIXTURE

TAMIL MAN
SOUTHERN INDIA
WHITE-NEGRO
MIXTURE

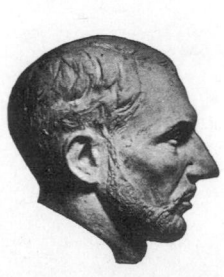

KASHMIRI MAN
KASHMIR PROVINCE
NORTHWEST INDIA
WHITE STOCK

TODA MAN
TODA TRIBE
VERY OLD
EAST INDIAN TYPE
SOUTHERN INDIA
AUSTRALOID STOCK
WHITE-NEGRO
MIXTURE

AFGHAN MAN
PESHAWAR
NORTHWEST INDIA
WHITE STOCK

ARAB MAN
HILLA
IRAQ
WHITE STOCK

BEDOUIN MAN
NORTH AFRICA
WHITE STOCK

Benares; and a man and a woman from Bengal. These sculptures show the refined features of the people of northern India. There is also the head of a beautiful Jaipur lady carved from limestone. It is exceptional for the regularity of her pleasing features.

The Andaman Islands, located in the Indian Ocean, are inhabited by members of the Negrito group, which comprises the Semang of the Malay Peninsula and eastern Sumatra, the Aëta of the Philippine Islands, and the Tapiro of New Guinea. The Andamanese are represented by a Pygmy hunter seated on a rock with his large bow held in his left hand and an arrow drawn back to his right cheek. He possesses the characteristic features of his group, which are short, black hair (sometimes with a reddish tinge), black skin, well-proportioned body, a small, round head, and small hands. The face is broad, the lips full but not everted, and there is no projection of the jaws.

The inhabitants of Burma represent southern Mongoloid types, possessing black hair (almost absent on the face and body), round heads, broad faces and noses, and frequently oblique eyes. The color of the skin varies from yellow to brown according to locality. For example, the farther removed from China, the less yellow is the color of the skin. As a representative of these people, the head of a Burmese man is interesting in comparison with the peoples of India and China.

## SOUTHEASTERN ASIA
### MALAY PENINSULA AND MALAY ARCHIPELAGO

The population of this region may be divided into two sections—a large southern Mongoloid group and a group not included in this classification. In the dense jungles of the Malay Peninsula live the Semang and the Sakai. The former belong to the Negrito or Pygmy group, since they are five feet or less in stature. The hair is short and frizzy, black in color with a reddish tinge and sparse on the face and body. The skin is dark chocolate brown in color. The shape of the head tends to be round; the lips are generally thin; the nose is short, flat, and extremely broad. The Semang also inhabit the eastern portion of the island of Sumatra. The representative of this group is a Pygmy hunter with his long blow-gun held upright beside him.

In the southern part of the Malay Peninsula also live the Sakai, who represent the second element among the aboriginal tribes of this region. They have intermarried considerably with the Negritos in the north and the Proto-Malays in the south. They differ from the Negritos in the lighter color of their skins, in their greater stature, and in their long, wavy, or curly hair, which is black with a reddish tinge. The Sakai belong to the pre-Dravidian group, being related to the Veddas of Ceylon and to the primitive jungle tribes of southern India.

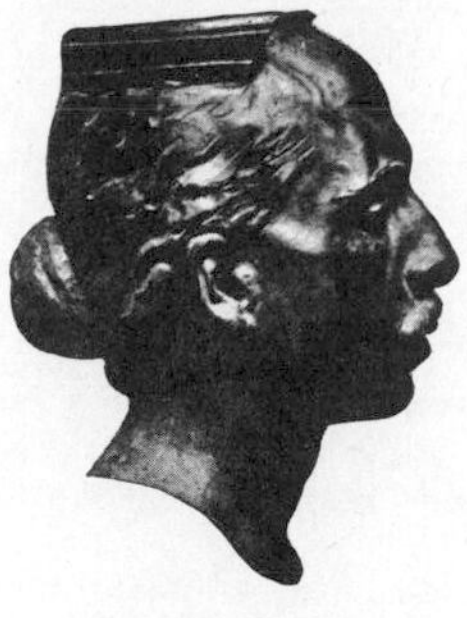

SINGHALESE MAN
CEYLON
WHITE STOCK

BENARES MAN
BENARES
NORTH CENTRAL INDIA
WHITE STOCK

JAIPUR WOMAN
RAJPUTANA PROVINCE
NORTHWEST INDIA
WHITE STOCK

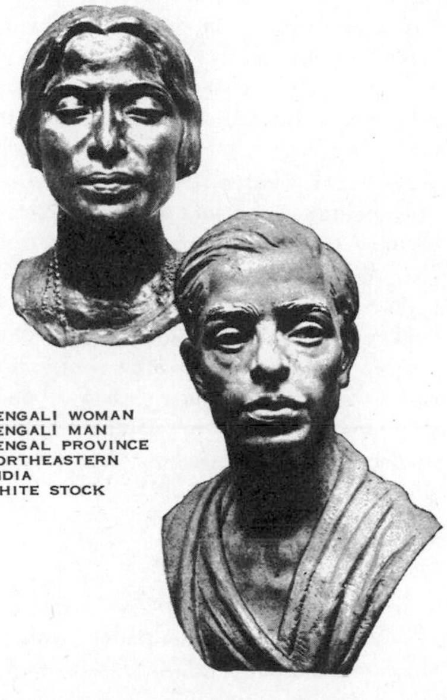

BENGALI WOMAN
BENGALI MAN
BENGAL PROVINCE
NORTHEASTERN
INDIA
WHITE STOCK

BURMESE MAN
BURMA
MONGOLOID STOCK

PADAUNG WOMAN
PADAUNG TRIBE
UPPER BURMA
MONGOLOID STOCK

SAKAI MAN
SAKAI TRIBE
TAPAH
MALAY PENINSULA
AUSTRALOID STOCK
WHITE-NEGRO
MIXTURE

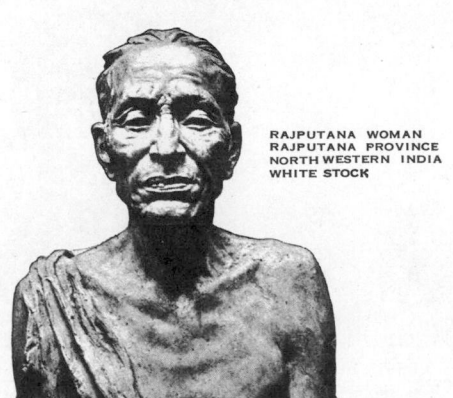

RAJPUTANA WOMAN
RAJPUTANA PROVINCE
NORTH WESTERN INDIA
WHITE STOCK

PYGMY MAN
SEMANG TRIBE
MALAY PENINSULA
NEGRO STOCK

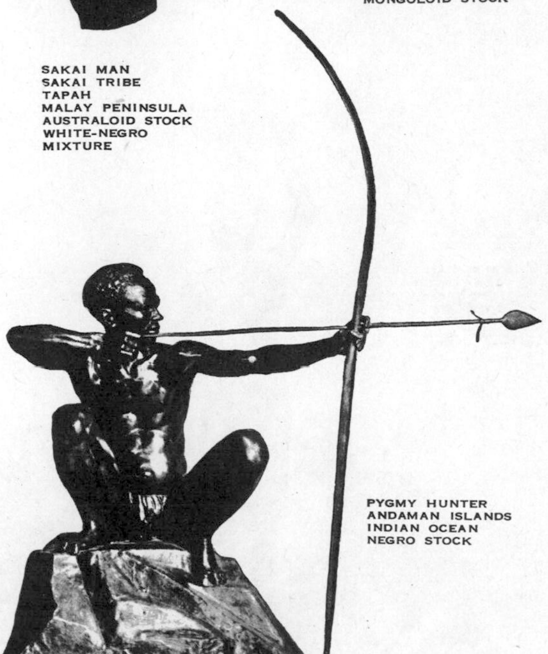

PYGMY HUNTER
ANDAMAN ISLANDS
INDIAN OCEAN
NEGRO STOCK

JAKUN GIRL
JAKUN MAN
JAKUN TRIBE
MALAY PENINSULA
MONGOLOID STOCK

MALAY MAN
MALAY PENINSULA
MONGOLOID STOCK

BONTOC IGOROT
MAN
LUZON
PHILIPPINES
MONGOLOID STOCK

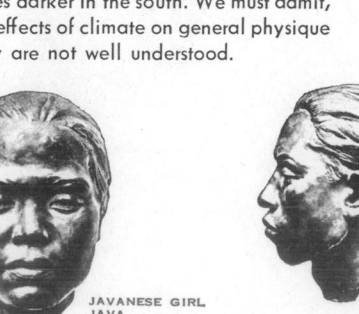

MALAYSIAN
COCKFIGHTERS
WOMAN FROM BALI
BOY FROM JAVA
LEFT, MAN FROM MADURA
RIGHT, MAN FROM BORNEO
MALAY ARCHIPELAGO
MONGOLOID STOCK

There is still a third primitive group in the Malay Peninsula. The Jakun, sometimes called "Savage Malays," possess a dark red or copper-brown skin and straight, dark, coarse hair. The head is round with high cheekbones and dark eyes with a tendency to obliquity. Busts of a Jakun man and girl are shown.

In marked contrast to these primitive types, there is a pure type of Malay, whose features express a high grade of intelligence compared with the Jakun.

The Malayan family (or, as it is also called, Indonesian) is distributed over the greater portion of the Malay Archipelago. It may be divided into the following groups: the Malay proper of the Malay Peninsula; the aborigines of the Philippines, Borneo, and Celebes; the Javanese and Sundanese of Java and Bali; and the Bataks of Sumatra. There are also scattered members of this family in Formosa and Madagascar. A typical Malayan is rather short in stature and has dark, wavy hair, tawny yellow-colored skin, lozenge-shaped face, prominent cheekbones, and slight-projecting jaws. The shape of the head varies markedly from long to round, with the former as the probable basic shape.

The types selected from the peoples of the Malay Archipelago represent a Dyak from Sarawak in Borneo, and a boy and a young girl from Java. There is also a composite group of figures representing various people of the Archipelago. These are two cockfighters intent on their national sport, watched by a girl from Bali who balances a platter of fruit on her head, and a small boy from Java eating a banana. In physical type the two men are similar, although one is from Borneo and the other from the island of Madura, situated off the north coast of Java.

## EASTERN ASIA
### CHINA AND JAPAN

The present Republic of China extends over an area of several million square miles, with a population roughly estimated at 400,000,000. The Chinese represent a single racial unit, which has had sufficient strength to maintain its culture and traditions in the face of numerous invaders. The Chinese as a whole are medium in stature. The shape of the head is intermediate between long and round, the skin yellowish brown in color, eyes oblique with the Mongolian fold, and hair straight and black.

There are, according to L. H. Dudley Buxton, two types of northern Chinese, one of which appears to be allied to the southern Chinese, and the other to the eastern Tibetans. From statistical data it can be shown that there is a tall element in the population, paralleled only among the neighboring Tibetans. The people of southern China belong to the same group as the northerners, but there are certain remarkable differences. In southern China the stature is less, and the head is shorter in length, which increases the cephalic index as the breadth remains fairly constant. The width of the nose appears slightly greater, which may be due to the increase of heat and moisture of the climate. The color of the skin becomes darker in the south. We must admit, however, that the effects of climate on general physique and physiognomy are not well understood.

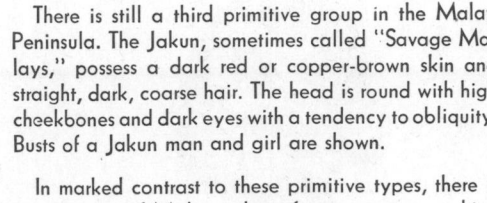

CANTONESE WOMAN
CANTON
SOUTH CHINA
MONGOLOID STOCK

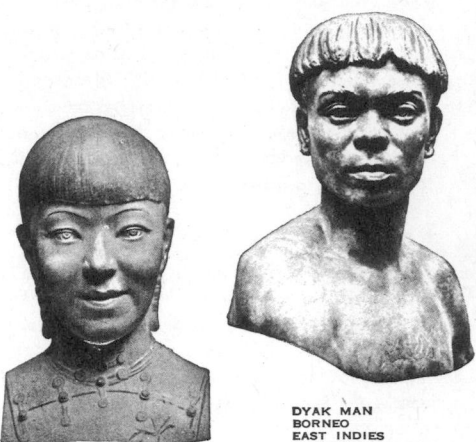

CHINESE WOMAN
SOUTHERN CHINA
MONGOLOID STOCK

DYAK MAN
BORNEO
EAST INDIES
MONGOLOID STOCK

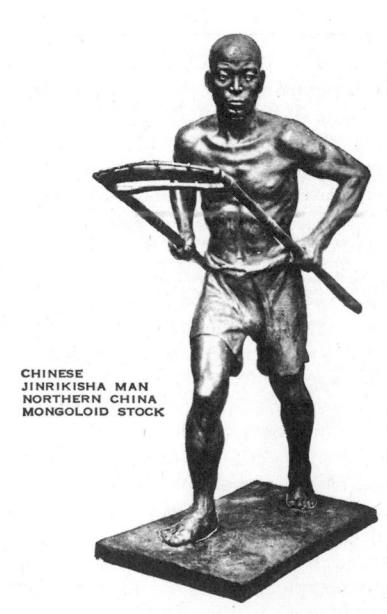

CHINESE
JINRIKISHA MAN
NORTHERN CHINA
MONGOLOID STOCK

JAVANESE GIRL
JAVA
EAST INDIES
MONGOLOID STOCK

JAVANESE BOY
JAVA
EAST INDIES
MONGOLOID STOCK

CHINESE MAN
SHANGHAI
CHINA
MONGOLOID STOCK

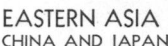

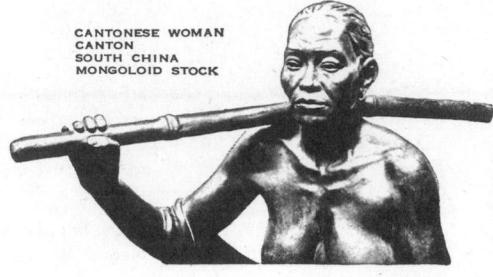

JAPANESE MAN
TOKYO
JAPAN
MONGOLOID STOCK

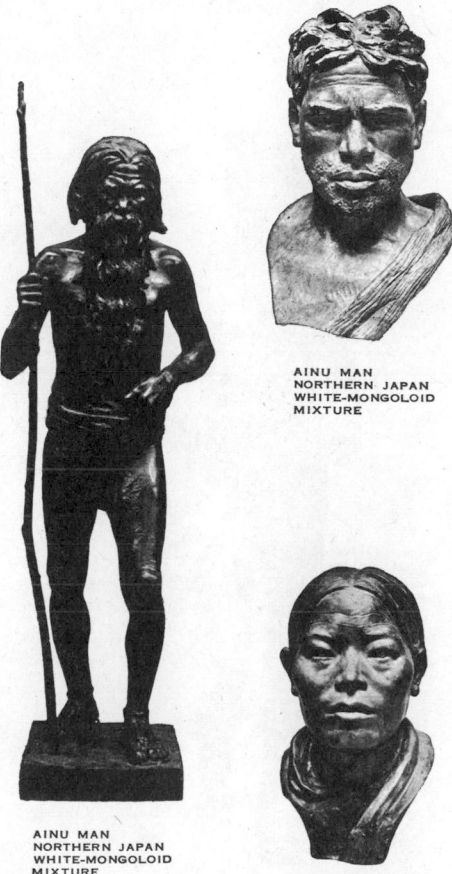

AINU MAN
NORTHERN JAPAN
WHITE-MONGOLOID
MIXTURE

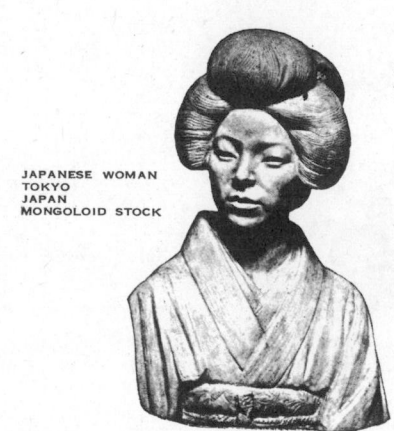

TIBETAN WOMAN
LHASA
TIBET
MONGOLOID STOCK

AINU MAN
NORTHERN JAPAN
WHITE-MONGOLOID
MIXTURE

JAPANESE WOMAN
TOKYO
JAPAN
MONGOLOID STOCK

MONGOL MAN
CENTRAL ASIA
OUTER MONGOLIA
MONGOLOID STOCK

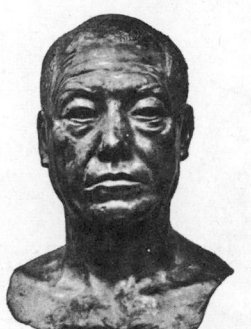

CHINESE MAN
NORTHERN CHINA
MONGOLOID STOCK

KOREAN MAN
NORTHEASTERN ASIA
MONGOLOID STOCK

TIBETAN MAN
LHASA
TIBET
MONGOLOID STOCK

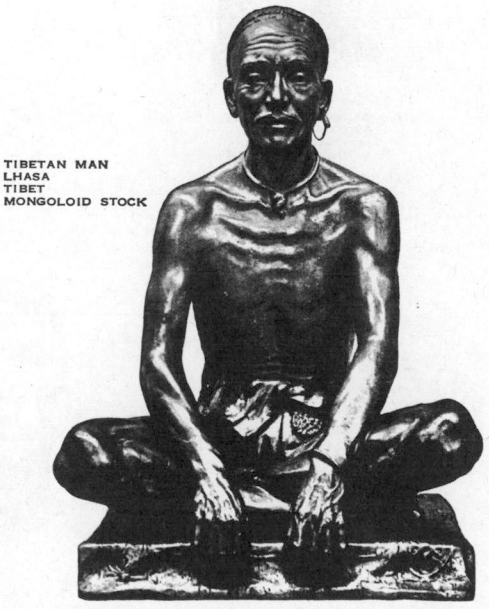

As representatives of the racial types of China, the following are shown: the full-length figure of a Chinese coolie posed between the shafts of his jinrikisha; and the bust of a Cantonese woman of the peasant class, with a bamboo pole, which is used for carrying loads, over her shoulder. There are also a bronze bust of a Chinese student and a stone bust of an attractive lady in her ornamented robe.

In prehistoric times the Ainus inhabited the islands which now comprise the Japanese Empire. At present confined to the northern island of Hokkaido, the Kuriles, and the southern portion of Sakhalin Island, they differ from all Mongolian races in their luxuriant black beards, the bushy and wavy head hair, and the general hairiness of other parts of the body. The color of the skin resembles that of the tanned Central European. Medium in stature, the average Ainu is thickset, with a head intermediate in shape between long and round, and a broad face, which does not project markedly. The narrow nose is short and concave. The large horizontal eyes are usually dark brown in color. The racial position of the Ainus is a question of considerable interest. They represent an ancient prehistoric stock, which has been greatly specialized.

There are two distinct types of modern Japanese, one of which possesses relatively fine features, while the other is more coarse in type. Both possess certain traits in common. The hair is always black and may be curly in form, where influenced by Ainu blood. In general, the stature is short, although there is considerable variation. The cephalic index and skin color are also variable characters. The color of the eyes is dark brown.

The fine or aristocratic type is taller and more slender, with an elongated face, and a prominent, narrow, arched nose. The eyes are either straight or oblique, and the epicanthic fold may be present. The coarse type, which may represent immigrants from southeastern Asia, is short and stocky, with a broad face, short, concave nose, and rounded nostrils, oblique eyes, usually an epicanthic fold, and a darker complexion than the other group.

As representatives of these islands are shown the busts of a Japanese man and a young woman. The life-size statue of an Ainu is an important contribution to the study of this racial type. Miss Hoffman modeled an aged Ainu and the head of a young man of this primitive tribe.

## CENTRAL AND NORTHERN ASIA

Central Asia comprises Tibet, Chinese Turkestan, and Mongolia. Northern Asia is practically identical with Siberia, which covers approximately one-quarter of the entire continent. The vast area of northern Asia is divided by the Yenisei River into western and eastern Siberia. The inhabitants may be grouped as Paleo-Siberians and Neo-Siberians. The latter, who inhabit chiefly the western geographical division, are a miscellaneous group including the Finnish-speaking tribes.

Among the Paleo-Asiatics are the Chukchi of northeastern Siberia; the Koryaks, who live between the Anadyr River and Kamchatka; and the Kamchadales. The Giliaks, Ainus, and those Eskimos who live on the Asiatic side of Bering Strait, are sometimes included in this division. The physical characters are black hair, brown- or reddish-colored sparse beard, yellowish white or brown skin, sometimes with a flat face, prominent cheekbones, oblique eyes, and a straight or concave nose. The head form varies from intermediate to round, although traces of a very ancient long-headed stock are present.

Included in this section is a seated figure of a Tibetan merchant from Lhasa. There are also the head of a Tibetan woman from Lhasa, and that of a Mongol priest from Outer Mongolia.

SAN ILDEFONSO
INDIAN WOMAN
NEW MEXICO U.S.A.
MONGOLOID STOCK

JICARILLA
APACHE INDIAN
MAN
NEW MEXICO U.S.A.
MONGOLOID STOCK

# AMERICA

Before the advent of European peoples the population of the Americas consisted of aborigines, called Indians by Columbus. From a historical point of view they are the true Americans. Moreover, up to the present time, there is no definite archaeological evidence for the existence of any pre-Indian peoples or cultures. It is generally conceded that the Indians are of Mongoloid stock. They entered the New World possibly 15,000 years ago, or even more remotely, in a series of migrations extending over many years. Small groups probably crossed Bering Strait, either because of pressure from hostile tribes or in search of new hunting grounds. Traveling south and east, they gradually spread over North, Central, and South America. The theory of waves of migration is corroborated by the fact that on either side of Bering Strait the country is incapable of supporting a large population, and by the fact that the American Indians, while possessing many traits in common, often show great variability in physical characters. And again we may speculate on the effects of climate and other environmental factors in producing physical differences.

The constant physical characters of the American Indians consist of a brown skin which frequently bears a reddish or yellowish tinge; dark eyes; straight, coarse, black hair; a minimum of beard and body hair; and a broad face with high and prominent cheekbones. The head is usually round, although there are certain groups in which long heads predominate. The stature also varies in different groups. The nose varies from flat to aquiline. The tallest people inhabited the region of the Mississippi Valley and extended for some distance to the north and east.

Among the Plains Indians and the tribes of the Northern and Eastern Woodlands there is little variation of the above characters. The Northwest Coast Indians, however, possess lighter skin and hair than do the other groups. They are medium in stature, with short bodies and long arms, and apparently are closely allied to the natives of northeastern Asia. The tribes north of this general region, including the Tlingit, Haida, and Tsimshian, are above the average in stature. They have large heads with extremely broad faces and concave or straight noses. In the southern part of this region, as, for example, among the Kwakiutl, the people are less tall, and are round-headed, with broad, high faces, and very long, narrow noses, which are frequently convex in shape. These Indians inhabit the Northwest Coast from latitude 60° north to the northern boundary of the state of Washington. Among the accompanying pictures are shown a magnificent Blackfoot Indian in the pose he adopts at the end of a successful hunt, and the head of a Sioux brave. To illustrate additional types of North American Indians several individuals from New Mexico have been portrayed, including a full-length figure of a Navaho, a Pueblo woman from San Ildefonso, New Mexico, and a Jicarilla Apache.

NAVAHO MAN
NAVAHO INDIANS
NEW MEXICO U.S.A.
MONGOLOID STOCK

BLACKFOOT
INDIAN MAN
MONTANA U.S.A.
MONGOLOID STOCK

SIOUX INDIAN
MAN
SOUTH DAKOTA U.S.A.
MONGOLOID STOCK

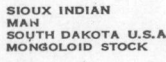

SIOUX INDIAN
MAN
SOUTH DAKOTA U.S.A.
MONGOLOID STOCK

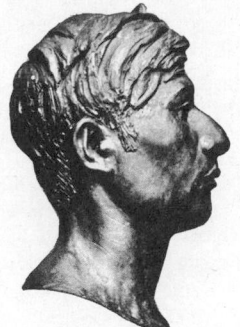

MAYA INDIAN
MAN
YUCATAN
MEXICO
MONGOLOID STOCK

The Eskimos form a definite group, clearly of Asiatic origin. In many respects they are the most Mongoloid of all Americans. They are distinguished by a short, stocky build, markedly long heads combined with very broad faces (an unusual feature in a people with a long skull), massive jaws, and moderately narrow noses. The sides of the head are often flat, and a ridge may be present along the dome of the skull. The eyes frequently show the Mongoloid fold. The head of an Eskimo man and that of an Eskimo woman are shown.

In Mexico and Central America the average stature is medium to short, and round heads predominate, although the evidence suggests that the first inhabitants were long-headed and were conquered by these later invaders. The head of a Yucatecan Maya is shown as an example.

The Indians of South America bear, in general, the physical characters common to the whole race. It is believed that they entered that continent through a succession of migrations by way of the Isthmus of Panama. The bust of a Tehuelche from Patagonia and the head of a Carib of the Amazon Basin illustrate two types from South America.

From time to time it has been asserted that ancient pre-Indian human remains have been discovered in America; for example, in Argentina, primitive types of Tertiary fossil man were reported to have been found. All alleged evidence of this character has so far been discredited.

CARIB INDIAN
MAN
AMAZON BASIN
SOUTH AMERICA
MONGOLOID STOCK

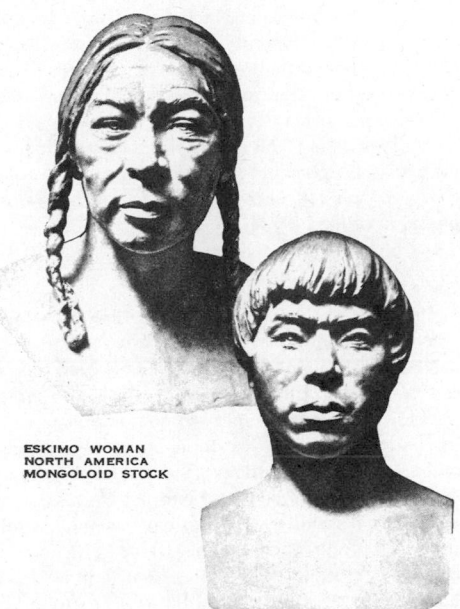

ESKIMO WOMAN
NORTH AMERICA
MONGOLOID STOCK

## OCEANIA

Oceania is the area which extends from Australia to Easter Island and from New Zealand northward to Hawaii, including all the island groups of the Pacific Ocean. The consensus of opinion is that man first entered the Pacific area from southeastern Asia. There have also been several important waves of migration, which add to the complexity of the racial problems involved. The six principal racial divisions in Oceania include the inhabitants of Australia, Tasmania, Melanesia, New Guinea, Polynesia, and Micronesia.

### AUSTRALIA

Australia is the smallest continent, with an area approximately the same size as the United States. In general, the physical traits of the Australian aborigines are uniform throughout the continent, although there are numerous minor variations. Archaeological evidence suggests that man entered this continent at a very early date and that he remained but little changed by outside factors until the arrival of the first Europeans in 1606.

The physical characters of the aboriginal Australian are jet black, wavy or curly hair, which is often heavy on the face; dark chocolate brown skin; medium stature with slim limbs; and a long head with a flat, retreating forehead, prominent brow ridges, projecting face, and a deeply set, broad nose.

### TASMANIA

The Tasmanians became extinct during the latter part of the nineteenth century. They were of medium height, had black to dark brown skins, woolly hair, and heavy brow ridges. The face was long, and oval or pentagonal in shape, while the head was sloping and small in size. The nose was short and broad, and the teeth were large. Tasmanian skulls and living heads show resemblance to Negritos, Melanesians, and Australian aborigines. In general, the physical characters of the Tasmanians were similar to those of the Australians. But Tasmanians were more Negroid than are the Australians. The original migratory route of these people is still under discussion.

ESKIMO MAN
NORTH AMERICA
MONGOLOID STOCK

AUSTRALIAN
ABORIGINAL WOMAN
AND BOY
NORTHEASTERN
AUSTRALIA
AUSTRALOID STOCK
WHITE-NEGRO
MIXTURE

TEHUELCHE
INDIAN MAN
PATAGONIA
SOUTH AMERICA
MONGOLOID STOCK

AUSTRALIAN
ABORIGINAL MAN
NORTHEAST
AUSTRALIA
AUSTRALOID STOCK
WHITE-NEGRO
MIXTURE

SOLOMON ISLANDER
SOLOMON ISLANDS
MELANESIA
NEGRO STOCK

## MELANESIA

The name is derived from the dark skin color of the peoples who inhabit these islands. This area embraces the Bismarck Archipelago, northeast of New Guinea, the Louisiade, Solomon, Santa Cruz, New Hebrides and Loyalty Islands, New Caledonia, Fiji, and small intervening groups. While a large Papuan element prevails throughout the population of Melanesia, there have also been several movements of racial stocks from Indonesia. The result of this mingling of peoples is that the modern population shows considerable variation and is by no means homogenous in character. The hair of the Melanesians is usually woolly, but may be either curly or wavy. The skin ranges from very dark to light brown. The stature varies from short to medium. The head is usually long in shape, but there are isolated round-headed groups. The forehead is commonly rounded, and the brow ridges are fairly prominent. The nose is broad, sometimes straight, and broader than that of the Papuan. In Melanesians there are Australoid and Negroid elements.

## NEW GUINEA

The inhabitants of New Guinea and the adjacent island groups belong to the woolly-haired (Negro) branch of mankind. There is considerable variety of racial type, which is subdivided into Negritos, Papuans, and Melanesians. Typical Negritos are the Tapiro Pygmies of the western mountains in Dutch New Guinea, who can be compared with the inhabitants of the Andaman Islands, the Semang Pygmies of the central part of the Malay Peninsula and eastern Sumatra, and the Negritos of the Philippines.

The hair of the Tapiro is short, black in color, and abundant on face and body. The skin is yellowish brown in color. In stature the average Tapiro is four feet nine inches. The head shows considerable variation in shape, the nose is straight and of medium breadth. A trait frequent among them and among other Negritos is a deep and convex upper lip.

The Papuans are dark-skinned, medium in stature, and long-headed. The black hair is often long and may be abundant on the face. The forehead is retreating, the brow ridges are prominent, and the lower part of the face projects. The broad nose is often prominent and convex, while the tip is sometimes turned down. The Papuans now inhabit the greater part of New Guinea, and were originally distributed throughout Melanesia. The words Papuan and Melanesian have geographical, linguistic, and physical connotations. We may speak of Papua and of Melanesia, of a Papuan and of a Melanesian. Both are of basic Negro stock with Australoid elements here and there.

## MICRONESIA

To the north of Melanesia lie countless islands including the Marianas, Caroline, Marshall, and Gilbert groups, which together form the area known as Micronesia. The population is extremely mixed, containing certain Melanesian, Polynesian, and Malaysian influences. The skin color ranges from brown to nearly yellow, and the hair is wavy or straight, but in the west some individuals are very dark-skinned with frizzly hair, while others are light-skinned with wavy or straight hair. The eyes are almost black and the cheekbones relatively prominent. In stature the Micronesians are medium and are not as robust as the Polynesians.

Among the illustrations various individuals of the peoples of Oceania are shown. Australia is represented by the full-length figures of a man, a woman and child. The man is shown in a characteristic pose as though throwing a spear. On his body are deep scars caused by cutting the flesh with a stone implement. The Solomon Islander in the act of climbing a date palm represents the Melanesian group. Around his neck is a crescent-shaped shell, and he wears a nose ring.

Two men from Hawaii and the bust of a Samoan are characteristic of the Polynesian group. There is a full-length Hawaiian on his surf-board as he speeds toward the beach. The Samoan, who holds a large knife against his right shoulder, also illustrates the well-developed physique of the Polynesian.

## POLYNESIA

This area of the central Pacific region includes the numerous groups and small islands situated mostly south of the equator. The two islands of New Zealand are the largest of the entire area, which also includes the Hawaiian, Society, and Marquesan groups, as well as Tonga and Samoa. The origin of the Polynesians remains in considerable doubt, but it is believed that at an early date they migrated into this large area from southeastern Asia. The Polynesian is average to tall in stature, the hair being straight or wavy in form and black in color. The skin varies from that of a South European to several shades of brown. The shape of the head is round, but there are smaller divisions of people with long or intermediate-shaped heads. In general form the face is elliptical with relatively prominent cheekbones, and a prominent nose, generally straight as among the Maori, but sometimes convex. Skull measurements show very few close resemblances to those of Melanesians and Australian aborigines.

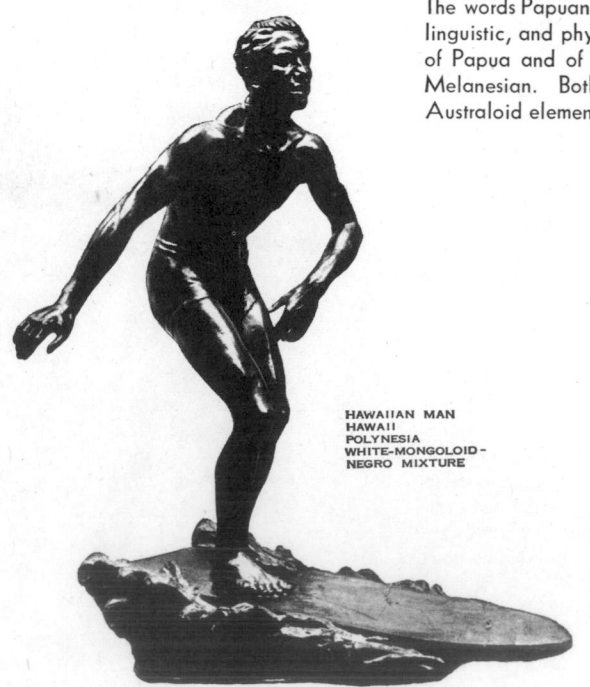

HAWAIIAN MAN
HAWAII
POLYNESIA
WHITE-MONGOLOID-
NEGRO MIXTURE

SAMOAN MAN
SAMOA
POLYNESIA
WHITE-MONGOLOID-
NEGRO MIXTURE

HAWAIIAN MAN
HAWAII
POLYNESIA
WHITE-MONGOLOID-
NEGRO MIXTURE

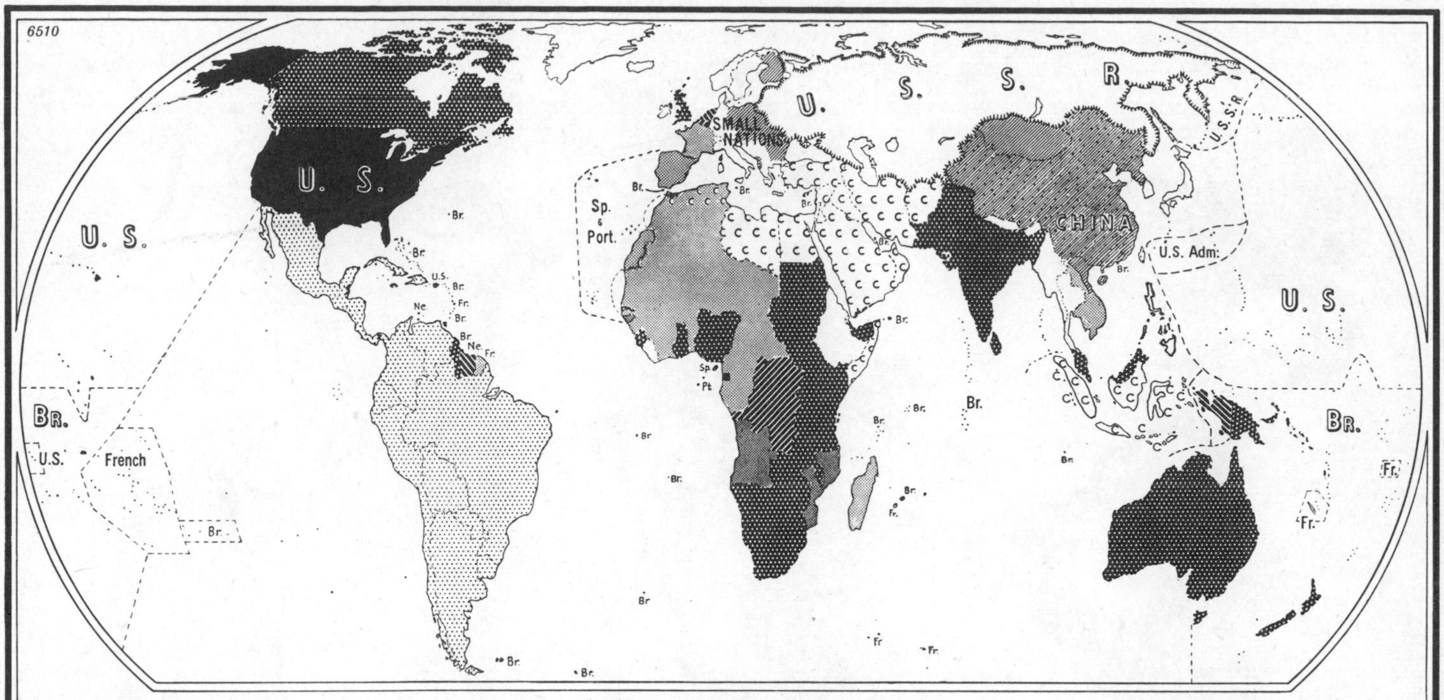

6510

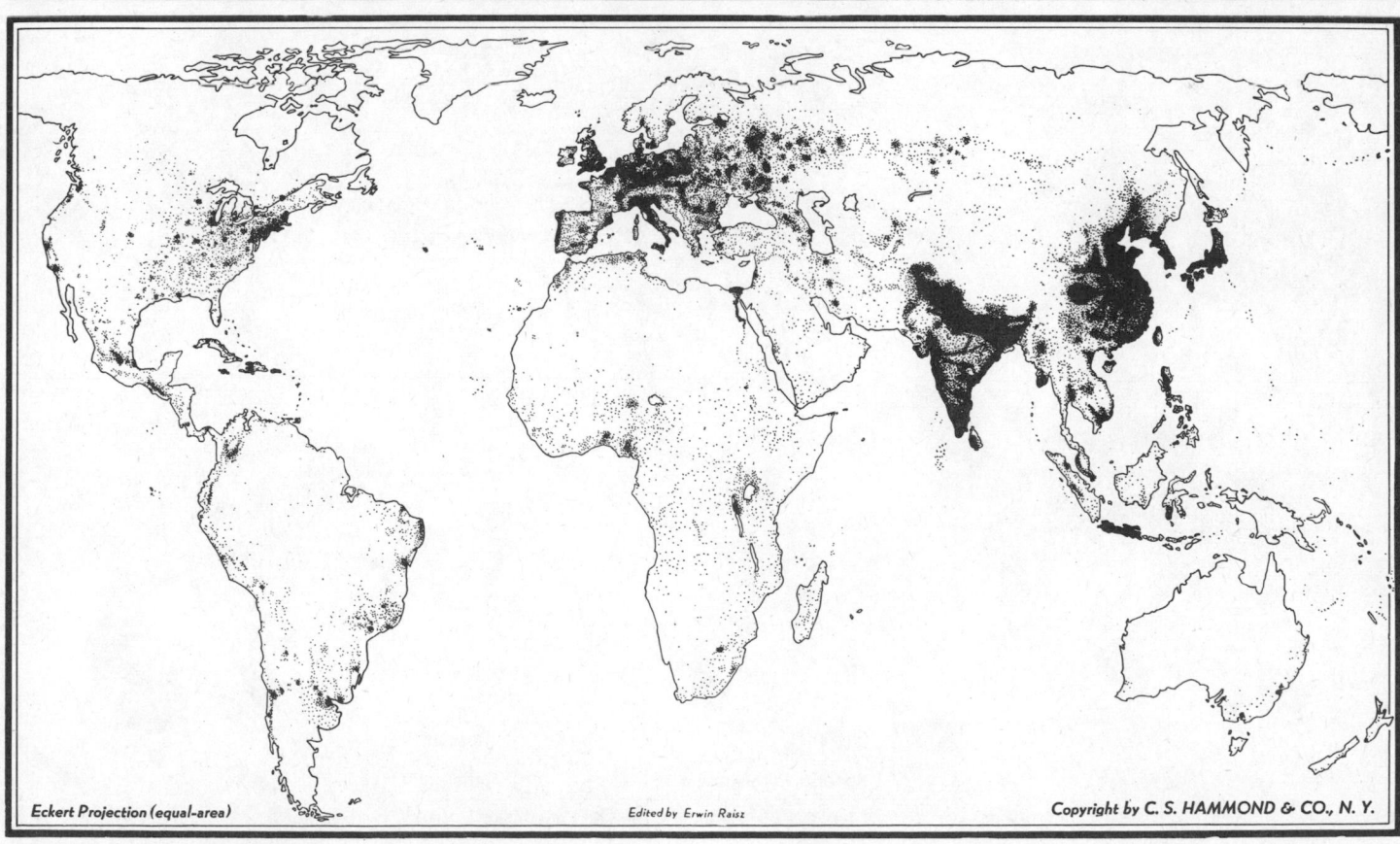

## POLITICAL ASSOCIATIONS FOLLOWING WORLD WAR II

**Legend:**

- United States
- British Commonwealth of Nations
- Belgium and Netherlands
- Spain and Portugal
- French Union
- U. S. S. R.
- China
- Islamic Group
- Small Nations
- Latin America
- Soviet Sphere of Influence

*Eckert Projection (equal-area)*

**POLITICAL ASSOCIATIONS FOLLOWING WORLD WAR II** The present divisions of the world into nations are the result of historical developments, and do not correspond entirely to cultural, geographical and economic units. Furthermore, the populations range from a half billion (China) to a few thousands (Andorra). More than half of the small nations have fewer people than the New York metropolitan area, yet each of the fifty-odd countries has a vote in the assembly of the United Nations. Representation in the United Nations will knit the lives of all peoples more closely together.

Over three quarters of the world's people live in countries which are members of the United Nations. One half of these are in the Big Five; the United States, the British Commonwealth of Nations, the U.S.S.R., China and France.

*Edited by Erwin Ra*

*Copyright by C. S. Hammond & Co., N. Y.*

*Eckert Projection (equal-area)*                *Edited by Erwin Raisz*                *Copyright by C. S. HAMMOND & CO., N. Y.*

**DENSITY OF POPULATION.** One of the most outstanding facts of human geography is the extremely uneven distribution of people over the Earth. One-half of the Earth's surface has less than 3 people per square mile, while in the lowlands of India, China, Java and Japan rural density reaches the incredible congestion of 2000-3000 per square mile. Three-fourths of the Earth's population live in four relatively small areas; Northeastern United States, North-Central Europe, India and the Far East.

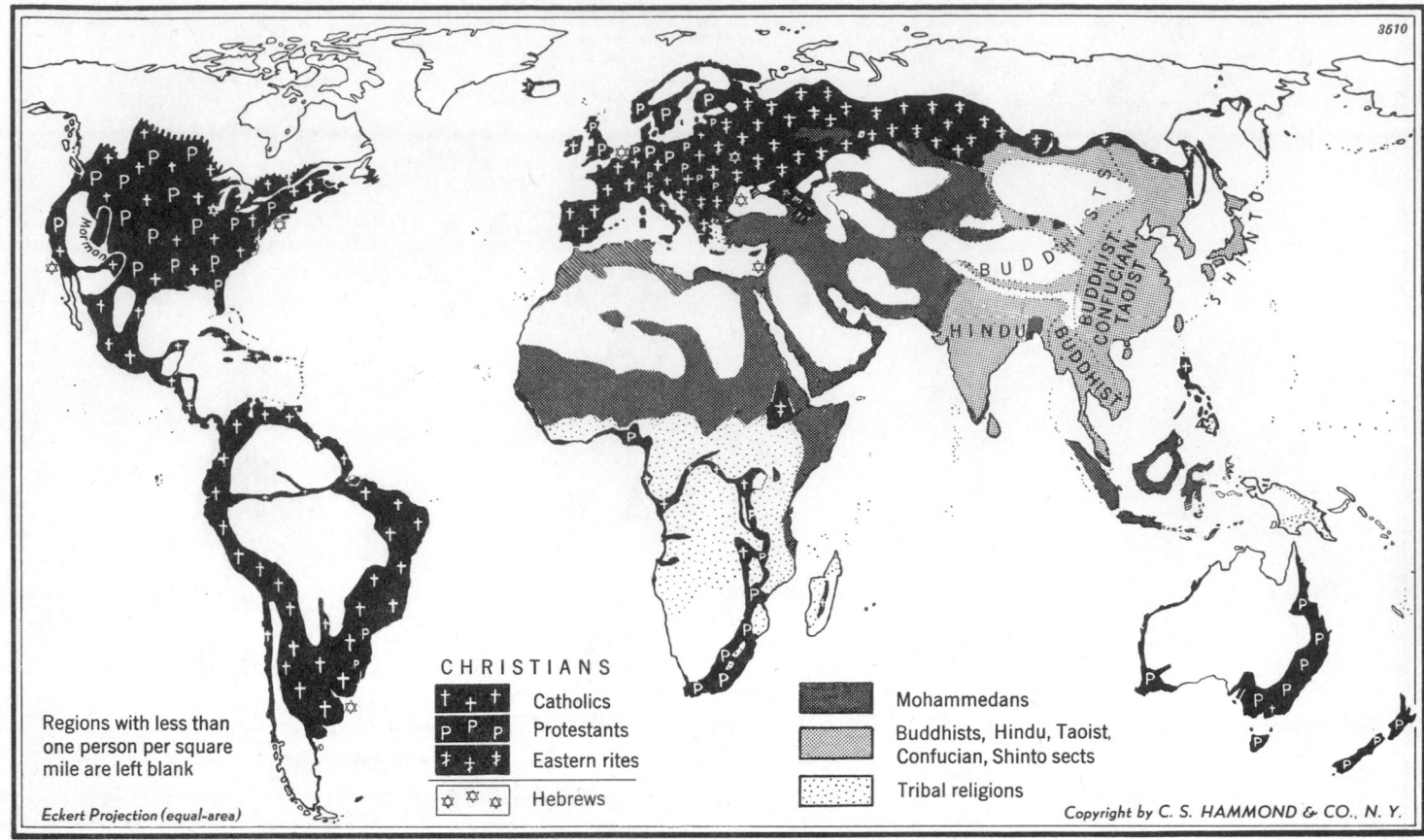

CHRISTIANS

† † † Catholics

P P P Protestants

‡ † ‡ Eastern rites

☆ ✡ ☆ Hebrews

Regions with less than
one person per square
mile are left blank

Mohammedans

Buddhists, Hindu, Taoist,
Confucian, Shinto sects

Tribal religions

*Eckert Projection (equal-area)*

Copyright by C. S. HAMMOND & CO., N. Y.

*Edited by Erwin Raisz*

**RELIGIONS.** *Most people of the Earth belong to four major religions: Christians, Mohammedans, Brahmans, Buddhists and derivatives. The Eastern rites of the Christians include the Greek Orthodox, Greek Catholic, Armenian, Syrian, Coptic and more minor churches. The lamaism of Tibet and Mongolia differs a great deal from Buddhism in Burma and Thailand. In the religion of China the teachings of Buddha, Confucius and Tao are mixed, while in Shinto a great deal of ancestor and emperor worship is added. About 11 million Hebrews live scattered over the globe, chiefly in cities and in the state of Israel.*

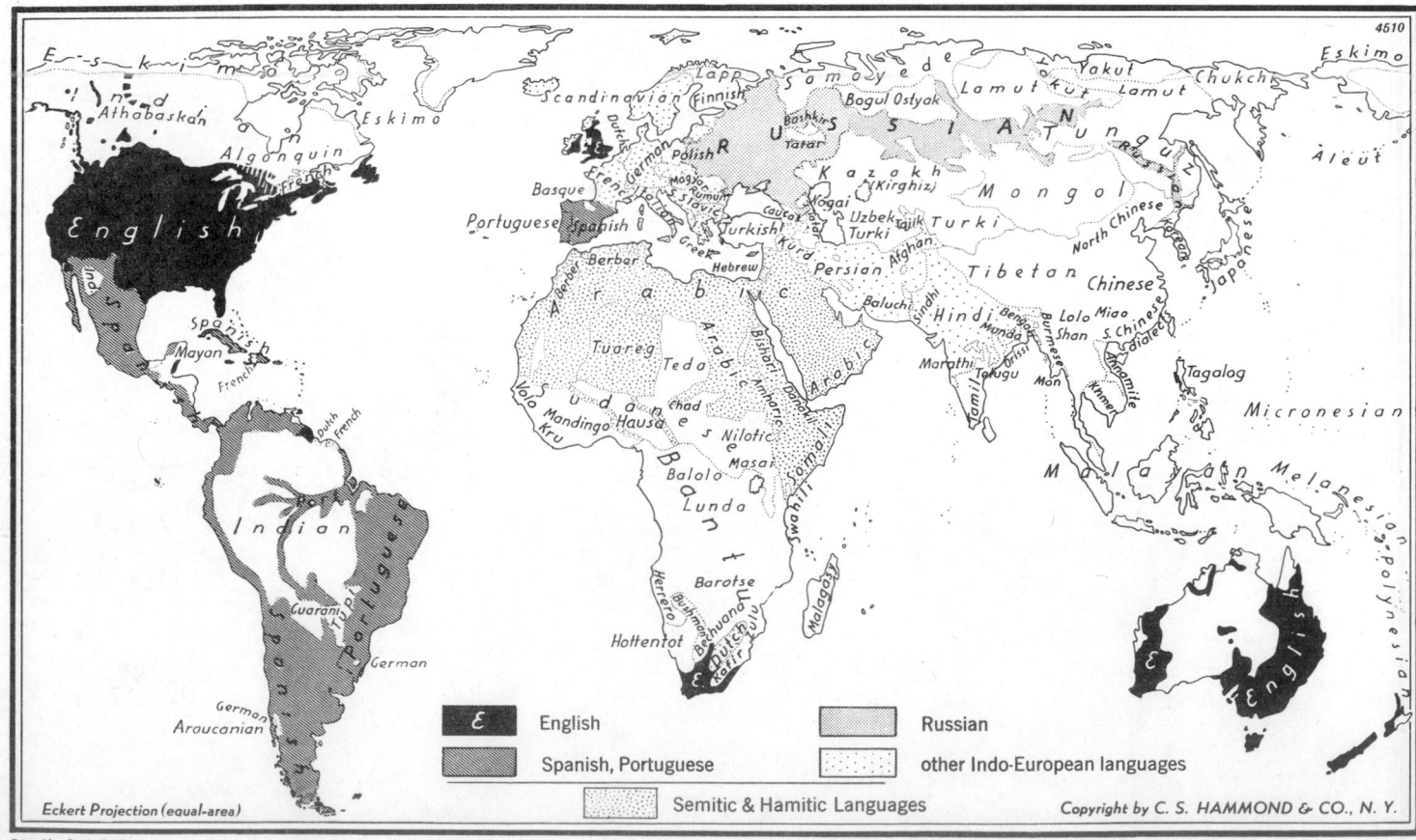

𝓔 English

Spanish, Portuguese

Russian

other Indo-European languages

Semitic & Hamitic Languages

*Eckert Projection (equal-area)*

Copyright by C. S. HAMMOND & CO., N. Y.

*Edited by Erwin Raisz*

**LANGUAGES.** *Several hundred different languages are spoken in the World, and in many places two or more languages are spoken, sometimes by the same people. The map above shows the dominant languages in each locality. English, French, Spanish, Russian, Arabic and Swahili are spoken by many people as a second language for commerce or travel.*

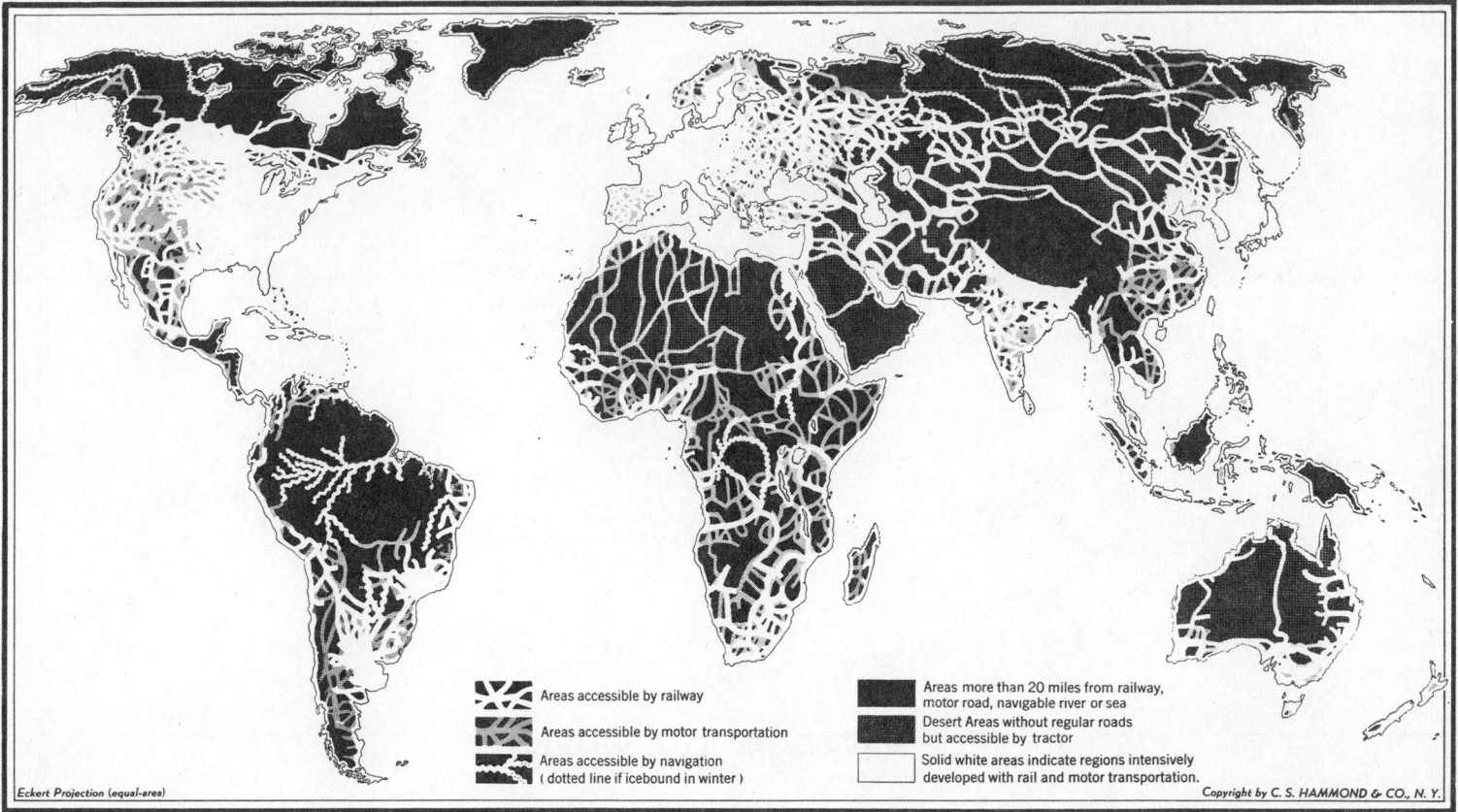

Areas accessible by railway

Areas accessible by motor transportation

Areas accessible by navigation
( dotted line if icebound in winter )

Areas more than 20 miles from railway,
motor road, navigable river or sea

Desert Areas without regular roads
but accessible by tractor

Solid white areas indicate regions intensively
developed with rail and motor transportation.

*Eckert Projection (equal-area)*

Copyright by C. S. HAMMOND & CO., N. Y.

*Edited by Erwin Raisz*

**ACCESSIBILITY.** *Many regions in the world are far from railways, roads, navigable rivers or the seas. Their economic development is retarded because their products can be brought to the world's markets only at great expense. Such areas are in the tundra (alpine), the boreal forest and in the equatorial rain forest regions. Desert areas, if not too mountainous, can be crossed by tractors. The largest inaccessible area is in Tibet, on account of high mountains, the alpine climate and isolationist attitude of the people. Airplane transportation will help to bring inaccessible areas into the orbit of civilization.*

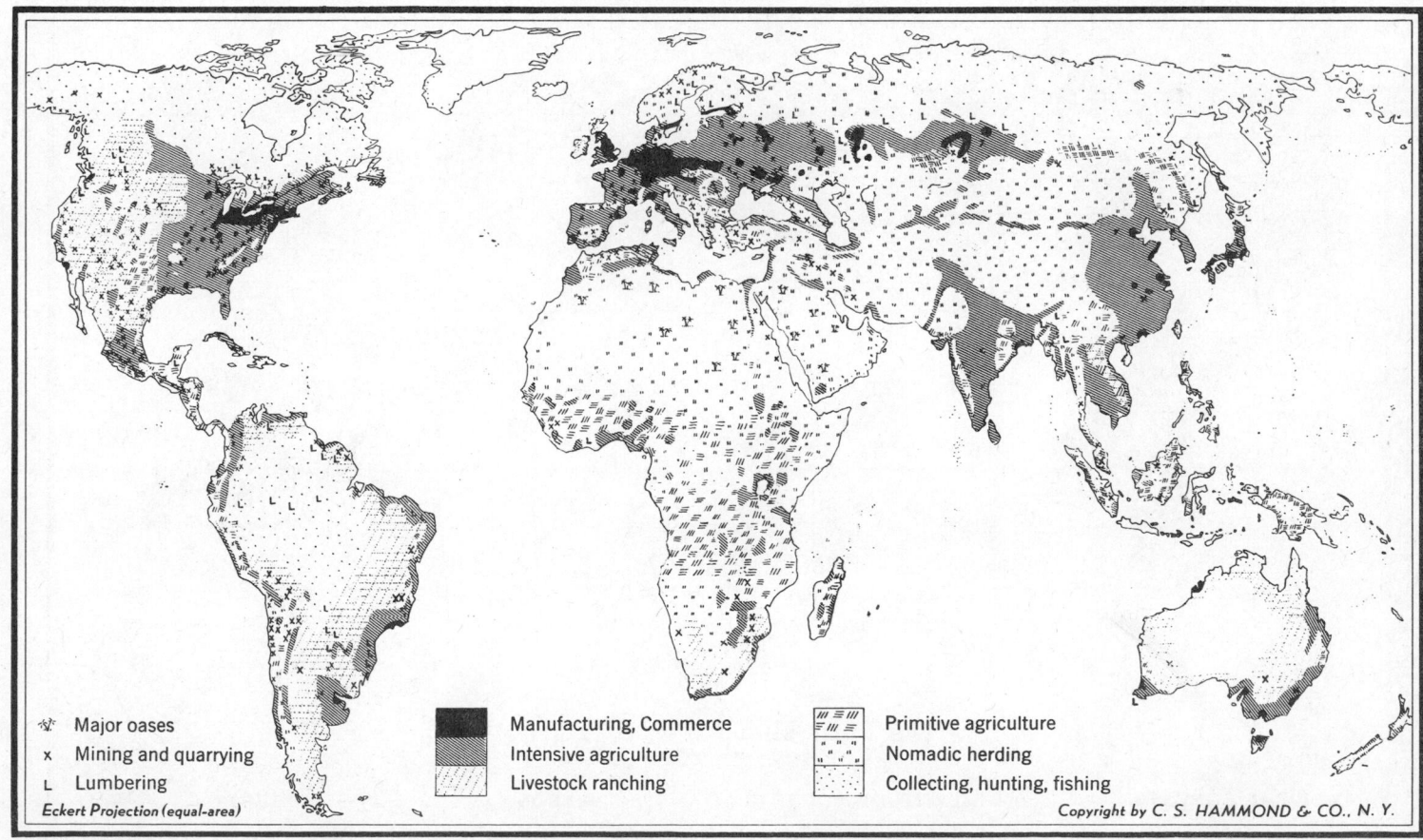

Major oases

x   Mining and quarrying

L   Lumbering

Manufacturing, Commerce

Intensive agriculture

Livestock ranching

Primitive agriculture

Nomadic herding

Collecting, hunting, fishing

*Eckert Projection (equal-area)*

Copyright by C. S. HAMMOND & CO.. N. Y.

*Edited by Erwin Raisz*

**OCCUPATIONS.** *Correlation with the density of population shows that the most densely populated areas fall into the regions of manufacturing and intensive farming. All other economies require considerable space. The most sparsely inhabited areas are those of collecting, hunting and fishing. Areas with practically no habitation are left blank.*

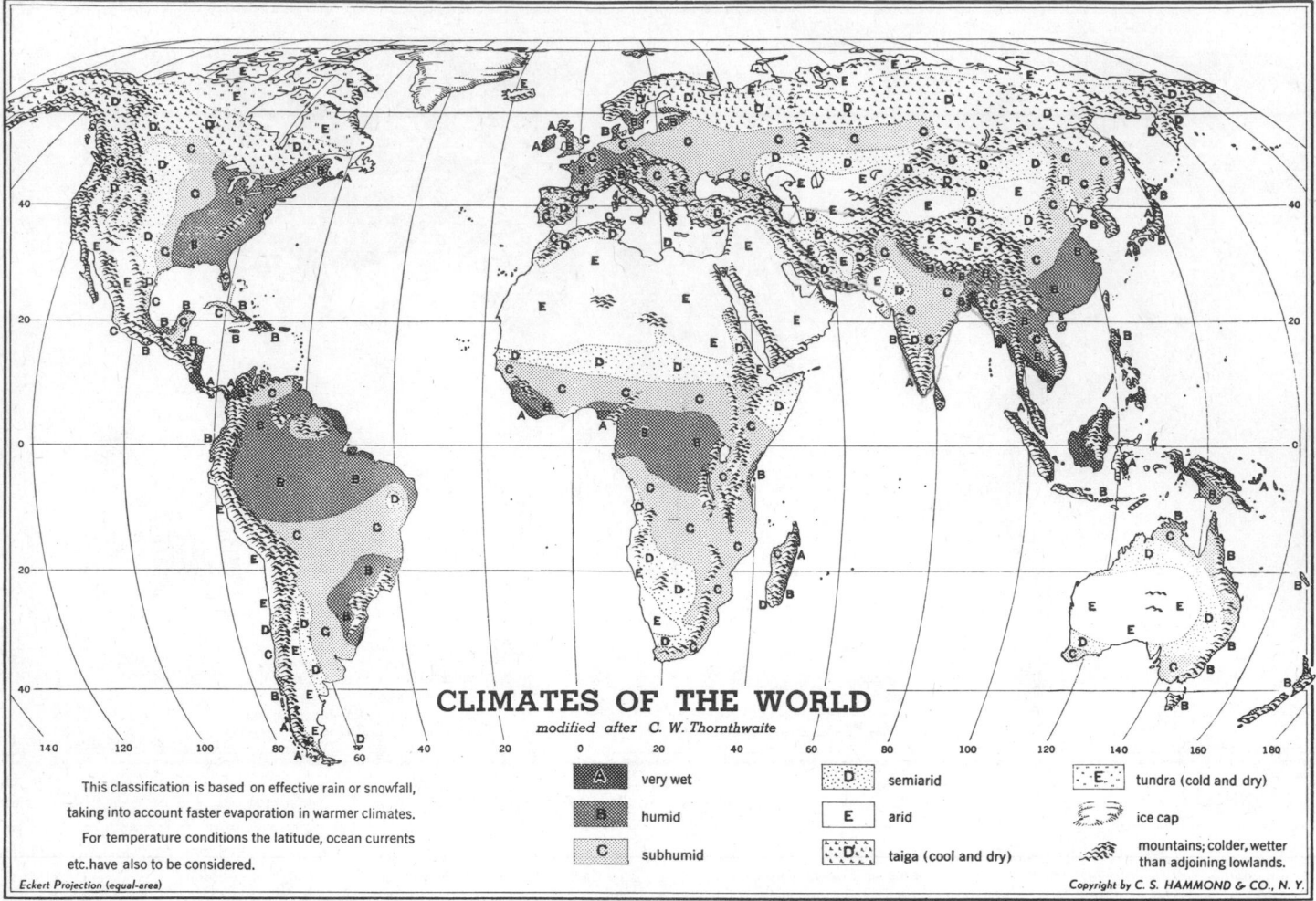

## CLIMATES OF THE WORLD

*modified after C. W. Thornthwaite*

| | | |
|---|---|---|
| A | very wet | D | semiarid | E | tundra (cold and dry) |
| B | humid | E | arid | | ice cap |
| C | subhumid | D | taiga (cool and dry) | | mountains; colder, wetter than adjoining lowlands. |

This classification is based on effective rain or snowfall, taking into account faster evaporation in warmer climates. For temperature conditions the latitude, ocean currents etc. have also to be considered.

*Eckert Projection (equal-area)*

Copyright by C. S. HAMMOND & CO., N. Y.

*Edited by Erwin Raisz*

## NATURAL VEGETATION

*after various sources*

**TROPICAL FORESTS**
- Tropical Rain Forest
- Lighter Tropical Forest (jungle)
- Scrub and Thorn Forest (dry)

**MIDLATITUDE FORESTS**
- Mediterranean Mixed Forest
- Broadleaf Forest (also pine, cedar etc.)
- Boreal Forest (mostly conifers)

**GRASSLANDS**
- Savanna or Parkland
- Prairie
- Steppe (shortgrass)

**DESERT etc.**
- Desert Shrub and Waste
- Tundra
- Mountains

*Eckert Projection (equal-area)*

Copyright by C. S. HAMMOND & CO., N. Y.

*Edited by Erwin Raisz*

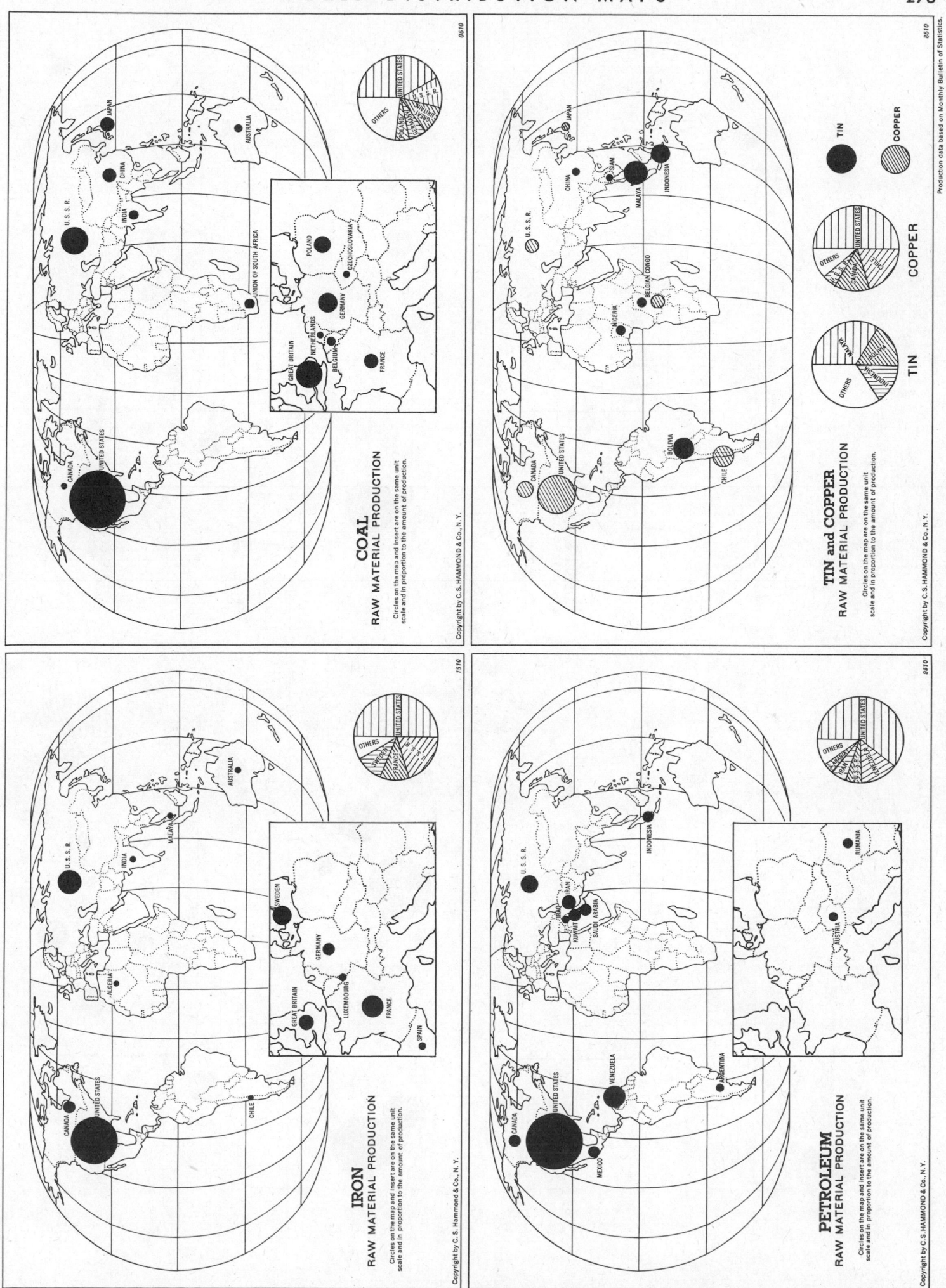

**COAL**
RAW MATERIAL PRODUCTION

Circles on the map and insert are on the same unit scale and in proportion to the amount of production.

Copyright by C. S. HAMMOND & Co., N.Y.

**TIN and COPPER**
RAW MATERIAL PRODUCTION

Circles on the map are on the same unit scale and in proportion to the amount of production.

Copyright by C. S. HAMMOND & Co., N.Y.

Production data based on Monthly Bulletin of Statistics, Statistical Office of the United Nations.

TIN

COPPER

**IRON**
RAW MATERIAL PRODUCTION

Circles on the map and insert are on the same unit scale and in proportion to the amount of production.

Copyright by C. S. Hammond & Co., N.Y.

**PETROLEUM**
RAW MATERIAL PRODUCTION

Circles on the map and insert are on the same unit scale and in proportion to the amount of production.

Copyright by C. S. HAMMOND & Co., N.Y.

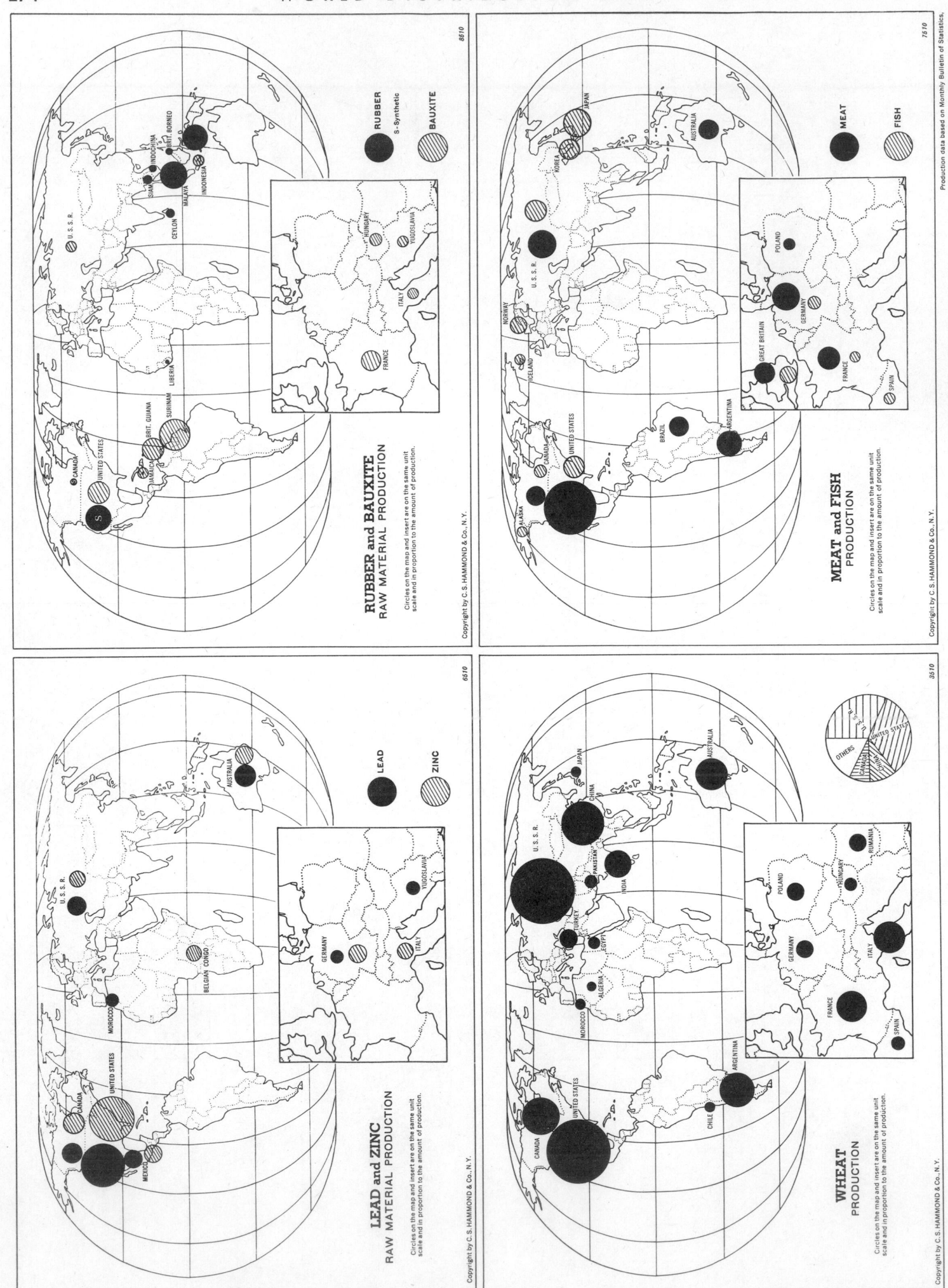

**RUBBER and BAUXITE**
RAW MATERIAL PRODUCTION

Circles on the map and insert are on the same unit scale and in proportion to the amount of production.

Copyright by C. S. HAMMOND & Co., N.Y.

RUBBER
S-Synthetic
BAUXITE

**MEAT and FISH**
PRODUCTION

Circles on the map and insert are on the same unit scale and in proportion to the amount of production.

Copyright by C. S. HAMMOND & Co., N.Y.

MEAT
FISH

Production data based on Monthly Bulletin of Statistics, Statistical Office of the United Nations.

**LEAD and ZINC**
RAW MATERIAL PRODUCTION

Circles on the map and insert are on the same unit scale and in proportion to the amount of production.

Copyright by C. S. HAMMOND & Co., N.Y.

LEAD
ZINC

**WHEAT**
PRODUCTION

Circles on the map and insert are on the same unit scale and in proportion to the amount of production.

Copyright by C. S. HAMMOND & Co., N.Y.

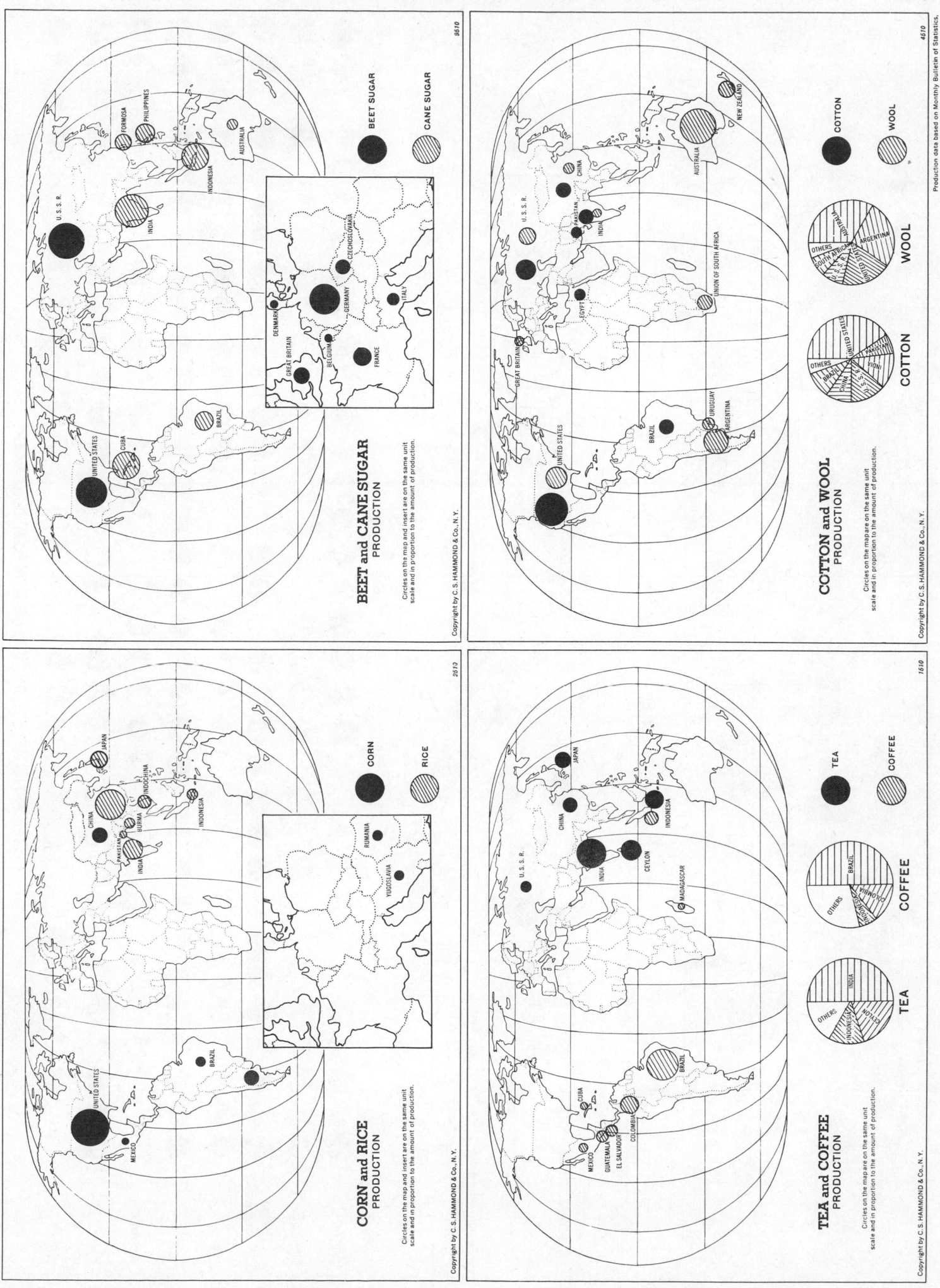

**BEET and CANE SUGAR**
PRODUCTION

Circles on the map and insert are on the same unit
scale and in proportion to the amount of production.

BEET SUGAR
CANE SUGAR

Copyright by C. S. HAMMOND & Co., N. Y.

9810

**COTTON and WOOL**
PRODUCTION

Circles on the map are on the same unit
scale and in proportion to the amount of production.

COTTON
WOOL
WOOL
COTTON

Production data based on Monthly Bulletin of Statistics,
Statistical Office of the United Nations.

Copyright by C. S. HAMMOND & Co., N. Y.

4810

**CORN and RICE**
PRODUCTION

Circles on the map and insert are on the same unit
scale and in proportion to the amount of production.

CORN
RICE

Copyright by C. S. HAMMOND & Co., N. Y.

2610

**TEA and COFFEE**
PRODUCTION

Circles on the map are on the same unit
scale and in proportion to the amount of production.

TEA
COFFEE
COFFEE
TEA

Copyright by C. S. HAMMOND & Co., N. Y.

1610

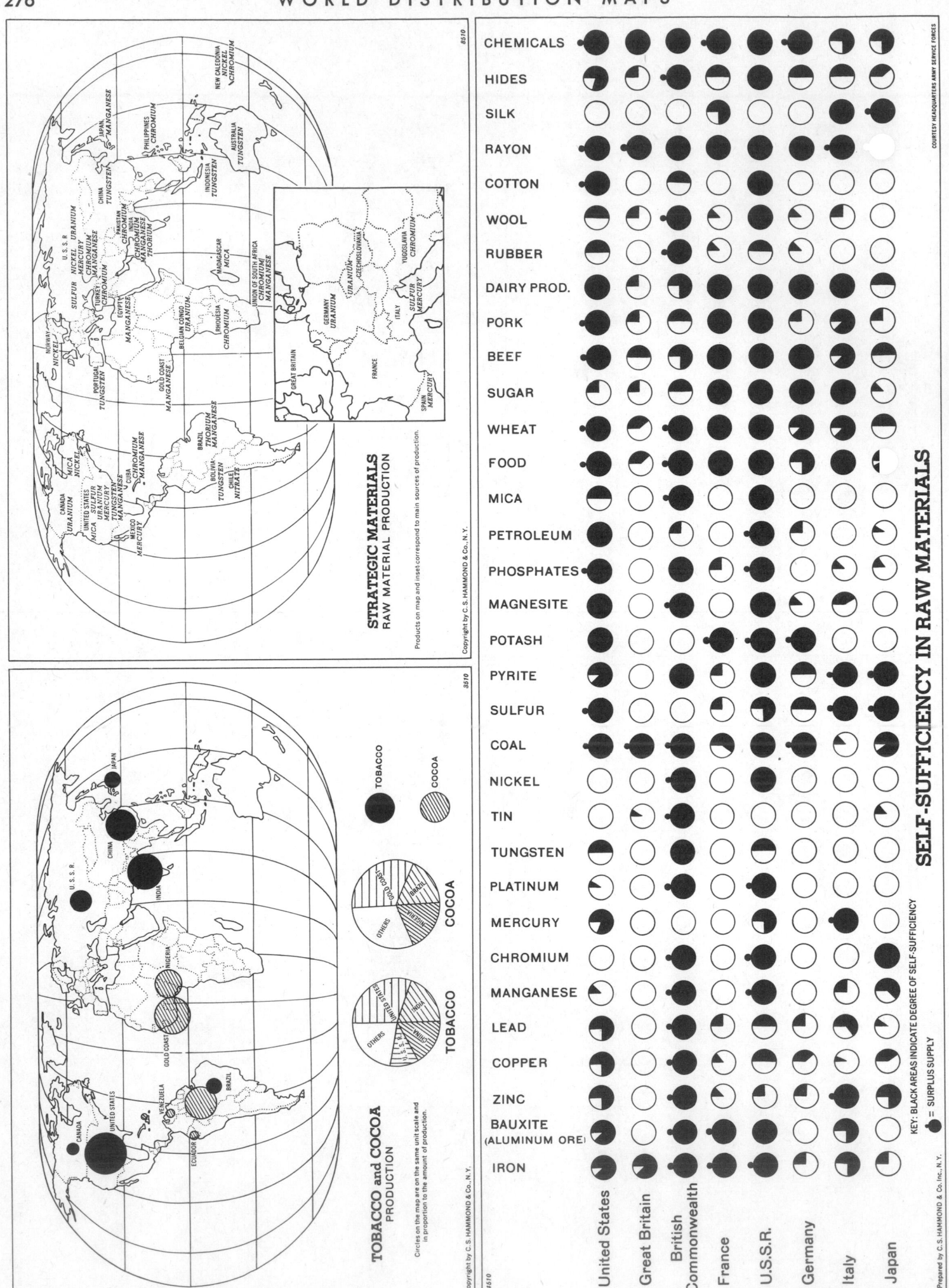

**STRATEGIC MATERIALS**
RAW MATERIAL PRODUCTION

Products on map and inset correspond to main sources of production.

Copyright by C. S. HAMMOND & Co., N.Y.

**TOBACCO and COCOA**
PRODUCTION

Circles on the map are on the same unit scale and in proportion to the amount of production.

Copyright by C. S. HAMMOND & Co., N.Y.

**SELF-SUFFICIENCY IN RAW MATERIALS**

KEY: BLACK AREAS INDICATE DEGREE OF SELF-SUFFICIENCY
● = SURPLUS SUPPLY

COURTESY HEADQUARTERS ARMY SERVICE FORCES

Prepared by C. S. HAMMOND & Co., Inc., N.Y.

# EARTH AND SOLAR SYSTEM

# PRINCIPAL LAKES AND INLAND SEAS

## Elements of the Solar System

| PLANETS | DISTANCE FROM SUN IN MILES MAXIMUM | MINIMUM | PERIOD OF REVOLUTION AROUND SUN IN DAYS | DIAMETER IN MILES | DENSITY (EARTH=1) |
|---|---|---|---|---|---|
| Sun | .... | .... | .... | 865,390 | 0.26 |
| Mercury | 43,404,000 | 28,599,000 | 87.87 | 3,009 | 0.68 |
| Venus | 67,730,000 | 66,814,000 | 224.70 | 7,575 | 0.94 |
| Earth | 94,560,000 | 91,446,000 | 365.26 | 7,927 | 1.00 |
| Mars | 154,936,000 | 128,476,000 | 686.98 | 4,216 | 0.71 |
| Jupiter | 507,289,000 | 460,465,000 | 4,332.59 | 88,698 | 0.24 |
| Saturn | 936,637,000 | 837,655,000 | 10,759.20 | 75,060 | 0.12 |
| Uranus | 1,868,930,000 | 1,700,745,000 | 30,685.93 | 30,878 | 0.25 |
| Neptune | 2,820,610,000 | 2,773,510,000 | 60,187.64 | 27,700 | 0.41 |
| Pluto | 4,585,000,000 | 2,753,000,000 | 90,470.23 | 3,600 approx. | 0.7 |

## Dimensions of the Earth

| | | |
|---|---|---|
| Superficial area | 196,950,000 | sq. miles |
| Land surface | 57,510,000 | " " |
| North America | 8,500,000 | " " |
| South America | 6,814,000 | " " |
| Europe | 3,872,000 | " " |
| Asia | 16,990,000 | " " |
| Africa | 11,500,000 | " " |
| Australia | 2,974,581 | " " |
| Water surface | 139,440,000 | " " |
| Atlantic Ocean | 31,830,000 | " " |
| Pacific Ocean | 63,801,000 | " " |
| Indian Ocean | 28,356,000 | " " |
| Arctic Ocean | 5,440,000 | " " |
| Equatorial circumference | 24,902 | miles |
| Meridional circumference | 24,860 | " |
| Equatorial diameter | 7,926.677 | " |
| Polar diameter | 7,899.988 | " |
| Equatorial radius | 3,963.34 | " |
| Polar radius | 3,949.99 | " |
| Volume of the Earth | 260,000,000,000 | cubic miles |
| Mass, or weight | 6,592,000,000,000,000,000,000 | tons |
| Mean distance from the Sun | 92,897,416 | miles |

The Moon, the only satellite of the Earth, from which her mean distance is 238,857 miles, occupies an average period, in her revolution round the earth, of 29 days, 12 hours, 44 minutes, 3 seconds; her diameter is 2,160 miles, and her mean density 0.60.

| | AREA IN SQ. MILES |
|---|---|
| Caspian Sea | 163,800 |
| Lake Superior | 31,820 |
| Lake Victoria | 26,828 |
| Lake Aral | 24,900 |
| Lake Huron | 23,010 |
| Lake Michigan | 22,400 |
| Lake Tanganyika | 12,700 |
| Lake Baikal | 12,150 |
| Great Bear Lake | 12,000 |
| Great Slave Lake | 11,170 |
| Lake Nyasa | 11,000 |
| Lake Erie | 9,940 |
| Lake Winnipeg | 9,398 |
| Lake Ontario | 7,540 |
| Lake Ladoga | 7,100 |
| Lake Balkhash | 6,700 |
| Lake Tchad (Chad) | 6,500 |
| Lake Onega | 3,765 |
| Lake Titicaca | 3,200 |
| Lake Nicaragua | 3,100 |
| Lake Athabaska | 3,058 |
| Reindeer Lake | 2,444 |
| Issyk-kul | 2,276 |
| Vänern | 2,149 |
| Lake Urmia | 1,795 |
| Great Salt Lake | 1,700 |
| Lake Albert | 1,640 |
| Lake Van | 1,453 |
| Lake Peipus | 1,400 |
| Lake Tana | 1,219 |
| Lake Bangweulu Approx. | 1,000 |
| Vättern | 733 |
| Dead Sea | 405 |
| Lake Balaton | 266 |
| Lake Geneva | 225 |
| Lake Constance | 208 |
| Lough Neagh | 153 |
| Lake Garda | 143 |
| Lake Neuchâtel | 83 |
| Lake Maggiore | 82 |
| Lough Corrib | 71 |
| Lake Como | 56 |
| Lake Lucerne | 44½ |
| Lake Zürich | 34 |

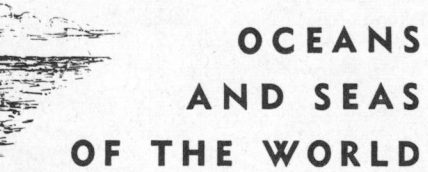

# OCEANS AND SEAS OF THE WORLD

| | AREA IN SQ. MILES | GREATEST DEPTH FEET | VOLUME IN CUBIC MILES |
|---|---|---|---|
| Pacific Ocean | 63,801,000 | 35,400 | 162,870,600 |
| Atlantic Ocean | 31,830,000 | 30,246 | 75,533,900 |
| Indian Ocean | 28,356,000 | 22,968 | 69,225,200 |
| Arctic Ocean | 5,440,000 | 17,850 | 4,029,400 |
| Mediterranean Sea | 1,145,000 | 15,197 | 1,019,400 |
| Bering Sea | 876,000 | 13,422 | 788,500 |
| Caribbean Sea | 750,000 | 23,748 | 2,298,400 |
| Sea of Okhotsk | 590,000 | 11,070 | 454,700 |
| East China Sea | 482,000 | 10,500 | 52,700 |
| Hudson Bay | 475,000 | 1,500 | 37,590 |
| Japan Sea | 389,000 | 13,242 | 383,200 |
| North Sea | 222,000 | 2,654 | 12,890 |
| Red Sea | 169,000 | 7,254 | 53,700 |
| Black Sea | 165,000 | 7,200 | .... |
| Baltic Sea | 163,000 | 1,506 | 5,360 |

# GREAT SHIP CANALS

| | LENGTH IN MILES | DEPTH IN FEET |
|---|---|---|
| Baltic-White Sea, U.S.S.R. | 141 | .... |
| Suez, Egypt | 100.76 | 34 |
| Albert, Belgium | 81 | 16.5 |
| Moscow-Volga, U.S.S.R. | 80 | 18 |
| Kiel, Germany | 61 | 37 |
| Göta, Sweden | 54 | 10 |
| Panama, Canal Zone, U.S.A. | 50.72 | 41 |
| Houston, U.S.A. | 50 | 36 |
| Amsterdam-Rhine, Netherlands | 45 | 41 |
| Beaumont-Port Arthur, U.S.A. | 40 | 32 |
| Manchester, England | 35.5 | 28 |
| Chicago Sanitary and Ship, U.S.A. | 30 | 22 |
| Welland, Canada | 27.6 | 25 |
| Juliana, Netherlands | 21 | 11.8 |
| Chesapeake-Delaware, U.S.A. | 19 | 27 |
| Cape Cod, U.S.A. | 13 | 25 |
| Lake Washington, U.S.A. | 8 | 30 |
| Corinth, Greece | 4 | 26.25 |
| Sault Ste. Marie, U.S.A. | 1.6 | 24.5 |
| Sault Ste. Marie, Canada | 1.4 | 18.25 |

# PRINCIPAL ISLANDS OF THE WORLD

| | AREA IN SQ. MILES | | AREA IN SQ. MILES | | AREA IN SQ. MILES | | AREA IN SQ. MILES |
|---|---|---|---|---|---|---|---|
| Greenland | 839,999 | Devon | 22,000 | Canary Islands | 2,894 | Martinique | 425 |
| New Guinea | 345,054 | Bismarck Arch. | 19,660 | Wrangel | 2,819 | Pemba | 380 |
| Borneo | 289,859 | Solomon Islands | 18,670 | Kerguelen | 2,700 | Orkney Islands | 376 |
| Madagascar | 241,094 | Tierra del Fuego | 18,500 | Prince Edward | 2,184 | Madeira Islands | 308 |
| Baffin | 201,600 | Southampton | 16,936 | Balearic Islands | 1,935 | Dominica | 305 |
| Sumatra | 164,148 | Melville | 16,503 | Trinidad | 1,864 | Tonga or Friendly Islands | 269 |
| Philippines | 115,600 | New Britain | 14,600 | Madura | 1,752 | Molokai | 261 |
| New Zealand, North and South Islands | 103,934 | Formosa (Taiwan) | 13,885 | South Georgia | 1,600 | St. Lucia | 233 |
| | | Kyushu | 13,770 | Cape Verde Islands | 1,557 | Corfu | 229 |
| England-Scotland-Wales | 88,745 | Prince of Wales | 13,736 | Long I., New York | 1,401 | Bornholm | 227 |
| Honshu | 87,426 | Vancouver | 13,020 | Socotra | 1,400 | Isle of Man | 221 |
| Victoria | 80,450 | Hainan | 13,000 | Gotland | 1,225 | Singapore | 220 |
| Ellesmere | 77,392 | Sicily | 9,926 | Samoa | 1,209 | Isle Royale | 209 |
| Celebes | 72,986 | Somerset | 9,594 | Isle of Pines | 1,180 | Guam | 203 |
| Java | 49,280 | Sardinia | 9,301 | Réunion | 970 | Virgin Islands | 190 |
| Cuba | 42,857 | New Caledonia | 7,202 | Azores | 890 | Curacao | 173 |
| Newfoundland | 42,734 | Fiji Islands | 7,036 | Fernando Poo | 810 | Barbados | 166 |
| Luzon | 40,420 | New Hebrides | 5,700 | Tenerife | 785 | Seychelles | 157 |
| Iceland | 39,709 | Kuril Islands | 5,700 | Maui | 728 | St. Vincent | 150 |
| Mindanao | 36,537 | Falkland Islands | 4,618 | Mauritius | 720 | Isle of Wight | 147 |
| Sakhalin | 35,400 | Jamaica | 4,411 | Zanzibar | 640 | Lanai | 141 |
| Novaya Zemlya | 35,000 | Bahama Islands | 4,404 | Tahiti | 600 | Grenada | 133 |
| Ireland | 31,839 | Hawaii | 4,021 | Oahu | 589 | Malta | 122 |
| Molucca Islands | 30,168 | Cape Breton | 3,975 | Guadeloupe | 583 | Martha's Vineyard | 120 |
| Hispaniola | 29,843 | New Ireland | 3,800 | Ahvenanmaa (Aland Is.) | 564 | Tobago | 116 |
| Hokkaido | 29,600 | Cyprus | 3,572 | Kauai | 551 | Channel Islands | 75 |
| Tasmania | 26,219 | Puerto Rico | 3,423 | Shetland Islands | 550 | Nantucket | 60 |
| Banks | 26,000 | Corsica | 3,367 | Rhodes | 542 | St. Helena | 47 |
| Ceylon | 25,332 | Crete | 3,235 | Faeröe Islands | 540 | Ascension | 34 |
| Timor Arch | 24,450 | Galápagos Islands | 3,042 | Caroline Islands | 525 | Hong Kong | 32 |
| Svalbard (Spitsbergen) | 24,294 | Hebrides | 3,000 | Marquesas Islands | 480 | Manhattan, New York | 22 |
| | | | | | | Bermudas | 21 |

# PRINCIPAL MOUNTAINS OF THE WORLD

| | FEET | | FEET |
|---|---|---|---|
| Mt. Everest, Nepal-Tibet | 29,028 | Dikh-Tau, U.S.S.R. | 17,085 |
| Mt. Godwin Austen (K2), India | 28,250 | Mt. Kenya, Kenya | 17,040 |
| Kanchenjunga, Nepal-Ind. | 28,146 | Mt. Ararat, Turkey | 16,916 |
| Mt. Makalu, Tibet-Nepal | 27,790 | Ruwenzori, Uganda | 16,787 |
| Dhaulagiri, Nepal | 26,795 | Klyuchevskaya Volcano, U.S.S.R. | 15,912 |
| Nanga Parbat, India | 26,620 | Mont Blanc, France | 15,781 |
| Annapurna, Nepal | 26,492 | Carstensz Toppen, New Guinea | 15,709 |
| Nanda Devi, India | 25,645 | Mt. Kazbek, U.S.S.R. | 15,545 |
| Mt. Kamet, India | 25,447 | Monte Rosa, Switzerland | 15,217 |
| Tirich-Mir, Pakistan | 25,263 | Mt. Belukha, U.S.S.R. | 15,154 |
| Anne Machin, China | 25,000 | Mt. Markham, Antarctica | 15,102 |
| Minya Konka, China | 24,900 | Matterhorn, Switzerland | 14,780 |
| Stalin Peak, U.S.S.R. | 24,589 | Ras Dashan, Ethiopia | 14,760 |
| Pobedy Peak, U.S.S.R. | 24,403 | Mt. Morrison, Formosa | 14,720 |
| Mt. Chomo Lhari, Bhutan | 23,997 | Mt. Whitney, California | 14,495 |
| Muztagh, Sinkiang | 23,885 | Mt. Elbert, Colorado | 14,431 |
| Tengri Khan, U.S.S.R. | 23,600 | Mt. Rainier, Washington | 14,408 |
| Aconcagua Volcano, Arg. | 23,080 | Mt. Shasta, California | 14,162 |
| Cerro Ojas del Salado, Argentina | 22,402 | Pikes Peak, Colorado | 14,110 |
| Cerro Huascarán, Peru | 22,180 | Finsteraarhorn, Switzerland | 14,026 |
| Llullaillaco Volcano, Chile | 22,145 | Mauna Loa, Hawaii | 13,680 |
| Cerro Mercedario, Arg. | 21,870 | Jungfrau, Switzerland | 13,667 |
| Tupungato, Chile | 21,810 | Jebel Toubkal, Morocco | 13,665 |
| Mt. Illampú, Bolivia | 21,489 | Mt. Kinabalu, No. Borneo | 13,451 |
| Sajama Volcano, Bolivia | 21,320 | Cameroon Mt., Cameroon | 13,349 |
| Mt. Illimani, Bolivia | 21,151 | Gran Paradiso, Italy | 13,323 |
| Chimborazo, Ecuador | 20,702 | Mt. Robson, Br. Columbia | 12,972 |
| Mt. McKinley, Alaska | 20,300 | Gross Glockner, Austria | 12,461 |
| Mt. Logan, Yukon | 19,850 | Fujisan, Japan | 12,395 |
| Cotopaxi Volcano, Ecuador | 19,498 | Mt. Cook, New Zealand | 12,349 |
| | | Pico de Teyde, Tenerife | 12,200 |
| Kilimanjaro, Tanganyika Terr. | 19,319 | Mt. Semeru, Java | 12,057 |
| Misti Volcano, Peru | 19,200 | Mulhacén, Spain | 11,417 |
| Citlaltepetl, Mexico | 18,696 | Mt. Leuser, Sumatra | 11,093 |
| Mt. Demavend, Iran | 18,550 | Mt. Etna, Sicily | 10,741 |
| Mt. Elbrus, U.S.S.R. | 18,468 | Lassen Peak, California | 10,453 |
| Mt. Tolima, Colombia | 18,438 | Mt. Tina, Dominican Rep. | 10,301 |
| Mt. St. Elias, Alaska | 18,008 | Volcano Irazu, Costa Rica | 10,525 |
| Mt. Popocatepetl, Mexico | 17,888 | Mt. Kosciusco, Australia | 7,352 |
| | | Mt. Mitchell, No. Carolina | 6,684 |

# LONGEST RIVERS OF THE WORLD

| | LENGTH IN MILES | | LENGTH IN MILES |
|---|---|---|---|
| Nile, Africa | 4,149 | Japurá, S. A. | 1,500 |
| Amazon, S. A. | 4,000 | Arkansas, U.S.A. | 1,450 |
| Mississippi-Missouri, U.S.A. | 3,892 | Dneiper, U.S.S.R. | 1,418 |
| Ob-Irtish, U.S.S.R. | 3,200 | Rio Negro, S. A. | 1,400 |
| Yangtze, China | 3,100 | Colorado, Ariz., U.S.A. | 1,360 |
| Congo, Africa | 2,900 | Kolyma, U.S.S.R. | 1,335 |
| Amur, Asia | 2,704 | Ohio, U.S.A. | 1,306 |
| Hwang (Yellow), China | 2,700 | Orange, Africa | 1,300 |
| Lena, U.S.S.R. | 2,648 | Red, Texas, U.S.A. | 1,300 |
| Mekong, Asia | 2,600 | Kama, U.S.S.R. | 1,262 |
| Niger, Africa | 2,600 | Irrawaddy, Burma | 1,250 |
| Mackenzie, Canada | 2,514 | Don, U.S.S.R. | 1,222 |
| Paraná, S. A. | 2,450 | Columbia, U.S.-Canada | 1,214 |
| Yenisei, U.S.S.R. | 2,364 | Saskatchewan, Canada | 1,205 |
| Murray, Australia | 2,310 | Darling, Australia | 1,160 |
| Volga, U.S.S.R. | 2,290 | Angara, U.S.S.R. | 1,151 |
| Madeira, S. A. | 2,000 | Tigris, Iraq | 1,150 |
| Yukon, Alaska | 1,979 | Sungari, Asia | 1,130 |
| St. Lawrence, Canada | 1,900 | Pechora, U.S.S.R. | 1,111 |
| Purus, S. A. | 1,850 | Peace, Canada | 1,054 |
| Rio Grande, U.S.A. | 1,800 | Snake, U.S.A. | 1,038 |
| São Francisco, S. A. | 1,800 | Churchill, Canada | 1,000 |
| Salween, Burma | 1,750 | Pilcomayo, S. A. | 1,000 |
| Danube, Europe | 1,725 | Uruguay, S. A. | 1,000 |
| Euphrates, Iraq | 1,700 | Magdalena, S. A. | 950 |
| Indus, Pakistan | 1,700 | Platte, U.S.A. | 928 |
| Orinoco, S. A. | 1,700 | Oka, U.S.S.R. | 918 |
| Tocantins, S. A. | 1,700 | Canadian, U.S.A. | 906 |
| Brahmaputra, India | 1,680 | Tennessee, U.S.A. | 900 |
| Syr Darya, U.S.S.R. | 1,680 | Brazos, U.S.A. | 870 |
| Si, China | 1,650 | Dneister, U.S.S.R. | 852 |
| Nelson, Canada | 1,600 | Frazer, Canada | 850 |
| Zambezi, Africa | 1,600 | Colorado, Tex., U.S.A. | 840 |
| Ural, U.S.S.R. | 1,574 | Northern Dvina, U.S.S.R. | 803 |
| Amu Darya, U.S.S.R. | 1,550 | Tisza, Europe | 800 |
| Ganges, India | 1,540 | Athabaska, Canada | 765 |
| Olenek, U.S.S.R. | 1,500 | North Canadian, U.S.A. | 760 |
| Paraguay, S. A. | 1,500 | North Saskatchewan, Can. | 760 |

# MAP PROJECTIONS
## *by Erwin Raisz*

Our earth is rotating around its *axis* once a day. The two end points of its axis are the *poles*; the line circling the earth midway between the poles is the *equator*. The arc from either of the poles to the equator is divided into 90 *degrees*. The distance, expressed in degrees, from the equator to any point is its *latitude* and circles of equal latitude are the *parallels*. On maps it is customary to show parallels of evenly-spaced degrees such as every fifth or every tenth.

The equator is divided into 360 degrees. Lines circling from pole to pole through the degree points on the equator are called *meridians*. They are all equal in length but by international agreement the meridian passing through the Greenwich Observatory in London has been chosen as *prime meridian*. The distance, expressed in degrees, from the prime meridian to any point is its *longitude*. While meridians are all equal in length, parallels become shorter and shorter as they approach the poles. Whereas one degree of latitude represents everywhere approximately 69 miles, one degree of longitude varies from 69 miles at the equator to nothing at the poles.

Each degree is divided into 60 minutes and each minute into 60 seconds. One minute of latitude equals a nautical mile.

The map is flat but the earth is nearly spherical. Neither a rubber ball nor any part of a rubber ball may be flattened without stretching or tearing unless the part is very small. To present the curved surface of the earth on a flat map is not difficult as long as the areas under consideration are small, but the mapping of countries, continents, or the whole earth requires some kind of *projection*. Any regular set of parallels and meridians upon which a map can be drawn makes a map projection. Many systems are used.

In any projection only the parallels or the meridians or some other set of lines can be *true* (the same length as on the globe of corresponding scale); all other lines are too long or too short. Only on a globe is it possible to have both the parallels and the meridians true. The scale given on a flat map can not be true everywhere. The construction of the various projections begins usually with laying out the parallels or meridians which have true lengths.

**RECTANGULAR PROJECTION.** This is a set of evenly-placed meridians and horizontal parallels. The central or *standard parallel* and all meridians are true. All other parallels are either too long or too short. The projection is used for simple maps of small areas, as city plans, etc.

**MERCATOR PROJECTION.** In this projection the meridians are evenly spaced vertical lines. The parallels are horizon-

tal, spaced so that their length has the same relation to the meridians as on a globe. As the meridians converge at higher latitudes on the globe, while on the map they do not, the parallels have to be drawn also farther and farther apart

to maintain the correct relationship. When every very small area has the same shape as on a globe we call the projection *conformal*. The most interesting quality of this projection is that all *compass directions* appear as straight lines. For this reason it is generally used for marine charts. It is also frequently used for world maps in spite of the fact that the high latitudes are very much exaggerated in size. Only the equator is true to scale; all other parallels and meridians are too long. The Mercator projection did *not* derive from projecting a globe upon a cylinder.

**SINUSOIDAL PROJECTION.** The parallels are truly-spaced horizontal lines. They are divided truly and the connecting  curves make the meridians. It does not make a good world map because the outer regions are distorted, but the central portion is good and this part is often used for maps of Africa and South America. Every part of the map has the same area as the corresponding area on the globe. It is an *equal-area* projection.

**MOLLWEIDE PROJECTION.** The meridians are equally-spaced ellipses; the parallels are horizontal lines spaced so that every belt of latitude should have the same area as on a globe. This projection is popular for world maps, especially in European atlases.

**GOODE'S INTERRUPTED PROJECTIONS.** Only the good central part of the Mollweide or  sinusoidal (or both) projection is used and the oceans are cut. This makes an equal-area map with little distortion of shape. It is commonly used for world maps.

**ECKERT PROJECTIONS.** These are similar to the sinusoidal or the Mollweide projections, but the poles are shown as lines half the length of the equator. There are several variants; the meridians are either sine curves or ellipses; the parallels are horizontal and spaced either 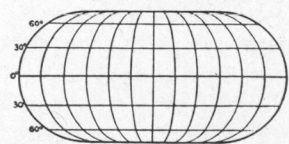 evenly or so as to make the projection equal area. Their use for world maps is increasing. The figure shows the elliptical equal-area variant.

**CONIC PROJECTION.** The original idea of the conic projection is that of capping the globe by a cone upon which both the parallels and meridians are projected from the

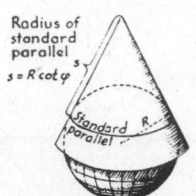

center of the globe. The cone is then cut open and laid flat. A cone can be made tangent to any chosen *standard parallel*.

The actually-used conic projection is a modification of this idea. The radius of the standard parallel is obtained as above. The meridians are straight radiating lines spaced truly on the standard parallel. The parallels are concentric circles spaced at true distances. All parallels except the standard are too long. The projection is used for maps of countries in middle latitudes, as it presents good shapes with small scale error.

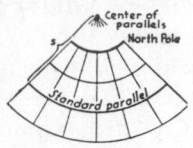

There are several variants: The use of *two standard parallels*, one near the top, the other near the bottom of the map, reduces the scale error. In the *Albers projection* the parallels are spaced unevenly, to make the projection equal-area. This is a good projection for the United States. In the *Lambert conformal conic projection* the parallels are spaced so that any small quadrangle of the grid should have the same shape as on the globe. This is the best projection for air-navigation charts as it has relatively straight azimuths.

An *azimuth* is a great-circle direction reckoned clockwise from north. A *great-circle direction* points to a place along the shortest line on the earth's surface. This is not the same as compass direction. The center of a great circle is the center of the globe.

**BONNE PROJECTION.** The parallels are laid out exactly as in the conic projection. All parallels are divided truly and the connecting curves make the meridians. It is an equal-area projection. It is used for maps of the northern continents, as Asia, Europe, and North America.

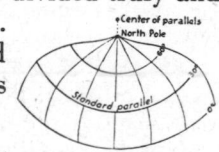

**POLYCONIC PROJECTION.** The central meridian is divided truly. The parallels are non-concentric circles, the radii of which are obtained by drawing tangents to the globe as

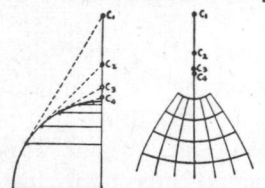

though the globe were covered by several cones rather than by only one. Each parallel is divided truly and the connecting curves make the meridians. All meridians except the central one are too long. This projection is used for large-scale topographic sheets—less often for countries or continents.

**THE AZIMUTHAL PROJECTIONS.** In this group a part of the globe is projected from an eyepoint onto a plane. The eyepoint can be at different distances, making different projections. The plane of projection can be tangent at the equator, at a pole, or at any other point on which we want to focus attention. The most important quality of all azimuthal projections is that they show every point at its true direction (azimuth) from the center point and all points equally distant from the center point will be equally distant on the map also.

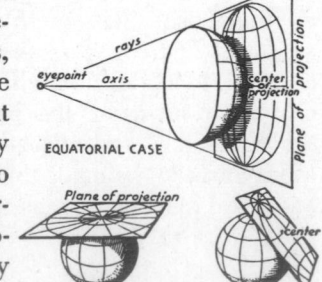

In the **GNOMONIC PROJECTION** the eyepoint is at the center of the globe. Only the central part is good; the outer regions are badly distorted. Yet the projection has one important quality, all great circles being shown as straight lines. For this reason it is used for laying out the routes for long range flying or trans-oceanic navigation.

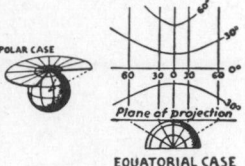

The **ORTHOGRAPHIC PROJECTION** has the eyepoint at

infinite distance and the projecting rays are parallel. The polar or equatorial varieties are rare but the oblique case became very popular on account of its visual quality. It looks like a picture of a globe. Although the distortion on the peripheries is extreme, we see it correctly because the eye perceives it not as a map but as a picture of a three-dimensional globe. Obviously only a hemisphere (half globe) can be shown.

Some azimuthal projections do not derive from the actual process of projecting from an eyepoint, but are arrived at by other means:

**AZIMUTHAL EQUIDISTANT PROJECTION.** This is the only projection in which every point is shown both at true great-circle direction and at true distance from the center point, but all other directions and distances are distorted. The principle of the projection can best be understood from the polar case. Most polar maps are in this projection. The oblique case is used for radio direction finding, for earthquake research, and in long-distance flying. A separate map has to be constructed for each central point selected.

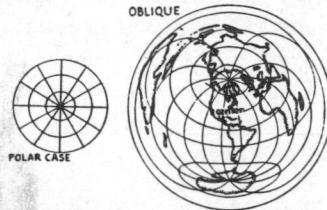

**LAMBERT AZIMUTHAL EQUAL-AREA PROJECTION.** The construction of this projection can best be understood from the polar case. All three cases are widely used. It makes a

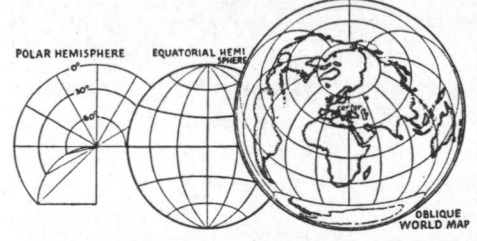

good polar map and it is often extended to include the southern continents. It is the most common projection used for maps of the Eastern and Western Hemispheres, and it is a good projection for continents as it shows correct areas with relatively little distortion of shape. Most of the continent maps in this atlas are in this projection.

**IN THIS ATLAS,** on almost all maps, parallels and meridians have been marked because they are useful for the following:

(a) They show the north-south and east-west directions which appear on many maps at oblique angles especially near the margins.

(b) With the help of parallels and meridians every place can be exactly located; for instance, New York City is at 41° N and 74° W on any map.

(c) They help to measure distances even in the distorted parts of the map. The scale given on each map is true only along certain lines which are specified in the foregoing discussion for each projection. One degree of latitude equals nearly 69 statute miles or 60 nautical miles. The length of one degree of longitude varies (1° long. = 1° lat. × cos lat.).

# Index of
# THE WORLD

## *Introduction*

THE INDEX OF THE WORLD gives the principal cities, towns and geographical features of the world (such as mountains, rivers, bays and islands) exclusive of the cities of the United States, Alaska and Hawaii which are covered in THE INDEX OF THE UNITED STATES. Each entry gives the index reference and the plate number on which the name is found. The name is found within the square formed by the two lines of latitude or longitude which enclose each of the co-ordinates — i.e. the marginal letters and numbers. In the case of maps consisting entirely of insets, the name is found near the intersecting point of the imaginary lines connecting the co-ordinates.

Where space on the map has not permitted giving the complete form of a name, the extended form is shown in the index. Where a place may be known under different names or by various spellings of the name, the different forms have been included to a large extent in the index.

The population figures given are the latest census figures or the latest official estimates.

In the belief that a geographical index should primarily serve to enable the reader to locate names quickly and accurately, we have employed the system of indexing followed in all government publications and telephone directories. All indexes sorted by mechanical means, such as the I. B. M. method, employ this system. Therefore, in alphabetizing, all those compound names with a common first part are grouped together, even though the first letter of the second part of the name may succeed the corresponding letter in a simple name. The three examples shown below are offered to illustrate this system in comparison with the less convenient alternate system of indexing.

INDEXING SYSTEM USED IN THIS ATLAS

| | | |
|---|---|---|
| San Cristobal | La Ceiba | Bac Kan |
| San Francisco | La Spezia | Bac Lieu |
| San Jose | Labe | Bac Ninh |
| Sanchez | Lachlan | Bacabal |
| Sandakan | | Backang |

ALTERNATE INDEXING SYSTEM

| | | |
|---|---|---|
| Sanchez | Labe | Bacabal |
| San Cristobal | La Ceiba | Bac Kan |
| Sandakan | Lachlan | Backang |
| San Francisco | La Spezia | Bac Lieu |
| San Jose | | Bac Ninh |

As a special feature translations of foreign geographical terms have been incorporated directly into the body of the index. For example: Rio will be found in the index with its English translation. All physical features are listed under their proper names and not according to their generic terms; that is to say, Rio Negro will be found under Negro and not under Rio Negro.

# INDEX OF THE WORLD

Capitals of Countries, States and Provinces are designated by asterisks (*). Dagger (†) designates Population figure including suburbs.

*Index Plate Ref. No.*

## A

Aabenraa, Denmark, 13,017.........F 9 13
Aachen (Aix la Chapelle), Germany, 129,811.........B 3 14
Aalborg, Denmark, 79,806.........G 8 13
Aalen, Germany, 25,375.........D 4 14
Aalst (Alost), Belgium, 41,960.........D 7 15
Aarau, Switzerland, 14,280.........F 2 19
Aarhus, Denmark, 116,167.........F 8 13
Aarlon (Arlon), Belgium, 11,180..H 9 15
Abadan with Khorramshahr, Iran 64,889.........F 5 27
Abadeh, Iran, 8,000.........H 5 27
Abakaliki, Nigeria, 4,307.........H10 34
Abakan, U.S.S.R., 36,135.........L 4 22
Abancay, Peru, 5,332.........F 6 46
Abashiri, Japan, 39,218.........M 1 33
Abau, Papua.........C 7 31
Abbazia (Opatija) Yugo., 11,737..A 3 21
Abbeville, France, 18,932.........D 2 16
Abbotsdale, C. of Good Hope, 618.D18 35
Abbottabad, Pakistan, 27,602.........B 2 29
Abdulino, U.S.S.R., 13,636.........G 4 22
Abécher, Fr. Eq. Africa.........L 9 34
Abeokuta, Nigeria, 56,600.........G10 34
Abercorn, N. Rhodesia, 1,177.........N13 35
Aberdare, Wales, 40,916.........D 6 10
Aberdeen (lake), Canada.........L 2 40
Aberdeen, Scotland, 182,729.........N 5 11
Abertillery, England, 27,617.........E 6 10
Abha, Saudi Arabia, 15,000.........D 6 26
Abidjan, Fr. W. Africa, 56,000....F10 34
Abitibi (lake), Canada.........D 4 41
Abitibi (river), Canada.........D 3 41
Åbo (Turku), Finland, 101,239......N 6 13
Abomey, Fr. W. Africa, 16,906.....G10 34
Abony, Hungary, 15,299.........E 3 20
Abu Arish, Saudi Arabia, 5,000.....D 6 26
Abu Dhabi, Tr. Oman, 5,000.........F 5 26
Abu Road, India, 9,935.........B 4 29
Abunã, Brazil.........H 5 46
Acadia Valley, Alta., 99.........H 4 40
Acambaro, Mex., 23,038.........J 7 44
Acapulco, Mexico, 28,512.........J 8 44
Accra,* Ghana, 135,192.........G11 34
Accrington, England, 40,671.........E 4 10
Achill (island), Ireland.........A 4 12
Achill Head (cape), Ireland.........A 4 12
Achinsk, U.S.S.R. .........L 4 22
Acireale, Italy 34,330.........E 6 18
Acklins (island), W. I., 1,744.......C 2 45
Aconcagua (mountain), Arg. .......F10 47
Acqui, Italy, 12,328.........B 2 18
Acre, Israel, 12,200.........C 2 24
Acre (river), Brazil.........G 6 46
Adalar, Turkey, 15,446.........D 6 28
Adana (Seyhan), Turkey, 117,799.F 4 28
Adapazari, Turkey, 36,210.........D 2 28
Adaut, Indonesia.........J 7 31
Addanki, India, 11,310.........C 5 29
Addis Ababa,* Ethiopia, 250,000...O10 34
Addis Alam, Ethiopia, 1,000.........O10 34
Adelaide, Australia, †483,585.......D 7 36
Adelboden, Switzerland, 2,873.......E 3 19
Aden,* Aden, †97,760.........E 7 26
Adilabad, India, 11,128.........C 5 29
Adirondack (mountains), U.S. .....P 3 43
Adiyaman, Turkey, 11,681.........H 4 28
Admiralty (gulf), Australia.........C 2 36
Admiralty (islands), Territory N.G., 14,420.........E 6 37
Adoni, India, 35,431.........C 5 29
Adrano, Italy, 26,952.........E 6 18
Adrar, Algeria, 1,722.........G 6 34
Adria, Italy, 22,990.........D 2 18
Adrianople (Edirne), Turkey 30,245.........B 2 28
Adriatic (sea).........E 3 18
Adua, Ethiopia, 6,000.........O 9 34
Aegean (sea).........G 6 21
Afgoi, Somaliland, 10,500.........P11 35
Afmadu, Somaliland, 2,000.........P11 35
Afyon, Turkey, 29,881.........D 3 28
Agadés, Fr. W. Africa, 4,300.........H 8 34
Agadir, Morocco, 29,879.........D 5 34
Agana,* Guam, 1,330.........E 4 37
Agartala, India, 17,693.........F 4 29
Agedabia, Libya, 7,000.........L 5 34
Agen, France, 28,591.........D 5 16
Aginskoye, U.S.S.R. .........N 4 23
Agira, Italy, 15,677.........E 6 18
Agordat, Eritrea, Ethiopia, 2,000..O 8 34
Agra, India, 375,665.........C 3 29
Ağri (Karaköse), Turkey, 10,013...K 3 28
Agrigento, Italy, 37,506.........D 6 18
Agrínion, Greece, 20,981.........E 6 21
Agua Prieta, Mexico, 10,471.........E 1 44
Aguadas, Colombia, 7,631.........F 2 46
Aguadilla, P.R., 18,181.........F 1 45
Aguascalientes, Mexico, 93,432.....H 6 44
Aguilar, Spain, 15,275.........D 4 17
Aguilas, Spain, 11,829.........F 4 17
Aguja (point), S.A. .........D 5 47
Agulhas (cape), U.S. Africa.........K19 35
Ahaggar (plateau), Fr. W. Afr. ..H 7 34
Ahar, Iran, 20,047.........E 1 27
Ahlen, Germany, 33,141.........B 3 14
Ahmadabad, India, 788,333.........B 4 29
Ahmadnagar, India, 70,418.........B 5 29
Ahmadpur East, Pakistan, 20,404.........B 3 29
Ahmedabad (Ahmadabad), India, 788,333.........B 4 29
Ahuachapán, El Salvador, 10,294..B 4 39
Ahvenanmaa (Aland) (isls.), Finland, 21,650.........L 6 13
Ahwar, Aden Pr., 5,000.........E 7 26
Ahwaz, Iran, 49,336.........F 5 27
Aígion, Greece, 15,070.........F 6 21
Aigun, China.........L 2 32
Ain es Sir, Jordan, 6,641.........D 4 24
Ain Karim, Israel, 1,700.........C 4 24
Ain Sefra, Algeria, 3,500.........G 5 34
Air (Asben) (mountains), Fr. W. Africa.........H 8 34
Airdrie, Scotland, 30,308.........D 2 11
Aire (river), England.........F 4 10
Aitape, Terr. N. G. 161.........B 6 31
Aitutake (island), Pacific, 2,356...K 7 37
Aiud, Rumania, 9,535.........F 2 21
Aiún, Sp. W. A., 3,142.........D 6 34
Aix, France, 32,076.........F 6 16
Aix-les-Bains, France, 10,720.........G 5 16
Ajaccio, France, 28,732.........F 7 16
Ajana, Australia, 80.........B 5 36
Ajmer, India, 196,633.........B 3 29
Akaroa, New Zealand, 556.........L 7 36
Akashi, Japan, 65,642.........H 8 33
Aken, Germany, 14,624.........D 3 14
Aketi, Belgian Congo, 6,616.........L11 35
Akhdhar (mt.), Sult. of Oman......G 5 26
Akhisar, Turkey, 23,579.........B 3 28
Akhmim, Egypt, 32,071.........N 6 34
Akhty, U.S.S.R., 3,886.........F 5 22
Akimiski (island), Canada.........D 3 41
Akita, Japan, 126,074.........J 4 33
Aklavik, N. W. Territory, 900.......C 1 40
Akmolinsk, U.S.S.R., 90,000.........J 4 22
Akola, India, 62,564.........C 4 29
Akpatok, (island), Canada.........G 1 41
Aksaray, Turkey, 10,936.........F 3 28
Akşehir, Turkey, 13,305.........D 3 28
Aktyubinsk, U.S.S.R., 45,000.........G 4 22
Akureyri, Iceland 7,143.........C 2 9
Akyab, Burma, 41,589.........B 2 30
Al Kadhimain, Iraq, 65,000.........C 4 27
Al Kuwait,* Kuwait, 80,000.........E 4 26
Al Qunfidha, Saudi Ar., 4,500.......D 6 26
Alabama (river), U.S. .........M 7 43
Alaçehir, Turkey, 10,738.........C 3 28
Alagir, U.S.S.R., 4,192.........F 5 22
Alagoinhas, Brazil, 21,283.........N 6 46
Alajuela, Costa Rica, 13,903.........E 6 39
Alanya, Turkey, 6,636.........D 4 28
Alapayevsk, U.S.S.R., 30,000.........P 6 23
Alatyr', U.S.S.R., 25,567.........F 4 22
Alausí, Ecuador, 4,812.........E 4 46
Alba, Italy, 13,807.........B 2 18
Alba Iulia, Rumania, 14,420.........F 2 21
Albacete, Spain, 71,822.........F 3 17
Albany, Australia, 4,761.........B 6 36
Albany (river), Canada.........D 3 41
Albatross (bay), Australia.........G 2 36
Albatross (island), Tas., Aust. ....G 7 36
Alberga (river), Australia.........E 5 36
Alberni, B. C., 3,947.........E 5 40
Albert, France, 8,742.........E 2 16
Albert (lake), Africa.........M11 35
Alberton, P.E.I., 820.........H 4 41
Albertville, Belgian Congo, 27,931.........M13 35
Albi, France, 27,768.........E 6 16
Albina, Surinam, 370.........K 2 46
Albury, Australia, 14,412.........H 7 36
Albury, New Zealand.........L 7 36
Alcalá de Guadaira, Spain, 17,844.D 4 17
Alcalá de Henares, Spain, 14,651..G 4 17
Alcamo, Italy, 41,471.........D 6 18
Alcântara, Brazil, 1,453.........M 4 46
Alcázar de San Juan, Spain, 22,964.........E 3 17
Alcira, Spain, 21,059.........F 3 17
Alcobaça, Brazil, 1,307.........K 4 46
Alcoy, Spain, 39,417.........F 3 17
Aldabra (island), Seychelles, 47....R13 35
Aldan, U.S.S.R. .........O 4 23
Aldan (river), U.S.S.R. .........O 4 23
Aldershot, England, 36,184.........G 6 10
Aleg, Fr. West Africa, 352.........D 8 34
Alegrete, Brazil, 20,160.........J 9 47
'Aleih, Lebanon, 5,271.........F 6 28
Aleksandrovsk-Sakhalinskiy, U.S.S.R., 100,000.........R 4 23
Aleksandrovskiy Zavod, U.S.S.R., 2,097.........N 4 23
Aleksinac, Yugoslavia, 7,383.........E 4 21
Alençon, France, 19,427.........D 3 16
Aleppo (Haleb), Syria, 324,899.....G 4 28
Alès, France, 20,259.........E 5 16
Alessandria, Italy, 70,238.........B 2 18
Alesund, Norway, 18,527.........D 5 13
Alexandra, New Zealand, 1,413.....K 7 36
Alexandretta (Iskenderun), Turkey, 22,946.........G 4 28
Alexandria (El Iskandariya), Egypt, 925,081.........M 5 34
Alexandria, Rumania, 17,840.........G 3 21
Alexandroupolis, Greece, 17,081....H 5 21
Alfeld, Germany, 12,287.........C 2 14
Alfreton, England, 23,388.........F 4 10
Algeciras, Spain, 20,610.........D 4 17
Algemesí, Spain, 15,510.........F 3 17
Alger,* Algeria, 329,700.........G 4 34
Algés, Portugal, 9,826.........A 1 17
Alghero, Italy, 18,602.........B 4 18
Alicante, Spain, †101,741.........F 3 17
Alice Arm, Br. Columbia, 75.........E 3 40
Alice Springs (Stuart), Aust., 1,871.........E 4 36
Aligarh, India, 141,618.........C 3 29
Alipore, India, 46,332.........E 2 29
Aliwal North, C. of G.H., 8,754....M18 35
Alkmaar, Netherlands, 37,827.........F 3 15
Allahabad, India, 332,295.........D 3 29
Allen (lake), Ireland.........E 3 12
Allen, Bog of, Ireland.........H 5 12
Allenstein (Olsztyn), Poland, 29,053.........E 2 24
Alleppey, India, 116,278.........C 7 29
Alloa, Scotland, 13,436.........E 1 11
Alma-Ata, U.S.S.R., 330,000.........J 5 22
Almada, Portugal, 11,995.........A 1 17
Almadén, Spain, 12,069.........D 3 17
Almaguer, Colombia, 830.........E 3 46
Almansa, Spain, 14,942.........F 3 17
Almeirim, Portugal, 7,104.........B 3 17
Almelo, Netherlands, 40,118.........K 4 15
Almendralejo, Spain, 21,363.........C 3 17
Almería, Spain, 75,861.........E 4 17
Almora, India, 10,995.........C 3 29
Alofi, Niue Island, 884.........K 7 37
Alon, Burma.........B 2 30
Alor Star, Mal. Fed., 32,424.........D 6 30
Alsack, Sask., 232.........J 4 40
Alsdorf, Germany, 22,205.........B 3 14
Alta Gracia, Argentina, 11,570....H10 47
Altagracia, Venezuela, 3,987.........F 1 46
Altai (mountains), Mon. Rep. .....D 2 32
Altamira, Brazil, 1,988.........K 4 46
Altamura, Italy, 38,231.........F 4 18
Altan Bulak, Mon. Rep., 8,000.......F 2 32
Altayskoye, U.S.S.R., 7,555.........K 4 22
Altena, Germany, 22,162.........B 3 14
Altenburg, Germany, 51,805.........E 3 14
Altin (mt. range), China.........C 4 32
Alto de Boa Vista, Brazil.........O15 47
Altona, Germany.........C 2 14
Altona, Man., 1,698.........L 5 40
Alty-Aryk, U.S.S.R., 5,706.........T 2 23
Alula, Som., 2,000.........S 9 34
Alv (means river) (Swedish).........
Alvaro Obregón (Frontera), Mex., 8,466.........N 7 44
Alwar, India, 54,143.........C 3 29
Amadeus (lake), Australia.........E 4 36
Amadjuak (lake), Canada.........F26 8
Amagasaki, Japan, 279,264.........H 8 33
Amaliás, Greece, 15,189.........E 7 21
Amalner, India, 34,694.........B 4 29
Amapá, Brazil, 1,267.........K 3 46
Amapala, Honduras, 2,934.........D 4 39
'Amara, Iraq, 48,915.........E 5 27
Amarante, Brazil, 2,545.........M 5 46
Amarapura, Burma.........B 2 30
Amargosa, Brazil, 4,858.........N 6 46
Amasya, Turkey, 14,446.........F 2 28
Amatitlán, Guat., 6,683.........B 3 39
Amazonas (river), Brazil.........K 4 46
Ambala, India, 107,383.........C 2 29
Ambalavao, Madag., 2,183.........R16 35
Ambarawa, Indonesia, 19,480.........J 2 31
Ambarchik, U.S.S.R. .........T 3 23
Ambato, Ecuador, 33,908.........E 4 46
Ambatondrazaka, Madag., 2,919...S15 35
Amberg, Germany, 37,920.........E 4 14
Ambodifotofra, Madag., 2,194.......S15 35
Amboina (Ambon), Indonesia, 23,066.........H 6 31
Ambositra, Madag., 4,516.........R16 35
Ambre (cape), Madagascar.........R14 35
Ambriz, Angola, 2,196.........J13 35
Ambrizete, Angola, 1,147.........J13 35
Ambunti, Terr. N.G. .........B 6 31
Amderma, U.S.S.R. .........H 3 22
Ameca, Mexico, 13,589.........H 6 44
American Falls (res.), U.S. .........E 4 42
Amersfoort, Neth., 55,996.........G 4 15
Amery, Manitoba, 25.........M 3 40
Amherst, Burma.........C 3 30
Amherst, N. S., 10,301.........H 4 41
Amherstburg, Ont., 4,099.........D 5 41
Amiens, France, 87,126.........D 3 16
Amman,* Jordan, 90,000.........D 4 24
Amne Machin (mt.).........E 5 32
Amos, Quebec, 5,145.........E 4 41
Amoy, China, 138,032.........J 7 32
Ampana, Indonesia.........G 6 31
Amparo, Brazil, 10,699.........L 8 46
Amran, Yemen, 5,000.........D 6 26
Amraoti, India, 61,971.........C 4 29
Amreli, India, 25,485.........B 4 29
Amritsar, India, 325,747.........B 2 29
Amsterdam,* Neth., 803,847.........B 4 15
Amstetten, Austria, 11,341.........C 2 20
Amu Dar'ya (river), U.S.S.R., .....H 5 22
Amul, Iran, 16,119.........H 2 27
Amundsen (gulf), Canada.........D31 8
Amuntai, Indonesia.........F 6 31
Amur (river), U.S.S.R. .........P 5 23
Amurang, Indonesia.........G 5 31
Amya, Burma.........C 4 30
An Khe, Vietnam.........F 4 30
An Najef, Iraq, 35,000.........C 5 27
An Nasiriya, Iraq, 15,000.........D 5 27
An Uaimh (Navan), Ireland, 4,102.........H 4 12
Anadyr,' U.S.S.R. .........U 3 23
Anadyr (mt. range), U.S.S.R. .....U 3 23
Anagni, Italy, 14,262.........F 6 18
Anaiza, Saudi Arabia, 20,000.........D 4 26
Anakapalle, India, 29,249.........D 5 29
Analalava, Madag., 1,170.........R14 35
Anantapur, India, 21,482.........C 6 29
Anantnag, Kash., 11,985.........C 2 29
Anápolis, Brazil, 18,350.........L 7 46
Anatolia (plateau), Turkey.........C 3 28
Añatuya, Arg., 9,310.........H 9 47
Anchieta, Brazil, 1,328.........M14 47
Ancona, Italy, 68,501.........D 3 18
Ancud, Chile, 6,410.........F12 47
Andaman (islands), India, 21,316.........F 6 29
Anderlecht, Belgium, 86,412.........B 9 15
Andermatt, Switz., 1,231.........G 3 18
Andernach, Germany, 15,879.........B 3 14
Anderson (river), Canada.........E 1 40
Andheri, India, 38,493.........B 7 29
Andizhan, U.S.S.R., 115,000.........U 2 23
Andkhui, Afghan., 18,438.........J 2 26
Andong, Korea, 35,275.........D 5 33
Andorra La Vieja,* Andorra, 1,100.........G 1 17
Andria, Italy, 63,937.........F 4 18
Andros (island), W.I., 6,718.........B 1 45
Andújar, Spain, 22,906.........D 3 17
Andulo, Angola, 2,631.........K14 35
Aneto (mountain), Spain.........G 1 17

Index Ref. Plate No.

Játiva, Spain, 17,164 F 3 17
Jaú, Brazil, 18,936 L 8 46
Jauf, Saudi Arabia, 7,500 C 4 26
Jauja, Peru, 7,713 E 6 46
Jaunpur, India, 44,833 D 3 29
Java (island), Indonesia, 51,097,747 D 7 31
Java (sea) D 6 31
Javarí (Yavarí) (river), S.A. F 4 36
Jawor (Jauer), Poland, 9,690 C 3 24
Jaworzno, Poland, 17,506 D 3 24
Jebel (means mt.) (Arab.)
Jedrezejów, Poland, 10,998 E 3 24
Jelenia Góra, Poland, 39,050 B 3 24
Jelgava (Yelgava), U.S.S.R., 34,099 D 4 22
Jemappes, Belg., 12,902 D 8 15
Jena, Germany, 82,722 D 3 14
Jequié, Brazil, 20,652 M 6 46
Jérémie, Haiti, 11,138 A 6 48
Jerez de la Frontera, Spain, †107,770 C 4 17
Jerez de los Caballeros, Spain, 12,738 C 3 17
Jericho, Australia, 302 H 4 36
Jerusalem (New City),* Israel, 120,000 C 4 24
Jesenice, Yugoslavia, 15,811 A 2 21
Jesselton,* No. Borneo, 11,704 F 4 31
Jessore, Pakistan, 23,867 E 4 29
Jette, Belgium, 29,484 B 9 15
Jeypore, India, 12,504 D 5 29
Jhang-Maghiana, Pak., 73,397 B 2 29
Jhansi, India, 127,365 C 3 29
Jhelum, Pakistan, 38,567 B 2 29
Jhunjhunu, India, 16,874 C 3 29
Jibhalanta (Uliassutai), Mon. Rep., 6,000 E 2 32
Jidda, Saudi Arabia, 80,000 C 5 26
Jihlava, Czech., 21,797 C 2 20
Jima (means island) (Jap.)
Jind, India, 14,909 C 3 29
Jinja, Uganda, 8,410 N11 35
Jinotepe, Nicaragua, 7,128 D 5 39
Jinsen (Inch'ŏn), Korea, 265,767 C 5 33
Jirgalanta (Kobdo), Mon. Rep. 10,000 D 2 32
Jish, Israel, 1,304 C 1 24
João Pessoa (Paraíba), Brazil, 89,517 O 5 46
Jódar, Spain, 11,980 E 4 17
Jodhpur, India, 180,717 B 3 29
Jogjakarta (Djokjakarta), Indonesia, 244,379 J 2 31
Johannesburg, Transv., †880,573 M17 35
Johnston (island), Hawaii, 69 K 4 37
Johnstone, Scotland, 16,660 B 2 11
Johore Bahru, Mal. Fed., 38,826 B 2 11
Joinville, Brazil, 20,915 L 9 47
Joki (means river) (Finnish)
Joliette, Quebec, 16,940 F 4 41
Jones (cape), Canada D 3 41
Jönköping, Sweden, 44,685 H 8 13
Jonquière, Quebec, 25,550 F 4 41
Jorhat, India, 11,664 F 3 29
Jos, Nigeria, 11,854 H10 34
Joseph Bonaparte (gulf), Aust. D 2 36
Juan de Fuca (strait), No. Amer. B 2 42
Juan Fernández (islands), Chile D10 47
Juárez (Ciudad Mante), Mexico, 21,291 K 5 44
Juàzeiro do Norte, Brazil, 41,999 N 5 46
Juba, Sudan, 7,900 N11 34
Jubbulpore, India, 256,998 D 4 29
Juchitán, Mexico, 13,819 M 8 44
Judenburg, Austria, 9,821 C 3 20
Juiz de Fora, Brazil, 84,999 M 8 46
Jujuy, Argentina, 31,091 G 8 46
Juli, Peru, 2,266 G 7 46
Juliaca, Peru, 6,034 F 7 46
Julianehaab, Greenland, 954 F23 8
Jülich, Germany 6,831 B 3 14
Julis, Israel, 1,019 B 4 24
Jullundur, India, 168,816 C 2 29
Jumet, Belgium, 28,569 E 8 15
Jumilla, Spain, 15,745 F 3 17
Jumna (river), India C 3 29
Junagadh, India, 58,111 B 4 29
Junan, China H 5 32
Juncos, Puerto Rico, 8,285 G 1 45
Jundiaí, Brazil, 39,560 L 8 47
Junee, Australia, 4,065 H 6 36
Junín, Argentina, 36,149 M12 47
Junín, Chile G 7 46
Juquiá, Brazil, 899 L 8 47
Jur (river), Sudan M10 34
Jura (island), Scotland, 258 E 8 11
Jura (mountains) F 4 16
Juruena (river), Brazil J 5 46
Jutaí (river), Brazil G 4 46
Jüterbog, Germany, 15,137 E 3 14
Jutiapa, Guatemala, 5,141 B 3 39
Jyväskylä, Finland, 24,050 O 5 13

# K

K 2 (Godwin Austen) (mt.) C 1 29
Kaakhka, U.S.S.R., 2,072 G 6 22
Kabala, S. Leone, 3,064 D10 34
Kabale, Uganda, 2,469 N12 35
Kabansk, U.S.S.R., 2,233 M 4 23
Kabba, Nigeria, 9,221 H10 34
Kabul,* Afghanistan, 206,208 J 3 26
Kadayanallur, India, 29,652 C 7 29
Kadiköy, Turkey, 77,675 D 6 28
Kadima, Israel, 1,309 B 3 24
Kadina, Australia, 1,272 F 6 36
Kadiri, India, 11,885 C 6 29
Kadiyevka, U.S.S.R., 170,000 M 1 23
Kadjang, Indonesia G 7 31
Kaduna, Nigeria, 10,628 H 9 34
Kaédi, Fr. West Africa, 5,030 D 8 34
Kaesong, Korea, 88,708 C 5 33
Kafr Kanna, Israel, 2,478 C 2 24
Kafue (river), N. Rhodesia M15 35
Kagoshima, Japan, 229,462 E 8 33
Kagul, U.S.S.R., 7,375 D 5 22
Kaiapit, Terr. N.G. B 7 31
Kaiapoi, New Zealand, 2,246 L 7 36
Kaifeng, China, 303,422 J 5 32
Kaihwa (Wenshan), China F 7 32
Kaikoura, New Zealand, 1,119 L 6 36
Kairouan, Tunisia, 32,299 H 4 34
Kairuku, Papua B 7 31
Kaiserslautern, Germany, 62,761 B 4 14
Kaishu (Haeju), Korea, 82,135 B 4 33
Kaitaia, New Zealand, 1,799 L 5 36
Kaitung, China K 3 32
Kaizuka, Japan, 53,586 H 8 33
Kajaani, Finland, 11,040 P 4 13
Kakabeka Falls, Ontario, 422 B 4 41
Kakhk, Iran, 4,978 L 3 27
Kakinada, India, 100,054 D 5 29
Käkisalmi (Priozersk), U.S.S.R. 4,132 D 3 22
Kalabahi, Indonesia G 7 31
Kalachinsk, U.S.S.R., 4,243 J 4 22
Kalámai, Greece, 37,781 F 7 21
Kalannie, Australia, 128 B 6 36
Kalat (Khelat), Pak., 2,009 A 3 29
Kalbe, Germany, 15,161 D 3 14
Kalewa, Burma B 2 30
Kalgan (Wanchuan), China, 151,234 J 3 32
Kalgoorlie, Australia, †22,834 C 6 36
Kalianda, Indonesia D 7 31
Kalinin, U.S.S.R., 240,000 E 4 22
Kaliningrad, U.S.S.R., 188,000 D 4 22
Kalisz, Poland, 55,146 D 3 24
Kalmar, Sweden, 27,049 K 8 13
Kalmykovo, U.S.S.R., 1,329 G 5 22
Kaluga, U.S.S.R., 89,484 E 4 22
Kalutara, Ceylon, 18,801 C 7 29
Kalyan, India, 31,356 B 5 29
Kálymnos, Greece, 9,683 H 7 21
Kama (river), U.S.S.R. G 4 22
Kamaishi, Japan, 35,231 L 4 33
Kamakura, Japan, 85,391 O 3 33
Kamarhati, India, 42,545 E 1 29
Kambove, B. Congo, 9,195 M14 35
Kamchatka (peninsula), U.S.S.R., 135,000 S 4 23
Kamen', U.S.S.R., 22,982 K 4 22
Kamenets Podolskiy, U.S.S.R., 33,035 D 5 22
Kamensk-Shakhtinskiy, U.S.S.R., 50,897 F 5 22
Kamensk-Ural'skiy, U.S.S.R., 50,897 G 4 22
Kamenskoye, U.S.S.R., 216 T 3 23
Kamenz, Germany, 13,862 F 3 14
Kamienna Góra, Poland, 12,754 C 3 24
Kamina, B. Congo, 1,020 L13 35
Kamloops, British Col., 9,096 F 4 40
Kamo, Japan, 27,741 J 5 33
Kampala, Uganda, 22,094 N11 35
Kampar, Malayan Fed., 15,302 D 6 30
Kampen, Netherlands, 23,095 H 3 15
Kampot, Cambodia E 5 30
Kamptee, India, 26,930 C 4 29
Kamsack, Saskatchewan, 2,843 K 4 40
Kamyshin, U.S.S.R., 29,800 F 4 22
Kamyshlov, U.S.S.R., 20,000 H 4 22
Kanazawa, Japan, 252,017 H 5 33
Kanchanaburi, Thailand, 7,342 C 4 30
Kanchenjunga (mt.), Nepal E 3 29
Kanchipuram, India, 74,635 D 6 29
Kandagach, U.S.S.R. G 5 22
Kandahar, Afghan., 77,186 J 3 26
Kandalaksha, U.S.S.R., 7,799 E 3 22
Kandangan, Indonesia, 9,774 F 6 31
Kandi, Fr. West Africa, 5,917 G 9 34
Kandukur, India, 10,396 C 5 29
Kandy, Ceylon, 57,013 D 7 29
Kangaroo (island), Australia F 7 36
Kangavar, Iran, 7,037 F 3 27
Kanggye, Korea, 30,013 C 3 33
Kanggyŏng, Korea, 20,327 C 5 33
Kangnŭng, Korea, 31,820 D 5 33
Kanhsien, China, 50,000 H 6 32
Kaniapiskau (river), Canada G 2 41
Kanibadam, U.S.S.R., 16,450 S 2 23
Kanin (peninsula), U.S.S.R. F 3 22
Kanjiža, Yugoslavia, 12,404 D 2 21
Kankan, Fr. West Africa, 16,000 E 9 34
Kanko (Hamhŭng), Korea, 112,184 C 4 33
Kannauj, India, 21,994 C 3 29
Kano, Nigeria, 130,173 H 9 34
Kanpur, India, 705,383 D 3 29
Kansas (river), U.S. J 5 42
Kansk, U.S.S.R. L 4 23
Kanye, Bech. Pr., 22,922 L16 35
Kaoan, China J 6 32
Kaohsiung, China, 166,058 J 7 32
Kaoka (Veld), S.W. Africa J15 35
Kaolak, Fr. West Africa, 33,000 C 9 34
Kaolan (Lanchow), China, 203,722 F 4 32
Kapfenberg, Austria, 23,843 C 3 20
Kapingamarangi (islands), Pacific, 454 F 5 37
Kaposvár, Hungary, 33,076 D 3 20
Kapsan, Korea, 58,077 C 3 33
Kapuskasing, Ontario, 5,463 D 4 41
Kara (Karskiye) (strait), U.S.S.R. G 2 22
Kara-Bogaz-Gol, U.S.S.R., 4,000 G 5 22
Kara-Kum (des.), U.S.S.R. G 5 22
Karacabey, Turkey, 11,105 C 2 28
Karachi,* Pakistan, 1,409,138 A 4 29
Karad, India, 17,996 B 5 29
Karadeniz Boğazi (Bosporus) (strait), Turkey C 2 28
Karaganda, U.S.S.R., 350,000 J 5 22
Karaginski (island), U.S.S.R. T 4 23
Karaikudi, India, 28,908 C 7 29
Karakorum (mts.), Kashmir C 1 29
Karaköse (Ağri), Turkey, 10,013 K 3 28
Karaman, Turkey, 13,605 E 4 28
Karamea, New Zealand, 171 L 6 36
Karanja, India, 18,126 C 4 29
Karapinar, Turkey, 7,426 E 4 28
Karasburg, S.W. Africa, 1,092 K17 35
Karasuk, U.S.S.R., 2,682 J 4 22
Karatsu, Japan, 51,820 D 7 33
Karauli, India, 19,177 C 3 29
Karbala, Iraq, 122,719 D 2 27
Karcag, Hungary, 25,031 F 3 20
Kardítsa, Greece, 18,543 E 6 21
Kargopol', U.S.S.R., 3,449 E 3 22
Karibib, South West Africa, 875 K16 35
Karikal, India, 70,541 D 6 29
Karimata (strait), Indonesia D 6 31
Karisimbi (mt.), Africa M12 35
Karkala, India, 9,012 B 6 29
Karlo (island), Finland O 4 13
Karlovac, Yugoslavia, 31,738 B 3 21
Karlovo, Bulgaria, 8,862 G 4 21
Karlovy Vary, Czech., 26,922 B 1 20
Karlshamn, Sweden, 10,691 J 9 13
Karlskoga, Sweden, 31,303 J 7 13
Karlskrona, Sweden, 30,997 K 8 13
Karlsruhe, Germany, 198,840 C 4 14
Karlstad, Sweden, 35,651 H 7 13
Karmakchi, U.S.S.R., 2,280 H 5 22
Karnal, India, 37,444 C 3 29
Karnobat, Bulgaria, 10,225 H 4 21
Karonga, Nyas. Pr., 300 N13 35
Karosa, Indonesia F 6 31
Karpinsk, U.S.S.R. R 5 23
Karpogory, U.S.S.R., 684 F 3 22
Karragullen, Australia, 307 B 2 36
Kars, Turkey, 20,524 K 2 28
Karsakpay, U.S.S.R., 15,000 H 5 22
Karshi, U.S.S.R., 20,400 H 6 22
Kartaly, U.S.S.R., 13,500 G 4 22
Karur, India, 27,575 C 6 29
Karviná, Czech., 33,905 E 2 20
Karwar, India, 15,812 B 6 29
Kasaba (Turgutlu), Turkey, 22,719 B 3 28
Kasai (river), Belgian Congo L13 35
Kasama, N. Rhodesia, 1,383 N14 35
Kasaragod, India, 11,566 B 6 29
Kasba (lake), Canada K 2 40
Kaschau (Košice), Czech., 60,658 F 2 20
Kasganj, India, 28,465 C 3 29
Kashan, Iran, 53,525 G 3 27
Kashgar (Shufu), China, 50,000 C 7 32
Kashing, China, 102,329 K 5 32
Kashiwazaki, Japan, 38,142 J 5 33
Kasimov, U.S.S.R., 13,007 F 4 22
Kaslo, British Columbia, 669 G 4 40
Kassa (Košice), Czech., 60,658 F 2 20
Kassala, Sudan, 39,074 O 8 34
Kassan, U.S.S.R., 6,224 H 6 22
Kassansay, U.S.S.R., 18,705 U 2 23
Kassel (Cassel), Germany, 162,132 C 3 14
Kastamonu, Turkey, 13,688 E 2 28
Kastoria, Greece, 9,468 E 5 21
Kastrup, Denmark, 5,343 H 9 13
Kasur, Pakistan, 63,086 B 2 29
Katahdin (mountain), U.S. R 3 43
Katanning, Australia, 2,863 B 6 36
Kateríne, Greece, 24,604 F 5 21
Katha, Burma B 1 30
Katherine, Australia, 596 E 2 36
Katihar, India, 26,326 E 3 29
Katiola, Fr. West Africa, 7,215 E10 34
Katmandu,* Nepal, 108,805 D 3 29
Katni, India, 24,630 D 4 29
Katoomba, Australia, 8,778 H 6 36
Katowice (Kattowitz), Poland, 170,036 B 4 24
Katrineholm, Sweden, 14,492 K 7 13
Katsena Ala, Nigeria, 1,138 J10 34
Katsina, Nigeria, 52,672 H 9 34
Katta-Kurgan, U.S.S.R., 18,500 H 5 22
Kattegat (strait) G 8 13
Kattowitz (Stalinogrod), Poland, 170,036 B 4 24
Katwijk, Netherlands, 19,859 E 4 15
Kau, Indonesia H 5 31
Kaufbeuren, Germany, 19,866 D 5 14
Kaulakapuas, Indonesia, 8,682 E 6 31
Kaulakurun, Indonesia E 6 31
Kaunas, U.S.S.R., 195,000 D 4 22
Kaura Namoda, Nigeria, 13,068 H 9 34
Kavadarci, Yugoslavia, 6,053 E 5 21
Kavaje, Albania, 9,689 D 5 21
Kavali, India, 11,969 D 6 29
Kávalla, Greece, 42,102 G 5 21
Kavieng, Terr. N.G., 715 E 6 37
Kavír (desert), Iran J 3 27
Kawagoe, Japan, 52,820 O 2 33
Kawaguchi, Japan, 124,783 O 2 33
Kawasaki, Japan, 319,226 O 2 33
Kawhia, New Zealand, 289 L 6 36
Kaya, Fr. West Africa, 3,610 F 9 34
Kayes, Fr. West Africa, 25,000 D 9 34
Kayseri, Turkey, 65,489 F 3 28
Kazalinsk, U.S.S.R. H 5 22
Kazan (river), Canada K 2 40
Kazan', U.S.S.R., 565,000 G 4 22
Kazandzhik, U.S.S.R., 2,600 G 6 22
Kazanlŭk, Bulgaria, 19,386 G 4 21
Kazerun, Iran, 25,831 G 6 27
Kazvin, Iran, 77,269 F 2 27
Kebumen, Indonesia, 14,102 J 2 31
Kecskemét, Hungary, 88,374 E 3 20
Kediri, Indonesia, 48,567 K 2 31
Kedougou, Fr. West Africa, 822 D 9 34
Keele (peak), Canada E 2 40
Keelung (Chilung), China, 99,623 K 6 32
Keeper (mountain), Ireland E 6 12
Keer-weer (cape), Australia G 2 36
Keetmanshoop, S. W. Afr., 4,477 K17 35
Keewatin, Ontario, 1,949 B 3 41
Kefar Atta, Israel, 5,700 C 2 24
Kefar Yehud, Israel, 3,100 B 3 24
Keighley, England, 56,944 F 4 10
Keijo (Seoul),* Korea, 1,446,019 C 5 33
Kellett (cape), Canada D31 8
Kelliher, Saskatchewan, 461 K 4 40
Kelowna, Br. Columbia, 9,181 G 5 40
Kelvington, Saskatchewan, 819 K 4 40
Kem, U.S.S.R., 16,700 E 3 22
Kemerovo, U.S.S.R., 240,000 O 5 23
Kemi, Finland, 23,524 O 4 13
Kemi (river), Finland O 3 13
Kempsey, Australia, 7,484 J 6 36
Kempten, Germany, 39,821 D 5 14
Kenadsa, Algeria, 7,840 F 5 34
Kendal, England, 18,541 E 3 10
Kendal, Indonesia, 13,804 J 2 31
Kendari, Indonesia G 6 31
Kendawangan, Indonesia D 6 31
Kendrapara, India, 11,880 E 4 29
Keng Tung, Burma C 2 30
Kenifra, Morocco, 11,549 E 5 34
Kenitra (Port-Lyautey), Morocco, 55,954 E 5 34
Kenjiho (Kyŏmip'o), Korea, 53,035 C 4 33
Kenmare (river), Ireland A 8 12
Kenn (reef), Australia K 4 36
Kennet (river), England F 6 10
Keno Hill, Yukon, 100 C 2 40
Kénogami, Quebec, 11,309 F 4 41
Kenora, Ontario, 10,278 B 4 41
Kensington, P.E.I., 854 H 4 41

# ILLUSTRATED GAZETTEER

*Ottawa, seat of the Canadian Government, is dominated by the splendid Gothic Parliament Buildings.*

# *of* Canada

A DESCRIPTION OF THE PROVINCES AND TERRITORIES GIVING FACTS ABOUT THE AREA,
CLIMATE, NATURAL RESOURCES, OCCUPATIONS AND INDUSTRIAL DEVELOPMENT.

### PRINCE EDWARD ISLAND

Prince Edward Island is the smallest of the Canadian provinces. Extending only 140 miles in length and from 4 to 40 miles in width, with a total area of 2,184 square miles, it lies in a great semi-circle in the Gulf of St. Lawrence.

Charlottetown, the capital, is the only city on the island and there are only seven towns. Of the total population almost three-fourths live in rural communities.

The island's situation close to the mainland on the west and Nova Scotia on the south and east affords it protection from the full fury of Atlantic storms. The well protected harbours, mild climate and fertile soil have made fishing and agriculture the two main industries of Prince Edward Island. A large amount of canned lobster is exported. The chief agricultural crops are oats and potatoes. Fox farming and ship-building are also important sources of income to the province.

The island, which was called St. Jean during the French regime, was later named Prince Edward in honour of the Duke of Kent, father of Queen Victoria. It joined with the other provinces in 1873.

### NEWFOUNDLAND

Newfoundland, the oldest colony in the British Empire and once a dominion itself, became in 1949, the tenth province of Canada, moving the easternmost point of Canada 200 miles nearer England. With an area of 155,364 square miles, Newfoundland lies one-third of the way on the airline route from New York to London. Gander, one of the great airports established on it, has come to be a well-known news date-line. St. John's, the capital, is the most easterly city of the North American continent. It has a harbour completely free of ocean swell.

# GAZETTEER OF CANADA

## NOVA SCOTIA

*Drying codfish is one of Newfoundland's major industries.*

Newfoundland's inhabitants are mostly of western English stock, with an admixture of Scottish and Irish elements. They are skilled in open-air crafts, and their talents are in great demand in New England and the St. Lawrence Valley.

The new province gives Canada easier access to one of the world's greatest fishing grounds, and adds its lumber resources and its paper mills to the country's wood and pulp industry.

Labrador, Newfoundland's bleak coastal dependency, stretches along the North American mainland to Hudson Strait. Along the Quebec border are fields of iron ore more extensive and at least as rich as the famous Minnesota Mesabi range. Although the deposits are now coming into initial production, cod-fishery remains the staple industry of the 7,000 inhabitants.

Nova Scotia, rich in historical interest, is one of the most picturesque of the provinces. The peninsula, jutting out into the Atlantic Ocean from the southeastern tip of the mainland, has a total land area of 20,743 square miles which includes Cape Breton Island. The population is almost equally divided between rural and urban life.

The province is divided approximately in half by a low, mountainous ridge. The coast along the Atlantic, although broken and rocky, affords innumerable harbours for the famous fishing fleets of Nova Scotia. During the summer months this coast is often engulfed in heavy rainstorms accompanied by severe gales which are caused by semi-tropical air currents sweeping north along the Atlantic seaboard. But, for the most part, the peninsula enjoys a cool, healthy climate.

The northern slope of the land has many fertile plains and rich, alluvial valleys. This area is dotted with many farms. There are large orchards as well as general farms. In the Annapolis Valley are grown apples that are world famous for their flavour and quality. Halifax, the capital, with its six mile long, year 'round harbour, is Canada's chief eastern winter port and point of entry.

The four main industries of Nova Scotia are shipbuilding, iron and steel production, fishing and allied industries, and agriculture, which includes fruit production and dairy output. The fishing industries of Nova Scotia are second in importance only to those of British Columbia among the provinces. There are also many sawmills and a quantity of pulp and paper is produced.

Close to the coast are abundant fishing grounds, which make Nova Scotia a fisherman's paradise for the amateur as well as the professional. The supply of swordfish and tuna have attracted big game anglers from all over the globe.

Just a mile from the mainland is Cape Breton

*Waterfront scene at Halifax, Nova Scotia.*

Island which abounds in wild, natural beauty.

The province was called Acadia under the French occupation. It was first named Nova

*Shipbuilding is an essential industry in Nova Scotia, as in the other Maritime Provinces.*

Scotia, Latin for New Scotland, in a patent granted to Sir William Alexander in 1621 by James I. The right to an elective, representative government was granted it in 1758.

## NEW BRUNSWICK

New Brunswick, almost as large as Scotland, has a total land area of 27,473 square miles. Its population is about two-thirds rural. Much of the land is wild and rugged, covered with forests, rushing streams, and lakes. However, there is fertile farm land in the valleys and coastal plains in the south and east.

New Brunswick has three cities. Fredericton, the smallest of these, is the capital and seat of the University of New Brunswick. Saint John is the largest city in the province. It is an important port, and like Halifax, has a year 'round harbour. Moncton, a port on the Petitcodiac River, is the home of the main offices and workshops of the Canadian National Railway. All three cities are important to the commerce of the province.

Production of pulp and paper, and sawmilling are the leading industries of New

*A typical Newfoundland fishing community stands on the rocky coast. Fishing is the major industry of the region.*

1. A raft of logs being floated to the mill.

2. Charlo River Falls in northern New Brunswick, typical of the many beautiful scenes in the province.

3. Potatoes are one of the chief crops of New Brunswick.

4. Logs entering the mill to be converted into pulp.

5. Along the Restigouche, an excellent salmon stream.

6. Southern Cross Cape, Grand Manan, New Brunswick.

7. Pulp logs being ground at the paper mill.

Brunswick. Other industries of importance are shipbuilding and repairs, production of miscellaneous foods, and fishing and allied industries.

Excellent hunting and fishing grounds which are easily accessible from the modern cities of the province attract sportsmen throughout the year. Red deer and black bear are plentiful. It is an ideal vacation place for those who love the outdoors, and the good modern highway system gives one the advantage of being able to reach the wild, beautiful country without the inconvenience of travelling over slow country roads.

New Brunswick, part of the territory originally called Acadia became a separate province in 1784.

## QUEBEC

As a mirror of the past, Québec, the largest of the provinces, remains, to-day, full of old world flavour. Throughout the province—despite the constant growth of modern cities, excellent highways, and marked industrial progress—the quaint and picturesque customs of old have been retained. The population is about 60% urban and is concentrated in the southern part of the province.

The total area of Québec is 594,860 square miles, 71,000 of which is fresh water area. This water area, formed mainly by many big rivers, represents the tremendous water-power available to serve the province in her great pulp and paper industry.

Québec City, capital, is an old city built on two levels, the upper and lower level being connected by steeply inclined, twisting streets and by an elevator. The older, lower part of the city with its irregular, narrow streets, reminiscent of old French provincial towns, is still the financial centre and main business section.

Montreal, an important port on the St. Lawrence River, is the largest city of Canada, and remains the second greatest French speaking

*Bread is still baked in open-air ovens in the picturesque Gaspe region of Quebec.*

city in the world. Amid modern skyscrapers and the busy whirl of a large manufacturing centre, the traveller sees landmarks of the day of Maisonneuve, founder of the first permanent colony on Montreal Island, and many historical buildings and monuments.

The province is richly endowed in natural resources. Its hydro-electric power development, greatest of all the provinces, is equal to that of Ontario and Manitoba combined. This great source of power, combined with the good supply of timber, forms the basis of Québec's dominant industry—pulp and paper production.

*Montreal on the St. Lawrence river is one of the world's largest inland ports.*

Québec is responsible for approximately fifty percent of the total value of this industry in Canada. Non-ferrous metal smelting and refining and petroleum refining have become the leading industries. Production of miscellaneous chemicals is important. Québec manufactures over 70% of the country's cotton yarn and cloth. The manufacture of railway rolling-stock and shipbuilding and repairs are two other important industries of the province. Extensive deposits of high quality asbestos and gold are found in its southeastern part. In this area many modern cities have developed as a result of the increase in mineral production. Iron mining is important in the northeast.

In the upper St. Lawrence Valley, as well as in the eastern sections, the climate and soil provide excellent farming country. There are many dairy farms and many commercial vegetable farms throughout this area. Québec

produces about 87% of the country's tobacco products.

Québec is unique in its mixture of the old and the new. In some sections, oxen are still being used to some extent as draught animals. In many districts country-women use hand looms and spinning wheels, and outdoor clay or stone bake ovens are still employed.

From the time of its founding, when it was called New France, the name of the province underwent many changes before it became officially known as the Province of Québec in 1867.

*Fraser Falls in Québec, which has the greatest hydro-electric power development of all the provinces.*

## ONTARIO

Between the Great Lakes on the south and Hudson and James Bays on the north, lies Ontario, the greatest manufacturing province of Canada. It covers a total land area of 333,835 square miles. The population is about 60% urban.

In the southwest, fertile soil and an ideal climate for farming provide one of the richest agricultural districts in Canada. The seasons here are comparatively mild and pleasant, and there is abundant rainfall. The cultivation of fruit has been highly and successfully developed, especially throughout the Niagara Belt on the Ontario Peninsula. Ontario is second in fruit production among the provinces.

Toronto, the second largest city in Canada, and capital of the province, is a beautiful, spreading city covering an area of about forty

square miles. It is the home of the University of Toronto and has many other important schools and colleges. The city is spaciously laid out. Toronto is the publishing centre of the country, and is the financial centre for the northern mining district. It has the largest mining exchange in the world.

In the northeast, is Ottawa, the capital of Canada, built on a group of hills overlooking the Ottawa River. From Parliament Hill, where the government buildings are located, one gets a magnificent view up and down the river, from the Chaudière Falls to the Rideau Falls. The city is divided approximately in half by the Rideau Canal—Upper Town being occupied by the English and Lower Town, by the French.

Ontario has a wider range of industrial activity than any other province. By virtue of its position on the Great Lakes which gives ready accessibility to the coal and iron ore from the United States, its large, industrious population, and a wealth of natural resources — minerals, forests, agriculture and water power, it has steadily maintained its leadership in Canadian industry.

The leading industries of Ontario include the manufacture of automobiles and parts, smelting and refining of non-ferrous metals, and primary iron and steel production and manufactures. Slaughtering and meat-packing and pulp and paper production are also important. In addition to these, Ontario produces almost the entire supply of Canada's agricultural implements and starch; operates about 80% of the country's leather tanneries; and supplies two-thirds of the fruit and vegetable preparations. It produces about one-half of the minerals of Canada.

All of southern Ontario enjoys a healthy invigorating climate. The climate in the north and northwest, where most of the good timberland is located, varies from that of the remainder of the province. During the winter there is an extremely heavy snowfall, which accumulates on the ground and often reaches a depth of as much as one hundred and forty inches before the late spring thaws. This heavy snow is of great value in hauling timber from the forest.

## MANITOBA

Manitoba, originally a part of the old district called Assiniboia, is known as the Keystone province. Located in the centre of Canada, it has a land area of 219,723 square miles.

*Grain elevators at Winnipeg store the golden harvest of Manitoba's fertile prairies.*

1. Pulp logs being loaded for shipment to one of Ontario's many papermills.

2. A gold mine in operation at Kirkland Lake, Ontario, one of the world's great gold producing areas.

3. Twin locks in the Welland Ship Canal which connects Lake Erie with Lake Ontario.

4. The supplying of dairy products to the large urban centres is a major industry of southern Ontario.

5. Heavy snows are valuable in hauling timber from the northern forests.

6. Cultivating peach trees near Grimsby in the Niagara Belt.

7. Scene on the Rideau Canal, Ottawa.

Although regarded principally as agricultural, Manitoba has an appreciable amount of ready water-power — ranking fourth in this resource — and large forests in the north. In recent years, the discovery of rich mineral deposits in the north and northwest have enabled the province to take its place in the great mining industry of Canada.

Manitoba has a continental type climate. The average precipitation is less than twenty inches annually. However, about 70% of this occurs during the summer months and is, thus, profitably used for the growing of crops. Strong gales and blizzards often occur during the cold winter months. The one redeeming feature of the extreme weather is its dryness.

Winnipeg, the capital of Manitoba, is an important distribution centre, forming the link between eastern and western Canada. All the grain from the western provinces passes through Winnipeg before being shipped east. It is also a big fur centre, and buyers from all over the North American continent go each year to the fur auctions held there. Both the Canadian National and the Canadian Pacific Railways have their western headquarters in this city.

The development of inexpensive electric

*Excellent grazing land throughout the Prairie Provinces makes livestock raising a major industry.*

power on the Winnipeg River has fostered the city's industrial progress. There are now many factories and plants and it is rapidly developing into an industrial centre.

Agriculture is still one of the leading occupations of Manitoba's people. The soil in the Red River Valley, in the southern part of the province, is exceptionally fertile, and long, sunny days facilitate the rapid growth of vegetation. Hard spring wheat is the leading crop. Oats, rye and barley are the next important ones.

The raising of livestock provides a great portion of Manitoba's income. Slaughtering and meat-packing recently attained first place among Manitoba's industries. Butter and cheese production is second. Close to these in importance is the manufacture of railway rolling stock, milling of flour and feed, and the making of chemical products.

The development of the mineral industry dates back to 1915 when the great Flin Flon mine was discovered in northern Manitoba. Since that time, there have been extensive mining operations and the province now mines quantities of gold, silver, copper, nickel and zinc.

A large part of the forest area of Manitoba

is classed as unproductive land, being covered with scrub growth. However, the province still possesses large, valuable forests and obtains much of its wealth from this resource. Fur trapping is carried on in the north.

*Sheep farming in western Canada is an important part of the livestock industry.*

## SASKATCHEWAN

Saskatchewan, named for the river, the full Indian name of which, *Sis-Sis-Katche-Wan-Sepie*, means the Big Angry Water, lies between Alberta and Manitoba, and has an area of 251,700 square miles. Almost all of the population, which is predominately rural, lives in the southern part of the province.

This is the most completely agricultural of all the provinces. Very little of the potential water power has been developed, but the discovery of large ore bodies along the Manitoba border has greatly increased the mineral output of the province.

The climate of Saskatchewan is continental in type, but the temperature does not reach quite the extremes found in Manitoba. The average precipitation is under twenty inches annually, 60% of it in the growing season.

Regina, the capital of Saskatchewan, formerly capital of the Northwest Territories, has a large distributing trade and is a central market

for its agricultural region. It contains many mills, banks, factories, wholesale houses, and a large oil refinery. Here is the western headquarters of the Royal Canadian Mounted Police. Both the Canadian Pacific and Canadian National Railways pass through Regina, and there are twelve radiating lines.

There are over 125,000 square miles—more than half the total land area—of prairie land in the province suitable for agriculture. Spring wheat is the leading crop, and oats comes second. Manufacturing has materially increased, but still consists chiefly of localized industries.

Although almost half of the entire wooded area is unproductive, there are many sawmills and planing mills in the province. The leading industry is slaughtering and meat-packing. Flour and feed milling and butter and cheese production and petroleum production are other important industries of the province.

Prince Albert National Park, a recreational area of 1,869 square miles of forested slopes, lakes with fine beaches, and streams is one of the many parks in the province.

## ALBERTA

Alberta, the furthest west of the three prairie provinces, contains a large and picturesque part of the Canadian Rockies. It has a land area of 248,800 square miles. Of its total population, 52% is rural.

The climate of Alberta is continental, modified somewhat by the Rocky Mountains. The winter climate in Alberta is one of the most variable in the world. Annual precipitation averages about twenty inches, or slightly higher than Manitoba and Saskatchewan, and occurs largely in summer.

Edmonton, the capital of the province, was originally the head of navigation on the North Saskatchewan River, and a centre of the fur trade for both the Hudson's Bay and North West Fur companies. Now, it is a centre of an important coal mining and mixed farming area and a distribution point for both these and the extensive mining areas to the north. It is also a railway centre, served by both transcontinental lines, and is the site of the

*Perhaps the most exciting scenery in Canada's National Parks is found in Alberta.*

University of Alberta. Edmonton was the first city of Canada to establish a municipal airport, and now has one of the most modern in the country. It is on the great circle air route to the Orient and connects directly by both railway and plane with the Alaska highway.

Agriculture in Alberta has been greatly aided by extensive irrigation, the chief crop being spring wheat, with oats second and barley third. Some rye is planted; and the sugar beet is beginning to be raised successfully. The provincial department of agriculture gives extensive aid to farmers. There are 85,560 square miles of non-forested land, suitable for agriculture.

Alberta is well suited to the development of ranches, and livestock is an important source of wealth. Meat-packing is first among the industries. Other important industries are the production of petroleum products, flour and feed, bread and bakery goods, and sawn lumber.

Alberta contains a coal reserve estimated at over a trillion tons, produces 97% of the Canadian output of petroleum, and leads in the production of natural gas.

At Fort McMurray are immense tar sands deposits, largest known reservoir of oil in the British Commonwealth of Nations. Natural gas comes from the coal fields of Viking, Kinsella and Fabyan in the eastern part of the province.

There are over 100,000 square miles of forested land. Five of the most famous national parks of Canada are located in Alberta, including Jasper, Banff, and Waterton Lakes.

## BRITISH COLUMBIA

Almost all of British Columbia, the third largest province, is mountainous. It covers 366,255 square miles including Vancouver, Queen Charlotte and other islands in the Pacific. Over

*Farm scene in the rich oil lands at Redwater, Alberta.*

half the population is urban.

The climate varies according to the geographical position of the various sections of the province. Vancouver, off the coast, has a climate very like England—the winters are warm and the summers, long, and cool. The western coast of the island has an average of more than 100 inches of precipitation annually. On the eastern side the precipitation is considerably lighter, averaging only about 29 inches.

On the southeast tip of Vancouver Island is Victoria, the capital of British Columbia. It is one of the most beautiful cities in Canada. There are many fine gardens, which because of the exceptionally mild climate, bloom most of the year. It has a good harbour and is the fourth important port of Canada. The Royal Canadian Navy has its headquarters here.

*The rocks of Canada's mines yield a king's ransom in valuable minerals daily.*

Victoria is an industrial centre and maintains a steady trade with other coastal cities, Australia, and the East.

Vancouver is the largest city in British Columbia and one of the principal ports of Canada. The University of British Columbia is located here. This city is also a large industrial centre and exports great quantities of lumber, wheat, flour, fish and apples.

British Columbia leads in the production of the following: lumber, shingles, fish, silver and fruit.

Shipbuilding and repairs is one of the chief industries of the province. Other leading industries are: Sawmilling; fish curing and packing; pulp and paper production; slaughtering and meat packing; mining and manufacture of petroleum products; aluminum refining.

The coastal area of the mainland enjoys a mild and wet climate. In the fertile valleys between the parallel mountain ranges, the climate is ideal and, although the rainfall is light there are numerous mountain streams which afford irrigation for the extensive fruit farming in this area. Almost all the common fruits such

*British Columbia is the leading producer of lumber among the provinces.*

as apples, cherries, plums, pears, peaches, etc. are grown here with great success. Cattle and

*View of Mt. Robson, British Columbia, showing the tumbling glacier.*

sheep are raised in some areas, and fur farming has been increasing steadily. Throughout the farming country, there are grains and mixed vegetable crops.

Salmon from the waters around British Columbia is famous the world over and this one fish accounts for a large portion of the value of the province's fishing industry. The main salmon waters are around Vancouver and Queen Charlotte Islands and the Fraser River. Other important fish are: halibut, herring and cod.

The province has an immense mineral wealth. Gold, silver, lead, copper, coal and zinc are found in large deposits.

The scenery of British Columbia is magnificent; 20,000 miles of highway lead through this beautiful country of majestic mountains and fertile valleys.

Intensive settlement began with the discovery of gold and led to British Columbia becoming a British colony in 1858. United with the colony of Vancouver, British Columbia became a province of Canada in 1871.

*Cleaning fish for market at Prince Rupert, British Columbia.*

## YUKON TERRITORY

The Yukon Territory has a total land area of 205,346 square miles.

Until the great Klondike gold strike in 1896, the Territory was inhabited by only a few tribes of Indians. During the boom years in the gold-mining industry there was a great influx of people to the area. In 1898, two years after the big strike, it was created a separate Territory and Dawson was selected as its capital. In 1953, however, the territorial capital was transferred to White Horse.

The climate of the Yukon is similar to that of the Northwest Territories. The summers are short, but the days are long and sunny, often averaging as much as twenty hours of light making possible farming on a small scale; the winters are about seven months long and are quite cold—the temperature often dropping as low as sixty-five degrees below zero.

There is great potential mineral wealth in this Territory. Gold is still mined in considerable quantity. Since the great placer deposits were depleted, lode mining has been the principal method of production.

The interior of the Yukon is principally a large plain surrounded by the St. Elias Mountain Range on the southwest and the Rocky Mountains on the south and southeast. Through the whole Territory runs the mighty Yukon River, and in the valleys and sand flats formed by it and its tributaries, are many dense forests. In the forest areas are many fur bearing animals and a variety of big game. Fox farming has become one of the important industries of the Territory.

The construction of the Alaska highway now links the great northwest areas, which were formerly inaccessible, with the cities of the Prairie Provinces and other parts of Canada. Opening of this highway and the advent of air traffic, have made the Yukon and Northwest Territories new frontiers for industrial development. Already new mining operations and prospecting expeditions have been planned and are being put into operation.

## NORTHWEST TERRITORIES

The Northwest Territories, by far the largest section of Canada, with 1,304,903 square miles, includes the many large islands between the mainland and the North Pole. The North Magnetic Polar Area has been located just north of Boothia Peninsula.

Very little land is fitted for agriculture, most of it being in the Mackenzie basin, but it is usual to raise the more common vegetables at most posts, taking advantage of the long daylight of summer. The broad northeastern stretch is known as the Barren Lands, or the Arctic Prairies. The shallow, tundra soil grows almost 800 species of flowering plants, and in a few sheltered spots, mainly along rivers, are found stunted willows. A sparse, Arctic forest of balsam, spruce, tamarack, poplar, white birch and Jack pine cover most of the rest of the mainland of the Territories.

There is great potential wealth of natural resources. At Great Bear Lake is the silver pitchblend mine, important as a source of radium and uranium. Silver, copper, cobalt and lead are also recovered from the ores dug at Port Radium. Gold and silver are mined at Yellowknife, on Great Slave Lake. Underlying the lower Mackenzie Valley are extensive oil and natural gas deposits. Expansion of the mining industry has been increased through the development of hydro-electric power.

South of Great Slave Lake is the northern part of Wood Buffalo National Park, a sanctuary for the North American bison. Muskoxen are protected throughout the Territories, and reindeer herding, as a native industry, has been introduced principally along the Mackenzie River.

The origin of the Territories is the 1670 grant of land to the Hudson's Bay Company. This area was much larger than the present one, and included almost all of Canada from the Rocky Mountains to the St. Lawrence watershed. The Territories as they exist today were practically unexplored, and most of the company's posts were entirely within the present borders of Manitoba and Saskatchewan.

Samuel Hearne and Alexander Mackenzie, travelling for the Hudson's Bay and Northwest Fur Companies, respectively, explored the Arctic regions in the latter part of the eighteenth century. Important trading posts in the present Territories were set up soon thereafter. By 1869 Canada gained total jurisdiction, and the province of Manitoba was cut from the Territories in 1870. The Northwest Mounted Police was established shortly thereafter and a lieutenant governor and council set up for the Territories.

By 1882, the area below the 60th parallel had become the provisional districts of Assiniboia, Saskatchewan, Athabaska and Alberta. From these, the three prairie provinces were later carved.

The Yukon Territory was separated in 1898. By 1906 Alberta and Saskatchewan became provinces, and Manitoba was extended to Hudson Bay in 1912, while Ontario and Quebec received the rest of the southern and eastern shores of the bay.

*Recent discoveries of uranium are opening the vast regions of northern Canada to development.*

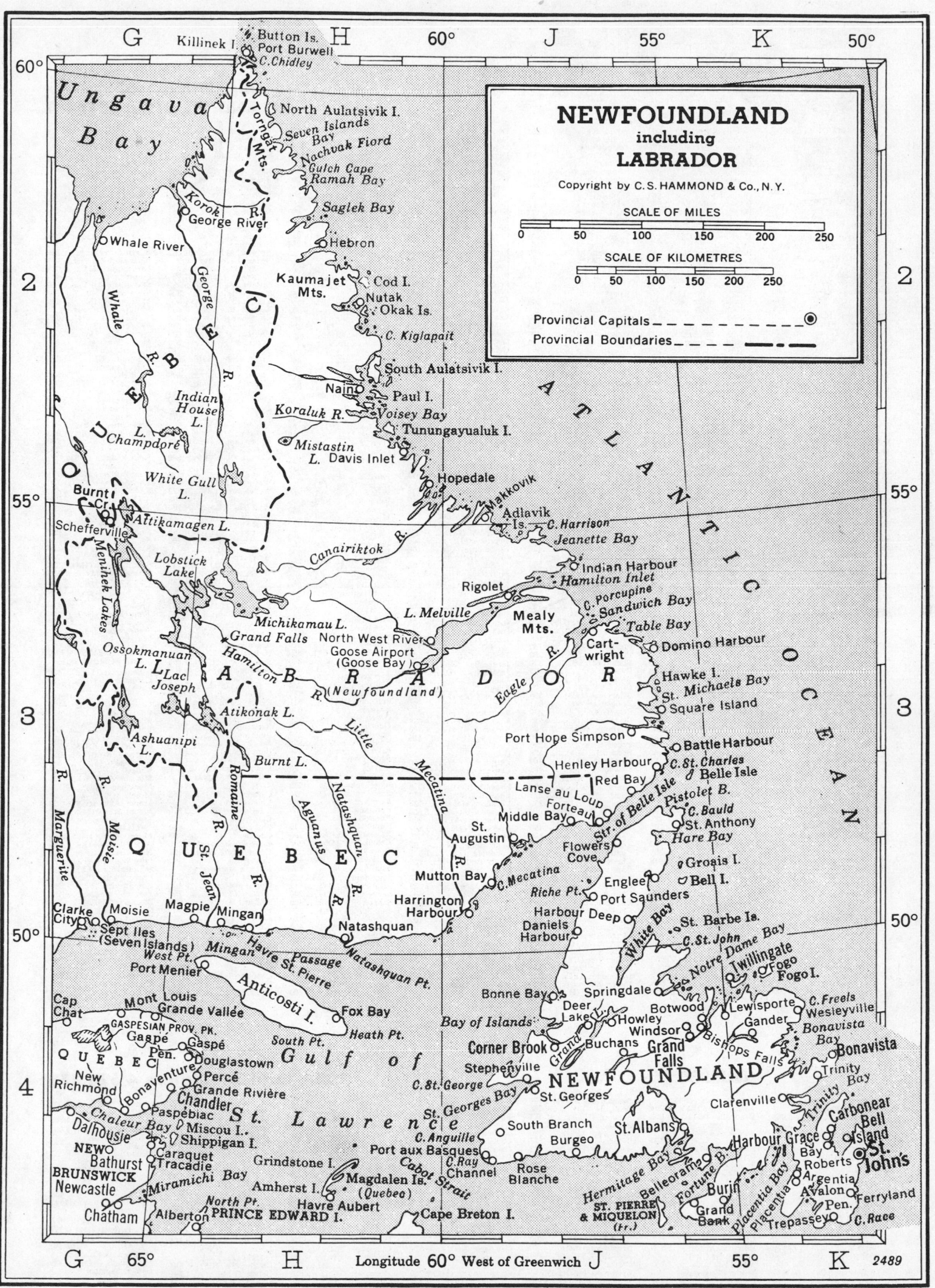

# NEWFOUNDLAND
## including
## LABRADOR

Copyright by C.S. HAMMOND & Co., N.Y.

SCALE OF MILES

0  50  100  150  200  250

SCALE OF KILOMETRES

0  50  100  150  200  250

Provincial Capitals ___ ___ ⊙

Provincial Boundaries ___ ___ ___

NEW BRUNSWICK NOVA SCOTIA PRINCE EDWARD I. NEWFOUNDLAND

# MARITIME PROVINCES AND NEWFOUNDLAND

**MAGDALEN ISLANDS**
**Total Population 11,556**
Etang du Nord (G2) ... 300
Grand Entry (H2)... 714
Grindstone Island (H2) ... 738
Havre Aubert (H2).1,200
House Harbour (H2) ... 425
Leslie (H2)... 140
Pointe Basse (H2)...

**NEW BRUNSWICK**
**Total Population 559,616**
Albert (E4)... 250
Alma (D4)... 500
Anagance (D4)... 150
Andover (B3)... 321
Apohaqui (D4)... 200
Arthurette (B3)... 125
Baie Verte (E3)... 100
Balmoral (C2)... 300
Barnaby River (D3) 300
Bath (B3)... 400
Bathurst ◉(D2)...5,267
Bay du Vin (D2)... 25
Beaver Brook Sta. (D2) ... 54
Beersville (E3)... 100
Belledune (D2)... 125
Belleisle Creek (D4) ... 125
Belleville (B3)... 50
Ben Lomond (D4)..
Benton (B3)... 100
Beresford (D2)... 127
Berry Mill Sta. (E3) 150
Black's Harbour (C4) ... 600
Blackville (D3) ... 500
Bloomfield Sta. (D4) ... 100
Boiestown (C3)... 225
Bonney River (C4).. 25
Buctouche (E3)... 800
Burnsville (D2)... 100
Burnt Church (D2) 100
Burton ◉(C4)...
Butternut Ridge (D4) ...1,000
Campbellton (C2)..8,389
Canaan Station (E3) 88
Canterbury Sta. (B4) ... 400
Cap Pele (E3)... 250
Sape Tormentine (E3) ... 127
Caraquet (D2)...1,500
Caron Brook (A2).. 200
Central Blissville (C4) ... 45
Centreville (B3)... 250
Chatham (D2)...6,332
Chelmsford (D3)... 30
Chipman (D3)...1,200
Clair (A2)... 400
Clifton (D2)... 150
Clifton (C4)... 100
Coal Branch Sta. (D3) ... 188
Cocagne (E3)... 200
Connors (A2)... 150
Cork Station (C4)... 15
Corn Hill (D4)... 100
Cross Creek (C3)... 200
Cumberland Bay (D3) ... 70
Dalhousie ◉(C1)...5,468
Debec (B3)... 139
Derby (D3)... 100
Doaktown (C3)... 270
Dorchester ◉(E4)..1,080
Douglas (C3)... 209
Douglastown (D2).. 481
Edgett's Landing (E4) ... 150
Edmundston ◉(A2) ...11,997
Elgin (D4)... 280
Fairville (C4)...12,307
Five Fingers (B2)... 15
Flatlands (B2)... 300
Florenceville (B3)... 490
Forest City (B4)...
FREDERICTON (C4) ...18,303
Fredericton Junction (C4) ... 175
Gagetown ◉(C4)... 312
Glassville (B3)... 150
Grand Bay (C4)... 207
Grand Falls (B2)...3,672
Grand Harbour (C5) ... 200
Grande Anse (D2).. 400
Hampstead (C4)... 200
Hampton ◉(D4)... 175
Harcourt (D3)... 250
Hartland (B3)...1,022
Harvey (E4)... 200
Harvey Station (B4) ... 200
Hatfield Point (D4) 150
Hillsborough (E4)...1,000
Hillsdale (D4)... 125
Hopewell Cape ◉(E4) ... 25
Hoyt Station (C4)... 75
Inkerman (E2)... 300
Jacquet River (C2). 316
Janeville (D2)... 30
Jemseg (C4)... 100
Juniper (B3)... 96
Kedgwick (B2)... 500
Kent Junction (D3) 77
Keswick Ridge (B4) 25
Kilburn (B3)... 177
Kingston (C4)... 125
Kouchibouguac (D3) ... 200
Lakeville Corner (C4) ... 250
Lepreau (C4)... 125
Little Rocher (E4).. 25
Loggieville (D2)... 437
Lorneville (C4)... 50
Ludlow (C3)... 100
Marysville (C3)...2,538
Maugerville (C4)... 50
Mc Adam (B4)...2,100
McNamee (C3)... 150
Memramcook (E4). 400
Millerton (D3)... 300
Millstream (D4)... 250
Milltown (B4)...1,975
Millville (B3)... 350
Moncton (Metropolitan Area) (E3)...49,496
Moore's Mills (B4). 150
Musquash (C4)... 188
Napudogan (C3)... 180
Nash Creek (C2)... 175
Nashwaaksis (C3)... 238
Neguac (D2)... 400
Nerepis (C4)... 25
New Denmark (B3) 90
New Mills (C2)... 250
Newcastle ◉(D2)...4,670
North Head (C5)... 800
Norton (D4)... 550
Notre-Dame (E3)... 335
Oak Bay (B4)... 100
Oromocto (C4)... 661
Paquetville (D2)... 233
Peel (B3)... 125
Pennfield (C4)... 200
Penobsquis (D4)... 150
Perth ◉(B3)... 706
Petersville (C4)... 100
Petit Rocher (D2)... 500
Petitcodiac (D4)... 900
Plaster Rock (B3)... 900
Plourd (A2)... 50
Pointe du Chêne (E3) ... 250
Port Elgin (F3)... 717
Portage River (E2). 150
Prince William (B4) 80
Quarryville (D3)... 150
Renous (D3)... 100
Rexton (E3)... 400
Richibucto ◉(D3)...1,158
Richibucto Village (E3) ... 50
Riley Brook (B2)... 50
River Charlo (C2).. 200
River de Chute (B3) ... 100
Riverside (E4)... 125
Rivière Verte (A2).. 700
Robichaud (E3)... 300
Rogersville (D3)... 700
Rothesay (D4)... 800
Sackville (E4)...2,849
Saint Andrews ◉(B4) ...1,534
Saint Antoine de Kent (E3)... 300
Saint Basile (A2)... 250
Saint George (C4)...1,322
Saint Ignace (D3)... 50
Saint Isidore (D2).. 300
Saint Jacques (A2).. 200
Saint John ◉(D4)..52,491
Saint John (Metropolitan Area) (D4)...77,553
Saint Leonard (B2).1,593
Saint Louis de Kent (D3) ... 500
Saint Martin's (D4) 547
Saint Stephen (B4)..3,491
Sainte Anne de Madawaska (B2).1,750
Sainte Croix (B4)... 90
Salisbury (D3)... 340
Salmon Beach (D2). 100
Salmon Creek (C3)...
Shediac (E3)...2,173
Sheffield (C4)... 250
Shippigan (E2)...1,362
South Nelson (D3). 477
Springfield (D4)... 66
Stanley (C3)... 300
Sussex (D4)...3,403
Tabusintac (D2)... 150
Taymouth (C3)... 97
Tilley (B3)... 25
Tracadie (D2)...1,500
Tracy (C4)... 100
Upham (D4)... 100
Upper Blackville (C3) ... 200
Waterford (D4)... 125
Watt (B4)... 40
Welsford (C4)... 300
Welshpool (C5)... 400
Wirral (C4)... 50
Woodstock ◉(B3)...4,308

**NOVA SCOTIA**
**Total Population 694,717**
Advocate Harbour (E4) ...
Amherst ◉(E4)...10,301
Annapolis Royal (D5) ... 765
Antigonish ◉(G4)..3,592
Apple River (E4)... 300
Arcadia (C6)... 300
Argyle (D6)... 30
Arichat ◉(J4)... 700
Aspen (G4)... 50
Athol (E4)... 50
Auburn (E4)... 100
Aylesford (E4)... 500
Baccaro (D6)... 75
Baddeck ◉(J3)... 650
Ballantyne's Cove (G4) ... 200
Barrington (D6)... 400
Barton (D5)... 300
Bass River (F4)... 450
Bay Saint Lawrence (J3) ... 200
Bayfield (H4)...
Bear River (D5)...1,200
Beaver Bank (F5)... 250
Bedford (F5)... 925
Belleisle (D5)... 400
Belleville (D6)... 75
Belliveau Cove (D5) 350
Belmont (F4)... 300
Berwick (E4)...1,134
Big Pond (J4)... 150
Birchtown (D6)... 250
Blandford (F5)... 250
Boisdale (J3)... 125
Boylston (H4)... 500
Brazil Lake (C5)... 75
Bridgeport (K3)... 500
Bridgetown ◉(D5)..1,041
Bridgeville (G4)... 200
Bridgewater (E5)...4,445
Brighton (C5)... 75
Briton Cove (J3)... 40
Broad Cove (E5)... 250
Brookfield (F4)... 175
Caledonia (G4)... 100
Caledonia (D5)... 482
Cambridge Sta. (E4) 200
Canning (E4)... 800
Canso (H4)...1,261
Cape North (J3)... 350
Cariboo Gold Mines (G4) ...
Carleton (D5)... 450
Catalone (J4)... 100
Centreville (C5)... 300
Centreville (E4)... 222
Chester (E5)...1,000
Chester Basin (E5)... 300
Cheticamp (H3)... 600
Cheverie (E4)... 200
Church Point (C5). 500
Clarence (D5)... 100
Clark's Harbour (D6) ... 945
Clarksville (F4)... 83
Clementsport (D5).. 290
Clementsvale (D5).. 550
Corberrie (D5)... 125
Craigmore (H4)... 30
Dalhousie East (E5) 140
Dartmouth (F5)...21,093
Debert Station (F4) 300
Deep Brook (D5)... 400
Denmark (F4)... 200
Digby ◉(D5)...2,145
Dingwall (J3)... 132
Dominion (K3)...2,964
Dublin Shore (E5).. 200
Earltown (F4)... 250
East Bay (J3)... 300
Eastern Passage (F5) ... 750
Economy (E4)... 200
Ecum Secum (G4).. 300
Elderbank (F5)... 200
Elmsdale (F5)... 300
Englishtown (J3)... 125
Falmouth (E5)... 300
Five Islands (E4)... 400
Fourchu (J4)... 343
Framboise (J4)... 275
Frankville (H4)... 300
Freeport (C5)... 700
Frizzleton (J3)... 100
Gabarouse (J4)... 500
Glace Bay (K3)...24,416
Glace Bay-Sydney (Metropolitan Area) (K3)...107,124
Goffs (F5)...
Goldsboro (H4)... 354
Goldenville (G4)... 800
Goshen (H4)... 150
Grand Etang (H3)... 300
Grand Narrows (J4) 100
Grand River (J4)... 300
Granville Centre (D5) ... 100
Granville Ferry (D5) 344
Great Village (F4).. 654
Greenfield (D5)... 250
Guysborough ◉(H4) 800
Guysborough Intervale (H4)... 250
Hackett's Cove (F5) 150
HALIFAX (F5)...93,301
Halifax (Metropolitan Area) (F5)...159,678
Hall's Harbour (E4) 105
Hantsport (E4)...1,298
Harbourville (D4)... 175
Havre Boucher (H4) 300
Hazel Hill (J4)... 300
Hebron (C6)... 500
Hectanooga (C5)... 100
Miscou Harbour (E2) ... 30
Moncton (E3)...36,003
Hemford (E5)... 130
Hopewell (G4)... 365
Hubbards (E5)... 450
Ingonish (J3)... 400
Inverness (H3)...2,026
Iona (J3)... 160
Irish Cove (J4)... 50
Isaac's Harbour (H4) ... 377
Joggins (E4)...1,102
Jordan Bay (D6)... 100
Jordan Falls (D6)... 225
Judique (H4)...
Kempt (D5)... 225
Kempt Town (F4)... 110
Kemptville (D5)... 75
Kennetcook (F4)... 200
Kentville ◉(E4)...4,937
Kingsport (E4)... 200
Kingston (E5)... 500
Lake Ramsay (E5).. 20
L'Ardoise (J4)... 450
Larry's River (H4).. 400
Lawrencetown (D5) 600
Lequille (D5)... 350
Liscomb (G4)... 209
Lismore (G4)... 100
Litchfield (D5)... 125
Liverpool ◉(E5)...3,500
Lochaber (G4)... 200
Lockeport (D6)...1,207
Londonderry (F4)... 625
Long Point (H4)... 80
Louisburg (K4)...1,314
Lower Argyle (D6). 125
Lower Wood Harbour (C6)... 482
Lunenburg ◉(E5)...2,859
Mabou (H3)... 600
Mahone Bay (E5)...1,109
Main-à-Dieu (K4).. 216
Maitland (F4)... 400
Malignant Cove (H4) ... 20
Margaree Harbour (H3) ... 400
Margaretsville (D4) 200
Mc Kinnon's Harbour (J3)... 100
Meagher's Grant (F5) ... 150
Merigomish (G4)... 200
Meteghan (C5)... 750
Meteghan River (C5) ... 400
Middle River (J3)... 300
Middle Stewiacke (F4) ... 200
Middleton (D5)...1,769
Milford Sta. (F4)... 300
Mill Village (E5)... 150
Milton (E5)...1,000
Mooseland (G5)... 50
Moser's River (G5) 230
Mount Uniacke (F5) 230
Mulgrave (H4)...1,227
Musquodoboit Harbour (F5)... 500
Neil's Harbour (J3) 300
New Annan (F4)... 350
New Campbellton (J3) ... 68
New Germany (E5). 900
New Glasgow (G4).9,998
New Harbour (H4). 100
New Haven (J3)... 100
New Ross (E5)... 500
New Waterford (K3) ...10,381
Newport (F5)... 400
Newport Sta. (E5).. 300
Nictaux Falls (E5).. 250
Noel (F4)... 500
North East Margaree (H3) ... 700
North River (F4)... 800
North Shore (J3)... 225
North Sydney (J3)...8,125
Nyanza (J3)... 50
Ohio (G4)... 150
Oldham (F5)...
Orangedale (H4)... 233
Oxford (E4)...1,545
Parrsboro (E4)...1,849
Peggy's Cove (F5).. 75
Petit Etang (J3)... 360
Petite Rivière Bridge (E5) ... 350
Pictou ◉(G4)...4,564
Pictou Landing (G4) (G4) ... 240
Pleasant Bay (H3).. 200
Plympton (D5)... 300
Point Tupper (H4). 290
Pomquet (H4)... 160
Port Clyde (D6)... 200
Port Greville (E4)... 350
Port Hastings (H4).. 300
Port Hawkesbury (H4) ...1,078
Port Hillford (H4).. 125
Port Hood ◉(H3)... 636
Port Lorne (D5)... 200
Port Maitland (C6) 500
Port Medway (E5)... 369
Port Morien (K3)... 800
Port Mouton (E6)... 200
Port Williams (E4).. 500
Poulamon (J4)... 350
Prospect (F5)... 500
Pubnico (D6)... 331
Pugwash (F4)... 930
Queensport (H4)... 250
Quinan (D6)... 500
Rawdon (F4)... 250
Reserve Mines (K3).1,300
River Bourgeois (J4) 300
River Denys Sta. (H4) ... 75
River Hébert (E4)..1,100
River John (G4)... 700
River Philip (F4)... 75
Riverport (E5)... 200
Rockdale (J4)... 600
Roseway (D6)... 50
Roslin (F4)... 15
Rossway (C5)... 190
Round Hill (D5)... 100
Sable River (D6)... 100
Saint Andrews (H4) 400
Saint Anns (J3)... 100
Saint Bernard (D5).1,000
Saint Peter's (J4)... 812
Sainte Croix (F5)...1,200
Salmon River (C5).. 800
Salt Springs (F4)... 150
Sambro (F5)... 150
Sandy Cove (C5)... 400
Saulnierville (C5)... 200
Scotsburn (F4)... 200
Scotsville (H3)... 75
Shag Harbour (D6) 200
Sheet Harbour (G5).1,500
Sheffield Mills (E4) 266
Shelburne ◉(D6)...2,337
Sherbrooke (H4)... 500
Ship Harbour (G5) 500
Shubenacadie (F4).. 785
Shunacadie (J3)...
South Brookfield (D5) ... 250
South Ohio (C6)... 350
Southampton (E4).. 150
Spencer's Island (E4) 188
Springfield (D5)... 200
Springhill (F4)...7,348
Stellarton (G4)...5,445
Stewiacke (F4)...1,024
Strathlorne (H3)... 100
Summerville (E4)... 350
Sunnybrae (G4)... 260
Sydney ◉(J3)...32,162
Sydney-Glace Bay (Metropolitan Area) (J3)...107,124
Sydney Mines (J3).8,731
Tangier (G5)... 300
Tatamagouche (F4) 1,000
Terence Bay (F5).. 300
Thorburn (G4)...1,200
Tidnish (E4)... 350
Tiverton (C5)... 400
Tracadie (H4)... 200
Trenton (G4)...3,240
Trout River (H3)...
Truro ◉(F4)...12,250
Tusket (C6)... 400
Upper Kennetcook (F4) ... 97
Upper La Have (E5) 300
Upper Musquodoboit (G4) ... 475
Upper Stewiacke (G4) ... 800
Upper Tantallon (E5) 132
Victoria Vale (D4).. 25
Voglers Cove (E5).. 300
Wallace (F4)... 300
Walton (F4)... 250
Waverly (F5)... 200
Wedgeport (C6)...1,322
Wentworth (F4)... 95
West Bay (H4)... 100
West Berlin (E5)... 30
West Pubnico (D6). 200
West River Sta. (G4) 50
Westchester Sta. (F4) 100
Weston (E4)...
Westport (C5)... 400
Westville (G4)...4,247
Weymouth (D5)...1,500
Whitehead (H4)... 132
Whycocomagh (H4) 400
Windsor ◉(E5)...3,651
Wolfville (E4)...2,497
Yarmouth ◉(C6)...8,095

**NEWFOUNDLAND**
**Total Population 415,074**
Argentia (J6)... 900
Badger (J5)... 500
Bay Roberts (J6)...1,306
Beaumont (J5)... 400
Bell Island (Wabana) (K6)...7,837
Belleoram (J6)... 570
Bishop's Falls (J5)..2,522
Bonavista (K5)...4,078
Bonne Bay (H5)... 800
Botwood (J5)...2,744
Buchans (H5)...1,800
Burgeo (H6)...1,138
Burin (J6)...1,116
Calvert (K6)... 350
Campbellton (J5)... 350
Cape Saint George (H5)...
Carbonear (K6)...3,955
Channel-Port aux Basques (H6)...3,320
Clarenville (J6)...1,195
Codroy (H6)... 450
Conche (J5)... 25
Cook's Harbour (J4) 250
Corner Brook (H5) 23,225
Cow Head (H5)... 343
Daniel's Harbour (H5) ... 257
Deer Lake (H5)...3,481
Elliston (K5)... 750
Englee (J5)... 677
Ferryland (K6)... 500
Fleur de Lys (J5)... 300
Flower's Cove (J4).. 800
Fogo (J5)...1,184
Fortune (J6)...1,194
Fortune Harbour (J5) ... 275
Gambo (J5)... 600
Gander (J5)...3,000
Garnish (J6)... 666
Glovertown (J5)... 604
Grand Bank (J6)...2,430
Grand Falls (J5)...5,508
Greenspond (K5)... 784
Griguet (J4)... 300
Hampden (H5)... 150
Harbour Deep (J5). 214
Harbour Grace (J6) 2,545
Heart's Content (K6) 1,000
Howley (J5)... 500
Humbermouth (H5) 1,914
Jackson's Arm (H5) 350
Joe Batt's Arm (K5) 800
King's Point (J5)... 275
La Scie (J5)... 450
Lamaline (J6)... 500
Lark Harbour (H5) 400
Lewisporte (J5)...2,076
Lumsden (K5)... 470
Marystown (J6)...1,460
Merasheen (J6)... 346
Millertown (J5)... 400
Musgrave Harbour (K5) ... 385
Newtown (K5)... 450
Norris Arm (J5)...1,000
Norris Point (H5)... 464
Pacquet (J5)... 175
Placentia (K6)...1,223
Point Leamington (J5) ... 500
Port au Port (H5).. 500
Port aux Basques-Channel (H6)...3,320
Port Blandford (J5). 600
Port Saunders (J5).. 350
Port Union (K5)... 625
Pouch Cove (K6)...1,090
Renews (K6)... 450
Robinsons (H5)... 200
Rose Blanche (H6). 950
Saint Alban's (J6)... 800
Saint Anthony (J4).1,761
Saint George's (H5) 750
SAINT JOHN'S (K6) ...57,078
Saint John's (Metropolitan Area) (K6)...85,121
Saint Lawrence (J6) 1,837
Saint Mary's (K6)... 660
Saint Vincent's (J6). 400
Sop's Arm (H5)... 150
South Branch (H6).. 200
Springdale (J5)... 800
Stephenville (H5)...3,762
Torbay (K6)...1,475
Trepassey (K6)... 570
Trinity (K5)... 250
Trout River (H5)... 500
Twillingate (J5)...2,100
Wesleyville (J5)...1,313
Windsor (J5)...4,520

**PRINCE EDWARD ISLAND**
**Total Population 99,285**
Alberton (E3)... 820
Cardigan (G3)... 210
CHARLOTTETOWN (F3) ...16,446
Crapaud (F3)... 178
Ellerslie (E3)... 125
Elmira (G3)... 100
Emerald (F3)... 100
Freetown (F3)... 300
Georgetown ◉(G3). 754
Hunter's River (F3). 375
Kensington (F3)... 855
Midgell (G3)... 75
Miscouche (E3)... 175
Montague (G3)...1,152
Morell (G3)... 309
Mount Albion (G3). 75
Mount Stewart (G3) 439
Murray Harbour (G4) ... 405
Murray River (G3). 450
New Glasgow (F3). 150
New London (F3)... 50
New Wiltshire (F3). 175
O'Leary Sta. (E3)... 639
Peake Station (G3) 100
Port Borden (F3)... 695
Port Hill (F3)... 150
Pownal (G3)... 60
Rustico (F3)... 100
Saint Louis (E3)... 200
Saint Peter's Bay (G3) ... 308
Souris East (G3)...1,449
South Lake (G3)... 75
Stanley Bridge (F3) 65
Sturgeon (G3)... 100
Summerside ◉(E3)..7,242
Tignish (E3)... 914
Vernon Bridge (G3) 100

◉ County Seat

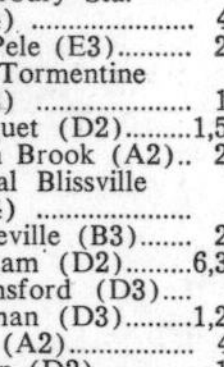

# QUEBEC

## 1956 Total Population 4,628,378

Abbotsford (E4)... 533
Abord-à-Plouffe (H4) ...8,068
Acton Vale (E4)...3,547
Albertville (B2)... 500
Alma (Ville-d'Alma) (F1) ...10,822
Amqui ◉(B2)...3,247
Ancienne-Lorette (H3) ...1,000
Ange-Gardien (F3). 333
Ange-Gardien-de-Rouville (E4)... 387
Anse-au-Griffon (D1) ... 500
Armagh (G3)... 839
Arthabaska ◉(F3)..2,399
Arundel (C4)... 350
Arvida (F1)...12,919
Asbestos (F4)...8,969
Aston Jct. (E3)... 401
Athelstan (C4)... 325
Ayer's Cliff ◉(E4).. 718
Aylmer (lake) (F4).
Aylmer East (B4)...5,294
Bagotville (G1)...4,822
Baie-Comeau (A1)..4,332
Baie-des-Capucins (B1) ... 300
Baie-des-Sables (A1) ... 735
Baie-d'Urfé (G4)...1,838
Baie-Saint-Paul ◉ (G2) ...4,052
Barachois-de-Malbaie (D1)... 515
Barré (G3)...1,000
Baskatong (lake) (B3)
Batiscan (E3)... 750
Batiscan (riv.) (E2)
Beaconsfield (H4)...5,496
Beauceville-Est ◉ (G3) ...1,709
Beauceville-Ouest (G3) ...1,459
Beauharnois ◉(D4).6,774
Beauport (J3)...6,735
Beaupré (G2)...2,377
Beaurepaire (G4)...2,500
Beaurivage (F3)... 396
Bécancour ◉(E3)... 312
Bedford ◉(E4)...2,272
Beebe (E4)...1,363
Beloeil (D4)...3,966
Berthierville ◉(D3).3,504
Bic (J1)...1,142
Black Lake (F3)...3,685
Boischatel (J3)...1,461
Boisvert (point) (J1)
Bolduc (G4)...1,000
Bonaventure (C2)...2,500
Boucherville (J4)...3,911
Bouchette (A3)... 400
Breakeyville (J3)... 500
Brébeuf (C3)... 500
Brome (lake) (E4).
Brompton (lake) (E4)
Bromptonville (F4).2,316
Brownsburg (C4)...3,412
Buckingham (B4)...6,781
Buckland (G3)... 500
Bury (F4)... 600
Cabano (J2)...2,350
Cacouna (H2)... 782
Calumet (C4)... 826
Canrobert (Ange-Gardien-de-Rouville) (E4). 387
Canton-Bégin (F1)...1,000
Cap-à-l'Aigle (G2).. 595
Cap-Chat (B1)...1,954
Cap-de-la-Madeleine (E3) ...22,943
Cap-Rouge (H3)... 350
Cap-Saint-Ignace (G2) ... 915
Cap-Santé ◉(F3)... 528
Cascapédia (riv.) (C1)
Caughnawaga (H4).2,240
Causapscal (B2)...2,957
Chaleur (bay) (C2).
Chambly (J4)...2,817
Chambord (E1)...1,091
Champlain (E3)... 710
Champlain (lake) (D4)
Chandler (D2)...3,338
Charette (D3)... 800
Charlemagne (H4)..2,428
Charlesbourg (J3)...8,202
Charny (J3)...3,622
Château-Richer ◉ (F3) ... 700
Châteauguay (H4).3,265
Châteauguay-Basin (H4) ...3,250
Chaudière (riv.) (G4)
Chénéville (B4)... 706
Chicoutimi ◉(G1).24,878
Chicoutimi (riv.) (F2)
Clermont (G2)...2,628
Cloridorme (D1)... 600
Coaticook (F4)...6,441
Commissioners (lake) (E1)
Compton (F4)... 481
Contrecoeur (D4)...1,662
Cookshire ◉(F4)...1,315
Corner of the Beach (D1) ... 300
Côte-St.-Michel (H4) ...24,706
Coteau-Landing ◉ (C4) ... 551
Coudres (isl.) (G2).
Courcelles (G4)... 498
Cowansville (E4)...5,242
Crabtree Mills (D4) ...1,103
Danville (E4)...2,296
Dartmouth (riv.) (D1)
Daveluyville (E3)... 591
Delisle (F1)...1,261
Delson (H4)... 816
Desbiens (F1)...2,021
Deschaillons (E3) ...1,759
Deschambault (E3).1,002
Deschênes (lake) (A4)
Deux-Rivières (St.-Stanislas-de-Champlain) (E3) 628
Disraeli (F4)...2,437
Dixville (F4) ... 458
Donnacona (F3)...4,147
Dosquet (F3) ... 600
Douglastown (D1).. 779
Drummondville ◉ (E4) ...26,284
Dunham (E4)... 399
East Angus (F4)...4,239
East Broughton (F3) ...1,868

## QUEBEC (Continued)

East Broughton Station (F3).........1,060
Eastman (E4)............ 651
Edouard (lake) (E2)
Farnham (E4).........5,843
Fassett (C4)............. 500
Ferme-Neuve (B3)..1,891
Fontenelle (D1)....... 430
Forestville (H1).......1,117
Fort-Chambly (J4)..1,864
Fortierville (F3)...... 600
Foster (E4).............. 436
Frampton (G3)......... 888
Garthby Sta. (F4)... 497
Gaspé (D1)..............2,194
Gaspé (bay) (D1)....
Gaspé (cape) (D1)..
Gaspé (pen.) (D2)..
Gaspesian Prov. Park (C1) ...........
Gatineau (B4).........8,423
Gatineau (riv.) (B3)
Gentilly (E3)........... 664
Giffard (J3)..............9,964
Godbout (B1)........... 663
Gracefield (A3)........ 639
Granby (E4)............27,095
Grande-Cascapédia (C2) ........... 513
Grand'Mère (E3)..14,023
Grande-Ligne (D4). 600
Grand-Rivière (D2) ...........1,024
Grande-Vallée (D1) 459
Grandes-Bergeronnes (H1) 810
Grandes-Piles (E3).. 650
Grenville (C4).........1,277
Grosses-Roches (B1) ........... 501
Ha! Ha! (riv.) (G1)
Ham-Nord (F4)....... 800
Hébertville (F1)......1,509
Hébertville-Station (F1) ...........1,189
Hemmingford (D4). 682
Henryville (D4)....... 644
Hérouxville (E3)...... 500
Honfleur (G3).......... 388
Howick (D4)............ 560
Huberdeau (C4)....... 900
Hudson (C4)............1,549
Hull ◉(B4)............49,243
Huntingdon ◉ (C4) ...........2,995
Iberville ◉(D4).......6,270
Ile-Bizard (H4)........ 900
Ile-Maligne (F1)......1,761
Ile-Perrot-Nord (G4) ........... 450
Ile-Perrot-Sud (H4).2,600
Iles (lake) (B3)..........
Inverness ◉(F3)...... 321
Isle-aux-Grues (H1) ...........1,000
Isle-Verte (H1)........1,000
Jacques-Cartier (Ville-Jacques-Cartier) (J4)....33,132
Jacques-Cartier (mt.) (C1).........
Jacques-Cartier (riv.) (F2)...........
Jesus (isl.) (H4)......
Joliette ◉(D3)........16,940
Jonquière (F1).......25,550
Kamouraska (H2)... 500
Kénogami (F1)......11,309
Kénogami (lake) (F1) ...........
Kiamika (B3)........... 400
Kiamika(lake) (B3)
Kildare (D3)........... 450
Kingsey Falls (E4).. 596
Knowlton ◉(E4).....1,328
La Baie (E3)............ 658
La Conception (C3) 400
La Decharge (F1)... 400
La Durantaye (G3). 412
La Guadeloupe (F4) ...........1,482
La Malbaie ◉(G2)..2,817
La Minerve (C3)...... 350
La Patrie (F4)........ 535
La Petite Rivière St. François (G2)...... 454
La Salle (H4).........18,867
La Tuque (E2)........11,096
La Vérendrye Prov. Park (A3)...........
Labelle (C3)............1,150
Lac-au-Saumon (B2) ...........1,681
Lac-aux-Sables (E3) 500
Lac-Bouchette (E1). 781
Lac-Carré (C3)........ 601
Lac-Edouard (E2)... 250
Lac-Etchemin (G3).1,380
Lac-Frontière (H3). 619
Lac-Humqui (B2).... 500
Lac-Masson (D3)... 650
Lac-Mégantic ◉ (G4) ...........6,864
Lac-Saguay (B3)...... 295
Lac-Sainte-Marie (B4) ........... 450
L'Acadie (J4)........... 550
Lachine (H4).........34,494
Lachute ◉(C4).........6,866
Lachute Mills (C4).3,000
Lacolle (D4)............1,141
Lamartine (G2).......1,000
Lambton (F4).......... 701
Langevin (G3)......... 552
L'Annonciation (C3) 783
Lanoraie (D4).......... 900
L'Anse-Saint-Jean (G1) ........... 250
Laprairie ◉(J4)........5,271
Larochelle (St.-Grégoire) (E3).... 625
Larouche (F1)......... 350
L'Assomption ◉ (D4) ...........3,683
L'Assomption (riv.) (D3) ...........
Laterrière (F1)........ 658
Laurentides Prov. Park (F2)...........
Laurierville (F3)...... 767
Lauzon (F3)............10,265
Laval-des-Rapides (H4) ...........11,248
Lavaltrie (D4)......... 917
L'Avenir (E4).......... 357
Leeds Village (F3).. 500
Lennoxville (F4)......3,149
L'Epiphanie (D4)....2,671
Les Eboulements (G2) ........... 500
Les Escoumins(H1) 750
Les Etroits (J2)....... 500
Les Hauteurs de Rimouski (J1). 750
Les Méchins (B1).... 600
Lévis (J3)................13,644
Lièvre (riv.) (B4)....
Linière (G3)...........1,149
L'Islet (G2)............. 823
Longueuil ◉(J4)....14,332
Loretteville ◉(H3)..4,957
Louiseville ◉(E3)....4,392
Loup (riv.) (H2)......
Low (B4).................. 500
Luceville (J1) ........1,265
Lyster Station (F3).1,010
Madeleine (cape) (D1) ...........
Magog (E4)...........12,638
Malbaie (riv.) (G2)
Manicouagan (point) (B1)..........
Maniwaki ◉(B3).....5,399
Manseau (E3)......... 846
Mansonville (E4).... 700
Marbleton (F4)....... 750
Maria (C2).............. 500
Marieville ◉(D4)....3,478
Mascouche (H4)......1,000
Maskinongé (E3).... 800
Maskinongé (riv.) (D3) ...........
Masson (B4)...........1,656
Massueville (St.-Aimé) (E4)......... 644
Matane ◉(B1)..........8,069
Matapédia (B2)....... 500
Matapédia (lake) (B1) ...........
Mattawin (riv.) (D3)
Mégantic (Lac-Mégantic) ◉(G4)6,864
Mégantic(lake) (G4)
Mekinac (lake) (E2)
Melocheville (C4)...1,422
Memphremagog (lake) (E4)...........
Metabetchouan (riv.) (F1)..........
Mille Isles (riv.) (H4) ...........
Mistassini(riv.) (E1)
Mont-Joli (J1)..........6,179
Mont-Laurier ◉ (B3) ...........5,486
Mont-Louis (C1)...... 500
Mont-Rolland (C4) ...........1,000
Mont-Saint-Grégoire (D4) ........... 594
Mont-Tremblant Prov. Park (C3)...
Montauban (E3)....... 336
Montebello (B4)......1,287
Montmagny ◉(G3).6,405
Montmorency (J3)..6,077
Montmorency (riv.) (F2) ...........
Montréal ◉ (H4) ...........1,109,439
Montréal (Metropolitan Area) (H4).1,395,400
Morin Heights (C4) 600
Mount Royal (H4)16,990
Namur (C4)............ 300
Napierville ◉(D4)..1,510
Neuville (F3)......... 727
New Carlisle ◉ (D2) ...........1,000
New Richmond (C2) ...........1,000
Newport (D2)........ 500
Nicolet (E3)...........4,084
Nicolet (riv.) (E3)..
Nominingue (B3)..... 733
Normandin (E1)......1,918
North (riv.) (C4).....
North Coaticook (F4) ........... 500
North Hatley (E4).. 671
Notre-Dame-de-Ham (F4) ........... 500
Notre-Dame-des-Bois (G4)............ 822
Notre-Dame-du-Lac ◉(J2)...........1,512
Notre-Dame-du-Laus (B3) ........... 650
Notre-Dame-du-Rosaire (G3)......... 800
Oies (isl.) (G2).......
Oka (C4)................1,084
Orléans (isl.) (F3)..
Ormstown (D4).......1,347
Ottawa (riv.) (B4)...
Ouareau (riv.) (D3)
Outremont (H4)...29,990
Panet (G3)..............2,100
Papineau (lake) (C4)
Papineauville ◉ (C4) ...........1,141
Parisville (F3)......... 500
Pespébiac (D2)........ 800
Patapedia (riv.) (B2)
Percé ◉(D1)........... 700
Péribonca (E1)........ 500
Petit-Saguenay (G1) 500
Petite-Nation (riv.) (B4) ...........
Pierreville (E3).......1,589
Plaisance (B4)........ 500
Plessisville (F3)......5,829
Pointe-au-Pic (G2)..1,220
Pointe-aux-Trembles (J4) ...........11,981
Pointe-Claire (H4)15,208
Pointe-Gatineau (B4)6,175
Poisson-Blanc (lake) (B4) ...........
Poltimore (B4)........ 400
Pont-Rouge (F3).....2,631
Pont-Viau (H4).......8,218
Pontbriand (F3)....... 450
Port-Alfred (G1).....7,986
Port-Daniel (D2)..... 800
Portneuf (F3)..........1,256
Prairies (riv.) (H4)
Price (A1)...............3,140
Princeville (F3).......2,841
QUÉBEC (H3).....170,703
Québec (Metropolitan Area) (H3)....301,108
Ravignan (G3)......... 807
Rawdon (D3)...........2,049
Restigouche (C2).... 532
Restigouche (riv.) (B2) ...........
Richelieu (Village-Richelieu) (D4)...1,398
Richmond ◉(E4)....3,849
Rigaud (C4)...........1,784
Rimouski ◉(J1)....14,630
Rimouski (riv.) (J1)
Rimouski Est (J1)...1,209
Ripon (B4).............. 549
Rivière-à-Pierre (E3) ........... 817
Rivière-au-Doré (E1)
Rivière-au-Renard (D1) ........... 850
Rivière-Beaudette (C4) ........... 270
Rivière-Bleue (J2)...1,481
Rivière-Caplan (C2) 317
Rivière-des-Prairies (H4) ...........6,806
Rivière-du-Loup ◉ (H2) ...........9,964
Rivière-du-Moulin (G1) ...........4,138
Rivière-la-Madeleine (C1) ........... 225
Rivière-Mailloux (G2) ........... 550
Rivière-Ouelle (G2). 600
Rivière-Trois-Pistoles (J1) ........... 400
Robertsonville (F3) 1,030
Roberval ◉(E1).......6,643
Rock Island (E4)....1,608
Rouge (riv.) (C3)....
Roxton Falls (E4)...1,023
Roxton Pond (E4).. 735
Saguenay(riv.) (G1) 53
St.-Adalbert (H3).... 600
St.-Adelphe-de-Champlain (E3)... 750
St.-Adolphe-de-Howard (C4)....... 350
St.-Adolphe-de-Dudswell (F4)...... 400
St.-Aimé (E4)......... 644
St.-Alban (E3)........ 815
St.-Albert (E3)........ 375
St.-Alexandre-d'Iberville (D4)..... 375
St.-Alexandre-de-Kamouraska(H2) 904
St.-Alexis-de-Montcalm (D4).... 489
St.-Alexis-de-Matapédia (B2).... 500
St.-Alexis-des-Monts (D3) ........... 700
St.-Alphonse-de-Caplan (C2)......... 600
St.-Ambroise-de-Chicoutimi (F1)..1,305
St.-Anaclet (J1)...... 800
St.-André-de-Kamouraska(H2) 539
St. Andrews (C4).... 811
St.-Anselme (F3).....1,086
St.-Antoine-Abbé (D4) ........... 275
St.-Antoine-Lotbinière (F3) ........... 300
St.-Antoine-sur-Richelieu (D4)..... 500
St.-Antonin (H2)..... 500
St. Apollinaire (F3) 824
St.-Arsène (H2)...... 400
St.-Athanase (H2).... 250
St.-Aubert (G2)....... 550
St.-Augustin (G4).... 393
St.-Augustin-de-Québec (H3)........ 550
St.-Barnabé-Sud (D4) ........... 300
St.-Barthélémy (D3) 900
St.-Basile (J4)......... 700
St.-Basile (F3).........1,635
St.-Benjamin (G3).. 700
St.-Benoît (C4)....... 467
St.-Benoît-Labre (G3) ........... 600
St.-Bernard-de-Dorchester (F3)..... 500
St.-Bonaventure(E4) 500
St.-Boniface-de-Shawinigan (D3). 880
St.-Bruno (J4)......... 800
St.-Bruno-de-Kamouraska(H2) 800
St.-Calixte-de-Kilkenny (D4)..... 400
St.-Camille (F4)....... 375
St.-Camille-de-Bellechasse (G3).. 650
St.-Casimir (E3)......1,447
St.-Césaire (D4)......1,739
St.-Charles-de-Bellechasse (G3). 946
St.-Charles-River-Richelieu (D4)...... 287
St.-Chrysostome (D4) ........... 866
St.-Clément (H2)..... 500
St.-Clet (C4)........... 308
St.-Côme (D3)......... 525
St.-Constant (H4).... 500
St.-Cuthbert (D3).... 600
St.-Cyprien (J2)...... 575
St.-Cyrille-de-Wendover (E4)....1,198
St.-Cyrille-de-L'Islet (G3).......... 700
St.-Damase (D4)...... 450
St.-Damase-de-Matane (B1)......... 700
St.-Damase des-Aulnaies (G2)...... 737
St.-Damien-de-Brandon (D3)....... 400
St.-Damien-de-Buckland (G3).... 500
St.-David-de-Lévis (J3) ........... 400
St.-David-d'Yamaska (E4) ........... 800
St.-Denis-Rivière-Richelieu (D4).... 944
St.-Denis-de-la-Bouteillerie (G2). 450
St.-Didace (D3)....... 472
St.-Dominique-de-Bagot (E4).......... 483
St.-Donat-de-Rimouski (J1)...... 476
St.-Edouard-de-Napierville (D4). 350
St.-Eleuthère (H2)... 650
St.-Elie (E3)........... 775
St.-Eloi (H1)........... 650
St.-Emile-de-Québec (H3).........1,645
St.-Emile-de-Suffolk (B4) ........... 450
St.-Emilien (Desbiens) (F1)..2,021
St.-Ephrem-de-Beauce (G3)......... 831
St.-Esprit (D4)........ 850
St.-Etienne-des-Grès (E3) ........... 500
St.-Eugène-de-Grantham (E4).... 400
St.-Eusèbe (J2)........ 308
St.-Eustache (H4)...3,740
St.-Fabien (J1)........1,200
St.-Félicien (E1).......4,152
St.-Félix-de-Valois (D3)..........1,323
St.-Ferdinand (F3)..2,431
St.-Féréol (G2)........ 330
St.-Fidèle (H2)........ 390
St. Flavien (F3)....... 634
St.-Fortunat (F4).... 400
St.-Francis (riv.) (E4) ...........
St.-François-Montmagny (G3). 600
St.-François (lake) (C4) ...........
St.-François (lake) (F4) ...........
St.-François-du-Lac ◉(E3)............ 826
St.-Frédéric (G3).... 375
St.-Fulgence (G1)....1,054
St.-Gabriel-de-Brandon (D3).....3,265
St.-Gabriel-de-Rimouski (J1)...... 575
St.-Gédéon (F1)...... 873
St.-Gédéon-de-Beauce (G4)......... 857
St.-Georges-de-Cacouna(Cacouna) (H2) ........... 782
St.-Georges-de-Windsor (F4)....... 400
St.-Georges-Ouest (G3) ...........3,597
St.-Gérard (F4)....... 665
St.-Germain-de-Grantham (E4).... 919
St.-Gervais (G3)...........1,000
St.-Gilles (F3)........ 400
St.-Godefroi (D2).... 400
St.-Grégoire (E3).... 625
St.-Guillaume (E4).. 802
St.-Henri (J3)......... 661
St.-Hermas (C4)...... 400
St.-Herménégilde (F4) ........... 236
St.-Hilarion (G2)..... 400
St.-Hilaire-Village (D4) ...........2,000
St.-Honoré (G4)...... 650
St.-Honoré-de-Témiscouta (H2). 891
St. Hubert (J4) ........... 400
St.-Hubert-de-Temiscouata (J2). 800
St.-Hugues (E4)...... 487
St.-Hyacinthe ◉ (D4) ...........20,439
St.-Irénée (G2)....... 500
St.-Isidore-d'Auckland (F4). 468
St.-Isidore-Dorchester (F3)... 688
St.-Jacques (D4)......1,979
St.-Janvier (H4)....... 650
St.-Jean ◉(D4)......24,367
St.-Jean (G3).......... 600
St.-Jean-Chrysostome-de-Lévis (J3)........ 500
St.-Jean-de-Boischatel (Boischatel) (J3).1,461
St.-Jean-de-Dieu (J1) ........... 998
St.-Jean-de-Matha (D3) ...........1,016
St.-Jean-des-Piles (E3) ........... 350
St.-Jean-Port-Joli ◉ (G2) ........... 900
St.-Jérôme ◉(H4)..20,645
St.-Joachim-de-Montmorency (G2) ........... 568
St.-John (lake) (E1)
St.-Joseph(lake) (F3)
St.-Joseph-de-Beauce (G3) ...........2,484
St.-Joseph-de-la-Rivière-Bleue (J2) ...........1,481
St.-Joseph-de-Sorel (D3) ...........3,530
St.-Joseph-du-Lac (C4) ........... 400
St.-Jovite (C3).........1,613
St.-Jude (E4)........... 700
St.-Just-de-Bretenières (H3).......... 400
St.-Justin (D3)........ 585
St.-Lambert (J4)...12,224
St.-Laurent (H4)...38,291
St.-Laurent-d'Orléans (G3) ........... 450
St.-Lawrence (gulf) (D2)..........
St.-Lawrence (riv.) (H1)..........
St.-Lazare-Village (G3) ........... 466
St.-Léandre (B1)...... 450
St.-Léon-le-Grand (B2) ........... 500
St.-Léonard-de-Portneuf (F3)........ 636
St.- Léonard-d'Aston E3 ........... 752
St.-Liboire ◉(E4).... 613
St.-Liguori (D3)...... 250
St.-Louis (lake) (H4)
St.-Louis-de-Gonzague (D4)...... 500
St.-Louis-du-Ha!-Ha! (H2) ........... 800
St.-Luc-de-Matane (B1) ........... 624
St.-Ludger (G4)....... 301
St.-Magloire (G3).... 772
St.-Malachie (G3).... 500
St.-Marc (D4)......... 322
St.-Marc-des-Carrières (E3)......2,457
St.-Marcel-de-l'Islet (G3) ........... 495
St.-Marcellin (J1)..... 350
St.-Martin (H4).......6,440
St.-Mathieu (J1)....... 550
St.-Maurice (riv.) (E2) ...........
St.-Méthode-de-Frontenac (F3)....1,000
St.-Michel-de-Bellechasse (G3).. 660
St.-Michel (Côte-St.-Michel) (H4)....24,706
St.-Michel-des-Saints (D3) ........... 800
St.-Modeste (H2)..... 300
St.-Nazaire (E4)...... 500
St.-Nérée (G3)........ 530
St.-Nicolas (H3)...... 350
St.-Noël (B1)..........1,027
St.-Norbert-d'Arthabaska(F3) 248
St.-Octave (B1)...... 500
St.-Odilon (G3)....... 450
St.-Omer (C3)......... 275
St.-Ours (D4)......... 691
St.-Pacôme (G2).....1,283
St.-Pamphile (H3)...1,000
St.-Pascal ◉(H2).....1,962
St. Paul-de-Chester (F4) ........... 267
St. Paul-de-Montminy (G3)...... 850
St. Paul-du-Nord (H1) ........... 300
St.-Paul-l'Ermite (J4) ...........2,002
St.-Paulin (D3)....... 943
St.-Peter (lake) (E3)
St.-Philémon (G3)... 500
St.-Philippe-de-Laprairie (J4)....... 498
St.-Philippe-de-Néri (H2) ........... 635
St.-Pie (E4)............1,229
St. Pierre-Baptiste (F3) ........... 750
St.-Pierre-Les-Becquets (E3)....... 393
St.-Pierre-Montmagny (G3) ...........1,200
St.-Pierre(point) (D1)
St.-Placide (C4)...... 305
St.-Polycarpe (C4).. 554
St.-Prime (E1)........ 629
St.-Prosper (E3)..... 418
St.-Prosper-de-Dorchester (G3).. 998
St.-Raphaël-Bellechasse ◉(G3)1,059
St.-Raymond (F3)...3,502
St.-Rémi (D4)........2,303
St.-Rémi-d'Amherst (C3) ........... 750
St.-Robert (E4)....... 500
St.-Roch-des-Aulnaies (G2)...... 350
St.-Roch-de-l'Achigan (D4)...... 700
St.-Roch-de-Richelieu (D4) ........... 700
St.-Romain (F4)...... 800
St.-Romuald-d'Etchemin (J3)..4,502
St.-Samuel-de-Gayhurst (G4)...... 550
St.-Sauveur-des-Montagnes (C4)..1,316
St.-Sébastien-de-Beauce (G4)......... 473
St.-Sévère (E3)........ 250
St.-Siméon (G2)......1,114
St.-Simon (E4)........ 436
St.-Simon (H1)........ 528
St. Stanislas-de-Champlain (E3)... 620
St.-Sylvestre (F3).... 476
St.-Télesphore (C4). 275
St.-Théophile (G4). 388
St.-Thuribe (E3)...... 500
St.-Timothée (D4).. 688
St.-Tite (E3)...........3,183
St.-Tite-des-Caps (G2) ........... 650
St.-Ubald (E3)........... 775
St.-Ulric (B1).......... 980
St.-Urbain-de-Charlevoix (G2).. 690
St.-Valère-de-Bulstrode (E3)...... 300
St.-Valérien (E4).... 348
St.-Valérien-de-Charlevoix (J1)... 450
St.-Vallier (G3)...... 533
St.-Victor-de-Beauce (G3) ........... 684
St.-Vincent-de-Paul (H4) ...........6,784
St.-Wenceslas (E3).. 315
St.-Zacharie (G3).... 400
St.-Zénon (D3)....... 850
St.-Zéphirin (E3).... 430
Ste.-Adelaide-de-Pabos (D2)......... 300
Ste.-Adèle (C4).......1,309
Ste.-Agathe-de-Lotbinière (F3).... 559
Ste.-Agathe-des-Monts (C3)........5,173
Ste.-Agnès-de-Charlevoix (G2).. 500
Ste.-Angèle-de-Monnoir (D4)...... 580
Ste.-Angèle-de-Mérici (J1)......... 655
Ste.-Angèle-de-Laval (E3)......... 542
Ste.-Anne(riv.) (G2)
Ste.-Anne(riv.) (F3)
Ste.-Anne-de-Beaupré (F2) ...........1,865
Ste.-Anne-de-Bellevue (H4)......3,647
Ste.-Anne-de-la-Pérade (E3).........1,282
Ste.-Anne-de-la-Pocatière (H2)..... 300
Ste.-Anne-des-Monts (C1) ...........1,000
Ste.-Anne-des-Plaines (H4) ........... 949
Ste.-Anne-du-Lac (B3) ........... 528
Ste.-Apolline-de-Patton (H3)......... 650
Ste.-Béatrix (D3).... 375
Ste.-Blandine (J1).... 508
Ste.-Catherine (F3) ........... 450
Ste.-Cécile-de-Frontenac (G4)..... 375
Ste.-Cécile-de-Masham (B4)......... 300
Ste.-Claire (G3)...... 828
Ste.-Clothilde (E4).. 450
Ste.-Croix ◉(F3).....1,241
Ste.-Edwidge (F4)... 450
Ste.-Elizabeth (D3). 554
Ste.-Emélie-de-l'Energie (D3)...... 700
Ste.-Emmélie (F3).. 500
Ste.-Eulalie (E3)..... 450
Ste.-Euphémie (G3) ........... 500
Ste.-Famille (G3).... 300
Ste.-Félicité (B1).... 812
Ste.-Florence (B2).. 370
Ste.-Flore (E3)....... 500
Ste.-Foy (H3).......14,615
Ste.-Geneviève-de-Batiscan ◉(E3).... 550
Ste.-Geneviève-de-Pierrefonds (H4).2,041
Ste.-Gertrude (E3).. 379
Ste.-Hélène-de-Kamouraska(H2) 800
Ste.-Hélène-de-Bagot (E4) ........... 290
Ste.-Hénédine ◉ (F3) ........... 606
Ste.-Julie-de-Verchères (J4)..... 400
Ste.-Julienne ◉(D4) 700
Ste.-Justine-de-Newton (C4)....... 487
Ste.-Louise (G2)...... 558
Ste.-Lucie-de-Beauregard (H3). 350
Ste.-Lucie-de-Doncaster (C3).... 484
Ste.-Marguerite-de-Dorchester (G3).. 350
Ste.-Marie-Beauce (G3) ...........3,094
Ste.-Marthe (C4).... 773
Ste.-Martine (D4).... 573
Ste.-Perpétue (E3)... 488
Ste.-Perpétue-de-l'Islet (H2)......... 500
Ste.-Pudentienne (Roxton Pond) (E4) ........... 735
Ste.-Rosalie (D4).....1,120
Ste.-Rose ◉(H4).....4,948
Ste.-Rose-de-Lima (B4) ...........1,714
Ste.-Rose-de-Watford (G3) ........... 450
Ste.-Rose-du-Dégelé (J2) ...........1,400
Ste.-Sabine (G3)..... 400
Ste.-Scholastique ◉ (C4) ........... 865
Ste.-Sophie-de-Lévrard (E3)....... 450
Ste.-Sophie-de-Mégantic (F3)..... 575
Ste.-Thérèse-de-Blainville (H4)....8,266
Ste.-Thérèse (isl.) (J4) ...........
Ste.-Ursule (D3)...... 486
Ste.-Véronique (C3) 400
Ste.-Victoire (D4)... 450
Salmon (riv.) (F4).
Sault-au-Mouton (H1) ........... 873
Sawyerville (F4)..... 823
Sayabec (B2)..........2,281
Scotstown (F4)........1,347
Scott-Jonction (F3) ........... 477
Senneville (G4)....... 979
Shawbridge (C4)..... 680
Shawinigan (riv.) (E3) ...........
Shawinigan Falls (D3) ...........28,597
Shawinigan Falls (Metropolitan Area) (D3)...58,328
Sherbrooke ◉(E4).58,668
Sherbrooke (Metropolitan Area) (E4)......63,694
Sillery (J3)...........13,154
Sorel ◉(D4)..........16,342
South Durham (E4) ........... 416
South Roxton (E4). 480
Squatteck (J2)....... 300
Stanstead (Stanstead Plain) (F4)..........1,134
Stoneham (F2)....... 472
Stratford Centre (F4) ........... 400
Sully (H2).............. 500
Sutton (E4)............1,407
Sweetsburg (E4)..... 879
Tadoussac ◉(H1)....1,066
Taureau (res.) (D3)
Témiscouata (lake) (H2) ...........
Templeton (B4).......2,475
Terrebonne (H4).....4,097
Thetford Mines (F3) ...........19,511
Thirty One Mile (lake) (B3)...........
Thurso (B4)............2,324
Ticouape (E1)........ 600
Tingwick (F4)......... 500
Tourelle (C1).......... 700
Tourville (H2)........ 713
Tring Jonction (F3)1,083
Trois-Pistoles (H1).4,039
Trois-Rivières (E3) ...........50,483
Trois-Rivières (Metropolitan Area) (E3).....77,961
Two Mountains (lake) (C4).........
Upton (E4)............. 797
Val-Alain (F3)........ 600
Val-Barrette (B3).... 568
Val-Brilliant (B1).... 939
Val-David (C3).......1,016
Valcartier-Village (F3) ........... 800
Valcourt (E4)......... 753
Vallée-Jonction (G3) ...........1,340
Valleyfield (C4)....23,584
Valmont (E3)......... 520
Varennes (J4).........2,047
Vaudreuil ◉(C4)..... 778
Verchères ◉(J4).....1,412
Verdun (H4)..........78,262
Victoriaville (E3)...16,031
Viger (H2)............. 450
Village Richelieu (D4) ...........1,398
Ville-d'Alma ◉ (F1) ...........10,822
Ville-Jacques-Cartier (J4) ...........33,132
Ville-St. Georges (G3) ...........3,142
Villeneuve (J3)......1,417
Villers(Ste.-Gertrude) (E3) ........... 379
Wakefield (B4)....... 376
Warwick (F4).........1,498
Waterloo ◉(E4).....4,266
Waterville (F4)......1,373
Weedon (F4)..........1,287
West Shefford (E4). 369
Westmount (H4)...24,800
Wickham Ouest (E4) ........... 393
Windsor (F4).........5,886
Wotton (F4)........... 751
Yamachiche ◉(E3). 900
Yamaska (riv.)(E4)

◉ County Seat

## ONTARIO

## 1956 Total Population 5,404,933

Abitibi (riv.) (J5)...
Actinolite (G3)....... 200
Acton (D4).............3,578
Agincourt (J4)........ 350
Ailsa Craig (C4)..... 533
Ajax (F4)...............5,683
Alexandria (K2).....2,487
Alfred (K2)...........1,257
Algoma Mills (B1).. 100
Algonquin Park (F2) 100
Algonquin Prov. Park (F2)..........
Allenford (C3)....... 200
Alliston (E3)..........2,426
Alma (D4).............. 195
Almonte (H2)........2,960
Alton (E4).............. 500
Alvinston (B5)....... 652
Amherst (isl.) (H3)
Amherstburg (A5)...4,099
Angus (E3)............. 400
Ansonville (K5)......1,335
Appin (C5)............. 125
Apple Hill (K2)...... 370
Apsley (F3)........... 175
Arden (G3)............ 300
Arkona (C4)........... 447
Armstrong Sta.(H4) 375
Arnprior (H2)........5,137
Arthur (D4)...........1,124
Athens (J3)........... 935
Atherly (E3).......... 250
Atikokan (G5).......2,400
Atwood (D4)......... 500
Auburn (C4)......... 175
Auden (H4)........... 444
Aultsville (J3)....... 350
Aurora (J3)...........3,957
Avening (D3)......... 94
Avonmore (K2)...... 500
Aylmer West (C5)...4,201
Ayr (D4)............... 939

Ayton (D3)...... 500
Baden (D4)......1,000
Bala (E2)...... 452
Balsam (lake) (F3).
Baltimore (F3)...... 200
Bancroft (G2)......1,669
Bannockburn (G3).. 200
Baptiste (lake) (G2)
Barrie ◉(E3)......16,851
Barrys Bay (G2)......1,366
Bath (H3)...... 637
Battersea (H3)...... 100
Bayfield (C4)...... 321
Bayfield (sound) (B2)......
Bays (lake) (F2)......
Baysville (E2)...... 125
Beachburg (H2)...... 450
Beachville (D4)...... 700
Beamsville (E4)......2,198
Beardmore (H5)...... 450
Beaverton (E3)......1,099
Beeton (E3)...... 675
Belgrave (C4)...... 125
Bellamys (J3)...... 96
Belle River (B5)......1,814
Belleville ◉(G3)......20,605
Belmont (C5)...... 500
Belwood (D4)...... 200
Berkeley (D3)...... 200
Bervie (C3)...... 300
Bethany (F3)...... 294
Birch Cliff (K4)......1,000
Biscotasing (J5)...... 200
Bishops Mills (J3) ...150
Blackstock (F3)...... 300
Blenheim (C5)......2,844
Blind River (A1)......3,633
Bloomfield (G4)...... 769
Bluevale (C4)...... 235
Blyth (C4)...... 757
Blytheswood (B5)...... 100
Bobcaygeon (F3)......1,242
Bolton (J4)......1,093
Bonfield (E1)...... 609
Bothwell (C5)...... 765
Bourget (J2)...... 612
Bowmanville (F4)...6,544
Bracebridge ◉(E2)..2,849
Bradford (E3)......2,010
Braeside (H2)...... 506
Brampton ◉(J4)......12,587
Brantford ◉(D4)..51,869
Brantford (Metropolitan Area) (D4)......55,740
Brechin (E3)...... 225
Brigden (B5)...... 500
Brighton (G3)......2,182
Britt (D2)...... 225
Brockville ◉(J3)......13,885
Bronte (E4)......2,024
Brooklin (E4)...... 650
Brougham (K3)...... 300
Bruce Mines (J5)... 451
Brucefield (C4)...... 200
Brussels (C4)...... 782
Buckhorn (F3)...... 150
Burford (D4)...... 700
Burgesville (D4)...... 300
Burks Falls (E2)...... 902
Burlington (E4)......9,127
Burlington Beach (E4)......3,314
Burnt (riv.) (F3)......
Burnt River (F3)...... 200
Burwash (D1)...... 125
Byng Inlet (D2)...... 647
Cabot Head (prom.) (C2)......
Cache Bay (D1)...... 894
Calabogie (H2)...... 428
Caledon East (E4). 337
Caledonia (E4)......2,078
Callander (E1)...... 750
Camlachie (B4)...... 147
Camp Borden (E3).1,000
Campbellford (G3).3,425
Canfield (E4)...... 138
Cannington (E3)...... 926
Capreol (K5)......2,394
Caradoc (C5)...... 477
Cardinal (J3)......1,994
Cargill (C3)...... 300
Carleton Place (H2)......4,790
Carp (H2)...... 400
Carrying Place (G3) 150
Cartier (J5)...... 507
Casselman (J2)......1,241
Castleton (F3)...... 400
Cavan (F3)...... 95
Cayuga ◉(E5)...... 772
Centralia (C4)...... 230
Centreville (H3)...... 100
Ceylon (D3)...... 150
Chalk River (G1)... 946
Chapleau (J5)......2,750
Charing Cross (B5) 135
Chatham ◉(B5)......22,262
Chatsworth (D3)...... 410
Chelmsford (K5)......2,142
Cherry Valley (G4) 125
Chesley (C3)......1,672
Chesterville (J2)......1,169
Chippawa (E4)......2,039
Christian (isl.) (D3)
Chute à Blondeau (K2)...... 225
Clandeboye (C4)...... 175
Claremont (K3)...... 400
Clarence (J2)...... 175
Clarence Creek (J2) 335
Clarendon Sta. (H3) 66
Clarksburg (D3)...... 478
Clarkson (J4)......1,450
Clear (lake) (F3)......
Clifford (D4)...... 533
Clinton (C4)......2,896
Cobalt ◉(K5)......2,367
Cobden (H2)...... 913
Coboconk (F3)...... 500
Cobourg ◉(F4)......9,399
Cockburn Island (A2)...... 210

Cochrane ◉(K5)......3,695
Cockburn (isl.) (A2)
Coe Hill (G3)...... 288
Colborne (G4)......1,240
Coldwater (E3)...... 693
Collingwood (D3)...7,978
Comber (B5)...... 608
Combermere (G2).. 150
Coniston (D1)......2,478
Consecon (G3)...... 500
Cookstown (E3)...... 600
Cooksville (J4)......1,800
Copetown (E4)...... 300
Copper Cliff (D1)...3,801
Coral Rapids (J4).. 51
Cordova Mines (G3)...... 10
Corinth (D5)...... 200
Cornwall ◉(K2)......18,158
Corunna (B5)...... 232
Couchiching (lake) (E3)......
Courtland (D5)...... 341
Courtright (B5)...... 581
Craighurst (E3)...... 190
Crediton (C4)...... 500
Creemore (D3)...... 838
Creighton Mine (C1)......1,240
Crosby (H3)...... 125
Crysler (J2)...... 333
Crystal Beach (E5).1,850
Crystal Falls (D1)..
Cumberland (J2)...... 300
Cutler (B1)...... 175
Dashwood (C4)...... 500
Dean Lake (A1)...... 80
Deep River (G1)......1,750
Delamere (D1)......
Delaware (C5)...... 257
Delhi (D5)......3,002
Deloro (G3)...... 253
Delta (H3)...... 500
Denbigh (G2)...... 100
Denfield (C4)......
Depot Harbour (D2)...... 457
Desbarats (J5)...... 200
Desboro (C3)...... 100
Deseronto (G3)......1,729
Detlor (G2)...... 90
Deux Rivières (F1).
Devlin (F5)...... 262
Dixie (J4)...... 325
Dorchester Sta. (C5)...... 400
Dorset (F2)...... 131
Douglas (H2)...... 500
Drayton (D4)...... 573
Dresden (B5)......2,260
Drumbo (D4)...... 500
Dryden (G4)......4,428
Dublin (C4)...... 300
Dunchurch (E2)...... 200
Dundalk (D3)...... 847
Dundas (D4)......9,507
Dungannon (C4)...... 435
Dunnville (E5)......4,478
Duntroon (D3)...... 166
Durham (D3)......2,067
Dutton (C5)...... 784
Dyment (G5)...... 158
Eastview (J2)......1,909
Eastwood (D4)...... 150
Eau Claire (F1)...... 150
Echo Bay (J5)...... 290
Edy's Mills (B5)...... 75
Eganville (G2)......1,598
Elgin (H3)...... 300
Elk Lake (K5)...... 350
Elmira (D4)......2,916
Elmvale (E3)...... 897
Elmwood (C3)...... 406
Elora (D4)......1,457
Elsas (J5)...... 150
Embro (C4)...... 529
Embrun (J2)...... 500
Emo (F5)...... 653
Emsdale (E2)...... 180
Englehart (K5)......1,705
English River (G5).
Enterprise (H3)...... 400
Erie (lake) (E5)......
Erieau (C5)...... 475
Erin (D4)...... 885
Espanola (C1)......4,000
Essex (B5)......3,348
Ethel (C4)...... 250
Everett (E3)...... 190
Exeter (C4)......2,655
Falkenburg Station (E2)...... 60
Fallbrook (H3)...... 250
Farran's Point (K3) 296
Fauquier (J5)...... 500
Fenelon Falls (F3) 1,137
Fergus (D4)......3,677
Fesserton (E3)...... 150
Feversham (D3)...... 200
Field (E1)...... 372
Finch (J2)...... 389
Fingal (C5)...... 350
Fisherville (E5)...... 200
Fitzroy Harbour (H2)...... 150
Fitzwilliam (isl.) (C2)......
Flanders (G5)...... 188
Flesherton (D3)...... 471
Florence (B5)...... 350
Flowerpot (isl.) (C2)
Foleyet (J5)...... 500
Fonthill (E4)......1,845
Fordwich (C4)...... 400
Forest (C4)......2,035
Forest Hill (J4)......19,480
Foresters Falls (H2)...... 150
Formosa (C3)...... 300
Fort Erie (E5)......8,632
Fort Frances ◉(F5) 9,005
Fort William (G5) 39,464
Fort William-Pt. Arthur (Metropolitan Area) (G5)......83,597

Fournier (K2)...... 250
Foxboro (G3)...... 319
Frankford (G3)......1,491
Franktown (H2)...... 100
Fraserdale (J5)...... 150
French (riv.) (D1).
Galetta (H2)...... 177
Galt (D4)......23,738
Gananoque (H3)......4,981
Gelert (F3)...... 200
Georgetown (E4)......5,942
Georgian (bay) (D2)
Georgian Bay Is. Nat'l Park (D3)..
Geraldton (H5)......3,263
Glammis (C3)...... 150
Glen Huron (D3)...... 95
Glen Robertson (K2)...... 560
Glen Williams (D4) 394
Glencoe (C5)......1,044
Goderich ◉(C4)......5,886
Gogama (J5)...... 500
Golden Lake (G2).. 100
Gooderham (F3)...... 100
Goodwood (E3)...... 333
Gore Bay ◉(B2)...... 731
Gormley (J3)...... 75
Gorrie (C4)...... 500
Goudreau (J5)...... 135
Grafton (G4)...... 430
Grand (riv.) (D4)..
Grand Bend (C4) ... 939
Grand Valley (D4). 655
Granton (C4)...... 306
Gravenhurst (E4)......3,014
Grimsby (E4)......3,805
Guelph ◉(D4)......33,860
Guelph (Metropolitan Area) (D4)......36,641
Hagersville (D5)......1,964
Haileybury (K5)......2,654
Haley Sta. (H2)...... 300
Haliburton (F2)...... 983
Haliburton (lake) (F2)......
Hamilton ◉(E4)..239,625
Hamilton (Metropolitan Area) (E4)......325,579
Hammond (J2)...... 200
Hampton (F4)...... 233
Hanover (C3)......3,943
Harriston (D4)......1,592
Harrow (B5)......1,851
Harrowsmith (H3).. 400
Harty (J5)...... 200
Harwood (F3)...... 190
Hastings (G3)...... 816
Hatchley (D4)...... 100
Havelock (G3)......1,205
Hawk Jct. (J5)...... 195
Hawkesbury (K2)...7,929
Hawkestone (E3)...... 195
Hearst (J5)......2,214
Heathcote (D3)...... 100
Hensall (C4)...... 829
Hepworth (C3)...... 356
Heron Bay (H5)...... 175
Hespeler (D4)......3,876
Hickson (D4)...... 250
Highgate (C5)...... 378
Highland Creek (K4)......1,200
Hillsburgh (D4)...... 500
Hillsdale (E3)...... 413
Holland Centre (D3)...... 300
Holland Landing (E3)...... 326
Holstein (D3)...... 300
Hornepayne (J4)......1,400
Hornings Mills (D3)...... 311
Hudson (G4)...... 700
Huntsville (E2)......3,051
Hurd (cape) (C2)...
Huron (lake) (B3)..
Hyde Park (C4)...... 200
Ignace (G5)...... 300
Ilderton (C4)...... 190
Ingersoll (C4)......6,811
Inglewood (E4)...... 400
Inkerman (J2)...... 250
Innerkip (D4)...... 335
Inwood (C5)...... 395
Iona (C5)...... 100
Ipperwash Prov. Park (C4)......
Iroquois (J3)...... 1,078
Iroquois Falls (K5).1,478
Islington (J4)......2,735
Ivanhoe (G3)...... 130
Jamestown (H5)......1,400
Jarvis (D5)...... 733
Jasper (J3)...... 300
Jeannettes Creek (B5)...... 138
Jellicoe (H5)...... 344
Joseph (lake) (E2).
Kagawong (B2)...... 200
Kakabeka Falls (G5) 422
Kaladar (H3)...... 200
Kaministikwia (G5) 120
Kapuskasing (J5)......5,463
Kapuskasing (riv.) (J5)......
Kearney (E2)...... 454
Keene (F3)...... 333
Keewatin (F5)......1,949
Kemptville (J2)......1,730
Kenilworth (D4)...... 200
Kenmore (J2)...... 200
Kenogami (riv.) (H4)
Kenora ◉(F4)......10,278
Kent Bridge (B5)...... 166
Kerwood (C5)...... 166
Keswick (E3)...... 248
Killaloe Sta. (G2)... 854
Kimberley (D3)...... 200
Kinburn (H2)...... 174
Kincardine (C3)......2,667
King City (J3)...... 530
Kingston ◉ (H3)......48,618

Kingston (Metropolitan Area) (H3)......57,600
Kingsville (B5)......2,884
Kinmount (F3)...... 488
Kippen (C4)...... 112
Kirkfield (E3)...... 412
Kirkland Lake (K5)......18,459
Kitchener ◉(D4)...59,562
Kitchener (Metropolitan Area) (D4)......79,429
Kleinburg (J4)...... 227
Komoka (C5)...... 188
La Passe (H2)...... 137
La Salle (A5)......2,703
Lake of the Woods (lake) (F5)......
Lake Superior Prov. Park (J5)......
Lakefield (F3)......1,938
Lakeport (G4)...... 200
Lakeview (J4)......1,400
L'Amable (G3)...... 88
Lambeth (C5)...... 333
Lanark (H2)...... 871
Lancaster (K2)...... 594
Lansdowne (H3)...... 490
Lansing (J4)......4,000
Latchford (K5)...... 508
Laurel (D4)...... 130
Leamington (B5)......7,856
Leaside (J4)......16,538
Lefaivre (K2)...... 200
Levack (J5)......2,929
Limoges (J2)...... 329
Lindsay ◉(F3)......10,110
Linwood (D4)...... 503
Lion's Head (C2)...... 413
Listowel (D4)......3,644
Little Britain (F3)... 300
Little Current (B2).1,514
Lloydtown (J3)...... 200
Lochalsh (J5)...... 300
Lombardy (H3)...... 125
London ◉(C5)......101,693
London (Metropolitan Area) (C5)......153,491
Long (point) (D5).
Long Branch (J4).10,249
Longford Mills (E3) 360
Longlac (H5)...... 250
L'Original ◉(K2)......1,067
Loring (D2)...... 200
Lorne Park (J4)...... 540
Low Bush River (K5)...... 150
Lucan (C4)...... 924
Lucknow (C4)...... 908
Lyn (J3)...... 255
Lynden (D4)...... 500
Lyndhurst (H3)...... 295
Mac Tier (E2)...... 500
Madawaska (F2)...... 400
Madawaska (riv.) (G2)......
Madoc (G3)......1,325
Magnetawan (E2)...... 197
Maidstone (B5)...... 190
Mallorytown (J3)...... 300
Malton (J4)......1,500
Malvern (J4)...... 175
Manitouwadge (H5)
Manitoulin (isl.) (B2)
Manitowaning (C2). 726
Manotick (J2)...... 500
Maple (J4)...... 400
Marathon (H5)......3,500
Markdale (D3)...... 986
Markham (K4)......2,873
Markstay (D1)...... 375
Marlbank (G3)...... 350
Marmora (G3)......1,428
Martintown (K2)...... 357
Massey (C1)......1,068
Matachewan (J5)......1,000
Matheson (K5)...... 758
Mattagami (riv.) (J5)
Mattawa (F1)......3,208
Mattice (J5)...... 225
Maxville (K2)...... 782
Maynooth (G2)...... 290
Mc Gregor (B5)...... 175
Mc Kellar (D2)...... 697
Mc Kerrow (C1)...... 190
Meadowvale (J4)...... 150
Meaford (D3)......3,643
Melbourne (C5)...... 360
Merlin (B5)...... 500
Merrickville (J3)...... 859
Merritton (E4)......5,404
Metcalfe (J2)...... 400
Michipicoten (isl.) (H5)......
Michipicoten Harbour (H5)...... 164
Middleville (H2)...... 192
Midhurst (E3)...... 166
Midland (D3)......8,250
Mildmay (C3)...... 860
Mill Bridge (G3)...... 150
Millbank (D4)...... 450
Millbrook (F3)...... 807
Mille Lacs (lake) (G5)......
Mille Roches (K2).. 729
Milton West ◉(E4).4,294
Milverton (C4)......1,070
Mimico (J4)......13,687
Minaki (F4)...... 150
Minden ◉(F3)...... 600
Missinaibi (riv.) (J5)
Mississagi (str.) (A2)
Mississippi (lake) H2)......
Mississippi Station (H3)...... 88
Mitchell (C4)......2,146
Monkton (C4)...... 350
Moonbeam (J5)...... 500
Moorefield (D4)...... 400
Moose Creek (K2).. 600
Morewood (J2)...... 195

Morpeth (C5)...... 200
Morrisburg (J3)......2,131
Morton (H3)...... 109
Moulinette (K2)...... 250
Mount Albert (E3). 600
Mount Brydges (C5)...... 577
Mount Dennis (J4).9,000
Mount Forest (D4).2,438
Mount Pleasant (D4)...... 300
Mountain Grove (H3)...... 200
Muncey (C5)...... 83
Muskoka (lake) (E2)...... 130
Myrtle (E3)...... 130
Nakina (H4)...... 500
Nanticoke (E5)...... 100
Napanee ◉(G3)......4,273
Neustadt (D3)...... 490
New Hamburg (D4)......1,939
New Liskeard (K5).4,619
New Lowell (E3)...... 300
New Toronto (J4).11,560
Newboro (H3)...... 270
Newburgh (H3)...... 603
Newbury (C5)...... 331
Newcastle (F3)......1,098
Newington (K2)...... 300
Newmarket (E3)......7,368
Newtonbrook (J4)..1,500
Newtonville (F4)...... 733
Niagara (riv.) (E4).
Niagara Falls (E4) 23,563
Niagara-on-the-Lake (E4)......2,740
Nipigon (H5)...... 700
Nipigon (lake) (H5)
Nipissing (lake) (E1)
Nobel (D2)...... 600
Nobleton (J3)...... 200
Noelville (D1)...... 200
North (chanl.) (A1)
North Augusta (J3).. 500
North Bay ◉(E1).21,020
North Gower (J2).. 469
Norval (E4)...... 300
Norwich (D5)......1,611
Norwood (F3)......1,017
Nottawa (D3)...... 211
Nottawasaga (bay) (D3)......
Novar (E2)...... 250
Oak Ridges (J3)...... 150
Oakville (E4)......9,983
Oakwood (F3)...... 250
Odessa (H3)...... 600
Oil City (B5)...... 175
Oil Springs (B5)...... 481
Omemee (F3)...... 837
Ontario (lake) (G4)
Opeongo (lake) (F2)
Orangeville ◉(D4)..3,887
Orillia (E3)......13,857
Orono (F4)...... 800
Osgoode Sta. (J2).. 390
Oshawa (F4)......50,412
Oshawa (Metropolitan Area) (F4)......64,428
OTTAWA (J2)......222,129
Ottawa (Metropolitan Area) (J2)......335,507
Ottawa (riv.) (H2)..
Otterville (D5)...... 500
Owen Sound ◉ (D3)......16,976
Oxford Mills (J3)... 225
Paisley (C3)...... 730
Pakenham (H2)...... 500
Palmerston (D4)......1,550
Paris (D4)......5,504
Park Hill (C4)......1,043
Parry (isl.) (D2)......
Parry Sound ◉(E2).5,378
Pefferlaw (E3)...... 184
Pelée (point) (B5)..
Pembroke ◉(G2)..15,434
Penetanguishene (D3)......5,420
Perth ◉(H3)......5,145
Petawawa (G2)...... 300
Peterborough ◉ (F3)......42,698
Peterborough (Metropolitan Area) (F3)......45,410
Petrolia (B5)......3,426
Pickering (K4)......1,150
Picton ◉(G3)......4,998
Plantagenet (J2)...... 583
Plattsville (D4)...... 700
Point Edward (B4).2,558
Point Pelée Nat'l Park (B5)......
Pointe-au-Baril (D2) 200
Pointe-aux-Roches (B5)...... 240
Pontypool (F3)...... 190
Porcupine (J5)...... 500
Port Arthur ◉ (H5)......38,136
Port Arthur-Ft. William (Metropolitan Area) (H5)......83,597
Port Burwell (D5)... 722
Port Carling (E2)...... 510
Port Colborne (E5) 14,028
Port Credit (J4)......6,350
Port Dalhousie (E4) 3,087
Port Dover (D5)......2,790
Port Elgin (C3)......1,558
Port Hope ◉(F4)......7,522
Port Lambton (B5). 300
Port Maitland (E5) 150
Port McNicoll (E3) 932
Port Perry (E3)......2,121
Port Rowan (D5)...... 766
Port Stanley (C5)......1,480
Port Sydney (E2)...... 185
Port Union (K4)...... 500

Portland (H3)...... 250
Powassan (E1)...... 935
Prescott ◉(J3)......4,920
Preston (D4)......9,387
Priceville (D3) ......231
Princeton (D4)...... 450
Proton Station (D3) 130
Providence Bay (B2)...... 350
Queensborough (G3)...... 188
Quetico Prov. Park (G5)......
Quibell (F4)...... 170
Rainy (lake) (G5)...
Rainy River (F5)......1,354
Red Rock (H5)......1,200
Redditt (F4)...... 300
Renfrew (H2)......8,634
Rice (lake) (F3)......
Richmond (J2)...... 772
Richmond Hill (J4)......6,677
Rideau (lake) (H3).
Rideau (riv.) (J2)...
Ridgetown (C5)......2,483
Ridgeway (E5)...... 864
Ripley (C3)...... 450
Riverside (B5)......13,325
Rockland (J2)......2,757
Rockcliffe Park (H2)......2,097
Rockport (J3)...... 200
Rockwood (D4)...... 600
Rodney (C5)......1,026
Rondeau Prov. Park (C5)......
Roseneath (G3)...... 200
Rosseau (E2)...... 223
Rosseau (lake) (E2)
Rossport (H5)...... 190
Rostock (C4)...... 100
Russell (J2)...... 600
Rutherglen (F1)...... 300
Ruthven (B5)...... 275
Saint Albert (J2)...... 222
Saint Catharines ◉ (E4)......39,708
Saint Catharines (Metropolitan Area) (E4)......84,493
Saint Clair (lake) (B5)......
Saint Clair (riv.) (B5)
Saint Clair Beach (B5)...... 831
Saint Davids (F4)... 250
Saint Eugene (K2).. 791
Saint George (D4)... 569
Saint Isidore (K2)... 450
Saint Jacobs (D4)...... 548
Saint Lawrence (riv.) (J3)......
Saint Marys (C4)......4,185
Saint Thomas ◉ (C5)......19,129
Saint Williams (D5) 377
Sainte Anne de Prescott (K2)...... 250
Salem (D4)...... 244
Salford (D4)...... 150
Sarnia ◉(B5)......43,447
Sarnia (Metropolitan Area) (B5)......52,493
Saugeen (riv.) (C3).
Sault Sainte Marie ◉ (J5)......37,329
Sault Ste. Marie (Metropolitan Area) (J5)......50,436
Savant Lake (G4)...... 97
Scarborough Village (K4)......
Scarborough Bluffs (K4)......1,475
Schreiber (H5)......1,850
Schumacher (K5)......3,002
Scotia (E2)...... 98
Scotland (D4)...... 444
Scugog (lake) (F3).
Seaforth (C4)......2,128
Sebringville (C4)...... 546
Seeleys Bay (H3)...... 285
Selkirk (E5)...... 421
Seul (lake) (G4)......
Severn (riv.) (E3)...
Severn Bridge (E3). 333
Shallow Lake (C3).. 366
Shannonville (G3)... 237
Sharbot Lake (H3). 533
Shedden (C5)...... 209
Sheguiandah (C2)... 250
Shelburne (D3)......1,245
Simcoe ◉(D5)......8,078
Simcoe (lake) (E3).
Singhampton (D3)... 177
Sioux Lookout (G4)......2,504
Smiths Falls (H3)...8,967
Smithville (E4)...... 754
Smooth Rock Falls (J5)......1,104
Sombra (B5)...... 388
South Mountain (J3)...... 278
South Porcupine (K5)......5,618
South River (E2)...... 995
Southampton (C3)..1,640
Spanish (B1)...... 194
Spanish (riv.) (C1)
Sparta (C5)...... 330
Spencerville (J3)...... 400
Spring Brook (G3).. 200
Springfield (C5)...... 482
Sprucedale (E2)...... 266
Stayner (E3)......1,429
Steep Rock Lake (G5)......1,450
Stella (H3)...... 200
Stirling (G3)......1,191
Stittsville (J2)...... 250
Stonecliffe (F1)...... 189
Stoney Creek (E4)..4,506
Stony (lake) (G3)...

Stouffville (J3)......2,307
Straffordville (D5).. 267
Stratford ◉(C4)......19,972
Strathroy (C5)......4,240
Stratton (F5)...... 450
Streetsville (J4)......2,643
Sturgeon Falls (D1).5,874
Sudbury ◉(C1)......46,482
Sudbury (Metropolitan Area) (C1)......93,755
Sulphide (G3)...... 198
Sultan (J5)...... 125
Sunderland (E3)...... 793
Sundridge (E2)...... 697
Superior (lake) (H5)
Sutton West (E3)......1,310
Swansea (J4)......8,595
Swastika (K5)...... 935
Sydenham (H3)...... 550
Tamworth (H3)...... 500
Tara (C3)...... 515
Tavistock (D4)......1,155
Tecumseh (B5)......4,177
Teeswater (C3)...... 852
Terrace Bay (H5).... 600
Thames (riv.) (B5).
Thamesford (C4)...... 500
Thamesville (C5)......1,074
Thedford (C4)...... 717
Thessalon (J5)......1,716
Thornbury (D3)......1,037
Thorndale (C4)...... 290
Thornhill (J4)...... 850
Thornton (E3)...... 288
Thorold (E4)......8,053
Thousand (isls.) (H3)
Tillbury (B5)......3,138
Tillsonburg (D5)......6,216
Timagami (K5)...... 500
Timagami (lake) (K5)......
Timmins (J5)......27,551
Tiverton (C3)...... 252
Tobermory (C2)...... 400
Toledo (H3)...... 275
TORONTO (K4).667,706
Toronto (Metropolitan Area) (K4)..1,347,905
Tottenham (E3)...... 702
Trenton (G3)......11,492
Trout Creek (E2).... 389
Tweed (G3)......1,634
Tyrone (F3)...... 145
Underwood (C3)...... 250
Unionville (K4)...... 565
Upsala (G5)...... 190
Utterson (E2)...... 300
Uxbridge (E3)......2,065
Vankleek Hill (K2) 1,647
Varney (D3)...... 100
Vars (J2)...... 300
Vermillion Bay (G4) 98
Verner (D1)...... 800
Vernon (J2)...... 200
Vernon (lake) (E2).
Verona (H3)...... 275
Victoria Harbour (E3)......1,012
Victoria Road (F3). 228
Vienna (D5)...... 362
Vineland (E4)...... 475
Vittoria (D5)...... 300
Wahnapitae (D1)...... 269
Wales (K2)...... 250
Walford Sta. (B1)... 140
Walkerton ◉(C3)......3,698
Wallaceburg (B5)......7,892
Walters Falls (D3).. 193
Walton (C4)...... 200
Wanup (D1)...... 133
Wardsville (C5)...... 318
Warren (D1)...... 500
Warsaw (F3)...... 233
Wasaga Beach (D3) 529
Washago (E3)...... 332
Waterdown (D4)......1,754
Waterford (D5)......1,908
Watford (C5)......1,217
Waterloo (D4)......16,373
Waubaushene (E3).. 557
Webbwood (C1)...... 500
Welland ◉(E4)......16,405
Wellesley (D4)...... 750
Wellington (G4)......1,077
West Hill (K4)......2,000
West Lorne (C5)......1,088
Westmeath (H2)...... 375
Weston (J4)......9,543
Westport (H3)...... 704
Wheatley (B5)......1,196
Whitby ◉(F4)......9,995
White Lake (H2)...... 150
White River (J5)...... 401
Whitefish (C1)...... 137
Whitney (F2)...... 247
Wiarton (C3)......1,954
Widdifield (E1)...... 96
Wikwemikong (C2). 452
Wilberforce (F3)...... 100
Williamsburg (J3)... 350
Williamstown (K2).. 531
Willowdale (J4)......9,500
Wilno (G2)...... 166
Winchester (J2)......1,338
Windermere (E2).... 158
Windsor ◉(B5)......121,980
Windsor (Metropolitan Area) (B5)......184,045
Wingham (C4)......2,766
Wolfe Island (H3).. 300
Woodbridge (J4)......1,958
Woodstock ◉(D4).18,347
Woodville (F3)...... 406
Wooler (G3)...... 250
Worthington (C1).... 150
Wroxeter (C4)...... 437
Wyevale (E3)...... 145
Wyoming (B5)...... 792
Yarker (H3)...... 365
York (E4)...... 150
Zephyr (E3)...... 150
Zurich (C4)...... 549

◉County Seat

## MANITOBA

## 1956 Total Population 850,040

Aikens (lake) (G3).
Alexander (B5)...... 500
Alexander Slough (marsh) (B5)......
Allegra (F4)...... 10
Alonsa (C4)...... 132
Altamont (D5)...... 125
Altona (E5)......1,698
Amaranth (D4)...... 100
Amery (J2)...... 25
Anderson (lake) (D2)......
Angusville (A4)...... 452
Anola (F5)......
Arbakka (F5)......
Arborg (E4)...... 450
Arden (C4)...... 300
Argyle (E4)...... 100
Armit (lake) (A2)...
Arnaud (E5)...... 590
Arnes (E4)...... 10
Arrow River (B4).... 150
Ashern (D3)...... 333
Ashville (B3)...... 20
Assapan (riv.) (G2)
Assiniboine (riv.) (C5)......
Assinika (lake) (G2)

| | |
|---|---|
| Aubigny (E5) | 150 |
| Austin (D5) | 300 |
| Badger (G5) | 110 |
| Bagot (D5) | 100 |
| Baldur (C5) | 550 |
| Balmoral (E4) | 200 |
| Balsam Bay (F4) | 100 |
| Bannerman (C5) | 118 |
| Baralzon (lake) (J1) | |
| Barkfield (F5) | |
| Barrows (A2) | |
| Basket (lake) (C3) | |
| Basswood (B4) | 144 |
| Bayton (D3) | |
| Beaconia (F4) | |
| Beauséjour (F4) | 1,523 |
| Beaver (D4) | |
| Beaverhill (lake) (J3) | |
| Bede (B5) | |
| Belair (F4) | |
| Belleview (B5) | |
| Bellhampton (C4) | |
| Bellsite (A2) | 300 |
| Belmont (C5) | 350 |
| Bénard (E5) | |
| Benito (A3) | 487 |
| Berens (isl.) (E2) | |
| Berens (riv.) (F2) | |
| Berens River (F2) | 200 |
| Beresford (B5) | 55 |
| Beresford Lake (G4) | |
| Berlo (E4) | |
| Bethany (C4) | 133 |
| Bethel (C4) | |
| Beulah (A4) | 74 |
| Bield (A3) | |
| Big Stone (point) (E2) | |
| Bigstone (riv.) (J3) | |
| Binscarth (A4) | 452 |
| Birch (isl.) (C2) | |
| Birch Bay (D3) | |
| Birch River (A2) | 273 |
| Birchview (B3) | |
| Bird River (G4) | |
| Birds Hill (F4) | 190 |
| Birdtail (B4) | |
| Birnie (C4) | 97 |
| Birtle (B4) | 806 |
| Bissett (G4) | 250 |
| Black (isl.) (F3) | |
| Bloodvein (riv.) (F3) | |
| Bluewing (A3) | |
| Bluff Creek (D4) | |
| Bodhan (B3) | |
| Boggy Creek (A3) | 350 |
| Boissevain (C5) | 1,115 |
| Bonnet (lake) (G4) | |
| Bonnie Doon (D4) | |
| Bowsman (A2) | 519 |
| Bradwardine (B5) | 100 |
| Brandon (C5) | 24,796 |
| Brightstone (F4) | |
| Broad Valley (E3) | 150 |
| Brochet (H2) | 100 |
| Brokenhead (F4) | |
| Brookdale (C4) | 100 |
| Broomhill (B5) | 30 |
| Brunkild (E5) | 77 |
| Bruxelles (C5) | 150 |
| Buchan (F4) | |
| Buffalo (bay) (G5) | |
| Bunclody (B5) | 12 |
| Burntwood (riv.) (J2) | |
| Butler (A5) | 32 |
| Caliento (F5) | |
| Camp Morton (F4) | 350 |
| Camper (D3) | 30 |
| Camperville (B2) | 25 |
| Carberry (C5) | 1,065 |
| Cardale (B4) | 77 |
| Cardinal (D5) | 117 |
| Carey (E5) | 47 |
| Carlowrie (E5) | 50 |
| Carman (D5) | 1,884 |
| Carnegie (B5) | |
| Carroll (B5) | 88 |
| Carroll (lake) (G3) | |
| Cartwright (C5) | 459 |
| Castle Point (C5) | 16 |
| Cayer (D3) | |
| Cedar (lake) (B1) | |
| Channel (isl.) (B2) | |
| Channing (H3) | |
| Charron (lake) (G2) | |
| Chater (C5) | 44 |
| Chatfield (E4) | 100 |
| Childs (lake) (A3) | |
| Chitek (lake) (C2) | |
| Chortitz (F5) | 150 |
| Churchill (K2) | 500 |
| Churchill (cape) (K2) | |
| Churchill (riv.) (J2) | |
| Clandeboye (E4) | |
| Clanwilliam (C4) | 188 |
| Clarkleigh (D4) | |
| Clear (lake) (C4) | |
| Clearwater (D5) | 500 |
| Clematis (E4) | |
| Cloverleaf (F5) | |
| Cochrane (riv.) (H2) | |
| Commissioner (isl.) (E3) | |
| Cooks Creek (F4) | |
| Cordova (C4) | |
| Cormorant (H3) | |
| Cormorant (lake) (H3) | |
| Coulter (B5) | 48 |
| Cowan (B2) | |
| Cracknell (A4) | 10 |
| Cranberry Portage (H3) | 350 |
| Crandall (B4) | 190 |
| Crane River (C3) | 750 |
| Crocus (C4) | |
| Croll (B5) | |
| Cromer (A5) | 88 |
| Cross (lake) (C1) | |
| Cross (lake) (J3) | |
| Crow Duck (lake) (G4) | |
| Crystal City (C5) | 505 |
| Culross (E5) | |
| Cypress River (D5) | 505 |
| Dallas (E3) | 480 |
| Dand (B5) | 20 |
| Darlingford (D5) | 190 |
| Dauphin (B3) | 6,190 |
| Dauphin (lake) (C3) | |
| Davis Point (D3) | |
| Dawson (bay) (B2) | |
| Decimal (G5) | |
| Decker (B4) | 95 |
| Deepdale (A3) | 77 |
| Deer Horn (E4) | |
| Deerwood (D5) | |
| Deleau (B5) | 188 |
| Deloraine (B5) | 900 |
| Delta Station (D4) | 70 |
| Dennis (lake) (E4) | |
| Desford (C5) | |
| Dog (lake) (D3) | |
| Dogskin (lake) (G3) | |
| Domain (E5) | 47 |
| Dominion City (E5) | 700 |
| Douglas Sta. (C5) | 150 |
| Drifting River (B3) | |
| Dropmore (A3) | 47 |
| Dry River (C5) | |
| Duck (mt.) (B3) | |
| Duck River (B3) | 73 |
| Dufresne (F5) | |
| Dufrost (E5) | 150 |
| Dunnottar (E4) | 178 |
| Dunrea (C5) | 250 |
| Durban (A3) | 77 |
| Eardley (lake) (F2) | |
| East Bay (C3) | |
| East Braintree (G5) | |
| East Selkirk (F4) | 390 |
| East Shoal (lake) (E4) | |
| Ebb and Flow (lake) (C3) | |
| Ebor (A5) | 25 |
| Eddystone (C3) | |
| Eden (C4) | 175 |
| Edrans (C4) | 67 |
| Edwin (D5) | |
| Egg (isl.) (E3) | |
| Ekhart (E4) | |
| Elbow (lake) (G4) | |
| Elgin (B5) | 400 |
| Elie (E5) | 150 |
| Elk (isl.) (F4) | |
| Elk Ranch (C4) | |
| Elkhorn (A5) | 673 |
| Elliot (lake) (G2) | |
| Elm Creek (E5) | 400 |
| Elphinstone (B4) | 275 |
| Elva (A5) | 97 |
| Emerson (E5) | 896 |
| Endcliffe (A4) | |
| Erickson (C4) | 488 |
| Eriksdale (D4) | 260 |
| Erinview (E4) | |
| Etawney (lake) (J2) | |
| Ethelbert (B3) | 505 |
| Ewart (A5) | |
| Fairfax (B5) | 63 |
| Fairford (D3) | 25 |
| Falcon (lake) (G5) | |
| Fallison (D5) | |
| Family (lake) (G3) | |
| Fannystelle (E5) | 166 |
| Faulkner (D3) | |
| Findlay (B5) | 25 |
| Firdale (C5) | |
| Fisher (bay) (E3) | |
| Fisher Branch (E3) | 637 |
| Fisherton (E3) | |
| Fishing (lake) (G2) | |
| Fishing River (C3) | |
| Flin Flon (H3) | 10,234 |
| Flintstone (lake) (G4) | |
| Foley (E4) | |
| Fork River (B3) | 174 |
| Forrest Station (C5) | 66 |
| Fort Alexander (F4) | 1,000 |
| Fort Garry (E5) | 1,485 |
| Fort Whyte (E5) | 800 |
| Fortier (E5) | |
| Fox (riv.) (K2) | |
| Foxwarren (A4) | 270 |
| Franklin (C4) | 166 |
| Fraserwood (E4) | 94 |
| Gammon (riv.) (G3) | |
| Gardenton (F5) | 500 |
| Garland (B3) | |
| Garner (lake) (G4) | |
| Garson (F4) | 277 |
| Geillini (lake) (J1) | |
| Gem (lake) (G4) | |
| Genthon (F5) | 150 |
| George (isl.) (E2) | |
| George (lake) (G4) | |
| Geyser (E4) | |
| Gilbert Plains (B3) | 859 |
| Gilchrist (lake) (G2) | |
| Gillam (K2) | 95 |
| Gimli (F4) | 1,660 |
| Giroux (F5) | 95 |
| Gladstone (D4) | 882 |
| Glen Elmo (B4) | |
| Glen Souris (C5) | |
| Glenboro (C5) | 765 |
| Glencairn (C4) | |
| Glenella (C4) | 195 |
| Glenhope (C4) | |
| Glenlea (E5) | 22 |
| Glenora (C5) | 35 |
| Gods (lake) (K3) | |
| Gods (riv.) (K3) | |
| God's Lake (J3) | 200 |
| Golden Stream (D4) | |
| Gonor (F4) | |
| Goodlands (B5) | 120 |
| Grahamdale (D3) | |
| Grand Beach (F4) | |
| Grand Marais (F4) | |
| Grand Rapids (C1) | 300 |
| Grand View (B3) | 963 |
| Grande Clairière (B5) | |
| Granville (lake) (H2) | |
| Grass (riv.) (J3) | |
| Grass River (D4) | |
| Graysville (D5) | 115 |
| Great Falls (F4) | 150 |
| Green Ridge (F5) | |
| Greenwald (F4) | |
| Greenway (C5) | 133 |
| Gregg (C5) | 36 |
| Gretna (E5) | 603 |
| Grifton (B3) | |
| Griswold (B5) | 200 |
| Grosse Isle (E4) | 63 |
| Grunthal (F5) | 870 |
| Gunton (E4) | 178 |
| Guynemer (C3) | |
| Gypsum (lake) (D3) | |
| Gypsumville (D3) | 212 |
| Hadashville (G5) | |
| Halbstadt (E5) | 450 |
| Halicz (B3) | |
| Hallboro (C4) | 86 |
| Hamiota (B4) | 690 |
| Hamrlik (E4) | |
| Harcus (D4) | 20 |
| Harding (B5) | 67 |
| Hargrave (A5) | 75 |
| Harlington (A2) | |
| Harmsworth (B5) | |
| Harperville (E4) | |
| Harrop (lake) (G2) | |
| Harrowby (A4) | 70 |
| Harte (C4) | |
| Hartney (B5) | 554 |
| Harwill (E3) | |
| Haskett (E5) | 72 |
| Hayes (riv.) (K3) | |
| Hayfield (B5) | 87 |
| Hayland (D3) | |
| Haywood (D5) | 134 |
| Hazelridge (F5) | 95 |
| Heaslip Sta. (C5) | |
| Hecla (F3) | 300 |
| Hecla (isl.) (F3) | |
| Helston (C4) | |
| Herb Lake (H3) | 225 |
| High Bluff (D4) | 96 |
| Hilbre (D3) | |
| Hillside Beach (F4) | |
| Hilltop (C4) | |
| Hilton (C5) | |
| Hnausa (F4) | 250 |
| Hodgson (E3) | 600 |
| Holland (D5) | 361 |
| Holmfield (C5) | 175 |
| Homebrook (C3) | |
| Homewood (E5) | 63 |
| Horndean (E5) | |
| Horod (B4) | |
| Horseshoe (lake) (G2) | |
| Horton (B5) | 12 |
| Hubbart (point) (K2) | |
| Hudson (bay) (K2) | |
| Hudwin (lake) (G1) | |
| Husavick (F4) | |
| Ideal (E4) | |
| Ile des Chênes (F5) | |
| Ilford (J2) | 97 |
| Indian Bay (G5) | |
| Indian Springs (D5) | |
| Ingelow (C5) | |
| Inglis (A4) | 212 |
| Inland (lake) (C2) | |
| International Peace Garden (B5) | |
| Inwood (E4) | 95 |
| Isabella (B4) | 86 |
| Island (lake) (K3) | |
| Janow (G5) | 230 |
| Jaroslaw (F4) | |
| Julius (F5) | 54 |
| Justice (C4) | 45 |
| Kaleida (D5) | |
| Kane (E5) | |
| Katimik (lake) (C2) | |
| Katrime (D4) | |
| Kawinaw (lake) (C2) | |
| Kazanjerri (lake) (H2) | |
| Kelloe (B4) | 86 |
| Kelwood (C4) | 222 |
| Kemnay (B5) | 66 |
| Kenton (B5) | 126 |
| Kenville (A3) | 139 |
| Kergwenan (C4) | |
| Keyes (C4) | 64 |
| Killarney (C5) | 1,434 |
| Kinosota (D4) | |
| Kinwow (bay) (E2) | |
| Kirkella (A4) | 65 |
| Kississing (H3) | 500 |
| Kississing (lake) (H2) | |
| Kleefeld (F5) | 625 |
| Knee (lake) (J3) | |
| Komarno (E4) | 133 |
| Koostatak (E3) | |
| Kulish (B3) | |
| La Broquerie (F5) | 800 |
| La Rivière (D5) | 256 |
| La Rochelle (F5) | 120 |
| La Salle (E5) | 99 |
| Lac du Bonnet (G4) | 523 |
| Ladywood (F4) | 25 |
| Lake Francis (E4) | |
| Lake of the Woods (lake) (H5) | |
| Lakeland (D4) | |
| Landseer (C5) | 8 |
| Langruth (D4) | 150 |
| Lauder (B5) | 184 |
| Laurie (lake) (A3) | |
| Laurier (C4) | 225 |
| Lavenham (D5) | |
| Lavinia (B4) | |
| Layland (D5) | |
| Learys (D5) | |
| Ledwyn (E4) | |
| Lena (C5) | 25 |
| Lennard (A3) | |
| Lenore (B5) | 166 |
| Lenswood (B2) | 300 |
| Letellier (E5) | 772 |
| Lettonia (G4) | |
| Lewis (F5) | |
| Lewis (lake) (G2) | |
| Libau (F4) | 162 |
| Lillesve (E4) | |
| Lily Bay (D4) | |
| Little Bullhead (F3) | |
| Loch Monar (E4) | |
| Lockport (E4) | 250 |
| Lonely (lake) (C3) | |
| Lonely Lake (D3) | |
| Long (lake) (G4) | |
| Long (point) (D1) | |
| Long (point) (D4) | |
| Lorette (F5) | 500 |
| Lowe Farm (E5) | 150 |
| Lundar (D4) | 800 |
| Lydiatt (F5) | 50 |
| Lyleton (A5) | 150 |
| Lynn Lake (H2) | 1,700 |
| Macdonald (D4) | 200 |
| MacGregor (D5) | 611 |
| Macross (D4) | |
| Mafeking (B2) | 278 |
| Magnet (C3) | 50 |
| Makaroff (A3) | 25 |
| Makinak (C4) | 130 |
| Malonton (E4) | 55 |
| Manigotagan (F3) | |
| Manigotagan (lake) (G4) | |
| Manitoba (lake) (D4) | |
| Manitou (D5) | 795 |
| Manson (A4) | 30 |
| Mantagao (riv.) (E3) | |
| Marchand (F5) | 96 |
| Marco (B4) | |
| Margaret (C5) | 70 |
| Mariapolis (C5) | 100 |
| Marius (D4) | 800 |
| Markland (E4) | |
| Marquette (E4) | 50 |
| Marshy (lake) (B5) | |
| Mather (C5) | 150 |
| Matheson Island (E3) | 150 |
| Matlock (F4) | 500 |
| Mayfeld (C4) | |
| Mc Auley (A4) | 158 |
| Mc Connell (B4) | 65 |
| Mc Creary (C4) | 365 |
| Mc Kay (lake) (C2) | |
| Mc Munn (G5) | |
| Mc Phail (riv.) (F2) | |
| Mc Tavish (E5) | 139 |
| Meadow Portage (C3) | |
| Meadowlands (C3) | |
| Meadows (E4) | 65 |
| Mears (B4) | |
| Medika (G5) | 450 |
| Medora (B5) | 150 |
| Mekiwin (C4) | |
| Melbourne (C5) | 78 |
| Meleb (E4) | 97 |
| Melita (A5) | 926 |
| Melrose (F4) | 300 |
| Menisino (F5) | |
| Mentmore (C4) | 20 |
| Menzie (B4) | |
| Merridale (A3) | |
| Methley (C3) | |
| Methven (C5) | 50 |
| Miami (D5) | 390 |
| Middle Church (E5) | |
| Middlebro (G5) | |
| Million (C3) | |
| Millwood (A4) | |
| Milner Ridge (F4) | |
| Miniota (B4) | 300 |
| Minitonas (B2) | 663 |
| Mink Creek (B3) | |
| Minnedosa (B4) | 2,306 |
| Minnedosa (riv.) (B4) | |
| Minnewakan (D4) | |
| Minto (B5) | 175 |
| Moar (lake) (G2) | |
| Moline (B4) | |
| Molson (F4) | 95 |
| Molson (lake) (J3) | |
| Monominto (F5) | |
| Moore Dale (C3) | |
| Moorepark (C4) | 166 |
| Moose (isl.) (E3) | |
| Moose (lake) (H3) | |
| Moose Bay (C3) | |
| Moose Lake (H3) | |
| Moosehorn (D3) | 223 |
| Morden (D5) | 2,237 |
| Morris (E5) | 1,260 |
| Morrison (lake) (C1) | |
| Mossy (riv.) (C3) | |
| Mountain Road (C4) | |
| Mountainside (B5) | |
| Mowbray (D5) | 75 |
| Muir (D4) | |
| Mukutawa (riv.) (E1) | |
| Mulvihill (D4) | 169 |
| Myrtle (E5) | 110 |
| Napinka (B5) | 181 |
| Narcisse (E4) | |
| Narol (F4) | |
| National Mills (A2) | |
| Neelin (C5) | 86 |
| Neepawa (C4) | 3,109 |
| Nejanilini (lake) (J2) | |
| Nelson (riv.) (J2) | |
| Nesbitt (C5) | 100 |
| Netley (E4) | |
| Neveton (E4) | |
| Newdale (B4) | 350 |
| Newton Siding (D5) | |
| Ninette (C5) | 160 |
| Ninga (C5) | 300 |
| Niverville (F5) | 600 |
| Norgate (C4) | |
| North Birch (lake) (E3) | |
| North Indian (lake) (J2) | |
| North Shoal (lake) (E4) | |
| Norway House (J3) | 1,200 |
| Notre Dame de Lourdes (D5) | 400 |
| Novra (A2) | |
| Nueltin (lake) (J1) | |
| Oak (lake) (B5) | |
| Oak Brae (C3) | |
| Oak Island (lake) (E4) | |
| Oak Lake (B5) | 471 |
| Oak Point (D4) | 138 |
| Oak River (B4) | 175 |
| Oakbank (F5) | 150 |
| Oakburn (B4) | 266 |
| Oakland (D4) | 10 |
| Oakner (B4) | 120 |
| Oakview (D3) | |
| Oakville (D5) | 190 |
| Oatfield (D4) | |
| Oberon (C4) | 10 |
| Obukowin (lake) (G3) | |
| Ochre River (C3) | 300 |
| Ogilvie (D4) | 20 |
| Oiseau (riv.) (G4) | |
| Olha (B4) | |
| Onanole (C4) | 210 |
| Osborne (E5) | |
| Ostenfeld (F5) | |
| Otterburne (E5) | 335 |
| Otto (E4) | |
| Overflowing (riv.) (A1) | |
| Overton (D4) | |
| Owl (riv.) (K2) | |
| Oxford (lake) (J3) | |
| Ozerna (B4) | |
| Paint (lake) (J2) | |
| Palsen (riv.) (G2) | |
| Pebble Beach (D3) | |
| Peguis (F4) | |
| Pelican (lake) (B2) | |
| Pelican (lake) (C5) | |
| Pelican Rapids (B2) | |
| Pembina (mt.) (D5) | |
| Pembina (riv.) (C5) | |
| Peonan (pen.) (D3) | |
| Petersfield (E4) | 200 |
| Petlura (B3) | |
| Petrel (C5) | |
| Pettapiece (M4) | 30 |
| Pickerel (lake) (C2) | |
| Pierson (A5) | 200 |
| Pigeon (riv.) (F2) | |
| Pikwitonei (J3) | 150 |
| Pilot Mound (D5) | 785 |
| Pinawa (G4) | 75 |
| Pine Falls (F4) | 600 |
| Pine River (B3) | 150 |
| Pine View (D4) | |
| Piney (F5) | 350 |
| Pipestone (B5) | 230 |
| Pipestone (creek) (A5) | |
| Pleasant Home (E4) | |
| Plum (lake) (B5) | |
| Plum Coulee (E5) | 498 |
| Plumas (D4) | 300 |
| Pointe du Bois (G4) | 222 |
| Polonia (C4) | |
| Pope (B4) | 50 |
| Poplar (point) (E2) | |
| Poplar Park (F4) | 300 |
| Poplar Point (D4) | 98 |
| Poplarfield (E4) | 116 |
| Port Nelson (K2) | |
| Portage (bay) (D3) | |
| Portage la Prairie (D4) | 10,525 |
| Powerview (F4) | 1,078 |
| Prairie Grove (F5) | 300 |
| Pratt (D5) | |
| Pulp River (B3) | |
| Punk (isl.) (F3) | |
| Purves (D5) | 66 |
| Quesnel (lake) (G4) | |
| Rackham (B4) | |
| Rapid City (B4) | 434 |
| Rat (riv.) (F5) | |
| Rathwell (D5) | 250 |
| Reaburn (E4) | 10 |
| Red (riv.) (E5) | |
| Red Deer (lake) (A2) | |
| Red Rose (E3) | 50 |
| Reedy Creek (C4) | |
| Regent (B5) | 50 |
| Reindeer (isl.) (E2) | |
| Reindeer (lake) (H2) | |
| Reinland (E5) | |
| Rembrandt (E4) | 25 |
| Rennie (G5) | 100 |
| Renwer (B2) | |
| Reston (A5) | 516 |
| Reykjavik (D3) | |
| Rice Creek (A2) | |
| Richer (F5) | 500 |
| Ridgely (E4) | |
| Ridgeville (E5) | 500 |
| Riding (mt.) (B4) | |
| Riding Mountain (C4) | 50 |
| Riding Mountain Nat'l Park (B4) | |
| Riding Park (B3) | |
| Ridley (D3) | |
| Riel (E5) | |
| Rita (F5) | |
| Rivers (B4) | 1,422 |
| Riverton (E3) | 795 |
| Roblin (A3) | 1,173 |
| Rock (lake) (C5) | |
| Roland (D5) | 500 |
| Rorketon (C3) | 150 |
| Rosa (F5) | |
| Rosebank (D5) | 44 |
| Roseisle (D5) | 166 |
| Rosenburg (E3) | |
| Rosenfeld (E5) | 175 |
| Rosenort (E5) | 148 |
| Ross (F5) | |
| Rossburn (B4) | 589 |
| Rossburn Junction (C4) | |
| Rossendale (D5) | 137 |
| Rosser (E5) | 117 |
| Rounthwaite (C5) | 7 |
| Routledge (B5) | |
| Russell (A4) | 1,227 |
| Ruthenia (A4) | |
| Sadlow (G5) | 100 |
| Saint Adolphe (E5) | 500 |
| Saint Alphonse (C5) | 40 |
| Saint Ambroise (E4) | 400 |
| Saint Andrew (lake) (E3) | |
| Saint Andrews (E4) | 850 |
| Saint Boniface (F5) | 28,851 |
| Saint Charles (E5) | 500 |
| Saint Claude (D5) | 300 |
| Saint Eustache (E5) | 122 |
| Saint François Xavier (E5) | 450 |
| Saint George (F4) | 40 |
| Saint George (lake) (E3) | |
| Saint James (E5) | 26,502 |
| Saint Jean-Baptiste (E5) | 1,200 |
| Saint Joseph (E5) | |
| Saint Labre (G5) | |
| Saint Laurent (D4) | 281 |
| Saint Lazare (A4) | 323 |
| Saint Léon (D5) | |
| Saint Lupicin (D5) | 268 |
| Saint Malo (F5) | 500 |
| Saint Marks (E4) | 80 |
| Saint Martin (lake) (D3) | |
| Saint Martin Station (D3) | |
| Saint Norbert (E5) | 813 |
| Saint Pierre-Jolys (F5) | 838 |
| Sainte Agathe (E5) | 500 |
| Sainte Amelie (C4) | 100 |
| Sainte Anne des Chênes (F5) | 800 |
| Sainte Elizabeth (E5) | 300 |
| Sainte Geneviève (F5) | |
| Sainte Madeleine (A4) | |
| Sainte Rose du Lac (C3) | 740 |
| Sale (riv.) (E5) | |
| San Clara (A3) | 300 |
| Sandilands (F5) | |
| Sandridge (E4) | |
| Sandy Lake (B4) | 287 |
| Sanford (E5) | 98 |
| Sarto (F5) | |
| Sasaginnigak (lake) (G3) | |
| Scandinavia (C4) | |
| Scanterbury (F4) | 97 |
| Scarth (B5) | 94 |
| Sclater (B3) | |
| Scotch Bay (D4) | |
| Seal (riv.) (J2) | |
| Seech (B4) | |
| Selkirk (F4) | 7,413 |
| Senkiw (F5) | 150 |
| Setting (lake) (H3) | |
| Seven Sisters Falls (G4) | |
| Sewell (E5) | 50 |
| Sharpewood (E4) | |
| Shell Valley (A3) | |
| Shellmouth (A4) | 86 |
| Shergrove (C3) | 150 |
| Sherridon (H3) | 1,500 |
| Shevlin (A3) | |
| Shoal (lake) (B4) | |
| Shoal (lake) (G5) | |
| Shoal Lake (B4) | 751 |
| Shorncliffe (E3) | |
| Shortdale (A3) | |
| Sidney (C5) | 162 |
| Sifton (B3) | 1,000 |
| Siglunes (D4) | |
| Silver (E4) | |
| Silver Bay (D3) | |
| Silver Plains (E5) | |
| Silverton Sta. (A4) | 6 |
| Sinclair (A5) | 92 |
| Sipiwesk (lake) (J3) | |
| Sirko (F5) | 5 |
| Sisib (lake) (C2) | |
| Skownan (C3) | |
| Skylake (E4) | 140 |
| Sleeve (lake) (E3) | |
| Slemon (lake) (G1) | |
| Smith Hill (C5) | |
| Snowflake (D5) | 122 |
| Snowshoe (lake) (G4) | |
| Solsgirth (B4) | 85 |
| Somerset (D5) | 600 |
| Souris (B5) | 1,759 |
| Souris (riv.) (B5) | |
| South Junction (G5) | 250 |
| Southern Indian (lake) (H2) | |
| Spearhill (D3) | |
| Sperling (E5) | 214 |
| Split (lake) (J2) | |
| Split Lake (J2) | 500 |
| Sprague (G5) | 400 |
| Springstein (E5) | |
| Spruce (isl.) (B1) | |
| Spurgrave (G5) | 140 |
| Starbuck (E5) | 230 |
| Stead (F4) | |
| Steep Rock (D3) | 88 |
| Steinbach (F5) | 2,688 |
| Stephenfield (D5) | 10 |
| Stevenson (lake) (J3) | |
| Stockton (C5) | 124 |
| Stonewall (E4) | 1,110 |
| Stony Hill (E4) | |
| Stony Mountain (E4) | 200 |
| Strathclair (B4) | 245 |
| Sturgeon (bay) (E3) | |
| Suffren (E4) | |
| Sundown (F5) | 600 |
| Swan (lake) (B2) | |
| Swan (lake) (D5) | |
| Swan Lake (D5) | 325 |
| Swan River (A2) | 2,644 |
| Sylvan (E3) | 250 |
| Tamarac (isl.) (F3) | |
| Tatnam (cape) (K2) | |
| Tenby (C4) | 20 |
| Terence (B5) | 41 |
| Teulon (E4) | 634 |
| Thalberg (F4) | |
| The Narrows (D3) | |
| The Pas (H3) | 3,971 |
| Thicket Portage (J3) | |
| Thornhill (D5) | 133 |
| Tilston (A5) | 125 |
| Todatara (lake) (J1) | |
| Tolstoi (F5) | 572 |
| Toutes-Aides (C3) | |
| Transcona (F5) | 8,312 |
| Traverse Bay (F4) | 120 |
| Treesbank (C5) | |
| Treherne (D5) | 551 |
| Trentham (F5) | 500 |
| Tummel (A3) | |
| Turtle (mt.) (B5) | |
| Turtle (riv.) (C3) | |
| Two Creeks (B4) | 86 |
| Tyndall (F4) | 270 |
| Ukraina (B3) | |
| Underhill (B5) | 4 |
| Union Point (E5) | 78 |
| Uno (B4) | |
| Valley (riv.) (B3) | |
| Valley River (B3) | |
| Valpoy (C3) | |
| Vannes (E4) | |
| Vassar (G5) | 95 |
| Venlaw (B3) | |
| Vestfold (E4) | |
| Vickers (lake) (F3) | |
| Victoria Beach (F4) | |
| Vidir (E3) | |
| Viking (lake) (G3) | |
| Virden (A5) | 3,225 |
| Vista (B4) | 88 |
| Vita (F5) | 404 |
| Vivian (F5) | 333 |
| Vogar (D4) | |
| Volga (C3) | |
| Wabowden (J3) | 88 |
| Wakopa (C5) | 62 |
| Waldersee (D4) | |
| Walkerburn (A3) | |
| Wallace (lake) (G3) | |
| Wampum (G5) | |
| Wanipigow (riv.) (G3) | |
| Wanless (H3) | 100 |
| Wapah (D3) | |
| Ward (B3) | |
| Warrenton (E4) | 122 |
| Wasagaming (C4) | |
| Washow (bay) (F3) | |
| Waskada (B5) | 357 |
| Waterhen (C3) | |
| Waterhen (lake) (C2) | |
| Wawanesa (C5) | 440 |
| Weaver (lake) (F2) | |
| Weiden (C3) | |
| Wekusko (H3) | 150 |
| Wellman (lake) (B3) | |
| Wellwood (C4) | 160 |
| West Hawk (lake) (G5) | |
| West Shoal (lake) (E4) | |
| Westbourne (D4) | 150 |
| Westgate (A2) | |
| Wheatland (B4) | 60 |
| Whitemouth (G5) | 300 |
| Whitemouth (lake) (G5) | |
| Whitemouth (riv.) (G5) | |
| Whitewater (B5) | 93 |
| Whitewater (lake) (B5) | |
| Wicked (point) (D2) | |
| Willen (A4) | |
| Windygates (D5) | |
| Winkler (E5) | 1,634 |
| WINNIPEG (E5) | 255,093 |
| Winnipeg (Metropolitan Area) (E5) | 409,687 |
| Winnipeg (lake) (E2) | |
| Winnipeg (riv.) (G4) | |
| Winnipeg Beach (F4) | 805 |
| Winnipegosis (B3) | 984 |
| Winnipegosis (lake) (C2) | |
| Wood Bay (D5) | 10 |
| Woodlands (E4) | |
| Woodmore (F5) | |
| Woodnorth (A5) | 55 |
| Woodridge (G5) | 600 |
| Woodside (D4) | |
| Wrong (lake) (F2) | |
| York Factory (K2) | |
| Zalicia (B3) | |
| Zant (D3) | |
| Zbaraz (E4) | |
| Zelena (A3) | |
| Zhoda (F5) | |

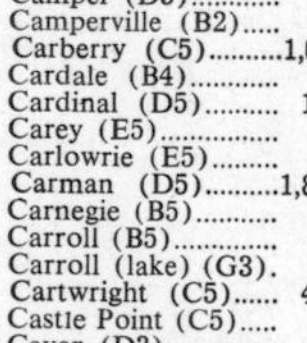

## SASKATCHEWAN

## 1956 Total Population 880,665

| | |
|---|---|
| Abbey (C5) | 305 |
| Aberdeen (E3) | 284 |
| Abernethy (H5) | 290 |
| Abound (F5) | 30 |
| Adanac (B3) | 47 |
| Admiral (C6) | 152 |
| Alameda (J6) | 304 |
| Albertown (D3) | 5 |
| Albertville (F2) | 35 |
| Alida (K6) | 168 |
| Allan (E4) | 337 |
| Allan (hills) (E4) | |
| Alsask (B4) | 232 |
| Altawan (B5) | |
| Alticane (D3) | 75 |
| Alvena (E3) | 176 |
| Amisk (lake) (M4) | |
| Amulet (G6) | 91 |
| Anerley (D4) | 44 |
| Aneroid (D6) | 350 |
| Anglia (C4) | 110 |

# ALBERTA

## 1956 Total Poulation 1,123,116

| | |
|---|---|
| Abee (D2) | 75 |
| Abilene (E2) | 30 |
| Acadia Valley (E4) | 99 |
| Acme (D4) | 292 |
| Aden (E5) | 150 |
| Aetna (D5) | 64 |
| Airdrie (C4) | 327 |
| Airways (E3) | |
| Alberta (mt.)(B3) | |
| Alberta Beach (C3) | 127 |
| Alcomdale (C3) | 100 |
| Alder Flats (C3) | 53 |
| Alderson (E4) | 81 |
| Aldersyde (C4) | 50 |
| Alexo (C3) | |
| Alhambra (C3) | |
| Alix (D3) | 517 |
| Allerston (E5) | |
| Alliance (E3) | 313 |
| Alpen Siding (D2) | |
| Altario (E4) | 75 |
| Amber Valley (D2) | |
| Amesbury (D2) | |
| Amisk (E3) | 151 |
| Analta (D2) | |
| Andrew (D3) | 602 |
| Angle Lake (E3) | |
| Anton Lake (D2) | |
| Anzac (E1) | |
| Ardley (D3) | 88 |
| Ardmore (E2) | 120 |
| Ardrossan (D3) | 41 |
| Armada (D4) | 65 |
| Armena (D3) | 37 |
| Arrowwood (D4) | 240 |
| Ashmont (E2) | 100 |
| Aspen Beach (D3) | |
| Assiniboine (mt.)(C4) | |
| Athabasca (D2) | 1,293 |
| Athabasca (lake)(C5) | |
| Athabasca (riv.)(D1) | |
| Atikameg (C2) | |
| Atlee (E4) | 65 |
| Bad Heart (A2) | |
| Badger Lake (D4) | |
| Balzac (C4) | |
| Banff (C4) | 2,518 |
| Banff Nat'l Park (B-C4) | |
| Barich (D2) | |
| Barnegat (E2) | |
| Barnwell (D5) | 200 |
| Barons (D4) | 352 |
| Barrhead (C2) | 1,610 |
| Bashaw (D3) | 597 |
| Bassano (D4) | 753 |
| Battle (riv.)(D3) | |
| Battle Lake (C3) | |
| Battle Ridge (E3) | |
| Battlebend (E3) | 4 |
| Bawlf (D3) | 287 |
| Bay Tree (A2) | 3 |
| Beacon Mines (B3) | |
| Beaumont (D3) | 75 |
| Beauvallon (E3) | 175 |
| Beaver Mines (C5) | |
| Beaverdam (E2) | |
| Beaverhill (lake)(D3) | |
| Beaverlodge (A2) | 768 |
| Beazer (D5) | |
| Beiseker (D4) | 321 |
| Bellevue (C5) | 863 |
| Bellis (D2) | 127 |
| Belloy (A2) | 100 |
| Benalto (C3) | 100 |
| Bentley (C3) | 536 |
| Benton Station (E4) | 87 |
| Berkinshaw (E3) | |
| Berry Creek (E4) | |
| Berwyn (B1) | 342 |
| Beverly (D3) | 4,602 |
| Beynon (D4) | |
| Bezanson (A2) | |
| Biche (lake)(E2) | |
| Bickerdike (B3) | 190 |
| Big Prairie (C4) | |
| Big Valley (D3) | 354 |
| Bitumount (E1) | |
| Birch (lake) (E3) | |
| Bindloss (E4) | 100 |
| Birch (mt.)(B5) | |
| Bircham (D4) | 25 |
| Bittern (lake)(D3) | |
| Bittern Lake (D3) | 45 |
| Black Diamond (C4) | 991 |
| Blackfalds (D3) | 340 |
| Blackfoot (E3) | 100 |
| Blackie (D4) | 198 |
| Blacktail (C4) | |
| Blairmore (C5) | 1,973 |
| Bloomsbury (C2) | |
| Blue Ridge (C2) | |
| Blueberry Mt. (A2) | |
| Bluesky (A1) | 315 |
| Bluffton (C3) | 400 |
| Bodo (E3) | |
| Bon Accord (D3) | 125 |
| Bonanza (A2) | |
| Bondiss (D2) | |
| Bonnyville (E2) | 1,495 |
| Boscombe (E2) | |
| Botha (D3) | 102 |
| Bottrel (C4) | |
| Bow (riv.)(D4) | |
| Bow Island (E5) | 1,001 |
| Bowden (C4) | 296 |
| Bowell (E4) | 15 |
| Bowmanton (E4) | |
| Bowness (C4) | 6,217 |
| Boyle (D2) | 304 |
| Bragg Creek (C4) | |
| Brant (D4) | 100 |
| Brazeau (mt.)(B3) | |
| Brazeau (riv.)(B3) | |
| Breton (C3) | 500 |
| Breynat (D2) | 50 |
| Brightview (D3) | |
| Brocket (D5) | 100 |
| Brooks (E4) | 2,320 |
| Brosseau (D3) | |
| Brownvale (B1) | 200 |
| Bruce (E3) | 150 |
| Bruderheim (D3) | 290 |
| Buck Lake (C3) | |
| Buffalo (E4) | 75 |
| Buffalo (lake)(D3) | |
| Buffalo Head (hills) (B5) | |
| Burdett (E5) | 225 |
| Burmis (C5) | 166 |
| Busby (C3) | 150 |
| Byemoor (D4) | 80 |
| Cabin Lake (E4) | |
| Cadogan (E3) | 97 |
| Cadomin (B3) | 800 |
| Cadron (D2) | |
| Cairns (E3) | |
| Calais (B2) | |
| Caldwell (D5) | |
| Calgary (C4) | 181,780 |
| Calgary (Metropolitan Area) (C4) | 196,152 |
| Calling (lake)(D2) | |
| Calmar (D3) | 730 |
| Camp Creek (C2) | |
| Campsie (C2) | 12 |
| Camrose (D3) | 5,817 |
| Canmore (C4) | 754 |
| Canyon Creek (C2) | |
| Cappon (E4) | |
| Carbon (D4) | 354 |
| Carbondale (D3) | 60 |
| Carcajou (B5) | |
| Cardiff (D3) | 150 |
| Cardston (D5) | 2,607 |
| Caribou (mts.)(B5) | |
| Carmangay (D4) | 299 |
| Caroline (C3) | 296 |
| Carolside (E4) | 3 |
| Carrot Creek (B3) | |
| Carseland (D4) | 125 |
| Carstairs (D4) | 449 |
| Caslan (D2) | 25 |
| Cassils (D4) | |
| Castor (D3) | 958 |
| Cavendish (E4) | 66 |
| Cayley (D4) | 146 |
| Cereal (E4) | 154 |
| Cessford (E4) | 150 |
| Champion (D4) | 402 |
| Chancellor (D4) | |
| Chard (E2) | |
| Chauvin (E3) | 353 |
| Cheadle (D4) | 50 |
| Chedderville (C3) | |
| Cherhill (C3) | 100 |
| Cherry Grove (E2) | 150 |
| Cherry Point (A1) | |
| Chigwell (D3) | 25 |
| Chin (D5) | 40 |
| Chinook (E4) | 154 |
| Chinook Valley (B1) | |
| Chipman (D3) | 192 |
| Chisholm Mills (C2) | 200 |
| Claire (lake)(B5) | |
| Clairmont (A2) | 98 |
| Clandonald (E3) | 350 |
| Claresholm (D4) | 2,431 |
| Clarkson Valley (B2) | |
| Clear Prairie (A1) | |
| Clive (D3) | 249 |
| Clover Bar (D3) | |
| Cluny (D4) | 197 |
| Clyde (D2) | 221 |
| Coal Valley (B3) | |
| Coaldale (D5) | 2,327 |
| Coalhurst (D5) | 105 |
| Coalspur (B3) | |
| Cochrane (C4) | 707 |
| Codesa (B2) | 50 |
| Cold (lake)(E2) | |
| Cold Lake (E2) | 1,097 |
| Coleman (C5) | 1,566 |
| Coleridge (E4) | 188 |
| Colinton (D2) | 200 |
| Columbia (mt.)(B3) | |
| Compeer (E4) | 138 |
| Condor (C3) | 175 |
| Conklin (E2) | 130 |
| Connor Creek (C2) | |
| Consort (E3) | 434 |
| Cooking Lake (D3) | |
| Cork (E2) | |
| Coronado (D3) | |
| Coronation (E3) | 784 |
| Countess (D4) | 8 |
| Cousins (E3) | |
| Coutts (D5) | 350 |
| Cowley (D5) | 92 |
| Craigend (E2) | 300 |
| Craigmyle (D4) | 138 |
| Craigower (E5) | |
| Crammond (C3) | |
| Cremona (C4) | 192 |
| Crooked Creek (B2) | |
| Crossfield (C4) | 459 |
| Crowfoot (D4) | |
| Crowsnest (pass)(C5) | |
| Czar (E3) | 153 |
| Dalemead (D4) | 36 |
| Dalroy (D4) | 45 |
| Dapp (C2) | 150 |
| Darling (D2) | |
| Darwell (C3) | 25 |
| Daysland (D3) | 499 |
| DeWinton (C4) | 100 |
| Deadwood (B1) | |
| Delacour (D4) | |
| Delburne (D3) | 429 |
| Delia (D4) | 282 |
| Delph (D3) | |
| Demmitt (A2) | |
| Derwent (E3) | 289 |
| Desmarais (D2) | |
| Deville (D3) | |
| Devon (D3) | 1,429 |
| Dewberry (E3) | 150 |
| Diamond City (D5) | 143 |
| Dickson (C3) | |
| Didsbury (C4) | 1,227 |
| Dimsdale (A2) | |
| Dixonville (B1) | |
| Dodds (D3) | 35 |
| Dog Pound (C4) | |
| Donalda (D3) | 256 |
| Donatville (D2) | |
| Donnelly (B2) | 265 |
| Dorenlee (D3) | 66 |
| Doris (C2) | |
| Dorothy (D4) | |
| Dowling (E4) | |
| Drayton Valley (C3) | 2,588 |
| Dreau (B2) | |
| Driftpile (C2) | |
| Drinnan (B3) | |
| Drumheller (D4) | 2,632 |
| Duchess (E4) | 177 |
| Duffield (C3) | |
| Duhamel (D3) | |
| Dunvegan (A2) | |
| Duvernay (E3) | |
| Eagle Butte (E5) | 68 |
| Eagle Hill (C4) | |
| Eaglesham (B2) | 250 |
| Earlie (E3) | |
| East Coulee (D4) | 1,350 |
| Easyford (C3) | 13 |
| Eckville (C3) | 456 |
| Edberg (D3) | 167 |
| Edgerton (E3) | 292 |
| EDMONTON (D3) | 226,002 |
| Edmonton (Metropolitan Area) (D3) | 248,949 |
| Edson (B3) | 2,560 |
| Edwand (D2) | 99 |
| Egg Lake (D2) | 135 |
| Egremont (D2) | 122 |
| Eldorena (D2) | 300 |
| Elk Island Nat'l Park (D3) | |
| Elk Point (E3) | 594 |
| Elmworth (A2) | |
| Elnora (D3) | 177 |
| Embarrass Portage (C5) | |
| Empress (E4) | 480 |
| Enchant (D4) | 73 |
| Endiang (D4) | 165 |
| Enilda (B2) | 350 |
| Ensign (D4) | 60 |
| Entrance (B3) | 50 |
| Entwistle (C3) | 354 |
| Erith (B3) | |
| Erskine (D3) | 164 |
| Etzikom (E5) | 95 |
| Etzikom Coulee (riv.) (E5) | |
| Eureka River (A1) | |
| Evansburg (C3) | 350 |
| Evergreen (C3) | |
| Excel (E4) | 95 |
| Exshaw (C4) | 250 |
| Fabyan (E3) | |
| Fairview (A1) | 1,260 |
| Faith (E5) | |
| Falher (B2) | 802 |
| Faust (C2) | 600 |
| Fawcett (C2) | |
| Federal (E3) | 20 |
| Fedorah (D3) | |
| Ferguson Flats (E2) | |
| Ferintosh (D3) | 195 |
| Fern Creek (C3) | |
| Ferrier (C3) | |
| Finnegan (E4) | |
| Fifth Meridian (B5) | |
| Flat Lake (E2) | |
| Flatbush (C2) | 125 |
| Fleet (E3) | 100 |
| Florann (E5) | |
| Foothills (B3) | 250 |
| Forbes (mt.)(B4) | |
| Foreman (D3) | |
| Foremost (E5) | 456 |
| Forest Lawn (D4) | 3,150 |
| Forestburg (E3) | 552 |
| Forestview (B2) | |
| Fork Lake (E2) | |
| Forshee (C3) | |
| Ft. Assiniboine (C2) | 75 |
| Ft. Chipewyan (C5) | |
| Ft. Fitzgerald (C4) | |
| Ft. Kent (E2) | |
| Ft. Macleod (D5) | 2,103 |
| Ft. MacKay (E1) | |
| Ft. Saskatchewan (D3) | 2,582 |
| Ft. Vermilion (B5) | 350 |
| Fox (E5) | |
| Frains (D2) | 73 |
| Franchere (E2) | 36 |
| Frank (C5) | 221 |
| Freemen River (C2) | |
| Frog (lake)(E3) | |
| Gadsby (D3) | 145 |
| Gage (A1) | |
| Gahern (E5) | |
| Gainford (C3) | 75 |
| Galahad (E3) | 215 |
| Garfield (C4) | |
| Garrington (C4) | |
| Gelkie (A3) | |
| Genesee (C3) | |
| Ghost Pine Creek (D4) | |
| Gibbons (D3) | 100 |
| Gilt Edge (E3) | |
| Gilwood (B2) | 2 |
| Girouxville (B2) | 300 |
| Gleichen (D4) | 581 |
| Glen Leslie (A2) | |
| Glendon (E2) | 314 |
| Glenevis (C3) | |
| Glenford (C3) | |
| Glenwoodville (D5) | 96 |
| Golden Spike (D3) | |
| Goodfish Lake (D2) | |
| Goose Lake (E2) | |
| Gordon (lake)(E1) | |
| Gordondale (A2) | 171 |
| Graham (lake)(C1) | |
| Grainger (D4) | 45 |
| Grand Centre (E2) | |
| Grande Prairie (A2) | 6,302 |
| Granlea (E5) | |
| Grantham (E4) | 25 |
| Granum (D5) | 322 |
| Granum (E2) | |
| Grassland (D2) | |
| Grassy Lake (E5) | 282 |
| Gratz (E3) | |
| Green Court (C2) | 60 |
| Greenshields (E3) | |
| Grimshaw (B1) | 904 |
| Grosmont (D2) | |
| Groton (E5) | |
| Grouard Mission (C2) | 328 |
| Gull (lake)(C3) | |
| Guy (B2) | |
| Gwynne (D3) | 100 |
| Habay (A5) | 450 |
| Hackett (D3) | |
| Haddock (B3) | |
| Haight (D3) | |
| Hairy Hill (D3) | 183 |
| Halcourt (A2) | |
| Halkirk (D3) | 209 |
| Hamlin (D2) | |
| Hanna (E4) | 2,327 |
| Hardieville (D5) | 100 |
| Hardisty (E3) | 628 |
| Harmattan (C4) | |
| Hartell (C4) | 500 |
| Hattonford (C3) | |
| Hay (lake)(A5) | |
| Hay (riv.) (A5) | |
| Hay Lakes (D3) | 193 |
| Haynes (D3) | 94 |
| Hays (E4) | |
| Hayter (E3) | 95 |
| Hazeldine (E3) | 75 |
| Hazelmere (A2) | |
| Heart Valley (A2) | |
| Heath (E3) | 31 |
| Heathdale (E4) | |
| Heinsburg (E3) | 135 |
| Heisler (D3) | 166 |
| Heldar (C2) | 100 |
| Helmsdale (E4) | |
| Hemaruka (E4) | 61 |
| Henry House (B3) | |
| Hercules (D3) | 18 |
| Herronton (D4) | |
| Hespero (C3) | |
| High Level (A5) | |
| High Prairie (B2) | 1,743 |
| High River (D4) | 2,102 |
| Highland Park (A1) | |
| Highridge (D2) | 50 |
| Highvale (C3) | |
| Highway (C3) | |
| Hilda (E4) | 285 |
| Hill Spring (D5) | 350 |
| Hillcrest Mines (C5) | 1,000 |
| Hilliard (D3) | 178 |
| Hillsdown (D3) | |
| Hindville (E3) | |
| Hines Creek (A1) | 360 |
| Hinton (B3) | |
| Hinton Trail (A2) | |
| Hoadley (C3) | |
| Hobbema (D3) | 122 |
| Holden (D3) | 544 |
| Holyoke (E2) | |
| Homeglen (D3) | |
| Hondo (D2) | |
| Hope Valley (E3) | |
| Horburg (C3) | |
| Hotchkiss (B1) | |
| Huallen (A2) | |
| Hubalta (D4) | 350 |
| Huggett (C3) | |
| Hughenden (E3) | 212 |
| Hussar (D4) | 168 |
| Hutton (E4) | |
| Huxley (D4) | 87 |
| Hylo (D2) | |
| Hythe (A2) | 481 |
| Idamay (E4) | |
| Iddesleigh (E4) | 35 |
| Imperial Mills (E2) | |
| Indus (D4) | 46 |
| Inland (D3) | |
| Innisfail (D3) | 1,883 |
| Innisfree (E3) | 318 |
| Iola (C3) | |
| Irma (E3) | 421 |
| Iron River (E2) | |
| Iron Springs (D5) | |
| Irricana (D4) | 158 |
| Irvine (E5) | 232 |
| Islay (E3) | 125 |
| James River Bridge (C4) | 10 |
| Jarrow (E3) | 66 |
| Jarvie (D2) | 145 |
| Jasper (B3) | 2,105 |
| Jasper Nat'l Park (A-B3) | |
| Jasper Place (D3) | 15,957 |
| Jaydot (E5) | |
| Jean-Coté (B2) | |
| Jenner (E4) | 24 |
| Joffre (D3) | |
| Jumping Pound (C4) | |
| Kahwin (D3) | |
| Kaleland (D3) | |
| Kathleen (B2) | |
| Kathryn (D4) | 44 |
| Kavanagh (D3) | |
| Keg River (A5) | |
| Kelsey (D3) | 55 |
| Keoma (D4) | |
| Kickinghorse (pass) (B4) | |
| Killam (E3) | 524 |
| Kimball (D5) | |
| Kingman (D3) | 97 |
| Kinikinik (D2) | |
| Kinmundy (E4) | |
| Kinsella (E3) | 93 |
| Kinuso (C2) | 306 |
| Kipp (D5) | 88 |
| Kirkcaldy (D4) | 47 |
| Kirriemuir (E4) | 77 |
| Kitchener (mt.)(B3) | |
| Kitscoty (E3) | 283 |
| Kleskun Hill (A2) | |
| Knob Hill (C3) | |
| Koknee (E3) | |
| Ksituan (A2) | |
| La Corey (E2) | |
| La Crête (B5) | |
| La Glace (A2) | |
| Lac Cardinal (A1) | |
| Lac la Biche (E2) | 967 |
| Lacombe (D3) | 2,747 |
| Lafond (E3) | |
| Lake Eliza (E3) | |
| Lake Isle (C3) | |
| Lake Louise (C4) | 113 |
| Lake Majeau (C3) | |
| Lake Thelma (E3) | |
| Lamont (D3) | 632 |
| Landonville (E3) | |
| Lanfine (E4) | 44 |
| Langdon (D4) | 92 |
| Larkspur (D2) | |
| Last Lake (A1) | |
| Lathom (D4) | |
| Lavoy (E3) | 127 |
| Lawton (C2) | |
| Le Goff (E2) | |
| Leaman (C3) | |
| Leduc (D3) | 2,008 |
| Leedale (C3) | |
| Legal (D3) | 457 |
| Legend (lake)(D1) | |
| Leicester (B2) | |
| Leighmore (A2) | |
| Leighton (E3) | |
| Leslieville (C3) | 153 |
| Lessard (E2) | |
| Lesser Slave (lake) (C2) | |
| Lethbridge (D5) | 29,462 |
| Leyland (B3) | 53 |
| Lindbergh (E3) | |
| Lindbrook (D3) | |
| Lisburn (C3) | |
| Little Plume (E5) | |
| Little Red River (B5) | |
| Lloydminster (E3) | 2,506 |
| Lloyds Hill (E3) | |
| Lobley (C4) | |
| Lomond (D4) | 189 |
| Lone Pine (C2) | |
| Lone Star (B1) | |
| Lonebutte (E4) | |
| Longview (C4) | 1,250 |
| Lonira (C2) | |
| Looma (D3) | |
| Lougheed (E3) | 201 |
| Lousana (D3) | 93 |
| Loyalist (E4) | 69 |
| Lucky Strike (E5) | |
| Lundbreck (C5) | 100 |
| Lundemo (D3) | |
| Luscar (B3) | 500 |
| Luzan (D3) | |
| Lyell (mt.)(B4) | |
| Lyndon (C4) | |
| Ma-Me-O Beach (D3) | 137 |
| MacKay (C3) | |
| Mackenzie Highway (B1) | |
| Madden (C4) | |
| Magrath (D5) | 1,382 |
| Mahaska (B3) | |
| Majorville (D4) | |
| Makepeace (D4) | |
| Maligne (lake)(B3) | |
| Mallaig (E2) | 450 |
| Maloy (E2) | |
| Manning (B1) | 726 |
| Mannville (E3) | 599 |
| Manola (C2) | |
| Manyberries (E5) | 130 |
| Mapova (D2) | |
| Marina (A1) | |
| Markerville (C3) | |
| Marlboro (B3) | 75 |
| Marwayne (E3) | 337 |
| Masinasin (E5) | |
| Maughan (E3) | |
| Maycroft (C5) | |
| Mayerthorpe (C3) | 563 |
| Mazeppa (D4) | 48 |
| McDonaldville (E3) | |
| McLaughlin (E3) | 95 |
| McLennan (B2) | 1,092 |
| McMurray (E1) | 1,110 |
| McRac (E2) | |
| McLeod Valley (C3) | |
| Meadowbrook (D2) | |
| Meadowview (C3) | |
| Meander River (A5) | 265 |
| Meanook (D2) | |
| Medicine Hat (E4) | 20,826 |
| Meeting Creek (D3) | 150 |
| Menaik (D3) | |
| Mercoal (B3) | 600 |
| Metiskow (E3) | 95 |
| Michichi (D4) | 100 |
| Midlandvale (D4) | 700 |
| Midnapore (C4) | 250 |
| Miette (B3) | |
| Milk (riv.)(D5) | |
| Milk River (D5) | 642 |
| Millet (D3) | 427 |
| Millicent (E4) | 77 |
| Milo (D4) | 167 |
| Minburn (E3) | 150 |
| Mirror (D3) | 591 |
| Mirror Landing (D2) | 344 |
| Monarch (D5) | 74 |
| Monitor (E4) | 79 |
| Moon Lake (C3) | |
| Moose Portage (D2) | |
| Morecambe (E3) | |
| Morinville (D3) | 957 |
| Morley (C4) | 75 |
| Morningside (D3) | |
| Morrin (D4) | 267 |
| Mosside (C2) | |
| Mossleigh (D4) | 50 |
| Mound (C4) | |
| Mountain Park (B3) | 400 |
| Mountain View (D5) | 250 |
| Moyerton (E3) | |
| Muirhead (C4) | |
| Mundare (D3) | 650 |
| Munson (D4) | 82 |
| Muriel (lake)(E2) | |
| Musidora (E3) | |
| Myrnam (E3) | 440 |
| Mystery Lake (C2) | |
| Naco (E4) | |
| Namaka (D4) | 34 |
| Nampa (B1) | |
| Nanton (D4) | 1,047 |
| Neerlandia (C2) | |
| Nemiskam (E5) | |
| Nestow (D2) | |
| Neutral Hills (E3) | |
| Nevis (D3) | 75 |
| New Brigden (E4) | 96 |
| New Dayton (D5) | 100 |
| New Kiew (E3) | |
| New Lindsay (E3) | |
| New Norway (D3) | 273 |
| New Sarepta (D3) | |
| Newbrook (D2) | 129 |
| Newcastle Mine (D4) | 1,078 |
| Nightingale (D4) | |
| Nilrem (E3) | |
| Nisbet (D4) | |
| Nisku (D3) | 250 |
| Niton (C3) | |
| Nobleford (D5) | 263 |
| Noral (D2) | |
| Norbuck (C3) | |
| Nordegg (B3) | 1,014 |
| Normandeau (E2) | |
| North Fork (D5) | |
| N. Saskatchewan (riv.)(E3) | |
| North Star (B1) | |
| N. Wabiskaw (lake) (D1) | |
| Norton (E5) | |
| Norway Valley (E3) | |
| Obed (B3) | |
| Ohaton (D3) | 46 |
| Okotoks (C4) | 764 |
| Oldman (riv.)(D5) | |
| Olds (D4) | 1,980 |
| Onefour (E5) | |
| Onoway (C3) | 190 |
| Opal (D3) | 128 |
| Oras (C3) | |
| Orion (E5) | 75 |
| Owl River (E2) | |
| Owlseye Lake (E2) | |
| Oyen (E4) | 562 |
| Ozada (C4) | 250 |
| Pakan (D2) | |
| Paradise Valley (E3) | 200 |
| Park Court (C3) | |
| Parkland (D4) | 130 |
| Pashley (E5) | |
| Patience (D3) | |
| Patricia (E4) | 130 |
| Paxson (D2) | |
| Peace (riv.)(B1) | |
| Peace River (B1) | 2,034 |
| Pearce (D5) | 60 |
| Peavine (C2) | |
| Peerless (lake)(C1) | |
| Peers (B3) | 55 |
| Pembina (riv.)(C3) | |
| Pemukan (E3) | |
| Pendant d'Oreille (E5) | |
| Pendryl (C3) | |
| Penhold (D3) | 213 |
| Peno (D3) | |
| Peoria (A2) | |
| Philips (E3) | |
| Philomena (E2) | |
| Pibroch (D2) | 122 |
| Pickardville (D2) | 425 |
| Picture Butte (D5) | 881 |
| Pigeon (lake)(D3) | |
| Pincher (C5) | 98 |
| Pincher Creek (D5) | 1,729 |
| Pine Lake (D3) | |
| Pinedale (B3) | |
| Pinhorn (E5) | |
| Pipestone Creek (A2) | |
| Pivot (E4) | |
| Plain Lake (E3) | |
| Plamondon (D2) | 100 |
| Poe (D3) | |
| Pollockville (E4) | 66 |
| Ponoka (D3) | 3,387 |
| Poplar Hill (A2) | |
| Porcupine (hills) (C4) | |
| Prairie Echo (B2) | |
| Prestville (A2) | |
| Priddis (C4) | |
| Primrose (E3) | |
| Prosperity (D2) | |
| Provost (E3) | 878 |
| Puffer (E3) | |
| Purple Springs (E5) | 40 |
| Queenstown (D4) | 166 |
| Radway (D2) | 203 |
| Rainier (E4) | |
| Raley (D5) | |
| Ranch (D2) | |
| Ranchville (E5) | |
| Ranfurly (E3) | 222 |
| Rangeton (C3) | |
| Ravine (C3) | |
| Raymond (D5) | 2,399 |
| Rearville (E4) | |
| Red Deer (D3) | 12,338 |
| Red Deer (riv.) (D4) | |
| Red Willow (D3) | 54 |
| Redcliff (E4) | 2,001 |
| Redland (D4) | 39 |
| Redwater (D3) | 1,065 |
| Reist (E4) | |
| Reno (B2) | |
| Retlaw (D4) | 60 |
| Ribstone (E3) | 90 |
| Rich Lake (E2) | |
| Richdale (E4) | 38 |
| Richmond Park (D2) | |
| Ricinus (C3) | |
| Rimbey (C3) | 980 |
| Rio Grande (A2) | |
| Robinson (E5) | |
| Rochester (D2) | 195 |
| Rochfort Bridge (C3) | 150 |
| Rocky (mts.)(B-C4) | |
| Rocky Mountain House (C3) | 1,285 |
| Rocky Rapids (C3) | |
| Rockyford (D4) | 226 |
| Rodef (D3) | |
| Rodino (E3) | |
| Roma (B1) | |
| Rosalind (D3) | 96 |
| Rose Lynn (E4) | |
| Rosebeg (E5) | |
| Rosebud (D4) | 93 |
| Rosedale (D4) | 1,400 |
| Roseglen (E4) | |
| Rosemary (E4) | 158 |
| Rosenheim (E3) | |
| Rosevear (B3) | |
| Rosyth (E3) | |
| Round Hill (D3) | 177 |
| Round Valley (C3) | |
| Rowley (D4) | 95 |
| Royal Park (D3) | |
| Royalties (C4) | 600 |
| Rumsey (D4) | 104 |
| Rusylvia (E3) | |
| Rycroft (A2) | 424 |
| Ryley (D3) | 495 |
| Saddle Lake (E2) | |
| Saint Albert (D3) | 1,320 |
| Saint Edouard (E3) | |
| Saint Kilda (E5) | |
| Saint Lina (E2) | |
| Saint Michael (D3) | 200 |
| Saint Paul (E3) | 2,229 |
| Saint Vincent (E2) | |
| Sandy Rapids (E2) | |
| Sangudo (C3) | 331 |
| Saunders (C3) | 159 |
| Sawdy (D2) | 130 |
| Scandia (E4) | |
| Scapa (D4) | |
| Schuler (E4) | 188 |
| Scollard (D4) | 66 |
| Scotfield (E4) | |
| Scotswood (A1) | |
| Seba Beach (C3) | 141 |
| Sedalia (E4) | 66 |
| Sedgewick (E3) | 608 |
| Seebe (C4) | |
| Seven Persons (E5) | 97 |
| Sexsmith (A2) | 345 |
| Shamrock Valley (E2) | |
| Sheerness (E4) | 100 |
| Shepard (D4) | 114 |
| Shining Bank (B3) | |
| Shouldice (D4) | |
| Sibbald (E4) | 88 |
| Silver Heights (E3) | |
| Sion (C3) | |
| Slave (riv.)(C5) | |
| Slave Lake (C2) | 90 |
| Smith (D2) | |
| Smoky (riv.)(A2) | |
| Smoky Heights (A2) | |
| Smoky Lake (D2) | 563 |
| S. Saskatchewan (riv.)(E4) | |
| S. Wabiskaw (lake) (D2) | |
| Sounding Lake (E3) | |
| Spedden (E2) | 150 |
| Spirit River (A2) | 743 |
| Spring Coulee (D5) | 125 |
| Springburn (B2) | |
| Spruce Grove (C3) | 309 |
| Stand Off (D5) | |
| Standard (D4) | 230 |
| Stanger (C3) | |
| Stanmore (E4) | 45 |
| Star (D3) | |
| Stauffer (C3) | |
| Stavely (D4) | 338 |
| Sterco (B3) | 175 |
| Stettler (D3) | 3,359 |
| Steveville (E4) | |
| Stirling (D5) | 430 |
| Stony Plain (C3) | 1,098 |
| Strachan (C3) | |
| Strathmore (D4) | 727 |
| Streamstown (E3) | 90 |
| Strome (E3) | 306 |
| Stubno (E3) | |
| Sturgeon Heights (B2) | |
| Styal (C3) | |
| Suffield (E4) | 76 |
| Sullivan (lake)(D3) | |
| Sundre (C4) | 923 |
| Sunnybrook (C3) | 200 |
| Sunnydale (E4) | |
| Sunnynook (E4) | 100 |
| Sunnyslope (D4) | 97 |
| Sunset House (B2) | |
| Swalwell (D4) | 117 |
| Sylvan Lake (C3) | 1,114 |
| Taber (E5) | 3,688 |
| Talbot (E3) | 50 |
| Tawatinaw (D2) | 125 |
| Teepee Creek (A2) | |
| Tees (D3) | 69 |
| Temple (mt.)(B4) | |
| The Twins (mt.) (B3) | |
| Thérien (E2) | 520 |
| Thickwood (hills) (D1) | |
| Thorhild (D2) | 288 |
| Thorsby (C3) | 411 |
| Three Hills (D4) | 1,095 |
| Throne (E3) | |
| Tiger Lily (C2) | |
| Tilley (E4) | 240 |
| Timeu (C2) | |
| Tod Creek (C5) | |
| Tofield (D3) | 800 |
| Tolland (E3) | |
| Tomahawk (C3) | |
| Torlea (E3) | |
| Torrington (D4) | 125 |
| Tothill (E5) | |
| Travers (D4) | 66 |
| Trefoil (D4) | |
| Triangle (B2) | |
| Trochu (D4) | 680 |
| Tudor (D4) | |
| Tulliby Lake (E3) | |
| Turin (D5) | 132 |
| Turner Valley (C4) | 704 |
| Twin Butte (C5) | |
| Twin River (D5) | |
| Twining (D4) | |
| Ukalta (D3) | |
| Usona (D3) | |
| Utikuma (lake)(C2) | |
| Vanesti (E3) | |
| Vanrena (A1) | |
| Vauxhall (D4) | 713 |
| Vega (C2) | |
| Vegreville (E3) | 2,574 |
| Venice (E2) | |
| Vermilion (E3) | 2,196 |
| Veteran (E3) | 241 |
| Viewpoint (D3) | |
| Viking (E3) | 897 |
| Vilna (E2) | 374 |
| Violet Grove (C3) | |
| Vulcan (D4) | 1,204 |
| Wabamun (C3) | 198 |
| Wabasca (D2) | |
| Wabiskaw (riv.) (C1) | |
| Wainwright (E3) | 2,653 |
| Wallace (mt.)(C2) | |
| Walsh (E5) | 142 |
| Wanham (A2) | 162 |
| Wapiti (A2) | |
| Warburg (C3) | 257 |
| Warden Jc. (D3) | 76 |
| Wardlow (E4) | |
| Warner (D5) | 450 |
| Warrensville (B1) | |
| Warspite (D2) | 159 |
| Warwick (D3) | |

Waskatenau (D2) 289
Wastina (E4)
Waterglen (D3)
Waterton Lakes Nat'l Park (C5)
Waterton Park (D5) 300
Waterways (E1) 400
Watino (B2) 62
Watts (D4)
Waybrook (D3)
Wayne (D4) 700
Weasel Creek (D2) 20
Webster (A2)
Welling (D5)
Wembley (A2) 272
West Wingham (E4)
Westcott (C4)
Westlock (C2) 1,136
Westward Ho (C4)
Wetaskiwin (D3) 4,476
Whatcheer (E4)
Wheat Centre (D4)
Whiskey Gap (D5) 100
Whitburn (A2)
White Court (C2) 130
Whitelaw (A1) 477
Whitemud Creek (B2)
Whitla (E5) 67
Wild Horse (E5)
Wildmere (E3)
Wildwood (C3) 547
Willesden Green (C3)
Willingdon (E3) 431
Willow Creek (D4)
Willow Trail (E2)
Willowlea (E3)
Wimborne (D4) 88
Windsor Creek (A2)
Winefred (lake) (E2)
Winfield (C3) 362
Winnifred (E5) 96
Withrow (C3)
Woking (A2) 325
Wolf Creek (B3)
Wood Buffalo (Nat'l Park) (B5)
Wood River (D3)
Woodhouse (D5)
Woolchester (E5)
Wostok (D3) 150
Wrentham (D5) 87
Yates (B3)
Yellowhead (pass) (A3)
Yeoford (C3)
Youngstown (E4) 305

## BRITISH COLUMBIA

## 1956 Total Population 1,398,464

Abbotsford (L3) 830
Aero (B3)
Agassiz (M3) 600
Ainsworth (J5) 250
Aiyansh (C2) 250
Alberni (H3) 3,947
Alberni (inlet) (H3)
Albert Canyon (J4) 50
Albreda (H4) 50
Alert Bay (D5) 695
Alexandria (F4) 70
Alexis Creek (F4) 50
Aleza Lake (G3) 250
Alice Arm (C2) 75
Alkali Lake (F4) 125
Allenby (G5) 250
Alta Lake (F5) 50
Alvin (L2)
Anahim Lake (E4)
Anvil Island (K2)
Anyox (C2)
Appledale (J5) 275
Argenta (J5)
Aristazabal (isl.) (C4)
Armstrong (H5) 1,197
Arrow Park (H5)
Arrowhead (H5) 200
Ashcroft (G5) 805
Aspen Grove (G5) 50
Assiniboine (mt.) (K5)
Athalmer (K5) 225
Atlin (J2) 500
Atlin (lake) (J1)
Attachie (G2)
Australian (F4)
Avola (H4) 97
Babine (D2) 10
Babine (lake) (E3)
Babine (riv.) (D2)
Baldonnel (G2)
Balfour (J5) 100
Bamfield (E6) 250
Bankeir (G5)
Banks (isl.) (B3)
Barkerville (G3) 300
Barkley (sound) (E6)
Barrett Lake (D3)
Barriere (H4) 50
Baynes Lake (K5) 100
Bear Flat (G2)
Beaton (J5) 100
Beatton (riv.) (G1)
Beatton River (F1)
Beavermouth (J4)
Beaver Creek (H3)
Beaverdell (H5) 98
Beaverley (F3)
Bella Bella (D4)
Bella Coola (D4) 350
Bella Coola (riv.) (D4)
Birch Island (H4) 72
Birken (F5) 50
Blind Channel (E5) 50
Bloedel (E5)
Blue River (H4) 500
Blueberry (G2)
Boat Basin (D5)
Boston Bar (G5) 135
Boswell (J5) 205
Boulder (G4)
Bowen Island (K3) 98
Bowser (H2) 50
Brackendale (F5) 175
Bralorne (F5) 500
Bridesville (H6) 113
Bridge Lake (G4) 200
Brilliant (J5) 712
Brisco (J5) 100
Britannia Beach (K2) 1,500
Brookmere (G5) 127
Brooks (pen.) (D5)
Brouse (J5) 150
Bryce (mt.) (J4)
Bulkley (mts.) (D3)
Bull Harbour (C5)
Burns Lake (D3) 1,016
Burton (H5) 250
Bute (inlet) (E5)
Butedale (C3) 350
Caamaño (sound) (C4)
Cache Creek (G5) 45
Calvert (isl.) (C4)
Campbell Island (C4) 200
Campbell River (E5) 3,069
Canal Flats (K5) 175
Canford (G5) 50
Canim Lake (G4) 50
Canoe (H5) 166
Cape Scott (C5)
Capilano (K3) 950
Cariboo (mts.) (G3)
Carmi (H5) 50
Cascade (H6) 175
Cassiar (mts.) (K2)
Cassidy (J3) 400
Castlegar (J5) 1,705
Cawston (H5) 350
Cecil Lake (G2)
Cedar (J3) 200
Cedarvale (C2) 100
Ceepeecee (D5) 100
Celista (H5) 175
Chamiss Bay (D5)
Chapman Camp (J5) 560
Chase (H5) 700
Chatham (sound) (B3)
Cheam View (M3) 35
Chemainus (J3) 2,250
Chief Lake (F3) 84
Chilkat (mt.) (H1)
Chilko (lake) (F4)
Chilkoot (pass) (J1)
Chilliwack (M3) 7,297
Chu Chua (H4) 77
Cinema (F3) 30
Claxton (C3)
Clayburn (L3) 350
Clayoquot (D5) 10
Clearwater Station (G4) 300
Cliffside (J3) 50
Clinton (G4) 300
Cloverdale (L3) 1,300
Coal Creek (K5) 150
Coal Harbour (D5) 20
Coal River (L2)
Coalmont (G5) 244
Coast (mts.) (D3)
Cobble Hill (K3) 300
Colquitz (K3) 150
Columbia (mt.) (J4)
Columbia (riv.) (H4)
Colwood (J4) 350
Comox (H2) 1,151
Continental Divide (D2)
Coombs (H3) 150
Copper Mountain (G5) 200
Copper River (C3)
Cornel Mills (G3)
Cottonwood (G3) 10
Courtenay (E5) 3,025
Cowichan Station (J3) 214
Cranbrook (K5) 4,562
Creston (J5) 1,844
Criss Creek (G4)
Crofton (J3) 100
Crowsnest (K5) 250
Crowsnest (pass) (K5)
Croydon Station (G3)
Cumberland (E5) 1,039
D'Arcy (F5) 50
Dawson Creek (G2) 7,531
Dean (chan.) (D4)
Dean (riv.) (D4)
Dease Lake (K2)
Dease (lake) (K2)
Decker Lake (E3) 250
Deer Park (H5) 100
Denman Island (H2) 150
Deroche (L3) 150
Devil's Thumb (mt.) (A1)
Dewdney (L3) 300
Dixon Entrance (str.) (A3)
Doe River (G2) 280
Dog Creek (G4) 35
Dome Creek (G3) 110
Dorreen (C3) 75
Douglas Lake (H5) 65
Duncan (J3) 3,247
Dunster (G3) 125
East Arrow Park (J5) 60
East Kelowna (H5) 350
East Pine (G2)
East Wellington (J3) 200
Eburne (K3) 1,100
Edgewater (J5) 55
Edgewood (H5) 190
Eholt (H5) 80
Elko (K5) 200
Endako (E3) 74
Enderby (H5) 965
Engen (E3)
Englewood (D5) 150
Esquimalt (K4) 10,353
Eutsuk (lake) (D3)
Ewings Landing (H5) 85
Extension (J3) 178
Fairmont Hot Springs (J5)
Fairweather (mt.) (H1)
Falkland (H5) 203
Fanny Bay (H2) 200
Farmington (G2)
Farrell Creek (G2)
Fawn (G4) 150
Ferguson (J5)
Fernie (K5) 2,808
Field (J4) 400
Finlay (riv.) (E1)
Finmoore (F3) 100
Flagstone (K5) 225
Flathead (K5) 68
Forest Grove (G4) 100
Fort Fraser (E3) 325
Fort Langley (L3) 560
Fort Nelson (M2) 350
Fort Saint John (G2) 1,908
Fort Saint James (E3) 615
Fort Steele (K5) 276
François (lake) (D3)
François Lake (D3) 250
Fraser (riv.) (F4)
Fraser Lake (E3) 250
Fraser Mills (K3) 633
Fruitvale (J5) 870
Fulford Harbour (K3) 205
Gabriola (J3) 200
Galiano (K3) 100
Gang Ranch (F4) 75
Ganges (K3) 500
Gardner (canal) (C3)
Garibaldi (F5) 50
Garibaldi Park (L2)
Georgia (str.) (J3)
Germansen Landing (E2)
Gerrard (J5) 30
Gibsons (J3) 990
Giscome (F3) 90
Glacier (J4) 50
Glacier Nat'l Pk. (J4)
Glendale Cove (E5)
Gold Bridge (F5) 400
Golden (J4) 750
Goldstream (J4) 100
Graham (isl.) (A3)
Grand Forks (H6) 1,995
Granite Bay (E5) 50
Granthams Landing (J3) 40
Grassy Plains (E3) 100
Great Central (H2) 200
Greenville (C2)
Greenwood (H5) 815
Gundy (G2)
Hagensborg (D4) 250
Halcyon Hot Springs (J5) 30
Halfmoon Bay (J2)
Hamber Park (J4)
Hanceville (F4) 50
Haney (L3) 2,250
Hansard (G3) 92
Harrison (lake) (M2)
Harrison Hot Springs (M3) 613
Harrison Mills (L3) 200
Harrogate (J5)
Hatzic (L3) 500
Haynes (H5)
Haysport (C3) 50
Hazelton (D2) 279
Headquarters (E5)
Hecate (str.) (B3)
Hedley (G5) 600
Heffley Creek (G5) 140
Holberg (C5) 50
Honeymoon Bay (J3)
Hope (M3) 2,226
Hopkins Landing (K2) 50
Hornby Island (H2) 150
Horsefly (G4) 110
Horseshoe Bay (K3) 150
Hosmer (K5) 100
Hot Springs Cove (D5) 66
Houston (D3) 200
Howser (J5) 36
Hudson Hope (F2) 50
Hulatt (F3) 50
Huntingdon (L3) 200
Hutton Mills (G3)
Hydraulic (F4) 50
Invermere (J5) 543
Ioco (K3) 900
Irvine's Landing (J2) 500
Iskut (riv.) (B2)
Isle Pierre (F3) 150
Jaffray (K5) 110
James Island (K3) 500
Johnson's Landing (J5) 35
Juan de Fuca (str.) (J4)
Kaleden (H5) 109
Kamloops (G5) 9,096
Kaslo (J5) 669
Kates Needle (mt.) (A1)
Keefer's (G5) 50
Keithley Creek (G4) 75
Kelowna (H5) 9,181
Kemano (D2)
Keremeos (G5) 666
Kettle Valley (H5) 100
Kickinghorse (pass) (J4)
Kimberley (K5) 5,774
Kincolith (B2) 125
King (isl.) (D4)
Kingsgate (K5) 35
Kinnaird (J5) 1,267
Kisgegas (D2)
Kitchener (J5) 185
Kitimat (C3) 8,000
Kitwanga (C2) 175
Klemtu (C4) 150
Klinaklini (riv.) (E4)
Knight Inlet (E5) 40
Kokanee Glacier Park (J5)
Koksilah (J3) 200
Kootenay (lake) (J5)
Kootenay (Nat'l Park) (J4)
Kootenay (riv.) (K5)
Kyuquot (D5) 125
Lac la Hache (G4) 50
Ladner (K3) 2,000
Ladysmith (J3) 2,107
Laidlaw (M3) 60
Lake Cowichan (J3) 1,949
Lake Hill (K3)
Langford Station (J3) 450
Langley (L3) 2,131
Lantzville (J3)
Lardeau (J5) 175
Lavington (H5) 150
Lempriere (H4)
Liard (riv.) (L2)
Lillooet (G5) 1,083
Lister (J5)
Little Fort (G4) 150
Longworth (G3) 175
Loos (G3) 50
Louis Creek (H4) 240
Lower Arrow (lake) (H5)
Lower Post (K1)
Lumby (H5) 786
Lund (E5) 210
Lyell (mt.) (J4)
Lynn Creek (K3) 1,000
Lytton (G5) 329
Mabel Lake (H5)
Macalister (F4) 85
Magna Bay (H4) 100
Malakwa (H5) 178
Manning, E. C., Park (G5)
Manson Creek (E2) 285
Mapes (E3)
Mara (H5) 150
Margaret Bay (D4) 50
Marguerite (F4) 10
Marysville (K5) 918
Masset (B3) 400
Matsqui (L3) 250
Mayne (K3) 250
McBride (G3) 489
McDame (K2)
McGuire (F5)
McLeod Lake (F2)
McLure (H4)
McMurdo (J4)
McMurphy (H4)
Merritt (G5) 1,790
Merville (E5) 175
Metchosin (K4) 250
Metlakatla (B3) 30
Michel (K5) 800
Midway (H5) 250
Milner (L3) 366
Milne's Landing (J4) 50
Minstrel Island (D5) 50
Minto Mine (F5) 50
Miocene (G4)
Mission City (L3) 3,010
Monashee (mts.) (H4)
Monte Creek (G5) 75
Monte Lake (G5)
Montney (G2)
Moose Heights (F3)
Moresby (isl.) (B4)
Mount Assiniboine Park (K5)
Mount Cartier (J5)
Mount Currie (F5)
Mount Lehman (L3) 150
Mt. Revelstoke Nat'l Park (H4)
Mount Robson (H3)
Mount Robson Park (H4)
Moyie (K5) 200
Mud River (F3)
Murrayville (L3) 390
Muskwa (M2)
Nadina River (D3) 100
Nakusp (J5) 1,750
Namu (D4) 100
Nanaimo (J3) 12,705
Nanika (dam) (D3)
Nanoose Bay (J3) 250
Naramata (H5) 450
Nass (riv.) (C2)
Nass Harbour (C3)
Natal (K5) 1,200
Nazko (F3)
Needles (H5) 100
Nelson (J5) 7,226
Nelson Forks (M2)
New Brighton (K2)
New Denver (J5) 736
New Hazelton (D2) 200
New Westminster (K3) 31,665
Newgate (K5) 60
Newlands (F3) 125
Newton Station (K3) 650
Nicola (G5) 170
Nithi River (E3)
North Bend (G5) 276
North Galiano (K3) 50
North Kamloops (G5) 4,351
North Pine (G2)
North Vancouver (K3) 19,951
Northfield (J3) 175
Notch Hill (H5) 75
Observatory (inlet) (C2)
Ocean Falls (D4) 2,650
Okanagan (lake) (H5)
Okanagan Centre (H5) 150
Okanagan Falls (H5) 125
Okanagan Landing (H5) 175
Okanagan Mission (H5) 250
Oliver (H5) 1,147
150 Mile House (G4) 177
Oona River (C3)
Ootsa Lake (E3) 50
Osoyoos (H6) 860
Oyama (H5) 100
Pacific (C3) 50
Parksville (J3) 1,112
Parsnip (riv.) (F2)
Parson (J4) 100
Pavilion (G5) 50
Peace (riv.) (F2)
Peachland (G5) 500
Pemberton (F5) 25
Pemberton Meadows (F5) 100
Pender Island (K3) 300
Penny (G3) 100
Penticton (H5) 11,894
Perow (D3) 50
Pink Mountain (F1)
Pioneer Mine (F5) 450
Pitt (isl.) (C3)
Pitt (lake) (L3)
Poplar Creek (J5) 33
Porcher (isl.) (B3)
Port Alberni (H3) 10,373
Port Albion (E6)
Port Alice (D5) 350
Port Clements (B3) 250
Port Coquitlam (L3) 4,632
Port Edward (B3) 250
Port Essington (C3) 225
Port Hammond (L3) 2,000
Port Hardy (D5) 175
Port Mann (L3) 500
Port Moody (L3) 2,713
Port Renfrew (J3) 100
Port Simpson (B3) 750
Portland (canal) (B2)
Pouce-Coupé (G2) 585
Powell River (E5) 5,174
Premier (C2) 400
Price (isl.) (C4)
Prince George (F3) 10,563
Prince Rupert (B3) 10,498
Princess Royal (isl.) (C3)
Princeton (G5) 2,245
Procter (J5) 250
Provincial Cannery (C4)
Punchaw (F3)
Purcell (mts.) (J5)
Qualicum Beach (J3) 726
Quathiaski Cove (E5) 175
Quatsino (D5) 300
Quatsino (sound) (C5)
Queen Charlotte (A3) 250
Queen Charlotte (isls.) (B3)
Queen Charlotte (sound) (C4)
Queen Charlotte (str.) (D5)
Quesnel (F4) 1,941
Quesnel (lake) (G4)
Quick (D3) 200
Quilchena (G5) 100
Radium Hot Springs (J5) 75
Red Pass (H4) 36
Redstone (F4) 10
Refuge Cove (E5) 300
Reid Lake (F3) 100
Remo (C3)
Renata (H5) 125
Revelstoke (J5) 3,469
Riske Creek (F4) 100
Rivers Inlet (D4) 250
Roberts Creek (J3) 150
Robson (J5) 200
Robson (mt.) (H3)
Rock Bay (E5) 100
Rock Creek (H6) 100
Rocky (mts.) (G3)
Rolla (G2) 950
Rose Lake (E3) 50
Rosebery (J5) 130
Rosedale (M3) 337
Rossland (H6) 4,344
Royal Oak (K3) 100
Royston (H2) 250
Ruby Creek (M3) 77
Ruskin (L3) 190
Rutland (H5) 500
Ryder Lake (M3)
Saanichton (K3) 500
Salmo (J5) 846
Salmon Arm (H5) 1,344
Salmon Valley (F3)
Saltair (J3)
San Josef Bay (C5)
Sandon (J5) 200
Sandspit (B3) 25
Sardis (M3) 500
Saturna (K3) 50
Savona (G5) 194
Sayward (D5)
Sechelt (J2) 439
Seechelt (pen.) (J2)
Selkirk (mts.) (J4)
Seton Portage (F5) 50
Seventy Mile House (G4) 25
Seymour (inlet) (D4)
Seymour Arm (H4)
Shalalth (F5) 250
Shawnigan Lake (J3) 398
Telkwa (D3) 580
Shelley (F3) 100
Shere (H4)
Shoreacres (J5) 500
Shushartie Bay (C5) 25
Shuswap (H5) 90
Shuswap (lake) (H4)
Sicamous (H5) 200
Sidmouth (J5) 100
Sidney (K3) 1,371
Sikanni Chief (F1)
Silverdale (L3) 250
Silverton (J5) 347
Similkameen (G5)
Simoom Sound (D5) 244
Sinclair Mills (G3)
Sir Sandford (mt.) (H4)
Sirdar (J5) 76
Skeena (riv.) (C3)
Skeena Crossing (D2) 15
Skidegate (B3) 400
Slocan (J5) 326
Slocan Park (J5) 100
Smith (sound) (C4)
Smith River (L1)
Smithers (D3) 1,962
Snowshoe (G3)
Soda Creek (G4) 50
Sointula (D5) 450
Solsqua (H5) 150
Somenos (J3) 200
Sooke (J4) 500
South Fort George (F3) 250
South Hazelton (C2) 150
South Pender (K3) 25
South Slocan (J5) 190
South Wellington (J3) 200
Southbank (E3) 100
Spences Bridge (G5) 400
Spuzzum (G5) 150
Squamish (K2) 1,292
Squilax (H5) 200
Stave (lake) (L3)
Steveston (K3) 1,100
Stewart (C2) 435
Stikine (mts.) (K2)
Stikine (riv.) (B1)
Stillwater (E5) 150
Stoner (F3)
Strathcona Park (E5)
Strathnaver (F3)
Stuart (lake) (E3)
Stuart Island (E5) 75
Sullivan Bay (D5) 150
Summerland (G5) 3,000
Summit Lake (F3)
Swift Creek (H4)
Taft (H4) 40
Tagish (lake) (J1)
Tahsis (D5)
Takla (lake) (D2)
Takla Landing (E2)
Taku (riv.) (J2)
Tatalrose (D3)
Tatla Lake (E4)
Taylor (G2)
Teidemann (peak) (E4)
Telegraph Creek (K2) 75
Terrace (C3) 1,473
Tête Jaune Cache (H4)
Texada (isl.) (J2)
Thetis Island (J3) 25
Thompson (riv.) (G5)
Thurlow (E5) 75
Tintagel (E3) 50
Tlell (B3)
Tofino (E5) 389
Topley (D3) 75
Trail (J6) 11,395
Trout Lake (J5) 100
Tulameen (G5) 100
Tupper (G2) 250
Tweedsmuir Park (D3)
Two Rivers (G2)
Ucluelet (E6) 520
Union Bay (H2) 500
Upper Arrow (lake) (H5)
Usk (C3) 150
Valemount (H4) 200
Vallican (J5) 50
Vananda (E5) 150
Vancouver (K3) 365,844
Vancouver (Metropolitan Area) (K3) 530,728
Vancouver (isl.) (J3)
Vanderhoof (E3) 1,085
Vavenby (H4) 75
Vernon (H5) 8,998
VICTORIA (K4) 54,584
Victoria (Metropolitan Area) (K4) 104,303
Waddington (mt.) (E4)
Wadhams (D4)
Waldo (K5) 100
Walhachin G5) 100
Waneta (J5) 75
Wardner (K5) 175
Ware (E1)
Warfield (J5) 2,051
Wellington (J3) 391
Wells (G3) 1,250
West Summerland (G5) 3,000
West Vancouver (K3)
Westbank (H5) 575
Westbridge (H5)
Westholme (J3) 150
Westview (E5) 3,499
Westwold (G5) 200
Whaletown (E5) 50
White Rock (K3) 2,000
Whonock (L3) 695
Williams Lake (F4) 1,790
Willow River (F3) 200
Wilmer (J5) 225
Wilson Creek (J2) 25
Windermere (K5) 95
Winlaw (J5) 248
Woodfibre (K2) 560
Woodpecker (F3) 75
Wynndel (J5) 200
Yale (M2) 176
Yellowhead (pass) (H4)
Ymir (J5) 190
Yoho Nat'l Park (J4)
Youbou (J3) 266
Zeballos (D5) 154

# NORTH AMERICAN HISTORICAL ATLAS

### On the written story of history which tells WHAT happened, this atlas superimposes maps showing WHERE it happened.

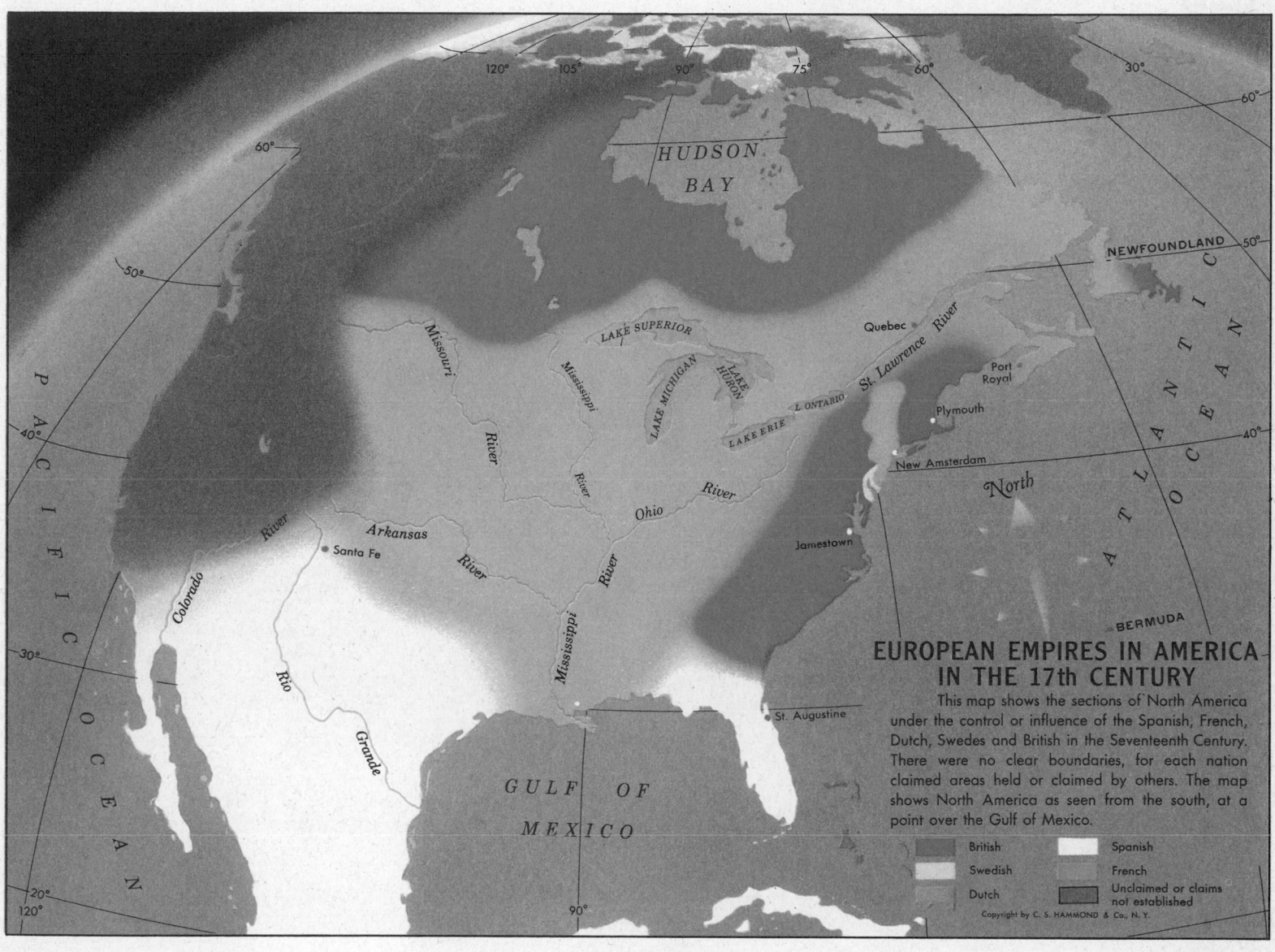

### EUROPEAN EMPIRES IN AMERICA IN THE 17th CENTURY

This map shows the sections of North America under the control or influence of the Spanish, French, Dutch, Swedes and British in the Seventeenth Century. There were no clear boundaries, for each nation claimed areas held or claimed by others. The map shows North America as seen from the south, at a point over the Gulf of Mexico.

British  Spanish
Swedish  French
Dutch  Unclaimed or claims not established

Copyright by C. S. HAMMOND & Co., N. Y.

## CONTENTS

Entire Contents Copyrighted MCMLV BY C. S. HAMMOND & CO. INC. Maplewood, N. J.

Printed in U.S.A.

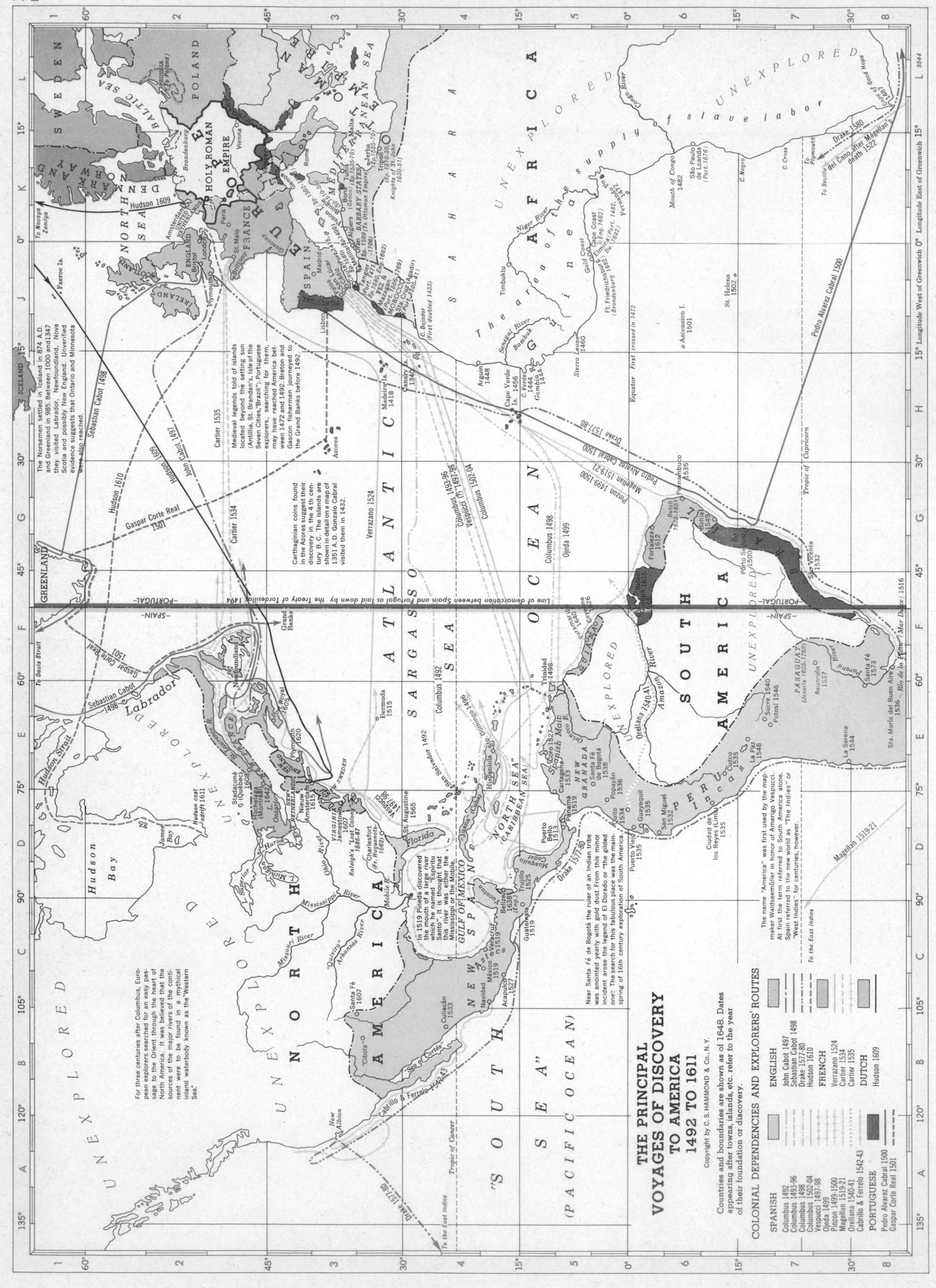

# THE PRINCIPAL
# VOYAGES OF DISCOVERY
# TO AMERICA
# 1492 TO 1611

Copyright by C. S. HAMMOND & Co., N.Y.

Countries and boundaries are shown as of 1648. Dates appearing after towns, islands, etc. refer to the year of their foundation or discovery.

## COLONIAL DEPENDENCIES AND EXPLORERS' ROUTES

| SPANISH | ENGLISH |
|---|---|
| Columbus 1492 | John Cabot 1497 |
| Columbus 1493-96 | Sebastian Cabot 1498 |
| Columbus 1498 | Drake 1577-80 |
| Vespuci 1497-98 | Hudson 1610 |
| Ojeda 1499 | FRENCH |
| Pinzon 1499-1500 | Verrazano 1524 |
| Magellan 1519-21 | Cartier 1534 |
| Orellana 1540-41 | Cartier 1535 |
| Cabrillo & Ferrelo 1542-43 | DUTCH |
| PORTUGUESE | Hudson 1609 |
| Pedro Alvarez Cabral 1500 | |
| Gaspar Corte Real 1501 | |

For three centuries after Columbus, European explorers searched for an easy passage to the Orient through the heart of North America. It was believed that the sources of the major rivers of the continent were to be found in a mythical inland waterbody known as the "Western Sea."

In 1519 Pineda discovered the mouth of a large river which he named "Espiritu Santo". It is thought that this river was either the Mississippi or the Mobile.

Near Santa Fé de Bogota the ruler of an Indian tribe was anointed yearly with gold dust. From this minor incident arose the legend of El Dorado or "the gilded one." The search for this fabulous place was the mainspring of 16th century exploration of South America.

The name "America" was first used by the map-maker Waldseemüller in honor of Amerigo Vespucci. At first the term referred to South America alone. Spain referred to the new world as "The Indies" or "West Indies" for centuries, however.

The Norsemen settled in Iceland in 874 A.D. and Greenland in 985. Between 1000 and 1347 they visited Labrador, Newfoundland, Nova Scotia and possibly New England. Unverified evidence suggests that Ontario and Minnesota were also reached.

Medieval legends told of islands located beyond the setting sun (Antillia, St. Brandan's, Isle of the Seven Cities, "Brazil"). Portuguese explorers, searching for them, may have reached America between 1472 and 1492. Breton and Gascon fishermen journeyed to the Grand Banks before 1492.

Carthaginian coins found in the Azores suggest their discovery in the 4th century B.C. The islands are shown in detail on a map of 1351 A.D. Gonzalo Cabral visited them in 1432.

The area of the supply of slave labor

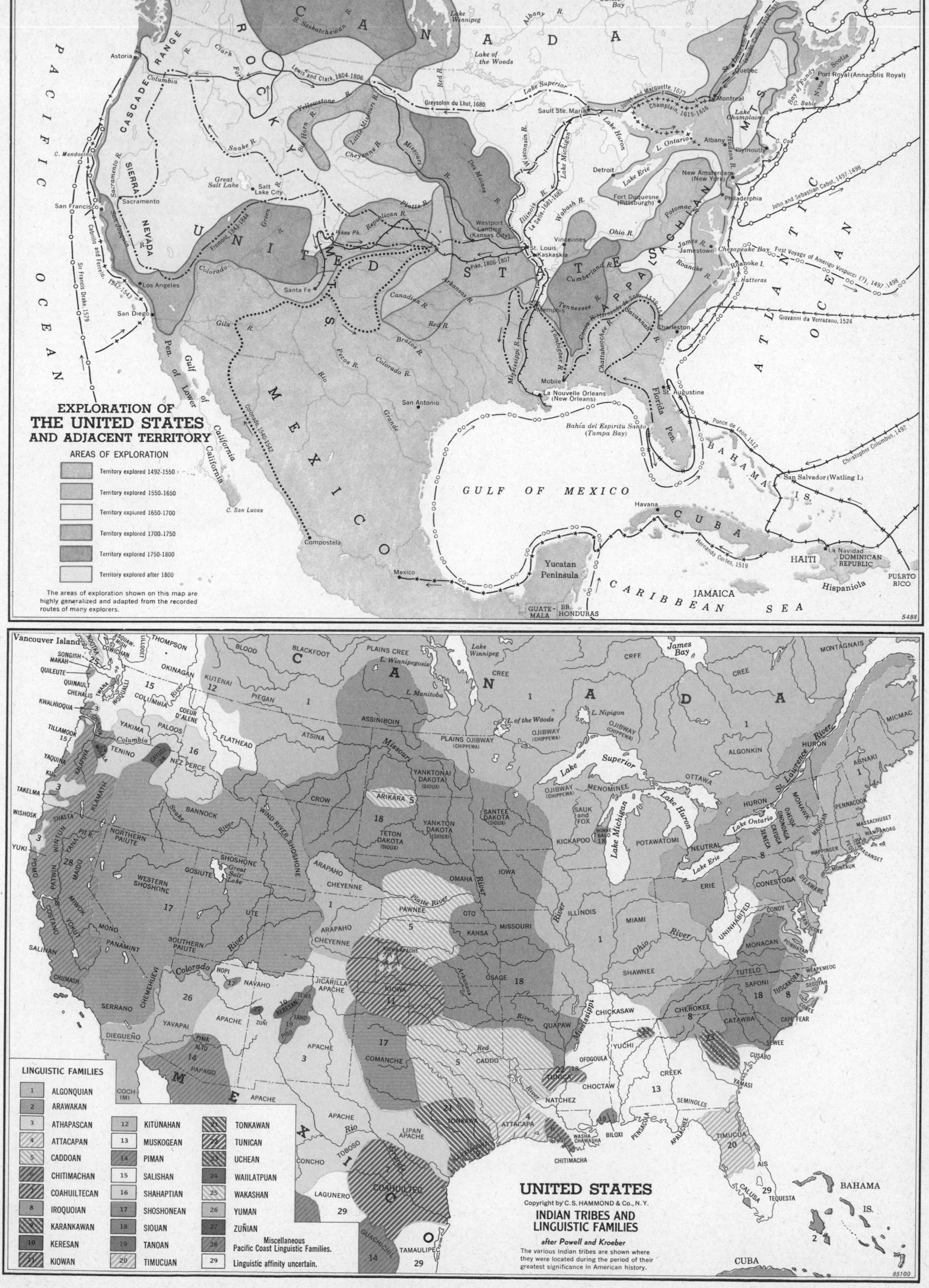

## EXPLORATION OF THE UNITED STATES AND ADJACENT TERRITORY

### AREAS OF EXPLORATION

Territory explored 1492-1550
Territory explored 1550-1650
Territory explored 1650-1700
Territory explored 1700-1750
Territory explored 1750-1800
Territory explored after 1800

The areas of exploration shown on this map are highly generalized and adapted from the recorded routes of many explorers.

## UNITED STATES

Copyright by C.S. Hammond & Co., N.Y.

### INDIAN TRIBES AND LINGUISTIC FAMILIES

*after Powell and Kroeber*

The various Indian tribes are shown where they were located during the period of their greatest significance in American history.

### LINGUISTIC FAMILIES

| 1 | ALGONQUIAN | | | | |
| 2 | ARAWAKAN | | | | |
| 3 | ATHAPASCAN | 12 | KITUNAHAN | | TONKAWAN |
| 4 | ATTACAPAN | 13 | MUSKOGEAN | | TUNICAN |
| 5 | CADDOAN | 14 | PIMAN | | UCHEAN |
| | CHITIMACHAN | 15 | SALISHAN | 24 | WAIILATPUAN |
| | COAHUILTECAN | 16 | SHAHAPTIAN | 25 | WAKASHAN |
| 8 | IROQUOIAN | 17 | SHOSHONEAN | 26 | YUMAN |
| | KARANKAWAN | 18 | SIOUAN | 27 | ZUÑIAN |
| 10 | KERESAN | 19 | TANOAN | 28 | Miscellaneous Pacific Coast Linguistic Families. |
| | KIOWAN | 20 | TIMUCUAN | 29 | Linguistic affinity uncertain. |

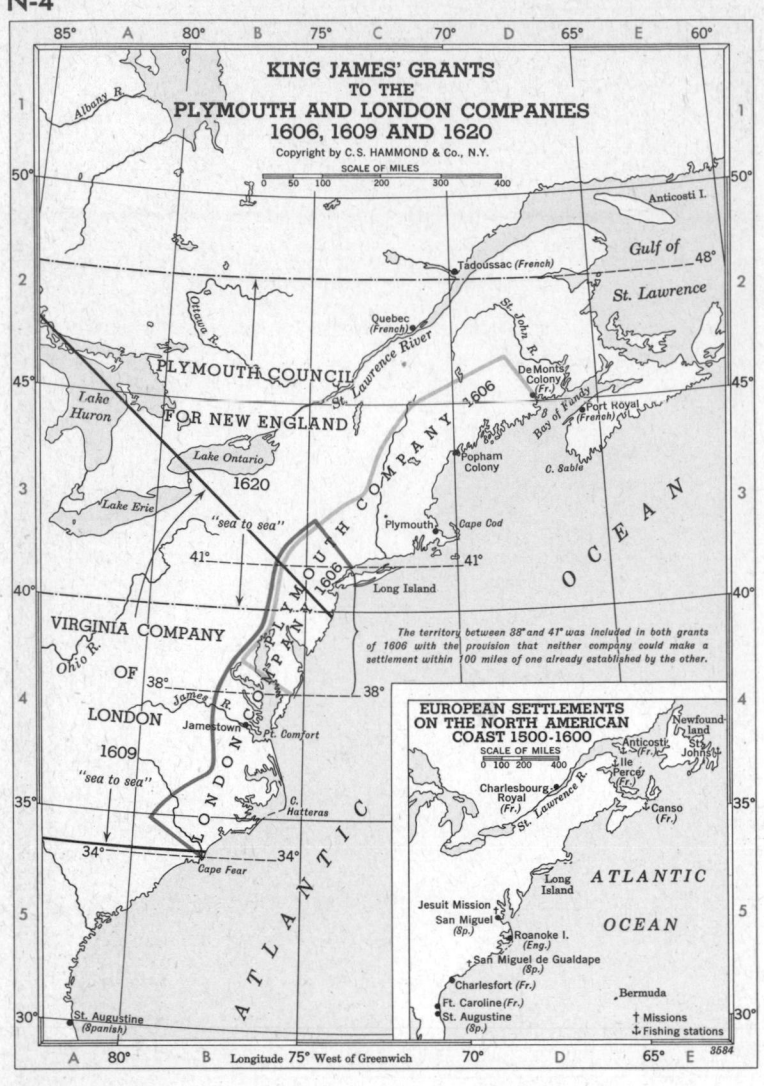

### KING JAMES' GRANTS TO THE PLYMOUTH AND LONDON COMPANIES 1606, 1609 AND 1620

Copyright by C.S. Hammond & Co., N.Y.

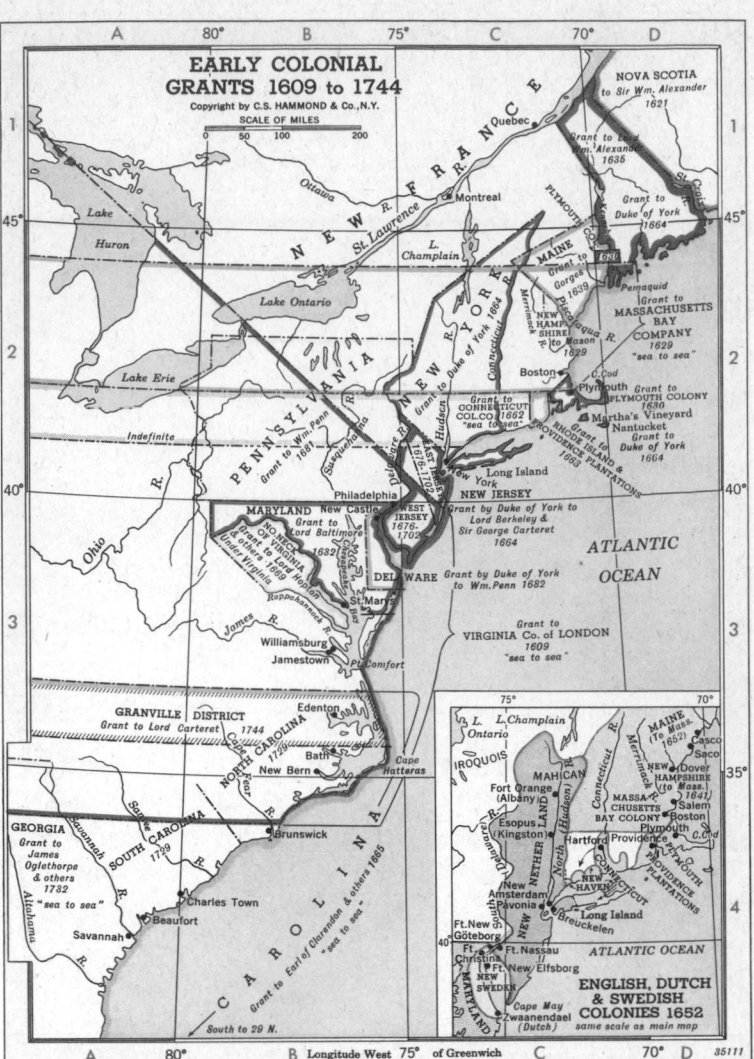

### EARLY COLONIAL GRANTS 1609 to 1744

Copyright by C.S. Hammond & Co., N.Y.

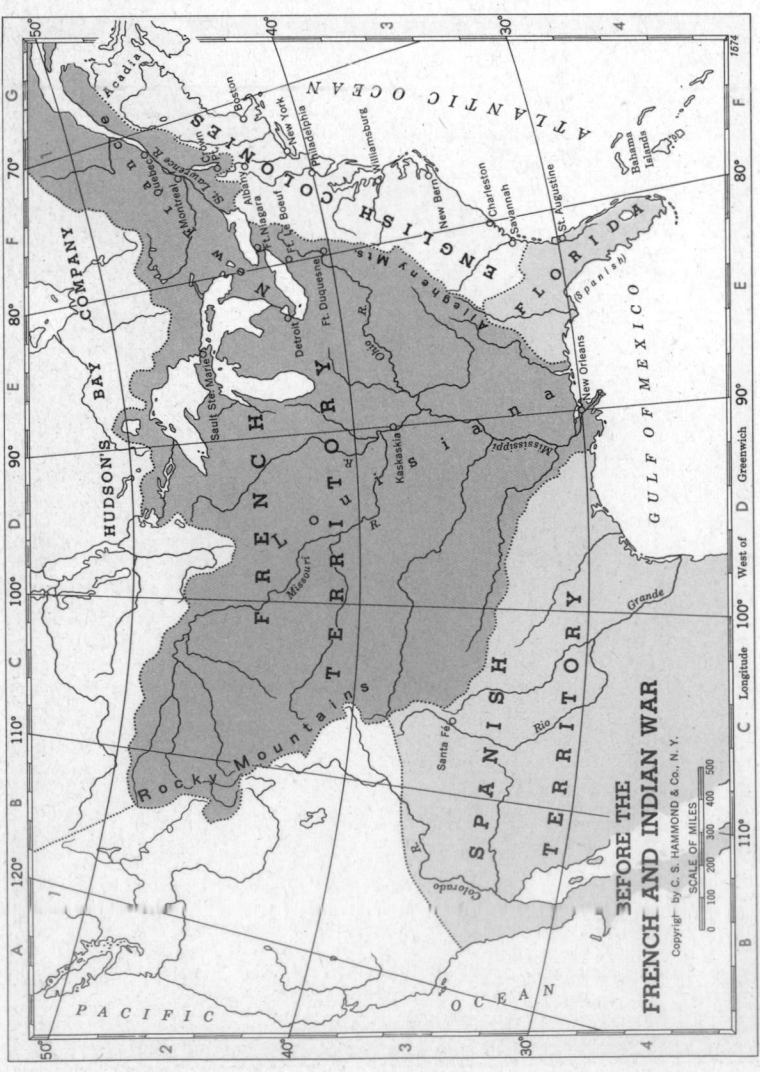

### BEFORE THE FRENCH AND INDIAN WAR

Copyright by C.S. Hammond & Co., N.Y.

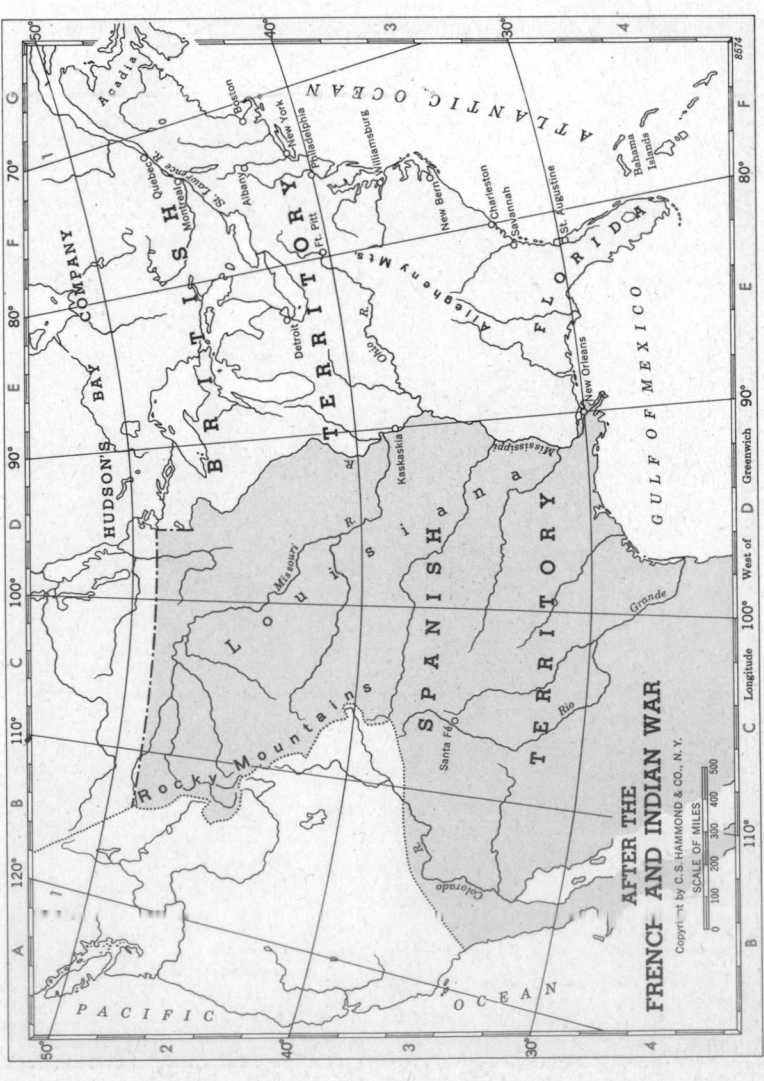

### AFTER THE FRENCH AND INDIAN WAR

Copyright by C.S. Hammond & Co., N.Y.

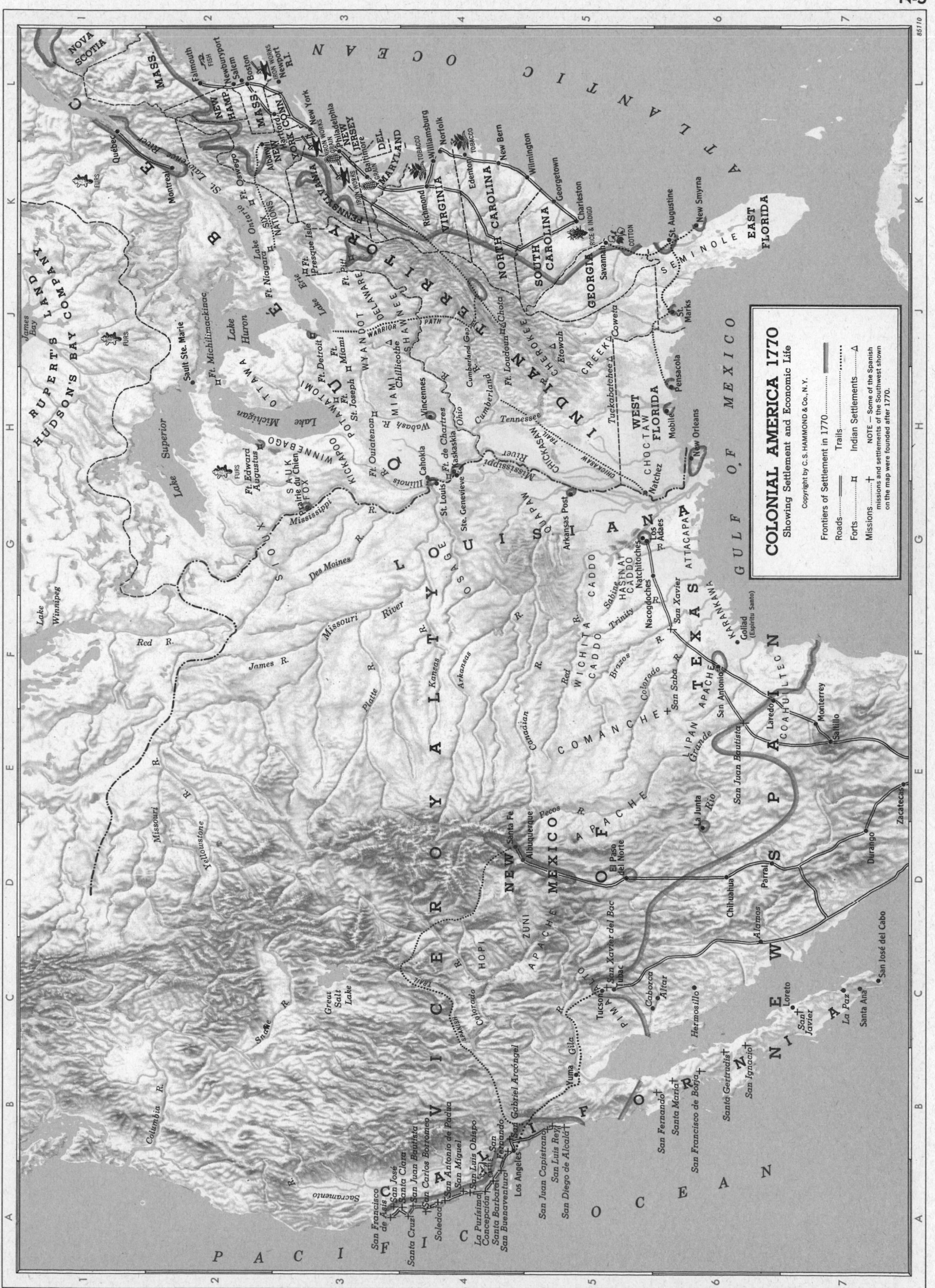

**COLONIAL AMERICA 1770**
Showing Settlement and Economic Life

Copyright by C.S. HAMMOND & Co., N.Y.

| | |
|---|---|
| Frontiers of Settlement in 1770 ............... | Trails ................. |
| Roads ................. | Indian Settlements ... △ |
| Forts ................. ⊔ | |
| Missions ................. + | NOTE — Some of the Spanish missions and settlements of the Southwest shown on the map were founded after 1770. |

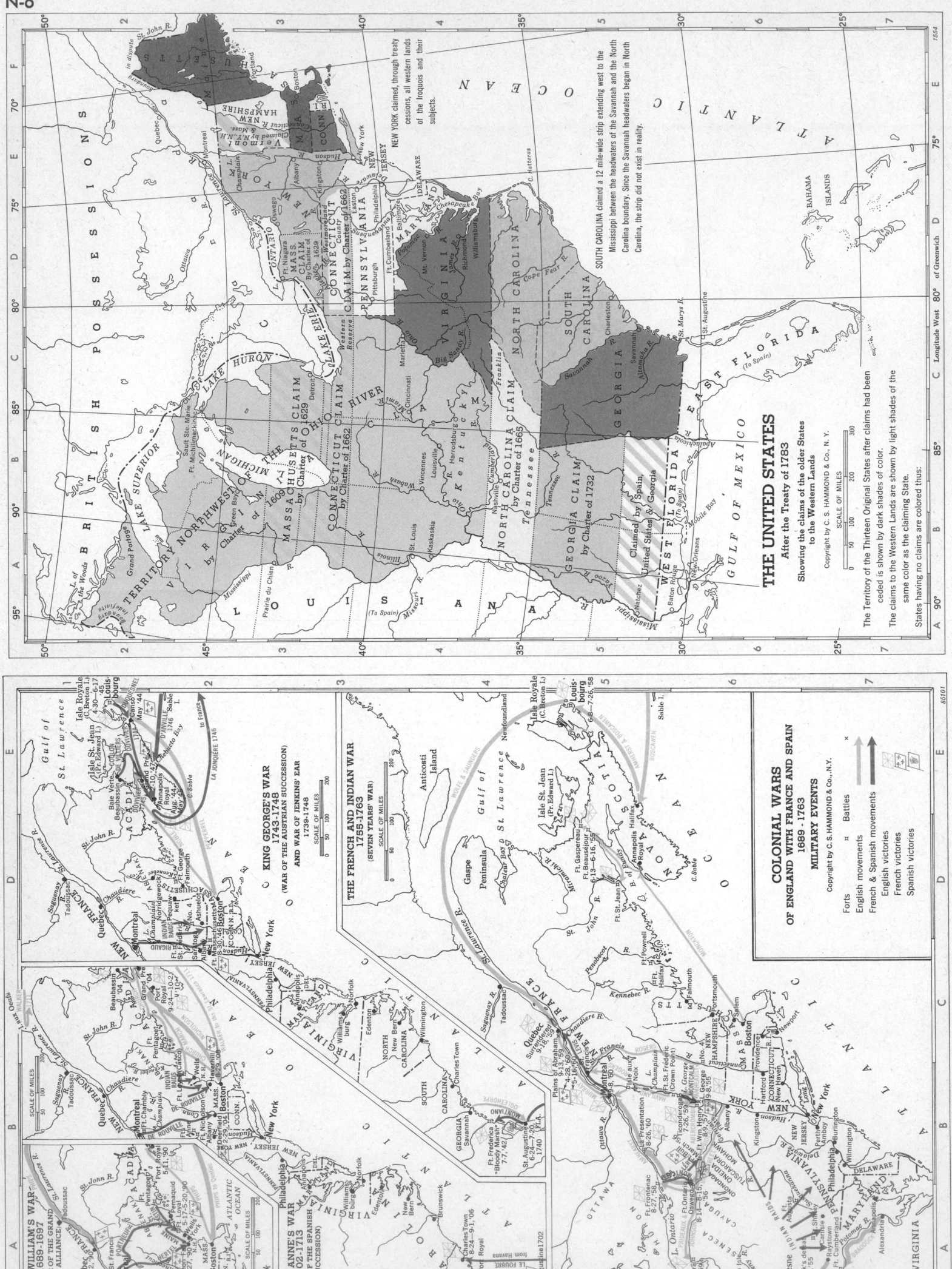

## THE UNITED STATES
### After the Treaty of 1783
Showing the claims of the older States to the Western Lands

Copyright by C. S. HAMMOND & Co., N. Y.

SCALE OF MILES

The Territory of the Thirteen Original States after claims had been ceded is shown by dark shades of color.

The claims to the Western Lands are shown by light shades of the same color as the claiming State.

States having no claims are colored thus:

## COLONIAL WARS
### OF ENGLAND WITH FRANCE AND SPAIN
1689 - 1763
### MILITARY EVENTS

Copyright by C. S. HAMMOND & Co., N.Y.

Forts ⚐   ⌧ Battles
English movements ✕
French & Spanish movements
English victories
French victories
Spanish victories

## KING WILLIAM'S WAR
1689-1697
(WAR OF THE GRAND ALLIANCE)

SCALE OF MILES

## QUEEN ANNE'S WAR
1702-1713
(WAR OF THE SPANISH SUCCESSION)

SCALE OF MILES

## KING GEORGE'S WAR
1743-1748
(WAR OF THE AUSTRIAN SUCCESSION)
AND WAR OF JENKINS' EAR
1739-1748

SCALE OF MILES

## THE FRENCH AND INDIAN WAR
1755-1763
(SEVEN YEARS' WAR)

SCALE OF MILES

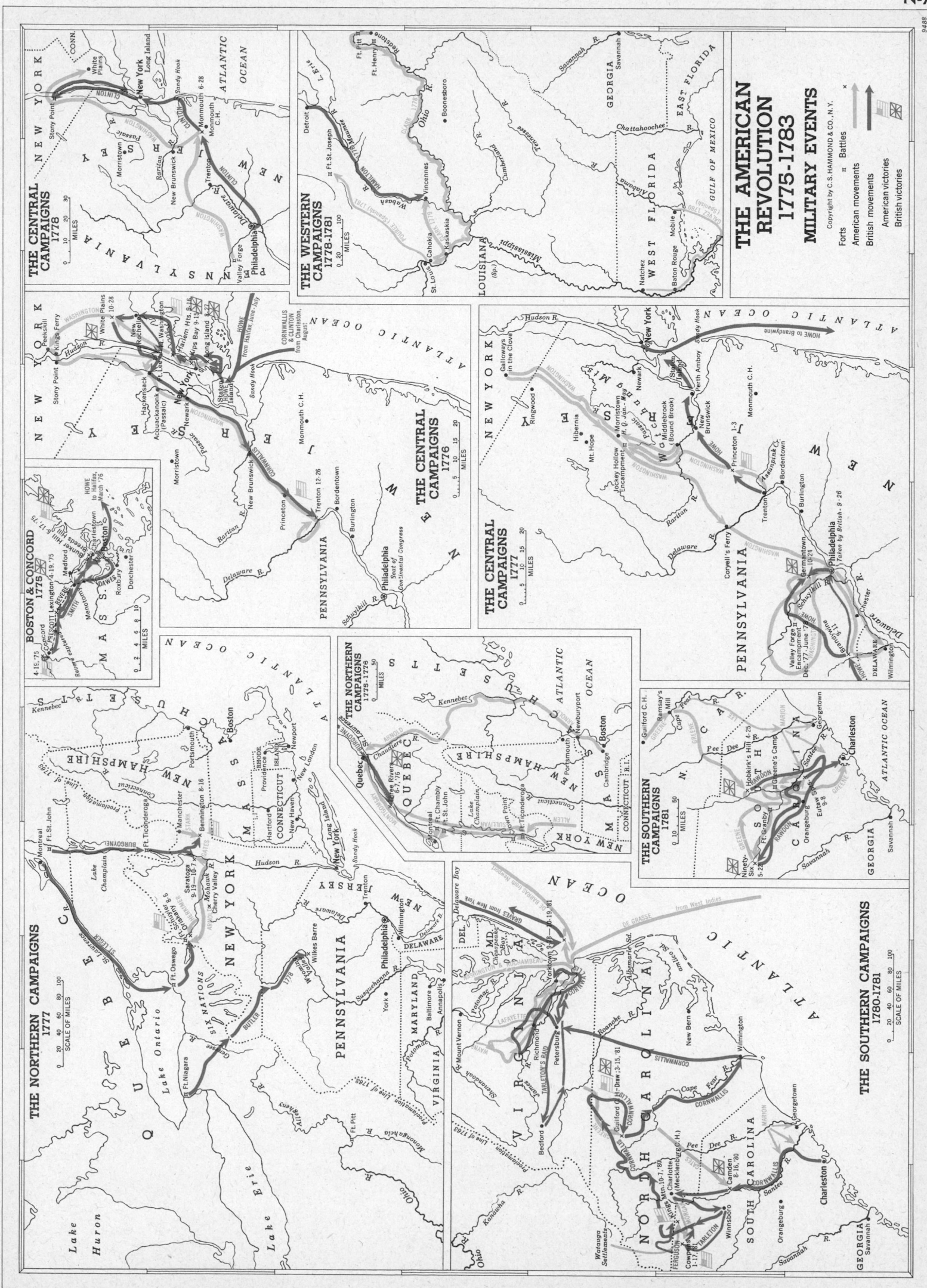

# THE AMERICAN REVOLUTION 1775-1783 MILITARY EVENTS

Copyright by C.S. HAMMOND & CO., N.Y.

Forts
× Battles
American movements
British movements
American victories
British victories

## THE CENTRAL CAMPAIGNS 1778

## THE WESTERN CAMPAIGNS 1778-1781

## BOSTON & CONCORD 1775

## NEW YORK & THE CENTRAL CAMPAIGNS 1776

## THE CENTRAL CAMPAIGNS 1777

## PENNSYLVANIA

## THE NORTHERN CAMPAIGNS 1775-1776

## THE NORTHERN CAMPAIGNS 1777

## THE SOUTHERN CAMPAIGNS 1781

## THE SOUTHERN CAMPAIGNS 1780-1781

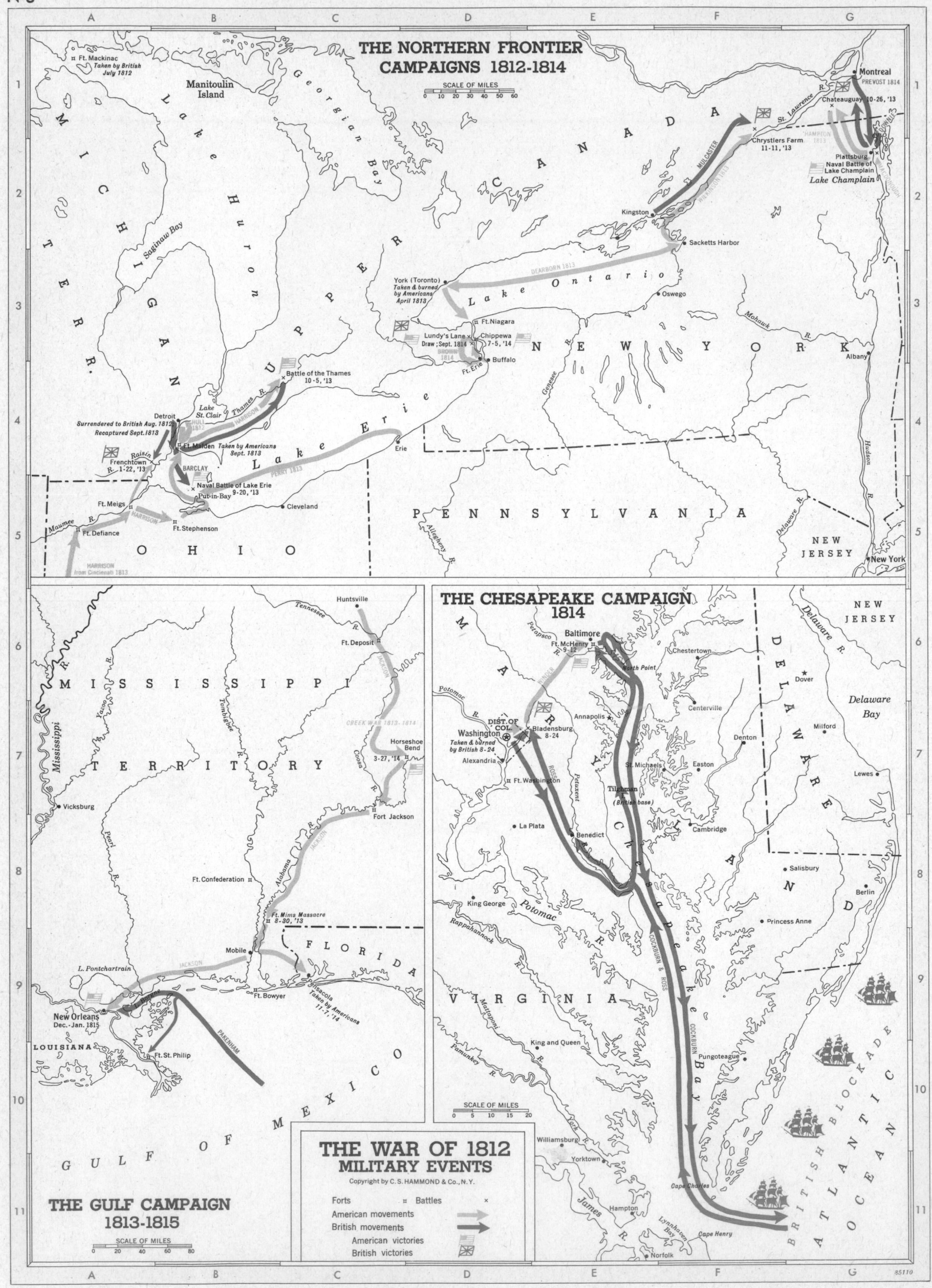

## THE NORTHERN FRONTIER CAMPAIGNS 1812-1814

SCALE OF MILES
0 10 20 30 40 50 60

MICHIGAN TERR.

Ft. Mackinac *Taken by British July 1812*

Manitoulin Island

Georgian Bay

Lake Huron

Saginaw Bay

UPPER CANADA

Montreal
PREVOST 1814
Chateauguay 10-26, '13
Chrystlers Farm 11-11, '13
St. Lawrence
HAMPTON 1813
Plattsburg
Naval Battle of Lake Champlain
Lake Champlain

MULCASTER
WILKINSON 1813

Kingston
Sacketts Harbor

DEARBORN 1813

Lake Ontario
Oswego

York (Toronto) *Taken & burned by Americans April 1813*

NEW YORK

Mohawk R.

Ft. Niagara
Lundy's Lane *Draw; Sept. 1814*
Chippewa 7-5, '14
1814
Ft. Erie
Buffalo

Genesee R.

Albany

Battle of the Thames 10-5, '13

Thames R.
HARRISON

Detroit *Surrendered to British Aug. 1812. Recaptured Sept. 1813*
Lake St. Clair
HULL 1812
Ft. Ft. Malden *Taken by Americans Sept. 1813*
BARCLAY
Lake Erie
PERRY 1813
Erie
Naval Battle of Lake Erie *Put-in-Bay 9-20, '13*
Cleveland

Raisin R.
Frenchtown *R. 1-22, '13*

Ft. Meigs
Maumee R.
HARRISON
Ft. Defiance
Ft. Stephenson

OHIO

PENNSYLVANIA

Allegheny R.

Delaware R.

NEW JERSEY

NEW YORK

Hudson R.

HARRISON *from Cincinnati 1813*

## THE CHESAPEAKE CAMPAIGN 1814

NEW JERSEY

Delaware R.

MARYLAND

Patapsco R.

Baltimore
Ft. McHenry *9-12*
North Point

Chestertown

Dover

Delaware Bay

Potomac R.

DIST. OF COL.
Washington *Taken & burned by British 8-24*
Bladensburg 8-24
Alexandria

Annapolis
Centerville

DELAWARE

Milford

ROSS

Ft. Washington
St. Michaels
Tilghman *(British base)*
Patuxent R.

Easton

Denton

Lewes

Benedict
La Plata

COCKBURN & ROSS

Cambridge

Salisbury

Berlin

VIRGINIA

King George
Potomac R.
JACKSON

Princess Anne

Rappahannock R.

Mattaponi R.

King and Queen
Pamunkey R.

Pungoteague

COCKBURN Bay

Chesapeake Bay

BRITISH BLOCKADE

ATLANTIC OCEAN

Cape Charles

Williamsburg
Yorktown
James R.
Hampton
Norfolk

Lynnhaven Bay
Cape Henry

SCALE OF MILES
0 5 10 15 20

## THE GULF CAMPAIGN 1813-1815

Huntsville
Tennessee R.
Ft. Deposit

MISSISSIPPI TERRITORY

Yazoo R.
Tombigbee R.

JACKSON

CREEK WAR 1813-1814

Horseshoe Bend 3-27, '14

Coosa R.
Alabama R.

Fort Jackson

Vicksburg
Pearl R.

Ft. Confederation

Ft. Mims Massacre *8-30, '13*

FLORIDA

Mississippi R.

Mobile
JACKSON
L. Pontchartrain

Ft. Bowyer
Pensacola *Taken by Americans 11-7, '14*

New Orleans *Dec.-Jan. 1815*
PAKENHAM
LOUISIANA
Ft. St. Philip

GULF OF MEXICO

## THE WAR OF 1812 MILITARY EVENTS

Copyright by C. S. HAMMOND & Co., N.Y.

Forts ⌂          Battles ×
American movements →
British movements →
American victories
British victories

35110

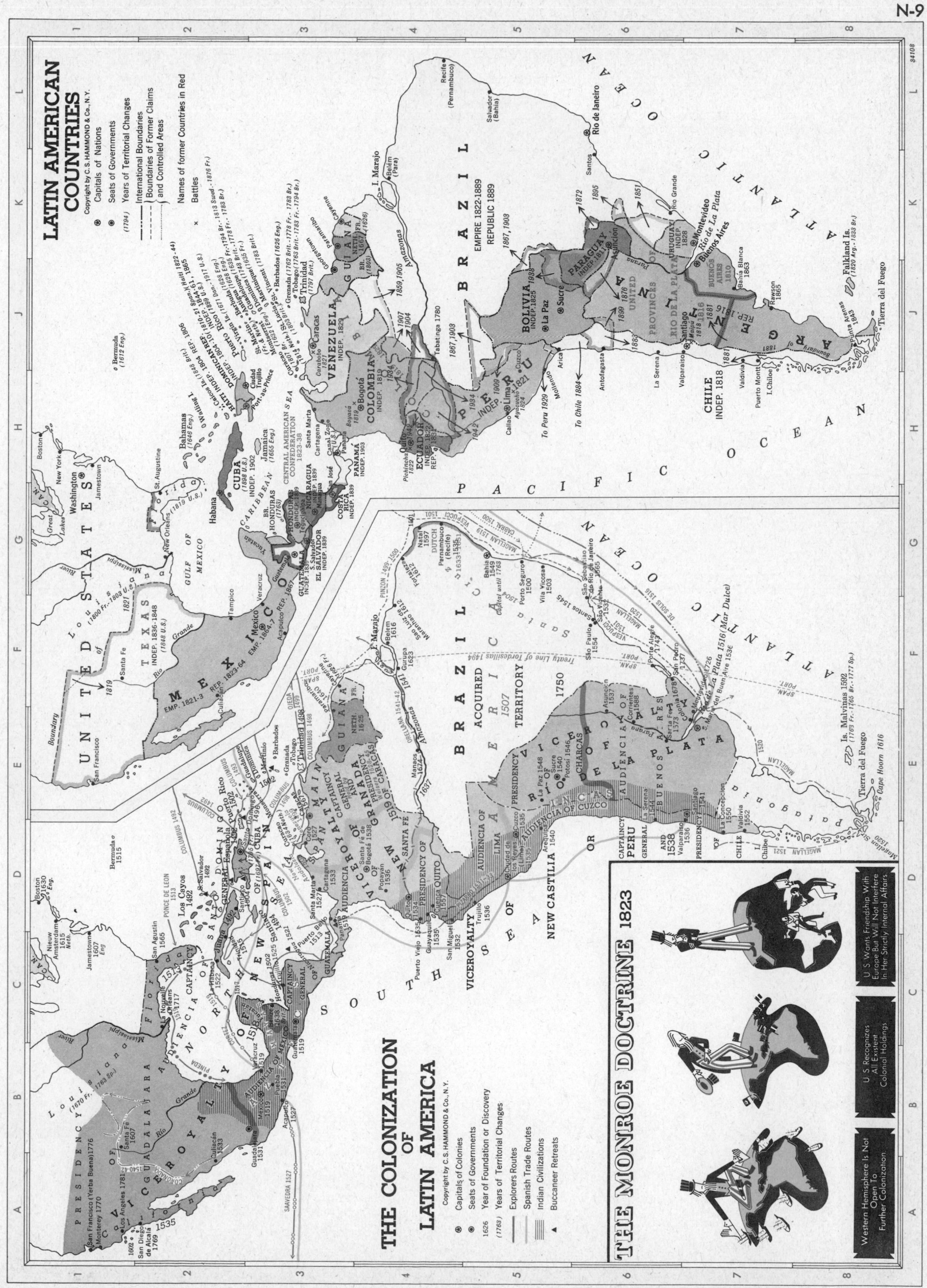

## LATIN AMERICAN COUNTRIES

Copyright by C. S. HAMMOND & Co., N.Y.

⊛  Capitals of Nations
⊛  Seats of Governments
(1794)  Years of Territorial Changes
———  International Boundaries
- - -  Boundaries of Former Claims
         and Controlled Areas
×  Battles

Names of former Countries in Red

## THE COLONIZATION OF LATIN AMERICA

Copyright by C. S. HAMMOND & Co., N.Y.

⊛  Capitals of Colonies
⊛  Seats of Governments
1626  Year of Foundation or Discovery
(1769)  Years of Territorial Changes
———  Explorers Routes
———  Spanish Trade Routes
▲  Indian Civilizations
▲  Buccaneer Retreats

## THE MONROE DOCTRINE 1823

Western Hemisphere Is Not Open To Further Colonization

U. S. Recognizes All Existent Colonial Holdings.

U. S. Wants Friendship With Europe But Will Not Interfere In Her Strictly Internal Affairs

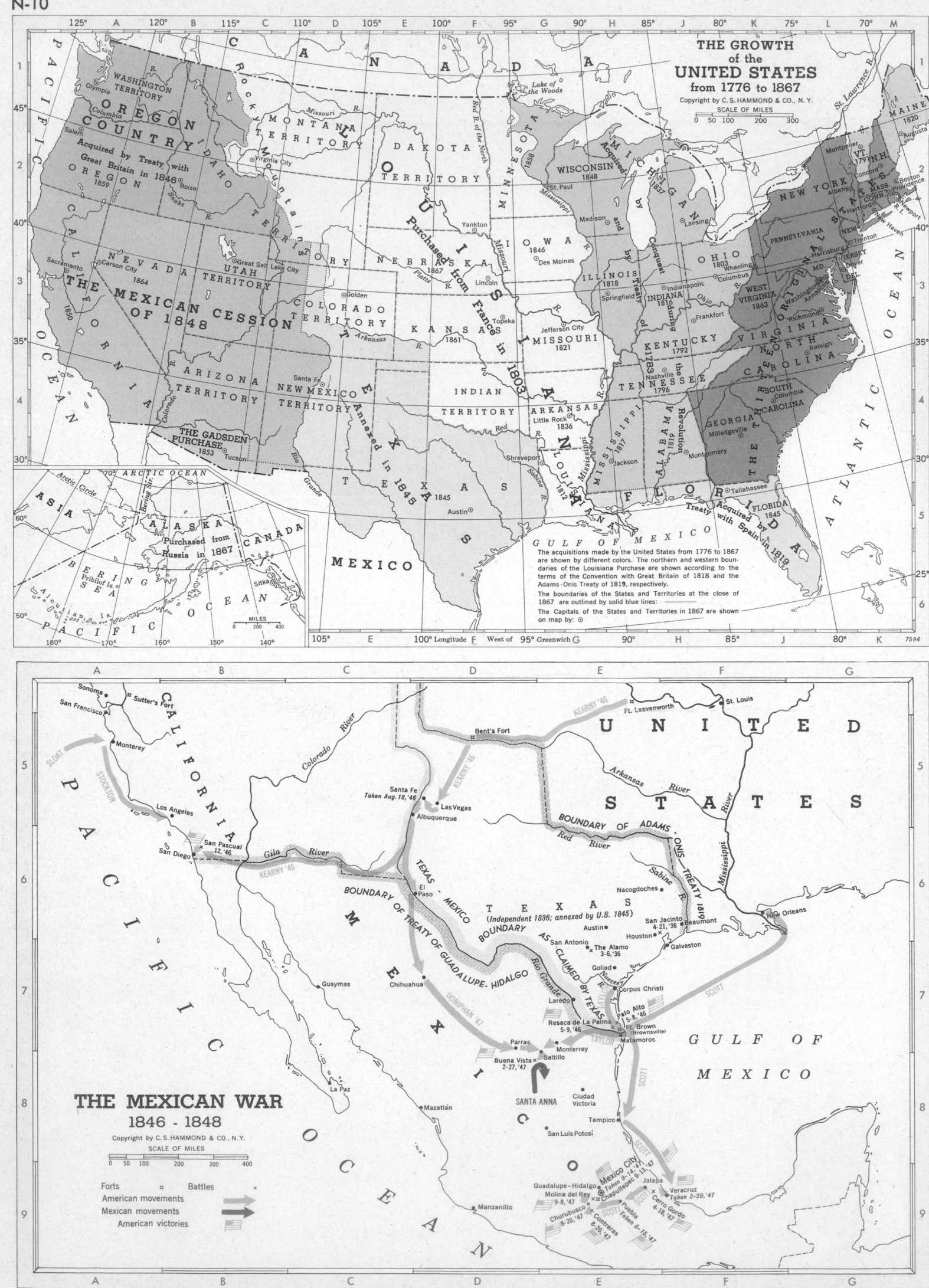

# THE GROWTH
## of the
## UNITED STATES
### from 1776 to 1867

Copyright by C.S. HAMMOND & CO., N.Y.

SCALE OF MILES
0 50 100 200 300

The acquisitions made by the United States from 1776 to 1867 are shown by different colors. The northern and western boundaries of the Louisiana Purchase are shown according to the terms of the Convention with Great Britain of 1818 and the Adams-Onis Treaty of 1819, respectively.

The boundaries of the States and Territories at the close of 1867 are outlined by solid blue lines:

The Capitals of the States and Territories in 1867 are shown on map by: ⊙

# THE MEXICAN WAR
## 1846 - 1848

Copyright by C.S. HAMMOND & CO., N.Y.
SCALE OF MILES
0 50 100 200 300 400

Forts □         Battles ×
American movements →
Mexican movements ⇒
American victories ⊠

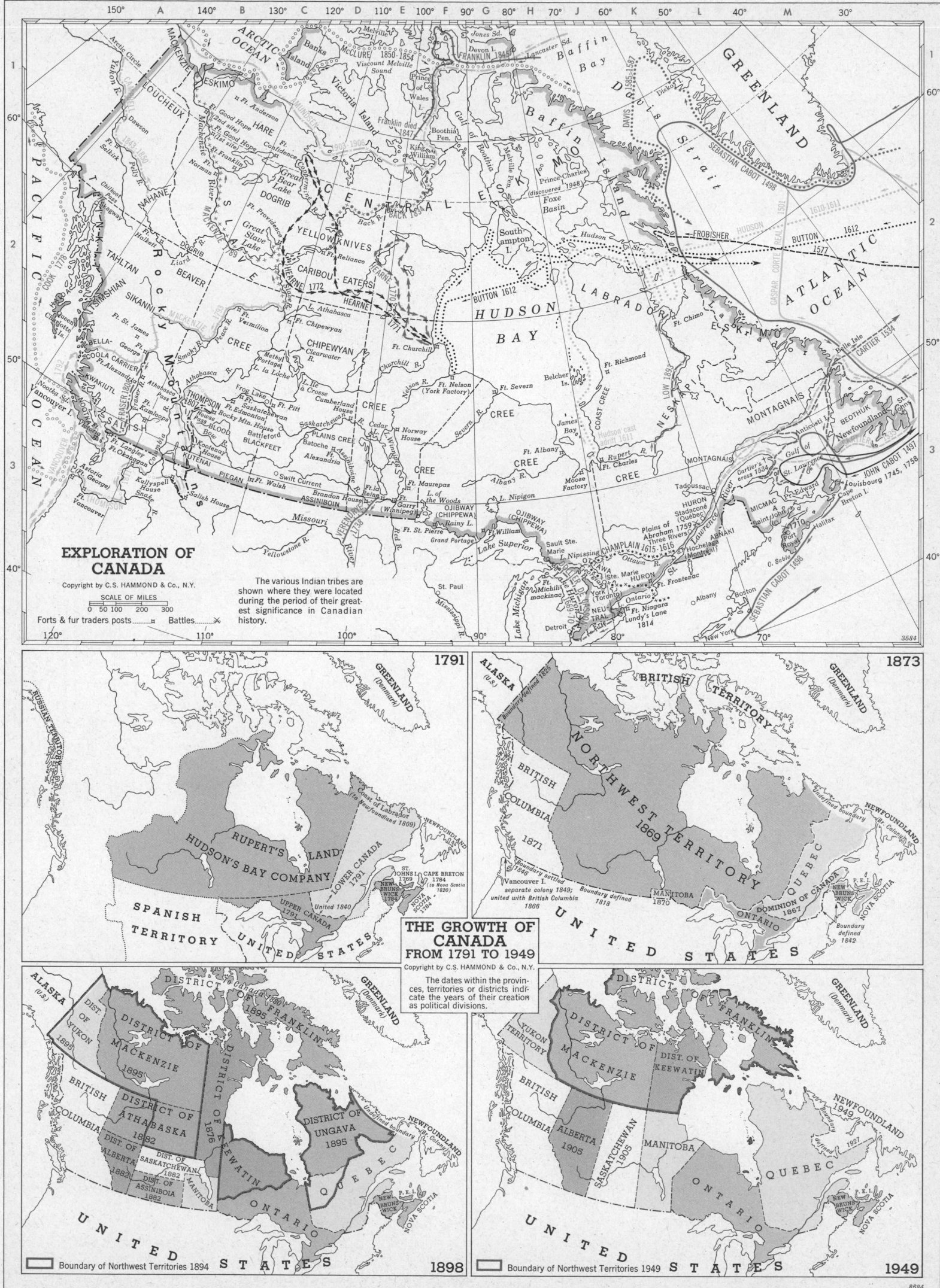

# EXPLORATION OF CANADA

Copyright by C.S. HAMMOND & Co., N.Y.

SCALE OF MILES
0 50 100 200 300

Forts & fur traders posts □    Battles ✕

The various Indian tribes are shown where they were located during the period of their greatest significance in Canadian history.

**1791**

**1873**

# THE GROWTH OF CANADA
### FROM 1791 TO 1949

Copyright by C.S. HAMMOND & Co., N.Y.

The dates within the provinces, territories or districts indicate the years of their creation as political divisions.

**1898**

Boundary of Northwest Territories 1894

**1949**

Boundary of Northwest Territories 1949

ROUTES TO THE WEST
1760-1860

Copyright by C.S. Hammond & Co., N.Y.

SCALE OF MILES

Individual roads and pioneer trails are shown
by means of distinguishing line symbols. The road
and trail names appear along the line symbols.

Canals ———  Forts ⌂  Indian Battles ✕

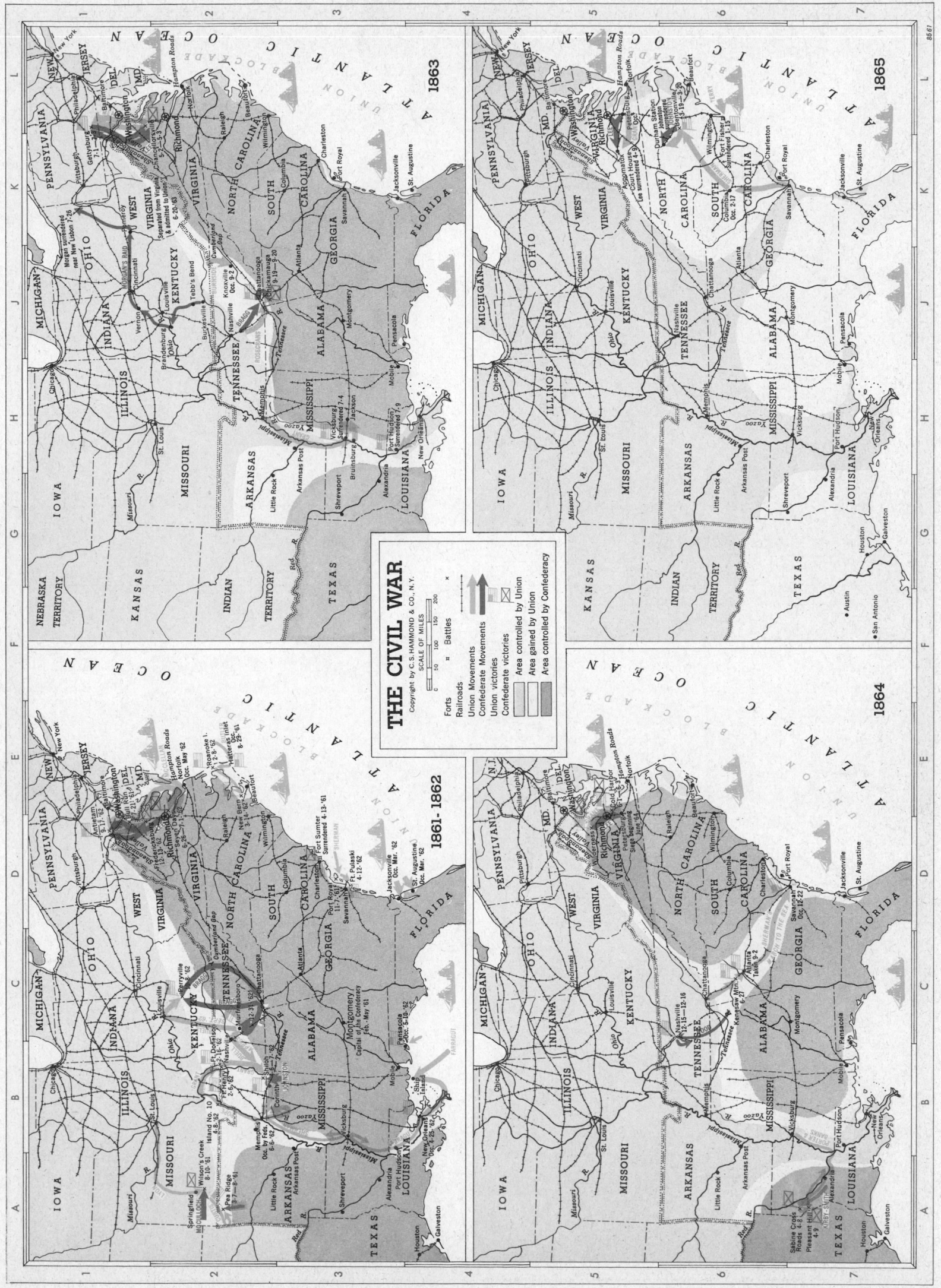

## THE CIVIL WAR

Copyright by C. S. HAMMOND & CO., N.Y.

SCALE OF MILES

0 50 100 150 200

× Battles

⌐ Forts

Railroads

Union Movements

Confederate Movements

Union victories

Confederate victories

Area controlled by Union

Area gained by Union

Area controlled by Confederacy

1861-1862

1863

1864

1865

THE WEST 1860-1910
Showing Railroads and Federal Land Grants

Copyright by C.S. HAMMOND & Co., N.Y.

| TRANSCONTINENTAL RAILROADS | |
|---|---|
| Constructed 1860-1870 | Constructed 1870-1880 |
| Constructed 1880-1890 | Constructed 1890-1900 |
| Constructed 1900-1910 | |

Major Federal land grants to railroads.

NOTE:-Within land-grant areas, no more than half the land-grant sections belonged to the railroad.

Frontiers of Settlement in 1860.

Forts ........... ⌂

Trails ...........

Indian Battles ........... ✗

Pony Express ...........

# DISTRIBUTION OF FOREIGN BORN
### PER CENT OF POPULATION OF EACH
### STATE BORN IN PRINCIPAL FOREIGN
### COUNTRIES

*Immigration to the United States in the nineteenth century was largely made up of Western European peoples—Germans, Irish, Swedes, English, etc. In the twentieth century the largest number of immigrants came from Southern and Eastern Europe—Italians, Poles and natives of the Russian and Austro-Hungarian Empires. Therefore, the year 1910 has been chosen as a base year for these maps because at that time both groups were present in sufficient numbers to be statistically significant.*

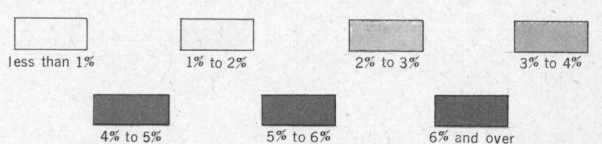

less than 1%    1% to 2%    2% to 3%    3% to 4%

4% to 5%    5% to 6%    6% and over

## ENGLAND, SCOTLAND & WALES

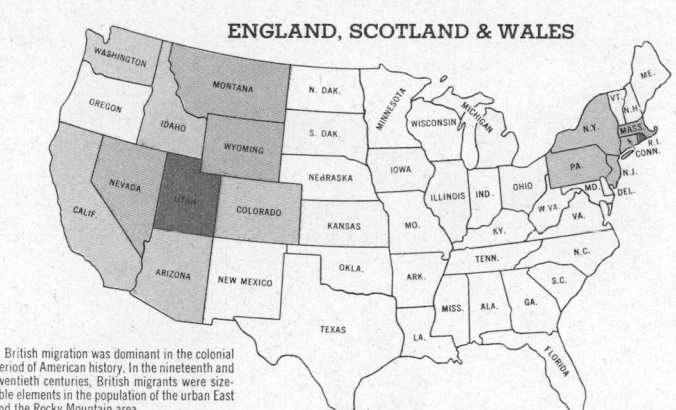

British migration was dominant in the colonial period of American history. In the nineteenth and twentieth centuries, British migrants were sizeable elements in the population of the urban East and the Rocky Mountain area.

## IRELAND

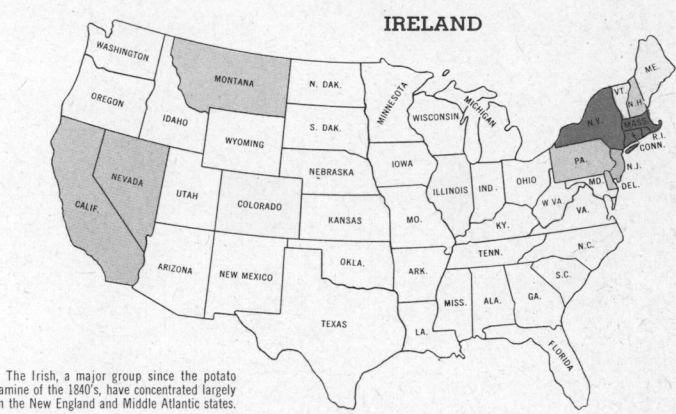

The Irish, a major group since the potato famine of the 1840's, have concentrated largely in the New England and Middle Atlantic states.

## GERMANY

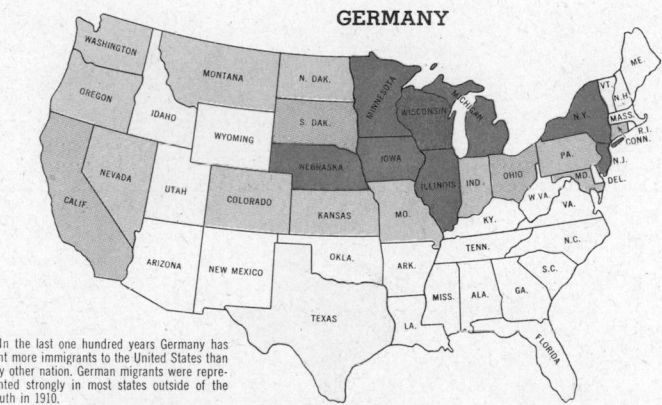

In the last one hundred years Germany has sent more immigrants to the United States than any other nation. German migrants were represented strongly in most states outside of the South in 1910.

## CANADA & NEWFOUNDLAND

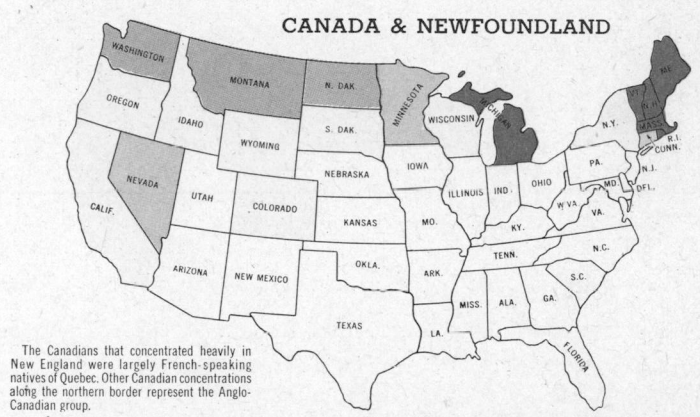

The Canadians that concentrated heavily in New England were largely French-speaking natives of Quebec. Other Canadian concentrations along the northern border represent the Anglo-Canadian group.

## NORWAY, SWEDEN & DENMARK

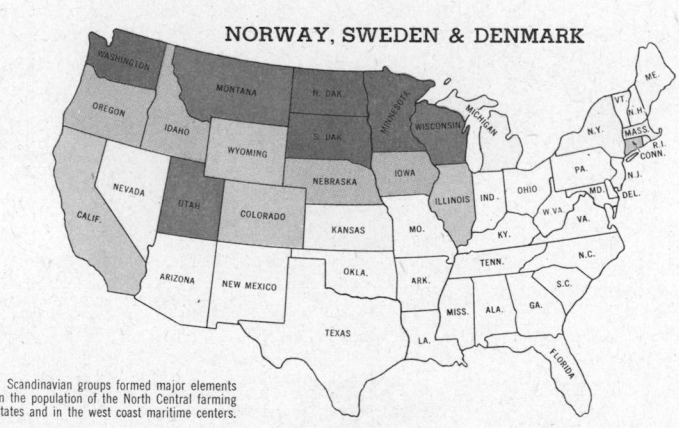

Scandinavian groups formed major elements in the population of the North Central farming states and in the west coast maritime centers.

## AUSTRO-HUNGARIAN MONARCHY

Immigrants from the Austro-Hungarian Monarchy were largely drawn from the Slavic peoples of that dominion—Czechs, Slovaks, Poles from Galicia, Croats and Slovenes.

## RUSSIAN EMPIRE

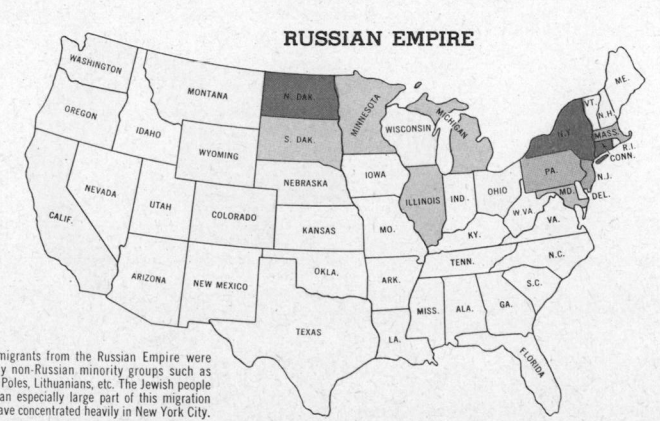

Immigrants from the Russian Empire were largely non-Russian minority groups such as Jews, Poles, Lithuanians, etc. The Jewish people were an especially large part of this migration and have concentrated heavily in New York City.

## ITALY

Italians arrived in great numbers after 1900. The majority have concentrated in the urban centers of the Northeast.

4561

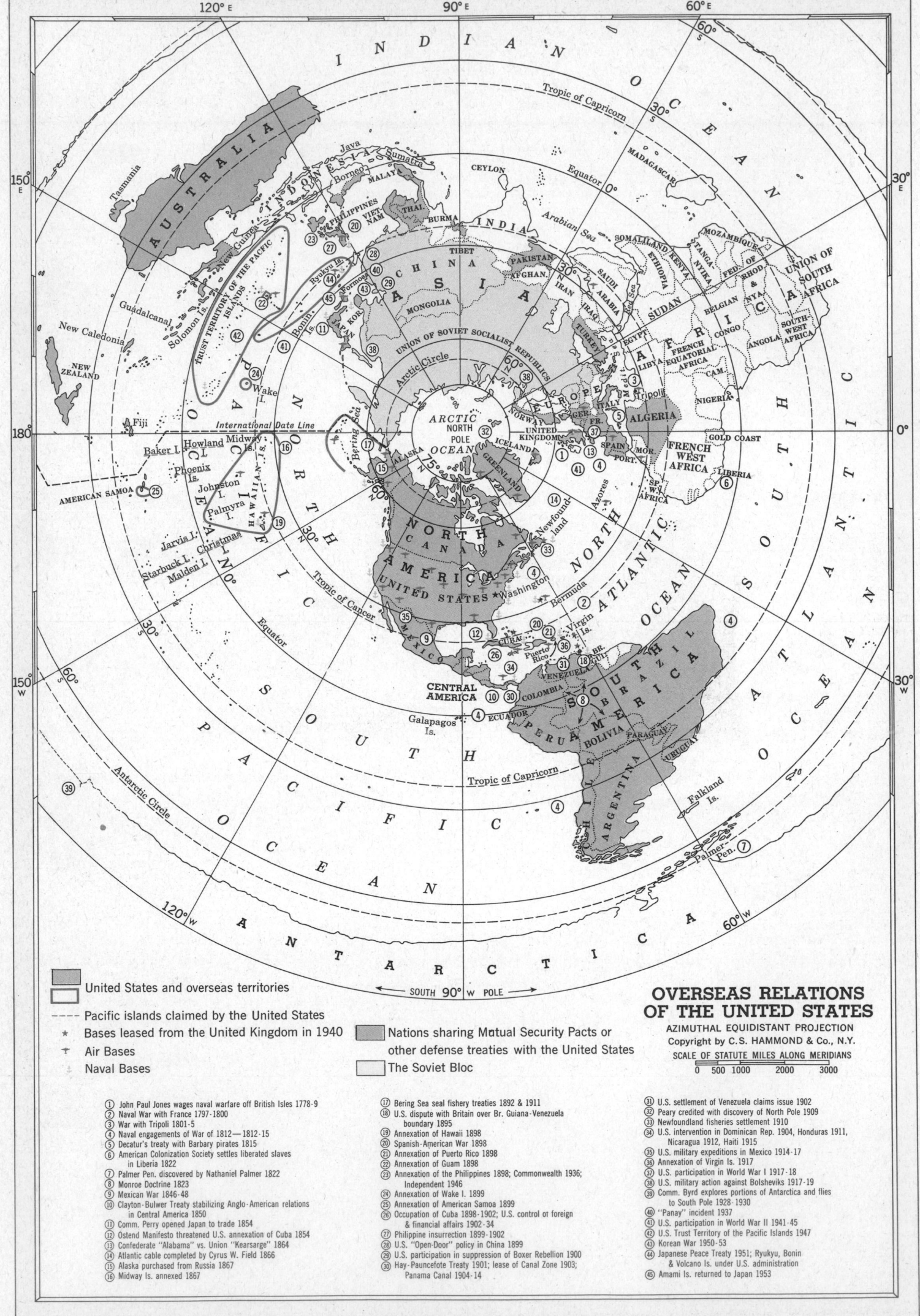

120° E     90° E     60° E

United States and overseas territories

Pacific islands claimed by the United States

★ Bases leased from the United Kingdom in 1940

⊤ Air Bases

⌄ Naval Bases

Nations sharing Mutual Security Pacts or other defense treaties with the United States

The Soviet Bloc

## OVERSEAS RELATIONS OF THE UNITED STATES

AZIMUTHAL EQUIDISTANT PROJECTION
Copyright by C.S. HAMMOND & Co., N.Y.

SCALE OF STATUTE MILES ALONG MERIDIANS

0   500   1000     2000     3000

① John Paul Jones wages naval warfare off British Isles 1778-9
② Naval War with France 1797-1800
③ War with Tripoli 1801-5
④ Naval engagements of War of 1812—1812-15
⑤ Decatur's treaty with Barbary pirates 1815
⑥ American Colonization Society settles liberated slaves in Liberia 1822
⑦ Palmer Pen. discovered by Nathaniel Palmer 1822
⑧ Monroe Doctrine 1823
⑨ Mexican War 1846-48
⑩ Clayton-Bulwer Treaty stabilizing Anglo-American relations in Central America 1850
⑪ Comm. Perry opened Japan to trade 1854
⑫ Ostend Manifesto threatened U.S. annexation of Cuba 1854
⑬ Confederate "Alabama" vs. Union "Kearsarge" 1864
⑭ Atlantic cable completed by Cyrus W. Field 1866
⑮ Alaska purchased from Russia 1867
⑯ Midway Is. annexed 1867

⑰ Bering Sea seal fishery treaties 1892 & 1911
⑱ U.S. dispute with Britain over Br. Guiana-Venezuela boundary 1895
⑲ Annexation of Hawaii 1898
⑳ Spanish-American War 1898
㉑ Annexation of Puerto Rico 1898
㉒ Annexation of Guam 1898
㉓ Annexation of the Philippines 1898; Commonwealth 1936; Independent 1946
㉔ Annexation of Wake I. 1899
㉕ Annexation of American Samoa 1899
㉖ Occupation of Cuba 1898-1902; U.S. control of foreign & financial affairs 1902-34
㉗ Philippine insurrection 1899-1902
㉘ U.S. "Open-Door" policy in China 1899
㉙ U.S. participation in suppression of Boxer Rebellion 1900
㉚ Hay-Pauncefote Treaty 1901; lease of Canal Zone 1903; Panama Canal 1904-14

㉛ U.S. settlement of Venezuela claims issue 1902
㉜ Peary credited with discovery of North Pole 1909
㉝ Newfoundland fisheries settlement 1910
㉞ U.S. intervention in Dominican Rep. 1904, Honduras 1911, Nicaragua 1912, Haiti 1915
㉟ U.S. military expeditions in Mexico 1914-17
㊱ Annexation of Virgin Is. 1917
㊲ U.S. participation in World War I 1917-18
㊳ U.S. military action against Bolsheviks 1917-19
㊴ Comm. Byrd explores portions of Antarctica and flies to South Pole 1928-1930
㊵ "Panay" incident 1937
㊶ U.S. participation in World War II 1941-45
㊷ U.S. Trust Territory of the Pacific Islands 1947
㊸ Korean War 1950-53
㊹ Japanese Peace Treaty 1951; Ryukyu, Bonin & Volcano Is. under U.S. administration
㊺ Amami Is. returned to Japan 1953

# HAMMOND'S
# HISTORICAL ATLAS

A collection of maps illustrating geographically the most significant periods and events in the development of Western Civilization.

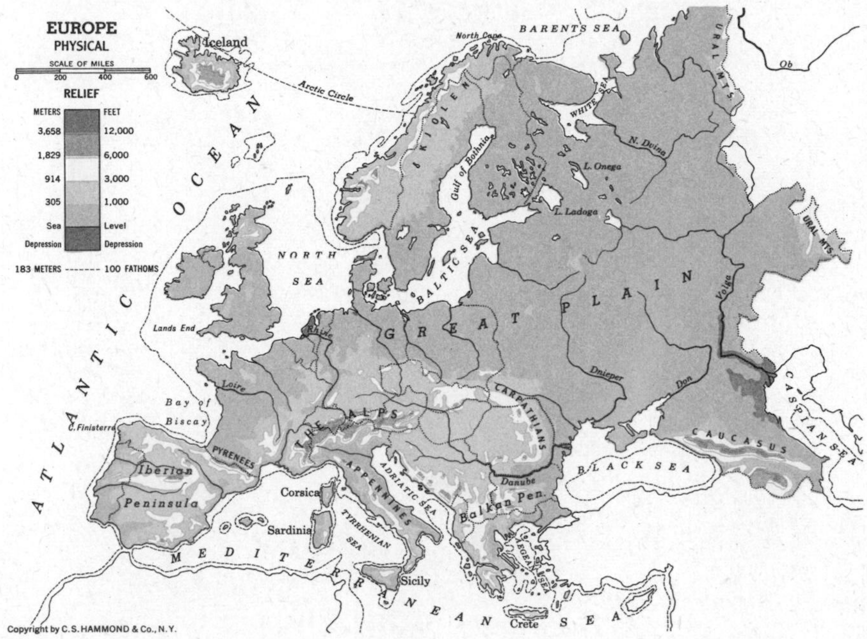

EUROPE
PHYSICAL
SCALE OF MILES
0   200   400   600
RELIEF

| METERS | FEET |
|---|---|
| 3,658 | 12,000 |
| 1,829 | 6,000 |
| 914 | 3,000 |
| 305 | 1,000 |
| Sea | Level |
| Depression | Depression |

183 METERS ------ 100 FATHOMS

Copyright by C. S. HAMMOND & Co., N. Y.

## TABLE OF CONTENTS

Published by

## C. S. HAMMOND & CO.

Printed in U. S. A.          MAPLEWOOD, N. J.          Copyright by C. S. Hammond & Co., MCMLVII

## MAP A

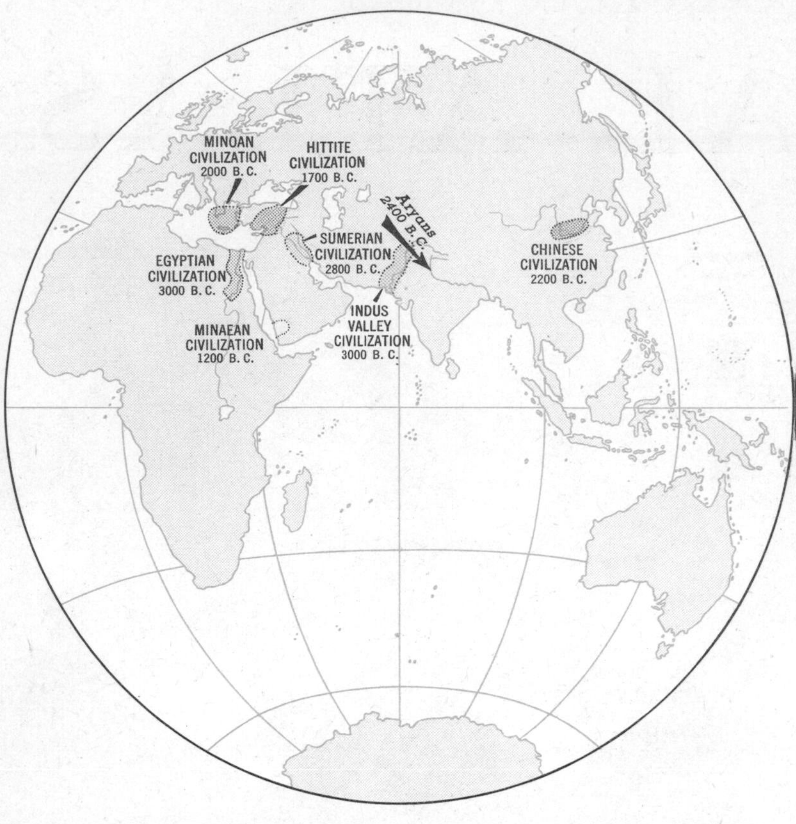

MINOAN CIVILIZATION 2000 B.C.
HITTITE CIVILIZATION 1700 B.C.
Aryans 2400 B.C.
SUMERIAN CIVILIZATION 2800 B.C.
EGYPTIAN CIVILIZATION 3000 B.C.
CHINESE CIVILIZATION 2200 B.C.
INDUS VALLEY CIVILIZATION 3000 B.C.
MINAEAN CIVILIZATION 1200 B.C.

*The Cradles of Civilization*
*3000-1000 B.C.*

## MAP B

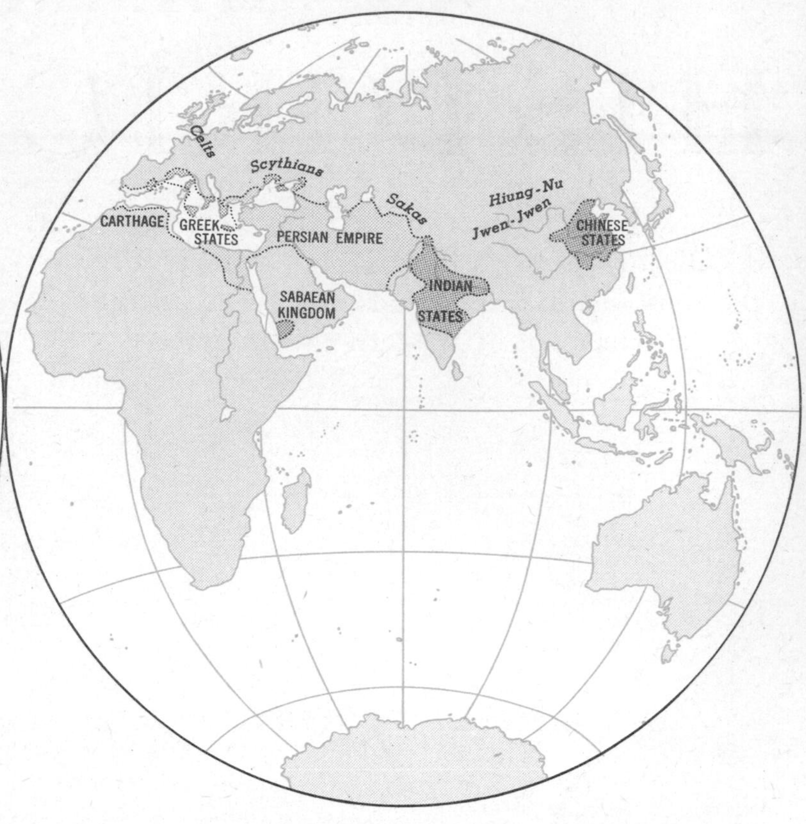

Celts
Scythians
Sakas
Hiung-Nu Jwen-Jwen
CARTHAGE
GREEK STATES
PERSIAN EMPIRE
CHINESE STATES
SABAEAN KINGDOM
INDIAN STATES

*Major States and Empires*
*in 500 B.C.*

## MAP C

MAYAN STATES
Huns
Germans
Slavs
White Huns
Kanggü
WESTERN ROMAN
EASTERN EMPIRE
Berbers
KINGDOM OF GHANA
Nubians
AXUMITE KINGDOM
HIMYARITIC KINGDOM
SASSANID EMPIRE
KUSHAN STATES
GUPTA EMPIRE
PALLAVA CONFEDERACY
Hindus
SINHALA
PYU
FUNAN
LANGKASUKA
YAVADWIPA
TARUMA
Hindus
K. OF MULAVARMAN
KOKURYO
WEI EMPIRE
SUNG EMPIRE
JAPANESE EMPIRE

*Major States and Empires*
*in 400 A.D.*

## MAP D

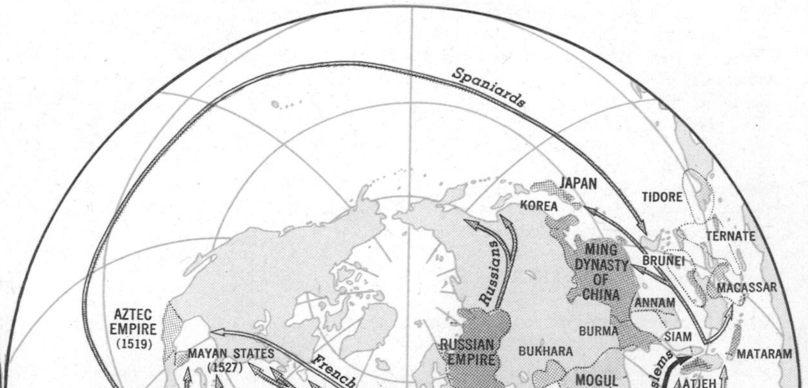

Spaniards
JAPAN
KOREA
TIDORE
MING DYNASTY OF CHINA
TERNATE
BRUNEI
MACASSAR
AZTEC EMPIRE (1519)
MAYAN STATES (1527)
French
English
Russians
RUSSIAN EMPIRE
BUKHARA
ANNAM
SIAM
MATARAM
Spaniards
Spaniards
INCA EMPIRE (1533)
MOROCCO
PERSIA
OTTOMAN EMPIRE
BURMA
MOGUL EMPIRE
Moslems
ATJEH
SONGHOY EMPIRE
HAUSA
BORNU
BAGUIRMI
DARFUR
ETHIOPIA
Portuguese
Dutch
Portuguese
Dutch

*The Expansion*
*of Western Civilization*
*1600 A.D.*

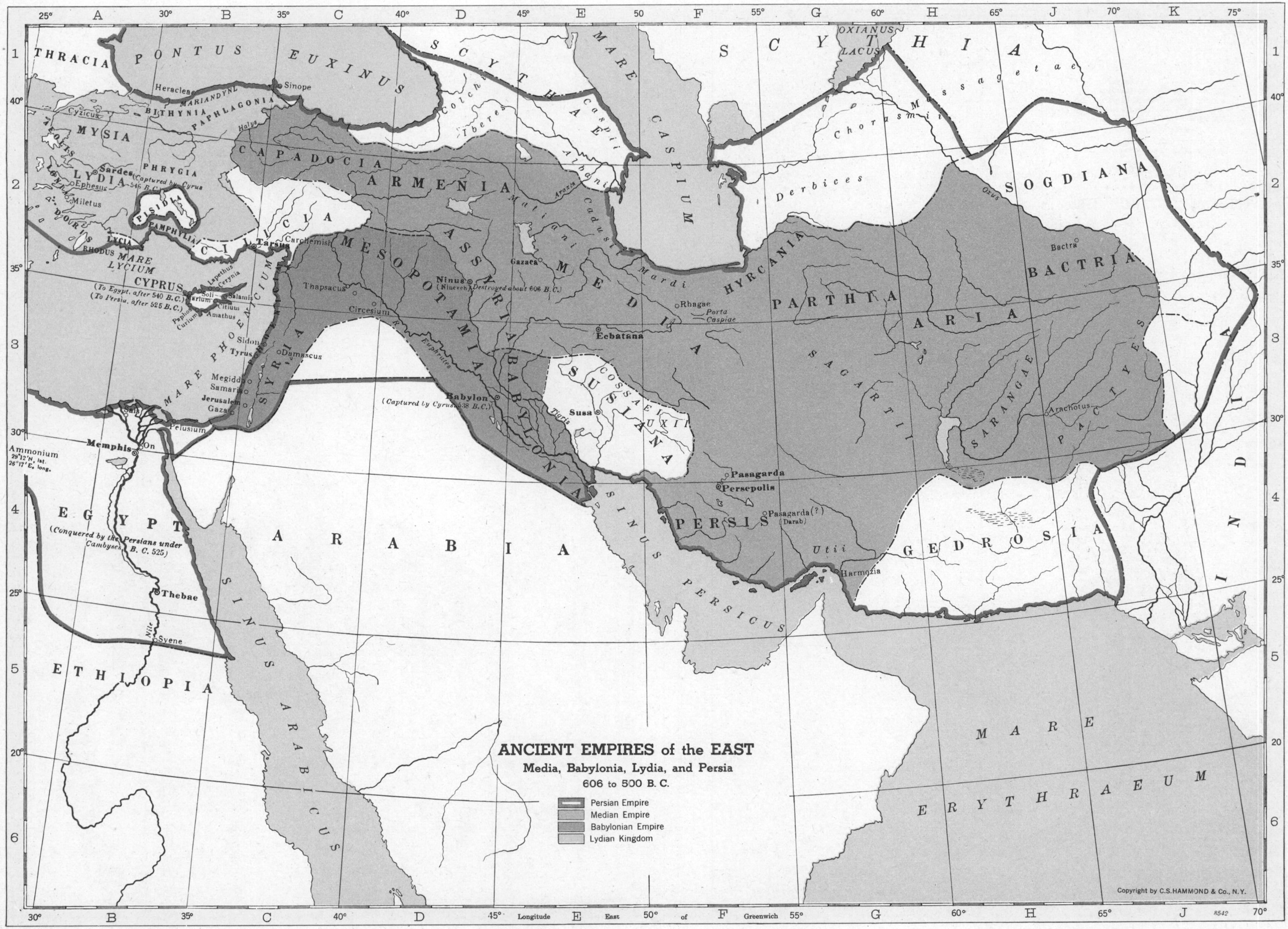

H-3

Copyright by C.S. HAMMOND & Co., N.Y.

1842

**ANCIENT EMPIRES of the EAST**
Media, Babylonia, Lydia, and Persia
606 to 500 B.C.

Persian Empire
Median Empire
Babylonian Empire
Lydian Kingdom

THRACIA
PONTUS EUXINUS
Sinope
Heraclea
MARIANDYNI
BITHYNIA PAPHLAGONIA
Halys
MYSIA
PHRYGIA
LYDIA
Sardes (Captured 546 B.C.)
Ephesus
Miletus
Aeolis
CARIA
Rhodus
LYCIA
MARE LYCIUM
PISIDIA
PAMPHYLIA
CILICIA
Tarsus
CAPADOCIA
ARMENIA
CYPRUS
Salamis
Citium
Paphos
Amathus
PHOENICIA
Sidon
Tyrus
Damascus
SYRIA
Megiddo
Samaria
Jerusalem
Gaza
MARE
Pelusium
On
Memphis
EGYPT
(Conquered by the Persians under Cambyses, B.C. 525)
Thebae
Syene
ETHIOPIA
Ammonium

SCYTHIA
SOGDIANA
BACTRIA
Bactra
ARIA
PARTHIA
HYRCANIA
MARE CASPIUM
MEDIA
Ecbatana
Rhagae
ASSYRIA
Ninus (Nineveh Destroyed about 606 B.C.)
MESOPOTAMIA
Euphrates
Tigris
Babylon (Captured by Cyrus 538 B.C.)
BABYLONIA
Thapsacus
Circesium
SUSIANA
Susa
COSSAEI
SAGARTII
PERSIS
Persepolis
Pasargada
SINUS PERSICUS
ARABIA
CARMANIA
GEDROSIA
Harmozia
PARAETACENE
SARANGAE
INDIA
MARE ERYTHRAEUM
SINUS ARABICUS

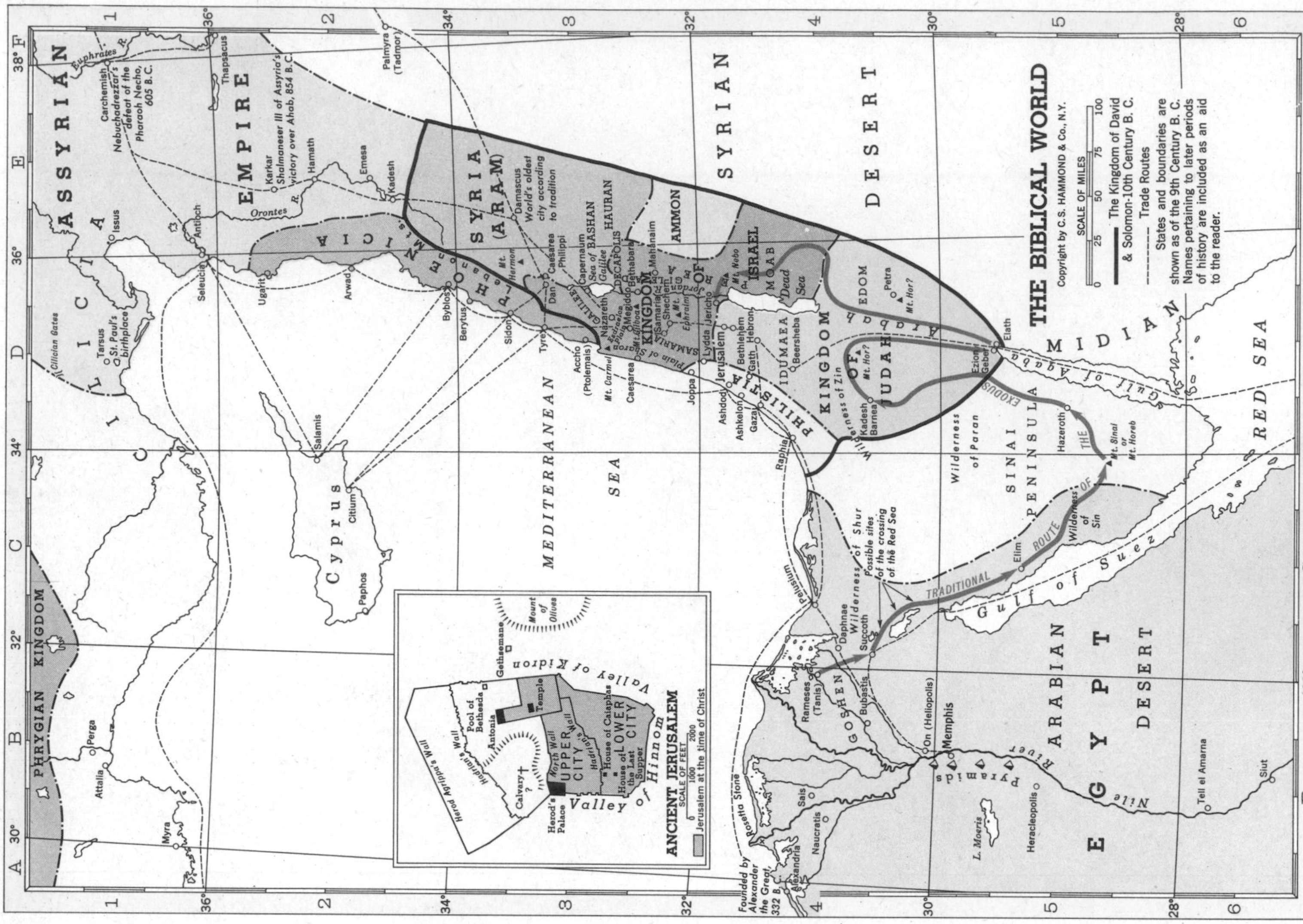

## THE BIBLICAL WORLD

Copyright by C.S. HAMMOND & Co., N.Y.

SCALE OF MILES

The Kingdom of David & Solomon-10th Century B.C.

Trade Routes

States and boundaries are shown as of the 9th Century B.C. Names pertaining to later periods of history are included as an aid to the reader.

### Major regions

ASSYRIAN EMPIRE — CILICIA — PHRYGIAN KINGDOM — CYPRUS — PHOENICIA — SYRIA (ARAM) — MEDITERRANEAN SEA — SYRIAN DESERT — KINGDOM OF ISRAEL — KINGDOM OF JUDAH — PHILISTIA — AMMON — MOAB — EDOM — IDUMAEA — MIDIAN — SINAI PENINSULA — EGYPT — ARABIAN DESERT — RED SEA — GOSHEN — Gulf of Suez — Gulf of Aqaba

### Selected place names
Euphrates R., Thapsacus, Carchemish, Nebuchadnezzar's defeat of Pharaoh Necho, 605 B.C., Palmyra (Tadmor), Emesa, Hamath, Karkar, Shalmaneser III of Assyria's victory over Ahab, 854 B.C., Issus, Antioch, Seleucia, Tarsus, St. Paul's birthplace, Cilician Gates, Salamis, Citium, Paphos, Perge, Attalia, Myra, Orontes R., Kadesh, Ugarit, Arwad, Byblos, Berytus, Sidon, Damascus, World's oldest city according to tradition, Mt. Hermon, Dan, Caesarea Philippi, Capernaum, Tyre, Accho (Ptolemais), Mt. Carmel, Caesarea, Joppa, Ashdod, Ashkelon, Gaza, Raphia, Megiddo, Samaria, Shechem, Jericho, Jerusalem, Bethlehem, Hebron, Gath, Beersheba, Dead Sea, Mt. Nebo, Petra, Mt. Hor?, Elath, Ezion Geber, Kadesh Barnea, Wilderness of Zin, Wilderness of Paran, Memphis, On (Heliopolis), Bubastis, Ramses (Tanis), Pelusium, Pyramids, Naucratis, Sais, Alexandria, Heracleopolis, L. Moeris, Siut, Tell el Amarna, Nile River, Wilderness of Sin, Wilderness of Shur, Mt. Sinai or Mt. Horeb, THE EXODUS, TRADITIONAL ROUTE

#### ANCIENT JERUSALEM
SCALE OF FEET

Jerusalem at the time of Christ

Mount of Olives, Gethsemane, Valley of Kidron, Temple, Pool of Bethesda, Antonia, House of Caiaphas, House of the Last Supper, UPPER CITY, LOWER CITY, Calvary, Herod's Palace, Royal Well, Gihon Well, Hezekiah's Wall, Herod Agrippa's Wall, Valley of Hinnom, Founded by Alexander the Great, 332 B.C.

---

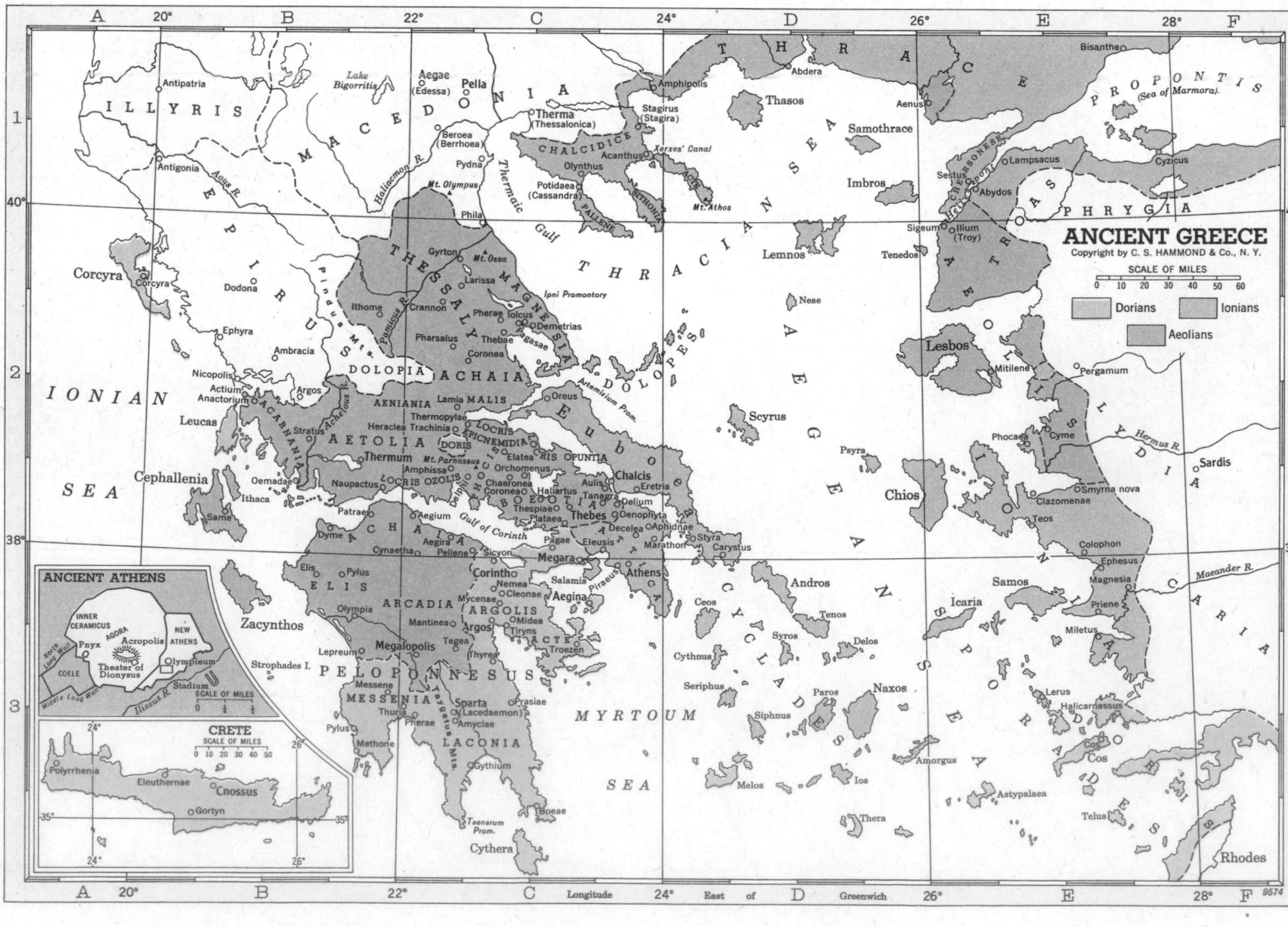

## ANCIENT GREECE

Copyright by C.S. HAMMOND & Co., N.Y.

SCALE OF MILES

Dorians · Ionians · Aeolians

### Regions
ILLYRIS — MACEDONIA — EPIRUS — THESSALY — THRACE — PHRYGIA — LYDIA — CARIA — AETOLIA — ACARNANIA — ACHAIA — BOEOTIA — ATTICA — ARCADIA — ELIS — MESSENIA — LACONIA — ARGOLIS — PELOPONNESUS — DOLOPIA — MAGNESIA — LOCRIS — PHOCIS — DORIS — AENIANIA — MALIS

### Seas
IONIAN SEA — MEDITERRANEAN — THRACIAN SEA — AEGEAN SEA — MYRTOUM SEA — PROPONTIS (Sea of Marmora) — Gulf of Corinth — Thermaic Gulf — Thermaic Gulf

### Places
Antipatria, Antigonia, Lake Bigorritis, Aegae (Edessa), Pella, Beroea (Berrhoea), Pydna, Mt. Olympus, Phila, Corcyra, Dodona, Ephyra, Ambracia, Nicopolis, Actium, Anactorium, Leucas, Cephallenia, Ithaca, Same, Patrae, Dyme, Zacynthos, Strophades I., Pylus, Olympia, Lepreum, Megalopolis, Messene, Methone, Sparta (Lacedaemon), Amyclae, Gythium, Taenarum Prom., Cythera, Boeae, Prasiae, Thyrea, Tegea, Mantinea, Argos, Mycenae, Midea, Tiryns, Troezen, Epidaurus, Cleonae, Nemea, Corinth, Sicyon, Pellene, Aegira, Aegium, Cynaetha, Stratus, Oeniadae, Naupactus, Thermum, Amphissa, Delphi, Mt. Parnassus, Crissa, Cirrha, Chaeronea, Coronea, Orchomenus, Thebes, Plataea, Thespiae, Leuctra, Tanagra, Oenophyta, Aulis, Chalcis, Eretria, Oreus, Artemisium Prom., Carystus, Styra, Marathon, Decelea, Aphidnae, Eleusis, Megara, Salamis, Piraeus, Athens, Aegina, Andros, Ceos, Cythnus, Seriphus, Siphnus, Paros, Naxos, Syros, Delos, Tenos, Mykonos, Ios, Amorgus, Melos, Thera, Astypalaea, Telus, Cos, Rhodes, Carpathos, Cnidus, Halicarnassus, Miletus, Priene, Magnesia, Ephesus, Colophon, Teos, Clazomenae, Smyrna nova, Phocaea, Cyme, Sardis, Maeander R., Hermus R., Chios, Samos, Icaria, Lerus, Patmos, Lesbos, Mitilene, Pergamum, Phocaea, Sigeum, Ilium (Troy), Tenedos, Lemnos, Imbros, Samothrace, Thasos, Abdera, Aenus, Bisanthe, Perinthus, Byzantium, Cyzicus, Lampsacus, Sestus, Abydos, Chersonesus, Amphipolis, Stagirus (Stagira), Acanthus, Olynthus, Potidaea (Cassandra), Therma (Thessalonica), Mt. Athos, PALLENE, CHALCIDICE, Xerxes' Canal, Neae, Scyrus, Psyra, Larissa, Gyrton, Crannon, Pherae, Pharsalus, Iolcus, Demetrias, Pagasae, Mt. Ossa, Mt. Pelion, Ithome, Thebae, Coronea, Lamia, Thermopylae, Heraclea Trachinia, Amphissa, Calydon, Pleuron, Halos

#### ANCIENT ATHENS
INNER CERAMICUS, AGORA, Pnyx, Acropolis, NEW ATHENS, Theater of Dionysus, Olympium, Stadium, North Long Wall, Middle Long Wall, South Long Wall, COELE, Ilissus R.

SCALE OF MILES

#### CRETE
SCALE OF MILES

Polyrrhenia, Eleuthernae, Cnossus, Gortyn

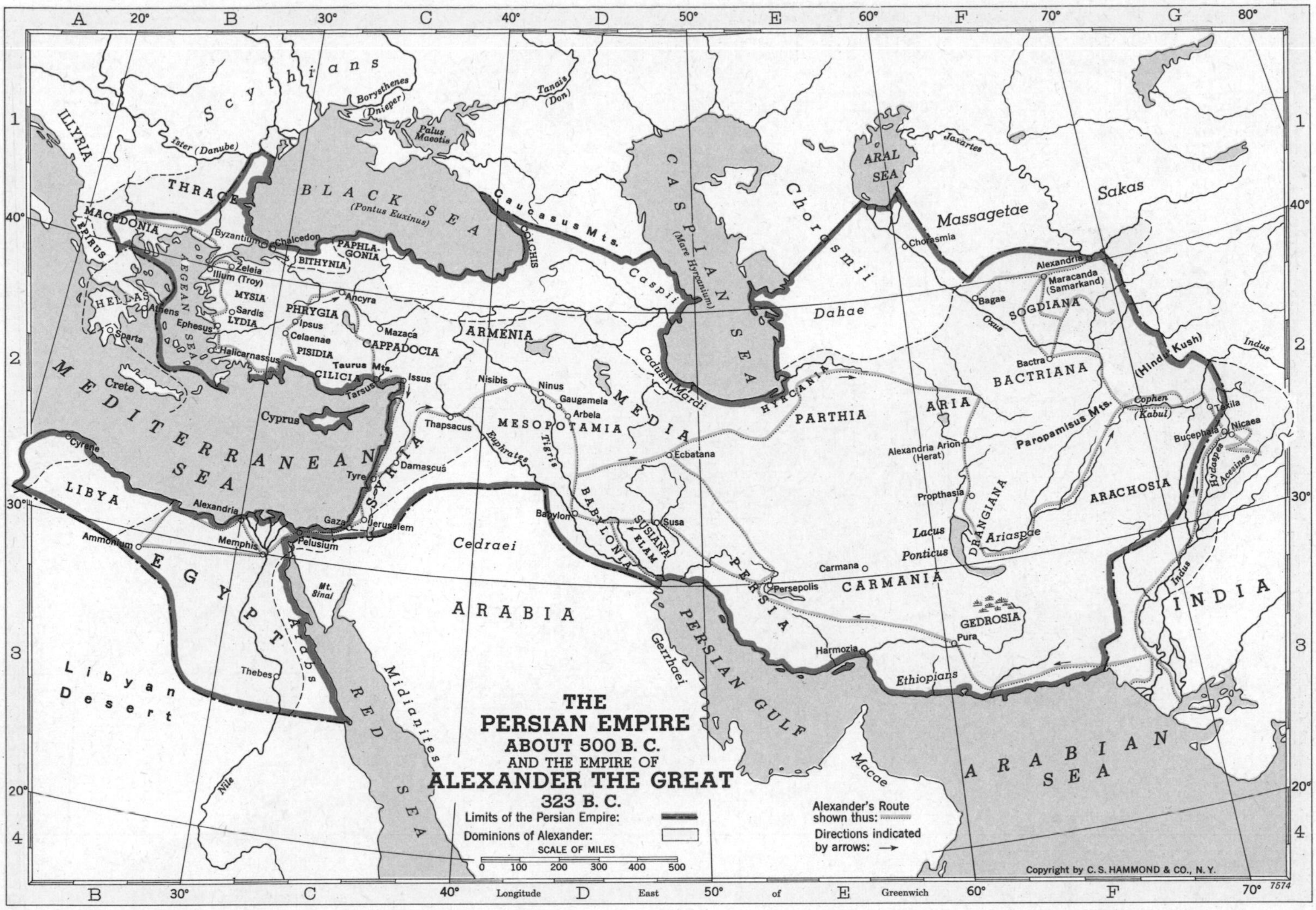
THE PERSIAN EMPIRE ABOUT 500 B. C. AND THE EMPIRE OF ALEXANDER THE GREAT 323 B. C.
Limits of the Persian Empire:
Dominions of Alexander:
Alexander's Route shown thus:
Directions indicated by arrows:
SCALE OF MILES
0 100 200 300 400 500
Copyright by C. S. HAMMOND & CO., N. Y.
Longitude East of Greenwich
7574
Scythians
ILLYRIA
Ister (Danube)
Borysthenes (Dnieper)
Palus Maeotis
Tanais (Don)
THRACE
BLACK SEA (Pontus Euxinus)
MACEDONIA
EPIRUS
Byzantium
Chalcedon
PAPHLAGONIA
BITHYNIA
Zeleia
Ilium (Troy)
MYSIA
Sardis
LYDIA
HELLAS
Athens
Ephesus
Sparta
AEGEAN SEA
PHRYGIA
Ancyra
Ipsus
Celaenae
PISIDIA
Halicarnassus
Mazaca
CAPPADOCIA
Taurus Mts.
CILICIA
Tarsus
Issus
Crete
Cyprus
MEDITERRANEAN SEA
Cyrene
LIBYA
Alexandria
Ammonium
Memphis
Pelusium
Gaza
Jerusalem
Tyre
Damascus
SYRIA
Thapsacus
EGYPT
Arabs
Mt. Sinai
Thebes
Nile
Libyan Desert
RED SEA
Midianites
ARABIA
Cedraei
Caucasus Mts.
COLCHIS
ARMENIA
Nisibis
Ninus
Gaugamela
Arbela
MESOPOTAMIA
Euphrates
Tigris
MEDIA
Ecbatana
Babylon
BABYLONIA
ELAM
SUSIANA
Susa
PERSIA
Persepolis
PERSIAN GULF
Gerrhaei
Cadusii
Mardi
CASPIAN SEA (Mare Hyrcanium)
Caspii
HYRCANIA
PARTHIA
Dahae
Chorasmii
ARAL SEA
Chorasmia
Massagetae
Sakas
Jaxartes
Alexandria
Maracanda (Samarkand)
Bagae
SOGDIANA
Oxus
Bactra
BACTRIANA
ARIA
Alexandria Arion (Herat)
Paropamisus Mts.
Hindu Kush
Cophen (Kabul)
Taxila
Nicaea
Bucephala
Hydaspes
Acesines
Indus
Propthasia
DRANGIANA
Ariaspae
ARACHOSIA
Lacus Ponticus
Carmana
CARMANIA
GEDROSIA
Pura
Harmozia
Ethiopians
INDIA
Macae
ARABIAN SEA

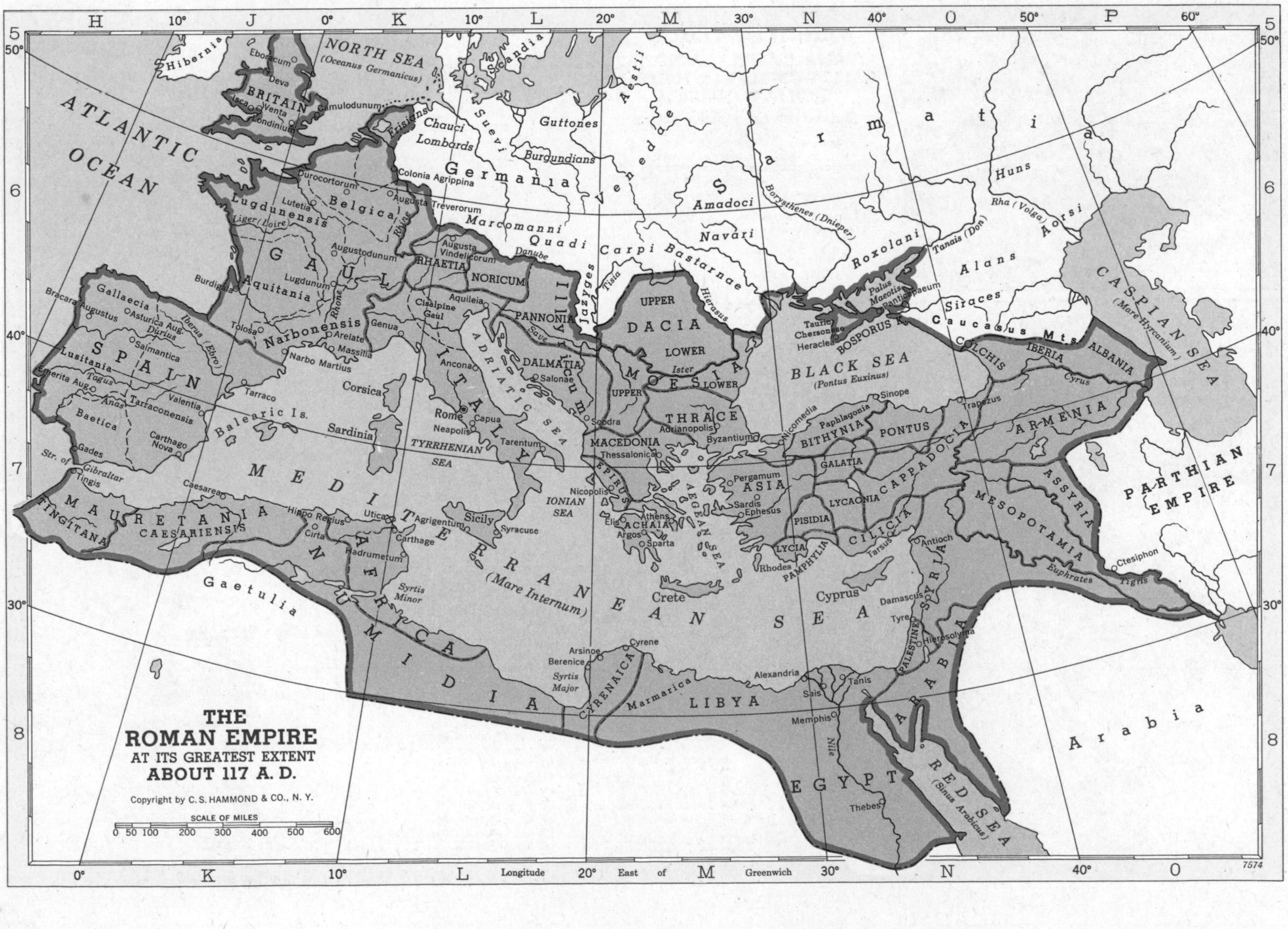
THE ROMAN EMPIRE AT ITS GREATEST EXTENT ABOUT 117 A. D.
Copyright by C. S. HAMMOND & CO., N. Y.
SCALE OF MILES
0 50 100 200 300 400 500 600
Longitude East of Greenwich
7574
Hibernia
Eboracum
Deva
BRITAIN
Isca
Venta
Londinium
Camulodunum
NORTH SEA (Oceanus Germanicus)
Scandia
ATLANTIC OCEAN
Frisians
Chauci
Lombards
Suevi
Guttones
Burgundians
Germania
Colonia Agrippina
Durocortorum
Lutetia
Belgica
Augusta Treverorum
Lugdunensis
Liger (Loire)
Rhine
Marcomanni
Quadi
Danube
GAUL
Augustodunum
Lugdunum
Aquitania
Burdigala
RHAETIA
Augusta Vindelicorum
NORICUM
PANNONIA
Aquileia
Cisalpine Gaul
Genua
Narbonensis
Tolosa
Arelate
Massilia
Narbo Martius
Gallaecia
Bracara Augustus
Asturica Aug.
Durius
Iberus (Ebro)
Salmantica
SPAIN
Lusitania
Emerita Aug.
Tagus
Anas
Tarraconensis
Valentia
Tarraco
Baetica
Carthago Nova
Gades
Str. of Gibraltar
Tingis
Balearic Is.
Corsica
Sardinia
ITALY
Ancona
Rome
Capua
Neapolis
Tarentum
ADRIATIC SEA
DALMATIA
Salonae
Illyricum
TYRRHENIAN SEA
Sicily
Syracuse
IONIAN SEA
MEDITERRANEAN SEA (Mare Internum)
MAURETANIA TINGITANA
MAURETANIA CAESARIENSIS
Caesarea
Hippo Regius
Cirta
Utica
Carthage
Agrigentum
Hadrumetum
NUMIDIA
AFRICA
Syrtis Minor
Gaetulia
Arsinoe
Berenice
Syrtis Major
Cyrene
CYRENAICA
Marmarica
LIBYA
Alexandria
Sais
Tanis
Memphis
Nile
EGYPT
Thebes
RED SEA (Sinus Arabicus)
ARABIA
Arabia
PALESTINE
Jerusalem
Hierosolyma
Tyre
Damascus
SYRIA
Cyprus
Crete
Aestii
Venedae
Sarmatia
Amadoci
Navari
Carpi
Bastarnae
Borysthenes (Dnieper)
Tisia
Jazyges
Hierasus
UPPER DACIA
LOWER
Ister
MOESIA
UPPER
LOWER
THRACE
Adrianopolis
Byzantium
MACEDONIA
Thessalonica
Scodra
EPIRUS
Nicopolis
ACHAIA
Athens
Elis
Argos
Sparta
AEGEAN SEA
Rhodes
Roxolani
Tanais (Don)
Huns
Rha (Volga)
Aorsi
Alans
Siraces
Palus Maeotis
Panticapaeum
Tauric Chersonese
Heraclea
BOSPORUS K.
BLACK SEA (Pontus Euxinus)
Caucasus Mts.
COLCHIS
IBERIA
ALBANIA
Cyrus
CASPIAN SEA (Mare Hyrcanium)
Sinope
Trapezus
Paphlagonia
Nicomedia
BITHYNIA
PONTUS
ARMENIA
GALATIA
CAPPADOCIA
Pergamum
ASIA
Sardis
Ephesus
LYCAONIA
PISIDIA
LYCIA
PAMPHYLIA
CILICIA
Tarsus
Antioch
MESOPOTAMIA
ASSYRIA
Euphrates
Tigris
Ctesiphon
PARTHIAN EMPIRE

## ANCIENT ITALY
### ITALIA, LIGURIA, VENETIA, GALLIA-CISALPINA, HISTRIA, SICILIA & CORSICA
**Before the time of Augustus**

Copyright by C.S. HAMMOND & CO., N.Y.

SCALE OF MILES

Roman Colonies, thus: ———————— Ostia
Greek Colonies, thus: **SYRACUSAE** (G)
Carthaginian Colonies, thus: ........... Eryx (C)
Dotted lines show the Modern shore line

### THE FORUM CAPITOLIUM and PALATIUM
1. Templum Saturni
2. Templum Concordiae
3. Scalae Gemoniae
4. Carcer (Tullianum)
5. Senaculum
6. Graecostasis
7. Rostra
8. Templum Jani

### IMPERIAL FORA
1. Scalae Gemoniae
2. Templum Vespasiani
3. Porticus Deorum Consentium
4. Equus Caesaris
5. T. Castoris et Pollucis
6. Templum Divi Julii
7. Arcus Augusti
8. Arcus Titi
9. Templum Antonini et Faustinae

## ROME
### Under the Emperors
1. Templum Jovis Capitolini
2. Arx
3. Forum Romanum
4. Templum Aesculapii
5. Forum Trajani
6. Forum Augusti
7. Porta Carmentalis
8. Arcus Septimii Severi
9. Arcus Constantini
10. Arcus Titi
11. Arcus Claudii
12. Arcus Tiberii
13. Arcus Gallieni
14. Arcus Marci Aurelii
15. Arcus Diocletiani
16. Porta Flumentara
17. Templum Mercurii
18. Theatrum Marcelli

### REGIONES AUGUSTI
I. Porta Capena
II. Caelimontium
III. Isis et Serapis
IV. Templum Pacis
V. Esquiliae
VI. Alta Semita
VII. Via Lata
VIII. Forum Romanum
IX. Circus Flaminius
X. Palatium
XI. Circus Maximus
XII. Piscina Publica
XIII. Aventinus
XIV. Trans Tiberim

### ROME
In the time of the Republic

7572

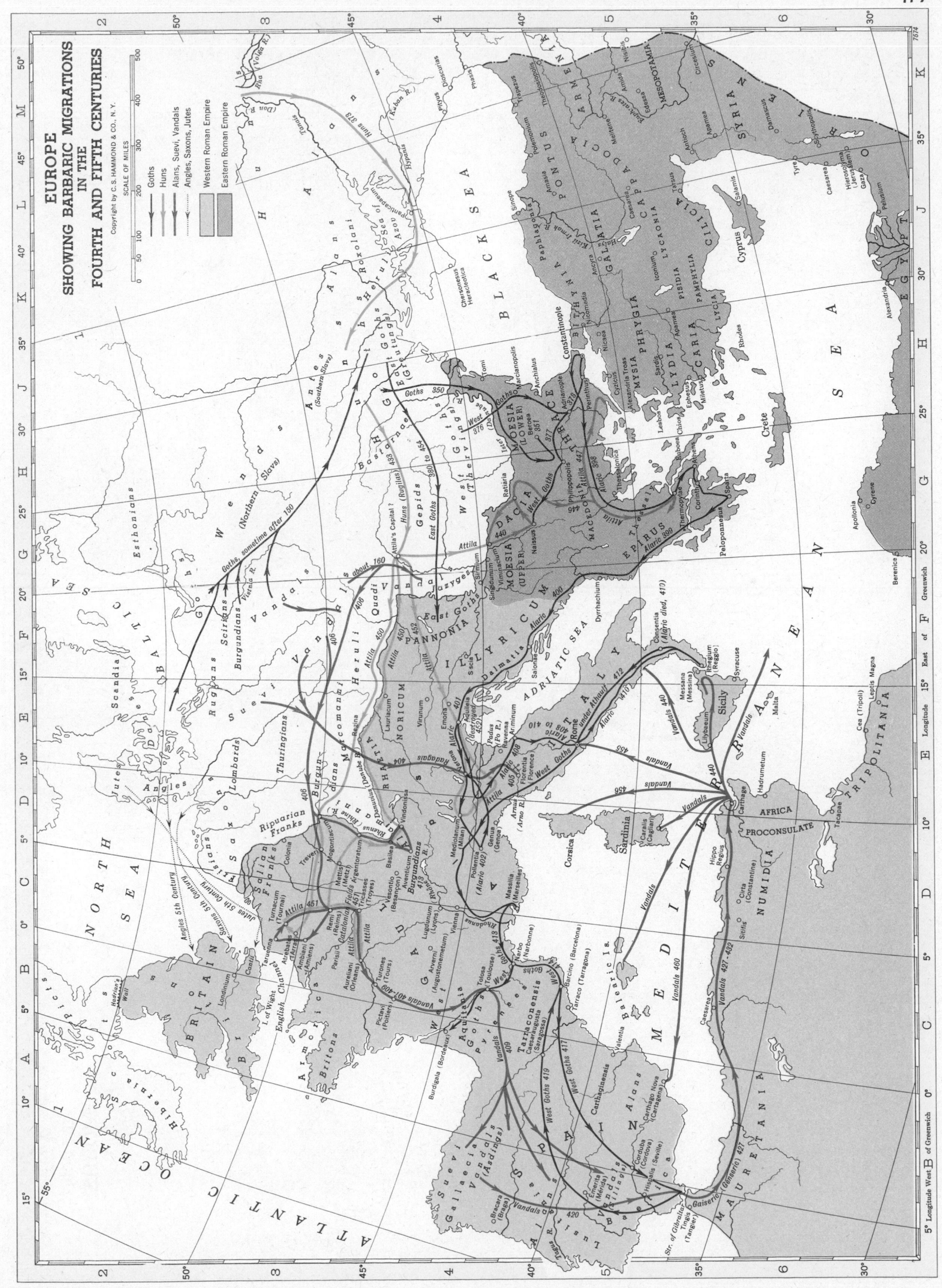

EUROPE
SHOWING BARBARIC MIGRATIONS
IN THE
FOURTH AND FIFTH CENTURIES

Copyright by C.S. Hammond & Co., N.Y.

SCALE OF MILES

Goths
Huns
Alans, Suevi, Vandals
Angles, Saxons, Jutes
Western Roman Empire
Eastern Roman Empire

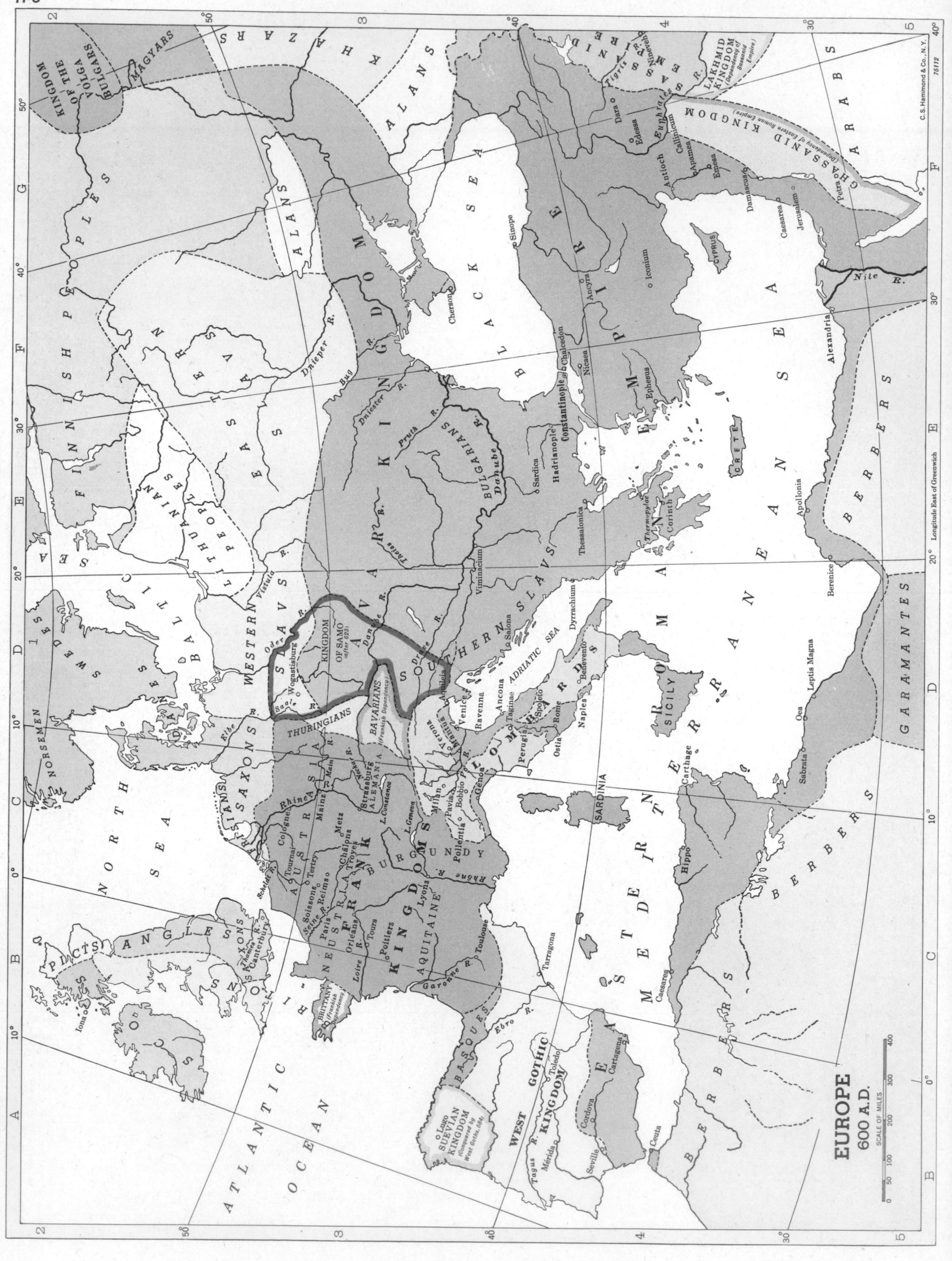

**EUROPE**
**600 A.D.**

SCALE OF MILES

0  50  100    200    300    400

KINGDOM OF THE VOLGA BULGARS

MAGYARS

KHAZARS

ALANS

FINNISH PEOPLES

LITHUANIAN PEOPLES

EASTERN SLAVS

WESTERN SLAVS

AVAR KINGDOM

BULGARIANS

SOUTHERN SLAVS

EASTERN ROMAN EMPIRE

GHASSANID KINGDOM (Dependency of Eastern Roman Empire)

LAKHMID KINGDOM (Dependency of Sassanid Empire)

SASSANID EMPIRE

ARABS

BERBERS

GARAMANTES

KINGDOM OF SAMO (after 623)

THURINGIANS

BAVARIANS (Frankish Dependency)

SAXONS

FRISIANS

AUSTRASIA

NEUSTRIA

ALEMANIA

BURGUNDY

FRANK KINGDOM

AQUITAINE

BRITTANY (Frankish Dependency)

BASQUES

WEST GOTHIC KINGDOM

SUEVIAN KINGDOM (Conquered by West Goths, 585)

LOMBARDS

SWEDES

NORSEMEN

PICTS

ANGLES

SAXONS

SCOTS

NORTH SEA

BALTIC SEA

ATLANTIC OCEAN

BLACK SEA

MEDITERRANEAN SEA

ADRIATIC SEA

Wogastisburg

Sala R.

Oder R.

Elbe R.

Rhine R.

Mainz

Main R.

Neckar R.

Strasburg

L. Constance

L. Geneva

Milan

Pavia

Genoa

Bobbio

Pollentia

Lyons

Rhône R.

Saône R.

Tournai

Soissons

Reims

Terfy

Metz

Châlons

Troyes

Paris

Orléans

Tours

Poitiers

Seine R.

Loire R.

Garonne R.

Toulouse

Ebro R.

Tarragona

Tarragona

Seville

Cordova

Toledo

Merida

Lugo

Tagus R.

Ceuta

Caesarea

Hippo

Carthage

Sabrata

Oea

Leptis Magna

Berenice

Apollonia

Sardinia

Sicily

Corsica

Naples

Rome

Ostia

Perugia

Spoleto

Benevento

Ancona

Ravenna

Venice

Verona

Aquileia

Salona

Dyrrachium

Corinth

Thermopylae

Thessalonica

Crete

Cyprus

Alexandria

Nile R.

Jerusalem

Caesarea

Damascus

Emesa

Apamea

Antioch

Callinicum

Edessa

Dara

Nineveh

Tigris R.

Euphrates R.

Petra

Berenice

Ephesus

Nicaea

Chalcedon

Constantinople

Hadrianople

Sardica

Viminacium

Naissus

Sava R.

Drina R.

Drave R.

Danube R.

Morava R.

Danube R.

Sinope

Cherson

Ancyra

Iconium

Ardea R.

Pruth R.

Dniester R.

Bug R.

Dnieper R.

Vistula R.

Don R.

Iona

Whithern

Canterbury

St. Davids

Thanet

Schedt R.

Cologne

Bordeaux

C.S. Hammond & Co., N.Y.

Longitude East of Greenwich

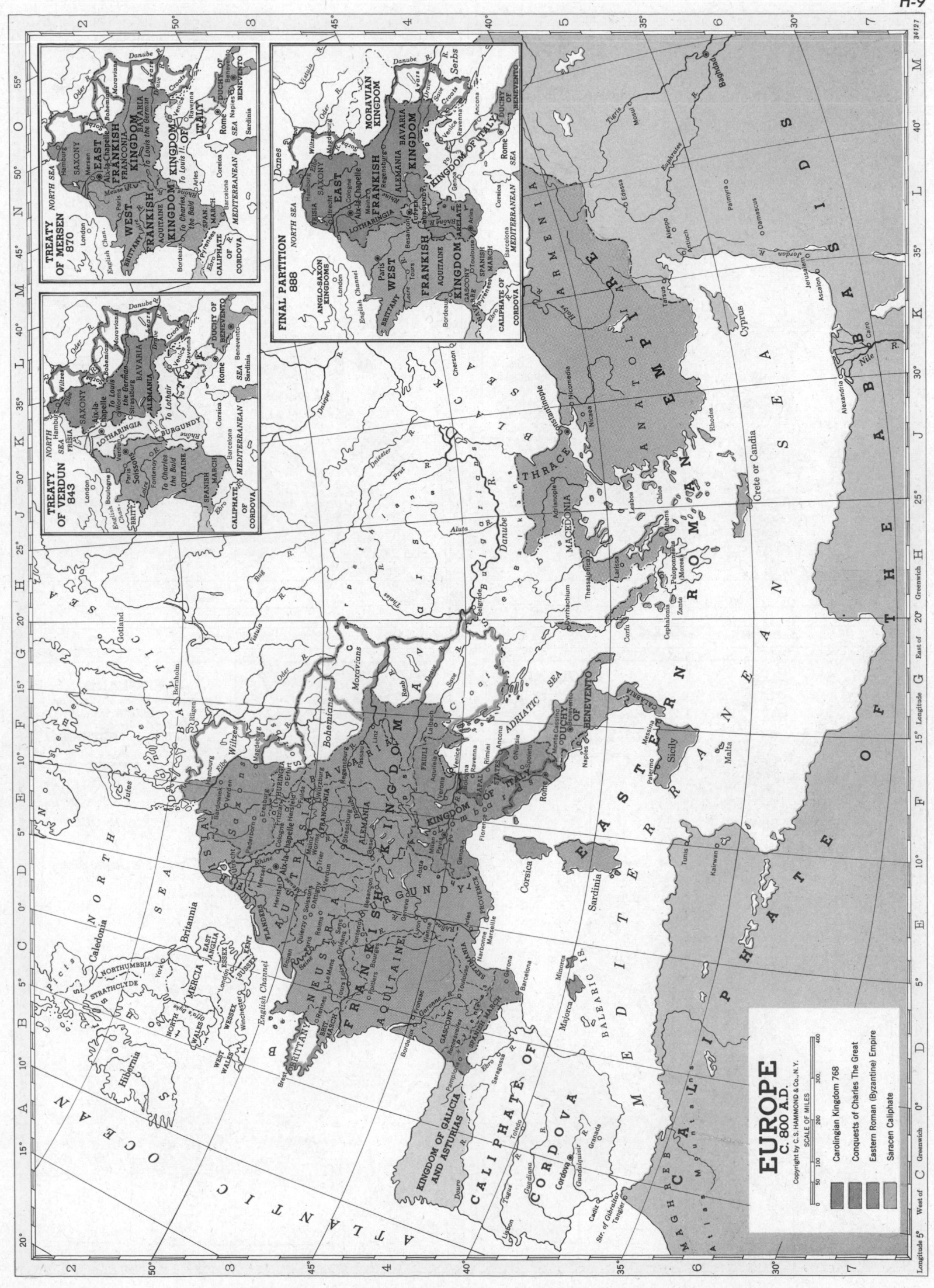

**TREATY OF MERSEN 870**

**TREATY OF VERDUN 843**

**FINAL PARTITION 888**

**EUROPE**
C. 800 A.D.

Copyright by C. S. HAMMOND & CO., N.Y.

SCALE OF MILES

Carolingian Kingdom 768

Conquests of Charles The Great

Eastern Roman (Byzantine) Empire

Saracen Caliphate

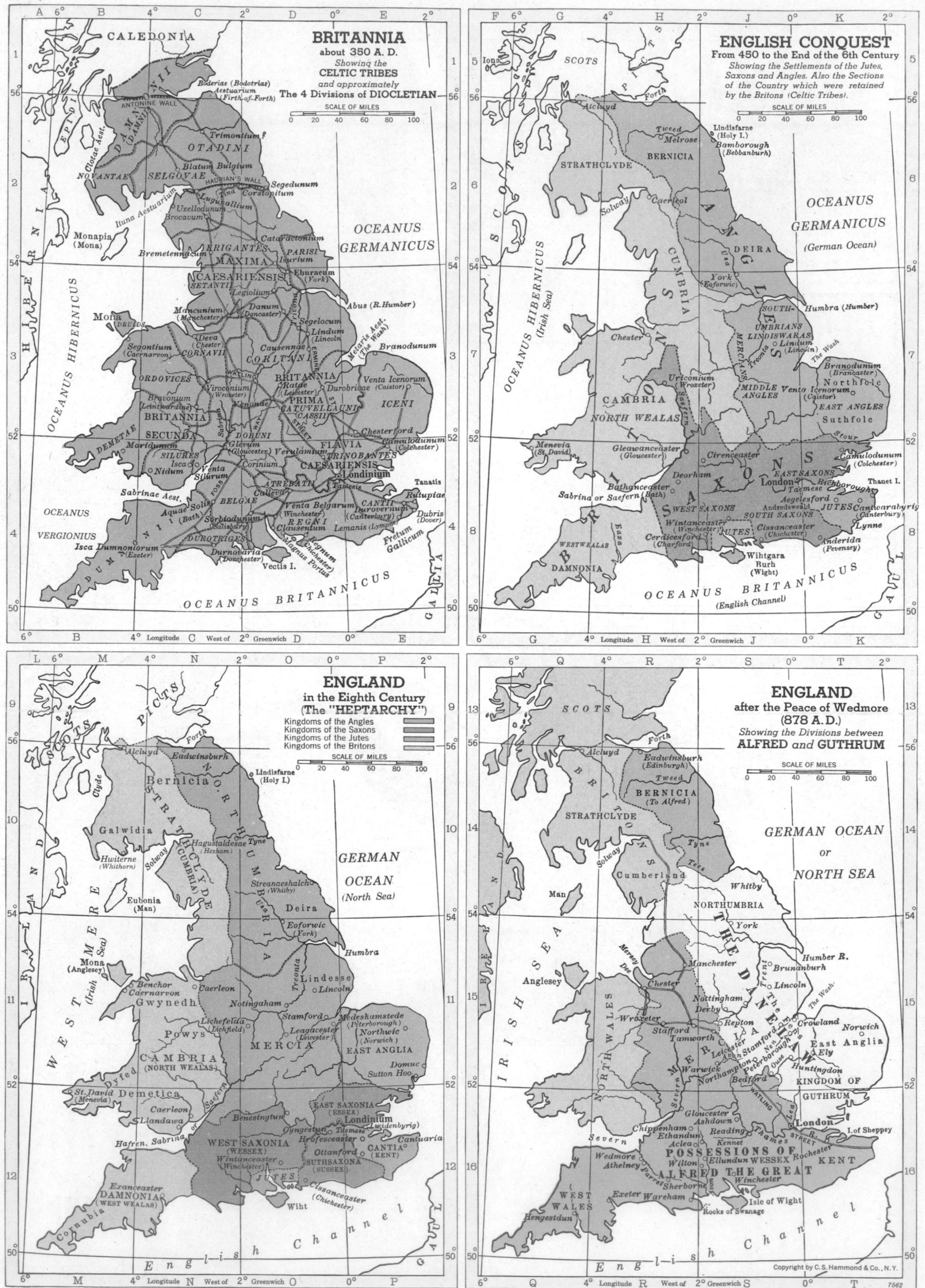

**BRITANNIA**
about 350 A.D.
*Showing the*
**CELTIC TRIBES**
*and approximately*
The 4 Divisions of DIOCLETIAN

SCALE OF MILES
0  20  40  60  80  100

**ENGLISH CONQUEST**
From 450 to the End of the 6th Century
*Showing the Settlements of the Jutes,
Saxons and Angles. Also the Sections
of the Country which were retained
by the Britons (Celtic Tribes).*

SCALE OF MILES
0  20  40  60  80  100

**ENGLAND**
in the Eighth Century
(The "HEPTARCHY")

Kingdoms of the Angles
Kingdoms of the Saxons
Kingdoms of the Jutes
Kingdoms of the Britons

SCALE OF MILES
0  20  40  60  80  100

**ENGLAND**
after the Peace of Wedmore
(878 A.D.)
*Showing the Divisions between*
**ALFRED and GUTHRUM**

SCALE OF MILES
0  20  40  60  80  100

Copyright by C. S. Hammond & Co., N.Y.

7562

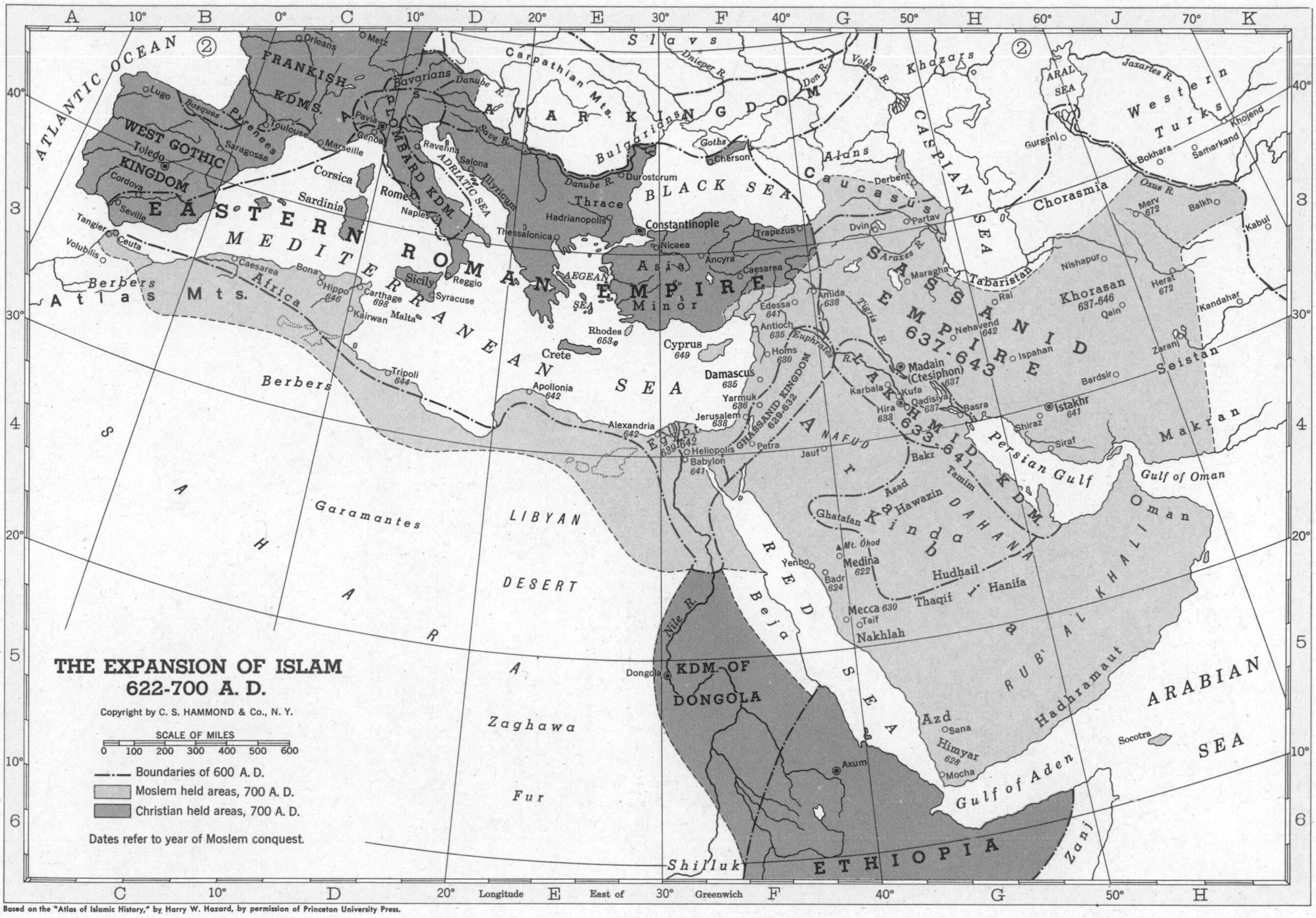

## THE EXPANSION OF ISLAM 622-700 A.D.

Copyright by C. S. HAMMOND & Co., N. Y.

SCALE OF MILES
0 100 200 300 400 500 600

- · - · Boundaries of 600 A.D.
Moslem held areas, 700 A.D.
Christian held areas, 700 A.D.

Dates refer to year of Moslem conquest.

Based on the "Atlas of Islamic History," by Harry W. Hazard, by permission of Princeton University Press.

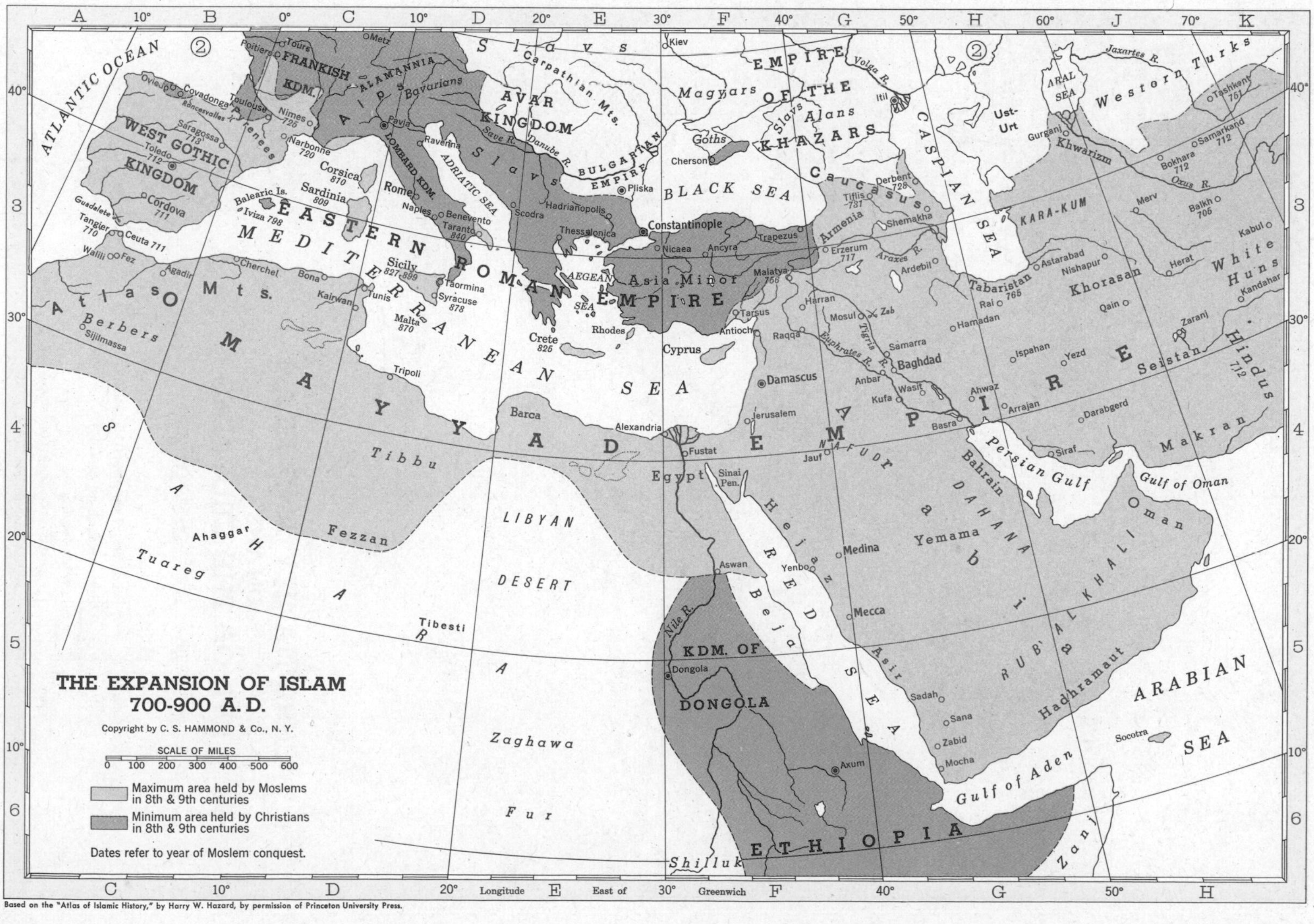

## THE EXPANSION OF ISLAM 700-900 A.D.

Copyright by C. S. HAMMOND & Co., N. Y.

SCALE OF MILES
0 100 200 300 400 500 600

Maximum area held by Moslems in 8th & 9th centuries
Minimum area held by Christians in 8th & 9th centuries

Dates refer to year of Moslem conquest.

Based on the "Atlas of Islamic History," by Harry W. Hazard, by permission of Princeton University Press.

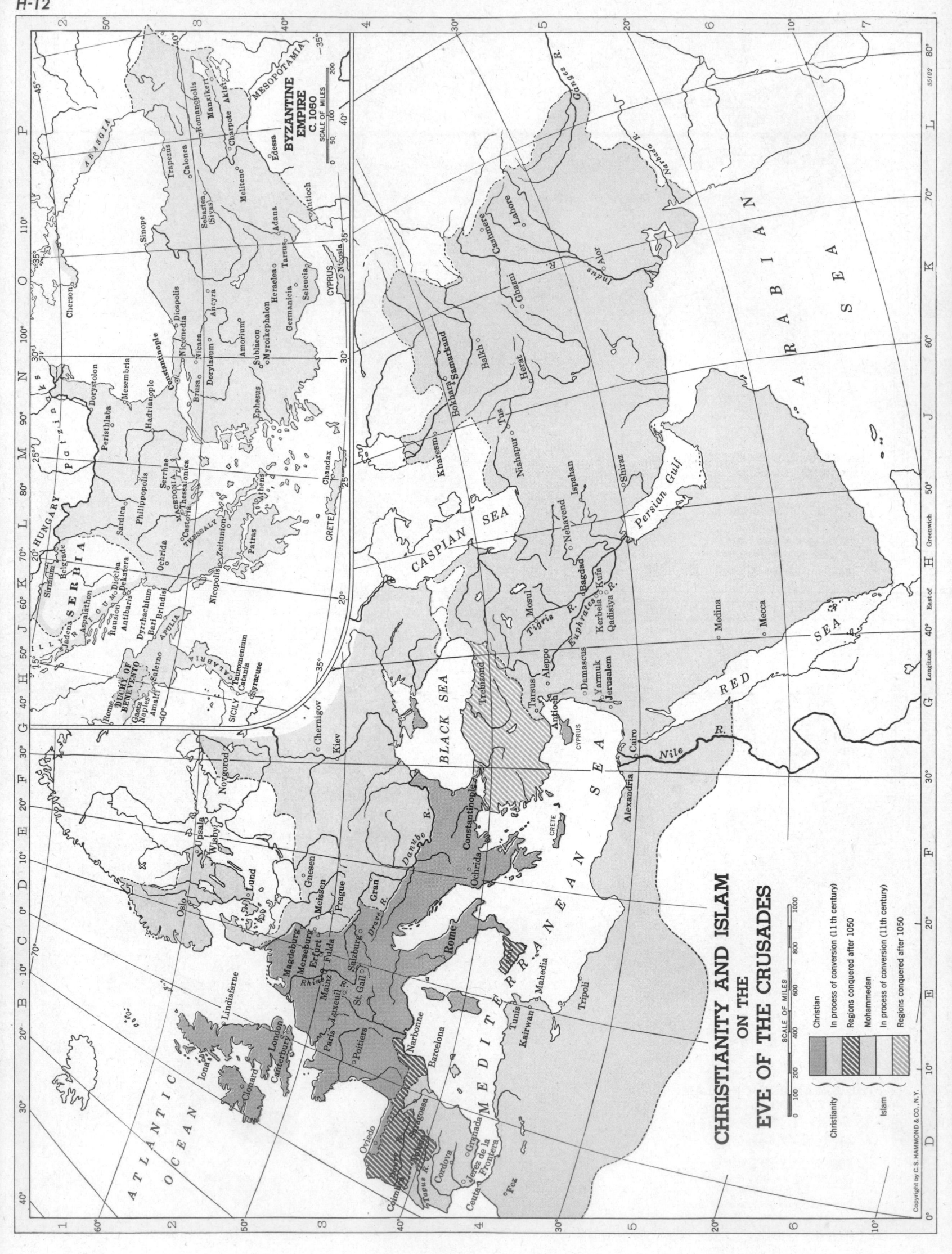

## CHRISTIANITY AND ISLAM
### ON THE
## EVE OF THE CRUSADES

SCALE OF MILES
0   100  200   400    600    800   1000

Christianity
- Christian
- In process of conversion (11th century)
- Regions conquered after 1050

Islam
- Mohammedan
- In process of conversion (11th century)
- Regions conquered after 1050

BYZANTINE
EMPIRE
C. 1050
SCALE OF MILES
0   50   100    200

Copyright by C. S. HAMMOND & CO., N.Y.

35102

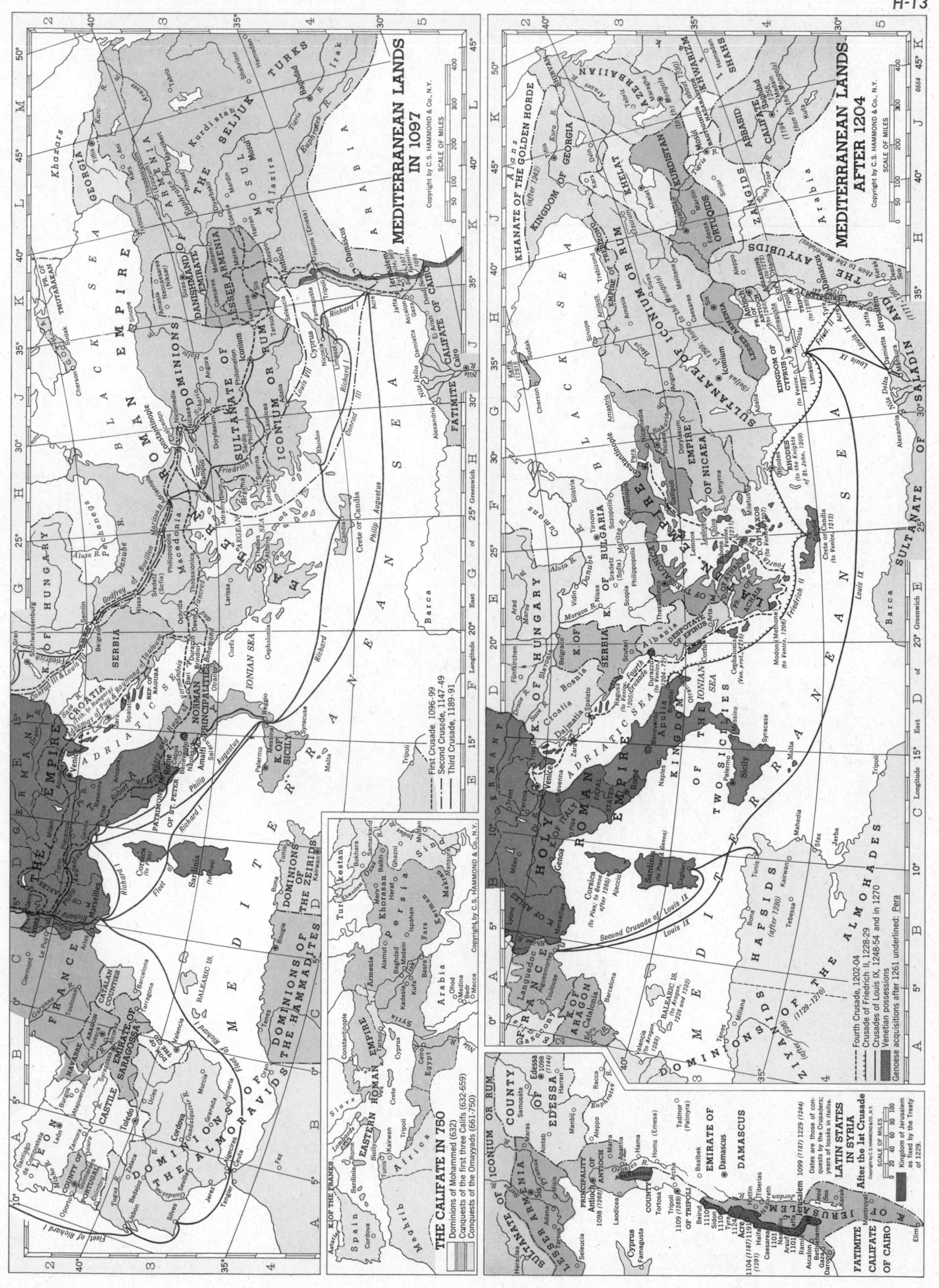

MEDITERRANEAN LANDS IN 1097

MEDITERRANEAN LANDS AFTER 1204

THE CALIFATE IN 750

LATIN STATES IN SYRIA After the 1st Crusade

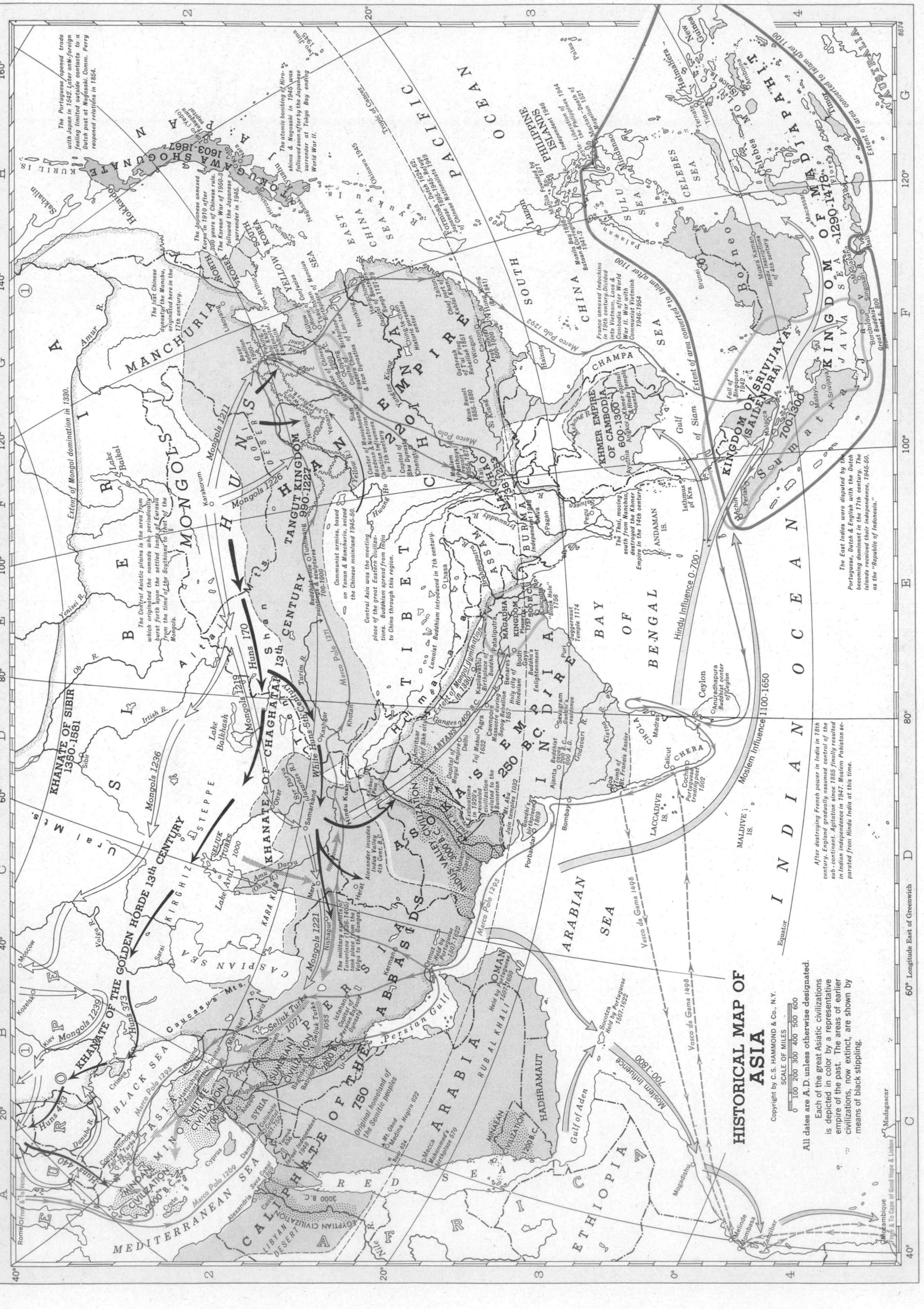

## HISTORICAL MAP OF ASIA

Copyright by C.S. HAMMOND & Co., N.Y.

SCALE OF MILES

0 100 200 300 400 500 600

All dates are A.D. unless otherwise designated. Each of the great Asiatic civilizations is depicted in color by a representative empire of the past. The areas of earlier civilizations, now extinct, are shown by means of black stippling.

SIBERIA

MANCHURIA

MONGOLS

KHANATE OF SIBIR 1350-1581

KHANATE OF THE GOLDEN HORDE 13th CENTURY

KHANATE OF CHAGHATAI 13th CENTURY

HUNS

TANGUT KINGDOM 990-1227

TIBET

HAN EMPIRE

CHINA

EMPIRE OF INDO-CHINA

KHMER EMPIRE OF CAMBODIA 600-1300

CHAMPA

BURMA

KINGDOM OF SRIVIJAYA (SAILENDRA) 700-1300

KINGDOM OF MAJAPAHIT 1290-1478

PHILIPPINE ISLANDS

PACIFIC OCEAN

SOUTH CHINA SEA

BAY OF BENGAL

INDIAN OCEAN

ARABIAN SEA

INDIA

ASOKA'S EMPIRE 250 B.C.

CALIPHATE OF THE ABBASIDS 750

PERSIA

ARABIA

HADHRAMAUT

RUB AL KHALI

OMAN

RED SEA

ETHIOPIA

AFRICA

MEDITERRANEAN SEA

BLACK SEA

CASPIAN SEA

EUROPE

RUSSIA

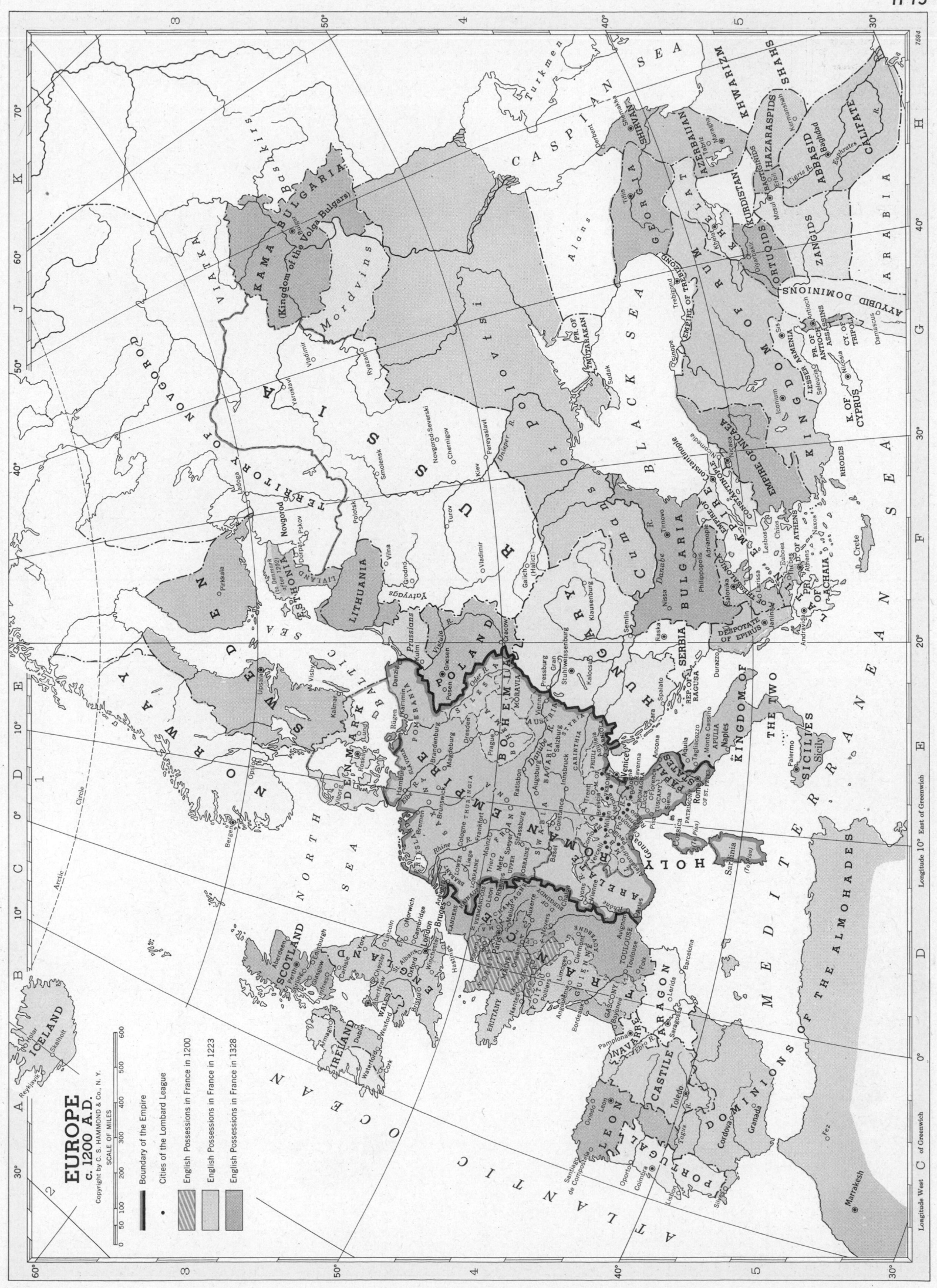

## EUROPE
### c. 1200 A.D.

Copyright by C. S. HAMMOND & Co., N.Y.

SCALE OF MILES

Boundary of the Empire

Cities of the Lombard League

English Possessions in France in 1200

English Possessions in France in 1223

English Possessions in France in 1328

GREENLAND

Gardar
(To Trondjem)

*Same scale as main map*

## ECCLESIASTICAL MAP OF
# EUROPE
### c. 1300 A.D.

SCALE OF MILES

| | | | | |
|---|---|---|---|---|
| 0 | 100 | 200 | 300 | 400 |

Archbishoprics
Bishoprics
Monasteries
Universities
*The Archepiscopal provinces are colored*

Longitude    West    0°    East    of    Greenwich

C.S. HAMMOND & CO., N.Y.

7572

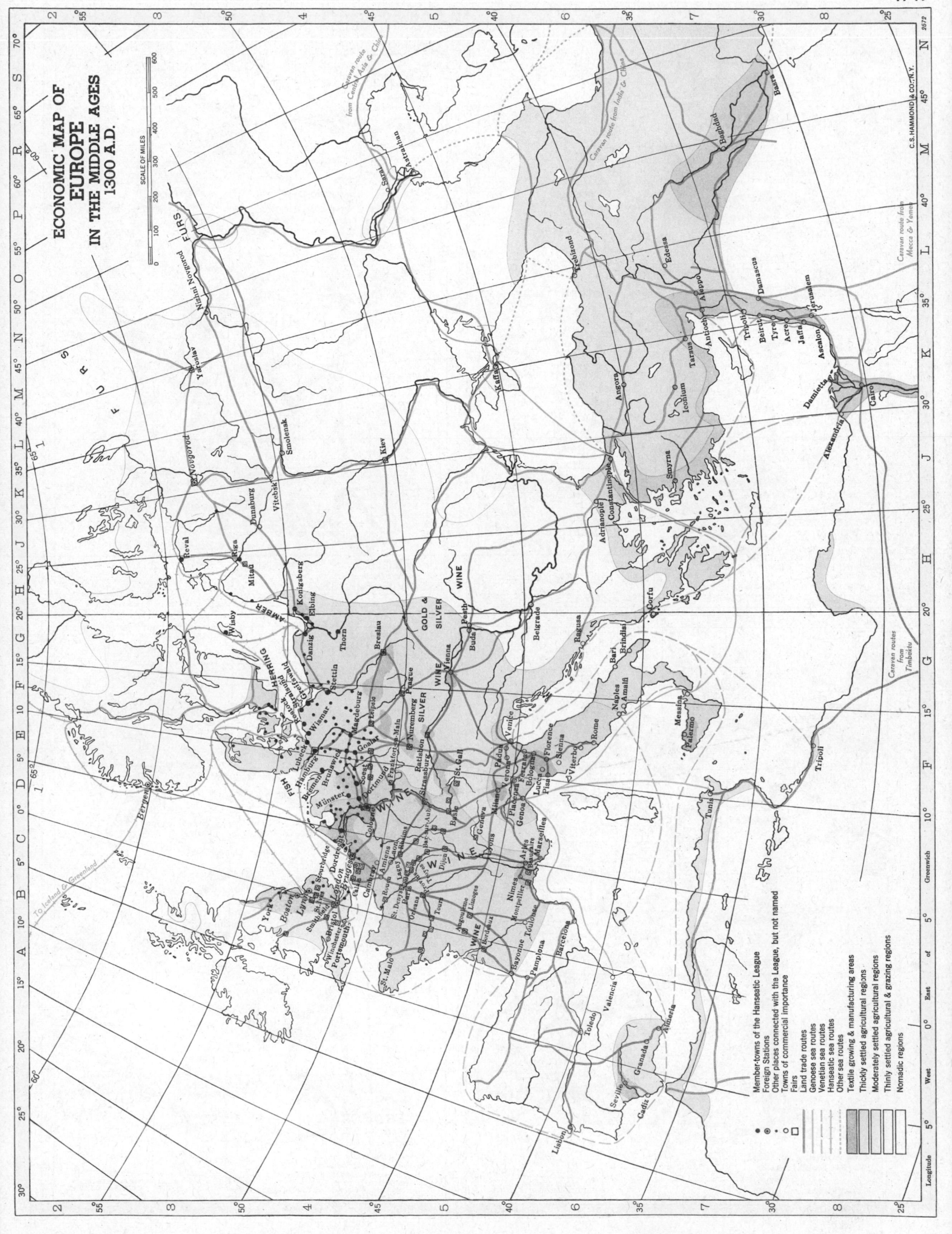

ECONOMIC MAP OF
EUROPE
IN THE MIDDLE AGES
1300 A.D.

SCALE OF MILES
0   100   200   300   400   500   600

C.S. HAMMOND & CO.-N.Y.

Member-towns of the Hanseatic League
Foreign Stations
Other places connected with the League, but not named
Towns of commercial importance
Fairs
Land trade routes
Genoese sea routes
Venetian sea routes
Hanseatic sea routes
Other sea routes

Textile growing & manufacturing areas
Thickly settled agricultural regions
Moderately settled agricultural regions
Thinly settled agricultural & grazing regions
Nomadic regions

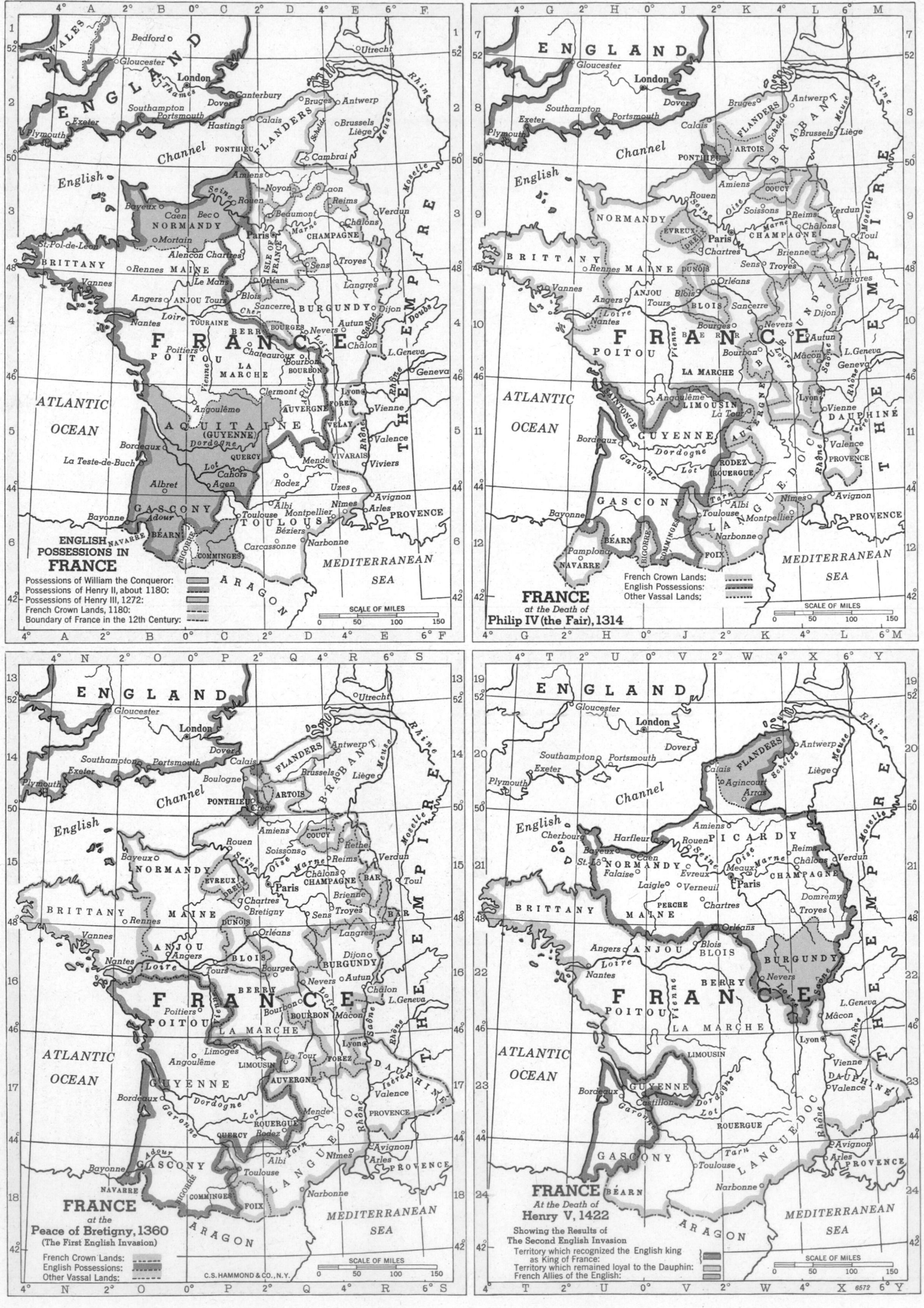

**ENGLISH POSSESSIONS IN FRANCE**

Possessions of William the Conqueror:
Possessions of Henry II, about 1180:
Possessions of Henry III, 1272:
French Crown Lands, 1180:
Boundary of France in the 12th Century: ---

**FRANCE**
*at the Death of*
**Philip IV (the Fair), 1314**

French Crown Lands:
English Possessions:
Other Vassal Lands:

**FRANCE**
*at the*
**Peace of Bretigny, 1360**
*(The First English Invasion)*

French Crown Lands:
English Possessions:
Other Vassal Lands:

C.S. HAMMOND & CO., N.Y.

**FRANCE**
*At the Death of*
**Henry V, 1422**

Showing the Results of
The Second English Invasion
Territory which recognized the English king
as King of France:
Territory which remained loyal to the Dauphin:
French Allies of the English:

SCALE OF MILES
0    50    100    150

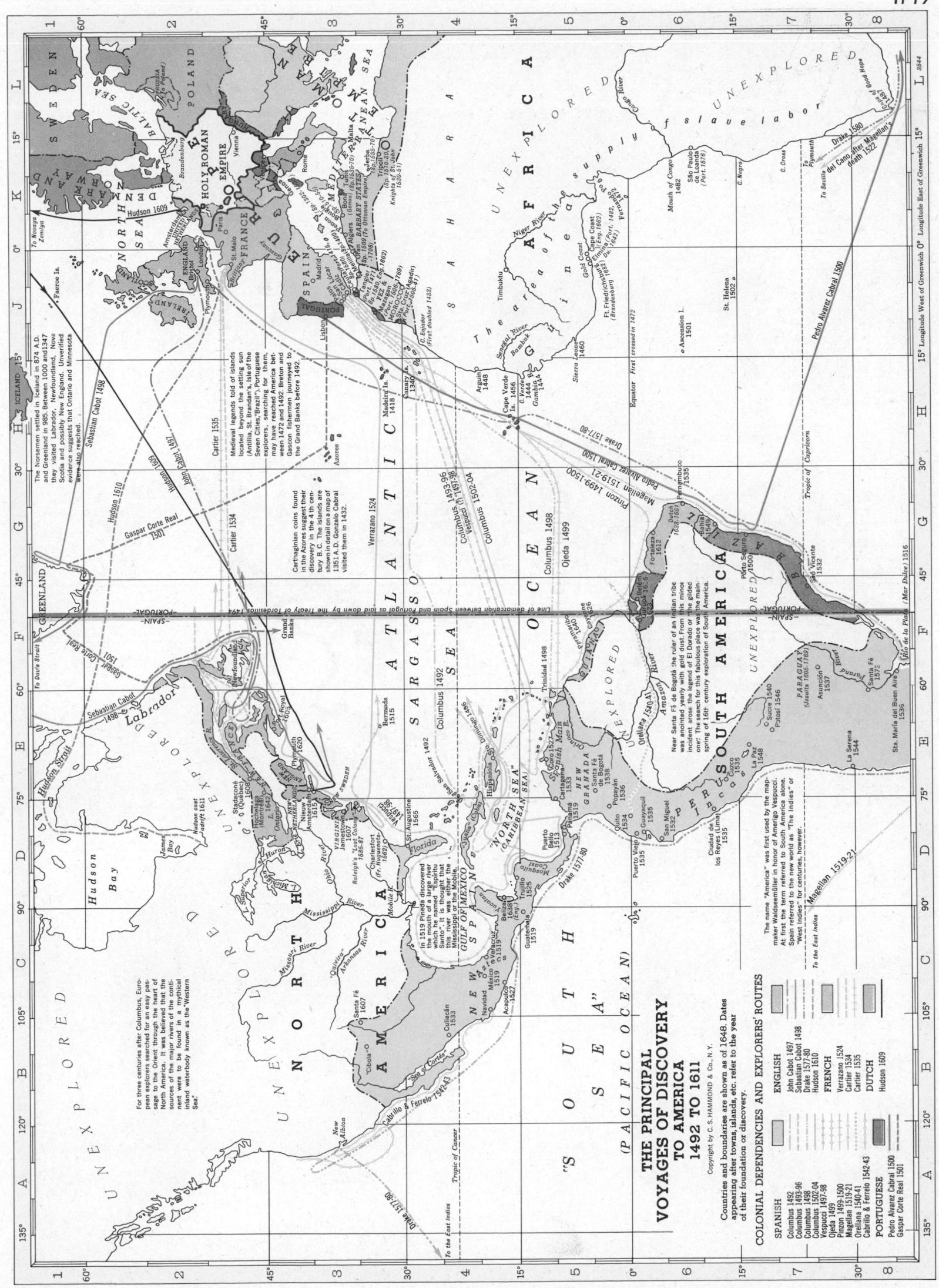

THE PRINCIPAL
VOYAGES OF DISCOVERY
TO AMERICA
1492 TO 1611

Copyright by C. S. HAMMOND & Co., N. Y.

Countries and boundaries are shown as of 1648. Dates
appearing after towns, islands, etc. refer to the year
of their foundation or discovery.

**COLONIAL DEPENDENCIES AND EXPLORERS' ROUTES**

SPANISH
Columbus 1492
Columbus 1493-96
Columbus 1498
Columbus 1502-04
Vespucci 1497-98
Ojeda 1499
Pinzon 1499-1500
Magellan 1519-21
Orellana 1540-41
Cabrillo & Ferrelo 1542-43

ENGLISH
John Cabot 1497
Sebastian Cabot 1498
Drake 1577-80
Hudson 1610

FRENCH
Verrazano 1524
Cartier 1534
Cartier 1535

DUTCH
Hudson 1609

PORTUGUESE
Pedro Alvarez Cabral 1500
Gaspar Corte Real 1501

The name "America" was first used by the map-
maker Waldseemüller in honor of Amerigo Vespucci.
At first the term referred to South America alone.
Spain referred to the new world as "The Indies" or
"West Indies" for centuries, however.

In 1519 Pineda discovered
the mouth of a large river
which he named "Espiritu
Santo". It is thought that
this river was either the
Mississippi or the Mobile.

Near Santa Fé de Bogotá the ruler of an Indian tribe
was anointed yearly with gold dust. From this minor
incident arose the legend of El Dorado or "the gilded
one". The search for this fabulous place was the mainspring of 16th century exploration of South America.

For three centuries after Columbus, European explorers searched for an easy passage to the Orient through the heart of
North America. It was believed that the
sources of the major rivers of the continent were to be found in a mythical
inland waterbody known as the "Western
Sea".

The Norsemen settled in Iceland in 874 A.D.
and Greenland in 985. Between 1000 and 1347
they visited Labrador, Newfoundland, Nova
Scotia and possibly New England. Unverified
evidence suggests that Ontario and Minnesota
were also reached.

Medieval legends told of islands
located beyond the setting sun
(Antilia, St. Brandan's, Isle of the
Seven Cities, "Brazil"). Portuguese
explorers, searching for them,
may have reached America between 1472 and 1492. Breton and
Gascon fishermen journeyed to
the Grand Banks before 1492.

Carthaginian coins found
in the Azores suggest their
discovery in the 4th cen-
tury B.C. The islands are
shown in detail on a map of
1351 A.D. Gonzalo Cabral
visited them in 1432.

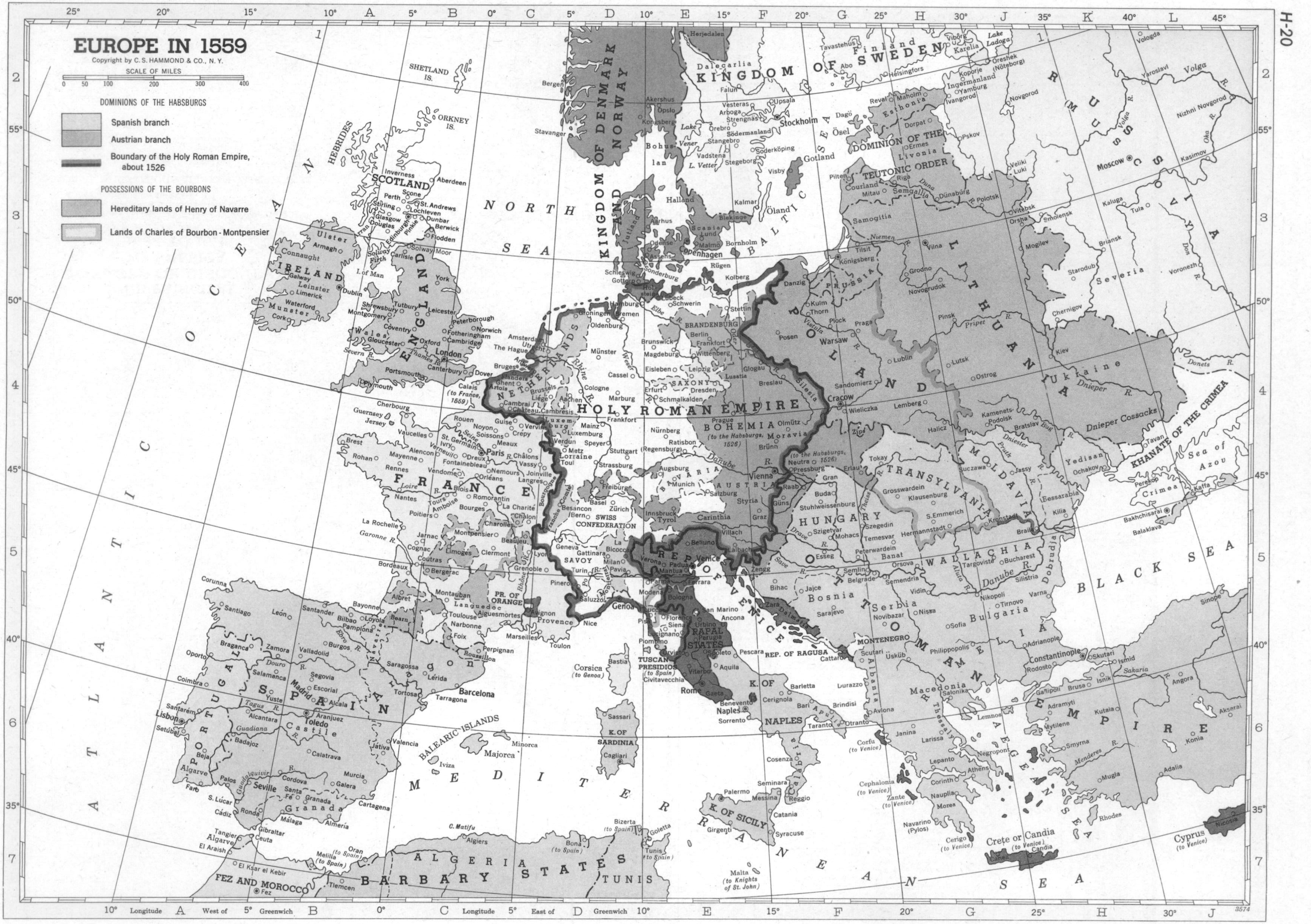

# EUROPE IN 1559

Copyright by C. S. HAMMOND & CO., N.Y.

SCALE OF MILES

0   50   100   200   300   400

DOMINIONS OF THE HABSBURGS

Spanish branch

Austrian branch

Boundary of the Holy Roman Empire, about 1526

POSSESSIONS OF THE BOURBONS

Hereditary lands of Henry of Navarre

Lands of Charles of Bourbon - Montpensier

## Major regions and seas

RUSSIA (MUSCOVY)

KINGDOM OF SWEDEN

KINGDOM OF DENMARK AND NORWAY

DOMINION OF THE TEUTONIC ORDER

LITHUANIA

POLAND

PRUSSIA

HOLY ROMAN EMPIRE

BOHEMIA

SAXONY

BRANDENBURG

NETHERLANDS

FRANCE

ENGLAND

SCOTLAND

IRELAND

WALES

SPAIN

PORTUGAL

SWISS CONFEDERATION

SAVOY

PR. OF ORANGE

REP. OF VENICE

TUSCANY

PAPAL STATES

K. OF NAPLES

K. OF SICILY

K. OF SARDINIA

HUNGARY

TRANSYLVANIA

MOLDAVIA

WALLACHIA

SERBIA

BOSNIA

BULGARIA

MONTENEGRO

ALBANIA

MACEDONIA

THESSALY

OTTOMAN EMPIRE

KHANATE OF THE CRIMEA

REP. OF RAGUSA

BARBARY STATES

ALGERIA

TUNIS

FEZ AND MOROCCO

NORTH SEA

BALTIC SEA

BLACK SEA

SEA OF AZOV

MEDITERRANEAN SEA

AEGEAN SEA

ATLANTIC OCEAN

Crete or Candia (to Venice)

Cyprus (to Venice)

Corsica (to Genoa)

BALEARIC ISLANDS

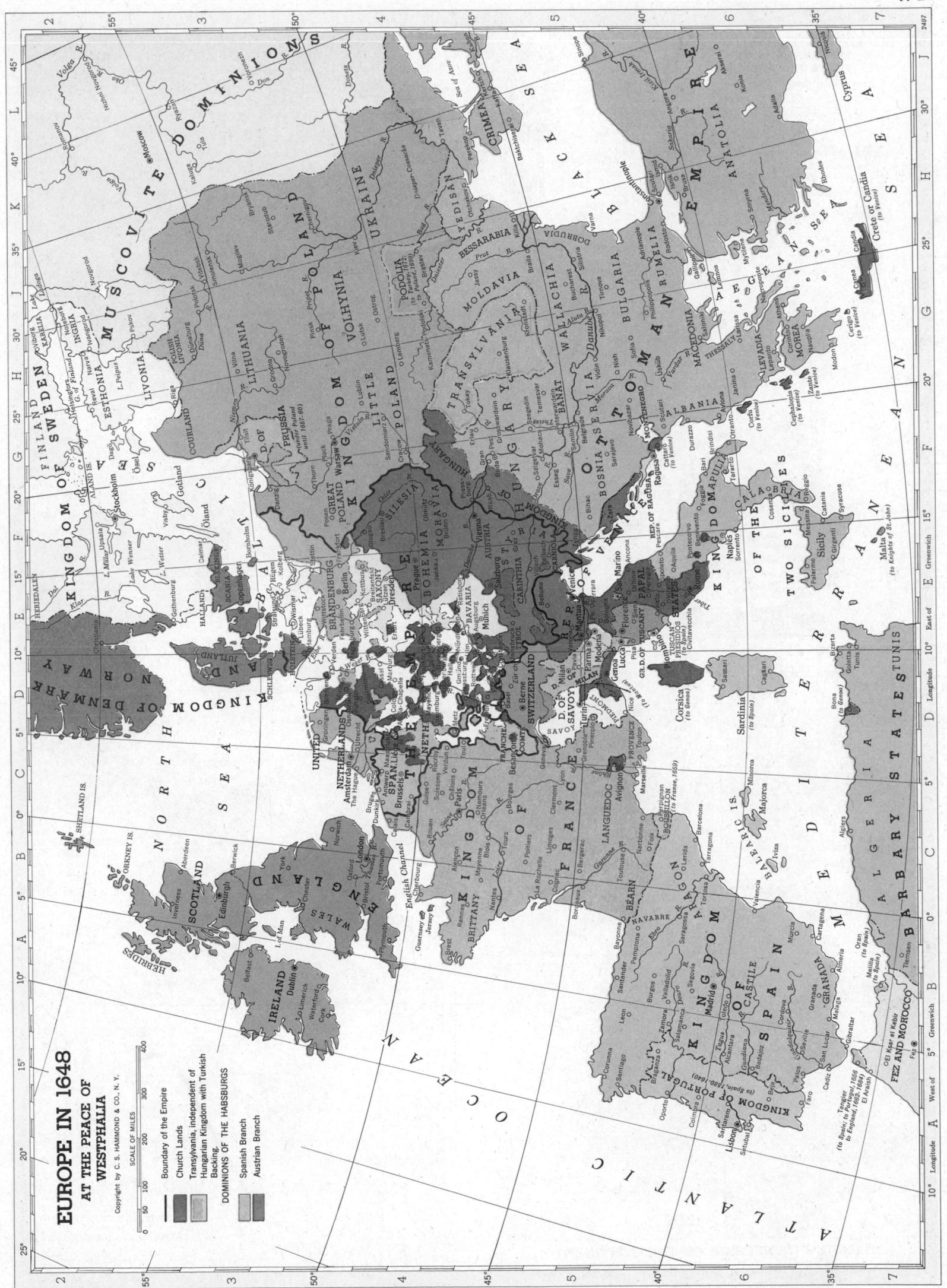

# EUROPE IN 1648
## AT THE PEACE OF WESTPHALIA

Copyright by C. S. HAMMOND & CO., N.Y.

SCALE OF MILES

0   50  100   200   300   400

— Boundary of the Empire

Church Lands

Transylvania, independent of
Hungarian Kingdom with Turkish
Backing.

DOMINIONS OF THE HABSBURGS

Spanish Branch

Austrian Branch

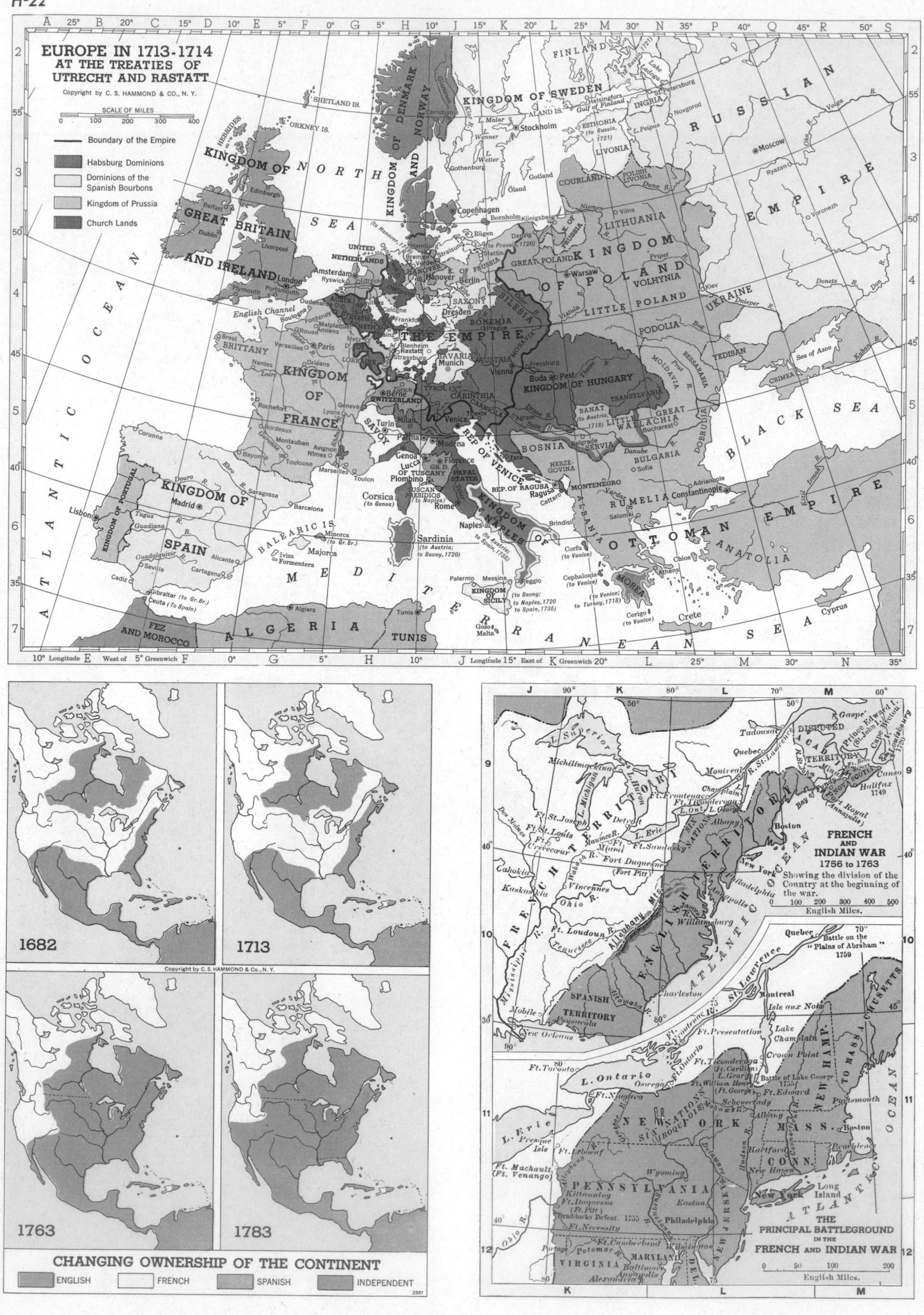

## EUROPE IN 1713-1714 AT THE TREATIES OF UTRECHT AND RASTATT

Copyright by C. S. HAMMOND & CO., N.Y.

SCALE OF MILES
0    100   200   300   400

Boundary of the Empire

Habsburg Dominions

Dominions of the Spanish Bourbons

Kingdom of Prussia

Church Lands

CHANGING OWNERSHIP OF THE CONTINENT

1682    1713    1763    1783

Copyright by C. S. HAMMOND & CO., N.Y.

ENGLISH    FRENCH    SPANISH    INDEPENDENT

## FRENCH AND INDIAN WAR 1756 to 1763

Showing the division of the Country at the beginning of the war.

0   100   200   300   400   500
English Miles

THE PRINCIPAL BATTLEGROUND IN THE FRENCH AND INDIAN WAR

0   50   100   200
English Miles

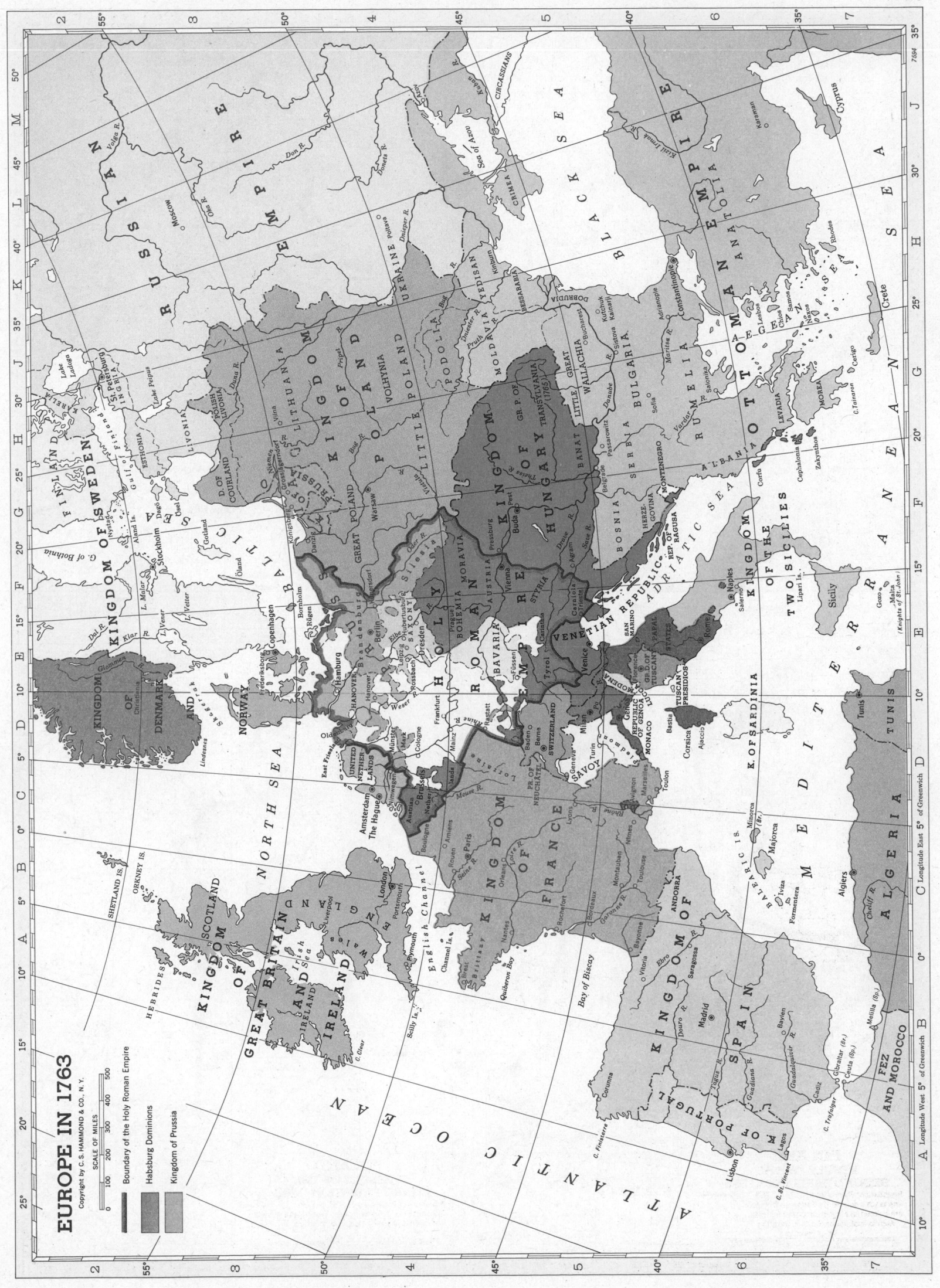

EUROPE IN 1763

Copyright by C.S. HAMMOND & CO., N.Y.

SCALE OF MILES
0  100  200  300  400  500

Boundary of the Holy Roman Empire
Habsburg Dominions
Kingdom of Prussia

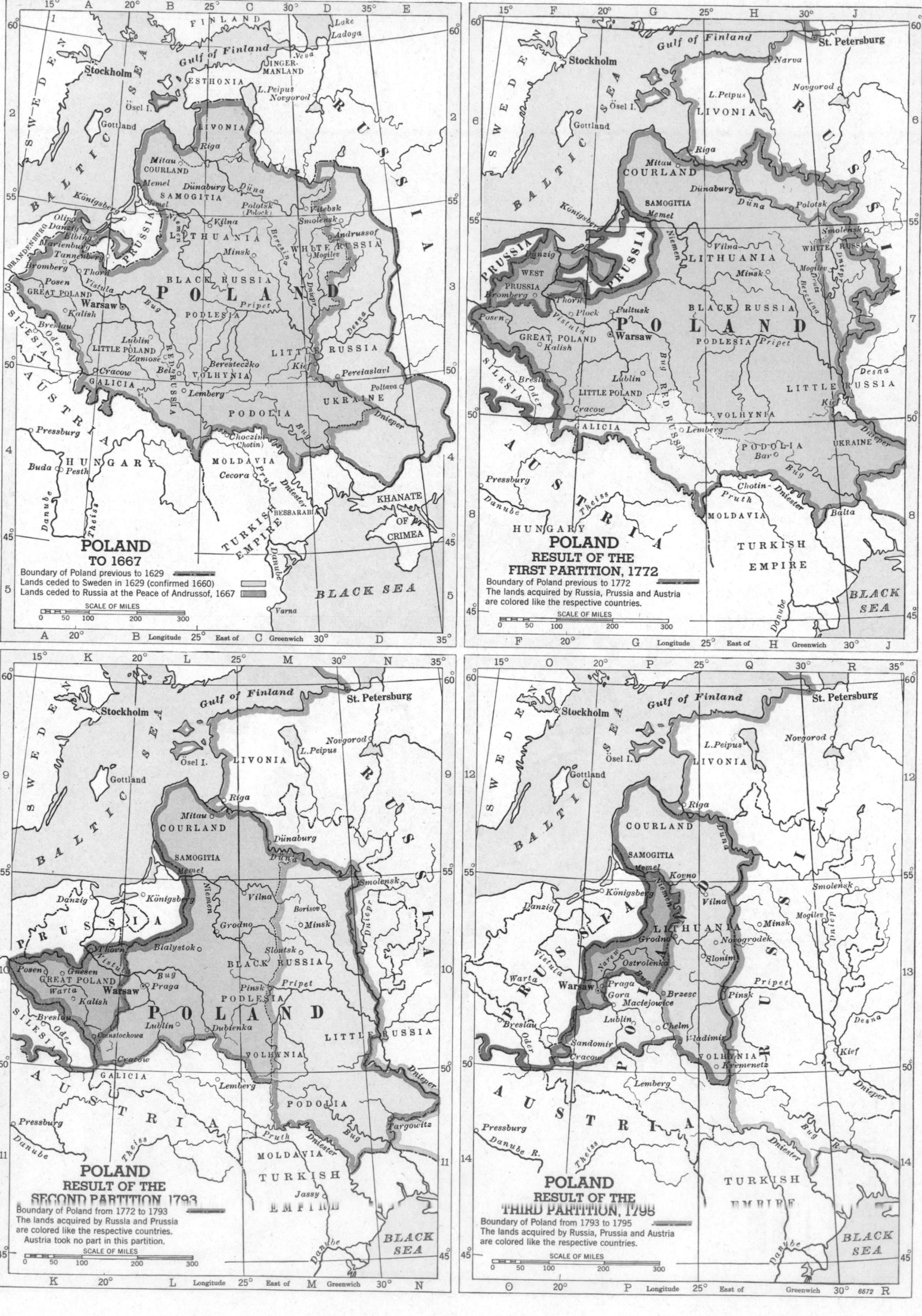

**POLAND**
TO 1667

Boundary of Poland previous to 1629
Lands ceded to Sweden in 1629 (confirmed 1660)
Lands ceded to Russia at the Peace of Andrussof, 1667

SCALE OF MILES
0    50   100        200        300

**POLAND**
RESULT OF THE
FIRST PARTITION, 1772

Boundary of Poland previous to 1772
The lands acquired by Russia, Prussia and Austria
are colored like the respective countries.

SCALE OF MILES
0    50   100        200        300

**POLAND**
RESULT OF THE
SECOND PARTITION, 1793

Boundary of Poland from 1772 to 1793
The lands acquired by Russia and Prussia
are colored like the respective countries.
Austria took no part in this partition.

SCALE OF MILES
0    50   100        200        300

**POLAND**
RESULT OF THE
THIRD PARTITION, 1795

Boundary of Poland from 1793 to 1795
The lands acquired by Russia, Prussia and Austria
are colored like the respective countries.

SCALE OF MILES
0    50   100        200        300

6572

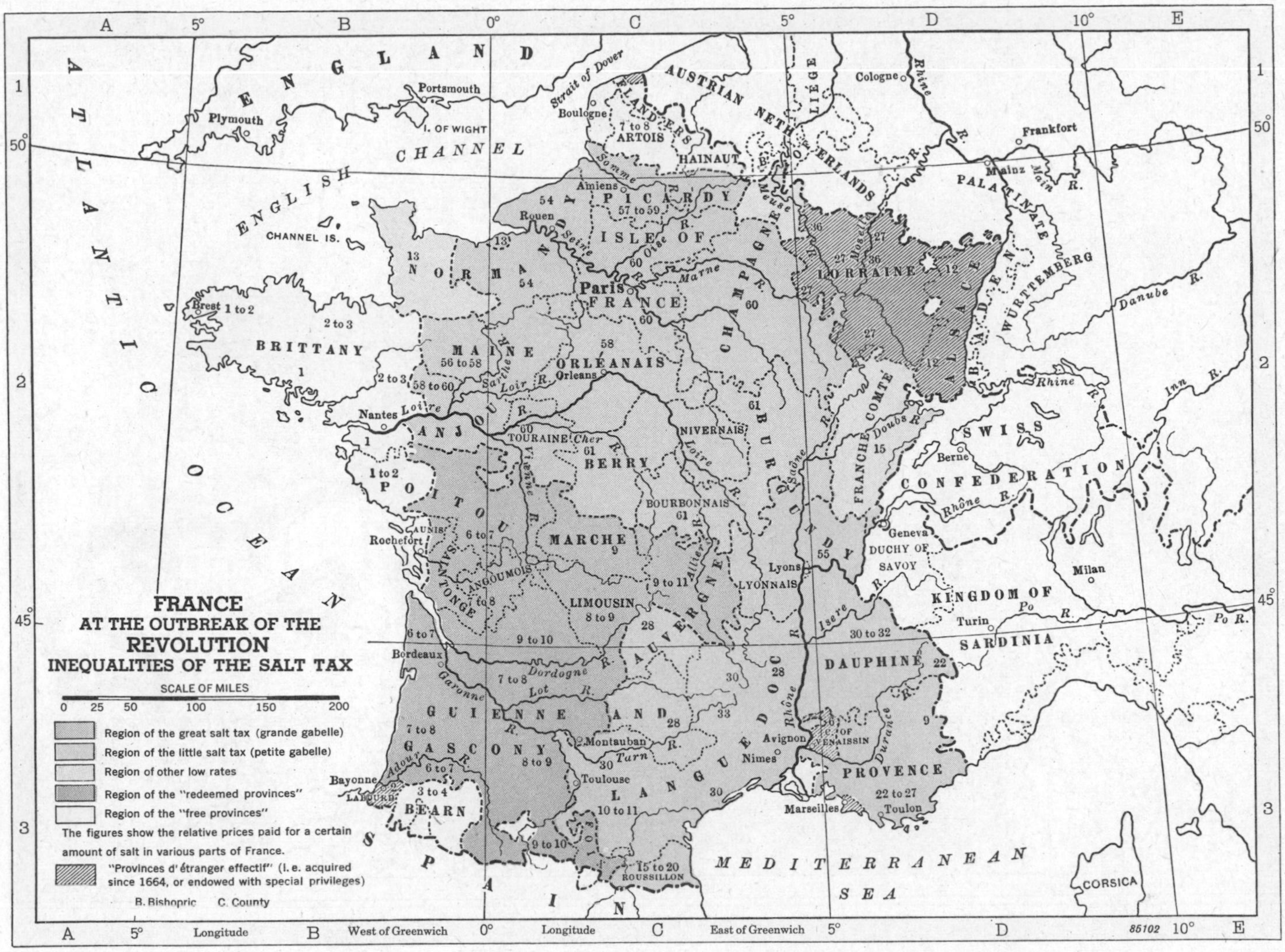

**FRANCE**
AT THE OUTBREAK OF THE
**REVOLUTION**
INEQUALITIES OF THE SALT TAX

SCALE OF MILES
0  25  50  100  150  200

Region of the great salt tax (grande gabelle)
Region of the little salt tax (petite gabelle)
Region of other low rates
Region of the "redeemed provinces"
Region of the "free provinces"

The figures show the relative prices paid for a certain amount of salt in various parts of France.

"Provinces d'étranger effectif" (i.e. acquired since 1664, or endowed with special privileges)

B. Bishopric  C. County

ATLANTIC OCEAN
ENGLAND
ENGLISH CHANNEL
CHANNEL IS.
Plymouth
Portsmouth
I. OF WIGHT
Boulogne
Strait of Dover
AUSTRIAN NETHERLANDS
FLANDERS
ARTOIS
HAINAUT
LIÈGE
Cologne
Frankfort
PALATINATE
Mainz
NORMANDY
PICARDY
ISLE OF FRANCE
Amiens
Rouen
Paris
Seine
Oise R.
Marne
CHAMPAGNE
LORRAINE
ALSACE
WÜRTTEMBERG
BADEN
Danube R.
BRITTANY
MAINE
ORLÉANAIS
Orleans
BURGUNDY
FRANCHE COMTE
Doubs R.
SWISS CONFEDERATION
Berne
Rhine
Brest
Nantes
Loire R.
ANJOU
TOURAINE
Cher R.
BERRY
NIVERNAIS
Loire R.
Geneva
DUCHY OF SAVOY
POITOU
MARCHE
BOURBONNAIS
LYONNAIS
Lyons
Milan
KINGDOM OF SARDINIA
Turin
Po R.
Rochefort
AUNIS
SAINTONGE
ANGOUMOIS
LIMOUSIN
AUVERGNE
Rhône R.
Isere R.
DAUPHINE
Bordeaux
Garonne R.
GUIENNE
Dordogne R.
Lot R.
QUERCY
ROUERGUE
LANGUEDOC
Rhône R.
Durance R.
PROVENCE
GASCONY
Montauban
Tarn R.
Toulouse
Nimes
Avignon
C.OF VENAISSIN
Marseilles
Toulon
Bayonne
Adour R.
LABOURD
BÉARN
ROUSSILLON
SPAIN
MEDITERRANEAN SEA
CORSICA
ATLANTIC OCEAN

A  5°  Longitude  B  West of Greenwich  0°  Longitude  C  East of Greenwich  5°  D  10°  E
85102

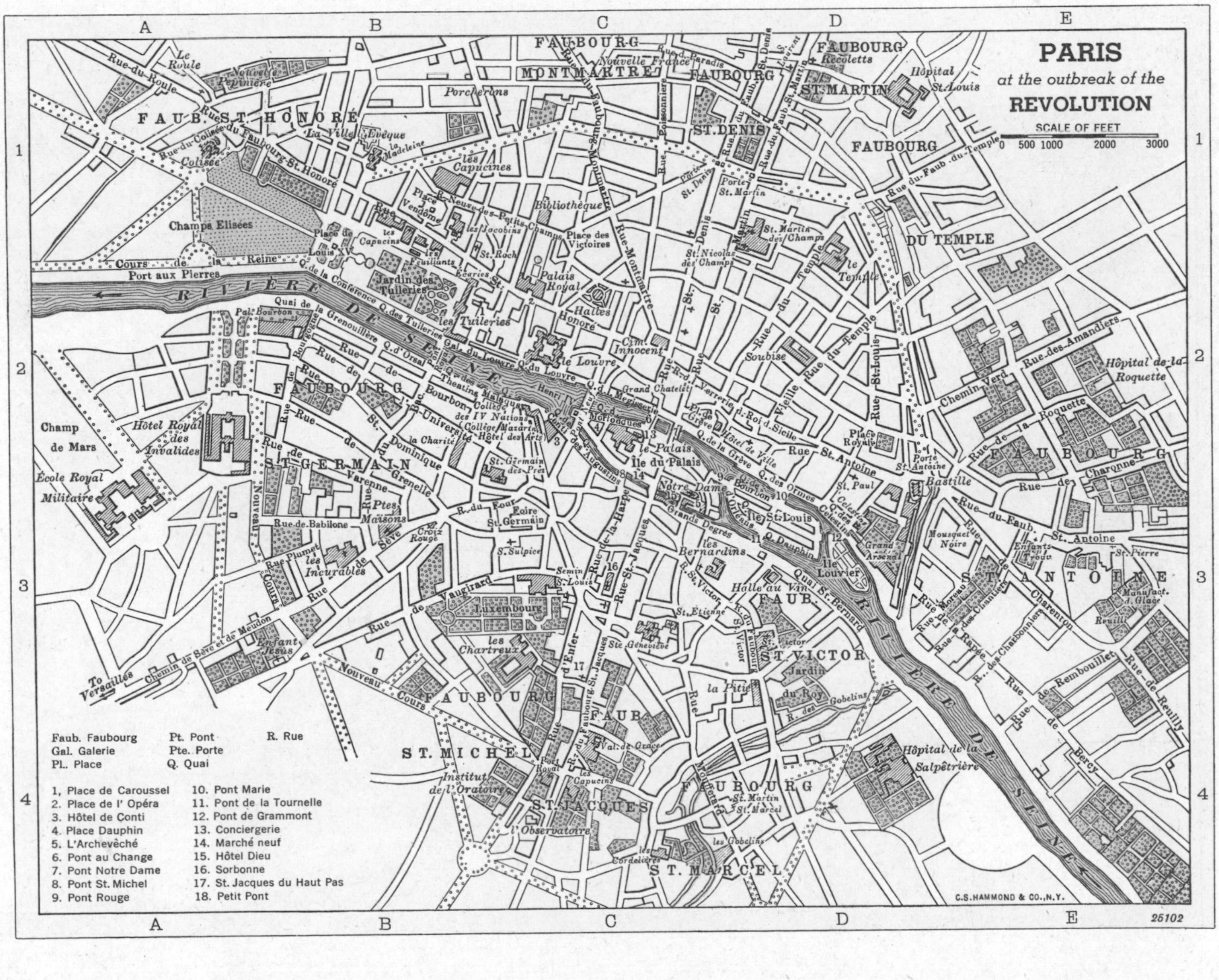

**PARIS**
at the outbreak of the
**REVOLUTION**

SCALE OF FEET
0  500  1000  2000  3000

Faub. Faubourg     Pt. Pont        R. Rue
Gal. Galerie       Pte. Porte
Pl. Place          Q. Quai

1. Place de Caroussel
2. Place de l' Opéra
3. Hôtel de Conti
4. Place Dauphin
5. L'Archevêché
6. Pont au Change
7. Pont Notre Dame
8. Pont St. Michel
9. Pont Rouge
10. Pont Marie
11. Pont de la Tournelle
12. Pont de Grammont
13. Conciergerie
14. Marché neuf
15. Hôtel Dieu
16. Sorbonne
17. St. Jacques du Haut Pas
18. Petit Pont

C.S. HAMMOND & CO., N.Y.

25102

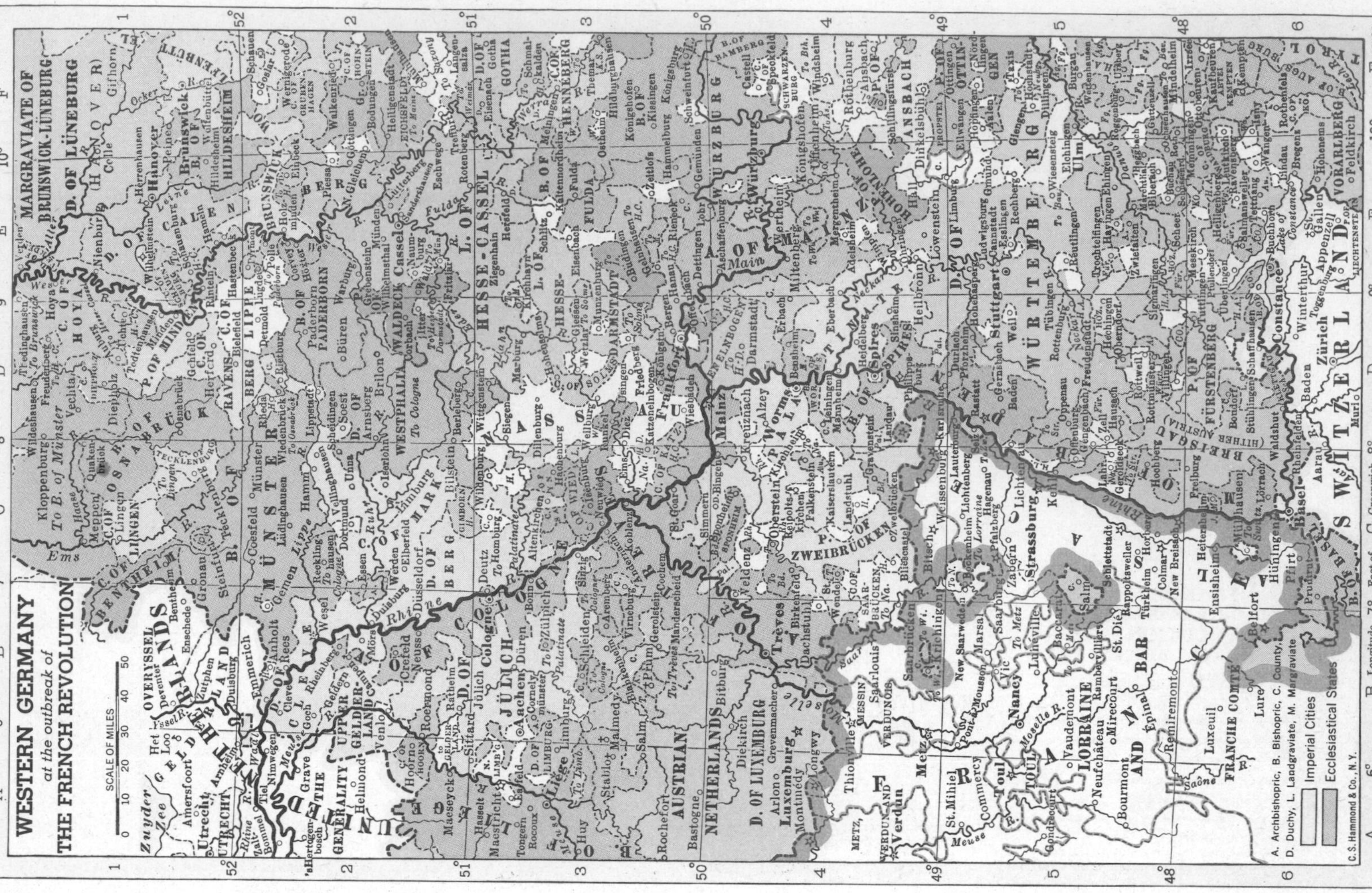

## WESTERN GERMANY
### at the outbreak of
### THE FRENCH REVOLUTION

SCALE OF MILES
0  10  20  30  40  50

MARGRAVIATE OF
BRUNSWICK-LÜNEBURG
D. OF LÜNEBURG (HANOVER)

C.S. Hammond & Co., N.Y.

A. Archbishopric, B. Bishopric, C. County.
D. Duchy, L. Landgraviate, M. Margraviate
Imperial Cities
Ecclesiastical States

F 35102

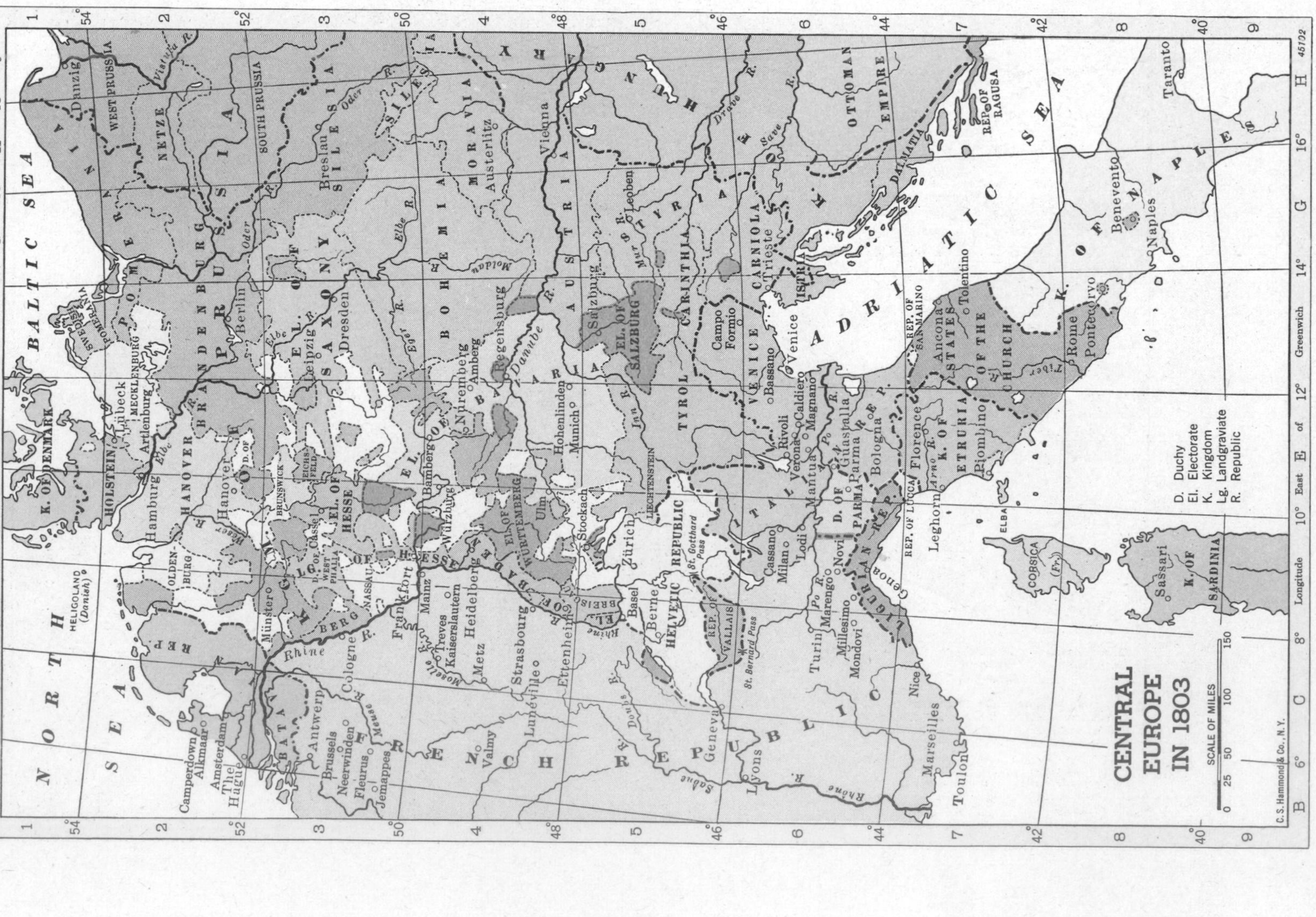

## CENTRAL EUROPE
### IN 1803

SCALE OF MILES
0  25  50  100  150

D. Duchy        El. Electorate
K. Kingdom      Lg. Landgraviate
R. Republic

C.S. Hammond & Co., N.Y.

45122

BALTIC SEA
NORTH SEA
ADRIATIC SEA

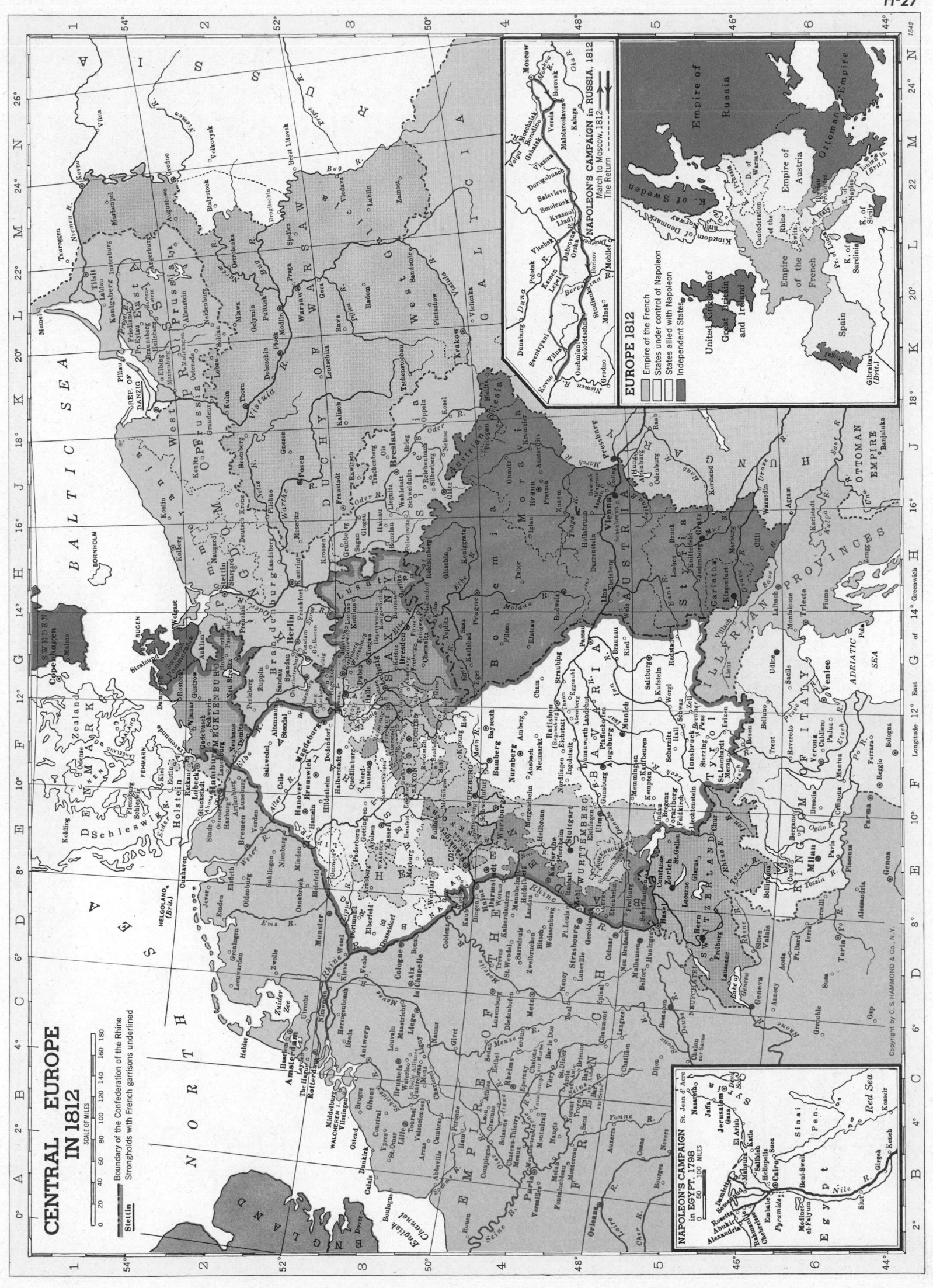

# CENTRAL EUROPE IN 1812

SCALE OF MILES
0 20 40 60 80 100 120 140 160 180

Boundary of the Confederation of the Rhine
**Stettin** Strongholds with French garrisons underlined

**NAPOLEON'S CAMPAIGN in RUSSIA, 1812**
March to Moscow, 1812
The Return

**EUROPE 1812**
Empire of the French
States under control of Napoleon
States allied with Napoleon
Independent States

**NAPOLEON'S CAMPAIGN in EGYPT, 1798**
0 50 100 MILES

Copyright by C. S. HAMMOND & Co., N.Y.

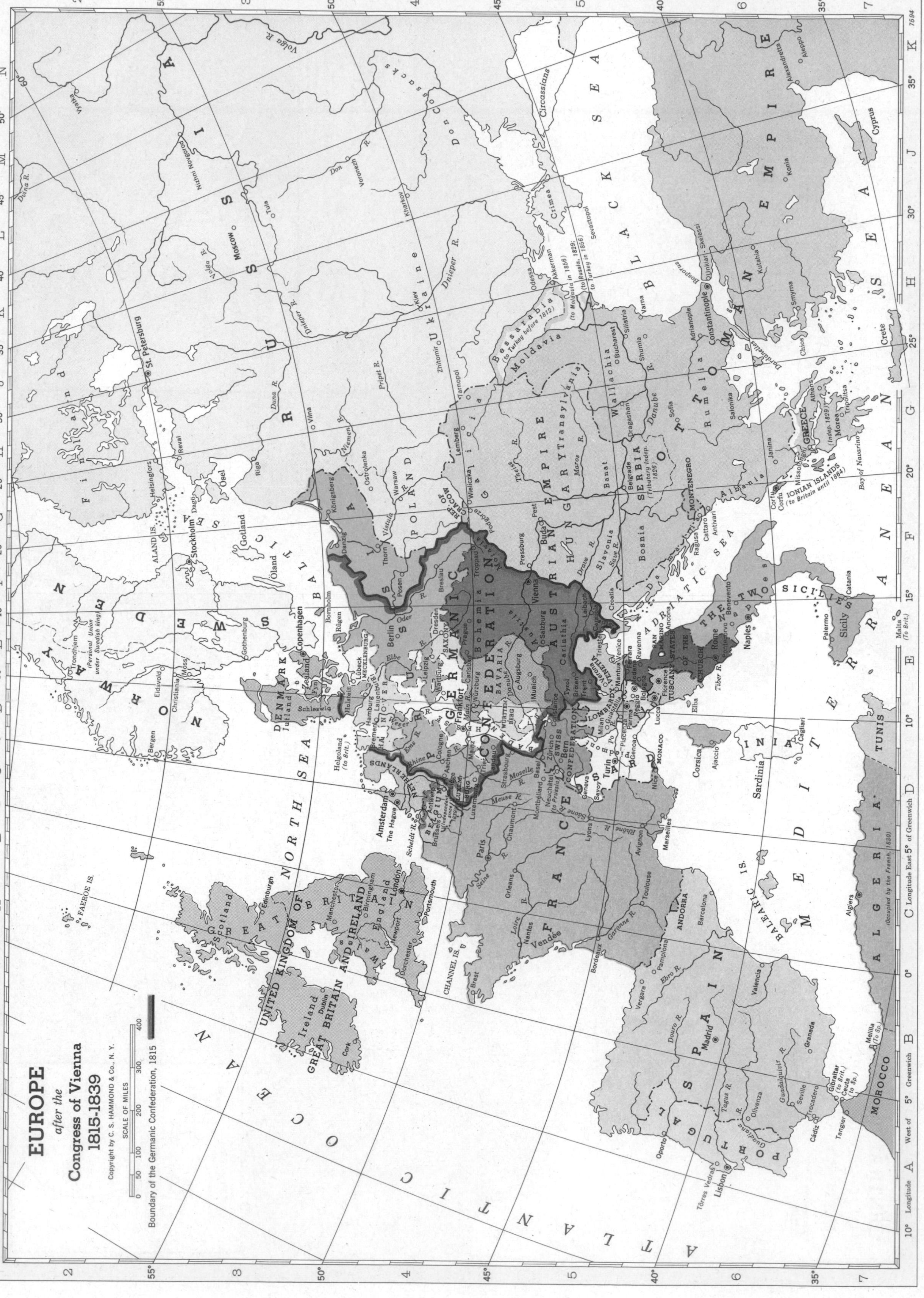

# EUROPE
### after the
## Congress of Vienna
### 1815-1839

Copyright by C. S. HAMMOND & Co. N.Y.

SCALE OF MILES
50 100 200 300 400

Boundary of the Germanic Confederation, 1815

RUSSIA

SWEDEN

NORWAY

FINLAND

DENMARK

GREAT BRITAIN AND IRELAND
UNITED KINGDOM OF

Scotland
Ireland
England

GERMANIC CONFEDERATION

POLAND
REP. OF KRAKOW

AUSTRIAN EMPIRE
HUNGARY
Transylvania
Bohemia
Galicia
Bavaria
Moravia
Carinthia

FRANCE

SPAIN

PORTUGAL

SWISS CONFEDERATION

LOMBARDY
VENETIA

CHURCH STATE OF THE

TUSCANY

Sardinia
Corsica

THE TWO SICILIES
Naples
Sicily

OTTOMAN EMPIRE
SERVIA
BOSNIA
MONTENEGRO
ALBANIA
WALLACHIA
Moldavia
Bessarabia
(to Turkey before 1812)
RUMELIA
Ukraine
Crimea
Circassians

GREECE
(Indep. 1829)
Morea
IONIAN ISLANDS
(to Britain until 1864)

MOROCCO
ALGERIA
(Occupied by the French, 1830)
TUNIS

NETHERLANDS
Amsterdam
The Hague
Brussels

ANDORRA
MONACO

NORTH SEA
BALTIC SEA
BLACK SEA
ADRIATIC SEA
MEDITERRANEAN SEA
ATLANTIC OCEAN

St. Petersburg
Moscow
Vienna
Berlin
Paris
London
Madrid
Lisbon
Copenhagen
Stockholm
Constantinople

BALEARIC IS.

Malta (To Brit.)
Gibraltar (to Brit.)
Helgoland (to Brit.)

Cyprus
Crete

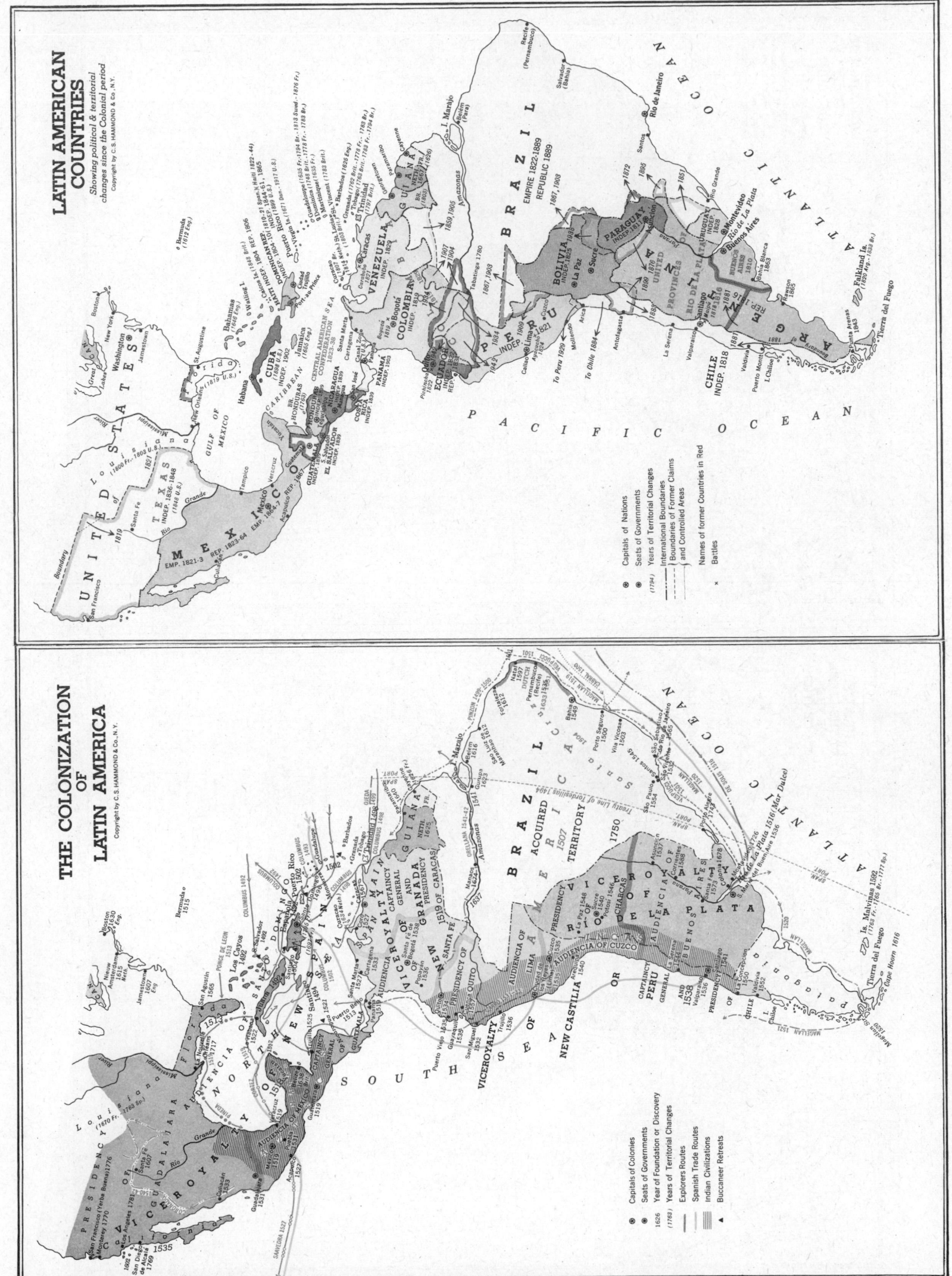

## LATIN AMERICAN COUNTRIES

Showing political & territorial
changes since the Colonial period

Copyright by C.S. HAMMOND & Co., N.Y.

### THE COLONIZATION OF LATIN AMERICA

Copyright by C.S. HAMMOND & Co., N.Y.

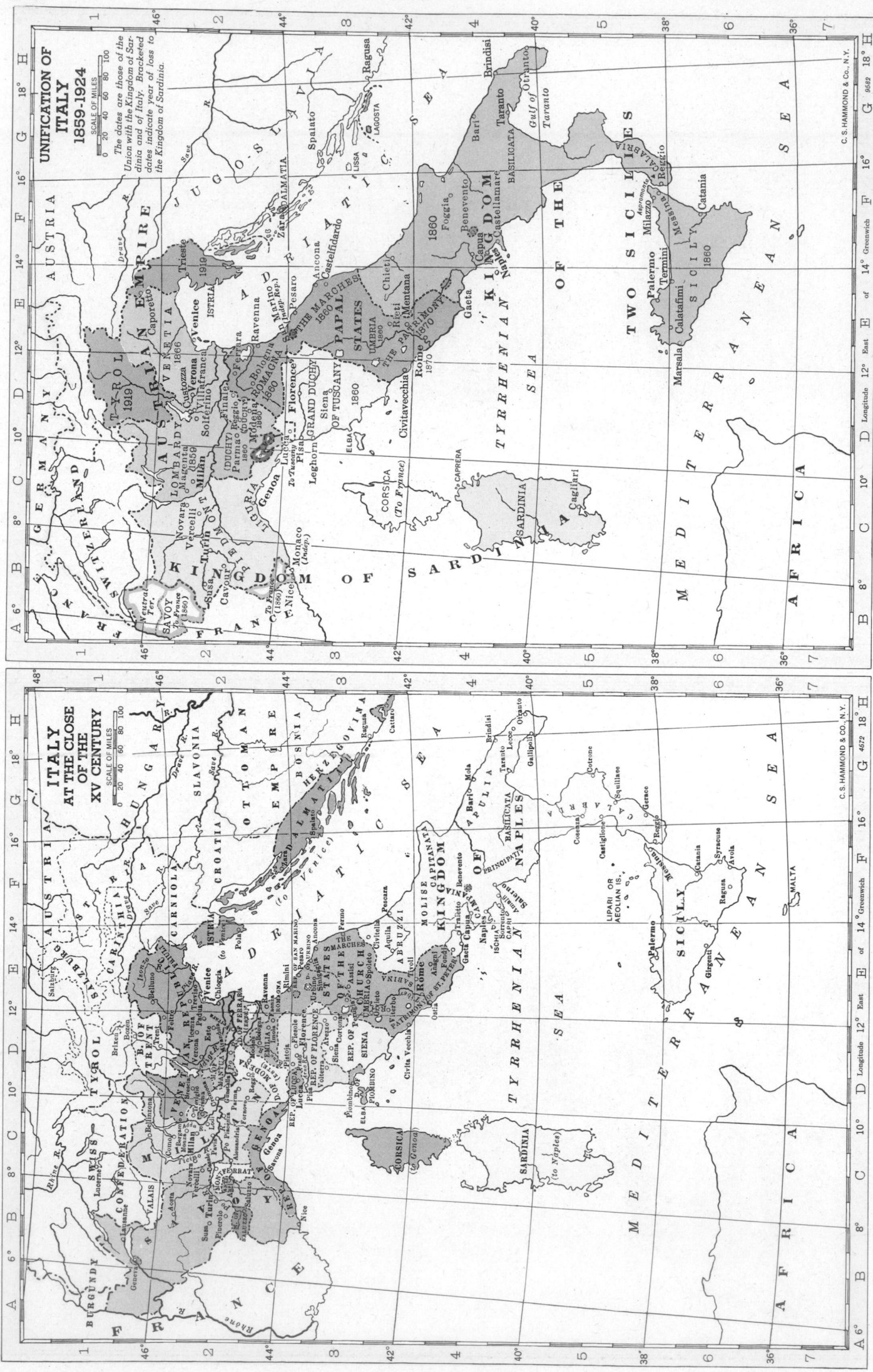

UNIFICATION OF ITALY
1859-1924

SCALE OF MILES

The dates are those of the
Union with the Kingdom of Sardinia and of Italy. Bracketed
dates indicate year of loss to
the Kingdom of Sardinia.

ITALY
AT THE CLOSE OF THE
XV CENTURY

SCALE OF MILES

C. S. HAMMOND & CO., N.Y.

## CENTRAL EUROPE
### 1815-1871

Boundary of German Confederation 1815-1866
Boundary of North German Confederation 1860-1871
Boundary of German Empire in 1871

SCALE OF MILES
0   25   50      100      150      200

## LANGUAGE MAP OF
## EUROPE
### 1910

Copyright by C.S. Hammond & Co., N.Y.

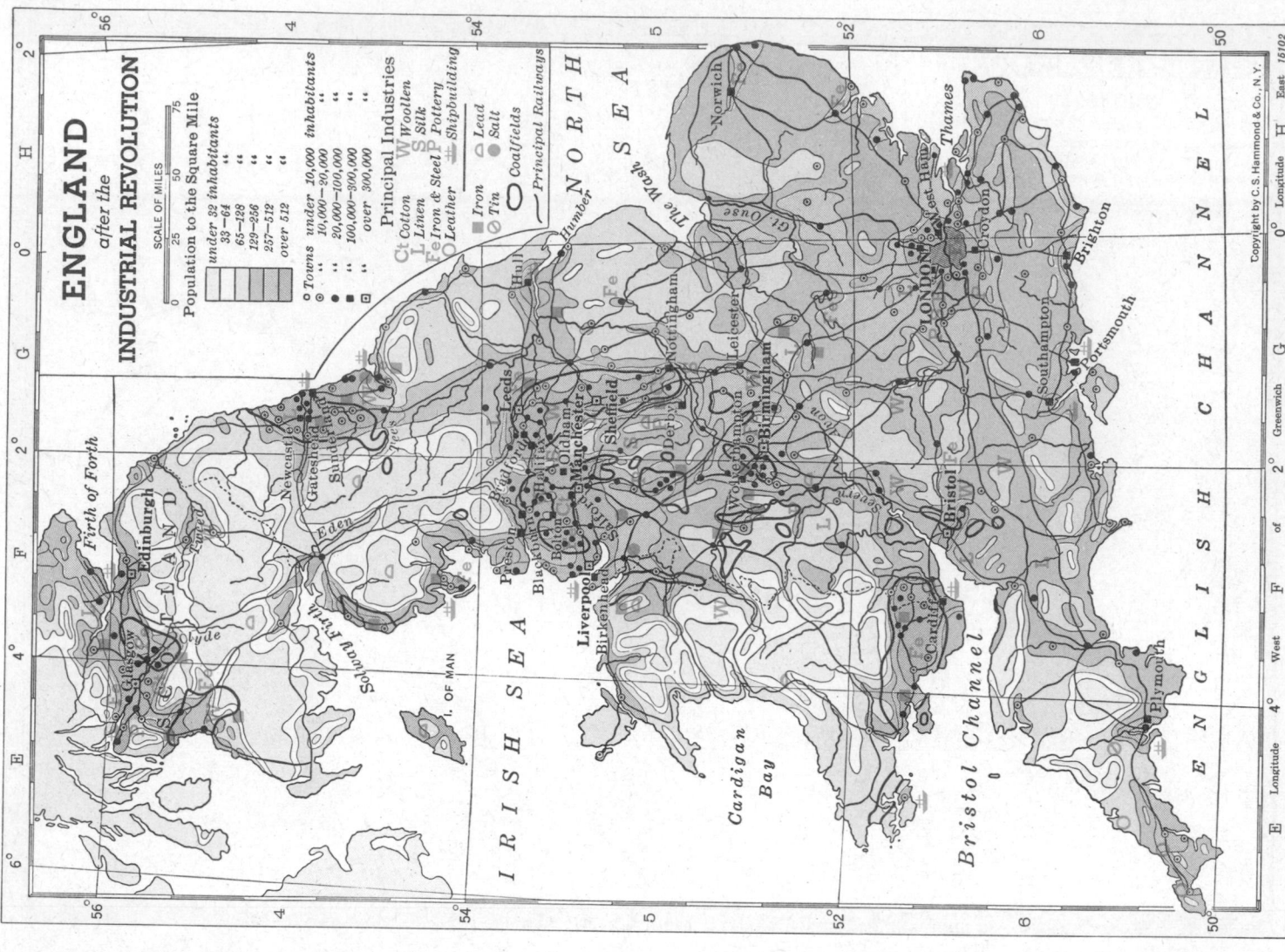

**ENGLAND**
*before the*
**INDUSTRIAL REVOLUTION**
c. 1701

**ENGLAND**
*after the*
**INDUSTRIAL REVOLUTION**

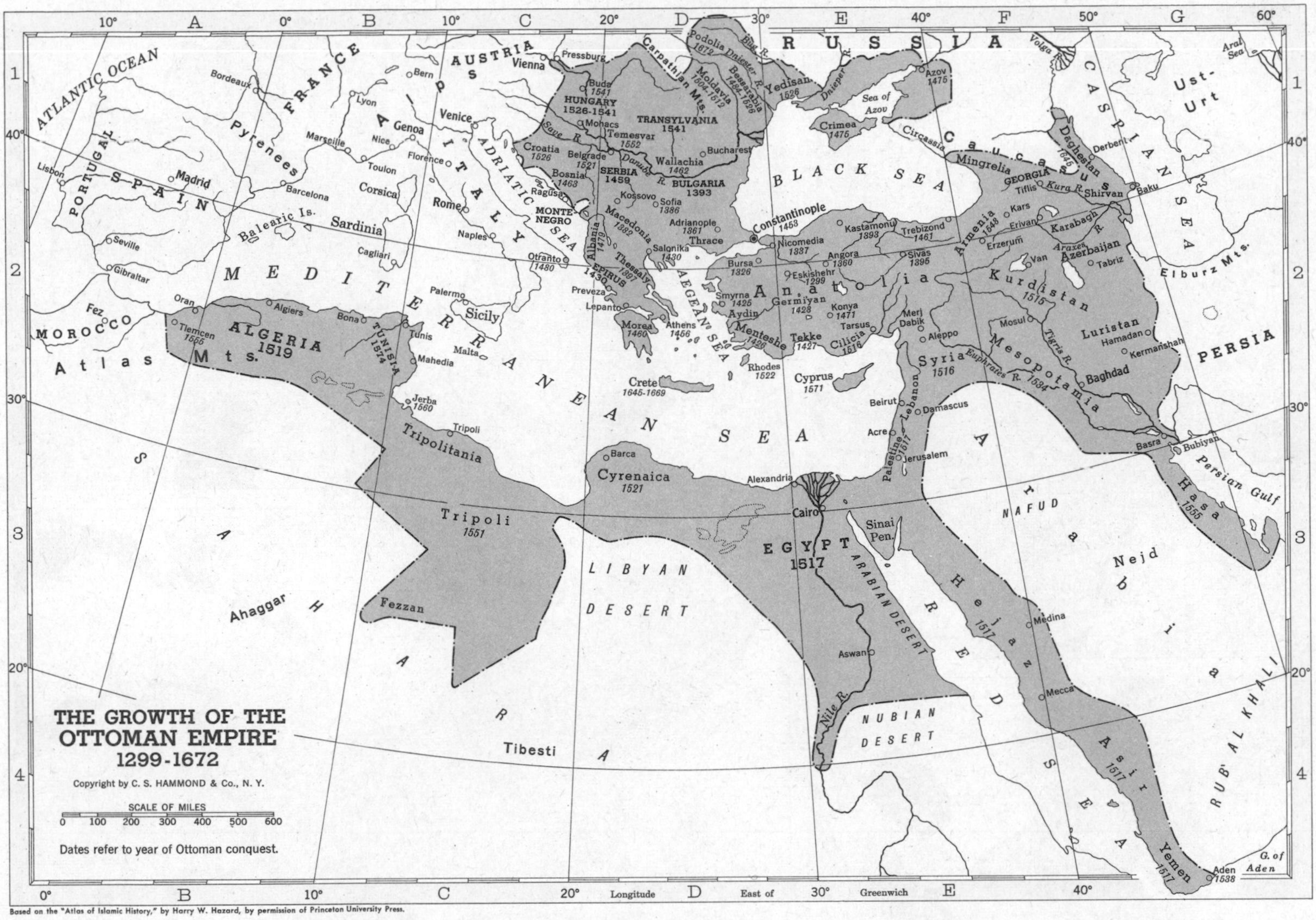

# THE GROWTH OF THE OTTOMAN EMPIRE 1299-1672

Copyright by C. S. HAMMOND & Co., N.Y.

SCALE OF MILES
0 100 200 300 400 500 600

Dates refer to year of Ottoman conquest.

Based on the "Atlas of Islamic History," by Harry W. Hazard, by permission of Princeton University Press.

**Map 1 labels:**

ATLANTIC OCEAN · FRANCE · AUSTRIA · RUSSIA · Ust-Urt · Bordeaux · Bern · Vienna · Pressburg · Podolia 1672 · Azov 1475 · Volga · Aral Sea · Lyon · Venice · Carpathian Mts. · Moldavia 1504 1711 · Bessarabia 1484 · Yedisan 1526 · Dnieper · CASPIAN SEA · Marseille · Nice · Genoa · HUNGARY 1526-1541 · Buda 1541 · TRANSYLVANIA 1541 · Temesvar 1552 · Mohacs 1526 · Wallachia 1462 · Bucharest · Crimea 1475 · Sea of Azov · Circassia · Daghestan 1578 · Derbent · Toulon · Corsica · Florence · Rome · Croatia 1526 · Belgrade 1521 · Danube R. · SERBIA 1459 · BULGARIA 1393 · BLACK SEA · Caucasus · Mingrelia · GEORGIA 1578 · Tiflis · Kura R. · Shirvan · Baku · Lisbon · Madrid · Barcelona · Bosnia 1463 · Ragusa · Kossovo · Sofia 1386 · Adrianople 1361 · Constantinople 1453 · Kastamonu 1393 · Trebizond 1461 · Armenia · Erivan · Kars · Karabagh 1639 · Erzerum · PORTUGAL · SPAIN · ITALY · MONTE NEGRO · Macedonia 1380 · Nicomedia 1337 · Thrace · Nicomedia · Bursa 1326 · Angora 1360 · Sivas 1396 · Van 1548 · Tabriz · Elburz Mts. · Seville · Gibraltar · Naples · Sicily · Thessaly 1397 · Smyrna 1425 · Anatolia · Germiyan 1428 · Konya 1471 · Meri Dabik · Mesopotamia · Kurdistan 1515 · Luristan · Kermanshah · PERSIA · Fez · Madrid · Balearic Is. · Sardinia · Cagliari · Palermo · Malta · Mahedia · Lepanto · Morea 1460 · Athens 1456 · Menteshe 1425 · Takke 1427 · Cilicia 1515 · Aleppo · Mosul 1555 · Hamadan · MOROCCO · Atlas Mts. · ALGERIA 1519 · Tlemcen 1555 · Algiers · Bona 1560 · TUNISIA 1574 · Tunis · Crete 1645-1669 · Rhodes 1522 · Cyprus 1571 · Syria 1516 · Euphrates R. 1534 · Baghdad · Basra · Bubiyan · MEDITERRANEAN SEA · Jerba 1560 · Tripoli 1551 · Tripolitania · Cyrenaica 1521 · Alexandria · Cairo · Beirut · Damascus · Acre · Palestine 1517 · Lebanon · Jerusalem · NAFUD · Persian Gulf · Hasa 1555 · Atlas · SAHARA · Ahaggar · Fezzan · LIBYAN DESERT · EGYPT 1517 · Sinai Pen. · Nejd · RUB' AL KHALI · Tibesti · Nile R. · Aswan · NUBIAN DESERT · Hejaz 1517 · Medina · Mecca · Asir 1517 · Yemen 1517 · Aden 1538 · G. of Aden · RED SEA · ARABIAN DESERT

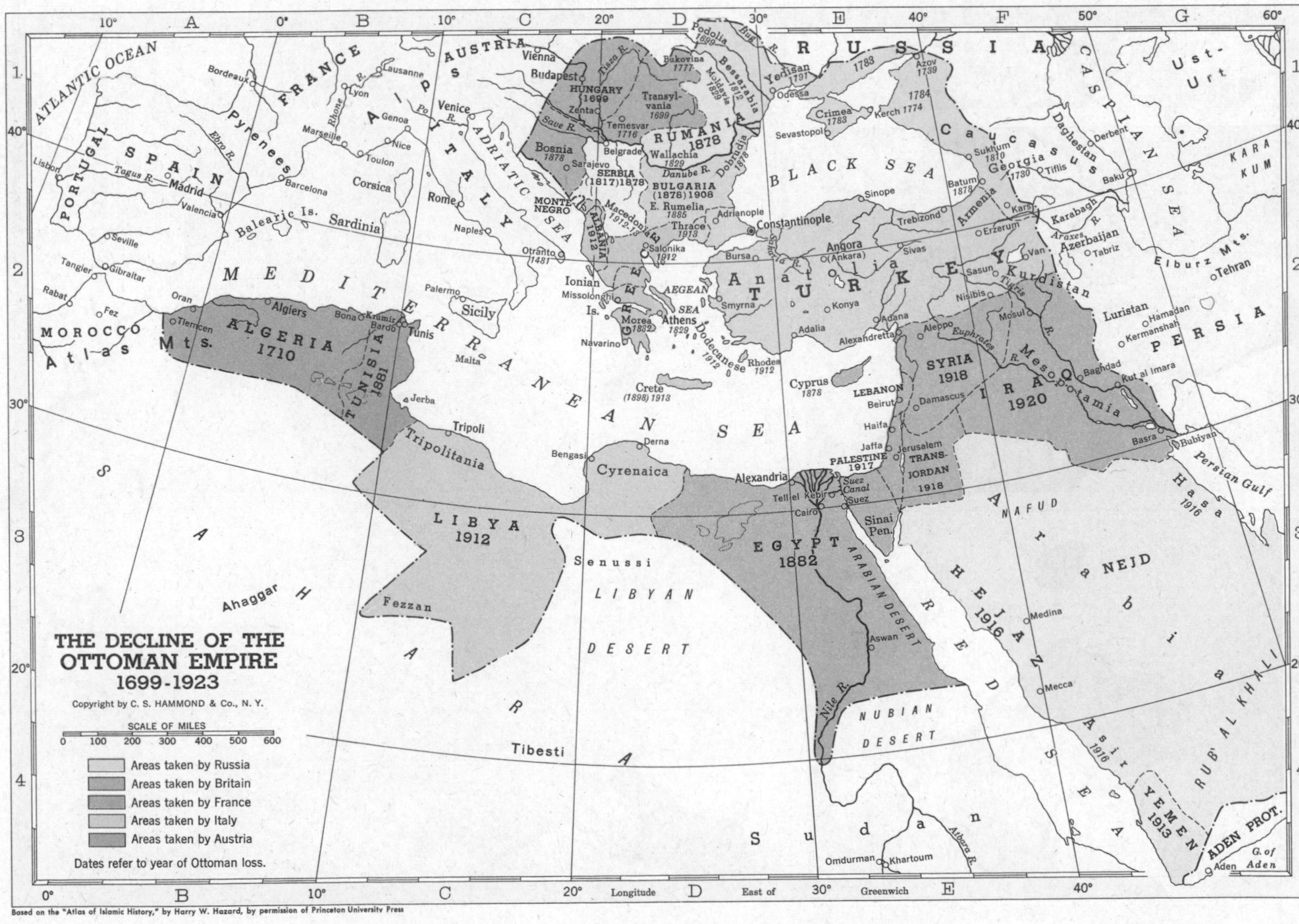

# THE DECLINE OF THE OTTOMAN EMPIRE 1699-1923

Copyright by C. S. HAMMOND & Co., N.Y.

SCALE OF MILES
0 100 200 300 400 500 600

Areas taken by Russia
Areas taken by Britain
Areas taken by France
Areas taken by Italy
Areas taken by Austria

Dates refer to year of Ottoman loss.

Based on the "Atlas of Islamic History," by Harry W. Hazard, by permission of Princeton University Press.

**Map 2 labels:**

ATLANTIC OCEAN · FRANCE · AUSTRIA · RUSSIA · Ust-Urt · Bordeaux · Lausanne · Vienna · Budapest · Bukovina 1777 · Moldavia 1812 · Bessarabia 1812 · Yedisan 1791 · 1783 · Azov 1739 · KARA KUM · Lyon · Geneva · HUNGARY 1699 · Zenta · Transylvania 1716 · Temesvar 1716 · RUMANIA 1878 · Wallachia · Danube R. · Kerch 1774 · Crimea 1783 · CASPIAN SEA · Marseille · Nice · Venice · Bosnia 1878 · Sarajevo · Belgrade · SERBIA (1817) 1878 · BULGARIA (1878) 1908 · Sevastopol · BLACK SEA · Caucasus · Sukhum 1810 · Batum 1878 · Georgia 1730 · Tiflis · Baku · Barcelona · Valencia · Corsica · Rome · MONTE NEGRO 1878 · ALBANIA 1913 · Macedonia 1912 · E. Rumelia 1885 · Thrace 1912 · Adrianople · Constantinople · Sinope · Trebizond · Armenia · Erzerum · Kars · Derbent · Elburz Mts. · Tehran · PORTUGAL · SPAIN · ITALY · Otranto 1481 · Salonika 1912 · Bursa · Anatolia · Angora (Ankara) · Sivas · Sasun · Van · Kurdistan · Azerbaijan · Araxes R. · Tabriz · Seville · Tangier · Gibraltar · Rabat · Fez · Naples · Sicily · Malta · Ionian Is. · Missolonghi 1829 · Morea 1829 · AEGEAN SEA · Athens · Smyrna · Konya · Adana · Adalia · Nisibis · Mosul · Luristan · Hamadan · Kermanshah · PERSIA · MOROCCO · Atlas Mts. · ALGERIA 1710 · Tlemcen · Oran · Algiers · Bona · Kroumir · TUNISIA 1881 · Bardo · Tunis · Navarino · Crete (1898) 1913 · Dodecanese 1912 · Rhodes 1912 · Cyprus 1878 · SYRIA 1918 · Aleppo · Euphrates · IRAQ 1920 · Baghdad · Kut el Imara · Basra 1916 · Bubiyan · MEDITERRANEAN SEA · Jerba · Tripoli · Tripolitania · Bengasi · Derna · Cyrenaica · Alexandria · Tell el Kebir · LEBANON 1918 · Beirut · Damascus · Haifa · Jaffa · PALESTINE 1917 · Jerusalem · TRANS-JORDAN 1918 · NAFUD · Mesopotamia · Persian Gulf · Hasa 1916 · SAHARA · Ahaggar · Fezzan · LIBYA 1912 · Senussi · LIBYAN DESERT · Suez Canal · Suez · Sinai Pen. · EGYPT 1882 · Cairo · NEJD · RUB' AL KHALI · Tibesti · Nile R. · Aswan · NUBIAN DESERT · Hejaz 1916 · Medina · Mecca · Asir 1916 · Yemen 1913 · ADEN PROT. · Aden · G. of Aden · RED SEA · ARABIAN DESERT · Sudan · Omdurman · Khartoum · Atbara R.

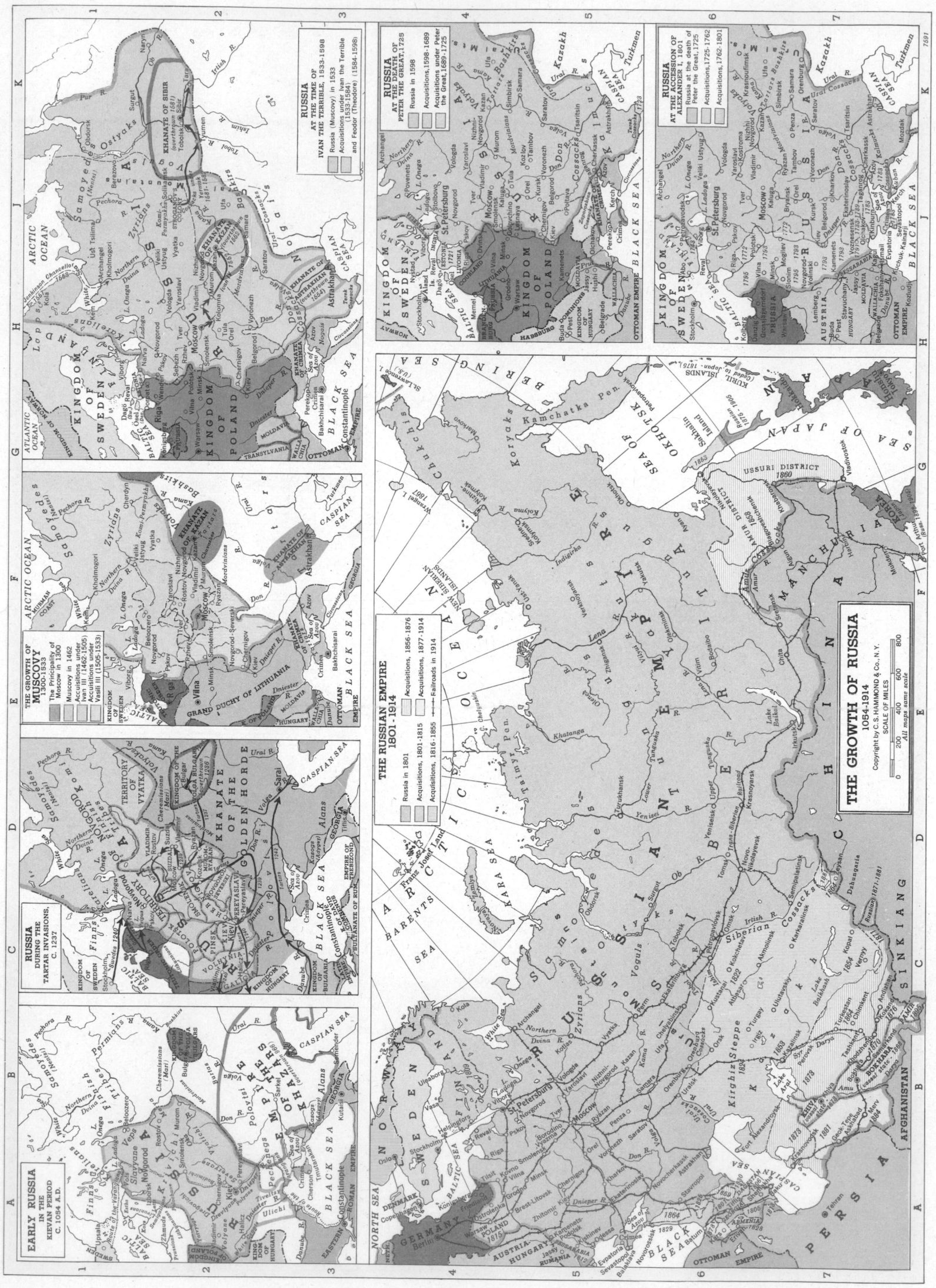

EARLY RUSSIA
IN THE
KIEVAN PERIOD
C. 1054 A.D.

RUSSIA
DURING THE
TARTAR INVASIONS.
C. 1237

THE GROWTH OF
MUSCOVY
1300-1533
The Principality of Moscow in 1300
Acquisitions under Ivan III (1462-1505)
Acquisitions under Vasilii III (1505-1533)

RUSSIA
AT THE TIME OF
IVAN THE TERRIBLE, 1533-1598
Russia (Muscovy) in 1533
Acquisitions under Ivan the Terrible (1533-1584) and Feodor (Theodore) (1584-1598)

RUSSIA
AT THE DEATH OF
PETER THE GREAT, 1725
Russia in 1598
Acquisitions under Peter the Great, 1689-1725

RUSSIA
AT THE ACCESSION OF
ALEXANDER I, 1801
Russia at the death of Peter the Great, 1725
Acquisitions, 1725-1762, 1762-1801

THE RUSSIAN EMPIRE
1801-1914
Russia in 1801
Acquisitions, 1801-1815
Acquisitions, 1816-1855
Acquisitions, 1856-1876
Acquisitions, 1877-1914
Railroads in 1914

THE GROWTH OF RUSSIA
1054-1914
Copyright by C. S. HAMMOND & Co., N.Y.
SCALE OF MILES
0   200   400   600   800
All maps same scale

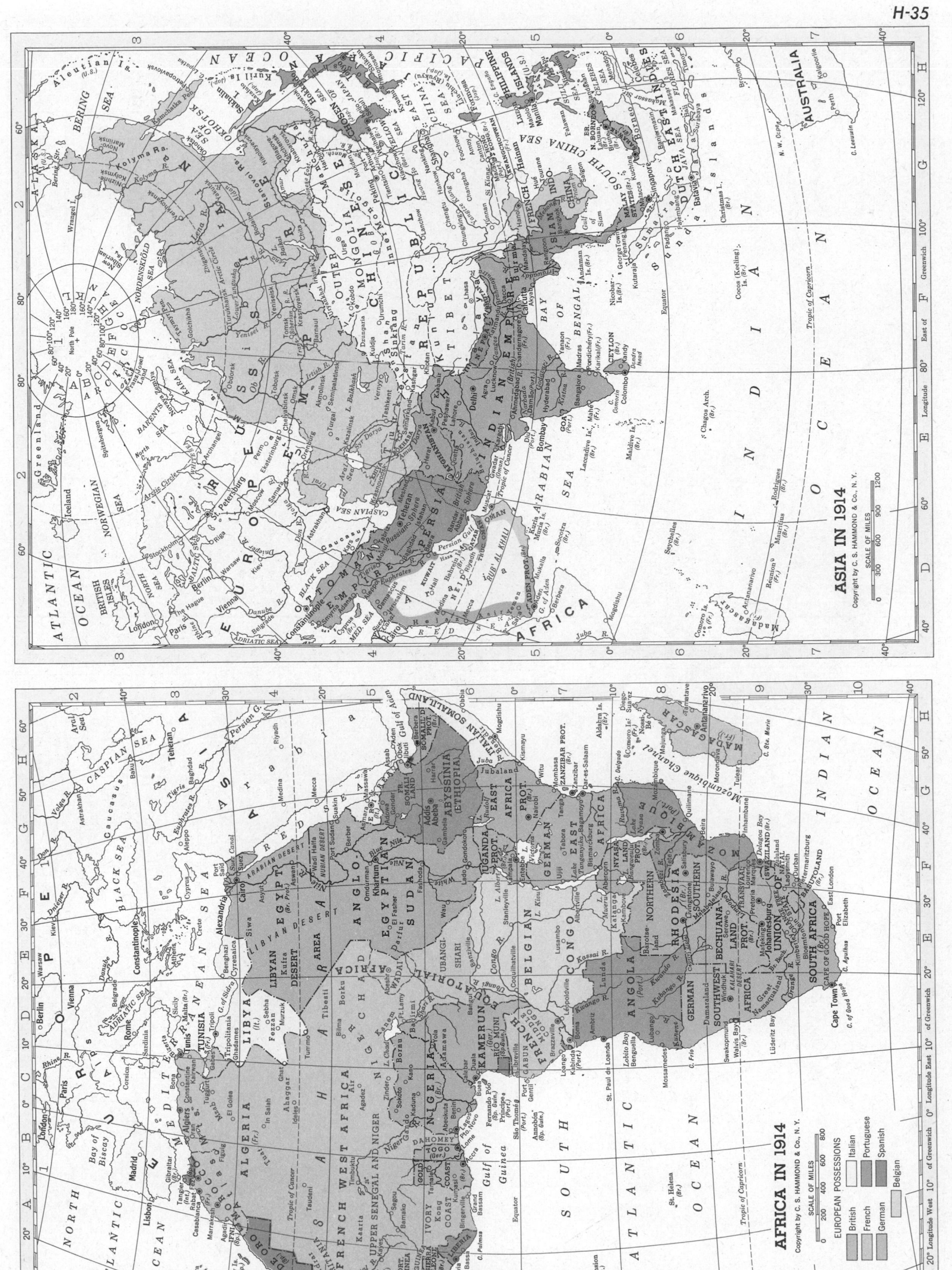

**ASIA IN 1914**

Copyright by C. S. HAMMOND & Co., N. Y.

SCALE OF MILES
0   300   600   900   1200

**AFRICA IN 1914**

Copyright by C. S. HAMMOND & Co., N. Y.

SCALE OF MILES
0   200   400   600   800

EUROPEAN POSSESSIONS

British
French
German
Italian
Portuguese
Spanish
Belgian

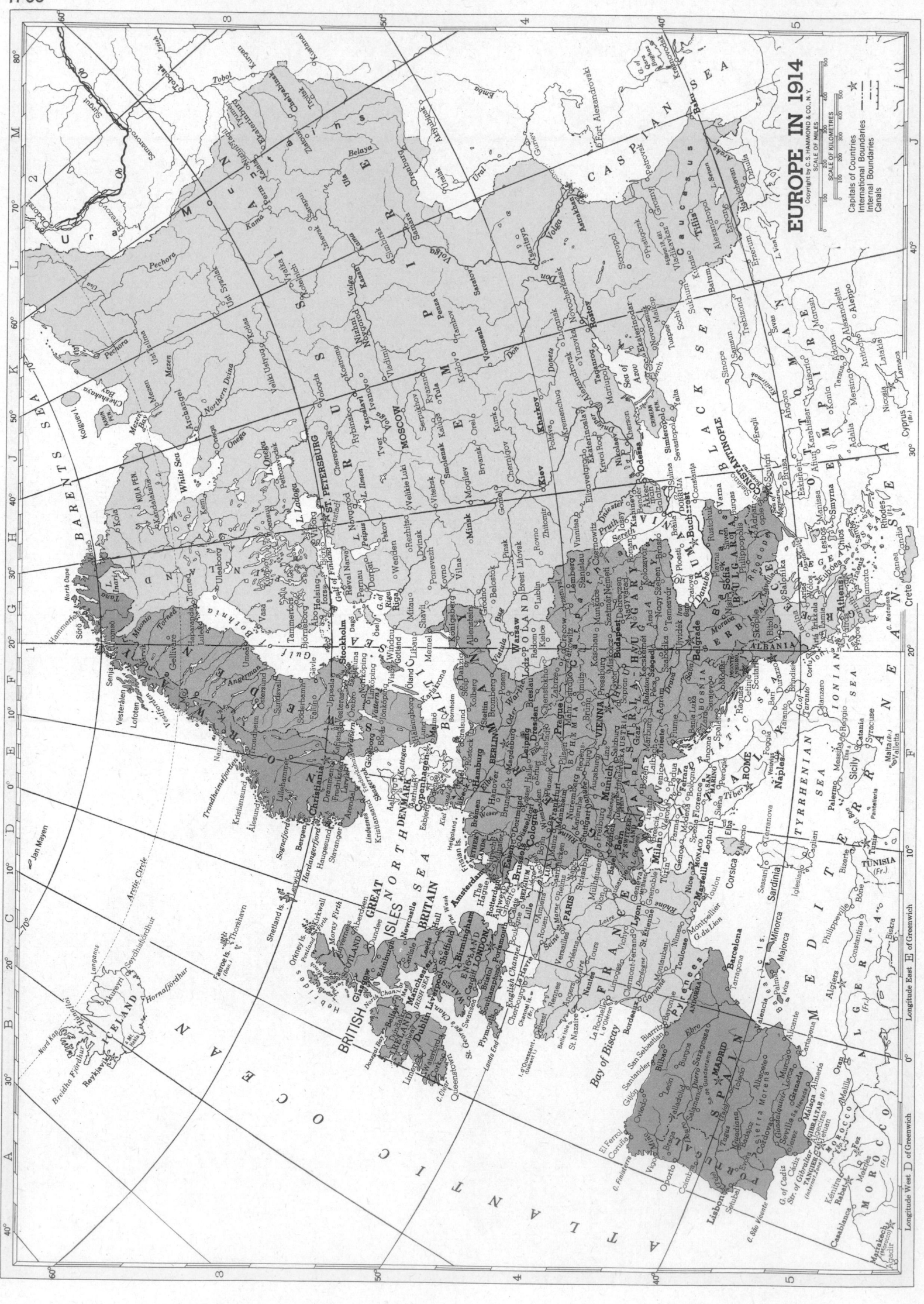

**EUROPE IN 1914**

Copyright by C. S. HAMMOND & CO., N.Y.

SCALE OF KILOMETRES

SCALE OF MILES

Capitals of Countries ✶
International Boundaries — · —
Internal Boundaries — - —
Canals

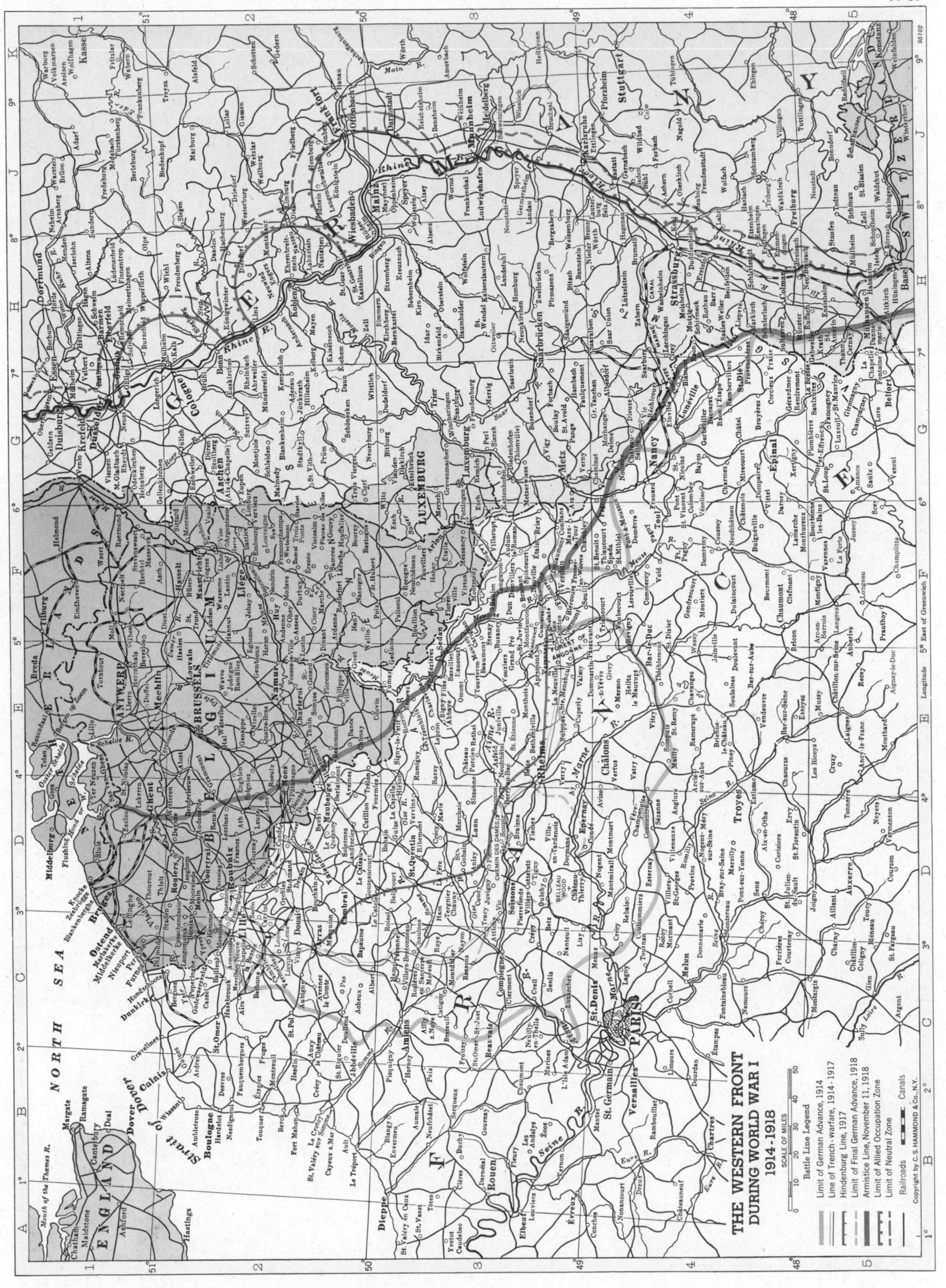

THE WESTERN FRONT
DURING WORLD WAR I
1914-1918

SCALE OF MILES

Battle Line Legend
Limit of German Advance, 1914
Line of Trench-warfare, 1914-1917
Hindenburg Line, 1917
Limit of Final German Advance, 1918
Armistice Line, November 11, 1918
Limit of Allied Occupation Zone
Limit of Neutral Zone
Railroads          Canals

Copyright by C.S. HAMMOND & Co., N.Y.

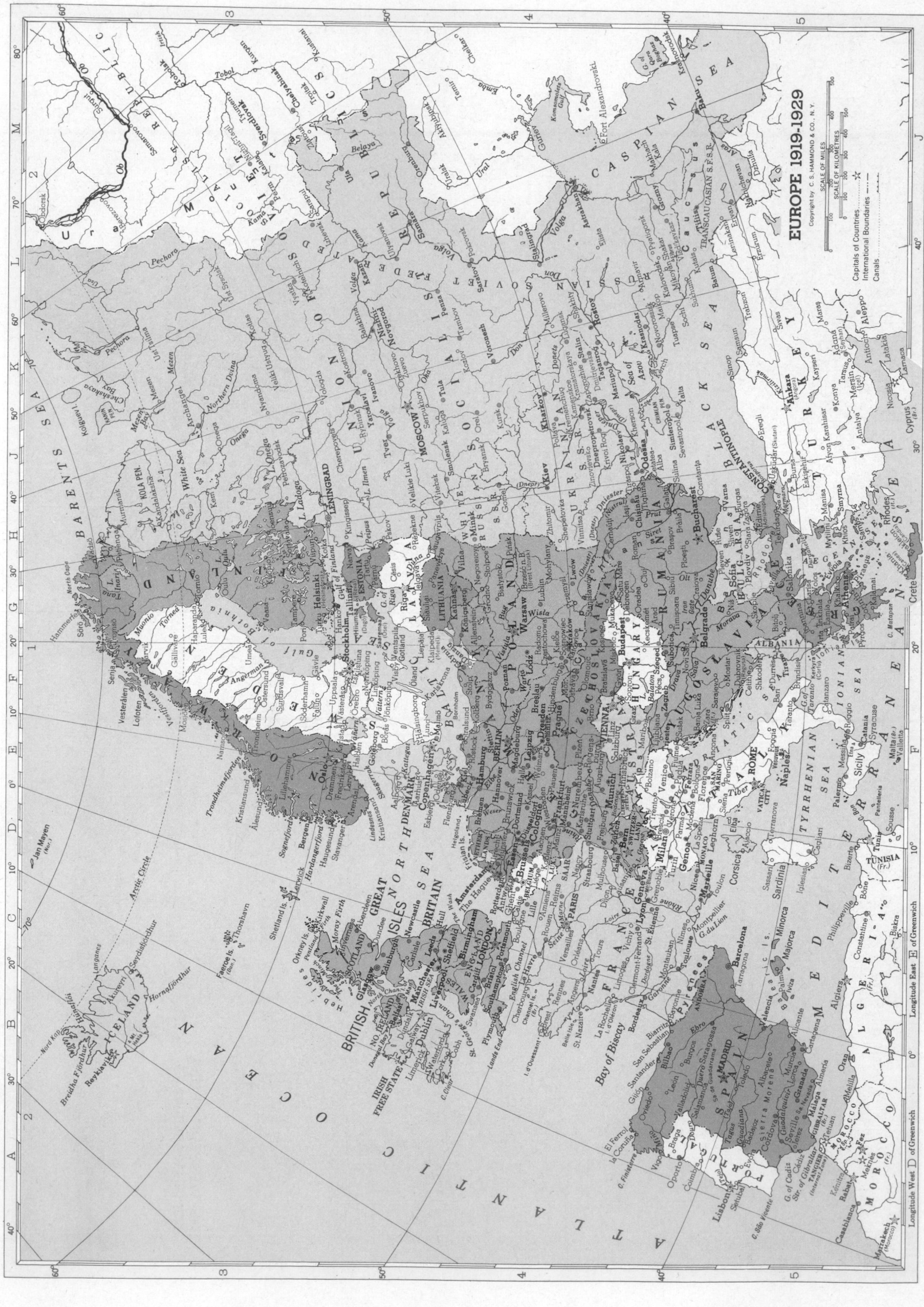

EUROPE 1919-1929

Copyright by C. S. HAMMOND & CO., N. Y.

SCALE OF MILES

SCALE OF KILOMETRES

Capitals of Countries............ ★
International Boundaries ........ -----
Canals ......................... ‑‑‑‑

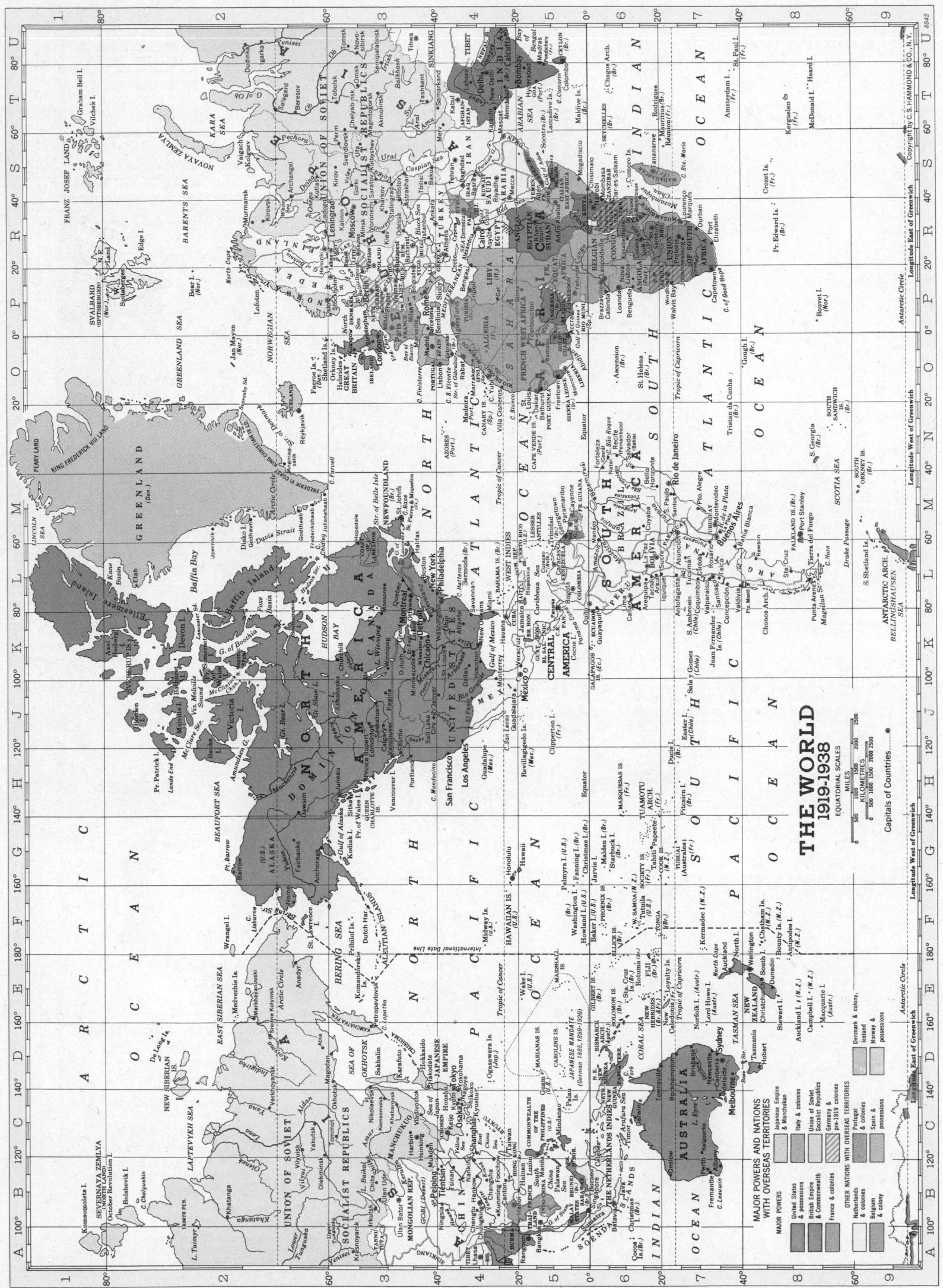

# THE WORLD
## 1919-1938

EQUATORIAL SCALES

MILES

KILOMETRES

Capitals of Countries........ ●

**MAJOR POWERS AND NATIONS
WITH OVERSEAS TERRITORIES**

MAJOR POWERS

United States & possessions
British Empire & Commonwealth
France & colonies

Japanese Empire & Manchukuo
Italy & colonies
Union of Soviet Socialist Republics
Germany & pre-1919 colonies

OTHER NATIONS WITH OVERSEAS TERRITORIES

Netherlands & colonies
Belgium & colony

Portugal & colonies
Spain & possessions

Denmark & colony
Iceland
Norway & possessions

Copyright by C. S. HAMMOND & CO., N.Y.

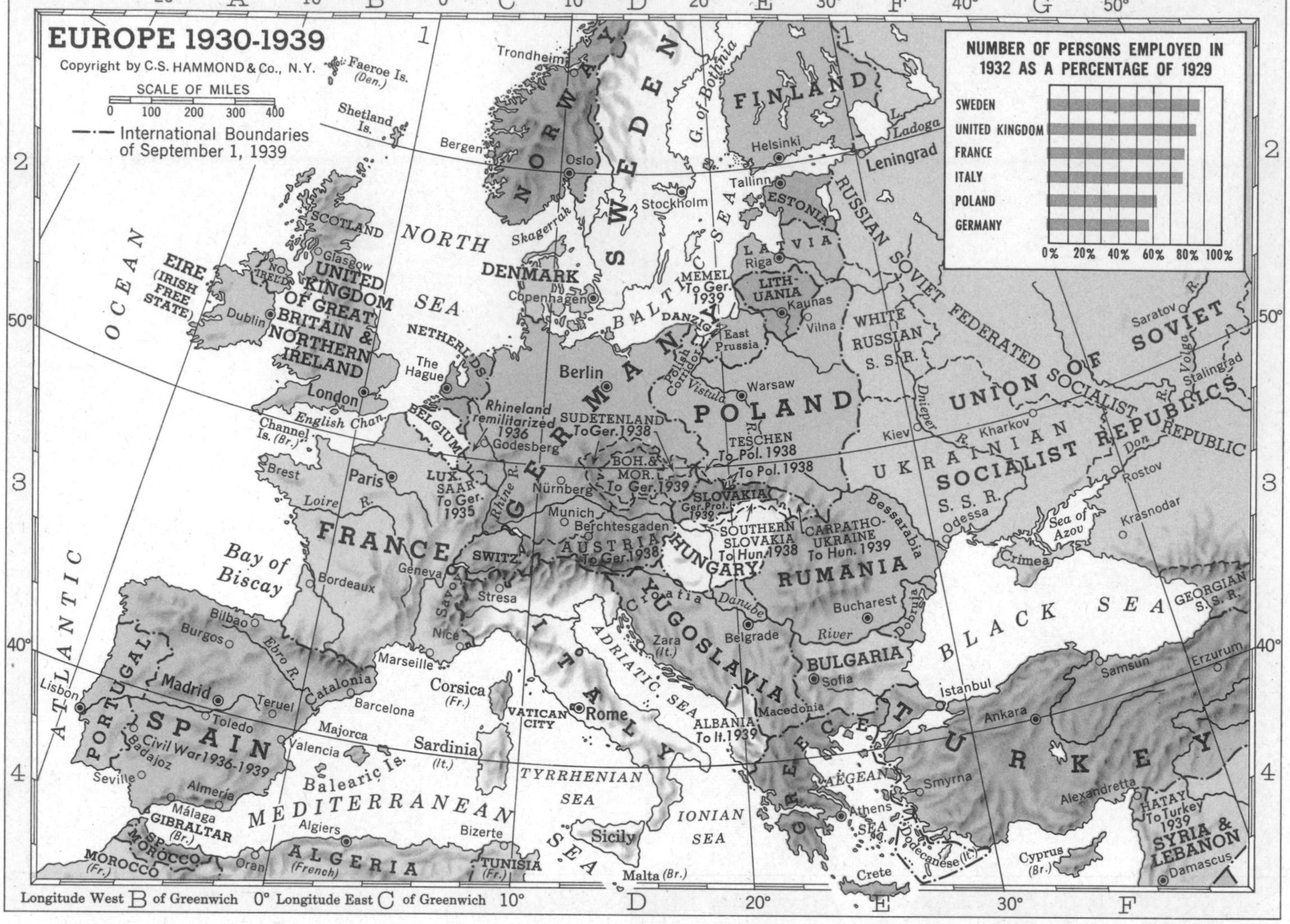

# EUROPE 1930-1939

Copyright by C.S. HAMMOND & Co., N.Y.

SCALE OF MILES
0 100 200 300 400

—— International Boundaries of September 1, 1939

### NUMBER OF PERSONS EMPLOYED IN 1932 AS A PERCENTAGE OF 1929

SWEDEN
UNITED KINGDOM
FRANCE
ITALY
POLAND
GERMANY

0% 20% 40% 60% 80% 100%

Faeroe Is. (Den.)
Shetland Is.
Trondheim
Bergen
NORWAY
SWEDEN
FINLAND
Helsinki
Leningrad
G. of Bothnia
Oslo
Stockholm
Skagerrak
NORTH SEA
SCOTLAND
Glasgow
DENMARK
Copenhagen
BALTIC SEA
Tallinn
ESTONIA
Ladoga
RUSSIAN SOVIET FEDERATED
EIRE (IRISH FREE STATE)
Dublin
UNITED KINGDOM OF GREAT BRITAIN & NORTHERN IRELAND
London
NETHERL'DS
The Hague
MEMEL To Ger. 1939
Riga
LATVIA
Vilna
LITH-UANIA
Kaunas
WHITE RUSSIAN S.S.R.
SOCIALIST REPUBLICS
UNION OF SOVIET
Saratov
Volga R.
Stalingrad
English Chan.
Channel Is. (Br.)
BELGIUM
Berlin
GERMANY
DANZIG
East Prussia
Corridor
Warsaw
POLAND
Vistula
Kiev
UKRAINIAN S.S.R.
Kharkov
Don R.
Rostov
SOCIALIST REPUBLICS
Brest
Paris
LUX.
SAAR To Ger. 1935
Rhineland remilitarized 1936
Godesberg
SUDETENLAND To Ger. 1938
TESCHEN To Pol. 1938
BOH. & MOR. To Ger. 1939
Dnieper
Odessa
Bessarabia
Krasnodar
FRANCE
Loire R.
Nürnberg
Munich
Berchtesgaden
SLOVAKIA
SOUTHERN SLOVAKIA To Hun. 1938
CARPATHO-UKRAINE To Hun. 1939
RUMANIA
Sea of Azov
Crimea
SWITZ.
AUSTRIA To Ger. 1938
HUNGARY
Bay of Biscay
Bordeaux
Geneva
Stresa
Nice
CROATIA
Danube River
Belgrade
Bucharest
GEORGIAN S.S.R.
BLACK SEA
Erzurum
SPAIN
Madrid
Toledo
Teruel
Barcelona
Catalonia
Marseille
Corsica (Fr.)
ITALY
Rome
Zara (It.)
ADRIATIC SEA
YUGOSLAVIA
BULGARIA
Sofia
Istanbul
Samsun
Ankara
Portugal
Lisbon
Badajoz
Civil War 1936-1939
Majorca
Valencia
Balearic Is.
Sardinia (It.)
VATICAN CITY
TYRRHENIAN SEA
Albania To It.1939
Macedonia
GREECE
Smyrna
TURKEY
HATAY To Turkey 1939
Alexandretta
Seville
Málaga
GIBRALTAR (Br.)
MOROCCO
Algiers
ALGERIA (French)
MEDITERRANEAN SEA
Bizerte
Sicily
IONIAN SEA
TUNISIA (Fr.)
Malta (Br.)
Crete
Athens
AEGEAN SEA
Dodecanese (It.)
Cyprus (Br.)
SYRIA & LEBANON
Damascus

Longitude West B of Greenwich 0° Longitude East C of Greenwich 10°

# THE FAR EAST 1930-1941

Copyright by C.S. HAMMOND & Co., N.Y.

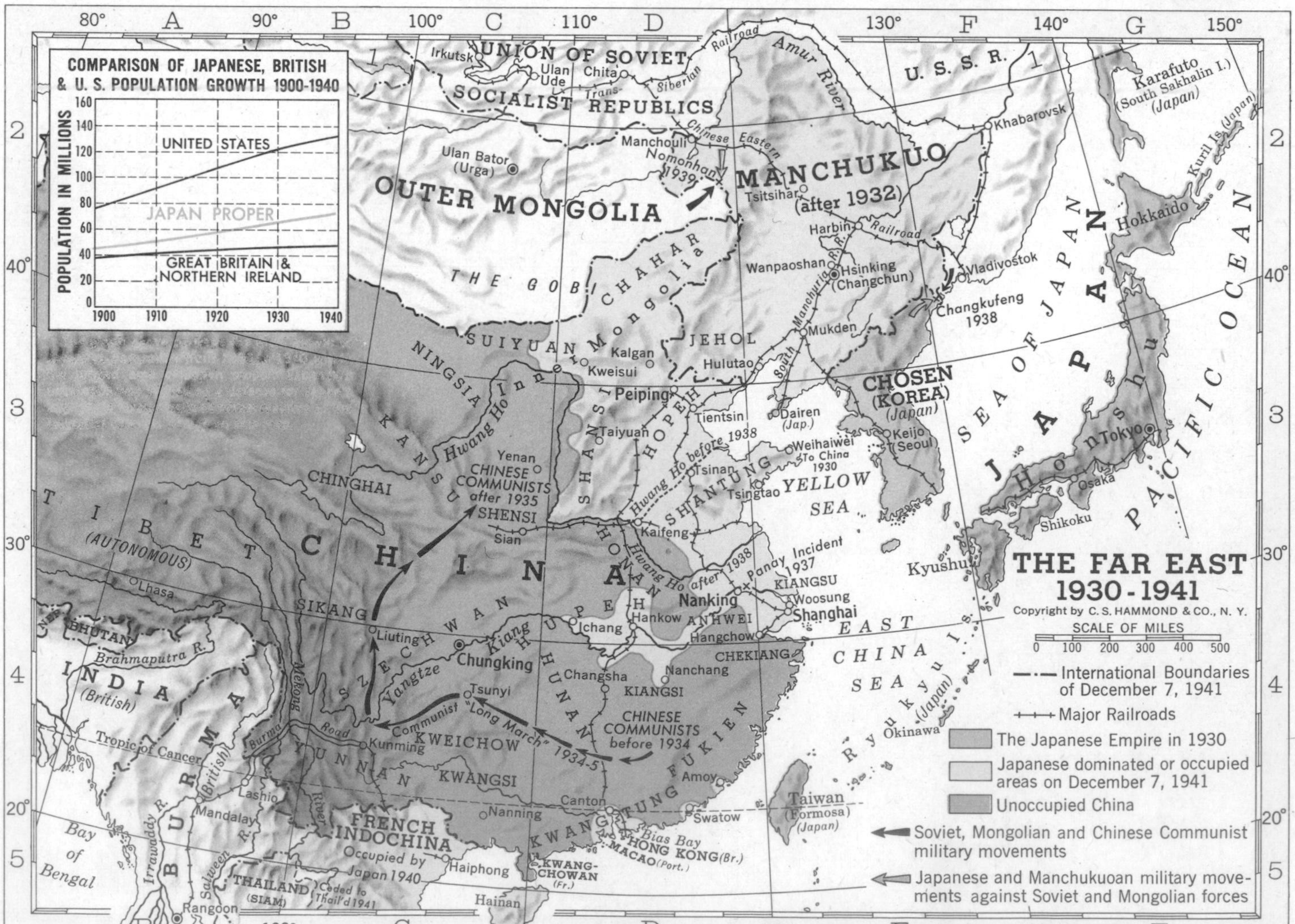

### COMPARISON OF JAPANESE, BRITISH & U.S. POPULATION GROWTH 1900-1940

POPULATION IN MILLIONS
UNITED STATES
JAPAN PROPER
GREAT BRITAIN & NORTHERN IRELAND
1900 1910 1920 1930 1940

Irkutsk
Ulan Ude
Chita
UNION OF SOVIET SOCIALIST REPUBLICS
Trans Siberian Railroad
Amur River
U.S.S.R.
Khabarovsk
Karafuto (South Sakhalin I.) (Japan)
Manchouli
Chinese Eastern Railroad
Nomonhan 1939
MANCHUKUO (after 1932)
Tsitsihar
Ulan Bator (Urga)
OUTER MONGOLIA
THE GOBI
Harbin
Hsinking (Changchun)
Vladivostok
Kuril Is. (Japan)
Hokkaido
Wanpaoshan
Mukden
Changkufeng 1938
Inner Mongolia
CHAHAR
JEHOL
Hulutao
Manchuria
South Manchurian Railroad
SEA OF JAPAN
CHINGHAI
TIBET (AUTONOMOUS)
Lhasa
NINGSIA
KANSU
SUIYUAN
Kalgan
Kweisui
SHANSI
Peiping
HOPEH
Tientsin
Dairen (Jap.)
Weihaiwei To China 1930
Keijo (Seoul)
CHOSEN (KOREA) (Japan)
JAPAN
Tokyo
Yenan
CHINESE COMMUNISTS after 1935
SHENSI
Sian
Taiyuan
Huang Ho before 1938
Tsinan
SHANTUNG
Tsingtao
YELLOW SEA
Osaka
Shikoku
SIKANG
CHINA
Kaifeng
Huang Ho after 1938
KIANGSU
Nanking
Woosung
Shanghai
Kyushu
SZECHWAN
Liuting
Kiang
HUPEH
Ichang
Hankow
ANHWEI
Hangchow
CHEKIANG
Panay Incident 1937
EAST CHINA SEA
INDIA (British)
Brahmaputra R.
BHUTAN
Chungking
HUNAN
Changsha
Nanchang
KIANGSI
Okinawa
Ryukyu
Tsunyi
"Long March" 1934-5
KWEICHOW
CHINESE COMMUNISTS before 1934
FUKIEN
Taiwan (Formosa) (Japan)
BURMA (British)
Burma Road
Kunming
YUNNAN
Communist Long March
KWANGSI
KWANGTUNG
Canton
Amoy
Swatow
Bias Bay
HONG KONG (Br.)
MACAO (Port.)
PACIFIC OCEAN
Tropic of Cancer
Mandalay
Lashio
Salween
Mekong
THAILAND (SIAM)
FRENCH INDOCHINA
Occupied by Japan 1940
Nanning
KWANG-CHOWAN (Fr.)
Hainan
Irrawaddy R.
Bay of Bengal
Rangoon
Haiphong

SCALE OF MILES
0 100 200 300 400 500

—·— International Boundaries of December 7, 1941
+++ Major Railroads
The Japanese Empire in 1930
Japanese dominated or occupied areas on December 7, 1941
Unoccupied China
→ Soviet, Mongolian and Chinese Communist military movements
→ Japanese and Manchukuoan military movements against Soviet and Mongolian forces

120° Longitude East of 130° Greenwich

# THE WORLD AT WAR 1939-1945

**ECKERT PROJECTION**
SCALE OF MILES ALONG EQUATOR
0    500    1000    1500    2000    2500

The following states, neutral throughout the greater part of the war, joined the conflict against the Axis after 1944:

| | | |
|---|---|---|
| ARGENTINA | LEBANON | SYRIA |
| CHILE | PARAGUAY | TURKEY |
| ECUADOR | PERU | URUGUAY |
| EGYPT | SAUDI ARABIA | VENEZUELA |

Legend:

- - - - - International Boundaries of September 1, 1939 (December 7, 1941 in Far East)
- - - - - Allied Maritime Supply Routes
———— U. S. Military Airways
The Allies

Sphere of German U-boat Operations
Neutral States
Allied Advances
Naval & air bases obtained by U.S. from Great Britain are underlined.

Areas Occupied by the Allies
The Axis Powers (including Thailand and Japanese-occupied areas on Dec. 7, 1941)
Areas Occupied by the Axis Powers
Vichy-controlled Areas (later to Allies)

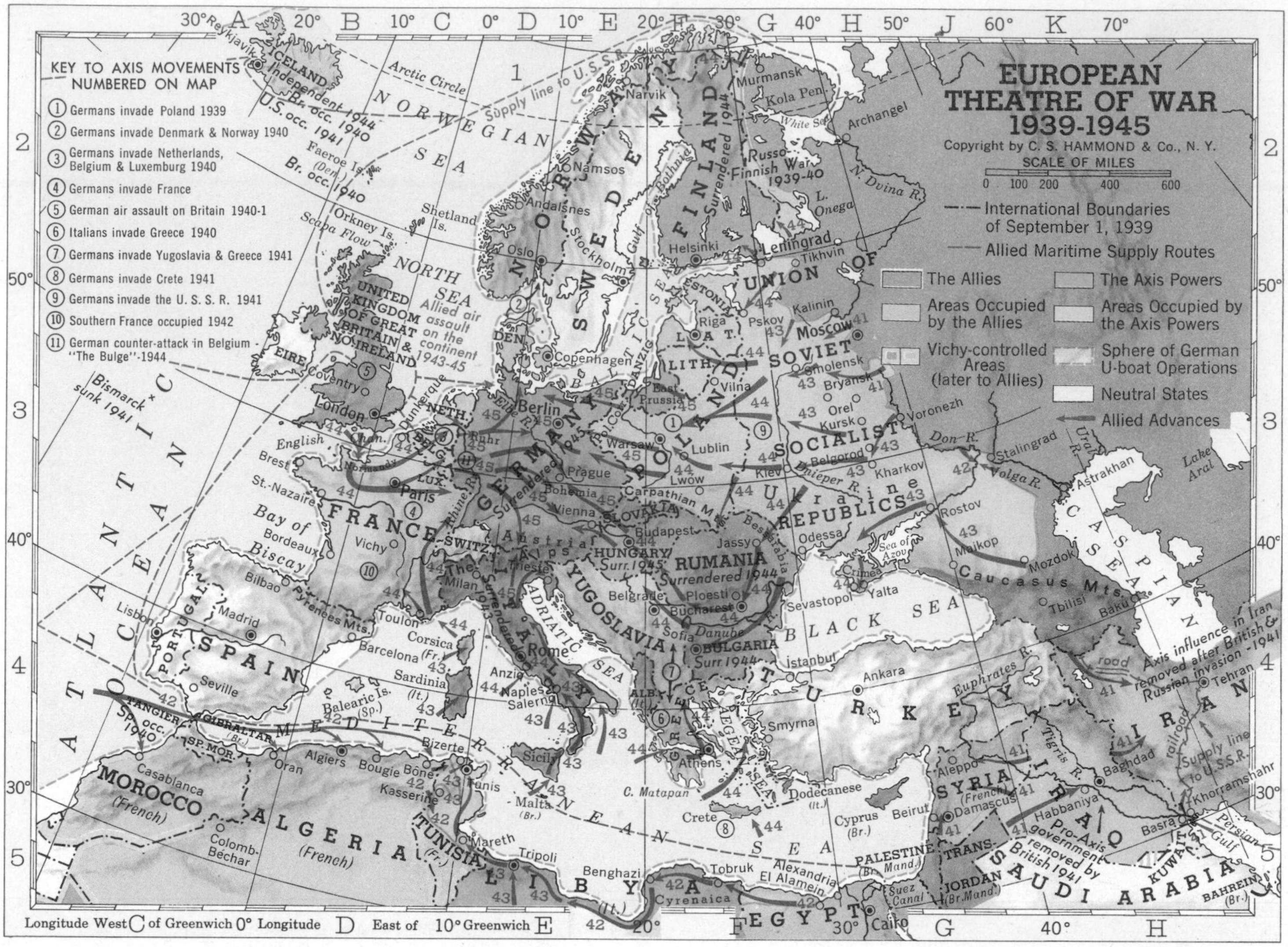

## EUROPEAN THEATRE OF WAR 1939-1945

Copyright by C. S. Hammond & Co., N.Y.

SCALE OF MILES
0 100 200 400 600

- – – International Boundaries of September 1, 1939
- – – Allied Maritime Supply Routes

The Allies
Areas Occupied by the Allies
Vichy-controlled Areas (later to Allies)

The Axis Powers
Areas Occupied by the Axis Powers
Sphere of German U-boat Operations
Neutral States

→ Allied Advances

**KEY TO AXIS MOVEMENTS NUMBERED ON MAP**

1. Germans invade Poland 1939
2. Germans invade Denmark & Norway 1940
3. Germans invade Netherlands, Belgium & Luxemburg 1940
4. Germans invade France
5. German air assault on Britain 1940-1
6. Italians invade Greece 1940
7. Germans invade Yugoslavia & Greece 1941
8. Germans invade Crete 1941
9. Germans invade the U.S.S.R. 1941
10. Southern France occupied 1942
11. German counter-attack in Belgium - "The Bulge" -1944

Longitude West C of Greenwich 0° Longitude D East of 10° Greenwich E

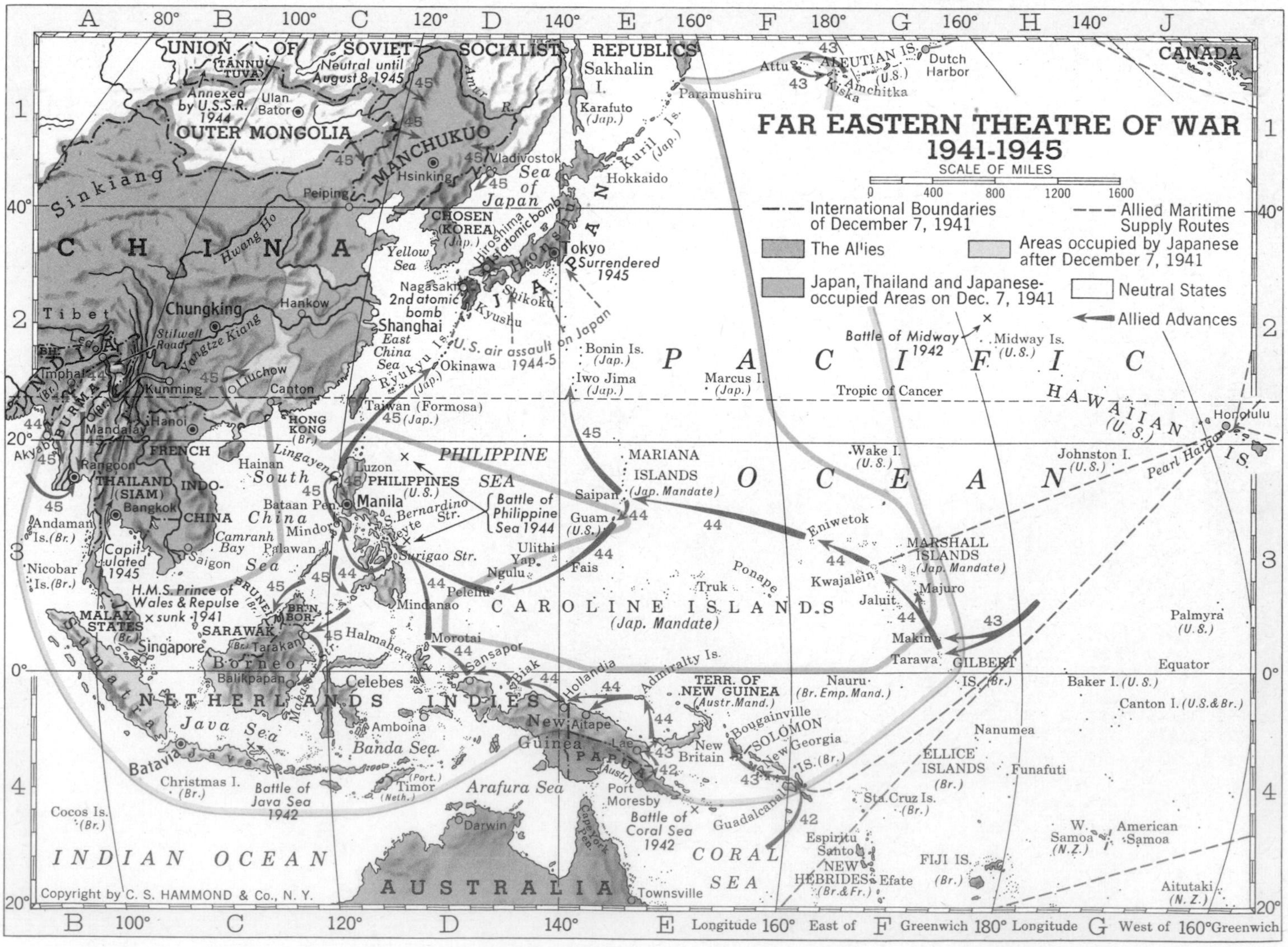

## FAR EASTERN THEATRE OF WAR 1941-1945

SCALE OF MILES
0 400 800 1200 1600

- – – International Boundaries of December 7, 1941
- – – Allied Maritime Supply Routes

The Allies
Japan, Thailand and Japanese-occupied Areas on Dec. 7, 1941

Areas occupied by Japanese after December 7, 1941
Neutral States

→ Allied Advances

Copyright by C. S. HAMMOND & Co., N.Y.

Longitude 160° East of Greenwich 180° Longitude West of 160° Greenwich

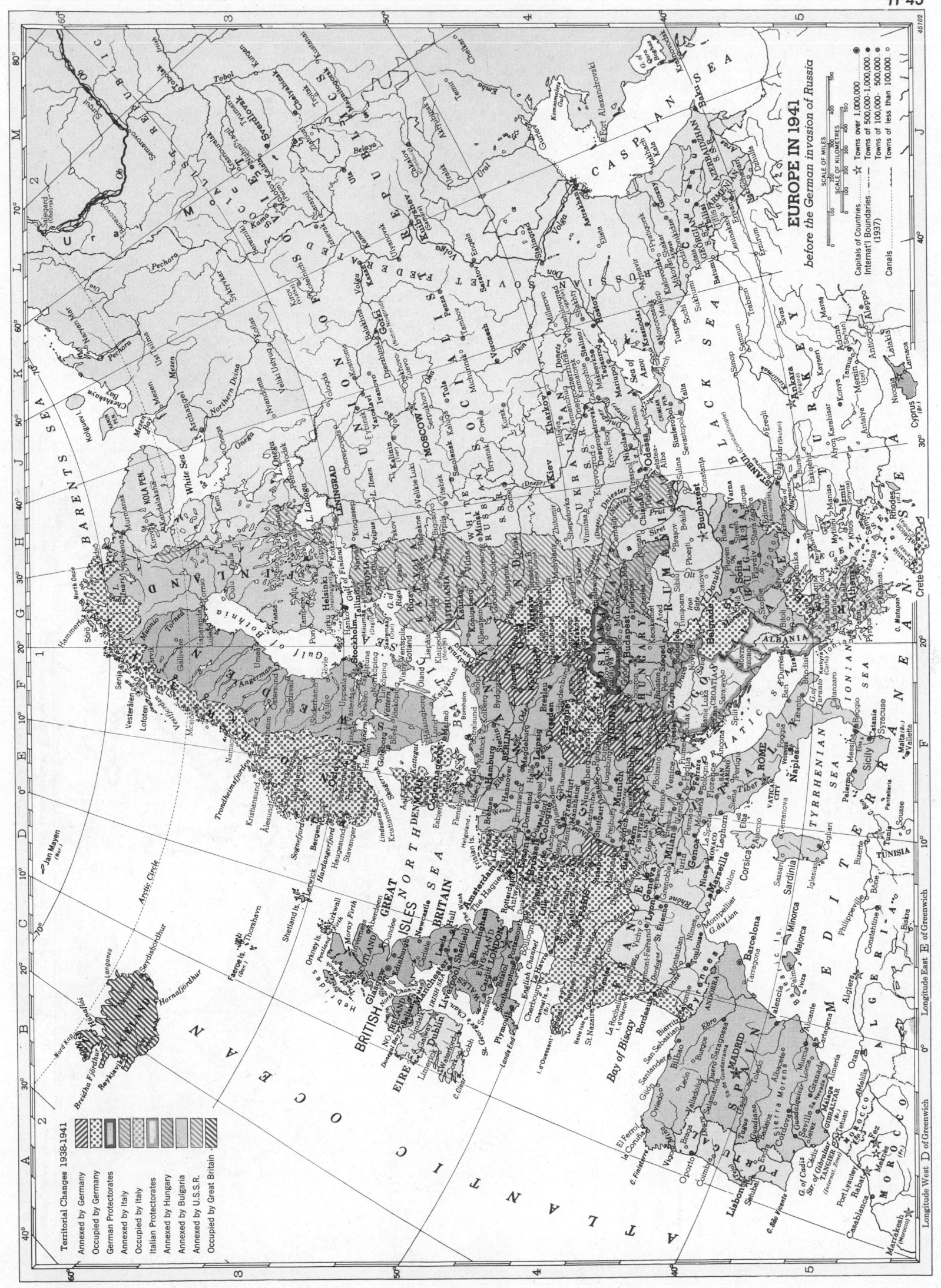

**EUROPE IN 1941**
*before the German invasion of Russia*

Territorial Changes 1938-1941

Annexed by Germany
Occupied by Germany
German Protectorates
Annexed by Italy
Occupied by Italy
Italian Protectorates
Annexed by Hungary
Annexed by Bulgaria
Annexed by U.S.S.R.
Occupied by Great Britain

Capitals of Countries
Intern'l Boundaries (1937)
Canals

Towns over 1,000,000
Towns of 500,000–1,000,000
Towns of 100,000–500,000
Towns of less than 100,000

SCALE OF KILOMETERS
SCALE OF MILES

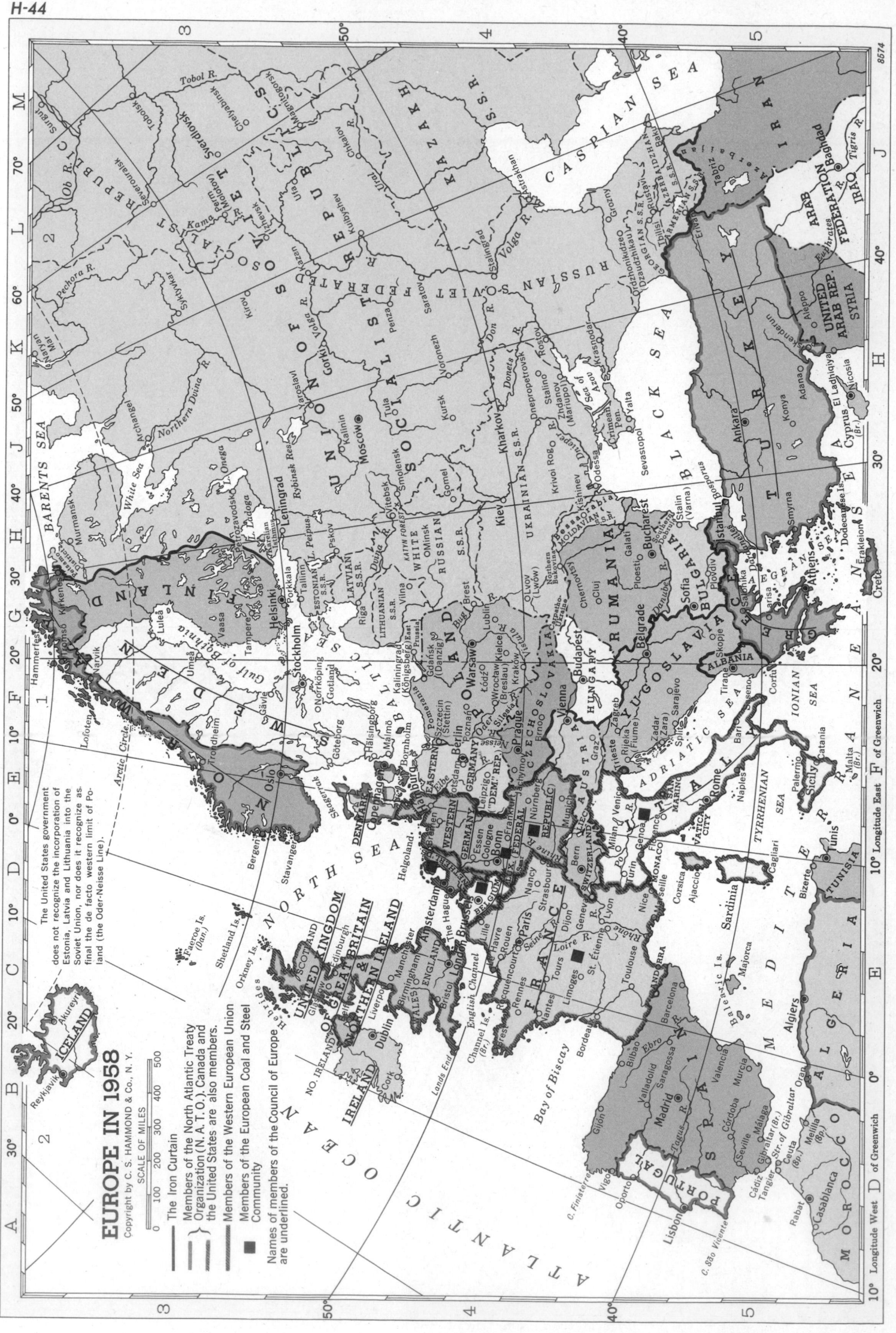

## EUROPE IN 1958

Copyright by C. S. HAMMOND & Co., N. Y.

SCALE OF MILES

0  100  200  300  400  500

The Iron Curtain

Members of the North Atlantic Treaty
Organization (N. A. T. O.) Canada and
the United States are also members.

Members of the Western European Union

Members of the European Coal and Steel
Community

Members of members of the Council of Europe

Names of members of the Council of Europe
are underlined.

The United States government
does not recognize the incorporation of
Estonia, Latvia and Lithuania into the
Soviet Union, nor does it recognize as
final the de facto western limit of Poland (the Oder-Neisse Line).

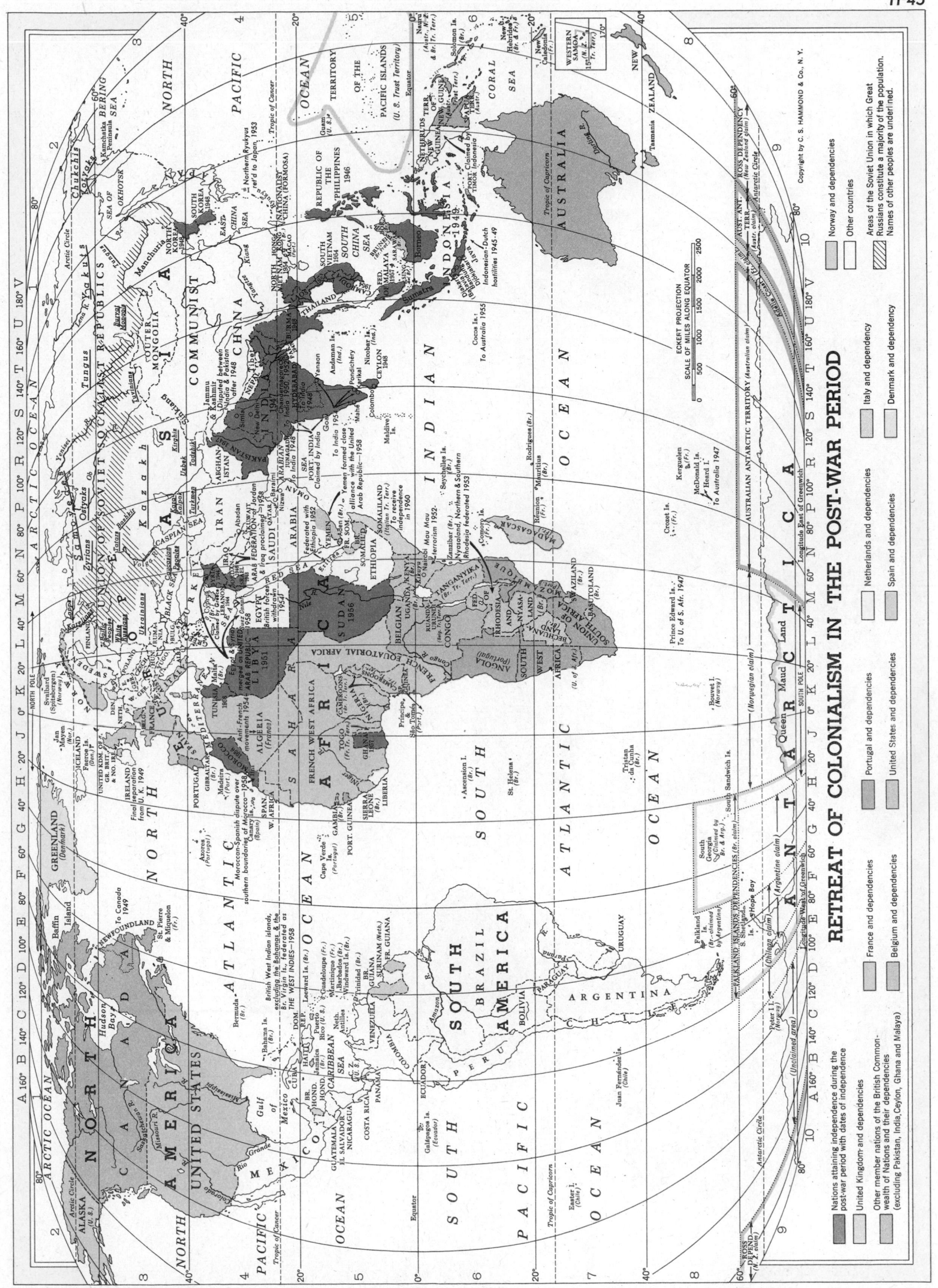

RETREAT OF COLONIALISM IN THE POST-WAR PERIOD

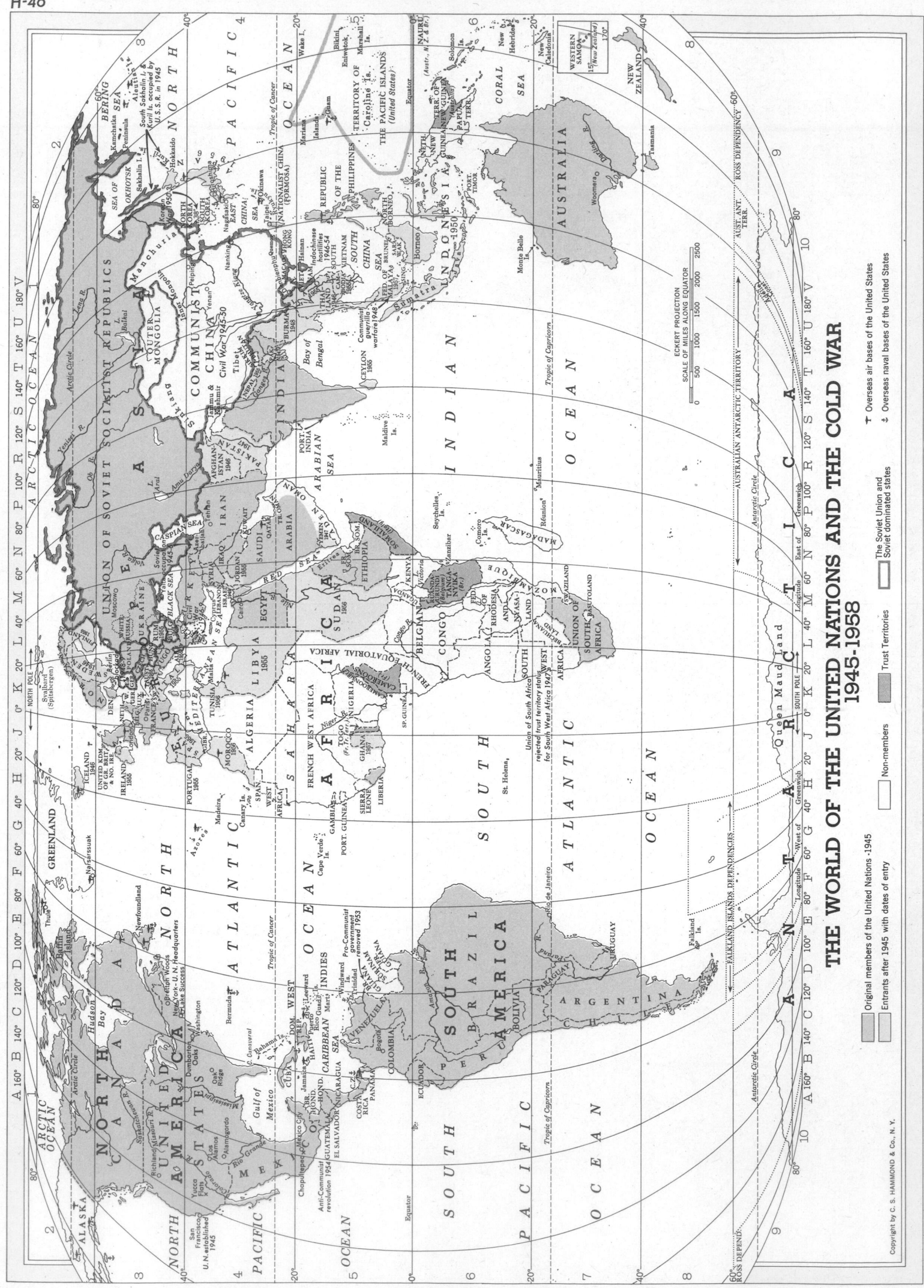

THE WORLD OF THE UNITED NATIONS AND THE COLD WAR
1945-1958

Original members of the United Nations -1945

Entrants after 1945 with dates of entry

Non-members

Trust Territories

The Soviet Union and
Soviet dominated states

⊤ Overseas air bases of the United States

⊥ Overseas naval bases of the United States

ECKERT PROJECTION
SCALE OF MILES ALONG EQUATOR
0   500   1000   1500   2000   2500

Copyright by C. S. HAMMOND & Co., N. Y.

# INDEX

# INDEX Continued